Red Hat® Linux® 7.1 Secrets®

Red Hat® Linux® 7.1 Secrets®

Naba Barkakati

Hungry Minds™

Hungry Minds, Inc.

Chicago, IL ♦ Indianapolis, IN ♦ New York, NY

Red Hat® Linux® 7.1 Secrets®

Published by
Hungry Minds, Inc.
909 Third Avenue
New York, NY 10022
www.hungryminds.com

ISBN: 0-7645-4771-2

Library of Congress Control Number: 2001089107

Printed in the United States of America

10 9 8 7 6 5 4 3 2 1

1B/RY/QU/QR/IN

Distributed in the United States by Hungry Minds, Inc.

Distributed by CDG Books Canada Inc. for Canada; by Transworld Publishers Limited in the United Kingdom; by IDG Norge Books for Norway; by IDG Sweden Books for Sweden; by IDG Books Australia Publishing Corporation Pty. Ltd. for Australia and New Zealand; by TransQuest Publishers Pte Ltd. for Singapore, Malaysia, Thailand, Indonesia, and Hong Kong; by Gotop Information Inc. for Taiwan; by ICG Muse, Inc. for Japan; by Intersoft for South Africa; by Eyrolles for France; by International Thomson Publishing for Germany, Austria, and Switzerland; by Distribuidora Cuspide for Argentina; by LR International for Brazil; by Galileo Libros for Chile; by Ediciones ZETA S.C.R. Ltda. for Peru; by WS Computer Publishing Corporation, Inc., for the Philippines; by Contemporanea de Ediciones for Venezuela; by Express Computer Distributors for the Caribbean and West Indies; by Micronesia Media Distributor, Inc. for Micronesia; by Chips Computadoras S.A. de C.V. for Mexico; by Editorial Norma de Panama S.A. for Panama; by American Bookshops for Finland.

For general information on Hungry Minds' products and services please contact our Customer Care department within the U.S. at 800-762-2974, outside the U.S. at 317-572-3993 or fax 317-572-4002.

For sales inquiries and reseller information, including discounts, premium and bulk quantity sales, and foreign-language translations, please contact our Customer Care department at 800-434-3422, fax 317-572-4002 or write to Hungry Minds, Inc., Attn: Customer Care Department, 10475 Crosspoint Boulevard, Indianapolis, IN 46256.

For information on licensing foreign or domestic rights, please contact our Sub-Rights Customer Care department at 212-884-5000.

For information on using Hungry Minds' products and services in the classroom or for ordering examination copies, please contact our Educational Sales department at 800-434-2086 or fax 317-572-4005.

For press review copies, author interviews, or other publicity information, please contact our Public Relations department at 650-653-7000 or fax 650-653-7500.

For authorization to photocopy items for corporate, personal, or educational use, please contact Copyright Clearance Center, 222 Rosewood Drive, Danvers, MA 01923, or fax 978-750-4470.

 is a trademark of Hungry Minds, Inc.

Credits

Acquisitions Editors
Terri Varveris
Greg Croy

Project Editor
Gus A. Miklos

Technical Editor
Kurt Wall

Copy Editors
Sarah B. Kleinman
Luann Rouff
Victoria Lee O'Malley

Project Coordinator
Maridee Ennis

Graphics and Production Specialists
Karl Brandt
Joe Bucki
LeAndra Johnson
Gabriele McCann
Brian Torwelle

Quality Control Technicians
Laura Albert
Andy Hollandbeck
Linda Quigley
Susan Moritz
Charles Spencer

Media Development Coordinator
Marisa Pearman

Proofreading and Indexing
York Production Services

About the Author

Naba Barkakati is an electrical engineer and a successful computer-book author who has experience in a wide variety of systems, ranging from MS-DOS and Windows to UNIX and the X Window System. He bought his first personal computer — an IBM PC-AT — in 1984 after graduating with a Ph.D. in electrical engineering from the University of Maryland. While pursuing a full-time career in engineering, Naba dreamed of writing software for the emerging PC software market. As luck would have it, instead of building a software empire like Microsoft, he ended up writing successful computer books.

Over the past 12 years, Naba has written over 25 computer books on a number of topics ranging from Windows programming with C++ to Linux. He has authored several best-selling titles such as *The Waite Group's Turbo C++ Bible, Object-Oriented Programming in C++, X Window System Programming, Visual C++ Developer's Guide,* and *Borland C++ 4 Developer's Guide.* His books have been translated into many languages, including Spanish, French, Polish, Greek, Italian, Chinese, Japanese, and Korean. Naba's most recent book is *Red Hat Linux 7 Weekend Crash Course,* also published by Hungry Minds.

Naba lives in North Potomac, Maryland, with his wife, Leha, and their children, Ivy, Emily, and Ashley.

This book is dedicated to my wife Leha, and daughters Ivy, Emily, and Ashley.

Preface

If you are just beginning to use Linux, what you need is a practical guide that not only gets you going with the installation and setup of Linux, but also shows you how to use Linux for a specific task, such as an Internet host or a software development platform.

The third edition of this book was a technical guide designed to address these needs. That book contained the standard installation and setup information and included version 6.2 of the popular Red Hat Linux on CD-ROMs.

A lot has happened in the year since the third edition was published. Linux is fast becoming a mainstream operating system with support from many major hardware and software vendors. Many commercial database vendors such as Oracle, IBM, Informix, and Sybase have announced support for, or already released, Linux versions of their databases. Some businesses have formally announced their intent to use Linux on their workstations and servers. IBM has thrown its support wholeheartedly behind Linux; there is even a version of Linux for the IBM S/390 mainframe. Prominent PC vendor Dell has teamed up with Red Hat and started shipping Red Hat Linux preinstalled on selected servers and workstations. Red Hat continues to improve its version of Linux. The recently released Red Hat Linux 7.1 includes many new system components including the Linux 2.4 kernel, XFree86 4.0.2, GCC 2.96 compiler, and the glibc 2.2 system libraries. The system now supports USB keyboards and mice. Additionally, there are many security-related enhancements such as the inclusion of secure shell and support of Kerberos authentication.

Red Hat Linux 7.1 Secrets follows the successful model of the previous edition except for the addition of several new chapters and reorganization of the content into a more logical progression. All of these changes are based on reader feedback. In addition to the improved content, this edition includes Red Hat Linux 7.1, with the 2.4 kernel, on the companion CD-ROMs. As in previous editions, this book provides detailed technical information on installing and customizing Linux for use with various types of computers and peripherals.

The information in this book then goes a step beyond existing books and demonstrates how to use Linux as a solution to specific problems. In addition, it provides information on software packages — such as e-mail, Web, and news, plus graphics and text utilities — that are included on the book's companion CD-ROMs.

The unique aspects of *Red Hat Linux 7.1 Secrets* are the tips, techniques, shortcuts, and little-known facts about using Linux in various real-world tasks that range from simply learning UNIX to setting up a Web server for your business.

By reading this book you can:

■ Learn how to install and set up Red Hat Linux from the CD-ROMs included with the book

- Learn how to use various peripherals (video cards, hard disks, and network cards) in Red Hat Linux
- Learn about dial-up networking (with SLIP and PPP) under Red Hat Linux
- Get tips, techniques, and shortcuts for specific uses of Red Hat Linux, such as:
  - Learn how to set up and use Internet services such as Web, Mail, News, FTP, NFS, NIS, and DNS
  - Understand how to set up a Windows server using Samba
  - Learn UNIX on Red Hat Linux
  - Learn Perl, shell, and Tcl/Tk programming on Red Hat Linux
  - Learn X and Motif programming on Red Hat Linux
- Understand the basics of system and network security
- Learn to perform system and network administration tasks
- Receive many Red Hat Linux tools and utilities
- Learn about Linux resources that can serve as continuing sources of information in the ever-changing world of Linux

Organization of the Book

Red Hat Linux 7.1 Secrets has 30 chapters, organized into five parts, plus three appendixes:

Part I: Setting Up Red Hat Linux

Part I includes nine chapters that introduce you to Linux, guide you through Red Hat Linux installation, and show you how to use various hardware in Linux. The first chapter provides an overview of Linux in general. The second chapter takes you through the steps needed to install Red Hat Linux from this book's companion CD-ROMs. The next seven chapters explain how to configure and use various types of PC hardware in Linux—a key feature of the Secrets book that differentiates this book from other Linux books. The hardware descriptions cover everything from the computer (processor, memory, and bus) to serial ports and PC cards (that use the PCMCIA interface).

Part II: Exploring Red Hat Linux

This part gets you acquainted with Red Hat Linux. The six chapters in this part describe the popular GNU utilities, the GUI desktops—GNOME and KDE, and the applications included with Red Hat Linux on the companion CD-ROMS. You also learn how to edit text files and perform basic system administration functions.

Part III: Internetworking Red Hat Linux

The chapters in Part III focus on connecting the Red Hat Linux system to the Internet and setting up various Internet services on the system. After describing dial-up networking, the chapters in this part walk you through the setup and configuration of a number of servers, including Web, FTP, SMTP (mail), news, DNS, NIS, NFS, and Samba.

Part IV: Managing Red Hat Linux

The four chapters in Part IV cover system administration and security. The first chapter in this part — Chapter 23 — starts by discussing a number of advanced system administration topics. The next three chapters show you how to install and upgrade software using the Red Hat Package Manager (RPM), how to rebuild and install a new kernel, and how to secure the system and the network.

Part V: Programming Red Hat Linux

Part V turns to the subject of programming in Linux. The first chapter — Chapter 27 — covers a number of software development tools and the GNU Public License that affects software developed in Linux. Then that chapter briefly touches on C and C++ programming. The next two chapters cover scripting using the shell, Perl, and Tcl/Tk. Finally, the last chapter introduces the reader to writing applications with graphical interfaces using X and Motif.

Appendixes

- Appendix A, "Linux Commands" presents alphabetically arranged reference entries for the many commonly used Linux commands.

- Appendix B, "Linux Resources" lists resources on the Internet where you can obtain the latest information about Linux.

- Appendix C, "About the CD-ROMs" summarizes the contents of the book's companion CD-ROMs.

If you are a new user, you should start in Part I with the installation of Red Hat Linux from the CD-ROMs. If you have specific hardware questions, you should go directly to a relevant chapter in Part I. If you have already installed Red Hat Linux, you might want to begin with Part II, learning how to make the most of Red Hat Linux in everyday use. For questions related to Internet services, consult the appropriate chapter in Part III. Part IV gets you going with various system administration tasks and explains how to maintain system and network security. To learn about programming in specific languages, consult the relevant chapters in Part V. When you need information on a specific Linux command, turn to Appendix A and look for that command in the alphabetically arranged reference entries.

Conventions Used in This Book

Red Hat Linux 7.1 Secrets uses a simple notational style. All listings, filenames, function names, variable names, and keywords are typeset in a `monospace font` for ease of reading. The first occurrences of new terms and concepts are in *italic*. Text you are directed to type is in `boldface`.

Each chapter starts with a short list of all the neat things that you learn in that chapter. The summary at the end of the chapter tells you a bit more about what the chapter covered.

Following the time-honored tradition of the Hungry Minds *Secrets* series, I use icons to help you quickly pinpoint useful information. The icons include the following:

Note
The Note icon marks a general interesting fact — something that I thought you'd like to know.

Tip
The Tip icon marks things that you can do to make your job easier.

Caution
The Caution icon highlights potential pitfalls. With this icon, I'm telling you: "Watch out! This could hurt your system!"

CD
The CD-ROM icon points to specific programs or documentation that can be found on the companion CD-ROM.

Cross-Reference
The Cross-Reference icon points out other chapters in the book for a deeper discussion of a specific topic.

Secret
The Secret icon marks facts that are not well-documented, but are important to know. It's not that no one knows this fact — it's just hard to find; and knowing this fact usually clears up many other questions that you may have. This icon also marks technical information that will be of interest to an advanced user.

Sidebars

I use sidebars throughout the book to highlight interesting, but not critical information. Sidebars explain concepts you may not have encountered before or give a little insight into a related topic. If you're in a hurry, you can safely skip the sidebars. On the other hand, if you find yourself flipping through the book looking for interesting information, reading the sidebars is a good idea.

About the Companion CD-ROMs

Red Hat Linux 7.1 Secrets addresses the needs of new users who want to put Red Hat Linux to some productive use on their home or office PC. To ensure that readers have everything they need to start using Red Hat Linux, this book includes a copy of Red Hat Linux 7.1 (with Linux kernel 2.4) on the companion CD-ROMs. Red Hat Linux is easy to install and is well supported by Red Hat (www.redhat.com).

See Appendix C for a summary description of the contents of the companion CD-ROMs. As you browse the contents of the CD-ROMs, you'll notice that there is a huge amount of software included in Red Hat Linux. The long list of software shouldn't overwhelm you. You only have to learn to use what you need. Besides, this book will show you how to install Red Hat Linux and use most of this software.

If you have enough space available on your PC's hard disk (or, better yet, a spare second hard disk), Red Hat Linux installation can be as simple as creating a boot disk, booting the PC, and filling up information in a series of dialog boxes. You don't have to take my word for it — you can see for yourself.

It's time to get started on your Linux adventure. Take out the first companion CD-ROM, turn to Chapter 1, and let the fun begin. Before you know it, you'll be a Linux expert!

I hope you enjoy this book as much as I enjoyed writing it!

Reach Out

The publisher and I would like your feedback. After you have had a chance to use this book, please take a moment to register this book on the http://my2cents.hungryminds.com Web site. (Details are listed on the my2cents page in the back of the book.)

Also, feel free to contact me directly at:

naba@ieee.org

Acknowledgments

I am grateful to Greg Croy and Terri Varveris for getting me started on *Red Hat Linux 7.1 Secrets,* which is now a fourth edition. As the project editor, Gus Miklos guided me through the manuscript-submission process and kept everything moving. I appreciate the guidance and support that Greg, Terri, and Gus gave me during this project.

I would like to thank Kurt Wall for reviewing the manuscript for technical accuracy and providing many useful suggestions for improving the book's content.

Thanks to everyone at Hungry Minds for transforming my raw manuscript into this well-edited and beautifully packaged book.

Of course, there would be no reason for this book if it were not for Linux. For this, we have Linus Torvalds and the legions of Linux developers around the world to thank.

Finally, and as always, my greatest thanks go to my wife, Leha, and our daughters, Ivy, Emily, and Ashley — it is their love and support that keeps me going. Thanks for being there!

Contents at a Glance

Contents

Introduction

Linux is truly amazing when you consider how it originated and how it continues to evolve. From its modest beginning as the hobby of one person — Linus Torvalds of Finland — Linux has grown into a full-fledged 32-bit operating system (it's 64-bit on 64-bit processors) with features that rival those of commercial UNIX operating systems such as Solaris and SCO UNIX. To top it off, Linux — with all of its source code — is available free of cost to anyone. All one has to do is download it from an Internet site or get it on a CD for a nominal fee from one of many Linux CD vendors.

Linux certainly is an exception to the rule "you get what you pay for." Even though Linux is free, it is no slouch when it comes to performance, features, and reliability. The robustness of Linux has to do with the way that it was developed. Many developers around the world collaborated over the Internet to add features. Incremental versions are continually being downloaded by users and tested in a variety of system configurations. Linux revisions go through much more rigorous beta testing than any commercial software does.

Since the release of Linux 1.0 on March 14, 1994, the number of Linux users around the world has grown exponentially. Based on data gathered by the Linux Counter (`http://counter.li.org/`), the estimated installed base is around sixteen million users worldwide. The same data provides some other interesting statistics about Linux:

- Most Linux users are in United States, Canada, and Europe.

- 88% of Linux users use it at home. 43% use it at work. Some use it both at work and home.

- 20% of users get Linux via FTP. About 30% of users buy Linux on a CD, typically from a vendor such as Red Hat or InfoMagic.

- Red Hat Linux (29%) is the most popular Linux distribution. Slackware (26%) and Debian (20%) are the other two prominent distributions.

- 40% of users run Linux on Intel Pentium and Pentium II systems; 15% on 486 processors. Systems typically have 32 to 128MB of memory and a 1GB to 10GB disk.

- 72% of the Linux systems use the Ethernet network while 34% use dial-up networking with SLIP and PPP.

- Most Linux systems have anywhere from one to nine users.

- Most Linux systems are used as Internet servers (WWW, FTP, Mail, firewall, and even as routers).

The Linux distributions — Red Hat, Slackware, Debian, and Caldera — differ in the way each handles the installation process. Because installation is the most difficult step in getting started with Linux, it helps to select a Linux distribution that makes installation easy. Red Hat Linux excels when it comes to the installation process. Red Hat provides an installation program that guides new users through critical parts of the installation process, including disk partitioning. The ease of installation makes Red Hat Linux a good choice for all users, especially new users.

Red Hat Linux comes with extensive online information on topics such as installing and configuring the operating system for a wide variety of PCs and peripherals. Although expert users can manage to install and run Red Hat Linux with the online documentation alone, new users find consulting a book (such as this one) helpful for detailed guidance on Red Hat Linux installation. Typically, users also move to Linux with some specific purpose in mind (such as setting up a World Wide Web server or learning Motif programming). The online documentation does not cover the specific uses of Linux that the user may have in mind. This book is designed to address these needs.

Part I

Setting Up Red Hat Linux

Chapter 1

An Overview of Red Hat Linux

In This Chapter

▶ Looking at Red Hat Linux and Linux kernel version numbers

▶ Taking stock of Linux's suitability as a UNIX platform

▶ Understanding how X, GNOME, and KDE provide a graphical interface to Linux

▶ Understanding the built-in networking capabilities of Linux

▶ Looking at Linux's implications for network managers and system administrators

▶ Making Windows coexist with Linux

▶ Looking at the software-development tools in Linux

▶ Using Linux as your Internet on-ramp

Starting with the Intel 80386 processor, continuing with the 80486, and now with the Pentium and the 64-bit Itanium, the computing power of PC processors continues to grow steadily. Processor clock speeds have increased from 16 MHz of the 80386 (several years ago) to the 1GHz of today's Pentium III processors. The IBM PC-AT-based Industry Standard Architecture (ISA) bus has been supplanted by the high-performance Peripheral Component Interconnect (PCI) bus. The hardware performance of a modern run-of-the-mill PC is clearly on a par with that of UNIX workstations, such as those from IBM, Sun Microsystems, and Hewlett-Packard.

When it comes to operating systems, however, PCs have not kept up with workstations. PCs running Microsoft Windows often do not take full advantage of the processing capabilities of the processors. Workstations, on the other hand, run UNIX — a multitasking, multi-user operating system. (This means that the operating system can run several programs simultaneously and support more than one user at a time.) Typically, UNIX workstations also use the X Window System for a graphical user interface.

UNIX has been available for PCs for quite some time, but until recently you had to pay nearly as much for a fully configured commercial PC UNIX operating system as you had to pay for the PC itself. This situation changed, however, when Linus Torvalds of the University of Helsinki in Finland decided to build a UNIX-like operating system for the PC. What started as a simple task-switching example, with two processes that printed AAAA . . . and BBBB . . .

on a dumb terminal, has grown into a full-fledged multitasking, multi-user operating system that rivals commercially available UNIX systems for Intel 80x86 systems. Many programmers around the world contributed code and collaborated to bring Linux to its current state. With the release of version 1.0 in March 1994, Linux became an operating system of choice for UNIX enthusiasts, as well as for people looking for a low-cost UNIX platform for a specific purpose, such as developing software or running an Internet host.

This chapter provides a broad-brushstroke picture of Red Hat Linux, one of several well-known Linux distributions (other well-known Linux distributions include Slackware, Debian, S.u.S.E., Caldera OpenLinux, and TurboLinux). The chapter describes how you can get the most out of the built-in capabilities of Red Hat Linux, such as networking, developing software, and running applications.

After you overcome your initial fear of the unknown and install Linux, you will see how you can use it to turn your PC into a UNIX workstation. The best part is that you can get Linux for free—just download it from one of several Internet sites (for example, you'll find links to many Linux distributions from the Linux Online Web site at `http://www.linux.org/dist/`). The best way for beginners and experts alike to get started, though, is to buy a book (such as this one) that comes with a Linux distribution on CD-ROM. This book is your complete guide to Red Hat Linux. In the next chapter, I discuss installation and then move on to specific tasks (such as developing software or connecting to the Internet) that you may want to perform with your Red Hat Linux PC.

What Is Red Hat Linux?

Linux is a freely available UNIX-like operating system that runs on a wide variety of systems. Linus Torvalds and other programmers originally developed Linux for the Intel 80x86 processor. Nowadays Linux is also available for systems based on other processors, such as the Motorola 68000 family, Alpha AXP processor, Sun SPARC processor, Hewlett-Packard's HP PA-RISC processor, the PowerPC processor, and the MIPS R4x00 and R5x00 processors. Work is in progress on porting Linux to the new 64-bit IA-64 architecture processors, the first of which has been named Itanium by Intel. More recently, IBM has announced Linux for its S/390 mainframe. This book covers Red Hat Linux for Intel 80x86 and Pentium processors (these are known as the IA-32 architecture processors).

Red Hat Linux is a specific Linux distribution. A *Linux distribution* is essentially a package consisting of the Linux operating system and a collection of applications, together with an easy-to-use installation program. All Linux distributions include the core Linux operating system (the *kernel*); the XFree86 X Window System for *x*86 systems; one or more graphical desktops, such as GNOME and KDE; and a large selection of applications. Everything comes in ready-to-run binary format, but the source and documentation are also included. By now, each Linux distribution has so much software that it comes on multiple CD-ROMs. For example, this book comes with three CD-ROMs containing the binaries and documentation packages of Red Hat Linux. The source CD-ROM is not included, but is available upon request (see coupon inside the back cover).

Like many other Linux distributions, Red Hat Linux is a commercial distribution of Linux. You can buy Red Hat Linux in computer stores and bookstores. The GNU (which stands for "GNU's Not UNIX") General Public License that applies to Linux allows for such commercial, for-profit distribution, but requires that the software be distributed in source-code form, and stipulates that anyone can copy and distribute the software in source-code form to anyone else.

Both the Linux kernel and Red Hat Linux have gone through a number of versions. The version numbers are unrelated, but each has some meaning.

Linux Kernel Version Numbers

After Linux version 1.0 was released on March 14, 1994, the loosely organized Linux development community adopted a version-number scheme. Versions 1.x.y and 2.x.y, wherein x is an even number, are stable versions. The number y is the *patch level*, which is incremented as problems are fixed. Notice that these version numbers are of the form *Major.Minor.Patch* where *Major* and *Minor* are integers denoting the major and minor version numbers, and *Patch* is another integer representing the patch level.

Versions 2.x.y with an odd x number are beta releases for developers only; they may be unstable, so you should not adopt these versions for day-to-day use. Developers add new features to these odd-numbered versions of Linux.

When this book was written, the latest stable version of the Linux kernel was 2.2.16, and developers were getting ready to release version 2.4.0 (note that information about the latest version of the Linux kernel is available at http://www.kernel.org/). This book's companion CD-ROMs contain version 2.4 of the Linux kernel, which became available in January 2001. This version of the Linux kernel supports symmetric multiprocessing (SMP) — which means that the operating system can automatically detect and make use of multiple processors on the motherboard.

**Cross-
Reference**

If you hear about a later version of Linux or about helpful patches (minor corrections) to the current version, you can obtain the patches and rebuild the kernel by following the instructions in Chapter 25.

Red Hat Linux Version Numbers

The Red Hat Linux version numbers, such as 6.3 or 7.0, are assigned by Red Hat. They are of the form x.y where x is the major version and y the minor version. Unlike with the Linux kernel version numbers, there is no special meaning associated with odd and even minor versions. Each version of Red Hat Linux includes specific versions of the Linux kernel and other major components, such as the XFree86, GNOME, KDE, and various applications.

Red Hat releases new versions of Red Hat Linux on a regular basis. For example, Red Hat Linux 5.2 came out in November 1998, 6.0 in April 1999, and 7.0 in September 2000. Typically, each new major version of Red Hat Linux includes significant new features. Red Hat Linux 6.*x* brought in the GNOME and KDE graphical desktops; Red Hat Linux 7.0 includes features such as support for the Universal Serial Bus (USB) keyboard and mice, XFree86 4.0, and strengthened network security with Kerberos.

Linux as a UNIX Platform

Like other UNIX systems, Linux is a multi-user multitasking operating system, which means that it enables multiple users to log in and run more than one program at the same time.

Linux is designed to comply with IEEE Std 1003.1 1996 Edition (POSIX). This standard defines the functions that applications written in the C programming language use to access the services of the operating system — for tasks ranging from opening a file to allocating memory. On March 8, 1996, the Computer Systems Laboratory of the National Institute of Standards and Technology (NIST), a U.S. Government agency, confirmed that Linux version 1.2.13, as packaged by Open Linux Ltd., conforms to the POSIX standard. To see a list of POSIX-validated products, point your World Wide Web browser to `http://www.nist.gov/itl/div897/ctg/posix/finalreg4.htm`. Note that the NIST POSIX testing program ended on December 31, 1997.

Along with POSIX conformance, Linux includes many features of other UNIX standards, such as the System V Interface Document (SVID), and the Berkeley Software Distribution (BSD) version of UNIX. Linux takes an eclectic approach, picking the most-needed features of several standard flavors of UNIX.

In addition to POSIX (IEEE 1003.1) compliance, Linux supports the IEEE 1003.2 standard that focuses on the operating system's command interpreter (commonly referred to as the *shell*), and a standard set of utility programs. If you know UNIX or you've had some exposure to it, you know that UNIX takes a tools-oriented view of the operating system. It provides a tool for almost anything that you might want to do, and the shell enables you to combine several tools to perform tasks more complicated than those handled by the basic tools. The IEEE 1003.2 standard maintains this tools-oriented view, providing the following features:

- A shell with a specified set of built-in commands and a programming syntax that can be used to write *shell programs*, or *scripts*.

- A standard set of utility programs — such as `sed`, `tr`, and `awk` — that can be called by shell scripts and applications. Even the `vi` editor and the `mail` electronic-mail program are part of the standard set. You learn more about these utilities in Chapters 11, 13, and 14.

- A set of C functions, such as `system` and `getenv`, that applications can use to access features of the shell.

- A set of utilities for developing shell applications.

A Short History of UNIX

UNIX was developed in the early 1970s at the AT&T Bell Laboratories. Its development came on the heels of another operating system called MULTICS; the developers are said to have come up with the name UNIX by changing the MULT in MULTICS to UN (meaning one). Bell Laboratories continued to develop UNIX and released several versions: System III followed by System V Release 1, or SVR1, and SVR2, SVR3, and SVR4.

As it maintained and enhanced UNIX, Bell Laboratories distributed the source code to educational institutions. The University of California at Berkeley was one of the schools that received a copy of UNIX and added many new features to the operating system. Eventually, UC Berkeley released its version of UNIX, called Berkeley Software Distribution (BSD) UNIX. The most widely used versions of BSD UNIX are 4.3 and 4.4 (known as 4.4BSD).

By the time 4.4BSD UNIX came out, UC Berkeley realized that there was very little original Bell Laboratories UNIX code in the source code. Soon several groups wrote new code to replace the small amount of leftover Bell Laboratories code and adapted BSD UNIX to the Intel 386 processor. This resulted in the FreeBSD and NetBSD versions of freely available BSD UNIX for Intel PCs.

Note that UNIX System V Release 4, or SVR4, combines all features of System V and BSD UNIX.

The default Linux shell is called *Bash,* which stands for *Bourne-Again Shell* — a reference to the *Bourne shell,* which has been the standard UNIX shell since the early days of UNIX. Bash incorporates many of the features required by IEEE 1003.2, and then some. It essentially inherits the features and functionality of the Bourne shell. In case of any discrepancy between the Bourne shell and IEEE 1003.2, Bash follows IEEE 1003.2. For stricter IEEE 1003.2 compliance, Bash even includes a POSIX mode.

All in all, Linux serves as a good platform for learning UNIX, because it offers a standard set of UNIX commands (the IEEE 1003.2 standard, as well as the best features of both System V and BSD UNIX).

Linux's support for POSIX and other common UNIX *system calls* (the functions applications call) makes it an excellent system for software development. Another ingredient of modern workstation software, the X Window System, is also available in Linux, in the form of XFree86.

Providing common productivity software — such as word processing, spreadsheet, and database applications — is an area in which Linux used to be lacking. This situation has changed, though. Both GNOME and KDE come with some office-productivity applications. Additionally, there are several prominent commercially available office-productivity applications for Linux that are not included on the companion CD-ROMs. Applixware Office is a good example of productivity software for Linux (http://www.vistasource.com/). Other well-known productivity-software packages include WordPerfect Office 2000 for Linux from Corel Corporation (http://linux.corel.com/) and StarOffice

The POSIX Standard

POSIX stands for *Portable Operating System Interface* (abbreviated as POSIX to make it sound like UNIX). The Institute of Electrical and Electronics Engineers (IEEE) began developing the POSIX standards to promote the portability of applications across UNIX environments. POSIX is not limited to UNIX, however. Many other operating systems, such as Compaq OpenVMS and Microsoft Windows NT, implement POSIX—in particular, IEEE Std. 1003.1 1996 Edition, or POSIX.1, which provides a source-level C-language Application Program Interface (API) to the services of the operating system, such as reading and writing files. POSIX.1 has been accepted by the International Standards Organization (ISO) and is known as the ISO/IEC 9945-1:1996 standard.

Incidentally, the term POSIX is used interchangeably with the IEEE 1003 and 2003 family of standards. There are several other IEEE standards besides the 1003 and 2003 family—such as 1224 and 1228—that also provide APIs for developing portable applications. For the latest information on all IEEE standards, visit the IEEE Standards Home Page at `http://standards.ieee.org/`. To read summary information about the POSIX standards, visit the IEEE Web page at `http://standards.ieee.org/reading/ieee/std_public/description/posix/`.

from Sun Microsystems (`http://www.sun.com/staroffice/`). Additionally, many existing software packages (designed for UNIX workstations with the X Window System) can be readily ported to Linux, thanks to Linux's support for portable standards, such as POSIX and the X Window System.

The X Window System in Linux

Let's face it—typing cryptic UNIX commands on a terminal is boring. Those of us who know the commands by heart may not realize it, but the installed base of UNIX is not going to increase significantly if we don't make the system easy to use. This is where the X Window System, or X, comes to the rescue.

X provides a standard mechanism for displaying device-independent bitmapped graphics. In other words, an X application can display its graphics output on many different machines that use different methods to display text, graphics, and images on the monitor. X is also a windowing system, meaning that it enables applications to organize their output in separate windows.

Although X provides the mechanism for windowed output, it does not offer any specific look or feel for applications. The look and feel come from graphical user interfaces (GUIs), such as GNOME and KDE, which are based on the X Window System.

Cross-Reference

The Red Hat Linux distribution on this book's CD-ROM comes with the X Window System in the form of XFree86 4.0 — an implementation of X11R6 (X Window System version 11, release 6, which is the latest release of X) for 80x86 systems. A key feature of XFree86 is its support for a wide variety of video cards available for today's PCs. As you learn in Chapter 3, XFree86 supports literally hundreds of PC video cards, ranging from the run-of-the-mill Super Video Graphics Adapter (SVGA) to accelerated graphics cards, such as the ones based on the S3, Mach64, and Weitek P9000 video chipsets.

As for the GUI, Linux includes two powerful graphical desktop environments: KDE (K Desktop Environment) and GNOME (GNU Object Model Environment). When you install Red Hat Linux, you can choose which desktop you want. KDE and GNOME provide desktops that are similar to the ones in Microsoft Windows and the Macintosh OS. With GNOME or KDE, you can begin using your Linux workstation without having to learn UNIX commands. However, if you should ever need to use UNIX commands, all you have to do is open a terminal window and type the commands at the shell prompt.

Red Hat Linux also comes with many graphical applications that run under X. The most noteworthy programs relate to image display and editing. The first is GIMP — the GNU Image Manipulation Program — a program with capabilities on a par with Adobe Photoshop, the second is ImageMagick, and the third is xpaint by David Koblas.

Another important aspect of the X Window System is that you can run applications across the network. For example, you might run a graphical application on a server on the network, but view that application's output and interact with it from your Linux desktop. In other words, with X, your Linux PC becomes a gateway to all the other systems on the network.

Although Motif is the dominant GUI in the UNIX marketplace, it is not packaged with Linux because the Open Software Foundation does not give away Motif for free. Motif has a look and feel similar to those of Microsoft Windows and includes the Motif Window Manager (mwm), and the Motif toolkit for programmers. You can download OpenMotif for Linux from http://www.motifzone.net/.

If you need Motif for a project, using a Linux PC with a copy of OpenMotif installed is still an economical way to set up a software-development platform. If you have a consulting business, or if you want to develop X and Motif software at home, Linux is definitely the way to go.

Along with GNOME and KDE, you get two more options for developing GUI applications in Linux. GNOME comes with a toolkit called Gtk+ (GIMP toolkit), and KDE comes with the Qt toolkit. If you do not want to learn Motif, you may want to use Gtk+ or Qt for your GUI applications.

Cross-Reference

Chapter 3 shows you how to set up XFree86 on your system, Chapter 12 presents the GNOME and KDE desktops, and Chapter 30 explains how to develop Motif applications on a Linux system.

Linux Networking

Networking refers to all aspects of data exchange between one or more computers, ranging from the physical connection, to the protocol for the actual data exchange. A *network protocol* is the method agreed upon by the sender and receiver for exchanging data across a network.

Different network protocols are used at different levels of the network. At the physical level — the level at which the data bits travel through a medium, such as a cable — Ethernet and token ring are two commonly used protocols. Application programs don't really work at this physical level, however. Instead, they rely on protocols that operate on blocks of data. These protocols include Novell's Internet Packet Exchange (IPX) and the well-known Transmission Control Protocol/Internet Protocol (TCP/IP).

Cross-Reference

The different levels of network protocols can be represented by a networking model, such as the seven-layer Open Systems Interconnection (OSI) reference model, developed by the International Standards Organization (ISO). Chapter 8 includes a discussion of this model.

Standard network protocols, such as TCP/IP have been key to the growth of interconnected computers, resulting in local-area networks (LANs), as well as wide-area networks (WANs). Protocols have enabled these smaller networks to communicate with each other, and we now have interconnected networks that form an internetwork: the Internet.

TCP/IP

The ability to network has been one of the strengths of UNIX since its early days. In particular, the well-known TCP/IP protocol suite has been an integral part of UNIX ever since TCP/IP appeared in BSD UNIX around 1982. By now, TCP/IP is the wide-area-networking protocol of choice in the global Internet.

Linux supports the TCP/IP protocol suite and includes all common network applications, such as `telnet`, `ftp`, and `rlogin`. At the physical-network level, Linux includes drivers for many Ethernet cards. Token ring is also an integral part of the Linux kernel source; all you have to do is rebuild the kernel and enable support for token-ring.

Cross-Reference

You might say that Linux's support for TCP/IP — the dominant protocol suite of the Internet — comes naturally. The rapid development of Linux itself would not have been possible without the collaboration of so many developers from Europe and America. That collaboration, in turn, has been possible only because of the Internet. Chapters 16 through 22 show you how to set up TCP/IP networking and use the network software.

Linux also includes the Berkeley Sockets programming interface (so named because the socket interface was introduced in Berkeley UNIX around 1982), a popular interface for network programming in TCP/IP networks. For those of you with C programming experience, the Sockets interface consists of several C header files and several C functions that you call to set up connections and to send and receive data.

You can use the Berkeley Sockets programming interface to develop Internet tools, such as World Wide Web (WWW) browsers. Because most TCP/IP programs (including those available for free at various Internet sites) use the Sockets programming interface, it is easy to get these programs up and running on Linux, because Linux includes the Sockets interface.

PPP and SLIP

Not everyone has an Ethernet connection to the Internet — in particular, few of us do who use Linux on our home PCs. There is, however, a way to connect to the Internet and communicate using the TCP/IP protocol over a phone line and a modem. What you need is a *server* — a system that has an Internet connection and that accepts a dial-in connection from your system.

Nowadays, commercial outfits known as *Internet service providers* (ISP) offer this type of service for a fee. If you don't want to pay for such a connection, find out whether a computer at your place of business provides this access. That option may not be unreasonable, especially if you are doing UNIX software development (for your company) on your Linux PC at home.

When you access the Internet through a server, that server runs either of two protocols:

- Serial Line Internet Protocol (SLIP)
- Point-to-Point Protocol (PPP)

Both protocols support TCP/IP over a dial-up line. SLIP is a simpler and older protocol than PPP, which has more features for establishing a connection. However, nearly everyone uses PPP nowadays. To establish a connection, your system must run the same protocol as the ISP's system.

Cross-Reference

Linux supports both SLIP and PPP for dial-up Internet connections. You can also turn your Linux system into a SLIP or PPP server so that other computers can dial into your computer and establish a TCP/IP connection over the phone line. Chapter 16 explains how to set up PPP dial-up Internet connection on your Red Hat Linux system.

File Sharing with NFS

In the MS-DOS and Microsoft Windows world, you may be familiar with the concept of a *file server* — a system that maintains important files and allows all other systems on the network to access those files. Essentially, all PCs on the network share one or more central disks. In DOS and Windows, users see the file server's disk as being just another drive, with its own drive letter (such as U). In PC networks, you typically implement file sharing with Novell NetWare or Microsoft LAN Manager protocols.

The concept of file sharing exists in UNIX as well. The Network File System (NFS) provides a standard way for a system to access another system's files over the network. To the user, the remote system's files appear to be in a directory on the local system.

Cross-Reference

NFS is available in Linux; you can share your Linux system's directories with other systems that support NFS. The other systems that access your Linux system's files via NFS do not necessarily have to run UNIX; NFS is available for DOS, Windows, OS/2, and Netware as well. Therefore, you can use a Linux PC as the file server for a small workgroup of PCs that run DOS and/or Windows. Chapter 22 further explores the use of a Linux PC as a file server.

Linux System Administration

System administration refers to tasks that someone must perform in order to keep a computer system up and running properly. Now that almost all computers are networked, it's necessary to perform another set of tasks to keep the network up and running. All these tasks are collectively called *network administration*. A site with many computers probably has a full-time *system administrator* who takes care of all system- and network-administration tasks. Really large sites may have separate system-administration and network-administration personnel. If you are running Linux on a home PC or on a few systems in a small company, you are probably both the system administrator and the network administrator.

Cross-Reference

Linux includes all the basic commands and utilities you need for system and network administration. Chapters 15 and 23 briefly cover some of these commands. Chapter 8 describes the network-administration tools.

Note

Red Hat Linux comes with the `Linuxconf` utility — an X application that enables you to perform most system and network administration tasks, without having to manually edit configuration files or type cryptic commands.

System-Administration Tasks

As a system administrator, your tasks will typically include the following:

- *Installing, configuring, and upgrading the operating system and various utilities.* You learn how to install Red Hat Linux and other software packages in Chapter 2. Chapter 3 tells you how to install the X Window System, and Chapter 25 shows you how to upgrade the operating system — the Linux kernel.

- *Adding and removing users.* As shown in Chapter 15, you can use Red Hat's graphical `Linuxconf` tool to add a new user after you install Linux. If a user forgets a password, you can change the password from the `Linuxconf` tool or use the `passwd` command to change it.

- *Installing new software.* For the typical Linux software, which you get in source-code form, this task involves using tools such as `gunzip` (to uncompress the software), `tar` (to unpack the archive), and `make` (to build the executable programs). For software distributed by Red Hat in Red Hat Package Manager (RPM) files, you have to use the `rpm` command to install the software. Chapter 24 describes RPM.

- *Making backups.* You can use the `tar` program to archive one or more directories and to copy the archive to a floppy disk (if the archive is small enough), or to a tape (if you have a tape drive). Chapter 23 covers backing up and restoring files and directories.

- *Mounting and unmounting file systems.* When you want to read an MS-DOS floppy disk, for example, you have to mount that disk's MS-DOS file system on one of the directories of the Linux file system. You have to use the `mount` command to do this. You can also use `Linuxconf` to mount a file system.

- *Monitoring the system's performance.* You have to use a few utilities, such as `top` (to see where the processor is spending most of its time) and `free` (to see the amount of free and used memory in the system).

- *Starting and shutting down the system.* Although starting the system typically involves nothing more than powering up the PC, you do have to take some care when you want to shut down your Linux system. You should use the `shutdown` command to stop all programs before turning off your PC's power switch. If your system is set up for a graphical login screen, you can perform the shutdown operation by selecting a menu item from the login screen.

Network-Administration Tasks

Typical network-administration tasks include the following:

- *Maintaining the network configuration files.* In Linux (as well as in other UNIX systems), several text files hold the configuration information for the TCP/IP network. You may have to edit these files in order to make networking work. You may have to edit one or more of the following files: `/etc/hosts`, `/etc/networks`, `/etc/host.conf`, `/etc/resolv.conf`, `/etc/HOSTNAME`, `/etc/hosts.allow`, `/etc/hosts.deny`, and the scripts in the `/etc/sysconfig/network-scripts` directory. You can either edit these files manually, or use `Linuxconf` to configure them.

- *Setting up PPP and SLIP.* You may use tools such as `chat` and `dip` to set up PPP and SLIP connections. You can also use the Red Hat Dialup Configuration Tool to set up PPP connections.

- *Monitoring network status.* You have to use tools such as `netstat` (to view information about active network connections), `/sbin/ifconfig` (to check the status of various network interfaces), and `ping` (to make sure that a connection is working).

- *Securing Internet services.* If your system is connected to the Internet (or if it is on an internal network), you have to secure the system against anyone who might use one of many Internet services to gain access to your system. Each service — such as e-mail, Web, or FTP — requires running a server program that responds to client requests arriving over the TCP/IP network. Some of these server programs have weaknesses that may enable an outsider to log into your system — maybe with root privileges. You have to turn off services that you do not need and also edit configuration files to restrict access to those services you are running.

Windows and Linux

As you probably know, MS-DOS and Microsoft Windows happen to be the most popular operating systems for 80386, 80486, and Pentium PCs. Because Linux started on 80386/80486 PCs, a connection between DOS/Windows and Linux has always existed. Typically, you start the Linux installation with some steps in DOS.

Linux has maintained its connection to DOS in several ways:

- Linux supports the older MS-DOS file system called FAT (file allocation table), as well as the newer Windows VFAT (long filenames) and FAT32 file systems. From Linux you can access MS-DOS and Windows files on the hard disk or a floppy disk.

- Linux includes a set of tools (called `mtools`) that manipulate MS-DOS files from within Linux.

- The DOSEMU project is building an MS-DOS emulator (see `http://www.dosemu.org/`) that uses the virtual 8086 mode of 80386 or better processors, much as Windows 95 and Windows 98 enable the user to run a DOS session within a window.

The DOSEMU project has already had some success, and many DOS applications (including WordPerfect 5.1 and FoxPro 2.0) can run under the DOS emulator.

An ongoing project called WINE is developing a free implementation of Windows for the X Window System under UNIX. Actually, WINE enables you to use your existing Windows 3.1/95/NT installation and run Windows 3.1/95/NT programs that you have installed on your PC's DOS partition. WINE works on many versions of UNIX, including Linux, FreeBSD, and Solaris.

Cross-Reference

Chapter 13 describes how you can access DOS from Linux, and explains the use of the `mtools` utilities.

Software Development in Linux

Of all its potential uses, Linux is particularly well suited to software development. Software-development tools, such as the compiler and libraries are included, because you need them anyway when you rebuild the Linux kernel. If you are a UNIX software developer, you already know UNIX, so you will feel right at home in Linux.

As far as the development environment goes, you have the same basic tools (such as an editor, a compiler, and a debugger) that you might use on other UNIX workstations, such as those from IBM, Sun Microsystems, and Hewlett-Packard (HP). Therefore, if you work by day on one of the mainstream UNIX workstations, you can use a Linux PC at home to duplicate that development environment at a fraction of the cost. Then you can either complete work projects at home or devote your time to software that you write for fun and then share on the Internet.

Just to give you a sense of Linux's software-development support, the following is a list of various features that make Linux a productive software-development environment:

- GNU's C compiler, gcc, which can compile ANSI-standard C programs.

- GNU's C++ compiler g++, which supports ANSI-standard C++ features.

- The GNU debugger, gdb, which enables you to step through your program to find problems and to determine where and how a program failed. (The failed program's memory image is saved in a file named core; gdb can examine this file.)

- The GNU profiling utility, gprof, which enables you to determine the degree to which a piece of software uses your computer's processor time.

- The GNU make utility, which enables you to compile and link large programs.

- Concurrent Versions System (CVS) and Revision Control System (RCS), which maintain version information and control access to the source files, so that two programmers don't modify the same source file inadvertently.

- The GNU Emacs editor, which prepares source files and even launches a compile-link process to build the program.

- The Perl scripting language, which you can use to write scripts that tie together many smaller programs with UNIX commands to accomplish a specific task.

- The Tool Command Language and its X toolkit (Tcl/Tk), which enable you to prototype X applications rapidly.

- The Python language, which is an interpreted language comparable to Perl and Tcl (the Red Hat Linux installation program, called anaconda, is written in Python).

- Dynamically linked shared libraries, which allow the actual program files to be much smaller, because all the library code that several programs may use is shared, with only one copy loaded in the system's memory.

- POSIX header files and libraries, which enable you to write portable programs.

Cross-Reference

Chapter 27 covers software development in Linux. Read Chapters 28 and 29 to learn about Perl and Tcl/Tk programming.

Linux as an Internet On-Ramp

You probably already have access to the Internet and have experienced what the Internet has to offer:

Electronic mail, newsgroups, and the World Wide Web (*WWW* or *the Web*). Whether you are in the "Been there, done that" camp or the "What's the Web?" camp, you may be happy to learn that a Red Hat Linux system includes everything you need to access the Internet. In fact, your PC can become a first-class citizen of the Internet, with its own Web server, on which you can publish any information you want.

Although Linux includes TCP/IP and supporting network software with which you can set up your PC as an Internet host, there is one catch: First, you have to obtain a physical connection to the Internet. Your Linux PC has to be connected to another *node* (which can be another computer or a networking device, such as a router) on the Internet. This requirement is the stumbling block for many people — an Internet connection costs money, with the price proportional to the data-transfer rate.

Many commercial ISPs provide various forms of physical connections to the Internet. In the U.S., if you are willing to spend between $15 and $30 a month, you can get an account on a PPP server. Then you can run PPP software on your Linux system, dial in, via a modem, and connect to the Internet at data-transfer rates ranging from 28,800 bits per second (bps) to 56,000 bps, depending on your modem.

Although a dial-up connection is adequate for accessing the Internet, receiving e-mail, and reading news, it may not be adequate if you want your system to provide information to other people through the Web or FTP (File Transfer Protocol). For that purpose, you need a connection that is available 24 hours a day, because other systems may try to access your system at any time of day. For a few hundred dollars a month you can get a dedicated PPP connection and make your system a permanent presence on the Internet. Other options that offer higher-capacity Internet connections than dial-up modems include cable modems and Digital Subscriber Line (DSL).

Another option for a small business — or for anyone who has a few networked PCs — is connecting a local-area network (LAN) to the Internet. You can run Linux on one of the PCs to accomplish this task. Typically, you would have an Ethernet LAN running TCP/IP connected to all of the PCs on the network, including the Linux machine. The Linux PC would set up a PPP connection to the Internet (via a dial-up or dedicated connection). You would then set up the Linux PC to act as a gateway between the Ethernet LAN and the Internet, so that the PCs on your LAN could access other systems on the Internet.

Cross-Reference

In Chapter 16 you learn how to configure your Linux system to access the Internet. More importantly, you learn how to use a Linux PC as your local network's gateway to the Internet.

Summary

Once you get Linux going on your PC, you can turn your attention to the work that you plan to do with it. Whether you want to develop software, or set up your PC as an Internet host, you can use Linux wisely if you know its overall capabilities. Accordingly, this chapter provides an overview of various aspects of Linux, ranging from software development to networking and system administration. In the next chapter, I show you how to install Red Hat Linux from this book's companion CD-ROMs and get started using Linux.

By reading this chapter, you learn the following:

▶ Linux is a freely available UNIX-like operating system that runs on a wide variety of systems. Red Hat Linux is a specific Linux distribution — a package incorporating the Linux operating system and a huge collection of applications, together with an easy-to-use installation program.

▶ Linux developers use a version number scheme to help you understand what the various versions of Linux kernel — the core operating system — mean. Kernel versions 2.$x.y$, where x is an even number, are stable versions. The number y is the *patch level,* which is incremented as problems are fixed. Versions 2.$x.y$, where x is an odd number, are beta releases for developers only — they may be unstable.

▶ POSIX stands for Portable Operating System Interface (abbreviated as POSIX to make it sound like UNIX). The Institute of Electrical and Electronics Engineers (IEEE) began developing the POSIX standards to promote the portability of applications across UNIX environments.

▶ This book's Red Hat Linux distribution comes with XFree86 (X Window System Version 11 Release 6, or X11R6), GNOME, and KDE software. After you install XFree86 and GNOME or KDE, you have a graphical user interface (GUI) for Linux. Additionally, X enables you to run applications across the network — which means that you can run applications on another system on the network and have the output appear on your Linux PC's display.

▶ Linux supports TCP/IP networking well. TCP/IP is the networking protocol of choice on the Internet. Therefore, a Linux PC is ideal as an Internet host providing services, such as FTP and the World Wide Web. You can also use the Linux PC as your Internet ramp by connecting to an Internet service provider through a dial-up TCP/IP connection and running a Web browser to surf the Net.

▶ The Red Hat Linux distribution on the companion CD-ROM also includes the `Linuxconf` tool, which enables you to perform most system- and network-administration tasks from a graphical user interface.

▶ Red Hat Linux includes all the software development tools you need to write UNIX and X applications. You'll find the GNU C and C++ compiler for compiling source files, `make` for automating the compiling, the `gdb` debugger for finding bugs, and Concurrent Versions System (CVS) and Revision Control System (RCS) for managing various revisions of a file. Thus, a Linux PC serves as the software developer's ideal workstation.

Chapter 2

Red Hat Linux Installation

In This Chapter

▶ Understanding the installation process for the Red Hat Linux CD-ROMs that accompany this book

▶ Learning what you need to know about your PC's hardware before installing Red Hat Linux

▶ Performing initial installation steps under MS-DOS or Windows

▶ Installing Red Hat Linux from the companion CD-ROMs

▶ Recovering from installation problems

Installation can be one of the trickier aspects of getting started with Red Hat Linux, especially if you have a no-name IBM-compatible PC. You need some specific information about hardware, such as the type of disk controller, video card, and CD-ROM drive. The Linux operating system controls the hardware through drivers (software through which the operating system accesses the hardware), so you need to make sure that the current release of Linux includes drivers for your hardware. If your hardware is popular enough, there's a good chance that someone has developed a driver for it. The version of Red Hat Linux on the companion CD-ROMs supports a wide variety of hardware, so all of your PC's peripherals are probably supported.

In this chapter, you learn how to install Red Hat Linux from the companion CD-ROMs. The chapter starts with an overview of the entire installation process; then it guides you step-by-step through the installation process.

Cross-Reference

If you have installed Red Hat Linux already, Chapter 10 shows you how to get started with Red Hat Linux.

Understanding the Red Hat Linux Installation Process

Before starting a big job, I always find it helpful to visualize the entire sequence of tasks that I must perform. The process is similar to studying a map before you drive to a place where you have never been. Red Hat Linux installation can be a big job, especially if you run into snags. This section shows you the road map for the installation process. After reading this section, you should be mentally prepared to install Red Hat Linux.

This chapter shows you the installation steps for the companion Red Hat Linux CD-ROMs. Here are the general steps for installing Red Hat Linux:

1. Gather information about your PC's hardware before you install Red Hat Linux. The Linux operating system accesses and uses various PC peripherals through software components called *drivers*. You have to make sure that the version of Red Hat Linux that you are about to install has the necessary drivers for your system's hardware configuration. Conversely, if you do not have a system yet, look at the list of hardware supported by Linux, and make sure that you buy a PC with components that Red Hat Linux supports.

2. Because most PCs come with Windows pre-installed on the hard disk, you will have to perform a process known as *partitioning* to allocate parts of your hard disk for use by Linux. If you have a spare hard disk, you may decide to keep MS-DOS and Windows on the first hard disk, and install Linux on the second hard disk. With a spare second disk, you don't need to worry about partitioning under DOS or Windows. If you have only one hard disk, however, you have to partition that disk into several parts. Use a part for DOS and Windows, and leave the rest for Linux. You should use the nondestructive repartitioning program FIPS to repartition your hard disk without destroying the existing contents. FIPS essentially creates a new partition, by shrinking the existing DOS partition. You can, of course, install Linux as the sole operating system on a PC; in that case, you can ignore this step and simply partition the disk under Linux. Finally, if you just want to try out Linux, you can also opt for the partionless installation method, where you can install Linux within a DOS/Windows partition. To do this, you simply specify / as the mount point for a DOS/Windows partition in the Disk Druid partitioning screen.

3. Under DOS or Windows, create a Linux boot disk. The boot disk is used to boot your PC and start an initial version of the Linux operating system. If you boot your PC under MS-DOS (it has to be MS-DOS only; not an MS-DOS prompt window in Windows 95/98/NT/2000), you can skip this step — instead, you can boot Linux directly from the CD-ROM. When you want to install directly from the CD-ROM, you must add the appropriate commands in AUTOEXEC.BAT and CONFIG.SYS, so that the CD-ROM drive is accessible from DOS.

4. Boot your PC with the Linux boot disk (or start MS-DOS and run a command from the CD-ROM). This procedure automatically loads the Linux kernel and runs, Anaconda, the Red Hat Linux installation program. From this point on, you will respond to a number of dialog boxes as the Red Hat installation program takes you through the steps. You have the option of using a text mode, or a graphical user interface (GUI). You have to use the text mode if, for some reason, the installation program fails to start the X Window System. Additionally, you have to use expert mode

installation if you want to exercise greater control over the installation, or if the Linux kernel does not detect some of the hardware, such as the SCSI controller and network adapter installed in your system. In expert mode, you have to identify your SCSI controller and network adapter by selecting them from a list of supported devices.

5. Respond to the dialog box that asks you to choose a language. From subsequent dialog boxes, you select the keyboard type and the mouse type. If you have already placed the CD-ROM in the CD-ROM drive, the installation program uses the CD-ROM as the source of all Red Hat Linux files. Otherwise, the installation program starts in text mode and displays a dialog box from which you have to select the storage medium in which the Red Hat Linux files are located.

6. Select whether you want to install a new system, or upgrade an existing installation. For a new installation, you also have to decide whether you want to set up a workstation, a server, a laptop, or a custom system. Select a custom installation for maximum flexibility.

7. Prepare the hard disk partitions on which you plan to install Linux. If you have created space for Linux by reducing the size of an existing DOS partition, now you have to create the partitions for Linux. Typically, you need at least two partitions: one for the Linux files and the other for use as the *swap partition*, which is a form of virtual memory. To perform this step, the installation program runs Red Hat's disk-management utility called Disk Druid. The installation program gives you the option of using the Linux `fdisk` command, or Disk Druid. You should use Disk Druid, because it's easier to use than `fdisk`.

8. Using Disk Druid, create the necessary hard disk partitions, indicate which partition is the swap partition, and specify the partition on which you want to install Linux (this is called the *root partition*). You also get a chance to mount other disk partitions, such as any existing DOS partitions. Mounting a partition associates a physical disk partition with a directory in the Linux file system.

9. Select the partitions that you want to format for Red Hat Linux.

10. Specify options for installing the Linux Loader (LILO) program on your hard disk, so you can boot Linux when you power up your PC after shutting it down. You can also enable an option to create a boot disk that you can use to boot your Linux system if you have problems booting from the hard disk.

11. If the initial Linux kernel detects a network card (assuming you have one installed on your system), the installation program lets you configure the network (the local area network, not the dial-up network). If the Linux kernel does not detect your network card, you can use expert mode and select your network card from a list. To configure the network, you specify a number of parameters, including an IP address, a host name, IP address of name servers, and a domain name for your Linux system. You also configure the firewall security level for your system.

12. Specify the local time zone.

13. Select a root password. The root user is the super user — a user who can do anything — in Linux. You can also add one or more other users.

14. Select various software package groups to install. Each package represents a part of Red Hat Linux, from the base operating system, to components such as the GNOME and KDE graphical desktops, the Emacs editor, programming tools, the Perl scripting language, and the X Window System (a graphical windowing system that is required by GNOME and KDE). You simply select the packages you need and let the Red Hat installation program do its job.

15. Configure the X Window System. In response to dialog boxes presented by the installation program, you provide information about your video card and monitor. In most cases, the installation program automatically detects the video card and the monitor. The installation program also lets you enable graphical login, so that when you boot your Linux system, it will display a graphical login window and, after you enter your user name and password, start the GNOME or KDE graphical desktop after successful login.

16. The installation program formats the disk partitions and installs the selected packages.

17. Create a boot disk that you can use to boot your Red Hat Linux system if the Linux kernel on the hard disk is damaged, or if LILO — the Linux Loader — does not work.

18. If you find that Linux does not work properly with one or more of your system components (such as the network card or sound card), you may have to reconfigure the Linux operating system to add support for those system components.

The following sections guide you through the basic installation steps and the initial booting of Linux.

Note

Your PC must have a CD-ROM drive — one that is supported by Linux — in order to install Linux from this book's companion CD-ROM. If your PC does not have a CD-ROM drive, but your PC is on a network, you can use another PC's CD-ROM drive and install Linux over the network using NFS or FTP. To install over the network, you must use a different boot disk — one that contains the `bootnet.img` file from the `\images` directory of the Red Hat Linux CD-ROM.

Preparing Your PC for Linux Installation

Before you install Linux, you should prepare your PC for the installation. You can be in either of two situations:

- You already have a PC that runs one of the popular PC operating systems, such as MS-DOS, Microsoft Windows 3.1, Windows 95/98/NT/2000, or OS/2.

- You are about to buy a new PC, and you plan to run Red Hat Linux on that PC, at least some of the time.

If you are about to purchase a PC, you are lucky because you can get a PC configured with peripherals that Red Hat Linux supports. To pick a Red Hat Linux-compatible configuration, simply consult the current list of hardware that Red Hat Linux supports, and then select a PC that includes supported hardware components. You may have to ask the PC vendor explicitly for detailed information about peripherals, such as the video card, CD-ROM drive, and networking card, to ensure that you can use the peripherals under Red Hat Linux. Selecting a PC with Red Hat Linux-supported hardware greatly minimizes the potential for problems installing Red Hat Linux. The next few sections list the hardware that Red Hat Linux supports.

You can also buy a PC with Red Hat Linux already installed on it. For example, Dell sells Red Hat Linux PCs, Hewlett-Packard offers Red Hat Linux on its NetServer systems, and IBM has been offering Red Hat Linux on its NetFinity Internet servers.

If you want to install Red Hat Linux on an existing PC, verify that the latest Red Hat Linux distribution supports all of the hardware on your PC. In other words, you have to take an inventory of your PC's hardware components and determine whether Red Hat Linux currently supports any of them.

Taking Stock of Your PC's Components

Like many other operating systems, Linux supports various types of hardware through device drivers. For each type of peripheral device, such as a networking card or a CD-ROM drive, Linux needs a driver. In fact, each kind of peripheral needs a separate driver. Because Linux is available free (or relatively inexpensively), and because many programmers scattered throughout the world cooperate to develop Linux, you cannot demand support for a specific kind of hardware. You can only hope that someone who can write a Linux driver has the same hardware that you do. In all likelihood, that person will write a driver, which eventually will find its way into a version of Linux; then you can use that hardware under Linux. It may take a while for Linux to support new interfaces.

Check the list of hardware that the version of Red Hat Linux on the companion CD-ROM supports (this list is summarized in the next few sections). You can install and run Linux, even if no Linux drivers are available for certain peripherals. At minimum, however, to install Red Hat Linux from the companion CD-ROM, you must have a Linux-compatible processor, bus type, hard disk, keyboard, and CD-ROM drive. If you want to run the X Window System and graphical desktops, such as GNOME or KDE, you also must ensure that XFree86 (the X server for Linux) supports the mouse, the video card, and the monitor. (Chapter 3 tells you all about X.)

Red Hat categorizes all hardware into three tiers:

- *Tier 1* hardware is fully supported. The installation program automatically detects Tier 1 hardware and installs the appropriate drivers.

- *Tier 2* hardware should be detected and is usable in Linux, but some users have reported problems, such as the Linux kernel not being able to detect some versions of the hardware. To support Tier 2 hardware, you may have to perform some explicit steps, such as manually loading the driver module or editing the /etc/modules.conf file.

- *Tier 3* hardware may be compatible with Linux, but is not officially supported by Red Hat Linux.

Finally, Red Hat also has an *Incompatible* category that includes hardware that is known to not work with Red Hat Linux.

The following sections provide an overview of the hardware that the version of Red Hat Linux on the companion CD-ROMs supports. The list of hardware is not grouped according to Red Hat's three tiers. For the most recent (and more detailed) list of hardware supported by Red Hat Linux, as well as the tier in which a specific hardware belongs, visit Red Hat's Web site at http://www.redhat.com/support/hardware/.

Cross-Reference

Chapters 3 through 9 cover all PC hardware in detail. Turn to those chapters for more information about whether Linux supports your system's unique hardware configuration. In these chapters, you also can find information about how to get the most from your PC's hardware under Linux.

Processor

The *processor* is the central processing unit (CPU) — the integrated circuit chip that performs all the processing in the PC. At minimum, you need an Intel 80386 processor to run Linux. Any Intel 80386-, 80486-, Celeron-, and Pentium-compatible processor can run the Linux operating system. Among the compatibles, Linux can run on AMD K5, K6, Athlon, and Cyrix, and IBM processors. Linux also supports motherboards with multiple processors. The installation program detects multiprocessor systems and installs the correct Symmetric Multiprocessing (SMP) Linux kernel on the system.

The 80x86 family of processors uses a *floating-point processor* (also known as a *math coprocessor*) to speed floating-point computations. In many 486 and Pentium processors, the floating-point processor is part of the basic processor. Linux uses the hardware floating-point processor, if available. Otherwise, Linux emulates the floating-point processor with software that is part of the Linux kernel.

Bus

The *bus* is the standard electrical connection between the processor and its peripherals. Several types of PC buses exist. After the processor, the bus is the most critical hardware characteristic of a PC. Each type of bus specifies the meaning of various signals, and the *protocol* (the order and timing of signals) for transferring data over the bus.

Each bus has a maximum rate of data transfer, which depends on how many bits of data the bus can carry at a time and on the *clock rate* — how many times a second the signal can change between two states (0 and 1). Like a processor's internal clock rate, the bus clock rate is expressed in megahertz (MHz). One megahertz means a million times a second.

Each bus type specifies the physical dimensions of the controller card, the number and purpose of the connectors, and the slot on the motherboard in which you plug in the card. Your system's hard disk, for example, is connected to the motherboard by means of a disk-controller card that is compatible with the bus type of that motherboard.

Following are several popular bus types:

■ The *Industry Standard Architecture (ISA)* bus was once the most widely used bus (until the PCI bus came along); the ISA bus was used in the original IBM PC-AT. The ISA bus can transfer data 16 bits at a time; it operates at an 8-MHz clock rate, which is slow compared with today's processors, which have clock rates in the 200–500 MHz range. Typically, the ISA bus can achieve a data-transfer rate of 5MB/sec (5 megabytes per second).

■ The *Video Electronics Standard Association (VESA) Local Bus*, or *VLB*, was designed for high-performance data transfer between the processor and the video card. The typical VLB transfer rate is 30MB/sec. Note that early VLB systems often have a nonstandard implementation of the VESA local bus, which may cause problems with Linux.

■ The *Micro Channel Architecture (MCA)* bus is IBM's proprietary bus, which first appeared in the PS/2 PCs. IBM designed this bus as a high-speed bus, but its proprietary nature kept it from being widely used in PCs.

■ The *Extended Industry Standard Architecture (EISA)* bus came about as an alternative to the MCA bus, with performance comparable to that of the MCA. The EISA bus is not widely used because the EISA bus peripheral cards are more expensive than their ISA bus counterparts. EISA bus performance is comparable to that of the VLB, transferring data at rates of 30MB/sec.

■ The *Peripheral Component Interconnect (PCI)* bus is the latest high-performance bus; it operates at a clock rate of 33 MHz and can transfer up to 64 bits of data at a time (newer versions of the PCI bus can operate at clock speeds of 66 or 100 MHz). When a PCI bus is used to transfer 32 bits at a time, the 33-MHz clock rate implies that the bus can transfer data at the rate of $33 \times 4 = 132$MB per second (notice that 32 bits = 4 bytes). PCI is the up-and-coming standard; the current crop of Pentium PCs use the PCI bus, but also offer ISA bus slots, so that you can continue to use ISA cards. Typically, the PCI bus achieves a data-transfer rate of 60MB/sec.

■ The *Accelerated Graphics Port (AGP)* is designed for the movement of large blocks of data between the PC's video card and the system's memory. AGP provides a peak data transfer rate of 528MB/sec in 32-bit blocks. AGP is widely used in high-performance 3D video cards.

- The *Universal Serial Bus (USB)* is a serial bus designed to connect devices such as a keyboard, mouse, and joystick to PCs. With USB, you can connect up to 127 peripherals to a computer without using different interrupts and IO addresses. USB supports a data transmission rate of 12Mbps (12 million bits per second), although many peripherals use a lower 1.5Mbps rate.

Linux supports ISA, VLB, EISA, PCI, AGP, and USB buses; the version of Linux on the companion CD-ROM can be installed and run on systems that have any of these buses. Because a bus is meant for connecting peripherals to the system, support for a bus implies that you can use peripherals that use controller cards of that bus type.

Cross-Reference

Of course, not all peripheral hardware (such as the video card and disk controller) for all these buses works under Linux. Each peripheral requires a driver, and the driver may not yet exist for some newer video cards or disk controllers. You can find more information about specific devices in Chapters 3 through 9.

Memory

Commonly referred to as *random-access memory* or *RAM*, memory is not a factor in compatibility. You do, however, need at least 32MB of RAM to get good performance. Although you may be able to install and run Linux on a PC that has 16MB RAM, you cannot run the X Window System efficiently on that PC. The X Window System manages the graphical user interface through an *X server*, which is a large program that needs a lot of memory to run efficiently.

Tip

Red Hat recommends a minimum of 16MB RAM for the text-mode installation, and 24MB or more for the graphical installation program. To run a graphical desktop, such as GNOME or KDE, Red Hat suggests that you have 48MB or more RAM.

Secret

If you are buying a new PC, it'll probably come with at least 32MB of RAM, if not 64MB or more. If you have an old PC with less than 16MB of RAM, you may want to add some more memory to bring the total up to at least 32MB. The more physical memory a system has, the more efficiently it runs multiple programs, because the programs can all fit in memory. Although Linux can use a part of the hard disk as virtual memory, such disk-based memory is much slower than physical memory. The amount of physical memory required depends on the size of the Linux operating system and on any other software that you have to run all the time, such as the X Window System. Although Linux alone would run on 16MB of memory, you need at least 32MB to run X. Add to this any applications (such as editor or compiler) that you might run, and you'll soon see why you need at least 32MB of RAM for adequate performance. Of course, the more physical memory, the better the system performs. For example, a Linux system with 128MB of RAM will perform better than one with 64MB, or less. When setting up a Linux system as a server (for example, a mail server), you should configure the system with at least 128 or 256MB of RAM.

Video card and monitor

Most PCs have what is known as *Super VGA (Video Graphics Array)* video cards. Linux works fine with all video cards in text mode. But when it comes to XFree86 — the Linux version of the X Window System — the story is quite different. If XFree86 does not support your video card explicitly, you have to work hard to get XFree86 configured for your video card.

The kind of monitor that you use is not particularly critical, but it must be capable of displaying at the screen resolutions that the video card uses, which are expressed in terms of the number of picture elements, or *pixels*, horizontally and vertically (such as $1,024 \times 768$).

Generally, XFree86's support for a video card depends on the *video chipset* — the integrated circuit that controls the monitor and causes the monitor to display output. You can find out the name of the video chipset used in a video card from the card's documentation. A video-card manufacturer, however, may use a video chipset in a nonstandard manner. In such a case, you need a special XFree86 server to support that video card.

Red Hat Linux 7.1 comes with both XFree86 3.3.6 servers and XFree86 4.0.3 servers. XFree86 3.3.6 supports a wide variety of video cards and chipsets by using a number of different X servers. XFree86 4.0.3 uses a single X server that can load video drivers and other modules. The X server supports a specific card by loading a video driver designed for that card. Unfortunately, XFree86 4.0.3 does not yet come with video drivers for as many video cards. As you install Red Hat Linux, the Red Hat Linux installation program automatically detects the video chipset as it sets up the X Window System. The Red Hat installation program selects from version 3.3.6 or 4.0.3 the X server that best supports your video card.

To see a list of video cards that XFree86 version 3.3.6 supports, check the Web page at `http://www.xfree86.org/cardlist.html`. To learn about the status of driver and video card support in XFree86 4.0.3 compared with that in XFree86 3.3.6, visit the Web page at `http://www.xfree86.org/4.0.3/Status.html`. That page provides links to XFree86 4.0.3 driver status information for the following video card and chipset vendors: 3Dfx, 3Dlabs, Alliance, ARK Logic, ATI, Avance Logic, Chips and Technologies, Cirrus Logic, Compaq/Digital, Cyrix, Epson, Genoa, IBM, IIT, Intel, Matrox, MX, NCR, NeoMagic, NVIDIA, Number Nine, Oak Technologies Inc, Paradise/Western Digital, RealTek, Rendition/Micron, S3, Silicon Integrated Systems (SiS), Silicon Motion, Inc., Trident Microsystems, Tseng Labs, Video 7, and Weitek.

Cross-Reference

Although you will go through an X configuration step during Red Hat Linux installation, you will find further details on configuring XFree86 in Chapter 3.

Hard drive

Linux supports any hard drive that your PC's *Basic Input and Output System (BIOS)* supports. In many older 386 and 486 PCs, you had to use a separate driver to access large hard drives — the system BIOS could not handle these drives. You can't install Linux on such systems. In short, Linux supports your hard drive only if the system BIOS supports the hard drive without any additional drivers.

For hard drives connected to your PC through a SCSI controller card, Linux must have a driver that enables the SCSI controller to access and use the hard drive (for more information, see the "SCSI controllers" section of this chapter).

Tip

The only key decision about the hard drive is its capacity. To install a reasonable selection of packages from the Red Hat Linux distribution, you need at least 1GB of hard drive space. You need more space if you want to leave Windows installed on the PC. Therefore, if your PC has an IDE interface and one small hard disk (1GB or smaller), you may want to add a second hard drive because most IDE controllers can support two hard drives. If you have a SCSI card, you can connect as many as seven or fifteen SCSI devices to it.

If you are buying a new PC, keep in mind that a complete Linux installation (with all the Red Hat packages) takes nearly 1.7GB of disk space. On top of that, you'll need some disk space for your work. Luckily, most new PCs come with disk sizes ranging anywhere from 2GB to 20GB. Any of these disk sizes is large enough, so you can keep Windows on one of the partitions, and then have the option of booting either Windows or Linux.

Tip

Consider buying a second hard drive for Linux. A second drive makes the installation process considerably less risky, because you do not have to use FDISK or FIPS partition the drive on which Windows 95/98 may be installed.

Floppy disk drive

As they do for the hard drive, Linux drivers use the PC BIOS to access the floppy disk drive. Therefore, your floppy disk drive is compatible with Linux. You may, however, have to boot Linux from a floppy disk drive during the installation. For this purpose, you need a high-density 3.5" (1.44MB-capacity) floppy disk drive. You can avoid booting from a floppy, provided you can boot your PC under MS-DOS (not an MS-DOS window under Windows 95/98/NT/2000), and you can access the CD-ROM from the DOS command prompt.

Keyboard and mouse

Linux supports any keyboard that already works with your PC. The mouse, however, needs explicit support in Linux. You need a mouse if you want to configure and run XFree86, the X Window System for Linux.

Linux supports the following popular mice:

- Any PS/2 (auxiliary device) mouse
- ATI XL Inport bus mouse
- Logitech bus mouse
- Logitech Mouseman serial mouse

- Logitech serial mouse
- Microsoft bus mouse
- Microsoft Intellimouse
- Microsoft serial mouse
- Mouse Systems serial mouse
- QuickPort (C&T 82C710) mouse (used on TI Travelmate and Toshiba laptop PCs)

Linux also supports touchpad devices, such as Alps Glidepoint, as long as they are compatible with one of the supported mice.

SCSI controller

The Small Computer System Interface, commonly called *SCSI* (and pronounced *scuzzy*), is a standard way of connecting many types of peripheral devices to a computer. SCSI is used in many kinds of computers, from high-end UNIX workstations to PCs. To use a SCSI device on your PC, you need a SCSI controller card that plugs into one of the connector slots on your PC's bus. Typically, you connect hard drives and CD-ROM drives through a *SCSI controller*. A single SCSI controller supports device addresses 0 through 7, with 7 usually assigned to the controller itself. This means that you can connect as many as seven to fifteen SCSI devices to your PC. If you want to access and use a SCSI device under Linux, you have to make sure that Linux supports your SCSI controller card.

The Red Hat Linux release on the companion CD-ROMs supports many popular SCSI controllers through loadable driver modules. For the latest list of supported SCSI controllers, visit http://www.redhat.com/support/hardware/.

The PC BIOS

All IBM-compatible PCs come with a Basic Input and Output System (BIOS) built into read-only memory (ROM). The BIOS contains a set of input/output (I/O) functions for accessing the PC's peripheral devices, such as the keyboard, display, printer, serial port, and floppy disk or hard drive.

The BIOS is essentially software stored on ROM and, as such, PC vendors revise and update the BIOS just like any software. Typically, the BIOS is revised to handle new devices, such as new hard drives with much larger capacities than originally envisioned, or even new bus types such as PCI. BIOS revisions may also improve performance, by doing various tasks more efficiently.

Because the BIOS is a crucial element in getting Linux to work with a PC's peripherals, you might consider a BIOS upgrade to get Linux going on an older 386 or 486 PC. The upgrade process involves replacing a pair of chips with new ones — you'll have to contact your BIOS's manufacturer to get new revisions of the BIOS chips compatible with your PC.

Note that you may need to know such settings as the interrupt request number (IRQ) and I/O port address of your SCSI controller. The Red Hat Linux installation program loads a SCSI driver module for your SCSI controller, and the installation program is supposed to find the settings by probing the controller. However, if it fails to probe correctly, you have to specify the settings yourself.

CD-ROM drive

CD-ROM (Compact Disc Read-Only Memory) drives are popular because each CD-ROM can hold up to 650MB of data. This is a relatively large amount of storage, compared to a floppy disk. CD-ROMs are reliable and inexpensive to manufacture. Vendors can use a CD-ROM to distribute a large amount of information at a reasonable cost.

This book provides Linux on a CD-ROM, so you need a CD-ROM drive to install the software. Most new PCs come with a CD-ROM drive. If the basic configuration does not include a CD-ROM drive, you can add one at a fraction of the cost of your PC — usually around one hundred U.S. dollars. If you have an older PC that doesn't have a CD-ROM drive, you need to buy one to install Linux from this book's companion CD-ROM.

CD-ROM drives became popular over the past few years when users went for the multimedia experience. As you may know, in the context of the PC, *multimedia* refers to the use of multiple media — sound, images, animation, and video — in software applications. The sound card and CD-ROM drive were the two common elements of all multimedia software.

The combination of sound cards and CD-ROM drives has been so popular that many sound cards (such as Creative Labs' Sound Blaster Pro) were sold with a CD-ROM drive. You had to connect the CD-ROM drive with a cable to the sound card, which included the appropriate hardware connector. Linux supports CD-ROM drives (such as the Sound Blaster Pro CD) that connect to a sound card.

Nowadays, most CD-ROM drives use the *Enhanced Integrated Drive Electronics (EIDE)* interface that also connects hard disk drives to the PC. Linux supports all EIDE CD-ROM drives. The EIDE interface is also referred to as the *AT Attachment Packet Interface (ATAPI, or simply ATA)*.

Some CD-ROM drives are SCSI devices that connect to a SCSI controller card. Linux supports a SCSI CD-ROM drive, as long as it has a driver for the SCSI controller.

The Red Hat Linux installation program can automatically detect and support the following common CD-ROM drives (all CD-ROM drives besides the first two types are proprietary drives that require special drivers):

- Any EIDE CD-ROM drive (also referred to as ATAPI or ATA drives)
- Any SCSI CD-ROM drive that can transfer data in blocks of 512 or 2,048 bytes (this includes most of the CD-ROM drives on the market)
- Creative Labs CD-200(F)

- Funai E2550UA/MK4015

- IBM External ISA CD-ROM drive

- Kotobuki/Matsushita/Panasonic CD-ROM drive models CR-521, CR-522, CR-523, CR-562, and CR-563 (the CD-ROM drives bundled with the Sound Blaster Pro sound card)

- Longshine LCS-7260

- Sound Blaster (SBPCD for NON-IDE)

- Teac CD-55A SuperQuad

The following proprietary CD-ROM drives should also work, but you may have to specify install-time options to load the appropriate driver:

- Aztech CDA268-01A, Orchid CDS-3110, and Okano/Wearnes CDD-110, Conrad TXC, CyCDROM CR520ie, CyCDROM CR540ie, CyCDROM CR940ie

- GoldStar R420

- ISP16, MAD16, or Mozart sound card (OPTi 82C928 and OPTi 82C929) with Sanyo/Panasonic, Sony, or Mitsumi drives

- Lasermate CR328A

- LMS/Philips internal CD-ROM drive 206 connected to a cm260 host adapter card

- Mitsumi CD-ROM drive (CR DC LU05S, FX001D/F)

- NEC CDR-260

- Optics Storage Dolphin 8000AT

- Sanyo CDR-H94A

- Sony CDU-31A, CDU-33A, CDU-510, CDU-515, CDU-535, CDU-531

Tip

The Sound Blaster 16 sound card features one of two CD-ROM interfaces: a proprietary interface and a SCSI interface. Linux supports both interfaces, but you need to know which interface your Sound Blaster 16 board provides. You can find this information in the manual that accompanies the Sound Blaster 16 board.

Note that you can connect an ATAPI CD-ROM drive to an IDE controller and treat it as a second hard drive. If you want a simple way to attach a CD-ROM drive to your PC and you don't need an additional hard drive, you might consider installing an ATAPI CD-ROM drive as a slave of the boot hard drive.

Sound card

On PCs, sound cards and CD-ROM drives go hand-in-hand because most CD-ROM-based multimedia programs include sound effects that you can enjoy only if you have a sound card. Under Linux, you also can play sound on the sound card. If you have a sound card, you can play audio CDs.

The sndconfig tool in Red Hat Linux can configure the following sound cards:

- Acer Notebook Sound
- AdLib
- Advance Logic ALS-007
- Compaq Deskpro XL sound
- Crystal CS423x sound chip
- Ensoniq Audio PCI 1370 (SoundBlaster 64/128 PCI), Creative/ Ensoniq Audio PCI 1371, Ensoniq SoundScape
- ESS688 AudioDrive, ESS1688 AudioDrive, ESS1868 AudioDrive
- Gravis UltraSound, Gravis UltraSound MAX, Gravis UltraSound PnP
- Logitech SoundMan Games (not SM16 or SM Wave)
- MediaTrix AudioTrix Pro (MT-0002-PC Control Chip)
- MediaVision Jazz16 (ProSonic, SoundMan Wave)
- Mozart/MAD16 (OPTi 82C928)
- MAD16 Pro (OPTi 82C929/82C930)
- miroSOUND PCM12
- OPL3-SA1 sound chip and OPL3-SA2/3/x sound chip
- Pro Audio Spectrum/Studio 16, Logitech SoundMan 16
- PSS (Orchid SW32, Cardinal DSP16)
- S3 SonicVibes
- Sound Blaster , Sound Blaster DS, Sound Blaster Pro, Sound Blaster 16/PNP, Sound Blaster 32/64 AWE
- Turtle Beach MultiSound Classic/Monterey/Tahiti, Turtle Beach MultiSound Pinnacle/Fiji
- Windows Sound System (AD1848/CS4248/CS4231)

Network adapter

A network adapter is necessary only if you are going to connect your Linux PC to a local area network (usually an Ethernet network). Linux supports a variety of Ethernet network adapters. Arcnet and IBM's token-ring network are also supported.

The Red Hat Linux installation program automatically detects and loads the driver for the following Ethernet cards:

- 3Com Etherlink III (3c509 EISA)
- 3Com 3c59x, 3c900, 3c905, 3c579 (3c905B and 3c905C are reported to work when the autonegotiation feature is disabled and the card is set for 10Mbps)

- Digital DE425, DE434, DE435, DE450, DE500 (uses DE4x5)

- Digital 2104x, 2114x Tulip chip cards: Digital 21x4x Tulip PCI Ethernet cards, SMC EtherPower 10 PCI(8432T/8432BT), SMC EtherPower 10/100 PCI(9332DST), DEC EtherWorks 100/10 PCI(DE500-XA), DEC EtherWorks 10 PCI(DE450), DEC QSILVER's, Znyx 312 etherarray, D-Link DFE500-Tx (21140-A with DP83840 transceiver), D-Link DFE-540TX, C-NET CNE-935 (21041), Allied Telesis LA100PCI-T, Danpex EN-9400, Cogent EM110, Lite-On Communications LNE100TX, Kingston EtherX KNT40T (21040), Kingston EtherX KNE100TX (21140AE), Kingston EtherX CP 10/100TX PCI, KNE-1100-TX, Netgear FA-310-TX

- Intel 82559 EEpro100 cards (Pro/100+ Server adapter, Pro/100+ Management adapter, Intel Pro/100+ Dual Port adapter), EtherExpress i82557/i82558 PCI Pro/10+

You can also use any of the following Ethernet cards, but you have to use the expert mode installation and manually select the card from a list:

- 3Com 3c503, 3c503/16, 3c505, 3Com Etherlink 16 (3c507)

- 100VG-AnyLan Network Adapters, HP J2585B, J2585A, J2970, J2973, J2573,Compex ReadyLink ENET100-VG4 & FreedomLine 100/VG

- Aironet Arlan 655

- Allied Telesis AT1500 (uses Lance driver), AMD Lance/PCnet, HP J2405A, NE2100, NE2500

- Allied Telesis AT1700

- Alteon AceNIC Gigabit Ethernet Driver

- AMD PCnet32 and AMD PCnetPCI

- Ansel Communications AC3200 EISA

- Apricot Xen-II, 680x0 VME (82596 chipset)

- AT&T GIS WaveLAN ISA

- Cabletron E21xx

- Compaq Netelligent 10/100 TX PCI UTP, 10 T PCI UTP, Compaq Integrated NetFlex 3/P, Compaq Netelligent Dual 10/100 TX PCI UTP, Compaq Netelligent Integrated 10/100 TX UTP, Compaq Netelligent 10/100 TX Embedded UTP, Compaq Netelligent 10 T/2 PCI UTP/Coax, Compaq Netelligent 10/100 TX UTP, Compaq NetFlex 3/P

- Comtrol Hostess SV11

- Crystal LAN CS8900/CS8920

- Digi Intl. RightSwitch SE-X EISA and PCI

- Digital 2104x,2114x Tulip chip cards: Accton EtherDuo PCI, Accton EN1207, Cogent EM100, Cogent EM110, Cogent EM400, Cogent EM960, Cogent EM964 Quartet (Four ports), Danpex EN-9400P3, Adaptec

ANA6901/C, Adaptec ANA6911/TX, Linksys EtherPCI, Surecom EP-320X, DEC 21140, Thomas Conrad TC5048, Znyx ZX312, Znyx ZX314, Znyx ZX315 EtherArray, Znyx ZX342, ZNYX ZX344, Znyx ZX345, Znyx ZX346, ZNYX ZX348, ZNYX ZX351

- Digital DEPCA & EtherWORKS, DE100, DE101, DE200 Turbo, DE201 Turbo, DE202 Turbo, DE210, DE422

- D-Link DE600, DE620 pocket adapters

- D-Link DFE-530-TX PCI 10/100, VIA Rhine PCI Fast Ethernet cards with either the VIA VT86c100A Rhine-II PC or 3043 Rhine-I

- EtherWORKS 3 (DE203, DE204, and DE205)

- Fujitsu FMV-181/182/183/184

- G-NIC PCI Gigabit Ethernet adapterZ8530 based HDLC cards for AX.25

- HP AnyLAN, 10/100VG, PCLAN (J2577, J2573, 27248B)

- HP PC-LAN Plus, HP PC-LAN (27245B and 27xxx series)

- ICL Etherteam 16i/32 EISA

- Intel EtherExpress 16

- Intel EtherExpress i82595 Pro10/10+ (ISA only)

- MiCom-Interlan NI5010 ethercard

- Mylex LNE390 EISA cards (LNE390A, LNE390B)

- NE1000/2000 and compatible ISA cards

- NE2000 (PCI), RealTEk RTL-8029, Winbond 89C940, Compex RL2000, KTI ET32P2, NetVin NV5000SC, Via 82C926, SureCom NE3

- NI5210 card (i82586 Ethernet chip), NI6510, ni6510 EtherBlaster

- Novell NE3210 EISA Network Adapter

- Packet Engines Yellowfin (and compatibles)

- Racal-Interlan ES3210 EISA Network Adapter

- RealTek cards using RTL8129 or RTL8139 Fast Ethernet chipsets

- RedCreek Communications PCI

- Sangoma S502/S508 multi-protocol FR, Sangoma S502A, ES502A, S502E, S503, S507, S508, S509

- SMC Ultra/EtherEZ (ISA, 8k 83c790), SMC 9000 series, SMC 9000 series, SMC Ultra32 EISA (32K) SMC EtherPower II 9432 PCI (83c170/175 EPIC series)

- Tangent ATB-II, Novel NL-10000, Daystar Digital LT-200, Dayna DL2000, DaynaTalk PC (HL), COPS LT-95, Farallon PhoneNET PC II & III

- Western Digital WD8003, WD8013

Cross-Reference

If you plan to use Linux on a stand-alone PC at home, you can use Point-to-Point Protocol (PPP) to connect to the Internet over a dial-up connection through an Internet Service Provider (ISP). See Chapter 16 for details.

Making a Hardware Checklist

Now that you have seen a summary of various hardware peripherals that Red Hat Linux supports, you should have a rough idea of whether you have the right PC hardware to use it. If you are buying a new PC to run Red Hat Linux, the hardware list should help you decide the hardware configuration of your new PC.

To summarize, go through the following checklist to see whether or not you are ready to install Red Hat Linux:

- Does your PC have an 80386 or better processor, with the ISA, EISA, VLB, MCA, or PCI bus; at least 32MB of RAM; a high-density floppy disk drive; and a large hard drive (at least 1GB)? Remember that if you plan to run both Windows 95 and Red Hat Linux on your PC, you need at least 2GB of disk space.

- Does your PC have a CD-ROM drive that Red Hat Linux supports? (You need a CD-ROM drive to install Red Hat Linux from this book's companion CD-ROM.)

- Can you get a second hard drive? (If so, you can install Red Hat Linux on that hard drive. Installing Red Hat Linux on a second drive prevents you from having to repartition your first hard drive, which usually has MS-DOS or Windows loaded on it.)

- If you have a SCSI controller with any SCSI devices that you want to use under Red Linux, is the SCSI controller supported by Linux?

- Is your video card supported by XFree86? (If not, you won't be able to set up and run the X Window System.)

- Does XFree86 support your mouse? (If not, you won't be able to set up and run the X Window System.)

As the comments after the questions indicate, you do not necessarily have to answer yes to each question. You must answer yes to the first two items, however, because without that basic hardware configuration, Red Hat Linux cannot run on your system.

Note

If you plan to install Red Hat Linux on an empty second hard disk or you want to install Linux in an existing DOS/Windows partition, you do not have to go through the process of partitioning (dividing) your hard disk under MS-DOS. You can skip the next few sections and proceed to "Creating the Red Hat Boot Disk." Then you can boot Linux from the boot disk and partition the second hard drive for use under Linux.

Repartitioning Your Hard Drive with FIPS

If your PC has a single hard disk drive, chances are good that you have Microsoft Windows 95/98/2000 (maybe even Windows 3.1) installed on that drive. If your hard drive is at least 2GB, I recommend that you keep Windows installed on your system, even if you want to work mostly in Linux. After all, you have to perform some of the Linux installation steps under MS-DOS or Windows. Moreover, you can access the Windows files from Linux. You get the best of both worlds if you keep MS-DOS and Windows around when you install Linux.

Typically, your PC hard disk is set up as a single large drive, designated by the drive letter C. Unless you can scrounge up a second hard disk for your PC, or you already have a second disk, your first task is to divide your one and only hard disk to make room for Linux.

There are two ways to repartition your hard disk:

- Destroy the existing partition and create two smaller, new partitions — one for Windows and the other for Linux. This requires you to back up and restore the existing Windows files. This is the hard way to repartition a hard disk.

- Use the FIPS program (included on the first companion CD-ROM) to resize the existing partition and free up space for a second partition on which you can install Linux.

In this section, you learn how to repartition your hard disk using FIPS (the easiest way to create a new partition for Linux). The idea is to shrink the existing DOS partition and create room for the Linux partition. Later on, during Linux installation, you have to further divide the partition meant for Linux into two parts: one for the Linux root file system and the other for swap space.

Working in MS-DOS or Windows Before You Install Linux

If you are an MS-DOS or Windows beginner, you may find it difficult to follow some of the Linux installation steps that you have to perform under MS-DOS. Following are some of the terms and concepts that you need to understand in order to perform the necessary installation steps:

- **Boot floppy drive** — The first floppy drive (A) is the boot floppy drive. If you put a floppy disk in the A drive and turn on the

power, your PC automatically tries to start from the floppy disk. (Many new PCs allow you to set the boot device; however, by default, nearly all PCs come configured with the first, and in many cases the only, floppy drive as the boot device.) This feature is built into the computer and does not depend on which operating system is installed on your system's hard disk. In most new systems, the A drive is a

3.5-inch floppy drive. Many older systems, however, use a 5.25-inch floppy drive as A. To install Linux, you need a high-density, 3.5-inch boot floppy drive (a 5.25-inch high-density floppy does not have enough storage space for the Linux boot file).

- **Partitions** — A physical hard drive can be divided into several parts, each of which can be treated as a separate logical hard drive. Although most new PCs use the entire hard disk as a single drive, you can partition the disk into up to four sections, called the *four primary partitions*. To install Linux on your hard disk, you have to create at least two partitions for Linux — one partition for the Linux file system and the other for swap space (virtual memory in which the contents of the physical memory can be stored temporarily). If you want to keep Windows in one partition and also install Linux, you need three partitions.

- **Repartitioning a hard disk** — If your hard disk has only one partition, the process of creating more partitions is referred to as *repartitioning*. To repartition a disk, you have to back up its contents. Then you need to use the MS-DOS FDISK command to delete the old partition and create several new ones, and finally restore the old contents to one of the partitions. The Red Hat Linux distribution (on this book's CD-ROM) includes an MS-DOS program called FIPS that you can use to repartition a hard disk without destroying the contents of the old partition. The utility is not guaranteed to work perfectly, however. Therefore, you still need to back up your important files before attempting to repartition the hard disk with FIPS.

- **Formatting a disk** — The MS-DOS FDISK program only defines a section of the physical disk to be used by an operating system, such as MS-DOS. You still have to prepare that section of disk before

MS-DOS can use it to store files and directories. Formatting is the process of making a partition ready for a file system.

- **Directories and files** — In MS-DOS, a drive is divided into directories. Each directory, in turn, can contain other directories and files. The file is where actual information is stored. The directories help you organize your documents and programs. All files for the Windows operating system, for example, are usually in the C:\WINDOWS directory. The directory C:\WINDOWS\SYSTEM contains some special files that Windows needs. As you can see, the backslash character is used as a separator between names of directories. The directory C:\ is known as the *root directory*; WINDOWS is a subdirectory of the root directory, and SYSTEM is a subdirectory of WINDOWS. Therefore, C:\WINDOWS\SYSTEM is two levels down from the root directory.

- **Filenames** — An MS-DOS filename consists of 1 to 8 characters, followed by a period and then an optional extension, which can have 0 to 3 characters. Therefore, README.TXT is an MS-DOS filename with the name README and the extension TXT. Executable programs have the COM or EXE extension, whereas DOC typically represents a document that can be opened by a word-processing program.

- **MS-DOS commands** — You use MS-DOS through commands you enter at a prompt. The MS-DOS command interpreter displays a prompt (usually the current drive and directory name, followed by a greater-than sign, such as C:\>). MS-DOS commands often have options that start with a slash. You can use the /S option with the FORMAT command, for example, to format and copy the system files to a disk. Note that you can use the MS-DOS commands even under Windows 95 in an MS-DOS window.

Red Hat Linux comes with a utility program called FIPS (The **F**irst **N**ondestructive **I**nteractive **P**artition **S**plitting Program) that can split an existing primary DOS partition into two partitions. FIPS cordons off the unused part of a hard disk, making a new partition out of it, without destroying any existing data.

Tip

Although you have no guarantee that FIPS will split a DOS partition successfully, you may consider using it to create room for Red Hat Linux, especially if you have a brand-new PC with only DOS and Windows installed on the hard disk. In this case, even if something goes wrong with FIPS, you can reinstall Windows and the applications. I always use FIPS to split the DOS partition on a new PC's hard disk and create room for Linux. Before using FIPS, make sure that the hard disk has enough free space to install Linux. You need 1GB to 2GB of free space for a useful Red Hat Linux installation.

The FIPS.EXE program and related files are located in the \DOSUTIL subdirectory of the first CD-ROM. To use FIPS, follow these steps:

1. For FIPS to work, all used areas of the disk must be contiguous, or at least as tightly packed as possible. You can prepare the disk for FIPS by running a defragmenter. In MS-DOS 6.0 or later, use the program DEFRAG to defragment the disk. In Windows 95/98, click the right mouse button on the disk symbol in the Explorer window, select Properties from the pop-up menu, click the Properties tab, and then click the Defragment Now button. Another way to start the defragmenter is to select Start ➪ Programs ➪ Accessories ➪ System Tools ➪ Disk Defragmenter. You also should check the hard disk for errors by running a program such as Norton Disk Doctor (in Windows 95/98, use SCANDISK). If you happen to have it, use Norton Speed Disk to defragment the hard disk because it's significantly faster than the DEFRAG utility.

2. Create a bootable disk, using the command FORMAT A: /S. In Windows 95/98, create a startup disk by using the Add/Remove Programs option in the Control Panel, and then following the instructions in the Startup Disk tab.

3. Copy the following files from the CD-ROM to the formatted disk (the following example assumes that D: is the CD-ROM drive):

```
COPY D:\DOSUTILS\FIPS.EXE A:

COPY D:\DOSUTILS\RESTORRB.EXE A:

COPY D:\DOSUTILS\FIPSDOCS\ERRORS.TXT A:
```

   FIPS.EXE is the program that splits partitions. ERRORS.TXT is a list of FIPS error messages. You consult this list for an explanation of any error messages displayed by FIPS. RESTORRB.EXE is a program that allows you to restore certain important parts of your hard disk from a backup of those areas created by FIPS.

4. Leave the bootable disk in the A drive, and restart the PC. The PC boots from A and displays the A\> prompt.

5. Type FIPS. The FIPS program runs and shows you information about your hard disk. FIPS gives you an opportunity to save a backup copy of important disk areas before proceeding. After that, FIPS displays the first free cylinder on which the new partition can start (as well as the size of the partition, in megabytes). Figure 2-1 shows the output of the FIPS program at this stage.

```
Sectors per FAT: 256
Sectors per track: 63
Drive heads: 255
Hidden sectors: 63
Number of sectors (long): 4192902
Physical drive number: 80h
Signature: 29h

Checking boot sector ... OK
Checking FAT ... OK
Searching for free space ... OK

Do you want to make a backup copy of your root and boot sector before
proceeding (y/n)? y
Do you have a bootable floppy disk in drive A: as described in the
documentation (y/n)? y

Writing file a:\rootboot.000

Enter start cylinder for new partition (17 - 260):

Use the cursor keys to choose the cylinder, <enter> to continue

Old partition     Cylinder     New Partition
 1059.0 MB           135          988.4 MB
```

Figure 2-1: The FIPS program, prompting the user for a new partition size

6. Use the left and right arrow keys to adjust the starting cylinder of the new partition (the one that results from splitting the existing partition) to change the partition size. Press the right arrow to increase the starting cylinder number (this leaves more room in the existing partition and reduces the size of the new partition you are creating).

7. When you are satisfied with the size of the new partition, press Enter. FIPS displays the modified partition table and prompts you to enter **C** to continue or **R** to reedit the partition table.

8. Press **C** to continue. FIPS displays some information about the disk and asks whether you want to write the new partition information to the disk.

9. Press **Y**. FIPS writes the new partition table to the hard disk and then exits.

Remove the disk from the A drive, and reboot the PC. When the system comes up, everything in your hard disk should be intact, but the C drive will be smaller. You have created a new partition from the unused parts of the old C drive.

You needn't do anything with the newly created partition under DOS. Later, in the "Partitioning and Using the Hard Disk" section, you'll learn how to use the new partition under Linux.

Creating the Red Hat Boot Disk

After you repartition the hard disk and make room for Linux, you can begin the next step of installing Linux from this book's CD-ROM: creating the Red Hat boot disk. (For this step, you should turn on your PC without any disk in the A drive, and then run Windows as usual.)

Tip

You do not need the Red Hat boot disk if you can boot your PC from the CD-ROM. You may have to go into the SETUP mode as the PC powers up and change the boot device to the CD-ROM. If you can boot directly from the first companion CD-ROM, skip this section and proceed to the section entitled "Booting Linux for Installation."

Like the MS-DOS or Windows boot disk, the Red Hat boot disk is used to start your PC, start Linux, and run the Red Hat installation program. Once you have installed Red Hat Linux, you will no longer need the Red Hat boot disk (except in an emergency when you need to reinstall Red Hat Linux from the CD-ROMs).

The Red Hat boot disk contains an initial version of Linux that you use to start Linux, prepare the hard disk, and load the rest of the files from the CD-ROMs to the hard disk. Creating the Red Hat boot disk involves using a utility program called RAWRITE.EXE to copy a special file called the Red Hat Linux *boot image* to a disk.

To create the Red Hat boot disk under Windows, follow these steps:

1. Open an MS-DOS window (select Start ⇨ Programs ⇨ MS-DOS Prompt).

2. In the MS-DOS window, enter the following commands at the MS-DOS prompt (my comments are in parentheses, and your input is in boldface):

   d: *(use the drive letter for the CD-ROM drive)*

   cd \dosutils

   rawrite

   Enter disk image source file name: **\images\boot.img**

   Enter target diskette drive: **a**

   Please insert a formatted diskette into drive A: and press -ENTER-:

3. As instructed, you should put a formatted disk into your PC's A drive and then press Enter. RAWRITE copies the boot-image file to the disk.

After you see the DOS prompt again, you can take the Red Hat boot disk out of the A drive and (if you haven't done so already) label it appropriately. A label such as *Red Hat Linux Boot Disk* would work.

Secret

If you are installing Red Hat Linux on a laptop and the CD-ROM drive is connected to a PCMCIA adapter, you must prepare a different boot disk for PCMCIA support. To prepare the PCMCIA boot disk, follow the same steps as the ones for the Red Hat boot disk, but specify \images\pcmcia.img as the image filename. Note that you do not need the PCMCIA boot disk if you are installing on a laptop using the laptop's built-in CD-ROM drive.

Installing Linux over a Network Using NFS

You can install Linux from another system on a network, provided both systems are on the network, and the other system has the Red Hat distribution on a directory that's exported through the Network File System (NFS). This installation option is useful if your PC does not have a CD-ROM drive, but does have network access. In that case, you can mount the Red Hat Linux CD-ROM on another system that has a CD-ROM drive and that supports NFS.

To perform an NFS installation, you must be knowledgeable about NFS, or ask for the help of someone who manages the network. You have to create a boot floppy disk with the `bootnet.img` file (instead of the `boot.img` file used for CD-ROM installation). After you use that boot floppy, designate NFS as the installation method and provide information about your network card and the network, including the IP addresses of your PC, gateway, and name server. Next, specify the NFS server's name or IP address and the server's directory containing the Red Hat distribution. Then, you can proceed with the usual installation steps.

Booting Linux for Installation

The Red Hat Linux installation program runs under Linux; therefore, you need to run Linux on your PC before you can go through the installation steps. This initial version of Linux can come from a boot floppy, or the CD-ROM itself. The initial Linux operating system, in turn, runs the installation program, which prepares the disk partitions and copies all necessary files from the CD-ROM to the disk.

You can boot your PC with an initial version of the Linux operating system in one of the following ways:

- Boot your PC from the first CD-ROM (this works only if your PC is bootable from the CD-ROM).

- Load Linux by executing the AUTOBOOT.BAT command file (from the DOSUTILS directory of the CD-ROM) while your PC is running MS-DOS. Boot your PC from the Linux boot floppy you created earlier.

The following sections describe these two approaches to booting Linux and initiating the Red Hat installation.

Booting Linux from the Red Hat CD-ROM

Most new PCs can boot directly from the CD-ROM. To do so, you have to go into SETUP as the PC powers up. The exact steps for entering SETUP depends on the PC, but it typically involves pressing a key such as F2. As the PC powers up, a brief message should tell you what key to press to enter SETUP. Once in SETUP, you can designate the CD-ROM drive as the boot device.

After your PC is set up to boot directly from the CD-ROM drive, place the first Red Hat Linux CD-ROM into the CD-ROM drive and reboot the PC. The PC should power up and start the Linux kernel from the CD-ROM. After Linux starts from the CD-ROM, the Red Hat installation program begins to run. The section "Installing Linux from the Red Hat CD-ROM" describes this process in detail.

Starting Linux from the Red Hat CD-ROM

You can start Linux directly from the CD-ROM while your PC is running MS-DOS. An MS-DOS program called LOADLIN.EXE can load a Linux kernel into memory and begin running Linux. The Linux kernel itself is in another file. You do not need to understand all of the details about how LOADLIN starts Linux. In fact, the Red Hat CD-ROM provides a DOS batch file, AUTOBOOT.BAT, in the \DOSUTILS directory that runs LOADLIN with appropriate arguments.

Note

You can use AUTOBOOT to start Linux directly from the CD-ROM only if your PC is running MS-DOS alone (not an MS-DOS window under Windows 95). In addition, you must be able to use the CD-ROM from MS-DOS. If your PC runs Windows 95, select Shutdown from the Start menu and then click the button labeled Restart the Computer in MS-DOS Mode. From the DOS prompt, try to see the directory of the CD-ROM with the command DIR *D*: where *D* is the drive letter of the CD-ROM drive. If this works, then you can start Linux directly from the CD-ROM. Otherwise, you have to use a boot floppy.

To start Linux, place the Red Hat CD-ROM in the CD-ROM drive and use the following commands from the DOS prompt:

```
D:              (use the drive letter for the CD-ROM drive)
cd \dosutils
autoboot
```

After Linux starts, the Red Hat installation program begins to run. The section "Installing Linux from the Red Hat CD-ROM" describes this process in detail.

Secret

The AUTOBOOT.BAT file runs the LOADLIN program with two arguments: the name of a Linux kernel file and a file that contains an initial file system (known as initial RAM disk, or *initrd,* because this file system is loaded into memory). If the autoboot command gives you an error message, type the following command to run loadlin and start Linux from the CD-ROM:

```
loadlin autoboot\vmlinuz initrd=autoboot\initrd.img
```

Booting from a Floppy

To start Linux for installation, put the Linux boot floppy in your PC's A drive and restart your PC (press the reset button, or press Ctrl+Alt+Delete, or in Windows 95/98, select Start ⇨ Shutdown and then select Restart from the dialog box). Your PC will go through its normal startup sequence, such as checking memory and running the ROM BIOS code. Then the PC loads Linux from the floppy and begins running the Red Hat installation program.

Watching the Boot Process

A few moments after you start the boot process, an initial screen appears — the screen displays a welcome message and ends with a `boot:` prompt. The welcome message tells you that help is available by pressing one of the function keys, F1 through F5.

If you want to read the help screens, press the function key corresponding to the help you want. If you don't press any keys, after a minute the boot process will proceed with the loading of the Linux kernel into the PC's memory. To start booting Linux immediately, press Enter. After the Linux kernel loads, it automatically starts the Red Hat Linux installation program, which, in turn, starts the X Window System and provides a graphical user interface (GUI) for the installation.

Tip

As the Linux kernel begins to run, various messages appear on the screen. These boot messages tell you whether the Linux kernel has detected your hardware. The messages typically flash by too quickly for you to follow. Afterwards, the screen shows a dialog box with a welcome message and some helpful information about the installation. At this point, you can read the messages about your hardware by pressing Alt+F4 — this switches the display to another virtual screen where all kernel messages appear in a form slightly different than what you see on the main installation screen. In particular, look for a message about the CD-ROM, because the kernel has to detect the CD-ROM in order to proceed with the rest of the installation. To return to the main installation screen, press Alt+F1.

Installing Linux from the Red Hat CD-ROM

After you start the initial version of Linux following the procedures described in the section "Booting Linux for Installation," Linux runs the Red Hat Linux installation program from the CD-ROM. The rest of the installation occurs under the control of the installation program.

Interacting with the Red Hat Installation Program

The default Red Hat installation program uses a graphical user interface. You can go through the installation steps by pointing and clicking with the mouse.

If the X Window System-based graphical interface fails to start, type `text` at the boot prompt to activate the text-mode interface that was common to the pre-6.1 versions of Red Hat Linux. In text mode, the Red Hat installation program uses a full-screen text-based interface. Each screen typically presents a dialog box with various elements, such as lists of items from which you select one or more buttons to indicate action. Typically, the buttons are labeled OK and Cancel. The bottom of the screen displays a help message that shows you how to navigate around the text screen.

Instead of a mouse, you use specific keys to move the text cursor. Consult Table 2-1 for the keystrokes to use for specific actions.

Table 2-1	Interacting with the Red Hat Installation Program in Text Mode
Keystrokes	*Action*
Arrow keys	Moves from one item to the next in a dialog box
Tab	Moves forward to the next item in a dialog box
Alt+Tab	Moves backward to the previous item in a dialog box
Spacebar	Selects the item on which the cursor rests. If the item is already selected, it turns the selection off. Thus, the spacebar toggles the selection.
Enter	Presses the button on which the cursor rests. If the dialog box has a single button, pressing Enter is equivalent to pressing that button.
F12	Accepts current values and proceeds to the next dialog box. This is equivalent to pressing the OK button.

Monitoring the Installation Process

As the installation progresses, you will primarily be responding to various dialog boxes, entering information the installation program needs. The installation program displays useful information about a number of virtual consoles — these are screens of text in memory that you can view on the physical screen, by pressing the key sequences shown in Table 2-2.

Tip

You will work mostly in the main console — virtual console 1. To switch to another virtual console, press the appropriate keystroke shown in Table 2-2. For example, to view the install log on virtual console 3, press Ctrl+Alt+F3. After you are done viewing the log, press Ctrl+Alt+F1 to return to the main console so you can continue with the installation.

Typically, you will get by without ever having to switch to the other screens, but if something goes wrong, you can switch to the install log screen, by pressing Ctrl+Alt+F3, where you can get more information about the problem.

Table 2-2   Virtual Consoles During Red Hat Linux Installation

Virtual Console	Keystroke	Description
1	Ctrl+Alt+F1	This is the main console on which the installation program displays the text-based user interface through which you install Linux.
2	Ctrl+Alt+F2	This console displays a shell prompt from which you can use Linux commands to monitor the progress of installation. The shell prompt appears only after you insert the CD-ROM and press Enter in response to a dialog box displayed by the installation program.
3	Ctrl+Alt+F3	This is the install log. Messages from the installation program appear here.
4	Ctrl+Alt+F4	The Linux kernel displays its messages on this console. After Linux initially boots, you may want to switch to this console to see the kernel messages, because they include information about hardware that Linux detects in your PC.
5	Ctrl+Alt+F5	This console shows the output of any other programs run during the installation process.
7	Ctrl+Alt+F7	This is where the installation program displays the X Window System-based graphical user interface.

Understanding the Red Hat Installation Phases

Installing Linux is a lengthy process with the following major phases:

1. **Getting Ready to Install** — Choose the language to be used during the installation process. Indicate the type of keyboard. If you haven't already placed the first Red Hat CD-ROM into the CD-ROM drive, you also have to specify the media from which Red Hat Linux is to be loaded (for example, the CD-ROM). After the graphical installation screen appears, you have to configure the mouse. Then specify whether you are installing or upgrading and, if you are installing, the type of installation: workstation, server, or custom. I show a custom system installation in this chapter.

2. **Partitioning and Using the Hard Disk** — This step is to prepare the hard disk space that you plan to use for Red Hat Linux. Partition the disk using Disk Druid or the Linux `fdisk` command. At minimum, you have two partitions — you should specify one of the partitions to be used as swap area; the other partition will hold the Linux root directory (represented

by /). The partitions are also formatted before use. Red Hat includes the Disk Druid program to perform all the steps in this phase of installation.

3. **Configuring Linux** — In this phase you specify where the Linux Loader (LILO) should be loaded and decide whether to create a boot disk. You set up the TCP/IP network, the firewall, the language support, the time zone, and specify a password for the root — the super user. You can also add other users when you set the root password. The final configuration step is to set up the authentication mechanism.

4. **Selecting the Package Groups to Install** — Select which packages of Red Hat Linux — such as X Window System, GNOME desktop, Emacs editor, and Web server — you want to install. After you select the packages, the installation program configures the X Window System and then installs the selected packages on the hard disk.

5. **Completing the Installation** — Configure the X Window System. This is the X configuration that will be used when you reboot the system after the installation finishes. You conclude this configuration step by creating a boot disk.

If you have all configuration information handy (such as video card, monitor, network card details, IP addresses, and host names for the TCP/IP network configuration), and all goes well, installing Linux from the companion CD-ROM on a fast (166MHz or better) Pentium PC should take approximately an hour (assuming that you select nearly all packages). For example, on a 200MHz Pentium PC with 64MB RAM and a 2GB-disk partition devoted to Linux, the entire installation took about 40 minutes. On older 486 PCs, the installation process may take somewhat longer.

The Red Hat installation program probes — attempts to determine the presence of — specific hardware, and tailors the installation steps accordingly. For example, if the installation program detects a network card, the program automatically displays the screens on which you can configure the TCP/IP network. Therefore, you may see some variation in the sequence of steps, depending on your specific hardware configuration.

The following sections describe each of the Red Hat Linux installation phases in detail.

Getting Ready to Install

In this phase, you perform the following steps before moving on to disk setup and the actual installation of Linux:

1. A text screen appears with a welcome message. The message tells you what to do to start the installation in several different modes. You can press Enter to begin installing in GUI mode or type text to install in text mode. If you have a SCSI controller or network card that the Linux kernel may not automatically detect, you should type expert isa to install in

expert mode (in this case, you have to select the hardware from a list, or provide a driver disk). Typically, you would press Enter to continue the installation in GUI mode.

2. The installation program starts the X Window System and displays a list of languages to be used during the installation (see Figure 2-2). The list includes languages such as English, French, German, Icelandic, Italian, Norwegian, Romanian, Russian, Slovak, Spanish, and Ukrainian. Use your mouse to select the language you want to use for the installation screens.

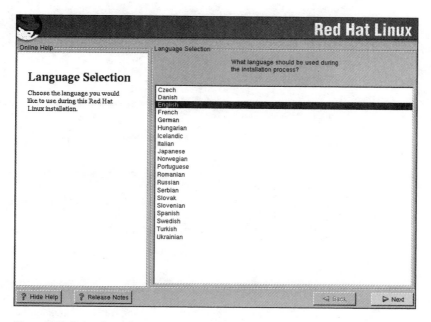

Figure 2-2: Selecting a language at the beginning of Red Hat Linux installation

When you're done, click the Next button to proceed to the next step.

Note that in the graphical mode installation, each screen has online help available on the left side of the screen. You can read the help message to learn more about what you are supposed to select in a specific screen.

3. The installation program displays a list of keyboard types, as shown in Figure 2-3.

Select a keyboard model that closely matches your PC's keyboard. If you don't see your keyboard model listed, select one of the generic models: Generic 101-key PC or Generic 104-key PC (newer keyboards with the Windows keys match this model). Next, select a keyboard layout that depends on your language's character set (for example, U.S. English in the United States). Finally, select the Enable Dead Keys option if the language you selected has special characters that have to be composed by pressing multiple keys in sequence. For English, you can safely disable dead keys.

Note that you can always reconfigure your keyboard after finishing the installation. Simply log in as root at a text console (you can get one by pressing, for example, Ctrl+Alt+F2) and type setup. This runs a text-mode setup utility that enables you to configure, among other things, the keyboard, the mouse, and the X Window System.

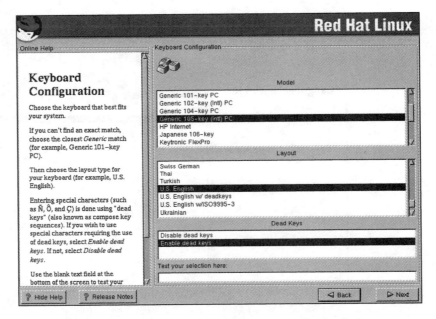

Figure 2-3: Selecting a keyboard type during Red Hat Linux installation

4. The installation program displays a screen (see Figure 2-4) from which you can configure the mouse in your system.

   The various mouse types are listed in a tree structure organized alphabetically by manufacturer. You need to know your mouse type and whether it is connected to the PC's serial port or the PS/2 port (this uses a small round connector). If your mouse type appears in the list, select it. Otherwise, select a generic mouse type. Most new PCs have a PS/2 mouse. Finally, for a two-button mouse, you should select the Emulate 3 Buttons option. Because many X applications assume that you are using a three-button mouse, go ahead and select this option. On a typical two-button mouse, you can simulate a middle-button click, by pressing both buttons simultaneously. On a Microsoft Intellimouse, the wheel acts as the middle button.

If you select a mouse with a serial interface, you have to specify the serial port where the mouse is connected. For COM1, specify /dev/ttyS0 as the device; for COM2, the device name is /dev/ttyS1.

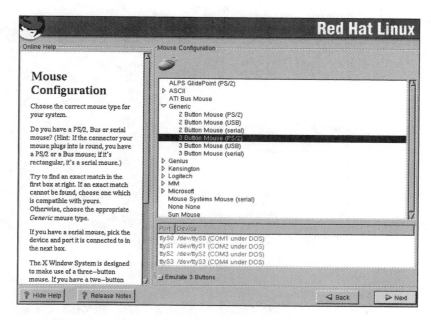

Figure 2-4: Configuring your mouse

5. The installation program displays a welcome message that provides some helpful information, including a suggestion that online manuals are available at http://www.redhat.com.

6. The installation program displays a screen (see Figure 2-5) asking if you want to install a new system, or upgrade an older Red Hat installation. Assuming that you are installing for the first time, make sure the cursor is on the Install button, and press Enter.

   For a full installation, the installation program requires you to select the installation class: Workstation, Server, Laptop, or Custom. The Workstation and Server installations simplify the installation process by partitioning the disk in a predefined manner. A Workstation-class installation deletes all currently existing Linux-related partitions and creates new partitions for the Linux root file system and swap space. A Server-class installation deletes all existing disk partitions, including any Windows partitions, and creates new partitions for Linux. All in all, the Server-class installation requires approximately 1.6GB of disk space. A Laptop installation is similar to a Workstation installation, except that it's for a laptop PC. For maximum flexibility, select the Custom installation.

   The next major phase of installation involves partitioning the hard disk for use in Linux.

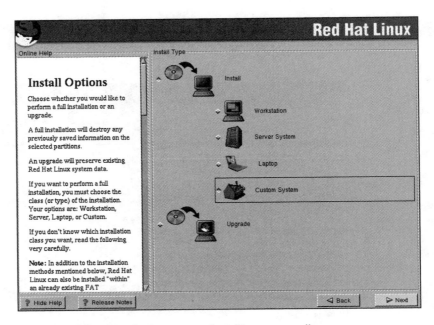

Figure 2-5: Selecting whether you are installing or upgrading

Partitioning and Using the Hard Disk

Like MS-DOS, Linux requires you to partition and prepare a hard disk before you can install Linux. You usually do not perform this step, because when you buy your PC from a vendor, the vendor takes care of preparing the hard disk and installing Windows and all other applications on the hard disk. Because you are installing Linux from scratch, however, you have to perform this crucial step yourself. As you see in the following sections, this task is just a matter of following instructions.

When the Red Hat Linux installation program reaches the disk partitioning phase, it displays a screen that gives you three options to partition and use the hard disk:

- **Automatic partition** — This option causes the Red Hat installation program to remove all existing Linux partitions on all disks and then create new partitions for installing Linux.

- **Disk Druid** — This is a Red Hat utility program that uses a graphical user interface to enable you to partition the disk and, at the same time, specify which parts of the Linux file system are to be loaded on which partition.

- **fdisk** — This is the Linux disk partitioning program, similar in concept to the DOS FDISK command, but with many more capabilities. When you use the Linux fdisk program, you have to type cryptic one-letter commands to manipulate disk partitions. Once you learn the commands, however, you may find `fdisk` more powerful than Disk Druid. For example, Disk Druid does not easily let you change the partition type, which indicates the type of file system to be stored on the partition, but you can easily change the partition type with `fdisk`.

Cross-Reference

This chapter explains how to use Disk Druid to prepare and use the disk partitions for Red Hat Linux installation. You will learn about `fdisk` in Chapter 4.

Before you begin to use Disk Druid to partition your disk, you need to know how to refer to the disk drives and partitions in Linux. You should also understand the terms *mount points* and *swap partition*. The next three sections describe these terms and concepts and, then proceed to describe Disk Druid.

Disk names in Linux

The first step is to understand how Linux refers to the various disks. Linux treats all devices as files and has actual files that represent each device. In Linux, these *device files* are located in the /dev directory. If you are new to UNIX, you may not yet know about UNIX filenames, but you will learn more as you continue to use Linux. Linux filenames are similar to MS-DOS filenames, except they do not use drive letters (such as A and C) and they substitute the slash (/) for the MS-DOS backslash (\) as the separator between directory names.

Because Linux treats a device as a file in the /dev directory, the hard disk names start with /dev. Table 2-3 lists the hard disk and floppy drive names that you may have to use.

Table 2-3   Hard Disk and Floppy Drive Names

Name	Description
/dev/hda	First Integrated Drive Electronics (IDE) hard drive (the C drive in DOS and Windows)
/dev/hdb	Second IDE hard drive
/dev/sda	First Small Computer System Interface (SCSI) drive
/dev/sdb	Second SCSI drive
/dev/fd0	First floppy drive (the A drive in DOS)
/dev/fd1	Second floppy drive (the B drive in DOS)

When you use the Red Hat Disk Druid or Linux `fdisk` program to prepare the Linux partitions, you have to identify the disk drive by its name, such as /dev/hda.

Tip

When Disk Druid or `fdisk` displays the list of partitions, the partition names are of the form /dev/hda1, /dev/hda2, etc. Linux constructs each partition name by appending the partition number (1 through 4 for the four primary partitions on a hard disk) to the disk's name. Therefore, if your PC's single IDE hard drive has two partitions, the installation program uses /dev/hda1 and /dev/hda2 as the names of these partitions. Table 2-4 shows some more examples of hard disk partition names in Linux.

Table 2-4   Hard Disk Partition Names

Name	Partition
/dev/hda1	First primary partition of first IDE drive
/dev/hda2	Second primary partition of first IDE drive
/dev/hda3	Third primary partition of first IDE drive
/dev/hda4	Fourth primary partition of first IDE drive
/dev/hda5	First logical partition of first IDE drive
/dev/hda6	Second logical partition of first IDE drive
/dev/hdb1	First primary partition of second IDE drive
/dev/sda1	First primary partition of first SCSI drive
/dev/sda2	Second primary partition of first SCSI drive
/dev/sdb1	First primary partition of second SCSI drive
/dev/sdc1	First primary partition of third SCSI drive

Mount point

In Linux, you use a physical disk partition by associating it with a specific part of the file system, which is a hierarchical arrangement of directories — a directory tree. If you have more than one disk partition (you may have a second disk with a Linux partition), you can use all of them in Linux under a single directory tree. All you have to do is decide which part of the Linux directory tree should be located on each partition — a process known in Linux as *mounting a file system on a device* (the disk partition is a device).

Note

The term *mount point* refers to the directory you associate with a disk partition, or any other device.

Suppose that you have two disks on your PC, and you have created Linux partitions on both disks. Figure 2-6 illustrates how you can mount different parts of the Linux directory tree (the file system) on these two partitions.

Swap partition

Most advanced operating systems support the concept of *virtual memory*, in which part of your system's hard disk is used as an extension of the physical memory (RAM). When the operating system runs out of physical memory, it can move (or swap out) the contents of currently unneeded parts of RAM to make room for a program that needs more memory. As soon as the time comes to access anything in the swapped-out data, the operating system has to find something else to swap out, and then it swaps in the required data from disk. This process of swapping data back and forth between the RAM and the disk is also known as *paging*.

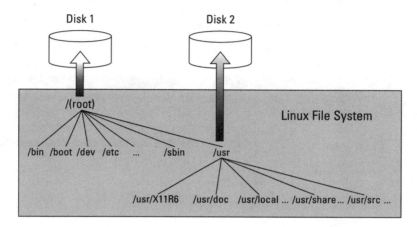

Figure 2-6: An example of mounting the Linux file system on two disk partitions

Because the disk is much slower than RAM, the system's performance is slower when the operating system has to perform a lot of paging, but virtual memory enables you to run programs that you wouldn't otherwise be able to run.

Linux supports virtual memory and can make use of a swap partition. When you create the Linux partitions, you should create a swap partition too. With the Disk Druid utility program, described in the next section, it is simple to create a swap partition. Simply mark a partition type as a swap device and Disk Druid will perform the necessary tasks.

Disk preparation

As you get ready to prepare the disk for Linux installation, you should see the Disk Druid screen, as shown in Figure 2-7. The exact appearance of this screen depends on your hard disk's current partitions.

Disk Druid gathers information about the hard drives on your system and displays a list of disk drives and the current partition information for one of the drives, as shown in Figure 2-7. For each partition, Disk Druid shows five fields:

- **Mount Point** indicates the directory in which the partition will be mounted. For example, if you have only one partition for the entire Linux file system, the mount point will be the root directory (/). For the swap partition, this field shows <Swap>. If this field appears as <not set>, you have to specify a mount point. To do so, select the partition and click the Edit button.

- **Device** refers to the partition's device name. For example, hda1 is the first partition on the first IDE drive.

- **Requested** shows how much space the partition has. For example, if the partition has 256MB of space, this field appears as 256M.

- **Actual** shows the amount of disk space the partition is using. Usually, the Requested and Actual fields are the same, but they may be different for partitions that can grow in size.

- **Type** shows the partition's type, such as Linux Native or DOS.

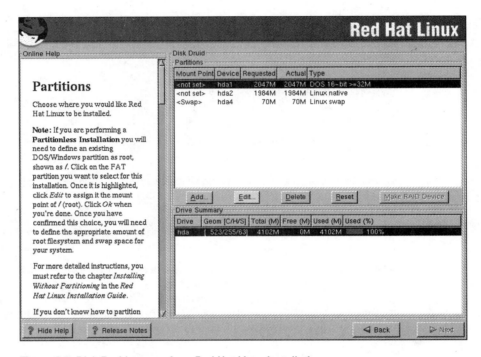

Figure 2-7: Disk Druid screen from Red Hat Linux installation program

You perform specific disk setup tasks in Disk Druid through the five buttons that run across the bottom of the dialog box. Specifically, the buttons perform the following actions:

- **Add** lets you create a new partition, assuming there is enough free disk space available to create a partition. When you click this button, another dialog box appears, in which you can fill in information necessary to create a partition.

- **Edit** lets you alter the attributes of the partition currently highlighted in the Partitions list. You make changes to the current attribute in another dialog box that appears when you click the Edit button.

- **Delete** is used to delete the partition currently highlighted in the Partitions list.

- **Reset** causes Disk Druid to ignore any changes that you may have made.

- **Make RAID Device** is used to set up a RAID (Redundant Array of Independent Disks) device — a technique that combines multiple disks to improve reliability and data transfer rates. There are several types of RAID configurations. This button is active only if your system has the hardware necessary to support a RAID device.

Tip

Exactly what you do in Disk Druid depends on the hard drives in your PC and the partitions they already have. If you want to install Linux in an existing DOS/Windows partition, click on that partition in the list and then click the Edit button. In the resulting Edition Partition dialog box, specify / as the mount point for that partition. You should also indicate the number of megabytes you want to allocate for the Linux file system.

For this discussion, I will assume that you want to install Linux in a dedicated hard disk partition and that you have created the necessary hard disk space for Linux by one of the following methods:

- You started with a single hard drive with a single partition (only the C drive in Windows). Then you used FIPS to split that partition into two (refer to the "Repartitioning Your Hard Drive with FIPS" section). After partitioning, you ended up with two DOS partitions.

- Your PC had a single large hard drive (greater than 2GB) that had two partitions (the C and D drives in Windows). In this case, the second partition is an empty extended partition that contains the logical drive D. You want to install Linux on the extended partition that used to be the D drive in Windows.

Both of these situations call for the same sequence of steps:

1. Delete the DOS partition — the one with enough space for Linux installation, not the one on which Windows is installed.

2. Create two Linux partitions out of the available disk space — one for swap space and the other for the Linux file system.

The next section covers the specific steps that you perform in Disk Druid to set up the minimum number of partitions that Linux needs. You can prepare other disk partitions (if you have a second hard drive, for example) following the steps outlined in the next section.

Setting up the partitions

To prepare an existing DOS partition for Linux, you have to perform the following steps in Disk Druid (for further guidance on setting up the partitions, see the sidebar "Setting Aside Space for the Linux File System"):

1. Delete the DOS partition that you want to use for Linux. To do this, select the partition (this will typically be the one with device name hda2 or hda3) from the Partitions list and then click the Delete button. Before

deleting the partition, remember to make a note of the partition's size from the Partitions list.

2. Create a new partition for the Linux file system. To do this, press the Add button. You will see a dialog box (see Figure 2-8) in which you should fill in / as the mount point and enter the size in megabytes. To compute the size, simply subtract the size of the swap space (32MB or the amount of RAM in your PC, whichever is more) from the original size of the partition. Select the OK button, and then press Enter to complete this step and return to the Disk Druid's main dialog box.

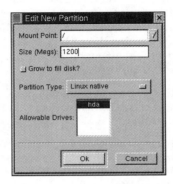

Figure 2-8: Dialog box in which you fill in the attributes of a new partition

3. Create another new partition and set it as a Linux swap space. To do this, click the Add button in the Disk Druid screen (refer to Figure 2-7). Then, in the dialog box (refer to Figure 2-8) enter the size of the partition. Click the list of partition types and use the mouse to select Linux Swap as the type. When you do so, the text <Swap Partition> appears in the Mount Point field. Next, click the OK button to define the new partition and return to the Disk Druid screen.

4. If you want to access the DOS partition under Linux, make sure you assign a mount point for this partition. Basically, you will assign a Linux directory name in which the DOS partition will appear. For example, you can use /dosc as the mount point for the DOS partition; then you can access the DOS files in the /dosc directory in Linux. This mnemonic is good because the name dosc should remind you that this drive is the C drive under DOS or Windows. To assign the mount point, select the DOS partition (typically, this will be listed as device hda1 in the Partitions list) and click the Edit button to edit the attributes. The Edit dialog box appears (see Figure 2-9). Type the mount point (for example, /dosc), and click the OK button to return to the Disk Druid screen.

5. After making the changes, click the Next button in the Disk Druid screen to proceed to the next installation step.

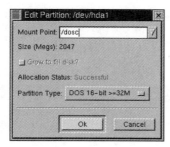

Figure 2-9: The Edit Partition dialog box enables you to change the attributes of a partition.

Setting Aside Space for the Linux File System

Although you can get by with a single large partition for the entire Linux file system and another for the swap space, you can better manage the disk space if you create separate partitions for the key parts of the Linux file system. The key directories in the Linux file system hierarchy and their purpose are as follows (you can learn more about the Filesystem Hierarchy Standard by visiting http://www.pathname.com/fhs/):

- /bin contains binary files for essential user commands (for use by all users)

- /boot contains the files needed to boot Linux

- /dev contains device files

- /etc contains host-specific system configuration files

- /home is for the user home directories (optional)

- /lib contains essential shared libraries and kernel modules needed to boot the system

- /mnt contains mount points, for temporarily mounted file systems

- /opt is for add-on application software packages

- /root is the home directory of the root user (optional)

- /sbin contains binary files for commands used by root

- /tmp is for temporary files

- /usr contains a host of software, such as the X Window System, libraries, binary files for application software, and so on

- /var is for log files and spool directories

You do not have to make a separate partition for each of these key directories. A typical partition layout might look as follows:

- / = 128MB for /bin, /dev, /etc, /lib, /opt, /root, and /sbin

- /boot = 16MB

- /home = 512MB (may have to be larger if you have more users)

- /tmp = 256MB

- /usr = 512MB

- /var = 256MB

- Swap partition = 32MB, or as much as the amount of RAM

After you finish specifying the partitions in Disk Druid, the Red Hat installation program displays a screen that lists the partitions that you may have to format for use in Linux. If you have only one disk partition for Linux, the list shows only that partition (see Figure 2-10).

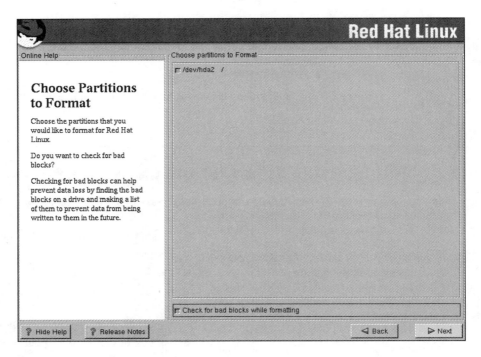

Figure 2-10: Formatting partitions for use in Linux

To format the partition, click the button next to the partition's name. You should also click the button next to the item marked Check for bad blocks while formatting so that the formatting process marks any areas of the disk that may be physically defective.

Note If you have multiple disk partitions mounted on different directories of the Linux file system and you are upgrading an existing installation, you do not have to format any partitions in which you want to preserve existing data. For example, if you have all user directories on a separate disk partition mounted on the /home directory, you do not have to format that partition.

Configuring Linux

When the installation program finishes loading all of the selected packages, it moves on to some configuration steps. The typical configuration steps are as follows:

- Install LILO
- Configure the network
- Configure the firewall
- Select languages to support
- Set the time zone
- Set the root password and add user accounts
- Configure password authentication

The following sections describe each of these configuration steps.

Installing LILO

LILO stands for *Linux Loader*—a program that resides on your hard disk and starts Linux from the hard disk. If you have Windows or OS/2 on your hard disk, you can configure LILO to load any of these operating systems as well.

The Red Hat installation program displays a screen (see Figure 2-11) that asks you where you want to install LILO, which is also known as the bootloader.

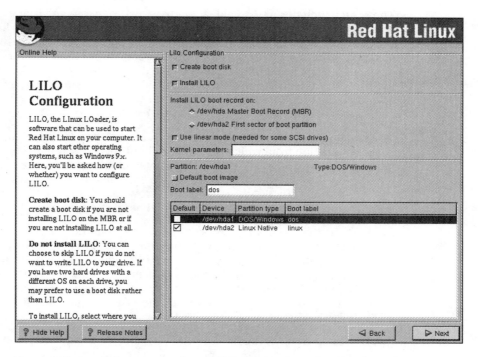

Figure 2-11: Specifying where to install LILO and whether to create a boot disk

The first button on this screen asks if you want to create a boot disk. You can use this disk to boot your Linux system if the Linux kernel on the hard disk is damaged, or if the Linux Loader (described in the next section) does not work. This button is selected by default and you should leave it that way. Later, the installation program prompts you to insert a blank floppy into your PC's A drive.

You can use the next checkbox, labeled `Install LILO`, to turn LILO installation on or off. If you choose not to install LILO, you should definitely create a boot disk. Otherwise, you won't be able to start Linux when you reboot the PC.

The next part of the LILO configuration screen gives you the option to install LILO in one of two locations:

- Master Boot Record (MBR), which is located in the first sector of your PC's hard disk (the C drive)

- First sector of the partition in which you loaded Linux

You should install LILO in the Master Boot Record, unless you are using another operating system loader, such as System Commander or OS/2 Boot Manager.

The screen includes a text field labeled `Kernel parameters` that enables you to enter any special options that may be needed by Linux as it boots. Whether you need any special options or not depends on what hardware you have. For example, on my system I have a 3Com 3C503 Ethernet card that is connected to the local Ethernet using an external transceiver. When Linux loads the driver software for the 3Com 3C503 card, I need to specify the option `xcvr=1` to make sure that the driver uses the external transceiver. I enter that option in the `Kernel parameters` text field.

The remainder of the LILO configuration screen gives you the option to select the disk partition from which you want to boot the PC. A table lists the Linux partition and any other partitions that may contain another operating system. On my system, the table includes two entries: the Linux partition and the DOS partition (which actually has Windows 95/98 installed on it). Each entry in that table is an operating system that LILO can boot.

After you install LILO, whenever your PC boots from the hard disk, LILO runs and displays a `boot:` prompt. At the prompt, you may type the name of an operating system to boot (the last column of the table in the bottom right section of Figure 2-11 shows the names you may enter at the LILO prompt). If the list shows two entries labeled `linux` and `dos`, you type `linux` to boot Linux and `dos` to boot from the DOS partition (which should start Windows 95/98, if that's what you have installed on that partition).

If you enter nothing at the LILO prompt, it waits for a few seconds and boots the default operating system. The default operating system is the one with a check mark in the Default column in Figure 2-11 (in this case, Linux is the default operating system).

After you configure LILO and enable creation of a boot disk, click the Next button to proceed to the next configuration step.

Configuring the network

Assuming the Linux kernel detected a network card, the Red Hat installation program displays the network configuration screen (see Figure 2-12) that enables you to configure the local area network (LAN) parameters for your Linux system.

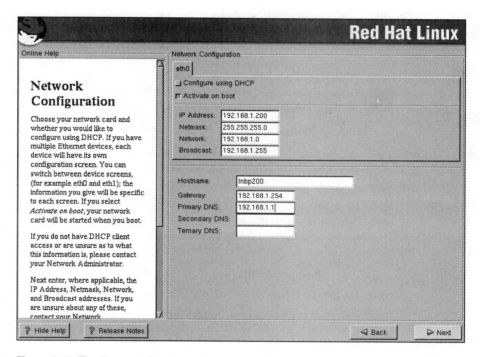

Figure 2-12: The Network Configuration screen enables you to configure the local area network.

This step is not for configuring the dial-up networking. You need to perform this step if your Linux system is connected to a TCP/IP LAN, through an Ethernet card.

Cross-Reference

If the Red Hat installation program does not detect your network card, you should restart the installation and type **expert isa** at the boot prompt. Then you will be able to manually select your network card. See the "Troubleshooting" section for more information.

The Network Configuration screen (shown in Figure 2-12) displays tabbed dialog boxes — one for each network card installed on your system and detected by the Linux kernel. These tabs are labeled `eth0`, `eth1`, and so on. If your system has only one Ethernet card, you will see only the `eth0` tab. Each tab offers two options for specifying the IP (Internet Protocol) address for the network interface:

- **Configure using DHCP** — Enable this option if your PC obtains its IP address and other network information from a Dynamic Host Configuration Protocol (DHCP) server.

- **Activate on boot** — Enable this option to turn on the network when your system boots.

You should select DHCP only if a DHCP server is running on your local area network. If you choose DHCP, your network configuration will be set automatically, and you can skip the rest of this section.

If you do not select the Configure using DHCP option, you have to provide a static IP address and other network information. You do this by entering certain parameters for TCP/IP configuration in the text input fields that appear on the Network Configuration screen (refer to Figure 2-12).

The Network Configuration screen asks for the following key network parameters:

- IP address of the Ethernet interface

- Network mask

- Host name for your Linux system (for a private LAN, you can assign your own host name without worrying about conflicting with any other existing systems on the Internet)

- IP address of the gateway (the system or device such as a router through which you might access any outside network)

- IP address of the primary name server

- IP address of a secondary name server

- IP address of a ternary name server

Cross-Reference

If you have a private LAN (one that is not directly connected to the Internet), you may use an IP address from a range that has been designated for private use. Common IP addresses for private LANs are in the range 192.168.1.1 through 192.168.1.254. You will learn more about TCP/IP networking and IP addresses in Chapter 8.

After you enter the requested parameters, click the Next button to proceed to the firewall configuration step.

Configuring the firewall

In this step, you select a predefined level of security from the Firewall Configuration screen (see Figure 2-13) and customize these security levels to suit your needs.

The Firewall Configuration screen enables you to configure the security levels of your Red Hat Linux system. You can select from one of the following predefined security levels:

- **High** security means your system will not accept any connections other than those that you explicitly enable. By default, a system with high security accepts only domain name service (DNS) requests and DHCP requests.

- **Medium** security means the system does not accept any connection requests for ports numbered 1023 and less; connections to NFS server at port 2049, and remote connections to the X Window System.

- **No firewall** security means your system accepts connections at all ports and it does not perform any security checking. You would use this option only if your system runs in a trusted network or if you plan to set up a more elaborate firewall configuration later on.

After you select a predefined security level, you can click the Customize button and then select other services that you might want to enable. When you're done configuring the firewall, click the Next button to proceed to the next step.

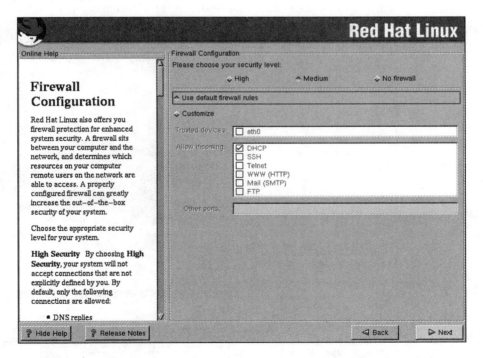

Figure 2-13: The Firewall Configuration screen enables you to configure the security level of your system.

Select languages to support

In this step you select one or more languages that your Red Hat Linux system will support once the installation is complete. This step is similar to the language selection step you had performed at the beginning of the installation when you selected the language to be used during the installation. Now you have to select the languages the system will support when you reboot the PC after completing the Red Hat Linux installation. From the Language Support Selection screen, select one or more languages to support. You must also select a default language. Then click the Next button to continue.

Setting the time zone

After completing the network configuration, you have to select the *time zone* — the difference between the local time and the current time in Greenwich, England, which is the standard reference time (also known as Greenwich Mean Time, or GMT; also known as UTC or Universal Coordinated Time). The installation program shows you a screen (see Figure 2-14) from which you can select the time zone, either in terms of a geographic location or as an offset from the UTC.

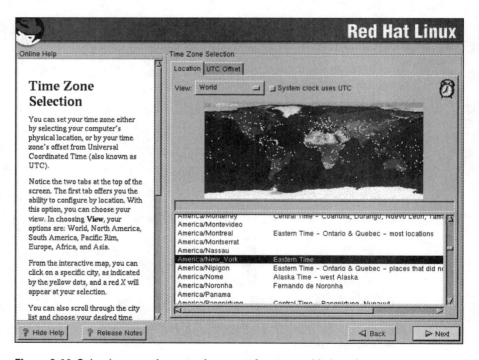

Figure 2-14: Selecting your time zone in terms of a geographic location

Notice that there are two tabs — Location and UTC Offset — from which you can select the time zone. Initially, the screen shows the Location tab. This tab lets you pick a time zone by simply clicking on your geographic location. As you move the mouse over the map, the currently selected location's name appears in a text field. If you want, you can also select your location from a long list of countries and regions. If you live on the East Coast of the United States, for example, you would select USA/Eastern. Of course, the easiest way is to simply click on the eastern United States on the map.

If the World view of the map is too large for you to select your location, click the View button on top of the map. A drop-down list of views appears with the following options: World, North America, South America, Pacific Rim, Europe, Africa, and Asia. You can then click the view appropriate for your location.

The other way to set a time zone is to specify the time difference between your local time and UTC. Click the UTC Offset tab to select the time zone this way. For example, if you are in the eastern part of the United States, you would select UTC-05:00 as the time zone. This tab also allows you to enable Daylight Saving Time, which applies to the United States only.

After you select your time zone, click the Next button to proceed to the next configuration step.

Setting the root password and adding user accounts

After completing the time zone selection, the installation program displays a screen (see Figure 2-15) from which you can set the root password and add one or more user accounts.

The root user is the super user in Linux. Because the super user can do any-thing in the system, you should assign a password that you can remember, but that others cannot guess easily. Make the password at least eight charac-ters long, include a mix of letters and numbers, and, for good measure, throw in some special characters, such as + or *.

Type the password on the first line and then reenter the password on the next line. Each character in the password appears as an asterisk (*) on the screen. You have to type the password in twice, and both entries must match before the installation program accepts it. This ensures that you did not make any typing mistakes. After you type the root password twice, you might also want to add one or more user accounts.

To add a user account, fill in the Account Name, Password, and Full Name fields and then click the Add button. The new account information then appears in the table underneath the Add button.

Click the Edit button to edit any accounts you have already created. To remove an account, select that account and click the Delete button. You do not have to add all the user accounts at this time. Later on, you can use the Linuxconf tool to add more user accounts.

Note that you must enter the root password before you can proceed with the rest of the installation. After you have done so and added any other user accounts you need, click the Next button to continue with the installation.

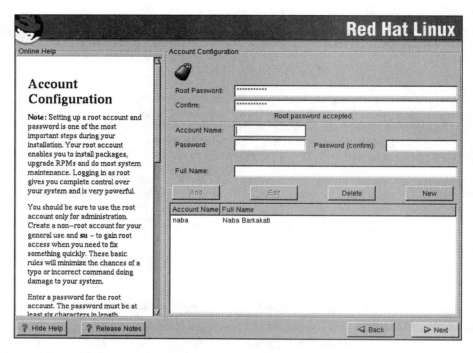

Figure 2-15: Setting the root password and adding other user accounts

Configuring password authentication

The installation program displays a screen from which you can enable or disable five password authentication options:

- **Enable MD5 passwords**—Select this option to enable users to use long passwords of up to 256 characters, instead of the standard password that can be, at most, eight characters long. Note that MD5 refers to Message Digest 5, an algorithm developed by RSA, Inc., to compute the digest of the entire data of a message. Essentially, MD5 reduces a message to a digest consisting of four 32-bit numbers.

- **Enable shadow passwords**—This option causes the /etc/psswd file to be replaced by /etc/shadow, which can only be read by the super user (root). This provides an added level of security.

- **Enable NIS**—Select this option to authenticate users on multiple systems in the same Network Information Service (NIS) domain with a common password and group file. Select the NIS domain option to specify the domain to which your system belongs. Otherwise, select the NIS server option to use a specific NIS server for authentication. To enable NIS, your Linux system must be connected to a network with an NIS server.

- **Enable LDAP**—Select this option to use Lightweight Directory Access Protocol (LDAP) as a unified authentication mechanism for logging into your Linux system, as well as other systems on the network. If you enable LDAP, you have to specify the LDAP Server and LDAP Base DN. For LDAP Server, specify the full domain name of a server running LDAP. In the LDAP Base DN text field, enter the distinguished name (DN) to look up the authentication information. To learn more about using LDAP in Linux, consult the LDAP Linux HOWTO on the Web (`http://www.linuxdoc.org/HOWTO/LDAP-HOWTO.html`).

- **Enable Kerberos**—Select this option to use Kerberos for secure, network-based authentication. If you enable Kerberos, you have to specify the Realm, KDC, and Admin Server. The Realm is the network that uses Kerberos. KDC is the Key Distribution Center, also known as the Ticket Granting Server, or TGS. Admin Server is the server that runs `kadmind`, through which the Kerberos realm is managed. To learn more about Kerberos, visit the Kerberos home page at MIT's Web site (`http://web.mit.edu/kerberos/www/`).

By default, only the Enable Shadow Passwords and Enable MD5 Passwords options are selected. Unless you plan to use LDAP or Kerberos, you should use these default settings for authentication; and click the Next button to proceed to the next configuration step.

Selecting the Package Groups to Install

After you complete the key configuration steps, the installation program displays a screen from which you can select the Red Hat Linux package groups that you want to install. After you select the package groups, you can take a coffee break and the Red Hat installation program can format the disk partitions and copy all selected files to those partitions.

Cross-Reference

Red Hat uses special files called *packages* to bundle a number of files that make up specific software. For example, all configuration files, documentation, and binary files for the Perl programming language come in a Red Hat package. You use a special program called Red Hat Package Manager (RPM) to install, uninstall, and get information about packages. Chapter 24 shows you how to use RPM. For now, just remember that a *package group* is made up of several Red Hat packages.

Figure 2-16 shows the screen from which you select the package groups that you elect to install. An icon, a descriptive label, and a button prefix identify each package group

Some of the package groups are already selected, as indicated by the pressed-in buttons. This is the minimal set of packages that Red Hat recommends for installation for the class of installation (Workstation, Server, or Custom) you have chosen. You can, however, choose to install any or all of the package groups. Use the mouse to scroll up and down the list, and click on an entry to select or deselect that package group.

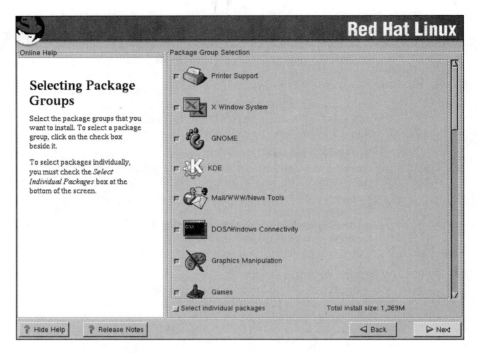

Figure 2-16: GUI screen from which you select the package groups to install

Table 2-5 shows the package groups included in the list. In addition to these user-selectable components, the Red Hat installation program automatically installs a number of packages that are needed to run Linux and the applications you select. In other words, even if you do not select any of the components on this screen, the installation program will install a number of packages that are needed simply to run the core Linux operating system and a minimal set of utilities.

Tip

Each component requires specific packages to run. The Red Hat installation program automatically checks for any package dependencies and shows you a list of packages that are required, but that you have not selected. In this case, you should install the required packages.

Because each package group is a collection of many different Red Hat packages, the installation program also gives you the option to select individual packages. If you select the button labeled Select Individual Packages that appears below the list in Figure 2-16 and then click the Next button, the installation program takes you to other screens from which you can select individual packages.

From those screens, you can select one or more packages you want to install. The bottom part of the screen then shows detailed information about the selected package. If you are installing Linux for the first time, you do not need to go down to this level of detail to install specific packages. Simply pick the package groups that you think you need from Table 2-5. You can always install additional packages later on with the RPM utility program, described in Chapter 24.

Table 2-5   List of Package Groups in Red Hat Linux

Package Group	Description
Printer Support	Packages needed to print from the system. Includes the LPRng package and utilities such as `groff` and Ghostscript.
X Window System	Packages that make up XFree86, the X Window System for Intel x86 systems. Includes all fonts, libraries, Ghostscript, Tcl/Tk, Perl, Python, and many utility programs, such as the Xconfigurator utility for configuring X.
GNOME	Packages for the GNOME (GNU Network Object Model Environment) graphical desktop, including the Sawfish window manager.
KDE	Packages for the K Desktop Environment — another graphical desktop for Linux.
Mail/WWW/News Tools	Packages such as `elm`, `pine`, and `trn` for reading e-mail and newsgroups. Also includes many packages for X Window System, Perl, Tcl/Tk, and printer support.
DOS/Windows Connectivity	Packages such as Samba, `mtools`, `zip`, and `unzip` that are useful for accessing DOS and Windows files from Linux.
Graphics Manipulation	Image manipulation packages such as ImageMagick, `gimp`, and Xpaint.
Games	Games such as `xbill`, `xboard`, `xboing`, `xgammon`, `xjewel`, `xpat2`, and `xpilot`. If GNOME is selected, this includes `gnome-games`. If KDE is selected, this includes `kdegames` and `kdetoys`.
Multimedia Support	Packages for sound and animation under X, GNOME, and KDE. Also includes other sound and animation support packages such as `aumix`, `sndconfig`, `mpg123`, `cdp`, and `playmidi`.
Laptop Support	Packages to support infrared wireless communication based on the IrDA™ standard.
Networked Workstation	TCP/IP networking packages such as FTP (File Transfer Protocol), Telnet, and NFS (Network File System).

Continued

Table 2-5 *(continued)*

Package Group	Description
Dialup Workstation	TCP/IP networking packages, as well as packages such as `ppp` and `dip` needed for dial-up networking. Also includes communication packages such as `minicom` and `lrzsz` (for sending and receiving files).
News Server	Perl and INN (Internet News server) packages needed to make the Linux system a server for newsgroups.
NFS Server	Packages such as `portmap` and `nfs-server`, which make the Linux system a NFS server.
SMB (Samba) Server	Samba and other supporting packages that are needed to use the Linux PC as a LAN Manager server. Includes many other packages, such as TCP/IP networking and printer support.
IPX/Netware™ Connectivity	Packages needed to use the Linux PC as a Novell Netware server. Includes much of the TCP/IP networking packages as well.
Anonymous FTP Server	The `wu-ftpd` and `anonftp` packages, along with all TCP/IP networking packages needed to support anonymous FTP in Linux.
Web Server	The Apache Web server and other networking packages needed to use the Linux system as a Web server.
DNS Name Server	The `bind`, `bind-utils`, and `caching-nameserver` packages, along with other support packages needed to provide Domain Name Service (DNS) on the Linux system.
Postgres (SQL) Server	The `postgresql`, `postgresql-data`, and `postgresql-devel` packages, along with many support packages to implement the Postgres SQL server (a database) on the Linux system.
Network Management Workstation	Packages to support network management through SNMP (Simple Network Management Protocol). Also includes many networking packages required by the network management tools.
Authoring/Publishing	Packages needed for the TeX (pronounced "tech") document-formatting system.

Package Group	Description
Emacs	Version of GNU Emacs editor that runs in X. Also includes the X Window System component and the version of Emacs that does not require X.
Development	The GNU C and C++ compilers, the gdb debugger, Revision Control System (RCS), Concurrent Version System (CVS), various header files, and other utilities for C and ++ programming. Includes various libraries needed for developing software that uses X. If GNOME is selected, includes header files and libraries such as gtk+ for developing applications for the GNOME desktop. If KDE is selected, includes the Qt library and other header files needed to develop KDE applications.
Kernel Development	The header files and source code for the Linux kernel. (You need this component to recompile the kernel.)
Utilities	A number of utilities for X and networking.
Everything	Select this item to install all of the components.

After you have selected the components you want, click the Next button to
continue with the rest of the installation.

Completing the Installation

After you complete the key configuration steps and select the components to
install, the installation program configures the X Window System. The installation program uses an X server with minimal capability that can work on all
video cards. In this step, the installation program prepares the configuration
file to be used by the X server when your system reboots.

The installation program tries to detect the video card and displays the result
in a screen. The detected card appears as the selected item in a long list of
video cards, as shown in Figure 2-17.

If you know the exact name of the video card, or the name of the video
chipset used in the video card, select that item from the list.

After selecting the video card, the installation program tries to detect the
monitor, displaying a screen with the results, whether successful or not (see
Figure 2-18).

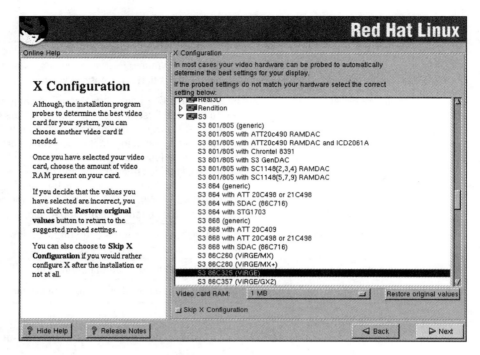

Figure 2-17: The result of detecting the video card is displayed in the X Configuration screen.

If the installation program displays a wrong monitor or a generic one as the choice, you should enter a range of values for the two parameters that appear along the bottom of the screen:

- **Horizontal Sync** — This is the number of times per second that the monitor can display a horizontal raster line, in kilohertz (kHz). A typical range might be 30–64 kHz.

- **Vertical Sync** — This is how many times a second the monitor can display the entire screen, in Hertz (Hz). Also known as *vertical refresh rate*, the typical range is 50–90 Hz.

Typically, the monitor's documentation includes all this information. If you bought your PC recently, you may still have the documentation. If you lost your monitor's documentation, one way to find the information might be from your Microsoft Windows setup. If your system came with a Windows driver for the display, that driver may display information about the monitor. Also, the Norton System Information tool may provide this information as well. Another possibility is to visit your computer vendor's Web site and look for the technical specification of the monitor. I was able to locate useful information about my system's monitor from the vendor's Web site.

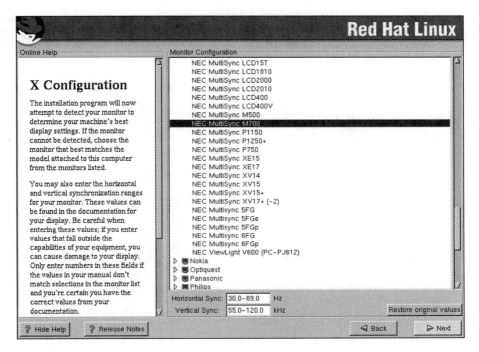

Figure 2-18: The result of detecting the monitor is displayed in the X Configuration screen.

Caution

Do not specify a horizontal synchronization range that is beyond the capabilities of your monitor. A wrong value can damage the monitor.

Next, the installation program displays a screen from which you can customize the system's graphical user interface (see Figure 2-19).

You can select the color depth and screen resolution from drop-down lists. Two checkboxes — GNOME and KDE — enable you to select the default GUI. Finally, you can select from two more checkboxes — Text and Graphical — to obtain a text or graphical login screen when the system restarts.

After you finish selecting X configuration options, click the Next button. The installation program displays a dialog box informing you that a log of the installation will be in the `/tmp/install.log` file. That file essentially lists all the Red Hat packages that are installed in your system. You can review the install log later and move the file to another directory for future reference. The content of the install log depends on the exact packages you choose to install.

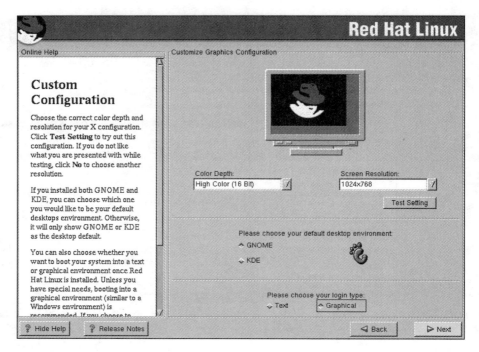

Figure 2-19: Customizing the GUI

Click the Next button to proceed with the installation. The Red Hat installation program formats the disk partitions and then installs the packages. As it installs packages, the installation program displays a status screen showing the progress of the installation, including information such as total number of packages to install, number installed so far, estimated amount of disk space needed, and estimated time remaining to install.

Tip

The formatting and installation takes quite a few minutes — so you can take a break and check back in ten minutes or so. When you come back, you should be able to get a sense of the time remaining from the status screen, which updates continually.

After all the packages are installed, the installation program displays a screen that asks you to insert a blank floppy into your PC's A drive. This floppy would be the boot disk that you can use to start Linux if something happens to the hard disk, or you did not install the LILO.

Insert a blank floppy into your PC's A drive and click the Next button (note that all data on the floppy will be destroyed). The installation program copies the Linux kernel and some other files to the floppy. After preparing the boot disk, the installation program displays a message informing you that installation is complete. The message reminds you to remove the floppy from drive

A before exiting the installation program. Do so and label the floppy appropriately, and save it for future use. Then click the Exit button to reboot your PC.

Troubleshooting the Installation

The Red Hat Linux installation program attempts to automatically detect hardware, instead of requiring you to manually select the make and model of key hardware components, such as SCSI controller and network card. If the installation program cannot detect a SCSI controller or network card, you can still install Red Hat Linux. The following sections describe a few troubleshooting approaches for some common installation problems.

Cross-Reference

If you have problems with specific hardware components, consult Chapters 3 through 9 for more information. In particular, Chapter 3 shows you how to configure X. Chapters 3 through 9 also include information about configuring specific devices. For example, Chapter 5 describes how to configure sound cards, and Chapter 6 shows you how to set up printers.

Using Text Mode Installation

The Red Hat installation program attempts to use a minimal X Window System (X) to display the graphical user installation screens. If the program fails to detect a video card, X does not start. If — for this reason or any other reason — it fails to start X, you can always fall back on the text mode installation program to specify the video card manually.

To use text mode installation, type `text` at the `boot:` prompt after you start the PC from the Red Hat Linux boot floppy. From then on, the basic sequence is similar to that of the graphical installation described earlier in this chapter. However, many small details are different. You should be able to respond to the prompts and perform the installation.

In text mode, when the installation program fails to detect the video card, it displays a list of video cards from which you can select one. By selecting the video card, X may work when you install in text mode. If it does not, you can configure X using the information in Chapter 3.

Using Expert Mode Installation

If the Red Hat installation program does not detect your SCSI controller or network card, you can specify these devices manually by running the installation in expert mode. Look for any indication of SCSI or network devices in the messages displayed by the Linux kernel as it boots. To view these boot messages during installation, press Ctrl+Alt+F4. This switches to a text-mode virtual console on which the messages appear. (A *virtual console* is a screen of text or graphical information stored in memory that you can view on the physical screen by pressing the appropriate key sequence.)

Another sign of undetected hardware is when the installation program skips a step. For example, if the Linux kernel does not detect the network card, the installation program skips the network configuration step.

To run the installation in expert mode, type `expert isa` at the `boot:` prompt in the initial text screen. The installation program then displays another text screen (see Figure 2-20) that asks for a driver disk, if you have one.

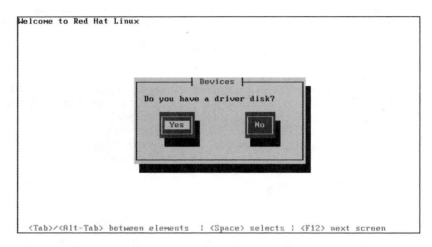

Figure 2-20: Prompt for driver disk during expert mode installation

The idea is that you receive a floppy disk with Linux drivers from the hardware vendor and you insert that floppy into the A: drive. If you have a driver disk, press Enter and a dialog box prompts you to insert the disk into the A: drive. After you do so, press Enter and the installation program loads the driver and guides you through steps necessary to install the driver.

If you do not have a driver disk, select Cancel. The installation program then goes through two more screens from which you select the language and the keyboard layout. Then the installation program prompts for the media containing the packages to be installed, as shown in Figure 2-21.

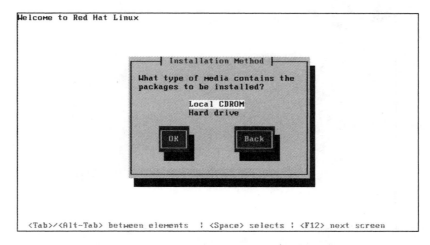

Figure 2-21: Specifying installation media during expert mode installation

Next, the installation program displays a dialog box that gives you another opportunity to add devices, as shown in Figure 2-22.

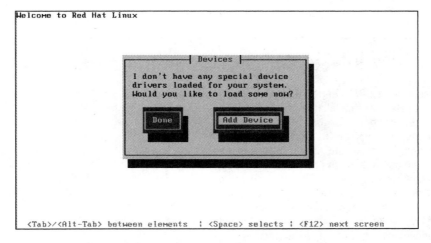

Figure 2-22: Adding devices during expert mode installation

Press Tab to highlight the Add Device button and then press Enter. The installation program then displays a dialog box that prompts for the type of device — SCSI or Network (see Figure 2-23).

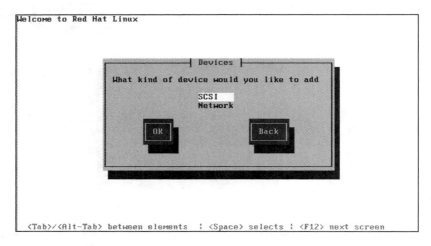

Figure 2-23: Selecting device type during expert mode installation

If you have any SCSI device, such as a SCSI hard drive, you select SCSI and press Enter. The installation program displays a list of SCSI controllers (see Figure 2-24) from which you should select the one on your system and press Enter. The installation program then loads that driver module.

Specifying SCSI Controller Settings

If you have a SCSI controller in your system, the Red Hat Linux installation program loads a SCSI driver module for that adapter. You have to identify the type of SCSI controller (such as Adaptec 1542 or Adaptec 2940). The installation program can attempt to determine the adapter settings such as IRQ and I/O port address by probing various I/O port addresses. However, if the installation program fails to determine the SCSI controller settings, you have to specify them as options for the driver module. The exact format of these options varies from one module to another. For example, the driver for

Adaptec AHA 152x cards accepts the options in the following format:

```
aha152x=IOPORT,IRQ,SCSI_ID[,
Reconnect,Parity]
```

where *IOPORT* is the I/O port address, *IRQ* is the interrupt request number, and *SCSI_ID* is the SCSI ID of the SCSI controller. The last two items are optional. A typical module option for the aha152x module might be as follows:

```
aha152x=0x340,11,7
```

See Chapter 4 for more information on SCSI controllers.

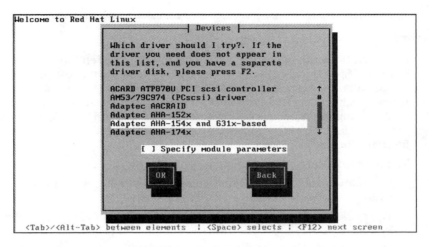

Figure 2-24: Selecting a SCSI controller in expert mode installation

The SCSI driver automatically probes and determines the SCSI controller's settings, such as interrupt request (IRQ) and I/O port address. If the driver has problems detecting the SCSI controller's settings, you can specify these parameters manually. To do so, select the checkbox labeled `Specify module parameters` and press Enter. The installation program then prompts you for the module parameters.

You can then enter a line such as `aha152x=0x340,11,7` to specify the parameters for the driver module. See the sidebar "Specifying SCSI Controller Settings" for more information on these settings.

After you add any SCSI controllers, you will be back at the dialog box shown in Figure 2-23. You can add network cards from this dialog box as well. In the dialog box shown in Figure 2-23, select Network from the list and press Enter. The installation program then displays a list of network cards from which you can select your network card.

When you press Enter, the installation program loads the driver module for the selected network card. That driver probes and determines the network card settings.

Once you get back to the screen shown in Figure 2-22, select Done and press Enter. The installation program then switches to graphics mode and guides you through the rest of the installation, as described earlier in this chapter.

Summary

Linux is a UNIX-like operating system for Intel 80x86, Pentium, and compatible systems. The CD-ROMs that accompany this book include the latest version of the popular Red Hat Linux distribution. This chapter guides you through the process of installing Red Hat Linux on your PC. The next chapter turns to another configuration task — how to configure and run the X Window System on your Red Hat Linux PC. You need X because with X you'll have a graphical user interface for Red Hat Linux.

The detailed information in this chapter includes the following:

▶ Information about your PC that you should gather before installing Red Hat Linux

▶ The overall process of installing Red Hat Linux (including the X Window System, GNOME, and KDE) from the companion CD-ROMs

▶ Steps that you need to perform under MS-DOS or Microsoft Windows before installing Linux

▶ How to boot Linux initially, partition the hard disk, and load the various software components from the companion CD-ROMs using the Red Hat installation program

▶ How to recover from some common installation problems

Chapter 3

Video Cards, Monitors, and the X Window System

If you have used Apple Macintosh or Microsoft Windows, you are familiar with the convenience of a graphical user interface (GUI — pronounced *gooey*). In Linux, the GUI is not an integral part of the operating system. Instead, Linux distributions, such as Red Hat Linux, typically provide GNOME and KDE as the GUI. GNOME and KDE are in turn built on a windowing system called the *X Window System,* or *X.* Red Hat Linux includes a version of X called XFree86, which is designed to work with your PC's video card and monitor. Which video card and monitor you use do not matter much if you work only with text. In order to install XFree86, you need detailed information about your video card and monitor.

The companion CD-ROMs contain the XFree86 software, which you might have installed on your hard disk during the installation process shown in Chapter 2. At that time, the Red Hat installation program would have detected your video card and monitor and configured XFree86. This chapter describes the attributes of video cards and monitors, and explains the X Window System. It also tells you how to use tools, such as `Xconfigurator` and `xf86config`, to manually prepare a configuration file, in case the installation program fails to properly configure XFree86 on your PC.

Video Cards and Monitors

The video card or graphics adapter contains the electronics that control the monitor. On most systems the video card takes the form of a circuit board that plugs into a slot on your PC's motherboard. On many new systems, however, the motherboard itself contains the necessary graphics chipsets.

Raster-Scan Display

All video cards operate on the same principle: They store an image in video memory (also called *video RAM*, or *VRAM* for short) and generate the appropriate signals to display the image on the monitor's screen.

The *monitor* is the physical device that contains the display screen, where the graphic and text output appears. The *display screen* is typically a phosphor-coated glass tube on which an electron beam traces the output image. On laptop computers, the display screen is a *liquid crystal display* (LCD) screen. More expensive laptops use active-matrix LCD-display screens.

The image that appears on the monitor is made up of many horizontal lines, known as *raster lines*. An electron beam in the monitor generates the raster lines by sweeping back and forth on a phosphor-coated screen, as illustrated in Figure 3-1.

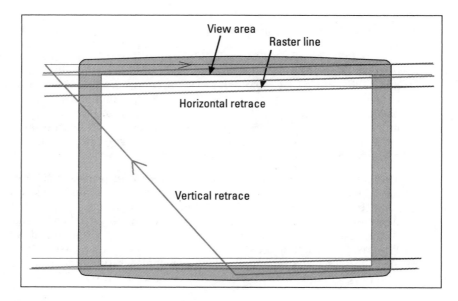

Figure 3-1: A typical raster-scan display

The phosphor on the screen glows in proportion to the intensity of the electron beam. The glowing dot on the screen represents a picture element, or *pixel*. Thus, a line of the image is generated by controlling the intensity of the beam as it scans across the screen. The phosphor fades in a while, but if the lines are redrawn repeatedly, our persistence of vision creates an illusion of a steady image. Most PC monitors redraw an entire screenful of raster lines 50 to 90 times per second.

As Figure 3-1 shows, the electron beam scans an area larger than the actual view area of the display screen, but the electron beam is active only when the beam is in the viewable area. Also, after reaching the end of a line, the beam has to return to the start of the next raster line. This part of the beam's motion is known as the *horizontal retrace*. Similarly, when the beam reaches the bottom of the screen, it has to return to the first line to start another cycle of drawing. This period is known as the *vertical retrace*. The beam's intensity is reduced (the beam is *blanked*) during horizontal and vertical retrace, so that those lines do not appear on the screen.

The video card generates the signals necessary to sweep the electron beam across the display and refresh the display at a rapid rate. There are two types of refresh: *interlaced* and *noninterlaced*. In interlaced refresh, each screen is drawn in two steps. First the electron beam sweeps across the screen drawing all the odd-numbered raster lines. Then the electron beam goes back to the beginning of the screen and draws all the even-numbered raster lines. Broadcast television uses interlaced refresh. Noninterlaced refresh involves drawing all raster lines in a single step. Most video cards refresh the screen 60 times, or more, per second and use a noninterlaced refresh.

Color Display

Color display screens represent any color with a combination of the three primary colors: red (R), green (G), and blue (B). Most color displays use three electron beams, one for each primary color.

The screen in a color display has a repeated triangular pattern of red, green, and blue phosphor dots. Each phosphor dot glows in its color when the electron beam impinges on it. A perforated metal screen, known as a *shadow mask*, ensures that each electron beam strikes the phosphor of the intended color. The video card varies the intensity of the red, green, and blue electron beams, thereby displaying many colors.

Color palette and resolution

Typically, a video card allows a palette of 256 colors, in which case each pixel's color is stored in an 8-bit value. The actual color (in terms of R, G, B components) that corresponds to a pixel's 8-bit value is determined by consulting a color lookup table, or *colormap*.

Today's high-performance video cards allow three bytes of storage per pixel, so that each pixel's value can directly specify the RGB components that determine that pixel's color. These so-called 24-bit video cards provide true color display, but require more video memory to store the entire image.

The resolution of a display screen is expressed in terms of the number of visible dots (pixels) across a raster line and the total raster lines. A common resolution is 640 dots across by 480 lines vertically, which is commonly expressed as 640 × 480. Other common screen resolutions are 800 × 600, 1,024 × 768, and 1,280 × 1,024.

Video RAM

The video card stores the contents of the pixels in random-access memory (RAM), known as video RAM. The number of colors and the display resolution supported by a video card depends on the amount of video RAM. To store the information content of a 256-color 1,024 × 768 display screen, for example, the video card needs 1,024 × 768, or 786,432 bytes of video RAM (because an 8-bit pixel value represents 256 colors and 1 byte = 8 bits). On the other hand, to display 24-bit color at 1,024 × 768 resolution, the video card needs three times as much video RAM: 3 × 786,432 = 2,359,296 bytes, or about 2.3MB of video RAM (because 24 bit = 3 bytes).

Typical video cards have one, two, four, eight, or 16 MB of video RAM. A video card with one MB of video RAM can comfortably handle a 256-color, 1,024 × 768-resolution display.

Dot clock

You will run across the term *dot clock* when you configure a video card to work with XFree86 (the X Window System). This term refers to the rate at which the video card can traverse the raster lines that make up a complete display screen. The value of the dot clock is expressed in terms of the number of dots drawn per second.

To get a rough idea of the dot clock, consider a 640 × 480 display, which has 640 × 480 = 307,200 dots (visible ones, anyway). To produce the appearance of a steady display, these dots should be repainted at least 72 times per second. Thus, the video card has to paint 640 × 480 × 72 = 22,118,400 dots a second. This rate amounts to approximately 22 million dots a second, which is expressed as a dot clock of 22 MHz (1 MHz = a million times per second).

In reality, an even higher dot clock is required for a 640 × 480 display refreshed at 72 Hz (which means 72 times per second), because the electron beam cannot turn around on a dime. As illustrated in Figure 3-1, the electron beam has to traverse a scan line beyond the visible number of dots, before it can snap back to the beginning of the next line. The required dot clock for a 640 × 480 display at a 72-Hz refresh rate, for example, is 25.2 MHz.

As you must realize by now, a higher-resolution display requires an even higher dot clock. A 1,024 × 768 display at a 72-Hz refresh rate implies 1,024 × 768 × 72 = 56,623,104 dots per second, at minimum. Thus, you can tell that the dot clock necessary for a 1,024 × 768 display will be somewhat higher than 56.6 MHz.

Older video cards support a fixed set of dot clocks, but many advanced video cards include a programmable dot clock. When a video card has a programmable dot clock, the X server can set the video card to operate at any dot clock that lies in a range of acceptable values. For a video card with a programmable dot clock, however, you may need to specify the name of the chip that controls the dot clock (known as the *clock chip*).

Importance of video card and monitor

Linux will work with any video card/monitor combination in text mode. If a video card and monitor work under MS-DOS or Windows, the combination will also work under Linux in text mode. The story is different when you install XFree86, the X Window System for Linux. Because XFree86 controls the video card directly (MS-DOS typically uses standard predefined modes of the video card), getting XFree86 running with a specific video card takes more work.

The monitor also is important for XFree86. Electrical signals from the video card control the monitor, so the monitor must be compatible with the video card. The output on the monitor is the result of a rapidly moving electron beam that the video card's signals control. A monitor's compatibility with a video card has to do with how fast the video card attempts to move the electron beam on the display screen.

The resolutions supported by a video card/monitor combination depend on the amount of video memory on the card and on how fast the monitor's electron beam can move. XFree86 gets the necessary information about the monitor and the video card from a special text file named `XF86Config` or `XF86Config-4` in the `/etc/X11` directory.

Understanding the X Window System

The name *X Window System*, or *X* for short, is loosely applied to several components that facilitate window-based graphics output (or a graphical interface) on a variety of bitmapped displays. A bitmapped display has two distinct components: a *video monitor* on which the graphics output appears and a *video card* (or *graphics card*) — either a plug-in card or some circuitry built into the system's motherboard — that causes the output to appear on the monitor.

At the heart of X is the *X server* — a process (computer program) running on a computer that has a bitmapped display, a keyboard, and a mouse. Applications — *X clients* — which need to display output, do so by communicating with the X server via one of several possible interprocess communication mechanisms. The communications between the X clients and the X server follow a well-defined protocol: the *X protocol*. In addition to the X server, the clients, and the X protocol, the term *X* encompasses a library of routines known as *Xlib*, which constitutes the C-language interface to the facilities of the X server.

X Server and Clients

When you run X on your system, the X server runs on your computer and controls the monitor, keyboard, and mouse. The server responds to commands sent by X clients that open windows and draw in those windows. The X clients may run locally or on remote systems. This arrangement is known as the *client/server model*. As the name implies, the server provides a service that the client requests. Usually, clients communicate with the server through a network, with client and server exchanging data using a protocol that both understand.

You may already have seen the client/server model in action. A *file server*, for example, stores files and allows clients to access and manipulate those files. Another common application, the *database server*, provides a centralized database from which clients retrieve data by sending queries. Similarly, the X display server offers graphics-display services to clients that send X protocol requests to the server.

One major difference exists between the X server and other servers, such as file and database servers. File servers and database servers are usually processes executing on remote machines, but the X server is a process executing on the computer where the monitor is located. The X clients may run locally or on remote systems.

In the PC LAN's client/server model, applications are typically stored on a central server. Users access these server-based applications from client PCs. When you run an application from a PC, the application executes in your PC's processor. In the X client/server model, the situation is different. When you run an application, it actually runs in the server's processor — only the output appears on your Linux PC (which runs the X server). In other words, the X server runs in a location you typically associate with the client (as in the client PC in a PC LAN). You should keep this distinction in mind when working with the X client/server model.

Graphical User Interfaces and X

An application's user interface determines its appearance (look) and behavior (feel). When the user interface uses graphic objects, such as windows and menus, we call it a *graphical user interface* (many call it GUI — pronounced *gooey* — for short). You can also call a GUI a point-and-click user interface, because users generally interact with a GUI by moving the mouse pointer onscreen and clicking the mouse button. To confirm the closing of a file, for example, the user may click the mouse button while the mouse pointer is inside a button labeled OK.

Graphical user interfaces were originally developed at the Xerox Palo Alto Research Center (PARC). Subsequently, Apple Computer made such interfaces popular in its Lisa and Macintosh systems. Today, graphical user interfaces are available for most systems. Microsoft Windows is available for most IBM-compatible PCs with 386 or better processors; Presentation Manager for OS/2; and Motif, GNOME, and KDE (built on X) for UNIX.

Most GUIs, including Motif, GNOME, and KDE, have three components:

- A window system
- A window manager
- A toolkit

The graphical *window system* organizes graphics output on the display screen and performs basic text- and graphics-drawing functions. The X Window System is the window system used by all X-based GUIs, such as GNOME and KDE.

The *window manager* enables the user to move and resize windows. The window manager is also partly responsible for the appearance of the windows, because it usually adds a decorative frame to them. The window manager also manages *input focus*, the mechanism by which the user can select one of several windows onscreen and make that one the current *active window* (the window with which the user intends to interact). This process is called giving the input focus to a window. For GUIs based on the X Window System, a window manager is an X client, just like any other X application. For example, GNOME comes with the Sawfish window manager.

The third component, the *toolkit*, is a library of routines with a well-defined programming interface. This toolkit is primarily of interest to programmers, because it enables them to write applications that use the facilities of the window system and that have a consistent look and feel. For example, GNOME comes with a toolkit named Gtk+ (GIMP toolkit), and KDE comes with the Qt toolkit.

A Short History of X

The development of the X Window System started in 1984 at the Massachusetts Institute of Technology (MIT), under the auspices of the MIT Laboratory for Computer Science and MIT/Project Athena. X had industry support from the beginning, because DEC and IBM were involved in Project Athena. By early 1986, DEC had introduced the first commer-cial implementation of X running on the VAXstation-II/GPX under the Ultrix operating system: X version 10, release 3 (X10R3). Soon X attracted the attention of other prominent workstation vendors, such as Hewlett-Packard, Apollo Computer (which has since merged with Hewlett-Packard), Sun Microsystems, and Tektronix.

Feedback from users of X10 urged project members to start a major redesign of the X protocol. While the design of what would become X version 11 (X11) proceeded, X10R4 was released in December 1986. X10R4 was the last release of X version 10.

In January 1987, during the first X technical conference, 11 major computer vendors announced a joint effort to support and standardize on X11. The first release of X11—X11R1—became available in September 1987. To ensure the continued evolution of X under the control of an open organization, the MIT X Consortium was formed in January 1988. Under the leadership of Robert W. Scheifler, one of the principal architects of X, the consortium was a major cause of the success of X. Since then, control of the X Window System has been passed on to the X Consortium, Inc., a not-for-profit corporation.

In March 1988, release 2 of X11—X11R2—became available. X11 release 3—X11R3—appeared in late October 1988. In January 1990, the MIT X Consortium released X11R4; X11R5 followed in August 1991. X11R6—the latest release of X—was released April 1994. Throughout these releases, the X11 protocol has remained unchanged. All enhancements have been made through the X11 protocol's ability to support extensions.

X on Red Hat Linux

The X Window System for Red Hat Linux comes from the *XFree86 project* — a cooperative project of programmers who bring X to the PC. (You can access the XFree86 home page at http://www.xfree86.org/.) As a result, the Linux version of X is called XFree86.

Note

The X server configures the display (number of colors, resolution in terms of number of pixels horizontally and vertically), mouse, and keyboard based on information stored in a configuration file. Red Hat Linux comes with two versions of XFree86 — 3.3.6 and 4.0.2. XFree86 3.3.6 uses different X servers for different video cards, whereas XFree86 4.0.2 has a single X server that loads different driver modules to support different video cards. Depending on your video card, the installation program selects an X server from one of these versions of XFree86. Each version has a different configuration file. For XFree86 3.3.6, the configuration file is /etc/X11/XF86Config and for XFree86 4.0.2 it's /etc/XFree86Config-42.

In order to configure X, you must prepare the configuration file. The configuration file contains information about your video card, monitor, keyboard, and mouse. Red Hat Linux comes with a utility program called xf86config (which is the same as the name of the configuration file, but in lower case) that enables you to create the XF86Config working configuration file. You can also use the Xconfigurator utility to create the configuration file.

Setting Up X on Red Hat Linux

You want to get X set up and going quickly, because without it Red Hat Linux has no GUI. If you are used to other graphical environments (perhaps on another UNIX workstation, or on a PC running Microsoft Windows), you probably want a similar graphical environment on Red Hat Linux.

If you plan to develop software on your Red Hat Linux system, chances are good that your software has a graphical component that must be implemented and tested under X. You have to set up and run X to perform this implementation and testing.

No matter what your purpose, if you want to set up XFree86, you have to prepare a special configuration file named XF86Config (that must be present in the /etc/X11 directory), that contains information about your hardware. You can use one of two utilities — Xconfigurator or xf86config — to create the XF86Config file. The next few sections guide you through the process of configuring XFree86 and starting X on your Red Hat Linux PC.

Note

You do not have to configure XFree86 if you have already successfully installed X during the Red Hat Linux installation, as explained in Chapter 2.

Knowing Your Hardware before Configuring XFree86

To configure XFree86 you must know the hardware that X must access and use. From this chapter's brief introduction to X, you know that the X server controls the following hardware:

- The video card
- The monitor
- The keyboard
- The mouse

The X server needs information about these components to work properly.

The monitor

XFree86 controls the monitor through the video card. This means that an XFree86 server can cause a video card to send a wide range of signals to the monitor (to control how fast a raster line is drawn, for example, or how often the entire screen is redrawn). If a video card causes the monitor to perform some task beyond its capabilities (drawing each raster line much faster than it was designed to do, for example), the monitor may actually be damaged. To ensure that the signals from the video card are within the acceptable range for a monitor, XFree86 needs information about some key characteristics of the monitor.

At minimum, you have to provide the following information about the monitor:

- The range of acceptable horizontal synchronization frequencies. A typical range might be 30–64 kHz.
- The range of allowable vertical synchronization rates (also known as *vertical refresh rates*), such as 50–90 Hz.
- If available, the bandwidth in megahertz, such as 75 MHz.

Typically, the monitor's documentation includes all this information. If you bought your PC recently, you may still have the documentation. If you lost your monitor's documentation, one way to find the information might be from your Microsoft Windows setup. If your system came with a Windows driver for the display, that driver may display information about the monitor. Also, the Norton System Information tool may provide this information as well. Another possibility is to visit your computer vendor's Web site and look for the technical specification of the monitor. I found useful information about my system's monitor on the vendor's Web site.

The video card

XFree86 already provides X servers that are designed to work with a particular video chipset (the integrated circuit chips that generate the signals needed to control the monitor). To select the correct X server, you have to indicate what video chipset your video card uses.

Even within a family of video cards based on a specific chipset, many configurable parameters may vary from one card to another. Therefore, you also must specify the vendor name and the model of your video card.

At a minimum, you have to provide the following information about the video card:

- Video chipset, such as S3, NVidia RIVA TNT, or ATI Mach64.

- Vendor name and model, such as Diamond Stealth 64 VRAM, Diamond Viper V550, Number Nine GXE64, or ATI Graphics Xpression.

- Amount of video RAM (random-access memory), such as 2MB or 4MB.

Most PC vendors indicate only the make and model of the video card in advertisements; the ads rarely mention the video chipset. You should ask explicitly about the video chipset and for as much information as the vendor can provide about the video card's model.

Tip

If you are going to use an old PC to run Linux, you could try to find the video chipset information by opening your computer's case and looking at the video card. The vendor name and model number may be inscribed on the card. For the video chipset, you have to look at the markings on the different chips on the video card and try to guess. You may find a chip with the following markings (only part of the markings are shown here):

```
S3 Trio 64 (GACC 2)
86C764 - P
```

You might guess that this card uses the S3 chipset. In fact, markings on the chip show the 86C764 number as well (either in the full form or as the number 764). Now, if you can locate the vendor name and model of this card, you may be all set to configure the X server to run properly on your PC.

To find out if your video card or chipset is supported by XFree86 4.0.2, visit the Web page at `http://www.xfree86.org/4.0.2/Status.html`. This Web page provides links to information on XFree86 support for specific video cards or chipsets from the following vendors (I briefly summarize the information here):

- *3Dfx* — All hardware supported in 3.3.6, such as Voodoo Banshee and Voodoo 3, is also supported in 4.0.2.

- *3Dlabs* — All hardware supported in 3.3.6, such as GLINT 500TX and Permedia, is also supported in 4.0.2. Permedia 3 is only supported in 4.0.2.

- *Alliance* — The AP6422 is supported in 3.3.6 but not fully supported in 4.0.2. On the other hand, the AT25 is supported in 4.0.2 but not in 3.3.6.

- *ARK Logic* — All hardware supported in 3.3.6, such as ARK1000PV, ARK2000PV, and ARK2000MT, is also supported in 4.0.2.

- *ATI* — All chipsets supported in 3.3.6 are supported in 4.0.2, except for Mach8 and some old Mach32 chips.

- *Avance Logic* — These chipsets are not supported in 4.0.2, but 3.3.6 supports the AL2101, ALI2228, ALI2301, ALI2302, ALI2308, and ALI2401 chipsets.

- *Chips and Technologies* — All chipsets (such as 65520, 65525, 65530, 65535, 65540, 65545, 65546, 65548, 65550, 65554, 65555, 68554, 69000, 64200, and 64300) are supported in both 3.3.6 and 4.0.2.

- *Cirrus Logic* — XFree86 3.3.6 supports the 6410, 6412, 6420, 6440, 5420, 5422, 5424, 5426, 5428, 5429, 5430, 5434, 5436, 5446, 5480, 5462, 5464, 5465, 6205, 6215, 6225, 6235, 7541, 7542, 7543, 7548, 7555, and 7556 chipsets. XFree86 4.0.2 also supports these chipsets except 6410, 6412, 6420, 6440, 5420, 5422, 5424, 5426, 5428, 5429, 6205, 6215, 6225, 6235, 7541, 7542, 7543, 7548, 7555, and 7556.

- *Compaq/Digital* — Compaq AVGA chipset is not supported in 4.0.2, but DEC TGA is supported in both 3.3.6 and 4.0.2.

- *Cyrix* — These chipsets are not yet well supported in 4.0.2, but 3.3.6 supports the Cyrix MediaGX chipset.

- *Epson* — These chipsets are not supported in 4.0.2, but 3.3.6 supports the Epson SPC8110 chipset.

- *Genoa* — These chipsets are not supported in 4.0.2, but 3.3.6 supports the old Genoa GVGA chipset.

- *IBM* — XFree86 3.3.6 supports the standard VGA chip, as well as 8514/A and XGA-2, but 4.0.2 supports only the VGA chip.

- *IIT* — These chipsets are not supported in 4.0.2, but 3.3.6 supports the AGX-016, AGX-015 and AGX-014 chipsets.

- *Integrated Micro Solutions (IMS)* — All hardware supported in 3.3.6, such as the IMS Twin Turbo 128, is also supported in 4.0.2.

- *Intel* — The i740 and i810 are supported in both versions.

- *Matrox* — All chipsets that are supported in 3.3.6, such as Millennium and Mystique, are also supported in 4.0.2.

- *MX* — These chipsets are not supported in 4.0.2, but 3.3.6 supports the MX68000 and MX68010 chipsets.

- *NCR* — These chipsets are not supported in 4.0.2, but 3.3.6 supports the NCR 77C22 and 77C22E chipsets.

- *NeoMagic* — All chipsets that are supported in 3.3.6, such as NM2070, NM2090, NM2093, NM2097, NM2160, and NM2200, are also supported in 4.0.2. The NM2230 and later chips are only supported in 4.0.2.

- NVIDIA — All chipsets that are supported in 3.3.6, such as Riva 128, 128ZX, TNT, TNT2 (Ultra, Vanta, M64), GeForce (DDR, 256) and Quadro, are also supported in 4.0.2. The NV1 is supported in 3.3.6 and newer chipsets — GeForce 2 or later — are supported only in 4.0.2.

- *Number Nine* — All chipsets supported in 3.3.6, such as Number Nine Imagine 128, Ticket 2 Ride, Revolution 3D, and Revolution IV, are also supported in 4.0.2.

- *Oak Technologies, Inc.* — These chipsets are not supported in 4.0.2, but 3.3.6 supports the OTI067, OTI077, and OTI087 chipsets.

- *Paradise/Western Digital* — These chipsets are not supported in 4.0.2, but 3.3.6 supports the Paradise PVGA1 and the Western Digital WD90C00, 90C10, 90C30, 90C24, 90C31, and 90C33 chipsets.

- *RealTek* — These chipsets are not supported in 4.0.2, but 3.3.6 supports the RealTek RTG3106 chipset.

- *Rendition/Micron* — All chipsets supported in 3.3.6, such as Verite 1000, 2100, and 2200, are also supported in 4.0.2.

- *S3* — XFree86 3.3.6 supports the 911, 924, 801, 805, 928, 864, 868, 964, 968, Trio32, Trio64, Trio64V+, Trio64UV+, Aurora64V+, Trio64V2, PLATO/PX, ViRGE, ViRGE/VX, ViRGE/DX, ViRGE/GX, ViRGE/GX2, ViRGE/MX, ViRGE/MX+, Trio3D, Trio3D/2X, Savage3D, Savage3D/MV, Savage4, Savage2000, Savage/MX-MV, Savage/MX, Savage/IX-MV, and Savage/IX chipsets. XFree86 4.0.2 supports only the ViRGE, Trio3D, and Savage chipsets.

- *Silicon Graphics, Inc. (SGI)* — SGI Indy's Newport cards are supported only in 4.0.2.

- *Silicon Integrated Systems (SiS)* — Both 3.3.6 and 4.0.2 support the SiS 86C205, 6326, 530, 620, 300, 630, and 540 chipsets. Support for the SiS 86C201, 86C202, 86C215, 86C225, 5597, and 5598 is currently available only in 3.3.6.

- *Silicon Motion, Inc* — All chipsets supported in 3.3.6, such as the Lynx, LynxE, Lynx3D, LynxEM, LynxEM+, and Lynx3DM, are also supported in 4.0.2.

- *Sun Microsystems* — Sun graphics hardware is supported only in 4.0.2.

- *Trident Microsystems* — Both 3.3.6 and 4.0.2 support the TVGA8900D, TGUI9420DGi, TGUI9440AGi, TGUI9660, TGUI9680, ProVidia 9682, ProVidia 9685, Cyber9320, Cyber9382, Cyber9385, Cyber9388, Cyber9397, Cyber9520, Cyber9525, 3DImage975, 3DImage985, Cyber9397/DVD, Blade3D, CyberBlade/i7, CyberBlade/DSTN/i7, and CyberBlade/i1 chipsets. Support for the older TVGA8200LX, TVGA8800CS, TVGA8900B, TVGA8900C, TVGA8900CL, TVGA9000, TVGA9000i, TVGA9100B, TVGA9200CXr, TGUI9400CXi, TGUI9420, and TGUI9430DGi chipsets are currently available only in 3.3.6.

- *Tseng Labs* — XFree86 3.3.6 supports the ET3000, ET4000AX, ET4000/W32, ET4000/W32i, ET4000/W32p, ET6000, and ET6100 chipsets. XFree86 4.0.2 supports all of these chipsets except the ET3000.

- *Video 7* — This chipset is not supported by 4.0.2, but 3.3.6 supports it.

- *Weitek* — These chipsets are not supported by 4.0.2, but 3.3.6 supports the P9000 and P9100 chipsets.

The mouse

The *mouse* is an integral part of a GUI, because users indicate choices and perform tasks by pointing and clicking. The X server moves an onscreen pointer as you move the mouse. The X server monitors all mouse clicks and sends these *mouse-click events* to the appropriate X client application — the one whose window contains the mouse pointer.

Although you may have set up the mouse during Linux installation, you still have to provide information about the mouse to the X server. The XFree86 X server needs a mouse to start; if the X server cannot access and control the mouse, it won't start.

To specify the mouse, you need to know the following things:

- The mouse type, such as Microsoft, Logitech, BusMouse, or PS/2-style mouse.

- The type of connection between your mouse and the system (serial or bus).

- The mouse device name. You can leave this as the generic name /dev/mouse, because the Red Hat installation program sets up a link between /dev/mouse and the actual mouse device; the actual device name depends on the type of mouse and where it is connected — the exact serial port for a serial mouse, for example.

You should not have any problem with the mouse, as long as the mouse type and device names are correct.

Configuring XFree86 with Xconfigurator

The XFree86 X servers read and interpret the XF86Config file to find detailed information about your PC's monitor, video card, keyboard, and mouse. Additionally, the XF86Config file specifies the types of video modes that you want to use. You can use the Xconfigurator utility program to create a configuration file that the X server needs. Log in as root and type Xconfigurator in a text console to run the utility.

The Xconfigurator program starts with a welcome dialog that informs you that the program will create a configuration file named XF86Config (usually placed in the /etc/X11 directory). After reading the message, press Enter to continue with the configuration process.

Xconfigurator automatically detects the chipset used by your video card and displays a summary message, as shown in Figure 3-2.

Because the dialog box in Figure 3-2 is for your information only, press Enter to continue with the rest of the configuration. The next step is to select your monitor from a list. Use the up and down arrow keys to browse through the list. If you find your monitor model listed, position the cursor on that monitor, and then press Enter. Otherwise, select Custom and press Enter. If you choose Custom, Xconfigurator displays another dialog box that prompts you for two critical parameters of your monitor:

■ *Horizontal synchronization frequency*—the number of times per second that the monitor can display a horizontal raster line, in kilohertz (kHz).

■ *Vertical synchronization rate* or *vertical refresh rate*—how many times per second the monitor can display the entire screen.

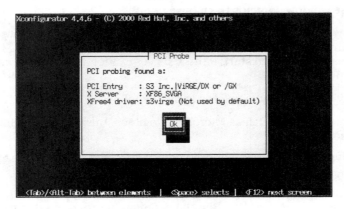

Figure 3-2: Result of probing the video card

You can find this information in your monitor's manual.

After entering the required information, press Enter to continue. Xconfigurator displays a list of predefined monitor capabilities.

Caution

Typically, one of the items from this list should match your monitor's specifications. If you need to guess your monitor's capabilities, be conservative. Do not specify a horizontal synchronization range that is beyond the capabilities of your monitor. An incorrect value can damage your monitor.

For example, if your monitor's manual says that it is capable of displaying 1,280 by 1,024 resolution at 60 Hz, then you should pick the item that matches this specification. After selecting the horizontal synchronization capabilities, press Enter.

Xconfigurator now prompts you for the vertical synchronization rate of your monitor. Pick the vertical synchronization range that is nearest to your monitor's specifications and press Enter.

If Xconfigurator is unable to detect the amount of video memory on your video card, it displays a dialog box that prompts you to select the amount of video memory from a list. Select the amount closest to your video card's memory and press Enter.

Xconfigurator prompts you to identify the clock chip—a timing device on the video card. You can safely press Enter to accept the default selection labeled *No Clockchip Setting (recommended)*.

Xconfigurator then displays a dialog box listing video modes in terms of pixel resolution, such as 1,280 × 1,024, and color, such as 16 bits per pixel, as shown in Figure 3-3.

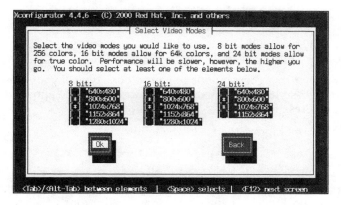

Figure 3-3: Selecting a video mode you would like to use

Press the tab key to move the cursor to a video mode, and press the space-bar to select that mode. You can choose as many modes as you want. Then press Tab to select the OK button and press Enter.

Next Xconfigurator gives you the option of starting X to test your configuration. You should press Enter. A graphical X screen appears and Xconfigurator shows a dialog box that asks if you can read the text. Close the dialog box.

Xconfigurator then displays a dialog box that asks if you want a graphical login screen. Select Yes and press Enter. This ensures that when the system reboots you will get a graphical login dialog, instead of a text screen.

Xconfigurator then writes the XF86Config file in the /etc/X11 directory and completes the X configuration.

Configuring XFree86 Using xf86config

You can also use a utility program called xf86config to generate a usable XF86Config file. The xf86config program asks you questions. You need to have some information about your PC's video card and monitor to answer these questions.

To run xf86config, log in as root and type xf86config at the shell command prompt. The xf86config program displays a screen of text with some helpful information. Press Enter to continue.

The xf86config program asks you to specify a mouse protocol that determines how the X server will communicate with the mouse. The program shows you the following list of options:

```
1.  Microsoft compatible (2-button protocol)
2.  Mouse Systems (3-button protocol)
3.  Bus Mouse
4.  PS/2 Mouse
5.  Logitech Mouse (serial, old type, Logitech protocol)
6.  Logitech MouseMan (Microsoft compatible)
7.  MM Series
8.  MM HitTablet
9.  Microsoft IntelliMouse
```

Type the number that corresponds to your mouse type. If your mouse is connected to a PS/2-style port, for example, select 4. Type the appropriate number, and then press Enter.

The xf86config program then asks the following:

```
Please answer the following question with either 'y' or 'n'.
Do you want to enable Emulate3Buttons?
```

If your mouse has two buttons, xf86config suggests that you enable Emulate3Buttons. Enter y. If you enable Emulate3Buttons you can simulate a middle-button click by pressing both buttons simultaneously. Many X applications assume that the mouse has three buttons, so this feature comes in handy in the PC world where a mouse typically has only two buttons.

Next you have to specify the full device name for the mouse. During Red Hat Linux installation, you configure the mouse and the installation program creates a link between your mouse device and the standard name /dev/mouse. Therefore, you can press Enter.

The xf86config program displays a list of keyboard types and prompts you for the one that matches your keyboard. Enter the number from the list. If none of the types matches, you can always select 1, which represents the Generic 101-key PC keyboard.

The xf86config program then asks you for the country for which the keyboard should be configured. Again, you have to pick from a list displayed by the program.

Next, xf86config informs you that it needs the horizontal and the vertical synchronization rates (or frequencies) of your monitor. Press Enter to continue. The xf86config program offers you the following options:

```
    hsync in kHz; monitor type with characteristic modes
 1   31.5; Standard VGA, 640x480 @ 60 Hz
 2   31.5 - 35.1; Super VGA, 800x600 @ 56 Hz
 3   31.5, 35.5; 8514 Compatible, 1024x768 @ 87 Hz interlaced (no
800x600)
 4   31.5, 35.15, 35.5; Super VGA, 1024x768 @ 87 Hz interlaced, 800x600
@ 56 Hz
 5   31.5 - 37.9; Extended Super VGA, 800x600 @ 60 Hz, 640x480 @ 72 Hz
 6   31.5 - 48.5; Non-Interlaced SVGA, 1024x768 @ 60 Hz, 800x600 @ 72
Hz
 7   31.5 - 57.0; High Frequency SVGA, 1024x768 @ 70 Hz
```

```
 8  31.5 - 64.3; Monitor that can do 1280x1024 @ 60 Hz
 9  31.5 - 79.0; Monitor that can do 1280x1024 @ 74 Hz
10  31.5 - 82.0; Monitor that can do 1280x1024 @ 76 Hz
11  Enter your own horizontal sync range
```

```
Enter your choice (1-11): 11
```

You can enter the number that corresponds to your monitor or type 11 to specify a range.

Caution

Do not specify a horizontal synchronization range that is beyond the capabilities of your monitor. An incorrect value can damage the monitor.

Many monitor manuals provide a range of values for the horizontal synchronization rate. To enter a range of values, type 11, and then press Enter. The program prompts you for the range. Enter the range as two values separated by a minus sign (-). My monitor's documentation, for example, says that the horizontal synchronization range is 30–69 kHz, so I enter the following:

```
Horizontal sync range: 30-69
```

Next xf86config prompts you for the vertical synchronization rate and gives you the following options:

```
1  50-70
2  50-90
3  50-100
4  40-150
5  Enter your own vertical sync range
```

```
Enter your choice: 5
```

If you know the range, type 5, and then press Enter. At the next prompt, enter the range for the vertical synchronization. My monitor's documentation shows this range to be 50–120 Hz, so I enter the following:

```
Vertical sync range: 50-120
```

Next you have to enter an identifier for your monitor's definition. Typically, you enter your monitor's make and model. You can enter anything here. This identifier is used to refer to the monitor in another part of the XF86Config configuration file. For my system's monitor, I respond as follows:

```
Enter an identifier for your monitor definition: Micron700FGx
```

The next task is to configure the video-card settings. The xf86config program displays an explanatory message and asks this question:

```
Do you want to look at the card database? y
```

Type y, and then press Enter. The program then displays a list of video cards, one screen at a time. Press Enter after each screen to see the entire list. The make, model, and chipset of the video card are crucial pieces of information that you need to configure XFree86 properly.

One of my PCs, for example, has a Diamond Stealth 3D 2000 PRO video card with the S3 ViRGE/DX chipset. I notice the following line on one of the screens:

```
239  Diamond Multimedia Stealth 3D 2000 PRO      S3 ViRGE/DX
```

I type 239 — the number corresponding to my video card — and press Enter.

Tip

Each new release of XFree86 supports more video cards. For example, XFree86 4.0.2 supports 751 cards. (As a point of reference, version 3.1.2 supported only 124 cards; version 3.3.1 supported 382 cards; and version 3.3.6 supported 671 cards.) If your video card's vendor and model do not appear in the list, but you know the video chipset, try selecting the entry that corresponds to the generic chipset. If you have a video card based on the S3-Trio64 chipset, for example, but you do not know the make and model of the card, select 456 from the list.

After you enter your selection, xf86config displays some information (and any appropriate instructions) about the video card that you selected. When I select card number 241, for example, xf86config displays the following:

```
Your selected card definition:

Identifier: Diamond Multimedia Stealth 3D 2000 PRO
Chipset:    S3 ViRGE/DX
Driver:     s3virge
Do NOT probe clocks or use any Clocks line.
This card is basically UNSUPPORTED. It may only work as a generic
VGA-compatible card. If you have an XFree86 version more recent than
what
this card definition was based on, there's a chance that it is now
supported.

Press enter to continue, or ctrl-c to abort.
```

Tip

Notice the instruction that I should not probe clocks or use any Clocks line. If you see any instruction like this, keep it in mind as you continue with xf86config. If the program offers to probe clocks, for example, you should answer no. You don't really have to understand what the instruction means; simply follow it, and you should have an XF86Config file that works properly.

After you press Enter to continue, xf86config asks how much video memory your video card has. Most current video cards have anywhere from 4MB (4,096KB) to 32MB (32,768KB) of video memory. You need at least 1MB of video memory to display 256 colors at 1,024 × 768 resolution (1,024 pixels horizontally by 768 pixels vertically). Type the number that corresponds to the amount of memory in your video card, and then press Enter.

Now you have to provide an identifier for your video card. The following is what I enter for my PC's video card:

```
Enter an identifier for your video card definition: Diamond Stealth 3D
2000 PRO
```

The program next asks you to enter the default color depth, in terms of number of bits per pixel. The choices range from monochrome (one bit per pixel), to millions of colors (24 bits per pixel). Enter the number corresponding to the depth you want, and then press Enter.

This step completes your session with xf86config. The program displays a message asking whether it can write the XF86Config file to the /etc/X11 directory. Type y and press Enter. The xf86config program writes the configuration file and exits.

If you are lucky, the XF86Config file generated by xf86config may be all that you need to run X with your PC's video card and monitor. Because of the potential for monitor damage if you make incorrect settings in the XF86Config file, however, you should use an editor to look through the configuration file (Chapter 14 describes the vi and GNU Emacs editors).

Checking the XF86Config file

The XF86Config file describes your video card, monitor, and mouse to the X server. By default, the X server first looks for the configuration file in the /etc/X11 directory (/etc/X11/XF86Config), which is where you should save the configuration file.

Secret

In Red Hat Linux, the XFree86 3.3.6 server uses the configuration file /etc/X11/XF86Config, whereas the XFree 4.0.2 server uses the /etc/X11/ XF86Config-4 file. Type ls -l **/etc/X11/X** to determine which version of XFree86 server you are running. If /etc/X11/X is a symbolic link to ../../ usr/X11R6/bin/XFree86, then you are running the XFree86 4.0.2 server; otherwise you are running the XFree86 3.3.6 server. For example, the symbolic link for a Red Hat Linux PC running XFree86 3.3.6 appears as

```
lrwxrwxrwx  1 root  root   29 Aug 31 13:33 /etc/X11/X ->
../../usr/X11R6/bin/XF86_SVGA
```

You can also check for the X server's version number with the xdpyinfo command. Type xdpyinfo | more in a terminal window and look for the vendor release number. For an XFree86 3.3.6 server, the vendor release number appears as follows:

```
vendor release number:    3360
```

If you study the /etc/X11/XF86Config-4 file (I refer to this file generically as XF86Config), you see that the configuration file consists of several sections. Each section has the following format:

```
# This a comment
Section "SectionName"
    EntryName   EntryValue
    ...
    ...
    Subsection "SubsectionName"
```

```
        EntryName EntryValue
        ...
        ...
    EndSubsection
EndSection
```

Sections consist of a sequence of entries; each entry has a name and a value. A section may contain one or more subsections. A hash mark (#) at the beginning of a line marks a comment line.

In XFree86 4.0.2, the XF86Config file contains one or more of the following sections:

- *Files* — This section lists the *pathnames* (full directory names) of font files and the file that contains the color database, called the *RGB file*. RGB stands for red, green, and blue — the three primary components of color.

- *ServerFlags* — This section lists various X server options, such as DontZap (which means "do not allow the Ctrl-Alt-Backspace keystroke to terminate the X server") and DontZoom (which means "do not accept special keystrokes to change screen resolution").

- *Module* — This section specifies which X server extension modules and font modules should be loaded. The modules are object code and libraries that add specific functionality to the X server.

- *InputDevice* — This section lists information about the keyboard and the mouse or pointer. (In the X Window System's terminology, the mouse is known as the *pointer*.)

- *Device* — This section describes the characteristics of a video card (or *graphics device*). The configuration file may have more than one Device section. The Driver entry in the Device section specifies the XFree86 4.0.2 driver for the video card.

- *Monitor* — This section includes the specifications of a monitor (such as horizontal and vertical synchronization rates) and a list of video modes that the monitor supports. In XFree86 4.0.2, a set of VESA modes is defined internally in the server, so for most monitors it isn't necessary to specify any modes explicitly in the Monitor section.

- *Modes* — This section enables you to define video modes outside the Monitor sections. The configuration file can have multiple Modes sections, or none. Modes sections are not usually necessary, because the monitor's built-in set of VESA standard modes is usually sufficient.

- *Screen* — This section describes a combination of a video card and monitor to be used by the X server. Typically, the configuration file has several Screen sections.

- *ServerLayout* — This section combines one or more Screen sections and one or more InputDevice sections to specify the complete layout of the display screens and input devices.

- *DRI*—This optional section provides information for the Direct Rendering Infrastructure. (To learn more about DRI, read the DRI User Guide online at `http://www.xfree86.org/current/DRI.html`.)

- *Vendor*—This optional section contains vendor-specific configuration information.

You should not have to learn all the details of these sections, and you need not change the configuration file manually. If you need to edit the configuration file, start with an `XF86Config` file generated by one of the configuration utilities, such as `Xconfigurator` or `xf86config`.

Three sections in `XF86Config` deal with the video card and monitor:

- The `Screen` section combines a video card and monitor with the video modes to be used by the X server for that screen. Typically, `XF86Config` contains several Screen sections, one for each display screen.

- The `Device` section describes the characteristics of a video card (also known as a *graphics device*). The configuration file can have several Device sections, one for each video card, if the system has multiple video cards.

- The `Monitor` section lists the technical specifications of a monitor (such as the horizontal and vertical synchronization rates) and includes a list of video modes that the monitor supports.

As you learned earlier in this chapter, you can create the `XF86Config` file by running the `xf86config` utility program. If you have your monitor's technical specifications handy, and your video card appears in the list that `xf86config` displays, the generated `XF86Config` file may work as is. You will typically run into problems only when you attempt to use the full capabilities of advanced video cards.

Screen Section

The X server determines the settings of the video card and the monitor from the `Screen` section meant for that server. The `Screen` section specifies the names of a `Device` (video card) and a `Monitor` that make up this screen. Following is a `Screen` section from a typical XFree86 4.0.2 configuration file:

```
Section "Screen"
    Identifier   "Screen0"
    Device       "S3 ViRGE/DX (generic)"
    Monitor      "Monitor0"
    DefaultDepth 16

    Subsection "Display"
        Depth    8
        Modes    "1024x768" "800x600" "640x480"
        ViewPort 0 0
        Virtual  1024 768
```

```
EndSubsection

Subsection "Display"
    Depth       16
    Modes       "1024x768" "800x600" "640x480"
EndSubsection
... other Display subsections ...
EndSection
```

Comment lines start with the hash mark (#). The section's definition is enclosed in the `Section . . . EndSection` block.

The Identifier line gives a name to this screen. This name is used to refer to the screen in the ServerLayout section. Following the `Device` and `Monitor` names are several `Display` subsections. Each `Display` subsection applies to a specific `Depth` (the number of bits of storage per pixel, which also determines the number of colors that can be displayed at a time).

Secret

The X server automatically uses the first `Display` subsection in the `Screen` definition, but you can start the server with command-line options that specify a different `Depth`. If you have set up your Red Hat Linux system for a graphical login screen, you can start the X server with a `Depth` of 24 by having the following line in the `[servers]` section of the `/etc/X11/gdm/gdm.conf` file:

```
0=/usr/bin/X11/X -bpp 24
```

The `-bpp` option for the X server program stands for bits per pixel, which is the same as `Depth`. Selecting a value for the `Depth` works, provided that the video card and the monitor are capable of supporting that `Depth`. You can also specify a default depth through the DefaultDepth entry in the `Screen` section.

The `Modes` line in the `Display` subsection lists the names of video modes that the monitor and video card can support. The names of these modes appear in the `Monitor` section of the `XF86Config` file.

For some video cards, if the card has more memory than is needed to hold the information for all visible pixels in a specific mode, the X server can use the leftover memory to give the appearance of a much larger array of pixels than the 640×480 or $1{,}024 \times 768$ that may be specified by a video mode. In other words, you get a large virtual screen from which you can select a smaller area to view. The `Virtual` line indicates the size of this virtual screen, whereas `ViewPort` specifies which part of the virtual screen is mapped to the physical display.

Device Section

The `Device` section of the `XF86Config` file provides information about the video card. For a video card based on the S3 ViRGE/DX chipset, `XF86Config` has a `Device` section that looks like this:

```
Section "Device"
    Identifier    "S3 ViRGE/DX (generic)"
    Driver        "s3virge"
    VendorName    "S3 ViRGE/DX (generic)"
    BoardName     "S3 ViRGE/DX (generic)"
EndSection
```

Each line in the section provides some information about the video card. In this case, the Identifier indicates the name assigned to this video card; this identifier is used in the Screen section to refer to this specific video card. If the information is available, the VendorName and BoardName further identify the video card.

For older video cards that do not have a programmable dot clock, an important line in the Device section is the Clocks line. The values in this line indicate the dot clocks that the video card supports. A typical Clocks line looks like this:

```
    Clocks    25.2 28.3
```

Nowadays most video cards do not require the Clocks line, because the cards have programmable dot clocks.

If your PC has more than one video card, you also need a BusID line identifying the location of this particular video card on the bus. For PCI bus video cards, you can find this information with the lspci command; look for the video card's name in the output, and use the number at the beginning of the line. For example, a typical BusID line might look like this:

```
    BusID    "PCI:00:0d:00"
```

In addition to the Clocks line, you can specify one or more flags meant for the X server for the type of video card that you are specifying in the Device section.

Monitor Section

The Monitor section lists the technical specifications of the monitor: the horizontal synchronization (or *horizontal sync*), frequency, and vertical refresh rate. You can get these values from your monitor's manual.

Secret

The horizontal-sync signal occurs at the end of each raster line; this signal moves the electron beam from the end of one line, to the beginning of the next raster line. The horizontal-sync frequency is essentially the number of times per second that the monitor can trace a raster line on the display screen. If the monitor can display 480 lines (at 640 × 480 resolution, for example) and repaint the screen 72 times per second (a vertical refresh rate of 72 Hz), the horizontal-sync frequency is at least 480 × 72 = 34,560 times per second = 34,560 Hz = 34.56 kHz. The actual value is higher, because the monitor always has to trace more lines than are displayed.

Caution

You have to be careful with the values of horizontal sync and vertical refresh, because the X server uses these values to select what signals are sent from the video card. A monitor may be physically damaged if the video card sends signals that are beyond the monitor's specifications.

When you use the xf86config program to create the XF86Config file, the xf86config program gives you the option to select the horizontal-synchronization frequencies from a general list. If you have no information about a monitor, you may want to start with a conservative setting for the horizontal sync, such as the value for a standard VGA monitor. (You do not have to enter the exact value of horizontal sync; just select the monitor type.)

Most new monitors are multisync monitors that support a range of horizontal-synchronization frequencies (as opposed to a fixed value). If you have the monitor's manual, you can specify the range of frequencies for the horizontal sync.

In XFree86 3.3.6, the most important entries in the Monitor section are the Modeline lines, which list the video modes that are suitable for use with the monitor. In XFree86 4.0.2, a set of VESA standard video modes is defined internally in the X server, and there is therefore no need to specify any video modes explicitly in the Monitor section, for most monitors.

Following is a typical Monitor section (comments show the format of video-mode specification):

```
Section "Monitor"
    Identifier    "Monitor0"
    VendorName    "Monitor Vendor"
    ModelName     "Monitor Model"
    HorizSync     30.0-69.0
    VertRefresh   55.0-120.0
# Modes can be specified in two formats. A compact one-line format, or
# a multi-line format.

# The following two are equivalent

#ModeLine "1024x768i" 45 1024 1048 1208 1264 768 776 784 817 Interlace

#   Mode "1024x768i"
#     DotClock   45
#     HTimings   1024 1048 1208 1264
#     VTimings   768 776 784 817
#     Flags      "Interlace"
#   EndMode

EndSection
```

The Monitor section's Identifier field gives a name to this monitor; this name is used in the Screen section to refer to this monitor. You should fill in the HorizSync and VertRefresh lines with information from the monitor's manual (or select conservatively from the typical values that the xf86config program displays).

ModeLine Computation

Although you can live with the VESA standard video modes defined in the XFree86 4.0.2 server, you may sometimes have to manually add a ModeLine to get a video mode to work for a video card/monitor combination.

You typically specify a ModeLine on a single line with the following syntax:

```
ModeLine "name"  CLK  HRES HSS HSE HTOT  VRES VSS VSE VTOT  flags
```

You must fill in all arguments that appear in italics, except the last argument, which is an optional keyword that indicates the type of the mode. The *flags* field, for example, can be Interlace for an interlaced mode (alternative raster lines are drawn through the image each time) or DoubleScan (each scan line is doubled). Other flags indicate the polarity of the sync signal. The values can be +HSync, -HSync, +VSync, or -VSync, depending on the polarities you are specifying.

The meanings of the arguments on the ModeLine are as follows:

- "*name*" is the name of this mode, in double quotes. Usually the resolution of the mode is used as its name. Thus, you'll see mode names such as "640x480" and "1024x768". These mode names are used in the Display subsection of the Screen section.

- *CLK* is the dot clock to be used for this mode. For a video card with a fixed set of dot clocks, the dot clock should be one of the values on the Clocks line in the Device section of the XF86Config file.

- *HRES HSS HSE HTOT* are the horizontal timing parameters. *HRES* is the horizontal resolution in terms of the number of pixels visible on a raster line. As Figure 3-1 shows, the actual number of pixels on a raster line exceeds the number of visible pixels. *HTOT* is the total pixels on the line. *HSS* is where the horizontal-sync signal begins, and *HSE* is the pixel number where the horizontal-sync signal ends. The horizontal-sync signal moves the electron beam from one line to the next. For a 640 × 480 video mode, these four parameters might be 640 680 720 864. That sequence of numbers says that 864 pixels are on the raster lines, but only 640 are visible. The horizontal-sync signal begins at pixel 680 and ends at pixel 864.

- *VRES VSS VSE VTOT* are the vertical timing parameters. *VRES* is the vertical resolution in terms of the number of visible raster lines on the display screen. As Figure 3-1 shows, the actual number of raster lines exceeds the number of visible raster lines. *VTOT* is the total raster lines. *VSS* is the line number where the vertical-sync signal begins, and *VSE* is the line number where the vertical-sync signal ends. The vertical-sync signal moves the electron beam from the bottom of the screen to the beginning of the first line. For a 640 × 480 video mode, these four parameters might be 480 488 491 521.

From a monitor's manual you can get two key parameters: the vertical refresh rate (in Hz) and the horizontal synchronization frequency (in kHz). The monitor's manual provides these two values as ranges of valid values. The vertical refresh rate is typically between 50 Hz and 90 Hz; the horizontal sync frequency can be anywhere from 30 kHz to 135 kHz. Following are two equations that define the relationship between the dot clock and some of the horizontal and vertical timing parameters on the ModeLine:

```
CLK = RR * HTOT * VTOT
CLK = HSF * HTOT
```

In these equations, RR is a screen refresh rate that is within the range of vertical refresh rate of the monitor, and HSF is a horizontal-scan frequency supported by the monitor. Remember to convert everything to a common unit (for example, make sure that all values are in Hz) when you apply these formulas.

To define a mode, you can start with a desired refresh rate (RR), such as 72 Hz. For a given dot clock, you then can compute the product HTOT * VTOT from the first equation. Next, plug in a value for HSF that is within the range of supported horizontal-scan frequencies for the monitor. Because the dot clock is already known, you can compute HTOT from the second equation. After you know HTOT, you can determine VTOT, because you already computed the product of HTOT * VTOT.

At this point, you know HTOT and VTOT. What you have to select are the arguments HSS, HSE, VSS, and VSE, which you need for the ModeLine. Unfortunately, figuring out these four parameters requires some trial and error. You can pick the HRES and VRES values first (HRES and VRES determine the resolution of the mode). Then you have to select HSS and HSE to lie between HRES and HTOT and ensure that HSE > HSS. Similarly, VSS and VSE should be between VRES and VTOT and make sure that VSE > VSS.

If the display area looks small or not centered, you have to alter the values HSS, HSE, VSS, and VSE to tweak the display. Given that the default XF86Config file already includes the ModeLines for many common video modes, you should simply provide the allowable ranges of vertical refresh rates and horizontal-sync frequencies for your monitor, and settle for one of the predefined modes.

Another way to correct minor display problems is to run the xvidtune utility that comes with XFree86. If your X display is working, but if the display does not look as good as you think it should (for example, if it does not fill the whole screen, or it is skewed to one side), type xvidtune in a terminal window. The program prints a few lines of information about the monitor on the terminal window. The xvidtune window and a dialog box appear. The dialog box (see Figure 3-4) displays a message that warns you about the possibility of damaging your monitor and video card if you use the xvidtune program improperly.

If you decide to proceed, click OK to dismiss the dialog box. You have to use xvidtune through the buttons on its main window, as shown in Figure 3-5.

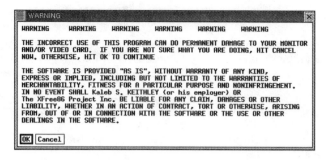

Figure 3-4: Warning message from xvidtune

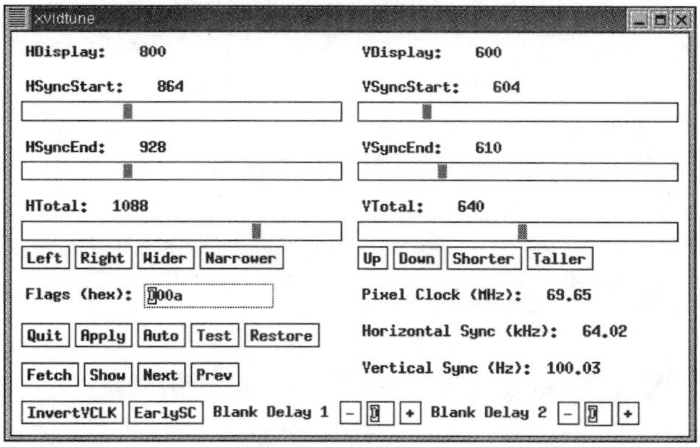

Figure 3-5: Main window for xvidtune

Click the Auto button. Then click the appropriate buttons (Up, Down, Left, Right, Shorter, Taller, Wider, Narrower) to adjust the display. After each click, the display will change. After you have adjusted the display to your liking, click the Show button. This prints out a ModeLine of the following form on the terminal window:

```
"800x600"     69.65    800  864  928 1088    600  604  610  640 -hsync -vsync
```

The idea is that you can use this ModeLine in the Monitor section of the /etc/X11/XF86Config file and then restart the X display (press Ctrl-Alt-Backspace to kill the X server).

If you want to adjust the other video modes, you can click the Next and Prev buttons to switch modes. The effect of these buttons is equivalent to pressing Ctrl-Alt-Keypad+ and Ctrl-Alt-Keypad–, respectively.

When you are through using xvidtune, click the Quit button to exit the program.

Running X

After you have a complete XF86Config file, your X server should be ready to run. Typically you will have already selected a graphical login option during installation, so that X starts automatically whenever your system restarts.

If you did not opt for a graphical login option, you can start the X server by running the startx script, which is a file that contains Linux commands. This script is in the /usr/X11R6/bin directory, but that directory should be in your PATH environment variable. Therefore, to run that script, type startx at the shell prompt.

The startx script looks for another script file, named .xinitrc, in your home directory. If startx does not find any .xinitrc file in your home directory, it runs the xinit command with the default script /etc/X11/xinit/xinitrc. Notice that unlike the .xinitrc file in your home directory, the default script file does not have a period as the first character of its name.

The result of running startx depends on the commands in .xinitrc in your home directory, if you have one. Otherwise, the result depends on the commands in the /etc/X11/xinit/xinitrc file.

There are some special keystrokes you can use to control the X server. The following sections describe these methods of controlling X.

Aborting X Using Ctrl-Alt-Backspace

If you have created a new XF86Config file to try out some new video modes, you can abort the X server, by pressing Ctrl-Alt-Backspace to kill the X server. (In Linux, the term *kill* refers to abnormally exiting a program. Linux even has a kill command that stops errant programs.)

If you have selected the graphical login option, the X server immediately restarts, but this time with the configuration options in the new XF86Config file. If your system is not set up for a graphical login screen, you will go back to the text display.

Secret

If you have enabled the graphical login screen and X does not work properly because of erroneous configuration options in the XF86Config file, press Ctrl-Alt-F1 to get a text-mode login screen. Log in as root and run xf86config to configure X, carefully selecting the options for monitor, video card, and the video mode (resolution and depth). After preparing the new XF86Config file, press Ctrl-Alt-F7 to get back to the graphical login screen, and press Ctrl-Alt-Backspace to kill the X server and force it to restart with the new configuration options.

Trying Different Screen Modes

In your XF86Config file, if you look at the Screen section that applies to your X server, you notice several Display subsections. Each Display subsection lists the video modes that are supported for a specific depth — the number of bits in each pixel's value. An X server typically supports a depth of 8, which means that each pixel has an eight-bit value and that the server can display up to $2^8 = 256$ distinct colors. The Display subsection lists the video modes in terms of the display resolution, which in turn is expressed in terms of the number of pixels horizontally and vertically. For example, here is a partial listing of a Screen section of the X configuration file:

```
Section "Screen"
    Identifier    "Screen0"
    Device        "S3 ViRGE/DX (generic)"
    Monitor       "Monitor0"
    DefaultDepth  16

    Subsection "Display"
        Depth       8
        Modes       "640x480" "800x600" "1024x768"
        ViewPort    0 0
        Virtual     1024 768
    EndSubsection
    ... other Display subsections ...
EndSection
```

When the X server starts, it configures the video card at the resolution (in this case, 640 × 480, or 640 pixels horizontally by 480 pixels vertically) that corresponds to the first mode shown in the Modes entry, as follows:

```
Modes       "640x480" "800x600" "1024x768"
```

You can try the other modes without having to exit the X server. Press Ctrl-Alt-Keypad+ (*Keypad+* means the plus key in the numeric keypad). The X server switches to the next mode — in this case 800 × 600. Press Ctrl-Alt-Keypad+ again, and the X server switches to 1,024 × 768 mode. When you press Ctrl-Alt-Keypad+, the X server cycles forward to the next mode listed in the Modes entry.

Tip

Press Ctrl-Alt-Keypad+ several times to make sure that the X server works in all video modes.

To cycle backward to the preceding mode, press Ctrl-Alt-Keypad– (*Keypad–* means the minus key in the numeric keypad). Therefore, if the X server is displaying in 800 × 600 mode and you press Ctrl-Alt-Keypad–, the server switches to 640 × 480 mode.

You can make the X server start in any of the supported modes. If you want the X server to start at the highest-resolution mode, simply change the Modes entry in the Screen section that corresponds to your X server (the Driver entry in the Screen section indicates the X server type) to the following:

```
Modes       "1024x768" "800x600" "640x480"
```

This change makes X start in 1,024 × 768 mode, which gives you much more screen area than 640 × 480 mode.

The screen resolutions in the `Modes` entry determine several things:

- The first resolution is the default resolution (the resolution in which the X server starts).

- When you alter screen resolutions, the X server scrolls through the resolutions in the order shown in the `Modes` entry. When you press Ctrl-Alt-Keypad+, the X server changes resolutions in the left-to-right order; the order is reversed when you press Ctrl-Alt-Keypad–.

Some applications, such as the Applixware office suite, require you to run the X server in 16 bits per pixel mode (also referred to as a 16-bit color depth). To make the X server start with a 16-bit color depth, perform the following steps:

1. Open the `/etc/X11/XF86Config` file using your favorite text editor.

2. Locate the `Screen` section corresponding to the X section that corresponds to your X server. For example, if you use the SVGA server, look for the Screen section that has `svga` as the `Driver` entry.

3. Just before the first `Display` subsection, insert the following line:

   ```
   DefaultColorDepth 16
   ```

   This forces the X server to use a 16-bit color depth. The server uses the information from the `Display` subsection that specifies `Depth` as 16.

4. Save the `XF86Config` file.

5. If X is running (and assuming you have enabled the graphical login screen), press Ctrl-Alt-Backspace to stop the X server and force it to restart. It should now use a 16-bit color depth.

Summary

Video cards and monitors don't matter much if you use Linux in text mode only. If you want to use the XFree86 X Window System, however, you have to pay attention to the video card and monitor. The X Window System, or X, is a popular window system that serves as the basis of graphical user interfaces and graphical output on most UNIX workstations. XFree86 is a free implementation of X for Intel 80x86 and compatible PCs. XFree86 works with a variety of video cards, but you have to configure it to use the appropriate parameters for your video card and monitor. This chapter shows you how to configure and run X on your Red Hat Linux system.

By reading this chapter, you learn the following:

▶ In a PC, the video card stores the array of pixels that constitutes the image that you see onscreen. The video card converts the pixel values to analog signals that drive the red (R), green (G), and blue (B) electron guns in a monitor. These RGB electron beams, in turn, paint the color image on the phosphor-coated display screen. The combination of the video card and monitor is important to the X Window System, because the X server controls the video card directly, and because the monitor must be capable of handling the signals that the video card generates.

▶ X Window System is a network-transparent windowing system based on the client/server model. The X server, running on a workstation with a bit-mapped graphics display, manages regions of screen known as *windows*, where the output from X client applications appears. The X clients often run on remote systems, but their output appears on the local X display.

▶ The term *graphical user interface* (GUI — pronounced *gooey*) describes a user interface that makes use of windows, menus, and other graphical objects, so that users can interact with the application by pointing with the mouse pointer and clicking mouse buttons. From an application developer's point of view, a GUI is a combination of a window manager, a style guide, and a library of routines or *toolkit* that can be used to build the user interface.

▶ X provides the basic functions that can be used to build a GUI. Many GUIs are built upon X. Motif, GNOME, and KDE are examples of such GUIs. GNOME and KDE are popular GUIs for Linux systems.

▶ XFree86 is the X Window System for Linux PCs; it comes on this book's companion CD-ROM. When you install Red Hat Linux from the CD-ROMs, you also install XFree86.

▶ When the X server runs, it consults a configuration file named `XF86Config` (in the `/etc/X11` directory) to select an appropriate video mode and to configure the video card and monitor for proper operation. Computing the valid video-mode parameters is complicated. As long as you know the technical specification of your monitor (such as horizontal-synchronization frequency and refresh rate), you do not need to compute the video-mode information.

▶ You configure XFree86 as you install Red Hat Linux. However, you can reconfigure XFree86 by running the `Xconfigurator` or `xf86config` program. These programs prompt you for some technical information about your PC's video card, monitor, and mouse.

▶ You should specify the correct information about your monitor, because incorrect information may cause damage to the monitor.

▶ You can kill the X server by pressing Ctrl-Alt-Backspace. If you have a graphical login screen, this key combination restarts the X server.

▶ You can switch among different modes (screen resolutions such as 1,024 × 768 and 800 × 600) by pressing special key combinations: Ctrl-Alt-Keypad+ and Ctrl-Alt-Keypad–.

Chapter 4

SCSI and IDE Drives

In This Chapter

▶ Surveying the types of disk controllers Linux supports

▶ Understanding disk drive concepts: cylinder, heads, and sectors (CHS)

▶ Understanding disk drive operations: partitioning and booting with LILO

▶ Understanding the 1,024-cylinder limit of BIOS

▶ Surveying SCSI disks that Linux supports

▶ Troubleshooting SCSI

▶ Using Iomega Zip drives in Linux

W hen it comes to disk drives and Linux, what matters is whether Linux
supports the *disk controller:* the card that connects the disk drive to
your PC's motherboard. Linux supports most common disk controllers. This
chapter gives you information about different disk controllers and offers specific details about how to install and run Linux on a system that has one or
more of these controllers.

Disk Controller Types

The disk controller is the adapter card that acts as an intermediary between
your PC's motherboard and one or more hard disk drives. Typically, you can
connect up to two hard drives and two floppy drives to a single disk controller. The Small Computer System Interface (SCSI) controller is an exception
to this norm; you can connect as many as 7 or 15 SCSI devices (anything that
has a SCSI interface, such as a disk drive, CD-ROM drive, tape drive, or scanner) in a series.

Over the years, several types of hard disk controllers have appeared for the
PC. Following are some of the disk controllers that you may find in a PC:

■ *ST-506* disk controllers, which originally appeared in IBM XT and AT computers, became the common disk controller of the PC industry in its early
years (remember that the IBM PC-AT came out in 1984). Many PCs have
disk controllers that are compatible with the ST-506. Seagate's ST-506
was the original hard drive for PCs; Western Digital's WD1003 was the
controller card. Thus, these controllers are often referred to as being
WD1003-compatible controllers. The original ST-506 drives used a

recording method known as *modified frequency modulation (MFM)*. Many ST-506 disk controllers also support drives that use another type of data-recording technique known as *run length limited (RLL)*.

■ The *Integrated Drive Electronics (IDE)* interface emulates the ST-506 interface. IDE drives, however, have the necessary controller circuitry built into them. The motherboard typically contains an IDE interface for connecting the drive to the motherboard. For many years now, IDE drives have been the most widespread in PCs. Nowadays, the term *AT attachment (ATA)* is used to refer to IDE. The original IDE interface could support only two drives, and it limited the maximum disk size to approximately 500MB. You needed third-party drivers to use disks larger than 500MB. Today's PCs with large disk drives use the Enhanced IDE interface (described next).

■ The *Enhanced IDE (EIDE)* interface supports up to four internal IDE devices, (which include hard drives as well as CD-ROM drives), higher-capacity drives, and higher speeds of data transfer. Typical EIDE interfaces consist of two IDE interfaces: primary and secondary, each of which is capable of supporting up to two drives. EIDE interfaces are popular because of their low cost. Many PCs use the EIDE interface to connect both the hard disk and the CD-ROM drive to the PC's motherboard.

■ The *Enhanced Small Device Interface (ESDI)* controllers emulate the ST-506 interface, but provide higher data-transfer rates.

■ *Small Computer System Interface (SCSI)* controllers provide a separate bus onto which you can connect up to seven SCSI devices. You will find hard drives, CD-ROM drives, tape drives, and scanners that support SCSI. You can connect multiple SCSI devices to the computer by daisy-chaining (connecting first to second, second to third, and so on) the devices with a SCSI cable. All UNIX workstations (such as the ones from Hewlett-Packard, IBM, and Sun Microsystems) use SCSI. Lately, SCSI is becoming popular on PCs as well. The only drawback is the fact that SCSI controllers are relatively expensive compared with EIDE controllers.

 Linux supports all these common disk controllers. Even though several disk controllers appear in the preceding list, there are essentially two types of controllers: IDE or ATA (where IDE refers to all ST-506-compatible interfaces), and SCSI.

Most Pentium systems use a motherboard that supports the Peripheral Component Interconnect (PCI) bus. These PCI systems need SCSI adapter cards that plug into PCI bus slots, and an IDE interface that connects to the PCI bus. Linux supports the PCI bus. The PCI bus is now the dominant bus in the PC marketplace, replacing the old and outdated ISA bus.

Disk Drive Concepts

When you read about disk drives, you'll run into some terms and concepts that are unique to the world of hard disks. The following sections explain some of these concepts.

Cylinders, Heads, and Sectors

The physical organization of the disk is expressed in terms of cylinders, heads, and sectors. A hard disk consists of several platters of magnetic material. In physical terms, you can think of *cylinder, head,* and *sector* as follows:

- A *cylinder* is a set of matching tracks on both sides of all the platters in the disk drive, where each *track* is one of a series of concentric rings on one side of a disk platter.

- The total number of *heads* is the number of sides of all the magnetic platters.

- A *sector* is a pie-shaped wedge on the platter. Each cylinder is divided into sectors.

Any location on the disk can be expressed in terms of the cylinder, the head, and the sector. Identifying a disk location in terms of cylinder (C), head (H), and sector (S) is known as *CHS addressing.*

Secret

The physical *geometry* of a hard disk usually is expressed in terms of cylinders, heads, and sectors (CHS). A disk may have a geometry of CHS = 8,894/15/63, which means that the disk has 8,894 cylinders, 15 heads, and 63 sectors. Usually, each sector can store 512 bytes (or half a kilobyte) of data. Thus, the capacity of this disk is $(8,894 \times 15 \times 63) \div 2$ kilobytes, or 4,202,415 kilobytes (about 4,103MB).

Note

PC hard disk controllers include a read-only memory (ROM) basic input/output system (BIOS) on the controller. By convention (and for compatibility with the original IBM PC architecture), the BIOS uses CHS addressing to access the hard disk. The disk BIOS, however, uses a 10-bit value as the cylinder address. Because 10 bits can hold numbers between 0 and 1,023, the BIOS can address, at most, 1,024 cylinders.

Many large disks have more than 1,024 cylinders. To accommodate the 1,024-cylinder limit, the disk controllers have to resort to some tricks to handle disks with more than 1,024 cylinders. Later, in the "Disks with more than 1,024 cylinders" section, you will learn more about problems with disks that have more than 1,024 cylinders.

Master Boot Record (MBR)

The first sector of the hard disk (cylinder 0, head 0, sector 1) is called the *master boot record (MBR).* This 512-byte storage area contains important information about the disk, such as the partition table; and a small amount of code that the PC's BIOS loads and runs when you boot the PC.

The small program in the MBR reads the partition table; determines which partition is active (that's just an attribute of a partition); reads the active partition's first sector, or *boot sector*; and runs whatever program resides in that boot sector. The program in a partition's boot sector usually loads whatever operating system is installed on that partition.

When you install the Linux Loader (LILO) on the hard disk, the LILO program resides on the hard disk's MBR, or the boot sector of the partition on which the Linux root directory (/) is located.

Partitions

Partitions are a way of dividing up a hard disk and treating each part separately. By dividing your PC's hard disk into partitions, you can install different operating systems in different partitions. Even if you use the entire disk for Linux, you would, at minimum, need a partition that Linux can use as *swap space* — an extension of memory, so that you can have more virtual memory than the physical memory on your system.

Secret

The master boot record contains the partition table, starting at byte 446 (0x1be, which means 1be in hexadecimal). The partition table can have up to four 16-byte entries. Each 16-byte value defines a partition. Each partition is specified by a starting and ending cylinder number. The partition entry also includes a type that identifies the operating system that created the partition. The concept of partitions is a convention that all PC-based operating systems, ranging from MS-DOS to Linux, follow.

In MS-DOS, you use the FDISK program to manipulate the partitions. Linux includes a program with the same name — fdisk (lowercase) — to alter the disk partitions. In addition to fdisk, Linux includes several disk-partitioning programs such as sfdisk, cfdisk, and Red Hat's Disk Druid.

Linux Device Names for Disks

In Linux, each device is represented by a device file in the /dev directory. The device name for the hard disk depends on the type of disk controller. For IDE and EIDE drives, the device name is /dev/hda for the first disk, /dev/hdb for the second disk, and so on.

On an EIDE interface, if you have a hard disk on the primary interface and a CD-ROM drive as the first device on the secondary interface, the device names are /dev/hda for the hard disk drive and /dev/hdc for the CD-ROM drive.

The Linux disk drivers treat each disk partition as being a separate device. The first partition in the first IDE disk is /dev/hda1, the second partition is /dev/hda2, the third one is /dev/hda3, and so on. Similarly, the device names for the partitions on the second IDE drive are /dev/hdb1, /dev/hdb2, and so on.

The SCSI disk devices are named /dev/sda, /dev/sdb, and so on. If a SCSI device is a hard disk, its partitions are named by appending the partition number to the device name. Thus, the partitions of the first SCSI hard disk are named /dev/sda1, /dev/sda2, /dev/sda3, and so on.

Floppy Disks in Linux

Chapter 13 describes several ways to access MS-DOS floppy disks under Linux; you can mount the floppy and use Linux commands, or use the `mtools` utility programs to read from or write to the floppy. You also can create a Linux file system on a floppy disk. In fact, you'll find Linux file systems on the boot and root floppies that you use to install Linux.

Formatting and creating a Linux file system on a floppy is a straightforward process. To format a 3.5-inch high-density floppy in the A drive, for example, use the following command (for more on floppy drive naming conventions, see the "How to Format a DOS Floppy" section in Chapter 15):

```
fdformat /dev/fd0H1440
```

If you have an old PC with a 5.25-inch high-density floppy as the A drive, you can access that floppy with the device name `/dev/fd0h1200`. On the B drive, change the first 0 in the device name to 1.

Secret

After you format the floppy, use the following command to create a Linux file system on the floppy:

```
mke2fs -m 0 /dev/fd0H1440 1440
```

The `-m` option is used to specify what percentage of blocks should be reserved for use by the *super user* (root). By specifying the `-m 0` option, you ensure that `mke2fs` does not reserve any space on the floppy disk for the super user. If you do not explicitly specify the `-m` option, `mke2fs` reserves five percent of the disk space for the super user.

After you create the file system on the floppy drive, you can mount the floppy at a *mount point* (an empty directory) in the Linux file system. The following example shows how you would mount the floppy drive at the `/mnt/floppy` directory:

```
mount /dev/fd0H1440 /mnt/floppy
```

Now you can use Linux commands, such as `cp` and `mv`, to copy or move files to the floppy disk. Before you eject the floppy disk from the drive, use the following command to dismount the floppy:

```
umount /dev/fd0H1440
```

Hard Disk Operations in Linux

You must perform some disk operations to install and use Linux on your system. Chapter 2 explains some of the disk operations that you perform when you set up Linux. The next few sections provide some additional information about these disk operations.

When you first get a PC, the hard disk usually is set up as one huge partition, and DOS and Windows are already installed on it. (If you bought your PC recently, it probably came with Windows 95 or Windows 98 preinstalled.) To install Red Hat Linux, you have to start by creating at least two partitions for Linux: one for the swap space and the other for the Linux file system.

If you have original disks to reinstall the current operating system again (be it Windows 95/98 or MS-DOS and Windows 3.1), you can simply go ahead and repartition the disk. To do this, boot the PC using a DOS boot floppy, and run the MS-DOS version of the FDISK program to delete the current partition and create new ones. Create three new partitions: one for DOS and Windows, one for the Linux swap space, and one for the Linux file system. Then you have to reinstall DOS and Windows in their partitions, and install Linux on the other partition.

Tip

If you do not want to go through the trouble of reinstalling DOS and Windows or Windows 95, you have to alter the existing partition somehow. FIPS, which can split an existing DOS partition into two separate partitions, enables you to perform this task. Chapter 2 describes how to use FIPS. You can also use PowerQuest's PartitionMagic utility (http://www.powerquest.com/) to repartition your hard disk without destroying existing data.

Partitioning Using fdisk

Partitioning the disk involves creating several smaller logical devices within a single hard disk. Under MS-DOS, you would use the FDISK program to view and alter a disk's partition table. In Linux, the partitioning program is called fdisk.

Even if you have already partitioned your hard disk, you can always run fdisk just to see the current partition table of a hard disk. If you have an IDE disk drive with the device name /dev/hda, for example, you can look at its partition table with fdisk as follows:

```
/sbin/fdisk /dev/hda
Command (m for help): m
Command action
   a   toggle a bootable flag
   b   edit bsd disklabel
   c   toggle the dos compatibility flag
   d   delete a partition
   l   list known partition types
   m   print this menu
   n   add a new partition
   o   create a new empty DOS partition table
   p   print the partition table
   q   quit without saving changes
   s   create a new empty Sun disklabel
   t   change a partition's system id
   u   change display/entry units
   v   verify the partition table
   w   write table to disk and exit
   x   extra functionality (experts only)
```

```
Command (m for help): p

Disk /dev/hda: 255 heads, 63 sectors, 523 cylinders
Units = cylinders of 16065 * 512 bytes

    Device Boot      Start       End    Blocks   Id  System
/dev/hda1     *          1       261   2096451    6  FAT16
/dev/hda2              262       396   1084387+   5  Extended
/dev/hda3              397       514    947835   83  Linux
/dev/hda4              515       523     72292+  82  Linux swap
/dev/hda5              262       396   1084356    6  FAT16

Command (m for help): q
```

The m command shows you a list of the single-letter commands that fdisk accepts. You can see the current partition table with a p command. This example's IDE disk has five partitions: three for DOS (one primary DOS partition and another extended DOS partition with a DOS drive in the extended partition), and two for Linux.

The Id field in the table of partitions printed by the fdisk program (when you type **p** at the fdisk prompt) is a number that denotes a partition type. That partition ID is a hexadecimal number. If you want to see a list of all known partition IDs, type **l** (a lowercase L) at the fdisk prompt, as follows:

```
Command (m for help): l

 0  Empty             16  Hidden FAT16    61  SpeedStor         a6  OpenBSD
 1  FAT12             17  Hidden HPFS/NTF 63  GNU HURD or Sys   a7  NeXTSTEP
 2  XENIX root        18  AST Windows swa 64  Novell Netware    b7  BSDI fs
 3  XENIX usr         24  NEC DOS         65  Novell Netware    b8  BSDI swap
 4  FAT16 <32M        3c  PartitionMagic  70  DiskSecure Mult   c1  DRDOS/sec (FAT-
 5  Extended          40  Venix 80286     75  PC/IX             c4  DRDOS/sec (FAT-
 6  FAT16             41  PPC PReP Boot   80  Old Minix         c6  DRDOS/sec (FAT-
 7  HPFS/NTFS         42  SFS             81  Minix / old Lin   c7  Syrinx
 8  AIX               4d  QNX4.x          82  Linux swap        db  CP/M / CTOS / .
 9  AIX bootable      4e  QNX4.x 2nd part 83  Linux             e1  DOS access
 a  OS/2 Boot Manag   4f  QNX4.x 3rd part 84  OS/2 hidden C:    e3  DOS R/O
 b  Win95 FAT32       50  OnTrack DM      85  Linux extended    e4  SpeedStor
 c  Win95 FAT32 (LB   51  OnTrack DM6 Aux 86  NTFS volume set   eb  BeOS fs
 e  Win95 FAT16 (LB   52  CP/M            87  NTFS volume set   f1  SpeedStor
 f  Win95 Ext'd (LB   53  OnTrack DM6 Aux 93  Amoeba            f4  SpeedStor
10  OPUS              54  OnTrackDM6      94  Amoeba BBT        f2  DOS secondary
11  Hidden FAT12      55  EZ-Drive        a0  IBM Thinkpad hi   fe  LANstep
12  Compaq diagnost   56  Golden Bow      a5  BSD/386           ff  BBT
14  Hidden FAT16 <3   5c  Priam Edisk
```

Booting from the Hard Disk Using LILO

To automatically boot Linux from a hard disk, you need the Linux Loader (LILO). LILO is a boot loader program; OS/2 has an equivalent program, called Boot Manager. These programs usually reside in the master boot record of a disk and are the first to be loaded. The boot loader program, in turn, prompts you for the name of an operating system to start (which typically means a disk partition from which to boot). Starting an operating system basically involves loading that operating system's main program into memory and running it. For Linux, this step involves loading the Linux kernel into memory and giving control to the kernel.

Cross-Reference

LILO is much more than just the Linux Loader; it also serves as a general-purpose boot manager that is capable of booting MS-DOS, OS/2, or Windows 95. Chapter 2 describes how you can install LILO on your hard disk during the Red Hat Linux installation process. This section summarizes the LILO installation process, if you do it outside the Red Hat Linux installation program described in Chapter 2.

Tip

You'll find the LILO documentation in the /usr/share/doc directory on your system. Type cd /usr/share/doc/lilo* to change to the LILO documentation directory (the exact name depends on the current version of LILO). You should consult the README file in that directory for the latest word on installing and configuring LILO. The following section provides an overview only.

Installing LILO

Typically, you install LILO as part of the Red Hat Linux installation process described in Chapter 2. The only time you have to repeat LILO configuration and installation is when you update the kernel, or add a new operating system that you want to boot through LILO.

Installing LILO involves two basic steps:

1. Prepare the LILO configuration file, which contains information that is necessary for installing LILO. The default LILO configuration file is /etc/lilo.conf.

2. Run the /sbin/lilo program (referred to as the *map installer* in LILO's README file) to update the boot sector and create the /boot/map file, which contains information that LILO uses during the boot process.

Cross-Reference

To prepare the LILO configuration file, you have to log in as root and edit the /etc/lilo.conf file. Chapter 25 briefly describes how to edit this file. Essentially, you add or edit information about the operating systems that you want to boot with Linux and the names of the disk partitions on which those operating systems reside.

When the LILO configuration file — /etc/lilo.conf — is ready, you can install LILO with the following command:

```
/sbin/lilo
```

The lilo program looks for the lilo.conf file in the /etc directory, interprets its contents, prepares the necessary boot and map files, and initializes the boot record of the device specified (by the boot line) in the configuration file. If the boot device is specified as a hard disk partition, for example, LILO sets up the boot sector of that disk partition.

Using LILO's boot prompt

As LILO starts, it displays the `boot:` prompt and waits for the name of a boot image to load. If you do not respond within a specified period (this value is stored in the `/etc/lilo.conf` file), LILO loads the default boot image (the first image in the `/etc/lilo.conf` file).

Secret

When you use LILO to boot Linux, you can specify the name of the Linux boot image, followed by one or more options. LILO passes these boot command-line options directly to the Linux kernel. As you read descriptions of various disk controllers, you'll find information on boot command-line options that you can use to specify various parameters of a device. These parameters typically include the I/O port address, the IRQ, and the DMA of a device. Notice that boot command-line options are always case-sensitive.

In Red Hat Linux 7.0, instead of the LILO boot prompt, you see a graphics screen that lists the names of all the boot images that LILO can boot. If you do not want to boot from the default boot image, use the up and down arrow keys to select another boot image. If you need the text-mode LILO prompt (in case you want to provide some boot options for a driver), press Ctrl+X. The following prompt appears:

```
LILO boot:
```

You can then type the name of the boot image followed by any boot options for the kernel or drivers.

Examining the LILO configuration file

The configuration file `/etc/lilo.conf` lists the kernel binary that LILO runs. You can examine the contents of the LILO configuration file by typing the following command:

```
cat /etc/lilo.conf
```

Here is what I see when I try this command on a Red Hat Linux PC with a SCSI adapter:

```
boot=/dev/hda
map=/boot/map
install=/boot/boot.b
prompt
timeout=50
message=/boot/message
linear
default=linux

image=/boot/vmlinuz-2.4.0-0.43.12
        label=linux
        root=/dev/hda3
        initrd=/boot/initrd-2.4.0-0.43.12.img
        read-only

other=/dev/hda1
        label=dos
        table=/dev/hda
```

To understand the LILO configuration file, note the following:

■ The first eight lines are the global options that apply, regardless of the specific kernel that LILO boots. The boot option specifies the device that contains the boot sector (in this case, the first IDE drive, /dev/hda). The prompt option forces LILO to display the boot prompt, and timeout specifies the time (in tenth of seconds) to wait before booting the default kernel. In this case, LILO waits for five seconds. The message option specifies a file that LILO displays before the boot prompt.

■ The last three lines are for booting from the DOS partition. (Microsoft Windows is installed in that partition.)

■ The five lines starting with image=/boot/vmlinuz-2.4.0-0.43.12 identify a specific kernel file (also called *boot image*) that LILO can boot. You can make LILO boot another kernel by adding a similar section to the configuration file.

■ The image=/boot/vmlinuz-2.4.0-0.43.12 line identifies the kernel that LILO loads. In this case, the kernel file is vmlinuz-2.4.0-0.43.12, located in the /boot directory.

■ The label=linux line names the kernel. In this case, you can type linux at the boot: prompt to make LILO boot this particular kernel.

■ The root=/dev/hda3 line specifies the disk partition on which the root Linux file system is located. This may be different on your system.

■ The initrd=/boot/initrd-2.4.0-0.43.12.img line specifies a file containing an initial RAM disk image that serves as a file system before the disks are available. You will see the initrd line only if your system has a SCSI adapter and the kernel uses a modular SCSI driver. In this case, the kernel uses the RAM disk—a block of memory used as a disk—to get started initially; then it loads the SCSI driver module and begins using the SCSI hard disk. You do not need the initrd line if you create a kernel with the SCSI adapter support built into the kernel.

You can learn more about the LILO configuration file by reading the LILO man page—type man lilo.conf to view this man page.

Removing LILO

If you set up LILO on the hard disk's master boot record but later want to remove it, you can do so easily, provided that you have MS-DOS version 5.0 or later. All you have to do is boot from a DOS boot floppy (place the boot floppy in drive A and then power up the PC) and run FDISK with the /MBR option. The FDISK /MBR command essentially restores the master boot record to the format that MS-DOS uses. The next time you boot the PC, MS-DOS should start immediately.

Another way to uninstall LILO is to use LILO itself as follows:

```
/sbin/lilo -u
```

LILO replaces the MBR from a saved copy of the old boot sector, which LILO saves when you first install LILO.

Caution

Use the /sbin/lilo -u command only if you have installed LILO on your hard disk's MBR. When you use the -u option, LILO simply copies a file named /boot/boot.*nnnn* to the disk's MBR (*nnnn* is the device number, such as 0300 for the /dev/hda and 0800 for /dev/sda). If you have been playing with LILO and an old boot file happens to be left over in the /boot directory, LILO might copy that file to the MBR. A bad MBR, of course, makes the disk unbootable. In such a case, boot from a DOS floppy and use the FDISK /MBR command to restore the MBR to boot DOS.

Creating Swap Space

Swap space is a disk partition that Linux uses as an extension of its memory. When some memory-resident data is not needed immediately, Linux stores that data in the swap space. To create the swap space, you have to create a disk partition using fdisk. Make sure that you set the type of that disk partition to Linux swap (partition ID 82 in hexadecimal). Typically, you would set up the swap partition and turn on swapping as you install Red Hat Linux from this book's CD-ROM.

If you have to set up the swap space outside the installation program, you have to use the mkswap command to initialize the swap partition. You need the size of the swap partition (in number of blocks) before you use the mkswap command. Use the Linux fdisk program and type the p command at the fdisk prompt to find the size of the swap partition.

For example, to initialize the /dev/hda4 partition as a swap partition, type the following command:

```
/sbin/mkswap -c /dev/hda4 72292
```

In this case, 72292 is the block size of the swap partition. You can skip the size parameter because the mkswap command can determine the size from the partition table.

The size of the swap partition depends on the amount of virtual memory you need. To Linux, the total amount of memory in your PC is the combined total of the swap partition's size and the amount of physical RAM. Although there is no formula to tell you how much virtual memory you need, the conventional wisdom is that you should have at least as much swap space as physical memory. If you have less than 16MB of RAM, make the swap space at least 16MB.

You can have a swap partition as large as 2GB, and you can have up to eight swap partitions. All you have to do is run the mkswap command for each swap partition that you create.

After mkswap finishes, use the /sbin/swapon command to turn on swapping. Linux then begins to use the swap space.

The /proc/swaps file contains information about the swap spaces your Linux system is using. For example, here's what I get when I check /proc/swaps on my system:

```
cat /proc/swaps
Filename                Type            Size    Used    Priority
/dev/hda4               partition       72288   1008    -1
```

The output shows the current swap spaces. Although it is customary to use a disk partition as the swap space, you can also use a file as swap space. The first column in the list of swap spaces is labeled `Filename` because the swap space can be a file. If you want to use a file as swap space, create the file with a command, such as the following:

```
dd if=/dev/zero of=swapfile bs=1024 count=65536
```

This creates a file named `swapfile` of size 65,536KB. Type `/sbin/mkswap -c swapfile` to initialize that file, and then type `/sbin/swapon swapfile` to use the file for swapping.

Tip

To ensure that Linux uses the swap space every time it boots, you need a line in the `/etc/fstab` file that indicates the swap partition's name. If the swap partition is `/dev/hda4`, for example, you would add the following line to `/etc/fstab`:

```
/dev/hda2       swap        swap       defaults     0 0
```

If you created a swap space when you installed Linux, the installation program adds the appropriate line in the `/etc/fstab` file. You may need to add such a line if you create additional swap spaces later.

Secret

If you put a partition's name in `/etc/fstab` but forget to run `mkswap` on that partition, Linux displays the following error message:

```
Unable to find swap-space signature
```

The fix is to run `mkswap` to initialize the swap partition.

Creating File Systems

To use a disk partition in Linux, you have to create a file system on that partition. You can think of this procedure as formatting the partition for Linux. When you install Linux by following the steps described in Chapter 2, one of the steps creates the file system; the setup program actually asks you whether you want to format a partition. For a Linux partition, the setup program uses the `mk2efs` command to create a Linux file system.

Linux supports several types of file systems, including the following:

- *MS-DOS file system* — This DOS file system is based on the file allocation table (FAT). This file system type is designated by the keyword `msdos`.

- *Microsoft Windows file system with support for long filenames* — This is a DOS-compatible FAT file system with support for long filenames. This file type is identified by the keyword `vfat`. You should use this file system to access all DOS/Windows disks from Linux.

- *Minix file system* — Minix is the original UNIX clone that inspired the creation of Linux. Linux started by using the Minix file system, which limits filenames to 14 or 30 characters. The `minix` keyword identifies this file-system type.

- *Extended file system* — This old Linux file system goes by the keyword `ext`. You should not use this file system anymore.

- *Second extended file system* — This system is the latest and greatest Linux file system. The keyword `ext2` refers to this file-system type. You can use longer filenames in this file system.

Tip

The installation program automatically creates an `ext2` file system on the Linux partition. To create an `ext2` file system manually, you have to use the `mke2fs` command as follows:

```
/sbin/mke2fs -c /dev/hda3
```

This command creates an `ext2` file system on the `/dev/hda3` partition. The `mke2fs` command automatically figures out the size of the partition and uses it to size the file system. The `-c` option forces `mke2fs` to check for bad blocks (using a fast read-only test), before creating the file system.

Tip

When you install Linux on a hard disk that uses standard IDE, MFM, or RLL controllers, always install the `ext2` file system and use the bad-block-checking options when you create the file system.

Specific Disk Problems in Linux

For most hard drives, installing Linux amounts to booting a Linux kernel that supports your system's hard disk controller, partitioning the disk under Linux, and loading the operating system and associated software onto the hard disk. You notice the hard disk only when you create the partitions (as explained in Chapter 2).

Whenever some aspect of the hard disk is out of the ordinary, however, you may run into problems when installing Linux. This section describes some of these potential problems and their solutions.

Windows 95/98 and LILO

On a PC that has both Linux and Windows 3.1 installed in separate partitions, you can use the Linux Loader (LILO) program to boot one or the other operating system. If you upgrade Windows 95 or 98, you'll notice that Windows 95/98 wipes out LILO. Windows 95/98 overwrites the master boot record with its own program, and LILO typically resides on the master boot record. In this case, all you have to do is boot Linux using a boot floppy (you should have created the boot floppy during Linux installation), and then run `/sbin/lilo` to reinstall LILO.

If you bought a new PC with Windows 98 preinstalled, all you have to do is install Linux by following the steps described in Chapter 2 (start with repartitioning the hard disk). When you come to the step that installs LILO, specify the operating systems and the disk partitions that LILO should configure for booting. When you specify partitions to boot, treat the Windows 95 disk partition as a DOS partition. After you finish installing Linux and LILO, you should be able to boot Windows 98 (assuming that you left it installed) or Linux by entering the name of the appropriate boot image at LILO's boot prompt.

Disks with More Than 1,024 Cylinders

Disks that have more than 1,024 cylinders were a problem in older Linux kernels. The version of Linux on the companion disk, however, should work fine with EIDE disks that have more than 1,024 cylinders.

Earlier versions of the Linux Loader (LILO) had a problem if the Linux boot partition was not located within the first 1,024 cylinders. LILO has been updated and can now handle situations where Linux is installed beyond the 1,024-cylinder limit. Also, the GNU boot loader, GRUB, easily handles booting from such situations .

EIDE Problems on PCI Systems

The current crop of Pentium PCs uses the PCI bus. With this new bus come new interfaces for disks. A common interface is the PCI EIDE controller to connect EIDE devices, such as hard disks and CD-ROM drives, to the PCI motherboard.

When the PCI bus first became popular in 1995, some users reported data corruption in EIDE disks with some PCI EIDE controllers. Specifically, the affected systems have PCI motherboards with PCI EIDE controllers that use one of the following chips:

- RZ 1000

- CMD 640

To determine what type of PCI EIDE controller your system has, use the `cat/proc/pci` or `/sbin/lspci` command (assuming, of course, that your system has a PCI bus).

The version of Linux on the companion CD-ROMs detects and works around these problems automatically. The only remaining indication of the problem is that when you type `cat /proc/pci`, the listing shows the CMD 640 controller as being buggy (assuming you have the CMD 640 interface on your system). For example, here are the first few lines of output I get when I type the `cat /proc/pci` command on an old PC with the CMD 640 interface:

```
cat /proc/pci
PCI devices found:
  Bus  0, device  13, function  0:
    IDE interface: CMD 640 (buggy) (rev 2).
      Medium devsel.  IRQ 14.
(other lines deleted)
```

Notice how the CMD 640 interface is reported to be buggy.

Error Messages about Inodes and Blocks

If you get error messages about bad inodes or blocks during system startup, chances are good that you did not shut down the system properly. Before powering off a Linux system, you should always log in as `root` and use the `shutdown` command to halt the system, as follows:

`/sbin/shutdown -h now`

After that, you must wait until you see a message that says that the system has halted. Only then should you turn the power off.

From a GNOME or KDE GUI session, log out first. Then, from the graphical login dialog box, select Option ⇨ System ⇨ Halt to halt the system.

Because of our typical DOS experience of simply turning the power switch off, most of us are tempted to reach for the power switch to shut down the system.

If the system is not shut down properly, the file system may be damaged. When you boot the system the next time, it runs a file-system-check program (`e2fsck`) that may fix the file system and boot the system. In some cases, however, `e2fsck` won't be able to fix the file-system damage. You have no option but to reinitialize the file system, using the `mke2fs` command.

SCSI Disk Controllers and Linux

The remainder of this chapter explains how to use SCSI controllers under Linux.

SCSI (pronounced "scuzzy") is an increasingly popular interface for connecting up to seven different devices on the SCSI bus. Each device, and the SCSI controller, has a unique SCSI identifier (ID) in the range 0 through 7. The controller usually is set to SCSI ID 7; the other devices use numbers between 0 and 6 (that means you can connect up to seven devices to a SCSI controller). Typically, a SCSI hard disk is set to SCSI ID 0.

Table 4-1 lists the SCSI controllers that the version of Linux kernel on the companion CD-ROMs supports. The table also shows the name of the driver module that supports a specific set of controllers.

Table 4-1   Supported SCSI Controllers

SCSI Controller	Linux Driver Module
ACARD ATP870U	atp870u
Adaptec AHA-1510/152x (ISA)	aha152x
Adaptec AHA-154x (ISA) (all models)	aha1542
Adaptec AHA-174x (EISA) (in enhanced mode)	aha1740
Adaptec AHA-274x/274xT (EISA), AHA-284x (VLB), AHA-2910B (PCI), AHA-2920C (PCI), AHA-2930/U/U2/CU, AHA-2940/U/W/AU/UW/U2W (PCI), AHA-294160M, AHA-2944D/WD/ UD/UWD (PCI), AHA-2950U2/ U2W/U2B, AHA-39160M, AHA-3940/ U/W/UW (PCI), AHA-3950U2D, AHA-3960D, AHA-398x/U/W/UW (PCI)	aic7xxx
Adaptec AHA-2920A (PCI) with Future Domain chipset	fdomain
Adaptec AVA-1502E (ISA/VLB) (Adaptec AHA-1520–compatible)	
Adaptec AVA-1505/1515 (ISA) (Adaptec AHA-152x compatible)	
AdvanSys ABP510/5150 Bus-Master ISA, ABP5140 Bus-Master ISA PnP (Plug and Play), ABP5142 Bus-Master ISA PnP with floppy, ABP542 Bus-Master ISA with floppy (single channel), ABP742 Bus-Master EISA (single channel), ABP752 Dual Channel Bus-Master EISA (dual channel), ABP842 Bus-Master VL (single channel), ABP852 Dual Channel Bus-Master VL (dual channel), ABP920 Bus-Master PCI, ABP930/U Bus-Master PCI/Ultra, ABP940/U Bus-Master PCI/Ultra (single channel), ABP950 Dual Channel Bus-Master PCI (dual channel), ABP960/U Bus-Master PCI/ULTRA MAC/PC, ABP970/U Bus-Master PCI/Ultra MAC/PC (single channel),	advansys
AIC-777x, AIC-785x, AIC-786x, AIC-787x, AIC-788x, AIC-789x, and AIC-3860 chipsets	aic7xxx
Always IN2000 (ISA)	in2000

SCSI Controller	Linux Driver Module
AMD AM53/79C974	`AM53C974`
AMI Fast Disk VLB/EISA (BusLogic-compatible)	
BusLogic FlashPoint LT/DL/LW/DW PCI	`BusLogic`
DPT PM2001, PM2012A (EATA-PIO), Smartcache/ SmartRAID Plus,III,IV families (ISA/EISA/PCI)	`eata`
Data Technology Corp DTC 3180/3280	`dtc`
DTC 329x (EISA) (Adaptec 154x-compatible)	`aha1542`
Future Domain TMC-1800, TMC-18C50, TMC-18C30, TMC-36C70, TMC-16x0, TMC-3260 (PCI)	`fdomain`
Future Domain TMC-8xx, TMC-950	`seagate`
ICP-Vortex GDT ISA and EISA SCSI Controllers, GDT PCI SCSI Disk Array Controllers (many RAID levels supported)	`gdth`
Initio INI-9X00U/UW SCSI host adapters	`initio`
Intraserver ITI-6200U2 Dual Channel Ultra2 SCSI Host Adapter (uses the NCR53C896 chipset)	`ncr53c8xx`
Iomega PPA3 parallel-port SCSI Host Bus Adapter embedded in ZIP drive	`ppa`
Mylex (formerly BusLogic) A Series (ISA/EISA), C Series (ISA/EISA/VLB/PCI), S Series (ISA/EISA/VLB), W Series (PCI)	`BusLogic`
NCR 5380 and 53C400 generic cards	`g_NCR5380`
NCR 53C406a (Acculogic ISApport / Media Vision Premium 3D SCSI)	`NCR53c406a`
NCR 53c810, 53c810A, 53c815, 53c825, 53c825A, 53c860, 53c875, 53c876 53c895 53c400, NCR5380, 53c810, 53c810A, 53c815, 53c820, 53c825, 53c810, 53c820, 53c720, 53c700, 53c710 (PCI), 53c700-66	`53c7,8xx`
NCR 53C875 and 53C876 chipsets	`ncr53c8xx`
Perceptive Solutions PSI-240I EIDE	`psi240i`
Pro Audio Spectrum/Studio 16 (ISA)	`pas16`
Qlogic / Control Concepts ISP2100 SCSI-FCP	`qlogicfc`
Qlogic Fast SCSI FASXXX family of chips (ISA/VLB/PCMCIA)	`qlogicfas`
QLogic ISP1020 Intelligent SCSI cards IQ-PCI, IQ-PCI-10, IQ-PCI-D (PCI)	`qlogicisp`
Quantum ISA-200S, ISA-250MG	`fdomain`

Continued

Table 4-1 *(continued)*

SCSI Controller	Linux Driver Module
Seagate ST-01/ST-02 (ISA)	`seagate`
SoundBlaster 16 SCSI-2 (Adaptec 152x–compatible) (ISA)	`aha152x`
Tekram DC-390, DC-390W/U/F (AMD53C974 chipset)	`tmscsim`
Trantor T128/T128F/T228 (ISA)	`t128`
Trantor T130B (NCR 53C400 chipset)	`g_NCR5380`
UltraStor 14F (ISA), 24F (EISA), 34F (VLB)	`u14-34f`
Western Digital WD7000-FAST, WD7000-FASST2, WD7000-ASC, WD7000-AX/MX/EX	`wd7000`

Cable and Termination Problems

The SCSI bus needs terminators at both ends to work reliably. A *terminator* is a set of resistors that indicate the end of the SCSI bus. One end is the controller card itself, which typically has the terminator. Often a SCSI device has two SCSI connectors, so that you can daisy-chain several external SCSI devices. You are supposed to place a terminator on the last connector on the chain.

Secret

Some SCSI controllers — such as Adaptec AHA 154xC, 154xCF, and 274x (x is any digit) — are sensitive to the type of cable and terminator you use. If the cables are not perfect, or the terminator is not used properly, these SCSI cards may fail intermittently, or may not work at all.

To avoid problems with overly sensitive SCSI cards, use cables that come from a reputable vendor, and use cables from the same vendor to connect all SCSI devices. The cables should be SCSI-2-compliant and should have an impedance of 132 ohms (a characteristic of the cable; all you have to do is make sure that the specified value is 132 ohms).

Adaptec AHA 151x, AHA 152x, and Sound Blaster 16 SCSI

These ISA-bus SCSI cards include all SCSI controllers based on the AIC 6260 or 6360 chipset. Typical hardware parameters for these controllers include the following:

- BIOS addresses — 0xd8000, 0xdc000, 0xd0000, 0xd4000, 0xc8000, 0xcc000, 0xe0000, and 0xe4000
- I/O ports — 0x140 and 0x340

- IRQs — 9, 10, 11, and 12

- DMA channels — not used

Secret

Autoprobe works with boards that have a BIOS installed. For other boards, such as Adaptec 1510 and Sound Blaster 16 SCSI, use the boot option in the following format:

```
aha152x=IOPORT,IRQ,SCSI-ID,RECONNECT
```

All right-side arguments are numbers. `IOPORT` is the I/O address, and if `RECONNECT` is nonzero, the driver is allowed to disconnect and reconnect the device. Usually, the `SCSI-ID` is 7, and `RECONNECT` is specified as 1. If an Adaptec AHA1510 card has I/O address 0x340 and IRQ 11, the boot option will be the following:

```
aha152x=0x340,11,7,1
```

Adaptec AHA154x, AMI FastDisk VLB, BusLogic, and DTC 329x

Typical hardware parameters of these ISA-bus SCSI controllers include the following:

- I/O ports — 0x330 and 0x334

- IRQs — 9, 10, 11, 12, 14, and 15

- DMA channels — 5, 6, and 7

Autoprobe works with these controllers; there is no need for a BIOS on the controller. The BusLogic SCSI controllers are software-compatible with the Adaptec 1542. ISA, VLB, and EISA versions of BusLogic cards are available.

Secret

Adaptec AHA 154xC and AHA 154xCF controller cards often generate unexpected errors; these controllers are very sensitive to the cable and termination details.

If you encounter infinite timeout errors with Adaptec AHA 154xC and 154xCF controllers, you may have to run the Adaptec setup program (which you do by pressing a specified key during power-up) and enable synchronous negotiation.

Adaptec AHA 174x

This controller is an EISA-bus SCSI controller that Adaptec no longer sells. Older EISA bus systems may have this card. Following are the hardware parameters of the AHA 174x card:

- Bus slots — 1–8

- I/O ports — The EISA bus does not require pre-assigned I/O ports

- IRQs — 9, 10, 11, 12, 14, and 15

- DMA channels — The EISA bus does not require pre-assigned DMA channels

The Linux driver can detect the card automatically without any problems. The driver also expects the card to be running in enhanced mode, as opposed to standard AHA 1542 mode.

Adaptec AHA 274x, AHA 284x, and AHA 294x

The Adaptec AHA 274x controller is an EISA bus card; AHA 284x is a VLB card; and AHA 294x is a new PCI bus card. The aic7xxx driver supports all three cards. You should enable the BIOS on these controller cards.

For the PCI controller to work, you must enable PCI support (CONFIG_PCI) during kernel configuration.

Always IN2000

The Always IN2000 is an ISA-bus controller card with the following parameters:

- I/O ports — 0x100, 0x110, 0x200, and 0x220
- IRQs — 10, 11, 14, and 15
- DMA — not used

The driver can detect the card automatically without any need for BIOS.

EATA DPT Smartcache

The Linux eata_dma SCSI driver supports all SCSI controllers that support the EATA-DMA protocol. The controllers include DPT PM2011, PM2012A, PM2012B, PM2021, PM2022, PM2024, PM2122, PM2124, PM2322, PM3021, PM3222, and PM3224.

Secret

The driver's autoprobe function works with all supported DPT cards. A common problem, however, is that the IDE driver detects the ST-506 interface of the EATA controller. If the IDE driver has a problem with the detected parameters and fails, you won't be able to access your IDE hardware. In this case, you should change the EATA board's parameters, such as the I/O address and the IRQ. In particular, don't use IRQs of 14 or 15, which are the IRQs of the primary and secondary IDE interfaces.

If you have a PCI controller, such as DPT PM2024, PM2124, or PM3224, remember to enable PCI BIOS when you configure the kernel.

Future Domain 16x0

The Future Domain 16x0 SCSI controller uses the TMC-1800, TMC-18C30, TMC-8C50, or TMC-36C70 chip. These ISA-bus cards typically have the following configurations:

- BIOS addresses — 0xc8000, 0xca000, 0xce000, and 0xde000
- I/O ports — 0x140, 0x150, 0x160, and 0x170
- IRQs — 3, 5, 10, 11, 12, 14, and 15
- DMA — not used

The driver can probe and detect the hardware automatically, provided that the controller has a BIOS installed.

NCR53c8xx SCSI Chip (PCI)

NCR53c8xx refers to NCR53c810, NCR53c815, NCR53c820, and NCR53c825 — a series of low-cost SCSI chips for PCI motherboards. The version of Linux on the companion CD-ROM supports the NCR53c8xx. The driver can detect SCSI devices automatically, provided that the PCI BIOS is present. In fact, the driver needs the BIOS, because it uses BIOS-initialized values in the registers of the NCR53c8xx.

A reported problem with the NCR53c8xx is that the chip works under DOS, but fails under Linux, because it times out on a test due to a lost interrupt. A typical cause of this error is a mismatch between the IRQ setting in the hardware (typically set with a jumper) and the IRQ value stored in the CMOS setup (the setup program of your PC, the one that you can run during power-up). To correct the problem, check the following things:

- Make sure that the hardware IRQ setting matches that in the CMOS setup.
- If the NCR 53c8xx is on a board that has jumpers for selecting PCI inter-rupt lines (PCI has interrupt lines INTA, INTB, INTC, and INTD), make sure that only INTA is being used.
- If the PCI board has jumpers for selecting level-sensitive and edge-triggered interrupts, make sure that the board is using "level-sensitive" interrupts.

Secret

Another reported problem with the driver auto-detecting an NCR53c8xx SCSI chip, is system lockup when an S3 928 or Tseng ET4000/W32 PCI video chipset is used, due to problems in the video chipsets.

Secret

On a system that has an NCR53c8xx SCSI chip, you may encounter the following message:

```
scsi%d: IRQ0 not free, detaching
```

This message indicates that the PCI configuration register contains a zero. The reason may be a mismatch between the hardware IRQ and the value in CMOS, or a defective BIOS.

Because the NCR53c8xx is a PCI device, you must enable PCI support when you rebuild the Linux kernel.

Seagate ST0x and Future Domain TMC-8xx and TMC-9xx

Typical hardware parameters of these ISA-bus SCSI controllers include the following:

- BIOS addresses — 0xc8000, 0xca000, 0xcc000, 0xce000, 0xdc000, and 0xde000
- IRQs — 3 and 5
- DMA channels — not used

When it tries to probe for the controller automatically, the driver probes only the BIOS addresses; it assumes that the IRQ is 5. Note that autoprobe works only if a BIOS is installed.

During boot, you can provide one of the following command lines to force detection of the controller:

```
st0x=BIOS-ADDRESS,IRQ
tmc8xx=BIOS-ADDRESS,IRQ
```

BIOS_ADDRESS is the BIOS address of the board, and *IRQ* is the interrupt-request channel.

Secret

Common problems with the ST01 or ST02 SCSI controller are timeouts when Linux accesses the disk connected to the controller, because the board's default settings disable interrupts. You should set jumpers (W3 on ST01 and JP3 on ST02) on the board to reenable interrupts. You also should select IRQ 5.

Secret

If you get errors when you try to run `fdisk` on a drive that is connected to a Seagate or Future Domain controller, you should use `fdisk`'s Extra Functions menu to specify the disk geometry (cylinders, heads, and sectors).

Pro Audio Spectrum PAS16 SCSI

The PAS16 SCSI refers to the SCSI interface on a Pro Audio Spectrum sound card. Following are the hardware-configuration parameters for the PAS16 SCSI:

- I/O ports — 0x388, 0x384, 0x38x, and 0x288
- IRQs — 10, 12, 14, and 15 (must be different from the IRQs used for sound)
- DMA — not used for the SCSI portion of the card

Secret

The autoprobe function does not require a BIOS. You can provide a command line at the boot prompt to specify the parameters of your PAS 16 SCSI. For a PAS 16 SCSI at I/O address 0x388 and IRQ 10, for example, use the following command line:

```
pas16=0x388,10
```

Trantor T128, T128F, and T228

These Trantor ISA-bus SCSI cards have the following configuration parameters:

- BIOS addresses — 0xcc000, 00xc8000, 0xdc000, and 0xd8000
- IRQs — on all boards, none, 3, 5, and 7; on T128F, 10, 12, 14, and 15
- DMA — not used

Secret

The driver can autoprobe as long as a BIOS is installed. If one of these SCSI controllers does not have a BIOS, or if the BIOS is disabled, you can specify the controller through a command line such as the following:

```
t128=BIOS-ADDRESS,IRQ
```

BIOS-ADDRESS is the base address (not I/O address). For a controller with a BIOS address 0xcc000 and IRQ 5, for example, the command line is

```
t128=0xcc000,5
```

Use –1 for the IRQ if a controller does not have an IRQ; use –2 to make the driver probe the IRQ.

Ultrastor 14f (ISA), 24f (EISA), and 34f (VLB)

The Ultrastor SCSI cards have the following configuration parameters:

- I/O ports — 0x130, 0x140, 0x210, 0x230, 0x240, 0x310, 0x330, and 0x340
- IRQs — 10, 11, 14, and 15
- DMA channels — 5, 6, and 7

The autoprobe function works in all cases, except when the I/O port address is 0x310. Because I/O port 0x310 is not supported by the autoprobe code, you should select a different I/O port address for the Ultrastor controller.

Secret

If you have a sound card, I/O port address 0x330 typically is used by the MIDI device. Use a different I/O port address for the Ultrastor card if you have a sound card in your PC. A good I/O port for the Ultrastor cards is 0x340.

The Ultrastor controllers support a WD1003 emulation mode, in which they can work with ST-506-interface disk drives. If you happen to have your Ultrastor controller in WD1003 mode, the Ultrastor SCSI driver will fail, displaying the following error message:

```
hd.c: ST-506 interface disk with more than 16 heads detected,
  probably due to non-standard sector translation.  Giving up.
  (disk %d: cyl=%d, sect=63, head=64)
```

You can fix this problem by setting the Ultrastor controller to its native SCSI mode.

Western Digital 7000

The hardware configurations for this ISA-bus SCSI controller are as follows:

- BIOS address — 0xce000
- I/O port — 0x350
- IRQ — 15
- DMA channel — 6

The driver can probe and detect the SCSI controller automatically, provided the BIOS is installed.

Some revisions of the Western Digital 7000 controller may not work with the driver. Reportedly, revision 5 and later controllers work fine. In addition, on the working controllers, the onboard SCSI chip should have an A suffix.

Iomega Zip Drive (SCSI)

The Iomega Zip drive is a low-cost, removable disk drive that enables you to use floppy-like disks, each of which is capable of holding 100 million characters. If you consider a megabyte to be $1,024 \times 1,024 = 1,048,576$ bytes, 100 million characters will be about 95MB. Unlike floppies, the Zip disks do not have a hardware write-protect tab, which means that you have to be careful when you initialize a disk or delete files.

The Zip drive comes in three versions: SCSI interface for Macintosh or MS-DOS, ATAPI, and a parallel-port version. The current Linux kernel supports all versions of the Zip drive.

Tip

The ATAPI version of the Iomega Zip drive is treated like another IDE hard drive. If your ATAPI Zip drive is connected as a slave to the second controller, its device name is `/dev/hdd4`. The following command mounts the ATAPI Zip drive on the `/mnt/zip` directory. (If the directory does not exist, create it with the `mkdir /mnt/zip` command):

```
mount /dev/hdd4 /mnt/zip
```

Both the DOS and Macintosh versions of the SCSI Iomega Zip drive should work under Linux. You can use an existing Linux-supported SCSI card (preferably, a simple Adaptec AHA152x–compatible card) to connect the Zip drive to your PC. The Zip drive has switches to turn on termination (if it's the last device in the chain) and select SCSI ID (one of 5 or 6).

You also can connect the Zip drive to a separately sold Zip Zoom interface card — a low-end SCSI card that's compatible with the Adaptec AHA152x card. If you have a kernel that supports the AHA152x, and you use LILO, you can use the Zip drive with the following line added to the `/etc/lilo.conf` file:

```
append="aha152x=0x340,11,7,1"
```

Tip

To prepare the Zip disk for use under Linux, you should try it under DOS. Run the \SCSI\INSTALL program on the Iomega Tools disk. After that, the Zip disk should work under Linux.

Log in as `root`, and run `/sbin/fdisk` on the SCSI device that represents the Zip drive. If the Zip drive is the only SCSI device, it will be `/dev/sda`, so you type the following:

```
/sbin/fdisk /dev/sda
```

Check the current partition, and set the type to Linux native. Then create an `ext2` file system with the following command:

```
/sbin/mke2fs /dev/sda1
```

The preceding command assumes that you are using the first partition of the Zip disk. Create a `zip` subdirectory in `/mnt` with the `mkdir /mnt/zip` command. You then can mount the Zip disk at an appropriate mount point and use the disk, as follows:

```
mount -t ext2 /dev/sda1 /mnt/zip
```

The contents of the Zip disk will be in the `/mnt/zip` directory. Before ejecting the disk, use the command `umount /mnt/zip` to dismount the Zip disk.

SCSI Troubleshooting

Most SCSI problems are due to bad cables or improper termination. You should check the cables and the terminator before trying anything else. The following sections list other common SCSI problems and their suggested fixes.

Problems booting with LILO

When booting from a SCSI hard disk, LILO may hang after displaying the letters `LI`. This problem occurs if the SCSI controller's BIOS and the Linux SCSI driver interpret the disk geometry differently.

Secret

To fix this problem, add the `linear` keyword on a single line in the `/etc/lilo.conf` file. This keyword causes LILO to use linear block addresses (LBAs) instead of the physical cylinder-head-sector (CHS) addresses when it accesses the disk. LILO will use the disk geometry supplied by the BIOS and compute physical addresses at run time, which should work properly.

SCSI device at all SCSI IDs

If a SCSI device shows up at all possible SCSI IDs, you must have configured that device with the same SCSI ID as the SCSI controller (usually, 7). Change the ID of that device to another value. (Many devices have a simple switch for setting the SCSI ID; on others, you have to change a jumper.)

SCSI device at all LUNs

If a SCSI device shows up at all possible SCSI logical unit numbers (LUNs), the device probably has errors in the *firmware* — the built-in code in the device's SCSI interface. To verify these errors, first use the following command line during boot:

```
max_scsi_luns=1
```

If the device works with this option, you can add it to the list of blacklisted SCSI devices in the array of structures named device_list in the file /usr/src/linux-2.4.0/drivers/scsi/scsi_scan.c. The definition of that structure and some parts of the array are as follows:

```
struct dev_info{
    const char * vendor;
    const char * model;
    const char * revision; /* Latest revision known to be bad. Not
used yet */
    unsigned flags;
};
Here
/*
 * This is what was previously known as the blacklist.  The concept
 * has been expanded so that we can specify other types of things we
 * need to be aware of.
 */
static struct dev_info device_list[] =

struct dev_info{
{
{"Aashima","IMAGERY 2400SP","1.03",BLIST_NOLUN},/* Locks up if polled
for lun !=
 0 */
{"CHINON","CD-ROM CDS-431","H42", BLIST_NOLUN}, /* Locks up if polled
for lun !=
 0 */
{"CHINON","CD-ROM CDS-535","Q14", BLIST_NOLUN}, /* Locks up if polled
for lun !=
 0 */
{"DENON","DRD-25X","V", BLIST_NOLUN},            /* Locks up if probed
for lun !=
 0 */
{"HITACHI","DK312C","CM81", BLIST_NOLUN},        /* Responds to all lun
- dtg */
{"HITACHI","DK314C","CR21" , BLIST_NOLUN},       /* responds to all lun
*/
{"IMS", "CDD521/10","2.06", BLIST_NOLUN},        /* Locks-up when LUN>0
polled. *
/
{"MAXTOR","XT-3280","PR02", BLIST_NOLUN},        /* Locks-up when LUN>0
polled. *
/
... lines deleted ...
```

```
{"DELL", "PV530F", "*", BLIST_SPARSELUN},
{"SONY", "TSL", "*", BLIST_FORCELUN},
/*
 * Must be at end of list...
 */
{NULL, NULL, NULL}
};
```

From this list, you can get an idea of the types of SCSI devices that have the problem of showing up at all LUNs. If you have the same problem with a SCSI device, you can add that device's name to this list before the last line before rebuilding the kernel. You may not want to do this, however, if you are not familiar with the C programming language.

Sense errors on an error-free SCSI device

The cause of this problem usually is bad cables or improper termination. Check all cables, and make sure that the SCSI bus is terminated at both ends.

Networking kernel problems with a SCSI device

If a Linux kernel with networking support does not work with SCSI devices, the problem may be the autoprobe function of the networking drivers. The autoprobe capability is meant to detect the type of networking hardware automatically; the network drivers read from and write to specific I/O addresses during autoprobing. If an I/O address happens to be the same as that used by a SCSI device, the system may have a problem. In this case, you have to check the I/O address, IRQ, and DMA values of the network cards and of the SCSI controller, and make sure that no conflicts exist. Most SCSI controllers (and even network adapters) allow you to configure these parameters (I/O address, IRQ, and DMA) through setup software that comes with the adapter.

Device is detected but not accessible

If the kernel detects a SCSI device (as reported in the boot messages, which you can see with dmesg | more) but you cannot access the device, the device file is missing from the /dev directory.

Secret

To add the device file, log in as root, change the directory to /dev, and then use the MAKEDEV script to create the device file. To add a device for a SCSI tape drive, for example, you would use the following command:

```
cd /dev
./MAKEDEV st0
```

When you log in as root, the current directory is typically not in the PATH environment variable. That's why you need to add the ./ prefix when executing the MAKEDEV script. You can find more information about the MAKEDEV script with the following command:

```
man MAKEDEV
```

SCSI lockup

If the SCSI system locks up, check the SCSI controller card, using any diagnostic software that came with the card (usually, the diagnostic software runs under DOS). Look for conflicts in I/O address, IRQ, or DMA with other cards. Some sound cards, for example, use a 16-bit DMA channel in addition to an 8-bit DMA; make sure that you did not inadvertently use the same 16-bit DMA for the SCSI card.

Secret

The Linux SCSI driver for some SCSI cards supports only one outstanding SCSI command at a time. With such a SCSI card, if a device such as a tape drive is busy rewinding, the system may not be able to access other SCSI devices (such as a hard disk or a CD-ROM drive) that are daisy-chained with that tape drive. A solution to this problem is to add a second SCSI controller to take care of the tape drives.

SCSI devices not found

If the Linux kernel does not detect your SCSI devices at startup, you get the following message when Linux boots:

```
scsi : 0 hosts
scsi : detected total
```

If you see this message, but you know that the SCSI devices are there (and that they work under DOS), the problem may be the lack of a BIOS on the SCSI controller; the autoprobe routines that detect SCSI devices rely on the BIOS.

This problem occurs for the following SCSI cards:

- Adaptec 152x, 151x, AIC-6260, and AIC-6360
- Future Domain 1680, TMC-950, and TMC-8xx
- Trantor T128, T128F, and T228F
- Seagate ST01 and ST02
- Western Digital 7000

Secret

Even if a SCSI controller has a BIOS, jumpers often are available for disabling the BIOS. If you disabled the BIOS for some reason, you may want to reenable it (read the documentation of your SCSI controller for directions), so that Linux can detect the SCSI devices automatically.

For a SCSI card, such as the Adaptec 151x, that does not have any BIOS, use the following command line during boot to force detection of the card:

```
aha152x=0x340,11,7,1
```

Summary

You need a hard disk to install Linux on your PC. In particular, to successfully install Linux, your PC's hard disk controller must be supported by Linux. This should not be a problem, because Linux supports the popular IDE and Enhanced IDE interfaces, as well as the SCSI interface. This chapter describes how to use IDE and SCSI hard disks in Linux.

By reading this chapter, you learn the following things:

▶ Linux's support for a specific hard disk drive depends on the disk controller used to connect that drive to the PC's motherboard. Linux supports the popular IDE (Integrated Drive Electronics); Enhanced IDE (EIDE); and SCSI disk controllers for ISA, EISA, VLB, and PCI buses. These disk controllers cover nearly all types of disks that PCs typically use.

▶ You have to partition a disk to install Linux, and when you install Linux, you have to create a swap space and set up a mechanism to boot Linux. You can use LILO to manage the boot process, even if you have multiple operating systems (such as DOS and Windows 95/98) on the disk.

▶ The disk controller sees the disk as a collection of 512-byte sectors on magnetic platters that are mounted on a spindle and rotate under read/write heads. This physical construction of a hard disk has led to the view of a disk as a collection of cylinders, heads, and sectors (CHS). Linux views the disk as a sequence of sectors that can be addressed sequentially (a linear block address, or LBA).

▶ SCSI is popular because you can connect up to seven devices through a single SCSI controller. The only drawback is that the SCSI controller is relatively expensive compared with EIDE controllers.

▶ Linux supports a wide variety of SCSI controllers, including the popular Adaptec and BusLogic SCSI controllers.

▶ Linux supports all three types of Iomega Zip drives (ATAPI, SCSI, and parallel port).

Chapter 5

CD-ROM Drives and Sound

In This Chapter

▶ Understanding the different types of interfaces for CD-ROM drives

▶ Specifying Linux device names for CD-ROM drives and sound cards

▶ Using specific CD-ROM drives in Linux

▶ Fixing common problems with CD-ROM drives in Linux

▶ Understanding the brands of sound cards that Linux supports

▶ Configuring the sound card in Red Hat Linux

▶ Playing audio CDs in Red Hat Linux

▶ Testing and troubleshooting sound cards in Linux

If you have installed, or are planning to install Red Hat Linux from this book's companion CD-ROMs, chances are good that your system already has a CD-ROM drive. You are probably reading this chapter because you have questions about using your CD-ROM drive to install Linux. You should find answers to your questions in this chapter. As with other peripheral devices (such as disk drives), the CD-ROM drive connects to your PC's motherboard through a controller board. Thus, the real issue of how to use a CD-ROM drive under Linux boils down to whether Linux includes a driver for that CD-ROM drive's interface. This chapter discusses various CD-ROM interfaces and explains which ones are supported under Linux.

I grouped CD-ROM drives with sound cards, because many CD-ROM drives used to connect to the PC through interfaces built into sound cards. Initially, vendors bundled CD-ROM drives and sound cards as a package, because you need both types of devices to enjoy multimedia software that uses sound, video, and animation. The CD-ROM provides the storage space you need to store the video clips, images, and sound files in a typical multimedia application. The sound card allows the PC to generate professional-quality sound — the other must-have ingredient in a multimedia application.

This chapter describes specific types of Linux-supported CD-ROM drives, categorized by interface type. You'll also find information about how to include support for specific sound cards in Red Hat Linux.

CD-ROM Drives

Each CD-ROM can hold up to 650MB of data (the equivalent of about 450 high-density 3.5-inch floppy disks) and does not cost much to produce. The physical medium of the CD-ROM is the same as that used for audio compact discs (CDs): a polycarbonate disc with an aluminized layer. A laser reads the data, which is encoded in microscopic pits on the aluminized layer. CD-ROM media are more robust and reliable than other magnetic media, such as floppy disks. All these factors make CD-ROM an attractive medium for distributing data and programs. In fact, most Linux books (including this one) bundle CD-ROMs with a complete Linux distribution that includes the operating system and lots of popular software. In this case, the CD-ROMs contain Red Hat Linux — a popular Linux distribution.

In that list of good properties of a CD-ROM — high capacity, low cost, and reliability — you don't see any mention of speed, because the data-transfer rates of CD-ROM drives are not as fast as those of hard disk drives. When CD-ROM drives first appeared, the drives could transfer data at rates of approximately 150KB per second. These drives were known as *single-speed* (also referred to as *1X*) CD-ROM drives. *Double-speed* (or *2X*) CD-ROM drives, which provide data-transfer rates of 300KB per second, were soon widely available. Currently, most systems come with 24X, 32X, or even 40X CD-ROM drives, which can sustain data-transfer rates of up to 3,600KB per second, and average access times of 95 milliseconds (compare this with hard-drive access times of around 10 milliseconds).

Note

Most CD-ROMs contain information in an ISO-9660 file system (formerly known as High Sierra). This file system supports only the MS-DOS-style 8.3 filenames, such as README.TXT, which have names up to eight characters in length and optional three-character filename extensions, such as .DOC or .TXT. An extension to the ISO-9660 file system, called the Rock Ridge Extensions, uses unused fields to support longer filenames and additional UNIX-style file attributes, such as ownership and symbolic links.

Most CD-ROM drives also typically enable you to play audio CDs via an external headphone jack. You also will find an output line that you can connect to the sound card, so that you can play an audio CD on the speakers attached to the sound card.

Supported CD-ROM Drives

As with hard disks, Linux's support for a CD-ROM drive depends on the interface through which that CD-ROM drive connects to the PC's motherboard. CD-ROM drives come with three popular types of interfaces:

- *IDE or AT Attachment Packet Interface (ATAPI)* — ATAPI is a recent specification for accessing and controlling a CD-ROM drive that is connected to the PC through the AT Attachment (ATA). ATAPI is gaining popularity, because it is built on the cheaper IDE interface. (ATA is the new name for IDE.)

- *Small Computer System Interface (SCSI)* — SCSI is popular because of its relatively high data rates and because it can support multiple devices. The only drawback is that you need a relatively expensive SCSI controller card for the PC.

- *Proprietary interfaces* — Many CD-ROM vendors provide their own proprietary interfaces between the CD-ROM drive and the PC's motherboard. Many sound cards include a built-in CD-ROM-drive interface, which is typically a proprietary interface. The problem with proprietary interfaces is that someone has to develop a Linux driver specifically for each interface, whereas with a SCSI interface you can use a SCSI driver to access any SCSI device.

ATAPI CD-ROM drives

ATA (AT Attachment) is the official ANSI (American National Standards Institute) standard name for the commonplace IDE interface, which is commonly used to connect hard-disk drives to the PC. ATAPI (ATA Packet Interface) is a protocol (similar to SCSI) for controlling storage devices, such as CD-ROM drives and tape drives. Although ATAPI is relatively new, it is rapidly becoming the most popular type of interface for CD-ROM drives, because ATAPI is based on the ATA (or IDE) interface and does not need any expensive controller card or cable. Also, an ATAPI CD-ROM can simply be connected as the second drive on the same interface on which the PC's hard drive is connected. That means that the ATAPI CD-ROM drive does not require a separate interface card.

The Linux kernel includes an ATAPI driver that should work with any ATAPI CD-ROM drive. ATAPI CD-ROM drives are available from many vendors, such as Aztech, Mitsumi, NEC, Philips, Sony, and Toshiba. Nowadays most new PCs (such as those from Gateway and Dell) come configured with ATAPI CD-ROM drives.

SCSI CD-ROM drives

Linux supports a SCSI CD-ROM drive connected to one of the supported SCSI controller cards (see Chapter 4 for more information). The only restriction is that the block size (for data transfers) of the SCSI CD-ROM drive should be 512 or 2,048 bytes, which covers all CD-ROM drives on the market.

Some CD-ROM drives include a controller with a modified interface that's not fully SCSI-compatible. These interfaces are essentially proprietary, and you cannot use such CD-ROM drives with the SCSI driver.

SCSI CD-ROM drives are available from many vendors, such as Plextor, Sanyo, and Toshiba.

Proprietary CD-ROM drives

Although the ATAPI and SCSI CD-ROM drives fall into neat categories and work well in Linux, the situation is much more confusing when it comes to CD-ROM drives with a proprietary interface. Following are two of the biggest sources of confusion:

- Some vendors, such as Creative Labs (of Sound Blaster fame), have sold CD-ROM drives with all types of interfaces: ATAPI, SCSI, and proprietary interfaces on a sound card. Thus, the vendor name alone does not mean anything; you have to know what type of interface the CD-ROM drive uses.

- PC vendors sometimes categorize the CD-ROM-drive interface as being IDE, even though the interface is really proprietary. Like the IDE (or ATAPI) interface, the proprietary CD-ROM-drive interface is cheap and popular.

As you may have guessed, proprietary CD-ROM-drive interfaces are popular because they tend to be much simpler than SCSI, which was the primary alternative to proprietary interfaces before ATAPI came along. Because of the popularity of relatively inexpensive ATAPI, most new PCs do not use proprietary interfaces for CD-ROMs. Because a proprietary CD-ROM interface can be built into a sound card at little cost, however, some Linux users may have PCs with proprietary CD-ROM drives.

If you have a choice, avoid proprietary CD-ROM-drive interfaces. They're more trouble than they are worth.

Table 5-1 lists CD-ROM drives with proprietary interfaces and the drivers you need to support those drives.

Table 5-1	**CD-ROM Drives with Proprietary Interfaces**
Driver	*CD-ROM Drive*
Aztcd	Aztech CDA268-01A (other models are ATAPI drives), Orchid CDS-3110, Okano/Wearnes CDD-110, Conrad TXC, CyCDROM CR520ie/CR940ie
cdu31a	Sony CDU31A/CDU33A
cm206cd	Philips/LMS CM 206
Gscd	GoldStar R420 (may be sold as part of the Reveal Multimedia kit)
isp16	CD-ROM drives attached to the interface on an ISP16, MAD16, or Mozart sound card
Mcd	Mitsumi CRMC LU005S, FX001
Mcdx	Mitsumi CRMC LU005S, FX001 (new driver)
Optcd	Optics Storage Dolphin 8000AT, Lasermate CR328A
Sbpcd	Matsushita/Panasonic (Panasonic CR-521, CR-522, CR-523, CR-562, and CR-563), Kotobuki, Creative Labs (CD-200), Longshine LCS-7260, Teac CD-55A
sjcd	Sanyo H94A
sonycd535	Sony CDU-535/CDU-531

CD-ROM Troubleshooting

You need a CD-ROM drive that works under Linux to install Linux from this book's companion CD-ROM. The initial Linux kernel comes with CD-ROM driver modules for all supported CD-ROM drives; therefore you should not have any problem as long as your CD-ROM drive is supported by Linux. Remember that the CD-ROM drive's interface is what counts, not the brand name. For example, any CD-ROM drive with the IDE interface will work under Linux, because Linux supports the IDE interface.

If Linux does not seem to recognize the CD-ROM drive after you have rebuilt the kernel, try the following steps to fix the problem:

1. If you have rebuilt the kernel with support for your CD-ROM drive, verify that you are indeed running the new kernel. To see the version number, use the `uname -srv` (or `uname -a`) command. Following is typical output from the `uname -srv` command:

   ```
   Linux 2.4.0-0.43.12 #1 Wed Dec 27 17:44:32 EST 2000
   ```

   This output from the `uname` command shows the kernel's version number, as well as the date on which the kernel was built. If that date does not match the date on which you rebuilt the kernel, you may not be running the new kernel. Go through the steps outlined in Chapter 25, and make sure that you have really installed the new kernel. One common problem is forgetting to reboot, so try that as well.

2. Look at the contents of the `/proc/devices` file to verify that the CD-ROM device is present. Use the following procedure to view the contents of a `/proc/devices` file:

   ```
   cat /proc/devices
   Character devices:
     1 mem
     2 pty
     3 ttyp
     4 ttyS
     5 cua
     7 vcs
    10 misc
    29 fb
    36 netlink
    81 video_capture
   109 lvm
   128 ptm
   136 pts
   ```

```
162 raw
180 usb

Block devices:
  1 ramdisk
  2 fd
  3 ide0
  9 md
 22 ide1
 58 lvm
```

This listing corresponds to the devices on my system. It shows two lists of devices — *character devices*, such as serial ports that transfer data one or more characters at a time, and *block devices*, such as hard disks that transfer data in fixed-size blocks. You should look for the CD-ROM device in the list of block devices. I know that my CD-ROM drive is connected to the secondary IDE interface. The two IDE interfaces correspond to the devices ide0 and ide1 in /proc/devices. Because ide1 appears in the listing, I know that the CD-ROM driver is in the kernel.

If you have a CD-ROM connected to a Sound Blaster Pro or compatible interface, look for a device number of 25 and the device name sbpcd.

If you don't see a device that corresponds to your CD-ROM drive, you did not configure the kernel properly to include the CD-ROM driver. Reconfigure and rebuild the kernel, making sure that you include support for your CD-ROM drive.

Note that for some SCSI CD-ROM drives, you have to specify the SCSI adapter as a boot option before the Linux kernel can access the CD-ROM drive.

3. Verify that the CD-ROM driver detected the CD-ROM drive when the system started. Use the dmesg | more command to look at the boot messages and see whether a line reports that the CD-ROM drive was found (you can also use the more /var/log/dmesg command). On my system, which has an ATAPI CD-ROM drive, the message looks like this:

```
hdc: Pioneer CD-ROM ATAPI Model DR-A24X 0105, ATAPI CDROM drive
```

If you find no boot message about the CD-ROM drive, make sure that the CD-ROM is physically installed. For an external CD-ROM drive, make sure that the drive is powered on and the cables are connected. Check any drive ID or jumpers, and make sure that they are set correctly. You may want to first make sure that the CD-ROM drive works under DOS; if you see the CD-ROM work under DOS, you can be sure that the drive is physically sound. Next, verify that you have rebuilt the kernel with support for the correct CD-ROM-drive interface.

4. Verify that you can read from the CD-ROM drive. Try the following command and see whether the drive's activity light comes on (it should) and whether there are any error messages (there shouldn't be):

```
dd bs=1024 count=5000 < /dev/cdrom > /dev/null
5000+0 records in
5000+0 records out
```

The /dev/null device is what you might call the bit bucket. Output directed to /dev/null simply vanishes.

If the dd command does not work, the device file for the CD-ROM device may not be set properly. Use the ls -l command to view detailed information about your CD-ROM device. The Red Hat Linux installation program sets up /dev/cdrom as a symbolic link to the actual CD-ROM device. For an ATAPI CD-ROM drive on the secondary IDE interface, for example, I would look at the /dev/cdrom symbolic link to make sure it points to the real CD-ROM device (/dev/hdc in this case), as follows:

```
ls -l /dev/cdrom
lrwxrwxrwx   1 root    root    3 Sep 20 13:49 /dev/cdrom -> hdc
```

5. Verify that you can mount the CD-ROM. Place a good CD-ROM (such as the CD-ROM from this book) in the CD-ROM drive and try to mount using the following command:

```
mount -t iso9660 -r /dev/cdrom /mnt/cdrom
```

The -t iso9660 option specifies that the CD-ROM has an ISO 9660 file system and the -r option says that you want to mount the file system read-only.

If you can read from the CD-ROM drive with the dd command, but cannot mount the CD-ROM, then you may have configured the kernel without support for the ISO-9660 file system. To verify the currently supported file systems, use the following command:

```
cat /proc/filesystems
nodev   shm
nodev   sockfs
nodev   pipefs
nodev   proc
        ext2
        iso9660
nodev   devpts
nodev   usbdevfs
        vfat
```

If you do not see iso9660 listed, you have to rebuild the kernel and add support for the ISO-9660 file system.

6. If nothing works, you may want to read the latest CDROM-HOWTO document. To read the HOWTO documents, use Netscape Communicator to visit the Web page at `http://metalab.unc.edu/pub/Linux/docs/HOWTO/`. and then follow the links to the CDROM-HOWTO document (your Red Hat Linux system must be connected to the Internet for this to work).

Cross-Reference

If you still cannot get the CD-ROM drive to work under Linux, you may want to post a news item to one of the `comp.os.linux` newsgroups. Chapter 19 describes how to post to newsgroups.

The following sections suggest solutions for a few more common problems.

Kernel configuration for specific CD-ROM drives

If you are rebuilding the kernel and you have an ATAPI CD-ROM drive, you should answer yes to the following questions as you configure the kernel (see Chapter 25 for more on configuring the kernel):

```
Enhanced IDE/MFM/RLL disk/cdrom/tape/floppy support
(CONFIG_BLK_DEV_IDE) [Y/m/n/?] y
    Include IDE/ATAPI CDROM support (CONFIG_BLK_DEV_IDECD) [Y/m/n/?] y
```

The possible responses are shown in brackets; y means yes (that means include support in the kernel), m means use a driver module, and n means no.

For SCSI CD-ROM drives, answer yes to the following questions:

```
*
* SCSI support
*
SCSI support (CONFIG_SCSI) [Y/m/n/?] y
*
* SCSI support type (disk, tape, CD-ROM)
*
SCSI CD-ROM support (CONFIG_BLK_DEV_SR) [Y/m/n/?] y
```

Of course, you also must specify your SCSI controller type; otherwise, the SCSI CD-ROM won't work. If you have an Adaptec AHA1542 SCSI controller, for example, answer yes to the following question:

```
Adaptec AHA1542 support (CONFIG_SCSI_AHA1542) [M/n/y/?] y
```

If your CD-ROM drive has a proprietary interface, you must enable support for that specific CD-ROM drive interface. Start by answering yes to the following question during kernel configuration:

```
*
* Old CD-ROM drivers (not SCSI, not IDE)
*
Support non-SCSI/IDE/ATAPI CDROM drives (CONFIG_CD_NO_IDESCSI)
[Y/n/?] y
```

After that you have to answer yes to the question about the specific CD-ROM drive in your PC. If you have a Mitsumi CD-ROM drive (with a proprietary interface, not ATAPI), for example, answer yes to the line that starts with Mitsumi (standard).

Newer versions of the Linux kernel may support other types of proprietary CD-ROM-drive interfaces. Check the prompts carefully before answering the questions posed by the kernel-configuration program.

Because most CD-ROMs use the ISO-9660 file system, you must also enable support for this file system in the kernel. To do this, answer yes to the following question during kernel configuration:

```
ISO 9660 CDROM filesystem support (CONFIG_ISO9660_FS) [Y/m/n/?] y
```

IDE (ATAPI) CD-ROM troubles

When a PC has an ATAPI CD-ROM drive, its ATA (IDE) adapter has two interfaces, primary and secondary, each of which is capable of supporting two drives. In Linux, the two primary devices are /dev/hda and /dev/hdb, which are typically used for hard-disk drives. The secondary IDE devices are /dev/hdc and /dev/hdd. Thus, if you have an IDE hard drive connected to the primary interface and an IDE CD-ROM drive connected to the secondary interface, the hard drive will be /dev/hda and the CD-ROM drive will be /dev/hdc.

Secret

Often, of the two devices on an IDE interface, one is designated the *master* and the other the *slave*. When only one IDE device is attached to an interface, it must be designated the master (or *single*). Typically, the IDE device has a jumper (a connector that connects a pair of pins) to indicate whether the device is a master or a slave.

If Linux refuses to recognize your IDE CD-ROM drive, however, you should check the CD-ROM drive's parameters, making sure that the drive uses the secondary IDE interface (IRQ 15 and I/O address 170H) and that it is set to be the master.

Secret

Some interface cards support more than two IDE interfaces. In such a case you should know that the Linux IDE CD-ROM driver might not recognize anything but the primary and secondary IDE interfaces. The Creative Labs Sound Blaster 16 CD-ROM interface is, by default, set to be the fourth IDE interface. If you are connecting a CD-ROM drive to a Sound Blaster 16 for use in Linux, you have to set the jumpers on the Sound Blaster 16 so that the IDE interface is the secondary interface, instead of the fourth interface.

Boot-time parameters for CD-ROM drives

Linux drivers normally find CD-ROM drives (and other peripherals) by *probing*—reading from and writing to various I/O addresses. Linux drivers also use any available information from the PC's CMOS memory. CMOS stands for complementary metal-oxide semiconductor—a type of semiconductor. Each PC has a small amount of battery-backed, nonvolatile CMOS storage, where vital pieces of information about the PC, such as the number of types of disk drives, are stored. The real-time clock is also stored in the CMOS.

One problem with probing is that it involves reading from or writing to specific I/O addresses. Depending on what device uses that I/O address, probing can cause the system to *hang* (become unresponsive). When the Sound

Blaster Pro CD driver, sbpcd, probes for a CD-ROM drive, it may access an I/O address that is used in an NE2000 Ethernet card; if this happens, the system hangs.

To avoid probing at boot time, you can pass specific device parameters for the device corresponding to your CD-ROM drive.

If you have a CD-ROM drive with the Sound Blaster Pro CD interface, the device name is sbpcd, and you can provide settings at LILO's boot prompt as follows:

```
sbpcd=0x230,SoundBlaster
```

This command tells the sbpcd driver that the I/O address of the CD-ROM drive is 230H. The exact boot-time parameters for a device depend on that device driver. Later sections of this chapter provide specific boot-time parameters for CD-ROM device drivers.

Secret

If you use LILO, you can put the boot-time parameters in the /etc/lilo.conf file with the following command:

```
append = "sbpcd=0x230,SoundBlaster"
```

CD-ROM Device Names

Linux uses a unique device name for each type of CD-ROM interface. The CD-ROM devices are block devices like the disk device, such as /dev/hda and /dev/sda. Table 5-2 lists the CD-ROM device names.

Table 5-2   CD-ROM Device Names in Linux

Device Name	CD-ROM Type
/dev/aztcd	Aztech CD-ROM drive interface
/dev/cdu31a	Sony CDU31A/CDU33A CD-ROM drive interface
/dev/cm206cd	Philips/LMS CD-ROM drive interface
/dev/gscd	GoldStar CD-ROM interface
/dev/hdc	ATAPI CD-ROM drive on the secondary IDE interface on an EIDE controller
/dev/mcd	Mitsumi CD-ROM drive interface
/dev/optcd	Optics Storage CD-ROM drive interface
/dev/sbpcd	Sound Blaster Pro CD-ROM drive interface
/dev/sjcd	Sanyo CD-ROM drive interface
/dev/sonycd535	Sony CDU-535/CDU-531 CD-ROM drive interface

By convention, the generic CD-ROM device (/dev/cdrom) is set up as a link to the actual CD-ROM device on your system. On my system, which has an ATAPI CD-ROM drive, a detailed listing of /dev/cdrom shows the following:

```
ls -l /dev/cdrom
lrwxrwxrwx  1 root   root      3 Sep 20 13:49 /dev/cdrom -> hdc
```

The output from ls indicates that /dev/cdrom is a symbolic link to /dev/hdc, which is the IDE block device. (The same device name is used for a disk or a CD-ROM drive connected to the interface.)

On the other hand, on my old 486 PC, the CD-ROM drive is on a Sound Blaster Pro card. In this case, a detailed listing of /dev/cdrom shows the following:

```
ls -l /dev/cdrom
lrwxrwxrwx  1 root   root      3 Sep 20 13:49 /dev/cdrom -> sbpcd
```

The convention of defining a symbolic link from the generic /dev/cdrom device to the actual CD-ROM device means that programs that use the CD-ROM drive can simply refer to the CD-ROM as /dev/cdrom and not worry about the actual type of CD-ROM-drive interface. Because of the symbolic link between /dev/cdrom and the actual CD-ROM device, any input or output requests go directly to the actual CD-ROM driver that knows how to handle the request.

CD-ROM-Drive Use Under Linux

If you put a new CD-ROM in the drive, you must mount the CD-ROM before you can use it. Use the following command to mount the CD-ROM:

```
mount -t iso9660 -r /dev/cdrom /mnt/cdrom
```

The -t option indicates that the file system of the CD-ROM is ISO-9660 (which is true for a typical CD-ROM), and the -r option indicates that the CD-ROM is mounted as read-only.

Tip

If you want to eject the CD-ROM and load a new one, you must first dismount the CD-ROM's file system by using the umount command. Type umount/mnt/cdrom. You can dismount the CD-ROM only if no processes are currently accessing the CD-ROM, and no user has the CD-ROM file system as the default directory. If you get a "device busy" error message in response to the umount command, you should change the current directory (for instance, type cd /) and then try the umount command again. Then you can eject the CD-ROM, by pressing the CD-ROM drive's eject button.

Specific CD-ROM-Drive Information

The following sections summarize information specific to some common device drivers. This information includes the name of the device file (such as /dev/sbpcd for a CD-ROM drive with Sound Blaster Pro interface), any boot parameters that the driver accepts, and any unique capabilities of the driver.

For more information, read the section that covers the CD-ROM interface of your CD-ROM drive.

The SCSI CD-ROM driver

The scd driver supports CD-ROM drives that connect to the PC through SCSI controller cards. The scd driver has the following characteristics:

```
Allows multiple CD-ROM drives: yes
Supports loadable module: yes
Can read audio frames: no
Performs auto-probing: yes
Name of device file: /dev/scd0, major device number = 11
Device configuration file: /usr/include/linux/cdrom.h
Kernel option during make config: SCSI CD-ROM support?
Name of README file: /usr/src/linux/Documentation/scsi.txt
```

Secret

The scd driver supports multiple CD-ROM drives on the SCSI bus. The names of the device files are /dev/scd0, /dev/scd1, /dev/scd2, and so on, with corresponding minor device numbers 0, 1, 2, and so on. All devices have the same major device number: 11.

The IDE (ATAPI) CD-ROM driver

The IDE device driver supports all types of IDE devices, ranging from hard drives to CD-ROM drives. The driver finds the drives by autoprobing and assigns device names in sequence: /dev/hda and /dev/hdb for drives on the primary IDE interface, and /dev/hdc and /dev/hdd for drives on the secondary IDE interface. A CD-ROM drive on the secondary IDE interface has the device name /dev/hdc (because the CD-ROM drive is slower than the hard disk, CD-ROM drives are connected to a separate IDE interface, rather than being set up as slave drives on the primary IDE interface).

The IDE CD driver has the following characteristics:

```
Allows multiple CD-ROM drives: yes
Supports loadable module: no
Can read audio frames: yes (on some drives)
Performs auto-probing: yes
Name of device file: /dev/hdc or /dev/hdd, major device number = 22
Device configuration file: /usr/include/linux/cdrom.h
Kernel option during make config: Include IDE/ATAPI CDROM support?
Name of README file: /usr/src/linux/Documentation/cdrom/ide-cd
```

The IDE CD driver accepts the following boot parameter:

```
hdc=cdrom
```

This parameter tells the IDE device driver that the first drive on the secondary IDE interface is a CD-ROM drive. If you have another CD-ROM drive on that interface, you could include the following boot parameter:

```
hdd=cdrom
```

The same IDE driver is used for IDE hard disk drives, as well as IDE (ATAPI) CD-ROM drives. The boot parameters are different for a hard drive.

The sbpcd driver

The sbpcd driver supports a variety of CD-ROM drives that connect to the PC through an interface that conforms to the proprietary interface used in Creative Labs Sound Blaster Pro sound cards.

The sbpcd driver has the following characteristics:

```
Allows multiple CD-ROM drives: yes
Supports loadable module: yes
Can read audio frames: yes (CR-562, CR-563, CD-200 only)
Performs auto-probing: yes
Name of device file: /dev/sbpcd0, major device number = 25
Device configuration file: /usr/src/linux/drivers/cdrom/sbpcd.h
Kernel option during make config: Matsushita/Panasonic/ Creative,
Longshine, TEAC CDROM support?
Name of README file: /usr/src/linux/Documentation/cdrom/sbpcd
```

The sbpcd driver accepts a boot parameter in the following format:

```
sbpcd=IOPORT,interface-type
```

IOPORT is the I/O port address of the device, in hexadecimal format (such as 0x230). The interface-type value is a single word that indicates the type of CD-ROM interface: it must be SoundBlaster, LaserMate, or SPEA.

If the device file /dev/sbpcd is missing, create it with the following mknod command:

```
mknod /dev/sbpcd b 25 0
```

The last three parameters specify the device type (b for block device), major device number (25 is the assigned number for /dev/sbpcd), and minor device number (0 for the first CD-ROM drive on the controller).

Secret

You can *daisy-chain* (connect first to second, second to third, and so on) up to four drives per controller. Use minor device numbers 1 through 3 for the three drives that you daisy-chain to the first drive.

The sonycd535 driver

The sonycd535 driver supports Sony CDU-535 and CDU-531 CD-ROM drives that connect to the PC through Sony's proprietary interface card.

The sonycd535 driver has the following characteristics:

```
Allows multiple CD-ROM drives: no
Supports loadable module: yes
Can read audio frames: no
Performs auto-probing: no
Name of device file: /dev/sonycd535, major device number = 24
Device configuration file: /usr/src/linux/drivers/cdrom/sonycd535.h
Kernel option during make config: Sony CDU535 CDROM support?
Name of README file: /usr/src/linux/Documentation/cdrom/sonycd535
```

This driver accepts the following boot parameter:

```
sonycd535=IOPORT
```

$IOPORT$ is the I/O port address of the device in hexadecimal format (such as 0x320).

The aztcd driver

The aztcd driver supports Aztech CDA268-01A, Orchid CD-3110, and Okano/Wearnes CDD110 CD-ROM drives that use a proprietary interface. Other CD-ROM drives from these vendors, such as Aztech CDA269, have the IDE interface; you have to use the IDE CD driver for those drives. The aztcd driver is only for the proprietary interface.

The aztcd driver has the following characteristics:

```
Allows multiple CD-ROM drives: no
Supports loadable module: yes
Can read audio frames: no
Performs auto-probing: no
Name of device file: /dev/aztcd, major device number = 29
Device configuration file: /usr/src/linux/drivers/cdrom/aztcd.h
Kernel option during make config: Aztech/Orchid/Okano/Wearnes/TXC/CyDROM  CDROM
support?
Name of README file: /usr/src/linux/Documentation/cdrom/aztcd
```

This driver accepts the following boot parameter:

```
aztcd=IOPORT
```

$IOPORT$ is the I/O port address of the device in hexadecimal format (such as 0x340).

The mcd driver

The mcd driver supports Mitsumi CRMC-LU005S and CRMC-FX001 CD-ROM drives with the proprietary Mitsumi interface. Many new PCs use the Mitsumi CD-ROM drives, but not the proprietary interface; instead, the current trend is to use the Mitsumi drives with the IDE (ATAPI) interface. Therefore, you should check carefully before selecting the mcd driver as the CD-ROM driver. If your PC has a Mitsumi CD-ROM driver, it's more likely to be an ATAPI drive than it is to be one that has the proprietary Mitsumi interface.

The mcd driver has the following characteristics:

```
Allows multiple CD-ROM drives: no
Supports loadable module: yes
Can read audio frames: no
Performs auto-probing: no
Name of device file: /dev/mcd, major device number = 23
Device configuration file: /usr/src/linux/drivers/cdrom/mcd.h
Kernel option during make config: Mitsumi (standard) [no XA/Multisession] CDROM
support?
Name of README file: /usr/src/linux/Documentation/cdrom/mcd
```

This driver accepts the following boot parameter:

```
mcd=IOPORT,IRQ
```

Major and Minor Device Numbers

Linux applications use device files to communicate with the system's hardware and peripheral devices. When an application reads from or writes to a device file, the Linux kernel passes the read or write request to a device driver that handles the interaction with the physical device. There can be more than one instance of each type of device. Accordingly, two numbers—*major device number* and *minor device number*—are associated with each device file. The major device number indicates which driver the device file refers to, and the minor device number identifies the specific physical unit the driver should access. For example, the CD-ROM interface of the Sound Blaster Pro card has a major device number of 25. The card can handle up to four daisy-chained CD-ROM drives. These four drives are identified by the minor device numbers 0 through 3 (in keeping with UNIX and C programming conventions, the numbers start at 0).

IOPORT is the I/O port address of the Mitsumi interface card in hexadecimal format (such as 0x300). *IRQ* is the interrupt-request number (such as 11) used by that card.

Tip

Red Hat Linux also comes with another Mitsumi driver, mcdx, that provides additional capabilities. To include this driver, you should answer yes to the following question during kernel configuration:

```
Mitsumi [XA/MultiSession] CDROM support?
```

The cdu31a driver

The cdu31a driver supports the Sony CDU31A and CDU33A CD-ROM drives with proprietary interfaces. This driver has the following characteristics:

```
Allows multiple CD-ROM drives: no
Supports loadable module: yes
Can read audio frames: yes
Performs auto-probing: no
Name of device file: /dev/cdu31a, major device number = 15
Device configuration file: /usr/src/linux/drivers/cdrom/cdu31a.h
Kernel option during make config: Sony CDU31A/CDU33A CDROM support?
Name of README file: /usr/src/linux/Documentation/cdrom/cdu31a
```

The cdu31a driver accepts a kernel command line that takes the following form:

```
cdu31a=IOPORT,IRQ[,PAS]
```

IOPORT is the I/O port address of the interface card in hexadecimal format (such as 0x340). *IRQ* is the interrupt-request number (such as 11) used by that card. If the drive is connected to a Pro-Audio Spectrum 16 sound card, you must specify the optional third parameter (shown in square brackets), PAS.

If you load the driver as a module with the insmod command, you have to provide the I/O port address and interrupt-request number in the following format:

```
/sbin/insmod cdu31a cdu31a_port=IOPORT cdu31a_irq=IRQ
```

The gscd driver

The gscd driver supports the GoldStar R420 CD-ROM drive. This driver has the following characteristics:

```
Allows multiple CD-ROM drives: no
Supports loadable module: yes
Can read audio frames: no
Performs auto-probing: no
Name of device file: /dev/gscd, major device number = 16
Device configuration file: /usr/src/linux/drivers/cdrom/gscd.h
Kernel option during make config: Goldstar R420 CDROM support?
Name of README file: /usr/src/linux/Documentation/cdrom/gscd
```

This driver accepts the following boot parameter:

```
gscd=IOPORT
```

IOPORT is the I/O port address of the device in hexadecimal format (such as 0x340).

The cm206cd driver

The cm206cd driver supports the Philips/LMS CM 206 CD-ROM drive. The driver has the following characteristics:

```
Allows multiple CD-ROM drives: no
Supports loadable module: yes
Can read audio frames: no
Performs auto-probing: yes
Name of device file: /dev/cm206cd, major device number = 32
Device configuration file: /usr/src/linux/drivers/cdrom/cm206.h
Kernel option during make config: Philips/LMS CM206 CDROM support?
Name of README file: /usr/src/linux/Documentation/cdrom/cm206
```

This driver accepts the following boot parameter:

```
cm206=IOPORT,IRQ
```

IOPORT is the I/O port address of the interface card in hexadecimal format (such as 0x340). *IRQ* is the interrupt-request number (such as 11) used by that card.

The sjcd driver

The sjcd driver supports the Sanyo H94A CD-ROM drive. This driver has the following characteristics:

```
Allows multiple CD-ROM drives: no
Supports loadable module: yes
Can read audio frames: no
Performs auto-probing: no
Name of device file: /dev/sjcd, major device number = 18
Device configuration file: /usr/src/linux/drivers/cdrom/sjcd.h
Kernel option during make config: Sanyo CDR-H94A CDROM support?
Name of README file: /usr/src/linux/Documentation/cdrom/sjcd
```

This driver accepts the following boot parameter:

```
sjcd=IOPORT,IRQ,DMA
```

IOPORT is the I/O port address of the interface card in hexadecimal format (such as 0x340). *IRQ* is the interrupt-request number (such as 11) used by that card. *DMA* is the DMA channel number (such as 1) used by the card.

Sound Cards and Red Hat Linux

Compared with those of the Apple Macintosh, the built-in sound-generation capabilities of IBM-compatible PCs are rather limited. Essentially, all you can do with the PC's built-in speaker is play a single note; you can't even vary the loudness of the note.

You can greatly improve the sound-output capability of a PC by installing a *sound card*, such as the Sound Blaster, that can synthesize a wide range of sounds. The sound card is an adapter that plugs into a slot on your PC's motherboard and that includes the electronic circuitry needed to play and record sound. You can plug speakers and a microphone into the back of a sound card. Many sound cards also include an interface through which you can connect a CD-ROM drive.

When a microphone is hooked up to the sound card, the card can convert the *analog* (continuously varying) sound waves into 8-bit or 16-bit numbers, sampling the wave at rates ranging from 4 kHz (4,000 times a second) to 44 kHz (44,000 times a second). Higher sampling rates and a higher number of bits (16) provide better quality, but you need more disk space to store high-quality sound. Additionally, the sound card can convert digital sound samples to analog signals that you can play on a speaker.

Most sound cards, including the popular Sound Blaster, also support MIDI commands, in addition to recording and playing back waveform sound. MIDI, which stands for Musical Instrument Digital Interface, is commonly used to record and play back musical sounds that can be created by a synthesizer. (Most sound cards have built-in synthesizers.)

The following is a list of sound cards currently supported by Linux:

- 6850 UART MIDI
- Acer FX-3D
- AD1816/AD1816A–based cards
- AdLib (no longer manufactured)
- ADSP-2115
- ALS-007–based cards (Avance Logic)
- ATI Stereo F/X (no longer manufactured)
- Audio Excel DSP 16

- AudioDrive
- Aztech Sound Galaxy (non-PnP) cards
- CMI8330 sound chip
- Compaq Deskpro XL onboard sound
- Corel Netwinder WaveArtist
- Creative SBLive!
- Crystal CS423x (PnP) and Crystal SoundFusion (CS461x)
- Ensoniq AudioPCI (ES1370), AudioPCI 97 (ES1371)
- Ensoniq SoundScape (and compatible sound cards made by Reveal and Spea)
- ES1370, 1371 sound chips
- ESC614
- ESS1688, 1788, 1868, 1869, 1887, 1888, 688 sound chips
- Gallant SC-6000 and SC-6600
- Gravis Ultrasound GUS, Ultrasound ACE, Ultrasound Max, and Ultrasound with 16-bit-sampling option
- Highscreen Sound-Booster 32 Wave 3D
- HP Kayak
- IBM MWAVE
- Logitech Sound Man 16, SoundMan Games, and SoundMan Wave
- MAD16 Pro (OPTi 82C928, 82C929, 82C930, 82C924 chipsets)
- Media Vision Jazz16
- MediaTriX AudioTriX Pro
- Microsoft Windows Sound System (MSS/WSS)
- MiroSOUND PCM12
- Mozart (OAK OTI-601)
- OPTi 82C928, 82C929, and 82C931
- Orchid SW32
- Personal Sound System (PSS)
- Pinnacle MultiSound
- Pro Audio Spectrum 16 (PAS)
- Pro Audio Studio 16
- Pro Sonic 16
- Roland MPU-401 MIDI interface

- S3 SonicVibes
- Sound Blaster 1.0
- Sound Blaster 16
- Sound Blaster 16ASP
- Sound Blaster 2.0
- Sound Blaster 32
- Sound Blaster 64
- Sound Blaster AWE32
- Sound Blaster AWE64
- Sound Blaster PCI 128
- Sound Blaster Pro
- Sound Blaster Vibra16
- Sound Blaster Vibra16X
- SY-1816
- Terratec Base 1
- Terratec Base 64
- ThunderBoard
- TI TM4000M notebook
- Turtle Beach Maui, MultiSound Classic, MultiSound Fiji, MultiSound Hurricane, MultiSound Monterey, MultiSound Pinnacle, MultiSound Tahiti, WaveFront Maui, WaveFront Tropez, WaveFront Tropez+
- VIA chip set
- VIDC 16-bit sound
- Yamaha OPL2 sound chip
- Yamaha OPL3 sound chip
- Yamaha OPL3-SA1 sound chip
- Yamaha OPL3-SA2 sound chip
- Yamaha OPL3-SA3 sound chip
- Yamaha OPL3-SAx sound chip
- Yamaha OPL4 sound chip

Secret

Many sound cards include a built-in interface through which you can attach a CD-ROM drive. Linux needs a separate device driver to access a CD-ROM drive connected to a sound card; the sound driver does not have anything to do with the CD-ROM drive, even though the drive is attached to the sound card. By the same token, the sound driver has nothing to do with the joystick port that many sound cards include.

Configuring the Sound Card

Linux needs a driver to control the sound card. The initial Linux kernel (after you install Linux from the companion CD-ROM) does not load the sound driver. The sound drivers are provided as loadable modules that you can load after booting Linux. You will find the sound drivers in the /lib/modules/ VERSION/kernel/drivers/sound directory, where VERSION is the kernel version number. For kernel version 2.4.0-0.43.12, the sound-driver modules are in the /lib/modules/2.4.0-0.43.12/kernel/drivers/sound directory. If you look at the names of the module files, you see that each filename ends with the extension .o.

Although you can manually load the sound-driver modules with the /sbin/modprobe utility, in Red Hat Linux you can configure the sound card by running the /usr/sbin/sndconfig utility. This is a text-mode configuration program, so you should run it from a text console using the following procedure:

1. From the graphics screen, press Ctrl+Alt+F1. This brings you to a text-mode virtual terminal that displays a login prompt. Log in as root.

2. Type /usr/sbin/sndconfig. A message informs you that the utility will probe for plug-and-play (PnP) sound card. Press Enter to continue with the probing.

3. Figure 5-1 shows the result of probing for sound cards. In this case, sndconfig detected an OPL3-SA3 Sound System card. Press Enter to continue with the configuration.

Figure 5-1: The sndconfig utility enables you to detect and configure the sound card.

If sndconfig cannot detect any sound cards, you have to select your sound card from a list. You also have to specify the I/O port address, interrupt-request (IRQ) number, and DMA channel for the card.

4. The utility then displays one or more dialog boxes that inform you that existing configuration files will be replaced. Press Enter to continue with each step.

5. A dialog box informs you that `sndconfig` will play a sound sample. Press Enter.

6. If all goes well, you should hear the sound. A dialog box asks you if you heard the sound. If you heard the sound, press Enter to select Yes. Otherwise, press Tab to select No, and then press Enter.

7. If you select No, `sndconfig` shows a dialog box from which you can manually select the interrupt-request number (IRQ), I/O port addresses, and direct memory access (DMA) channels.

8. The utility then plays a MIDI — Musical Instrument Digital Interface — sound sample. You can listen to this sample and confirm this part as well. Note that you can play audio CDs and other sound files, even if you cannot hear the MIDI sample play.

9. After you exit from `sndconfig`, type `exit` to log out. Then press Ctrl+Alt+F7 to return to the graphical user interface.

Once you have configured the sound card for Linux, you can play audio CDs and other sound files in Linux.

Secret

The `sndconfig` utility probes for plug-and-play (PnP) sound cards (and other devices) that can dynamically set the I/O port addresses, the interrupt request numbers (IRQ), and the direct memory access (DMA) channel. The results of the probe are stored in the `/etc/isapnp.conf` file. The information in the `/etc/isapnp.conf` file include the I/O port addresses, IRQ, and DMA channel information for the sound card.

Secret

Once the `/etc/isapnp.conf` file is configured with the settings for any PnP device, the Red Hat Linux boot process automatically runs the `/sbin/isapnp` program to apply those settings. This happens when the shell script `/etc/rc.d/rc.sysinit` is executed as the system boots.

After configuring the `/etc/isapnp.conf` file, `sndconfig` adds appropriate lines to the `/etc/modules.conf` file so that the Linux kernel can load the sound driver when the system reboots, or whenever an application (such as the audio CD player) needs the sound driver.

The lines in `/etc/modules.conf` specify the name of the driver and its configuration options. For example, I have a Yamaha OPL3-SA*x* sound card on a PC running Red Hat Linux. This happens to be a PnP sound card for the ISA bus. For this card `sndconfig` adds the following lines to the `/etc/modules.conf` file:

```
alias sound-slot-0 opl3sa2
options sound dmabuf=1
alias midi opl3
options opl3 io=0x388
options opl3sa2 mss_io=0x530 irq=5 dma=0 dma2=1 mpu_io=0x330 io=0x370
```

If you do not have a PnP sound card, you have to specify the I/O address, the IRQ, and the DMA channel number of the sound card. You should provide the same values for these parameters as are set under DOS and Windows. You should be able to find the settings by reading the sound card's manual (a new PC with a sound card typically includes a small manual for it). In Windows 95/98, you can find the sound-card settings by opening the System Properties tab (double-click the System icon from Start ➪ Settings ➪ Control Panel) and looking under the item labeled Sound, video and game controller.

You can also find this information from the contents of the AUTOEXEC.BAT file in Windows 95/98 systems. For example, one of my systems has a Sound Blaster card, and its AUTOEXEC.BAT file contains the following command:

```
SET BLASTER=A220 I5 D1 H5 P300 T6
```

From my experience with Sound Blaster cards, I could determine from this SET command that the I/O address is 220 (hexadecimal), the IRQ is 5, the 8-bit DMA channel is 1, the 16-bit DMA channel is 5, and the I/O address of the MPU MIDI chip is 300 (hexadecimal). Thus, I provided these values when configuring the Sound Blaster card.

Learning Sound-Device Names

Like any other devices in Linux, the sound devices have files in the /dev directory with specific names. Table 5-3 lists the standard device filenames that provide sound capability in Linux (you may not have all devices on your system).

Table 5-3   Standard Sound Device Filenames in Linux

Device Filename	Description
/dev/audio	An audio device that is capable of playing Sun workstation–compatible audio files (typically with a .au extension). The device does not support all capabilities of the Sun workstation audio device, but can play Sun audio files.
/dev/audio1	A Sun workstation–compatible audio device for the second sound card (if any)
/dev/dsp	A digital signal-processing device that also can play Sun audio files
/dev/midi00 - 03	MIDI ports
/dev/mixer	A sound-mixer device
/dev/mixer1	A second sound-mixer device
/dev/sequencer	A MIDI sequencer device
/dev/sndstat	A device that provides information about the sound driver (see the example later in this chapter in the section "Checking sound-driver status")

Testing the Sound Card

If you rebuild the Linux kernel to include the sound-card driver into the kernel, you should reboot the system to use the updated kernel. If you used the sndconfig tool to add the appropriate lines to the /etc/modules.conf file, the sound driver should be loaded whenever it is needed. For a PnP sound card with appropriate settings in the /etc/isapnp.conf file, the isapnp utility should activate the card settings at boot time.

If you have a kernel with sound-driver support, you should see messages about the sound driver as Linux boots. The boot messages scroll by too fast to read, but you can look for them in the file /var/log/messages. Log in as root and use a text editor, such as vi or emacs to open the file /var/log/messages. Near the end of the file you should see the messages from the most recent system reboot. Look for one or more lines that mention your sound card's name or model number. If you have a PnP card, also note any occurrence of lines containing the word isapnp — these lines show the result of isapnp activating the PnP devices. On my system, for example, I have a Yamaha OPL3-SA3 PnP sound card. In this case, the boot messages include the following messages (I show only the relevant parts of each line):

```
isapnp: Board 1 has Identity cb 80 86 00 01 30 00 a8 65:  YMH0030 Serial No
2156265473 [checksum cb]
isapnp: YMH0030/2156265473[0]{OPL3-SA3 Snd System }: Ports 0x220 0x530 0x388
0x330 0x370; IRQ5 DMA0 DMA1 --- Enabled OK
isapnp: YMH0030/2156265473[1]{OPL3-SA3 Snd System }: Port 0x201; --- Enabled OK
rc.sysinit: Setting up ISA PNP devices succeeded
... (lines deleted)
kernel: Found OPL3-SA3 (YMF715)
kernel: YM3812 and OPL-3 driver Copyright (C) by Hannu Savolainen, Rob Hooft
1993-1996
```

Sometimes, the sound driver may print error or warning messages as it is loaded. When you browse the /var/log/messages file, you should look for these messages as well.

Trying the sound card

To test the sound driver, you should try playing a sound file. A good way to do this is to use an audio CD player to play a sound track from an audio CD. See the section "Playing Audio CDs" for more information about various CD Player applications.

If you don't have an audio CD handy, you can use the X Multimedia System (XMMS) to open a sound file and play it. XMMS can play many types of sound files, including MP3 and Windows WAV. You will find many WAV sound files — which usually have names that end with the .wav extension — in the /usr/share/sounds directory of your Red Hat Linux system.

You can start XMMS from the GNOME desktop by selecting Main Menu ⇨ Programs ⇨ Multimedia ⇨ XMMS. The X Multimedia System has a simple user interface. To open a sound file, select Window Menu ⇨ Play File, or press **L** to select a .wav file from the Open dialog box. Select a file from the /usr/share/sounds directory and XMMS starts playing the sound file, as shown in Figure 5-2.

Figure 5-2: Playing a sound file with the X Multimedia System

If you get an error message from XMMS, select Window Menu ➪ Options ➪ Preferences and select the OSS Driver as the Output Plugin. If you want to adjust the volume or other attributes of the sound, start the GMIX audio mixer, by selecting Main Menu ➪ Programs ➪ Multimedia ➪ Audio Mixer from the GNOME desktop.

If you have a microphone connected to your sound card, you also can try recording a 10-second sound file with the following command:

```
dd bs=8k count=10 </dev/audio >test.au
```

The dd command simply copies a specified amount of data from one file to another. In this case, the input file is the audio device (which records from the microphone), and the output file is the sound file. You may have to run the audio-mixer program to set the recording-gain level for the microphone. After recording the sound file, you can play it back by sending the data back to /dev/audio with the cat command.

Playing Audio CDs

You need a special application to play audio CDs in the CD-ROM drive. This book's companion CD-ROM comes with xplaycd, an X application that provides a graphical control panel for playing audio CDs. Additionally, both GNOME and KDE come with CD players.

Note

Before using any CD player program, make sure that you unmount any CD-ROM that is currently in the drive (use the umount /dev/cdrom command) and place an audio CD in the drive. To play the audio CD, you must also have a sound card and the appropriate sound drivers installed, as described in earlier sections of this chapter.

The xplaycd program needs the X Window System to run, so you should first log in at the graphical login screen and then select Main Menu ➪ Programs ➪ Multimedia ➪ XPlayCD from the GNOME desktop. You can also run xplaycd by typing xplaycd at the shell prompt in a terminal window. Figure 5-3 shows the graphical user interface of xplaycd.

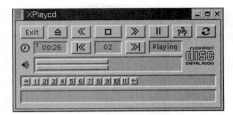

Figure 5-3: The graphical control panel of the xplaycd program for playing audio CDs

If you are using the GNOME desktop, you can play audio CDs using the CD Player application. You can launch the GNOME CD Player by selecting Main Menu (the Foot) ➪ Multimedia ➪ CD Player. Figure 5-4 shows this CD player playing a track from an audio CD.

Figure 5-4: The GNOME CD Player playing a track from an audio CD

As you can see, the GNOME CD Player displays the title of the CD and the name of the current track. The GNOME CD Player gets the song titles from CDDB — a CD database on the Internet. This means that you need an active Internet connection for the CD Player to download song information from the CD database. Once the CD Player downloads information about a particular CD, it caches that information in a local database for future use. The CD Player's user interface is intuitive, and you can learn it easily. One nice feature is that you have the ability to select a track by title, as shown in Figure 5-5.

Note

To learn more about CDDB, read the Frequently Asked Questions at `http://www.cddb.com/faq.html`.

If you want to log in as a normal user and play audio CDs on the CD-ROM drive, you should first log in as root and set the permissions settings on the CD-ROM device so that anyone can read it. (You have to set the permissions for the actual CD-ROM device, not the generic `/dev/cdrom` device.) To do this, follow these steps:

1. Log in as root. If you are already logged in, type the **su** command and enter the super user's password to assume the identity of root.

2. Make the CD-ROM device readable by all users using the `chmod` command as follows:

   ```
   chmod o+r /dev/cdrom
   ```

   Anyone who has access to your Red Hat Linux PC can now play audio CDs and access the CD-ROM drive.

Figure 5-5: Selecting a specific audio track to play with the GNOME CD Player

If you use KDE as your desktop, you find a similar audio CD player in KDE. You can start the KDE CD player by selecting K ➪ Multimedia ➪ CD Player. Figure 5-6 shows the KDE CD Player playing a track from an audio CD.

Figure 5-6: Playing an audio CD with the KDE CD Player

Troubleshooting Sound Cards

If, after you configure the sound driver, the sound card does not produce any sound when you play a sound file or an audio CD, try the following steps to diagnose and fix the problem:

1. If you have rebuilt the kernel, verify that you are running the kernel that you rebuilt with support for the sound card. To see the version number, use the `uname -srv` (or `uname -a`) command. Here is typical output from this command:

```
uname -srv
Linux 2.4.0-0.43.12 #1 Wed Dec 27 17:44:32 EST 2000
```

Cross-Reference

This string shows the kernel's version number, as well as the date when the kernel was built. If the date it shows does not match the date on which you rebuilt the kernel, you probably aren't running the new kernel. Go through the steps outlined in Chapter 25, and make sure that you really installed the new kernel. One common problem is forgetting to reboot, so try that step as well.

2. Check to see whether the sound driver is included in the kernel. One way to check is to look at the contents of the `/proc/devices` file. The following is an example:

```
cat /proc/devices
Character devices:
  1 mem
  2 pty
  3 ttyp
  4 ttyS
  5 cua
  7 vcs
 10 misc
 29 fb
 36 netlink
 81 video_capture
109 lvm
128 ptm
136 pts
162 raw
180 usb

Block devices:
  1 ramdisk
  2 fd
  3 ide0
  9 md
 22 ide1
 58 lvm
```

The listing should show character device 14, `sound`. If you don't see this device, either the kernel may not be configured properly, or the sound driver module may not be loaded properly.

3. Verify that the sound driver detected the sound card when the system started. Use `tail 100 /var/log/messages` to look at the boot messages, and check for a line reporting that the sound card was found. If the sound driver does not report the sound card, then it's possible that the sound card is not properly installed and configured. For a PnP sound card, also look for lines showing status reported by the `isapnp` program.

First, make sure that the sound card works under DOS or Windows. Determine the I/O address, IRQ, and DMA channel, and then reconfigure the kernel to include support for your sound card with the same parameters as under DOS.

4. If nothing works, you may want to read the latest Sound-HOWTO file. To read the HOWTO documents, double-click the LDP icon on the GNOME desktop and then follow the links to the Sound-HOWTO document (your Red Hat Linux system must be connected to the Internet for this to work). You can also find documentation for specific sound drivers in the `/usr/src/linux/Documentation/sound` directory. Note that this directory exists only if you have installed the Linux source code (see Chapter 25 for more information).

Cross-Reference

If you still cannot get the sound card to work under Linux, you may want to post a news item to one of the `comp.os.linux` newsgroups. Chapter 19 discusses how to connect to the Internet and access the newsgroups. You might also consider purchasing the low-cost ($20) commercial version of the Open Sound System (OSS) driver from 4Front Technologies (`http://www.opensound.com/`). The commercial OSS driver supports more sounds cards (in particular, sound cards with proprietary programming information) than the OSS driver included with the Linux kernel.

Summary

Unlike many UNIX workstations, a typical PC nowadays comes with a CD-ROM drive and a sound card. The popularity of multimedia software fuels the demand for CD-ROM drives and sound capability in PCs. Additionally, many software packages, including Linux, are available on CD-ROM. Linux supports CD-ROM drives and sound cards. This chapter describes the CD-ROM drives and sound cards that Linux supports, and shows you how to detect and correct some common sound-card and CD-ROM-drive installation problems.

By reading this chapter, you learn the following:

▶ Linux's support for a specific CD-ROM drive depends on the interface you use to connect that CD-ROM drive to the PC's motherboard. Linux supports the most popular ATAPI (IDE) and SCSI interfaces for CD-ROM drives, as well as many proprietary CD-ROM interfaces, such as Aztech, Sony, Mitsumi, and the Sound Blaster Pro CD-ROM interface.

▶ New users often mistakenly select a CD-ROM driver based on the brand name of the CD-ROM drive; instead, they should select the CD-ROM driver that matches the CD-ROM's interface. Thus, a Mitsumi CD-ROM drive with an ATAPI interface requires the IDE driver, not the Mitsumi driver.

▶ Sound cards often include interfaces for CD-ROM drives and joysticks. The sound driver supports only the sound card's sound capabilities; you need separate drivers for the CD-ROM drive and the joystick.

▶ To use a sound card, you have to load the sound driver module or rebuild the Linux kernel to include the sound driver. When you load a sound-driver module, you must provide information about the card's interrupt-request number (IRQ), I/O address, and direct memory access (DMA). You have to provide the same information when you build the kernel and include support for a sound card in the kernel.

▶ To ensure that the Linux kernel can load the sound driver module when needed, you have to provide the module-related information in the configuration file `/etc/modules.conf`.

▶ In Red Hat Linux you can configure a sound card using the `sndconfig` utility program. The `sndconfig` utility probes plug-and-play (PnP) sound cards and configures them by creating the `/etc/isapnp.conf` configuration file for the `/sbin/isapnp` program. The `sndconfig` utility also adds appropriate entries in the `/etc/modules.conf` file to load the sound driver when the system boots.

▶ Both GNOME and KDE come with CD Player applications that can play sound tracks from audio CDs. You can use these CD players to test your sound card.

Chapter 6

Printers

When you set up Red Hat Linux on a PC, the printer probably is the last thing on your mind. First, you want to get Red Hat Linux running on the PC. Then you may decide to make the modem work to dial up your office network, or your Internet service provider. When you begin to depend more on Red Hat Linux, however, you'll want to print text or PostScript files that you prepare or get from the Internet, and that's when you want to know how to make the printer work with Red Hat Linux.

As you might guess, physically connecting a printer to the PC's parallel port is straightforward; that part does not depend on the operating system. The software setup for printing is the part that takes some effort. Accordingly, this chapter provides information on setting up the printing environment in Red Hat Linux.

Setting Up Printers in Red Hat Linux

PCs typically come with one parallel port and two serial ports. The parallel port is so named because it can transfer eight bits of data in parallel. The serial port, however, has to send data in bit-oriented serial manner. For example, an eight-bit byte is transferred as a sequence of eight bits that go through the serial port, one after another. The upshot is that the parallel port is much faster than the serial port.

Although a printer can connect to the PC through either the serial port or the parallel port, most users connect the printer to the PC's parallel port.

Printer Device Names

In MS-DOS and Windows, the first parallel port is called *LPT1*; the second one is *LPT2*. The serial ports are *COM1* and *COM2*.

In Linux, the parallel ports have device names just like other devices, such as `/dev/ttyS0` for the PC's first serial port, or `/dev/hda` for the first IDE disk. The device names `/dev/lp0` and `/dev/lp1` refer to the first and second parallel ports, respectively.

Watch out, though — just because your PC has only one parallel port does not mean that Linux will use `/dev/lp0` as the device name for that parallel port. When Linux boots, it displays information about the parallel that it detects. Check the boot messages in the file `/var/log/messages` to see what parallel-port device Linux detects. On my PC, which has a single parallel port, the boot message includes the following (I show only the line with the type of message you should look for):

```
parport0: PC-style at 0x378 [PCSPP,TRISTATE]
```

In this case, the first line starts with the word `parport0`, which is "programmer speak" for parallel port zero, or the first parallel port. That line essentially indicates that the parallel port was detected by the operating system.

Note

The `parport0` device enables many device drivers to share a single parallel port. This enables other devices, such as Zip drives and backpack CD-ROM drives, to share the parallel port with the printer. Each device has its own driver, and each driver accesses the parallel port through the `parport0` device. The `parport0` device is the one that actually controls the physical parallel port.

Table 6-1 lists the parallel-port device names and device numbers in Linux:

Table 6-1   Parallel-Port Device Names and Numbers

Device Name	Major Device Number	Minor Device Number
/dev/lp0	6	0
/dev/lp1	6	1
/dev/lp2	6	2

Spooling and Print Jobs

You may already be familiar with the concept of spooling, from printing under Microsoft Windows. *Spooling* refers to the capability to print in the background. When you print from a word processor in Windows, for example, the output first goes to a file on the disk. Then, while you continue working with the word processor, a background process sends that output to the printer.

The Red Hat Linux printing environment, which consists of several programs described later in this chapter, also supports spooling. The *spool directory* refers to the directory that contains output files intended for the printer.

The term *print job* refers to what you print with a single print command. The printing environment queues print jobs by storing them in the spool directory. A background process periodically sends the print jobs from the spool directory to the printer.

Red Hat Linux uses the LPRng software for its printing environment. LPRng is an enhanced, portable implementation of the print spooler that was part of the Berkeley Software Distribution (BSD) UNIX. The BSD, or Berkeley print spooler, is called the *LPR print spooler*, because users use the `lpr` command to print on this spooler. As you become more knowledgeable about UNIX (or if you are a UNIX old-timer), you may find this bit of information to be useful, because it tells you the printing commands that you can use in Red Hat Linux. If you don't know anything about BSD UNIX, don't worry; you learn about the printing commands in the following section.

Note

To learn more about the LPRng print spooler, open the `/usr/share/doc/LPRng-3.6.26/LPRng-HOWTO.html` file in the Netscape Communicator. That file is a complete HOWTO for LPRng, and explains all of its features. For the latest news, visit the LPRng Web Page (`http://www.astart.com/LPRng.html`).

Configuring Printers

In Red Hat Linux, you can configure a printer using the LPRng Printer Tool. To configure printers with this tool, you must be running X. From the graphical login screen, log in as root and select Main Menu ⇨ Programs ⇨ System ⇨ LPRng Printer Tool from the GNOME desktop. (If you are not logged in as root, type `su` in a terminal window, enter the root password, and then type `lprngtool` to run the printer tool.)

The main window of the printer tool, formally known as the Red Hat Linux Print System Manager, appears (see Figure 6-1). If you have not installed the IPX/Netware Connectivity package group, you see a dialog box with a message informing you that a package named `ncpfs` is not installed and, therefore, you cannot print to a Netware printer. You can click the Ignore button to dismiss this dialog box. The first time you run the printer tool, it also displays a dialog box informing you that old printer configuration files will be converted to LPRng format. Click OK to dismiss this dialog box and work with the main window of the printer tool.

You can manage the printer queue and add a new printer through the printer tool utility. Click the Add button to configure a new printer. The printer tool displays the Add a Printer dialog box, from which you can select the type of printer, as shown in Figure 6-2.

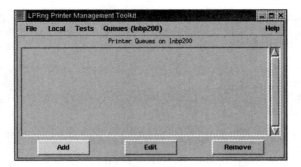

Figure 6-1: The main window of the LPRng Printer Tool

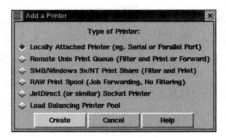

Figure 6-2: Selecting the type of printer

You can select from the following types of printers:

- **Locally Attached Printer**—Refers to a printer connected directly to the serial or parallel port of the PC on which you are installing Linux.

- **Remote UNIX Print Queue**—Refers to a printer physically connected to another Linux system on the local network.

- **SMB/Windows 9x/NT Print Share**—Refers to a printer connected to another PC that is on the local network and that runs the LAN Manager protocol (typically used to share resources, such as disks and printers among PCs running Windows 95/98 or Windows NT/2000).

- **RAW Print Spool**—Refers to a printer connected to this Linux PC that accepts jobs sent by other systems on the local area network. The term "RAW" means that the printer expects all processing, such as conversion of images and text into PostScript, to be done by the systems that send the print jobs.

- **JetDirect (or similar) Printer**—Refers to a network-connected printer that prints data received at a specific TCP/IP port (typically, port number 9100). The HP JetDirect cards use this method of printing.

- **Load Balancing Printer Pool** — Refers to a technique that assigns multiple printers to a single print queue. Documents sent to the print queue will be printed on one of the printers in the pool.

You should specify the printer connection that applies to your configuration. If you select the locally attached printer and click the Create button, the printer tool displays the Info dialog box, with information about the detected parallel ports, as shown in Figure 6-3.

Figure 6-3: Information about the parallel ports that have been detected

Click OK to continue with the printer configuration. Next, the Edit Locally Attached Printer (for example, Serial or Parallel Port) Entry dialog box prompts for various entries for the local printer, as shown in Figure 6-4.

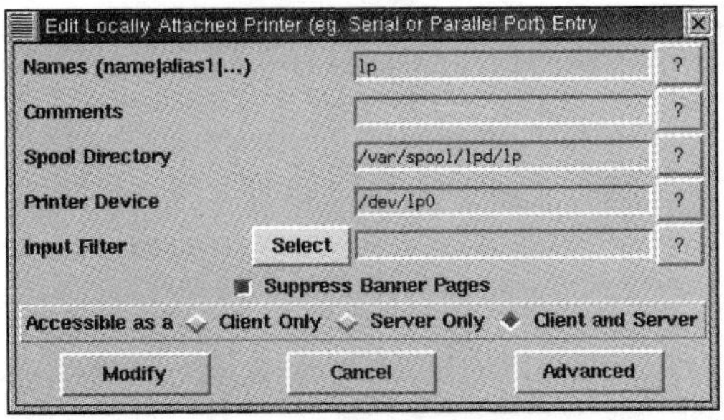

Figure 6-4: Providing information about a local printer

The text fields are already filled in and you can accept these as is. You do have to select the printer type. To do this, click the Select button next to the Input Filter text field. This brings up the Configure Filter dialog box (see Figure 6-5), which enables you to select the printer type and some other parameters, such as the paper size and the resolution of the printer (typically 600×600 dots per inch in many modern laser printers). You should select the appropriate values.

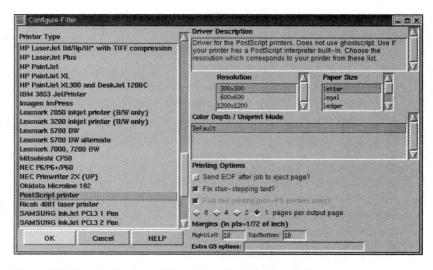

Figure 6-5: Use the Configure Filter dialog box to select printer type and options, such as paper size and resolution.

Another item in the Configure Filter dialog box shown in Figure 6-5 is an option labeled `Fix stair-stepping text?`. This refers to a problem that occurs when text files from Linux are sent to the printer. In Linux text files, each line ends with a single linefeed character, whereas DOS and Windows end each line with a carriage return, followed by a linefeed. The printer reacts to carriage returns and linefeeds the same way as old-fashioned typewriters — linefeed advances to the next line and carriage return moves to the beginning of a line. When printing a DOS text file, the lines print one after another, as you would expect. However, when the printer prints a Linux text file with lines ending in a linefeed only, the output looks something like the following:

```
Line 1 ends here
                Line 2 here
                            and so on
                                        like a staircase.
```

What Is a Daemon?

In UNIX, the term *daemon* is used for background processes that monitor and perform many critical system functions. Typically, a daemon is started when the system boots, and the daemon processes run as long as the system is up. Most daemons have the capability to restart copies of themselves to handle specific tasks. And although this is not a rule, most daemons have names that end with d, such as `crond`, `syslogd`, `klogd`, `inetd`, `lpd` (that's the printer daemon), `named`, and `httpd`. Another key characteristic of daemons is that they do not require any user interaction, so there are no terminal devices associated with a daemon.

To avoid this staircase effect, just check the box marked Fix stair-stepping of text in the Configure Filter dialog box, and Linux will take care of the problem by sending a carriage return before each linefeed whenever you print a text file.

After you select the options shown in Figure 6-5, click OK in successive dialog boxes, until you get back to the main window shown in Figure 6-1. This window should now show the information about the new printer.

After you finish adding the printer, select File ⇨ Restart LPRng from the print tool's menu. This restarts lpd — the print spooler daemon that takes care of printing (see the sidebar "What Is a Daemon?"). If you have a printer connected to the parallel port, turn the printer on, and then select Tests ⇨ Print ASCII test page to print a page. This will confirm that you have set up the printer correctly.

Note

The LPRng printer tool enables you to create an entry — called a printcap entry — in the /etc/printcap file for the new printer. For the printers listed in the tool (see Figure 6-5), you can use the tool to set up the printcap entry. If your printer is not on the list, you have to manually set up an entry in the printcap file.

The User's View of Printing in Linux

Now that you have set up a printer on your Red Hat Linux, the following sections provide an overview of the basic printing commands.

Printing with lpr

In Red Hat Linux, you use the lpr command to queue a print job. To print the file rfc1789.txt, you would type the following:

```
lpr rfc1789.txt
```

The lpr command places information about this print job in a control file, and then sends the control file and the rfc1789.txt file to lpd, the print spooler. By default, the lpd print spooler accepts files to be printed, holds them in the print queue, and then forwards them to the printer (or to another system, if the printer is a remote one).

You can embellish the simple lpr command with some options. A common option is to indicate the type of printer with -P. If you have a Hewlett-Packard LaserJet printer named hplj (later in the "Learning about /etc/printcap" section, you'll see that the printer name appears in the /etc/printcap file), and you print with the following command:

```
lpr -Phplj rfc1789.txt
```

In addition to the -P option of lpr, you can specify the default printer through the PRINTER environment variable. If your printer's name were hplj, you would use the following command to ensure that lpr sends all print jobs to the hplj printer:

```
export PRINTER=hplj
```

You may want to put the environment definition in the default login script for Bash. Just add the export PRINTER=hplj line to /etc/profile. This example assumes that your system's printer is named hplj; you should replace that name with whatever name you assign to your system's printer.

Because the default login script — /etc/profile — is common to all logins that use the Bash shell, defining the PRINTER environment variable in /etc/profile saves everyone the trouble of having to specify the printer explicitly.

Note

If you do not set the PRINTER environment variable, or specify a printer name through the -P option, lpr assumes that you want to print on the printer whose entry appears first in the /etc/printcap file.

Checking the Print Queue Using lpq

When lpr queues a print job, it does not print any messages. If you mistakenly print a large file and want to stop the print job before you waste too much paper, you have to use the lpq command to look at the current print jobs. Following is a typical listing of print jobs that you get with lpq:

```
lpq
Printer: lp@localhost
 Queue: 1 printable job
 Server: pid 5531 active
 Unspooler: pid 5532 active
 Status: processing 'dfA530localhost.localdomain', size 627, format
'f', IF filter 'filter' at 21:46:25.965
 Rank   Owner/ID        Class Job Files              Size Time
active root@localhost+530  A    530 /usr/lib/rhs/rhs-print 627 21:46:25
```

The word active in the Rank column indicates the job that's currently printing. The rest of the rows (if any) show jobs in the order in which they'll be printed. If you do not see your print job listed, it has finished printing. The Job column shows the job number of each print job; in this case, the job number is 530.

Canceling the Print Job Using lprm

To remove a job from the print queue, use the lprm command. To remove print job number 530, you would type the following:

```
lprm 530
```

Tip

If you are in a hurry and want to cancel all print jobs that you have submitted so far, use lprm with -a as the argument, as follows:

```
lprm -a
```

Checking the Printer Status Using lpc

To see the names of printers that are connected to your system, use the /usr/sbin/lpc status command. On a typical system, the lpc status command might show the following:

```
/usr/sbin/lpc status
 Printer        Printing Spooling Jobs  Server Subserver Redirect Status/(Debug)
 lp@localhost   enabled  enabled    0   none   none
```

This sample output shows the status of a printer named lp@localhost — the default printer name (because this printer is the first entry in the /etc/printcap file).

Don't worry about the fact that lpc status reports no daemon present for a printer; the daemon that controls a specific printer's queue goes away when the spool directory is empty. There is always a master copy of the printer daemon, lpd that monitors the spool directories. When you print anything on a specific printer with the lpr command, the master copy of lpd creates a new lpd process to take care of that printer's queue.

Employing Fancy Printing

So far, you've seen the commands for sending a file to the printer. If you have a PostScript printer, you can send it a PostScript file to produce nicely formatted output.

If you want to print a text file with some additional formatting, such as a header and a page number on each page, you can use the pr command. The idea is to use pr to format the text file, and then send that output to lpr. Following is an example:

```
pr -h"Web Server Access Statistics" -l60 webstat.txt | lpr
```

This command line prints the file webstat.txt with the text Web Server Access Statistics added to the top of each page. The -l60 option sets the length of each page to 60 lines.

Nowadays, PostScript is a common format for documentation files for software, especially software that you download from the Internet. If you have PostScript files, you can preview and print them with the Ghostview program. (To try the program, type **ghostview** in a terminal window. You need the X Window System to run Ghostview.)

A Behind-the-Scenes View of Printing

In Red Hat Linux, with the LPRng print spooling system, the user's view of printing is based on the basic printing commands: lpr, lpq, lprm, and lpc status. A bit more information will help you understand how printing works behind the scenes. As with so many things in Linux, support for printing is all a matter of having the right files in the right places. This becomes apparent after you have configured Linux for networking and set up dial-in modems, for example. In each case, you have to make sure that several configuration files appear in the correct places. The printing environment has the same requirement: configuration files that specify how printing occurs.

Although nowadays you can use graphical configuration tools to set up services, such as printing and dial-up networking, it is useful to know the names of the text configuration files, because you can then fix problems even if you do not have access to a graphical login.

If you have experience with MS-DOS, you might have printed files by simply copying them to the printer port (LPT1, for example). You might think that a similar approach would be good enough for Linux. As you will see in the next section, such a brute-force approach to copying a file to the physical printer port is not appropriate for a multi-user system like Linux. What you need is a way to queue print jobs and have a separate printing process take care of the printing.

Copying to the Printer: Brute-Force Printing

If you have a printer connected to the /dev/lp1 parallel port (you can find this information from the boot messages), you can print a text file simply by sending the file to the printer with the following command:

```
cat webstat.txt > /dev/lp0
```

This command would indeed produce a printout of the file webstat.txt, provided that the following conditions are true:

- You are logged in as root (Linux allows only root and certain processes direct access to physical devices, such as printers).
- The printer is connected to the /dev/lp0 port, powered up, and online.

The problem with copying a file directly to the printer device is that the command will complete only when the copying (which, in this case, is equivalent to printing) is done. For a large file, this process could take a while. In fact, if the printer is not turned on, the command will appear to hang (if this happens, just press Ctrl+C to abort the command).

Spooling: A Better Way to Print

On a multitasking and multi-user system such as Linux, a better way to print is to *spool* the data: Send the output to a file, and then have a separate process send the output to the printer. That way, you can continue with your work while the printing takes place in the background. In addition, if your system has more than one user, everyone can print on the same printer, without worrying about whether the printer is available; the background printing process can take care of all the details.

That's how the LPRng printing environment works. Users use a client program — lpr — to send the files to be printed to a server called lpd — the printer daemon — over a TCP/IP connection. The lpd server then queues the files and sends them to the printer.

Note

Although you typically would have only one printer connected to your PC, one advantage of the LPRng printing system is the capability to print on a printer that's connected to another system on a network. Printing to a remote printer is handled in the same fashion as printing to a local printer; the local lpr program simply sends the files to the remote system's lpd server.

As explained earlier, the user-level program for spooling a file is lpr. When lpr runs, it sends the data to the lpd server that manages the specified printer. Other user-level commands for working with print queues are lpq, lprm, and lpc. As this section describes, the program that completes the LPRng printing environment is the printer daemon: lpd.

In addition to the five programs lpd, lpr, lpq, lprm, and lpc, a file named /etc/printcap plays a crucial role in the Linux printing environment. The "Learning about /etc/printcap" section describes that file.

Controlling the Printer Using lpc

All users can use the lpc status command to check the status of printers. If you log in as root, you can use lpc to perform many more printer-control functions, such as starting and stopping spooling, enabling and disabling printers, and rearranging the order of print jobs. You can use the second argument to lpc to perform a specific task, or run lpc in interactive mode.

To run lpc in interactive mode, type /usr/sbin/lpc at the shell prompt. At the lpc> prompt, type help to see a list of commands that lpc understands. To get more help about a command, type help *command-name* (*command-name* is one of the lpc commands). Following is a sample session with lpc:

```
/usr/sbin/lpc
lpc> help
usage: lpc [-a][-Ddebuglevel][-Pprinter][-Shost][-Uusername][-V] [command]
 with no command, reads from stdin
  -a            - alias for -Pall
  -Ddebuglevel  - debug level
  -Pprinter     - printer or printer@host
  -Shost        - connect to lpd server on host
  -Uuser        - identify command as coming from user
  -V            - increase information verbosity
```

```
commands:
active    (printer[@host])          - check for active server
abort     (printer[@host] | all) - stop server
class     printer[@host] (class | off)        - show/set class printing
disable   (printer[@host] | all) - disable queueing
debug     (printer[@host] | all) debugparms - set debug level for printer
down      (printer[@host] | all) - disable printing and queueing
enable    (printer[@host] | all) - enable queueing
hold      (printer[@host] | all) (name[@host] | job | all)*   - hold job
holdall   (printer[@host] | all) - hold all jobs on
kill      (printer[@host] | all) - stop and restart server
lpd       (printer[@host]) - get LPD PID
lpq       (printer[@host] | all) (name[@host] | job | all)*   - invoke LPQ
lprm      (printer[@host] | all) (name[@host]|host|job| all)* - invoke LPRM
msg printer message text  - set status message
move printer (user|jobid)* target - move jobs to new queue
noholdall (printer[@host] | all) - hold all jobs off
printcap  (printer[@host] | all) - report printcap values
quit                             - exit LPC
redirect  (printer[@host] | all) (printer@host | off )*      - redirect jobs
redo      (printer[@host] | all) (name[@host] | job | all)*  - release job
release   (printer[@host] | all) (name[@host] | job | all)*  - release job
reread    (printer[@host])           - LPD reread database information
start     (printer[@host] | all) - start printing
status    (printer[@host] | all) - status of printers
stop      (printer[@host] | all) - stop  printing
topq      (printer[@host] | all) (name[@host] | job | all)*  - reorder job
up        (printer[@host] | all) - enable printing and queueing
  diagnostic:
    defaultq                - show default queue for LPD server
    defaults                - show default configuration values
    client  (printer | all) - client config and printcap information
    server (printer | all) - server config and printcap
lpc> q
```

Tip

For a specific operation, you can simply use the single-line syntax with lpc, followed by one of the lpc commands and any necessary arguments. To stop the print-spooling daemon (lpd), move print job 39 to the top of the queue, and start spooling again, you would use the following commands (the example assumes that the printer's name is hplj):

```
lpc stop hplj
lpc topq 39
lpc start hplj
```

Table 6-2 lists the lpc commands that anyone can use (provided the /usr/sbin directory is in the PATH environment variable; if not, type export PATH=$PATH:/usr/sbin to update PATH).

Table 6-2   lpc Commands That Anyone Can Use

Command	Description
status *printer-name*	Displays the status of the specified printer. If you do not provide a printer name, this command shows the status of the printer named lp—the default printer.
exit	Exits lpc (use in interactive mode only).
quit	Exits lpc (use in interactive mode only).

Table 6-3 lists the lpc commands that only root can use.

Table 6-3   lpc Commands That Only Root Can Use

Command	Description
abort *printer-name*	Behaves like stop, but does not allow the current job to complete. When printing is restarted, the current job prints again.
disable *printer-name*	Disables spooling of print jobs to a specified printer. When spooling is disabled, users can no longer use lpr to print.
down *printer-name*	Disables spooling and stops the printer daemon from printing the spooled print jobs (combines the actions of disable and stop).
enable *printer-name*	Enables spooling of print jobs to a specified printer.
reread *printer-name*	Sends a request to the printer daemon (lpd) to reread the configuration file (/etc/lpd.conf) and the /etc/printcap file. You might try this command if the printer appears to be fine but nothing is printed, even though lpq shows jobs waiting in the spool area.
start *printer-name*	Enables the printer daemon so that it can begin printing any jobs in that printer's spool directory.
stop *printer-name*	Waits for the current print job to complete, and then disables the printer daemon so that it stops printing the jobs in that printer's spool directory.
topq *printer-name job-id*	Moves the specified print job to the beginning of the printer's queue. If you use a user name in place of *job-id*, all jobs that belong to that user are moved to the beginning of the queue.
up *printer-name*	Reverses the action of the down command, enables spooling, and starts the printer daemon (combines the actions of enable and start).

Tracing a Print Request from lpr to the Printer

A good way to understand the LPRng print spooling system is to trace a print request from the lpr program, all the way to the actual output at the printer. The programs lpr and lpd and an optional filter program complete the printing process, as shown in Figure 6-6.

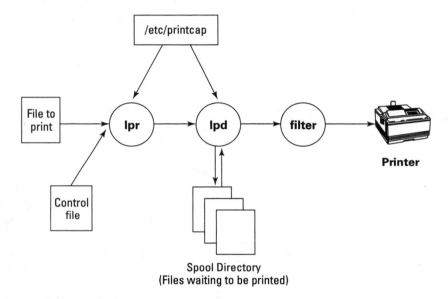

Figure 6-6: The LPRng print spooling system

As Figure 6-6 shows, the steps of the LPRng print spooling process are as follows:

1. The lpr program takes the file to be printed, prepares a control file with information about the print job, and sends both the files to the lpd server over a TCP/IP connection.

2. The lpd server stores the files for the print job temporarily in a spool directory. It sorts the queue and determines the print order.

3. For each print job, lpd sends the file through a filter program to convert the file into a format suitable for the printer, and then sends the filter's output to the printer. If there is no filter (this is specified in the /etc/printcap file), lpd sends the file directly to the printer.

Both the lpr and lpd programs consult the /etc/printcap file for information about the printer.

Learning about /etc/printcap

The /etc/printcap file is at the heart of the LPRng printing environment. This text file (with cryptic syntax) describes the capabilities of various printers. The file must contain information about every printer that you can access from your system (including printers that are on the same network as your PC). No harm is done if the /etc/printcap file contains descriptions of printers that you do not actually have; the lpr and lpd programs consult the /etc/printcap file only to look up information for a specified printer.

The basic structure of /etc/printcap

The /etc/printcap file is modeled after the /etc/termcap file, which describes the capabilities of various types of terminals. To understand the syntax of entries in /etc/printcap, examine the following sample entry for an HP LaserJet printer, generated by the Red Hat print tool:

```
# HP Laserjet printer
lp|hplj|Lasertjet-IRM|HP Laserjet 4M in IRM Division:\
  :lp=/dev/lp0:\
  :sd=/var/spool/lpd/lp:\
  :mx#0:\
  :if=/var/spool/lpd/lp/filter:\
  :lf=/var/spool/lpd/lp/hplj-log:\
  :sh:
```

This example is a reasonably readable layout of an entry in the /etc/printcap file. The entry says the following things:

- Send the print job to a printer device named /dev/lp0 (lp option).

- Store queued print jobs in the /var/spool/lpd/lp directory (sd option).

- Do not limit the size of print jobs (mx option).

- Pass the print file through the filter (a command that reads from standard input and generates output on the standard output) named /var/spool/lpd/lp/filter (if option).

- Log errors in a file named /var/spool/lpd/lp/hplj-log, which must already exist in order for the error logging to work (lf option).

- Suppress headers — a separator page between print jobs (sh option).

Notice that the print tool appends a backslash (\) at the end of each line. The backslash causes the next line to be appended to the current line. The older BSD print spooler required each /etc/printcap entry to be a single line, which is why the Red Hat print tool appends a backslash after each line. LPRng does not require the backslashes at the end of each line, but they are allowed for backward compatibility with the older BSD print spooler.

Make sure that there are no extra spaces after the backslash character at the end of a line. If a space or tab character appears after the backslash, the printing programs (lpr, lpd, and lpc) will not consider the following line to be a continuation. This error may cause printing to fail for a printer (even though the entry may look fine when you examine the /etc/printcap file).

As is true of most configuration files in Linux, the comment lines in /etc/printcap start with a pound-sign character (#).

Printer names

The first part of an entry (up to the first colon) lists the name of the printer and its aliases, separated by vertical bar (|) characters. Typically, each printer has three names:

- A short name with, at most, four characters (such as hplj)

- A longer name that indicates the printer's owner (such as LaserJet-IRM)

- A descriptive name that should fully identify the printer to the users on your system (for example, HP LaserJet 4M in IRM Division)

If you print something with lpr without specifying a printer, and the PRINTER environment variable is not defined, that print job automatically goes to the first printer in the /etc/printcap file.

Option types

After the names, the printer's entry has a sequence of options. If you examine the sample entry, you notice that colons (:) separate the fields. There are three types of options:

- *String options* — Such as lp (which specify the printer's device name), are specified by the following syntax:

  :option_name=string:

  You can embed special characters in the string by using the backslash notation from the C programming language. To specify the form-feed character (which might be used to eject a page on the printer), you would use \f.

- *Number options* — Such as mx (which specify the size of print-job files), are specified as follows:

  :option_name#number:

  This is an older syntax that is still accepted in LPRng, but the new recommended syntax is as follows:

  :option_name=number:

- *Boolean options* — Such as sh (which suppress printing of a header page separating consecutive print jobs), are true when they appear in the printer's entry; otherwise, they are false.

Each option has a specific meaning. Through these options, you control how output appears on the printer (for example, should the data file be processed by any intermediate program before output goes to the printer), and how errors are logged. The following sections further describe the options in /etc/printcap.

Although the contents of /etc/printcap appear cryptic at first, when you know the basic format and the meaning of the various options, you'll be able to understand and edit the file easily.

Tip

The subsequent sections provide all the information that you need to understand and add a new entry to the /etc/printcap file. If you need to look up information about the options in the /etc/printcap file, you can do so easily with the following command:

```
man printcap
```

Options in printcap entries

Before you learn about specific printcap options (I'll refer to the /etc/printcap file with the generic name printcap), consult Table 6-4, which provides an alphabetic list of some printcap options. The Option column shows the two-character name of an option. The Type column shows the type of the option (string, number, or Boolean). The Default column shows the value assumed by lpr and lpd when the printcap entry does not specify this option. The Description column briefly describes the option.

Table 6-4   Alphabetic List of Common printcap Options

Option	Type	Default	Description
af	string	NULL	Name of the accounting file
br	number	none	Baud rate (applies only if the lp option specifies a serial-port device)
cf	string	NULL	Name of the cifplot data filter
df	string	NULL	Name of the TeX data filter (DVI format)
ff	string	\f (form feed)	String to send for a form feed
fo	Boolean	false	If specified, prints a form feed when the device is opened
gf	string	NULL	Name of the graph data filter
hl	Boolean	false	If specified and if sh is not specified, prints the burst header page last. (The *burst header page* separates one print job from another.)

Continued

Table 6-4   *(continued)*

Option	Type	Default	Description
if	string	NULL	Name of the text filter, which is called once for each print job. (You can use this to interpret the file and convert it to a format that is suitable for your printer.)
lf	string	log	Name of the file where errors are logged
lockfile	string	/var/spool/ lpd/lpd	Name of the lock file
lp	string	/dev/lp	Device name to open to send output to the printer
mc	number	1	Maximum number of copies to print
mx	number	0	Maximum size of the print-job file (in KB); a value of 0 means unlimited size
nf	string	NULL	Name of the *ditroff* (device-independent *troff*) data filter
of	string	NULL	Name of the output-filtering program (called only if the *if* option is not specified, and called only once)
pl	number	66	Number of lines per page
pw	number	132	Page width, in number of characters
px	number	0	Page width in pixels (horizontal)
py	number	0	Page length in pixels (vertical)
rf	string	NULL	Name of the filter for printing FORTRAN-style text files
rg	string	NULL	Restricted group; only members of listed groups can access the printer
rm	string	NULL	Name of the system for the remote printer
rp	string	lp	Remote printer name
rw	Boolean	false	If specified, opens the printer device for reading and writing
sb	Boolean	false	If specified, prints a short banner (one line only)
sd	string	/var/ spool/ lpd/lp	Name of the spool directory
sf	Boolean	true	If specified, does not print form feeds
sh	Boolean	false	If specified, does not print the burst page header
st	string	status	Name of the status file
tr	string	NULL	Trailer string to print when the printer queue is emptied

As Table 6-4 shows, you can specify quite a few options for each `printcap` entry. LPRng allows many more options than the ones shown in Table 6-4. For a typical entry in the `/etc/printcap` file, however, you have to specify only a few options. Following are the most commonly used `printcap` options:

■ `if` — a string that specifies the input-filter name

■ `lf` — a string that specifies the file in which errors for this printer are logged

■ `lp` — a string that specifies the device name for the printer (such as `/dev/lp1`)

■ `mx` — a number that specifies the maximum allowable size (in 1KB blocks) of a print file

■ `rm` — a string that specifies the name of a remote computer

■ `rp` — a string that specifies the name of a remote printer

■ `sd` — a string that specifies the name of the spool directory for this printer

The next few sections further explain a few of these options.

Input-filter option

The *input filter* is a shell script, or an executable program that reads the print data from the standard input (`stdin`) and writes output to the standard output (`stdout`). The advantage of the input filter is that it enables you to process a text file and convert it to a format that your printer needs.

The print daemon calls the specified input filter once for each print job. Suppose that you specified the `if` option as follows:

```
:if=/var/spool/lpd/lp/hplj-if.pl:
```

If the file `/usr/spool/lp1/hplj-if.pl` is a Perl script, the script is invoked with a large number of options, where each option provides values from the `/etc/printcap` file and the job control file.

Table 6-5 shows some of the options you would assume the filter would receive as command-line arguments.

Table 6-5   Command-Line Argument Options

Argument	Description
`-c`	Passes control characters literally to the printer (if the first argument is `-c`, the filter should simply copy the standard input to the standard output)
`-wwidth`	Page width, in number of characters per line (from the `pw` option in the `printcap` file)

Continued

Table 6-5 *(continued)*

Argument	Description
-l*length*	Page length, in number of lines per page (from the pl option in the printcap file)
-i*indent*	Indents the output by printing *indent* number of blank spaces in front of each line
-n *login*	login name of the user who submitted the print job
-h *host*	Name of the system on which the user submitted the print job
-a *acct-file*	Name of the accounting file from the af option in printcap

You'll see the use of input filters in "How to avoid the staircase effect," which describes how to avoid a "staircase" pattern when you print UNIX text files on a PC printer, which expects a carriage return–line feed pair at the end of each line.

The printer device

The printer-device option, lp, should specify the Linux device name for the port to which you connected the printer. For a local printer on the PC's parallel port, this option is usually /dev/lp0.

If your printer is on a serial port, specify the serial port's device name— /dev/ttyS0 for COM1 and /dev/ttyS1 for COM2—as the string in the lp option.

When you set up a printcap entry for a remote printer, specify the lp option as follows:

`:lp=printer@host:`

where *printer* and *host* identify the printer and the remote host.

Another subtle use of the lp option is to set it to /dev/null—the universal "bit bucket" (nothing happens when data is sent to the null device). When you try a new printcap entry to see whether everything works, and you don't want to waste paper, just set the lp option of that printcap entry as follows:

`:lp=/dev/null:`

The log file

The log-file option, lf, specifies the file to which lpd sends error messages. If you don't specify any file, error messages go to a file named log in the same directory as the spool directory (specified by the sd option). Typically, you specify a log file in the spool directory for the printer, as follows:

`:lf=/var/spool/lpd/lp/hplj-log:`

You can specify any file you want, but the specified file must exist; if it does not, lpd will not log errors.

Suppressing headers and form feed

In the terminology of the LPRng printing environment, the *burst header page* or *banner page* refers to the page that precedes a print job. By default, lpd generates a banner page and also sends a form feed to make sure that every print job starts on a new page.

The two Boolean options, sh and sf, turn off the header page and form feed, respectively. All you have to do is place the two options in the printcap entry, as follows:

```
:sh:\
:sf:
```

Setting the maximum size of a print job

You can use the mx option to limit the size of a print job. The size refers to the number of bytes in the spooled file. Before the advent of graphics and laser printers, this limit may have made sense. Nowadays, it's better not to specify this limit, because graphics files can turn out to be huge, even though the output may be only a few pages. To make sure that the size of spool files is limited only by available disk space, specify zero as the value of the mx option, as follows:

```
:mx=0:
```

If you want to make sure that spool files do not take up all your available disk space, set the option minfree to the number of kilobytes that must be available for lpd to accept a print job and write spooled data in the spool directory.

Using multiple printcap entries for one printer

As you begin to understand the printcap entries, you'll see that an entry specifies various processing options for the data that goes to the physical printer. If a printer can handle both PostScript and HP's Printer Control Language (PCL), for example, you can have two separate printcap entries: one for PostScript output and the other for PCL. Programs that generate PostScript could use the PostScript printer name, whereas those that *speak* PCL can send the output to the PCL printer.

The following sections describe how to set up a printer manually. One of the first steps in configuring a printer is preparing the printcap entry for the printer. A good way to learn to prepare a printcap entry is to try a sample entry.

A printcap Template

In this section, I'll write a `printcap` entry for a printer named `sample`. Because the `/var/spool/lpd/lp` directory already exists, I decide to use that directory as the spool directory. To test the `printcap` entry without actually sending output to any printer, I'll use `/dev/null` as the printer device name and specify an input filter that copies the input data to a file.

With these assumptions, I wrote the following `printcap` entry and added it to the `/etc/printcap` file:

```
# A sample printcap template
sample|sample-printer|A sample printer that prints to a file:
  :sd=/var/spool/lpd/lp:
  :lp=/dev/null:
  :if=/var/spool/lpd/lp/sample-if.tcl:
  :lf=/var/spool/lpd/lp/sample-log:
  :mx=0:
  :sh:
```

For error logging, I created the `/var/spool/lpd/lp/sample-log` file with the following commands (while I was logged in as `root`):

```
cd /var/spool/lpd/lp
touch sample-log
chmod 600 sample-log
chown lp.lp sample-log
```

Next, I prepared the input filter, `/var/spool/lpd/lp/sample-if.tcl`. As you may have guessed from the filename, I wrote the input filter in Tcl. You can write the filter as a shell script or in Perl — whatever language you like. In fact, you can write the filter in C or C++. If you write the filter in C or C++, of course, you have to compile and link to create the executable file, the name of which you must specify in the `if` field of the `printcap` entry.

Following is the Tcl script file that serves as the input filter for the sample printer:

```
#!/usr/bin/tcl
#
# Sample input filter
#
# Place in printer's spool directory and make it
# executable by world.
# The filter is invoked with the following command line:
#
# <filter> [-c] -wWidth -lLength -iIndent -n Login -h Host AcctFile

# Open the file /tmp/sample.out
set outfile [open /tmp/sample.out w]

puts $outfile "----------------------------------------"
flush $outfile
exec date >@ $outfile
```

```
puts $outfile "-----------------------------------------"

# Read from stdin and write to outfile

while { [gets stdin line] != -1} {
  puts $outfile $line
}

close $outfile
```

This filter simply writes the standard input to the file /tmp/sample.out, adding a header that shows the date and time of printing. Because the device name for the sample printcap entry is set to /dev/null, the /tmp/sample. out file will be the only proof that printing worked.

Note that in a real input filter, the script would copy standard input to standard output, performing any necessary conversions (such as inserting extra characters on each line, or indenting a line by a specified number of blank spaces).

After you prepare the filter file, type the following commands to change the owner and permissions (the permission change is needed to make the script executable):

```
chown lp.lp sample-if.tcl
chmod +x sample-if.tcl
```

Next, restart the lpd print spooler with the following command:

```
/etc/rc.d/init.d/lpd restart
```

To see the printcap entry for the sample printer in action, try the following command:

```
ls -l /var/spool/lpd/lp | lpr -Psample
```

This command sends the directory listing of the /var/spool/lpd/lp directory to lpr. The lpr command then spools that listing for printing on the sample printer (because of the -Psample option). After the print job is spooled, the lpd daemon invokes the input filter for the printer named sample. That filter (/var/spool/lpd/lp/sample-if.tcl), in turn, copies the directory listing to the /tmp/sample.out file.

To see whether everything worked, check the contents of the /tmp/sample. out file, as follows:

```
cat /tmp/sample.out
-----------------------------------------
Thu Sep 28 20:32:54 EDT 2000
-----------------------------------------
total 52
-rw-------    1 lp       lp            482 Sep 28 20:31 acct
-rw-------    1 lp       lp             65 Sep 27 22:27 control.lp
-rw-------    1 lp       lp              0 Sep 28 20:23 control.sample
```

```
-rwx------    1 lp       lp            10074 Sep 25 21:44 filter
-rw-------    1 lp       lp              191 Sep 25 21:44 general.cfg
-rw-------    1 lp       lp                0 Sep 25 21:45 log
-rw-------    1 lp       lp                0 Sep 27 22:27 lp
-rw-------    1 lp       lp              351 Sep 25 21:44 postscript.cfg
-rw-------    1 lp       lp                0 Sep 28 20:31 sample
-rwx--x--x    1 lp       lp              579 Sep 28 20:11 sample-if.tcl
-rw-------    1 lp       lp                0 Sep 28 20:11 sample-log
-rw-------    1 lp       lp                0 Sep 25 21:45 status
-rw-------    1 lp       lp             1533 Sep 25 21:46 status.lp
-rw-------    1 lp       lp             1553 Sep 28 20:31 status.sample
-rw-------    1 lp       lp              147 Sep 25 21:44 textonly.cfg
-rw-------    1 lp       lp                5 Sep 25 21:46 unspooler.lp
-rw-------    1 lp       lp                5 Sep 28 20:31 unspooler.sample
```

As the output of the cat command shows, the /tmp/sample.out file appears to contain the expected output: the listing of the /var/spool/lpd/lp directory, with a date stamp as the header.

Specific Printing Problems and Solutions

Typically, you should be able to print text files readily. This section highlights some of the problems that you may encounter and suggests appropriate solutions.

Print Job Submitted, but No Output

This problem is one of the most frustrating. You submit a print job to a printer through lpr (making sure that you use the -P option to name the printer), and no error messages are reported, but nothing comes out of the printer. Try the following steps to identify the reason for the failure to print:

1. Type /usr/sbin/checkpc to make sure that the spool directories and files used by LPRng have the correct permissions and are in place. To fix any problems, type /usr/sbin/checkpc -f -V.

2. Check the physical printer. Make sure that it's connected to the PC, that the power is on, and that the printer is online.

3. Make sure that the printer is connected to the device specified in the lp field of the printer's printcap file. Also make sure that the device is not /dev/null.

4. Run lpq, and make sure that the printer's queue shows the job that you submitted.

5. Type /usr/sbin/lpc stat to see the status of the printers, and make sure that printing and queuing are enabled for the printer.

6. Make sure that the printer daemon, lpd, is running. If not, type /etc/rc.d/init.d/lpd start to start the daemon.

7. Check the file that you are trying to print. Some PostScript printers simply ignore plain-text files. (Filters are available that can convert plain text to PostScript. You may have to install such a filter.)

Problem Printing on a Remote Printer

If you submit a print job on a remote printer, and output does not appear on the remote printer, check the following fields in the /etc/printcap file on the remote system:

■ See whether the rg field specifies groups that are allowed to print. If your user name is not in that group, your job may not be processed.

■ See whether the rs field appears. If this field appears, you must have an account on the remote system in order to be able to print on the remote printer.

How to Avoid the Staircase Effect

In UNIX, each line in a text file ends with a *newline* (line-feed) character. On typewriters, pressing the line-feed key advances the paper to the next line, but does not bring the carriage to the edge of the paper; you have to press the carriage-return key to make that happen. If you were to print a UNIX text file on a typewriter-like device, the result would be something like the following:

```
First line
            Second line
                        Third line
                                    Fourth line
```

As you can see, the lines of text look like a staircase—the origin of the term *staircase effect*.

MS-DOS and many PC printers behave like typewriters; each line of text must have both a carriage return and a line feed to advance properly to the next line on the paper. When you send a UNIX text file to a printer that expects a carriage-return, line-feed ending for each line, the resulting output shows the staircase effect.

Note

You can avoid the staircase effect in two ways, both of which require an input filter:

Some printers can be set to treat a line-feed (LF) character as a carriage return, followed by a line feed (CR+LF). The HP LaserJet and Deskjet family of printers, for example, can be programmed to treat a CR as CR+LF by sending the sequence Esc &k2G (the Escape character followed by &k2G). You can use an input filter to send this sequence to the printer at the beginning of the file.

If the printer cannot be programmed to treat LF as CR+LF, you can write an input filter that converts each LF at the end of a line to CR, followed by LF.

Following is an input filter that sends the special printer command to LaserJet printers to enable the interpretation of LF as CR+LF:

```
#!/bin/bash
# Input filter for HP LaserJet and Deskjet printers
# to treat LF as CR+LF

# Send command to make printer interpret LF as CR+LF
echo -ne \\033\&k2G

# Next command sends stdin to stdout
cat

# Next command sends a form feed at the end of the file
echo -ne \\f
```

If you save this shell script in the file /var/spool/lpd/lp/hplj-if.sh (and make it executable with the chmod +x command), you can use the filter by placing the following field in that printer's printcap entry:

```
:if=/var/spool/lpd/lp/hplj-if.sh:
```

Avoiding Truncated Graphics Files

Graphics files can be quite large. If you have problems printing graphics files because they get truncated, check the printcap entry for the printer. Make sure that the entry does not have an mx option, limiting the maximum size of the file to be printed.

To avoid the truncation problem, add the following mx field to the printcap entry:

```
mx=0
```

This entry allows spool files to be as large as necessary. In practice, however, other factors may limit the maximum size of spool files. One obvious limit is available free space in the disk partition where the spool directory is located.

The lpr -i Command Does Not Indent Output

The -i option of the lpr command is supposed to indent the output by a specified amount. For that option to work, you must provide an input filter, because lpr simply passes the -i option to the input filter. You get indented output only if the input filter handles the -i option.

Printing PostScript Files

If your printer is a PostScript printer, you can print a PostScript file, simply by spooling the file to the printer. If you do not have a PostScript printer, you can use the Ghostscript program to print PostScript files on many types of printers. In fact, you can preview PostScript files with the Ghostview program, which uses Ghostscript to generate output suitable for displaying in an X window.

The Ghostscript software is included on the companion CD-ROM. You have the option to install Ghostscript when you install Linux, by following the steps outlined in Chapter 2.

Table 6-6 describes over 100 output devices that the companion CD-ROM's version of Ghostscript (version 5.50) supports. As you can see, the output devices include hardware devices, such as the display screen and printer, as well as many popular image-file formats, such as TIFF and PCX.

Table 6-6   Ghostscript Devices

Device Name	Description of Output Device
ap3250	Epson AP3250 printer
Bit	Monochrome bitmap
Bitcmyk	Bitmap with colors in CMYK (cyan-magenta-yellow-black) format
Bitrgb	Bitmap with colors in RGB (red-green-blue) format
bj10e	Canon BubbleJet BJ10e printer
bj200	Canon BubbleJet BJ200 printer
bjc600	Canon Color BubbleJet BJC-600, BJC-4000, and BJC-70 printers
bjc800	Canon Color BubbleJet BJC-800 printer
Cdeskjet	HP DeskJet 500C color printer in 1-bit-per-pixel mode
cdj500	HP DeskJet 500C printer (same as cdjcolor)
cdj550	H-P DeskJet 550C, 560C, 660C, and 660Cse printers
Cdjcolor	HP DeskJet 500C printer with 24-bits-per-pixel color and high-quality color (Floyd-Steinberg) dithering (also good for HP DeskJet 540C and Citizen Projet IIc printers)
Cdjmono	HP DeskJet 500C printer in black-and-white mode (also good for DeskJet 510, 520, and 540C in black-and-white mode)
cp50	Mitsubishi CP50 color printer
Deskjet	HP DeskJet and DeskJet Plus printers
Dfaxhigh	DigiFAX (from DigiBoard, Inc.) software format
Dfaxlow	Low- (normal) resolution DigiFAX format
djet500	HP DeskJet 500 printer
djet500c	HP DeskJet 500C printer (does not work on 550C or 560C)
dnj650c	HP DesignJet 650C printer

Continued

Table 6-6 *(continued)*

Device Name	Description of Output Device
eps9high	Epson-compatible 9-pin printer in triple-resolution (interleaved lines) mode
eps9mid	Epson-compatible 9-pin printer in intermediate-resolution (interleaved lines) mode
Epson	Epson-compatible dot-matrix printers (9-pin or 24-pin)
Epsonc	Epson LQ-2550 and Fujitsu 3400/2400/1200 color printers
Epswrite	Encapsulated PostScript (EPS) output
faxg3	International Telecommunications Union (ITU) standard Group 3 FAX file with EOLs (End of Lines), but no header or EOD
faxg32d	ITU standard Group 3 two-dimensional FAX file with EOLs, but no header or EOD
faxg4	ITU standard Group 4 FAX file with EOLs, but no header or EOD
Ibmpro	IBM 9-pin Proprinter
imagen	Imagen ImPress printers
iwhi	Apple Imagewriter in high-resolution mode
iwlo	Apple Imagewriter in low-resolution mode
iwlq	Apple Imagewriter LQ in 320×216 dpi mode
jetp3852	IBM Jetprinter (Model #3852) inkjet color printer
jpeg	Joint Photographic Experts Group (JPEG) format RGB output
jpeggray	JPEG format gray output
la50	DEC LA50 printer
la70	DEC LA70 printer
la70t	DEC LA70 printer with low-resolution text enhancement
la75	DEC LA75 printer
la75plus	DEC LA75plus printer
laserjet	HP LaserJet printer
lbp8	Canon LBP-8II laser printer
lj250	DEC LJ250 Companion color printer
lj4dith	HP LaserJet 4 with Floyd-Steinberg dithering
ljet2p	HP LaserJet IID/IIP/III with TIFF compression
ljet3	HP LaserJet III printer with Delta Row compression

Device Name	Description of Output Device
ljet3d	HP LaserJet IIID printer with duplex (two-sided printing) capability
ljet4	HP LaserJet 4 printer (default resolution of 600 dpi)
ljetplus	HP LaserJet Plus printer
ln03	DEC LN03 printer
lp2563	HP 2563B line printer
m8510	C. Itoh M8510 printer
necp6	NEC P6, P6+, and P60 printers at 360 × 360 dpi resolution
oce9050	OCE 9050 printer
paintjet	HP PaintJet color printer
pbm	Plain Portable Bitmap format
pbmraw	Raw Portable Bitmap format
pcx16	Older EGA/VGA 16-color PCX file format (4-bit planar format)
pcx24b	24-bit color PCX file format (three 8-bit planes)
pcx256	256-color PCX file format (8-bit chunky format)
pcxcmyk	PCX file format, 4-bit chunky CMYK color
pcxgray	8-bit gray scale PCX file format
pcxmono	Monochrome PCX file format (1 bit per pixel)
pdfwrite	Portable Document Format (PDF) output that can be read by Adobe Acrobat
pgm	Plain Portable Graymap format
pgmraw	Raw Portable Graymap format
pgnm	Portable Graymap (plain format)
pgnmraw	Portable Graymap (raw format)
pj	HP PaintJet XL printer
pjxl	HP PaintJet XL color printer
pjxl300	HP PaintJet XL300 color printer (also good for PaintJet 1200C)
png16	4-bit color Portable Network Graphics (PNG) format
png16m	24-bit color Portable Network Graphics (PNG) format
png256	8-bit color Portable Network Graphics (PNG) format
pnggray	8-bit gray Portable Network Graphics (PNG) format
pngmono	Monochrome Portable Network Graphics (PNG) format
pnm	Portable Pixmap (plain format) (RGB)

Continued

Table 6-6 *(continued)*

Device Name	Description of Output Device
pnmraw	Portable Pixmap (raw format) (RGB)
ppm	Plain Portable Pixmap format
ppmraw	Raw Portable Pixmap format
psgray	PostScript (Level 1) 8-bit gray image
psmono	PostScript (Level 1) monochrome image
pswrite	PostScript output
pxlcolor	HP color PCL XL printers
pxlmono	HP black-and-white PCL XL printers (LaserJet 5 and 6 family)
r4081	Ricoh 4081 laser printer
sj48	StarJet 48 inkjet printer
st800	Epson Stylus 800 printer
stcolor	Epson Stylus Color
t4693d2	Tektronix 4693d color printer, 2 bits per RGB component
t4693d4	Tektronix 4693d color printer, 4 bits per RGB component
t4693d8	Tektronix 4693d color printer, 8 bits per RGB component
tek4696	Tektronix 4695/4696 inkjet plotter
tiff12nc	Tagged Image File Format (TIFF) that uses 12-bit RGB, no compression
tiff24nc	TIFF that uses 24-bit RGB, no compression (NeXT standard format)
tiffcrle	TIFF that uses ITU standard one-dimensional Huffman Run Length Encoded (RLE) FAX format (Group 3 FAX, with no End of Lines)
tiffg3	TIFF file that uses ITU standard Group 3 FAX format (Group 3 FAX, with End of Lines)
tiffg32d	TIFF file that uses ITU standard two-dimensional Group 3 FAX format
tiffg4	TIFF file that uses ITU standard Group 4 FAX format
tifflzw	Tagged Image File Format that uses Lempel-Ziv Welch (LZW) compression
tiffpack	Tagged Image File Format that uses PackBits compression
uniprint	Unified printer driver that can be configured to work with Color ESC/P, ESC/P2, HP-RTL/PCL color and black-and-white printers

Device Name	Description of Output Device
x11	X Window driver (to display output in a window)
x11alpha	X Window driver with 4-bit alpha (transparency) capability
x11cmyk	X Window driver that accepts colors in CMYK (Cyan-Magenta-Yellow-Black) format
x11mono	Monochrome (black-and-white) X Window driver
xes	Xerox XES printers such as 2700, 3700, 4045, and so on

You run the Ghostscript program with the gs command. Use the sDEVICE=*devicename* option to specify a device name. To interpret the PostScript file testfile.ps and produce output for an HP LaserJet 4 printer, for example, you would type the following:

```
gs -sDEVICE=ljet4 testfile.ps
```

To print PostScript files, you would define a printcap entry for a PostScript printer (typically, with a name such as ps), and specify an input filter for that entry. Then, in the input filter, you would use gs to create the output for your printer. If you have an HP DeskJet 550C printer, you would place the following line in the body of a shell script that serves as the input filter for the printcap entry for the HP DeskJet 550C:

```
/usr/bin/gs -dSAFER -dNOPAUSE -q -sDEVICE=cdj550 -sOutputFile=-
```

The -sDEVICE=cdj550 option specifies that the output device is an HP DeskJet 550C. The -sOutputFile=- option sends the output to stdout, which is what the input filter should do: send its stream of output to the standard output (the printer daemon will send that output to the physical printer).

Summary

Printing under Red Hat Linux is simple, provided that the LPRng printing environment is set up properly. You do have to learn a small set of commands to submit a print job and check the status of pending print jobs. This chapter explains the LPRng printing environment from the user's point of view, and then explains how to set everything up as a system administrator.

By reading this chapter, you learn the following things:

▶ In Linux, the printer's device name depends on the port to which you connect the printer. For a typical printer connected to the parallel port, the device name is /dev/lp0 or /dev/lp1, depending on the I/O address of the parallel port. If the printer is connected to the serial port, the device name is /dev/ttyS0 (for COM1) or /dev/ttyS1 (for COM2).

▶ Red Hat Linux comes with the LPRng print spooling system, which is a portable, enhanced implementation of the Berkeley print spooler.

▶ As a user, you print with the `lpr` command, check the status of the print queue with `lpq`, cancel print jobs with `lprm`, and check the printer's status with `lpc status`.

▶ Behind the scenes, the `lpr` command sends the print file and a control file to the `lpd` server (the print daemon), which places the files in a holding directory called the *spool directory*. Then `lpd` sends the spooled print files to the printer.

▶ You can use the LPRng printer tool to set up the `/etc/printcap` entry for many popular printers.

▶ The `/etc/printcap` file essentially specifies what to do when a print job is sent to the printer. Fields in the `/etc/printcap` file control various aspects of printing, ranging from page size, to whether a burst header page is printed before each print job.

▶ In `/etc/printcap`, you can specify an input filter (a process that reads from standard input and writes to standard output) through which all print jobs must pass. The input filter can send special commands to the printer, or alter the print file as necessary.

▶ The staircase effect refers to the appearance of the printout when you print a UNIX text file (in which each line ends with a single line-feed character) on a PC printer, which expects lines to end with a carriage return–line feed pair. You can use an input filter to avoid the staircase effect.

▶ You can use the Ghostscript software (included on the companion CD-ROM) to view and print PostScript files. Many freely available software packages include documentation in PostScript format.

Chapter 7

Modems and Terminals

In This Chapter

▶ Learning the names of serial-port devices in Linux

▶ Understanding serial communications

▶ Looking at the RS-232C standard

▶ Understanding different types of modem standards, such as V.34 and V.90

▶ Using the Hayes-standard AT command set used by modems

▶ Dialing out with a modem in Linux

▶ Setting up Linux for dial-in use

▶ Using multiport serial I/O boards in Linux

If you have installed Red Hat Linux on your home PC, you may want to use a modem to dial out to your office system or a bulletin-board system (BBS). You also may want to connect to the Internet through the modem. To use a modem, you have to learn how Linux works with the PC's *serial ports* — the ports through which the modem communicates with the PC. You also need to get cables to connect the modem to the PC, select the proper serial device to use in Linux, and set up configuration files that control the communication parameters for the serial port.

Terminals — devices that have a display screen and a keyboard — also connect to the PC through the serial ports. In that sense, terminals are similar to modems. Terminals are ideal for simple data-entry tasks and are often used in point-of-sale systems. Linux also supports multiport serial boards that enable you to connect many terminals or modems to your PC running Linux.

This chapter explains how to connect, set up, and use modems and terminals. Much of the information applies to any device connected to the serial port, but some information is specific to modems. This chapter focuses primarily on modems because modems are more popular than dumb terminals connected to a Linux system.

PC and Serial Ports

If you have used communications software, such as Procomm or Crosstalk, under MS-DOS or Windows, you have used your PC's serial port. These communications programs transfer bytes of data from the PC to the modem over the serial port. The serial port is so named because each byte of data is sent *serially*—one bit at a time. Serial data communications comes with its own set of terminology. To understand how to set up the serial port, you need to understand the terminology.

UART

A chip named the *universal asynchronous receiver/transmitter* (UART), which is at the heart of all serial communications hardware, takes care of converting each byte to a stream of ones and zeros. That stream of ones and zeros is then sent over the communications medium (for example, the telephone line). At the receiving end, another UART reconstitutes bytes of data from the stream of ones and zeros.

The original IBM PC's motherboard did not include any serial communications capability. Instead, the serial communications function was provided through a separate serial adapter card (or *serial board*) called the IBM Asynchronous Communications Adapter. This serial board used National Semiconductor's INS8250 UART chip.

Later, PCs began including the serial communications hardware on the motherboard, but same 8250 or compatible UART was used for a long time. Still later, an improved version of the 8250—the 16450—was introduced, but the improvements were in the chip's fabrication details, not in its basic capability.

A problem with the 8250 and 16450 UARTs is that they do not have any way to buffer received characters. If the PC cannot keep up with the character stream, some characters may be lost. At high data-transfer rates (more than 9,600 bits per second), the PC may have trouble keeping up with the arrival of characters, especially with operating systems that keep the PC busy (such as Microsoft Windows).

The solution was to add a first-in-first-out (FIFO) buffer on the UART, enabling the PC to fall behind occasionally, without losing any incoming characters. The newer 16550A UARTs have send and receive buffers, each of which is capable of storing up to 16 characters. The 16550A UART is compatible with the old 8250 and 16450, but it can support higher data-transfer rates, because the built-in buffers can store incoming and outgoing characters directly on the UART.

On a historical note, National Semiconductor's original 16550 UART had the FIFO buffers, but the FIFO circuits had some bugs. The 16550A (and later versions of that UART) fixed the problems of the original 16550. By now, however, the 16550 name is often used to refer to any UART with an onboard receive and transmit buffer. You don't have to worry about the distinctions between the 16550 and 16550A, except in the case of the original 16550 UARTs from National Semiconductor; those chips are marked NS16550 (without an A).

Note

Linux supports PC serial ports and serial I/O boards that use a 8250, 16450, 16550, 16550A, or compatible UART. However, you really need a 16550A or better UART to keep up with today's high-speed modems, which can transfer data at rates of up to 56,000 bits per second. Most new Pentium PCs should already have 16550A UARTs. If you are buying a new PC to run Linux, you should check with the vendor and make sure that the serial interface uses 16550A UARTs. Newer UARTs, such as the 16654 and 16750, come with a 64-byte buffer. These UARTs should also work with Linux.

Communications Parameters

In serial communications, the transmission medium (such as the telephone line) is kept at a logical 1 when it is idle (1 is represented by the presence of a signal on the line). In this case, the line is said to be *marking*. On the other hand, when the line is at a logical 0, it is said to be *spacing*. Thus, logical 1 and 0 are also referred to as MARK and SPACE, respectively.

A sequence of ones and zeros makes up a single 8-bit character, as shown in Figure 7-1.

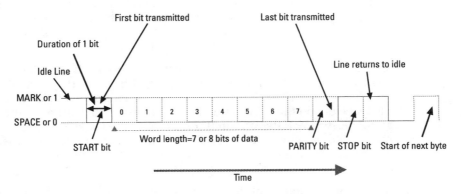

Figure 7-1: The format of a single character in serial communications

As Figure 7-1 shows, a change in the condition of the line from MARK to SPACE indicates the start of a character. That change in line condition is referred to as the START bit. Following the START bit is a pattern of bits that represents the character, and then a bit known as the PARITY bit. Finally, the line reverts to its idling MARK condition, which represents the STOP bit and indicates the end of the current character. The number of bits used to represent the character is known as the *word length* and is usually either seven or eight.

Baud versus BPS

The data-transfer rate is expressed in terms of *bits per second,* or *bps.* In the early days of modems, the data-transfer rate was the same as the baud rate — the rate of change of the line's state — because each line state carried a single bit of information. Nowadays, modems use different technology that can send several bits of information each time the line state changes. In other words, you can get a high bps with a relatively low baud rate. Even the fastest modems today use a baud rate of 2,400, even though the bits per second can be as high as 56,000.

Thus, the term *baud* and *bits per second* are not the same. Most of us, however, ignore the exact definition of *baud rate* and simply use the term *baud* to mean bits per second. Even though I'll stick to the term bps when I speak of data-transfer rates, you'll run across Linux settings that use the term *baud rate* to mean bps.

The PARITY bit is used to perform rudimentary error detection. When *even parity* is selected, for example, the parity bit is set so that the total number of ones in the current word is even (the logic is similar for odd parity). At the receiving end, the parity is recalculated and compared with the received parity bit. If the two disagree, the receiver declares a parity error. One problem of error detection with the parity check is that it can detect only errors that affect a single bit. The bit pattern 0100 0001 0 (the ASCII code for the letter *A*), for example, transmitted with an eight-bit word length and even parity, may change (due to noise in the telephone line) to 0100 0111 0 (ASCII *G*), but the receiver would not see the error, because the parity would still be even. Thus, parity error detection is rarely used nowadays.

In serial communications the transmitter and the receiver both must have some knowledge of how long each bit lasts; otherwise, they cannot detect the bits correctly. The duration of each bit is determined by data clocks at the receiver and the transmitter. Notice, however, that although the clocks at the receiver and the transmitter must have the same frequency, they do not have to be synchronized. The START bit signals the receiver that a new character follows; the receiver then begins detecting the bits until it sees the STOP bit.

A particular condition of the line is sometimes used to gain the attention of the receiver. The normal state of the line is MARK (1), and the beginning of a character is indicated by a SPACE (0). If the line stays in the SPACE condition for a period of time longer than it would have taken to receive all the bits of a character, a BREAK is assumed to have occurred. When the receiver sees the BREAK condition, it can get ready to receive characters again.

The selection of the clock frequency depends on the *baud rate* (or simply *baud*), which refers to the number of times that the line changes state every second. Typically, the serial I/O hardware uses a clock rate of 16 times the baud rate so that the line is sampled often enough to reliably detect.

Serial-Port IRQs and I/O Addresses

The PC typically has two serial ports, called COM1 and COM2 in MS-DOS parlance. The PC can also support two more serial ports: COM3 and COM4. Because of these port names, the serial ports are often referred to as *COM ports*.

Like other devices, the serial ports need interrupt-request (IRQ) numbers and I/O port addresses. Two IRQs — 3 and 4 — are shared among the four COM ports. Table 7-1 lists the IRQs and I/O port addresses assigned to the four serial ports.

Table 7-1   IRQ and I/O Port Addresses Assigned to Serial Ports

Port	IRQ	I/O Address
COM1	4	0x3f8
COM2	3	0x2f8
COM3	4	0x3e8
COM4	3	0x2e8

Serial-Device Names in Linux

Like other devices in Linux, the serial-port devices are represented by device files in the /dev directory. Each serial port has two names: one for incoming connections and one for outgoing connections. Table 7-2 lists the device names for incoming and outgoing serial ports, including the major and minor device numbers.

Table 7-2   Device Names for Incoming and Outgoing Serial Ports

COM Port	Device Name*	Major Device Number	Minor Device Number
Incoming COM1	/dev/ttyS0	4	64
Incoming COM2	/dev/ttyS1	4	65
Incoming COM3	/dev/ttyS2	4	66
Incoming COM4	/dev/ttyS3	4	67
Outgoing COM1	/dev/cua0	5	64
Outgoing COM2	/dev/cua1	5	65
Outgoing COM3	/dev/cua2	5	66
Outgoing COM4	/dev/cua3	5	67

* You should now use the /dev/ttySx devices for both incoming and outgoing serial communications. The /dev/cuax devices only exist to provide backwards compatibility with older programs. The plan is to abolish the /dev/cuax devices in the future.

If you installed Red Hat Linux from this book's companion CD-ROM, all these devices should already be in your system. If you check the /dev directory you'll find the /dev/ttyS* and /dev/cua* devices, where * is 0, 1, 2, 3, and so on.

Note

Historically, Linux used the /dev/ttyS* devices for dialing in and the /dev/cua* devices for dialing out. However, the current version of the Linux kernel does not distinguish between /dev/ttyS* and /dev/cua* devices. My recommendation is to use the /dev/ttyS* device names wherever you need to refer to serial devices.

Modems

The term *modem* is a contraction of *modulator/demodulator*—a hardware device that converts digital signals, consisting of ones and zeros, to continuously varying analog signals that can be transmitted over telephone lines and radio waves. Thus, the modem is the intermediary between the digital world of the PC and the analog world of telephones. (Note that Winmodems are largely software-based devices that are different from the traditional modems; see the sidebar "Winmodems and Linux" for more on Linux support for Winmodems.)

Inside the PC, ones and zeros are represented with voltage levels, but signals carried over telephone lines are usually tones of different frequencies. The modem sits between the UART and the telephone line and makes data communication possible over the phone lines. The modem converts information back and forth between the voltage/no voltage representation of digital circuits and different frequency tones that are appropriate for transmission over phone lines.

The communication between the PC and the modem follows the RS-232C standard (often stated as RS-232, without the C). The communications protocol between two modems also follows one of several international modem standards. The next few sections briefly describe these standards.

Winmodems and Linux

Many PCs and laptops come with Winmodems that turn over much of the modem's signal processing functions to the main CPU. These modems work only with special software that performs the necessary parts of the modem's functionality. For this reason they are often called *software modems*. Initially, such software modems came with special driver software for Microsoft Windows only; hence the name Winmodem (for *Windows modem*). Lately, the necessary Linux software to operate these modems has become available. If your system has a Winmodem, you should visit the Linux Winmodem Support homepage at http:// www.linmodems.org/ to learn more about Linux support for various models of Winmodems. For a list of Linux-compatible Winmodems — or Linmodems, as they are often called — visit the Web page at http://www.kcdata.com/~gromitkc/winmodem.html.

RS-232C Standard

The RS-232C standard, set forth by the Electronic Industries Association (EIA), specifies a prescribed method of information interchange between the modem and the PC's serial-communication hardware.

Note

In EIA terminology, the modem is Data Communications Equipment (DCE), and the PC is Data Terminal Equipment (DTE). You'll see references to DCE and DTE in discussions of the RS-232C standard.

A modem can communicate in one of two modes:

- *Half-duplex mode,* in which data transmission can occur in only one direction at a time.

- *Full-duplex mode,* which enables independent two-way communications.

Most modems communicate in full-duplex mode.

RS-232C cables

The RS-232C standard also provides control signals, such as Request to Send (RTS) and Clear to Send (CTS), that can be used to coordinate the transmission and reception of data between the PC and the modem. The term *handshaking* refers to the coordination of the data exchange.

The handshaking signals, as well as data transmission and reception, occurs through wires in the cable that connects the PC to the modem. The RS-232C specifies a 25-pin connector, with a specific function assigned to each pin.

A typical modem has a female 25-pin, D-shell connector (called the DB-25 connector), whereas the PC's serial port provides a male nine-pin, D-shell (DB-9) connector. Thus, to connect a PC's serial port to a modem, you need a cable with a female DB-9 connector at one end and a male DB-25 connector at the other end. Figure 7-2 illustrates a typical PC-to-modem cable (often sold in computer stores as an AT Modem Cable).

Some PCs have a DB-25 connector for the serial port. For these machines, you need a cable that has DB-25 connectors on both ends.

The RS-232C standard specifies the pins for the 25-pin connector. Figure 7-3 shows the DB-25 connector and pin assignments for IBM PC–compatible DB-25 male connectors.

Of the 25 pins available in a DB-25 connector, only nine are used in the PC's serial port. In the Serial/Parallel Adapter card for the PC-AT, IBM decided to save space by introducing a DB-9 connector. The pin assignments for the DB-9 connector are shown in Figure 7-4.

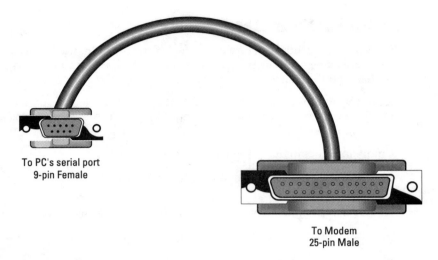

Figure 7-2: A typical cable for connecting a PC's serial port to a modem

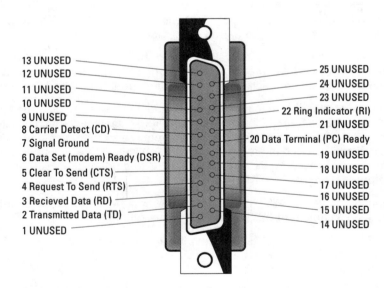

Figure 7-3: Pin assignments for the DB-25 serial connector

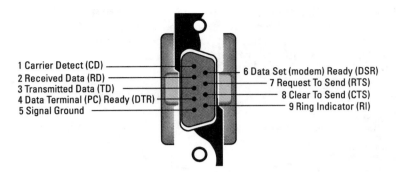

1 Carrier Detect (CD)
2 Received Data (RD)
3 Transmitted Data (TD)
4 Data Terminal (PC) Ready (DTR)
5 Signal Ground

6 Data Set (modem) Ready (DSR)
7 Request To Send (RTS)
8 Clear To Send (CTS)
9 Ring Indicator (RI)

Figure 7-4: Pin assignments for the DB-9 serial connector used in PC serial ports

Using modem cables (DTE to DCE)

When you connect a PC (DTE) to a modem (DCE), the cable should connect the like signals at both ends as follows (the arrow indicates the direction of data transfer on that line):

PC (DTE) DB-9		*Modem (DCE) DB-25*
Pin 3 TD (Transmit Data)	→	Pin 2 TD (Transmit Data)
Pin 2 RD (Receive Data)	←	Pin 3 RD (Receive Data)
Pin 7 RTS (Request to Send)	→	Pin 4 RTS (Request to Send)
Pin 8 CTS (Clear to Send)	←	Pin 5 CTS (Clear to Send)
Pin 6 DSR (Data Set Ready)	←	Pin 6 DSR (Data Set Ready)
Pin 5 Signal Ground	← →	Pin 7 Signal Ground
Pin 1 CD (Carrier Detect)	←	Pin 8 CD (Carrier Detect)
Pin 4 DTR (Data Terminal Ready)	→	Pin 20 DTR (Data Terminal Ready)
Pin 9 RI (Ring Indicator)	←	Pin 22 RI (Ring Indicator)

A cable that has such connections is often called a *straight-through cable,* because it connects like signals to each other. If the connector at one end is DB-25 and the other one is DB-9, all you have to do is look up the pin numbers for each type of connector in Figures 7-3 and 7-4.

Using null modem cables (DTE to DTE)

If you want to connect two PCs through the serial port you cannot use a straight-through cable like the one that connects the PC to a modem. The reason is that each PC expects to send data on the TD line and receive data on the RD line. If both PCs send data on the same line, neither PC can hear the other. A solution is to create a cable that connects one PC's output (TD) to the other one's input (RD), and vice versa. Such a cable is known as a *null modem* cable.

Figure 7-5 shows the signal interconnections in a typical null modem cable. Instead of showing the pin numbers, I have shown the RS-232C signal names. The exact pin numbers depend on the type of connectors. You should consult Figures 7-3 and 7-4 for the pin numbers.

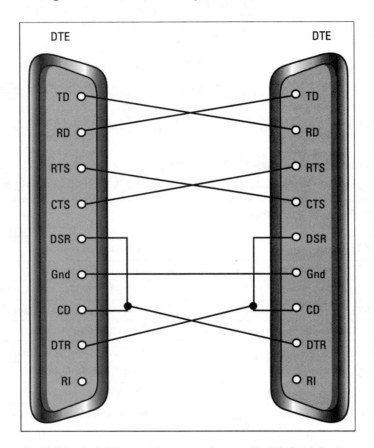

Figure 7-5: Signal interconnections in a typical null modem cable

Choosing cables

When you connect two devices that support RS-232C serial communications, the choice of cable depends on the type of each device: DTE or DCE. As I mentioned earlier, the PC is a DTE, and a modem is a DCE. Many printers and terminals are DTEs.

Use a straight-through modem cable to connect a DTE to a DCE. To connect a DTE to a DTE you need a null modem cable. Many computer stores sell null modem adapters. You can connect two DTE devices by using a modem cable with a null modem adapter.

Secret

Notice that the serial interface on the HP LaserJet family of printers is configured as a DTE. Thus, you need a null modem–style cable to connect a PC's serial port to a LaserJet printer. Unfortunately, serial printer cables (for connecting a printer to the serial port) introduce a further complication. Printer manufacturers interpret some of the RS-232C signals in a printer-specific way. Thus, you may have to connect various signals in a specific way to successfully use a printer with a serial interface.

Flow control

The RS-232C standard includes the RTS/CTS signals for hardware handshaking between the communicating devices (such as the PC and the modem). In addition to this hardware flow control, special ASCII control characters (Ctrl-Q/Ctrl-S, or XON/XOFF) are typically used to implement flow control in software. Flow control is necessary because sometimes the receiver may not be able to keep up with the rate of data arrival and should be able to inform the sender to stop data transmission while it catches up.

Suppose that a receiver has a buffer to store incoming characters. As the buffer gets full, the receiver can send the XOFF character (Ctrl-S) to the transmitter, indicating that transmission should stop. If the transmitter understands the meaning of the XOFF character, it can stop sending data.

Then, when the receiver empties the buffer, it can send an XON character (Ctrl-Q) to indicate that transmission can resume. This scheme of flow control is used in many communications programs, because it is simple. This is unfortunate because when the XON/XOFF protocol is used, the XON and XOFF characters cannot be part of the data because of their special meaning.

Note

The software-based XON/XOFF flow control is not used with modem speeds faster than 9600 bps because it slows down data transfers. Most high-speed modem connections use hardware flow control only.

Modem Standards

As the Internet and online services have grown in popularity, the demand for modems that offer high data-transfer rates has grown accordingly. Early modems transferred data at the rate of 300 bits per second (bps), whereas the latest modems can transfer at rates of up to 56,000 bps — which represents an increase of a hundredfold in modem performance. To achieve these high data-transfer rates, modems use many tricks, including compressing the data before sending it. As you might expect, two modems can communicate successfully only if both modems understand how to interpret the signal being exchanged between the two. This is where the standard modem protocols come into play.

Secret

The International Telecommunications Union (ITU) has ratified several modem standards in use today. These standards have names that start with V. The latest standard is V.90, which supports data-transfer rates of 56,000 bps (more precisely, 56,000 bps downstream and up to 33,600 bps upstream). The

V.90 standard is also called V.PCM because it uses a technique known as Pulse Coded Modulation (PCM). Table 7-3 lists some of the common modem standards used today.

Tip

If you need the exact text of the ITU Series V recommendations, as these data communication standards are called, you can purchase copies from ITU's Web site at `http://www.itu.ch/itudoc/itu-t/rec/v/`. The site offers the files in English, French, or Spanish, and in a number of file formats, including Microsoft Word for Windows, Adobe's Portable Document Format (PDF), and PostScript.

Table 7-3   Modem Standards

Standard Name	Maximum Data-transfer Rate (bps)
Bell 103	300
Bell 212A	1,200
V.17 (Group III Fax)	14,400
V.21	300
V.22	1,200
V.22bis	2,400
V.23	1,200
V.27ter (Group III Fax)	4,800
V.29 (Group III Fax)	9,600
V.32	9,600
V.32bis	14,400
V.34	28,800
V.90	56,000 downstream and up to 33,600 bps upstream

When you buy a modem, make sure that it conforms to these international standards. Nowadays, the ITU V.90–compliant 56K modems are the norm.

Modem Commands (AT Commands)

The now-famous AT command set first appeared in the 300-baud Hayes Smartmodem, a name coined and trademarked by Hayes Microcomputer Products, Inc. The Smartmodem worked in two distinct modes:

- *Command mode* — In this mode, characters sent from the PC (DTE) are interpreted as commands for the modem.

- *Online mode* — After receiving a dial command and establishing a connection, the modem sends all received data out on the phone lines.

The Hayes Smartmodem commands start with the characters AT (for attention). The initial command set included those to dial a number, turn the modem's speaker on or off, and set the modem to answer an incoming call.

The AT command system has been widely copied by modem manufacturers, making the AT command mechanism a de facto standard. Although virtually all modems use a core command set, each modem manufacturer has its own proprietary commands that control some of the exotic and advanced features of the modem.

The AT command line

I have found it very helpful to know at least a few of the AT commands for controlling a modem. Although many communications programs hide the details of the AT commands, you can end up in a situation in which the communications software is primitive — all the software does is send the other modem whatever you type. In such situations, you can enter AT commands to set up the modem, dial out, and establish a connection. The following sections briefly cover the AT command set.

As the name implies, each command in the AT command set starts with the letters AT. Following these letters, you can enter one or more valid commands and then end the command line with a carriage return (press Enter on the PC's keyboard). Thus, the command line has the following format:

`AT[command1][command2]...<CR>`

`[command1]` and `[command2]` denote optional commands, each of which has appropriate arguments. The ending `<CR>` is a required carriage return.

Suppose that you want to use the following commands:

- The E command with an argument of 1 to force the modem to echo the commands
- The V command with 1 as the argument to make the modem provide verbose result codes (instead of numeric codes)

You can send these commands to the modem with the following AT command line:

`ATE1V1`

As with any AT command line, of course, you have to end this command by pressing Enter. If you enter this command through a communications software package, you see that the modem replies with the string OK.

Secret

All modems accept a minimum of 40 characters per command line, in which the character count includes the AT and the final carriage return. Many modems, however, can accept up to 255 characters on an AT command line.

If an internal modem stops responding to the AT commands, you may have to shut down the system and power it off to reset the modem.

The A/ command

The A/ command is an exception to the AT command syntax. If you enter A/ as the only command on a line by itself (no need to press Enter), the modem immediately repeats the last command line that it received.

Configuration commands

These commands specify how the modem should operate and how it responds to commands. Following are some useful configuration commands:

- *Echo commands* — ATE1 causes the modem to display a command as you type it; ATE0 disables the display of the command.

- *Speaker volume* — The ATLn (n being a number between 0 and 3) command sets the volume of the modem's built-in speaker. ATL0 and ATL1 set the volume to low, ATL2 sets it to medium, and ATL3 sets it to high.

- *Speaker control* — ATMn (n being a number between 0 and 2) controls whether and when the modem's speaker is turned on. ATM0 turns the speaker off, ATM1 turns it on until a call is established, and ATM2 turns it on always.

- *Quiet mode* — When quiet mode is enabled, the modem does not acknowledge commands or report call status. ATQ0 disables quiet mode and causes the modem to respond to commands and show call status. ATQ1 enables quiet mode.

- *Verbose mode* — When verbose mode is enabled, the modem acknowledges commands and reports call status with words. Otherwise, it responds with numeric codes (which may be more suitable for communications software than for humans). The ATV1 command turns on verbose mode; ATV0 turns it off. A typical modem generates the nine responses listed in Table 7-4.

Table 7-4   Responses from a Typical Modem

Numeric Response	Word Response
0	OK
1	CONNECT
2	RING
3	NO CARRIER
4	ERROR
5	CONNECT 1200
6	NO DIALTONE
7	BUSY
8	NO ANSWER

- Most modems include several other responses for reporting successful connections at higher data rates.

- *Result code selection* — The ATX*n* command selects the type of reports that the modem should send back. The argument *n* can be one of the following:

  0   CONNECT

  1   CONNECT *bits-per-sec*

  2   CONNECT *bits-per-sec*, NO DIALTONE

  3   CONNECT *bits-per-sec*, BUSY

  4   CONNECT *bits-per-sec*, NO DIALTONE, BUSY

- *View stored profiles* — AT&V causes the modem to display the current values of a selected set of configuration parameters and the values of internal registers. Some modems have nonvolatile memory to store groups of settings, known as *profiles*. On such modems, AT&V displays the stored profiles.

Action commands

Each action command causes the modem to perform some action immediately. The most important action command is the dial command: ATDT*number*. Two other useful action commands are ATZ*n* and AT&F*n*, which reset the modem's configuration. Following are some of the important action commands:

- *Pulse dial* — The ATDP*number* command causes the modem to use the pulse dialing system to dial a specified phone number. The pulse dialing system was used by rotary telephones. Nowadays, you typically use the ATDT command to dial a number by using the tone dialing system.

- *Tone dial* — Use the ATDT*number* command to dial a specified phone number by using the tone dialing system. To dial the number 555-1234, for example, use the command ATDT555-1234. You should enter whatever other digits you may need to dial the number that you want to reach. If you need to dial 9 for an outside line, simply use ATDT9, 555-1234. The comma introduces a slight pause (typically, two seconds), which may be necessary to get an outside line.

- *Dial last number* — The ATDL command causes the modem to execute the last dial command.

- *Hook control* — The ATH command simulates the act of lifting or putting down the handset of a regular telephone. ATH0 hangs up the phone; ATH1 makes the modem go online (as though you had picked up the handset).

- *Answer call* — Use the ATA command to make the modem answer the phone. You can put the modem in answer mode (by setting register S0 — a storage area in the modem — to a nonzero value), so that it answers the phone when someone calls. With the ATA command, you can force the modem to answer the phone even if register S0 is set to 0 (which means that the modem won't answer the phone).

- *Return to online* — The AT0 command returns the modem to online mode. Use this command after you press +++ (rapidly enter three plus signs in sequence with some pause before and after the sequence) to take the modem offline.

- *Software reset* — If the modem stores configuration profiles in nonvolatile memory, you can recall one of the configuration profiles with the ATZ*n* command (*n* being the number of the configuration profile). If you enter ATZ without any argument, the modem is reset. The ATZ command terminates any existing connection.

- *Factory-default setting* — The AT&F command causes the modem to restore the factory-default settings. Some modems take a numeric argument with AT&F; consult your modem's documentation for more information on the meaning of the numeric argument.

The ATS*r=n* commands

In addition to the AT command set, Hayes Smartmodem pioneered the use of internal modem registers to configure the modem. All current modems have a set of registers, called the *S registers,* that control many aspects of the modem (including features that may be unique to a specific brand of modem).

Secret

A typical modem has anywhere from 30 to 60 S registers, denoted by S0, S1, S2, and so on. The ATS*r=n* command sets the S register numbered *r* to the value *n*. To view the current contents of the S register numbered *r,* use the ATS*r?* command.

Register S0, for example, contains the number of rings after which the modem answers the phone. When S0 is zero, the modem does not answer the phone at all. The following listing shows how you might query and set the S0 register with the ATS command:

```
ATS0?
000
OK
ATS0=1
OK
ATS0?
001
```

The exact set of S registers varies from one brand of modem to another, but most modems seem to provide and interpret the following 13 S registers consistently, as follows:

- *S0, ring to answer on* — The number of rings after which the modem answers the phone. When S0 is 0, the modem does not answer the phone.

- *S1, counts number of rings* — The count of incoming rings. When S1 equals S0, the modem answers the phone (assuming that S0 is nonzero). The modem resets S1 to 0 a few seconds after the last ring.

- *S2, escape code character* — The character used as the escape sequence to switch the modem from online mode to command mode. The default value is 43, which is the ASCII code for the plus (+) character. To go from online mode to command mode, enter this escape character three times in rapid succession.

- *S3, carriage-return character* — The ASCII code of the character used as the carriage return (this character terminates the AT command lines). The default value is 13.

- *S4, line-feed character* — The ASCII code of the character used as the line-feed character when the modem generates word responses to commands. The default value is 10.

- *S5, backspace character* — The ASCII code of the character used as the backspace character. The modem echoes this character to implement the "erase preceding character" function. The default value is 8.

- *S6, wait time for dial tone (seconds)* — The number of seconds to wait before dialing the first digit in a dial command. The default value is 2.

- *S7, wait time for carrier (seconds)* — The number of seconds that the modem waits for a carrier. If the modem does not detect a carrier after waiting for this many seconds, it displays the NO CARRIER message. The default value depends on the modem. Typically it will be anywhere from 30 to 60.

- *S8, comma time (seconds)* — The number of seconds to pause when the modem finds a comma in the phone number to dial. The default value is 2.

- *S9, carrier detect time (tenths of a second)* — The amount of time, in tenths of seconds, that the carrier must be present before the modem declares that a carrier has been detected. The default value is 6, which means that the carrier must be present for 0.6 seconds before the modem detects it.

- *S10, carrier loss time (tenths of a second)* — The amount of time, in tenths of seconds, that the carrier can be lost before the modem disconnects. The default value is anywhere from 7 to 15, which means that the carrier can be lost for 0.7 to 1.5 seconds before the modem disconnects.

- *S11, dial-tone spacing (milliseconds)* — The duration of each dial tone and the spacing between adjacent tones. The default value is typically somewhere between 50 and 100 milliseconds (50 is considered the minimum necessary for dial tones to be recognized by the phone system).

- *S12, escape sequence guard time (fiftieths of a second)* — The amount of guard time, in fiftieths of a second, that must occur before and after the escape-code sequence (the default sequence is +++) that switches the modem from online mode to command mode. The default value is 50, which means that the guard time is one second.

Online help

In response to the AT$ command, U.S. Robotics modems display online help information on the basic modem command sets. You'll find the help information instructive, because it shows you the breadth of commands that a typical modem accepts. You can enter the command in a serial communications program such as Minicom, which I describe briefly later in the "Dialing out with a communications program" section of this chapter.

Linux and Modems

If you're using Linux at home or in a small office, you probably want to use the modem for one or more of the following reasons:

- To dial out to another computer (such as a bulletin-board system), an online service (such as America Online), or another UNIX system, perhaps at your university or company.

- To enable other people to dial in and use your Linux system. If your home PC runs Linux and you have a modem set up, you might even dial in to your home system from work.

- To use dial-up networking with Serial Line Internet Protocol (SLIP) or Point-to-Point Protocol (PPP) to connect to the Internet (typically through an Internet service provider).

Cross-Reference
The following sections describe the first two uses of a modem: to dial in or dial out from your Linux PC. Dial-up networking with SLIP or PPP is an important topic in itself: Chapter 16 covers that subject in detail.

Dialing Out with a Modem

When you installed Red Hat Linux from this book's companion CD-ROM, you automatically installed some tools that you can use to dial out from your Linux system with a modem. Before you can dial out, however, you have to make sure that you have a modem properly connected to one of the serial ports of your PC and that the Linux devices for the serial ports are set up correctly.

Examining a modem's hardware setup

Make sure that your modem is properly connected to the power supply and the telephone line.

Buy the right type of cable to connect the modem to the PC. As explained in earlier sections of this chapter, you need a straight-through serial cable to connect the modem to the PC. The types of connectors at the ends of the cable depend on the type of serial connector on your PC. The modem end of the cable needs a male DB-25 connector. The PC end of the cable often is a female DB-9 connector, but some PCs need a female DB-25 connector at the PC end of the cable as well.

You can buy modem cables at most computer stores. In particular, the DB-9 to DB-25 modem cables are often sold as AT modem cables.

Caution

If your PC's serial port is a DB-25, the connector at the back of the PC (not the one on the cable) is a male DB-25 connector. Don't confuse this connector with the parallel port's DB-25 connector, which is female. If you do use the wrong connector no damage should occur, but serial communications won't work.

Tip

If your PC has an internal modem, all you have to do is make sure that the IRQ and I/O addresses are set properly (assuming that the modem card has jumpers for setting these values). For COM1, set the IRQ to 4 and the I/O address to 0x3f8; for COM2, set the IRQ to 3 and the I/O address to 0x2f8. You also have to connect the phone line to the phone jack at the back of the modem card.

Checking Linux's serial devices

When you install Red Hat Linux from this book's CD-ROM, following the directions in Chapter 2, the necessary Linux serial devices are automatically created for you. You should have the /dev/ttyS* devices for dialing in and out through the modem.

The installation process creates the /dev/ttyS* files with a permission setting that does not enable everyone to read the device. If you want any user to be able to dial out with the modem, type the following command while you are logged in as root:

```
chmod o+rw /dev/ttyS*
```

This command gives all users access to the dial-out devices.

Another approach is to create a group named ppp and make it the owner of the /dev/ttyS* files. Then you can add to the ppp group those users whom you trust to use the dial-out capability.

To verify that the Linux kernel detected the serial port correctly, check the boot messages by opening /var/log/dmesg in a text editor, or by typing **dmesg | grep ttyS** in a terminal window. If you see a message about the serial driver being loaded, the next few lines should show information about one or more serial ports on your system. For example, on my system I get the following message for the second serial port (COM2):

```
ttyS01 at 0x02f8 (irq = 3) is a 16550A
```

You can also check for the serial ports with the setserial command. Type **setserial -g /dev/ttyS*** to see detailed information about the serial ports. A telltale sign of a problem is a message from setserial of the form:

```
/dev/ttyS0, UART: unknown, Port: 0x03f8, IRQ: 4
```

Secret

If the UART is shown as unknown, this means that the serial port was not detected. This usually occurs because your PC's BIOS is set up to expect a plug-and-play (PnP) operating system. You should reboot your PC and, as it powers up, press a key (typically you have to press a function key such as F2, but the exact key depends on your PC's BIOS) to enter BIOS setup. In the setup screen, locate the option for PnP operating system (often labeled "Plug & Play O/S") and turn that option off. Then save the BIOS settings and exit. This causes the PC to reboot. This time, when Linux boots again, the kernel should be able to detect the PC's serial port correctly.

Dialing out with a communications program

After you complete the physical installation of the modem and verify that the necessary Linux device files exist, you can try to dial out through the modem. The best approach is to use the Minicom serial communications program included in the Linux distribution on this book's CD-ROM and installed in the /usr/bin directory. The Minicom program is a serial communications program with a text-based interface that emulates a VT102 terminal. Minicom is similar to other communications software, such as Procomm or Crosstalk, which you may have used under MS-DOS or Windows.

To run Minicom, type **minicom** at the shell prompt in a terminal window or a virtual console. If you run Minicom as a normal user (not root), Minicom may display the following error message and exit:

```
minicom
minicom: there is no global configuration file /etc/minirc.dfl
Ask your sysadm to create one (with minicom -s).
```

Log in as root and then type:

```
minicom -s
```

Minicom starts and displays a dialog that lets you configure various aspects of Minicom, including serial port and the modem dialing commands. To enter the modem-initialization commands, use the arrow key to highlight the Modem and dialing item, as shown in Figure 7-6.

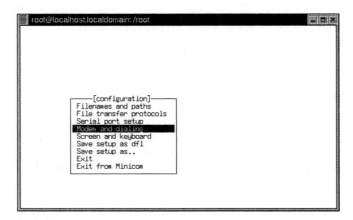

Figure 7-6: Minicom's setup menu

With the Modem and dialing entry highlighted, press Enter. Minicom displays another menu with a list of settings you can change. Press A to change the modem initialization string. Minicom places the cursor on the first line, as shown in Figure 7-7.

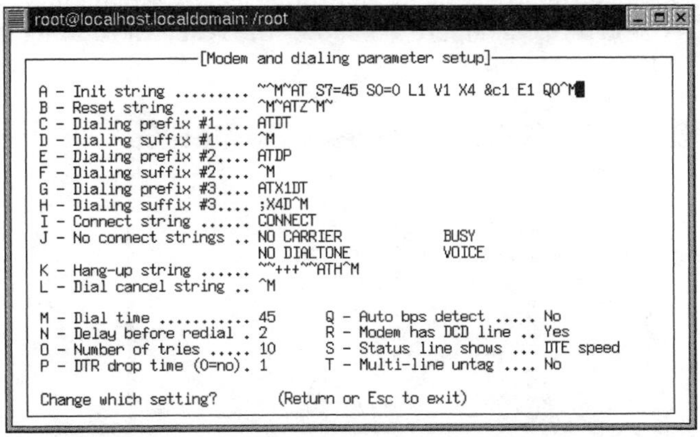

```
root@localhost.localdomain: /root                          _ □ ×
                    [Modem and dialing parameter setup]
    A - Init string ......... ~^M^AT S7=45 S0=0 L1 V1 X4 &c1 E1 Q0^M█
    B - Reset string ........ ^M^ATZ^M^
    C - Dialing prefix #1.... ATDT
    D - Dialing suffix #1.... ^M
    E - Dialing prefix #2.... ATDP
    F - Dialing suffix #2.... ^M
    G - Dialing prefix #3.... ATX1DT
    H - Dialing suffix #3.... ;X4D^M
    I - Connect string ...... CONNECT
    J - No connect strings .. NO CARRIER          BUSY
                              NO DIALTONE         VOICE
    K - Hang-up string ...... ~~+++~~ATH^M
    L - Dial cancel string .. ^M

    M - Dial time .......... 45    Q - Auto bps detect ..... No
    N - Delay before redial . 2    R - Modem has DCD line .. Yes
    O - Number of tries ..... 10   S - Status line shows ... DTE speed
    P - DTR drop time (0=no). 1    T - Multi-line untag .... No

    Change which setting?       (Return or Esc to exit)
```

Figure 7-7: Setting up modem and dialing parameters in Minicom

You can then use the backspace key to edit that line and type the AT command you need to initialize the modem. For example, I have a 56K modem that I initialize with the following AT command:

```
AT &F1 E1 V1
```

After you enter the modem initialization string, press Enter to return to the top-level menu.

If you have no more changes to make, use the up and down arrow keys to highlight the item labeled Save as dfl (meaning save as default) and then press Enter. Minicom saves the settings in the /etc/minirc.dfl file — the default configuration file for Minicom. After that, you can exit Minicom by selecting Exit from Minicom and pressing Enter.

You also need to do the following before any user can run Minicom:

■ Make sure that the text file /etc/minicom.users has a line containing the word ALL. (This enables all users to access Minicom's default configuration file.)

■ Assuming that you want all users to be able to dial out using the modem, enable any user to read from and write to the serial port where the modem is connected. For example, if the modem is on COM1 (/dev/ttyS0), type chmod o+rw /dev/ttyS0 to give everyone write permission for that device.

- Establish a link between the /dev/modem and the serial port device where the modem is connected. If the modem is on COM1 (/dev/ttyS0), you should type the following command:

```
ln -s /dev/ttyS0 /dev/modem
```

After that, you can run Minicom as an ordinary user. When Minicom first runs, it resets the modem. Figure 7-8 shows the result of running Minicom in a terminal window.

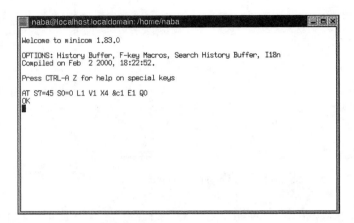

Figure 7-8: The initial Minicom screen

The Minicom program is something like another shareware communications program named Telix. As in that program, you can press Ctrl-A to get the attention of the Minicom program. After you press Ctrl-A, if you press Z, a help screen appears in the form of a text window, as shown in Figure 7-9.

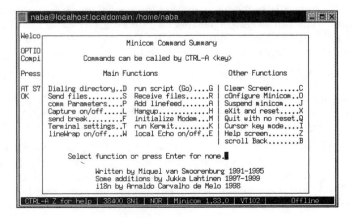

Figure 7-9: The Minicom help screen

In the help screen, you can get information about other Minicom commands. From the help screen, press Enter to return to online mode. In online mode you can use the modem's AT commands to dial out. In particular, you can use the ATDT command to dial the phone number of another modem (for example, your Internet service provider's computer or a system at work), as shown in Figure 7-10. Once you get the login prompt, you can log in as usual and use the remote system.

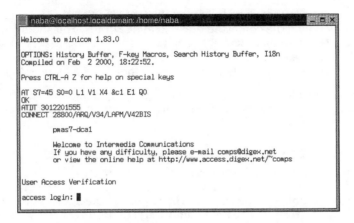

```
Welcome to minicom 1.83.0

OPTIONS: History Buffer, F-key Macros, Search History Buffer, I18n
Compiled on Feb  2 2000, 18:22:52.

Press CTRL-A Z for help on special keys

AT S7=45 S0=0 L1 V1 X4 &c1 E1 Q0
OK
ATDT 3012201555
CONNECT 28800/ARQ/V34/LAPM/V42BIS

        pmas7-dca1

        Welcome to Intermedia Communications
        If you have any difficulty, please e-mail comps@digex.net
        or view the online help at http://www.access.digex.net/~comps


User Access Verification

access login: █
```

Figure 7-10: Dialing a remote system using Minicom

When you log out of the other system and want to exit Minicom, press Ctrl-A and then type **X** to exit the program. Press Enter again in response to the Minicom prompt.

Setting Up Linux for Dial-In

You can set up the same modem for dial-in as well as dial-out use (only one operation is allowed at any one time, of course). Setting up a modem for dial-in use involves setting up a program that monitors the serial port for any incoming calls; this program provides the login prompt. The generic name for these programs is getty. You can use the uugetty program that comes as a part of the getty_ps package on the second companion CD-ROM of this book. The Red Hat installation program does not install uugetty, so you have to install it manually. To install uugetty, follow these steps:

1. Insert the second CD-ROM into the CD-ROM drive. If you are at the GUI screen, the CD-ROM should be mounted automatically (this is done by the magicdev program, which runs in the background). Otherwise, mount the CD-ROM with the mount /mnt/cdrom command.

2. Type the following commands to install uugetty:

```
cd /mnt/cdrom/RedHat/RPMS
rpm -ivh getty_ps*
```

These steps install the getty_ps package, which includes uugetty and the necessary configuration files.

Note that you can also use the newer mgetty package as the getty program for dial-in support. The mgetty package is on the second companion CD-ROM.

To learn more about the uugetty package, read the documentation that comes with the package. Type cd /usr/share/doc/getty* to change to the documentation directory and then read the text file README.linux in a text editor, or by typing the command more README.linux. You should also consult the latest Modem-HOWTO document. To read the HOWTO documents, use the Web browser to go the URL http://www.redhat.com/mirrors/LDP/. From there, click the HOWTOs link and look for the Modem-HOWTO.

The next few sections briefly explain how to set up a modem on COM1 for dial-in use. The Linux device name for that modem (when configured for incoming calls) is /dev/ttyS0.

Editing /etc/rc.d/rc.serial

When Linux starts, the init process executes the /etc/rc.d/rc.sysinit script, which, in turn, executes the /etc/rc.d/rc.serial script, if it exists. Thus, you can configure the serial ports by putting the appropriate commands in the /etc/rc.d/rc.serial file (simply create the /etc/rc.d/rc.serial file, if it does not exist).

If you have a high-speed modem, such as a 56K modem, you should put a command in the rc.serial file to run the setserial program, and set the spd_vhi flag for the serial port. When you set the spd_vhi flag you are enabling your PC to communicate with the modem at a much higher speed than the modem might be using to connect with a remote system. Put the following line in the rc.serial file:

```
/bin/setserial /dev/ttyS0 spd_vhi
```

If your modem supports hardware that uses the RTS (Request to Send) and CTS (Clear to Send) signals, you should make use of them. Enable hardware handshaking for the modem with the stty command, by placing the following command in the rc.serial file:

```
/bin/stty crtscts < /dev/ttyS0
```

Updating the uugetty configuration file

The uugetty program checks the /etc/gettydefs file for information on the speed and settings of a serial port (often referred to as a line). The entries in /etc/gettydefs also tell uugetty what login prompt it should display.

The existing /etc/gettydefs file should work as is. You may, however, want to edit the login prompt. I use the following setting for a modem:

```
# 57600 fixed-baud modem entry
F57600# B57600 CS8 CRTSCTS # B57600 SANE -ISTRIP HUPCL CRTSCTS #@S
login: #F57600
```

The /etc/gettydefs file has many more settings, but I use only this one. The label F57600 at the beginning of the line is what I specify when I run uugetty on the /dev/ttyS0 line. The CRTSCTS flag indicates that the modem uses hardware flow control with the RTS/CTS signals (which I enabled with the stty command in /etc/rc.d/rc.serial file).

Note

This entry already exists in the /etc/gettydefs file. The items near the end of the last line are for the login prompt. You can use the codes listed in Table 7-5 to further customize the login prompt.

Table 7-5   Some Useful /etc/gettydefs Codes

Code	Meaning
@B	The current data-transfer rate in bits per second
@D	The current date in MM/DD/YY format
@L	The serial line to which uugetty is attached (such as ttyS0)
@S	The name of the system (as shown by the uname -n command)
@T	The current time in HH:MM:SS (24-hour) format
@U	The number of currently logged-in users
@V	The value of VERSION specified in the uugetty configuration file (/etc/conf.uugetty.ttyS0 for uugetty running on the ttyS0 line)

To display a single @ character in the login prompt, use either \@ or @@. You can put other special characters in the login prompt by using the backslash escape. Table 7-6 lists some of the recognized escape characters. With these features, you can customize the login prompt to suit your needs.

Table 7-6   Escape Characters in /etc/gettydefs

Character	Meaning
\\	A single backslash
\b	Backspace character (Ctrl-H)
\c	Stops newline at the end of a string
\f	Form feed (Ctrl-L)
\n	Newline character (Ctrl-J)
\r	Carriage return (Ctrl-M)
\s	Single space
\t	Single tab (Ctrl-I)
\nnn	ASCII character whose decimal value is nnn (if the number begins with 0, the value is assumed to be octal; if it begins with 0x, it's considered hexadecimal)

Preparing the uugetty configuration file

The uugetty program has many parameters that you can tweak. In fact, you can specify separate options for uugetty on each line. These per-line configuration files are in the /etc/default directory. The name of each configuration file takes the form uugetty.*line,* in which *line* is the device name for the line (without the /dev part). Thus, /etc/conf.uugetty.ttyS0 is the configuration file for the copy of uugetty that runs on the /dev/ttyS0 line.

```
Here's a typical /etc/conf.uugetty.ttyS0 file on one of my Linux
PCs:
# Line to initialize (line name should not include /dev)
INITLINE=ttyS0
# Timeout to disconnect if idle...
TIMEOUT=60


# Modem initialization string. Sets the modem not to auto-answer.
# When a call comes, uugetty will issue an ATA command to make
# the modem go online
# Format of these entries:
#   <expect> <send> ... (chat sequence)
INIT="" \d+++\dAT\r OK\r\n ATH0\r OK\r\n
AT\sM0\sE1\sQ0\sV1\sX4\sS0=0\s&C1\s&S0\r OK\r\n


# Waitfor string. If this sequence of characters is received
# over the line, a call is detected.
WAITFOR=RING


# The following line is the connect chat sequence. This chat
# sequence is performed after the WAITFOR string is found.
# The \A character automatically sets the baud rate to the
# characters that are found, so if you get the message CONNECT 26400,
# the baud rate is set to 26400 baud.
#
# format: <expect> <send> ... (chat sequence)
CONNECT="" ATA\r CONNECT\s\A


# The next line sets the time to delay before sending the login banner
DELAY=1
```

The entries in this file control the way uugetty initializes the modem, waits for a call, and answers with a login prompt.

The uugetty process uses the INIT string to initialize the modem. In this case, the initialization sequence issues the typical modem commands shown in Table 7-7.

Table 7-7   Typical Modem Initialization Commands

Command	Purpose
ATM0	Turns speaker off
ATE1	Turns command echo on
ATQ0	Turns quiet mode off (so that the modem reports status)
ATV1	Turns verbose mode on
ATX4	Makes the modem report detailed result codes
ATS0=0	Turns auto-answer off (uugetty puts the modem on line at the right moment with an ATA command)
AT&C1	Enables the modem to control the carrier-detect (CD) line (which is turned on only after connect)
AT&S0	Turns the DSR (Data Set Ready) signal on and leaves it on

The uugetty process waits for the WAITFOR string before using the CONNECT string to initiate the connection. When the modem receives a call, it reports RING as the status. When uugetty receives the RING string, it issues the CONNECT string to the modem. The CONNECT string contains the command ATA, which puts the modem online.

After that, uugetty displays the contents of the file /etc/issue, followed by the login prompt. Then uugetty runs the /bin/login program to take care of the actual login.

Starting uugetty in /etc/inittab

To ensure that uugetty runs when Linux starts, you have to put a line in the /etc/inittab file so that the init process starts uugetty automatically. Following is what I put in the /etc/inittab file to start a copy of uugetty on the /dev/ttyS0 line (for the modem on COM1):

```
# Serial line with dial-in modem
s0:235:respawn:/sbin/uugetty ttyS0 F57600 vt100
```

Cross-Reference

This command ensures that uugetty runs in run levels 2, 3, and 5. (Refer to Chapter 23 for a discussion of run levels and /etc/inittab.)

The arguments to uugetty have the following meaning:

- ttyS0 specifies the line that uugetty monitors (ttyS0 means /dev/ttyS0).
- F57600 specifies the line speed (F57600 must appear in the /etc/gettydefs file).
- vt100 specifies the terminal type (the terminal type must be an entry from the /etc/termcap file).

Testing the dial-in setup

After you complete all the setup steps for uugetty and the modem, you have to make sure that the init process reexamines the /etc/inittab file and starts uugetty as specified in that file. To do this, log in as root and type the following command:

```
init q
```

After this command you can test the dial-in modem. You may want to have a friend call your system and see whether login works. If you have two phone lines (and more than one computer at home), you can dial out on one line and log into the Linux system set up on the other line.

Now your Linux system is all set for users to log in through the dial-in modem. When people dial into your Linux system, they should see a login prompt. At that point, they can enter a user name and password to log in to the system.

Terminals and Multiport Serial Boards

The previous sections showed you in detail how to set up and use a modem in Linux for dialing out and letting other people dial in. The rest of this chapter briefly describes the steps involved in setting up terminals connected to the PC's serial port. You'll also find a list of multiport serial boards that Linux supports.

Note

Note that you might want to use other MS-DOS PCs (especially older 286 and 386 PCs) as terminals connected to your Linux system. All you need on the PC is a serial communications package, such as Procomm Plus or Telix.

Setting Up a Terminal on a Serial Port

To set up a terminal on a serial port you have to set up a getty process, just as you do when you set up a dial-in modem. Follow these steps:

1. Make sure that you used the correct serial cable to connect the terminal to the serial port. Most terminals need a null modem cable in which the TD (transmit data) and RD (receive data) signal lines are reversed in going from one end of the cable to the other. (See earlier sections of this chapter for further discussions of serial cables.)

2. Set up the terminal's communication parameters. The exact steps depend on the terminal type.

3. Edit /etc/gettydefs and add a line for the terminal. If the terminal operates at 9,600 bps, specify a line such as the following (the line that begins with a # is a comment):

```
# 9600 bps connection to a terminal

T9600# B9600 CS8 CLOCAL # B9600 SANE -ISTRIP CLOCAL #@S login:
#T9600
```

The most important part is the CLOCAL flag, which tells the getty process to ignore modem-control signals.

4. Edit the /etc/inittab file and add a line to start a getty process on the line connected to the terminal. If you have a VT100-compatible terminal on the line ttyS1 (COM2), you might add the following line to your system's /etc/inittab:

```
s2:235:respawn:/sbin/getty ttyS1 T9600 vt100
```

5. Log in as root, and force the init process to reexamine the /etc/inittab file, as follows:

```
init q
```

6. A login prompt should appear on the terminal, and you should be able to log in.

Setting Up Multiport Serial Boards in Linux

If you plan to support a small business with a Linux PC and dumb terminals (terminals are cheaper than complete PCs, although you could also use old PCs as terminals), you want more than two serial ports. With another serial board, the PC can support four serial ports. If you want more than four serial ports, you have to buy special serial I/O boards known as *multiport serial boards*. These boards typically support anywhere from 4 to 32 serial ports. The serial ports share one IRQ, but each port has a unique I/O address.

Tip

Many multiport serial boards use the 16450 or 16550A UARTs. When you buy a board, you may want to make sure that the UART is 16550A-compatible.

To add support for a specific multiport serial board, you have to add appropriate lines in the /etc/rc.d/rc.serial file. For specific information, consult the multiport serial board's documentation or contact the vendor. The Linux kernel's serial port driver supports the following 16450 or 16550A UART–based multiport serial boards:

- AST FourPort and clones (4 ports)
- Accent Async-4 (4 ports)
- Arnet Multiport-8 (8 ports)
- Bell Technologies HUB6 (6 ports)
- Boca BB-1004 (4 ports), BB-1008 (8 ports), BB-2016 (16 ports)
- Boca IOAT66 (6 ports)
- Boca 2by4 (4 serial and 2 parallel ports)
- Computone ValuePort V4-ISA (AST FourPort-compatible)
- Digi PC/8 (8 ports)
- GTEK BBS-550 (8 ports)
- Longshine LCS-8880, Longshine LCS-8880+ (AST FourPort-compatible)

- Moxa C104, Moxa C104+ (AST FourPort-compatible)
- PC-COMM (4 ports)
- Sealevel Systems COMM-2 (2 ports), COMM-4 (4 ports), and COMM-8 (8 ports)
- SIIG I/O Expander 2S IO1812 (4 ports)
- STB-4COM (4 ports)
- Twincom ACI/550
- Usenet Serial Board II (4 ports)

The Boca BB-1004 and BB-1008 boards do not support the Carrier Detect (CD) and Ring Indicator (RI) signals that are necessary to make dial-in modems work. Thus, you cannot use the BB-1004 and BB-1008 boards with dial-in modems.

Some multiport serial boards use special processors instead of the 16450 or 16550A UART. Table 7-8 lists some intelligent multiport serial boards that Red Hat Linux supports. It also shows the name of the driver module that you must load to add support for a specific type of multiport serial board. These driver modules are located in the /lib/modules/*VERSION*/char directory of your Red Hat Linux system, *VERSION* being the Linux kernel version. Thus, for kernel version 2.4.0-0.43.12, these driver modules are in the /lib/modules/2.4.0-0.43.12/char directory.

Table 7-8 Linux Drivers for Intelligent Multiport Serial Boards

Multiport Serial Board	Linux Driver Module
SDL RISCom/8	riscom8
Comtrol RocketPort	rocket
Stallion multiport serial driver	stallion
Microgate SyncLink ISA and PCI high-speed multiprotocol serial adapters	synclink
Winbond W83977AF Super I/O chip multiport boards	w83977af_ir
Cyclades Cyclom-Y and Cyclades-Z series multiport serial boards	cyclades
Digi International PC/Xe, PC/Xi, PC/Xr, and PC/Xem	epca
Hayes ESP serial card	esp
ISI series of cards by MultiTech	isicom
Stallion Intelligent multiport serial boards	istallion
COSA or SRP synchronous serial card	cosa

Tip

To learn more about setting up a multiport serial board, you may want to read the latest Serial-HOWTO document. To read the HOWTO documents, click on the LDP icon on the GNOME desktop, or use the Web browser to go the URL `http://www.redhat.com/mirrors/LDP/`. On that Web page, click the HOWTOs link and look for the Serial-HOWTO.

Summary

Modems provide a convenient way to dial out and connect to other systems. You can also set up a modem to enable other people to dial into your Red Hat Linux system. This chapter describes the use of modems in Linux. By reading this chapter, you learn the following things:

▶ In Linux, the serial ports have two types of associated device files, depending on whether you use the serial ports as outgoing or incoming devices. When you access the serial port to dial out with a modem, the device names are `/dev/cua0` and `/dev/cua1` for COM1 and COM2, respectively. On the other hand, COM1 and COM2 go by the device names `/dev/ttyS0` and `/dev/ttyS1` when they are used as incoming devices. Although older versions of Linux distinguished between incoming and outgoing device names, nowadays you should use the `/dev/ttyS*` devices names for both dial in and dial out.

▶ The universal asynchronous receiver transmitter (UART) is at the heart of serial communications. The UART converts outgoing bytes into individual bits that the modem can convert to analog form and send over telephone lines; it also packs incoming bits into bytes. For high-speed communications you need a National Semiconductor 16550A or compatible UART; these UARTs have 16-byte receive and transmit buffers to allow reliable data transmission in multitasking operating systems such as Linux — operating systems that may not be capable of monitoring the serial ports constantly.

▶ Serial communications involves several parameters, including baud rate (or bit rate), word length, parity, and number of stop bits. *Baud rate* actually refers to the number of times that the state of the transmission line changes each second, but it is commonly used to refer to the data-transmission rate (in bits per second, or *bps*).

▶ The RS-232C standard specifies how serial communication takes place between two devices. RS-232C refers to the modem as Data Communications Equipment (DCE), whereas the PC is called Data Terminal Equipment (DTE). The RS-232C standard also defines the pins of a serial cable.

▶ Several standards define the way that modems transmit signals over telephone lines. The International Telecommunications Union (ITU) has ratified several modem standards, including V.34 for 28,800 bps and V.90 for 56,600 bps (or 56K) operation. You need two compatible modems at two ends of a line to establish a communications path.

▶ All modern modems understand a set of commands that start with the letters AT. This AT command set was developed by Hayes Microcomputer Products, Inc. You can set up a modem and dial out by using the AT commands.

▶ To dial out from Linux, you need a communications program. Red Hat Linux on the companion CD-ROMs includes the Minicom communications program.

▶ If you cannot seem to dial out on a modem connected to the serial port, your PC's BIOS may be set to use a plug-and-play (PnP) operating system. You have to turn off the PnP operating system option in the BIOS setup and then boot Linux. This enables Linux to correctly detect the serial ports.

▶ To enable other people to dial into your Linux system through a modem, you have to run uugetty (or some other getty process) on the serial line with the modem. You also must set up some parameters in the /etc/gettydefs file. You typically start uugetty in the /etc/inittab file.

▶ You can connect a terminal to the serial port as long as you use an appropriate cable. Linux also supports several types of multiport serial I/O boards that enable you to connect several terminals or modems to your Linux PC.

Chapter 8

Networks

UNIX and networking go hand in hand. In particular, TCP/IP (Transmission Control Protocol/Internet Protocol) networking is practically synonymous with UNIX. As a UNIX clone, Linux includes extensive built-in networking capabilities. In particular, Linux supports TCP/IP networking over several physical interfaces, such as Ethernet cards, serial ports, and parallel ports.

You typically would use an Ethernet network for your local area network (LAN) — at your office or even your home (if you happen to have several systems at home). TCP/IP networking over the serial port enables you to connect to other networks by dialing out over a modem. Linux supports both Serial Line Internet Protocol (SLIP) and Point-to-Point Protocol (PPP).

This chapter focuses on Linux's support for Ethernet and TCP/IP. Although much of this applies to TCP/IP over the serial line, this chapter does not dwell on the specific details of dial-up networking; that topic is the focus of Chapter 16.

The chapter starts with a discussion of networking in general and TCP/IP in particular; then it covers the physical setup of an Ethernet LAN, including information about specific brands of Ethernet cards. Finally, the chapter describes how to set up a TCP/IP network on a Linux system.

Laptops often use PCMCIA cards (also called PC cards) for networking. Chapter 9 describes the PC cards that Linux supports.

Networking Basics

Like any other technical subject, networking is full of terminology and jargon that a newcomer might find daunting. This section introduces some basic concepts of networking, starting with a layered model of networking and proceeding to details of Ethernet and TCP/IP network protocols.

The OSI Seven-Layer Model

A widely used conceptual model of networking is the seven-layer Open Systems Interconnection (OSI) reference model, developed by the International Standards Organization (ISO). The OSI reference model describes the flow of data between the physical connection to the network and the end-user application. Each layer is responsible for providing particular functionality, as shown in Figure 8-1.

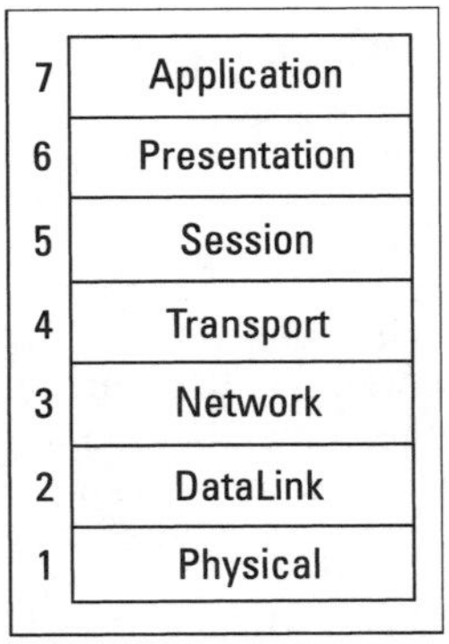

7	Application
6	Presentation
5	Session
4	Transport
3	Network
2	DataLink
1	Physical

Figure 8-1: The OSI seven-layer reference model of networking

As Figure 8-1 shows, the OSI layers are numbered from bottom to top. Basic functions, such as physically sending data bits through the network cable, are at the bottom; and functions that deal with higher-level abstractions of the data are at the top. The purpose of each layer is to provide services to the next-higher layer in a manner such that the higher layer does not have to know how the services are actually implemented. In fact, each layer is designed so that it does not have to know how the other layers work.

The purposes of the seven layers in the OSI reference model are as follows:

- The *physical layer* (Layer 1) transmits raw bits of data across the physical medium (the networking cable or electromagnetic waves, in the case of wireless networks). This layer carries the data generated by all the higher layers. The physical layer deals with three physical components:

- Network topology (such as bus or star), which specifies how various nodes of a network are physically connected

- Transmission medium (such as RG-58 coaxial cable, shielded or unshielded twisted pair, fiber-optic cable, and microwave) that carries the actual signals representing data

- Transmission technique (such as Carrier Sense Multiple Access with Collision Detection [CSMA/CD], used by Ethernet; and token-based techniques, used by token-ring and Fiber Distributed Data Interface [FDDI]), which defines the hardware protocols for data transfer

■ The *data-link layer* (Layer 2) deals with logical packets (or *frames*) of data. This layer packages raw bits from the physical layer into frames, the exact format of which depends on the type of network, such as Ethernet or token ring. The frames used by the data-link layer contain the physical addresses of the sender and the receiver of data.

■ The *network layer* (Layer 3) knows about the logical network addresses and how to translate logical addresses to physical ones. At the sending end, the network layer converts larger logical packets to smaller physical data frames. At the receiving end, the network layer reassembles the data frames into their original logical packet structure.

■ The *transport layer* (Layer 4) is responsible for the reliable delivery of messages that originate at the application layer. At the sending end, this layer divides long messages into several packets. At the receiving end, the transport layer reassembles the original messages and sends an acknowledgment of receipt. The transport layer also ensures that data is received in the correct order and in a timely manner. In case of errors, the transport layer requests retransmission of data.

■ The *session layer* (Layer 5) enables applications on different computers to initiate, use, and terminate a connection (the connection is called a *session*). The session layer translates the names of systems to appropriate addresses (for example, IP addresses in TCP/IP networks).

■ The *presentation layer* (Layer 6) manages the format used to exchange data between networked computers. Data encryption and decryption, for example, would be in this layer. Most network protocols do not have a presentation layer.

■ The *application layer* (Layer 7) is the gateway through which application processes access network services. This layer represents services (such as file transfers, database access, and electronic mail) that directly support applications.

The OSI model is not specific to any hardware or software; it simply provides an architectural framework and gives us a common terminology for discussing various networking capabilities.

A Simplified Four-Layer TCP/IP Network Model

The OSI seven-layer model is not a specification; it provides guidelines for organizing all network services. Most implementations adopt a layered model for networking services, and these layered models can be mapped to the OSI reference model. The TCP/IP networking model, for example, can be adequately represented by a simplified model.

Network-aware applications usually deal with the top three layers (session, presentation, and application) of the OSI seven-layer reference model. Thus, these three layers can be combined into a single layer called the *application layer*.

The bottom two layers of the OSI model — physical and data link — also can be combined into a single physical layer. These combinations result in a simplified four-layer model, as shown in Figure 8-2.

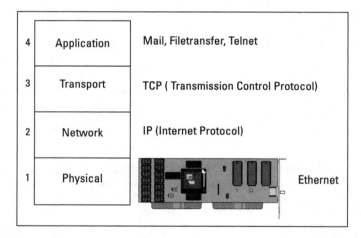

4	Application	Mail, Filetransfer, Telnet
3	Transport	TCP (Transmission Control Protocol)
2	Network	IP (Internet Protocol)
1	Physical	Ethernet

Figure 8-2: A simplified four-layer networking model

At each of these layers, information is exchanged through one of many network protocols.

Network Protocols

A *network protocol* refers to a detailed process agreed upon by the sender and receiver for exchanging data at a specific layer of the networking model. Thus, you would find the following protocols in the simplified four-layer network model of Figure 8-2:

- Physical-layer protocols, such as Ethernet, token ring, and FDDI

- Network-layer protocols, such as the Internet Protocol (IP), which is part of the TCP/IP protocol suite

- Transport-layer protocols, such as the Transmission Control Protocol (TCP) and User Datagram Protocol (UDP), that are part of the TCP/IP protocol suite

- Application-layer protocols — such as File Transfer Protocol (FTP), Simple Mail Transfer Protocol (SMTP), Domain Name Service (DNS), telnet, Hypertext Transfer Protocol (HTTP), and Simple Network Management Protocol (SNMP) — that are also part of the TCP/IP protocol suite

The term *protocol suite* refers to a collection of two or more protocols from these layers that form the basis of a network. Some of the well-known protocol suites are as follows:

- IPX/SPX (Internet Packet Exchange/Sequenced Packet Exchange) protocol suite, used by Novell NetWare

- NetBIOS and NetBEUI (Network BIOS Extended User Interface), used by Microsoft's operating systems

- TCP/IP protocol suite

Note

Of these protocol suites, you will probably be most interested in the TCP/IP protocol suite, because that's what Linux and other UNIX systems support well.

Cross-
Reference

In addition to the TCP/IP protocol, Linux also supports the IPX protocol, but not the SPX protocol necessary for NetWare. Linux's support for NetBIOS comes in the form of a software package named Samba, which is included on the companion CD-ROMs and described in the "LAN Manager server" section of Chapter 21.

More on TCP/IP

This chapter gives you an overview of TCP/IP and Ethernet networking and then moves on to Linux-specific instructions for setting up TCP/IP networking. A single chapter simply isn't enough to provide all available information about TCP/IP. For more information on TCP/IP, consult one of the following books:

- Douglas E. Comer, *The Internet Book: Everything You Need to Know About Computer Networking and How the Internet Works,* Prentice Hall, 2000

- Douglas E. Comer, *Internetworking with TCP/IP, Volume 1: Principles, Protocols, and Architecture,* Third Edition, Prentice Hall, 1995

- W. Richard Stevens, *UNIX Network Programming,* Second Edition, Prentice Hall, 1998

TCP/IP and the Internet

TCP/IP has become the protocol of choice on the Internet — the "network of networks" that evolved from ARPAnet, a packet-switching network that itself evolved from research initiated by the U.S. Government's Advanced Research Projects Agency (ARPA) in the1970s. Subsequently, ARPA acquired a *Defense* prefix and became DARPA. Under the auspices of DARPA, the TCP/IP protocols emerged as a popular collection of protocols for *internetworking* — a term used to describe communication among networks.

Note

TCP/IP has flourished for several reasons. A significant reason is because the protocol is an open one, which means that the technical descriptions of the protocol appear in public documents, so anyone can implement TCP/IP on specific hardware and software.

Another more important reason for TCP/IP's success is the availability of sample implementation. Instead of describing network architecture and protocols on paper, each component of the TCP/IP protocol suite began life as a specification with a sample implementation.

RFCs

The details of each TCP/IP protocol (including TCP and IP, as well as specific service protocols such as SMTP and FTP), are described in documents known as Requests for Comments (RFCs). These documents are freely distributed on the Internet. You can get RFCs from `http://www.cis.ohio-state.edu/hypertext/information/rfc.html` (click the Index link for a complete index of the RFC or search by keyword). Another good URL for RFCs is `http://www.faqs.org/rfcs/`.

In fact, this notation used to name Internet resources in a uniform manner is itself documented in an RFC. The notation, known as the Uniform Resource Locator (URL), is described in RFC 1738, "Uniform Resource Locators (URL)," written by, among others, T. Berners-Lee, the originator of the World Wide Web (WWW).

You can think of RFCs as the working papers of the Internet research-and-development community. All Internet standards are published as RFCs. However, many RFCs do not specify any standards; they are informational documents only.

The following are some RFCs that you may find interesting:

- RFC 768, "User Datagram Protocol (UDP)"
- RFC 791, "Internet Protocol (IP)"
- RFC 792, "Internet Control Message Protocol (ICMP)"
- RFC 793, "Transmission Control Protocol (TCP)"
- RFC 821, "Simple Mail Transfer Protocol (SMTP)"
- RFC 822, "Format for Electronic Mail Messages"

- RFC 854, "TELNET Protocol Specification"
- RFC 950, "Internet Standard Subnetting Procedure"
- RFC 959, "File Transfer Protocol (FTP)"
- RFC 1034, "Domain Names: Concepts and Facilities"
- RFC 1058, "Routing Information Protocol (RIP)"
- RFC 1112, "Host Extensions for IP Multicasting"
- RFC 1155, "Structure and Identification of Management Information for TCP/IP-based Internets"
- RFC 1157, "Simple Network Management Protocol (SNMP)"
- RFC 1519, "Classless Inter-Domain Routing (CIDR) Assignment and Aggregation Strategy"
- RFC 1541, "Dynamic Host Configuration Protocol (DHCP)"
- RFC 1661, "Point-to-Point Protocol (PPP)"
- RFC 1738, "Uniform Resource Locators (URL)"
- RFC 1796, "Not All RFCs Are Standards"
- RFC 1855, "Netiquette Guidelines"
- RFC 1866, "Hypertext Markup Language — 2.0"
- RFC 1886, "DNS Extensions to Support IP Version 6"
- RFC 1918, "Address Allocation for Private Internets"
- RFC 1939, "Post Office Protocol, Version 3 (POP3)"
- RFC 2026, "The Internet Standards Process — Revision 3"
- RFC 2028, "The Organizations Involved in the IETF Standards Process"
- RFC 2045 through 2049, "Multipurpose Internet Mail Extensions (MIME)" [Parts One through Five]
- RFC 2060, "Internet Message Access Protocol — Version 4rev1 (IMAP4)"
- RFC 2146, "U.S. Government Internet Domain Names"
- RFC 2151, "A Primer on Internet and TCP/IP Tools and Utilities"
- RFC 2305, "A Simple Mode of Facsimile Using Internet Mail"
- RFC 2328, "Open Shortest Path First Routing (OSPF) Version 2"
- RFC 2368, "The mailto URL scheme"
- RFC 2373, "IP Version 6 Addressing Architecture"
- RFC 2396, "Uniform Resource Identifiers (URI): Generic Syntax"
- RFC 2460, "Internet Protocol, Version 6 (IPv6) Specification"
- RFC 2535, "Domain Name System Security Extensions"
- RFC 2700, "Internet Official Protocol Standards"

- RFC 2853, "Generic Security Service API Version 2: Java Bindings"
- RFC 2865, "Remote Authentication Dial In User Service (RADIUS)"
- RFC 2870, "Root Name Server Operational Requirements"
- RFC 2871, "A Framework for Telephony Routing over IP"
- RFC 2935, "Internet Open Trading Protocol (IOTP) HTTP Supplement"

Tip   The RFCs continue to evolve as new technology and techniques emerge. If you work in the networking area, you should keep an eye on the RFCs to monitor emerging networking protocols. You can check up on the RFCs at http://www.faqs.org/rfcs/.

IP Addresses

When you have many computers on a network, you need a way to identify each one uniquely. In TCP/IP networking, the address of a computer is known as the *IP address*. Because TCP/IP deals with internetworking, the address is based on the concept of a network address and a host address. You might think of the idea of a network address and a host address as having to provide two addresses to uniquely identify a computer:

- The *network address,* which indicates the network on which the computer is located
- The *host address* of the computer on that network

Dotted-decimal addresses

The original IP address is a four-byte (32-bit) value. The convention is to write each byte as a decimal value and to put a dot (.) after each number. Thus, you see network addresses such as 140.90.141.131. This way of writing IP addresses is known as *dotted-decimal* notation.

Address classes

The bits in an IP address are interpreted in the following manner:

```
<Network Address, Host Address>
```

In other words, a specified number of bits of the 32-bit IP address are considered to be a network address; the rest of the bits are interpreted as being a host address. The host address identifies your PC, whereas the network address identifies the LAN to which your PC is connected.

To accommodate networks of various sizes (the network size is the number of computers in that network), the IP address includes the concept of several classes of network. There are five classes of IP addresses, named class A through class E, as shown in Figure 8-3.

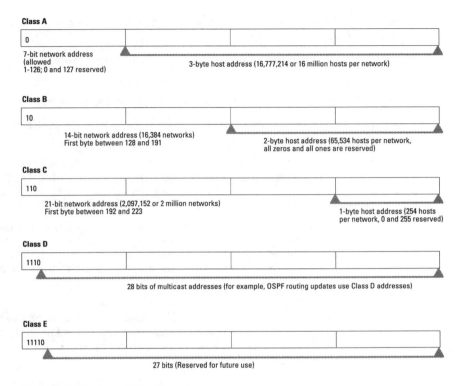

Figure 8-3: Classes of IP addresses

Of the five address classes, only classes A, B, and C are used for addressing networks and hosts; class D and E addresses are reserved for special use.

Class A addresses support 126 networks, each with up to 16 million hosts. Although the network address is 7-bit, two values (0 and 127) have special meaning; therefore, you can have only 1 through 126 as Class A network addresses. There can be approximately 2 billion class A hosts.

Class B addresses are for networks with up to 65,534 hosts. There can be, at most, 16,384 class B networks. All class B networks, taken together, can have approximately 1 billion hosts.

Class C addresses are for small organizations. Each class C address allows up to 254 hosts, and there can be approximately 2 million class C networks. Therefore, there can be at most approximately 500 million class C hosts. If you are in a small company, you probably have a class C address.

All together, class A, B, and C networks can support, at most, approximately 3.5 billion hosts.

You can tell the class of an IP address by the first number in the dotted-decimal notation, as follows:

- Class A addresses: 1.xxx.xxx.xxx through 126.xxx.xxx.xxx
- Class B addresses: 128.xxx.xxx.xxx through 191.xxx.xxx.xxx
- Class C addresses: 192.xxx.xxx.xxx through 223.xxx.xxx.xxx

Even within the five address classes, the following IP addresses have special meaning:

- An address with all zeros in the network portion of the address indicates the local network — the network where the message with this IP address originated. Thus, the address 0.0.0.200 means host number 200 on this class C network.

- The class A address 127.xxx.xxx.xxx is used for *loopback* — communications within the same host. Conventionally, 127.0.0.1 is used as the loopback address. Processes that need to communicate through TCP with other processes on the same host, use the loopback address to avoid having to send packets out on the network.

- Turning on all the bits in any part of the address indicates a broadcast message. The address 128.18.255.255, for example, means all hosts on the class B network 128.18. The address 255.255.255.255 is known as a limited broadcast; all workstations on the current network segment will receive the packet.

Getting an IP address for your network

If you are setting up an independent network of your own that will be connected to the Internet, you need unique IP addresses for your network. IP addresses are administered through the Internet Network Information Center (InterNIC). For a fee, you can get a domain name (a descriptive name for your network such as mycompany.com) and a range of IP addresses for your network. To learn more about InterNIC and how to obtain a domain name, point your Web browser to `http://rs.internic.net/`. You can also obtain domain names from Network Solutions located on the Web at `http://www.networksolutions.com/`.

If you get your Internet access through an Internet service provider (ISP), you need not worry about getting IP addresses for your systems; your ISP will provide the necessary IP addresses.

Next-generation IP (IPv6)

When the four-byte IP address was created, the number of addresses seemed to be adequate. By now, however, class A and class B addresses are running out, and class C addresses are depleting at a fast rate. In addition, the proliferation of class C addresses has introduced a unique problem. Each class C address needs an entry in the network routing tables — the tables that contain information about how to locate any network in the Internet. Too many class C addresses means too many entries in the routing tables. In fact, Classless Inter-Domain Routing (CIDR) — documented in RFC 1519 — was developed to alleviate the problems caused by too many class C addresses, and it is used in the Internet as the primary mechanism to improve scalability of the Internet routing system.

The Internet Engineering Task Force (IETF) recognized the potential for running out of IP addresses in 1991, and work began then on the next-generation IP addressing scheme, named IPng, which will eventually replace the old four-byte addressing scheme (called IPv4, for IP Version 4).

Note

Several alternative addressing schemes for IPng were proposed and debated. The final contender, with a 128-bit (16-byte) address, was dubbed IPv6 (for IP Version 6). On September 18, 1995, the IETF declared the core set of IPv6 addressing protocols to be an IETF Proposed Standard. By now, there are over 50 RFCs dealing with various aspects of IPv6, from IPv6 over PPP to transmission of IPv6 packets over Ethernet.

IPv6 is designed to be an evolutionary step from IPv4. The proposed standard provides direct interoperability between hosts using the older IPv4 addresses and any new IPv6 hosts. The idea is that users can upgrade their systems to use IPv6 when they want and that network operators are free to upgrade their network hardware to use IPv6 without affecting current users of IPv4. Sample implementations of IPv6 are being developed for many operating systems, including Linux. For more information about IPv6 in Linux, consult the Linux IPv6 FAQ/HOWTO at `http://www.linuxhq.com/IPv6/`.

Note

The IPv6 128-bit addressing scheme allows for 170,141,183,460,469,232,000, 000,000,000,000,000,000 unique hosts! That should last us for a while!

Private Networking Addresses

If you don't plan to connect your network to the Internet, you really don't need any unique IP address. RFC 1918 ("Address Allocation for Private Internets") provides guidance about what IP addresses you can use within private networks (the term *private internet* refers to any network that's not connected to the Internet). Three blocks of IP addresses are reserved for private internets:

- 10.0.0.0 to 10.255.255.255
- 172.16.0.0 to 172.31.255.255
- 192.168.0.0 to 192.168.255.255

You can use addresses from these blocks for your private network without having to coordinate with any organization. For example, I use the 192.168.1.0 Class C address for a small private network.

Network masks

The *network mask* is an IP address that has 1s in the bits that correspond to the network address, and 0s in all other bit positions. The class of your network address determines the network mask.

If you have a class C address, for example, the network mask is 255.255.255.0. Thus, class B networks have a network mask of 255.255.0.0, and class A networks have 255.0.0.0 as the network mask.

Network addresses

The *network address* is the bitwise-AND of the network mask with any IP address in your network. If the IP address of a system on your network is 206.197.168.200, and the network mask is 255.255.255.0, the network address is 206.197.168.0. As you may have noticed, the network address has a zero in the host-address area. When you request a domain name and an IP address from NIC, you get a network address.

Subnets

If your site has a class B address, you get one network number, and that network can have up to 65,534 hosts. Even if you work for a megacorporation that has thousands of hosts, you may want to divide your network into smaller subnetworks (or *subnets*). If your organization has offices in several locations, for example, you may want each office to be on a separate network. You can do this by taking some bits from the host-address portion of the IP address and assigning those bits to the network address. This procedure is known as *defining a subnet mask*.

Essentially, you add more bits to the network mask. If you have a class B network, for example, the network mask would be 255.255.0.0. Then, if you decide to divide your network into 128 subnetworks, each of which has 512 hosts, you would designate seven bits from the host address space as the subnet address. Thus, the subnet mask becomes 255.255.254.0.

TCP/IP Routing

Routing refers to the task of forwarding information from one network to another. Consider the two class C networks 206.197.168.0 and 164.109.10.0. You need a routing device to send packets from one of these networks to the other.

Because a routing device facilitates data exchange between two networks, it has two physical network connections, one on each network. Each network interface has its own IP address, and the routing device essentially passes packets back and forth between the two network interfaces. Figure 8-4 illustrates how a routing device has a physical presence in two networks and how each network interface has its own IP address.

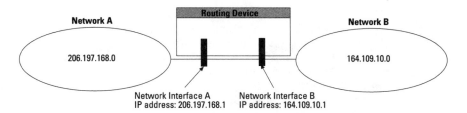

Figure 8-4: A routing device allows packet exchange between two networks.

The generic term *routing device* could be a general-purpose computer with two network interfaces, or a dedicated device designed specifically for routing. Such dedicated routing devices are known as *routers*.

Note

The generic term *gateway* also refers to any routing device. For good performance (a high packet-transfer rate), you want a *dedicated router,* whose sole purpose is to route packets of data in a network.

Later, when you learn how to set up a TCP/IP network in Linux, you'll run into the term *gateway,* which refers to a routing device, regardless of whether the device is another PC or a router. All you have to specify is the gateway's IP address on your network.

A single routing device, of course, does not connect all the networks in the world; packets get around in the Internet from one gateway to another. Any network connected to another network has a designated gateway. You can even have specific gateways for specific networks. As you'll learn later, a routing table keeps track of the gateway associated with an external network and the type of physical interface (such as Ethernet or Point-to-Point Protocol over serial lines) for that network. A default gateway gets packets that are addressed to any unknown network.

In your local area network, all packets addressed to another network go to your network's default gateway. If that gateway is physically connected to the destination network, the story ends there, because the gateway can physically send the packets to the destination host. If that gateway does not know the destination network, however, it sends the packets to the next default gateway (the gateway for the other network on which your gateway also "lives"). In this way, packets travel from one gateway to the next until they reach the destination network (or you get an error message saying that the destination network is unreachable).

To send packets around in the network efficiently, routers exchange information (in the form of routing tables), so that each router can have a "map" of the network in its vicinity. Routers exchange information by using a routing protocol from a family of protocols, known as Interior Gateway Protocol (IGP). A commonly used Interior Gateway Protocol is the Routing Information Protocol (RIP). Another, more recent, Interior Gateway Protocol is the Open Shortest Path First (OSPF).

Secret

In TCP/IP routing, any time a packet passes through a router, it's made what is considered a *hop*. In RIP, the maximum size of the Internet is 15 hops. A network is considered to be unreachable from your network if a packet does not reach the destination network within 15 hops. In other words, any network more than 15 routers away is considered to be unreachable. The newer OSPF routing protocol uses a different metric for measuring the quality of different network paths; therefore, it can have hops greater than 15.

Within a single network, you don't need a router, as long as you do not use any subnet mask to break the single IP network into several subnets. In that case, however, you have to set up routers to send packets from one subnet to another.

Domain Name System (DNS)

You can access any host computer in a TCP/IP network with an IP address. Remembering the IP addresses of even a few hosts of interest, however, is tedious. This fact was recognized from the beginning of TCP/IP, and the association between a host name and IP address was created. The concept is similar to that of a phone book, in which you can look up a telephone number by searching for a person's name.

In the beginning, the association between names and IP addresses was maintained in a text file named HOSTS.TXT at the Network Information Center (NIC), which was located in the Stanford Research Institute (SRI). This file contained the names and corresponding IP addresses of networks, hosts, and routers on the Internet. All hosts on the Internet used to transfer that file by FTP, or File Transfer Protocol. (Can you imagine all hosts getting a file from a single source in today's Internet?) As the number of Internet hosts increased, the single file idea became intractable. The hosts file was becoming difficult to maintain, and it was hard for all the hosts to update their hosts file in a timely manner. To alleviate the problem, RFCs 881, 882, and 883 introduced the concept and plans for *domain names* in November 1983. Eventually, this led to the Domain Name System (DNS) as we know it today (documented in RFCs 1032, 1033, 1034, and 1035).

The domain-name hierarchy

DNS provides a hierarchical naming system much like your postal address, which you can read as "your name" at "your street address" in "your city" in "your state" in "your country." If I know your full postal address, I would locate you by starting with your city in your country. Then I'd locate the street address to find your home, ring the doorbell, and ask for you by name.

Note

DNS essentially provides an addressing scheme for an Internet host that is much like the postal address. The entire Internet is subdivided into several domains, such as gov, edu, com, mil, and net. Each domain is further subdivided into subdomains. Finally, within a subdomain, each host is given a symbolic name. To write a host's *fully qualified domain name (FQDN),* you string together the host name, subdomain names, and domain name with dots (.) as separators. Following is the full domain name of a host named ADDLAB in the subdomain NWS within another subdomain NOAA in the GOV domain: ADDLAB.NWS.NOAA.GOV. Note that domain names are not case-sensitive. By the way, a single dot (.) represents the topmost level (root) of the domain name hierarchy.

Figure 8-5 illustrates part of the Internet Domain Name System, showing the location of the host ADDLAB.NWS.NOAA.GOV.

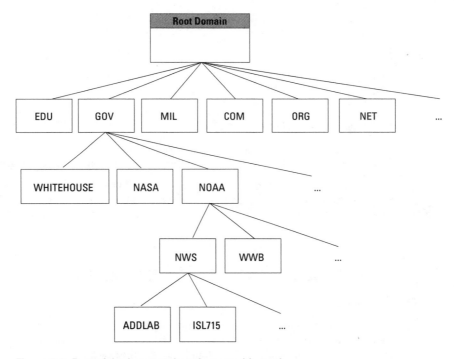

Figure 8-5: Part of the Internet domain-name hierarchy

For a commercial system in the COM domain, the name of a host might be as simple as METROLINK.COM.

Tip

You can refer to a user on a system by appending an at sign (@), followed by the host's domain name, to the user name (the name under which the user logs in). Thus, you would refer to the user named webmaster at the host gao.gov as webmaster@GAO.GOV (unlike host names, user names are case-sensitive).

That's how you refer to users when you send electronic mail.

Name servers

TCP/IP network applications resolve a host name to an IP address by consulting a *name server,* which is another host that's accessible from your network. If you decide to use the Domain Name System (DNS) on your network, you have to set up a name server in your network or indicate a name server (by an IP address).

Later sections of this chapter discuss the configuration files /etc/host.conf and /etc/resolv.conf, through which you specify how host names would be converted to IP addresses. In particular, you specify the IP addresses of a name server in the /etc/resolv.conf file.

If you do not use DNS, you still can have host name–to–IP address mapping through a text file named /etc/hosts. The entries in a typical /etc/hosts file might look like the following example:

```
# This is a comment
127.0.0.1       lnbp200 localhost.localdomain localhost
192.168.1.100   lnb486
192.168.1.50    lnbp133
192.168.1.60    lnbp600
192.168.1.200   lnbp200
192.168.1.233   lnbp233
192.168.1.40    lnbp400
192.168.1.25    mac       lnbmac
192.168.1.1     lnbp75
```

As the example shows, the file lists a host name for each IP address. The IP address and host names will be different for your system, of course.

Secret

One problem with relying on the /etc/hosts file for name lookup is the fact that you have to replicate this file on each system on your network. This procedure can become a nuisance even in a network that has only five or six systems.

TCP/IP Services and Client/Server Architecture

By design, a typical Internet service is implemented in two parts — a server that provides information and one or more clients that request information. Such client/server architecture has been gaining popularity as an approach for implementing distributed information systems. The client/server architecture typically consists of a collection of computers connected by a communication network. The functions of the information system are performed by processes (computer programs) that run on these computers and communicate through the network.

In recent years, the client/server architecture has become commonplace as the mechanism that brings the centralized corporate databases to desktop PCs on a network. In a client/server environment, one or more servers manage the centralized database and clients gain access to the data through the server.

Like a database server, an Internet service such as FTP or the Web also provides a service using the client/server model. A user who wants to access information uses a client (for example, a Web browser) to connect to a server and download information (for example, Web pages from a Web server). In this case, the Web server acts as a database manager — the data is the HTML files (Web pages).

Note

Client/server architecture requires clients to communicate with the servers. That's where TCP/IP comes in — TCP/IP provides a standard way for clients and servers to exchange packets of data. The next few sections explain how TCP/IP-based services communicate. From this discussion, you'll learn about the port numbers associated with many well-known Internet services.

TCP/IP and Sockets

Client/server applications such as Web servers and browsers use TCP/IP to communicate. These Internet applications perform TCP/IP communications using the Berkeley Sockets interface (so named because the socket interface was introduced in Berkeley UNIX around 1982). The sockets interface consists of a library of routines that an application developer can use to create applications that can communicate with other applications on the Internet. There is even a Windows Sockets API (Application Programming Interface — a fancy name for a library of functions) that's modeled after the Berkeley Sockets interface. The Winsock interface, as it's known, provides a standard API that Windows programmers can use to write network applications.

Note

Even if you do not write network applications using sockets, you have to use many network applications. Knowledge of sockets can help you understand how network-based applications work, which, in turn, helps you find and correct any problems with these applications.

Socket definition

Network applications use sockets to communicate over a TCP/IP network. A *socket* is an abstraction that represents a end-point of a connection. Data can be sent as well as received through it. A socket has three attributes:

- The network address (the IP address) of the system
- The port number identifying the process (a process is a computer program running on a computer) that exchanges data through the socket
- The type of socket (such as stream or datagram) identifying the protocol for data exchange

Essentially, the IP address identifies a network node; the port number identifies a process on the node; and the socket type determines the manner in which data is exchanged — through a connection-oriented or connectionless protocol.

Connection-oriented protocols

The socket type indicates the protocol being used to communicate through the socket. A connection-oriented protocol works like a normal phone conversation. When you want to talk to your friend, you have to first dial your friend's phone number and establish a connection before you can have a conversation. In the same way, connection-oriented data exchange requires both the sending and the receiving processes to establish a connection before data exchange can begin.

In the TCP/IP protocol suite, TCP — Transmission Control Protocol — supports a connection-oriented data transfer between two processes running on two computers on the Internet. TCP provides a reliable two-way data exchange between processes.

As the name TCP/IP suggests (and as the "Network protocols" section indicates), TCP relies on IP — Internet Protocol — for delivery of packets. IP does not guarantee delivery of packets; nor does it deliver packets in any particular sequence. IP does, however, efficiently deliver packets from one network to another. TCP is responsible for arranging the packets in the proper sequence, detecting whether errors occurred, and requesting retransmission of packets in case of any error.

TCP is useful for applications that plan to exchange large amounts of data at a time. In addition, applications that need reliable data exchange use TCP. For example, FTP uses TCP to transfer files.

In the sockets model, a socket that uses TCP is referred to as a *stream socket*.

Connectionless protocols

A connectionless data exchange protocol does not require the sender and receiver to explicitly establish a connection. It's like shouting to your friend in a crowded room — you can't be sure if your friend actually heard you.

In the TCP/IP protocol suite, the User Datagram Protocol (UDP) provides connectionless service for sending and receiving packets known as *datagrams*. Unlike TCP, UDP does not guarantee that datagrams ever reach their intended destination. Nor does UDP ensure that datagrams are delivered in the order they were sent.

UDP is used by applications that exchange small amounts of data at a time, or by applications that do not need the reliability and sequencing of data delivery. For example, SNMP (Simple Network Management Protocol) uses UDP to transfer data.

In the sockets model, a socket that uses UDP is referred to as a *datagram socket*.

Sockets and the client/server model

It takes two sockets to complete a communication path. When two processes communicate, they use the client/server model to establish the connection. The server application listens on a specific port on the system — the server is completely identified by the IP address of the system where it runs and the port number where it listens for connections. The client initiates connection from any available port and tries to connect to the server (identified by the IP address and port number). Once the connection is established, the client and the server can exchange data according to their own protocol.

The sequence of events in sockets-based data exchanges depends on whether the transfer is connection-oriented (TCP) or connectionless (UDP).

For a connection-oriented data transfer using sockets, the server "listens" on a specific port, waiting for clients to request connection. Data transfer begins only after a connection is established.

For connectionless data transfers, the server waits for a datagram to arrive at a specified port. The client does not wait to establish a connection; it simply sends a datagram to the server.

Client/Server Communications with TCP/IP

Client/server applications use the following basic steps to exchange data in a TCP/IP network:

1. Create a socket. If the socket already exists, you can skip this step.

2. Bind an IP address and port to the socket.

3. Listen for connections if the application is a server using a stream socket.

4. Establish connection if the application is a client using a stream socket.

5. Exchange data.

6. Close the socket when done.

Connectionless sockets (that implement data transfer using UDP) do not require Steps 3 and 4.

Regardless of whether it's a server or a client, each application first creates a socket. Then it associates (binds) the socket with the local computer's IP address and a port number. The IP address identifies the machine (where the application is running), and the port number identifies the application using the socket.

Note

Servers typically listen to a well-known port number so that clients can connect to that port to access the server. For a client application, the process of binding a socket to the IP address and port is the same as that for a server, but the client can use zero as the port number — the sockets library automatically uses an unused port number for the client.

For a connection-oriented stream socket, the communicating client and server applications have to establish a connection. The exact steps for establishing a connection depend on whether the application is a server or a client.

Note

In the client/server model, the server has to be up and running before the client can run. After creating a socket and binding the socket to a port, the server application sets up a queue of connections, which determines how many clients can connect to the server. Typically, a server listens to anywhere from one to five connections. However, the size of the listen queue is one of the parameters you can adjust (especially for a Web server) to ensure that the server responds to as many clients as possible.

After setting up the listen queue, the server waits for a connection from a client.

Establishing the connection from the client side is somewhat simpler. After creating a socket and binding the socket to a network address, the client establishes connection with the server. To make the connection, the client needs to know the network name or IP address of the server, as well as the port on which the server accepts connection. As the next section shows, all Internet services have well-known standard port numbers.

Note

After a client establishes connection to a server using a connection-oriented stream socket, the client and server can exchange data by calling appropriate sockets API functions. Like a conversation between two persons, the server and client alternately send and receive data—the meaning of the data depends on the message protocol used by the server and the clients. Usually, a server is designed for a specific task; inherent in that design is a message protocol that the server and clients use to exchange the necessary data. For example, the Web server and the Web browser (client) communicate using the Hypertext Transfer Protocol (HTTP).

Internet Services and Port Numbers

The TCP/IP protocol suite has become the lingua franca of the Internet, because many standard services are available on all systems that support TCP/IP. These services make the Internet tick by enabling the transfer of mail, news, and Web pages. These services go by well-known names such as the following:

- FTP (File Transfer Protocol) enables the transfer of files between computers on the Internet. FTP uses two ports—data is transferred on port 20, while control information is exchanged on port 21.

- HTTP (Hypertext Transfer Protocol) is a recent protocol for sending HTML documents from one system to another. HTTP is the underlying protocol of the Web. By default, the Web server and client communicate on port 80.

- SMTP (Simple Mail Transfer Protocol) is for exchanging e-mail messages between systems. SMTP uses port 25 for information exchange.

- NNTP (Network News Transfer Protocol) is for distribution of news articles in a store-and-forward fashion across the Internet. NNTP uses port 119.

- TELNET enables a user on one system to log into another system on the Internet (the user must provide a valid user ID and password to successfully log into the remote system). TELNET uses port 23 by default. However, the TELNET client can connect to any specified port.

- SNMP (Simple Network Management Protocol) is for managing all types of network devices on the Internet. Like FTP, SNMP uses two ports: 161 and 162.

- TFTP (Trivial File Transfer Protocol) is for transferring files from one system to another (typically used by X terminals and diskless workstations to download boot files from another host on the network). TFTP data transfer takes place on port 69.

- NFS (Network File System) is for sharing files among computers. NFS uses Sun's Remote Procedure Call (RPC) facility, which exchanges information through port 111.

A well-known port is associated with each of these services. The TCP protocol uses this port to locate a service on any system. (A server *process* — a computer program running on a system — implements each service.)

As with the /etc/hosts file, which stores the association between host names and IP addresses, the association between a service name and a port number (as well as a protocol) is stored in another text file, named /etc/services. Following is a small subset of entries in the /etc/services file in a Linux system:

```
ftp-data        20/tcp
ftp             21/tcp
ssh             22/tcp                              # SSH Remote Login Protocol
ssh             22/udp                              # SSH Remote Login Protocol
telnet          23/tcp
smtp            25/tcp          mail
time            37/tcp          timserver
time            37/udp          timserver
rlp             39/udp          resource            # resource location
nameserver      42/udp          name                # IEN 116
whois           43/tcp          nicname
re-mail-ck      50/tcp                              # Remote Mail Checking Protocol
re-mail-ck      50/udp                              # Remote Mail Checking Protocol
domain          53/tcp          nameserver          # name-domain server
domain          53/udp          nameserver
bootps          67/tcp                              # BOOTP server
bootps          67/udp
bootpc          68/tcp                              # BOOTP client
bootpc          68/udp
tftp            69/udp
gopher          70/tcp                              # Internet Gopher
rje             77/tcp          netrjs
finger          79/tcp
www             80/tcp          http                # WorldWideWeb HTTP
www             80/udp                              # HyperText Transfer Protocol
link            87/tcp          ttylink
kerberos        88/tcp          kerberos5 krb5      # Kerberos v5
kerberos        88/udp          kerberos5 krb5      # Kerberos v5
```

You'll find browsing through the entries in the /etc/services file to be instructive, because they show the breadth of networking services available under TCP/IP.

Note

Note that port number 80 is designated for World Wide Web service. In other words, if you set up a Web server on your system, that server listens to port 80. By the way, IANA — the Internet Assigned Numbers Authority (http://www.iana.org/) — is responsible for coordinating the assignment of port numbers below 1,024.

The xinetd Super Server

The client/server model requires that the server be up and running before a client makes a request for service. A simplistic idea would be to run all the servers all the time. However, this idea is not practical because each server process would use up system resources in the form of memory and processor time. Besides, you don't really need all the services up and ready at all times. A smart solution to this problem is to run a single server, xinetd, that listens to all the ports and then starts the appropriate server when a client request comes in. (The xinetd server is a replacement for an older server named inetd, but with improved accesses control and logging. The name xinetd stands for extended inetd.)

For example, when a client tries to connect to the FTP port, xinetd starts the FTP server and lets it communicate directly with the client (and the FTP server exits when the client disconnects).

Because it starts various servers on demand, xinetd is known as the Internet super server. Typically, a UNIX system starts xinetd when the system boots. The xinetd server reads a configuration file named /etc/xinetd.conf at startup. This file tells xinetd which ports to listen to and what server to start for each port. The file can contain instructions that include other configuration files. In Red Hat Linux, the /etc/xinetd.conf file looks like the following:

```
# Simple configuration file for xinetd
#
# Some defaults, and include /etc/xinetd.d/

defaults
{
        instances               = 60
        log_type                = SYSLOG authpriv
        log_on_success          = HOST PID
        log_on_failure          = HOST RECORD
}

includedir /etc/xinetd.d
```

Comment lines begin with the pound sign (#). The defaults block specifies default values for some attributes. These default values apply to all other services in the configuration file. The instances attribute is set to 60, which means there can be at most 60 servers simultaneously active for any service.

Secret

The last line in the /etc/xinetd.conf file uses the includedir directive to include all files inside the /etc/xinetd.d directory, excluding files that begin with a period (.). The idea is that the /etc/xinetd.d directory would contain all service configuration files — one file for each type of service that the xinetd server is expected to manage.

Here is the listing of files in the /etc/xinetd.d directory on a typical Red Hat Linux system:

```
ls -l /etc/xinetd.d
total 44
-rw-r--r--    1 root      root          302 Jul 22 15:04 finger
-rw-r--r--    1 root      root          344 Jul 24 09:41 linuxconf-web
-rw-r--r--    1 root      root          241 Jul 18 17:58 ntalk
-rw-r--r--    1 root      root          362 Jul 21 08:43 rexec
-rw-r--r--    1 root      root          361 Jul 21 08:43 rlogin
-rw-r--r--    1 root      root          414 Jul 21 08:43 rsh
-rw-r--r--    1 root      root          341 Jul 21 14:34 swat
-rw-r--r--    1 root      root          229 Jul 18 17:58 talk
-rw-r--r--    1 root      root          289 Jul 18 18:02 telnet
-rw-r--r--    1 root      root          498 Jul 25 13:42 tftp
-rw-r--r--    1 root      root          347 Jul 24 01:59 wu-ftp
```

Each file specifies the attributes for one service. For example, the following listing shows the contents of the /etc/xinetd.d/wu-ftpd file, which specifies the xinetd configuration for the ftp service:

```
# default: on
# description: The wu-ftpd FTP server serves FTP connections. It uses
# normal, unencrypted usernames and passwords for authentication.
service ftp
{
        socket_type              = stream
        wait                     = no
        user                     = root
        server                   = /usr/sbin/in.ftpd
        server_args              = -l -a
        log_on_success          += DURATION USERID
        log_on_failure          += USERID
        nice                     = 10
}
```

The filename (in this case, wu-ftpd) can be anything; what matters is the service name that appears next to the service keyword in the file. In this case, the line service ftp tells xinetd the name of the service. xinetd uses this name to look up the port number from the /etc/services file. If you use the grep command to look for ftp in the /etc/services file, here's what you'll find:

```
grep ftp /etc/services
ftp-data        20/tcp
ftp             21/tcp
tftp            69/udp
sftp            115/tcp
venus-se        2431/udp                # udp sftp side effect
codasrv-se      2433/udp                # udp sftp side effect
```

From this, you can see that the port number of the FTP service is 21. This tells `xinetd` to listen to port 21 for FTP service requests.

The attributes, enclosed in curly braces, have the following meanings:

- The `socket_type` attribute is set to `stream`, which tells `xinetd` that the FTP service uses a connection-oriented TCP socket to communicate with the client. For services that use the connectionless UDP sockets, this attribute would be set to `dgram`.

- The `wait` attribute is set to `no`, which tells `xinetd` to start a new server for each request. If this attribute is set to `yes`, `xinetd` waits until the server exits before starting the server again.

- The `user` attribute provides the user ID that `xinetd` uses to run the server. In this case, the server runs the FTP server as `root`.

- The `server` attribute specifies the program to run for this service, and the `server_args` attribute is the argument that `xinetd` passes to the server program. In this case, the `/usr/sbin/in.ftpd` program is pro-vided `-l -a` as an argument.

- The `log_on_success` attribute tells `xinetd` what information to log when a server is started and when the server exits. In this case, the attribute appends the `DURATION` and `USERID` flags to the default setting of `HOST` and `PID`. The result is that if the FTP service is successful, `xinetd` logs the name of the remote host that requested the service, the process ID of the FTP server (that it starts), the user ID of the remote user, and the duration of the service session. This setting for the `log_on_success` attribute results in entries in the `/var/log/secure` file of the following form:

  ```
  Sep 30 19:01:01 lnbp200 xinetd[521]: START: ftp pid=11171
  from=192.168.1.40

  Sep 30 19:01:41 lnbp200 xinetd[521]: EXIT: ftp pid=11171
  duration=40(sec)
  ```

- The `log_on_failure` attribute tells `xinetd` what information to log when it cannot start a server. In this case, the attribute appends the `USERID` flag to the default setting of `HOST` and `RECORD`. The result is that if the FTP service fails, `xinetd` logs the name of the remote host that requested the service, the user ID of the remote user, and some informa-tion about the remote host.

- The `nice` attribute determines the priority that `xinetd` assigns to the server (–20 is the highest priority; 19 is the lowest priority). Only privi-leged processes can set the priority to a negative value, which means higher priority.

Secret

Note that `xinetd` uses the facilities of the `libwrap` library (called the *TCP wrapper*), which provides an access control facility for Internet services. The TCP wrapper can start other services such as FTP and TELNET, but before starting the service, the wrapper consults the `/etc/hosts.allow` file to see if the host requesting service is allowed that service. If there is nothing in

/etc/hosts.allow about that host, the TCP wrapper checks the
/etc/hosts.deny file to see if the service should be denied. If both files
are empty, the TCP wrapper allows the host access to the requested service.
You can place the line ALL:ALL in the /etc/hosts.deny file to deny all
hosts access to any Internet services (see the "/etc/hosts.allow" and
"/etc/hosts.deny" sections to learn more about these access control files).

Browse through the files in the /etc/xinetd.d directory on your Red Hat
Linux system to find out the kinds of services xinetd is set up to start. Some
of these services, such as finger, provide information that may be used by
intruders to break into your system. You might want to turn off these services by placing the following line inside the curly braces that enclose all
attributes:

```
disable        = yes
```

When you make such a change to the xinetd configuration files, you must
restart the xinetd server by typing the following command:

```
/etc/rc.d/init.d/xinetd restart
```

Stand-Alone Servers

Although starting servers through xinetd is a smart approach, xinetd is not
efficient if a service has to be started very often. The Web server typically has
to be started often because every time a user clicks on a link on a Web page, a
request arrives at the Web server. For such high-demand services, it's best to
start the server in a stand-alone manner. Such stand-alone servers are designed
to run as *daemons* — processes that run continuously. That means the server
listens on the assigned port and whenever a request arrives, the server handles
the request by making a copy of itself. In this way, the server keeps running forever. A more efficient strategy, used for Web servers, is to run multiple copies of
the server and let each copy handle some of the incoming requests.

Ethernet and Linux

TCP/IP is a fine protocol suite for networking, but before you can use TCP/IP,
you have to set up the physical network. Ethernet is a good choice for the
physical data-transport mechanism, for the following reasons:

- Ethernet is proven technology (it has been in use since the early 1980s).

- Ethernet provides good data-transfer rates: typically 10 million bits per
  second (10 Mbps), although there is now 100 Mbps Ethernet and Gigabit
  Ethernet (1,000 Mbps).

- Ethernet hardware is relatively low-cost (PC Ethernet cards cost about
  $50 U.S.).

Typically, Linux supports affordable hardware well, and Ethernet is no exception. The following sections describe the Ethernet cards that Linux supports
and the physical setup of an Ethernet LAN.

Ethernet Basics

Ethernet is a standard way to move packets of data between two or more computers connected to a single cable. (Larger networks are constructed by connecting multiple Ethernet segments with gateways.) Because a single wire is used, a protocol has to be used for sending and receiving data, because only one data packet can exist on the cable at any time. An Ethernet LAN uses a data-transmission protocol known as *Carrier Sense Multiple Access/Collision Detection* (*CSMA/CD*) to ensure that multiple computers can share the single transmission cable. Ethernet controllers embedded in the computers follow the CSMA/CD protocol to transmit and receive Ethernet packets.

The idea behind the CSMA/CD protocol is similar to the way in which you have a conversation at a party. You listen for a pause (*carrier sense*) and talk when no one else is speaking. If you and another person begin talking at the same time, both of you realize the problem (*collision detection*) and pause for a moment; then one of you starts speaking again. As you know from experience, everything works out.

In an Ethernet LAN, each Ethernet controller checks the cable for the presence of signals — that's the carrier-sense part. If the signal level is low, a controller sends its packets on the cable; the packet contains information about the sender and the intended recipient. All Ethernet controllers on the LAN listen to the signal, and the recipient receives the packet. If two controllers send out a packet simultaneously, the signal level in the cable rises above a threshold, and the controllers know that a collision occurred (two packets were sent out at the same time). Both controllers wait for a random amount of time and then send their packets again.

Ethernet was invented in the early 1970s at the Xerox Palo Alto Research Center (PARC) by Robert M. Metcalfe. In the 1980s, Ethernet was standardized by the cooperative effort of three companies: Digital Equipment Corporation (DEC), Intel, and Xerox. Using the first initials of the company names, that Ethernet standard became known as the *DIX standard*. Later, the DIX standard was included in the 802-series standards developed by the Institute of Electrical and Electronics Engineers (IEEE). The final Ethernet specification is formally known as IEEE 802.3 CSMA/CD, but people continue to call it Ethernet.

Ethernet sends data in packets (also known as *frames*) with a standard format that consists of the following sequence of components:

- 8-byte preamble
- 6-byte destination address
- 6-byte source address
- 2-byte length of the data field
- 46- to 1,500-byte data field
- 4-byte frame-check sequence (used for error checking)

You don't need to know much about the innards of Ethernet packets except to note the 6-byte source and destination addresses. Each Ethernet controller has a unique 6-byte (48-bit) address. At the physical level, packets must be addressed with these 6-byte addresses.

Address Resolution Protocol

In an Ethernet LAN, two Ethernet controllers can communicate only if they know each other's 6-byte physical Ethernet address. You may wonder how IP addresses are mapped to physical addresses. This problem is solved by the Address Resolution Protocol (ARP), which specifies how to obtain the physical address that corresponds to an IP address. Essentially, when a packet has to be sent to an IP address, the TCP/IP protocol uses ARP to find the physical address of the destination.

When the packet is meant for an IP address outside your network, that packet is sent to the gateway that has a physical presence on your network. Therefore, it can respond to an ARP request for a physical address.

Ethernet Cables

The original Ethernet standard used a thick coaxial cable, nearly half an inch in diameter. That wiring is called *thickwire* or *thick Ethernet,* although the IEEE 802.3 standard calls it 10Base5. That designation means several things: The data-transmission rate is 10 megabits per second (10 Mbps); the transmission is baseband (which simply means that the cable's signal-carrying capacity is devoted to transmitting Ethernet packets only); and the total length of the cable can be no more than 500 meters. Thickwire was expensive, and the cable was rather unwieldy.

Nowadays, two other forms of Ethernet cabling are more popular. The first alternative to thick Ethernet cable is *thinwire,* or 10Base2, which uses a thin, flexible coaxial cable. A thinwire Ethernet segment can be, at most, 185 meters long. The other more recent alternative is Ethernet over unshielded twisted-pair cable (UTP), known as 10BaseT.

To set up a 10BaseT Ethernet, you need an Ethernet *hub* — a hardware box with RJ-45 jacks. You build the network by running twisted-pair wires (usually, Category 5, or Cat5, cables) from each PC's Ethernet card to this hub. Nowadays, you can get a 4-port 10BaseT hub for about $50 U.S. Figure 8-6 shows a typical small 10BaseT Ethernet LAN that you might set up at a small office or your home.

Thinwire has a feature that makes it attractive for small offices or home offices that have more than one PC. You can daisy-chain the thinwire cable from one PC to another and construct a small Ethernet LAN, as shown in Figure 8-7.

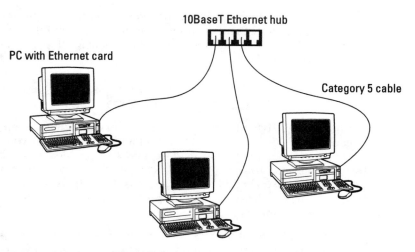

Figure 8-6: A 10BaseT Ethernet LAN using a hub

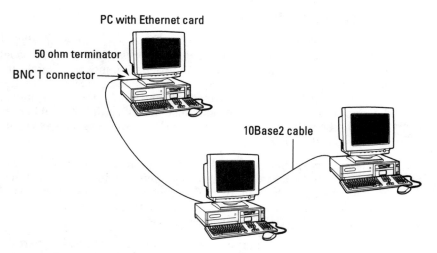

Figure 8-7: Constructing a small thinwire Ethernet LAN

As Figure 8-7 shows, you need Ethernet cards in the PCs. The cards should have thinwire connectors, known as BNC connectors. You also need segments of thinwire cable (technically known as RG-58 thin coaxial cables with 50-ohm impedance). For each Ethernet card's BNC connector, you need a BNC T connector (so called because the connector looks like a T), and you need two 50-ohm terminators for the two end-points of the Ethernet network. Then all you have to do to complete your own Ethernet LAN is connect the parts in the manner shown in Figure 8-7. I used this approach to connect several PCs and a workstation in my home office.

Thinwire is easy to set up, but it's not convenient to connect many PCs this way. One problem is that any break in the cable causes the entire network to come down.

You can also connect a 10Base2 LAN with a 10BaseT LAN by using a hub that has a 10Base2 port and multiple 10BaseT ports.

Caution

Remember that you have to use the BNC T connectors and 50-ohm terminators, even if you are connecting only two PCs on a 10Base2 LAN; you can't simply connect the two Ethernet cards with a cable.

Supported Ethernet Cards

To set up an Ethernet LAN, you need an Ethernet card for each PC. Linux supports a wide variety of Ethernet cards for the PC. Table 8-1 lists the supported Ethernet cards and their Linux drivers. The driver name is useful when you load the Ethernet driver module.

Table 8-1   Ethernet Cards and Their Linux Drivers

Ethernet Card	Driver Name
3Com 3C501* (obsolete and very slow)	3c501
3Com EtherLink II, 3C503, 3C503 (16-bit)	3c503 and 8390
3Com Etherlink Plus 3C505*	3c505
3Com Etherlink-16 3C507*	3c507
3Com Etherlink III, 3C509 / 3C509B (ISA)	3c509
3Com 3C515 Fast EtherLink Ethercard (ISA)	3c515
3Com 3C523*	3c523
3Com 3C529	3c509
3Com 3C579 (EISA)	3c509
3Com 3C562 PCMCIA Card	3c589
3Com 3C589* / 3C589B* PCMCIA Card	3c589
3Com Etherlink III Vortex (3C590, 3C592, 3C595, 3C597) (PCI)	3c59x
3Com Etherlink XL Boomerang Ethercards (3C900, 3C905) (PCI)	3c59x
3Com 3C985	acenic
Accton MPX	ne and 8390
Accton EN1203, EN1207, EtherDuo-PCI	de4x5, tulip

Continued

Table 8-1 *(continued)*

Ethernet Card	Driver Name
Allied Telesis AT1500	lance
Allied Telesis AT1700	at1700
Allied Telesis AT2450	pcnet32
Allied Telesis AT2500*	rtl8139
Allied Telesis AT2540FX*	eepro100
AMD LANCE (7990, 79C960/961/961A, PCnet-ISA)	lance
AMD 79C965 (PCnet-32) and 79C970/970A (PCnet-PCI)	pcnet32
AMD 79C971 (PCnet-FAST), 79C972 (PCnet-FAST+)	pcnet32
AMD 79C974 (PCnet-SCSI)	pcnet32
Ansel Communications AC3200* (EISA)	ac3200
Apricot Xen-II* (82596) onboard Ethernet	apricot
Boca BEN (ISA, VLB, PCI)	lance, pcnet32
Cabletron E21xx*	ne and 8390
Cabletron E2100*	e2100 and 8390
Cabletron E22xx*	lance
Cogent EM100* ISA/EISA	smc9194
Cogent eMASTER+, EM100-PCI, EM400, EM960, EM964	de4x5, tulip
Compaq Deskpro / Compaq XL (Embedded AMD Chip)	pcnet32
Compaq Nettelligent/NetFlex (Embedded TI ThunderLAN Chip)	tlan
Danpex EN9400	de4x5, tulip
D-Link DE-100, DE-200, DE-220-T, DE-250	ne and 8390
D-Link DE-520	pcnet32
D-Link DE-528	ne, ne2k-pci, and 8390
D-Link DE-530	de4x5, tulip
D-Link DE-600	de600
D-Link DE-620	de620
DFINET-300 and DFINET-400	ne and 8390
DEC DEPCA, DE100/1, DE200/1/2, DE210, DE422	depca
DEC EtherWorks 3 (DE203, DE204, DE205)	ewrk3
DEC DE425 EISA, DE434, DE435, DE500	de4x5, tulip

Ethernet Card	*Driver Name*
DEC 21040, 21041, 2114x, Tulip	de4x5, tulip
Farallon Etherwave	3c509
Fujitsu FMV-181/182/183/184	fmv18x
HP 27245A	hp and 8390
HP EtherTwist, PC LAN+ (27247, 27252A)	hp+ and 8390
HP-J2405A	lance
HP-Vectra On Board Ethernet	lance
HP 10/100 VG Any LAN (27248B, J2573, J2577, J2585, J970, J973)	hp100
HP NetServer 10/100TX PCI (D5013A)	eepro100
IBM Thinkpad 300 built-in adapter	znet
ICL EtherTeam 16i/32 (EISA)	eth16i
Intel EtherExpress	eexpress
Intel EtherExpress PRO 10/100B	eepro100
LinkSys Etherfast 10/100 cards	tulip
LinkSys Pocket Ethernet Adapter Plus	de620
Mylex LNE390A, LNE390B	lne390 and 8390
Mylex LNP101, LNP104*	de4x5, tulip
Novell Eagle NE1000, NE2000	ne and 8390
NE2000-PCI (RealTek/Winbond/Compex)	ne, ne2k-pci and 8390
NE1500, NE2100	lance
NE/2* MCA	ne2
NE3210	ne3210 and 8390
NE5500	pcnet32
Proteon P1370-EA	ne and 8390
Proteon P1670-EA	de4x5, tulip
Pure Data PDUC8028, PDI8023	wd and 8390
Racal-Interlan ES3210*	es3210
Racal-Interlan NI5010*	ni5010
Racal-Interlan NI5210	ni52
Racal-Interlan NI6510* (not EB)	ni65
Racal-Interlan EtherBlaster (also known as NI6510EB)	lance

Continued

Table 8-1 *(continued)*

Ethernet Card	Driver Name
RealTek RTL8002/8012 (AT-Lan-Tec) Pocket adaptor	atp
RealTek 8009, 8019	ne and 8390
RealTek 8029	ne, ne2k-pci and 8390
RealTek 8129*/8139*	rtl8139
Sager NP943*	3c501
Schneider & Koch SK G16	sk_g16
SEEQ 8005	seeq8005
SMC Elite Ultra/EtherEZ (ISA)	smc-ultra and 8390
SMC Elite Ultra32 EISA	smc-ultra32 and 8390
SMC PCI EtherPower 10/100	de4x5, tulip
SMC EtherPower II* PCI	epic100
SMC-9000 / SMC 91c92/4, 91c100	smc9194
Texas Instruments ThunderLAN	tlan
VIA 86C926 Amazon	ne, ne2k-pci and 8390
VIA 86C100A Rhine II (and 3043 Rhine I)	via-rhine
Western Digital WD8003 (SMC Elite) and WD8013 (SMC Elite Plus)	wd and 8390
Zenith Z-Note built-in adapter	znet
Znyx ZX342 (DEC 21040 based)	de4x5, tulip

*Cards marked with an asterisk have either buggy drivers or drivers that have not been fully tested.

If you have upgraded the Linux kernel, the new kernel may support even more cards than the ones shown in this list.

If you have not bought an Ethernet card yet, you want to buy a 16-bit card, not an 8-bit card. A 16-bit card transfers data faster and has a larger onboard buffer. The cards come with different types of connectors, as follows:

■ A DB-15 connector for thick Ethernet. (You need an additional transceiver to connect thickwire to other types of Ethernet, such as thinwire or 10BaseT.)

■ A thinwire BNC connector

■ An RJ-45 connector for 10BaseT. (The RJ-45 connector looks like a common RJ-11 phone jack, but the RJ-45 version has eight positions instead of six.)

Nowadays, most Ethernet cards come with a 10BaseT connector. If you have more than one PC with 10BaseT Ethernet cards, you can easily set up a small LAN — all you need is a 10BaseT Ethernet hub. A wire goes from each PC's Ethernet card to the hub, and the hub sets up the proper connections for Ethernet.

You can use Ethernet cards with a DB-15 thick Ethernet connector in a thin-wire or 10BaseT network. All you need is a transceiver that attaches to the DB-15 port and provides the right type of connector (BNC for thinwire, and RJ-45 for 10BaseT).

A better choice is to buy the newer "Combo" version of Ethernet cards that come with both thinwire and 10BaseT transceivers built in; there is a BNC connector for a thinwire network, and a RJ-45 jack for a 10BaseT network.

Ethernet Drivers as Modules

Red Hat Linux ships with very few drivers built into the kernel. Instead, most drivers, including Ethernet drivers, are provided in the form of dynamically loadable modules. When you set up networking during Red Hat Linux installation, the installation program adds appropriate entries to the text file `/etc/modules.conf`. These entries tell the `modprobe` command what modules to load. For Ethernet drivers, the important entries are lines that define the driver aliases `eth0`, `eth1`, and so on. If you have only one Ethernet card, the alias `eth0` should be set to the name of the driver for your Ethernet card (refer to Table 8-1 for a list of cards and their corresponding drivers).

For example, my PC has a 3Com 3C503 Ethernet card. For this card, the installation program adds the following alias entry in the `/etc/modules.conf` file:

```
alias eth0 3c503
```

You may also need another entry in the `/etc/modules.conf` file to specify various options, such as I/O port address and interrupt number (IRQ) for your Ethernet card. For example, I added the following line to `/etc/modules.conf` to specify an IRQ of 5 and an I/O port address of 0x300 (hexadecimal 300) for the 3Com 3C503 card:

```
options 3c503 irq=5 io=0x300
```

Tip

Most ISA Ethernet cards accept parameters of this form. Instead of letting the Ethernet driver probe for the card, it is best if you specify the IRQ and I/O port address through the option line in the `/etc/modules.conf` file. For PCI and EISA Ethernet cards, it is safe to let the driver probe for various parameters of the card. Consult the file `/usr/src/linux/Documentation/networking/net-modules.txt` for a list of all the options that each Ethernet driver module accepts.

Ethernet Autoprobing

At boot time, a kernel with Ethernet support or an Ethernet driver module (being loaded by `modprobe`) attempts to probe and detect the Ethernet card. The probing involves reading from and writing to specific I/O port addresses.

Although you specify a single I/O port address for a device, most devices use a block of I/O addresses for their operation. The I/O address that you specify is the *base address*; the rest of the I/O addresses are consecutive I/O ports, starting at the base address.

Secret

Depending on the number of I/O addresses used by a device, two devices may end up with overlaps in the range of I/O addresses that they use. The NE2000 card, for example, uses 32 I/O ports (that's 0x20 in hexadecimal notation). If you select 0x360 as the base I/O address for a NE2000 card, the card uses the ports from 0x360 to 0x37F. Unfortunately, the PC's parallel port (LPT1) uses the base I/O address of 0x378, and the secondary IDE controller uses the addresses 0x376–0x376. Thus, the NE2000 configured at 0x360 now has an overlap with the I/O addresses used by the first parallel port and the secondary IDE controller. In this case, you can prevent any problems by configuring the NE2000 card at a different I/O address, such as 0x280.

Overlapping I/O port addresses cause problems because during autoprobing, the kernel may perform operations that might be harmless for some devices, but that may cause another device to lock up the system. Typically, however, if your Ethernet card and other devices were working under DOS or Windows, you should have no problem with them under Linux (assuming, of course, that your Ethernet card is supported under Linux).

If your system hangs during autoprobing, you can exclude a specific range of I/O addresses from being probed. To exclude a range of addresses during autoprobing, use the `reserve` command during the LILO boot prompt. The `reserve` command has the following syntax:

```
reserve=BASE-IO-PORT1,NUMPORTS1[,BASE-IO-PORT2,NUMPORTS2,...]
```

Here, `BASE-IO-PORT1` is an I/O port address in hexadecimal notation (for example, `0x300`); and `NUMPORTS1` is the number of ports (for example, 32) to be excluded when autoprobing. The arguments in brackets are optional; they are used to specify additional exclusion regions.

If you prevent a range of I/O addresses from being autoprobed, a device that may be at that address may not be detected. Thus, you must specify that device's parameters explicitly on the boot command line.

For Linux kernels with Ethernet support linked into the kernel, the LILO command for specifying device parameters is `ether`, which takes the following format:

```
ether=IRQ,BASE-IO-PORT,PARAM-1,PARAM-2,NAME
```

Table 8-2 explains the meanings of the arguments. All arguments are optional. The Ethernet driver takes the first nonnumeric argument as *NAME*.

Table 8-2:   Arguments for ether

Argument	*Meaning*
IRQ	The IRQ of the Ethernet card. Specify a zero *IRQ* to make the driver autodetect the IRQ.
BASE-IO-PORT	The base I/O port address of the Ethernet card. Specify a zero *BASE-IO-PORT* to make the driver autodetect the base I/O port address.
PARAM-1	The meaning depends on the Ethernet driver. Some drivers use the least significant four bits of this value as the debug message level. The default is 0; set this argument to a value of 1 to 7 to indicate how verbose the debug messages should be (7 means most verbose). A value of 8 stops debug messages. The AMD LANCE driver uses the low-order four bits as the DMA channel.
PARAM-2	The meaning depends on the Ethernet driver. The 3Com 3c503 drivers use this value to select between an internal and external transceiver — 0 means the internal transceiver, and 1 means that the card uses an external transceiver connected to the DB-15 thick Ethernet port.
NAME	The name of the Ethernet driver (eth0, eth1, and so on). By default, the kernel uses eth0 as the name of the first Ethernet card that it autoprobes. The kernel does not probe for more than one Ethernet card, because that would increase any chance of conflicts with other devices during autoprobing.

If you have an Ethernet card at the I/O address 0x300 and do not want this card to be autoprobed, use a command line such as the following at the LILO boot prompt:

```
reserve=0x300,32 ether=0,0x300,eth0
```

The reserve command prevents 32 I/O ports starting at 0x300 from being autoprobed, whereas the ether command specifies the base I/O port address for the Ethernet card. The exact I/O addresses depend on your Ethernet card and the range of addresses for which an overlap with some other device exists. Most of the time, you should not have to use these commands.

Secret

The I/O addresses and IRQs of PCI cards are assigned by the PCI BIOS when the system powers up. Thus, you cannot set the I/O address or IRQ of any PCI card through the LILO command line. Even if you specify these parameters through LILO commands, they are ignored for a PCI device.

Network-Device Names

For most devices, Linux uses files in the /dev directory. The networking devices, however, have names that are defined internally in the kernel; no files for these devices exist in the /dev directory. Following are the common network-device names in Linux:

- lo — the loopback device. This device is used for efficient handling of network packets that are sent from your system to itself (when, for example, an X client communicates with the X server on the same system).

- eth0 — the first Ethernet card. If you have more Ethernet cards, they get device names eth1, eth2, and so on.

- ppp0 — the first serial port configured for a point-to-point link to another computer, using Point-to-Point Protocol (PPP). If you have more serial ports configured for PPP networking, they are assigned device names ppp1, ppp2, and so on.

- sl0 — the first serial port configured for Serial Line Internet Protocol (SLIP) networking. SLIP is used for establishing a point-to-point link to a TCP/IP network. If you use a second serial port for SLIP, it gets the device name sl1.

Secret

You always have a loopback device (lo), whether or not you have any network. The loopback device passes data from one process to another without having to go out to a network. In fact, the whole point of the loopback device is to allow network applications to work, as long as the communicating processes are on the same system.

Cross-
Reference

PPP is popular in dial-up networks, in which you use a modem to dial in to an Internet host (typically, a system at your work or your Internet service provider) and establish a connection to the Internet. Chapter 16 covers this subject in detail.

If you want to see the names of installed network devices on your system, try the following command:

```
cat /proc/net/dev
```

This command shows the network-device names, as well as statistics on the number of packets sent and received for a specific device.

Multiple Ethernet Cards

You might use a Linux PC as a gateway between two Ethernet networks. In that case, you might have two Ethernet cards in the PC. The Linux kernel can support more than one Ethernet card; what it does *not* do is detect multiple cards automatically. The kernel looks for only the first Ethernet card. If you happen to have two Ethernet cards, you should specify the parameters of the cards on the LILO boot command line. (The two cards must have different IRQs and I/O addresses, of course.) Following is a typical boot command line for two Ethernet cards:

```
ether=10,0x220,eth0 ether=5,0x300,eth1
```

If you happen to have two Ethernet cards, you can place the necessary LILO boot parameters in the /etc/lilo.conf file, so that you don't have to enter the arguments every time you boot Linux. For the preceding example, the line in /etc/lilo.conf looks like the following:

```
append="ether=10,0x220,eth0 ether=5,0x300,eth1"
```

If you plan to use a Linux PC with two network interfaces as a TCP/IP gateway, you have to recompile the kernel with IP forwarding enabled. Chapter 25 explains how to rebuild the kernel. During the rebuild process, when you use the make config command, you should enable CONFIG_NETFILTER, CONFIG_IP_ADVANCED_ROUTER, CONFIG_IP_MULTIPLE_TABLES, CONFIG_IP_ROUTE_NAT, and CONFIG_IP_ROUTE_FWMARK.

TCP/IP Setup in Linux

Like almost everything else in Linux, TCP/IP setup is a matter of preparing numerous configuration files (text files that you can edit with any text editor). Most of these configuration files are in the /etc directory. The Red Hat installation program helps by hiding the details of the TCP/IP configuration files. Nevertheless, it's better if you know the names of the files and their purposes, so that you can edit the files manually, if necessary.

Cross-Reference

The next few sections show you how to set up TCP/IP for an Ethernet LAN. Chapter 16 covers dial-up networking under Linux, including topics such as PPP.

Before you look at TCP/IP setup, make sure that your system's Ethernet card is properly installed and detected by the Linux kernel.

Configuring the Kernel for TCP/IP

The kernel configuration is the first step in setting up your system for TCP/IP. As shown in Chapter 25, the first step in kernel configuration involves the following commands:

```
cd /usr/src/linux
make config
```

The configuration program asks several questions about various system capabilities, some of which are about networking:

```
*
* Networking options
*
Packet socket (CONFIG_PACKET) [Y/m/n/?]
   Packet socket: mmapped IO (CONFIG_PACKET_MMAP) [Y/n/?]
Kernel/User netlink socket (CONFIG_NETLINK) [Y/n/?]
   Routing messages (CONFIG_RTNETLINK) [Y/n/?]
   Netlink device emulation (CONFIG_NETLINK_DEV) [Y/m/n/?]
```

```
Network packet filtering (replaces ipchains) (CONFIG_NETFILTER) [Y/n/?]
  Network packet filtering debugging (CONFIG_NETFILTER_DEBUG) [N/y/?]
Socket Filtering (CONFIG_FILTER) [Y/n/?]
Unix domain sockets (CONFIG_UNIX) [Y/m/n/?]
TCP/IP networking (CONFIG_INET) [Y/n/?]
  IP: multicasting (CONFIG_IP_MULTICAST) [Y/n/?]
  IP: advanced router (CONFIG_IP_ADVANCED_ROUTER) [N/y/?]
  IP: kernel level autoconfiguration (CONFIG_IP_PNP) [N/y/?]
  IP: tunneling (CONFIG_NET_IPIP) [M/n/y/?]
  IP: GRE tunnels over IP (CONFIG_NET_IPGRE) [M/n/y/?]
    IP: broadcast GRE over IP (CONFIG_NET_IPGRE_BROADCAST) [Y/n/?]
  IP: multicast routing (CONFIG_IP_MROUTE) [N/y/?]
  IP: ARP daemon support (EXPERIMENTAL) (CONFIG_ARPD) [N/y/?]
  IP: TCP Explicit Congestion Notification support (CONFIG_INET_ECN) [N/y/?]
  IP: TCP syncookie support (disabled per default) (CONFIG_SYN_COOKIES) [Y/n/?]
*
*   IP: Netfilter Configuration
*
Connection tracking (required for masq/NAT) (CONFIG_IP_NF_CONNTRACK) [M/n/y/?]
  FTP protocol support (CONFIG_IP_NF_FTP) [M/n/?]
Userspace queueing via NETLINK (EXPERIMENTAL) (CONFIG_IP_NF_QUEUE) [M/n/y/?]
IP tables support (required for filtering/masq/NAT) (CONFIG_IP_NF_IPTABLES)
[M/n/y/?]
  limit match support (CONFIG_IP_NF_MATCH_LIMIT) [M/n/?]
  MAC address match support (CONFIG_IP_NF_MATCH_MAC) [M/n/?]
  netfilter MARK match support (CONFIG_IP_NF_MATCH_MARK) [M/n/?]
  Multiple port match support (CONFIG_IP_NF_MATCH_MULTIPORT) [M/n/?]
  TOS match support (CONFIG_IP_NF_MATCH_TOS) [M/n/?]
  Connection state match support (CONFIG_IP_NF_MATCH_STATE) [M/n/?]
  Unclean match support (EXPERIMENTAL) (CONFIG_IP_NF_MATCH_UNCLEAN) [M/n/?]
  Owner match support (EXPERIMENTAL) (CONFIG_IP_NF_MATCH_OWNER) [M/n/?]
  Packet filtering (CONFIG_IP_NF_FILTER) [M/n/?]
    REJECT target support (CONFIG_IP_NF_TARGET_REJECT) [M/n/?]
    MIRROR target support (EXPERIMENTAL) (CONFIG_IP_NF_TARGET_MIRROR) [M/n/?]
  Full NAT (CONFIG_IP_NF_NAT) [M/n/?]
    MASQUERADE target support (CONFIG_IP_NF_TARGET_MASQUERADE) [M/n/?]
    REDIRECT target support (CONFIG_IP_NF_TARGET_REDIRECT) [M/n/?]
  Packet mangling (CONFIG_IP_NF_MANGLE) [M/n/?]
    TOS target support (CONFIG_IP_NF_TARGET_TOS) [M/n/?]
    MARK target support (CONFIG_IP_NF_TARGET_MARK) [M/n/?]
  LOG target support (CONFIG_IP_NF_TARGET_LOG) [M/n/?]
ipchains (2.2-style) support (CONFIG_IP_NF_COMPAT_IPCHAINS) [M/n/y/?]
ipfwadm (2.0-style) support (CONFIG_IP_NF_COMPAT_IPFWADM) [M/n/y/?]
  The IPv6 protocol (EXPERIMENTAL) (CONFIG_IPV6) [M/n/y/?]
    IPv6: enable EUI-64 token format (CONFIG_IPV6_EUI64) [N/y/?]
*
*   IPv6: Netfilter Configuration
*
IP6 tables support (required for filtering/masq/NAT) (CONFIG_IP6_NF_IPTABLES) [M
/n/y/?]
  limit match support (CONFIG_IP6_NF_MATCH_LIMIT) [M/n/?]
  netfilter MARK match support (CONFIG_IP6_NF_MATCH_MARK) [M/n/?]
```

```
   Packet filtering (CONFIG_IP6_NF_FILTER) [M/n/?]
   Packet mangling (CONFIG_IP6_NF_MANGLE) [M/n/?]
    MARK target support (CONFIG_IP6_NF_TARGET_MARK) [M/n/?]
   Kernel httpd acceleration (EXPERIMENTAL) (CONFIG_KHTTPD) [N/y/m/?]
Asynchronous Transfer Mode (ATM) (EXPERIMENTAL) (CONFIG_ATM) [Y/n/?]
   Classical IP over ATM (CONFIG_ATM_CLIP) [Y/n/?]
     Do NOT send ICMP if no neighbour (CONFIG_ATM_CLIP_NO_ICMP) [N/y/?]
   LAN Emulation (LANE) support (CONFIG_ATM_LANE) [M/n/y/?]
     Multi-Protocol Over ATM (MPOA) support (CONFIG_ATM_MPOA) [M/n/y/?]
*
*
*
The IPX protocol (CONFIG_IPX) [M/n/y/?]
```

You can accept the default answer (the first item shown in brackets at the end of each question) for almost all these questions. You should answer yes to enable IP forwarding if you want to use your Linux system as a gateway (or router) between two separate networks.

The following list explains some of these configuration questions:

- *Network packet filtering*—If you answer yes to this question, the kernel allows networking software to selectively enable or disable access to groups of TCP/IP ports. You need additional software to control access to specific TCP/IP ports. You should answer yes to this option if you want your Linux system to act as an intermediary through which a number of other systems on a LAN can access other systems on the Internet (assuming the Linux system is connected to the Internet through a second network interface, such as a PPP dial-up connection).

- *TCP/IP networking*—This option enables support for the TCP/IP protocol suite in the kernel. You should answer yes to this question, even if you do not plan to set up a LAN. TCP/IP can be used even within a single system; the loopback device lo provides the data-transport mechanism to support TCP/IP exchanges between processes on the same PC.

- *IP: multicasting*—This question refers to the capability of the system to send and receive network packets addressed to a subset of hosts on the network. Some new Internet services, such as Internet Talk Radio, rely on multicasting. Even if you enable this feature, you need additional software to use the multicasting capabilities.

- *IP: TCP syn cookie support*—If you answer yes to this question, the kernel includes code that provides protection against a type of network attack known as SYN flooding.

- *The IPX protocol*—Answer yes if you want to include support for the Internet Packet Exchange (IPX) protocol—part of the Xerox Network System (XNS) protocol. Novell NetWare uses IPX as its network layer. NetWare's transport layer is called Sequenced Packet Exchange (SPX); Linux does not include SPX support.

Running Red Hat's Network Configuration Tool

After you ensure that the Linux kernel is properly configured for TCP/IP, you have to make sure that the appropriate configuration files exist. Red Hat Linux includes a program named netcfg (in the /usr/bin directory) that helps you configure various network interfaces on your system for TCP/IP networking. You can run netcfg to add a new network interface, or alter information such as name servers and host names (you can also directly edit the configuration files listed in the "TCP/IP configuration files" section).

Log in as root and from the GNOME desktop, select Main Menu ⇨ Programs ⇨ System ⇨ Network Configuration to run the network configuration tool. You can also type netcfg in a terminal window to start that program.

The network configuration tool displays a dialog box, as shown in Figure 8-8.

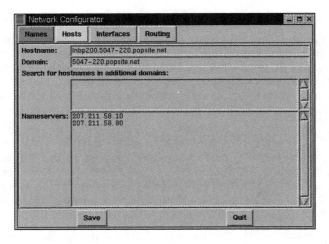

Figure 8-8: Configuring TCP/IP network with the Red Hat network configuration tool

You can configure various aspects of your network through the four buttons at the top of the dialog box. Specifically, the buttons enable you to do the following:

- *Names* lets you enter the host name for your system and enter the IP addresses of name servers. The name server addresses are stored in the /etc/resolv.conf file. The host name is stored in a variable in the /etc/sysconfig/network file.

- *Hosts* shows you the current contents of the /etc/hosts file and lets you add, remove, or edit entries.

- *Interfaces* lets you add a new network interface, specify the IP address of the interface; and activate the interface. This information is stored in various files in the /etc/sysconfig directory.

- *Routine* lets you add static routes (each route lists the gateway to use to reach a specified network).

Tip

To configure the network interfaces, you need to assign IP addresses to each interface. If you are running a private network, you may use IP addresses in the range 192.168.0.0 to 192.168.255.255. (There are other ranges of addresses reserved for private networks, but this range should suffice for most needs.) For example, I use the 192.168.1.0 address for a small private network.

Testing the network

After you run netcfg, you may want to check whether the network is up and running. If you have not rebooted your system yet, you have to run /sbin/ifconfig to configure the Ethernet interface for your IP address. On a system whose IP address is 192.168.1.200, you would type the following command (you have to be logged in as root to do this):

```
/sbin/ifconfig eth0 192.168.1 netmask 255.255.255.0 broadcast 192.168.1.255
```

Verifying another system's accessibility

Now you should use the ping utility program to verify whether another system on your network is accessible. On my PC, I might try the following:

```
ping 192.168.1.1
PING 192.168.1.1 (192.168.1.1): 56 data bytes
64 bytes from 192.168.1.1: icmp_seq=0 ttl=64 time=0.9 ms
64 bytes from 192.168.1.1: icmp_seq=1 ttl=64 time=0.9 ms
64 bytes from 192.168.1.1: icmp_seq=2 ttl=64 time=0.8 ms
64 bytes from 192.168.1.1: icmp_seq=3 ttl=64 time=0.9 ms
        (press Ctrl-C here)
--- 192.168.1.1 ping statistics ---
4 packets transmitted, 4 packets received, 0% packet loss
round-trip min/avg/max = 0.8/0.8/0.9 ms
```

If the ping command shows that other systems on your network are reachable, you can proceed to use other network programs, such as ftp and telnet.

Using TCP/IP Configuration Files

Running the Red Hat network configuration tool may be enough to get TCP/IP configured on your system. You may want to be familiar with the configuration files, however, so that you can edit the files if necessary. You can specify the name servers through the netcfg script, for example, but you may want to add an alternative name server. To do so, you need to know about the /etc/resolv.conf file, which stores the IP addresses of name servers.

The following sections describe the basic TCP/IP configuration files.

/etc/hosts

The /etc/hosts text file contains a list of IP addresses and host names for your local network. In the absence of a name server, any network program on your system consults this file to determine the IP address that corresponds to a host name.

Following is the /etc/hosts file from my system, showing the IP addresses and names of other hosts on my LAN:

```
127.0.0.1         localhost          localhost.localdomain
# Other hosts on the LAN
192.168.1.100     lnb486
192.168.1.50      lnbp133
192.168.1.200     lnbp200
192.168.1.233     lnbp233
192.168.1.40      lnbp400
192.168.1.25      mac        lnbmac
192.168.1.1       lnbp75
```

As the example shows, each line in the file starts with an IP address, followed by the host name for that IP address. You can have more than one host name for a given IP address.

/etc/networks

The /etc/networks file is another text file that contains the names and IP addresses of networks. These network names are commonly used in the routing command (/sbin/route) to specify a network by name, instead of by its IP address.

Don't be alarmed if your Linux PC does not have the /etc/networks file. Your TCP/IP network will work fine without this file. In fact, the Red Hat Linux installation program does not create any /etc/networks file.

/etc/host.conf

Linux uses a resolver library to obtain the IP address that corresponds to a host name. The /etc/host.conf file specifies how names are resolved. A typical /etc/host.conf file might contain the following lines:

```
order hosts, bind
multi on
```

The entries in the /etc/host.conf file tell the resolver library what services to use, and in which order, to resolve names.

The order option indicates the order of services. The sample entry specifies that the resolver library should first consult the /etc/hosts file, and then check the name server to resolve a name.

Secret

The multi option determines whether a host in the /etc/hosts file can have multiple IP addresses. Hosts that have more than one IP address are called *multihomed,* because the presence of multiple IP addresses implies that the host has several network interfaces (the host "lives" in several networks simultaneously).

/etc/resolv.conf

The /etc/resolv.conf file is another text file used by the resolver —
a library that determines the IP address for a host name. Following is a
sample /etc/resolv.conf file:

```
domain xyz.com
nameserver 164.109.1.3
nameserver 164.109.10.23
```

The first line specifies your system's domain name. The nameserver line provides the IP addresses of name servers for your domain. If you have multiple
name servers, you should list them on separate lines. They are queried in the
order in which they appear in the file.

If you do not have any name server for your network, you can safely ignore
this file. TCP/IP should still work, even though you may not be able to refer to
hosts by name.

/etc/hosts.allow

This file specifies which hosts are allowed to use the Internet services (such
as TELNET and FTP) running on your system. As explained in the section
"The xinetd super server," the TCP wrapper consults the /etc/hosts.allow
file before starting Internet services. It starts the service only if the entries in
the hosts.allow file imply that the requesting host is allowed to use the
services.

The entries in /etc/hosts.allow are in the form of a *server:IP address*
format, where *server* refers to the name of the program providing a specific
Internet service, and *IP address* identifies the host allowed to use that service. For example, if you want all hosts in your local network (which has the
class C address 192.168.1.0) to access the FTP service (which is provided by
the in.ftpd program), you would add the following line in the
/etc/hosts.allow file:

```
in.ftpd:192.168.1.
```

If you want to let all local hosts have access to all Internet services, you can
use the ALL keyword and rewrite the line as follows:

```
ALL:192.168.1.
```

Finally, to open up all Internet services to all hosts, you can replace the
IP address with ALL, as follows:

```
ALL:ALL
```

You can also use host names in place of IP addresses.

To learn the detailed syntax of the entries in the /etc/hosts.allow file, type
man hosts.allow at the Linux shell prompt.

/etc/hosts.deny

This file is just the opposite of /etc/hosts.allow—whereas hosts.allow specifies which hosts may access Internet services (such as TELNET and FTP) on your system, the hosts.deny file identifies the hosts that must be denied services. As explained in the section "The xinetd super server," the TCP wrapper consults the /etc/hosts.deny file if it does not find any rules in the /etc/hosts.allow file that apply to the requesting host. The tcpd program denies service if it finds in the hosts.deny file a rule that applies to the host.

The entries in /etc/hosts.deny file follow the same format as those in the /etc/hosts.allow file—they are in the form of a *server:IP address* format, where *server* refers to the name of the program providing a specific Internet service and *IP address* identifies the host allowed to use that service.

If you have already set up entries in the /etc/hosts.allow file to allow access to specific hosts, you can place the following line in /etc/hosts.deny to deny all other hosts access to any service on your system:

```
ALL:ALL
```

Tip

To learn the detailed syntax of the entries in the /etc/hosts.deny file, type man hosts.deny at the Linux shell prompt.

/etc/nsswitch.conf

This file, known as the name service switch (NSS) file, specifies how services such as the name resolver library, NIS, NIS+, and local configuration files, such as /etc/hosts and /etc/shadow interact. Newer versions of Linux that use GNU C Library version 2 (glibc 2) or later, rely on the /etc/nsswitch.conf file to determine what takes precedence: a local configuration file, or a service such as DNS or NIS (see Chapter 21 to learn more about DNS and NIS).

As an example, the following hosts entry in the /etc/nsswitch.conf file specifies that the resolver library should first try the /etc/hosts file, then try NIS+, and finally try DNS:

```
hosts:        files nisplus dns
```

You can learn more about the /etc/nsswitch.conf file and what it does by typing info libc "Name Service Switch" in a terminal window.

Configuring Networks at Boot Time

You want to start your network automatically every time you boot the system. For this to happen, you have to put the appropriate commands in one or more startup scripts. The init process runs immediately after Linux boots. The process consults the /etc/inittab file and then executes various commands (typically, shell scripts), depending on the current run level. In run level 3—the multi-user level—/etc/inittab specifies that init should run the script file /etc/rc.d/rc with the argument 3.

Essentially, the startup script ends up executing the script file /etc/rc.d/ init.d/network to activate all networking interfaces. If you consult the /etc/rc.d/init.d/network file, you will notice that network initialization is done by using another set of files in the /etc/sysconfig directory. The network activation script checks the variables defined in the /etc/sysconfig/network file to decide whether to activate the network. In /etc/ sysconfig/network, you should see a line with the NETWORKING variable as follows:

```
NETWORKING=yes
```

The network is activated only if the NETWORKING variable is set to yes.

The /etc/rc.d/init.d/network script, in turn, executes a number of scripts in the /etc/sysconfig/network-scripts directory to activate specific network interfaces. For example, to activate the Ethernet interface eth0, the /etc/sysconfig/network-scripts/ifup script is executed with /etc/sysconfig/network-scripts/ifcfg-eth0 as the configuration file. Here is what a typical /etc/sysconfig/network-scripts/ifcfg-eth0 file contains:

```
DEVICE=eth0
IPADDR=192.168.1.200
NETMASK=255.255.255.0
BROADCAST=192.168.1.255
ONBOOT=yes
BOOTPROTO=none
```

As you can see, this file contains the network device name, as well as the IP address of the interface and several other TCP/IP parameters. The ONBOOT variable indicates whether this network interface should be activated when Linux boots. If your PC has an Ethernet card, you would want to activate the interface at boot time; therefore, ONBOOT is set to yes.

Cross-Reference

The files in the /etc/sysconfig directory are created by the Red Hat Linux installation program as you install Linux, following the steps outlined in Chapter 2.

The /etc/sysconfig/network-scripts/ifup script essentially runs the following commands:

- /sbin/ifconfig, to configure the specified network interface; in this case, the Ethernet card (eth0)

- /sbin/route, to set up the routing table for the activated network interface

TCP/IP Diagnostics

After you configure Ethernet and TCP/IP (during Red Hat Linux installation or by running netcfg later on), you should be able to use various networking applications without any problem. The TCP/IP protocol suite includes several tools that help you monitor and diagnose problems.

Checking the Interfaces

Use the /sbin/ifconfig command to view the currently configured network interfaces. The ifconfig command is used to configure a network interface (that is, to associate an IP address with a network device). If you run ifconfig without any command-line arguments, the command displays information about the current network interfaces. Following are a typical invocation of ifconfig and the resulting output:

```
/sbin/ifconfig
eth0      Link encap:Ethernet   HWaddr 02:60:8C:8E:C6:A9
          inet addr:192.168.1.200  Bcast:192.168.1.255  Mask:255.255.255.0
          UP BROADCAST RUNNING MULTICAST  MTU:1500  Metric:1
          RX packets:3007 errors:0 dropped:0 overruns:0 frame:0
          TX packets:1140 errors:0 dropped:0 overruns:0 carrier:0
          collisions:0 txqueuelen:100
          Interrupt:5 Base address:0x300

lo        Link encap:Local Loopback
          inet addr:127.0.0.1  Mask:255.0.0.0
          UP LOOPBACK RUNNING  MTU:3924  Metric:1
          RX packets:54 errors:0 dropped:0 overruns:0 frame:0
          TX packets:54 errors:0 dropped:0 overruns:0 carrier:0
          collisions:0 txqueuelen:0
```

This output shows that two interfaces — the loopback interface (lo) and an Ethernet card (eth0) — are currently active on this system. For each interface, you can see the IP address, as well as statistics on packets delivered and sent. For the Ethernet card, ifconfig also reports the IRQ (shown as Interrupt: 5) and the base I/O port address (0x300). If the Red Hat Linux system had a dial-up PPP link up and running, you'd also see an item for the ppp0 interface in the output.

Checking the IP Routing Table

The other network configuration command, /sbin/route, also provides status information when it is run without any command-line argument. If you are having trouble checking a connection to another host (that you specify with an IP address), check the IP routing table to see whether a default gateway is specified. Then check the gateway's routing table to ensure that paths to an outside network appear in that routing table.

A typical output from the /sbin/route command looks like the following:

```
/sbin/route
Kernel IP routing table
Destination    Gateway        Genmask          Flags Metric Ref   Use Iface
192.168.1.200  *              255.255.255.255  UH    0      0     0 eth0
192.168.1.0    *              255.255.255.0    U     0      0     0 eth0
127.0.0.0      *              255.0.0.0        U     0      0     0 lo
default        192.168.1.1    0.0.0.0          UG    0      0     0 eth0
```

As this routing table shows, the local network uses the eth0 Ethernet interface, and the default gateway is also that Ethernet interface. The *default gateway* is a routing device that handles packets addressed to any network, other than the one in which the Linux system resides. In this example, packets addressed to any network address other than ones that begin with 192.168.1 are sent to the gateway — 192.168.1.1. The gateway forwards those packets to other networks (assuming, of course, that the gateway is connected to another network).

Checking Connectivity to a Host

To check for a network path to a specific host, use the ping command. Ping is a widely used TCP/IP tool that uses a series of Internet Control Message Protocol (ICMP, often pronounced as *eye-comp*) messages. (ICMP provides for an Echo message to which every host responds.) Using the ICMP messages and replies, Ping can determine whether the other system is alive, and can compute the round-trip delay in communicating with that system.

The following example shows how I run ping to see whether one of the systems on my network is alive:

```
ping 192.168.1.50
PING 192.168.1.50 (192.168.1.50): 56 data bytes
64 bytes from 192.168.1.50: icmp_seq=0 ttl=32 time=2.2 ms
64 bytes from 192.168.1.50: icmp_seq=1 ttl=32 time=1.2 ms
64 bytes from 192.168.1.50: icmp_seq=2 ttl=32 time=1.2 ms
64 bytes from 192.168.1.50: icmp_seq=3 ttl=32 time=0.8 ms

--- 192.168.1.50 ping statistics ---
4 packets transmitted, 4 packets received, 0% packet loss
round-trip min/avg/max = 0.8/1.3/2.2 ms
```

In Red Hat Linux, ping continues to run until you press Ctrl+C to stop it; then it displays summary statistics showing the typical time it takes to send a packet between the two systems. On some systems, ping simply reports that a remote host is alive. However, you can still get the timing information with appropriate command-line arguments.

Checking Network Status

To check the status of the network, use the netstat command. This command displays the status of network connections of various types (such as TCP and UDP connections). You can view the status of the interfaces quickly with the -i option, as follows:

```
netstat -i
Kernel Interface table
Iface MTU Met RX-OK RX-ERR RX-DRP RX-OVR  TX-OK TX-ERR TX-DRP TX-OVR Flg
eth0 1500  0  3279      0      0      0   1269      0      0      0 BRU
lo   3924  0    62      0      0      0     62      0      0      0 LRU
```

In this case, the output shows the current status of the loopback and Ethernet interfaces. Table 8-3 describes the meanings of the columns.

Table 8-3: Columns in the Kernel Interface Table

Column	Meaning
Iface	Name of the interface
MTU	Maximum Transfer Unit — the maximum number of bytes that a packet can contain
RX-OK, TX-OK (TX)	Number of error-free packets received (RX) or transmitted
RX-ERR, TX-ERR	Number of packets with errors
RX-DRP, TX-DRP	Number of dropped packets
RX-OVR, TX-OVR	Number of packets lost due to overflow
Flags	A = receive multicast, B = broadcast allowed, D = debugging turned on, L = loopback interface (notice the flag on lo), M = all packets received, N = trailers avoided, O = no ARP on this interface, P = point-to-point interface, R = interface is running, and U = interface is up

Another useful `netstat` option is `-t`, which shows all active TCP connections. Following is a typical result of `netstat -t` on one of my Linux PCs:

```
netstat -t
Active Internet connections (w/o servers)
Proto Recv-Q Send-Q Local Address           Foreign Address         State
tcp      624      0 lnbp200:1147            IWIN.nws.noaa.gov:www   CLOSE_WAIT
tcp        0      0 lnbp200:1146            tgftp.nws.noaa.gov:www  ESTABLISHED
tcp        0    126 lnbp200:telnet          lnbp400:1059            ESTABLISHED
```

In this case, the output columns show the protocol (`Proto`), the number of bytes in the receive and transmit queues (`Recv-Q`, `Send-Q`), the local TCP port in *hostname:service* format (`Local Address`), the remote port (`Foreign Address`), and the state of the connection.

Summary

Linux has extensive built-in support for TCP/IP and Ethernet networks. Thinwire Ethernet, which uses flexible RG-58 coaxial cables, provides a convenient way to set up a small network, because you can simply daisy-chain the PCs together. This chapter explains the basics of TCP/IP and Ethernet; it also shows you how to set up TCP/IP networking on your Linux PC.

By reading this chapter, you learn the following things:

▶ The OSI seven-layer model provides a framework for making various networks work together. The OSI layered model also sets the stage for various networking protocols.

▶ The Transmission Control Protocol and Internet Protocol (TCP/IP) originated from research initiated by the U.S. Government's Advanced Research Projects Agency (ARPA) in the 1970s. The modern Internet evolved from the networking technology developed during that time.

▶ All Internet protocols are documented in Requests for Comments (RFC) documents. The RFCs are available from the Internet resource `http://www.cis.ohio-state.edu/hypertext/information/rfc.html`. All standards are in RFCs, but many RFCs simply provide information to the Internet community.

▶ Internetworking is at the heart of the TCP/IP protocol; that is the purpose of the Internet Protocol. The TCP/IP protocol identifies a host with a 32-bit IP address that has two parts: a network address and a host address.

▶ An IP address typically is expressed in dotted-decimal notation, in which each byte's value is written in decimal format and separated from the adjacent byte by a dot (.). A typical IP address is 140.90.141.131.

▶ IP addresses are grouped in classes. Class A addresses use a one-byte network address and three bytes for the host address; class B addresses use a two-byte network and host address; and class C addresses use a three-byte network address and a single byte for the host address. The values of the first byte indicate the type of address: 1–126 are class A, 128–191 are class B, and 192–223 are class C.

▶ The IP address space is filling rapidly. To alleviate this problem, the Internet Engineering Task Force has adopted a new 16-byte (128-bit) addressing scheme known as IPv6 (or IP version 6). Hosts that use the new IPv6 addresses will work with hosts that use the older IPv4 (32-bit) addresses.

▶ Ethernet is a popular physical data-transport mechanism. Several Ethernet standards exist, each of which uses a different type of cable. The 10Base5 Ethernet (the original Ethernet) uses thick coaxial cables, 10Base2 uses thin coaxial cables, and 10BaseT uses unshielded twisted-pair (UTP), or telephone cables. Thinwire Ethernet (10Base2) is easy to implement and convenient for small office networks.

▶ You need an Ethernet card on your PC to connect to an Ethernet network. Linux supports a wide variety of Ethernet cards. You should buy a 16-bit Ethernet card for good performance.

▶ Setting up TCP/IP on Linux requires setting up various configuration files. The Red Hat network configuration program (`/usr/bin/netcfg`) provides a convenient way to set up these files. You need some information — such as an IP address, the address of a gateway, and the address of a name server — to set up TCP/IP networking on your system. If you do not plan to connect your local network to the Internet, you can use a range of IP addresses (such as 192.168.0.0 to 192.168.255.255) without having to coordinate with any organization.

▶ Linux comes with many TCP/IP utilities, such as `ftp` (File Transfer Protocol) and `telnet` (for logging in to another system on the network).

▶ To diagnose TCP/IP networking problems, you can use the `ping`, `route`, and `netstat` commands.

Chapter 9

Laptops and PC Cards

In This Chapter

▶ Introducing PCMCIA

▶ Understanding PC Cards

▶ Looking at typical uses of PC Cards

▶ Activating the PCMCIA Card Services for Linux

▶ Looking at PC Cards that Card Services for Linux supports

▶ Obtaining the latest information about Card Services for Linux

▶ Installing Red Hat Linux on laptop computers

Laptop computers typically include PCMCIA slots for attaching peripherals. PCMCIA stands for Personal Computer Memory Card International Association, a non-profit organization that has standardized the interface for adding memory cards to laptop computers. Although originally conceived for memory cards, PCMCIA devices became popular for a wide variety of add-ons for laptops. Today, laptop computers use many PCMCIA devices, such as modems, network cards, SCSI controllers, and sound cards. Using Linux on a laptop means having to deal with the PCMCIA devices, or PC Cards, as the popular press calls them nowadays. Thanks to the efforts of David Hinds, you can now use PCMCIA devices under Linux with his PCMCIA Card Services for Linux. This chapter briefly describes the PCMCIA support package for Linux and also provides information on running Linux on laptop computers.

Note

I refer to the actual cards as *PC Cards*, because that's the proper name for the devices. PCMCIA refers to the industry organization that specifies the standard for PC Cards. However, I use the term PCMCIA Card in one context — when referring to PCMCIA Card Services for Linux (or Card Services, for short), which is the software that supports PC Cards under Linux.

PC Card Basics

PC Cards originated as *static random access memory* (SRAM) and *flash RAM* cards that were used to store data on small laptop computers. The credit-card-sized cards fit into a slot on the side of the laptop. The flash memory cards used *electrically erasable programmable read-only memory* (EEPROM) to provide laptop storage capability that might have been too small for other conventional storage media.

Vendors soon realized the convenience of the memory-card slot as a general-purpose expansion slot for laptop computers. The Personal Computer Memory Card International Association (PCMCIA) standardized various aspects of PC Cards, including the electrical interface, card dimensions, and card-slot sizes. This standardization has contributed to the proliferation of PC Cards in the laptop market.

By now, PCMCIA slots are a feature of almost all laptops, and the memory card is a small part of the overall PC Card market. Most laptops provide PCMCIA slots, so that users can add hardware, such as fax/modems, sound cards, network cards, SCSI cards, and even hard disks.

Tip

To learn more about PCMCIA (the association) and PC Card specifications, point your favorite World Wide Web browser to `http://www.pc-card.com/`. Particularly, read the PC Card FAQ (Frequently Asked Questions) at `http://www.pc-card.com/faq.htm`.

PC Card Physical Specifications

PC Cards are divided into three different classifications, according to the thickness of the card. Following are the standard physical dimensions for each type of PC Card, in terms of width by length by thickness:

- Type I PC Card: 54 mm by 85.6 mm by 3.3 mm
- Type II PC Card: 54 mm by 85.6 mm by 5 mm
- Type III PC Card: 54 mm by 85.6 mm by 10.5 mm

All three types of PC Cards have the same length and width—the size of a standard credit card, except that credit card corners are rounded. The cards, however, are thicker than credit cards, and the card types are differentiated by thickness.

The term *form factor* is often used to refer to the dimensions of PC Cards.

All PC Cards use the same 68-pin connector. Because of this connector, a thinner card (Type I, for example) can be used in a thicker slot (Type II, for example). As you might guess, a thicker card cannot be used in a thinner slot, because you cannot physically insert a thick card into a thin slot.

PC-Card Use

Each type of PC Card is used for a specific type of application. Following are the typical applications of PC Cards, by card type:

- *Type I PC Card*—These thin cards are used for memory devices, such as static RAM (SRAM) and flash RAM.

- *Type II PC Card*—These cards are used for input and output (I/O) devices, such as fax/modems, network adapters, and sound cards.

- *Type III PC Card*—These cards are used for devices that need the added thickness, such as hard disks with rotating components (hard to believe, isn't it?).

A PC Card can have a maximum length of 135.6 mm (slightly longer than 5.25 inches), meaning that the card can extend outside the host. Such extended cards are used for devices such as removable media, transceivers, and antennas.

PCMCIA Standards

All these specifications are described in the PCMCIA Standard, of which there have been three major releases:

- *PCMCIA Standard Release 1.0 (June 1990)*—The initial standard defined the 68-pin connector and Type I and Type II PC Cards. This standard also defined the Card Information Structure (CIS) that has been the basis for interoperability of PC Cards. The first release of the PCMCIA Standard did not account for any I/O cards; only memory cards were considered.

- *PCMCIA Standard Release 2.0, 2.01, 2.1 (1991–94)*—The second release of the standard defined an I/O interface for the 68-pin connector. Release 2.01 added the PC Card AT Attachment (ATA) specification and provided an initial version of the Card and Socket Services (CSS) Specification. Release 2.1 further enhanced the CSS Specification.

- *PC Card Standard (February 1995)*—The current release of the standard has a new name: it is called the PC Card Standard, instead of the PCMCIA Standard. This release of the standard adds information to improve compatibility among different types of PC Cards and includes support for features, such as 3.3 volt operation, DMA support, and 32-bit CardBus bus mastering.

PC Card Terminology

As all laptop vendors adopt PC Card slots, the PC Card market has experienced explosive growth. Thanks to the PCMCIA Standards, the PC Card devices can be used in any PC Card slot. As you use PC Cards, you'll run into some special terms, including the following:

- *Card Information Structure (CIS)* describes the characteristics and capabilities of a PC Card, so that the operating system or driver software can configure the card.

- *CardBus* is an electrical specification that describes the use of 32-bit bus mastering technology and enables PC Cards to operate at up to 33 MHz.

- *Direct Memory Access (DMA)* has the same meaning as in other peripherals; now PC Cards can use DMA technology.

- *Execute In Place (XIP)* refers to the feature that enables operating-system and application software to run directly from the PC Card without having to be loaded into the system's RAM, which eliminates the need for too much system RAM.

- *Low Voltage Operation* refers to the capability of PC Cards to operate at 3.3 volts (as well as at five volts). The connector has a physical key to ensure that you cannot inadvertently insert a 3.3-volt card into a five-volt slot.

- *Multifunction Capability* enables a PC Card to support several functions. 3Com's 3C562, for example, is a 10Base-T Ethernet card and a 28,800-bps modem in a Type II form-factor PC Card.

- *Plug and Play* enables you to insert or remove a PC Card while the system is turned on (this is known as *hot-swapping*). You can hot-swap PC Cards by making the power-connection pins the longest, so that the data lines disconnect before the power.

- *Power Management* refers to the capability of PC Cards to interface with the Advanced Power Management (APM) capabilities of laptops through the Card Services Specification.

- *Zoomed Video (ZV)* refers to a connection between a PC Card and the system's video controller that enables the card to write video data directly to the video controller.

PCMCIA Card Services for Linux

The standardization of PC Cards means that Linux developers can get their hands on the programming information that they need to write device drivers for PC Cards. In particular, the Card Services Specification provides an Application Programming Interface (API) that's independent of the hardware that controls the PC Card sockets — the receptacles or slots for PC Cards.

The Socket Services Specification, a related specification, also provides an API that enables software applications to access the hardware that controls the sockets for PC Cards.

You do not have to learn about the PC Card and Socket Services APIs. David Hinds has already done the work in his PCMCIA Card Services for Linux, a software package that you can use to access PC Card devices under Linux. All you need to do is turn on the PCMCIA support when you need it.

Activating Card Services

PCMCIA Card Services software should already be installed on your system because Red Hat Linux includes PCMCIA support. In Red Hat Linux, the following files control the activation of the Card Services:

- `/etc/rc.d/init.d/pcmcia` is the shell script that starts the PCMCIA Card Services. Essentially, the command `/etc/rc.d/init.d/pcmcia start` activates the Card Services when you boot the system. The script loads the appropriate PCMCIA driver modules using the `/sbin/ insmod` command. Then the script runs the `/sbin/cardmgr` program, which handles all card-insertion and card-removal events. Running the `cardmgr` program enables you to hot-swap PC Cards, so that you can insert or eject a card at any time. To stop Card Services, type `/etc/rc.d/init.d/pcmcia stop`.

- `/etc/sysconfig/pcmcia` contains a number of variables that are used by the `/etc/rc.d/init.d/pcmcia` script. In particular, the Card Services are not activated unless the line `PCMCIA=yes` appears in the `/etc/sysconfig/pcmcia` file. If your system does not have any PCMCIA devices, you will find the line `PCMCIA=no`.

You can activate the Card Services at system startup by ensuring that the line `PCMCIA=yes` appears in the `/etc/sysconfig/pcmcia` file. Of course, you want to do this only if your PC has a PCMCIA slot (most laptop PCs do).

Using the cardctl Program

If you have PCMCIA Card Services running, you can use the `/sbin/cardctl` program to monitor and control a PCMCIA socket. To view the status of a PCMCIA slot, type:

```
/sbin/cardctl status
```

The output should show the current socket-status flags.

The `cardctl` program takes many more arguments. With different arguments, you can suspend a card, resume it, or view the configuration parameters, such as interrupts and configuration registers. To learn more about `cardctl` from the online manual, type `man cardctl` to view the manual page.

Using Supported PC Cards

In the PCMCIA Card Services documentation directory, you'll find a file named SUPPORTED.CARDS. (You can change to that directory by typing `cd /usr/share/doc/kernel-pcmcia*`.) That file lists all the PCMCIA Cards that are known to work with at least one system.

The list of supported cards has become too numerous to include here. The categories of cards supported by the Card Services are as follows:

- *Ethernet cards* — Close to a hundred different models of Ethernet cards are supported, including popular models such as 3Com 3c589, 3c589B, 3c589C, and 3c589D; Megahertz XJ10BT, and CC10BT; and Xircom CreditCard CE2.

- *Fast Ethernet (10/100BASET) cards* — Over 20 cards are supported, including 3Com 3c574TX, 3c575TX, 3CCFE575B, and 3CXFE575B; Linksys EtherFast 10/100; and Xircom CreditCard CE3.

- *Token Ring cards* — IBM Token Ring Adapter and 3Com 3c689 TokenLink III cards are supported.

- *Wireless network cards* — AT&T/NCR/Lucent WaveLAN version 2.0, DEC RoamAbout/DS, and Xircom CreditCard Netwave are supported.

- Modem and serial cards: All modem and serial-port cards should work. The only exceptions are modems such as Compaq 192, New Media WinSurfer, Megahertz XJ/CC2560, 3Com 3CXM356/3CCM356 and 3CXM656/3CCM656, and other WinModems that require special Windows drivers.

- *Memory cards* — All static RAM (SRAM) memory cards should work.

- *SCSI adapter cards* — Over 30 different models of SCSI cards are supported, including models such as Adaptec APA-1460, APA-1460A, APA-1450A, and APA-1460B SlimSCSI; IBM SCSI; Iomega Zip and Jaz Cards; NEC PC-9801N-J03R; and Toshiba NWB0107ABK and SCSC200B.

- *ATA/IDE disk drive cards* — All ATA/IDE disk-drive PC Cards are supported.

- *ATA/IDE CD-ROM adapter cards* — Many ATA/IDE CD-ROM adapters are supported, including Argosy EIDE CD-ROM; Caravelle CD-36N; Creative Technology CD-ROM; IBM Max 20X CD-ROM; Sony PCGA-CD5 CD-ROM; Digital Mobile Media CD-ROM; some EXP models; and several IO-DATA models.

- *Multifunction cards* — Several multifunction cards are supported, including 3Com 3c562, 3c562B/C/D, and 3c563B/C/D; IBM Home and Away Card; Linksys LANmodem 28.8, 33.6; Megahertz EM1144, EM3288, and EM3336; Motorola Mariner and Marquis; Ositech Jack of Diamonds; and Xircom CreditCard CEM28, CEM33, CEM56 models.

- *Other cards* — The Trimble Mobile GPS card is supported through the serial/modem driver.

For the latest list of supported cards, consult the SUPPORTED.CARDS file in the version of PCMCIA Card Services that you installed on your system (type `cd /usr/share/doc/kernel-pcmcia*` and then `more SUPPORTED_CARDS`).

Further Reading

To learn more about the PCMCIA Card Services software, you should consult the PCMCIA-HOWTO. To read this HOWTO document, type `cd /usr/share/doc/kernel-pcmcia*` to change to the directory where that HOWTO file is located (if you cannot find the file, type `locate PCMCIA-HOWTO` to find the file). Then type `more PCMCIA-HOWTO` to view the PCMCIA-HOWTO file. This file contains the latest information about the Card Services software, including common problems and suggested fixes.

In particular, you should look through the PCMCIA-HOWTO file for any information that applies to your specific PC Card.

Linux on Laptops

Laptops are more integrated than desktops are; a laptop's video card, monitor, and hard disk are all built into a compact package. In other words, you cannot easily mix and match components with laptops as you do with desktop systems, and so you have to make sure that Linux supports all components of your laptop system.

Most laptops with Intel 80386 or better processors should be able to run plain Linux. If you want to install XFree86 (X Window System), however, you may have some trouble, because the video card (on a laptop, video circuitry is built into the motherboard) and the pointing device must be supported by XFree86. With the Linux kernel versions 2.2 and later, you can use the VESA Frame Buffer console driver to get X working on most laptops, even if XFree86 doesn't natively support the laptop's graphics chipset. All you need to do is add a line such as vga=791 to the lilo.conf file to enable the VESA Frame Buffer console driver. Also, nowadays most laptop pointing devices can at least emulate a standard PS/2 Mouse, so all pointing devices should work with XFree86.

**Cross-
Reference**

Chapters 3 through 8 of this book cover individual components, such as the video card and monitors. This section provides some information about running Red Hat Linux on laptop PCs.

PCMCIA

Laptops typically include the PCMCIA interface through which you can connect many different peripheral devices to the laptop. As this chapter explains earlier, the version of Red Hat Linux on the companion CD-ROMs supports PCMCIA. The current PCMCIA drivers support many common PCMCIA controllers, such as Databook TCIC/2, Intel i82365SL, Cirrus PD67xx, and Vadem VG-468 chipsets. See previous sections in this chapter for a discussion of specific PC Cards that Linux supports.

More about Linux on Laptops

This chapter barely touches upon the subject of how to run Linux on laptops. As users install and run Linux on a variety of laptops, the user community's cumulative experience of Linux on laptops continues to grow. Much of this information is summarized and made available on the Web. For detailed information on how to install and run Linux on laptops, point your Web browser to the Linux on Laptops Home Page:

`http://www.cs.utexas.edu/users/kha rker/linux-laptop/`

This page includes links to many more Web pages, each documenting the details of how to install and run Linux on a specific laptop. In particular, you will find out if you have to do anything special to get Linux and X running on your laptop.

Advanced Power Management

Another laptop-specific feature is power management, which refers to the capability of a laptop to suspend its activities so as to conserve battery power. Laptops that have Advanced Power Management (APM) capability can suspend and resume power-consuming components (such as the display and hard drive), as well as provide information on battery life.

The version of Red Hat Linux on the companion CD-ROMs supports APM. You can learn more about how to support APM under Linux by visiting the Web site at http://www.worldvisions.ca/~apenwarr/apmd/.

Sound on Laptops

Many high-end laptops come with built-in sound. Using the sound capabilities under Linux is a straightforward process, provided that you can figure out what type of sound card your laptop has. Chapter 5 covers sound cards in detail.

As you learn in Chapter 5, the typical setup for Sound Blaster Pro is I/O address 0x220 (that's 220 in hexadecimal notation; the 0x prefix indicates hexadecimal in the C programming language), IRQ 5, and DMA 1. Thus, on any laptop (such as the NEC Versa P) with a SoundBlaster Pro–compatible sound card, you should configure the Linux kernel with a SoundBlaster Pro at I/O address 0x220, IRQ 5, and DMA 1. The Texas Instruments TravelMate 4000M has a built-in sound card that requires similar settings.

On the other hand, on a laptop (such as the NEC Versa M) with a Microsoft Sound System–compatible sound card, try the Microsoft Sound System at I/O address 0x530, IRQ 9, and DMA 3. As usual, you should check your laptop's documentation for clues about the make and model of the sound card before you set up sound support.

The bottom line is that you can set up Linux to support sound on a laptop the same way you can for a desktop PC. The first step is finding out what type of sound card your laptop has. Many laptops that have sound don't have sound hardware supported by Linux. For example, Linux does not have sound drivers for any of the laptops with Neomagic's combined video/sound chipsets. Of course, many laptops simply do not have sound capability, so this point may be moot for some laptop users.

X on Laptops

Users have reported success in running Linux together with XFree86 on many 386, 486, and Pentium laptops. Until recently, to run X on a laptop you had settle for the standard 16-color VGA server (XF86_VGA16), because XFree86 did not support many of the popular video chipsets used in laptops. Nowadays laptops support high-resolution LCD screens with capabilities on a par with those of desktop PCs, but the 16-color VGA server does not exploit the high-resolution capability. You have to be able to run the Super VGA X server (XF86_SVGA) to use 256 colors on a laptop.

Most laptops use one of the following types of video chipsets:

- NeoMagic NM20xx series chips
- Western Digital WD90C24 series chips
- Chips & Technology 655xx series chips
- Cirrus Logic CLGD6235, CLGD6440, CLGD7543, CLGD7548, and CLGD7555

Both XFree86 3.3.6 and XFree86 4.0.1 support most of these chipsets. The Chips & Technologies 65550 is popular on high-end laptops, such as NEC Versa 6200MMX. This chipset supports the Super VGA mode of 1,280 × 768 resolution with 64,000 colors.

Tip

If you plan to run X on a laptop, your best bet is to browse the list of laptops in the *Linux on Laptops* Web page (`http://www.cs.utexas.edu/users/kharker/linux-laptop/`) and select a laptop with a video chipset that XFree86 supports.

Summary

Developed as a way to attach memory cards to laptop computers, PC Cards have become a popular way to add new capabilities to laptops. If you use Linux on a laptop you need to access the PC Cards. Dave Hinds' PCMCIA Card Services for Linux provides you with a way to use PC Cards under Linux. This chapter described how to activate the Card Services for Linux software. In this chapter, you learned the following:

- ▶ PC Cards originated as credit-card-sized memory devices that plugged into a slot on the side of a laptop computer and provided a data-storage medium.

- ▶ The Personal Computer Memory Card International Association (PCMCIA) standardized various aspects of the PC Cards, including the electrical interface, the card dimensions, and the card-slot sizes.

- ▶ Nowadays, PC Cards are used widely in laptops as an expansion slot for many devices, such as network adapters, fax/modem cards, SCSI controllers, sound cards, and even hard disks.

- ▶ There are three types of PC Cards: Types I, II, and III. All types of cards have the same length and width (54 mm by 85.6 mm) — the length and width of a standard credit card. The types differ in thickness. Type I is the thinnest (3.3 mm), and Type III is the thickest (10.5 mm).

- ▶ Red Hat Linux includes Dave Hinds' PCMCIA Card Services for Linux. You can find a list of supported PC Cards in the SUPPORTED.CARDS file. (Type `cd/usr/share/doc/kernel-pcmcia*` to change to the relevant directory. Also read the PCMCIA-HOWTO file in that directory.)

▶ Laptops are a special breed of computer, because all parts of a laptop—from the hard disk to the video card—are tightly integrated. Linux runs on many laptops. The main problem with running Linux on laptops is support for laptop-specific features, such as Advanced Power Management (APM) and PCMCIA or PC Card interfaces. Another problem is running X on a laptop, because laptop video chipsets are not as well supported by XFree86 as desktop PCs' video cards are. Nevertheless, Linux and X run on a wide variety of laptops. In fact, Linux will run on almost any new laptop.

Part II

Exploring Red Hat Linux

# Chapter 10

Red Hat Linux Basics

In This Chapter

▶ Running Red Hat Linux for the first time

▶ Looking up online documentation

▶ Understanding the Linux directory structure

▶ Using Linux commands to work with files

▶ Understanding shells: the command interpreters of Linux

▶ Looking at Bash (the Bourne Again Shell)

Now that you have installed Red Hat Linux from this book's companion CD-ROMs, you are ready to explore and learn the basics of Red Hat Linux. This chapter shows you how to log in, log out, and shutdown your Linux system. Then you will power up again and learn about Linux commands.

Although Red Hat Linux comes with the GNOME and KDE graphical user interfaces, you can't do everything from the graphical environment. It's not impossible to design a graphical interface that enables you to perform most chores, but sometimes you may have to perform system administration tasks when the graphical environment is not available. You may be logged in through a terminal session, or you may have problems with X. In such cases, you have to use Linux commands to accomplish specific tasks.

This chapter also shows you how to work with files and directories in Red Hat Linux. To use files and directories, you need to understand the concept of a hierarchical file system. The chapter provides a quick introduction to the Linux file system. Then you learn to explore the file system with the graphical file manager (both GNOME and KDE comes with file managers). Finally, you learn several Linux commands that you can use to work with files and directories.

Starting Red Hat Linux for the First Time

After the installation is complete, the Red Hat Linux installation program automatically reboots the system. The PC goes through its normal power-up sequence and loads LILO from the C: drive. A graphical screen appears with

the names of the partitions that LILO can boot. You can press the up and
down arrow keys to select the partition from which LILO should boot. When
you installed LILO, if you specified the Linux partition as the default one, you
can simply wait; after a few seconds, LILO boots Linux.

To get the text-mode LILO prompt, press Ctrl+X. The following prompt
appears:

```
LILO boot:
```

You can view the names of the available bootable partitions by pressing the
Tab key. For example, a typical result of pressing Tab might be the following:

```
linux dos
```

Then you can type the name of the partition from which LILO should boot.

Sometimes you need the text-mode LILO boot prompt so that you can specify
boot-time arguments that LILO passes to the Linux kernel. For example, if you
want to mount your root file system read-only so that you can run the file system consistency checking program (called fsck), you can specify this by typing the following line in response to the LILO boot prompt:

```
linux ro
```

What Is BogoMIPS?

When your Linux system boots, you notice a
message that says `Calibrating delay loop... 398.13 BogoMIPS`, with some
number before `BogoMIPS`. BogoMIPS is one
of those words that confound new Linux users.
In this sidebar, you'll learn what it means.

As you may know, *MIPS* is an acronym for *millions of instructions per second* — a measure
of how fast your computer runs programs. As
such, MIPS is not a very good measure of
performance, because comparing the MIPS
of different types of computers is difficult.
BogoMIPS is *bogus MIPS*, which refers to an
indication of the computer's speed. Linux uses
the *BogoMIPS* number to calibrate a delay
loop, in which the computer processes
some instructions repeatedly, until a specified
amount of time has passed.

The *BogoMIPS* numbers can range anywhere
from 1 to 300 or more, depending on the type of
processor (386, 486, or Pentium). A typical
33MHz 80386DX system has a *BogoMIPS* of
about 6, whereas a 66MHz 80486DX2/66 system shows a *BogoMIPS* of about 33. The
BogoMIPS for older Pentium systems is on a
par with (or slightly less than) that of 80486
processors, because the *BogoMIPS* calcula-
tion does not take advantage of any advanced
features of the Pentium (such as the capability
to execute instructions in parallel). On an old
75MHz Pentium system, Linux reports a
BogoMIPS of 30.22. However, on a 200MHz
Pentium MMX system, the *BogoMIPS* is
398.13. It's higher yet on more recent 600 and
750MHz Pentium systems.

Secret

Note that after you boot your Linux system with the root file system mounted read-only, no processes can write to the file system until you remount the file system again with the `mount -w -n -o remount /` command. To learn more about LILO boot parameters, type `man bootparam`.

After LILO boots Linux, you should see a long list of opening messages, including the names of the devices that Linux detects. One of the first few messages says `Calibrating delay loop... 398.13 BogoMIPS`; the number that precedes `BogoMIPS` depends on your system's processor type. *BogoMIPS* is a Linux jargon term that is the subject of countless discussions in various newsgroups devoted to Linux. (You'll learn more about newsgroups in Chapter 19.) Linux uses the BogoMIPS measurement in situations in which the operating system has to wait for a specified period.

At the end of all the messages, you see a graphical login screen, such as the one shown in Figure 10-1.

The window in the middle of the screen displays a welcome message with your system's host name — the name you assign to your system when you configure the network. If the network is not configured, `localhost. localdomain` is used as the host name.

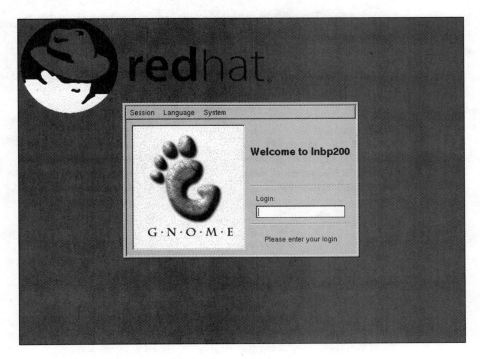

Figure 10-1: Graphical login screen in Red Hat Linux

You can log in using any of the accounts that you defined during the installation, including root. For example, to log in as root, type **root** in the first text field and press Enter (move the mouse over the login dialog box before you begin typing). Then type the root password (the one you set during installation) to log in as the super user.

Cross-Reference

If you forgot the root password, see Chapter 15 for a procedure that enables you to set up a new root password.

Because the default GUI is GNOME, the GNOME desktop appears, along with a warning dialog box from the GNOME File Manager. Click the OK button to dismiss the warning dialog box. The GNOME Hints window appears and you get a desktop (as shown in Figure 10-2) that's similar to the Windows desktop. Now you can perform a few initial chores and learn how to shut down your Red Hat Linux system.

Figure 10-2: Initial GNOME desktop after logging in as root

Take a moment to look at the initial GNOME desktop as it appears in Figure 10-2. The GNOME desktop is very much like the Windows 95/98/2000 desktop. The GNOME Panel — similar to the Windows taskbar — appears along the bottom edge of the screen. You can access various menus and launch applications from the GNOME Panel. The Panel also contains such applets as the Clock applet, which displays the time in a small area at the right edge of the Panel.

Cross-Reference

You will learn more about the GNOME desktop in Chapter 12. For now, all you need to know is that the stylized foot at the left edge of the GNOME Panel is the Main Menu button. This button is like the Start button in Windows 95/98/NT/2000. You can access many programs (including the Linuxconf tool for system configuration and the dialog box that enables you to log out) from the Main Menu button, or the "foot."

You learn more about the GNOME desktop later in this chapter and again in Chapter 12. The following sections show you how to log out of and shut down your Red Hat Linux system.

Logging Out

Now that you have seen how to log in, you should learn how to log out. To log out, select Main Menu (the foot icon) ⇨ Log Out. The screen is grayed out and a dialog box asks you if you really want to log out. Click the Yes button to log out.

After a few moments, the graphical login screen (refer to Figure 10-1) appears so that another user can log in and use the system.

Shutting Down Linux

When you are ready to shut down Red Hat Linux, you should do so in an orderly manner. Even if you are the sole user of a Linux system, several other programs are usually running in the background. In addition, operating systems such as Linux try to optimize the way in which they write data to the disk. Because disk access is relatively slow (compared with the time needed to access memory locations), data usually is held in memory and written to the disk in large chunks. Therefore, if you simply turn the power off, you run the risk that some files will not be updated properly.

Any user (you do not have to be logged in) can shut down the system from the graphical login screen. The System menu in the login window provides menu options for rebooting or halting the system. To shut down the system, simply select System → Halt, as shown in Figure 10-3.

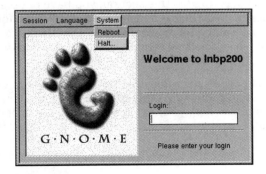

Figure 10-3: Selecting the menu option to halt your Red Hat Linux system

Another dialog box asks you to confirm if you really want to halt the system. Click the Yes button. The system then shuts down in an orderly manner.

As the system shuts down, you will see messages about processes being shut down. You may be surprised how many processes there are, even though no one is explicitly running any programs on the system. If your system does not automatically power off on shut down, you can manually turn the power off.

If you are already logged in as root, you can use the `shutdown` command to halt or reboot the system. If you are already logged in using another user name, you can become super user by typing the following command (your input is shown in boldface; my comments are in italic):

```
su
Password:    (type the root password and press Enter)
```

After you become super user, type the following command to halt the system:

```
/sbin/shutdown -h now
```

After a few moments, you see many more messages about processes being stopped. On older systems, you will see a message about the system being halted. You can then turn the power off. On newer systems, the shutdown process also turns the power off.

If you want to reboot the system instead of halting it, use the `shutdown` command with the `-r` option, as follows:

```
/sbin/shutdown -r now
```

Looking Up Online Documentation

You should familiarize yourself with an important source of information in Red Hat Linux. Every so often, you see instructions that ask you to enter a Linux command. After a while, you are bound to get to the point at which you vaguely recall a command's name, but you cannot remember the exact syntax of what you are supposed to type. This is a situation in which the Linux online manual pages can come to your rescue.

Tip

To try out the commands described in this section, you have to open a terminal window in GNOME. Click the terminal icon (next to the N for Netscape) in the Main Panel along the bottom edge of the GNOME desktop (see Figure 10-2). This opens a terminal window in which you can type Linux commands.

You can view the manual page — commonly referred to as the *man page* — for a command by using the `man` command. (You do have to remember *that* command in order to access online help.) For example, to view the man page for the `modprobe` command, type the following command in a terminal window:

```
man modprobe
```

The man command then displays the help information page-by-page. Press the Spacebar to move to the next page. Press **b** to move backward by a page. To look for a specific word in the man page, press the forward slash, type the word, and press Enter. For example, to search for the word "debug," type /debug and press Enter. When you finish reading the man page, press **q** to return to the Linux command prompt.

Having touted the usefulness of the online help pages, I must point out that the term *Linux command* refers to any executable file, ranging from a script file that contains other Linux commands, to standard Linux executable programs. Although man pages exist for most standard programs, many programs do not have any online help. Nevertheless, whenever you are having difficulty recalling some command, it is worthwhile to use the man command to see whether any online help for that command exists.

If you do not want to read the full man page, you can use whatis to read a one-line summary of a command. For example, here's how you use whatis to see a brief description of the modprobe command:

```
whatis modprobe
modprobe                (8)  - high level handling of loadable module
```

The number (8) indicates the man page section where the modprobe command is listed. You should try the whatis command to view one-line descriptions of a few other commands.

You can use the shell's wildcard feature and the whatis command to explore the files in various system directories such as /bin, /sbin, /usr/sbin, /usr/bin, and so on. Simply change the directory to one of interest and type whatis * to view one-line descriptions of the programs in that directory. (whatis displays information for those programs for which such information is available.) For example, here is how you can explore the /sbin directory:

```
cd /sbin; whatis * | more
arp                     (7)  - Linux ARP kernel module
arp                     (8)  - manipulate the system ARP cache
askrunlevel: nothing appropriate
badblocks               (8)  - search a device for bad blocks
cardctl                 (8)  - PCMCIA card control utility
cardmgr                 (8)  - PCMCIA device manager
... rest of the output not shown ...
```

As you can see, the output is an alphabetic list of all programs in the current directory, along with the one-line descriptions where available. The whatis command displays a message saying nothing appropriate if there is no information available for a program.

The man and whatis commands are useful when you know the name of a command. If you do not know the exact name of a command, you can use the apropos command to search for a command by a keyword (or even a part of a word). For example, if you remember that the command contains the word probe, type the following apropos command to search:

```
apropos probe
modprobe          (8)  - high level handling of loadable modules
pnpprobe          (8)  - scan ISA bus for PnP sound cards
SuperProbe        (1x) - probe for and identify installed video hardware
```

In this case, the search result shows three candidate commands, each with a brief description. You can then select the command that does what you want to do.

Tip

If `apropos` displays a long list of commands that scroll by too fast for you to read, you can type `apropos` *keyword* `| more` to view the output one screen at a time.

Another form of online documentation that you can refer to are the HOWTO files, which you can access by visiting the Linux Documentation Project (LDP) Web site `http://www.redhat.com/mirrors/LDP/`. (Click the big "N" icon on the GNOME Panel to launch Netscape Communicator.) On that Web page you'll find, among other things, links to Frequently Asked Questions (FAQs) and HOWTOs. You can click the HOWTOs link and download (or read) HOWTO documents in several formats, including text and HTML. For example, if you click to view plain-text HOWTOs, the Web browser shows a list of over 200 HOWTO files (see Figure 10-4).

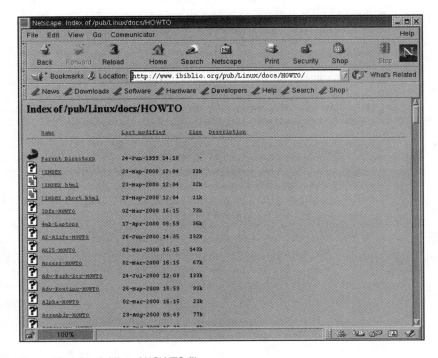

Figure10-4: Partial list of HOWTO files

Each HOWTO file contains information about some area of Linux, such as the hardware that it supports or how to create a boot disk. Table 10-1 lists some of the HOWTO files that you should be able to access through the `http://www.redhat.com/mirrors/LDP/` Web page. To view any of these files, click on the name, and the Web browser should load the full text file.

Tip

At the very end of the list of HOWTO files you will find a folder named `mini`. Click on that link to view a list of mini-HOWTOs, which cover many more narrowly focused topics.

Table 10-1	Some Linux HOWTO Files from Linux Documentation Project
HOWTO Filename	**Contents**
3Dfx-HOWTO	How to configure Linux to support the 3Dfx graphics accelerator chip
AX25-HOWTO	How to install and configure Linux to support the AX.25 packet radio protocol used by Amateur Radio Operators worldwide
Access-HOWTO	How to make Linux accessible to persons with disabilities
Alpha-HOWTO	Overview of Digital Equipment Corporation's 64-bit RISC architecture Alpha CPU (Linux runs on the Alpha)
Assembly-HOWTO	How to program in assembly language in Linux
Bash-Prompt-HOWTO	How to use the Bash shell (command processor)
Belgian-HOWTO	How to configure Linux for Belgian users
Benchmarking-HOWTO	How to benchmark a Linux system (measure how fast the system completes a computing task)
Beowulf-HOWTO	How to build and configure a Beowulf supercomputer by clustering multiple Linux systems
BootPrompt-HOWTO	A list of arguments that can be passed to Linux at boot time (at the LILO boot: prompt)
Bootdisk-HOWTO	How to create boot, root, and other utility disks for Linux
Busmouse-HOWTO	How to install, configure, and use a busmouse in Linux
C++ Programming-HOWTO	How to avoid memory problems, and program properly in C++ programming language
C-C++Beautifier-HOWTO	How to beautifully format C and C++ programs so that they are more readable

Continued

Table 10-1   *(continued)*

HOWTO Filename	*Contents*
Cable-Modem	How to connect a Linux system to a cable modem or cable Internet Service Provider
CD-Writing-HOWTO	How to record a CD using a CD Recorder installed in a Linux system
CDROM-HOWTO	How to install, configure, and use CD-ROM drives with Linux
CVS-RCS-HOWTO	How to set up CVS and RCS source code control systems
Cable-Modem-Providers-HOWTO	How to connect a Linux system with various cable modem–based Internet service providers
Chroot-BIND HOWTO	How to install and configure a BIND 8 name server in a secure manner
Commercial-HOWTO	A list of commercial software for Linux
Config-HOWTO	How to configure the most common applications in Linux
Consultants-HOWTO	A list of consultants or consulting firms that provide support for Linux
Cyrus-IMAP	How to install, configure, and run Cyrus IMAP (Internet Message Access Protocol) software for reading e-mail from many different locations and accounts
DB2-HOWTO	How to install DB2 Universal Database version 7.1 for Linux
DNS-HOWTO	How to set up Domain Name Service (DNS) on a Linux system
DOS-Win-to-Linux-HOWTO	How to apply your DOS and Windows knowledge to the Linux environment
DOS-to-Linux-HOWTO	How to apply your knowledge of MS-DOS in Linux
DOSEMU-HOWTO	How to set up and use the MS-DOS Emulator, DOSEMU
DSL-HOWTO	How to set up and use high-speed DSL (Digital Subscriber Loop) connections to the Internet
DVD-Playing-HOWTO	How to play DVD movies in Linux
Diskless-HOWTO	How to set up a diskless Linux system
Distribution-HOWTO	A list of Linux distributions, with particular focus on commercial CD-ROM distributions

HOWTO Filename	*Contents*
`Emacs-Beginner-HOWTO`	How to use the Emacs editor in Linux
`Enterprise-Java-for-Linux-HOWTO`	How to set up an Enterprise Java environment on Linux
`Ethernet-HOWTO`	How to configure and use Ethernet network adapters with Linux
`Filesystems-HOWTO`	How to access various file systems
`Finnish-HOWTO`	How to set up Linux for the Finnish language. (Except for the initial paragraph, the HOWTO itself is in Finnish.)
`Firewall-HOWTO`	How to set up an Internet firewall on a Linux system
`Framebuffer-HOWTO`	How to use framebuffer devices (an abstraction of graphics hardware) in Linux
`Francophones-HOWTO`	How to set up Linux for the French language. (This HOWTO is in French.)
`From-PowerUp-To-Bash-Prompt-HOWTO`	How Linux boots itself
`Ftape-HOWTO`	How to set up and use floppy tape drives (QIC-40, QIC-80, QIC-3010, and QIC-3020-compatible tape drives that connect to your PC through the floppy disk controller) in Linux
`GCC-HOWTO`	How to set up and use the GNU C compiler and development libraries in Linux
`German-HOWTO`	How to use Linux with the German character set. (This HOWTO is in German.)
`Glibc2-HOWTO`	How to install and use the GNU C Library version 2 (`libc 6`) on Linux systems
`Hardware-HOWTO`	A list of hardware known to work with Linux; and how to locate any necessary drivers
`Hebrew-HOWTO`	How to support the Hebrew character set in X Window System and text-mode screens
`HOWTO-HOWTO`	How to write a HOWTO document
`HOWTO-INDEX`	Index of all HOWTOs
`IP-Masquerade-HOWTO`	How to enable the IP Masquerading feature on a Linux system
`IPCHAINS-HOWTO`	How to obtain, install, and configure the enhanced IP firewall chains software for Linux, including some ideas about how you might use the `ipchains` tool (`ipchains` replaces the older `ipfwadm` tool)

Continued

Table 10-1 *(continued)*

HOWTO Filename	Contents
IPX-HOWTO	How to obtain, install, and configure various software that use the Linux support for IPX protocol (IPX is used by Novell Netware)
IR-HOWTO	How to use IrDA-compliant infrared devices in Linux (IrDA™ is a standard for infrared wireless communication at speeds ranging from 2400bps to 4Mbps)
ISP-Hookup-HOWTO	How to connect a Linux system to an Internet service provider (ISP) via a dial-up modem connection
ISP-Setup-RedHat	How to set up a Red Hat Linux system for dial-in, virtual Web hosting, e-mail, POP3, and FTP
IngresII-HOWTO	How to install the Ingres II Relational Database Management System on Linux
Installation-HOWTO	How to obtain and install Linux
Intranet-Server-HOWTO	How to use a Linux system in an Intranet that ties together Unix, Novell Netware, Windows NT, and Windows 95 systems
Italian-HOWTO	How to set up Linux for the Italian language. (This HOWTO is in Italian.)
Java-CGI-HOWTO	How to develop and use Java programs in Linux
Jaz-Drive-HOWTO	How to use 1GB and 2GB Iomega Jaz drives in Linux
Kernel-HOWTO	How to upgrade and rebuild the Linux kernel
Keyboard-and-Console-HOWTO	How to use various Linux utilities to configure the keyboard and the console (the text-mode screen)
Kickstart-HOWTO	How to use the RedHat Linux KickStart system to install an identical version of Linux on a large number of systems
Kiosk-HOWTO	How to set up a Web-based kiosk using Linux, X, Netscape Navigator, and a trackball
Kodak-Digitalcam-HOWTO	How to get a Kodak digital camera to work in Linux
LDAP-HOWTO	How to install, configure, run, and maintain a Lightweight Directory Access Protocol (LDAP) server on a Linux system
Laptop-HOWTO	How to install and use Linux on laptop computers
LinuxDoc+Emacs+Ispell-HOWTO	How to use Emacs and Ispell to write documents such as HOWTOs for the Linux Documentation Project

HOWTO Filename	*Contents*
MGR-HOWTO	How to use the MGR (ManaGeR) graphical windowing system in Linux
MILO-HOWTO	How to set up and use the Miniloader (MILO) for Linux on Alpha AXP-based systems. (Just as LILO loads and starts Linux on Intel-based PCs, MILO loads Linux on Alpha systems.)
MIPS-HOWTO	How to obtain and use the version of Linux for the MIPS processors from Silicon Graphics. (The MIPS processors are used in many systems, ranging from Silicon Graphics workstations to Nintendo 64 game consoles.)
MP3-HOWTO	How to encode and play MP3 sound files in Linux
Mail-Administrator-HOWTO	How to perform system administration tasks related to electronic mail (e-mail) systems in Linux
Mail-User-HOWTO	Information for users of the e-mail system
Majordomo-MajorCool-HOWTO	How to install Majordomo Mailing List Software and the MajorCool utility to manage Majordomo lists on Linux
Modem-HOWTO	How to select, connect, configure, and use modems in Linux
Multi-Disk-HOWTO	How to best use multiple disks and partitions in Linux
Multicast-HOWTO	Information about multicasting over TCP/IP networking
Mutt-GnuPG-PGP-HOWTO	How to configure Mutt-i, PGP, and various versions of GnuPG in order to set up a mail reader with encryption and digital signing capabilities
NET3-4-HOWTO	New version of the NET-3-HOWTO document
NFS-HOWTO	How to set up an NFS (Network File System) server and client in Linux
NIS-HOWTO	How to configure NIS (Network Information Service) in Linux
Networking-Overview-HOWTO	An overview of networking capabilities of Linux
Optical-Disk-HOWTO	How to install and configure optical disk drives in Linux (includes detailed coverage of the Panasonic LF1000 PD Phase change optical drive with the SCSI-II interface)

Continued

Table 10-1 *(continued)*

HOWTO Filename	Contents
Oracle-7-HOWTO	How to install and configure the Oracle Database Server on a Linux system
Oracle-8-HOWTO	How to install and get started with Oracle 8i Enterprise Edition for Linux
PCI-HOWTO	Information on Linux's support for the PCI (Peripheral Component Interconnect) bus architecture
PCMCIA-HOWTO	How to install and use PCMCIA (Personal Computer Memory Card International Association) Card Services in Linux
PHP-HOWTO	How to develop Web applications using PHP, a server-side HTML scripting language
PPP-HOWTO	How to set up and use Point-to-Point Protocol (PPP) networking in Linux
PalmOS-HOWTO	How to use a PalmOS device (such as Palm III) with Linux
Parallel-Processing-HOWTO	How to use parallel processing approaches such as SMP (Symmetric Multiprocessing) Linux systems, clusters of networked Linux systems, and parallel execution using multimedia instructions (i.e., MMX), and attached (parallel) processors hosted by a Linux system
Pilot-HOWTO	How to use the 3Com (U.S. Robotics) Palm Pilot personal digital assistant (PDA) with a Linux system
Plug-and-Play-HOWTO	How to support Plug-and-Play (PnP) devices in Linux
Polish-HOWTO	How to set up Linux for the Polish language. (This HOWTO is in Polish.)
Portuguese-HOWTO	How to set up Linux for the Portuguese language. (This HOWTO is in Portuguese.)
PostgreSQL-HOWTO	How to set up and use the PostgreSQL database engine in Linux
Printing-HOWTO	How to set up printing in Linux
Printing-Usage-HOWTO	How to use the print spooling system in Linux
Process-Monitor-HOWTO	How to monitor Linux processes; and how to restart them automatically if they die
Quake-HOWTO	How to install, run, and troubleshoot Quake, QuakeWorld and Quake II in Linux (these are 3D action games developed by id Software)

HOWTO Filename	*Contents*
RPM-HOWTO	How to use the Red Hat Package Manager (RPM) in Linux
Reading-List-HOWTO	List of books useful to a Linux user
RedHat-CD-HOWTO	How to make your own CDs from the Red Hat Linux distribution that are equivalent to the ones commercially available from Red Hat
Root-RAID-HOWTO	How to create a root-mounted RAID (Redundant Array of Inexpensive Disks) file system in Linux
SCSI-Programming-HOWTO	Information on programming the SCSI device driver in Linux (useful for programmers who want to add support for a new SCSI device in Linux)
SMB-HOWTO	How to use the Server Message Block (SMB) protocol, also called the NetBIOS or LAN Manager protocol, with Linux
SMP-HOWTO	Information on configuring Symmetric Multiprocessing (SMP) on Linux systems with multiple processors
SRM-HOWTO	How to boot an Alpha-based Linux system using the SRM (System Reference Manual) firmware, which is the firmware normally used to boot DEC Unix on Alpha
Secure-Programs-HOWTO	How to write secure programs for Linux and UNIX systems
Security-HOWTO	An overview of security issues in a Linux system
Serbian-HOWTO	How to configure Linux for Serbian users. (This HOWTO is in Serbian.)
Serial-HOWTO	How to set up serial communication devices in Linux
Serial-Programming-HOWTO	How to program the serial port in Linux
Shadow-Password-HOWTO	How to obtain, install, and configure the password Shadow Suite in Linux (password shadowing provides for more secure passwords than the ones stored in the /etc/passwd file)
Slovenian-HOWTO	How to configure Linux for Slovenian users. (This HOWTO is in Slovenian.)
Software-Building-HOWTO	How to build and install UNIX software distributions in Linux
Software-Release-Practice-HOWTO	Describes the good software release practices of Linux Open Source projects

Continued

Table 10-1 *(continued)*

HOWTO Filename	Contents
Sound-HOWTO	How to enable support for sound hardware in Linux
Sound-Playing-HOWTO	Lists many sound file formats and the applications that can be used to play sound in Linux
Spanish-HOWTO	How to configure Linux for Spanish-speaking users. (This HOWTO is in Spanish.)
TclTk-HOWTO	How to install, configure, and use the Tcl/Tk programming environment in Linux
TeTeX-HOWTO	How to install and use the teTeX TeX (pronounced *tech* as in technology) and LaTeX document formatting software in Linux
Text-Terminal-HOWTO	How to install and use text terminals (typically connected to multiport serial cards or a terminal server) with a Linux host
Thai-HOWTO	How to set up Linux for Thai-speaking users. (This HOWTO is in Thai)
Tips-HOWTO	Hints and tips to make Linux more useful and fun
UMSDOS-HOWTO	How to install and use the UMSDOS file system that lets you install Linux in an MS-DOS directory
UPS-HOWTO	How to use an uninterruptable power supply (UPS) with Linux
UUCP-HOWTO	How to set up and use the Unix-to-Unix Copy (UUCP) software in Linux
Unix-Internet-Fundamentals-HOWTO	Nontechnical description of how PCs, UNIX-like operating systems, and the Internet work
User-Authentication-HOWTO	How to secure user authentication in Linux
User-Group-HOWTO	How to establish and run a Linux User Group
VAR-HOWTO	Lists Linux Value Added Resellers (VARs)
VME-HOWTO	How to run Linux on VMEbus systems
VMS-to-Linux-HOWTO	How to transition from VMS to Linux. (VMS is an operating system that runs on VAX systems from Digital Equipment Corporation.)
VPN-HOWTO	How to configure a Linux system to support a Virtual Private Network (VPN)
VPN-Masquerade-HOWTO	How to configure a Linux firewall to masquerade IPsec and Point-to-Point Tunneling Protocol (PPTP) traffic to support a Virtual Private Network (VPN)

HOWTO Filename	*Contents*
Virtual-Services-HOWTO	How to support virtual services on a Linux system so that a single machine can recognize multiple IP addresses without multiple network cards
WWW-HOWTO	How to set up a World Wide Web (WWW) service in Linux
WWW-mSQL-HOWTO	How to use the mSQL database server with a Web server in Linux
Winmodems-and-Linux-HOWTO	How to get a Winmodem (which normally needs a Windows driver to work) working in Linux
XFree86-HOWTO	How to install and configure the XFree86 (X Window System version 11 Release 6 — X11R6) in Linux
XFree86-Video-Timings-HOWTO	How to create a modeline in the X configuration file for a specific video card. (See Chapter 3 for a description of modeline and the format of the X configuration file.)
XWindow-User-HOWTO	How to configure the X Window environment for a Linux user
Xinerama-HOWTO	How to configure XFree86 version 4.0 with multiple monitors and the Xinerama extension

Understanding the Linux File System

Like any other operating system, Linux organizes information in files and directories. The files, in turn, are contained in directories (a directory is a special file that can contain other files and directories). A directory can contain other directories, giving rise to a hierarchical structure. This hierarchical organization of files is called the *file system*.

The Linux file system provides a unified model of all storage in the system. The file system has a single root directory, indicated by a forward slash (/). Then there is a hierarchy of files and directories. Parts of the file system can reside in different physical media, such as hard disk, floppy disk, and CD-ROM. Figure 10-5 illustrates the concept of the Linux file system and how it spans multiple physical devices.

If you are familiar with MS-DOS or Windows 95/98/NT, you'll note that there is no concept of a drive letter in UNIX. In addition, filenames do not have a strict 8.3 name-extension format (the term *8.3 filename* results from the use of an eight-character name and a three-character extension in MS-DOS). In Linux, you can have long filenames (up to 256 characters), and filenames are case-sensitive. Often, UNIX filenames have multiple extensions, such as sample.tar.Z. Some UNIX filenames include the following: index.html, Makefile, kernel-2.2.15-2.5.0.i686.rpm, .bash_profile, and httpd_src.tar.gz.

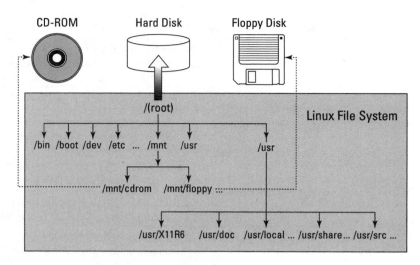

Figure 10-5: The Linux file system provides a unified view of storage that may span multiple Drives.

To locate a file, you need more than just the file's name; you also need information about the directory hierarchy. The term *pathname* refers to the complete specification necessary to locate a file — the complete hierarchy of directories leading to the file — and the filename. Figure 10-6 shows a typical Linux pathname for a file.

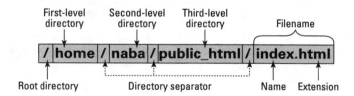

Figure 10-6: A typical Linux pathname

As you can see from Figure 10-6, a Linux pathname consists of the following parts:

1. The root directory, indicated by a forward slash (/) character.

2. The directory hierarchy, with each directory name separated from the previous one by a forward slash (/) character. A / appears after the last directory name.

3. The filename, with a name and one or more optional extensions.

Many directories have specific purposes. If you know the purpose of specific directories, finding your way around Linux directories is easier. Another benefit of knowing the typical use of directories is that you can guess where to look for specific types of files when you face a new situation. Table 10-2 briefly describes the directories in a Linux system:

Table 10-2   Linux System Directories

Directory	Description
/	The root directory that forms the base of the file system. All files and directories are contained logically in the root directory, regardless of their physical locations.
/bin	Contains the executable programs that are part of the Linux operating system. Many Linux commands, such as cat, cp, ls, more, and tar, are located in /bin.
/dev	Contains all device files. Linux treats each device as a special file; all such files are located in the device directory /dev.
/etc	Contains most system configuration files and the initialization scripts (in the /etc/rc.d subdirectory).
/home	Conventional location of the home directories of all users. User naba's home directory, for example, is /home/naba.
/lib	Contains library files, including the loadable driver modules, needed to boot the system.
/lost+	Directory for lost files. Every disk partition has a lost+found directory.found
/mnt	A directory, typically used to mount devices temporarily, such as floppy disks and disk partitions. Also contains the /mnt/floppy directory for mounting floppy disks, and the /mnt/cdrom directory for mounting the CD-ROM drive. (Of course, you can mount the CD-ROM drive on another directory as well.)
/proc	A special directory that contains information about various aspects of the Linux system.
/root	The home directory for the root user.
/sbin	Contains executable files representing commands that typically are used for system-administration tasks. Commands such as mount, halt, umount, and shutdown reside in the /sbin directory.
/tmp	Temporary directory that any user can use as a scratch directory, meaning that the contents of this directory are considered unimportant, and usually are deleted every time the system boots.
/usr	Contains the subdirectories for many important programs, such as the X Window System, and the online manual.
/var	Contains various system files (such as logs), as well as directories for holding other information, such as files for the Web server and anonymous FTP server.

The /usr directory also contains a host of useful subdirectories. Table 10-3 lists a few of the important subdirectories in /usr.

Table 10-3 Important /usr Subdirectories

Subdirectory	Description
/usr/X11R6	Contains the XFree86 (X Window System) software.
/usr/bin	Contains executable files for many more Linux commands, including utility programs commonly available in Linux, but not part of the core Linux operating system.
/usr/games	Contains some old Linux games such as fortune, banner, and trojka.
/usr/include	Contains the header files (files with names ending in .h) for the C and C++ programming languages; also includes the X11 header files in the /usr/include/X11 directory and the kernel header files in the /usr/include/linux directory.
/usr/lib	Contains the libraries for C and C++ programming languages; also contains many other libraries, such as database libraries, graphical toolkit libraries, and so on.
/usr/local	Contains local files. The /usr/local/bin directory, for example, is supposed to be the location for any executable program developed on your system.
/usr/sbin	Contains many administrative commands, such as commands for electronic mail and networking.
/usr/share	Contains shared data, such as default configuration files and images for many applications. For example, /usr/share/gnome contains various shared files for the GNOME desktop; and /usr/share/doc has the documentation files for many Linux applications (such as the Bash shell, mtools, the Sawfish window manager, and the GIMP image processing program).
/usr/share/man	Contains the online manual (which you can read by using the man command).
/usr/src	Contains the source code for the Linux kernel (the core operating system).

Using the GNOME File Manager

Now that you know the basics of the Linux file system, you can explore the file system. You can access the files and directories in two ways:

- By using a graphical file manager in the GNOME or KDE desktop

- By typing appropriate Linux commands in a terminal window or a text console

The graphical file manager is similar to Windows Explorer and is intuitive to use. You may want to spend a few minutes now exploring the file system, using the GNOME File Manager (the KDE file manager works in a similar manner, so it isn't covered here).

To start the GNOME File Manager, double-click the file folder icon in the upper-left corner of the GNOME desktop (see Figure 10-2). The GNOME File Manager runs and displays the contents of your home directory, as shown in Figure 10-7.

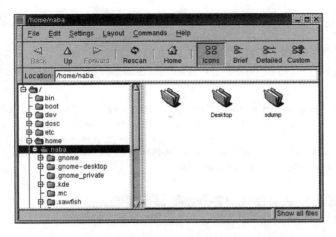

Figure 10-7: My home directory, as it appears in the GNOME file manager

The File Manager's window is vertically divided into two windows — the left side shows a tree view of the file system in a scrolling window; the right side shows the files and directories in the currently selected directory. As you can see from the tree view, Figure 10-7 shows the content of the /home/naba directory. The title bar shows the name of the currently selected directory.

If you have used Windows Explorer, you can use the GNOME File Manager in a similar manner. To view the contents of another directory, first locate the directory in the tree view. For example, to view the /etc/X11 directory, click the plus sign (+) next to the etc directory. This causes the File Manager to display the subdirectories in etc and change that plus sign to a minus sign. Now click the X11 directory. The right-hand window now shows the contents of the /etc/X11 directory, as shown in Figure 10-8.

The File Manager displays the contents of the selected directory, using icons. Each directory appears as a folder, with the name of the directory shown underneath the folder icon. Ordinary files, such as XF86Config, appear as a sheet of paper. The file named X is a link; its icon is similar to the icon used to show a shortcut in Windows. The prefdm file is an executable file.

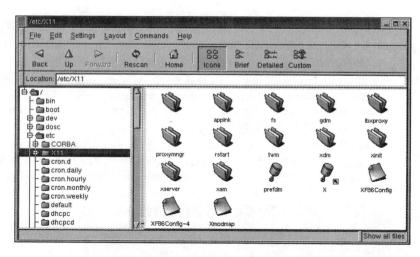

Figure 10-8: Viewing the contents of the /etc/X11 directory in the GNOME File Manager

The File Manager window has the usual menu bar and a toolbar. Notice that the toolbar button labeled Icons in Figure 10-8 is pressed in. That means the directory contents are being displayed using large icons. Click the Brief button; this causes the File Manager to display the contents using smaller icons in a list format, as shown in Figure 10-9.

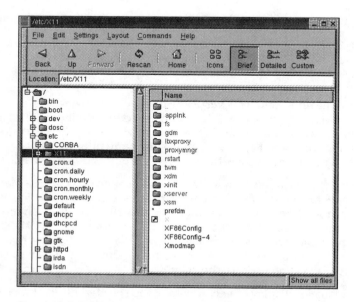

Figure 10-9: Brief view of the /etc/X11 directory

To view more information about each file, click the Detailed button on the toolbar. The File Manager now displays the size of each file or directory, and the time when each was last modified, as shown in Figure 10-10.

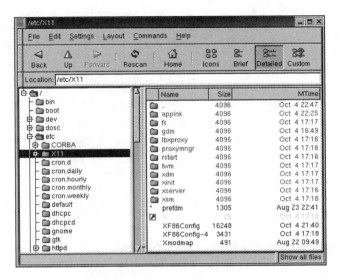

Figure 10-10: Detailed view of the /etc/X11 directory

If you click any of the information titles — Name, Size, or Mtime — along the top of the list view, the File Manager sorts the list according to the information. For example, click the MTime information title. The File Manager now displays the list of files and directories sorted, according to the time of last modification (that's what MTime means). Clicking the Name information title sorts the files and directories alphabetically. This feature works in the Brief and Custom view as well.

Finally, you can view the file permissions by clicking the Custom button. The File Manager then displays the icons, filenames, sizes, and file permissions, as shown in Figure 10-11.

For now, ignore the meaning of the permissions. You will learn about them in the next section when you learn the Linux commands to navigate the file system.

In addition to moving around the file system and viewing contents of directories, you can use the File Manager to perform tasks, such as moving a file from one directory to another and deleting a file. I won't outline each step, but you can take a few moments to try the following tasks:

- ■ To move a file to a different directory, drag and drop the file's icon on the directory where you want the file.

- To copy a file to a new location, select the file's icon and then select File ⇨ Copy. You can also right-click on the file's icon and select Copy from the pop-up menu. A dialog box prompts you for the name of the directory to which the file should be copied.

- To delete a file or directory, right-click on the icon and select Delete from the pop-up menu. A dialog box asks you to confirm if you really want to delete the file or directory. You can click Yes to delete the selected item, or click No to cancel the operation.

- To rename a file or a directory, click the name in the Icon view (see Figure 10-8). Then you can type the new name or edit the name.

- To create a new directory, right-click in an empty area of the right-hand window and select New Directory from the pop-up menu. A dialog box prompts you for the name of the new directory.

- To find files, select Commands ⇨ Find Files from the menu bar. A dialog box prompts you for what you want to find and where to start the search. After you enter this information, click OK to start the search. The results of the search appear in a new window.

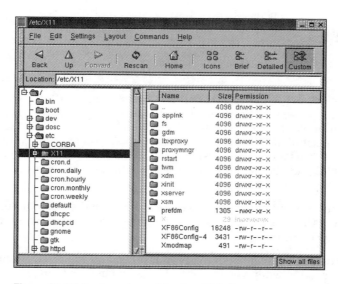

Figure 10-11: Custom view of the /etc/X11 directory

Navigating the File System with Linux Commands

Although the graphical file managers are easy to use, you can use them only if you have a graphical login. Sometimes, you may not have a graphical environment to run a graphical file manager. For example, you might be logged in through a text terminal, or X might not be working on your system. In those situations, you have to rely on Linux commands to work with files and directories. Of course, you can always use Linux commands, even in the graphical environment — all you have to do is open a terminal window and type the Linux commands. Click the terminal icon in the GNOME Panel (see Figure 10-2) to start a terminal emulation program that displays a terminal window.

Directory Navigation

In Red Hat Linux, when you log in as root, your home directory is /root. For other users, the home directory is usually in the /home directory. My home directory (when I log in as naba) is /home/naba. This information is stored in the /etc/passwd file. By default, only you have permission to save files in your home directory, and only you can create subdirectories in your home directory to further organize your files.

Linux supports the concept of a *current directory*, which is the directory on which all file and directory commands operate. After you log in, for example, your current directory is the home directory. To see the current directory, type the pwd command.

To change the current directory, use the cd command. To change the current directory to /usr/share/doc, type the following:

```
cd /usr/share/doc
```

Then, to change the directory to the bash-2.04 subdirectory in /usr/share/doc, type this command:

```
cd bash-2.04
```

Now, if you use the pwd command, that command shows /usr/share/doc/bash-2.04 as the current directory. Therefore, you can refer to a directory's name in two ways:

- An absolute pathname (such as /usr/share/doc) that specifies the exact directory in the directory tree
- A relative directory name (such as bash-2.04, which represents the bash-2.04 subdirectory of the current directory)

If you type cd bash-2.04 in /usr/share/doc, the current directory changes to /usr/share/doc/bash-2.04; but the same command in /home/naba tries to change the current directory to /home/naba/bash-2.04.

Tip

Use the cd command without any arguments to change the current directory to your home directory. Actually, the lone cd command changes the current directory to the directory listed in the HOME environment variable; but that environment variable contains your home directory by default.

Notice that the tilde character (~) also refers to the directory specified by the HOME environment variable. Thus, the command cd ~ changes the current directory to whatever directory the HOME environment variable specifies.

Tip

You can use a shortcut to refer to any user's home directory. Prefix a user's login name with a tilde (~) to refer to that user's home directory. Therefore, ~naba refers to the home directory of the user naba, and ~root refers to the home directory of the root user. If your system has a user with the login name emily, you can type cd ~emily to change to Emily's home directory.

The directory names . and .. have special meanings. A single period (.) indicates the current directory, whereas two periods (..) indicate the parent directory. If the current directory is /usr/share/doc, for example, you can change the current directory to /usr by using the following command:

```
cd ..
```

Essentially, this command takes you up one level in the file system hierarchy.

Shell Prompt and Current Directory

Note that you can display the current directory in the shell prompt. The Bash shell uses the value of the environment variable PS1 as the primary prompt. Another variable, PS2, functions as the secondary prompt when a command requires further input from the user. You can view these variables with the echo command (for example, type echo $PS1 to view the setting of PS1). By default, the PS1 variable is defined in Red Hat Linux as follows:

```
echo $PS1
[\u@\h \W]\$
```

With this setting for PS1, the prompt looks like this:

```
[username@hostname dirname]$
```

In this example, *username* is the name of the user; *hostname* is the system's name; and *dirname* is the last part of the current working directory. Thus, if the current directory is /usr/src/linux, the *dirname* is linux. Table 10-4 shows the character sequences you can use in the PS1 environment variable to customize your prompt.

Table 10-4   Character Sequences in the PS1 Environment

Code	What Appears in Prompt
\t	Current time in HH:MM:SS format
\d	Date in "Weekday Month Date" format, such as "Sat Jul 10"
\n	newline
\s	Name of the shell, such as bash
\w	Full name of the current working directory, such as /usr/src/linux

Code	What Appears in Prompt
\W	Basename of the current working directory, such as linux for /usr/src/linux
\u	User name of the current user
\h	Host name
\#	Command number of this command
\!	History number of this command
\$	# if the effective user ID is 0 (indicating the user is root); otherwise, a $
\nnn	Character corresponding to the octal number nnn
\\	A backslash
\[	Begins a sequence of nonprinting characters, which could be used to embed a terminal control sequence into the prompt
\]	Ends a sequence of nonprinting characters

Given this information, you can show the full directory name (enclosed in square brackets) in the prompt with the following command:

```
export PS1="[\w]"
```

If the current directory is /usr/src/linux-2.4, the prompt appears as follows:

```
[/usr/src/linux-2.4]
```

Directory Listings and Permissions

As you move around the Linux directories, you may want to know the contents of a directory. You can get a directory listing by using the ls command. By default, the ls command — without any options — displays the contents of the current directory in a compact, multicolumn format. For example, type the following commands to see the contents of the /etc/X11 directory. (You type the commands shown in boldface; I have omitted the command prompts from the listing):

```
cd /etc/X11
ls
X              XF86Config-4  applnk  gdm        prefdm    rstart  xdm    xserver
XF86Config     Xmodmap       fs      lbxproxy   proxymngr twm     xinit  xsm
```

From this listing, you cannot tell whether an entry is a file or a directory. To tell the directories and files apart, use the -F option with ls, as follows:

```
ls -F
X@             Xmodmap       gdm/      proxymngr/  xdm/      xsm/
XF86Config     applnk/       lbxproxy/ rstart/     xinit/
XF86Config-4   fs/           prefdm*   twm/        xserver/
```

Now the directory names have a slash (/) appended to them. Plain filenames appear as is. The at sign (@) appended to the first filename indicates that that file is actually a link to another file (in other words, this filename simply refers to another file). An asterisk (*) is appended to files that are executable (see, for example, the prefdm file in the listing).

You can see even more detailed information about the files and directories with the -l option:

ls -l

For the /etc/X11 directory, a typical output from ls -l looks like the following:

```
lrwxrwxrwx    1 root     root          29 Oct  4 17:18 X -> ../../usr/X11R6/bin
/XF86_SVGA
-rw-r--r--    1 root     root       16248 Oct  4 21:40 XF86Config
-rw-r--r--    1 root     root        3431 Oct  4 17:18 XF86Config-4
-rw-r--r--    1 root     root         491 Aug 22 09:49 Xmodmap
drwxr-xr-x   10 root     root        4096 Oct  4 22:25 applnk
drwxr-xr-x    2 root     root        4096 Oct  4 17:17 fs
drwxr-xr-x    6 root     root        4096 Oct  4 16:49 gdm
drwxr-xr-x    2 root     root        4096 Oct  4 17:16 lbxproxy
-rwxr-xr-x    1 root     root        1305 Aug 23 22:41 prefdm
drwxr-xr-x    2 root     root        4096 Oct  4 17:16 proxymngr
drwxr-xr-x    4 root     root        4096 Oct  4 17:16 rstart
drwxr-xr-x    2 root     root        4096 Oct  4 17:17 twm
drwxr-xr-x    3 root     root        4096 Oct  4 17:17 xdm
drwxr-xr-x    3 root     root        4096 Oct  4 17:17 xinit
drwxr-xr-x    2 root     root        4096 Oct  4 17:16 xserver
drwxr-xr-x    2 root     root        4096 Oct  4 17:16 xsm
```

This listing shows considerable information about each directory entry—which can be a file or another directory. Looking at a line from the right column to the left, you see that the rightmost column shows the name of the directory entry. The date and time before the name show when the last modifications to that file were made. Before the date and time is the size of the file, in bytes.

The file's group and owner appear to the left of the column that shows the file size. The next number to the left indicates the number of links to the file. (A link is like a shortcut in Windows.) Finally, the leftmost column shows the file's *permission settings*, which determine who can read, write, or execute the file.

The first letter of the leftmost column has a special meaning, as the following list shows:

- If the first letter is l, the file is a symbolic link to another file.
- If the first letter is d, the file is a directory.
- If the first letter is a dash (-), the file is a normal file.

- If the first letter is b, the file represents a block device, such as a disk drive.

- If the first letter is c, the file represents a character device, such as a serial port or a terminal.

After that first letter, the leftmost column shows a sequence of nine characters, which appears as rwxrwxrwx when each letter is present. Each letter indicates a specific permission; a hyphen in place of a letter indicates no permission for a specific operation on the file. Think of these nine letters as three groups of three letters (rwx), interpreted as follows:

- The leftmost group of rwx controls the read, write, and execute permission of the file's owner. In other words, if you see rwx in this position, the file's owner can read (r), write (w), and execute (x) the file. A hyphen in the place of a letter indicates no permission. Thus, the string rw- means that the owner has read and write permission, but no execute permission. Typically, executable programs (including shell programs) have execute permission. However, for directories, the execute permission is equivalent to a use permission — a user must have execute permission on a directory to open and read the contents of the directory.

- The middle three rwx letters control the read, write, and execute permission of any user belonging to that file's group.

- The rightmost group of rwx letters controls the read, write, and execute permission of all other users (collectively referred to as the *world*).

Thus, a file with the permission setting rwx------ is accessible only to the file's owner, whereas the permission setting rwxr--r-- makes the file readable by the world.

An interesting feature of the ls command is the fact that it does not list any file whose name begins with a period. To see these files, you must use the ls command with the -a option, as follows:

ls -a

Try this command in your home directory and compare the result with what you see when you don't use the -a option:

1. Type cd to change to your home directory.

2. Type ls -F to see the files and directories in your home directory.

3. Type ls -aF to see everything, including the hidden files.

Tip   Most Linux commands take single-character options, each with a minus sign (think of this sign as a hyphen) as a prefix. When you want to use several options, type a hyphen and concatenate the option letters one after another. Therefore, ls -al is equivalent to ls -a -l.

The Bash Shell

If you have used MS-DOS, you may be familiar with COMMAND.COM: the DOS command interpreter. That program displays the infamous C:\> prompt. Linux provides a command interpreter that resembles COMMAND.COM in DOS. In UNIX, the command interpreter traditionally is referred to as a shell. The original UNIX shell was called the *Bourne shell*, and its executable program was named sh. The default Linux shell is Bash, and its program name is bash (found in the /bin directory). Bash is compatible with the original sh, but includes many desirable features of other well-known shells, such as the C shell and the Korn shell. For example, Bash enables you to recall commands that you entered previously, and it even completes partial commands (this is called *command completion*).

The purpose of a shell such as Bash is to display a prompt and execute the command that you type at the keyboard. Some commands, such as cd (change directory) and pwd (print working directory), are built into Bash. Other commands, such as cp (copy) and ls (list directory), are separate programs (a file representing these commands resides in one of the directories on your system). As a user, however, you really do not have to know or care whether a command is built in, or is in the form of a separate executable program. Note than shell built-in commands are executed before executable files with the same name.

In addition to the standard Linux commands, Bash can execute any program stored in an executable file. Bash can even execute a shell script (a text file that contains one or more commands). As you learn in Chapter 28, you actually can use the shell's built-in commands to write programs (also known as *shell scripts*). Type help at the shell prompt to see a list of the built-in commands.

The shell enables you to run any Linux command, but you need to know the commands before you can run them. Because Linux is a UNIX clone, all Linux commands essentially are UNIX commands. Some of the most important commands, which were summarized earlier in the chapter, are for moving around the Linux file system. A large number of the Linux commands are GNU utilities — Chapter 11 provides an overview of GNU utilities.

Cross-Reference

Consult Appendix A for a Linux command reference to learn about many more Linux commands, including most GNU utilities.

The next few sections give you a feel for the various features of a shell, ranging from the general command syntax, to defining aliases for long commands.

Note

The discussions in this chapter assume that you use Bash as your shell, because Bash is the shell that you get when you install Linux from the CD-ROMs that accompany this book.

Shell Command Syntax

Because a shell interprets what you type, it is important to know how the shell processes the text that you enter. All shell commands have the following general format:

```
command option1 option2 ... optionN
```

A single line of command commonly is referred to as a *command line*. On a command line, you enter a command followed by one or more options (or *arguments*), known as *command-line options* (or *command-line arguments*).

One basic rule states that you have to use a space or a tab to separate the command from the options. You also must separate options with a space or a tab. If you want to use an option that contains embedded spaces, you have to put that option inside quotation marks. To search for my name in the password file, for example, I enter the grep command as follows:

```
grep "Naba Barkakati" /etc/passwd
```

When grep prints the line with my name, it looks like this:

```
naba:x:500:100:Naba Barkakati:/home/naba:/bin/bash
```

I use shadow passwords on my system. That's why the password field (the characters between the first and second colon) is a single letter x. Nevertheless, this line contains some useful information; the most interesting information (for the purposes of this discussion) is the field that follows the last colon (:). That field shows the name of the shell that I am running.

The number and the format of the command-line options, of course, depend on the actual command. When you learn more about the commands, you see that the command-line options that control the behavior of a command are of the form -X , in which X is a single character.

Because various GNU tools and utilities implement most Linux commands, you should know that GNU command-line options begin with two dashes followed by a descriptive word. Thus, the GNU options are of the form -*xxxx*, where *xxxx* is a word denoting the option. For example, the GNU ls --all command shows all directory entries, including those that begin with a period (.). This is the same as the ls -a command in all UNIX systems.

If a command is too long to fit on a single line, you can press the backslash (\) key, followed by Enter. Then, continue entering the command on the next line. Or, you can concatenate several shorter commands on a single line; just use the semicolon (;) as a separator between the commands. For example, when rebuilding the Linux kernel (as explained in Chapter 2), you can complete three sequential tasks by typing the following commands on a single line:

```
make dep; make clean; make zImage
```

Combining Commands

Linux follows the UNIX philosophy of giving the user a toolbox of many simple commands. You can, however, combine these simple commands to create a more sophisticated command. Suppose you want to determine whether a device file named sbpcd resides in your system's /dev directory because you need that device file for a Sound Blaster Pro CD-ROM drive. You can use the command `ls /dev` to get a directory listing of the `/dev` directory and see whether anything that contains `sbpcd` appears in the listing. Unfortunately, the `/dev` directory has a great many entries, and it may be difficult to locate any item that has `sbpcd` in its name. You can, however, combine the `ls` command with `grep` and come up with a command that does exactly what you want:

```
ls /dev | grep sbpcd
```

The shell sends the output of the `ls` command (the directory listing) to the `grep` command, which searches for the string `sbpcd`. That vertical bar (|) is known as a *pipe,* because it acts as a conduit between the two programs; the output of the first command becomes the input of the second one.

Note

Most Linux commands are designed in a way that enables the output of one command to be fed into the input of another. To do this, simply concatenate the commands, placing pipes between them.

I/O Redirection

Linux commands that are designed to work together have a common feature — they always read from the *standard input* (usually, the keyboard) and write to the *standard output* (usually, the screen). Error messages are sent to the *standard error* (usually, the screen). These three devices often are referred to as *stdout, stdin,* and *stderr.*

If you want a command to read from a file, you can redirect the standard input to come from that file. Similarly, to save the output of a command in a file, redirect the standard output to a file. These features of the shell are called *input* and *output redirection,* or *I/O redirection.*

Using the following command, for example, you can search through all files in the `/usr/include` directory for the occurrence of the string `typedef`, and then save that list in a file called `typedef.out`:

```
grep typedef /usr/include/* > typedef.out
```

This command also illustrates another feature of Bash. When you use an asterisk (*), Bash replaces the asterisk with a list of all the filenames in the specified directory. Thus, `/usr/include/*` means all the files in the `/usr/include` directory.

Table 10-5 shows the syntax of common I/O redirection commands.

Table 10-5   Common Standard I/O Redirections

Task	Command syntax
Send stdout to a file	`command > file`
Send stderr to file	`command 2> file`

Task	Command syntax
Send stdout and stderr to file	*command* > *file* 2>&1
Read stdin from a file	*command* < *file*
Append stdout to the end of a file	*command* >> *file*
Append stderr to the end of a file	*command* 2>> *file*
Append stdout and stderr to the end of a file	*command* >> *file* 2>&1
Read stdin from the keyboard until the character	*command* <<c
Pipe stdout to command2	*command* | *command2*
Pipe stdout and stderr to command2	*command* 2>&1 | *command2*

Environment Variables

The shell and other Linux commands need information to work properly. If you type a command that isn't one of that shell's built-in commands, the shell has to locate an executable file (whose name matches the command that you type). The shell needs to know which directories to search for those files. Similarly, a text editor, such as vi, needs to know the type of terminal (even if the terminal happens to be xterm, which essentially emulates a terminal in a window).

One way to provide this kind of information to a program is through command-line options. However, if you use that approach, you may have to enter many options every time you start a program. UNIX provides an elegant solution through *environment variables*.

An *environment variable* is nothing more than a name associated with a string. On my system, for example, the environment variable named PATH is defined as follows:

```
PATH=/usr/local/bin:/bin:/usr/bin:.:/usr/X11R6/bin
```

The string to the right of the equal sign is the value of the PATH environment variable. By convention, the PATH environment variable is a sequence of directory names, each name separated from the preceding one by a colon (:). The period in the list of directories also denotes a directory; it represents the current directory.

When the shell has to search for a file, it simply searches the directories listed in the PATH environment variable. The shell searches the directories in PATH in order of their appearance. Therefore, if two programs have the same name, the shell executes the one that it finds first.

In a fashion similar to the shell's use of the PATH environment variable, an editor such as vi uses the value of the TERM environment variable to figure out how to display the file that you are editing with vi. To see the current setting of TERM, type the following command at the shell prompt:

```
echo $TERM
```

If you type this command in an xterm window, the output is as follows:

```
xterm
```

In kvt (the KDE terminal), the TERM environment variable is defined as xterm-color.

To define an environment variable in Bash, use the following syntax:

```
export NAME=Value
```

Here, NAME denotes the name of the environment variable, and Value is the string representing its value. Therefore, you set TERM to the value xterm by using the following command:

```
export TERM=xterm
```

Tip

After you define an environment variable, you can change its value by simply specifying the new value with the syntax NAME=new-value. For example, to change the definition of TERM to vt100, type TERM=vt100 at the shell prompt.

With an environment variable such as PATH, you typically want to append a new directory name to the existing definition, rather than define the PATH from scratch. The following example shows how to accomplish this task:

```
export PATH="$PATH:/usr/games"
```

This command appends the string :/usr/games to the current definition of the PATH environment variable. The net effect is to add /usr/games to the list of directories in PATH.

Note that you also can write this export command as follows:

```
export PATH=${PATH}:/usr/games
```

PATH and TERM are only two of a handful of common environment variables. Table 10-6 lists some of the useful environment variables in Bash.

Table 10-6   Useful Bash Environment Variables

Environment Variable	Contents
BASH	The full path name of the Bash executable program (usually, /bin/bash)
BASH_VERSION	The version number of the Bash program
DISPLAY	The name of the display on which the X Window System displays output (typically set to :0.0)

Environment Variable	Contents
HOME	Your home directory
HOSTNAME	The host name of your system
LOGNAME	Your login name
MAIL	The location of your mail directory
PATH	The list of directories in which the shell looks for programs
PS1	The shell prompt. (The default is bash$ for all users except root; for root, the default prompt is bash#.)
SHELL	Your shell (SHELL=/bin/bash for Bash)
TERM	The type of terminal

Processes

Every time the shell acts on a command that you type, it starts a *process*. The shell itself is a process; so are any scripts or programs that the shell executes. Examples of such programs are the kwm window manager in the KDE environment and the Enlightenment window manager in GNOME. You can use the ps command to see a list of processes. When you type ps x, for example, Bash shows you the current set of processes. Following is a typical report that is displayed when you enter the ps x command in a terminal window (I also included the --cols 132 option to ensure that you can see each command in its entirety):

```
ps x --cols 132
  PID TTY     STAT   TIME COMMAND
    1 ?       S      0:05 init [5]
    2 ?       SW     0:01 [kflushd]
    3 ?       SW     0:00 [kupdate]
    4 ?       SW     0:00 [kpiod]
    5 ?       SW     0:01 [kswapd]
    6 ?       SW<    0:00 [mdrecoveryd]
   61 ?       SW     0:00 [khubd]
  334 ?       S      0:01 syslogd -m 0
  344 ?       S      0:00 klogd
  375 ?       SW     0:00 [lockd]
  376 ?       SW     0:00 [rpciod]
  401 ?       SW     0:00 [apmd]
  505 ?       S      0:00 xinetd -reuse -pidfile /var/run/xinetd.pid
  522 ?       S      0:01 /usr/sbin/sshd
  607 ?       S      0:00 gpm -t imps2
  759 ?       S      0:00 crond
  825 ?       S      0:00 rhnsd --interval 30
... lines deleted ...
```

```
  885 ?        S      0:00 /usr/bin/gdm -nodaemon
24713 ?        S    140:32 /etc/X11/X -auth /var/gdm/:0.Xauth :0
24714 ?        S      0:00 /usr/bin/gdm -nodaemon
24726 ?        S      0:01 /usr/bin/gnome-session
24759 ?        S      0:00 gnome-smproxy --sm-client-id default0
24763 ?        S      0:04 sawfish --sm-client-id=default2
24829 ?        S      0:00 magicdev --sm-client-id=default12
24839 ?        S      0:00 gnome-name-service
24843 ?        S      0:02 panel --sm-client-id default7
24846 ?        S      0:01 gmc --nowindows --sm-client-id default8
24856 ?        S      0:00 tasklist_applet --activate-goad-server
tasklist_applet --goad-fd 8
24858 ?        S      0:00 deskguide_applet --activate-goad-server
deskguide_applet --goad-fd 8
25107 ?        S      0:00 in.telnetd: lnbp400
25112 pts/1    S      0:00 login -- naba
26366 pts/1    R      0:00 ps x --cols 132
```

In the default output format, the COMMAND column shows the commands that created the processes. This list shows the bash shell and the ps command as the processes. Other processes include all the programs that the shell started when I logged in at the graphical login screen and started a GNOME session. In particular, the list includes the sawfish (window manager) process.

The default ps x command does not provide all the processes running on a Linux system. What ps x shows are the commands that you started, either directly or indirectly (through shell scripts that run automatically when you log in). To see the full complement of processes, use the a option of the ps command, together with the x option, as follows:

ps ax

Secret

The ps ax form of the command is the BSD UNIX format of the ps command. You also can write the command as ps -ax — with a hyphen prefix for the options as in most other Linux commands. The Linux ps command accepts options both with and without a hyphen prefix with the options. I don't show the output of the command because quite a few processes are running even when you are the only user on the system. You should expect to see anywhere from 60 to 80 processes in the list.

Secret

If you study the output of the ps command, you may find that the first column has the heading PID, and that it shows a number for each process. *PID* stands for *process ID* (identification), which is a sequential number assigned by the Linux kernel. If you look through the output of the ps ax command, you should see that the init command is the first process; it has a PID or process number of 1. That's why init is referred to as the *mother of all processes*.

Tip

The process ID or process number is useful when you have to forcibly stop an errant process. Look at the output of the ps ax command and note the PID of the offending process. Then, use the kill command with that process number. To stop process number 123, for example, type kill -9 123.

Secret

UNIX systems, including Linux, use signals to notify a process that a specific event has occurred. The `kill` command enables you to send a signal to a process (identified by a process number). The `-9` part of the `kill` command indicates the signal to be sent; 9 happens to be the number of the `SIGKILL` signal that causes a process to exit.

Background Commands and Virtual Consoles

When using MS-DOS, you have no choice but to wait for each command to complete before you enter the next command. (You can type ahead a bit, but the MS-DOS system can hold only a few characters in its internal buffer.) Linux, however, can handle multiple tasks simultaneously. The only problem you may have is that the terminal or console is tied up until a command completes.

If you work in a terminal window and a command takes too long to complete, you can open another terminal window and continue to enter other commands. If you work in text mode, however, and a command seems to take too long, you need some other way to access your system.

Several methods enable you to continue working while your Linux system handles a lengthy task:

- You can start a lengthy command *in the background*, which means that the shell starts the process corresponding to a command and immediately returns to accept more commands. The shell does not wait for the command to complete; the command runs as a distinct process in the background. To start a process in the background, you simply place an ampersand & at the end of a command line. When I want to run the `convpcx` shell script to convert an image file named `image1` to PCX format, for example, I run the script in the background by using the following command:

```
convpcx image1 &
```

- If a command (that you did not run in the background) seems to be taking a long time, press Ctrl+Z to stop it; then, type **bg** to put that process in the background.

- Use the *virtual-console* feature of Linux. Even though your Linux system has only one physical terminal or console (the combination of monitor and keyboard is called the *terminal* or *console*), it gives you the appearance of having multiple consoles. The initial text screen is the first virtual console. Press Alt+F2 to get to the second virtual console, Alt+F3 for the third virtual console, and so on. From the X Window System, you have to press Ctrl+Alt+F1 to get to the first virtual console, Ctrl+Alt+F2 for the second one, and so on.

Tip

To get back to the X display, press Ctrl+Alt+F7. You can use one of the virtual consoles to log in and kill processes that may be causing your X display screen to become unresponsive (e.g., if the mouse stops responding).

Filename Completion in Bash

Many commands take a filename as an argument. When you want to browse through a file named /etc/X11/XF86Config, for example, type the following:

```
more /etc/X11/XF86Config
```

That entry causes the more command to display the file /etc/X11/ XF86Config one screen at a time. For commands that take a filename as an argument, Bash includes a feature that enables you to type short filenames. All you have to type is the bare minimum—just the first few characters—to uniquely identify the file in its directory.

To see an example, type more /etc/X11/XF, but don't press Enter; press Tab instead. Bash automatically completes the filename, so that the command becomes more /etc/X11/XF86Config. Now press Enter to run the command.

Tip

Whenever you type a filename, press Tab after the first few characters. Bash probably can complete the filename, so that you don't have to type the entire name. If you don't enter enough characters to uniquely identify the file, Bash beeps. Just type a few more characters and press Tab again.

Wildcards

Another way to avoid typing too many filenames is to use *wildcards*, special characters, such as the asterisk (*) and question mark (?), that match zero or more characters in a string. If you are familiar with MS-DOS, you may use commands such as COPY *.* A: to copy all files from the current directory to the A drive. Bash accepts similar wildcards in filenames. In fact, Bash provides many more wildcard options than MS-DOS does.

Bash supports three types of wildcards:

- The asterisk (*) character matches zero or more characters in a filename. Therefore, * denotes all files in a directory.
- The question mark (?) matches any single character.
- A set of characters in brackets matches any single character from that set. The string [xX]*, for example, matches any filename that starts with x or X.

Wildcards are handy when you want to perform a task on a group of files. To copy all the files from a directory named /mnt/cdrom to the current directory, for example, type the following:

```
cp /mnt/cdrom/* .
```

Bash replaces the wildcard character * with the names of all the files in the /mnt/cdrom directory. The period at the end of the command represents the current directory.

You can use the asterisk with other parts of a filename to select a more specific group of files. Suppose that you want to use the grep command to search for the string typedef struct in all files of the /usr/include directory that meet the following criteria:

- The filename starts with s.
- The filename ends with .h.

The wildcard specification s*.h denotes all filenames that meet these criteria. Thus, you can perform the search with the following command:

```
grep "typedef struct" /usr/include/s*.h
```

The string contains a space that you want the grep command to find, so you have to enclose that string in quotation marks. This method ensures that Bash does not try to interpret each word in the string as a separate command-line argument.

Although the asterisk (*) matches any number of characters, the question mark (?) matches a single character. Suppose that you have four files — image1.pcx, image2.pcx, image3.pcx, and image4.pcx — in the current directory. To copy these files to the /mnt/floppy directory, use the following command:

```
cp image?.pcx /mnt/floppy
```

Bash replaces the single question mark with any single character, and copies the four files to /mnt.

The third wildcard format — [...] — matches a single character from a specific set. You may want to combine this format with other wildcards to narrow down the matching filenames to a smaller set. To see a list of all filenames in the /etc/X11/xdm directory that start with x or X, type the following command:

```
ls /etc/X11/xdm/[xX]*
```

When expanding the [...] wildcard format, if Bash does not find any filenames matching that format, it leaves the wildcard specification intact.

Command History

To make it easy for you to repeat long commands, Bash stores up to 500 old commands. Essentially, Bash maintains a *command history* (a list of old commands). To see the command history, type history. Bash displays a numbered list of the old commands, including those that you entered during previous logins. That list may resemble the following:

```
1   cd
2   ls -a
3   more /etc/X11/XF86Config
4   history
```

If the command list is very long, you may choose to see only the last few commands. To see the last ten commands only, type the following:

```
history 10
```

To repeat a command from the list generated by the `history` command, simply type an exclamation point (!), followed by that command's number. To repeat command number 3, type `!3`.

You also can repeat an old command without knowing its command number. Suppose you typed `more /usr/lib/X11/xdm/xdm-config` a while ago, and now you want to look at that file again. To repeat the previous `more` command, type the following:

```
!more
```

Often, you may want to repeat the last command that you typed, perhaps with a slight change. For example, you may have displayed the contents of the directory by using the `ls -l` command. To repeat that command, type two exclamation points as follows:

```
!!
```

Sometimes, you may want to repeat the previous command but add extra arguments to it. Suppose that `ls -l` shows too many files. Simply repeat that command, but pipe the output through the `more` command as follows:

```
!! | more
```

Bash replaces the two exclamation points with the previous command and then appends | `more` to that command.

Tip

An easy way to recall previous commands is to press the up arrow key, which causes Bash to go backward in the list of commands. To move forward in the command history, press the down arrow key.

Command Editing

After you recall a command, you do not have to use the command as is; you can edit the command. Bash supports a wide variety of command-line editing commands. These commands resemble those used by the `emacs` and `vi` editors.

Suppose you want to look at the file `/etc/X11/XF86Config`, but you type the following:

```
more /etc/X11/XF86config
```

After you press Enter and see an error message stating that there is no such file, you realize that the `c` in `config` should have been uppercase. Instead of typing the entire line, you can type the following editing command to fix the problem:

```
^con^Con
```

Bash interprets this command to mean that it should replace the string `con` with `Con` in the previous command.

By default, Bash enables you to edit the command line using a small subset of commands supported by the emacs editor.

Because I am already familiar with emacs, I use emacs commands to edit commands. To bring back a previous command line, for example, I press Ctrl-P. Then, I commonly use the following keystrokes to edit the command line:

- Ctrl-B to go backward a character
- Ctrl-F to go forward a character
- Ctrl-D to delete the character on which the text cursor rests

To insert text, I type the text. Although emacs has a huge selection of editing commands, you can edit Bash command lines adequately with the preceding small set.

Secret

By default, the Bash shell supports emacs-style editing of command lines. To edit the command line using the vi editor's commands, type set -o vi at the shell prompt. In vi mode, you have to press Esc to enter editing commands, and press i to switch back to interacting with the shell. From vi mode, you can return to emacs editing by typing set -o emacs at the shell prompt.

Aliases

While configuring the Linux kernel and creating a new Linux boot floppy, I found myself changing the directory to /usr/src/linux/arch/i386/boot quite a few times. After typing that directory name twice, I immediately set up a shortcut using Bash's alias feature:

```
alias goboot='cd /usr/src/linux/arch/i386/boot'
```

I intentionally did not use any underscore characters or uppercase letters in goboot, because I wanted the alias to be quick and easy to type (and it had to mean something to me only). Now that I've defined the alias, I can go to that directory by typing the following at the Bash prompt:

```
goboot
```

As you can see, an *alias* simply is an alternative (and, usually, shorter) name for a lengthy command. Bash replaces the alias with its definition and performs the equivalent command.

Tip

If you type the same long command often, you can define an alias for that command. To make sure that the alias is available whenever you log in, place the definition in the .bash_profile file in your home directory.

Many users use the alias feature to give more familiar names to common commands. If you are a DOS user, and you use the dir command to get a directory listing, you can simply define dir as an alias for ls (the Linux command that displays the directory listing), as follows:

```
alias dir=ls
```

Now you can type di r whenever you want to see a directory listing.

Another good use of an alias is to redefine a dangerous command, such as rm, to make it safer. By default, the rm command deletes one or more specified files. If you type rm * by mistake, rm deletes all files in your current directory. I learned this the hard way one day when I wanted to delete all files that ended with .xwd. (These files contained old screen images that I no longer needed.) I intended to type rm *.xwd, but somehow, I ended up typing rm * .xwd. I got the following message:

```
rm: .xwd: No such file or directory
```

At first I was puzzled by the message, so I typed **ls** to see the directory's contents again. When the listing showed nothing, I realized that I had an extra space between the * and .xwd. Of course, all the files in that directory were gone forever.

The rm command provides the -i option, which asks for confirmation before deleting a file. To make that option a default, add the following alias definition to the .bash_profile file in your home directory:

```
alias rm='rm -i'
```

That's it! From now on, when you use rm to delete a file, the command first asks for confirmation, as follows:

```
rm .bash_profile
rm: remove `.bash_profile'? n
```

Press **y** to delete the file; otherwise, press **n**.

Summary

Once you have installed Red Hat Linux on your PC, you can begin learning how to use and operate a Red Hat Linux system. Some of the basic steps are to log in, log out, and shut down the system. You also need to learn how to navigate the file system. At heart, Linux is still UNIX, and you have to learn to use a shell — a command interpreter — to perform many common tasks. Even when you use a graphical interface, you sometimes have to open a terminal window and type commands at the shell prompt. This chapter got you started with Red Hat Linux operations and Bash — the Bourne Again shell — and some Linux commands for navigating the file system. You also learned to use the GNOME File Manager to explore the file system.

By reading this chapter, you learn the following:

▶ With graphical login enabled, you can log in, log out, and shut down a Red Hat Linux system from the graphical screen. You can also use /sbin/ shutdown to shut down the system from the shell prompt.

▶ Online documentation is available to help with many aspects of the Linux operating system.

▶ The Linux directory structure is organized logically as a single tree, regardless of the physical location of subdirectories. Linux includes many commands for navigating directories and manipulating files.

▶ GNOME includes a graphical file manager that you can use to work with files and directories.

▶ Even when you stay in the graphical environment of the X Window System and GNOME (or KDE), you may have to type Linux commands in a terminal window to perform many routine tasks. This especially is true when you log in using TELNET, or when you have problems with X.

▶ A shell is a program that runs commands for you. Bash is the default shell in Linux. Bash is compatible with the Bourne shell that comes with all other UNIX systems.

Chapter 11

GNU Utilities

In This Chapter

▶ Understanding the role of the GNU Project

▶ Getting an overview of the GNU software packages

▶ Learning the shell utilities, file utilities, text utilities, and binary utilities

▶ Exploring bc, gzip, patch, and Midnight Commander

▶ Learning about the sed stream editor

Red Hat Linux includes the Linux kernel and a large collection of utilities and applications that make it a complete operating system. Most of these utilities and applications are from the GNU Project. In a way, Linux became a full-fledged UNIX-like operating system primarily because of the GNU software. The GNU Project provided everything from the software development tools — assembler, compiler, and make — to GNOME, the GUI desktop. This chapter gives you an overview of the GNU software and introduces you to some of the GNU utilities.

What Is the GNU Project?

GNU is a recursive acronym that stands for *GNU's Not Unix*. The GNU Project was launched in 1984 by Richard Stallman to develop a complete Unix-like operating system. The GNU Project developed nearly everything needed for a complete operating system except for the operating system kernel. All GNU software was distributed under the GNU General Public License (GPL). GPL essentially requires that the software is distributed in source-code form, and stipulates that any user can copy, modify, and distribute the software to anyone else in source-code form. Users may, however, have to pay for their copy of GNU software.

The Free Software Foundation (FSF) is a tax-exempt charity that raises funds for work on the GNU Project. To learn more about the GNU Project, visit their home page at http://www.gnu.org/. There you will find information about how to contact the Free Software Foundation and how you can help the GNU Project.

Cross-Reference

Chapter 13 describes several applications, such as The GIMP, Ghostscript, and Ghostview. Chapter 14 describes the GNU Emacs editor, one of the most well known software packages from the GNU Project. Other GNU software, such as the Bash shell, C/C++ compiler, the make utility, and other software packages, are described in several chapters throughout this book.

An Overview of GNU Software

As a Red Hat Linux user, you may not realize the extent to which Red Hat Linux (and, for that matter, all Linux distributions) relies on GNU software. Nearly all tasks that you perform in a Red Hat Linux system involve one or more GNU software packages. For example, the GNOME graphical user interface (GUI) and the Bash shell are both GNU software. If you rebuild the kernel or develop software, you will do so with the GNU C and C++ compiler and the make utility; both are parts of the GNU software packages that accompany all Linux distributions. If you edit text files with the ed or Emacs editor, you are again using a GNU software package. The list goes on and on.

Table 11-1 briefly describes some of the well-known GNU software packages that come with Red Hat Linux. You can browse the table to get a feel for the types of tasks you can perform with GNU software.

Table 11-1   Well-known GNU Software Packages

Software Package	Description
Autoconf	Generates shell scripts that automatically configure source code packages
Automake	Generates Makefile.in files for use with Autoconf
Bash	The default shell — command interpreter — in Red Hat Linux. (Bash is compatible with the UNIX sh shell and offers many extensions found in csh and ksh shells.)
bc	An interactive calculator with arbitrary precision numbers
Binutils	A package that includes several utilities for working with binary files: ar, as, gasp, gprof, ld, nm, objcopy, objdump, ranlib, readelf, size, strings, and strip.
GNU C Library	For use with all Linux programs
gnuchess	A chess-playing program
cpio	Copies file archives to and from disk, or to another part of the file system
diff	Compares files, showing line-by-line changes in several different formats

Software Package	*Description*
ed	A line-oriented text editor
Emacs	An extensible, customizable full-screen text editor and computing environment
Fileutils	A package that implements the following Linux commands: `chgrp`, `chmod`, `chown`, `cp`, `dd`, `df`, `dir`, `dircolors`, `du`, `install`, `ln`, `ls`, `mkdir`, `mkfifo`, `mknod`, `mv`, `rm`, `rmdir`, `sync`, `touch`, and `vdir`.
Findutils	A package that includes the `find`, `locate`, and `xargs` utilities
Finger	A utility program designed to enable users of UNIX systems (including Red Hat Linux) on the Internet to get information about one another
Gawk	The GNU Project's implementation of the AWK programming language that conforms to the definition of the language in the POSIX 1003.2 Command Language and Utilities Standard
GCC	Compilers for C, C++, Objective C, and other languages
gdb	Source-level debugger for C, C++ and Fortran
gdbm	A replacement for the traditional `dbm` and `ndbm` database libraries
gettext	A set of utilities that enables software maintainers to internationalize a software package's user messages
Ghostscript	An interpreter for the Postscript and Portable Document Format (PDF) languages
Ghostview	An X Window System application that provides a graphical front end to Ghostscript, and enables users to view Postscript or PDF files in a window
The GIMP	The GNU Image Manipulation Program is an Adobe Photoshop-like image-processing program
GNOME	Provides a graphical user interface (GUI) for a wide variety of tasks that a Linux user might perform
Gnumeric	A graphical spreadsheet (similar to Microsoft Excel) that works in GNOME
grep package	Includes the `grep`, `egrep`, and `fgrep` commands that are used to find lines that match a specified text pattern
Groff	A document formatting system similar to `troff`
GTK+	A GUI toolkit for the X Window System (used to develop GNOME applications)
gzip	A GNU utility for compressing and decompressing files

Continued

Table 11-1   *(continued)*

Software Package	*Description*
indent	Formats C source code by indenting it in one of several different styles
less	A page-by-page display program similar to more, but with additional capabilities
libpng	A library for image files in the Portable Network Graphics (PNG) format
m4	An implementation of the traditional UNIX macro processor
make	A utility that determines which files of a large software package need to be recompiled, and issues the commands to recompile them
mtools	A set of programs that enables users to read, write, and manipulate files on a DOS file system (typically a floppy disk)
ncurses	A package for displaying and updating text on text-only terminals
patch	A GNU version of Larry Wall's program to take the output of diff and apply those differences to an original file to generate the modified version
RCS	The Revision Control System is used for version control and management of source files in software projects
sed	A stream-oriented version of the ed text editor
Sharutils	A package that includes shar (used to make shell archives out of many files) and unshar (to unpack these shell archives)
Shellutils	A package that includes the following utilities, which are part of the Bash shell: basename, chroot, date, dirname, echo, env, expr, factor, false, groups, hostname, id, logname, nice, nohup, pathchk, printenv, printf, pwd, seq, sleep, stty, su, tee, test, true, tty, uname, uptime, users, who, whoami, **and** yes
tar	A tape archiving program that includes multi-volume support; the capability to archive sparse files, handle compression and decompression, and create remote archives; and other special features for incremental and full backups
texinfo	A set of utilities that generate printed manuals, plain ASCII text, and online hypertext documentation (called Info), and enables users to view and read online Info documents
textutils	A set of utilities such as cut, join, nl, split, tail, wc, and so on, for manipulating text
time	A utility that reports the user, system, and actual time used by a process

The remainder of this chapter introduces you to several categories of GNU utilities.

Shell Utilities

The shell utilities implement a number of shell commands that you can use interactively, or in shell scripts. Each utility program performs a very specific task. The idea is that you can combine these commands in shell scripts to perform more complicated tasks.

Table 11-2 briefly describes each shell utility. You can try out some of these utilities by typing the program name at the shell prompt. Each program takes command-line options. You should first type man `progname`, where `progname` is the name of the utility, to learn more about the command-line options. Then try the utility with appropriate options.

Cross-
Reference

You will encounter some of these shell utilities again in Chapter 28 in the section covering shell programming.

Table 11-2   GNU Shell Utilities

Program	Description
`[`	Evaluates an expression and returns zero if the result is true (same as `test`)
`basename`	Removes the path prefix from a given path name
`chroot`	Changes the root directory
`date`	Prints or sets the system date and time
`dirname`	Removes the last level or filename from a given path name
`echo`	Prints a line of text
`env`	Prints environment variables or runs a command with modified environment variables
`expr`	Evaluates expressions
`factor`	Prints prime factors of a number
`false`	Returns an unsuccessful exit status
`groups`	Prints the names of the groups to which a user belongs
`hostid`	Prints the numeric identifier for the host
`id`	Prints the real and effective user and group IDs
`logname`	Prints the current login name
`nice`	Runs a program with specified scheduling priority

Continued

Table 11-2 *(continued)*

Program	Description
nohup	Allows a command to continue running after the user logs out
pathchk	Checks whether filenames are valid and portable
pinky	Prints information about users. (This is similar to the finger program; in fact, the name pinky refers to a lightweight finger)
printenv	Prints environment variables
printf	Formats and prints data
pwd	Prints the working (current) directory
seq	Prints numeric sequences
sleep	Suspends execution for a specified time
stty	Prints or changes terminal settings
su	Enables the user to adopt the ID of another user, or the super user (root)
tee	Sends output to multiple files
test	Evaluates an expression and returns zero if the result is true
true	Returns a successful exit status
tty	Prints the terminal name
uname	Prints system information
users	Prints current user names
who	Prints a list of all users currently logged in
whoami	Prints the user name for the current effective user ID
yes	Prints a string repeatedly until the process is killed

File Utilities and the Find Command

The file utilities include programs that you can use to work with files and directories in your Red Hat Linux system. Table 11-3 briefly describes each of these programs. You can copy and delete files, create new directories, and change the file permissions and ownerships. You can also list directories and see the amount of disk space used by the files.

Because you need to use the file utilities often, the next few sections show you how to use some of them. Also provided is a brief introduction to the find command, which enables you to locate all files that meet specified criteria.

Table 11-3   GNU File Utilities

Program	Description
chgrp	Changes group ownership of files
chmod	Changes the permissions of files
chown	Changes the ownership of files
cp	Copies files
dd	Converts a file according to a specified format and then copies the file
df	Shows storage space (hard disk, CD-ROM, floppy, and so on) usage for the file systems
dir	Prints a brief directory listing
dircolors	Prints the command to set the LS_COLORS environment variable, used by the color version of the GNU ls program
du	Shows disk space used by files and directories
install	Copies files and sets permissions
ln	Creates links between files
ls	Lists the contents of a directory
mkdir	Creates directories, if they do not already exist
mkfifo	Creates named pipes, used for data transfer between programs (FIFO stands for first-in first-out, which is how the named pipes transfer data)
mknod	Creates special block or character device files (usually located in the /dev directory)
mv	Renames files
rm	Deletes files
rmdir	Deletes empty directories
shred	Deletes a file securely by first overwriting it to make it harder to recover the data
sync	Flushes file system buffers to disk, thereby synchronizing memory and disk
touch	Changes the timestamps of files
vdir	Prints detailed directory listings (similar to ls -l)

File Manipulation

You often may copy files from one directory to another. Use the `cp` command to perform this task. To copy the file `/usr/X11R6/lib/X11/xinit/Xclients` to the `Xclients.sample` file in the current directory (such as your home directory), type the following:

```
cp /usr/X11R6/lib/X11/xinit/Xclients Xclients.sample
```

If you want to copy a file to the current directory and retain the same name, use a period (.) as the second argument of the `cp` command. Thus, the following command copies the `XF86Config` file from the `/etc/X11` directory to the current directory (denoted by a single period):

```
cp /etc/X11/XF86Config .
```

The `cp` command makes a new copy of a file and leaves the original intact.

Tip

If you want to copy the entire contents of a directory — including all subdirectories and their contents — to another directory, use the command `cp -ar sourcedir destdir` (this copies everything under *sourcedir* directory to *destdir*). For example, to copy all files from the `/etc/X11` directory to the current directory, type the following command:

```
cp -ar /etc/X11 .
```

Another GNU utility command, `mv`, moves a file to a new location. The original copy is gone, and a new copy appears at the specified destination. You can use `mv` to rename a file. If you want to change the name of the `today.list` to `old.list`, use the `mv` command, as follows:

```
mv today.list old.list
```

On the other hand, if you want to move the `today.list` file to a subdirectory named `saved`, use this command:

```
mv today.list saved
```

Note

An interesting feature of `mv` is the fact that you can use it to move entire directories, with all their subdirectories and files, to a new location. If you have a directory named `data` that contains many files and subdirectories, you can move that entire directory structure to `old_data` with the following command:

```
mv data old_data
```

Another common file operation is deleting a file. Use the `rm` command to delete a file named `old.list`, for example, by typing the following command:

```
rm old.list
```

Caution

Be careful with the `rm` command — in particular, when you log in as `root`. Inadvertently deleting important files with `rm` is very common.

Directory Manipulation

To organize files in your home directory, you have to create new directories. Use the mkdir command to create a directory. For example, to create a directory named images in the current directory, type the following:

```
mkdir images
```

After you create the directory, you can use the cd images command to change to that directory.

You can create an entire directory tree by using the -p option of the mkdir command. For example, suppose your system has a /usr/src directory and you want to create the directory tree /usr/src/book/java/examples/applets. You can create this directory hierarchy by typing the following command:

```
mkdir -p /usr/src/book/java/examples/applets
```

When you no longer need a directory, use the rmdir command to delete it. You can delete a directory only when the directory is empty.

To remove an empty directory tree, you can use the –p option, like this:

```
rmdir -p /usr/src/book/java/examples/applets
```

This command removes the empty parent directories of applets. The command stops when it encounters a directory that's not empty.

Disk Copying with dd

The dd command is useful for copying binary data to a floppy disk (or other devices, such as tape). For example, if you want to make a Red Hat boot disk on a Linux system, you can use the dd command to prepare the boot disk before you install Red Hat Linux from this book's companion CD-ROMs. Perform the following steps to prepare the boot disk:

1. Log in as root and mount the first CD from this book's companion CD-ROMs on /mnt/cdrom (type mount /mnt/cdrom). Change to the directory with the boot images as follows:

   ```
   cd /mnt/cdrom/images
   ```

2. Place a formatted floppy disk in the floppy drive. Then type the following command to copy the boot.img file to the floppy disk:

   ```
   dd if=boot.img of=/dev/fd0 bs=1440k
   ```

If you want to copy another boot image to the floppy, replace boot.img with that file's name.

Disk Usage Information

Two programs in the GNU file utilities — df and du — enable you to check disk space usage. These commands are simple to use. The df command shows you a summary of disk space usage for all mounted devices, as shown in the following example:

```
df
Filesystem           1k-blocks      Used Available Use% Mounted on
/dev/hda2             2000236     1259140    639488  67% /
/dev/hda1             2096160     1915488    180672  92% /dosc
/dev/hdc              654848       654848         0 100% /mnt/cdrom
```

The output is a table that shows the device, the total kilobytes of storage, how much is in use, how much is available, the percentage being used, and the mount point. For example, on my system, the /dev/hda2 device (a disk partition) is mounted on the Linux file system's root directory; it has about 2GB of space, of which 1.2GB (or 67 percent) is being used, and 639MB is available. Similarly, you can see from the last line that the CD-ROM has about 654MB of storage in use.

The other command — du — is useful for finding out how much space a directory is using. For example, type the following command to view the contents of all the subdirectories in the /var/log directory (this directory contains various error logs):

```
du /var/log
4        /var/log/httpd
4        /var/log/news/OLD
8        /var/log/news
1260     /var/log/sa
4        /var/log/vbox
4        /var/log/samba
1576     /var/log
```

Each directory name is preceded by a number — that number denotes the number of kilobytes of disk space used by that directory. Thus, the /var/log directory, as a whole, uses 220KB of disk space, whereas the /var/log/httpd subdirectory uses 4KB.

You can use the -h option with the du command to view the disk space usage in human-readable format. For example, here's what you get when you use du -h to view the disk space used by the /var/log directory and its contents:

```
du -h /var/log
4.0k     /var/log/httpd
4.0k     /var/log/news/OLD
8.0k     /var/log/news
1.3M     /var/log/sa
4.0k     /var/log/vbox
4.0k     /var/log/samba
1.6M     /var/log
```

If you simply want the total disk space used by a directory (including all the files and subdirectories contained in that directory), use the -s option together with the -h option, as follows:

```
du -sh /var/log
1.6M    /var/log
```

Notice that the -s option causes du to print just the summary information for the /var/log directory.

The find Command

The find command is very useful for locating files (and directories) that meet specified search criteria. The Linux version of the find command also comes from GNU, and it has more extensive options than the standard UNIX version. I show the syntax for the standard UNIX find command, however, because that syntax works in GNU find, and you can use the same format on other UNIX systems.

I must admit that when I began using UNIX many years ago (Berkeley UNIX in the early 1980s), I was confounded by the find command. I stayed with one basic syntax of find for a long time before graduating to more complex forms. The basic syntax that I learned first was for finding a file anywhere in the file system.

Suppose that you want to find any file or directory with a name that starts with gnome. You can use find to perform this search, as follows:

```
find / -name "gnome*" -print
```

This command tells find to start looking at the root directory (/), to look for filenames that match gnome*, and to display the full path name of any matching file.

You can use variations of this simple form of find to locate a file in any directory (as well as any subdirectories contained in the directory). If you forget where in your home directory you stored all files named report* (names that start with the string report), you can search for the files by using the following command:

```
find ~ -name "report*" -print
```

When you become comfortable with this syntax of find, you can use other options of find. For example, to find only specific types of files (such as directories), use the -type option. The following command displays all top-level directory names in your Linux system:

```
find / -type d -maxdepth 1 -print
```

You probably do not have to use the complex forms of find in a typical Linux system, but you can look up the rest of the find options, by using the following command:

```
man find
```

Text Utilities

The GNU text utility package includes a large number of utilities to manipulate the contents of text files. These utilities are patterned after the UNIX commands of the same name. The GNU versions of the programs usually have additional options and are optimized for speed. In general, the GNU utilities do not have any of the arbitrary limitations of their UNIX counterparts.

Table 11-4 briefly describes each text utility. The best way to learn these utilities is to try each one out. Before trying out a program, type info *progname* or man *progname* (where *progname* is the name of the program) to view the online help information.

Cross-Reference

A few selected text utilities are described in the following sections. You will find reference pages for many of these utilities in Appendix A.

Table 11-4	**GNU Text Utilities**
Program	**Description**
cat	Concatenates files and writes them to standard output
Cksum	Prints the cyclic redundancy check (CRC) checksums and byte counts of files (used to verify that files have not been corrupted in transmission, by comparing the cksum output for the received files with the cksum output for the original files)
comm	Compares two sorted files line by line. (The sort command sorts files.)
csplit	Splits a file into sections determined by text patterns in the file and places each section in a separate file named xx00, xx01, and so on
cut	Removes sections from each line of files and writes them to standard output
expand	Converts tabs in each file to spaces and writes the result to standard output
fmt	Fills and joins lines, making each line roughly the same length, and writes the formatted lines to standard output
fold	Breaks lines in a file so that each line is no wider than a specified width, and writes the lines to standard output
head	Prints the first part of files
join	Joins corresponding lines of two files using a common field and writes each line to standard output
md5sum	Computes and checks the MD5 message digest (a 128-bit checksum using the MD5 algorithm)
nl	Numbers each line in a file and writes the lines to standard output

Program	Description
od	Writes the contents of files to standard output in octal and other formats. (This is used to view the contents of binary files.)
paste	Merges corresponding lines of one or more files into vertical columns separated by tabs, and writes each line to standard output
pr	Formats text files for printing
ptx	Produces a permuted index of file contents
sort	Sorts lines of text files
split	Splits a file into pieces
sum	Computes and prints a 16-bit checksum for each file and counts the number of 1,024-byte blocks in the file
tac	Writes each file to standard output, last line first
tail	Prints the last part of files
tr	Translates or deletes characters in files
tsort	Performs a topological sort (used to organize a library for efficient handling by the ar and ld commands)
unexpand	Converts spaces into tabs
uniq	Removes duplicate lines from a sorted file
wc	Prints the number of bytes, words, and lines in files

Counting Words and Lines in a Text File

For example, suppose you want to use the wc command to display the character, word, and line count of a text file. Try the following:

```
wc /etc/inittab
    57    244    1756 /etc/inittab
```

This causes wc to display the number of lines (57), words (244), and characters (1756) in the /etc/inittab file. If you simply want to see the number of lines in a file, use the -l option:

```
wc -l /etc/inittab
    57 /etc/inittab
```

As you can see, in this case, wc simply displays the line count.

If you don't specify a filename, the wc command expects input from the standard input. You can use the pipe feature of the shell to feed the output of another command to wc. This can be handy sometimes. Suppose you want a rough count of the processes running on your system. You can get a list of all processes with the ps ax command, but instead of manually counting the lines, just pipe the output of ps to wc and you can get a rough count, as follows:

```
ps ax | wc -l
      61
```

That means the ps command produced 61 lines of output. Because the first line simply shows the headings for the tabular columns, you can estimate that about 60 processes are running on your system. (Of course, this count probably includes the processes used to run the ps and wc commands as well, but who's counting?)

Sorting Text Files

You can sort the lines in a text file using the sort command. To see how the sort command works, first type more /etc/passwd to see the current contents of the /etc/passwd file. Now type sort /etc/passwd to see the lines sorted alphabetically. If you want to sort a file and save the sorted version in another file, you have to use the Bash shell's output redirection feature, as follows:

```
sort /etc/passwd > ~/sorted.text
```

This command sorts the lines in the /etc/passwd file and saves the output in a file named sorted.text in your home directory.

Substituting or Deleting Characters from a File

Another interesting command is tr — it substitutes one group of characters for another (or deletes a selected character), throughout a file. Suppose that you occasionally have to use MS-DOS text files on your Linux system. Although you might expect to use a text file on any system without any problems, there is one catch: DOS uses a carriage return followed by a line feed to mark the end of each line, whereas Linux (and other UNIX systems) use only a line feed. Therefore, if you use the vi editor with the -b option to open a DOS text file (for example, type vi -b *filename* to open the file), you see ^M at the end of each line. That ^M stands for Ctrl+M, which is the carriage-return character.

On your Linux system, you easily can rid the DOS text file of the extra carriage returns, by using the tr command with the -d option. Essentially, to convert the DOS text file *filename.dos* to a Linux text file named *filename.linux*, type the following:

```
tr -d '\015' < filename.dos > filename.linux
```

In this command, '\015' denotes the ASCII code for the carriage-return character in octal notation.

Note

You can use the `tr` command to translate or delete characters from the input. When you use `tr` with the `-d` option, it deletes all occurrences of a specific character from the input data. Following the `-d` option, you must specify the character to be deleted. Like many UNIX utilities, `tr` reads the standard input and writes its output to standard output. As the sample command shows, you must employ input and output redirection to use `tr` to delete all occurrences of a character in a file and save the output in another file.

Splitting a File into Several Smaller Files

The `split` command is handy for those times when you want to copy a file to a floppy disk, but the file is too large to fit on a single floppy. You can then use the `split` command to break up the file into smaller files, each of which can fit on a floppy.

By default, `split` puts 1,000 lines into each file. The files are named by groups of letters such as `aa`, `ab`, `ac`, and so on. You can specify a prefix for the filenames. For example, to split a large file called `hugefile.tar` into smaller files that fit onto several high-density 3.5-inch floppy disks, use `split` as follows:

```
split -b 1440k hugefile.tar part.
```

This command splits the `hugefile.tar` file into 1,440K chunks so that each can fit onto a floppy disk. The command creates files named `part.aa`, `part.ab`, `part.ac`, and so on.

To combine the split files back into a single file, use the `cat` command as follows:

```
cat part.?? > hugefile.tar
```

Binary Utilities

Just as the text utilities are meant for working with text files, the GNU binary utilities are meant for performing various tasks on binary files. Some of these utilities, such as ar, as, and ld, are used when building and managing object files that are generated when source files are compiled. A number of other binary utilities enable you to examine the contents of binary files. For example, the `strings` command prints all strings of printable characters in a file. Here is what the `strings` command displays for a simple C program that prints `Hello, World!` (the name of the binary executable is `a.out`):

```
strings a.out
/lib/ld-linux.so.2
__gmon_start__
```

```
libc.so.6
printf
__cxa_finalize
__deregister_frame_info
_IO_stdin_used
__libc_start_main
__register_frame_info
GLIBC_2.1.3
GLIBC_2.0
PTRh
QVh\
Hello World!
```

Notice that the output includes the `Hello World!` String, as well names of libraries (`/lib/ld-linux.so.2` and `libc.so.6`) and C functions (`printf`).

You can use the `size` command to look at the number of bytes that various sections (such as the code size, data area, and stack space) of a program would need. Here is the output of `size` for the `a.out` file that contains the `Hello, World!` program:

```
size a.out
   text     data      bss       dec     hex filename
   1003      232       24      1259     4eb a.out
```

In this case, the program requires 1,003 bytes for the code (called text, but it's the binary executable code of a program), 232 bytes for the data, and 24 bytes for stack. Thus, the program requires a total of 1,259 bytes of memory. Note that the actual size of the `a.out` file will be much larger than 1,259 bytes because other information, such as symbols, is included in the file. Programmers would find the output of the `size` command useful, because it tells them about the memory required to load and run a program.

Table 11-5 briefly describes the programs in the GNU binary utilities package. You can try some of these programs on any binary file in the system. For example, here's the result of running `size` on `/bin/bash`—the executable for the Bash shell:

```
size /bin/bash
   text     data      bss       dec     hex filename
 488691    22324    16912    527927   80e37 /bin/bash
```

Table 11-5   GNU Binary Utilities

Program	Description
addr2line	Uses debugging information in an executable file to translate program addresses into filenames and line numbers
ar	Creates and modifies archives and extracts from archives. (An archive is a library holding the object code of commonly needed subroutines.)

Program	Description
as	This is the portable GNU assembler
gasp	This is a filter program to translate encoded C++ symbols
gprof	This is the GNU profiler, used to determine which parts of a program are taking most of the execution time
ld	This the GNU linker, used to combine a number of object and archive files and create executable files
nm	Lists symbols from object files
objcopy	Copies the contents of an object file to another (can also translate the format, if required)
objdump	Displays information from object files
ranlib	Generates an index to the contents of an archive
readelf	Displays information about one or more Executable and Linking Format (ELF) object files
size	Lists the section sizes of an object or archive file
strings	Lists printable strings from files
strip	Discards symbols from object files

Other Utilities

This section introduces you to a few more utilities from the GNU software packages shown in Table 11-1. The list is not exhaustive; I included only a few selected utilities. Following are the utilities summarized in the following sections:

- GNU bc — an arbitrary precision calculator
- gzip — a utility for compressing and expanding files
- Midnight Commander — a file manager with a text-based interface
- patch — a utility for applying changes to a text file

GNU bc

GNU bc enables you to enter arbitrary precision numbers and perform various calculations with these numbers. GNU bc implements the arbitrary precision-calculation capability specified by the POSIX P1003.2/D11 draft standard.

GNU bc is installed as part of the base operating system during the Red Hat Linux installation that is on the companion CD-ROMs.

If you have GNU bc installed, you should be able to run it with the following command:

```
bc
bc 1.06
Copyright 1991-1994, 1997, 1998, 2000 Free Software Foundation, Inc.
This is free software with ABSOLUTELY NO WARRANTY.
For details type `warranty'.
```

After displaying the banner, bc waits for your input. Then you can enter numbers and expressions, using syntax similar to that of the C programming language.

Numbers are the basic elements in bc. A number is treated as an arbitrary precision number with an integral and fractional part. You can enter numbers and evaluate expressions just as you write expressions in C, as the following example shows:

```
1.000000000000000033 + 0.1
1.100000000000000033
```

As soon as you enter an expression, bc evaluates the expression and displays the result.

You also can define variables and use them in expressions, as follows:

```
cost=119.95
tax_rate=0.05
total=(1+tax_rate)*cost
total
125.94
```

If you check this result with your calculator, you'll notice that bc truncates the result of multiplication (it does the same with division). If you want, you can retain more significant digits by setting the scale variable, as follows:

```
scale=10
total=(1+tax_rate)*cost
total
125.9475
```

In this case, the result has more significant digits.

The bc utility supports an entire programming language with a C-style syntax. You can write loops and conditional statements, and even define new functions with the define keyword. The following example shows how you might define a factorial function:

```
define factorial (n) {
  if(n <= 1) return (1);
  return (factorial(n-1)*n);
}
```

As you can see, the `factorial` function is recursive; it calls itself. Entering the lines as shown in the example is important. In particular, `bc` needs the open brace on the first line because that brace tells `bc` to continue reading input, until it comes to a closing brace.

After you define the `factorial` function, you can use it just as you might call a C function. Following are some examples:

```
factorial(3)
6
factorial(4)
24
factorial(10)
3628800
factorial(40)
815915283247897734345611269596115894272000000000
factorial(50)
30414093201713378043612608166064768844377641568960512000000000000
factorial(100)
9332621544394415268169923885626670049071596826438162146859296389521759\
9999322991560894146397615651828625369792082722375825118521091686400000\
00000000000000000000
```

As the example shows, you can use `bc` to represent as large a number as you want; no limit exists. When necessary, `bc` displays the result on multiple lines, with each continuation line ending in a backslash followed by a new line.

To quit `bc`, type the following command:

```
quit
```

To learn more about `bc`, consult its man pages, by using the `man bc` command. After you learn about new features of `bc`, try them interactively.

gzip

The `gzip` program is the GNU zip compression utility that is used to compress all Linux software distributions. When you run `gzip` with a filename as an argument, it reduces the file's size by using the Lempel-Ziv (LZ77) compression algorithm, and stores the result in a file with the same name, but with an additional `.gz` extension. Thus, if you compress a file with the `gzip files.tar` command, the result is a compressed file with the name `files.tar.gz`.

The same `gzip` program can decompress any file that was previously compressed by `gzip`. To decompress the file `files.tar.gz`, for example, you can simply type the following:

```
gzip -d files.tar
```

Notice that you do not have to explicitly type the .gz extension; gzip automatically appends a .gz extension when it is looking for the compressed file. After decompressing, the utility creates a new file with the name files.tar.

Instead of gzip -d, you can use the gunzip command to decompress a file:

```
gunzip files.tar
```

This command also looks for a file named files.tar.gz and decompresses the file, if found.

By default, gzip stores the original filename and timestamp in the compressed file. You can decompress a file with the -N option to restore the original filename and timestamp.

Following is the basic syntax of the gzip command:

```
gzip [-cdfhlLnNrtvV19] [-S .xxx] [file ...]
```

The options have the following meanings:

- -c writes output to standard output
- -d decompresses the file
- -f forces compression or decompression, even if the file has multiple links or the corresponding file already exists
- -h displays a help screen and quits
- -l lists files sizes before and after compression
- -L displays the gzip license and quits
- -n stops gzip from storing the original filename in the compressed file
- -N restores the original filename during decompression
- -q suppresses all warnings
- -r causes gzip to traverse the directory structure recursively and operate on all files
- -S .xxx causes gzip to use the suffix .xxx instead of .gz
- -t tests the integrity of a compressed file
- -v displays the name and percentage of compression for each file
- -V displays the version number and the compiler options used to build that version of gzip
- -1 uses the fastest compression method (even though compression may not be as much)
- -9 uses the slowest compression method (provides the most compression)
- file ... specifies one or more filenames (the files to be compressed or decompressed)

The gzip utility is installed automatically when you install Red Hat Linux from the companion CD-ROMs.

Midnight Commander

Midnight Commander is a file manager with a text-based interface, similar to Norton Commander for MS-DOS. You can use Midnight Commander to manage files and directories, without having to learn UNIX commands. If you are not familiar with all the UNIX commands, you may want to use Midnight Commander to perform file operations, such as copy, rename, and delete. You can even view or edit a file with Midnight Commander.

When you install Red Hat Linux from the companion CD-ROMs, you can install Midnight Commander.

You can run Midnight Commander from the console or a terminal window. To start Midnight Commander, type **mc**.

Figure 11-1 shows typical output from Midnight Commander. In this case, the current directory happens to be the root directory (/).

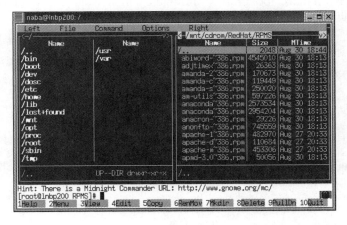

Figure 11-1: Midnight Commander running in a terminal window

The display has two side-by-side directory listings. You can change the directory on either listing. The two side-by-side views enable you to perform operations, such as copying or moving between two directories.

At the bottom of the Midnight Commander display are ten commands that vaguely resemble buttons in a graphical interface. These commands are the common operations that you can perform in the Midnight Commander window, by pressing the corresponding function key. For example, press F10 to quit Midnight Commander.

Midnight Commander responds to mouse input in a console window or a terminal window. This means that you can double-click a directory name to view that directory's contents in the Midnight Commander display. You can also click the commands (displayed in reverse video on the bottom edge of the Midnight Commander display) to activate them.

patch

The GNU patch utility is designed to apply *patches*, or corrections, to files. The basic idea behind patch is that when you want to distribute changes in a file, you run the standard UNIX diff command and generate a diff file that indicates how the file should be changed; then you distribute that diff file to everyone who has the original file. The recipient runs the patch utility with the diff file, as input and patch makes the changes in the original files.

Cross-Reference

The patch utility is installed automatically when you install Linux from the companion CD-ROMs. Chapter 28 discusses how to use patch to apply changes to the Linux kernel sources when you upgrade the kernel from one version to the next.

You can learn more about patch through a simple example. Assume that you have a file named original.txt that contains the following text:

```
Version: 1.0

Revision history:
  10/26/2000: Original file (NB)

This text file is used as an example to illustrate how to
use diff and patch to update a file.
```

Suppose that you already distributed this file to several users. (Pretend that the file is the source file of a computer program.) After a while, you make some changes in this file. The new file, named revised.txt, looks like the following:

```
Version: 1.1

Revision history:
  10/26/2000: Original file (NB)
  4/19/2001: Added a new line (LB)

This text file is used as an example to illustrate how to
use diff and patch to update a file.

Here is something new...
```

Now you want to provide these changes to your users so they can use the new file. Your first task is to create a diff file that captures the changes you have made.

To create the `diff` file, run `diff` with the `-u` option, and specify the two file-names as arguments — the original file, followed by the revised one. Thus, the following command creates the `diff` file for the current example:

```
diff -u original.txt revised.txt > patch-1.1
```

This command creates the file `patch-1.1`, which is what you would distribute to your users who are currently using the file `original.txt`. This `diff` file is also referred to as the *patch file*.

When a user receives the patch file, all that he or she needs to do is put the patch file in the same directory where the file `original.txt` resides, and then type the following command:

```
patch < patch-1.1
patching file 'original.txt'
```

First, `patch` copies the `original.txt` file to `original.txt.orig`; then it applies the changes directly to the file `original.txt`. After `patch` finishes, you'll find that the content of the `original.txt` file matches that of `revised.txt`. This example should give you a good idea of how to use the `patch` utility to update text files.

Stream Editor — sed

The `sed` program is a text editor similar to `ed` (described in Chapter 14), but unlike `ed`, `sed` is not interactive. Instead, `sed` is meant for editing a stream of input coming from standard input, and writing the edited text to standard output. The name `sed` stands for *stream editor* because it operates on a stream of text.

The `sed` editor is typically used to edit one or more files automatically through a shell script, or to simplify repetitive edits on multiple files. The following sections provide an overview of `sed`.

Running sed

The `sed` editor expects to read from the standard input and write to the standard output. You can provide a filename on the command line, but `sed` still writes the output to standard output. This means that `sed` does not change the file it edits. You can redirect the output to another file or the original file, thereby changing that file.

By default, `sed` applies each editing command globally to all lines in the file. You can, however, use line addresses or patterns to restrict the lines to which the editing commands apply.

To use `sed` on the fly from the shell prompt, you can run it as follows:

somecommand | sed *'editcommand'* | *anothercommand*

In this case, you feed the output of *somecommand* to sed, sed applies *editcommand* to each line, and then sed's output goes to *anothercommand*. For example, to see all the current processes that have gnome in their name, you can type the following command, which uses sed to edit the stream:

```
ps ax --cols 132 | sed -n '/gnome/p' | cut -c 28-132
/usr/bin/gnome-session
gnome-smproxy --sm-client-id default0
gnome-name-service
gnome-terminal --use-factory --start-factory-server
gnome-pty-helper
sed -n /gnome/p
```

In this case, each line in the output of the ps command is edited by sed, and then a part of each line is extracted, by using the cut command. Here, sed is invoked as follows:

```
sed -n '/gnome/p'
```

The -n option stops sed from printing each line to standard output. The '/gnome/p' part of the command line is an editing command—it means print each line containing the string gnome.

If you want to apply multiple sed commands, use the -e option to specify each editing command. For example, the following sed command takes the output of ps and deletes all lines that do not contain gnome (this is the edit command -e '/gnome/!d'), and then deletes any line that contains the string sed (this is done by -e '/sed/d'):

```
ps ax | sed -e '/gnome/!d' -e '/sed/d' | cut -c 28-80
/usr/bin/gnome-session
gnome-smproxy --sm-client-id default0
gnome-name-service
gnome-terminal --use-factory --start-factory-server
gnome-pty-helper
```

Of course, you typically do not type long sed commands at the shell prompt. Instead, sed is used in shell scripts. You can also place sed commands in a file and then edit a text file, by running sed with the -f option, as follows:

```
sed -f sedscriptfile myfile
```

This command edits *myfile* by using the sed commands in *sedscriptfile*, and writes the lines to standard output. If you want to save the output in another file, redirect the output as follows:

```
sed -f sedscriptfile myfile > editedfile
```

Learning the Basics of sed Commands

All sed commands have the following general form:

```
[address][,address][!]command[arguments]
```

The parts shown in square brackets are optional. The *command* is an editing command (similar to those for the ed editor) that specifies what action sed takes on a line. The *address* specifies the lines to which the commands apply. The exclamation mark (!) causes the command to be applied to all lines that do not match the address. The *arguments* are needed by some editing commands, such as the w or r command, that read a file for which you have to provide the filename as an argument.

Cross-Reference

As you can see, the basic syntax of sed commands is simple; but the address usually includes regular expressions, which cause the sed commands to appear very cryptic. Chapter 28 describes regular expressions.

Understanding the address is the key to learning sed. A sed command can have zero, one, or two addresses. The addresses identify lines to which sed commands are to be applied. An address is a regular expression or a line number, or a symbol such as $ that refers to a line number. Use the following guidelines to understand how addresses control what gets edited:

- If there are no addresses, sed applies the command to each line. For example, if a script has the command s/UNIX/Linux/, then sed changes every occurrence of UNIX to Linux.

- If there is only one address, sed applied the command to any lines matching the address. For example, 1d deletes the first line of the stream.

- If you specify two comma-separated addresses, sed applies the command to the first matching line and all subsequent lines up to and including the line matching the second address. Thus, the following command deletes everything from line 26, to the last line in the file:

  `26,$d`

- If you add an exclamation mark (!) after an address, the command applies to all lines that do not match the address. For example, the command /gnome/!d deletes all lines that do not contain the string gnome.

You can use curly braces to apply more than one editing command to an address. The syntax is as follows:

```
[/pattern/][,/pattern]{
command1
command2
...other commands...
}
```

Note that the opening curly brace ({) must end a line, and the closing curly brace (}) must be on a line by itself. You should ensure that there are no blank spaces after the curly braces.

Sometimes you need to delete a line, but hold it in temporary storage and insert it elsewhere in the output stream. There are sed commands, such as h and g for such operations. To use these commands, you need to understand the concept of *pattern space* and *hold space*. The pattern space is the buffer holding the current input line. The hold space is a separate set-aside buffer used for temporary storage. You can copy the contents of the hold space to the pattern space, and vice versa. For example, suppose you want to extract all lines containing the string Item: and move them to a location later in the file (assume that the place is a line that has the string List of items:). You can do this with the following sed script:

```
/Item:/{
H
d
}
/List of items:/G
```

The first four lines of the script apply the commands H and d to the lines that contain Item:. The H command appends the line to the hold space, and then the d command deletes it. Then the G command on the last line of the script inserts the contents of the hold space after the string List of Items:.

Because of limited space, this section does not show you all the sed commands in detail. However, Table 11-6 provides a summary of commonly used sed commands, grouped by function.

Table 11-6   Commonly Used sed Commands

Command	Meaning
Editing	
=	Prints the line number of a line. For example, /ORDER/= prints the line number of the lines containing the ORDER string (the line number is printed before each matching line).
a\	Appends text after a line. For example, the following script appends a few lines to the file at the end of the output: $a\ This line goes at the end of the file.\ Then this one.
c\	Replaces text. For example, the following script replaces the first 50 lines of text with a single line that says <50 lines deleted>: 1,50c\ <50 lines deleted>
i\	Inserts text before a line. For example, the following script inserts text before a line containing SKU 53055: /SKU 53055/i\ *** THE FOLLOWING ITEM IS OUT OF STOCK ***
d	Deletes lines. The command 1,20d deletes the first 20 lines.
l	Prints the line showing nonprinting characters as ASCII codes. For example, 5l prints the fifth line.

Command	Meaning

n	Skips the current line. For example, suppose a file contains section headers on a line right after a SECTION line. The following script extracts all section headers from the file (run this script with `sed -n -f scriptfile`, where *scriptfile* contains the following script):
	
	`/^SECTION/{`
	`n`
	`p`
	`}`

p	Prints a line. For example, the `/gnome/p` command prints the lines containing the string gnome. Because sed prints each line anyway, this will cause duplicate lines to be printed. You can use the p command with `sed -n` to print only selected lines (`-n` stops sed from printing lines by default).
q	Quits sed. For example, `/Detailed Report/q` quits the editor after printing the first line that contains this string.
s	Substitutes one pattern with another. For example, `s/UNIX/Linux/` replaces all occurrences of UNIX with Linux.
y	Translates characters (similar to what the tr command does). For example, `/^Appendix [1-9]/y/123456789/ABCDEFGHI/` replaces Appendix 1, 2, and so on, to Appendix A, B, and so on.

Working Multiple Lines

Command	Meaning

D	Deletes the first part of pattern space (up to a newline) created by the N command. For example, the following script deletes multiple blank lines:
	
	`/^$/{`
	`N`
	`/^\n$/D`
	`}`

N	Appends the next input line to the pattern space (a newline character separates the two lines). See the example for D.

Copying and Pasting

Command	Meaning

h	Copies the pattern space to the hold space, wiping out what was in the hold space earlier. For example, the following script finds an order number (assumed to be four digits) in a file and prints a note followed by the order number:
	
	`/Order/{`
	`h`
	`s/Order \#[0-9]\{4\}$/We have shipped your order:/`
	`p`
	`x`
	`}`

Continued

Table 11-6	*(continued)*	

Command	Meaning
H	Appends the pattern space to the hold space. See example earlier in the "Learning the basics of sed commands" section.
g	Pastes the contents of the hold space into the pattern space, overwriting the previous contents
G	Pastes the contents of the hold space after the current line. See example earlier in the "Learning the basics of sed commands" section.
x	Exchanges contents of pattern space with the contents of hold space. See example for h.
File Input and Output	
r	Reads a file into the input stream. For example, /^Dear/r letter inserts the contents of the letter file into the input stream after the line that begins with Dear.
w	Writes input lines to a file. For example, /^Order/w writes all lines that begin with Order to the file named orders.

Summary

Software from the GNU Project has helped make Linux a complete operating system. Many components of Linux—from the Bash shell to the GNOME graphical user interface (GUI)—come from the GNU Project. This chapter provides an overview of the GNU software packages and describes some of the utility programs in those packages. Other GNU software packages are covered in other parts of this book.

By reading this chapter, you learn the following things:

▶ The GNU Project, supported by the Free Software Foundation, provided many software packages that make Linux a complete operating system. More information about the GNU Project is available online at http://www.gnu.org/.

▶ The GNU software packages include such well-known software as the Bash shell, the GNOME GUI, the GIMP image-processing program, the gzip compression/decompression utility, the tar archiving program, the Emacs editor, as well as a large number of other utilities that Linux users and programmers use.

Chapter 12

GUI Desktops

In This Chapter

▶ Getting a graphical login screen in Linux

▶ Understanding the GNOME and KDE graphical environments

▶ Learning how to customize X applications through resources

By now, you have installed Red Hat Linux and X, and you have had your first taste of Red Hat Linux. During Red Hat Linux installation, the installation program configures X and gives you an option to use a graphical login screen. If you opted for the graphical login screen, X starts automatically, and you get a graphical screen with a login dialog box.

This chapter explains how Linux automatically starts in graphics mode. If you did not enable the graphical login screen, you can easily do so by reading this chapter. You also learn about GNOME and KDE — two graphical environments in Red Hat Linux. The last part of the chapter shows you the general techniques for customizing X applications, using X resources.

Cross-Reference

Turn to Chapter 2 if you have not installed Red Hat Linux and X yet. Turn to Chapter 3 if you have installed Red Hat Linux, but have not configured X yet. Then return to this chapter to learn how Linux automatically starts X and displays a graphical login screen.

Setting Up a Graphical Login

To log in on many UNIX workstations (such as those from Hewlett-Packard or IBM), you have to type the name and password in a login dialog window. Setting up your Linux workstation to display a graphical login screen is easy — all you have to do is make the appropriate selection during the installation. Even if you did not initially elect to have a graphical login screen, you can easily set it up once you know the details. The following sections explain how your Red Hat Linux system displays the graphical login screen.

The init Process and the Display Manager

A process named `init` starts the initial set of processes on your Red Hat Linux system. What `init` starts depends on the current run level, the contents of the `/etc/inittab` file, and the shell scripts located in the `/etc/rc.d` directory and its subdirectories. For now, you don't need to understand the details, except to know that the graphical login screen starts at run level 5.

Cross-Reference

Chapter 23 describes in detail the `init` process, the `/etc/inittab` file, and the Red Hat Linux boot process.

The last line of the `/etc/inittab` file is responsible for starting the graphical login process with the following entry (the number 5 denotes run level 5):

```
x:5:respawn:/etc/X11/prefdm -nodaemon
```

This command runs `/etc/X11/prefdm`, a shell script that starts a specific display manager, depending on your choice of the default GUI desktop, as indicated by the setting of the `DESKTOP` variable in the `/etc/sysconfig/desktop` file. The display manager is a program responsible for displaying the graphical login window, authenticating users who log in, running initialization scripts at the start of a session, and cleaning up after the session. As you can see from this brief description, the display manager process manages the display, making it available to the users and cleaning up after the user finishes a session. The exact steps that the display manager performs depend on your choice of the GUI desktop, whether it is GNOME or KDE.

For example, if your default desktop is GNOME, the `/etc/sysconfig/desktop` file contains the following line:

```
DESKTOP="GNOME"
```

For the GNOME graphical user interface, or GNOME GUI (the default in Red Hat Linux), `/etc/X11/prefdm` runs `/usr/bin/gdm`—the GNOME display manager. The "Switching from GNOME to KDE" section shows you how to switch to the KDE GUI. When you use KDE, `/etc/X11/prefdm` runs `/usr/bin/kdm`—the KDE display manager. This means that regardless of your choice of the GUI, at run level 5 `init` starts a display manager. The display manager, in turn, displays the graphical login dialog box, which enables you to log into the system.

Tip

If you did not enable the graphical login screen during Red Hat installation, you can do so by editing the `/etc/inittab` file. Locate the line containing `initdefault` and make sure that it reads as follows:

```
id:5:initdefault:
```

Caution

Before you edit the `/etc/inittab` file, you should know that any errors in this file may prevent Linux from starting up to a point at which you can log in. If you cannot log in, you cannot use your system.

The GNOME Display Manager (gdm)

The gdm program is written as a replacement for xdm, the X display manager. Like xdm, gdm starts an X server for each local display, displays a login dialog box, and enables the user to log into the system.

When gdm runs, it reads various configuration parameters from the configuration file /etc/X11/gdm/gdm.conf, which has a structure similar to a Windows INI file. For example, here is a typical gdm.conf file:

```
[daemon]
Chooser=/usr/bin/gdmchooser --disable-sound --disable-crash-dialog
DefaultPath=/usr/bin:/bin:/usr/X11R6/bin:/usr/local/bin:/opt/bin
DisplayInitDir=/etc/X11/gdm/Init
Greeter=/usr/bin/gdmlogin --disable-sound --disable-crash-dialog
Group=gdm
HaltCommand=/sbin/shutdown -h now
KillInitClients=1
LogDir=/var/gdm
PidFile=/var/run/gdm.pid
PostSessionScriptDir=/etc/X11/gdm/PostSession/
PreSessionScriptDir=/etc/X11/gdm/PreSession/
RebootCommand=/sbin/shutdown -r now
RootPath=/sbin:/usr/sbin:/usr/bin:/bin:/usr/X11R6/bin:/usr/local/bin:/
opt/bin
ServAuthDir=/var/gdm
SessionDir=/etc/X11/gdm/Sessions/
User=gdm
UserAuthDir=
UserAuthFBDir=/tmp
UserAuthFile=.Xauthority

[security]
AllowRoot=1
RelaxPermissions=1
RetryDelay=3
UserMaxFile=65536
VerboseAuth=1

[xdmcp]
Enable=0
HonorIndirect=0
MaxPending=4
MaxPendingIndirect=4
MaxSessions=16
MaxWait=30
MaxWaitIndirect=30
Port=177

[gui]
GtkRC=
MaxIconWidth=128
MaxIconHeight=128
```

```
[greeter]
Browser=0
DefaultFace=/usr/share/pixmaps/nobody.png
DefaultLocale=english
Exclude=bin,daemon,adm,lp,sync,shutdown,halt,mail,news,uucp,operator,n
obody
Font=-adobe-helvetica-bold-r-normal-*-*-180-*-*-*-*-*-*
GlobalFaceDir=/usr/share/faces/
Icon=/usr/share/pixmaps/gdm.xpm
LocaleFile=/etc/X11/gdm/locale.alias
Logo=/usr/share/pixmaps/gnome-logo-large.png
Quiver=0
SystemMenu=1
Welcome=Welcome to %n
Welcome[de]=Willkommen auf %n
Welcome[fr]=Bienvenue sur %n
Welcome[ja]=%n ¤Ø¤è¤_¤_¤1/2

[chooser]
DefaultHostImg=/usr/share/pixmaps/nohost.png
HostImageDir=/usr/share/hosts/
ScanTime=3

[debug]
Enable=0

[servers]
0=/usr/bin/X11/X
#1=/usr/bin/X11/X
```

The [servers] section of the file specifies the displays on which gdm
displays the login dialog box. Each line of this section starts with a display
number and shows the command needed to start the X server. Table 12-1
describes all the gdm configuration options.

Tip

Edit the Welcome= line to change the welcome message on the graphical
login screen. The default message says welcome to the hostname, which
can be somewhat cryptic. You can edit that line and change the message to
something more meaningful with the syntax Welcome=Welcome to XYZ Corp.

Table 12-1   The gdm Configuration Options

Configuration Option	Description
[daemon] Section	
Chooser=*chooserprogram*	Full path and name of the gdmchooser executable file (typically, this should be /usr/bin/gdmchooser)
DefaultPath=*pathname*	Path (names of directories separated by colons) to be used for the user's session

Configuration Option	Description
DisplayInitDir=*pathname*	Directory containing the initialization scripts (the default is /etc/X11/gdm/Init)
Greeter=*greeterprogram*	Full path and name of the greeter executable file, followed by arguments (typically, this should be /usr/bin/gdmlogin)
Group=*groupname*	Group name under which gdmlogin and gdmchooser are run (the default is gdm)
HaltCommand=*haltprogram*	Full path and arguments to the command to be executed when the user selects Halt from the System menu (typically, this should be /sbin/shutdown -h now)
KillInitClients=1 or 0	When set to 1, gdm kills the X clients started by the Init scripts after the user logs in (the default is 1)
LogDir=*pathname*	Directory containing the log files for the displays (by default, the value of this option is the same as that of the ServAuthDir option)
PidFile=*pidfile*	Name of the file where the process ID (pid) of the gdm process is stored (the default is /var/run/gdm.pid)
PostSessionScriptDir= *pathname*	Directory that contains the PostSession scripts — scripts run after the user logs out (the default is /etc/X11/gdm/PostSession/)
PreSessionScriptDir=*pathname*	Directory that contains the PreSession scripts — scripts run right after the user logs in (the default is /etc/X11/gdm/PreSession/)
RebootCommand=*rebootprogram*	Full path and arguments to the command to be executed when the user selects Reboot from the System menu (typically, this should be /sbin/shutdown -r now)
RootPath=*pathname*	Path (names of directories separated by colons) to be used for the root user's session
ServAuthDir=*pathname*	Directory (the default is /var/gdm) containing the X authentication files for the displays (this directory should be owned by user gdm, group gdm, with permission 750)

Continued

Table 12-1 *(continued)*

Configuration Option	Description
SessionDir=*pathname*	Directory containing scripts for all session types available on the system (the default is /etc/X11/gdm/Sessions)
User=*username*	User name under which gdmchooser and gdmlogin are run (the default is gdm)
UserAuthDir=*pathname*	Directory where the user's .Xauthority file should be saved. (if this field is empty, the user's home directory is used, which is the default)
UserAuthFBDir=*pathname*	Directory where a fallback cookie (which simply refers to the small amount of authentication information) is created if gdm fails to update the user's .Xauthority file (the default is /tmp)
UserAuthFile=*filename*	Name of the file for storing the user's authentication cookies (the default is .Xauthority)
[security] Section	
AllowRoot=1 or 0	When set to 1, the root user can log in (the default is 1)
RelaxPermissions=0, 1, or 2	0 = gdm only accepts files and directories owned by the user; 1 = gdm allows group writeable files and directories; 2 = gdm allows world writeable files and directories (the default is 1)
RetryDelay=*N*	Number of seconds to wait before gdm displays the login window again after a failed login (the default is 3 seconds)
UserMaxFile=*N*	Maximum size (in bytes) of files that gdm will read or write (the default is 64KB, or 65,536 bytes)
VerboseAuth=1 or 0	When set to 1, gdm prints authentication errors in the message field of the greeter — the login window (the default is 0)
[xdmcp] Section	
Enable=1 or 0	When set to 1, gdm supports the X Display Manager Control Protocol (XDMCP) that enables users to log into other hosts on the network (the default is 0)

Configuration Option	Description
HonorIndirect=1 or 0	When set to 1, gdm allows remote execution of the gdmchooser client on X terminals (the default is 0)
[xdmcp] Section	
MaxPending=N	Maximum number of pending connections (the default is 4) that gdm should allow (this helps avoid any denial of service attacks)
MaxPendingIndirect=N	Maximum number of gdmchooser clients that gdm will run simultaneously on remote displays (the default is 4)
MaxSessions=N	Maximum number of remote display connections that gdm will accept (the default is 16)
MaxWait=N	Maximum number of seconds gdm waits for a response from a display before assuming that the display is not active anymore (the default is 30 seconds)
MaxWaitIndirect=N	Maximum number of seconds gdm waits for a remote display to complete protocol negotiations after the display requests a chooser (the default is 30 seconds)
Port=177	The UDP port number where gdm listens for XDMCP requests (the default is 177)
[gui] Section	
GtkRC=pathname	Directory that contains the theme to be used by the gdmlogin and gdmchooser programs (the default is empty, which means no themes are used)
MaxIconWidth=N	Maximum width (the default is 128 pixels) of icons that the face browser will display (gdmlogin can display a face browser containing icons for all the users on a system; these icons can be installed globally by the system administrator or in the users' home directories)
MaxIconHeight=N	Maximum height (the default is 128 pixels) of icons that the face browser will display

Continued

Table 12-1 *(continued)*

Configuration Option	Description
`Browser=1 or 0`	When set to 1, displays a browser, called the *face browser*, where the faces of all system users are displayed (the default is 0)
`DefaultFace=imagefile`	A file, readable by the `gdm` user, containing an image that is to be displayed if a user does not have a personal picture in the `~/gnome/photo` directory (which refers to the `gnome/photo` subdirectory of the user's home directory). The default is the `/usr/share/pixmaps/nobody.png` file
`DefaultLocale=localename`	Language to be used for the session if nothing is specified in `~/.gnome/gdm` and the user did not select a language in the Locale menu in the greeter. (The default is `english`.)
`Exclude=usernames`	Comma-separated list of user names to be excluded from the face browser; the excluded users will still be able to log in
`Font=fontname`	Font to be used for the welcome message in the greeter
`GlobalImageDir=pathname`	Directory where face files (each containing an icon showing a user's face) are located (the default is `/usr/share/faces/`)
`Icon=imagefile`	A file, readable by the `gdm` user, containing the image to be displayed when the login window is in iconified state (the default is `/usr/share/pixmaps/gdm.xpm`)
`LocaleFile=localefile`	Full path name for the file in GNU locale format, with entries for all languages supported on the system (the default is `/etc/X11/gdm/locale.alias`)
`Logo=imagefile`	A file, readable by the `gdm` user, with the image to be displayed in the logo area (the default is `/usr/share/pixmaps/gnome-logo-large.png`).
`Quiver=1 or 0`	When set to 1, the `gdmlogin` program shakes the display (not physically, but by moving the graphics output) when a user enters an incorrect password (the default is 0)

Configuration Option	Description
[greeter] Section	
Welcome=*message*	The English welcome message that the gdmlogin program displays next to the logo on the login screen (the default message is Welcome= Welcome to %n, where %n means the node name — the hostname without the domain)
Welcome[*xx*]=*message*	The welcome message for the language indicated by the two-letter identifier *xx* (de for German, fr for French, and ja for Japanese)
[chooser] Section	
DefaultHostImg=*filename*	File containing an image to be displayed for those hosts that do not have a unique icon file (the default is /usr/share/pixmaps/nohost.png)
HostImageDir=*pathname*	Directory (the default is /usr/share/hosts/) that contains host icon files; each file name matches the host system's fully qualified domain name (such as yourhost.yourdomain.com).
ScanTime=*N*	Number of seconds the chooser should wait for replies to its XDMCP broadcast query (the default is 3 seconds)
[debug] Section	
Enable=1 or 0	When set to1, gdm saves information that can help isolate any bugs in gdm (the default is 0)
[servers] Section	
N=/usr/bin/X11/X	Command to start the X server for local display number *N* (if your system has a single monitor, *N* is 0)

For the default configuration (after you install Red Hat Linux and X from the companion CD-ROMs), gdm manages the login session as follows:

1. The gdm program starts the X server and looks for a script named after the local display's name (for the first display, the filename is :0) in the /etc/X11/gdm/Init directory. If it does not find that file, gdm executes the file named Default from that directory. The /etc/X11/gdm/Init/ Default script in Red Hat Linux contains the following commands:

```
#!/bin/sh
# Xsetup for Red Hat Linux
# Copyright (c) 1999, 2000 Red Hat, Inc.

/usr/X11R6/bin/xsetroot -solid "#356390"

/sbin/pidof -s kdm &> /dev/null && [ $? -eq 0 -a -x
/usr/bin/kdmdesktop ] && /usr/bin/kdmdesktop && sleep 1s

# only set the background if the xsri program is installed
if [ -x /usr/bin/xsri ]; then
    /usr/bin/xsri  -geometry +5+5 -avoid 300x250 -keep-aspect \
        /usr/share/pixmaps/redhat/redhat-transparent.png
fi
```

In this case, the script sets the background to a solid color and displays the Red Hat logo. The gdm program runs this script as root and waits until the commands finish.

2. The gdm program runs the /usr/bin/gdmlogin program, which displays a dialog box that contains fields in which the user can enter a name and a password.

3. After a user enters a name and password and presses Enter, gdm verifies the password and tries to execute the startup script /etc/X11/gdm/ PreSession/*DisplayName,* where *DisplayName* is :0 for the first display. If that file is not found, gdm executes the /etc/X11/gdm/ PreSession/Default script, if it exists.

4. The gdm program runs the session script from the /etc/X11/gdm/ Sessions directory. The exact script that gdm runs depends on the session that the user selects in the Sessions menu in the login dialog box that gdmlogin displays. If the user has not explicitly selected a specific type of session (GNOME or KDE), gdm runs the /etc/X11/gdm/Default script, which, in turn, executes the /etc/X11/xdm/Xsession script. This script looks for another script file, named .xsession, in the user's home directory and executes that script, if it exists. Next, it looks for the .Xclients script file in the user's home directory and executes that file, if it exists. Otherwise, Xsession executes the /etc/X11/xinit/ Xclients script. When you follow through these scripts, you find that the Xclients script executes the /usr/bin/gnome-session program. The gnome-session program then starts the GNOME session (which includes a set of applications and a window manager). Initially, gnome-session uses the session file /usr/share/gnome/default.session (a text file) to start the applications and the window manager. Later, the GNOME session is restored to the values saved in the ~/.gnome/

session file (this refers to the session file in the .gnome subdirectory in the user's home directory). The default session file specifies a window manager named Sawfish.

5. From this point on, the user can interact with the system through the X display and through the window manager (started by the gnome-session program based on the contents of the session file).

6. When the user ends the GNOME session (by selecting Log out from the Main Menu button), gdm attempts to run the script /etc/X11/gdm/ PostSession/*DisplayName*, where *DisplayName* is :0 for the first display. If that file does not exist, gdm executes the /etc/X11/gdm/ PostSession/Default script, if it exists.

Although this brief description of gdm does not show you all the details, gdm provides a user-friendly interface for user login and for starting a GNOME session. Moreover, like many other X programs, gdm is highly configurable. For example, the names of the script files in the preceding list are the typical ones, but you can specify other names through the file named gdm.conf, which, by default, also resides in the /etc/X11/gdm directory.

Switching from GNOME to KDE

GNOME and KDE are both capable GUI environments. Red Hat Linux comes with both of these GUIs, but you get GNOME as the default GUI. However, Red Hat also includes the utility script /usr/bin/switchdesk that enables you to easily switch from one GUI to another and vice versa. To switch from GNOME to KDE, follow these steps:

1. From your GNOME desktop, select Main Menu (foot) ⇨ Programs ⇨ System ⇨ Desktop Switching Tool. (You can also type switchdesk at the shell prompt in a terminal window.) The Desktop Switcher dialog box appears.

2. In the Desktop Switcher dialog box, click the KDE radio button to select it (see Figure 12-1). Then click the OK button. Another dialog box appears.

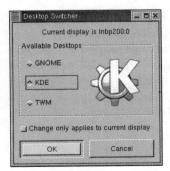

Figure 12-1: Switching to KDE using the switchdesk utility

3. A message informs you that the desktop configuration has been changed, but you must restart X. Click the OK button to dismiss the dialog box.

Although the message in Step 3 says you must restart X, all you need to do is log out of the session and log back in. To log out, select Main Menu ⇨ Log Out. When you log in again, you should get the KDE GUI, as shown in Figure 12-2.

As you can see, the KDE desktop looks very much like Windows 95/98/NT/2000. You can see that the desktop has icons of folders and devices (e.g., floppy and CD-ROM), as well as a trash can for storing deleted files. The bar along the bottom of the screen is the KDE panel, and the leftmost icon (marked K) is the K^ button, or simply K button. That button is like the Start button in Windows 95/98/NT/2000. You click the K button to get a menu of applications that you can start. You can explore the KDE desktop on your own and learn more about KDE in the section "Using KDE."

Getting back to the subject of switching GUIs, the `switchdesk` utility changes the GUI by creating the appropriate scripts in your home directory. It leaves the display manager unchanged. This means that you use the GNOME display manager, `gdm`, for login, even when you switch to the KDE GUI. After you log in, `gdm` executes a session script that eventually executes the `.Xclients` script in your home directory, if that script exists.

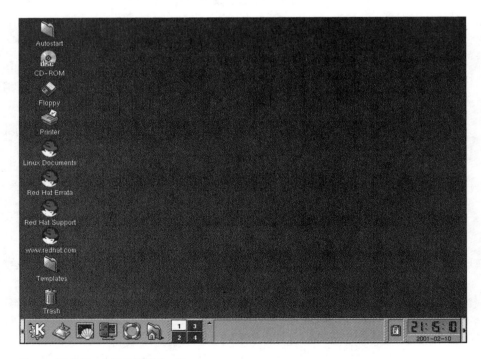

Figure 12-2: The initial KDE desktop

To switch from GNOME to KDE, the switchdesk utility creates a .Xclients script in your home directory with the following lines:

```
#!/bin/bash

# Created by Red Hat Desktop Switcher

if [ -e "$HOME/.Xclients-$HOSTNAME$DISPLAY" ]; then
    exec $HOME/.Xclients-$HOSTNAME$DISPLAY
else
    exec $HOME/.Xclients-default
fi
```

Then switchdesk creates an .Xclients-default script with the following commands:

```
# Created by Red Hat Desktop Switcher
exec startkde
```

The result of these changes is that when you log in, gdm executes the .Xclients script in your home directory, which, in turn, executes the startkde program (/usr/bin/startkde) to start a KDE session.

Because the switchdesk utility changes the GUI through the .Xclients and .Xclients-default scripts in a user's home directory, these changes only affect that particular user.

To switch from KDE to GNOME, log in as root, open a terminal window, and type switchdesk at the shell prompt. Then select GNOME as the desktop. After you log out of KDE and log back in, you should get GNOME as your desktop.

Note that if you want to use GNOME for one session only (as opposed to making it your default GUI), simply select Session ⇨ Gnome from the login window menu in the initial login screen, as shown in Figure 12-3.

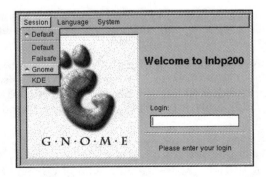

Figure 12-3: Switching to GNOME for the current session only

You should get the GNOME desktop for this session. The next time you log in, the system reverts to KDE.

Using GNOME

GNOME stands for GNU Network Object Model Environment; and GNU, as you probably know, stands for GNU's Not Unix. GNOME is a GUI and a programming environment. From the user's perspective, GNOME is like the Motif-based Common Desktop Environment (CDE) or Microsoft Windows. Behind the scenes, GNOME has many features that enable programmers to write graphical applications that work together well. The next few sections provide a quick overview of GNOME, highlighting the key features of the GNOME GUI. You can explore the details on your own.

You can always find out the latest information about GNOME, by visiting the GNOME home page at `http://www.gnome.org`.

Taking Stock of GNOME

Although what you see of GNOME is the GUI, there is much more to GNOME than the GUI. To help you appreciate it better, note the following points and key features of GNOME:

- GNOME is officially pronounced "guh-NOME," but many people pronounce the word as "NOME." Note that "guh-NOME" stems from "guh-NU," the way people pronounce GNU.

- GNOME runs on several UNIX systems, including Linux, BSD (FreeBSD, NetBSD, and OpenBSD), Solaris, HP-UX, AIX, and Silicon Graphics IRIX.

- GNOME uses the Gimp Tool Kit (GTK+) as the graphics toolkit for all graphical applications. GTK+ relies on X for output and supports multiple programming languages, including C, C++, Perl, and others. Users can easily change the look and feel of all GTK+ applications running on a system. GTK+ is licensed under the GNU Library General Public License (LGPL). See Chapter 27 for more information about the LGPL.

- GNOME also uses Imlib, another library that supports displaying images on an X display. Imlib supports many different image formats, including XPM and PNG (Portable Network Graphics).

- GNOME uses the Object Management Group's Common Object Request Broker Architecture (CORBA) Version 2.2 to enable GNOME software components to communicate with one another regardless of where the components are located, or what programming language is used to implement the components.

- The GNOME GUI works with any window manager designed for the X Window System. To support some GNOME features, such as session management and the GNOME pager (see the next section), you need a GNOME-compliant window manager. Several such window managers are available. Red Hat Linux comes with the Sawfish window manager. Other options for window managers include Window Maker and TWM.

- GNOME applications support drag-and-drop operations.

- GNOME application developers write documentation using DocBook, which is a Document Type Definition (DTD) based on Standard General Markup Language (SGML). This means that you can view the manual for a GNOME application on a Web browser, such as Netscape Communicator.

- GNOME supports standard internationalization and localization methods. This means that you can easily configure a GNOME application for a new native language.

- GNOME uses Mesa, an implementation of OpenGL (an application programming interface — API — for 3D graphics) to support 3D graphics.

Exploring GNOME

Assuming that you enabled a graphical login screen during Red Hat Linux installation, you should get the GNOME GUI whenever you log in to your Linux system. The exact appearance of the GNOME display depends on the current session. The session is nothing more than the set of applications (including a window manager) and the state of these applications. GNOME stores the session information in the file ~/.gnome/session (this file is in the .gnome subdirectory of your home directory). This is a text file; if you are curious, you can browse the file with the more command.

Initially, the GNOME session comes from the /usr/share/gnome/default. session file. However, as soon as the session starts, the GNOME session manager (/usr/bin/gnome-session) saves the current session information in the ~/.gnome/session file. A typical initial GNOME desktop produced by the session description in the default session file is shown in Figure 12-4.

As you can see from the icons on the left side of the GNOME desktop, GNOME enables you to place folders and applications directly on the desktop. This is similar to the way in which you can place icons directly on the Windows 95/98/NT/2000 desktop.

Secret

The default GNOME session also starts the magicdev daemon that is designed to monitor devices, such as the floppy drive and the CD-ROM drive, and to detect events, such as the user inserting a CD-ROM into the drive. When magicdev detects a new CD-ROM, it mounts the CD-ROM and communicates with the GNOME file manager to display the contents of the CD-ROM. You can configure magicdev through the GNOME Control Center, described later in this chapter.

Although by looking at Figure 12-4 you cannot readily tell that the Sawfish window manager is running, you need the window manager as part of your session. A *window manager* is a special X application that handles interactions for various applications that are displaying windows onscreen. You need a window manager to control the placement and size of each application's window. Without a window manager, you cannot change a window's location or alter its size.

Figure 12-4: The initial GNOME desktop, with the default session file

To see why a window manager is necessary, consider the case of two X applications — A and B — that are displaying on the same screen. Neither application has any idea of the other's needs. Suppose that you run application B after A, and B takes over the entire screen (the root window) as its output window. At this point, A's window is obscured underneath B's, and you have no way to reach A's window.

A window manager enables you to switch from B to A, even when B is ill-behaved. (For example, if B's window fills the entire screen, you have no way of accessing A's window without a window manager). The Sawfish window manager adds a decorative frame to the main window of each application. This frame enables you to move and resize the windows. You can click and drag a corner of the frame to shrink B's window. The Sawfish window manager shows an outline of the window that changes in size as you move the mouse. This outline enables you to make the topmost window smaller to expose windows underneath it. Additionally, with Sawfish, you can get a pull-down menu by clicking the upper-left corner of the window's frame (see Figure 12-5). This menu contains options that enable you to resize the window, reduce the window to an icon, and quit the application.

As in the window frames in Microsoft Windows 95/98/NT/2000, the right-hand corner of the title bar includes three buttons: The leftmost button reduces the window to an icon, the middle button maximizes the window to fill up the entire screen, and the rightmost button closes the window. Unlike Windows, the locations of these buttons, as well as the appearance of the entire window frame, are configurable in GNOME.

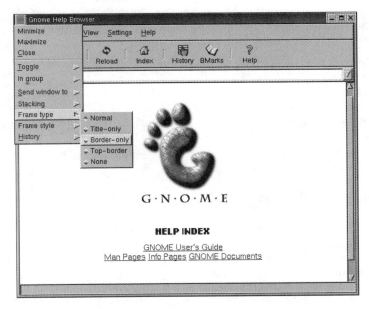

Figure 12-5: The Sawfish window manager adds a frame and menu to a window.

The GNOME panel

A key feature of the GNOME desktop is the long bar along the bottom edge of the screen. This is known as the GNOME panel, or simply the panel. The panel is a separate GNOME application. As Figure 12-6 shows, it provides a display area for menus and small panel applets. Each panel applet is a small program that is designed to work inside the panel. For example, the clock applet on the panel's far right displays the current date and time.

Figure 12-6: The GNOME panel

Tip

Notice the two outward-pointing arrows at the left and right ends of the panel. Click the arrow and the panel slides away, reducing its display area to a small sliver along the edge of the screen. This frees up more desktop area for windows. Click the arrow again and the panel reappears.

The GNOME panel in Figure 12-6 includes several other applets:

■ The GNOME Pager applet provides a virtual desktop that's larger than the physical dimensions of your system's screen. In Figure 12-6, the pager displays four pages in a small display area. Each page represents an area equal to the size of the X display screen. To go to a specific page, click that page in the pager window. If you want a window to always appear on each virtual screen page, simply select Toggle ⇨ Sticky from its window menu (see Figure 12-5). A sticky window always appears at the same location on each virtual screen page. The GNOME Pager applet also displays buttons for each window being displayed in the current virtual page.

■ Launcher applets display buttons with icons of applications. Clicking a button starts (launches) that application. For example, click the big "N" icon to launch Netscape Communicator.

■ The GNOME weather applet displays the local weather; you can start this applet by selecting Main Menu ⇨ Applets ⇨ GNOME Weather. In the Main Menu ⇨ Applets menu you will find many more categories of applets that you can try out.

The GNOME panel also displays the Main Menu button (the stylized foot) that behaves like the Windows Start menu.

The Main Menu button, or the "foot"

In Figure 12-6, the left-hand side of the panel includes a button with the image of a stylized foot (which happens to be the GNOME logo). That foot is the Main Menu button. As with the Start button in Windows 95/98/NT/2000, you can launch applications from the menu that pops up when you click the left mouse button on the foot. Typically, this menu lists items that start an application. Some of the menu items have an arrow; another pop-up menu appears when you place the mouse pointer on an item with an arrow. Figure 12-7 shows a typical view of the Main Menu on my system.

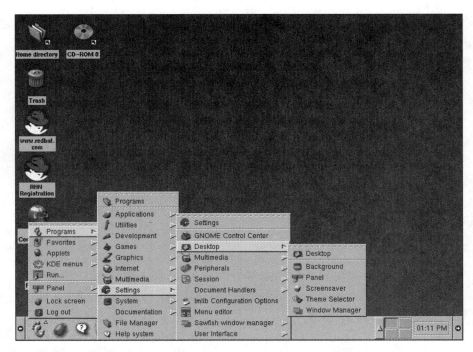

Figure 12-7: Click the left mouse button on the foot to view the Main menu.

Explore all the items in the Main menu to see all the tasks you can perform from this menu. In particular, move the mouse over the Main Menu ⇨ Settings item to see the menu that lists your options for changing the appearance of the desktop. For instance, you can change the desktop's background from this menu.

Secret

KDE applications can also run under GNOME. In fact, the KDE applications are organized under the KDE menus. Even if you use the GNOME desktop, you can always start a KDE application from the KDE menus (see Figure 12-8). Thus, you are in no way limited to running only GNOME applications when you use the GNOME GUI.

GNOME Control Center

You can configure certain aspects of the GNOME desktop from the GNOME Control Center. To launch the Control Center, select Main Menu ⇨ Settings ⇨ GNOME Control Center, or click the toolbox in the GNOME panel (refer to Figure 12-6).

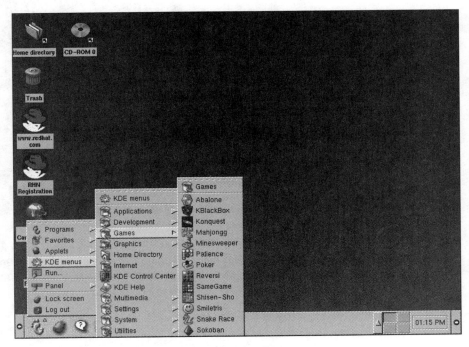

Figure 12-8: Selecting a KDE application from the KDE menus

The GNOME Control Center's user interface is somewhat similar to that of linuxconf (described in Chapter 15). The window is vertically divided into two parts: a narrower left side and a wider right side. The left side shows a tree menu of all the configuration items. The top-level items are organized into several categories, such as Desktop and Multimedia. You can click a category to see its subcategories. To configure an item, locate the item in the tree menu and click it. The right-hand area then displays a dialog box with the settings you can change. For example, Figure 12-9 shows the options for customizing the GNOME desktop's background.

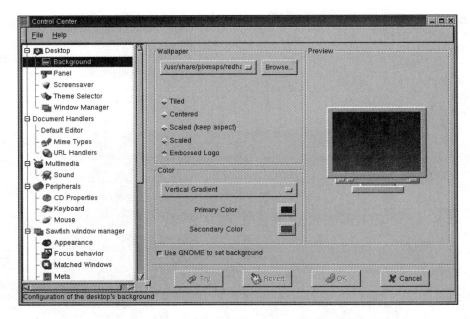

Figure 12-9: Customizing the GNOME desktop using the GNOME Control Center

In this case, the GNOME Control Center enables you to select a background of solid color, or pick a wallpaper (an image to be used as the background). When you are done making the changes, click OK to close the dialog box and apply the changes.

To quit the Control Center, select File ⇨ Exit.

Using KDE

KDE stands for the K Desktop Environment. The KDE project started in October 1996, with an intention to develop a common GUI for UNIX systems that use the X Window System. The first beta version of KDE was released a year later in October 1997, and KDE Version 1.0 was released in July 1998. KDE 2.0 was released on October 23, 2000. KDE 2.1 is now in beta and will be released by the time this book goes to print.

From the user's perspective, KDE provides a graphical desktop environment that includes a window manager, the Konqueror Web browser and file manager, a panel for starting applications, a help system, configuration tools, and many applications, including the KOffice office suite, image viewer, PostScript viewer, and mail and news programs.

From the developer's perspective, KDE has class libraries and object models for easy application development in C++. KDE is a large development project with many collaborators.

The following sections provide an overview of KDE, but the best way to learn about KDE is to use it for a while. Follow the instructions in the section "Switching from GNOME to KDE" to change your GUI to KDE. Then use it for a while to get a feel for KDE's capabilities.

You can always find out the latest information about KDE by visiting the KDE home page at `http://www.kde.org`.

Taking Stock of KDE

Like GNOME, KDE is meant to be a complete desktop environment for users, and a programming environment for application developers. Here are some key features of KDE:

- KDE runs on a number of UNIX-like systems, including Linux, FreeBSD, Solaris, HP-UX, and Silicon Graphics IRIX. KDE needs the X Window System.

- KDE is written in C++ and uses object-oriented development.

- KDE uses the *Qt Free Edition* GUI toolkit from a Norwegian company, Trolltech AS (`http://www.troll.no/`). Qt is a C++ class library for building GUIs; it provides the widgets such as menus, buttons, and sliders used in KDE applications. Earlier, there was some controversy over the Qt license, because its terms are not the same as the GNU General Public License. However, in September 2000, Trolltech announced that it would license Qt Free Edition, Version 2.2, under the GNU General Public License.

- KDE provides an application development framework built on the Object Management Group's CORBA 2.0 standard. Around CORBA, KDE adds an object model called KOM, that is similar to Microsoft's DCOM (Distributed Component Object Model) and IBM's System Object Model (SOM). KDE also includes the OpenParts compound document model built using the X Window System and KOM. OpenParts provides capabilities similar to those of IBM's OpenDoc model or Microsoft's Object Linking and Embedding (OLE) and ActiveX controls.

- KDE includes an office application suite based on the KOM/OpenParts technology. The office suite, named KOffice, includes a spreadsheet (KSpread), a FrameMaker-like word processor (KWord), a presentation application (KPresenter), and a drawing program (KIllustrator).

- KDE supports drag-and-drop operations.

■ KDE supports internationalization, and most KDE applications have been translated into over 25 different languages.

Exploring KDE

KDE is easy to use and has many similarities with the Windows 95/98/NT/ 2000 GUI. You can start applications from a menu that's similar to the Start menu in Windows. KDE also enables you to place folders and applications directly on the desktop.

The KDE GUI has three key parts: the window manager; a panel, for starting applications; and the Konqueror file manager cum Web browser. When your KDE session starts, you'll see a Windows 95/98-like desktop with a panel along the bottom edge of the screen, as shown in Figure 12-10.

Figure 12-10: The KDE panel

The left and right ends of the panel show outward-pointing arrows. You can click these arrows to hide the panel and make more room on the desktop for applications. When the panel is hidden, it still shows a small bar with an arrow. To view the entire panel again, click that arrow and the panel slides out.

The most important component of the panel is the K button on the left-hand side. That button is like the Start button in Windows 95/98/NT/2000. When you click the K button, a pop-up menu appears. From this menu, you can get to other menus by moving the mouse over items with a right-pointing arrow. For example, Figure 12-11 shows a typical menu hierarchy for changing some desktop settings.

You can start applications from this menu. That's why the KDE documentation calls the K button the *Application Starter*.

Next to the K button, the panel includes several other buttons. If you don't know what a button does, simply move the mouse over the button and a small pop-up window displays a brief message about that button. To read the online help about KDE, click the button with an icon of a book and a light-bulb. That button launches KDE Help, which enables you to read help information on many aspects of KDE.

To view the contents of your home directory (using the Konqueror file manager), click the button with the icon of a folder and a home. Figure 12-12 shows a typical KDE desktop, with KDE Help and the file manager displaying the home directory.

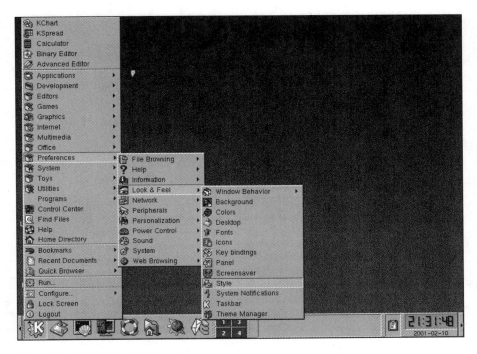

Figure 12-11: Click the K button for menus.

You should browse through the help information in KDE Help to learn more about various aspects of KDE. In particular, click the icon labeled "KDE user's manual" to learn more about the KDE desktop.

The KDE window manager adds borders, the title bar, and other decorations to each application's window. It also adds a window menu to each window. Click the button in the upper-left corner of a window to view the window menu, as shown in Figure 12-13.

The window menu lets you do things, such as maximize or iconify the window, change its size, and switch to a different desktop. Of course, the window border itself has other buttons to perform these tasks (for example, the buttons at the upper-right corner of the window).

KDE supports a virtual desktop. By default, you get four virtual desktops. You can click one of the buttons labeled One, Two, Three, and Four to switch to a specific desktop. Use the desktops to organize your application windows. You needn't clutter up a single desktop with many open windows. When a desktop gets crowded, simply switch to another desktop and open the applications there.

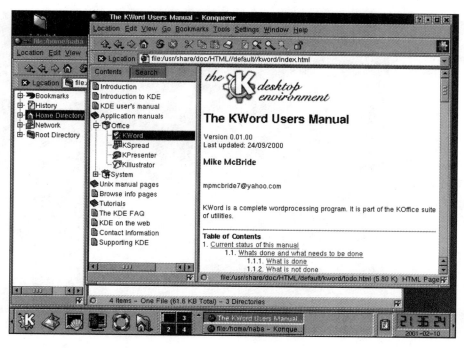

Figure 12-12: The KDE desktop with some applications running

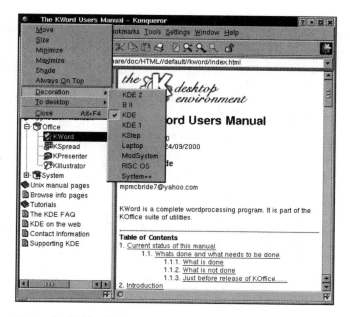

Figure 12-13: The KDE window manager adds window decorations and a window menu.

The KDE panel also includes a button with the icon of a terminal covered by a shell — in Figure 12-13 this is the button to the right of the desktop buttons (labeled One, Two, Three, and Four). Click this button to run konsole (a terminal emulation program) and get a terminal window, as shown in Figure 12-14.

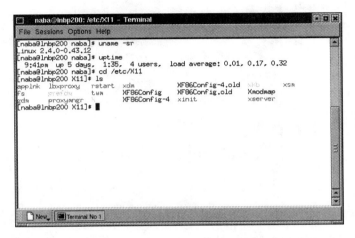

Figure 12-14: Typing Linux commands in the konsole terminal emulation window

You can type Linux commands at the shell prompt in the terminal emulation window. Chapter 10 describes the shell and some important Linux commands.

KDE includes a KDE Control Center that you can use to customize various aspects of KDE, including the desktop background, icons, and fonts. To start the KDE Control Center, select K ⇨ Control Center; or, from the panel, click the button with the icon of a monitor covered by a circuit board. The KDE Control Center main window has two parts. The left side of the window has a tree menu of items that you can control with this tool. The tree menu is organized into categories, such as Look & Feel, Network, Peripherals, Personalization, etc. Click an item to view the subcategories for that item. To change an item, go through the tree menu to locate the item, and then click it. That item's configuration options then appear in a dialog box on the right side of the window. For example, Figure 12-15 shows the options for customizing the desktop background.

You can choose the desktop whose background you want to customize. Then select either a solid color background or a wallpaper (an image used as a background). After making your selections, click OK to close the dialog box and make the change.

To log out of KDE, select K ⇨ Logout, and click the Logout button on the resulting dialog box.

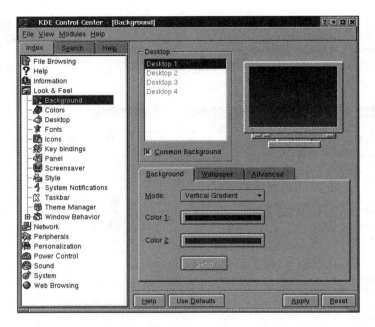

Figure 12-15: Customizing the desktop background with KDE Control Center

Customizing X

You can customize almost all aspects of the X display, ranging from the screen's background color to the default font for all applications. The basic philosophy of X (and of UNIX as well) is that the user should have the freedom to configure the software to suit his or her taste. Thus, X applications load various settings from a resource file. Each X application also accepts a set of standard command-line options. This section describes the general techniques for customizing X applications. These techniques apply to all X applications, such as the xterm and rxvt terminal emulators.

Root-Window Appearance

In X, the entire display screen is called the *root window*. A utility program named xsetroot enables you to tailor the appearance of the root window. With xsetroot, you can customize the screen as follows:

■ Use the -solid option to set the screen to a solid color. You can specify the color by name; the color names are in the text file /usr/lib/X11/rgb.txt.

■ Use the -bitmap option to set the background to a bitmapped graphic file.

■ Use the -cursor or the -cursor_name options to specify a cursor shape when the mouse pointer rests anywhere on the root window.

■ Use the -gray option to set the background to gray.

To customize the root window, you should run xsetroot from the command prompt and experiment with various options until you find an appearance that you like. Then you can put the appropriate xsetroot commands in your .Xclients file.

In GNOME and KDE, you can change the background color from a graphical control center. Each environment comes with a configuration tool that lets you customize the appearance of the desktop.

Screen color

You can set the screen's background color with the xsetroot program. To set the background to a solid NavyBlue color, for example, type the following command at a shell prompt in a terminal window:

```
xsetroot -solid NavyBlue
```

To try more colors, you have to know the names of the colors. The color definitions are in a text file named /usr/lib/X11/rgb.txt. To see a list of the color names, open that file with an editor, or type the following command in a terminal window:

```
more /usr/lib/X11/rgb.txt
```

You can also view the RGB color names with the command showrgb | more.

Following are some of the lines from the rgb.txt file:

```
255 255 255     white
  0   0   0     black
190 190 190     gray
 65 105 225     RoyalBlue
  0   0 128     NavyBlue
218 165  32     goldenrod
184 134  11     DarkGoldenrod
233 150 122     DarkSalmon
255 160 122     LightSalmon
```

As you might guess, the three numbers indicate the intensity levels of the red (R), green (G), and blue (B) components of the color. The intensity levels range between 0 and 255.

In addition to using the descriptive name for a color, you can specify a color as a hexadecimal number of six hexadecimal digits, which works out to two digits for each of the three components of a color: red (R), green (G), and blue (B). The digits in a six-digit hexadecimal RGB value of a color are interpreted from left to right, with the most significant pair of digits being assumed to be for R, the middle pair for G, and the least significant pair for B. The character # precedes the hexadecimal digits to signify a color specification in hexadecimal format. When you specify a color this way, you have to put the hexadecimal color value within quotation marks. You can use the hexadecimal format to specify any color that you want.

Table 12-2 lists some common colors expressed in hexadecimal format.

Table 12-2	Common Colors in Hexadecimal Format
Color	*Hexadecimal Value*
black	#000000
red	#ff0000
green	#00ff00
blue	#0000ff
yellow	#ffff00
cyan	#00ffff
magenta	#ff00ff
white	#ffffff

Now that you know how to specify any arbitrary color in hexadecimal RGB format, you can experiment with new colors. You can try a strange color for the screen background, for example, by using the following command:

```
xsetroot -solid "#ccb0b0"
```

If you want a simple gray background (which can be quite pleasing to the eye, if a bit unadventurous), you can get it by using this command:

```
xsetroot -gray
```

Screen-background image

You needn't use a solid color as the screen background. You can use xsetroot with the -bitmap option to tile a monochrome bitmap image over the screen background (tiling means that copies of the bitmap are laid out one next to the other until the whole screen is covered — similar to the way in which you would cover a floor with actual tiles). You can use the -fg and the -bg options to draw the image in the foreground color and fill the background with a selected background color.

Try the following command to set the screen background to an interesting pattern of the X logo:

```
xsetroot -bitmap /usr/include/X11/bitmaps/xlogo64 -fg "#cccccc" -bg
"#c0c0c0"
```

The /usr/include/X11/bitmaps directory contains many more bitmap files that you can try as background images. Note that xsetroot cannot display a color image as the screen background.

In GNOME and KDE, you can use their respective control centers to select a color image as the background for your desktop.

Hexadecimal Numbers

Although you may not be familiar with the term hexadecimal, you're familiar with one number system from your everyday experience — the decimal number system. We express decimal numbers using the digits 0 through 9; and when writing values, we use the concepts of ones, tens, hundreds, and thousands. For example, consider the number 3,495. Using the concept of ones, tens, hundreds, and thousands, we can write this as:

3,495 = 3 Thousands + 4 Hundreds + 9 Tens + 5 Ones

or

$3,495 = 3 \times 10^3 + 4 \times 10^2 + 9 \times 10^1 + 5 \times 10^0$

The last form represents the number in powers of 10, which is the *base* or *radix* of the decimal number system.

The hexadecimal number system is similar to the decimal number system, except that the base is 16. To write a number in hexadecimal, you need sixteen digits representing the values from 0 through 15, just as the decimal system uses the ten digits, 0 through 9. Here are the sixteen hexadecimal digits:

Hex	Decimal
0	0
1	1
2	2
3	3
4	4
5	5
6	6
7	7
8	8
9	9
A	10
B	11
C	12
D	13
E	14
F	15

As you can see, the letters A through F are used to represent the values 10 through 15, respectively. You can use either lowercase or uppercase letters for the hexadecimal digits.

Knowing the similarity between the decimal and hexadecimal number systems, you can easily find the decimal equivalent of a hexadecimal number. For example, 1b in hexadecimal is $1 \times 16^1 + 11 \times 16^0 = 16 + 11 = 27$ in decimal.

Tip

Avoid using colorful images as a screen background; other X programs will run out of colors if you display a too-colorful image as the background. Remember that an 8-bit video mode can display at most 256 colors. If the background image has anything more than 16 colors, you'll probably run into problems as you run other programs. In particular, programs such as the Netscape Communicator Web browser also need colors to display all those images that most Web pages have.

In addition to causing X to run out of colors, a color image background also uses up resources of the X server and may affect the system's performance. Therefore, the safe solution is to use a solid-color background for the screen background.

Cursor shape and color

With the xsetroot program, you can set the shape and color of the cursor when the pointer is resting anywhere on the root window. Inside an application's windows, the application controls the cursor shape and color.

Although you can use two bitmap files to define an arbitrarily shaped cursor, a simpler method is to select one of the predefined cursor shapes. You can use the -cursor_name option of the xsetroot program to specify a cursor. The cursor names are defined in the file /usr/include/X11/cursorfont.h. The names are meant for use in X programs, and each cursor name has an XC_ prefix. You have to omit the XC_ prefix when you use the cursor name with the xsetroot program.

Following are a few cursor names:

■ X_cursor—A cursor shaped like an X (the default cursor)

■ arrow—An arrow pointing to the upper-right corner

■ left_ptr—An arrow pointing to the upper-left corner

The default cursor is a black X_cursor. To change the cursor to a white left-pointing arrow, type the following command:

```
xsetroot -cursor_name left_ptr -fg white -bg black
```

In the Macintosh and Windows 95/98/NT/2000 graphical environments, the cursor is a left-pointing arrow. If you are familiar with those environments, you might want to change the cursor to the left-pointing arrow.

X Resources

Most X applications are highly configurable. You can alter the appearance and, to some extent, even the behavior of an X application in two ways:

■ Alter the application's default behavior through options you specify in the command line that starts the application.

■ Specify values for options in a text file called a *resource file*. (X programmers use the term *resource* to refer to any user-configurable option in an application.)

For small UNIX utilities, a handful of command-line options may be enough to specify all user-configurable parameters of the program. X applications tend, however, to have a large number of variables that the user can set. An X application may have several windows, each of which may have a border, a background color, and a foreground color. Although an X application provides default values for these parameters, the user can override most of these values. In addition, the user can change the font for any text that is to be displayed in windows. X applications simply have too many variables for the user to set through command-line options alone. The creators of X recognized this problem and devised a database of resources.

In an X application, the term *resource* refers to any parameter that affects the application's behavior or appearance. Accordingly, foreground and background colors, fonts, and size and placement of windows are typical resources. A resource does not have to be a parameter related to X; it can be anything that controls the behavior of an application and that can be specified by the user. An application might have a parameter named `verbose`, which, when set, enables the printing of detailed information as it runs. In addition to the application's window size and location, `verbose` qualifies as a resource of the application.

The resource file

You have to specify the resources for an X application in a text file known as a *resource file* or a *resource database*. The X resource database is a simple text file in which you can specify the value of various parameters in a well-defined format.

X resource files are not as complicated and sophisticated as a traditional database. The X resource database contains specifications of the form "all foreground colors are white," "`xterm`'s background is light cyan," and so on.

X applications use a set of utility routines, collectively known as the *X resource manager*, to extract the value of precisely identified individual parameters from this rather imprecise database. Consider the query "what is the foreground color of the `xterm` application?" If you specified the foreground color of `xterm` in the resource file, the resource manager returns this value. If, however, the only specification for foreground color in the database is the general statement "all foreground colors are black," the value returned for `xterm`'s foreground color is black.

X's resource-naming convention

To specify an X application's resource values, such as foreground color, you have to know how to name a resource and specify its value.

The name of a resource depends on the name of the application and the names of its components, which usually are the major child windows. For applications that were built with the *X toolkit* (essentially, a library of user interface components), the components would be the names of widgets used to build the application.

Note

A *widget* is nothing more than a user interface component, such as a push button, a list box, or a dialog box. An X toolkit, such as the Motif toolkit, provides the functions that programmers can use to create and use widgets in their programs.

The names of the application and its components can be of two types: *class name* and *instance name*. The class name indicates the general category of the application or component, whereas each individual copy has its own instance name.

Consider a concrete example: the `xterm` application. This application is of the class `XTerm`, and the instance goes by the name `xterm`. The `xterm` application uses a component named `vt100` of class `VT100` (the `VT100` component emulates a VT102, but the internal name is VT100), which contains a component named `scrollbar` of the class `Scrollbar`. Now consider the following resources: the foreground color of the VT100 window and the visibility of the scrollbar in that window. In `xterm`, as in most X applications, the foreground color resource has the class name `Foreground`, and the instance name `foreground`. The scrollbar's visibility is controlled by a Boolean variable named `on`.

Most X applications built with an X toolkit follow this convention of naming the class of a resource, by capitalizing the first letter of its instance name. Names of applications also follow this convention, which promotes some consistency among applications. The naming of the application, its components, and the resources, however, is entirely under the control of the application. (Toolkit-based applications, however, are somewhat constrained by the built-in names of predefined widgets.)

Now you can give these resources unique names in `xterm` and specify values for them. You can assign values for the foreground color of the VT100 window and the `on` variable of its scrollbar in the following manner:

```
xterm.vt100.foreground:    yellow
xterm.vt100.scrollbar.on:    true
```

This example illustrates the syntax of naming resources and specifying their values. The name of a resource starts with the name of the application, followed by names of the components, each of which is separated from the next by a period (`.`). The resource name comes last, and the value of the resource follows a colon (`:`). You specify the value as a text string; it is up to the application to interpret that string. The resource manager has utility routines that can help the programmer with this task.

The names illustrated so far in this section are full instance names, showing the application and all its components. You also can have full class names, which for `xterm.vt100.foreground` is `XTerm.VT100.Foreground`. You obtain this name by replacing the instance name of each component with the corresponding class name.

Partial names for resources

The preceding section explains how to specify a resource by its full name, but the resource specification can be imprecise. You might indicate, for example, that all components of class VT100 should have a yellow foreground. You can accomplish this task by making the following entry in the resource database:

```
*VT100.Foreground:    yellow
```

Because there is no application name, this specification of the foreground color applies to the VT100 component used in any application. Similarly, to specify that the background color of every component of the `xterm` application be Navy, you would include the following line in the resource file:

```
xterm*background:Navy
```

To understand the resource-naming scheme, you have to know something about the inner workings of the X resource manager. By now, you probably have guessed that the X resource manager locates a resource's value by matching a precisely specified resource name with the imprecise entries in the resource database. The search algorithm used by the resource manager follows certain rules for matching a full resource name with the partial names in the resource database. Knowing the following rules can help you understand what kind of specification for a resource is precise enough to suit your needs:

- An asterisk (*) matches zero or more components of the name. Therefore, the query for `xterm.vt100.foreground` matches the following entry:

  ```
  xterm*foreground:  yellow
  ```

- After the asterisk is accounted for, the application name, the component names, and the resource name (class or instance) must match the items present in the entry. Therefore, a query for `XTerm.VT100.Scrollbar.Background` matches the entry

  ```
  xterm.vt100.scrollbar.background: Navy
  ```

  but not

  ```
  xterm.vt100.scrollbar.on: true
  ```

- More specific resource specifications take precedence over less specific settings. Entries with a period (.) take precedence over ones that have an asterisk (*). If you specify the following, everything in `xterm` has a navy background, but the scrollbar has a white background:

  ```
  xterm*background: Navy
  ```

  ```
  xterm.vt100.scrollbar.background: white
  ```

- Instance names take precedence over class names. Thus, the specific entry `xterm*background` will override the one that uses class names: `XTerm*Background`.

- An entry with a class name or an instance name takes precedence over one that uses neither. In `xterm`, the value given in the entry `XTerm*Foreground` overrides one under the more general entry `*Foreground`.

- Names are matched from left to right, because the hierarchy of components of a resource name goes from left to right. In other words, when looking for the resource named `xterm.vt100.scrollbar.background`, the resource manager matches the entry

  ```
  xterm.vt100*background: white
  ```

  instead of

  ```
  xterm*scrollbar.background: Navy
  ```

  because `vt100` appears to the left of `scrollbar`.

The location of resource files

Most X toolkit applications, including Motif applications, load resource settings from several sources in a specific order. First, the applications look for a file named /usr/lib/X11/app-defaults/*AppClass*, in which *AppClass,* is the class name of the application. Thus, xterm looks for its resources in /usr/lib/X11/app-defaults/XTerm.

Next, the application looks for a string named RESOURCE_MANAGER, which is attached to (associated with) the root window of the display in which the application's window appears. In X, a string associated with the root window is known as a *property* of the root window.

Tip

You can use the utility program xprop to see whether this property exists on your display's root window. Simply type xprop -root, and look for an entry labeled RESOURCE_MANAGER(STRING) in the output. The xprop utility also can read a resource file and load the contents into this property (as a long string).

If the RESOURCE_MANAGER property does not exist, the application reads the resource specifications from the .Xdefaults file in your home directory. Next, the application loads the resources (if any) specified by the file indicated by the environment variable XENVIRONMENT. If this variable is not set, the next source for resources is a file named .Xdefaults-*hostname* in your home directory. In this file, *hostname* is the name of the system on which the application is running.

You can, of course, override any of the resource specifications through command-line options.

If you want to see the effects of resources, following is an example of how you might do it. In your current xterm window, use an editor to create the file xttest, containing the following lines:

```
xterm.vt100.scrollBar:        true
*VT100.Foreground:            yellow
xterm.vt100.background:       navy
xterm.vt100.scrollbar.background: white
```

Now type the following command, run the xrdb utility program, and load these settings into the RESOURCE_MANAGER property of the root window:

```
xrdb -load xttest
```

Type xprop -root to verify that the resources are loaded. Notice that the contents of the resource file are stored internally in the property RESOURCE_MANAGER as a very long string. Now start another xterm session with the command xterm &. You should see a new xterm window that has yellow characters on a navy background, except for the scrollbar, which has a white background.

Standard X resources

By convention, all X applications have a standard set of resources. These resources include parameters, such as foreground and background colors, window size and location (collectively known as *geometry*), and font. Table 12-3 lists some of the standard X resources.

Table 12-3   Standard X Resources

Instance Name	Class Name	Command-Line Option	Specifies
background	Background	-bg -background	Background color
borderColor	BorderColor	-bd -border	Border color
borderWidth	BorderWidth	-bw -borderwidth	Border width (in pixels)
display	Display	-d -display	Name of display
foreground	Foreground	-fg -foreground	Foreground color
font	Font	-fn -font	Font name
geometry	Geometry	-geometry	Size and location
title	Title	-title	Title string

Command-line options in X applications

In addition to resource databases, X applications accept command-line arguments. Table 12-3 shows the common command-line options for X applications. This section summarizes a few important command-line options.

The -display option

You use -display to specify the display on which the application's output should appear. (An X application can run on one system and display its output on a display connected to another system on a network.) If you are logged into a remote computer, for example, and you want to run the client xclock on that system, you can start it with a command, such as the following:

```
xclock -display sysname:0 &
```

Here, *sysname* is the name of your system (the name that you see when you type the command **hostname** on your system).

The -geometry option

Another common option is -geometry, which you use to specify the size and location of an application's window. You have to specify the geometry in a standard format, as follows:

```
width × height[+-]xoffset[+-]yoffset
```

In this format, *width, height, xoffset,* and *yoffset* are numbers, and you have to pick one of the two signs shown in the brackets. The *width* and *height* values specify the size of the window, in pixels (except for xterm, for which you specify these values as numbers of columns and rows of text). The *xoffset* and *yoffset* values are also in pixels. The meaning of these two numbers depends on the application. In xterm, for example, a positive *xoffset* indicates the number of pixels by which the left edge of the window is offset from the left edge of the screen. A negative *xoffset,* on the other hand, specifies the number of pixels by which the right edge of the window is offset from the right edge of the screen. Similarly, positive and negative *yoffset* indicate the offsets of the top and bottom edges of the window, respectively.

You would type the following command to place an 80-character by 25-line xterm window at the upper-right corner of your screen, with a 16-pixel gap between the window's frame and the screen's top and right edges:

```
xterm -geometry 80x25-16+16 &
```

Options for window appearance

Several other command-line options determine the appearance of an application's window. These options specify the foreground color (-fg); the background color (-bg); the border color (-bd); and the border width (-bw), in pixels. You specify the colors by names that appear in the /usr/lib/X11/rgb.txt file. To start xterm with yellow characters on a navy background, use the following command:

```
xterm -bg navy -fg yellow &
```

If a color name includes embedded space, enter the name in quotes. To specify light blue as the background for xterm, use the following command:

```
xterm -bg "light blue" &
```

As explained in the "Screen color" section earlier in this chapter, you also can specify the color as a hexadecimal number with six hexadecimal digits. The digits in a six-digit hexadecimal RGB value of a color are interpreted from left to right, with the most significant pair of digits assumed to be for red (R), the middle pair for green (G), and the least significant pair for blue (B). You have to place the # character in front of the hexadecimal digits to signify that the color specification is in hexadecimal format. You can try a strange color for xterm's background by using the following command:

```
xterm -bg "#ccb0b0" &
```

Font specification

The font resource of an application controls the appearance of the text output. Like colors, fonts are specified by names. In X, font names are very descriptive. Following is an example:

```
-adobe-courier-medium-r-normal--12-120-75-75-m-60-iso8859-1
```

For this font, adobe is the maker, courier is the family, and the font is of medium weight (it can be bold, for example). The r value indicates that the font is roman. An i at this position indicates italic, and o indicates oblique. The normal value is a parameter for character width and spacing between characters; it also can be condensed, narrow, or double.

The numbers that follow the two dashes (--) indicate the font's size: 12 indicates the pixel size of the font, and 120 gives the size in tenths of a printer's point. The next two numbers, 75-75, give the horizontal and vertical resolution for which the font is designed. The letter that follows the resolution (m) is the spacing; this value can be m for monospace or p for proportional. The next number, 60, is the average width of all characters in this font, measured in tenths of a pixel (in this case, 6 pixels). The string iso8859-1 identifies the character set of the font, as specified by the International Standards Organization (ISO). In this case, the character set is ISO Latin 1, a superset of the ASCII (American Standard Code for Information Interchange) character set.

Tip

You do not have to give the entire name when you specify a font in a resource file. You can use asterisks (*) for fields that can be arbitrary. Suppose that you want the VT100 window in xterm to use a medium-weight 12-point courier font. With a judicious sprinkling of asterisks, you can specify this font in the resource file as follows:

```
*VT100*Font: *courier-medium-r-normal--*120*
```

Summary

Newcomers and old-timers alike can benefit from a graphical point-and-click user interface. This chapter shows you how Red Hat Linux starts a graphical login screen so that you can stay in the graphical environment. This chapter also covers the GNOME and KDE graphical user interfaces and explains how to customize the appearance of X applications. The next chapter introduces you to common Linux applications.

By reading this chapter, you learn the following:

▶ After Linux boots, a process named init starts all the other processes. The exact set of initial processes depends on the run level, which typically is a number ranging from 0 to 6. The /etc/inittab file specifies the processes that start at each run level. The /etc/inittab file specifies that a graphical display manager starts at run level 5. In Red Hat Linux, the GNOME Display Manager (gdm) provides the graphical login prompt. The Red Hat Linux installation program can set up a graphical login for you.

▶ GNOME and KDE are two popular GUIs for Linux. Red Hat Linux comes with both GNOME and KDE, but your system starts with GNOME as the default GUI. You can use the switchdesk utility to change your default GUI to KDE.

▶ Both GNOME and KDE are similar to other modern desktop environments, such as Apple Macintosh and Microsoft Windows. Therefore, you can easily learn to use GNOME and KDE. Both include control centers from which you can customize various aspects of the desktop, including the appearance.

▶ You can easily customize most X applications. The customizable aspects of an X application are known as *resources*. You can specify the values of resources in the .Xresources file in your home directory. Through resources, you can specify parameters, such as background color, foreground color, and fonts.

Chapter 13

Linux Applications and Utilities

The Red Hat Linux distribution on this book's companion CD-ROMs includes many applications. The GNOME and KDE desktops come with a number of applications, such as calendars, calculators, CD players, and games. Red Hat Linux also comes with the GNU software packages, discussed in Chapter 11, which include applications, such as the GIMP, for working with images; and Ghostview, for viewing PostScript files.

Many more Linux applications are available on the Internet, or commercially from various Linux vendors. This chapter briefly describes some of the Linux applications included on the companion CD-ROMs. You are also introduced to several prominent commercially available office productivity applications for Linux that are not included on the companion CD-ROMs.

Applications on the Companion CD-ROMs

Table 13-1 shows a selected set of Linux applications on the CD-ROMs, organized by category.

Table 13-1	Linux Applications on the CD-ROMs
Category	*Applications*
Editors	GNU Emacs, JED, Joe, vim, GUI text editors, gnotepad+, KDE Binary Editor
GUI desktops	GNOME, KDE

Continued

Table 13-1 *(continued)*

Category	Applications
Office tools	Calendars, Calculators, Gnumeric spreadsheet, Spelling Checker
Utilities	GNU bc, gzip, Midnight Commander, patch, GnuPG (GNU Privacy Guard)
Graphics, images, and sound	The GIMP, XPaint, Xfig, Gnuplot, Ghostscript, Ghostview, ImageMagick, X Multimedia System, dia, gtv, CD Players
DOS/Windows	mtools
System administration	User Mount Tool, Time Tool, System Monitor, Gnome RPM, Linuxconf
Internet	dip, elm, imap, ircii, inn, pine, pppd, rdist, sendmail, tin, trn, x3270, xchat, Telnet, FTP, ssh, Netscape Communicator
Serial communications	Minicom
Database	PostgreSQL, MySQL
Programming	Bison, flex, Gawk, GCC, p2c, Perl, Python, RCS, CVS, Tcl/Tk, yacc
Text formatting	groff, TeX
Games	GNU Chess, Mahjongg, Reversi, Minesweeper, FreeCell, Gnobots, Snake Race, AisleRiot, fortune, xgammon, xpilot

This list is by no means comprehensive. The Red Hat Linux distribution comes with a plethora of standard GNU utilities that are not shown in the list.

This chapter provides a brief summary of a smaller subset of these applications. In particular, you will learn about some of the programs that were not covered in earlier chapters. Some applications, such as GNU Emacs and vi, are covered in detail elsewhere in the book. Also, entire categories of important applications, such as Internet applications, are covered in great detail in individual chapters within the book.

Quite a few of the listed applications are automatically installed during the Linux installation process. Other applications have to be installed from one of the companion CD-ROMs.

Note

You can start many of these applications from the GNOME or KDE desktop. The main menu button of each desktop provides a series of menus from which you can select the applications. In this chapter, I explain how to start applications, if available, from the GNOME Main Menu button, because the default GNOME menu also includes the KDE menus through which you can start any KDE application, as well.

Editors

You'll find the following text editors on the companion CD-ROMs:

- GNU Emacs — the one and only original Emacs
- JED — a GNU Emacs–like editor
- Joe — a text editor with commands similar to those of WordStar
- Vim — a `vi`-like editor
- GUI text editors that are part of GNOME and KDE
- `gnotepad+` — a graphical HTML editor
- KDE Binary Editor — a graphical editor for binary files

As you can see, most of these editors aspire to be either GNU Emacs or `vi`. The look-alikes typically are smaller in size and have fewer features.

The GUI text editors are part of GNOME and KDE. The `gnotepad+` application is for preparing and editing HTML files.

GNU Emacs

The companion CD-ROM includes GNU Emacs version 20.7. GNU Emacs, which is one of the best-known GNU products, is distributed by the Free Software Foundation. The CD-ROM includes two versions of GNU Emacs:

- The full version of GNU Emacs (`/usr/bin/emacs`), which works under X and provides menus for editing operations. You must have X installed to run this version. The binary is configured with the following options:

  ```
  --with-x11 --with-x-toolkit --prefix=/usr
  ```

- A version (`/usr/bin/emacs-nox`) that is somewhat smaller than the full version of GNU Emacs; offers the same functionality, but without the support for X.

You can type `emacs-nox` or `emacs -nw` to run the non-X version of GNU Emacs in a terminal window under X. The non-X version, however, is mainly for those users who do not have the X Window System installed on their systems.

Cross-Reference

Chapter 14 describes the features of GNU Emacs and how to use it for text-editing tasks.

JED

Like several of the other freely available text editors, this editor is named after its author, John E. Davis. JED is a small, but powerful GNU Emacs-like editor that supports editing modes and can read info files, like GNU Emacs. JED can also emulate other text editors, such as WordStar and the EDT editor of VAX/VMS systems. One of JED's unique features is the fact that you can actually edit binary files in JED.

You can find the RPM file for JED in the RedHat/RPMS directory of the second companion CD-ROM.

Joe

The companion CD-ROMs include the Joe text editor version 2.8. Joe is named after its creator, Joseph H. Allen. The Joe editor uses commands similar to those of WordStar, the popular PC word processor of yesteryear.

You will find the RPM file for the Joe editor in the RedHat/RPMS directory of the second companion CD-ROM.

Vim

Vim stands for *Vi IMproved*. As the name implies, Vim is an improved version of the standard UNIX text editor vi. The companion CD-ROMs include version 5.7 of Vim. In addition to the standard vi commands, Vim includes many new features, including several levels of undo, command-line history, and filename completion.

Cross-Reference

In Red Hat Linux, when you run the vi editor, you are actually running Vim. Chapter 14 shows you how to use the vi editor.

GUI Text Editors

Both of the Linux graphical desktops — GNOME and KDE — come with *GUI text editors* (text editors that have graphical user interfaces).

To try the GNOME text editor, gEdit, select Main Menu ⇨ Programs ⇨ Applications ⇨ gEdit from the GNOME desktop. You can open a file by clicking the Open button on the toolbar. This brings up the Open File dialog box. You can then change directories and select the file to edit, by clicking the OK button.

The gEdit editor then loads the file in its window. You can open more than one file and move among them as you edit the files. Figure 13-1 shows a typical editing session with gEdit.

In this case, the editor has four files open for editing: fstab, inittab, hosts, and modules.conf (all from the /etc directory). The filenames appear as tabs below the toolbar of the editor's window. You can switch between the files by clicking the tabs with the filenames.

The rest of the text-editing steps are intuitive. To enter new text, click to position the cursor and begin typing. You can select text and copy, or cut using the buttons on the toolbar above the text-editing area. To paste the text elsewhere in the file, position the cursor, and then click the Paste button.

KDE has two text editors: Advanced Editor and Simple Editor. Both editors have a similar user interface, but the menus have some differences. From the KDE desktop, you can start KEdit (the KDE text editor), by selecting K ⇨ Editors ⇨ Text Editor. To open a text file, select File ⇨ Open from the menu. A dialog box appears. From this dialog box, you can go to the desired directory, select the file to open, and click the OK button. The KDE text editor then opens the file and displays its contents in the window.

You can edit a text file with the Advanced Editor in a similar manner. To start the Advanced Editor, select K ⇨ Editors ⇨ Advanced Editor. Figure 13-2 shows the Advanced Editor editing the /etc/xinetd.conf file on a Red Hat Linux system.

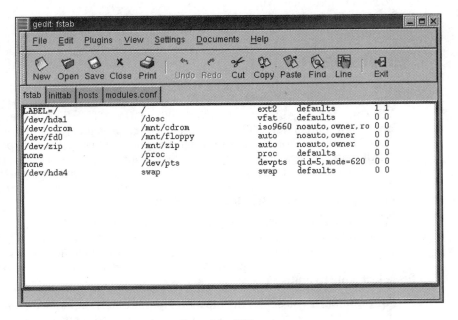

Figure 13-1: Editing several text files with gEdit

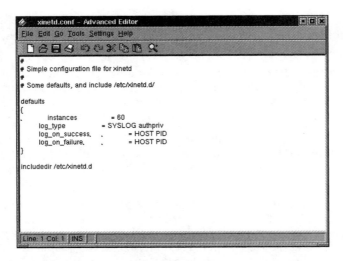

Figure 13-2: Editing a text file with the KDE Advanced Editor

The KDE editor also has a toolbar, but the buttons only show icons. If you do not know what a button does, move the mouse pointer over the button and a pop-up message appears with help.

You cannot open multiple files in the same editor window. Instead, you have to select File ⇨ New Window to open a new editor window, and then open another file in the new window.

gnotepad+

The gnotepad+ application is an HTML editor that comes with GNOME. To start gnotepad+, select Main Menu ⇨ Programs ⇨ Applications ⇨ gnotepad+. You can use gnotepad+ to open and edit existing HTML files or create a new one. To prepare a new HTML file, you can simply begin typing in the text window. The second toolbar has buttons that you can click to insert specific HTML tags. For example, if you click the H1 button, gnotepad+ inserts the string <H1></H1> in the window and places the cursor between the two tags, so you can type the header text. When you"re done, you can save the file by clicking the button with a disk icon (on the first toolbar).

To open an existing HTML file, click the Open button (the one that looks like an open file folder) from the toolbar, or select File ⇨ Open. An Open File dialog box appears. In that dialog box, you can change to a directory such as /var/www/html (where Apache Web server expects the HTML files) and select a file to edit.

For example, if you select the file /var/www/html/index.html, the gnotepad+ program loads this file in its window and displays it as HTML code, as shown in Figure 13-3.

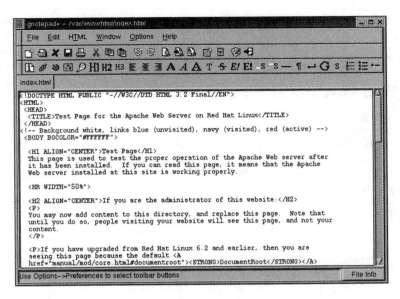

Figure 13-3: Editing an HTML file in gnotepad+

You can now edit the HTML code and add new text. To view the HTML file as a formatted document, select File ⇨ View HTML ⇨ View (Xm)HTML as doc. This causes gnotepad+ to display the formatted document in a new tab, as shown in Figure 13-4.

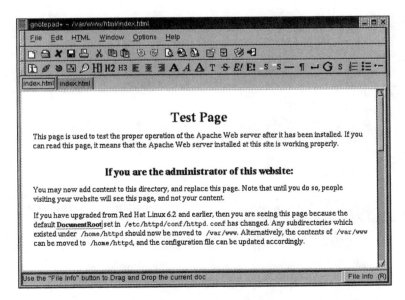

Figure 13-4: Viewing an HTML file as a formatted document in gnotepad+

You can go back and forth between the two views by clicking the tabs that appear above the document. You can edit the HTML tags and text in the HTML view, and then switch to the formatted document to see the results.

KDE Binary Editor

The KDE Binary Editor is a hexadecimal editor for binary files. You can open any file — text or binary — in the KDE Binary Editor to view the content as a string of hexadecimal digits as well as characters. To start the KDE Binary Editor, select K ⇨ Utilities ⇨ Binary Editor in the KDE desktop (from the GNOME desktop, select Main Menu ⇨ KDE menus ⇨ Utilities ⇨ Binary Editor). From the Binary Editor window, select File ⇨ Open. Then, from the resulting dialog box, select the file you want to open in the Binary Editor. For example, Figure 13-5 shows the Binary Editor editing the file /bin/bash — the binary executable file for the Bash shell.

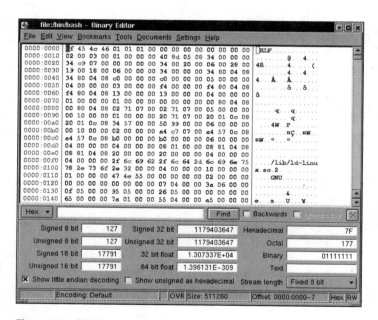

Figure 13-5: Editing a binary file in the KDE Binary Editor

As Figure 13-5 shows, the KDE Binary Editor displays the contents of the binary file in a split-window view. A wide window on the left shows the value of each byte as pairs of hexadecimal digits (each hexadecimal digit represents four bits of data and a byte has eight bits). The narrower window on the right shows the ASCII character corresponding to each byte. If the character is not printable, the byte is shown as a period (.).

You can see from Figure 13-5 that the binary file for Bash contains the string ELF near the beginning of the file. This means that the file is an ELF executable (see Chapter 27 for a brief discussion of the ELF format). Also note that the file contains the name of a shared library — /lib/ld-linux.so.2.

You might find it interesting to open other binary files in the KDE Binary Editor and see what they contain. For example, if you open a GIF image file, you would see that the file starts with the string GIF87a or GIF89a.

Caution

Always be extra careful when you use a binary editor to open and view executable and library files. Remember that you have the ability to ruin a binary if you inadvertently alter the data and save the changes.

Office Tools

This book's companion CD-ROMs include several office tools, such as calendars, calculators, and spell checkers. The following sections describe a few of these office tools:

- Gnumeric — a spreadsheet program
- Calendars — ical and GNOME Calendar
- Calculators — xcalc, GNOME calculator, and KDE calculator
- aspell — spelling checker

Gnumeric Spreadsheet

The GNOME desktop comes with *Gnumeric* — an X-based graphical spreadsheet program. To try out Gnumeric, select Main Menu ⇨ Programs ⇨ Applications ⇨ Gnumeric spreadsheet from the GNOME panel. The Gnumeric program displays its main window, which looks similar to Windows-based spreadsheets, such as Microsoft Excel. (In fact, Gnumeric can read and write Excel 95 format spreadsheet files.)

You use Gnumeric in the same way you use Microsoft Excel. You can type entries in cells, use formulas, and format the cells (such as specify the type of value and the number of digits after the decimal point). Figure 13-6 shows a typical spreadsheet in Gnumeric.

You might want to type in a similar spreadsheet. Use formulas that you'd normally use in Microsoft Excel. For example, use the formula SUM(D2:D6) to add up the entries from cell D2 to D6. To set cell D2 as the product of the entries A2 and C2, type **=A2*C2** in cell D2. To learn more about the functions available in Gnumeric, select Help ⇨ Gnumeric function reference from the menu. This brings up the Netscape Communicator, with information about the Gnumeric functions, as shown in Figure 13-7.

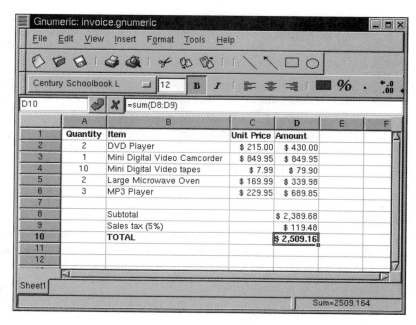

Figure 13-6: A typical spreadsheet in Gnumeric

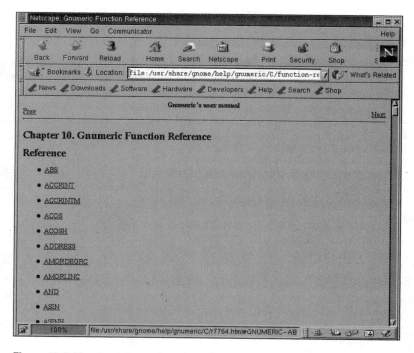

Figure 13-7: Viewing information about Gnumeric's functions in the GNOME Help Browser

You can browse the list of functions and click on a function to read more about that function.

When you're finished preparing the spreadsheet, select File ⇨ Save As to save it. A dialog box appears from which you can specify the file format, the directory location, and the name of the file. Gnumeric can save the file in a number of formats, including XML (eXtensible Markup Language), Excel 95, a simple text file, and Adobe's Portable Document Format (PDF) file. You cannot read the file back into Gnumeric unless you save it as an XML or Excel 95 file. Gnumeric's default file format is XML, which is a text-based format. However, Gnumeric compresses the resulting XML file using the GNU Zip (gzip) compression program. Gnumeric assigns a .gnumeric extension to files stored in the compressed XML format.

Save the spreadsheet in Excel 95 format. Then transfer that file to a Windows system and try to open it, using Microsoft Excel. Notice that the file loses some of the text styles (such as boldface and justification) in the translation, but the basic elements (the numbers and the formulas) stay intact.

Note

KDE comes with the KOffice suite of applications that includes the KSpread spreadsheet program, as well as the KWord word processor, KPresenter presentation software, KChart charting program, and KIllustrator drawing program. You can run KSpread by selecting K ⇨ Office ⇨ KSpread from the KDE desktop.

Calendars

The companion CD-ROMs contain several calendar programs. The GNOME desktop comes with its own calendar program. Additionally, when you install the X Window System following the steps outlined in Chapter 2, you also install ical — an X Window System–based calendar program. You can start both calendars from the GNOME panel's Main Menu button or the KDE main menu.

ical calendar

To start ical, select Main Menu ⇨ Programs ⇨ Applications ⇨ ical from the GNOME desktop. (You can also simply type ical in a terminal window.) The program displays a full-screen window from which you can click a date to view that day's schedule. Figure 13-8 shows a typical calendar.

To add appointments for a specific time, click the time, and type a brief description of the appointment.

You can go to a different month or year by clicking the arrows next to the month and the year. After you finish adding events and appointments, select File ⇨ Save to save the calendar.

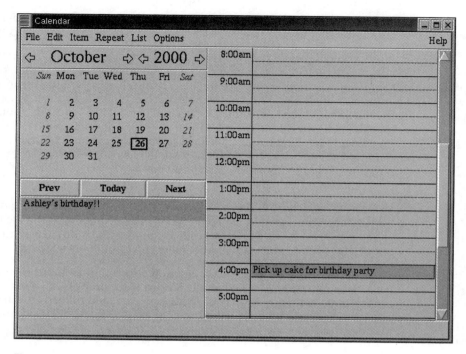

Figure 13-8: Viewing a calendar with ical

To add an event or to-do item for a specific date, select the date from the calendar, click in the blank area under the calendar, and type the description of the event.

To add appointments for a specific time, click the time and type a brief description of the appointment. After you finish adding events and appointments, select File ⇨ Save to save the calendar.

GNOME calendar

GNOME comes with a calendar program. To start the GNOME calendar, select Main Menu ⇨ Programs ⇨ Applications ⇨ Calendar from the GNOME panel. The GNOME calendar's main window appears. The GNOME calendar has a different user interface than the ical program, but it's still intuitive. Figure 13-9 shows a typical calendar in the GNOME calendar program's main window.

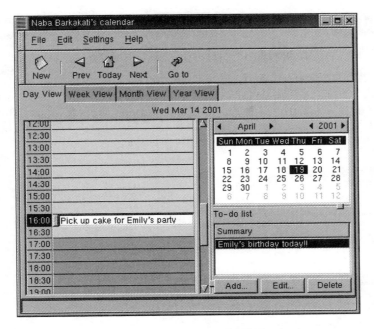

Figure 13-9: Viewing a calendar with the GNOME calendar program

As Figure 13-9 shows, the GNOME calendar program has a toolbar with a number of buttons for performing common tasks. Underneath the toolbar, a number of tabs display the appointments in four different views: daily, weekly, monthly, and yearly. If you are unsure about what a button does, simply place the mouse pointer on the button and a small pop-up help message gives you some information.

To add an appointment, you double-click the date in the right side of the window and then click the New button on the toolbar. This brings up a dialog box in which you can enter information about the appointment. Select File ➪ Save to store the calendar for future use.

Calculators

You have a choice of three calculators that you can use with Red Hat Linux:

- xcalc, the X calculator that comes with the X Window System
- GNOME calculator
- KDE calculator

All of these calculators are scientific calculators capable of performing typical calculations, such as square root and inverse, as well as trigonometric functions, such as sine, cosine, and tangent.

xcalc calculator

The xcalc calculator is styled after Texas Instrument's TI-30 model. To use the xcalc calculator, type xcalc & in a terminal window. Figure 13-10 shows the resulting calculator. You can use the calculator by clicking the buttons, or by entering the numbers on the keyboard.

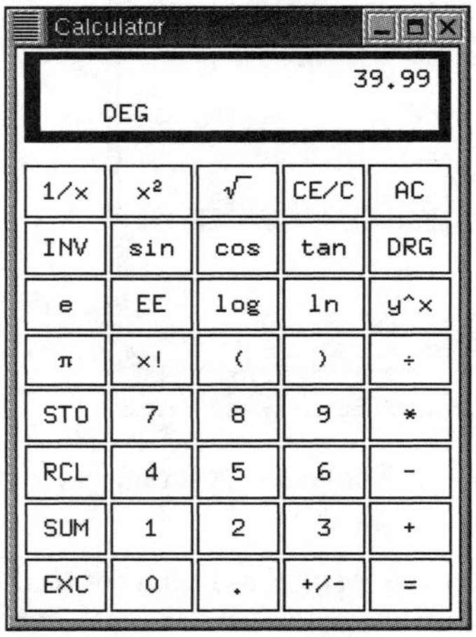

Figure 13-10: The TI-30-style calculator displayed by xcalc

If you prefer the Reverse Polish Notation (RPN) of the Hewlett-Packard calculators, you can get a calculator modeled after the HP-10C by typing the xcalc -rpn & command. In RPN, the operands precede the operation. For example, to add 2.25 to 9.95 on an HP-10C calculator, you press the keys in the following order: 2.25 ENTER 9.95 +. Figure 13-11 shows the HP-10C look-alike displayed by xcalc.

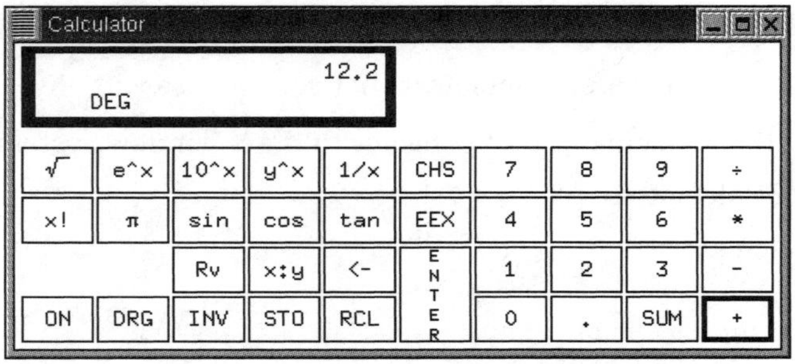

Figure 13-11: The HP-10C-style calculator displayed by xcalc

GNOME calculator

The GNOME calculator is based on xcalc, but with a nicer user interface. To run the GNOME calculator, select Main Menu ⇨ Programs ⇨ Utilities ⇨ Simple Calculator in the GNOME panel. Figure 13-12 shows the resulting display of the GNOME calculator.

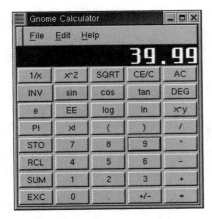

Figure 13-12: The Gnome calculator

If you compare Figure 13-12 with Figure 13-10, you see that both the TI-30 style xcalc and the GNOME calculator have the same set of buttons — except the buttons look better in the GNOME calculator.

KDE calculator

KDE also includes a scientific calculator with more features than xcalc and the GNOME calculator. For example, it can perform calculations in hexadecimal, decimal, octal, and binary format. From the KDE desktop, you can start the KDE calculator by selecting K ⇨ Utilities ⇨ Calculator (or Main Menu ⇨ KDE menus ⇨ Utilities ⇨ Calculator from the GNOME Panel). Figure 13-13 shows the KDE calculator.

With the KDE calculator, you can convert a number from one base to another by simply entering the number with one of the buttons selected, and then clicking the desired base. For example, to convert the hexadecimal value FF to decimal, click the Hex button and enter FF by pressing the F button twice. Then click the Dec button to see the answer, which should be 255.

Figure 13-13: The KDE calculator

aspell — Spelling Checker

The `aspell` utility is an interactive spelling checker. When you install Red Hat Linux from the companion CD-ROMs, you have the opportunity to install `ispell`.

Using `aspell` is simple. You use it to check the spelling of words in a text file. To do so, simply type `aspell check` *filename*. To try out `aspell`, type some notes and save them in a text file named `notes.txt`. To run the spelling checker on that file, type the following command in a terminal window:

```
aspell check notes.txt
This note describes the *concensus* reached during the August 16
meeting.
1) consensus                    6) consensus's
2) con census                   7) consensuses
3) con-census                   8) consciences
4) condenses                    9) condensers
5) concerns                     0) consensual
i) Ignore                       I) Ignore all
r) Replace                      R) Replace all
a) Add                          x) Exit
?
```

After `aspell` runs, it scans the file named `notes.txt` until it finds a mis-spelled word (any word that does not appear in `ispell`'s dictionary). As the output shows, `aspell` displays the sentence with the misspelled word (*concensus*) and highlights that word by enclosing it in a pair of asterisks. Below that sentence, `aspell` lists possible corrections, numbering them sequen-tially from 1. In this case, the utility lists *consensus* — the right choice — as the first correction for *concensus*. The list also includes a few items labeled with a letter; these refer to specific actions, such as ignore the misspelling, or accept the misspelling for the rest of the file.

At the end of the list of options, aspell displays a list of 16 other options — ten numbered 0 through 9 and six labeled with single letters i, r, a, I, R, and x — followed by a question mark prompt. You should press one of the numbers or letters from the list shown in aspell's output to indicate what you want aspell to do. The numbered options show ten possible replacement words for the misspelled word. Following are the meanings of the list of items that aspell displays for a misspelled word:

- Space means accept the word this time.

- N (where N is a number from 0 to 9) refers to the numbered item showing the suggested correction that you want to use. To replace the misspelled word with the correction numbered 0, simply type **0**.

- i means ignore the misspelled word.

- I means ignore all occurrences of the word.

- r means replace this occurrence. aspell prompts for a replacement word.

- R means replace all occurrences. aspell prompts for a replacement word.

- a means add. aspell accepts the word and adds it to the user's private dictionary.

- x causes aspell to save the rest of the file and exit, ignoring misspellings.

Note

To read the aspell manual, start the Web browser, select File ⇨ Open Page, and click the Choose File button from the Open Page dialog box. Go to the /usr/share/doc directory and look for a directory name that begins with aspell (the complete name depends on the aspell version number). From the man-html subdirectory of that directory, open the 1_Introduction. html file.

Graphics, Images, and Sound

The applications in this category enable you to work with images, graphics (line drawings and shapes), and sound. Chapter 5 describes the CD players that you can use to play audio CDs on your Red Hat Linux system. The following applications, summarized in this chapter, enable you to prepare, view, modify, and print graphics and images:

- The GIMP (the GNU Image Manipulation Program) — a program for viewing and performing image-manipulation tasks, such as photo retouching, image composition, and image creation

- Xpaint — a bitmap painting program patterned after MacPaint

- Xfig — a drawing program that is capable of producing engineering drawings

- Gnuplot — a plotting package
- Ghostscript — a PostScript interpreter that is capable of producing output on many devices, including output in various image-file formats
- Ghostview — an X application that serves as a front end to Ghostscript

The GIMP

The *GIMP* (*GNU Image Manipulation Program*) is an image-manipulation program written by Peter Mattis and Spencer Kimball and released under the GNU General Public License (GPL). It is installed if you select the Graphics Manipulation package when you install Red Hat Linux from this book's companion CD-ROMs. The GIMP is comparable to other image-manipulation programs, such as Adobe Photoshop and Corel Photopaint.

To try out the GIMP, select Main Menu ⇨ Programs ⇨ Graphics ⇨ The GIMP from the GNOME desktop (from the KDE desktop, select K ⇨ Red Hat ⇨ Graphics ⇨ The GIMP). The GIMP starts and displays a window with copyright and license information. Click the Continue button to proceed with the installation. The next screen shows the directories to be created when you proceed with a personal installation of the GIMP (see Figure 13-14).

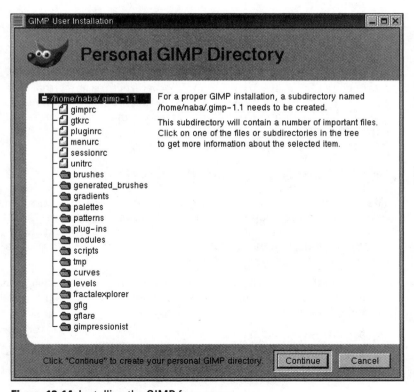

Figure 13-14: Installing the GIMP for a user

As you can see from Figure 13-14, GIMP installation involves creating a directory called .gimp-1.1 in your home directory and placing a number of files in that directory. This directory essentially holds information about any changes to user preferences that you might make to the GIMP. Go ahead and click the Continue button at the bottom of the window. The GIMP creates the necessary directories and copies the necessary files to those directories. Then it displays an installation log, as shown in Figure 13-15.

Figure 13-15: The user installation log displayed by the GIMP

After reading the installation log and ensuring that there are no error messages, click the Continue button. The GIMP then guides you through several screens from which you are asked to specify the values of some parameters; you can accept the defaults and click the Continue button in each screen until the installation window closes. From this time on, you won't see the installation window anymore; you have to deal with installation only once when you run the GIMP for the first time.

The GIMP then loads any plug-ins — external modules that enhance its functionality. It displays a startup window that shows a message about each plug-in as it has loaded. After finishing the startup, the GIMP displays a tip of the day in a window. You can browse the tips and then click the Close button to close the tip window. At the same time, the GIMP displays a number of windows, as shown in Figure 13-16.

These windows include a main toolbox window titled The GIMP, a Tool Options window, a Brush Selection window, and a Layers, Channels & Paths window. Of these, the main toolbox window is the most important — in fact, you can close the other windows and work using the menus and buttons in the toolbox.

The toolbox has three menus on the menu bar: File, Xtns (extensions), and Help. The File menu has options to create a new image, open an existing image, save and print an image, mail an image, and quit the GIMP. The Xtns menu gives you access to numerous extensions to the GIMP. The exact content of the Xtns menu depends on which extensions are installed on your system. The Help menu enables you to view tips and get help on the GIMP. For example, select Help ⇨ Help... to bring up the GIMP Help Browser with online information about the GIMP.

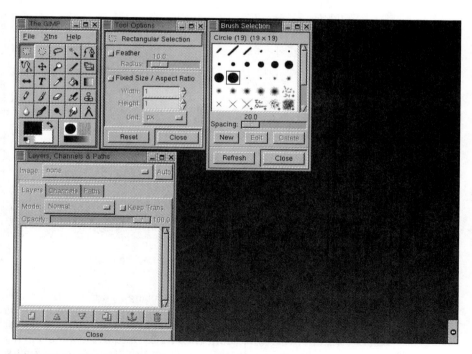

Figure 13-16: Initial windows displayed by the GIMP

To open an image file in the GIMP, select File ⇨ Open. This brings up the Load Image dialog box from which you can select an image file. You can change directories and select the image file you want to open. GIMP can read all common image-file formats, such as GIF, JPEG, TIFF, PCX, BMP, PNG, and PostScript. After you select the file and click the OK button, the GIMP loads the image into a new window. Figure 13-17 shows an image opened by the GIMP.

Figure 13-17: Opening an image with the GIMP

The toolbox also has a large number of buttons that represent the tools you use to edit the image and apply special effects. You can get pop-up help on each tool button by placing the mouse pointer on the button. You can select a tool by clicking the tool button, and then you can apply that tool's effects on the image.

For your convenience, the GIMP displays a pop-up menu when you right-click your mouse on the image window. The pop-up menu has most of the options from the File and Xtns menus in the toolbox. You can then select specific actions from these menus.

You can do much more than just load and view images with the GIMP, but a complete discussion of all its features is beyond the scope of this book. If you want to try the other features of the GIMP, you should consult the GIMP User Manual (GUM), available online at `http://manual.gimp.org/`. You can also select Xtns ⇨ Web Browser ⇨ GIMP.ORG ⇨ Documentation to access the online documentation for the GIMP (you will need an Internet connection for this to work).

Some documentation about the GIMP is installed in the `/usr/share/doc` directory. To go to that directory, type `cd /usr/share/doc/gimp*` (the actual directory name depends on the current version of the GIMP). The README file in that directory points you to other resources on the Web where you can learn more about the GIMP. In particular, visit the GIMP home page at `http://www.gimp.org/` to learn the latest news about the GIMP and to find links to other resources.

XPaint

XPaint is an image-display and image-editing program patterned after the venerable MacPaint program for the Apple Macintosh. XPaint runs under the X Window System and enables you to view and edit bitmapped images in several formats, including GIF, X11 Pixmap (xpm), X11 Bitmap (xbm), and TIFF.

XPaint is included on this book's companion CD-ROM. You can choose to install XPaint when you install Linux from the companion CD-ROM; it's in the *Graphics Manipulation* package.

To run XPaint, type xpaint & in a terminal window. From the GNOME desktop, you can also start XPaint by selecting Main Menu ➪ Programs ➪ Graphics ➪ Paint. XPaint runs and displays its toolbox window, as shown in Figure 13-18.

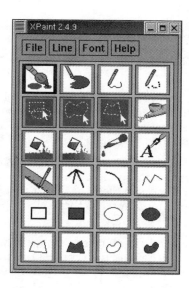

Figure 13-18: The image-editing toolbox in XPaint

All image-loading and image-editing operations start in the toolbox window. If you have used any image-editing program, you should not have any problem with the tools in the toolbox.

A menu bar that contains four items — File, Line, Font, and Help — appears at the top edge of the XPaint toolbox window. If you click any of these items, a pull-down menu appears, from which you can make further selections. The Help menu offers some online help information.

Figure 13-19 shows the result of selecting Help from the Help menu.

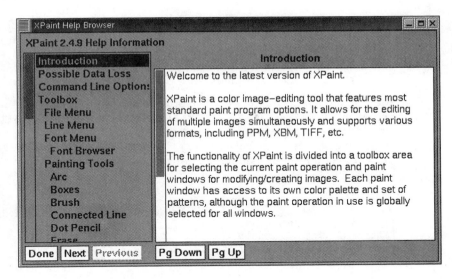

Figure 13-19: Online help in XPaint

This window provides information on how to use various features of XPaint. Click the Next and Previous buttons (at the bottom edge of the Help window) to select a topic and look at its help information.

xfig

The xfig program is an interactive drawing program that runs under X and can generate encapsulated PostScript files that are suitable for inclusion in documents. On the second companion CD-ROM, xfig is in the RedHat/RPMS subdirectory in two Red Hat Package Manager (RPM) files: xfig-3.2.3c-3.i386.rpm and transfig-3.2.3c-1.i386.rpm.

To install xfig, follow these steps:

1. Log in as root and mount the second CD-ROM with the following command:

   ```
   mount /mnt/cdrom
   ```

2. Change to the appropriate directory with the following command:

   ```
   cd /mnt/cdrom/RedHat/RPMS
   ```

3. Install the transfig program with the rpm command as follows:

   ```
   rpm -ivh transfig*.rpm
   ```

4. Install the xfig program with the rpm command as follows:

   ```
   rpm -ivh xfig*.rpm
   ```

To try xfig, type **xfig &** in a terminal window. This command causes a rather large xfig window to appear. At the top edge of the window, you'll find a menu bar. To open an xfig drawing, click the File button. That action brings up a file-selection dialog box, through which you can change directories and locate xfig files (they usually have the .fig extension).

You will find a large number of xfig drawings, organized into subdirectories in the /usr/lib/X11/xfig/Libraries directory of your Red Hat Linux system (these files are installed when you install xfig). You can open and view some of these drawing files in xfig. For example, Figure 13-20 shows the xfig window after loading the drawing file /usr/lib/X11/xfig/Libraries/twostory.fig.

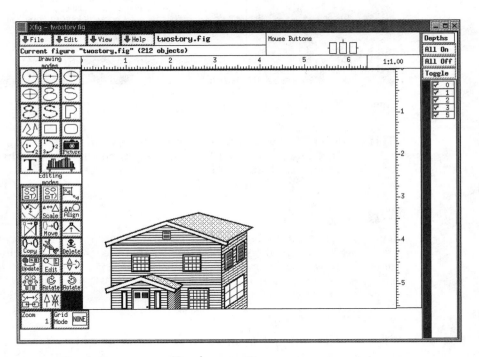

Figure 13-20: A sample drawing displayed by Xfig

As is true of any other tool, learning to use all of the features of xfig takes some practice. If you are familiar with other drawing software, such as MacDraw (Macintosh) or CorelDRAW (PC), you should be able to use xfig without much trouble.

Gnuplot

Gnuplot is an interactive plotting utility. You need to run Gnuplot under the X Window System, because it uses an X window as the output device. Gnuplot is a command-line-driven program; it prompts you and accepts your input commands. In response to those commands, Gnuplot displays various types of plots. The output appears in an X window.

Secret

Incidentally, although Gnuplot has "Gnu" in its name, it has nothing to do with GNU, or the Free Software Foundation.

On the second companion CD-ROM, Gnuplot is in the `RedHat/RPMS` subdirectory in the `gnuplot-3.7.1-12.i386.rpm` file.

To install Gnuplot, follow these steps:

1. Log in as `root` and mount the second CD-ROM with the following command:

   `mount /mnt/cdrom`

2. Change to the appropriate directory with the following command:

   `cd /mnt/cdrom/RedHat/RPMS`

3. Install Gnuplot with the following `rpm` command:

   `rpm -ivh gnuplot*.rpm`

After installing Gnuplot, you should be able to run it by typing `gnuplot &` in a terminal window. Gnuplot displays an opening message and waits for further input at the prompt, as shown in Figure 13-21.

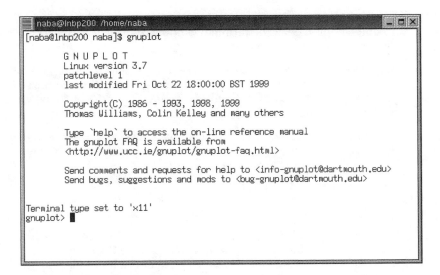

Figure 13-21: Running Gnuplot in a terminal window

To see an immediate result, type the following Gnuplot command at the prompt:

```
plot sin(x)
```

Gnuplot opens an output window and displays a plot of the sine function, as shown in Figure 13-22.

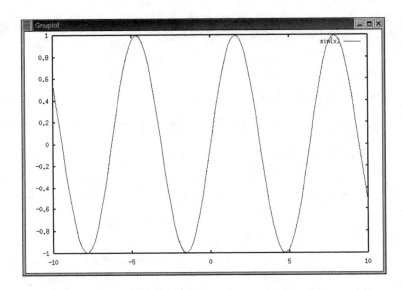

Figure 13-22: Plotting sin(x) in Gnuplot

To quit Gnuplot, click the terminal window to make it active; then type `quit`. This example is a simple illustration of Gnuplot's capabilities.

At any time in Gnuplot, you can ask for online help. The help is similar to that in DEC's VAX/VMS system. To learn more about the `plot` command, for example, type `help plot` at the Gnuplot prompt. Figure 13-23 shows the resulting help information.

Gnuplot also comes with several example files that appear in the `/usr/lib/gnuplot/demos` directory of your system. To try these demo files, type the following commands in a terminal window:

```
cd /usr/share/doc/gnuplot*
cd demo
gnuplot
```

When the Gnuplot prompt appears, load one of the demo files (the ones with the `.dem` extension) with the `load` command. To load the `world.dem` file, for example, type `load "world.dem"`. The demo Gnuplot file displays a map of the world, and then pauses until you press Enter. After you press Enter, Gnuplot displays the next plot, which happens to be a view of the earth in spherical coordinates, as shown in Figure 13-24.

```
naba@lnbp200: /home/naba                                            _ □ ×
gnuplot> help plot
 `plot` is the primary command for drawing plots with `gnuplot`. It creates
 plots of functions and data in many, many ways.  `plot` is used to draw 2-d
 functions and data; `splot` draws 2-d projections of 3-d surfaces and data.
 `plot` and `splot` contain many common features; see `splot` for differences.
 Note specifically that `splot`'s `binary` and `matrix` options do not exist
 for `plot`.

 Syntax:
      plot {<ranges>}
           {<function> | {"<datafile>" {datafile-modifiers}}}
           {axes <axes>} {<title-spec>} {with <style>}
           {, {definitions,} <function> ...}

 where either a <function> or the name of a data file enclosed in quotes is
 supplied.  A function is a mathematical expression or a pair of mathematical
 expressions in parametric mode.  The expressions may be defined completely or
 in part earlier in the stream of `gnuplot` commands (see `user-defined`).

 It is also possible to define functions and parameters on the `plot` command
 itself.  This is done merely by isolating them from other items with commas.

 There are four possible sets of axes available; the keyword <axes> is used to
Press return for more: █
```

Figure 13-23: Online help in Gnuplot

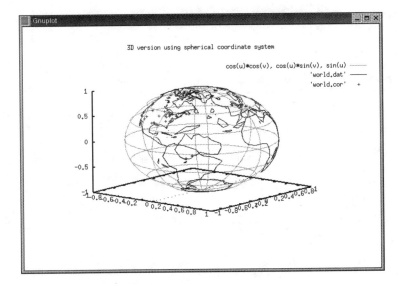

Figure 13-24: A 3D plot of the world in Gnuplot

If you are curious about the `world.dem` file, here's what that file contains:

```
#
# $Id: world.dem,v 1.1.1.1.2.2 1999/08/19 14:34:27 lhecking Exp $
#
#
set title "Gnuplot Correspondences"
set nokey
set noborder
set noyzeroaxis
set noxtics
set noytics
#
# plot world map and correspondent locations as a +
plot 'world.dat' with lines 3 4, 'world.cor' with points 1 2
set title ""
set key
set border
set yzeroaxis
set xtics
set ytics
pause -1 "Hit return to continue"
#
# plot a '3D version using spherical coordinate system' of the world.
set angles degrees
set title "3D version using spherical coordinate system"
set ticslevel 0
set view 70,40,0.8,1.2  # HBB: ,,2.0
set mapping spherical
set parametric
set samples 32
set isosamples 9
set urange [-90:90]
set vrange [0:360]
splot cos(u)*cos(v),cos(u)*sin(v),sin(u) with lines 5 6,\
'world.dat' with lines 3 4, 'world.cor' with points 1 2
pause -1 "Hit return to continue"
#
# plot a '3D version using cylindrical coordinate system' of the
world.
set title "3D version using cylindrical coordinate system"
set ticslevel 0.0
set view 70,40,0.8,1.2   #HBB: ,,2.0
set mapping cylindrical
set parametric
set samples 32
set isosamples 9
set urange [-180:180]
set vrange [-90:90]
splot cos(u),sin(u),v with lines 5 6,\
'world.dat' with lines 3 4, 'world.cor' with points 1 2
pause -1 "Hit return to continue"
```

```
#
# Clean up:
#
reset
```

As the listing shows, the `world.dem` file consists of Gnuplot commands. You can learn a great deal about Gnuplot by trying each file in the Gnuplot demo directory and then studying the commands in the file.

Ghostscript

Ghostscript is a utility for previewing and printing PostScript documents. Ghostscript enables you to print PostScript documents on many non-PostScript devices.

At its heart, Ghostscript is a nearly complete implementation of the PostScript language. Ghostscript includes the interpreter that processes PostScript input and generates output on an output device. A Ghostscript device can be a printer (or display screen), as well as an image-file format, such as BMP or PCX.

Ghostscript is distributed under the GNU GPL, but is copyrighted and maintained by Aladdin Enterprises. The latest version remains under Aladdin's control for one year after its release, at which point, it is transferred to the Free Software Foundation and can be distributed under GPL. Some Ghostscript documentation is installed in the `/usr/share/doc` directory. To change to the appropriate directory, type `cd /usr/share/doc/ghostscript*`. (The exact directory name depends on the version of Ghostscript installed on your system.) You can find the latest contact information by opening the `Readme.htm` file in Netscape Communicator. That directory also contains some other Ghostscript documentation. All of these documentation files are HTML files that you can view using the Netscape Communicator.

To run Ghostscript, type `gs` in a terminal window. Ghostscript brings up an empty window and displays the following text in the terminal window (the version number will be different if you are running a later version of Ghostscript):

```
GNU Ghostscript 5.50 (2000-2-13)
Copyright (C) 1998 Aladdin Enterprises, Menlo Park, CA.  All rights reserved.
This software comes with NO WARRANTY: see the file COPYING for details.
GS>
```

At this point, you are interacting with the Ghostscript interpreter. Unless you know the Ghostscript language (which is like PostScript), you'll feel lost at this prompt. It's kind of like the `C:>` prompt under MS-DOS, or the Linux shell prompt at a terminal.

If you do have a PostScript file available, you can load and view it with a simple command. For example, try the following command:

```
GS> (/usr/share/ghostscript/5.50/examples/golfer.ps) run
>>showpage, press <return> to continue<<
```

What you typed is a Ghostscript command that should cause Ghostscript to load the file /usr/share/ghostscript/5.50/examples/golfer.ps and process it. (If you are running a version of Ghostscript other than 5.50, you must change 5.50 to that version number.) The result is a picture in Ghostscript's output window. To exit Ghostscript, press Enter and type quit.

Fortunately, you do not have to use Ghostscript at the interpreter level (unless you know PostScript well and want to try PostScript commands interactively). You typically use Ghostscript to load and view a PostScript file.

Ghostscript takes several command-line arguments, including the file to be loaded. To see a list of Ghostscript options, type the gs -h command:

```
gs -h
GNU Ghostscript 5.50 (2000-2-13)
Copyright (C) 1998 Aladdin Enterprises, Menlo Park, CA.  All rights reserved.
Usage: gs [switches] [file1.ps file2.ps ...]
Most frequently used switches: (you can use # in place of =)
 -dNOPAUSE             no pause after page  | -q       `quiet', fewer messages
 -g<width>x<height>   page size in pixels   | -r<res>  pixels/inch resolution
 -sDEVICE=<devname>   select device         | -dBATCH  exit after last file
 -sOutputFile=<file>  select output file: - for stdout, |command for pipe,
                                            embed %d or %ld for page #
Input formats: PostScript PostScriptLevel1 PostScriptLevel2 PDF
Available devices:
   x11 x11alpha x11cmyk x11cmyk2 x11cmyk4 x11cmyk8 x11gray2 x11gray4 x11mono
   ap3250 imagen iwhi iwlo iwlq la50 la70 la75 la75plus lbp8 appledmp ccr
   lips3 lq850 ln03 lj250 lj4dith lp2563 m8510 necp6 oce9050 r4081 sj48
   st800 stcolor t4693d2 t4693d4 t4693d8 tek4696 xes lp8000 deskjet djet500
   djet500c dnj650c laserjet ljetplus ljet2p ljet3 ljet3d ljet4 cljet5
   lj5mono lj5gray declj250 hl7x0 cdeskjet cdjcolor cdjmono cdj500 cdj550
   paintjet pj pjxl pjxl300 pjetxl cdj850 cdj670 cdj880 cdj890 cdj1600 hpdj
   lex2050 lex3200 lex5700 lex7000 uniprint md2k md5k bj10e bj200 bjc600
   bjc800 epson eps9mid eps9high epsonc ibmpro jetp3852 lxm5700m oki182
   okiibm dfaxhigh dfaxlow faxg3 faxg32d faxg4 cp50 pcxmono pcxgray pcx16
   pcx256 pcx24b pcxcmyk pbm pbmraw pgm pgmraw pgnm pgnmraw pnm pnmraw ppm
   ppmraw tiffcrle tiffg3 tiffg32d tiffg4 tifflzw tiffpack tiff12nc tiff24nc
   bmp16m psmono psgray psrgb bit bitrgb bitcmyk pngmono pnggray png16
   png256 png16m jpeg jpeggray pdfwrite bbox pswrite epswrite pxlmono
   pxlcolor nullpage
Search path:
   . : /usr/share/ghostscript/5.50 : /usr/share/fonts/default/ghostscript :
   /usr/share/fonts/default/Type1
For more information, see /usr/doc/ghostscript-5.50/Use.htm.
Report bugs to ghost@aladdin.com, using the form in Bug-form.htm.
```

**Cross-
Reference**

The output — in this case, for Ghostscript version 5.50 — shows common command-line switches (which are the same as options), and a list of available devices. Table 6-5 in Chapter 6 describes what each device name means.

To see how Ghostscript renders a PostScript document, you can use any PostScript document that you may have available. You can view one of the sample PostScript files in the /usr/share/ghostscript/5.50/examples directory (replace 5.50 with whatever version of Ghostscript is installed on your system). Type the following command, for example, in a terminal window:

```
gs /usr/share/ghostscript/5.50/examples/golfer.ps
```

Ghostscript opens that file, processes its contents, and displays the output in another window, as shown in Figure 13-25.

Figure 13-25: Ghostscript displaying a PostScript file

In this case, the output happens to be a picture of a golfer. After displaying the output, Ghostscript displays the following message:

```
>>showpage, press <return> to continue<<
```

Press Enter to continue. For a multiple-page PostScript document, Ghostscript then shows the next page. After all the pages are displayed, you return to the Ghostscript prompt. Type `quit` to exit Ghostscript.

Ghostview

Ghostview is an X-based graphical front end to the Ghostscript interpreter. Ghostview is ideal for viewing and printing PostScript documents. For a long document, you can even print selected pages. You also can view the document at various levels of magnification, by zooming in or out.

To run Ghostview, select Main Menu ⇨ Programs ⇨ Graphics ⇨ Ghostview from the GNOME Panel, or type `ghostview &` in a terminal window. This causes the Ghostview window to appear. The window is divided into three parts:

- Along the top edge, you'll find eight buttons. The first six buttons are menu buttons — when you click any of these buttons, a menu appears. The last two buttons are initially empty.

- On the left side are several more buttons, text boxes for information display, and scrollbars for scrolling the image.

- The large area occupying most of the Ghostview window is the work area, where Ghostview displays the PostScript document.

To load and view a PostScript document in Ghostview, select File ⇨ Open, or click the Open button on the left side of the window. This action causes Ghostview to display a file-selection dialog box. Use this dialog box to select a PostScript file. You can select one of the PostScript files that come with Ghostview. For example, open the file `tiger.ps` in the `/usr/share/ghostscript/5.50/examples` directory. (If your system has a version of Ghostscript later than 5.50, you have to use the new version number in place of 5.50.)

To open the selected file, click the `Open File` button in the file-selection dialog box. Ghostview opens the selected file, processes its contents, and displays the output in its window, as shown in Figure 13-26.

In the last two buttons on the upper-right corner of the window, Ghostview displays the current filename and the date the file was created. Ghostview takes this information from the comments in the PostScript file itself, not from the timestamp of the file.

As you move the mouse over the image, Ghostview displays the coordinates of the mouse pointer in a button along the upper-left corner of the window.

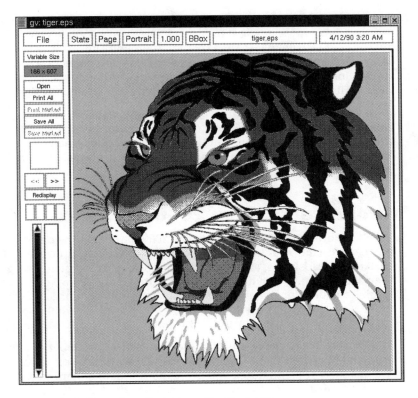

Figure 13-26: Ghostview displaying a PostScript file

Note

Ghostview is useful for viewing various kinds of documentation that come in PostScript format (these files typically have the `.ps` extension in their names). For example, I used Ghostview to view the documentation for the CVS program, which comes in several PostScript files that you can find in the `/usr/share/doc/cvs*` directory. When viewing such documents in Ghostview, I use the magnification button — the button labeled `1.000` in Figure 13-26. If you click that button, a menu appears with a number of magnification factors from 0.1 to 10.0. I had to select a magnification of 2.000 to make the document legible onscreen.

Commercially Available Office Applications for Linux

Most businesses need office applications: word processors, spreadsheets, and the like. Initially, Linux was lacking in this area; now, however, Linux users can choose from several commercial office productivity applications, such as WordPerfect Office 2000 for Linux (`http://linux.corel.com/`),

Applixware Office (`http://www.vistasource.com/`), and StarOffice (`http://www.sun.com/staroffice/`). These products do cost some money, but the cost is usually less than that for Microsoft Office — the leading office application suite for Windows. (Microsoft Office is a collection of several applications: Microsoft Word for word processing; Microsoft Excel for spreadsheets; Microsoft PowerPoint for presentation graphics; and Microsoft Access for databases.)

This book's companion CD-ROMs do not include any of these commercial office applications for Linux, but the next few sections briefly describe them. As you read the descriptions, you can visit each vendor's Web site for the products.

WordPerfect Office 2000 for Linux

Corel Corporation's WordPerfect Office 2000 for Linux is a complete office applications suite that includes WordPerfect 9 for word processing, Quattro Pro 9 for spreadsheets, and Corel Presentations 9 for presentation graphics. The product comes bundled with many more components, such as Adobe Acrobat Reader (for PDF files), as well as many clip art images. Corel even bundles a copy of Corel Linux (based on the Debian distribution), but you can also install and use WordPerfect Office 2000 on Red Hat Linux.

WordPerfect Office can open, edit, and save files in a number of Microsoft Word and Microsoft Excel formats, as well as WordPerfect formats from other systems. According to Corel, you need about 140MB of hard disk space for a typical installation of WordPerfect Office 2000; the full installation requires about 450MB.

You can learn more about the latest release of WordPerfect Office 2000 for Linux by visiting Corel's Web site at `http://linux.corel.com/`. The links at that Web site lead you to more information and to Corel's online store, where you can purchase the product.

Applixware Office

Applixware Office is another prominent office application suite for all Linux distributions, including Red Hat Linux. In April 2000, Applix, Inc., formed a separate group — VistaSource, Inc. — that focuses solely on Linux applications.

Like other office suites, Applixware Office includes Words (for word processing), Spreadsheets (for spreadsheets), and Graphics and Presents (for presentation graphics). Additionally, it also has Mail (an e-mail interface), and Data (an interactive relational database browsing tool). Applixware Office can also read and write documents in Microsoft Office and Corel WordPerfect formats, as well as several other file formats. Although trial versions are not offered, the entire Applixware Office suite is currently priced at less than $100 U.S. You can also purchase Words or Spreadsheets separately; each of these costs less than $50 U.S.

You can learn more about Applixware at VistaSource's Web site (`http://www.vistasource.com/`).

StarOffice

StarOffice is another commercial office applications suite, which was created by StarDivision of Hamburg, Germany, and recently purchased by Sun Microsystems. StarOffice is a cross-platform solution — you can run StarOffice on Linux, Windows 95/98/NT, Sun Solaris SPARC, Sun Solaris x86, and OS/2. Also, StarOffice is available in several languages: English, French, German, Spanish, Italian, Swedish, Dutch, and Portuguese. StarOffice 5.2 for Linux is provided in the form of a large tar file (a form of archive), which you can download for free.

StarOffice is unique in that it combines all of its components into a common desktop from which you can open new documents, drag-and-drop documents from one application to another, and access the Internet. StarOffice includes the following components:

- *StarOffice Writer* for word processing (Microsoft Word–compatible)
- *StarOffice Calc* for spreadsheets (Microsoft Excel–compatible)
- *StarOffice Impress* for presentations (Microsoft PowerPoint–compatible)
- *StarOffice Draw* for vector graphics drawing
- *StarOffice Base* for data management
- *StarOffice Schedule* for organizing events, tasks, contacts, and projects
- *StarOffice Mail* for electronic mail
- *StarOffice Discussion* for participating in Internet newsgroups

You can download a copy of StarOffice for free from `http://www.sun.com/staroffice/`. You can also find the details of Sun's StarOffice licensing policy at the same URL.

Note

In October 2000, Sun released the source code of StarOffice under open-source licenses. Further work on StarOffice is being done by OpenOffice.org, an open-source project sponsored by Sun. To learn more about OpenOffice.org and to participate in the project, visit `http://www.openoffice.org/`.

Summary

Red Hat Linux comes with a large number of applications and utilities. This chapter describes some of these applications, including common office tools — spreadsheet, calendars, calculators, and spelling checker — as well as graphics and imaging programs, such as the GIMP and Ghostview.

By reading this chapter, you learn the following:

- The companion CD-ROMs include a variety of applications and utilities. Many of these applications are installed when you install Red Hat Linux from the companion CD-ROMs, following the steps outlined in Chapter 2. You have to install some of the applications manually from the CD-ROMs.

- GNOME comes with the Gnumeric spreadsheet — a Microsoft Excel–like spreadsheet for Linux. Both GNOME and KDE come with calendar and calculator utilities.

- The `aspell` spelling checker can check the spelling in text files.

- The GIMP, Xpaint, Ghostscript, and Ghostview are useful for working with image files of various formats. In particular, the GIMP is image-processing software with capabilities on a par with commercial packages, such as Adobe Photoshop and Corel Photopaint. Ghostview is ideal for viewing and printing PostScript and PDF documents.

- There are several commercially available office application suites for Linux — WordPerfect Office 2000 for Linux, Applixware Office, and StarOffice. These commercial applications are not part of Red Hat Linux, but you can find out more about each product in case you need a Linux office suite for your home or business.

Chapter 14

Text Processing

In This Chapter

▶ Editing text in Linux

▶ Using ed, the line editor

▶ Using vi, the full-screen text editor

▶ Editing text files with GNU Emacs

▶ Getting online help in GNU Emacs

▶ Understanding the format of a man page

▶ Preparing a man page with groff

ext processing refers to all aspects of creating, editing, and formatting textual documents. The simplest form of text processing is preparing a plain-text file, which you have to do often, because most Red Hat Linux configuration files are plain-text files. For this purpose, Red Hat Linux offers a choice of text editors, ranging from the UNIX standard, vi, to the very powerful GNU Emacs.

To prepare formatted text in Red Hat Linux, you have to use a markup language, such as groff. Using a markup language, you place special formatting commands in a plain-text file, and a formatting program processes the marked-up text file to generate the formatted document for printing or viewing. You may already be familiar with a more recent markup language called Hypertext Markup Language (HTML), which is used as the standard document format on the World Wide Web.

Note

Even if you use a Microsoft Windows- or Macintosh-based "what you see is what you get" (often referred to as "whizzy whig" for the acronym WYSIWYG) application to prepare formatted text, you have to learn the rudiments of a markup language if you want to prepare a *man page* — online help text available through the man command.

This chapter describes the text-processing facilities in Linux. The chapter starts with the ed, vi, and GNU Emacs text editors. The second half of the chapter describes how to use the groff text-formatting program to prepare a man page.

Text Editing with ed and vi

Text editing is an important part of all operating systems, including Linux. In Linux, you need to create and edit a variety of text files:

- System configuration files, including /etc/fstab, /etc/hosts, /etc/inittab, /etc/X11/XF86Config, and many more
- User files, such as .newsrc and .bash_profile
- Mail messages and news articles
- Shell script files
- Perl and Tcl/Tk scripts
- C or C++ programs

All UNIX systems, including Linux, come with two text editors:

- ed — a line-oriented text editor
- vi — a full-screen text editor that supports the command set of an earlier editor named ex

In Red Hat Linux, vi and ex are emulated by another text editor named vim, but you can invoke the editor with the vi command.

Tip

Although ed and vi may be more cryptic than other more graphical text editors, you should learn the basic editing commands of these two editors, because there are times when these may be the only editors available. When you run into a system problem and Linux refuses to boot from the hard disk, for example, you may have to boot from a floppy. In this case, you have to edit system files with the ed editor, because that editor is small enough to fit on the floppy.

As shown in the following sections, it is easy to learn the basic text-editing commands of ed and vi.

Using ed

The ed text editor works with a *buffer*—an in-memory storage area where the actual text resides, until you explicitly store the text in a file. You have to use ed only when you boot a minimal version of Linux (for example, from a boot floppy) and the system does not support full-screen mode.

Starting ed

To start ed, use the following command syntax:

```
ed [-] [-G] [-s] [-pprompt-string] [filename]
```

The arguments shown in brackets are optional. The following list explains the arguments:

- - suppresses the printing of character counts and diagnostic messages
- -G forces backward compatibility with older versions of ed
- -s is the same as the single hyphen
- -p *prompt-string* sets the prompt string (the default is a null prompt string)
- *filename* is the name of the file to be edited

Learning ed

When you use the ed editor, you work in either command mode or text-input mode:

- *Command mode* is what you get by default. In this mode, anything that you type is interpreted as a command. As you learn in the "Summary of ed commands" section, ed has a simple command set, wherein each command consists of a single character.

- *Text-input mode* enables you to enter text into the buffer. You can enter input mode with the commands a (append), c (change), or i (insert). After entering lines of text, you can leave text-input mode by entering a period (.) on a line by itself.

Secret

The ed editor embodies the concept of the *current line* — the line to which ed applies the commands that you type. Each line has an address: the line number. You can apply a command to a range of lines, by prefixing the command with an address range. The p command, for example, prints (displays) the current line. To see the first 10 lines, use the following command:

```
1,10p
```

In a command, the period (.) refers to the current line, and the dollar sign ($) refers to the last line. Thus, the following command deletes all the lines from the current line to the last one:

```
.,$d
```

Examining a sample session with ed

The following example shows how to begin editing a file in ed:

```
ed -p: /etc/fstab
608
:
```

This example uses the -p option to set the prompt to the colon character (:), and opens the file /etc/fstab for editing. Turning on a prompt character is helpful, because without the prompt, it's difficult to tell whether ed is in input mode, or command mode.

The ed editor opens the file, reports the number of characters in the file (608), displays the prompt (:), and waits for a command.

After ed opens a file for editing, the current line is the last line of the file. To see the current line number, use the .= command:

```
:.=
10
```

This output tells you that the /etc/fstab file has 10 lines. (Your system's /etc/fstab file, of course, may have a different number of lines.) The following example shows how you can see all these lines:

```
:1,$p
LABEL=/         /                      ext2     defaults             1 1
/dev/hda1       /dosc                  vfat     defaults             0 0
/dev/cdrom      /mnt/cdrom             iso9660  noauto,owner,ro 0 0
/dev/fd0        /mnt/floppy            auto     noauto,owner         0 0
/dev/zip        /mnt/zip               auto     noauto,owner         0 0
none            /proc                  proc     defaults             0 0
none            /dev/pts               devpts   gid=5,mode=620       0 0
/dev/hda4       swap                   swap     defaults             0 0
:
```

To go to a specific line, type the line number:

```
:1
LABEL=/         /                      ext2     defaults             1 1
:
```

The editor responds by displaying that line.

Suppose that you want to delete the line that contains cdrom. To search for a string, type a slash (/) followed by the string that you want to locate:

```
:/cdrom
/dev/cdrom      /mnt/cdrom             iso9660 noauto,owner,ro 0 0
:
```

The editor locates the line that contains the string, and then displays it. That line becomes the current line. To delete the line, use the d command, as follows:

```
:d
:
```

To replace a string with another, use the s command. To replace cdrom with the string cd, for example, use this command:

```
:s/cdrom/cd/
:
```

To insert a line in front of the current line, use the i command:

```
:i
    (type the line you want to insert)
.   (type a single period)
:
```

You can enter as many lines as you want. After the last line, enter a period (.) on a line by itself. That period marks the end of text-input mode, and the editor switches to command mode. In this case, you can tell that ed has switched to command mode, because you see the prompt (:).

When you are happy with the changes, you can write them to the file with the w command. If you want to save the changes and exit, type wq to perform both steps at the same time:

```
:wq
632
```

The ed editor saves the changes in the file, displays the number of characters that it has saved, and exits.

If you want to quit the editor without saving any changes, use the Q command.

Summarizing ed commands

The sample session should give you an idea of how to use ed commands to perform the basic tasks of editing a text file. Table 14-1 lists all commonly used ed commands.

Table 14-1   Commonly Used ed Commands

Command	Meaning
!command	Execute a shell command
$	Go to the last line in the buffer
%	Apply the command that follows to all lines in the buffer (for example, %p prints all lines)
+	Go to the next line
+n	Go to n-th next line (n is a number)
,	Apply the command that follows to all lines in the buffer (for example, ,p prints all lines); similar to %
-	Go to the preceding line
-n	Go to nth previous line (n is a number)
.	Refer to the current line in the buffer
/regex/	Search forward for the specified regular expression. (See Chapter 28 for an introduction to regular expressions.)
;	Refer to a range of line (if no line numbers are specified, assume current through last line in the buffer)

Continued

Table 14-1 *(continued)*

Command	*Meaning*
=	Print the line number
?*regex*?	Search backward for the specified regular expression. (See Chapter 28 for an introduction to regular expressions.)
^	Go to the preceding line; also see the - command
^*n*	Go to the *n*th previous line (where *n* is a number); also see the -*n* command
a	Append after the current line
c	Change the specified lines
d	Delete the specified lines
e *file*	Edit the file
f *file*	Change the default filename
h	Display an explanation of the last error
H	Turn on verbose-mode error reporting
i	Insert text before the current line
j	Join contiguous lines
k*x*	Mark the line with letter *x* (later, the line can be referred to as '*x*)
l	Print (display) lines
m	Move lines
n	Go to line number *n*
newline	Display the next line and make that line current
P	Toggle prompt mode on or off
q	Quit the editor
Q	Quit the editor without saving changes
r *file*	Read and insert the contents of the file after the current line
s/*old*/*new*/	Replace *old* string with *new*
Space n	A space, followed by *n*; *n*th next line (*n* is a number)
u	Undo the last command
W *file*	Append the contents of the buffer to the end of the specified file
w *file*	Save the buffer in the specified file (if no file is named, save in the default file — the file whose contents ed is currently editing)

Most editing commands can be prefixed with a line number or an address range, expressed in terms of two line numbers separated by a comma; the command then applies to the specified lines. To append after the second line in the buffer, for example, use the following command:

```
2a
(Type lines of text. End with single period on a line.)
```

To print lines 3 through 15, use this command:

```
3,15p
```

Although you may not use ed often, much of the command syntax carries over to the vi editor. As the following section on vi shows, in its command mode, vi accepts ed commands.

Using vi

The vi editor is a full-screen text editor that enables you to view a file several lines at a time. Most UNIX systems, including Linux, come with vi. Therefore, if you learn the basic features of vi, you can edit text files on almost any UNIX system.

Like the ed editor, vi works with a buffer. When vi edits a file, it reads the file into a buffer—a block of memory—and enables you to change the text in the buffer. The vi editor also uses temporary files during editing, but the original file is not altered until you save the changes with a specific vi command.

Setting the terminal type

Before you start a full-screen text editor, such as vi, you have to set the TERM environment variable to the terminal type (such as vt100 or xterm). The vi editor uses the terminal type to look up the terminal's characteristics in the /etc/termcap file, and then control the terminal in full-screen mode.

When you run X and a graphical user interface, such as GNOME or KDE, you can use vi in a terminal window. The terminal window's terminal type is xterm (to verify this, type echo $TERM at the command prompt). When you start the terminal window, it automatically sets the TERM environment variable to xterm. Therefore, you should be able to use vi in an xterm window, without explicitly setting the TERM variable.

Starting vi

If you want to consult the online manual pages for vi, type the following command:

```
man vi
```

To start the editor, use the `vi` name and run it with the following command syntax:

`vi [flags] [+cmd] [filename]`

The arguments shown in brackets are optional. The following list explains the arguments:

- *flags* are single-character flags that control the way that `vi` runs.
- *+cmd* causes `vi` to run the specified command after it starts. (You learn more about the commands in the "The `vi` command summary" section.)
- *filename* is the name of the file to be edited.

The *flags* arguments can be one or more of the following:

- `-c` *cmd* executes the specified command before editing begins.
- `-e` starts in colon command mode (described in the following section).
- `-i` starts in input mode (described in the following section).
- `-m` causes the editor to search through the file for something that looks like an error message from a compiler.
- `-R` makes the file read-only, so that you cannot accidentally overwrite the file (you can also type `view filename` to start the editor in this mode to simply view a file).
- `-s` runs in safe mode, wherein many potentially harmful commands are turned off.
- `-v` starts in visual command mode (described in the following section).

Most of the time, however, `vi` starts with a filename as the only argument, as follows:

`vi /etc/hosts`

Another common way to start `vi` is to jump to a specific line number right at startup. To begin editing at line 296 of the file `/etc/X11/XF86Config`, for example, use the following command:

`vi +296 /etc/X11/XF86Config`

This way of starting `vi` is useful when you edit a source file after the compiler reports an error at a specific line number.

Learning vi concepts

When you edit a file with `vi`, the editor loads the file into a buffer, displays the first few lines of the file in a full-screen window, and positions the cursor on the first line. When you type the command **vi /etc/fstab** in a terminal window, for example, you get a full-screen text window, as shown in Figure 14-1.

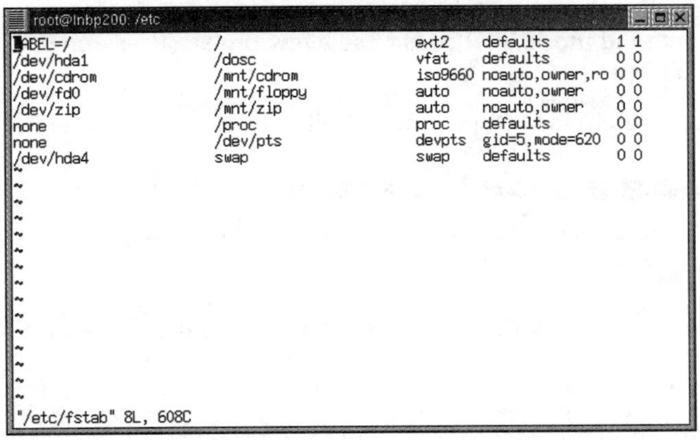

```
┌─ root@lnbp200: /etc ──────────────────────────────── _ □ X ─┐
│ ▌ABEL=/              /               ext2    defaults        1 1 │
│ /dev/hda1            /dosc           vfat    defaults         0 0 │
│ /dev/cdrom           /mnt/cdrom      iso9660 noauto,owner,ro  0 0 │
│ /dev/fd0             /mnt/floppy     auto    noauto,owner     0 0 │
│ /dev/zip             /mnt/zip        auto    noauto,owner     0 0 │
│ none                 /proc           proc    defaults         0 0 │
│ none                 /dev/pts        devpts  gid=5,mode=620   0 0 │
│ /dev/hda4            swap            swap    defaults         0 0 │
│ ~                                                               │
│ ~                                                               │
│ ~                                                               │
│ ~                                                               │
│ ~                                                               │
│ ~                                                               │
│ ~                                                               │
│ ~                                                               │
│ ~                                                               │
│ ~                                                               │
│ ~                                                               │
│ "/etc/fstab" 8L, 608C                                          │
└─────────────────────────────────────────────────────────────┘
```

Figure 14-1: A file displayed in a full-screen text window by the vi editor

The last line shows information about the file, including the number of lines and the number of characters in the file. Later, this area is used as a command-entry area. The rest of the lines are used to display the file. If the file contains fewer lines than the window, vi displays the empty lines with a tilde (~) in the first column.

The current line is marked by the cursor, which appears as a small black rectangle. The cursor appears on top of a character. In Figure 14-1, the cursor is on the first character of the first line.

In vi, you work in one of three modes:

■ *Visual-command mode* is what you get by default. In this mode, anything that you type is interpreted as a command that applies to the line containing the cursor. The vi commands are similar to those of ed and are listed in the section "The vi command summary."

■ *Colon-command mode* enables you to read or write files, set vi options, and quit. All colon commands start with a colon (:). When you enter the colon, vi positions the cursor at the last line and enables you to type a command. The command takes effect when you press Enter. Note that vi's colon-command mode relies on the ed editor.

■ *Text-input mode* enables you to enter text into the buffer. You can enter text-input mode with the command a (insert after cursor), A (append at end of line), or i (insert after cursor). After entering lines of text, you have to press Esc to leave text-input mode and re-enter visual-command mode.

One problem with all these modes is that you cannot easily determine vi's current mode. It can be frustrating to begin typing, only to realize that vi is not in text-input mode. The converse situation also is common — you may be typing text when you want to enter a command. If you want to ensure that vi is in command mode, just press Esc a few times. (Pressing Esc more than once doesn't hurt.)

Tip

To view online help in vi, type :help while in command mode.

Examining a sample session with vi

To begin editing the file /etc/fstab, enter the following command:

```
vi /etc/fstab
```

Figure 14-1, shown previously, shows the resulting display, with the first few lines of the file displayed in a full-screen text window. The last line shows the file's name and statistics: the number of lines and characters.

The vi editor initially positions the cursor on the first character. One of the first things that you need to learn is how to move the cursor around. Try the following commands (each command is a single letter; just type the letter, and vi responds):

- j moves the cursor one line down
- k moves the cursor one line up
- h moves the cursor one character to the left
- l moves the cursor one character to the right

You can also move the cursor using the arrow keys.

Instead of moving one line or one character at a time, you can move one word at a time. Try the following single-character commands for word-size cursor movement:

- w moves the cursor one word forward
- b moves the cursor one word backward

The last type of cursor movement affects several lines at a time. Try these commands and see what happens:

- Ctrl+D scrolls down half a screen
- Ctrl+U scrolls up half a screen

The last two commands, of course, are not necessary when the file contains only a few lines. When you are editing large files, however, it is handy to move several lines at a time.

You can go to a specific line number at any time. This is when a colon command comes in. To go to line 1, for example, type the following and then press Enter:

```
:1
```

When you type the colon, vi displays the colon on the last line of the screen. From then on, vi uses the text that you type as a command. You have to press Enter to submit the command to vi. In colon-command mode, vi accepts all the commands that the ed editor accepts — and then some.

To search for a string, first type a slash (/). The vi editor displays the slash on the last line of the screen. Type the search string, and then press Enter. The vi editor locates the string and positions the cursor at the beginning of that string. Thus, to locate the string dosc in the file /etc/fstab, type the following:

/dosc

To delete the line that contains the cursor, type dd . The vi editor deletes that line of text and makes the next line the current one.

Tip

To begin entering text in front of the cursor, type i. The vi editor switches to text-input mode. Now you can enter text. When you finish entering text, press Esc to return to visual-command mode.

After you finish editing the file, you can save the changes in the file with the :w command. If you want to save the changes and exit, you can type :wq to perform both steps at the same time. The vi editor saves the changes in the file and exits. You can also save the changes and exit the editor, by pressing Shift+zz (hold the Shift key down and press z twice).

To quit the editor without saving any changes, use the :q! command.

Summarizing the vi commands

The sample editing session should give you a feel for the vi commands, especially its three modes:

- visual-command mode (the default)
- text-input mode, which you enter by typing a, A, or i
- colon-command mode, in which you enter commands followed by a colon (:)

In addition to the few commands illustrated in the sample session, vi accepts a large number of commands. Table 14-2 lists the basic vi commands, organized by task.

Table 14-2   Basic vi Commands

Command	Meaning
Insert Text	
a	Insert text after the cursor
A	Insert text at the end of the current line

Continued

Table 14-2 *(continued)*

Command	Meaning
I	Insert text at the beginning of the current line
i	Insert text before the cursor
o	Open a line below the current line
O	Open a line above the current line
Ctrl-v	Insert any special character in input mode
Delete Text	
D	Delete up to the end of the current line
dd	Delete the current line
dw	Delete from the cursor to the end of the following word
x	Delete the character on which the cursor rests
Change Text	
C	Change up to the end of the current line
cc	Change the current line
cw	Change the word
J	Join the current line with the next one
rx	Replace the character under the cursor with x (x is any character)
~	Change the character under the cursor to the opposite case
Move Cursor	
$	Move to the end of the current line
;	Repeat the last f or F command
^	Move to the beginning of the current line
e	Move to the end of the current word
fx	Move the cursor to the first occurrence of character x on the current line
Fx	Move the cursor to the last occurrence of character x on the current line
H	Move the cursor to the top of the screen
h	Move one character to the left
j	Move one line down
k	Move one line up

Command	Meaning
L	Move the cursor to the end of the screen
l	Move one character to the right
M	Move the cursor to the middle of the screen
n|	Move the cursor to column n on current line
nG	Place cursor on line n
w	Move to the beginning of the following word

Mark a Location

Command	Meaning
'x x.	Move the cursor to the beginning of the line that contains mark
\`x	Move the cursor to mark x
mx	Mark the current location with the letter x

Scroll Text

Command	Meaning
Ctrl-b	Scroll backward by a full screen
Ctrl-d	Scroll forward by half a screen
Ctrl-f	Scroll forward by a full screen
Ctrl-u	Scroll backward by half a screen

Refresh Screen

Command	Meaning
Ctrl-L	Redraw the screen

Cut and Paste Text

Command	Meaning
"$x$ndd	Delete n lines and move them to buffer x (x is any single lowercase character)
"Xnyy	Yank n (a number) lines and append them to buffer x
"$x$nyy	Yank n (a number) lines into buffer x (x is any single uppercase character)
"xp	Put the yanked lines from buffer x after the current line
P	Put the yanked line above the current line
p	Put the yanked line below the current line
yy	Yank (copy) the current line into an unnamed buffer

Colon Commands

Command	Meaning
:!command	Execute the shell command
:e filename	Edit the file
:f	Display the filename and current line number

Continued

Table 14-2 *(continued)*

Command	Meaning
:N	Move to line *n* (*n* is a number)
:q	Quit the editor
:q!	Quit without saving changes
:r *filename*	Read the file and insert after the current line
:w *filename*	Write the buffer to the file
:wq	Save the changes and exit
Search Text	
/*string*	Search forward for *string*.
?*string*	Search backward for *string*.
n	Find the next string
View File Information	
Ctrl-g	Show the filename, size, and current line number
Miscellaneous	
u	Undo the last command
Esc	End text-input mode and enter visual-command mode
U	Undo recent changes to the current line

Working with GNU Emacs

Text editors are a matter of personal preference, and many UNIX users swear by GNU Emacs. Although it is intimidating at first, GNU Emacs is one of those software packages that grows on you; it has so many features that many users and programmers often perform all their tasks directly from within GNU Emacs.

A significant advantage of GNU Emacs is its availability on nearly every computer system imaginable, from MS-DOS PCs to any UNIX system. If a system does not have GNU Emacs, you can get it from any one of many sites on the Internet. For your Linux system, you get GNU Emacs on the companion CD-ROMs; you can choose to install it when you install Linux on your system. If you are just getting started with UNIX text editors, I recommend that you learn to use GNU Emacs and vi. That way, you acquire a skill that is usable on any UNIX system.

Because GNU Emacs is so versatile and powerful, describing it in detail could easily take an entire book, and there are quite a few books on GNU Emacs on the market. Most notably, O'Reilly & Associates has a GNU Emacs book, *Learning GNU Emacs* by Debra Cameron, Bill Rosenblatt, and Eric S. Raymond, that you may find useful.

On a text terminal, GNU Emacs runs in text-mode, full-screen display. Under X, GNU Emacs runs in a window. Either way, the basic commands remain the same. The X version also enables you to position the cursor with the mouse.

The next few sections provide a brief introduction to the text-editing features of GNU Emacs.

Starting GNU Emacs

On the Linux console, you can start GNU Emacs by typing emacs. If you are running X, type emacs & in an xterm window to start GNU Emacs. This command launches the X Window System version of GNU Emacs in the background and enables you to continue other work in the xterm window.

When first started, GNU Emacs creates a buffer named *scratch* and displays a help message, followed by a copyright message in a window, as shown in Figure 14-2.

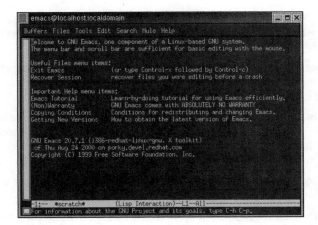

Figure 14-2: The initial window displayed by the X version of GNU Emacs

The initial GNU Emacs window also shows helpful information in the area where you normally edit the contents of a file. You can use the menus to get more help on Emacs.

One message also tells you that to quit GNU Emacs, you should press C-x C-c (that's Ctrl-x, followed by Ctrl-c). As you'll learn in the "Typing GNU Emacs commands" section, all GNU Emacs command keystrokes start with a control character or Escape (which is referred to as *Meta* and abbreviated as M in Emacs documentation). The left Alt key also works as the Meta key.

Note

To be consistent with the GNU Emacs notation, I use the notation C-*x* for Ctrl-*x* and M-*x* for Esc-*x* (*x* is any character).

Learning GNU Emacs

Although I have used GNU Emacs extensively for years, I feel that I have barely scratched the surface when it comes to using its full capabilities. As is true of anything else, your best bet is to start with a small subset of GNU Emacs commands. Then, as you become more proficient with the software, you can gradually add to your repertoire of GNU Emacs commands and features.

GNU Emacs employs some basic concepts that, if learned, are helpful. Some of those concepts include the following:

- Like other text editors (vi or ed), GNU Emacs uses a buffer to maintain the text that you enter and change. You have to explicitly save the buffer to update the contents of the file.

- Unlike vi and ed, GNU Emacs does not require typing any special command to enter text into the buffer. By default, anything that you type goes into the buffer.

- GNU Emacs uses the concept of a cursor marked by a block shape. When you type text, GNU Emacs inserts that text in front of the character on which the cursor rests.

- GNU Emacs has long, descriptive command names that are *bound to* (associated with) specific key sequences — these are the *key bindings* for the GNU Emacs commands. C-x C-c, for example, is bound to the GNU Emacs command save-buffers-kill-emacs.

- All GNU Emacs key bindings start with a control character (for which you simultaneously press Ctrl and a character) or Escape.

- GNU Emacs uses several modes, each of which provides a specific type of editing environment. (In C mode, for example, GNU Emacs indents the braces.)

- In the GNU Emacs window, the last screen line is called the *minibuffer*; it displays all commands and filenames that you type. The line second to the bottom is called the *mode line*. On this line, GNU Emacs displays the name of the buffer and the current mode (the default mode is called *fundamental*).

- You do not have to start GNU Emacs each time you want to edit a file. Rather, you start GNU Emacs, and then open one or more files for editing. You save and close files that you finish editing.

- You can use many buffers in GNU Emacs, and you can cut and paste between buffers.

Typing GNU Emacs Commands

GNU Emacs has an extensive set of commands in which each command has very long descriptive names, such as the following:

```
save-buffer save-buffers-kill-emacs scroll-up previous-line
```

Most of these commands, however, are bound to somewhat cryptic keystrokes. Otherwise, you'd have to type these long commands and wouldn't get much editing done.

Although you can enter any of the descriptive commands in the minibuffer (at the bottom of the GNU Emacs window), the basic means of entering the commands is through special keystrokes. These keystrokes begin with one of the following characters:

- A control character that you enter by simultaneously pressing the Ctrl key and the character. In GNU Emacs documentation, each control character is abbreviated as C-*x* (*x* is a letter). This book uses the notation Ctrl-*x* to denote the control character that corresponds to the letter *x*. In GNU Emacs online help, Ctrl-v is written as C-v.

- An Escape character. In GNU Emacs, the Esc key is abbreviated as the Meta key, or M. Thus, Esc v (Escape, followed by the letter v) is written as M-v. Note that, depending on the keyboard, the Meta key may also be the Alt key, or some other key such as the Windows key, on some Windows keyboard.

Most of the time, you enter the control commands, which require pressing the Ctrl key, together with a letter. Ctrl-v or C-v, for example, causes GNU Emacs to move forward one screen.

The commands with an Esc prefix are easier to enter, because you press the keys in sequence: first the Escape key, and then the letter. Esc v or M-v, for example, causes GNU Emacs to move backward one screen of text. To enter this command, press Esc first, and then press **v**. Although the Ctrl and Esc commands may sound complicated, you can learn a basic set very quickly.

Getting Help

The best source of information on GNU Emacs is GNU Emacs itself. For starters, GNU Emacs includes an online tutorial that teaches you its basics. To use the tutorial, type C-h t. GNU Emacs displays the initial screen of the tutorial in its window, as shown in Figure 14-3.

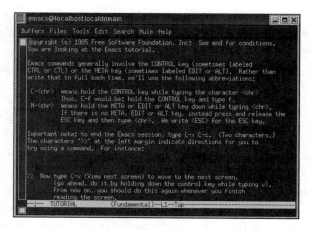

Figure 14-3: GNU Emacs displays the online tutorial when you press C-h t.

As the instructions near the bottom of Figure 14-3 show, the tutorial guides you through the steps and asks you to try GNU Emacs commands. If you are new to GNU Emacs, go through the tutorial. Because the tutorial is hands-on, it gives you a good feel for GNU Emacs.

In addition to the tutorial, you can look up the key bindings for various GNU Emacs commands. To see the key bindings, type C-h b. GNU Emacs splits the window and displays a list of key bindings in the bottom half, as shown in Figure 14-4.

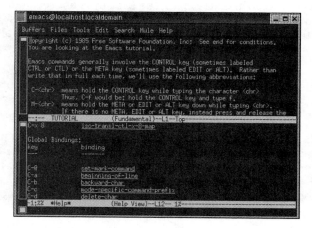

Figure 14-4: GNU Emacs displays the key bindings in a split window when you press C-h b.

Each line in the key binding shows the name of the key and the GNU Emacs command associated with that command. If you press the key, GNU Emacs executes the command that is bound to that key.

Figure 14-4 illustrates GNU Emacs' capability to split its window into two or more parts. After splitting, each part becomes a separate window with its own buffer.

In Figure 14-4, you can scroll the key-binding list with the following keystrokes:

- C-x o switches to the other window (the bottom window, which shows the Help buffer with its key-bindings list).

- C-v scrolls the contents of the Help buffer.

Table 14-3 lists other GNU Emacs help commands.

Table 14-3   GNU Emacs help Commands

Command	Meaning
C-h c	Prompts you for a key sequence and briefly describes that sequence
C-h f	Prompts you for a GNU Emacs command name and describes that command
C-h k	Prompts you for a key sequence and describes what that sequence does
C-h l	Displays the last 100 characters typed
C-h m	Displays the current GNU Emacs mode
C-h s	Displays the syntax table for the current buffer
C-h v	Prompts for a variable name and describes that variable
C-h w	Prompts for a command and shows that command's key binding

Reading a File

After you start GNU Emacs, you can read in a file with the C-x C-f command. To open the file /usr/src/linux/COPYING, for example, follow these steps:

1. Press C-x C-f. GNU Emacs prompts you for a filename.

2. Type the filename—/usr/src/linux/COPYING—and press Enter. GNU Emacs reads the file into a buffer and displays that buffer in the window.

To open a file in the current directory, you do not have to type the full directory name; just type the filename. By default, GNU Emacs looks for the file in the current working directory.

Tip

You do not have to type the full filename in GNU Emacs; just enter the first few characters of the filename and then press Tab. If the partial name uniquely identifies a file, GNU Emacs completes the filename for you. Thus, all you need to type is the first few characters of a filename—just enough to uniquely identify the file. You can use this shortcut feature to avoid typing long filenames.

Suppose that the current working directory contains the file `Makefile`, which is the only file whose name starts with the substring `Mak`. To load that file in GNU Emacs, press `C-x C-f`, type `Mak`, and press Tab. GNU Emacs completes the filename and reads the file `Makefile`.

Moving Around the Buffer

One of the first things that you have to do is move around the buffer. The cursor marks the current spot in the buffer; anything that you type goes into the buffer in front of the character under the cursor. Thus, to insert text into a file, you have to read in the file, move the cursor to the desired spot, and type the text.

To move around the buffer, you need to move the cursor. You have to use control keys to move the cursor in any direction. Following are the six basic cursor-movement commands:

- `C-b` moves the cursor backward one character.
- `C-f` moves the cursor forward one character.
- `C-n` moves the cursor to the following line (while trying to maintain the same column position as in the current line).
- `C-p` moves the cursor to the preceding line (while trying to maintain the same column position as in the current line).
- `C-a` moves the cursor to the beginning of the current line.
- `C-e` moves the cursor to the end of the current line.

If moving one character at a time is too slow, you can move one word at a time, using these commands:

- `M-f` moves the cursor forward one word.
- `M-b` moves the cursor backward one word.

You can move in even bigger chunks through the buffer. The following two commands enable you to move one screen at a time:

- `C-v` moves forward one screen.
- `M-v` moves backward one screen.

You can use two other simple cursor-movement commands for really big jumps:

- M-< (Esc followed by the less-than key) moves the cursor to the beginning of the buffer.

- M-> (Esc followed by the greater-than key) moves the cursor to the end of the buffer.

A timesaving feature of GNU Emacs lets you repeat a command a specified number of times. Suppose that you want to move 13 characters forward. You can do so by pressing C-f 13 times or by typing C-u 13 C-f. The C-u command accepts a repeat count and repeats the next command that many times. If you don't provide a count and simply type a command after C-u, GNU Emacs repeats the command four times. Thus, C-u C-f means "move forward four characters."

Secret

One exception to the behavior of the C-u command exists: When you use C-u with the M-v or C-v command, GNU Emacs does not repeat the screen-scrolling commands. Instead, GNU Emacs scrolls the screen up or down by the specified count. Thus, if you press C-u 10 C-v, GNU Emacs scrolls down 10 lines (not 10 screens).

Inserting and Deleting Text

Because GNU Emacs does not have special command and insert modes like vi, just begin typing to insert text in GNU Emacs. GNU Emacs inserts the text in front of the cursor. GNU Emacs, of course, interprets control characters and Esc as being the beginning of a command.

You can take advantage of the repeat-count feature to insert many copies of a character. I typically use the following line to separate sections of a C program:

```
/*-------------------------------------------------*/
```

I enter this line with the following key presses:

```
/* C-u 51 - */
```

Ignore the spaces; I don't manually type them. I first type /*. Then I press **C-u** and type 51. Finally, I press the hyphen (-), followed by the ending */.

You can delete text in GNU Emacs in the following ways:

- To delete the character in front of the cursor, press Del.

- To delete the character on which the cursor rests, press C-d.

- To delete the word after the cursor, press M-d.

- To delete the word immediately before the cursor, press M-Del.

- To delete from the cursor to the end of the line, press C-k. (GNU Emacs refers to this command as "kill the line.")

Tip

Whenever you delete anything longer than one character, GNU Emacs saves it for you. Press C-y to retrieve the saved text.

You can undo a change with the C-x u command. Each time you press C-x u, GNU Emacs performs the undo operation for a previous command. To undo the effects of the last two commands, for example, press C-x u twice.

Searching and Replacing

Every text editor has search-and-replace capability, and GNU Emacs is no exception. The two most common search commands are as follows:

- C-s *string*—incrementally searches forward for *string*
- C-r *string*—incrementally searches backward for *string*

When you press C-s to search forward, GNU Emacs prompts you for a search string in the minibuffer (the last line in the GNU Emacs window). As you enter the characters for the string, GNU Emacs jumps to the first occurrence of the string that you have typed so far. By the time you finish typing the search string, GNU Emacs will have positioned the cursor at the end of the next occurrence of the search string (provided, of course, that GNU Emacs finds the string).

To find the next occurrence of the string, press C-s again. To end the search, press Enter. You also can halt the search with cursor control commands, such as C-f or C-b.

Searching in the reverse direction works similarly; just press C-r instead of C-s.

GNU Emacs also enables you to replace an occurrence of one string with another. The two basic commands for replacing strings are replace-string and query-replace. The replace-string command replaces all occurrences of one string with another. The query-replace command works similarly, but GNU Emacs prompts you each time it's about to replace a string, enabling you to decide which strings actually are replaced.

The query-replace command is bound to the M-% (Esc, followed by %) key sequence. To perform a query-replace operation, first press M-%. GNU Emacs displays the following prompt in the minibuffer:

```
Query replace:
```

Enter the string that you want to replace—suppose that it's 2000—and then press Enter. GNU Emacs prompts you for the replacement string, as follows:

```
Query replace 2000 with:
```

Enter the replacement string—say, 2001—and press Enter. GNU Emacs moves the cursor to the next occurrence of the string to be replaced and displays a prompt in the minibuffer:

```
Query replacing 2000 with 2001: (? for help)
```

Type **y** or press the spacebar to enable GNU Emacs to replace the string. Otherwise, press **n** or Del to stop GNU Emacs from replacing the string. In either case, GNU Emacs moves to the next occurrence of the string and repeats the prompt. When no more strings are left, GNU Emacs displays a message in the minibuffer informing you how many occurrences of the string were replaced.

No key binding exists for the `replace-string` command. You can type any GNU Emacs command, however, by following these steps:

1. Type `M-x`. GNU Emacs displays `M-x` in the minibuffer and waits for more text.

2. Type the GNU Emacs command, and press Enter. To use the `replace-string` command, for example, type `replace-string`, and then press Enter.

3. For some commands, GNU Emacs prompts for further input; enter that input. When you use `replace-string`, for example, GNU Emacs first prompts for the string to be replaced, and then for the replacement string.

When you type a GNU Emacs command with `M-x`, you can press the spacebar or the Tab key for command completion. To enter the `replace-string` command, for example, you might start by typing `repl`, and then press the spacebar. That action causes GNU Emacs to display `replace-`, and then pause. Type **s** and press the spacebar again. GNU Emacs displays `replace-string`. You then can use the command, by pressing Enter. Try it; you'll see what I mean.

Copying and Moving

Another common editing function is copying blocks of text and moving that text to another location in the buffer. The first step in working with a block of text is to define the block.

In GNU Emacs, a *block* is defined as the text between a mark and the current cursor position. You can think of the *mark* as a physical marker placed in the buffer to mark a location. To set the mark, move the cursor to the beginning of the block, and then press `C-@` or `C-Space` (press the Ctrl key together, with the spacebar). GNU Emacs sets the mark at the current location and displays the following message in the minibuffer:

```
Mark set
```

After the mark is set, GNU Emacs treats the text between the mark and the current cursor location as a block. To copy the block, type the following:

```
M-w
```

That command copies the block to an internal storage area without deleting the block from the current buffer.

If you actually want to cut the block of text, type the following:

```
C-w
```

That command deletes the block of text from the buffer and moves it to an internal storage area.

To insert the cut (or copied) text at any location, move the cursor to the insertion point, and type the following:

```
C-y
```

That command causes GNU Emacs to paste the previously cut text in front of the cursor.

Between the cut and paste operations, you may switch from one buffer to another, and thereby cut from one file and paste in another. To cut from one file and paste into another, follow these steps:

1. Open the first file with the `Cx C-f` command. For this exercise, assume that the first file's name is `first.txt`.
2. Open the second file with the `C-x C-f` command. For this exercise, assume that the second file's name is `second.txt`.
3. Change to the first buffer with the `C-x b first.txt` command.
4. Move the cursor to the beginning of the text to be copied, and press `C-Space`.
5. Move the cursor to the end of the block, and press `C-w` to cut the text.
6. Change to the second buffer with the `C-x b second.txt` command.
7. Move the cursor to the location where you want to insert the text, and press `C-y`. GNU Emacs inserts the previously cut text from first buffer into the second one.

Saving Changes

After you edit a buffer, you have to write those changes to a file to make them permanent. The GNU Emacs command for saving a buffer to its file is `C-x C-s`. This command saves the buffer to the file with the same name.

To save the buffer in another file, use the command `C-x C-w`. GNU Emacs prompts you for a filename. Type the filename and press Enter to save the buffer in that file. Unlike many DOS or Windows word processors, GNU Emacs does not automatically add a file extension. You have to provide the full filename.

Running a Shell in GNU Emacs

GNU Emacs is versatile enough to enable you to access anything in Linux from within a GNU Emacs session. One way to access anything in Linux is to run a shell session. You can do so with the GNU Emacs command named shell. To see how the shell command works, use M-x (press Esc followed by **x**). GNU Emacs displays M-x in the minibuffer and waits for further input. Type shell and press Enter. GNU Emacs starts a new shell process and displays the shell prompt in the GNU Emacs window. Type any shell command that you want. The output appears in the GNU Emacs window.

You can continue to use the shell for as long as you need it. All output from the commands goes into the window where the shell prompt appears. When you no longer need the shell, type exit. That command terminates the shell process and returns you to GNU Emacs.

If you want to run a single shell command, use the M-! key binding. When you use M-!, GNU Emacs displays the following prompt in the minibuffer:

```
Shell command:
```

Type a shell command (such as ls -l) and press Enter. GNU Emacs executes that command and displays the resulting output in a separate window. To revert to a single-window display, type C-x 1. That command is Ctrl+x, followed by the number 1. The command instructs GNU Emacs to delete the other windows (excluding the one that contains the cursor).

Note

If you are in the mood for a lighthearted quote, type M-x yow and Emacs displays a quote from Zippy the Pinhead in the minibuffer. Each time you type this command, Emacs displays a different quote.

Writing Man Pages with groff

Before the days of graphical interfaces, typesetting with the computer meant preparing a text file with embedded typesetting commands, and then processing that marked-up text file with a computer program that generated commands for the output device: a printer or some other typesetter.

As you know, such markup languages still exist. A prime example is Hypertext Markup Language (HTML), which is used to prepare World Wide Web pages.

In the late 1970s and early 1980s, I prepared all my correspondence and reports on a DEC VAX/VMS system, using a program named RUNOFF. That program formatted output for a line printer or a daisy-wheel printer. That VAX/VMS RUNOFF program accepted embedded commands such as the following:

```
.page size 58,80
.spacing 2
.no autojustify
```

As you might guess, the first command sets the number of lines per page and the number of characters on each line. The second command generates double-spaced output. The last command turns off justification. Essentially, I would pepper a text file with these commands, run it through RUNOFF, and send RUNOFF's output to the line printer. The resulting output looked as good as a typewritten document, which was good enough for most work in those days.

UNIX came with a more advanced typesetting program called troff (which stands for *typesetting runoff*) that could send output to a special device called a *typesetter*. A typesetter could produce much better output than a line printer. troff enables you to choose different fonts and to print text in bold and italic.

To handle output on simpler printers, UNIX also included nroff (which stands for *nontypesetting runoff*) to process troff files and generate output, to ignore fancy output commands, and to generate output on a line printer. troff typesetting is versatile enough that many computer books have been typeset with troff.

Now that nearly every computer has some sort of graphical interface (Microsoft Windows, Apple Macintosh, or GNOME and KDE in Linux), most word-processing programs work in "what you see is what you get" mode, in which you get to work directly with the formatted document. Therefore, you probably won't have any reason to use troff for typesetting. nroff is still used for one important task, however: preparing man pages. The remainder of this chapter focuses on that aspect of using nroff.

Note

The groff program is the GNU version of troff and nroff. With appropriate flags, you can use groff to typeset for several output devices, including any typewriter-like device.

Even if you do not use groff to prepare formatted documents (because using a PC-based word processor is more convenient), you may end up using groff to write the man page for any program that you write.

Man pages are the files that contain the information users can view, by typing the command man *progname*. This command shows online help information on *progname*. The subject of a man page can be anything from an overview of a software package, to the programming information for a specific C function (for example, try man fopen on your Linux system).

After you go through an example, you'll realize that writing man pages in groff is quite simple.

Note

Before reading about the man page preparation process, understand that you do not really use the groff program to prepare the man page. The man page is just a text file containing embedded commands that groff recognizes. You might use groff to view a man page during preparation, but you can prepare a man page without ever running groff.

Trying an Existing man Page

Before you write a man page, look at an existing man page. A brief example is the man page for zless. Figure 14-5 shows the man page of zless in an xterm window.

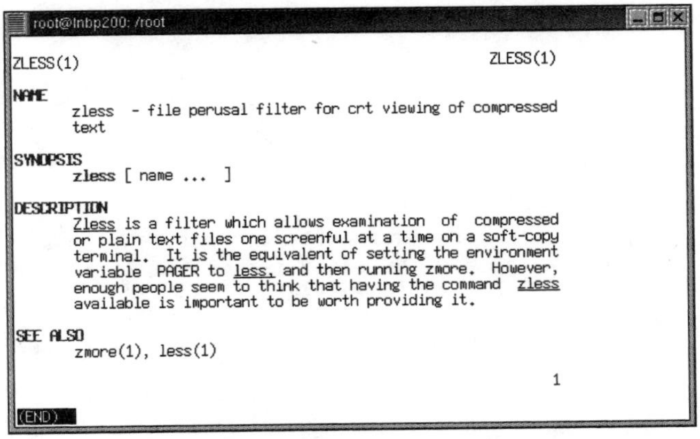

```
ZLESS(1)                                              ZLESS(1)

NAME
       zless  - file perusal filter for crt viewing of compressed
       text

SYNOPSIS
       zless [ name ... ]

DESCRIPTION
       Zless is a filter which allows examination  of  compressed
       or plain text files one screenful at a time on a soft-copy
       terminal.  It is the equivalent of setting the environment
       variable PAGER to less, and then running zmore.  However,
       enough people seem to think that having the command  zless
       available is important to be worth providing it.

SEE ALSO
       zmore(1), less(1)

                                                           1

(END)
```

Figure 14-5: Output of the man zless command in a terminal window

In this case, you don't really have to pay attention to the exact content of the man page; all you care about is the layout. Take a moment to look at the layout and note the following points:

- The name of the command appears at the top of the man page. The number 1 that appears in parentheses next to the command's name denotes the section of the UNIX manual where this command belongs.

- The man page contains several sections, each of which appears in boldface. The text within the section is indented.

- In this example, the sections are NAME, SYNOPSIS, DESCRIPTION, and SEE ALSO. If you try a few more man pages, you'll see that some man pages have many more sections. Almost all man pages, however, have these four sections.

- Some text appears in boldface.

Looking at a man Page Source

After you view a man page with the man command, you should look at the original source file from which the man command generates the output. In your Linux system, the man page source files are in several directories. These directory names are defined in the /etc/man.config file.

The source file for the `zless` man page is `/usr/share/man/man1/zless.1.gz`. Look at this file to see how the man page appears in its final form, which is shown in Figure 14-5. Here is how to look at the source file for the `zless` man page:

```
cd /usr/share/man/man1
zless zless.1
.TH ZLESS 1
.SH NAME
zless \- file perusal filter for crt viewing of compressed text
.SH SYNOPSIS
.B zless
[ name ...  ]
.SH DESCRIPTION
.I  Zless
is a filter which allows examination of compressed or plain text files
one screenful at a time on a soft-copy terminal.  It is the equivalent
of setting the environment variable PAGER to
.I less,
and then running zmore.  However, enough people seem to think that
having the
command
.I zless
available is important to be worth providing it.
.SH "SEE ALSO"
zmore(1), less(1)
```

One interesting feature of the marked-up text file for the man page is the haphazard manner in which lines break. The formatting program `groff` (the man command uses `groff` to process the marked-up text file) fills up the lines of text and makes everything presentable.

Most `groff` commands have to be on a line by themselves, and each such command starts with a period. You can, however, embed some `groff` font-control commands in the text; these embedded commands start with a backslash (\).

Here is a summary of the commands that you see in the `zless` man page source file:

- `.B` turns on boldface
- `.I` turns on italic
- `.SH` is the start of a new section
- `.TH` indicates the document title

If you use these dot commands (meaning commands that begin with a period or dot) to change the font, the man page source file tends to have many short lines, because each dot command has to appear on a separate line. As the following section shows, you can use embedded font-change commands to produce a more readable source file.

Writing a Sample man Page

This section shows you how to write a man page for a sample application named `satview`. Assume that the `satview` program displays a satellite image in a window. The program has some options for specifying the map projection, the zoom level, and the name of the file that contains the satellite image data.

Use a text editor to type the man page source code shown in the following listing, and save it in a file named `satview.1`:

```
.TH SATVIEW 1 "October 26, 2000" "Satview Version 10.1"
.SH NAME
satview \- View satellite images.
.SH SYNOPSIS
\fBsatview\fP [-p \fIprojection\fP] [-m] [-z \fIzoomlevel\fP]
\fIfilename\fP
.SH DESCRIPTION
\fBsatview\fP displays the satellite image from \fIfilename\fP.
.SS Options
.TP
\fB-p \fIprojection\fR
Set the map projection (can be \fBL\fR for Lambert Conformal or
\fBP\fR for Polar Stereographic). The default is Lambert Conformal.
.TP
\fB-m\fP
Include a map in the satellite image.
.TP
\fB-z \fIzoomlevel\fR
Set the zoom level (can be one of: 2, 4, or 8). The default
zoomlevel is 1.
.TP
\fIfilename\fR
File containing satellite data.
.SH FILES
.TP
\fC/etc/awips/satview.rc\fR
Initialization commands for \fBsatview\fR
.SH SEE ALSO
nexrad(1), contour(1)
.SH Bugs
At zoom levels greater than 2, map is not properly aligned with image.
```

The source file has the following significant features:

- The `.TH` tag indicates the man page title, as well as the date and a version-number string. In the formatted man page, the version and date strings appear at the bottom of each page.

- This man page has six sections — NAME, SYNOPSIS, DESCRIPTION, FILES, SEE ALSO, and Bugs — each of which starts with the `.SH` tag.

- The DESCRIPTION has an Options subsection. The `.SS` tag indicates the beginning of a subsection.

- In the `Options` subsection, each item is listed with the `.TP` tag.
- The `\fB` command changes the font to boldface.
- `\fI` changes the font to italic.
- `\fR` changes the font to roman.
- `\fP` changes the font to its preceding setting.

With this information in hand, you should understand the man page source listing.

Testing and Installing the man Page

As you prepare the man page file, you want to make sure that it is formatted correctly. To view the formatted output, use the following command:

```
groff -Tascii -man satview.1 | more
```

This command runs the `groff` command with the `ascii` typesetting device (which means that it produces plain ASCII output), and with the man page macro set (that's what the `-man` option does).

If you find any formatting discrepancies, check the dot commands and any embedded font-change commands, and make sure that everything looks right.

After you are satisfied with the man page format, you can make the man page available to everyone, by copying the file to one of the directories in which all man pages are located. Log in as root and install the man page with the following copy command:

```
cp satview.1 /usr/share/man/man1
```

After that, try the man page with this command:

```
man satview
```

Figure 14-6 shows the resulting output. Compare the output with the source file listing shown in the "Writing a sample man page" section to see the effects of the commands on the final output. The italic command generates underlined output, because the terminal window cannot display an italic font.

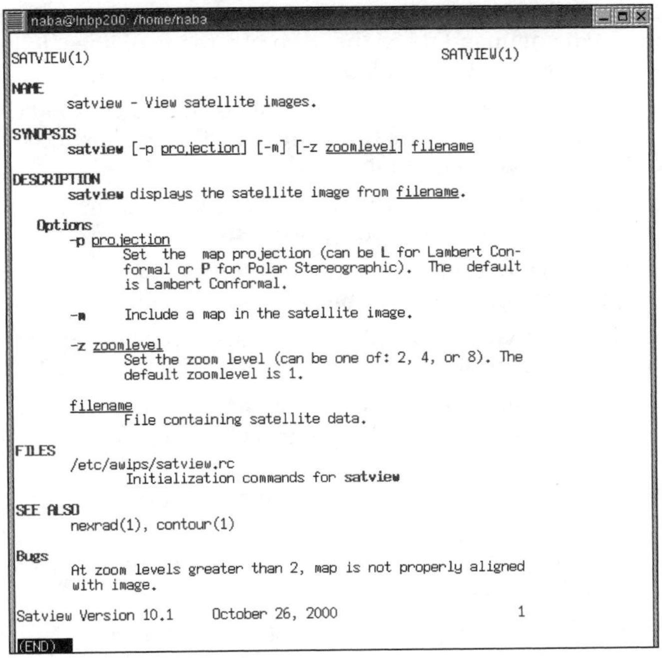

```
SATVIEW(1)                                                 SATVIEW(1)

NAME
       satview - View satellite images.

SYNOPSIS
       satview [-p projection] [-m] [-z zoomlevel] filename

DESCRIPTION
       satview displays the satellite image from filename.

    Options
       -p projection
              Set   the   map projection (can be L for Lambert Con-
              formal or P for Polar Stereographic).  The   default
              is Lambert Conformal.

       -m     Include a map in the satellite image.

       -z zoomlevel
              Set the zoom level (can be one of: 2, 4, or 8). The
              default zoomlevel is 1.

       filename
              File containing satellite data.

FILES
       /etc/awips/satview.rc
              Initialization commands for satview

SEE ALSO
       nexrad(1), contour(1)

Bugs
       At zoom levels greater than 2, map is not properly aligned
       with image.

Satview Version 10.1     October 26, 2000                    1

(END)
```

Figure 14-6: Output of the man satview command in an xterm window

Using the listing in this section as a guide, you can now write your own man pages.

Summary

The configuration of many Linux features depends on settings stored in text files. Therefore, you have to know how to edit text files in order to set up and maintain a Linux system. Another form of text processing involves type-setting and formatting text documents. Linux includes groff for this purpose. Nowadays, you're likely to use a PC to prepare formatted documents, but you still need to prepare one kind of formatted document: the man pages that pro-vide online help for any software that you write. Accordingly, this chapter shows you how to use several text editors. It also shows you how to prepare man pages by using groff.

By reading this chapter, you learn the following:

▶ Linux includes a variety of text editors. It's important to learn ed and vi, because all UNIX systems come with these editors. Although the ed editor may be cryptic, you may have to use it to edit files when no other editor is available.

▶ The `ed` editor works on a text file one line at a time (which is why it's called a line editor). Each command takes the form of a range of lines, followed by a one-character command that applies to that range of lines.

▶ The `vi` editor is a full-screen editor that enables you to view a file several lines at a time. The `vi` editor has three modes: visual-command mode, colon-command mode, and text-input mode.

▶ In text-input mode, you can enter text. To change to text-input mode, press **i**, **a**, or **A**. To return to command mode, press Esc.

▶ In `vi`'s colon command mode, you enter a colon (:) followed by a command that has the same syntax as `ed` commands.

▶ GNU Emacs is more than just an editor — it's also an environment from which you can perform most routine tasks.

▶ As an editor, GNU Emacs does not have any modes; whatever you type goes into the file. Commands begin with a control character (such as `Ctrl+x`) or Esc.

▶ To view the online tutorial, type `Ctrl-h t` in GNU Emacs.

▶ The `groff` utility is useful for formatting documents. `groff` provides the functionality of the standard UNIX `nroff` and `troff` utilities. You have to use `groff` to prepare man pages.

▶ The best way to learn to prepare a man page is to study an existing man page, and mimic its style in your own man page. This chapter provides an example of how you might prepare a typical man page.

# Chapter 15

Basic System Administration

This chapter introduces you to some Linux system administration tasks. You learn to perform these system administration tasks using Linuxconf, a graphical system administration tool that comes with Red Hat Linux. First you learn how to add user accounts using Linuxconf, and then you explore other tasks that Linuxconf enables you to perform. This overview of Linuxconf should help you perform other system administration tasks as the need arises.

Because you typically install Red Hat Linux on a PC that previously had DOS or Microsoft Windows installed on it, a common system administration task is to access the DOS/Windows files from Linux. This chapter shows you how to mount and access MS-DOS disks, including floppy disks. You'll also learn about a package called `mtools`, which enables you to access and use (copy, delete, and format) MS-DOS files (typically, on a floppy disk) in Red Hat Linux.

Revisiting Linux System Administration

Chapter 1 provides an overview of the tasks involved in Linux system administration. In this chapter, you briefly revisit the key tasks that you perform as a system administrator, learning where, in this book, you can find more information about a specific task.

You can group the tasks into two broad categories: system administration and network administration. The first one refers to keeping the system itself up and running, while network administration focuses on the LAN and Internet services.

Typical system administration tasks include the following:

- *Adding and removing users.* This chapter shows you how to add or remove user accounts using Linuxconf and the useradd and userdel commands.

- *Installing, configuring, and upgrading the operating system and various utilities.* Chapter 2 covers how to install Red Hat Linux, and Chapters 3 through 9 focus on how to configure and set up specific hardware in Red Hat Linux. Chapter 25 describes how to upgrade or reconfigure the Linux kernel.

- *Installing new software.* Chapter 24 shows you how to use the Red Hat Package Manager (RPM) to install software. In that chapter, you also learn how to unpack and build software from source archives that you may download from various Internet sites. This chapter briefly describes the Gnome RPM graphical utility that you can use to install RPM packages.

- *Making backups.* Chapter 23 covers backing up and restoring files and directories using the GNU tar utility.

- *Mounting and unmounting file systems.* The mount and umount commands appear in various chapters, such as Chapters 4 and 5. This chapter shows you how to mount MS-DOS file systems. You also learn to use the mtools utilities to access Windows/DOS files. This chapter also introduces you to the User Mount Tool for mounting file systems.

- *Monitoring the system's performance.* This chapter describes a few utilities for monitoring system performance. This topic is further described in Chapter 23.

- *Starting and shutting down the system.* Chapter 10 describes how you should start and shut down your Red Hat Linux system.

Typical network administration tasks include the following:

- *Maintaining the network configuration files.* Chapter 8 describes various TCP/IP configuration files.

- *Setting up PPP and SLIP.* You learn about PPP and SLIP in Chapter 16.

- *Monitoring network status.* Chapter 8 presents some utility programs that you can use as network diagnostic tools.

- *Securing Internet services.* Chapters 17 through 22 cover various Internet services such as mail, the Web, and FTP. Chapter 26 describes how to secure your system and Internet services.

Recovering from a Forgotten Root Password

To perform system administration tasks, you often have to become the root user by typing the su command, and then providing the root password. If you forget the root password, you can follow these steps to set up a new root password:

1. Power up your PC as usual. At the LILO boot prompt, type the name of the Linux boot partition followed by the word single, as follows (you type the text shown in boldface):

```
LILO boot: linux single
```

This causes Linux to start up as usual, but run in a single-user mode that does not require you to log in. After Linux starts, you will see the following command-line prompt:

```
bash#
```

2. Use the passwd command to change the root password as follows:

```
bash# passwd
New UNIX password:
```

Type the password that you want to use (it won't appear onscreen) and then press Enter. Linux asks for the password again, shown as follows:

```
Retype new UNIX password:
```

Type the password again, and press Enter. If you enter the same password both times, the passwd command changes the password and displays the following message:

```
passwd: all authentication tokens updated successfully
```

3. Now you reboot the PC by pressing Ctrl+Alt+Delete. After Linux starts, it displays the familiar login screen. Now you should be able to log in as root with the new password.

Adding User Accounts

Adding user accounts to the system is a key system administration function. You have a chance to add user accounts as you install Red Hat Linux, following the steps outlined in Chapter 2. If you did not add other user accounts during installation, you can do so now. You can use the Linuxconf tool or the useradd command to add a new user account on your system.

Tip

It is a good idea to create other user accounts besides root. Even if you are the only user of the system, logging in as a less-privileged user is good practice because you cannot damage any important system files inadvertently. When necessary, you can type the su - command to log in as root and perform any system-administration tasks.

Using Linuxconf to Add User Accounts

You can use the Linuxconf graphical system administration tool to add user accounts. To start Linuxconf, log in as root at the graphical login screen, and then select Main Menu (Foot) ⇨ Programs ⇨ System ⇨ LinuxConf from the GNOME desktop. If this is your first time running Linuxconf, it displays a Welcome message in a window. You can read the message and then click Quit to close the window. Then the initial Linuxconf window appears, as shown in Figure 15-1.

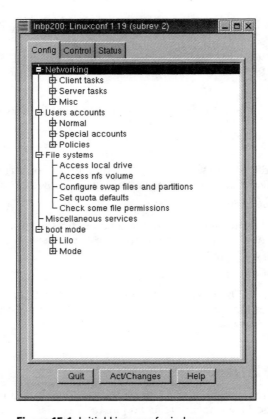

Figure 15-1: Initial Linuxconf window

The initial Linuxconf window shows three tabs: Config, Control, and Status (see Figure 15-1). Each tab includes a tree menu that you can use to perform various tasks with Linuxconf. Click the plus sign (+) next to an item to expand that item and view the submenu—the plus sign changes to a minus sign (–) when the menu is expanded. You can collapse an expanded menu and hide the details by clicking the minus sign. Menu items without any plus or minus signs next to them are the lowest-level items; you might think of each of these items as a *leaf*, in keeping with the tree analogy.

To perform a specific action, you click on the lowest level leaf in the tree menu (the label tells you what that menu selection does). When you click a specific leaf item in the tree menu, the configuration options for that item appear in a tabbed dialog box on the right-hand side of the window.

To add myself as a new user, I would follow these steps:

1. In the Config tab, select the User Accounts option, and then click the User Accounts item listed under Normal (see Figure 15-2). This tree menu selection can be written as User Accounts ⇨ Normal ⇨ User Accounts in the Config tab. Selecting this item causes Linuxconf to display the User Accounts tab in the right-hand panel, as shown in Figure 15-2.

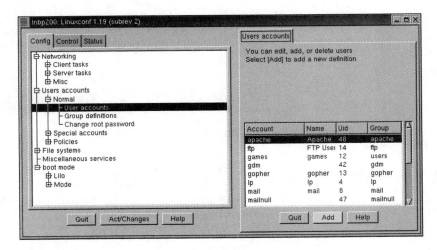

Figure 15-2: The User Accounts tab in Linuxconf

2. Click the Add button in the User Accounts tab shown in Figure 15-2. This brings up the User Account Creation tab, as shown in Figure 15-3.

3. Fill in the requested information. In particular, you must enter the login name and, optionally, the home directory. For my account I use /home/naba as the home directory. You can use a similar home directory for your account. After I fill in all of the fields, I click the Accept button. If the /home/naba directory does not exist, Linuxconf creates the directory.

4. Linuxconf displays the Changing Password dialog box, in which you enter the password for the new account and click the Accept button. Linuxconf then requires you to retype your password for confirmation. Note that Linuxconf rejects your choice of password as unacceptable, if the password is a combination of words that can be found in the dictionary. After entering the password, click the Quit button in the User Accounts dialog box.

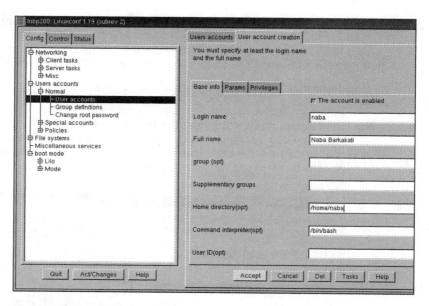

Figure 15-3: Entering information for a new user account

5. To quit Linuxconf, click the Quit button in the main window. The Linuxconf tool displays the Status of System dialog box, which asks you if you want to activate the changes. Click the Activate the Changes button to finish the task and exit Linuxconf.

Note

If you want to remove a user account, click on the user name in the tab that lists all user accounts (see Figure 15-2). Then click on the user account you want to delete. Linuxconf displays a User Information tab with that user's information — this tab looks like the User Account Creation tab shown in Figure 15-3. Click the Del button at the bottom of the tab. Linuxconf displays a dialog box asking you to confirm that you want to delete the account. You have the option to archive the account's data, delete it altogether, or leave the account data in place (but deactivate the account). You can make your selection and click the Accept button to delete the account.

Using useradd to Add User Accounts

If you are working from a text console, you can create a new user account by using the useradd command. For example, here are the steps I follow to add an account for a new user:

1. Type the following useradd command with the -c option to create the account:

```
useradd -c "Ashley Barkakati" ashley
```

2. Set Ashley's password using the `passwd` command:

`passwd ashley`

Changing password for user ashley

New UNIX password: *(Type the password, then press Enter.)*

Retype new UNIX password: *(Type the password again.)*

passwd: all authentication tokens updated successfully

Note that if you type a password that can be easily guessed, the `passwd` program rejects it with the following message:

BAD PASSWORD: it is based on a dictionary word

The `useradd` command consults the files `/etc/default/useradd` and `/etc/login.defs` to obtain default information on various parameters for the new user account. For example, the default shell (`/bin/bash`) and default home directory location (`/home`) are specified in `/etc/default/useradd`. The `/etc/login.defs` file provides system-wide defaults for automatic group and user Ids, as well as password expiration parameters.

Note

You can delete a user account with the `userdel` command. Simply type `userdel` *username* to delete a user's account. To wipe out that user's home directory as well, type `userdel -r` *username*.

To learn more about the `useradd` and `userdel` commands, type `man useadd`, or `man userdel` in a terminal window.

Exploring Linuxconf

You can perform many system and network administration tasks in Linux. You will find it helpful to explore the tree menus for the kinds of configuration tasks Linuxconf can perform. This section provides an overview of the tasks you can perform through these tree menus.

Note

This section's coverage of Linuxconf, however, is far from complete. It would take many more pages to thoroughly cover Linuxconf's features and explain each of the tasks it can perform. Linuxconf has its own home page on the Web at `http://www.solucorp.qc.ca/linuxconf/`. Visit the home page to learn the latest news about Linuxconf and read online documentation.

You can get online help while running Linuxconf. A Help window appears when you click the Help button that appears in the lower-right corner of the Linuxconf window (refer to Figure 15-1). This Help window provides an overview of Linuxconf.

Most Linuxconf tabs also include Help buttons that provide context-sensitive help — information that relates to the task you are about to perform (see, for example, Figure 15-2). If you need help at any time in Linuxconf, press the nearest Help button to read some relevant information about the task at hand. (Note, however, that in a few cases, Linuxconf displays a message saying that the Help file for that item has not yet been written.)

Getting back to the initial Linuxconf window (refer to Figure 15-1), note that the window shows three tabs — Config, Control, and Status — each with a tree menu. The Config tab is for configuring various system files, the Control tab includes options for starting and stopping services, and the Status tab is for examining various log files.

To explore the tree menus in the Config, Control, and Status tabs, click the plus signs to expand the menu. Then click on each of the lowest-level menu items to perform a specific task (these are the items without any plus or minus sign preceding them). Each item causes Linuxconf to display a tab to the right of the tree menu. Examine the contents of the tab and click Cancel (or Quit) to get rid of that tab. As you proceed through this Linuxconf exploration, consult Tables 15-1, 15-2, and 15-3 to learn about the tasks that you can perform through the Config, Control, and Status tabs, respectively. By studying these tables as you explore the tree menus, you can get a feel for what you can do with Linuxconf. For your convenience, the entries in Tables 15-1, 15-2, and 15-3 are arranged in the order in which you encounter those items in Linuxconf's tree menu.

Secret

The menu options listed in Tables 15-1, 15-2, and 15-3 are the default ones that you get when you install Red Hat Linux. You can, however, enable or disable Linuxconf modules, which, in turn, can change the menus. For example, see the Control files and Systems ⇨ Configure Linuxconf modules option in the Control tab (see Table 15-2).

Table 15-1   Tasks Performed Through the Config Tab

Option	Tasks Performed
Networking	
Client tasks	Set the host name and IP addresses of each network card on your system. Define the host-name search path. Set up default routes. Set up the Network Information Service (NIS). Set up IPX interface (Novell Netware), if any.
Server tasks	Specify file systems to export through Network File System (NFS). Set up alternate IP addresses for each network interface.
Miscellaneous	Add or edit entries with information about other hosts in the network. Specify parameters for accessing Linuxconf through a Web browser.
User Accounts	
Normal	Set up user accounts, define groups, and change the root password
Special accounts	Set up special accounts such as the PPP account, the UUCP account, and the POP account

Option	*Tasks Performed*
Policies	Specify policies for password and account (default home directory, minimum password length and password expiration), default user shell, default PPP shell, and default SLIP shell
File Systems	
Access local drive	Edit characteristics of the local file system (`/etc/fstab`), including the enabling of user and group disk quotas on selected partitions
Access NFS volume	Mount NFS file systems
Configure swap files	Edit, add, or delete swap files or partitions
Set quota defaults	Set the disk quota for partitions that have disk quota enabled
Check file permissions	Check permissions for selected files (Linuxconf reports if the permissions are acceptable)
Boot Mode	
Lilo	Configure the Linux Loader (LILO)
Mode	Select the default boot mode (graphics mode or text mode)

Table 15-2   Tasks Performed Through the Control Tab

Option	*Tasks Performed*
Control Panel	
Activate configuration	Preview and activate the changes made so far
Shutdown/Reboot	Force a reboot or shutdown of your system
Control service activity	Enable or disable any system service
Mount/unmount file systems	Mount or unmount local and NFS file systems
Configure super user tasks	Schedule cron jobs for the root user account (explained in Chapter 23)
Archive configurations	Save a system configuration
Switch system profile	Pick a new system profile to activate (the profile stores all the configurations you specify through Linuxconf)

Continued

Table 15-2 *(continued)*

Option	Tasks Performed
Control Files and Systems	
Configure all configuration files	Specify the configuration files managed by Linuxconf. The list includes such files as `/etc/X11/XF86Config`, `/etc/exports`, `/etc/hosts`, `/etc/modules.conf`, and `/etc/inittab`
Configure all commands and daemons	Specify the commands used to start various system services
Configure file permission and ownership	View and change permission settings of various configuration files managed by Linuxconf
Configure Linuxconf modules	Enable or disable Linuxconf modules to enhance its functionality
Configure system profiles	Save configurations and switch between saved configurations for this Linux system
Override Linuxconf add-ons	Add, modify, or delete new Linuxconf drop-ins that provide information on how to control add-on packages
Add Linuxconf add-ons	Perform the same tasks as "Override Linuxconf add-ons"
Date and time	Set date and time
Features	Define special behavior of Linuxconf, such as whether GUI mode is allowed and whether color may be used in text mode

Table 15-3   **Tasks Performed Through the Status Tab**

Option	Tasks Performed
Logs	
Kernel boot messages	View boot messages in a window
Linuxconf logs	View a log of configuration commands issued by Linuxconf

Using Other System Administration Tools

In addition to Linuxconf, Red Hat Linux also comes with several other system administration utilities that enable you to perform various system administration tasks through a graphical user interface. The following system administration tools are summarized in the following sections:

- **User Mount Tool** — a utility that enables users to mount devices
- **Time Tool** — a utility that enables you to set the date and time
- **System Monitor** — a tool that displays the current system load
- **Gnome RPM** — a utility for installing, uninstalling, and upgrading RPMs

User Mount Tool

To start the User Mount Tool, select Main Menu ⇨ Programs ⇨ System ⇨ Disk Management. This tool runs and displays the current status of all the devices listed in the /etc/fstab file. Figure 15-4 shows a typical output.

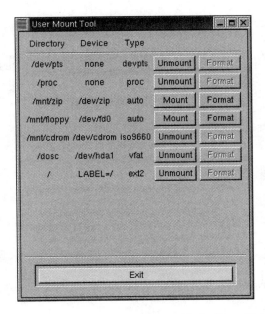

Figure 15-4: Mounting devices with the User Mount Tool

The User Mount Tool displays a list of devices that corresponds to the entries in the /etc/fstab file. For example, here is the /etc/fstab file corresponding to the output shown in Figure 15-4:

```
LABEL=/        /            ext2     defaults        1 1
/dev/hda1      /dosc        vfat     defaults        0 0
/dev/cdrom     /mnt/cdrom   iso9660  noauto,owner,ro 0 0
/dev/fd0       /mnt/floppy  auto     noauto,owner    0 0
/dev/zip       /mnt/zip     auto     noauto,owner    0 0
none           /proc        proc     defaults        0 0
none           /dev/pts     devpts   gid=5,mode=620  0 0
/dev/hda4      swap         swap     defaults        0 0
```

On your system, the display will likely be different, because you may not have all of the entries I have defined in my system's /etc/fstab file.

The User Mount Tool enables you to mount and unmount devices using buttons that appear next to the line describing a device and its mount point (the directory where the device is mounted). For example, to mount the CD-ROM on /mnt/cdrom, click the Mount button on the line that starts with /mnt/cdrom. The User Mount Tool mounts the CD-ROM and changes that button to Unmount (because once the device is mounted, the only logical action is to unmount it). The User Mount Tool shows a Format button for devices to which you have write access. To exit the User Mount Tool, click the Exit button.

Time Tool

Time Tool is a Tcl/Tk application that provides a graphical interface for setting the system clock. To start Time Tool, select Main Menu ⇨ Programs ⇨ System ⇨ Time Tool. Figure 15-5 shows a typical output from Time Tool.

Figure 15-5: Setting the system clock with Time Tool

Time Tool displays the current date and time—the time keeps updating as you use the tool. A brief help message tells you how to change the date and time. Click the part of the date or time you want to change and then use the up and down arrows to adjust it. For example, to change the date, click the date and then click an arrow.

After you have changed the date and time, you can set the system clock by pressing the Set System Clock button. Click Reset Time to revert the Time Tool's display back to the system clock. When done, click the Exit Time Machine button to quit Time Tool.

System Monitor

The GNOME System Monitor tool enables you to view the system load in terms of the number of processes that are currently running, their memory usage, and the free disk space on your system. To run the tool, select Main Menu ⇨ Programs ⇨ System ⇨ System Monitor. You can also start the tool by typing gtop in a terminal window. The tool starts and displays its output in a window, as shown in Figure 15-6.

The output is similar to the output you see when you type top in a text-mode console or a terminal window. As with the text-mode top, the display keeps updating to reflect the current state of the system.

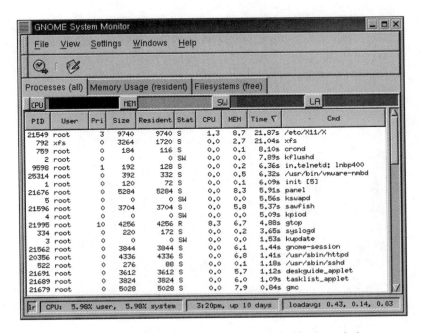

Figure 15-6: Viewing current processes in the System Monitor window

The current processes are shown in descending order of CPU usage. For each process, the System Monitor shows a number of details, including the process ID (PID), the user who started the process, the priority of the process, and the command used to start the process.

The GNOME System Monitor window has two more tabs that display the memory usage and the free space on the file system. To view this information, click the appropriate tab. For example, to see how various processes are using memory, click the Memory Usage tab. Figure 15-7 shows typical memory usage information.

The processes are listed in the order in which they are resident in memory. The multicolored rectangle on the left-hand side represents the physical memory. The memory used by each process is shaded with a color to help you see how much each process is using. The processes and the amount of memory used by each process are listed on the right side of the window.

The bottom edge of the window shows the system name, the CPU usage summary, system up time (how long the system has been up and running), and the load average (a number that represents the system's processing load).

Chapter 23 explains the load average and shows other ways of monitoring system performance.

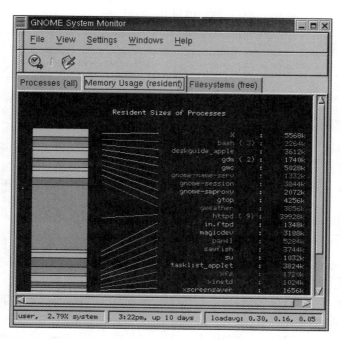

Figure 15-7: Viewing memory usage with System Monitor

Gnome RPM

Gnome RPM is a graphical front end to Red Hat's RPM (Red Hat Package Manager) tools. It is similar to an older Tcl/Tk-based front end called Glint, but Gnome RPM is a GNOME application that used the GTK+ and GNOME libraries for the graphical user interface.

To start Gnome RPM, log in as root, and then select Main Menu ⇨ Programs ⇨ System ⇨ GnoRPM. Gnome RPM has a standard GNOME user interface with a menu bar and a toolbar. The toolbar has buttons for common RPM operations, such as Install a New Package, Upgrade a Package, or Uninstall a Package. The tree menu on the left side of the window shows the currently installed packages organized in a hierarchy of package groups (a package group contains a number of packages or RPMs). You can click the plus signs to view the hierarchy. If you click a specific package group, Gnome RPM displays all of the packages in that group in the area to the right of the tree menu. For example, Figure 15-8 shows the packages in the package group named X.

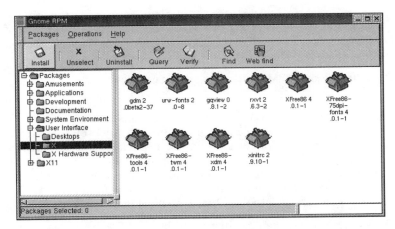

Figure 15-8: Gnome RPM displaying the contents of the X package group

As Figure 15-8 shows, the X package group contains the packages that make up XFree86 — the X Window System.

You typically select one or more packages and then perform tasks, such as uninstalling the package, querying the package (to see when it was installed and the files it contains), or verifying the package (to confirm that none of the files have changed). To perform these operations, open the package group and select the package by clicking the package icon. Then click the Uninstall, Query, or Verify button to initiate the operation. Each of these operations brings up a window in which Gnome RPM displays relevant information and provides buttons through which you can initiate further action. For example, when you query the gnuplot package (it's in the Applications ⇨ Engineering category of the tree menu), Gnome RPM displays the information in a window, as shown in Figure 15-9.

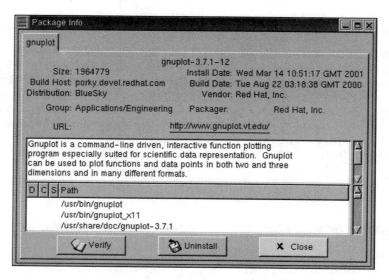

Figure 15-9: Gnome RPM querying the gnuplot package

This window includes buttons to verify or uninstall the package. As Figure 15-9 shows, you can learn a lot about a package by browsing the information in the query results. You can see when the package was installed, when it was built, its size in bytes, a brief description, and what files make up the package (including the full path name of each file). There is even a URL where you can find more information about the package. Gnome RPM displays the URL as a link that you can click to view that Web page in the Web browser.

Cross-Reference

The operations you can perform with Gnome RPM are similar to what you can do with the rpm command from the command line. The rpm commands are described in Chapter 24. Chapter 24 also shows you how to use Gnome RPM to perform other tasks, such as install new packages.

Mounting a DOS File System

If you have Microsoft Windows installed on your hard disk, you probably already have the DOS partition mounted under Linux. During installation (see Chapter 2), the Red Hat installation program runs the Disk Druid program, which asks whether you want to access any DOS hard disk partition under Linux. Disk Druid finds these DOS partitions (and OS/2 partitions, as well) by checking the hard disk's partition table.

Through the Disk Druid program, you can specify where you want to mount each DOS partition. (Mounting makes the DOS directory hierarchy appear as part of the Linux file system.) Commonly, you mount the first DOS partition as /dosc, the second one as /dosd, and so on. If you specify these mount points, Disk Druid performs the necessary steps to ensure that the DOS partitions are mounted automatically whenever you boot Linux.

Secret

To see whether your DOS hard disk partition is mounted automatically, follow these steps (you do not have to be the root user to do this):

1. Use the grep command to look for the string vfat in the file /etc/fstab. Note the result I get with grep on one of my Linux PCs:

   ```
   grep vfat /etc/fstab
   /dev/hda1   /dosc   vfat    defaults    0 0
   ```

   I explain the file /etc/fstab in the section "The /etc/fstab file" of this chapter.

2. If the output shows one or more lines that contain vfat, your Linux system mounts DOS/Windows hard disk partitions automatically. In this example, the output shows a matching line whose first field is the partition name /dev/hda1 (the first partition on the first IDE disk); the second field, /dosc, shows where that partition is mounted.

3. If the grep command does not show any lines that contain the string vfat in /etc/fstab, your system does not mount any DOS/Windows hard disk partitions automatically. An explanation, of course, may be that your hard disk does not have any DOS partitions.

Tip

Another quick way to find out about the mounted devices is to type mount (without any arguments) at the shell prompt. Following is the output of the mount command on my system:

```
/dev/hda2 on / type ext2 (rw)
none on /proc type proc (rw)
usbdevfs on /proc/bus/usb type usbdevfs (rw)
/dev/hda1 on /dosc type vfat (rw) (Windows partition mounted on /dosc)
none on /dev/pts type devpts (rw,gid=5,mode=620)
/dev/hdc on /mnt/cdrom type iso9660 (ro,nosuid,nodev,user=naba)
```

If you see any vfat in the output, those lines indicate MS-DOS file systems mounted on Linux. In this case, a MS-DOS partition is mounted on the Linux directory /dosc.

The following sections explain how the DOS partitions are mounted automatically. Even if you don't have any DOS partitions on your hard disk, you should learn how to access a DOS file system from Linux, because you may have to access a DOS floppy disk under Linux. Understanding the concept of mounting is key to using a DOS file system under Linux.

The mount Command

As Chapter 10 explains, Linux has a single file system that starts at the root directory, denoted by a single slash (/). Even if you have a separate hard disk (or multiple hard disk partitions on a single disk), the contents of those hard disks appear logically somewhere in the Linux file system. *Mounting* is the operation that you perform to cause a physical storage device (a hard disk partition or a CD-ROM) to appear as part of the Linux file system.

Many Linux systems have a small disk partition mounted on the root directory (/) and a larger partition mounted on the /usr directory. A larger partition is used for /usr because many software packages, including the X Window System, are installed under /usr.

You can use the mount command to mount a device on the Linux file system manually at a specified directory. That directory is referred to as the *mount point*. You can use any directory as the mount point. However, if you mount a device on a non-empty directory, you lose the capability to access the files in that directory until you unmount the device with the umount command. Therefore, you should always use an empty directory (such as /mnt) as the mount point.

Like any UNIX command, mount has quite a few options. You can, however, get by with just a few options.

Note

Because mounting makes a physical device part of the Linux file system, by default only the root user can run the mount command. However, the root user can set up entries in the /etc/fstab file to enable any user to mount a device. Consult the "Mounting DOS floppy disks" section to learn how you can enable any user to mount DOS floppy disks. If you try to mount a device when you are not logged in as root, you get the following message:

```
mount: only root can do that
```

That means that you have to log in as root first.

Tip

If you are not logged in as root, use the su - command to become root. When you type su - without any argument, the shell assumes that you want to become root and prompts you for the root password, as follows:

```
[naba@lnbp200 naba]$ su -   (Become the root user)
Password:                    (Enter root password)
[root@lnbp200 naba]#         (Now you are root)
```

After you enter the root password, the prompt changes to indicate that you are root. After you finish whatever you want to do as root, type exit to return to your normal login.

As root, suppose you want to mount the CD-ROM device on the mount point /mnt/cdrom (which should already exist on your system). To do so, type the following command:

```
mount /mnt/cdrom
```

You don't need to specify the CD-ROM device name because an entry exists in the /etc/fstab file for the /mnt/cdrom mount point. That entry specifies the CD-ROM device name and the file system type.

The mount command reports an error if the CD-ROM device is mounted already, or if there is not a CD-ROM in the drive. Otherwise, the mount operation succeeds, and you can access the CD-ROM's contents through the /mnt/cdrom directory.

To mount a DOS partition, use a similar format for the mount command, but also specify the type of file system on the DOS partition. If your DOS partition happens to be the first partition on your IDE (Integrated Drive Electronics) drive, and you want to mount it on /dosc, use the following mount command:

```
mount -t vfat /dev/hda1 /dosc
```

The -t vfat part of the mount command specifies that the device you mount — /dev/hda1 — has an MS-DOS file system. Linux has built-in support for MS-DOS files. Figure 15-10 illustrates the effect of this mount command.

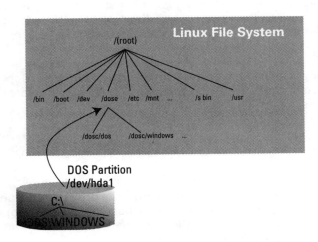

Figure 15-10: Mounting a DOS partition on the /dosc directory

Figure 15-10 also shows how directories in your DOS partition are mapped to the Linux file system. What was the C:\DOS directory under DOS becomes /dosc/dos under Linux. Similarly, C:\WINDOWS now is /dosc/windows. You probably can see the pattern. To convert a DOS filename to Linux (for this specific case, when you mount the DOS partition on /dosc), perform the following steps:

- Change the DOS names to lowercase.

- Change C:\ to /dosc/.

- Change all backslashes (\) to slashes (/).

Note that by typing the command `mount -a`, you can mount all file systems mentioned in the `/etc/fstab` file (except for those lines that contain the `noauto` keyword). See the section on `/etc/fstab` below.

Mounting DOS Floppy Disks

Just as you can mount a DOS hard disk partition under Linux, you can mount a DOS floppy disk. Usually, you have to log in as `root` to mount a floppy, but you can follow the steps shown in the latter part of this section to set up your system, so that any user can mount a DOS floppy disk. You also need to know the device name for the floppy drive. By default, Linux defines two generic floppy device names:

- `/dev/fd0`, which is the A drive (the first floppy drive)
- `/dev/fd1`, which is the B drive (the second floppy drive, if you have one)

As for the mount point, an existing directory named `/mnt/floppy` is created specifically for this type of temporary mount operation. Thus, you can mount the DOS floppy disk on the `/mnt/floppy` directory with the following command:

```
mount -t vfat /dev/fd0 /mnt/floppy
```

After the floppy is mounted, you can copy files to and from the floppy using Linux's copy command (cp). To copy the file `gnome1.pcx` from the current directory to the floppy, type the following:

```
cp gnome1.pcx /mnt/floppy
```

Similarly, to see the contents of the floppy disk, type the following:

```
ls /mnt/floppy
```

When you want to remove the floppy disk from the drive, first dismount the floppy drive. This action removes the association between the floppy disk's file system and the mount point on the Linux file system. Use the `umount` command to dismount a device, as follows:

```
umount /dev/fd0
```

Secret

You can set up your Linux system so that any user can mount a DOS floppy. You simply log in as `root` and add a line in the `/etc/fstab` file. For example, to enable users to mount a DOS floppy in the A drive on the `/a` directory, perform the following steps:

1. Log in as `root`.

2. Create the `/a` directory, with the following command:

   ```
   mkdir /a
   ```

3. Edit the `/etc/fstab` file in a text editor (such as `vi` or Emacs) and insert the following line; then save the file and quit the editor:

   ```
   /dev/fd0    /a    vfat    noauto,user    0 0
   ```

You'll learn more about the /etc/fstab file in the next section; the user option (which appears next to noauto) enables all users to mount DOS floppy disks. The first field in that line is the device name (/dev/fd0), the second field is the mount directory (/a), and the third field shows the type of file system (vfat).

4. Log out and log in as a normal (not root) user.

5. To confirm that you can mount a DOS floppy without being root, insert a DOS floppy in the A drive and type the following command:

   mount /a

   Notice that you use the mount directory as an argument for the mount command. The mount operation should succeed and you should see a listing of the DOS floppy when you type the command ls /a.

6. To unmount the DOS floppy, type umount /a.

The /etc/fstab File

In Linux, the /etc directory contains many text files that have configuration information for the system. As you learned in Chapter 5, for example, the /etc/inittab file contains information about what processes to start after Linux boots. The /etc/fstab file is one such configuration file — a text file containing information that the mount and umount commands use. Each line in the /etc/fstab file provides information about a device to be mounted on a directory in the Linux file system.

Following is the /etc/fstab file from a typical Linux system:

```
LABEL=/       /            ext2     defaults           1 1
/dev/hda1     /dosc        vfat     defaults           0 0
/dev/cdrom    /mnt/cdrom   iso9660  noauto,owner,ro    0 0
/dev/fd0      /mnt/floppy  auto     noauto,owner       0 0
/dev/zip      /mnt/zip     auto     noauto,owner       0 0
none          /proc        proc     defaults           0 0
none          /dev/pts     devpts   gid=5,mode=620     0 0
/dev/hda4     swap         swap     defaults           0 0
```

The first field on each line shows a device name, such as hard disk partition (or it identifies a partition by a LABEL keyword). The second field is the mount point, and the third field indicates the type of file system on the device. You can ignore the last three fields for now.

The sample /etc/fstab file shows that the /dev/hda4 device (the fourth partition on the first IDE hard disk) functions as a swap device for virtual memory, which is why both the mount point and the file-system type are set to swap. The line on which vfat is the file-system type specifies that the DOS partition /dev/hda1 should be mounted on /dosc.

Secret

The contents of the /etc/fstab file are used to mount various file systems in Linux automatically. During Linux startup, the init process executes a shell script that invokes mount with the -a option. This script causes mount to read the /etc/fstab file and mount all listed file systems (except those with the noauto option). Therefore, to mount a DOS partition automatically, add a line to the /etc/fstab file that contains the necessary information for mounting that partition. If you want to mount the DOS file system in the first partition of the first Small Computer System Interface (SCSI) disk on /dosd, for example, add the following line to /etc/fstab:

```
/dev/sda1    /dosd    vfat    defaults 0  0
```

The fourth field on each line of the /etc/fstab file shows a comma-separated list of options that apply to a specific device. Typically, you will find the defaults option in this field. The defaults option implies — among other things — that the device is mounted at boot time; that only the root user can mount the device; and that the device is mounted for reading and writing. If the options include noauto, the device is not mounted automatically when the system boots. Another useful option is user. Any user can mount a device in the /etc/fstab file that has the user option. For example, if you want to enable any user to mount the CD-ROM, log in as root and add the user option to the /dev/cdrom line in /etc/fstab as follows:

```
/dev/cdrom   /mnt/cdrom   iso9660 noauto,ro,user  0  0
```

With this line in place, any user can mount a CD-ROM with the following command:

```
mount /mnt/cdrom
```

Using mtools

The preceding sections showed you one way to access the MS-DOS file system: mount the DOS hard disk or floppy disk using the mount command, then use regular Linux commands, such as ls and cp. This approach to mounting a DOS file system is fine for hard disks. Linux can mount the DOS partition automatically at startup, and you can access the DOS directories on the hard disk anytime.

If you want a quick directory listing of a DOS floppy disk, however, mounting can be tedious. First, you have to mount the floppy drive. Then, you have to use the ls command. Finally, you must use the umount command before taking the floppy disk out of the drive.

This is where the mtools package comes to the rescue. The mtools package implements most common DOS commands; the commands have the same names as in DOS, except that you add an m prefix to each command. Thus, the command for getting a directory listing is mdir, and mcopy copies files. The best part of mtools is the fact that you do not have to mount the floppy disk to use the mtools commands.

Secret

Because the `mtools` commands write to and read from the physical device (floppy disk), you have to log in as `root` to perform these commands. If you want any user to access the `mtools` commands, you have to alter the permission settings for the floppy drive devices. Use the following command to permit anyone to read from and write to the first floppy drive:

```
chmod o+rw /dev/fd0
```

Determining If You Have mtools

The `mtools` package comes with the Red Hat Linux distribution on this book's companion CD-ROMs. When you install Linux, `mtools` is installed automatically as part of the base Linux. The `mtools` executable files are in the `/usr/bin` directory. To see whether you have `mtools` installed, type `ls /usr/bin/mdir` at the shell prompt. If the `ls` command shows that this file exists, you should have `mtools` available on your system.

You also can type the following `rpm` command to verify that `mtools` is installed on your system:

```
rpm -q mtools
mtools-3.9.7-3
```

If `mtools` is installed, the output shows you the full name of the `mtools` package. The sample output shows that `mtools` version 3.9.7 is installed on the system.

To try `mtools`, follow these steps:

1. Log in as `root`, or type `su`, and then enter the root password.

2. Place an MS-DOS floppy disk in your system's A drive.

3. Type `mdir`. You should see the directory of the floppy disk (in the standard DOS directory-listing format).

The /etc/mtools.conf File

The `mtools` package should work with the default setup, but if you get any errors, you should check the `/etc/mtools.conf` file. That file contains the definitions of the drives (such as A, B, and C) that the `mtools` utilities see. Following are a few lines from a typical `/etc/mtools.conf` file:

```
drive a: file="/dev/fd0" exclusive 1.44m mformat_only
drive b: file="/dev/fd1" exclusive 1.44m mformat_only

# First SCSI hard disk partition
#drive c: file="/dev/sda1"

# First IDE hard disk partition
drive c: file="/dev/hda1"
```

```
# IDE Zip drive
drive X: file="/dev/hdd4" exclusive
```

The pound sign (#) indicates the start of a comment. Each line defines a drive letter, the associated Linux device name, and some keywords that indicate how the device is accessed. In this example, the first two lines define drives A and B. The third noncomment line defines drive C as the first partition on the first IDE drive (/dev/hda1). If you have other DOS drives (D, for example), you can add another line that defines drive D as the appropriate disk partition.

If your system's A drive is a high-density, 3.5-inch drive, you should not have to change anything in the default /etc/mtools.conf file to access the floppy drive. If you also want to access any DOS partition in the hard drive, uncomment and edit an appropriate line for the C drive.

Typically, you use the mtools utilities to access the floppy disks. Although you can define C and D drives for your DOS hard disk partitions, you may want to access those partitions by mounting them with the Linux mount command. Because the hard disk partitions can be mounted automatically at startup, accessing them through the Linux commands should be just as easy.

Tip

You also can access Iomega Zip drives through mtools. Simply specify a drive letter and the appropriate device file name. For built-in IDE (ATAPI) Zip drives, try /dev/hdd4 as the device file.

The mtools Commands

As explained earlier in this chapter, the mtools package is a collection of utilities. So far, you have seen the command mdir — the mtools counterpart of the DIR command in DOS.

Tip

If you know the MS-DOS commands, you'll find that using the mtools commands is very easy. Type the DOS command in lowercase letters, and remember to add m in front of each command. Because the Linux commands and filenames are case-sensitive, you must use all lowercase letters when you type mtools commands.

Table 15-4 summarizes the commands available in mtools Version 3.9.7.

Table 15-4	The mtools Commands	
mtools Utility	**MS-DOS Command (If Any)**	**Action**
mattrib	ATTRIB	Changes MS-DOS file-attribute flags
mbadblocks		Tests a floppy disk, and marks the bad blocks in the file allocation table (FAT)

mtools Utility	MS-DOS Command (If Any)	Action
mcd	CD	Changes an MS-DOS directory
mcopy	COPY	Copies files between MS-DOS and Linux
mdel	DEL or ERASE	Deletes an MS-DOS file
mdeltree	DELTREE	Recursively deletes an MS-DOS directory
mdir	DIR	Displays an MS-DOS directory listing
mdu		Lists space occupied by a directory and its contents
mformat	FORMAT	Places an MS-DOS file system on a low-level-formatted floppy disk (use fdformat to low-level-format a floppy in Linux)
minfo		Gets information about an MS-DOS file system
mkmanifest		Makes a list of short name equivalents
mlabel	LABEL	Initializes an MS-DOS volume label
mmd	MD or MKDIR	Creates an MS-DOS directory
mmove		Moves or renames an MS-DOS file or subdirectory
mmount		Mounts an MS-DOS disk
mpartition		Creates an MS-DOS file system as a partition
mrd	RD or RMDIR	Deletes an MS-DOS directory
mren	REN or RENAME	Renames an existing MS-DOS file
mshowfat		Shows FAT entries for an MS-DOS file
mtoolstest		Tests and displays the current mtools configuration
mtype	TYPE	Displays the contents of an MS-DOS file
mwrite	COPY	Copies a Linux file to MS-DOS
mzip		Performs certain operations on SCSI Zip disks
xcopy	XCOPY	Recursively copies a DOS directory into another

You can use the mtools commands just as you would use the corresponding DOS commands. For example, the mdir command works like the DIR command in DOS. The same goes for all the other mtools commands shown in Table 15-4. With regard to wildcard characters (such as *), you have to remember that the Linux shell is the first program to see your command.

Therefore, if you do not want the shell to expand the wildcard character, you should use quotation marks around filenames that contain any wildcard characters. To copy all `*.txt` files from the A drive to your Linux directory, for example, use the following command:

```
mcopy "a:*.txt".
```

If you omit the quotation marks, the shell tries to expand the string `a:*.txt` with filenames from the current Linux directory. It also tries to copy those files (if any) from the DOS floppy disk.

On the other hand, when you want to copy files from the Linux directory to the DOS floppy disk, you *do* want the shell to expand any wildcard characters. To copy all `*.pcx` files from the current Linux directory to the DOS floppy disk, for example, invoke `mcopy` as follows:

```
mcopy *.jpg a:
```

The `mtools` utilities enable you to use the backslash character (\) as the directory separator, just as you would under DOS. Whenever you have a filename that contains the backslash character, you must enclose the string in double quotation marks. The following command copies a file from a subdirectory on the A drive to the current Linux directory:

```
mcopy "a:\test\sample.dat".
```

How to Format a DOS Floppy

Suppose that you run Linux on your home PC, and you no longer have MS-DOS installed on your system, but you have to copy some files on an MS-DOS floppy disk and take the disk to your office. If you already have a formatted MS-DOS floppy, you can simply mount that floppy and copy the file to the floppy using the Linux `cp` command. What if you do not have a formatted DOS floppy? The `mtools` package again comes to the rescue.

The `mtools` package provides the `mformat` utility, which can format a floppy disk for use under MS-DOS. Unlike the DOS `format` command that formats a floppy in a single step, the `mformat` command requires you to follow a two-step process:

1. Use the `fdformat` Linux command to low-level-format a floppy disk. The `fdformat` command expects the floppy device name to be the argument; the device name includes all the parameters necessary for formatting the floppy disk.

   Figure 15-11 illustrates the device-naming convention for the floppy drive device. Based on the information shown in Figure 15-11, you use the following command to format a 3.5-inch, high-density floppy disk in your system's A drive:

   ```
   fdformat /dev/fd0H1440
   ```

```
Double-sided, 80 tracks, 18 sec/track. Total capacity 1440 kB.
Formatting ... done
Verifying ... done
```

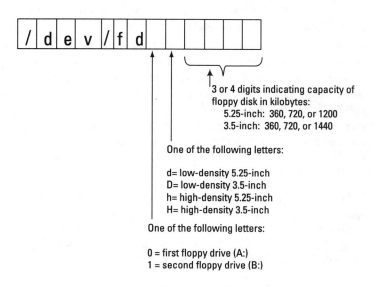

3 or 4 digits indicating capacity of
floppy disk in kilobytes:
    5.25-inch: 360, 720, or 1200
    3.5-inch: 360, 720, or 1440

One of the following letters:

d= low-density 5.25-inch
D= low-density 3.5-inch
h= high-density 5.25-inch
H= high-density 3.5-inch

One of the following letters:

0 = first floppy drive (A:)
1 = second floppy drive (B:)

Figure 15-11: Naming convention for the floppy disk drive in Linux

2. Use the mformat command to put an MS-DOS file system on the low-level-formatted floppy disk. If the floppy is in drive A, type the following command:

```
mformat a:
```

Summary

Even if you are the only user of your Red Hat Linux system, you have to perform some system administration tasks to keep the system up and running. Moreover, if your PC has a DOS partition in addition to the Linux partition, or if you work with DOS floppy disks, you may want to access the DOS files directly from Linux. This chapter provides an overview of Linux system administration and network administration tasks. It introduces Linuxconf and shows how to use the mtools utility programs to format and access a DOS floppy disk directly from Linux.

By reading this chapter, you learned the following:

▶ Red Hat Linux comes with the Linuxconf graphical system administration tool that enables you to configure system files and activate various services (start or stop processes that perform specific tasks). By exploring the three tabs — Config, Control, and Status — in the Linuxconf window, you can learn about the tasks you can perform with Linuxconf.

▶ You can add new user accounts using Linuxconf or the useradd command. To remove an account, you can either use Linuxconf or the userdel command.

▶ Red Hat Linux also includes several other graphical system administration tools besides Linuxconf. You learned to use the User Mount Tool, Time Tool, System Monitor, and Gnome RPM.

▶ Linux has built-in support for the MS-DOS file system. You can use the mount command to access a DOS partition, or a DOS floppy from Linux. After mounting a DOS file system at a directory in your Linux system, you can use Linux commands, such as ls and cp to manipulate the DOS files.

▶ When you install Linux (following the directions in Chapter 1), you also install a set of utility programs, known as mtools. The mtools programs provide a convenient way to access MS-DOS files, especially floppy disks, because you can use mtools commands without first having to mount the floppy disk. The mtools utilities include commands such as mdir and mcopy that work like the DOS commands, DIR and COPY.

Part III

Internetworking Red Hat Linux

Chapter 16

Internet Connection Setup

After installing Red Hat Linux, you may want to connect your Red Hat Linux PC (and perhaps your own LAN) to the Internet. Nowadays, you have the following popular options for connecting a small office or home office to the Internet:

- **Digital Subscriber Line (DSL)** — Various telecommunications companies offer DSL — a high-speed data transmission service over a regular phone line. You can use DSL to connect your Red Hat Linux system to the Internet. In this case, you must connect a special DSL modem to an Ethernet card on your Red Hat Linux system. Typical DSL offerings offer data-transfer rates from 128Kbps to over 1Mbps. When you use DSL, your Red Hat Linux system is always connected to the Internet.

- **Cable modem** — If the cable television company in your area offers Internet access over cable, you can use that service to hook up your Red Hat Linux system to the Internet. As with DSL, you connect a cable modem to an Ethernet card in your Red Hat Linux system. You get higher data-transfer rates than DSL — 10Mbps is typical, but a number of cable connections share this data rate. As with DSL, a cable modem connection provides an "always on" connection to the Internet.

- **Dial-up networking** — In this case, your Red Hat Linux system uses the Point-to-Point Protocol (PPP) or Serial Line Internet Protocol (SLIP) over a dial-up link to connect to another system already on the Internet. Usually that Internet-connected system belongs to your Internet Service Provider (ISP). This method of connection is referred to as *dial-up networking*—establishing a network connection between your Red Hat Linux PC and another network (such as the Internet) through a dial-up modem. In this case, the maximum data-transfer rate is 56Kbps.

As you might note, the first two options—DSL and cable modem— essentially involve connecting a special modem to an Ethernet card on your Linux system. In these cases, the setup procedures are the same as the ones in Chapter 8 for setting up Ethernet local area network (LAN).

This chapter focuses on the third option—dial-up networking—which involves setting up a PPP or SLIP connection from your Linux PC to your ISP's system. You also learn how you can use IP masquerading to share a Linux system's Internet connection with other systems on a LAN.

Cross-Reference

As you read this chapter, consult Chapter 8 for discussions of networking, TCP/IP, the Internet, as well as terms such as Request for Comments (RFC).

Learning the Basics of Dial-Up Networking

Dial-up networking refers to connecting a PC to a remote network through a dial-up modem. A significant difference exists between dial-up networking and plain old serial communication. Both approaches use a modem to dial up another computer and establish a communication path, but the serial com- munication software (such as `minicom`, described in Chapter 7) makes your computer act like a terminal connected to the remote computer. The serial communication software exclusively uses dial-up connection. You cannot run another copy of the communication software and use the same modem con- nection, for example.

In dial-up networking, you run TCP/IP or other network-protocol software on your PC, as well as on the remote system with which your PC has a dial-up communication path. That communication path simply forms one of the lay- ers in the OSI seven-layer network model. The network protocols exchange data packets over the dial-up connection. You simultaneously can use any number of network applications to communicate over the single dial-up con- nection. With dial-up networking, your PC truly is a part of the network to which the remote computer belongs. (If the remote computer is not on a net- work, dial-up networking creates a network that consists of the remote com- puter and your PC.) Thus, you can have any number of network applications (ranging from a Web browser to a `telnet` session) running at the same time, with all applications sharing the physical data-transport capabilities of the dial-up connection.

In this chapter, I describe TCP/IP over a dial-up connection because TCP/IP is the dominant protocol of the Internet, and Linux has built-in support for TCP/IP. More accurately, I should say that the discussion in this chapter applies to TCP/IP over any point-to-point serial communication link. The "dial-up" part simply reflects the fact that most people use a modem to establish the point-to-point communication link to a remote computer.

Like TCP/IP networking over Ethernet, TCP/IP networking over a dial-up link involves specifying the *protocol* — the convention — for packaging a network packet over the communication link. There are two popular protocols for TCP/IP networking over point-to-point serial communication links:

- *Serial Line Internet Protocol (SLIP)* is a simple protocol that specifies how to frame an IP packet on a serial line. RFC 1055 describes SLIP.

- *Point-to-Point Protocol (PPP)* is a more advanced protocol for establishing a TCP/IP connection over any point-to-point link, including dial-up serial links. RFC 1661 describes PPP.

I first provide an overview of SLIP and PPP; then, I show you how to use SLIP, as well as PPP, to set up a network connection to a remote system.

Serial Line Internet Protocol (SLIP)

SLIP originated as a simple protocol for framing an *IP packet* — an Internet Protocol packet that consists of an IP header (which includes the source and destination IP addresses), followed by data (the data sent from source to destination). RFC 1055, "A Nonstandard for Transmission of IP Datagrams over Serial Lines: SLIP," J. L. Romkey, June 1988, describes SLIP. As the title of RFC 1055 suggests, SLIP is not an official Internet standard; it's a de facto standard.

SLIP defines two special characters for framing — marking the beginning and ending — IP packets:

- SLIP-END is octal 300 (decimal 192); it marks the end of an IP packet.

- SLIP-ESC is octal 333 (decimal 219); it "escapes" any SLIP-END or SLIP-ESC characters that are embedded in the packet (for example, to ensure that a packet does not end prematurely because the IP packet happens to include a byte with decimal 192).

The protocol involves sending out the bytes of the IP packet one by one and marking the end of the packet with a SLIP-END character. The following convention handles any SLIP-END and SLIP-ESC characters that happen to appear in the IP packet:

- Replace a SLIP-END character with SLIP-ESC, followed by octal 334 (decimal 220).

- Replace a SLIP-ESC character with SLIP-ESC, followed by octal 335 (decimal 221).

That's it! Based on the most popular implementation of SLIP from Berkeley UNIX, SLIP also uses these conventions:

- Packets start and end with the SLIP-END character to ensure that each IP packet starts anew.

- The total size of the IP packet (including the IP header and data, but without the SLIP framing characters) is 1,006 bytes.

SLIP's simplicity led to its popularity (although PPP is used more widely). SLIP has several shortcomings, however:

- Both ends of the SLIP connection have to know their IP addresses. Although some schemes permit dynamic assignment of IP addresses, the protocol does not have any provisions for address negotiation.

- Both ends of SLIP must use the same packet size, because the protocol does not permit the two ends to negotiate the packet size.

- SLIP has no support for data compression. (As you learn later in this section, *Compressed SLIP*, or *CSLIP*, introduces compression in SLIP.)

- There is no way to identify the packet type in SLIP. Accordingly, SLIP can carry only one protocol — the one that both ends of SLIP are hard-wired to use. A transport mechanism such as SLIP should be capable of carrying packets of any protocol type.

Note

Compressed SLIP (CSLIP) addresses the lack of data compression in SLIP, as described in RFC 1144, "Compressing TCP/IP Headers for Low-Speed Serial Links," V. Jacobson, February 1990. CSLIP compresses TCP/IP header information, which tends to be repetitive in packets exchanged between the two ends of a SLIP connection. CSLIP does not compress the packet's data.

CSLIP often is referred to as the *Van Jacobson compression* in recognition of CSLIP's author. Incidentally, PPP also supports the Van Jacobson TCP/IP header compression.

Point-to-Point Protocol (PPP)

PPP fixes the shortcomings of SLIP and defines a more complex protocol. Unlike SLIP, PPP is an official Internet standard. It is documented in RFC 1661, "The Point-to-Point Protocol," W. Simpson, July 1994 (updated in RFC 2153, "PPP Vendor Extensions," W. Simpson, May 1997).

PPP includes the following main components:

- A packet-framing mechanism that uses a modified version of the well-known High-Level Data Link Control (HDLC) protocol

- A Link Control Protocol (LCP) to establish, configure, and test the data link

- A family of Network Control Protocols (NCP) that enables PPP to carry more than one type of network packet — such as IP, IPX, or NetBEUI (Network BIOS Extended User Interface) — over the same connection

PPP has replaced SLIP as the protocol of choice for transporting packets over point-to-point links. In addition to the ubiquitous serial link, some versions of PPP work over several other types of point-to-point links. Some of these point-to-point links include Frame Relay, SONET/SDH (Synchronous Optical Network/Synchronous Digital Hierarchy), X.25, and ISDN (Integrated Services Digital Network).

The PPP frame has a more complex structure than that of SLIP. The PPP frame structure is based on ISO (International Standards Organization) standard 3309, "Data Communications — High-Level Data Link Control Procedures — Frame Structure," 1979. The HDLC protocol uses a special flag character to mark the beginning and the end of a frame. Figure 16-1 shows the structure of a complete PPP frame.

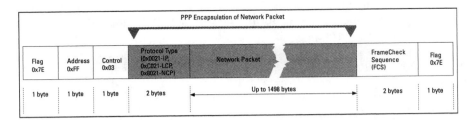

Figure 16-1: The format of a PPP frame

As Figure 16-1 shows, the PPP frames begin and end with a flag character whose value is always 0x7E (7E in hexadecimal notation). The Address and Control fields come from HDLC; they have the fixed values of 0xFF and 0x03, respectively. The PPP data consists of a 2-byte protocol field. (Actually, this field can be only 1 byte; the Link Control Protocol negotiates the length of the protocol field.)

Within the encapsulated network packet, PPP uses 0x7D as the escape character. To send a byte that has a special meaning (such as 0x7E, which marks the beginning and end of a frame), PPP follows these steps:

- Embeds 0x7D in the data
- Places the data byte being escaped
- Toggles the sixth bit of that data byte

Thus, if the PPP data includes 0x7E, that byte is replaced by the 2-byte sequence 0x7D, followed by 0x5E. (If you toggle the sixth bit of 0x7E, or 0111 1110 in binary, you get 0x5E, or 0101 1110 in binary.)

When you use PPP to set up a link between your Red Hat Linux PC and a remote computer, your PC first sends LCP packets to set up the data link. After the physical data link is established and any optional parameters are negotiated, your PC sends NCP packets to select one or more network protocols for use over that link. Thereafter, any of those network protocols can send packets over the PPP link.

Tip

You don't need to know the complete details of PPP to use it effectively. Later in this chapter, I describe how you can use PPP to establish a TCP/IP network connection to another computer.

Making a SLIP Connection

To set up a SLIP connection between your Linux PC and a remote system, both systems must support SLIP. Both ends also must run some SLIP software when the connection is up.

To include SLIP support in your Linux kernel, you should answer yes to the following questions during the kernel-configuration step (in which you type `make config`):

```
SLIP (serial line) support (CONFIG_SLIP) [M/n/y/?] y
 CSLIP compressed headers (CONFIG_SLIP_COMPRESSED) [Y/n/?]
 Keepalive and linefill (CONFIG_SLIP_SMART) [Y/n/?]
 Six bit SLIP encapsulation (CONFIG_SLIP_MODE_SLIP6) [Y/n/?]
```

Chapter 25 describes how to configure and rebuild the kernel. You also need TCP/IP support in the kernel, of course.

Secret

If you install Red Hat Linux from this book's companion CD-ROM, your system has SLIP support in the form of a module. That means whenever SLIP support is needed, the module loader automatically loads the SLIP module. To explicitly load the SLIP module, log in as `root` and type `/sbin/modprobe slip`.

Typically, you first establish a SLIP connection by dialing up the remote system, logging in, and starting SLIP on the remote system. Then, you must start SLIP at your end. After the two ends are running SLIP, the SLIP connection is up. To use that connection, you also have to configure the interface (with the `ifconfig` command) and set up the routing (with the `route` command), so that network packets originating on your PC can reach their destination. You can perform all these steps through a program called `dip` (Dial-up IP Protocol Driver), which automates the process of setting up a SLIP connection. You learn how to use `dip` in the following sections.

Verifying SLIP Support

Before trying SLIP, you should verify that your kernel includes SLIP support. Type `dmesg | more` to view the boot messages (or open the file `/var/log/messages` in a text editor). If your kernel has SLIP support, you should see a message such as the following:

```
CSLIP: code copyright 1989 Regents of the University of California
SLIP: version 0.8.4-NET3.019-NEWTTY-MODULAR (dynamic channels,
max=256).
SLIP linefill/keepalive option.
```

The first two lines refer to Compressed SLIP (CSLIP) and SLIP support, respectively. If you see these lines, you can assume that your kernel supports SLIP.

Tip

If SLIP support is in the form of a loadable module and you loaded the SLIP module with the `/sbin/modprobe slip` command, type `/sbin/lsmod` to verify that the SLIP module was loaded.

Obtaining Remote-System Information

The exact mechanics of establishing a SLIP connection to a remote system depend on that system's setup. If you obtain a SLIP account from an Internet Service Provider (ISP), the ISP should give you the needed information to establish a SLIP connection. At minimum, this information includes the following:

- The phone number that you must dial to connect to the remote computer.
- The user name and password to log in to the system.
- The IP addresses for both ends of the SLIP connection. Many ISPs provide a fixed (static) IP address, whereas other ISPs assign IP addresses dynamically.

You also get the IP addresses of name servers (which translate names to IP addresses), a mail server, and a news server. These IP addresses are necessary when you begin to use Internet applications on your system; you don't need them during SLIP-connection setup.

Typically, an ISP sets up a SLIP account for you in such a way that the SLIP software starts automatically when you log in. The ISP starts SLIP by specifying that the SLIP software run in place of a shell (such as `/bin/bash`) for that account name. An ordinary user may have an entry in `/etc/passwd` that looks like the following example:

```
naba:ZbWOxq2XGAO3g:501:100:Naba Barkakati:/home/naba:/bin/bash
```

Colons (:) separate the fields in that line in `/etc/passwd`. The first field is the user name; the last two fields are the home directory and the shell (the program to run after that user logs in), respectively. For a SLIP account, the entry may be the following:

```
slipxxx:ZbWOxq2XfLO3g:501:101:SLIP user xx:/tmp:/usr/bin/ppl
```

The user name may be something cryptic (`slipxxx`), and the home directory may be `/tmp`. The last field shows the name of the SLIP pro–gram on the remote system. On a Hewlett-Packard workstation, for example, `/usr/bin/ppl` is the point-to-point link software that establishes a SLIP connection.

If the remote system resides at your office, you may have a separate SLIP login—or you can log in as a normal user to start the SLIP software. You can automate this part of the process with the dip program that runs on your Linux PC.

Using dip to Establish a SLIP Connection

The dip (Dial-up IP Protocol Driver) program enables you to automate the steps involved in setting up a SLIP connection to a remote system. If you want, you can run dip in an interactive mode. The best way to use dip, however, is to prepare a *script file* (a text file that contains commands for dip) and then run dip with that script file as input. I show you how to set up a dip script later in this chapter. First, however, try using some of the dip commands interactively.

Running dip interactively

To get a feel for dip's commands, run dip interactively. Start dip with the -t option, as follows:

```
/usr/sbin/dip -t
DIP: Dialup IP Protocol Driver version 3.3.7o-uri (8 Feb 96)
Written by Fred N. van Kempen, MicroWalt Corporation.

DIP> help
DIP knows about the following commands:

        beep      bootp     break     chatkey   config
        databits  dec       default   dial      echo
        flush     get       goto      help      if
        inc       init      mode      modem     netmask
        onexit    parity    password  proxyarp  print
        psend     port      quit      reset     send
        shell     skey      sleep     speed     stopbits
        term      timeout   wait

DIP> quit
```

When you run dip in interactive mode, you can use the help command to see a list of commands that dip accepts. If you have all the information, such as IP addresses and the phone number to dial, you can use dip in interactive mode and issue appropriate commands to dial a remote system, log in, and complete the SLIP connection. Table 16-1 lists the available dip commands and shows the syntax and meaning of each command. You typically use these commands in a dip script file.

Table 16-1   The dip Commands

Command	Meaning
beep [*times*]	Beeps a specified number of times
bootp	Uses BOOTP protocol to determine the local IP address. BOOTP, or Bootstrap Protocol (defined in RFC 951), provides a way for a workstation to determine its IP address. The protocol was developed to enable a diskless workstation to find a host from which to download a boot file and execute.
break	Sends a BREAK. (Refer to Chapter 7 for an explanation of BREAK.)
chatkey *keyword* [*value*]	Adds a keyword (and an associated value) to the list of modem responses that dip recognizes. chatkey RING 10, for example, associates the value 10 with the modem response RING.
config [interface|routing] [pre|up|down|post] *arguments*	Uses the specified interface and routing-table disabled.
databits 7 | 8	Sets the number of data bits to 7 or 8. (You must specify one of the two values.) The number of data bits also is referred to as *word length* in serial communications.
dec $*variable* [*number* | $*var2*]	Decrements the specified variable (dip uses a dollar-sign prefix with a name to denote a variable). You can provide a number or another variable to indicate the amount to be decremented. If you do not provide a number or a second variable, dip decrements the value of the variable by 1.
default	Sets up the default route to the remote system with which dip has established connection. The default route forwards network packets that are addressed to any unknown network address.
dial *phonenum* [*num_seconds*]	Dials the specified phone number and waits the specified number of seconds to receive an answer. If you do not specify a number of seconds, dip uses 60 seconds as a timeout. After issuing the modem's dial command, dip parses the modem's reply and sets the variable named $errlvl according to the reply (0=OK, 1=CONNECT).

Continued

Table 16-1 *(continued)*

Command	Meaning
echo on | off	The command echo on enables the display of all modem replies and text sent to the modem. (This command can help you debug dip scripts.) The echo off command disables this feature so dip works in silence. I like to see what's going on, so I always use echo on in dip scripts.
exit [*status*]	Exits the dip script with the specified status code (leaves the current SLIP connection intact so dip remains running). You must exit a dip script in this manner after establishing a successful SLIP connection.
flush	Flushes the input read from the modem or terminal
get $*variable* [*number* | ask | remote [*timeout*] | $*var2*]	Gets the value of a specified variable. Use the ask keyword to prompt the user for a value. Employ a number to simply set the variable to that value. Use the remote keyword to read a value from the remote system. You also can provide the name of a second variable as the source of the value.
goto *label*	Jumps to a specified label in the script. The label marks a location in the script. The syntax for a label uses the label's text followed by a colon (:). You can see an example of this in the "Setting up a dip script" section later in this chapter.
help	Prints help information (used in interactive mode)
if *expression* goto *label*	Tests the *expression* and jumps to the *label* if the expression is true. The expression is a form of $*variable operator constant*, in which $*variable* denotes a dip variable and *operator* is ==, !=, <, >, <=, or >=. *constant* is a constant value.
inc $*variable* [*number* | $*var2*]	Increments the specified variable. You can provide a number or another variable to indicate the amount to be incremented. If you do not provide a number or a second variable, dip increments the value of the variable by 1.
init *init_string*	Specifies the initialization string to be sent to the modem before dip executes the dial command. The default *init_string* is ATE0 Q0 V1 X1. (Refer to Chapter 7 for a list of Hayes-modem commands.)
mode SLIP | CSLIP | PPP | TERM	Sets the protocol for use in the connection. The default is SLIP. If your ISP supports Compressed SLIP, use the CSLIP mode.

Command	Meaning
modem *modem_type*	Specifies the type of modem. The only acceptable value is HAYES, which dip assumes by default.
netmask *xxx.xxx.xxx.xxx*	Specifies the netmask for use in configuring the SLIP interface. (Refer to Chapter 8 for a discussion of TCP/IP terms, including netmask.)
parity E | O | N	Sets the parity for use in serial communication. Use E for even, O for odd, and N for none.
password	Prompts the user for a password and then sends that password to the modem
proxyarp	Sets up proxy ARP. (Described in RFC 1027, proxy ARP enables a host — which also must be a gateway — to stand in for other hosts.)
print *any_text* [*$variable*]	Prints the text, as well as the values, of any variables
port *device_name*	Specifies the device name of the serial port to which the modem is connected. You must provide the device name without the /dev/ prefix. Thus, use cua0 if the modem is on COM1.
quit	Exits dip with non-zero status
reset	Sends the string +++, followed by ATZ, to the modem. (The three plus signs get the modem's attention, and ATZ resets the modem.)
securidf *fixed_part*	Stores the fixed part of a SecureID password
securid	Prompts the user for the variable part of a password generated by an ACE System SecureID card
send *text* [*$variable*]	Sends the text, as well as the values of any variables, to the modem
skey [*timeout* | *$variable*]	Makes dip look for an S/Key challenge from the remote system. (Bellcore developed S/Key as an authentication system.)
sleep *num_seconds*	Waits the specified number of seconds
speed *bits_per_second*	Sets the serial port's speed. (You have to provide a number in bits-per-second units.)
stopbits 1 | 2	Sets the number of stop bits for serial communication
term	Makes dip go into terminal-emulation mode. This mode enables you to interact directly through the serial connection. You can press Ctrl+] to exit terminal mode.

Continued

Table 16-1 *(continued)*

Command	Meaning
timeout *num_seconds*	Sets the timeout value to a specified number of seconds. If no activity occurs for that number of seconds, dip breaks the connection and exits.
wait *text* [*timeout* | *$variable*]	Waits for the specified text to arrive. The optional argument indicates how long dip should wait.

In addition to these commands, dip provides several built-in variables. Table 16-2 lists the built-in variables in dip.

Table 16-2   Built-In dip Variables

Variable	Description
$errlvl	The result code of the last executed command. Zero indicates success; any other value indicates error.
$local	The host name of your Red Hat Linux PC (the local system)
$locip	The IP address of your Red Hat Linux PC
$modem	The name of the modem (The only supported value is HAYES.)
$mtu	The Maximum Transfer Unit—the maximum number of bytes that a packet can contain
$port	The name of the serial device (for example, cua0 for COM1) used for the SLIP connection
$remote	The host name of the remote system — the other end of the SLIP connection
$rmtip	The IP address of the remote end of the SLIP connection
$speed	The data-transfer rate between your PC and the modem (in bits per second)

When you first try a SLIP connection, you may want to run dip in interactive mode and use its term command to log in and establish the connection. The following example shows how I log in as root on my Linux system and establish a SLIP connection with a remote HP workstation. (My input is in boldface; my comments appear in italics.)

```
lnbsoft:/home/naba/slip# dip -t
DIP: Dialup IP Protocol Driver version 3.3.7o-uri (8 Feb 96)
Written by Fred N. van Kempen, MicroWalt Corporation.
```

```
DIP> get $locip 140.90.23.195
DIP> get $rmtip 140.90.23.194
DIP> port cua0
DIP> speed 38400
DIP> term
[ Entering TERMINAL mode. Use CTRL+] to get back ]

NO CARRIER
ATZ
OK
ATDT5551212    (use appropriate phone number here)
CONNECT 28800/ARQ/V34/LAPM/V42BIS

GenericSysName [Release] (see /etc/issue)
 dialin login: naba   (use your login name here)
Password:  (type your password here)

(extraneous messages deleted)

You have mail.
TERM = (hp)   (press Enter)
/users/naba 21 % ppl
 ppl: starting for naba at Thu Oct 26 20:45:55 2000

/dev/ttyd01 38400 Linet=140.90.23.194 Rinet=140.90.23.195 Mask=255.255.255.0
SLIP
initialization complete, running protocol
  (Press Ctrl+] here)
[ Back to LOCAL mode. ]
DIP> default
DIP> mode SLIP
```

After the final mode SLIP command, dip exits and the connection is completed. Now, I can use network applications, such as telnet or ftp, to access the remote system. When I no longer need the SLIP connection, I log in as root again and type dip -k cua0 to end the connection.

Notice that in dip's interactive mode, you have to switch to a terminal mode (with the term command) to send commands to the modem. You have to remain in terminal mode to send the dialing commands to the modem and to log in to the remote system when you see the login prompt.

After you enter any commands needed by the remote system, revert to dip's command mode by pressing Ctrl+]. Then, you can complete the SLIP setup by entering the default command followed by the mode SLIP command. The default command causes dip to set up a default route by using the SLIP connection (which means that any network packet with an unknown address goes to the SLIP connection). The mode SLIP command makes dip communicate with the remote end by using the SLIP protocol.

If your ISP supports Compressed SLIP, use the mode CSLIP command instead of mode SLIP.

Setting up a dip script

As the preceding section shows, you can establish a SLIP connection by running dip in interactive mode with the -t option. That approach is not convenient, however, if you want to make a SLIP connection regularly. If your ISP provides you with fixed IP addresses for both ends of the SLIP connection, you can set up a script file that sets up the connection automatically. The script file contains commands for the dip program; you have to write the script according to the syntax required by the dip program.

Tip

If your dip script file is named connect.dip (using the .dip extension for script files meant for dip is common), you can use that file with dip by typing dip connect. This command causes the dip program to read and execute commands from the script filenamed connect.dip.

The script file essentially is a sequence of commands for dip, much like the commands that you use when you run dip with the -t option. The only major difference is that you have to use the send command to send some text to the modem, and you must use the wait command to look for specific text coming back from the remote system. Following is a dip script file that I use to connect to a HP workstation. (I must use the ppl command manually to establish a point-to-point link that uses the SLIP protocol.)

```
# File: connect.dip
#
# Establishes a dial-up SLIP connection.
#
# Naba Barkakati, 10/20/00

main:
# Echo everything so we can debug easily
  echo on

# Set up my IP address
  get $locip 140.90.23.195

# Set up the remote IP address
# NOTE: These are test values only - you should use
# IP addresses specific to your case

  get $rmtip 140.90.23.194

# Set the netmask on sl0 to 255.255.255.0
  netmask 255.255.255.0

# Select the serial port and speed (my modem is on COM1, which
# is /dev/cua0 - select yours appropriately)
  port cua0
  speed 38400

# Send initialization sequence to modem
  send ATZ\r
  wait OK 2
```

```
  send ATE1M1V1X4L3S0=0\&c1Q0DT5551212\r
  wait CONNECT 75

# Check the "errlvl"
  if $errlvl != 0 goto error

# We are connected. Log in.
login:
  wait login: 30
if $errlvl != 0 goto no_login_prompt

# Send your user name (use your user ID on the next line)
  send your-username\r
  wait word: 10

# Send the passwrd (use your password on the next line)
  send your-password-here

# The following sequence depends on your system
# In this case, I am responding to a system's prompt for
# terminal name
  wait TERM 10
  send \r
  sleep 5
  send \r
  send \r
  wait some-text-in-the-prompt 30

# Start SLIP at the remote end
  print Sending command to start SLIP...
  send ppl\n
  wait some-text-indicating-SLIP-is-running 30

  default
  mode SLIP
# Print a message and exit
  print Connected... $locip -> $rmtip
  goto exit

no_login_prompt:
  print No login prompt...
  goto error

error:
  print CONNECT FAILED...
  quit 1

exit:
```

Notice that you must replace the items in italics with the text and numbers appropriate for your situation. In particular, if you obtain a SLIP account from an ISP, you must get the IP addresses and the phone number from the ISP.

Also, the exact steps for logging in to the remote system vary from one system to another.

Checking the SLIP connection

After the SLIP connection is set up, you can use the ifconfig command to see whether the SLIP device sl0 is configured (dip does this for you). Following is typical output from the ifconfig command once SLIP is up and running:

```
/sbin/ifconfig
lo        Link encap:Local Loopback
          inet addr:127.0.0.1 Bcast:127.255.255.255 Mask:255.0.0.0
          UP BROADCAST LOOPBACK RUNNING MTU:2000 Metric:1
          RX packets:0 errors:0 dropped:0 overruns:0
          TX packets:25 errors:0 dropped:0 overruns:0

sl0       Link encap:Serial Line IP
          inet addr:140.90.23.195 P-t-P:140.90.23.194 Mask:255.255.255.0
          UP POINTOPOINT RUNNING MTU:296 Metric:1
          RX packets:4 errors:0 dropped:0 overruns:0
          TX packets:4 errors:0 dropped:0 overruns:0

eth0      Link encap:10Mbps Ethernet HWaddr 00:20:AF:E8:A2:25
          inet addr:206.197.168.200 Bcast:206.197.168.255 Mask:255.255.255.0
          UP BROADCAST RUNNING MULTICAST MTU:1500 Metric:1
          RX packets:2087 errors:0 dropped:0 overruns:0
          TX packets:543 errors:0 dropped:0 overruns:0
          Interrupt:10 Base address:0x210
```

Secret

If you use the default command, dip adds a default route to the SLIP connection. To verify this, type the /sbin/route command and verify that the packets for the IP address 140.90.23.194 (in this case, the remote end of the SLIP connection) are sent to the sl0 device — the SLIP device. Packets meant for the default destination (any IP address other than the ones listed in the routing table) should be sent to the IP address 140.90.23.194 — the remote end of the SLIP connection. You need these routing-table entries so that your Linux system can communicate with the remote system.

Ending a SLIP connection

To end a SLIP connection, you have to use dip itself with the -k option, followed by the serial device used for the SLIP connection. Log in as root, and type the following command to close a SLIP connection on /dev/cua0:

```
dip -k cua0
DIP: Dialup IP Protocol Driver version 3.3.7o-uri (8 Feb 96)
Written by Fred N. van Kempen, MicroWalt Corporation.

DIP: process 951 killed.
```

Connecting to a Remote Network Using PPP

PPP is a more complex and versatile protocol than SLIP, but the mechanics of connecting to a remote network with PPP closely resemble the steps that you use for SLIP. You still get IP addresses for the two ends of the PPP connection, a phone number to dial, and a user name under which to log in to the remote system.

Note

Just as the `dip` program helps you automate SLIP setup, you use two other programs — `pppd` and `chat` — to set up and configure a PPP connection. Before you try anything, make sure your Linux kernel includes the PPP network devices.

Checking PPP Support

As with SLIP, to use PPP, you must have the Linux kernel configured with PPP support, or use the PPP module. In the `make config` step of rebuilding the Linux kernel (consult Chapter 25 for details), you should answer yes to the following question about PPP support:

```
PPP (point-to-point) support (CONFIG_PPP) [M/n/y/?]y
```

If you configure and rebuild the kernel with PPP support, you should see messages about PPP support as your system boots. You can view these messages with the `dmesg` command, or by browsing the file `/var/log/messages` in a text editor. Lines such as the following should appear:

```
IP Protocols: ICMP, UDP, TCP, IGMP
CSLIP: code copyright 1989 Regents of the University of California
PPP: version 2.3.7 (demand dialing)
PPP line discipline registered.
```

Secret

Nowadays, it is common practice to provide most drivers and support for protocols such as PPP, in the form of modules that the kernel can load after the system boots. The companion CD-ROMs include the `ppp.o` module for PPP. You do not have to do anything to load the module; the kernel loads whenever PPP support is needed. However, you also can manually load the PPP module; to do so, log in as `root` and type `/sbin/modprobe ppp`. Essentially, you do not have to rebuild the kernel to enable PPP support; it's already available in the form of a loadable module.

Gathering Information for a PPP Connection

Many ISPs provide PPP access to the Internet through one or more systems that the ISP maintains. If you sign up for such a service, the ISP should provide you the information that you need to make a PPP connection to the remote system. At minimum, this information should include the following:

- The IP address for your side of the connection. (This IP address is associated with your PC's PPP interface — the serial port.) Often this IP address is assigned dynamically (this means the IP address may change every time your system establishes a connection).

- The IP address of the ISP's PPP interface. (This address may be listed as the *gateway address* because this interface is your system's gateway to the Internet.) This IP address may be assigned dynamically.

- The phone number to dial to connect to the remote system.

- The user name and password that you must use to log in to the remote system.

Most ISPs also provide the IP addresses of a name server, mail server, and news server. These addresses, however, are not important for the mechanics of setting up a PPP connection.

Using pppd with chat to Make the PPP Connection

To set up a PPP networking connection between two systems, you must have PPP software running at both ends. Typically, your ISP provides you with an account already set up, so that the PPP software runs automatically upon login. In that case, you simply start the PPP software on your system after you log in to the remote system.

Following are the two basic steps for setting up a PPP connection:

1. Dial up and log in to the remote system. (I assume that when you log in, the remote system starts its PPP software automatically.)

2. Start the PPP software on your Red Hat Linux system.

Just as the dip program supports a SLIP connection, the pppd program takes care of communicating with PPP over a dial-up line. Therefore, after you log in and start PPP software at the remote system, you have to run pppd on your Linux system.

Secret

The pppd program's name stands for Point-to-Point Protocol daemon. (In UNIX, the term *daemon* refers to a program that runs in the background and performs some useful task.) The pppd program provides an option through which you can invoke another program that actually establishes the serial communication and completes the remote login process.

Note

In Linux, it is common practice to use pppd with the chat program. If you install Linux from this book's companion CD-ROMs, you can find both the pppd and chat programs in the /usr/sbin directory on your Linux system.

Using the chat program

You need to understand how `chat` works so that you can use it to dial up and log in to the remote system automatically. The `chat` program is designed to process a script that uses an *expect-send* pattern of text. The program looks for the *expect* string; when the program receives it, `chat` sends the *send* string.

Suppose that I want `chat` to look for the string `login:` (how most UNIX systems prompt for a user name), and then send my user name (`naba`). Following that, I want `chat` to expect the `Password:` prompt and send out my password. In this case, I use the following *expect-send* pairs:

```
login: naba word: my-password
```

You may notice the omission of the leading l in the login prompt and some parts of the password prompt; this is to avoid being too specific so that `chat` succeeds even if the received text differs slightly. After all, the first few characters of the login prompt or the `Password:` string may be garbled.

Timeouts

When it waits for an expected text string, `chat` uses a timeout feature. If the string does not arrive within the timeout period, `chat` moves to the next string. The default timeout value is 45 seconds. You can change the timeout with the `TIMEOUT` command, as follows:

```
TIMEOUT 10 login: naba TIMEOUT 5 word: my-password
```

In this case, `chat` waits for the `login:` prompt for a timeout period of 10 seconds. Then, the timeout changes to 5 seconds before `chat` looks for the `Password:` string.

Tip

Sometimes, modems (especially the 56K V.90 modems) can take awhile to establish a connection. This is because the modems go through a complex sequence of steps to arrive at optimum data-transfer rates. In this case, you want to include a longer timeout between the modem dialing command and the expected `CONNECT` message from the modem. This example permits up to two minutes (120 seconds) between the dialing command and a `CONNECT` response from the modem:

```
ATDT95551212 TIMEOUT 120 CONNECT
```

Sub-expect sequences

The typical login sequence illustrates a simple case. A more complex case is when `chat` looks for a login prompt, but none arrives within the timeout period. If you log in at a terminal, you press Enter to get another login prompt. You can simulate this behavior with `chat`'s *sub-expect sequences*, which start with two dashes. Following is an example:

```
login:--login: naba word: my-password
```

In this case, if chat does not receive the login: prompt within the timeout period, chat sends a single return (just as if you had pressed Enter at the keyboard) and then looks for the login: prompt again.

ABORT strings

Most modems report the status of a connection as a string. For example, the modem may report CONNECT (possibly followed by the speed of connection) when successfully connected, BUSY if the remote phone is busy, or NO CARRIER if the modem does not get a dial tone from the phone.

Stop the connection if the modem returns any status other than CONNECT. You can take care of this with chat's ABORT command. The idea is to specify strings that should cause chat to abort the phone call. Following is an example:

```
ABORT BUSY ABORT "NO CARRIER" "" ATZ OK ATDT5551212
```

The first ABORT BUSY pair defines the BUSY string as an abort string. The next pair, ABORT "NO CARRIER", defines another abort string. (Use quotation marks to enclose any string that contains spaces.)

After the two abort strings, you see two expect-send pairs. The first pair instructs chat to expect nothing (indicated by an empty string, "") and to send the ATZ command to reset the modem. The next expect-send pair causes chat to expect the string OK and to send the dialing command (ATDT, followed by a phone number) after the modem sends the OK string.

Escape sequences

You can use special characters in the expect-send strings. Most special characters are denoted by a backslash prefix, which serves as the escape character. These special character sequences traditionally are called *escape sequences*. Table 16-3 lists the escape sequences that you can use in scripts for the chat program.

Table 16-3	chat Escape Sequences
Sequence	*Description*
" "	Two consecutive quotes indicate an empty string. If you send an empty string, chat sends a single carriage-return character.
\b	A backspace character
\c	Stops the new-line character at the end of the send string. You can send \c only at the end of a string.
\d	Delays for one second. You cannot use this sequence in the expect string.
\ddd	A byte that contains the specified octal value

Sequence	Description
\K	Sends a BREAK signal (refer to Chapter 15). You cannot use this sequence in an expect string.
\n	A new-line (line-feed) character
\N	Sends a null character (a byte with all zero bits). You cannot use this sequence in an expect string.
\p	Pauses for a tenth of a second. You cannot use this sequence in an expect string.
\q	Suppresses writing of the string to the /var/adm/syslog file. This sequence is not valid in an expect string.
\r	A carriage return
\s	A space character. Use this sequence when you do not want to place quotes around the string.
\t	A tab character
^C	A control character that corresponds to the letter following the caret. Thus, ^X means Ctrl+X.

You can use all of these escape sequences in send strings; but as the comments indicate, you cannot use many of these sequences in expect strings.

Using pppd with a chat script

The PPP daemon program, pppd, handles the actual details of PPP networking. It uses the PPP driver code in the Linux kernel to exchange TCP/IP packets over the serial port.

You need to perform two basic steps to complete a PPP connection with a remote system:

1. Dial out, using your modem, and log in to the remote system using a user name and password provided by the remote system's owner. Typically, when you log in to the remote system, that action should start the necessary PPP software at the remote end.

2. Start the PPP daemon (pppd) on your system to initiate and conduct a PPP session with the remote system.

The pppd program is designed to take care of both of these steps. Essentially, you use the chat program to perform the first step: dialing up and logging in to the remote system. You do not have to run chat separately. Instead, provide a chat script in the pppd command line; pppd invokes chat to process that script.

A typical pppd command line

In its simplest form, you can run pppd with a long command line that can look like the following:

```
/usr/sbin/pppd connect "/usr/sbin/chat chat-script" crtscts lock \
defaultroute noipdefault passive /dev/modem 115200
```

The backslash at the end of the first line continues the command on the next line. The actual pppd command line is even longer because the chat-script part is a sequence of expect-send pairs. Here is what various parts of the pppd command line mean:

- The connect option instructs pppd to connect by executing the command within double quotes following the connect option. In this example, the command is shown without the enclosing quotation marks:

  ```
  /usr/sbin/chat chat-script
  ```

  The chat-script part may be a long sequence of expect-send pairs of strings that the chat program processes. You can implement a simple dial-up login script, by using the following command to start chat:

  ```
  /usr/sbin/chat "" ATZ OK ATDT5551212 CONNECT "" \
  login: my-username word: my-password
  ```

  This chat script sends ATZ to reset the modem, waits for an OK, and then sends a dial command (ATDTphone-number). It then waits for a CONNECT and sends an empty string (a carriage return). Then it waits for the login: string and sends my-username (which should be your PPP login name). Finally, the script waits for the word: string and sends my-password (the password for your PPP login account).

- The crtscts option instructs pppd to use the Request to Send (RTS) and Clear to Send (CTS) signals for hardware handshaking with the modem. (Consult Chapter 7 for more information on RTS and CTS signals.)

- The lock option causes pppd to create a UUCP-style lock file for the serial device to prevent other programs from using the modem. (UUCP was one of the first programs to use a lock file; that's why this is called a UUCP-style lock file.)

- The defaultroute option instructs pppd to set up a default route entry on your system to use the remote system as the gateway. The default route entry is removed when the PPP connection ends.

- The noipdefault option instructs pppd to wait for the IP address from the remote system.

- The device name tells pppd to dial out on the device /dev/modem. As explained in Chapter 7, the /dev/modem device should be a symbolic link to the serial port where the modem is attached. For example, if your modem is on COM1, /dev/modem is a symbolic link to /dev/ttyS0.

- The last option causes pppd to set the modem's data rate (often called the *baud rate*) to 115,200 bps. This is not the same as the data-transfer rate between the local and the remote modem; this simply sets the highest data rate for the UART. (See Chapter 7 for a discussion of UART.)

As this list shows, that single pppd command line packs a great deal of information. At the same time, that command does a great deal of work. After pppd establishes the connection to the remote system, your system is part of the remote network (provided that the remote system adds appropriate routing-table entries).

Caution

You should note one key point about the pppd command line: The entire chat command (which follows the connect option) is enclosed in quotes, but the chat command itself uses various strings in quotes. Remember to use a backslash-character prefix for those embedded quotes. The following example shows how a chat script looks in a pppd command line:

```
/usr/sbin/pppd connect "/usr/sbin/chat \"\" ATZ OK \
ATDT5551212 CONNECT \"\" login:--login: my-username \
word: my-password"    (rest of command line not shown)
```

As this example shows, all embedded quotes need a backslash prefix. If the modem's AT command includes ampersands (&), you need a backslash prefix for each ampersand. You can use single quotes around the chat command line; then, you don't need the backslash prefixes in front of the embedded double quotes.

A PPP dial-up script

If you use pppd routinely, you probably do not want to type the command. You should prepare a shell script and start pppd from the script. If you save the script in a filenamed ppp-on, for example, you can set up a PPP connection with the following command:

```
./ppp-on
```

This is how I connect my Linux PC to the Internet through my ISP. Here's a typical shell script to set up a PPP connection to a remote system:

```
#!/bin/sh
# A script to establish a dial-up PPP connection

# Other shell variables
  PHONE="301-555-1212"
  DEVICE="/dev/modem"
  SPEED="115200"
  PPP_LOGINNAME="my-username"
  PPP_PASSWORD="my-password"

/usr/sbin/pppd connect "/usr/sbin/chat -v REPORT CONNECT \
    ABORT \"NO CARRIER\" ABORT BUSY ABORT \"NO DIAL TONE\" \
    \"\" ATZ OK ATE1M1V1X4DT$PHONE TIMEOUT 120 CONNECT \"\" \
    login:--login: $PPP_LOGINNAME word: $PPP_PASSWORD" \
```

```
        crtscts lock defaultroute noipdefault $DEVICE $SPEED
# End of script
```

I replace some sensitive information (such as phone number, user name, password, and IP addresses) with phony values. In the script, this information appears in italics. Replace these parameters with ones that apply to your situation. If you have a PPP account with an ISP, the ISP should provide you with this information. You also must edit the AT command sequence so that it works with your modem.

Testing the PPP connection

If you have PPP access to another system (such as an ISP or a system at your employer's organization), you can set up a script as described in the preceding section and enjoy the benefits of full TCP/IP network access to another system. After you run the script, and after pppd completes the initial protocol exchanges to set up the connection, you can verify that the connection is up by typing the ifconfig command. This command shows a listing such as this:

```
/sbin/ifconfig
eth0      Link encap:Ethernet  HWaddr 02:60:8C:8E:C6:A9
          inet addr:192.168.1.200  Bcast:192.168.1.255  Mask:255.255.255.0
          UP BROADCAST RUNNING MULTICAST  MTU:1500  Metric:1
          RX packets:4363 errors:0 dropped:0 overruns:0 frame:0
          TX packets:2111 errors:0 dropped:0 overruns:0 carrier:0
          collisions:0 txqueuelen:100
          Interrupt:5 Base address:0x300

lo        Link encap:Local Loopback
          inet addr:127.0.0.1  Mask:255.0.0.0
          UP LOOPBACK RUNNING  MTU:3924  Metric:1
          RX packets:50 errors:0 dropped:0 overruns:0 frame:0
          TX packets:50 errors:0 dropped:0 overruns:0 carrier:0
          collisions:0 txqueuelen:0

ppp0      Link encap:Point-to-Point Protocol
          inet addr:209.100.18.220  P-t-P:209.100.18.4  Mask:255.255.255.255
          UP POINTOPOINT RUNNING NOARP MULTICAST  MTU:1500  Metric:1
          RX packets:132 errors:2 dropped:0 overruns:0 frame:2
          TX packets:146 errors:0 dropped:0 overruns:0 carrier:0
          collisions:0 txqueuelen:10
```

Find the ppp0 device listed in the output. The ifconfig output also shows the IP addresses of the local and remote ends of the PPP connection. This output confirms that the PPP device is up and running.

To verify that the routing table is set up correctly, use the /sbin/route command without any arguments, as follows:

```
/sbin/route
Kernel IP routing table
Destination     Gateway         Genmask            Flags Metric Ref Use Iface
```

```
209.100.18.4    *           255.255.255.255 UH   0     0     0 ppp0
192.168.1.200   *           255.255.255.255 UH   0     0     0 eth0
192.168.1.0     *           255.255.255.0   U    0     0     0 eth0
127.0.0.0       *           255.0.0.0       U    0     0     0 lo
default         209.100.18.4 0.0.0.0        UG   0     0     0 ppp0
```

In the routing table, the first line shows a route to the remote end of the PPP connection; this one should be set to the ppp0 device. Also, the default route should be set up so that the remote end of the PPP connection serves as the gateway for your system (as the last line of the routing table shows).

After checking the interface configuration (with the ifconfig command) and the routing table (with the route command), verify that you can reach some well-known host. If your ISP gives you the IP address of a name server or a mail server, you can try to ping those addresses. Otherwise, try to ping the IP address of a system at your workplace or university.

The following example displays the results of the ping command:

```
ping 140.90.23.100
PING 140.90.23.100 (140.90.23.100): 56 data bytes
64 bytes from 140.90.23.100: icmp_seq=0 ttl=241 time=244.3 ms
64 bytes from 140.90.23.100: icmp_seq=1 ttl=241 time=200.0 ms
64 bytes from 140.90.23.100: icmp_seq=2 ttl=241 time=220.0 ms
64 bytes from 140.90.23.100: icmp_seq=3 ttl=241 time=190.0 ms

--- 140.90.23.100 ping statistics ---
4 packets transmitted, 4 packets received, 0% packet loss
round-trip min/avg/max = 190.0/213.5/244.3 ms
```

The end of each line shows the round-trip time for a packet originating at your system to reach the designated IP address (140.90.23.100, in this case) and return to your system. For a PPP connection over dial-up lines, you can see times in hundreds of milliseconds.

Incidentally, you do not have to have an account on a system to ping its IP address. Although a system may disable the automatic response to ping messages (ping uses Internet Control Message Protocol or ICMP messages), most systems respond to ping.

Secret

To see your connection speed, type tail -100 /var/log/messages | grep V42BIS. This shows lines such as the following, with connection speeds reported by the modem:

```
Oct 26 17:31:27 lnbp200 chat[1533]:   42666/ARQ/V90/LAPM/V42BIS^M
Oct 26 17:32:24 lnbp200 chat[1579]:   33333/ARQ/V90/LAPM/V42BIS^M
```

Ending the PPP connection

After pppd establishes a PPP connection, the link stays up as long as the PPP software at both ends continues to run. When you no longer need the PPP connection, you can end it by stopping the pppd process.

After setting up a PPP link, pppd creates a file in the /var/run directory where it stores the process ID of pppd. The filename is based on the PPP device name. For the first PPP link, the PPP device is ppp0 and the process ID file is /var/run/ppp0.pid. You can write a shell script to kill the pppd process by using the process ID stored in the /var/run/ppp0.pid file.

In fact, you do not have to write your own shell script to end a PPP link. In the /usr/share/doc/ppp-2.3.11/scripts/ directory (the directory name may differ if you have a newer version of PPP), you can find a script named ppp-off that performs this task for you. Copy the /usr/share/doc/ppp-2.3.11/scripts/ppp-off file to the /usr/local/bin directory and make it executable (use the command chmod +x ppp-off). Then, whenever you want to bring down the PPP link, log in as root and type **/usr/local/bin/ppp-off**. This command ends the pppd process, which, in turn, cleans up the routing table.

The /usr/share/doc/ppp-2.3.11/scripts/ppp-off script looks like this:

```
#!/bin/sh
##############################################################################
#
# Determine the device to be terminated.
#
if [ "$1" = "" ]; then
        DEVICE=ppp0
else
        DEVICE=$1
fi


##############################################################################
#
# If the ppp0 pid file is present, then the program is running. Stop it.
if [ -r /var/run/$DEVICE.pid ]; then
        kill -INT `cat /var/run/$DEVICE.pid`
#
# If the kill did not work, then there is no process running for this
# pid. It also may mean that the lock file will be left. You may wish
# to delete the lock file at the same time.
        if [ ! "$?" = "0" ]; then
                rm -f /var/run/$DEVICE.pid
                echo "ERROR: Removed stale pid file"
                exit 1
        fi
#
# Success. Let pppd clean up its own junk.
        echo "PPP link to $DEVICE terminated."
        exit 0
fi
#
# The ppp process is not running for ppp0
echo "ERROR: PPP link is not active on $DEVICE"
exit 1
```

Notice that this script uses the command `cat /var/run/$DEVICE.pid` (`DEVICE` is defined as `ppp0`) to obtain the process ID of the `pppd` process. That process ID then functions as an argument in the `kill` command that terminates the `pppd` process.

Using Red Hat Tools to Set Up PPP

Red Hat Linux comes with two graphical tools—Dialup Configuration tool and RH PPP Dialer—that you can use to set up a PPP connection and establish a dial-up PPP connection.

To set up a PPP connection using Red Hat's graphical Dialup Configuration tool, log in as `root` and select Main Menu ⇨ Programs ⇨ Internet ⇨ Dialup Configuration Tool from the GNOME desktop. The Dialup Configuration tool displays the Add New Internet Connection dialog box, as shown in Figure 16-2.

The Add New Internet Connection dialog box is similar to the wizards that Microsoft provides for setting up various hardware and software in Microsoft Windows. Click the Next button. The Dialup Configuration Tool searches for any modems and displays the device name of the modem if it finds one. Otherwise, it displays a screen where you can enter the modem device name (such as `/dev/ttyS0` for a modem connected to the COM1 port) and the modem's baud rate.

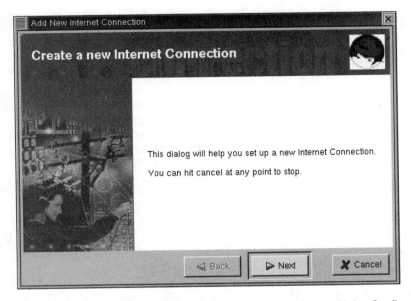

Figure 16-2: Creating a new Internet connection with Red Hat's Dialup Configuration Tool

The dialog box then guides you through successive screens where you provide information, such as the phone number of the ISP, your user name, and password (for your account on the ISP's system). You also assign a name for this dial-up account. When you finish with the Add New Internet Connection dialog box, the Dialup Configuration Tool displays the Internet Connections dialog box that lists the currently configured dial-up accounts (as shown in Figure 16-3).

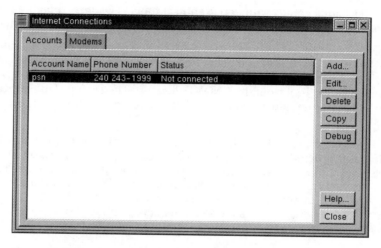

Figure 16-3: Viewing current dial-up accounts in Red Hat's Dialup Configuration Tool

For example, in this case, I configure one account with the name psn. You can view the information about the modem by clicking the Modems tab in the dialog box.

The Dialup Configuration Tool saves the configuration information in the `/etc/sysconfig/network-scripts/ifcfg-ppp0` and `/etc/wvdial.conf` files. For the psn dial-up account, the contents of the `/etc/sysconfig/network-scripts/ifcfg-ppp0` file contains the following:

```
DEVICE=ppp0
NAME=psn
WVDIALSECT=psn
MODEMPORT=/dev/ttyS1
LINESPEED=57600
PAPNAME=naba
USERCTL=true
ONBOOT=no
PERSIST=no
```

To establish a PPP connection, select Main Menu ⇨ Programs ⇨ Internet ⇨ RH PPP Dialer from the GNOME desktop. A dialog box appears with a list of the interfaces you can use to make a connection (Figure 16-4).

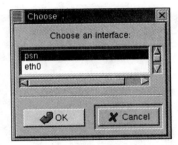

Figure 16-4: Selecting an interface to use for a dial-up connection

The dial-up interface is shown using the account name you assign when you configure that dial-up connection. For example, in my case, the dialog box lists psn as one of the interfaces. I then choose psn for my dial-up connection. Select the interface you define with the Dialup Configuration Tool and click the OK button to start the connection.

Secret

The RH PPP Dialer runs /usr/sbin/pppd with appropriate options to establish the PPP connection. For example, for the connection named psn, the PPP Dialer starts pppd with the following command:

```
/usr/sbin/pppd lock modem crtscts asyncmap 00000000 defaultroute
usepeerdns user naba remotename ppp0 nodetach /dev/ttyS1 57600 ipparam
ppp0 linkname ppp0 noauth connect /usr/bin/wvdial --remotename ppp0 --
chat psn
```

You can look up the meanings of the pppd options by reading the pppd man page with the man pppd command. This command specifies /usr/bin/wvdial as the program that dials the modem and handles the interaction with the remote system. The configuration file /etc/wvdial.conf contains the information used by the dialer. In particular, that file contains your user name and password (in plain text) for logging in to the remote system.

Once the connection is up and running, RH PPP Dialer displays a dialog box showing the status of the connection. You can verify the PPP connection by typing the /sbin/ifconfig command (and looking for the ppp0 interface in the output), or by running Netscape Communicator to access Web sites on the Internet.

Routing Through the PPP Connection

Commonly, a PPP connection connects two geographically separated networks or, more commonly, connects a small local area network (LAN) to the Internet. In a typical scenario, you have a small Ethernet LAN that you want to connect to the Internet. You can do this with a Linux PC that has both an Ethernet card and a modem. The Linux system has a presence on your Ethernet LAN through its Ethernet-card interface. If you can establish a PPP connection to a system on the Internet, you can use the Linux PC as the gateway between your LAN and the remote system (which, presumably, already is connected to the Internet). Figure 16-5 illustrates such a scenario.

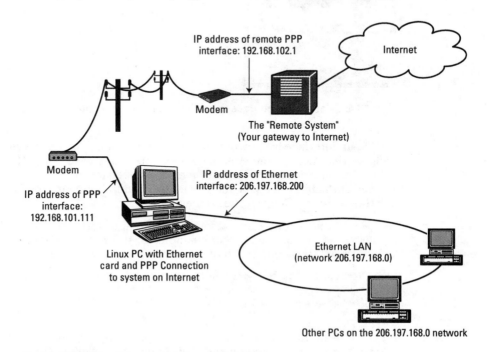

Figure 16-5: Connecting a LAN to the Internet

In this case, you have a small Ethernet LAN with a few PCs and a class C IP address of 206.197.168.0. You have 206.197.168.200 assigned as the IP address of your Linux PC's Ethernet-card interface.

The Linux PC also has a modem through which you establish a PPP connection to a remote system on the Internet. Both ends of the PPP connection have unique IP addresses. You want to ensure that the PCs on your Ethernet LAN can access the Internet. Use your Linux PC as a gateway to route network packets between the Ethernet LAN and the remote system, because the Linux PC is the only one that has both PPP and Ethernet interfaces. You can accomplish this goal in one of the following ways:

- **Use your Linux PC as a router**— Obtain a valid class C network address from an ISP and configure the Linux PC so that it acts as the gateway between your network and the Internet.

- **Use IP masquerading**—Set up your Ethernet LAN with private IP addresses (for example, use 192.168.1.0 as the network address) and use the Linux PC as a firewall. Enable IP masquerading in the Linux kernel, and use the `ipchains` program to enable the Linux PC to masquerade as any of the systems in your LAN. Essentially, each system on your Ethernet LAN ends up with access to the Internet even though it doesn't have a unique IP address.

The following sections further explain these two approaches.

Using Linux PC as a Router

To use your Linux PC as a router, perform the following major steps:

1. Log in as `root` and enable IP forwarding with the following command:

   ```
   echo 1 > /proc/sys/net/ipv4/ip_forward
   ```

   When IP forwarding is enabled, the Linux kernel automatically forwards packets from one interface to another.

2. Use the `route` command to set up a route to the remote system. A *route* specifies a path between two network nodes. A typical specification says something like this: "All packets for the 206.197.168.0 network should be sent to the Ethernet interface named `eth0`." The *gateway* IP address serves as the destination for any network address without an explicit route. If you do have a PPP link, you may want to say, "Send any packet with an unresolved address to the remote IP address of the PPP link." Use the IP address of the remote end of the PPP connection as the gateway on the Linux system. To learn more about the route command, type `man route` at the shell prompt.

3. Make sure that all systems on your LAN use the Linux PC as the default gateway for TCP/IP networking.

4. Ensure that the remote gateway has a route to your LAN. Without this step, TCP/IP packets from the Internet cannot reach your LAN. If you get your Internet connection from an ISP, the ISP (for a fee, of course) provides you with properly routed IP addresses for your LAN.

Note Although a Linux PC with a PPP connection can act as a gateway between a LAN and the Internet, a more economical solution uses a dial-up router specifically designed to connect your LAN to the Internet. In both cases, you need an ISP to provide you with access to a remote system already connected to the Internet.

Using IP Masquerading to Share an Internet Connection

Linux supports a feature called *IP masquerading*, which enables you to connect an Ethernet LAN with a private IP address to the Internet. This occurs through a Linux PC (with an officially assigned IP address) that has a connection to the Internet. The Linux PC may be connected to the Internet by dial-up PPP, or some other connection, such as DSL or cable modem.

With IP masquerading enabled, your Red Hat Linux PC acts as a stand-in for any of the other systems on the Ethernet LAN. As with the router setup, the Red Hat Linux PC is designated as the gateway for the Ethernet LAN. However, masquerading involves more than simply forwarding IP packets back and forth between the LAN and the Internet.

When the Red Hat Linux PC masquerades as another system on the LAN, it modifies outgoing packets so that they always appear to originate from the Red Hat Linux PC. When a response to one of the outgoing packets is received, the Red Hat Linux PC performs the reverse task — it modifies the packets so that they appear to come from the Internet, directly to the system that sends the outgoing packet. The end result is that each system on the Ethernet LAN appears to have full access to the Internet, even though the Ethernet LAN uses a non-unique, private IP address.

To enable and use IP masquerading, perform the following steps:

1. Make sure that the Linux kernel — the core operating system — supports IP firewall chains. This should be true for the version of Red Hat Linux you install from the companion CD-ROMs. If the file `/proc/net/ip_fwchains` exists, then the kernel supports IP firewall chains. (Type `ls /proc/net/ip_fwchains` to verify that the file exists.)

2. Make sure the Red Hat Linux PC has an Internet connection and a network connection to your LAN. Typically, the Linux PC has two network interfaces — an Ethernet card for the LAN and a dial-up PPP connection to the Internet (through an ISP).

3. Make sure that all other systems on your LAN use the Linux PC as the default gateway for TCP/IP networking. Use the same ISP-provided DNS addresses on all systems.

4. Enable IP forwarding in the kernel by typing the following command:

   ```
   echo "1" > /proc/sys/net/ipv4/ip_forward
   ```

   This is necessary because IP forwarding is disabled by default. To ensure that IP forwarding is enabled when you reboot your system, place this command in the `/etc/rc.d/rc.local` file.

5. Run `/sbin/ipchains` — the IPCHAINS firewall administration program — to set up the rules that enable the Linux PC to masquerade for your LAN.

For example, to enable masquerading for a LAN via the Linux PC's `ppp0` network interface, you can use the following commands:

```
/sbin/ipchains -P forward DENY
```

```
/sbin/ipchains -A forward -i ppp0 -j MASQ
```

If you want the IP masquerading set up at system startup, you should place these commands in the `/etc/rc.d/rc.local` file.

Tip

You may find IP masquerading a convenient way to provide Internet access to a small LAN (for example, a LAN at home or in the office). At home, I use IP masquerading to connect an Ethernet LAN to the Internet through a Linux system. The Linux PC has an Ethernet card for the LAN connection and a modem to connect to the Internet via an ISP. (The dial-up connection receives a dynamic IP address from the ISP.) With IP masquerading on the Linux PC, everyone in your family or small business can access the Internet from any of the other PCs on the LAN.

Setting Up a PPP Server

The preceding sections describe how your Linux PC can establish a PPP link with another system that offers PPP service. After a PPP link is set up, both ends of the PPP link behave as peers. Before a PPP link is established, you can think of the end that initiates the dial-up connection as the client, because that system asks for the connection. The other end provides the PPP connection when needed, so it's the PPP server.

If you want to enable other people to connect to your Linux PC by using PPP over a dial-up modem, follow these steps:

1. Follow the steps outlined in Chapter 7 to enable dial-up login on your system. Test this part to make sure that everything works by dialing into your system from another computer and logging in as a user. This step involves adding a line such as the following to the `/etc/inittab` file:

    ```
    s0:235:respawn:/sbin/uugetty ttyS0 F57600 vt100
    ```

2. Add a new user for the dial-up PPP connection — the user name under which the client system logs in. Upon login, the `pppd` program should run automatically. Specify `/usr/local/bin/ppp-login` as the shell for the user.

3. Prepare the `/usr/local/bin/ppp-login` script. This script is the "shell" for the PPP login account, which means this script executes when the PPP user logs in. Thus, the script should start the `pppd` program with appropriate options. After you prepare the script, remember to make it executable. Following is a typical `/usr/local/bin/ppp-login` script:

    ```
    #!/bin/sh
    ```

    ```
    # A script to start PPP service for a login account
    ```

```
# Shell variables with IP addresses
  RMTIP="192.168.111.111"
  LOCIP="192.168.111.222"


  exec /usr/sbin/pppd -detach silent modem \
          crtscts $LOCIP:$RMTIP
```

I tested this setup from a Windows 95 PC and it worked; however, I had to type in the user name and password manually in a terminal window. In Windows 95/98 dial-up networking, you can turn on an option that displays a terminal window after the modems establish connection. I typed in the PPP user name and password in that window.

Summary

Most of us do not have a direct connection to the high-bandwidth backbones of the Internet. Instead, we rely on dial-up modem connections to Internet Service Providers (ISPs), which, in turn, are connected to the backbones (typically provided by large telecommunications companies such as Sprint and AT&T). You can accomplish TCP/IP networking over serial lines with SLIP and PPP. Software for both SLIP and PPP comes with Linux. This chapter explains SLIP and PPP and shows you how to configure and use both of these protocols as data-transport mechanisms for TCP/IP networking.

Through this chapter, you learn the following:

▶ Serial communications with software such as minicom (or something like HyperTerminal, in the Windows world) enables your PC to become a terminal to a remote host. This type of serial communication does not get you a full network connection in which several network applications can use the same physical link to transfer data between your PC and the remote system.

▶ SLIP, or Serial Line Internet Protocol, was the first attempt at using the serial link as a data-transport layer for TCP/IP networking. Although simple, SLIP proved deficient in many ways. Both ends needed to know the IP addresses, for example, and only one type of protocol could use a SLIP connection for packet transport.

▶ PPP, or Point-to-Point Protocol, is a more complex protocol for packet transport over any point-to-point link. PPP can carry packets of many protocols over the same link. PPP is the preferred way to establish a dial-up TCP/IP network connection with ISPs.

▶ A program named dip establishes a SLIP connection with a remote system.

▶ Setting up a PPP link involves two basic steps. First, you must use a utility program to dial the modem and make the connection with the remote modem; then, you have to start the PPP software on your system. The `chat` program functions with the `pppd` program to perform these two steps.

▶ When you connect your Linux PC to a remote system by using PPP, the PPP link functions as the default route on the Linux PC, because the PPP connection is the gateway to the rest of the Internet.

▶ You can use the Red Hat Dialup Configuration Tool to set up a PPP connection, and you can use the RH PPP Dialer to run `pppd` and establish a PPP connection.

▶ You can use IP masquerading to provide Internet access to a private LAN through a Linux PC that has a PPP connection to an ISP.

▶ You also can set up your Linux PC as a PPP server so that others may dial in and establish a PPP connection with your system. This chapter describes the steps for setting up a PPP server.

Chapter 17

Web Server

Chapter 16 showed you how to connect your Red Hat Linux PC to the Internet (through an Internet Service Provider). This chapter addresses one of the reasons the Internet has become so popular in recent years: the World Wide Web (WWW, W3, or simply the Web), which provides an easy graphical way to browse and retrieve information from the Internet.

As a host on the Internet, all your Red Hat Linux system needs is a *Web browser*—an application that "knows" how to download and display Web documents—so that you can enjoy the benefits of the Web. You also can make information available to other users through *Web pages*—the common term for Web documents.

This chapter first explains what the World Wide Web is and describes the HyperText Transfer Protocol (HTTP)—the information exchange protocol that makes the Web work. Then it provides a brief introduction to the Netscape Communicator Web browser, which comes with Red Hat Linux on this book's companion CD-ROMs.

Next the chapter addresses the use of the Web as a popular way to publish information on the Internet. Red Hat Linux includes the Apache HTTP server (*HTTP server* being the technical term for a Web server), which you can use simply by placing your HTML files in the appropriate directory. This chapter shows you where various files should go and how to configure the Apache Web server.

Discovering the World Wide Web

If you have used a network file server of any kind, you know the convenience of being able to access files that reside at a shared location. Using a word processing application that runs on your computer, you can easily open a document that physically resides on the file server.

Now imagine a word processor that enables you to open and view a document that resides on any computer on the Internet. You can view the document in its full glory, with formatted text and graphics. If the document makes a reference to another document (possibly one that resides on yet another computer), you can open that linked document by clicking the reference. That kind of easy access to distributed documents is essentially what the World Wide Web provides.

Of course the documents have to be in a standard format, so that any computer (with appropriate Web software) can access and interpret them. Additionally, a standard protocol is necessary for transferring Web documents from one system to another.

The standard Web document format is HyperText Markup Language (HTML), and the standard protocol for exchanging Web documents is HyperText Transfer Protocol (HTTP).

Note

A Web server is the software that provides HTML documents to any client that makes the appropriate HTTP requests. A Web browser is the client software that actually downloads an HTML document from a Web server and displays the contents graphically.

Like a Giant Spiderweb

The World Wide Web is the combination of Web servers and HTML documents that contain a variety of information. Imagine the Web as a giant book whose pages are scattered throughout the Internet. You use a Web browser running on your computer to view the pages, as illustrated in Figure 17-1.

As Figure 17-1 shows, the pages — the HTML documents — are linked by network connections that resemble a giant spiderweb, so you can see how the Web got its name. The "World Wide" part refers to the fact that the Web pages are linked around the world.

Links and URLs

Like the pages of real books, Web pages contain text and graphics. Unlike the pages of real books, however, Web pages can contain multimedia information such as images, video clips, digitized sound, and cross-references, called *links*, that can actually take the user to the page referred to.

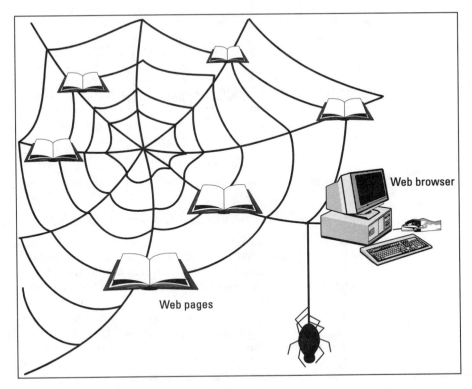

Figure 17-1: The World Wide Web is like millions of pages scattered across the Internet, which you can read from your computer by using a Web browser.

The *links* in a Web page are references to other Web pages that you follow (click) to go from one page to another. The Web browser typically displays these links as underlined text (in a different color), or as images. Each link is like an instruction to the reader — such as "for more information, please consult Chapter 17" — that you might find in a real book. In a Web page, all you have to do is click the link and the Web browser brings up the page referred to, even if it's on a different computer.

Note

The term *hypertext* refers to nonlinear organization of text (as opposed to the sequential, linear arrangement of text in most books or magazines). The links in a Web page are referred to as hypertext links, because by clicking a link you can jump to a different Web page, which is an example of nonlinear organization of text.

This arrangement raises a question. In a real book, you might ask the reader to go to a specific chapter or page. How does a hypertext link indicate the location of the Web page in question? In the World Wide Web each Web page has a special name, called a *Uniform Resource Locator (URL)*. A URL uniquely specifies the location of a file on a computer, as shown in Figure 17-2.

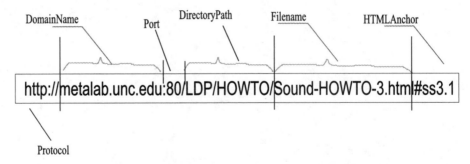

Figure 17-2: A Uniform Resource Locator (URL) is comprised of various parts.

As Figure 17-2 illustrates, a URL has this sequence of components:

1. *Protocol* — This is the name of the protocol that the Web browser will use to access the data that reside in the file specified by the URL. In Figure 17-2 the protocol is `http://`, which means that the URL specifies the location of a Web page. Following are the common protocol types and their meanings:

   - `file://` specifies the name of a local file that is to be opened and displayed. You can use this URL to view HTML files without having to connect to the Internet. For example, `file:///usr/share/doc/HTML/index.html` opens the file `/usr/share/doc/HTML/index.html` from your Red Hat Linux system.

   - `ftp://` specifies a file that is accessible through File Transfer Protocol (FTP). For example, `ftp://ftp.purdue.edu/pub/uns/NASA/nasa.jpg` refers to the image file `nasa.jpg` from the `/pub/uns/NASA/` directory of the FTP server `ftp.purdue.edu`.

   - `gopher://` specifies a document and the name of a host system that runs the Gopher server from which the document is to be retrieved. Gopher servers provide information by using a simple protocol. For example, `gopher://gopher.tc.umn.edu/` accesses the Gopher service at the University of Minnesota.

   - `http://` specifies a file that is accessible through the HyperText Transfer Protocol (HTTP). This is the well-known format of URLs for all Web sites, such as `http://www.redhat.com/` for Red Hat's home page.

   - `https://` specifies a file that is to be accessed through a Secure Sockets Layer (SSL) connection, which is a protocol designed by Netscape Communications for encrypted data transfers across the Internet. This form of URL is typically used when the Web browser sends sensitive information such as credit card number, user name, and password to a Web server. For example, a URL such as `https://some.site.com/secure/takeorder.html` might display an HTML form that requests credit card information and other personal information such as name, address, and phone number.

- `mailto://` specifies an e-mail address that you can use to send an e-mail message. For example, `mailto:webmaster@someplace.com` refers to the webmaster at the host `someplace.com`.

- `news://` specifies a newsgroup you can read by means of the Network News Transfer Protocol (NNTP). For example, `news://news.psn.net/comp.infosystems.www.authoring.html` accesses the `comp.infosystems.www.authoring.html` newsgroup at the news server `news.psn.net`. If you have a default news server configured for the Web browser, then you can omit the news server's name and use the URL `news:comp.infosystems.www.authoring.html` to access the newsgroup.

- `telnet://` specifies a user name and a system name for remote login. For example, the URL `telnet://guest:bemyguest@someplace.com/` logs into the host `someplace.com` with the user name `guest` and password `bemyguest`.

2. *Domain name* — This contains the fully qualified domain name of the computer on which resides the file specified by this URL. You can also specify an IP address in this field (see Chapter 8 for more information on IP addresses). The domain name is not case-sensitive.

3. *Port address* — This is the port address of the server that implements the protocol listed in the first part of the URL (see Chapter 8 for a discussion of port addresses). This part of the URL is optional, because there are default ports for all protocols. The default port for HTTP, for example, is 80. Some sites, however, may configure the Web server to listen to a different port. In such a case, the URL must include the port address.

4. *Directory path* — This is the directory path of the file being referred to in the URL. For Web pages, this field is the directory path of the HTML file. The directory path is case-sensitive.

5. *Filename* — This is the name of the file. For Web pages, the filename typically ends with `.htm` or `.html`. If you omit the filename, the Web server returns a default file (often named `index.html`). The filename is case sensitive.

6. *HTML anchor* — This optional part of the URL makes the Web browser jump to a specific location in the file. If this part starts with a question mark (?) instead of a hash mark (#), then the browser takes the text following the question mark to be a query. The Web server returns information based on such queries.

HyperText Transfer Protocol (HTTP)

The HyperText Transfer Protocol — the protocol that underlies the World Wide Web — is called *HyperText* because Web pages include hypertext links. The *Transfer Protocol* part refers to the standard conventions for transferring a Web page across the network from one computer to another. Although you really do not have to understand HTTP to set up a Web server or use a Web browser, I think you'll find it instructive to know how the Web works.

Before I explain anything about HTTP, you should get some firsthand experience of it. On most systems the Web server listens to port 80 and responds to any HTTP requests sent to that port. Therefore, you can use the telnet program to connect to port 80 of a system (if it has a Web server) to try some HTTP commands.

To see an example of HTTP at work, follow these steps:

1. Make sure that your Linux PC's connection to the Internet is up and running. (If you use SLIP or PPP, for example, make sure that you have established a connection.)

2. Type the following command:

   ```
   telnet www.gao.gov 80
   ```

3. After you see the Connected... message, type the following HTTP command:

   ```
   GET / HTTP/1.0
   ```

   and press Enter twice. In response to this HTTP command, the Web server returns some useful information, followed by the contents of the default HTML file (usually called index.html).

The following is what I got when I tried the GET command on the U. S. General Accounting Office's Web site:

```
telnet www.gao.gov 80
Trying 161.203.16.2...
Connected to www.gao.gov.
Escape character is '^]'.
GET / HTTP/1.0
........(Press Enter once more to send a blank line)
HTTP/1.1 200 OK
Date: Sat, 03 Feb 2001 20:00:15 GMT
Server: Apache/1.3.14 (Unix) PHP/4.0.1pl2
Last-Modified: Wed, 10 Jan 2001 19:49:21 GMT
ETag: "26001d-6e8-3a5cbcc1"
Accept-Ranges: bytes
Content-Length: 1768
Connection: close
Content-Type: text/html
```

```
<!DOCTYPE HTML PUBLIC "-//W3C//DTD HTML 4.0 Transitional//EN"
"http://www.w3.org/TR/REC-html40/loose.dtd">

<HTML>
<HEAD>
<TITLE>The United States General Accounting Office</TITLE>
...... (lines deleted)
</HEAD>

...... (lines deleted)

</BODY>
</html>
Connection closed by foreign host.
```

When you try this example with `telnet`, you see exactly what the Web server
sends back to the Web browser. The first few lines are administrative information for the browser. The server returns this information:

- A line that shows that the server uses HTTP protocol version 1.1 and a
  status code of 200 indicating success: `HTTP/1.1 200 OK`

- The current date and time. A sample date and time string looks like this:

  `Date: Sat, 03 Feb 2001 20:00:15 GMT`

- The name and version of the Web-server software. For example, for a site
  running the Apache Web server version 1.3.14 with the PHP hypertext
  processor version 4.0.1p12, the server returns the following string:

  `Server: Apache/1.3.14 (Unix) PHP/4.0.1p12`

- The type of document being returned by the Web server. For HTML documents, the content type is reported as follows:

  `Content-type: text/html`

- The date and time when the document was last modified in a line
  such as:

  `Last-Modified: Wed, 10 Jan 2001 19:49:21 GMT`

- The length of the document in number of bytes. In this case, the document is 1768 bytes long, so the server returns the following string:
  `Content-length: 1768`

The document itself follows the administrative information. An HTML document has the following general layout:

```
<title>Document's title goes here</title>
<html>
<body optional attributes go here >
... The rest of the document goes here
</body>
</html>
```

You can identify this layout by looking through the listing that shows what the Web server returns in response to the GET command. Because the example uses a telnet command to get the document, you see the HTML content as lines of text. If you were to access the same URL (http://www.gao.gov) with a Web browser (such as Netscape Navigator), you would see the page in its graphical form, as shown in Figure 17-3.

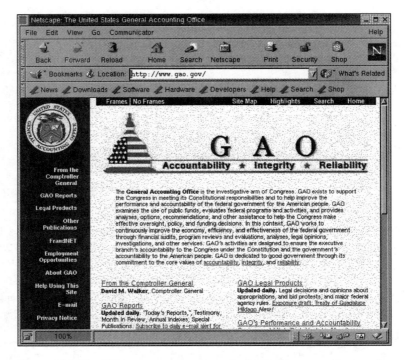

Figure 17-3: The URL www.gao.gov viewed with the Netscape Communicator Web browser

The example of HTTP commands shows the result of the GET command. GET is the most common HTTP command, because it causes the server to return a specified HTML document.

The other two HTTP commands are HEAD and POST. The HEAD command is almost like GET: it causes the server to return everything in the document except the body. The POST command sends information to the server; it's up to the server to decide how to act on the information.

Is HTTP an Internet Standard?

Despite its widespread use in the World Wide Web since 1990, the HyperText Transfer Protocol (HTTP) was not an Internet standard until recently. All Internet standards are distributed as a Request for Comment (RFC). The first HTTP-related RFC was RFC 1945, "HyperText Transfer Protocol — HTTP/1.0" (T. Berners-Lee, R. Fielding, and H. Frystyk, May 1996). However, RFC 1945 is considered an informational document, not a standard.

RFC 2616, "HyperText Transfer Protocol — HTTP/1.1" (R. Fielding, J. Gettys, J. Mogul, H. Frystyk, L. Masinter, P. Leach, T. Berners-Lee, June 1999) is the Draft Internet standard for HTTP.

To read these RFCs, point your Web browser to either www.rfc-editor.org/rfc.html or www.cis.ohiostate.edu/htbin/rfc/rfc-index.html.

To learn more about HTTP/1.1 and other Web-related standards, use a Web browser to access www.w3.org/pub/WWW/Protocols.

Surfing the Net

Like anything else, the World Wide Web is easier to understand after you have seen how it works. One of the best ways to learn about the Web is to "surf" with a Web browser. Browsing Web pages is fun, because the typical Web page contains both text and images. Also, browsing has an element of surprise; you can click the links and end up at unexpected Web pages. Links are the most curious aspect of the Web. You can start by looking at a page that shows today's weather; a click later, you can be reading this week's issue of *Time* magazine.

Before you can try anything, of course, you need a Web browser. (You must also have an Internet connection for your Red Hat Linux system, but I am assuming that you have already taken care of that part.)

In January 1998, Netscape Communications Corporation announced that it was making its Netscape Communicator product available for free (Netscape Communicator is an integrated Web browser, e-mail- and newsreader, and Web page composer — the Web browser is called Navigator). That means that anyone can now download, install, and use the Netscape Web browser on his or her system without paying any fee.

Note

The version of Red Hat Linux on this book's companion CD-ROM includes Netscape Communicator. When you follow the directions in Chapter 2 to install Red Hat Linux, Netscape Communicator is automatically installed provided you elect to install the Mail/WWW/News Tools component.

Starting Netscape Navigator

Netscape Navigator began as a successor to Mosaic, the original GUI-based Web browser from the National Center for Supercomputing Applications (NCSA) at the University of Illinois in Urbana-Champaign. One of Mosaic's primary developers, Marc Andreessen, was the force behind Netscape Navigator, as well. Netscape Navigator improved on Mosaic in several ways, the most significant being the way that Netscape Navigator loads a Web page.

When a Web page includes embedded images, the browser has to download each image separately. Mosaic displays a Web page only after everything on that page has been downloaded. Netscape Navigator, on the other hand, begins displaying the page as soon as parts of it are available.

Netscape Navigator also finishes downloading a page faster, because it makes multiple connections with the Web server to download separate parts of the page in parallel. (This process puts more of a load on the Web server, but it's beneficial to the user.)

From the GNOME desktop, you can start Netscape Communicator in one of three ways:

- Click the Netscape Communicator icon (the one with a big N) on the GNOME Panel, as shown in Figure 17-4.

- Select Main Menu ➪ Programs ➪ Internet ➪ Netscape Communicator. (Main Menu refers to the button with a stylized foot at the left edge of the GNOME Panel, as shown in Figure 17-4.)

- Type netscape at the shell prompt in a terminal window.

Figure 17-4: Clicking the icon with the big N starts Netscape Communicator.

When Netscape Communicator starts, it displays a Navigator window with a default home page (the main Web page on a Web server is known as the *home page*). In Red Hat Linux, the default home page is set in the URL file:/usr/ share/doc/HTML/index.html, which refers to the file /usr/share/doc/ HTML/index.html on your system. You can configure Navigator to use a different Web page as the default home page.

Secret

Compare the syntax of the URL http://www.redhat.com/ with the URL syntax shown earlier in this chapter — this URL does not appear to have a filename. When a URL does not have a filename, the Web server sends a default HTML file named index.html (that's the default filename for the popular UNIX-based Apache and NCSA Web servers; Windows NT-based Web servers use a different default filename).

Learning Netscape Navigator's User Interface

Figure 17-5 shows a Web page from the Hungry Minds Web site, as well as the main elements of the Netscape Navigator window.

The Netscape Navigator window sports a Motif user interface with a title bar that shows the current document title, as well as a menu bar that contains all the standard menus (File, Edit, and so forth).

The most important part of the Netscape window is the document window — the large area in which Netscape displays the Web page with its text and images.

Immediately above the document window are three items that you can turn on or off from the View menu:

- The *Navigation Toolbar* gives you quick access to some common menu items. The Back and Forward buttons are for moving between Web pages that you've already seen; Home takes you to the default home page (which is initially set to Netscape's home page); Reload forces the browser to download the current page again; Search takes you to a page from which you can search for information on the Internet; Print prints the current page; Security shows security information; and Stop stops loading of the current Web page.

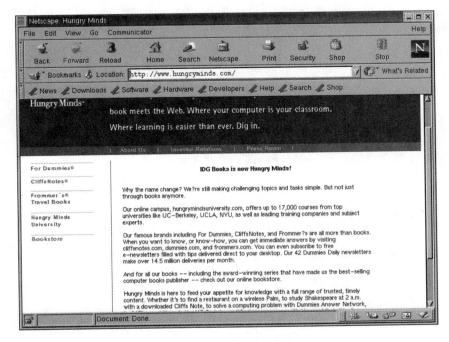

Figure 17-5: Elements of the Netscape Navigator window

- The *Location Toolbar* displays the location of the current Web page in the form of a URL and enables you to access your bookmarks (saved URLs). You can also click in this area and type in the URL of any page you want to see.

- The *Personal Toolbar* offers shortcuts to specific Web pages. In the version of Netscape Communicator that comes with Red Hat Linux, these shortcuts provide access to different Web pages on Red Hat's Web site. The Downloads button, for example, takes you to `http://www.redhat.com/browser/downloads.html`, from which you can download the latest version of Red Hat Linux.

In the upper right-hand corner of the Netscape window is the Activity Indicator button (marked with a large N). Netscape animates the Activity Indicator while it downloads a Web page. Clicking this button takes you to Netscape's home page.

Secret

In the upper left-hand corner of the Netscape window is a padlock — the security padlock. Netscape supports a secure version of the HTTP that uses Secure Sockets Layer (SSL) to transfer encrypted data. When Netscape connects to a Web server that supports secure HTTP, the security padlock appears locked. Otherwise the security padlock is open, signifying an insecure connection. The URL for secure HTTP transfers begins with `https://` instead of the usual `http://` (note the extra `s` in `https`).

Netscape displays status messages in the area to the right of the security key. When Netscape is busy downloading a Web page, it displays the percentage of the document that it has downloaded.

Along the upper right-hand edge of the window Netscape Navigator displays a number of icons. By clicking these icons, you can open other windows to perform tasks, such as reading e-mail messages, reading a newsgroup, or editing a Web page. To learn more about any of these icons, simply move the mouse pointer over the button and Netscape Navigator displays a help message in a small pop-up window (and also in the status message area).

Setting Up a Web Server

You probably already know how it feels to use the Web, but you may not know how to set up a Web server so that you, too, can provide information to the world through Web pages. To become an information provider on the Web you have to run a Web server on your Red Hat Linux PC on the Internet. You also have to prepare the Web pages for your Web site — a task that may be more demanding than the Web server setup.

Web servers provide information using HTTP. Web servers are also known as *HTTP daemons* (because continuously running server processes are called *daemons* in UNIX) or HTTPD for short. The Web server program is usually named `httpd`.

Among the available Web servers, the Apache Web server is the most popular. The Apache Web server started out as an improved version of the NCSA HTTPD server, but soon grew into a separate development effort. Like NCSA HTTPD, the Apache server is developed and maintained by a team of collaborators. Apache is freely available over the Internet.

The following sections describe the installation and configuration of the Apache Web server.

Installing the Apache Web Server

Installing Red Hat Linux from this book's companion CD-ROMs gives you the option to install the Apache Web server. As described in Chapter 2, simply select the Mail/WWW/News Tools component when you are prompted for the components to install. The WWW in the name of the component refers to the World Wide Web, and it includes the Apache Web server. If you install the Web server, everything should be set so that the Apache Web server (the server program is called httpd) is started automatically.

Perform these steps to verify that the Apache Web server software is installed on your system:

1. Use the rpm -q command to check whether the Apache package is installed:

```
rpm -q apache
apache-1.3.14-6
```

   If the output shows an apache package name, you have installed the Apache software.

2. Type the following command to check whether the httpd process (httpd is the name of the Apache Web server program) is running:

```
ps ax | grep httpd
```

   The output should show a number of httpd processes. It is common to run several Web server processes — one parent and several child processes — so that several HTTP requests can be handled efficiently by assigning each request to an httpd process. If there is no httpd process, log in as root and edit the /etc/httpd/conf/httpd.conf file. Make sure that the line that starts with the ServerName option is uncommented (no # character at the beginning of the line) and is set to your host's IP address or host name. For a private LAN, you can set the option to ServerName localhost. Then restart the httpd with the command /etc/init.d/httpd restart.

3. Use the telnet program on your Linux system and use the HTTP HEAD command to query the Web server, as follows:

```
telnet localhost 80
Trying 127.0.0.1...
Connected to localhost.
Escape character is '^]'.
HEAD / HTTP/1.0
... Press Enter once more to type a blank line
HTTP/1.1 200 OK
Date: Sat, 03 Feb 2001 20:42:46 GMT
Server: Apache/1.3.14 (Unix) (Red-Hat/Linux) mod_ssl/2.7.1
OpenSSL/0.9.5a DAV/1.0.2 PHP/4.0.4 mod_perl/1.24
Last-Modified: Wed, 06 Dec 2000 22:36:51 GMT
ETag: "c4e9-b4a-3a2ebf83"
Accept-Ranges: bytes
Content-Length: 2890
Connection: close
Content-Type: text/html


Connection closed by foreign host
```

If you get a response such as that in the preceding code, your system
already has the Apache Web server installed and set up correctly. All you
have to do is understand the configuration so that you can place the
HTML documents in the proper directory.

Tip

Use a Web server to load the homepage from your system. For instance, if
your system's IP address is 192.168.1.100, use the URL `http://192/168.
1.100/` and see what happens. You should see a Web page with the title
"Test Page for the Apache Web Server on Red Hat Linux."

Configuring the Apache Web Server

Red Hat Linux configures the Apache Web server software to use these
directories:

- The Web server program — `httpd` — is installed in the `/usr/sbin`
  directory.

- The Apache Web server configuration files are located in the `/etc/
  httpd/conf` directory. The configuration files are text files with direc-
  tives that specify various aspects of the Web server. There are three
  configuration files — `access.conf`, `httpd.conf`, and `srm.conf` — but
  all directives are placed in the `httpd.conf` file only (a later section
  describes the Apache directives). The `/etc/httpd/conf` directory also
  contains information needed by the Secure Sockets Layer (SSL) implementation that comes as part of the Apache Web server.

Why Is It Called Apache?

According to the information about the Apache Web server project on `http://www.apache.org/info.html`, the Apache group was formed in March 1995 by a number of people who provided patch files that had been written to fix bugs in NCSA HTTPD 1.3. The result after applying the patches to NCSA HTTPD was what they called *a patchy server*; that's how the name Apache came about.

According to the January 2001 Netcraft Web Server Survey at `http://www.netcraft.co.uk/Survey/`, the Apache Web server is the most popular — 58.75 percent of 27,585,719 sites reported using the Apache server. Microsoft Internet Information Server (IIS) is a distant second with 21.40 percent of the sites.

- The Apache Web server is set up to serve the HTML documents from the `/var/www/html` directory. Therefore, you should place your Web pages in this directory.

- If you have any Common Gateway Interface (CGI) programs — programs that the Web server can invoke to access other files and databases — you should place these in the `/var/www/cgi-bin/` directory.

- The `/var/log/httpd` directory is meant for Web server log files (access logs and error logs).

- The `/etc/init.d/httpd` script starts the `httpd` process as your Red Hat Linux system boots.

Apache configuration files

The Apache server's operation is controlled by three configuration files located in the `/etc/httpd/conf` directory. The configuration files control how the server runs, what documents it serves, and who can access these documents.

The following gives descriptions of the three configuration files:

- `httpd.conf` — Configuration file for the Apache server. The directives in the file specify general attributes of the server, such as the port number and the directory in which the server's directories are located. This is the most important configuration file for the Apache Web server, because everything, including directives that used to be in the `srm.conf` and `access.conf` files, is nowadays placed in `httpd.conf`.

- `srm.conf` — Configuration file for the server resources — the documents and other information that the Web server provides to the users. For example, the `srm.conf` file can specify where the documents are located (srm stands for *server resource map*). Note that nowadays all the options are placed in the `httpd.conf` file and that `srm.conf` is left empty.

Learning More about the Apache Web Server

The Apache Web server has too many options and configuration directives to describe in detail in this book. There are whole books devoted to configuring the Apache Web server. You should consult one of these books for more information:

- Mohammed J. Kabir, *Apache Server Bible*, IDG Books Worldwide, 1998.

- Mohammed J. Kabir, *Apache Server Administrator's Handbook*, IDG Books Worldwide, 1999.

- Ken A. L. Coar, *Apache Server For Dummies*, IDG Books Worldwide, 1998.

You can also find late-breaking news and detailed information about the latest version of Apache HTTPD from Apache's Web site at `http://www.apache.org/docs/`. In particular, you can browse through a complete list of Apache directives at `http://www.apache.org/docs/mod/directives.html`.

- `access.conf` — Configuration file that controls access to the Web server. You can control access to the entire Web server as well as to specific directories. Note that nowadays all access control options are placed in the `httpd.conf` file and this file is left empty.

The next few sections show you the key information about the `httpd.conf` configuration file. Typically you do not have to change anything in the configuration files to use the Apache Web server *except* for setting the `ServerName` in the `httpd.conf` file. However, it is useful to know the format of the configuration files and the meaning of the various keywords used in them.

As you study the configuration files in the `/etc/httpd/conf` directory, keep these syntax rules in mind:

- Each configuration file is a text file that you can edit with your favorite text editor and view with the `more` command.

- All comment lines begin with a #.

- Each line can have only one directive.

- Extra spaces and blank lines are ignored.

- All entries, except path names and URLs, are case-insensitive.

The httpd.conf configuration file

The `/etc/httpd/conf/httpd.conf` file is the basic HTTP daemon configuration file — it includes directives that control how the Apache Web server runs. For example, the `httpd.conf` file specifies the port number the server uses, the name of the Web site, and the e-mail address to which mail is sent in case of any problems with the server. Additionally, nowadays `httpd.conf` also includes all options that used to be in the other configuration files, `srm.conf` and `access.conf`. That means that `httpd.conf` also includes resource configuration directives and access control directives.

Although all the directives now reside in the same file, the following sections show the Apache directives grouped into three separate categories: general HTTPD directives, resource configuration directives, and access control directives.

General HTTPD directives

Some interesting items from the `httpd.conf` file are:

- `ServerName` specifies the host name of your Web site (of the form `www.your.domain`). The name should be a registered domain name that others can locate through their name servers. Here is an example:

  `ServerName   www.myhost.com`

- `ServerAdmin` is the e-mail address that the Web server provides to clients in case any errors occur. The default value for `ServerAdmin` is `root@localhost`. You should set this to a valid e-mail address that anyone on the Internet can use to report errors with your Web site.

Many more directives control the way that the Apache Web server works. The following list summarizes some of the directives that you can use in the `httpd.conf` file. You can leave most of these directives in their default settings, but it's important to know about them if you are maintaining a Web server.

- `ServerType type` — Specifies how Linux executes the HTTP server. The `type` can be `xinetd` (to run the server through the `xinetd` daemon) or `standalone` (to run the server as a stand-alone process). You should run the server as a stand-alone for better performance. Additionally, the latest Apache documentation states that the `xinetd` mode is no longer recommended and does not work properly.

- `Port num` — Specifies that the HTTP daemon should listen to port `num` (a number between 0 and 65,535) for requests from clients. The default port for HTTPD is 80. You should leave the port number at its default value, because clients will assume the HTTP port to be 80. If your server does not use port 80, the URL for your server must specify the port number.

- `User name [ #id]` — Specifies the user name (or ID) used by the HTTP daemon when it is running in stand-alone mode. You can leave this directive at the default setting (`apache`). If you specify a user ID, use a hash (#) prefix for the numeric ID.

- `Group name [ #id]` — Specifies the group name (or ID) of the HTTP daemon when running in stand-alone mode. The default group name is `apache`.

- `ServerRoot pathname` — Specifies the directory where the Web server is located. By default, the configuration and log files are expected to reside in subdirectories of this directory. In Red Hat Linux, `ServerRoot` is set to `/etc/httpd`.

- `ServerName www.company.com`—Sets the server's host name to `www.company.com` instead of its real host name. You cannot simply invent a name; the name must be a valid name from the Domain Name System (DNS) for your system.

- `StartServers num`—Sets the number of child processes that start as soon as the Apache Web server runs. The default value is 8.

- `MaxSpareServers num`—Sets the desired maximum number of idle child-server processes (a child process is considered idle if it is not handling an HTTP request). The default value is 20.

- `MinSpareServers num`—Sets the desired minimum number of idle child server processes (a child process is considered idle if it is not handling an HTTP request). A new spare process is created every second if the number falls below this threshold. The default value is 5.

- `Timeout numsec`—Sets the number of seconds that the server waits for a client to send a query after the client establishes connection. The default `Timeout` is 300 seconds (five minutes).

- `ErrorLog filename`—Sets the file where `httpd` logs the errors that it encounters. If the filename does not begin with a slash (/), the name is taken to be relative to `ServerRoot`. The default `ErrorLog` is `/var/log/httpd/error_log`. Typical error-log entries include events such as server restarts and any warning messages, such as the following:

```
[Sat Feb  3 15:57:16 2001] [notice] Apache/1.3.14 (Unix)  (Red-
Hat/Linux) mod_ssl/2.7.1 OpenSSL/0.9.5a DAV/1.0.2 PHP/4.0.4
mod_perl/1.24 configured - resuming normal operations

[Sat Feb  3 15:58:38 2001] [error] [client 192.168.1.40] File does
not exist: /var/www/html/manual/index.html

[Sat Feb  3 15:59:24 2001] [notice] caught SIGTERM, shutting down
```

- `TransferLog filename`—Sets the file where `httpd` records all client accesses (including failed accesses). The default `TransferLog` is `/var/log/httpd/access_log`. The following example shows how a typical access is recorded in the `TransferLog` file:

```
192.168.1.200 - - [03/Feb/2001:15:57:31 -0500] "GET / HTTP/1.0"
200 2890

192.168.1.200 - - [03/Feb/2001:15:57:32 -0500] "GET /poweredby.png
HTTP/1.0" 200 1154

192.168.1.200 - - [03/Feb/2001:15:57:32 -0500] "GET
/icons/apache_pb.gif HTTP/1.0" 200 2326
```

The first entry is for the text of the file; the second and third entries are for embedded images. The last two items on each line show the status code returned by the server, followed by the number of bytes sent by the server.

- `LogFormat formatstring formatname` — Specifies the format of log-file entries for the `TransferLog`. This format is also used by the `CustomLog` directive to produce logs in a specific format.

- `CustomLog filename formatname` — Sets the name of the custom log file where `httpd` records all client accesses (including failed accesses) in a format specified by `formatname` (which you define using a `LogFormat` directive).

- `PidFile filename` — Sets the file where `httpd` stores its process ID. The default `PidFile` is `/var/run/httpd.pid`. You can use this information to kill or restart the HTTP daemon. The following example shows how to restart `httpd`:

  ```
  kill -HUP `cat /var/run/httpd.pid`
  ```

- `MaxClients num` — Sets the limit on the number of clients that can simultaneously connect to the server. The default value is 150. The value of `MaxClients` cannot be more than 256.

- `LoadModule module modules/modfile.so` — Loads a module that was built as a Dynamic Shared Object (DSO). You have to specify the module name and the module's object file. Because the order in which modules are loaded is important, you should leave these directives as they appear in the default configuration file.

Resource configuration directives

The resource configuration directives specify the location of the Web pages, as well as how to specify the data types of various files. To get started, you can leave the directives at their default settings. These are some of the resource configuration directives for the Apache Web server:

- `DocumentRoot pathname` — Specifies the directory where the HTTP server finds the Web pages. In Red Hat Linux, the default `DocumentRoot` is `/var/www/html`. If you place your HTML documents in another directory, set `DocumentRoot` to that directory.

- `UserDir dirname` — Specifies the directory below a user's home directory where the HTTP server looks for the Web pages when a user name appears in the URL (in an URL such as `http://www.psn.net/~naba/`, for example, which includes a username with a tilde prefix). The default `UserDir` is `public_html`, which means that a user's Web pages are in the `public_html` subdirectory of that user's home directory. If you do not want to allow users to have any Web pages, specify `disabled` as the directory name in the `UserDir` directive.

- `DirectoryIndex filename1 filename2 ...` — Indicates the default file or files to be returned by the server when the client does not specify any document. The default `DirectoryIndex` is `index.html`. If `httpd` does not find this file, it returns an index (basically, a nice-looking listing of the files) of that directory.

- `AccessFileName filename`—Specifies the name of the file that may appear in each directory that contains documents and that indicates who has permission to access the contents of that directory. The default `AccessFileName` is `.htaccess`. The syntax of this file is the same as that of Apache access-control directives, which the following section discusses.

- `AddType type/subtype extension`—Associates a file extension with a MIME data type (of the form `type/subtype`, such as `text/plain` or `image/gif`). Thus, to have the server treat files with the `.lst` extension as plain-text files, specify the following:

  `AddType text/plain .lst`

  The default MIME types and extensions are listed in the `/etc/mime.types` file.

- `AddEncoding type extension`—Associates an encoding type with a file extension. To have the server mark files ending with `.gz` or `.tgz` as encoded with the `x-gzip` encoding method (the standard name for the GZIP encoding), specify the following:

  `AddEncoding x-gzip gz tgz`

- `DefaultType type/subtype`—Specifies the MIME type that the server should use if it cannot determine the type from the file extension. If you do not specify `DefaultType`, `httpd` assumes the MIME type to be `text/html`. In the default `httpd.conf` file that you get from the companion CD-ROMs, `DefaultType` is specified as `text/plain`.

- `Redirect requested-file actual-URL`—Specifies that any requests for `requested-file` are to be redirected to `actual-URL`.

- `Alias requested-dir actual-dir`—Specifies that the server use `actual-dir` to locate files in the `requested-dir` directory (in other words, `requested-dir` is an alias for `actual-dir`). To have requests for the `/icons` directory go to `/var/www/icons`, specify the following:

  `Alias /icons/ /var/www/icons/`

- `ScriptAlias requested-dir actual-dir`—Specifies the real name of the directory where scripts for the Common Gateway Interface (CGI) are located. The default srm.conf file contains this directive:

  `ScriptAlias /cgi-bin/ /var/www/cgi-bin/`

  This directive means that when a Web browser requests a script, such as `/cgi-bin/test-cgi`, the HTTP server runs the script `/var/www/cgi-bin/test-cgi`.

- `FancyIndexing on [off]`—Enables or disables the display of fancy directory listings, with icons and file sizes.

- `DefaultIcon iconfile`—Specifies the location of the default icon that the server should use for files that have no icon information. By default, `DefaultIcon` is `/icons/unknown.gif`.

- `ReadmeName filename`—Specifies the name of a README file whose contents are added to the end of an automatically generated directory listing. The default `ReadmeName` is `README`.

- `HeaderName filename`—Specifies the name a header file whose contents are prepended to an automatically generated directory listing. The default `HeaderName` is `HEADER`.

- `AddDescription "file description" filename`—Specifies that the `file description` string be displayed next to the specified `filename` in the directory listing. You can use a wildcard, such as `*.html`, as the `filename`. For example, the following directive describes files ending with `.tgz` as GZIP compressed `tar` archives:

  `AddDescription "GZIP compressed tar archive" .tgz`

- `AddIcon iconfile extension1 extension2 ...`—Associates an icon with one or more file extensions. The following directive associates the icon file `/icons/text.gif` with the file extension `.txt`:

  `AddIcon /icons/text.gif .txt`

- `AddIconByType iconfile MIME-types`—Associates an icon with a group of file types specified as a wildcard form of MIME types (such as `text/*` or `image/*`). To associate an icon file of `/icons/text.gif` with all `text` types, specify the following:

  `AddIconByType (TXT,/icons/text.gif) text/*`

  This directive also tells the server to use TXT in place of the icon for clients that cannot accept images. (Browsers tell the server what types of data they can accept.)

- `AddIconByEncoding iconfile encoding1 encoding2 ...`— Specifies an icon to be displayed for one or more encoding types (such as `x-compress` or `x-gzip`).

- `IndexIgnore filename1 filename2 ...`—Instructs the server to ignore the specified filenames (they typically contain wildcards) when preparing a directory listing. To leave out README, HEADER, and all files with names that begin with a period (.), a trailing tilde (~), or a trailing hash mark (#), specify the following:

  `IndexIgnore .??* *~ *# HEADER* README* RCS CVS *,v *,t`

- `IndexOptions option1 option2 ...`—Indicates the options that you want in the directory listing prepared by the server. Options can include one or more of the following:

  - `FancyIndexing` turns on the fancy directory listing that includes filenames and icons representing the files' types, sizes, and last-modified dates.

  - `IconHeight=N` specifies that icons are `N` pixels tall.

  - `IconWidth=N` specifies that icons are `N` pixels wide.

- `NameWidth=N` makes the filename column `N` characters wide.

- `IconsAreLinks` makes the icons act like links.

- `ScanHTMLTitles` shows a description of HTML files.

- `SuppressHTMLPreamble` does not add a standard HTML preamble to the header file (specified by the `HeaderName` directive).

- `SuppressLastModified` stops display of the last date of modification.

- `SuppressSize` stops display of the file size.

- `SuppressDescription` stops display of any file description.

- `SuppressColumnSorting` stops the column headings from being links that enable sorting the columns.

■ `ErrorDocument errortype filename`—Specifies a file that the server should send when an error of a specific type occurs. You can also provide a text message for an error. Here are some examples:

```
ErrorDocument 403 "Sorry, you cannot access this directory"

ErrorDocument 404 /cgi-bin/bad_link.pl

ErrorDocument 401 /new_subscriber.html
```

If you do not have this directive, the server sends a built-in error message. The `errortype` can be one of the following HTTP/1.1 error conditions (see RFC 2616 at `http://www.ietf.org/rfc/rfc2616.txt` or `http://www.cis.ohio-state.edu/htbin/rfc/rfc2616.html` for more information):

- 400—Bad Request
- 401—Unauthorized
- 402—Payment Required
- 403—Forbidden
- 404—Not Found
- 405—Method Not Allowed
- 406—Not Acceptable
- 407—Proxy Authentication Required
- 408—Request Timeout
- 409—Conflict
- 410—Gone
- 411—Length Required

- 412 — Precondition Failed
- 413 — Request Entity Too Large
- 414 — Request-URI Too Long
- 415 — Unsupported Media Type
- 416 — Requested Range Not Satisfiable
- 417 — Expectation Failed
- 500 — Internal Server Error
- 501 — Not Implemented
- 502 — Bad Gateway
- 503 — Service Unavailable
- 504 — Gateway Timeout
- 505 — HTTP Version Not Supported

■ `TypesConfig filename` — Specifies the file that contains the mapping of file extensions to MIME data types. (MIME stands for Multipurpose Internet Mail Extensions, which defines a way to package attachments in a single message file.) The server reports these MIME types to clients. If you do not specify a `TypesConfig` directive, `httpd` assumes that the `TypesConfig` file is `/etc/mime.types`. The following are a few selected lines from the default `/etc/mime.types` file:

```
application/msword          doc
application/pdf             pdf
application/postscript      ai eps ps
application/x-tcl           tcl
audio/mpeg                  mpga mp2 mp3
audio/x-pn-realaudio        ram rm
audio/x-wav                 wav
image/gif                   gif
image/jpeg                  jpeg jpg jpe
image/png                   png
text/html                   html htm
text/plain                  asc txt
video/mpeg                  mpeg mpg mpe
```

Each line shows the MIME type (such as `text/html`), followed by the file extensions for that type (`html` or `htm`).

Access control directives

The access control directives enable you to control who can access different directories in the system. These are the global access configuration directives. In each directory containing documents served by the Apache Web server, you can have another access configuration file with the name specified by the `AccessFileName` directive. (That per-directory access configuration file is named `.htaccess` by default.)

Stripped of most of the comment lines, the access control directive has this format:

```
# First, we configure the "default" to be a
# very restrictive set of permissions.
<Directory />
Options None
AllowOverride None
</Directory>

# The following directory name should
# match DocumentRoot in srm.conf
<Directory /var/www/html>
    Options Indexes Includes FollowSymLinks
    AllowOverride None
    order allow,deny
    allow from all
</Directory>

# The directory name should match the
# location of the cgi-bin directory
<Directory "/var/www/cgi-bin">
    AllowOverride None
    Options ExecCGI
    Order allow,deny
    Allow from all
</Directory>
```

The access control directives use a different syntax from the other Apache directives. The syntax is like that of HTML. Various access control directives are enclosed within pairs of tags, such as `<Directory>` ... `</Directory>`.

The following list describes some of the access control directives. In particular, notice the `AuthUserFile` directive; you can have password-based access control for specific directories.

■ `Options opt1 opt2 ...` —Specifies the access control options for the directory section in which this directive appears. The options can be one or more of the following:

  ● `None` disables all access control features.

  ● `All` turns on all features for the directory.

  ● `FollowSymLinks` enables the server to follow symbolic links.

- SymLinksIfOwnerMatch follows symbolic links, only if the same user of the directory owns the linked directory.

- ExecCGI enables execution of CGI scripts in the directory.

- Includes enables server-side include files in this directory (the term *server-side include* refers to directives, placed in an HTML file, that the Web server processes before returning the results to the Web browser).

- Indexes enables clients to request indexes (directory listings) for the directory.

- IncludesNOEXEC disables the #exec command in server-side includes.

- AllowOverride directive1 directive2 ... — Specifies which access control directives can be overridden on a per-directory basis. The directive list can contain one or more of the following:

- None stops any directive from being overridden.

- All enables overriding of any directive on a per-directory basis.

- Options enables the use of the Options directive in the directory-level file.

- FileInfo enables the use of directives controlling document type, such as AddType and AddEncoding.

- AuthConfig enables the use of authorization directives, such as AuthName, AuthType, AuthUserFile, and AuthGroupFile.

- Limit enables the use of Limit directives (allow, deny, and order) in a directory's access configuration file.

- AuthName name — Specifies the authorization name for a directory.

- AuthType type — Specifies the type of authorization to be used. The only supported authorization type is Basic.

- AuthUserFile filename — Specifies the file in which user names and passwords are stored for authorization. For example, the following directive sets the authorization file to /etc/httpd/conf/passwd:

```
AuthUserFile /etc/httpd/conf/passwd
```

You have to create the authorization file with the /usr/sbin/htpasswd support program. To create the authorization file and add the password for a user named jdoe, specify the following:

```
/usr/bin/htpasswd -c /etc/httpd/conf/passwd jdoe
New password: (type the password)
Re-type new password: (type the same password again)
Adding password for user jdoe
```

- `AuthGroupFile filename`—Specifies the file to consult for a list of user groups for authentication.

- `order ord`—Specifies the order in which two other directives—`allow` and `deny`—are evaluated. The order is one of the following:

  - `deny,allow` causes the Web server to evaluate the `deny` directive before `allow`.

  - `allow,deny` causes the Web server to evaluate the `allow` directive before `deny`.

  - `mutual-failure` enables only those hosts that are in the `allow` list.

- `deny from host1 host2...`—Specifies the hosts that are denied access.

- `allow from host1 host2...`—Specifies the hosts that are allowed access. To enable all hosts in a specific domain to access the Web documents in a directory, specify the following:

  ```
  order deny,allow
  allow from .nws.noaa.gov
  ```

- `require entity en1 en2...`—This directive specifies which users can access a directory. `entity` is one of the following:

  - `user` enables only a list of named users.

  - `group` enables only a list of named groups.

  - `valid-user` enables all users listed in the `AuthUserFile` access to the directory (provided that they enter the correct password).

Supporting Virtual Hosts with the Apache HTTP Server

A useful feature of the Apache HTTP server is its ability to handle virtual Web servers. This ability enables a single server to respond to many different IP addresses and serve Web pages from different directories, depending on the IP address. That means you can set up a single Web server to respond to both www.big.org and www.tiny.com and serve a unique home page for each host name. A server with this capability is known as *multi-homed Web server*, a *virtual Web server*, or a server with *virtual host support*.

As you might guess, Internet service providers use virtual host capability to offer virtual Web sites to their customers. You must meet the following requirements to support virtual hosts:

- The Web server must be able to respond to multiple IP addresses (each with a unique domain name) and must enable you to specify document directories, log files, and other configuration items for each IP address.

- The Linux system must associate multiple IP addresses with a single physical network interface. Red Hat Linux enables you to associate multiple IP addresses with a single physical interface.

- Each domain name associated with the IP address must be a unique registered domain name with proper DNS entries.

For the latest information on how to set up virtual hosts in an Apache HTTP server, consult the following URL:

`http://www.apache.org/docs/vhosts/index.html`

The Apache HTTP server can respond to different host names with different home pages. You have two options when supporting virtual hosts:

- *Run multiple copies of the* `httpd` *program, one for each IP address* — In this case, you create a separate copy of the `httpd.conf` configuration file for each host and use the `BindAddress` directive to make the server respond to a specific IP address.

- *Run a single copy of the* `httpd` *program with a single httpd.conf file* — In the configuration file, set `BindAddress` to * (so that the server responds to any IP address) and use the `VirtualHost` directive to configure the server for each virtual host.

You should run multiple HTTP daemons only if you do not expect heavy traffic on your system; the system may not able to respond well because of the overhead associated with running multiple daemons. However, you may need multiple HTTP daemons if each virtual host has a unique configuration need for the following directives:

- `ServerType` (specifies whether the server runs as a stand-alone process, or through `xinetd`)
- `UserId` and `GroupId` (the user and group ID for the HTTP daemon)
- `ServerRoot` (the root directory of the server)
- `TypesConfig` (the MIME type configuration file)

For a site with heavy traffic you should configure the Web server so that a single HTTP daemon can serve multiple virtual hosts. Of course, this recommendation implies that there is only one configuration file. In that configuration file, use the `VirtualHost` directive to configure each virtual host.

Most ISPs nowadays use the `VirtualHost` capability of Apache HTTP server to provide virtual Web sites to their customers. Unless you pay for a dedicated Web host, you typically get a virtual site where you have your own domain name, but share the server and the actual host with many other customers.

The syntax of the `VirtualHost` directive is as follows:

```
<VirtualHost hostaddr>
    ... directives that apply to this host
    ...
</VirtualHost>
```

With this syntax, you use `<VirtualHost>` and `</VirtualHost>` to enclose a group of directives that will apply only to the particular virtual host identified by the `hostaddr` parameter. The `hostaddr` can be an IP address, or the fully qualified domain name of the virtual host.

You can place almost any Apache directives within the `<VirtualHost>` block. At a minimum, Webmasters include the following directives in the `<VirtualHost>` block:

- `DocumentRoot`, which specifies where this virtual host's documents reside.

- `Servername`, which identifies the server to the outside world (this should be a registered domain name suported by DNS).

- `ServerAdmin`, the e-mail address of this virtual host's Webmaster.

- `Redirect`, which specifies any URLs that are to be redirected to other URLs.

- `ErrorLog`, which specifies the file where errors related to this virtual host are to be logged.

- `CustomLog`, which specifies the file where accesses to this virtual host are logged.

When the server receives a request for a document in a particular virtual host's `DocumentRoot` directory, it uses the configuration parameters within that server's `<VirtualHost>` block to handle that request.

Here is a typical example of a `<VirtualHost>` directive that sets up the virtual host `www.1nbsoft.com`:

```
<VirtualHost www.1nbsoft.com>
    DocumentRoot    /home/naba/httpd/htdocs
    ServerName    www.1nbsoft.com
    ServerAdmin    webmaster@1nbsoft.com
    ScriptAlias    /cgi-bin/    /home/naba/httpd/cgi-bin/
    ErrorLog    /usr/home/naba/httpd/logs/error_log
    CustomLog    /home/naba/httpd/logs/access_log common
</VirtualHost>
```

Here the name `common` in the `CustomLog` directive refers to the name of a format defined earlier in the `httpd.conf` file by the `LogFormat` directive, as follows:

```
LogFormat "%h %l %u %t \"%r\" %>s %b" common
```

This format string for the log produces lines in the log file that look like this:

```
dial236.dc.psn.net - - [29/Oct/2000:18:09:00 -0500] "GET / HTTP/1.0" 200 1243
```

The format string contains two letter tokens that start with a percent sign (%). The meaning of these tokens are shown in Table 17-1.

Table 17-1   LogFormat Tokens

Token	Meaning
%b	The number of bytes sent to the client, excluding header information
%h	The host name of the client machine
%l	The identity of the user, if available
%r	The HTTP request from the client (for example, `GET / HTTP/1.0`)
%s	The server response code from the Web server
%t	The current local date and time
%u	The user name supplied by the user (only when access control rules require user name/password authentication)

Summary

The World Wide Web (WWW or the Web) has propelled the Internet into the mainstream, because Web browsers make it easy for users to browse documents stored on various Internet hosts. Whether you run a small business, or manage computer systems and networks for a large company, chances are good that you have to set up and maintain a Web server. Because of its built-in networking support, a Red Hat Linux PC makes an affordable World Wide Web server. This chapter describes how to configure the Apache Web server on a Red Hat Linux PC.

By reading this chapter, you learn:

▶ The World Wide Web is possible because of the standard format for documents and the standard protocol for transferring a document across the network. The document format is HyperText Markup Language, or HTML. The standard document exchange protocol is HyperText Transfer Protocol, or HTTP.

▶ The Web has a client/server architecture, with Web servers providing the HTML documents (often referred to as *Web pages*) to Web-browser clients.

▶ The Uniform Resource Locator (URL) syntax uniquely identifies Web pages and other network resources. A URL identifies the location of the document (machine name and directory), as well as the protocol to be used to transfer the document (such as `http` or `ftp`).

▶ How to use Netscape Navigator, which comes on the CD-ROMs.

▶ Among Web servers, the most popular one is the Apache Web server. You can install the Apache Web server during Red Hat Linux installation. This chapter describes the Apache Web server configuration files and some of the configuration directives.

Chapter 18

Mail Server

You are probably familiar with electronic mail (or e-mail) — the mainstay of the Internet. E-mail enables you to exchange messages and documents with anyone on the Internet. One of the most common ways that people use the Internet is to keep in touch with friends, acquaintances, loved ones, and strangers through e-mail. You can send a message to a friend thousands of miles away and get a reply within a couple of minutes. Essentially, you can send messages anywhere in the world from an Internet host, and that message typically makes its way to its destination within minutes — something that you cannot do with regular paper mail.

Because e-mail can be stored and forwarded, you can arrange to send and receive e-mail without making your Linux system a full-time host on the Internet. You won't get the benefits of nearly immediate delivery of messages, however, if your system is not an Internet host.

This chapter introduces you to the mail software in Red Hat Linux, including mail readers such as `elm` and `pine`; and the `sendmail` mail server.

Installing Mail Software

During Red Hat Linux installation from this book's companion CD-ROMs, you have the option to install the necessary packages for World Wide Web, mail, and news. As described in Chapter 2, select the *Mail/WWW/News Tools* component when you are prompted for which components to install.

Cross-Reference

If you install the mail software during Red Hat Linux installation, you do not have to do much more to begin using the mail service. Otherwise, you can use the Red Hat Package Manager (RPM) to install individual packages. Chapter 24 describes how to use the `rpm` program to install new software.

To access the RPM files for mail, mount the CD-ROM with the following xcommand:

```
mount /mnt/cdrom
```

Then, change directory to `/mnt/cdrom/RedHat/RPMS`, where you will find the RPM files. Unless I explicitly indicate otherwise, the RPM file should be on the first CD-ROM. Some of the RPMs that you may want to install are as follows (I show the RPM name; the actual filename starts with the RPM name, has a version number, and ends with a `.rpm` extension):

- `elm` (a mail-user agent)
- `fetchmail` (a mail retrieval and forwarding utility)
- `imap` (an Internet Message Access Protocol server) — on the second CD-ROM
- `mailx` (a mail-user agent)
- `metamail` (software to handle MIME — Multipurpose Internet Mail Extensions)
- `pine` (a versatile mail and news program)
- `procmail` (a local mail-delivery package, meant to be invoked directly by `sendmail` or from a `.forward` file to automatically process mail; for example, to delete all mail from a specific address)
- `sendmail` (a complex mail-transport agent)
- `sendmail-cf` (configuration files for `sendmail`) — on the second CD-ROM
- `sendmail-doc` (documentation for `sendmail`) — on the second CD-ROM

You probably have already installed many of these packages. For this chapter, you should install `elm` and `sendmail` (as well as any other mail reader that you want to try).

To determine whether `sendmail` is installed on your system, type the following command:

```
rpm -q sendmail
sendmail-8.11.2-1
```

If the output shows `sendmail`, it's installed. In the preceding example, `sendmail` version 8.11 is installed on the system.

Understanding Electronic Mail

E-mail is one of the most popular services on the Internet. Everyone likes the convenience of being able to communicate without having to play the game of "phone tag," in which two people leave telephone messages for each other without successfully making contact. When you send an e-mail message, it waits in the recipient's mailbox to be read at the recipient's convenience.

E-mail started as a simple mechanism in which messages were copied to a user's mailbox file. That simple mechanism is still used. In Red Hat Linux, your mail messages are stored in the /var/spool/mail directory, in a text file with the same name as your user name.

Messages are addressed to a user name. That means that if John Doe logs in with the user name jdoe, e-mail to him is addressed to jdoe. The only other piece of information needed to uniquely identify the recipient is the *fully qualified domain name* of the recipient's system. Thus, if John Doe's system is named someplace.com, his complete e-mail address becomes jdoe@someplace.com. Given that address, anyone on the Internet can send e-mail to John Doe.

Red Hat Linux comes with all the software that you need to set up and use e-mail on your Linux system. The following sections guide you through various aspects of setting up and using e-mail on your Red Hat Linux system.

Mail Software

To set up and use e-mail on your Red Hat Linux PC, you need two types of mail software:

- *Mail-user agent* software enables you to read your mail messages, write replies, and compose new messages. Typically, the mail-user agent retrieves messages from the mail server using POP3 or IMAP4 protocol. POP3 is the Post Office Protocol Version 3 and IMAP4 is the Internet Message Access Protocol Version 4. Red Hat Linux comes with mail-user agents such as pine and elm. Netscape Communicator also includes a mail-user agent and a newsreader, besides the Web browser.

- *Mail-transport agent* software actually sends and receives mail-message text. The exact method used for mail transport depends on the underlying network. In TCP/IP networks, the mail-transport agent delivers mail using the Simple Mail Transfer Protocol (SMTP). Red Hat Linux includes sendmail, a powerful and popular mail-transport agent for TCP/IP networks.

Most mail-transport agents run as *daemons,* background processes that run as long as your system is up. Because you or another user on the system might send mail at any time, the transport agent has to be there to deliver the mail to its destination. The mail-user agent runs only when the user wants to check mail.

More on sendmail

This chapter shows you how to use a predefined sendmail configuration file to get e-mail going on your system. sendmail, however, is a very complex mail system. *Sendmail (Nutshell Handbook)* by Bryan Costales, Eric Allman, and Gigi Estabrook (O'Reilly & Associates, 1997) will help you learn to configure sendmail.

You should also visit www.sendmail.org and www.sendmail.net for a thorough

description of sendmail features and configuration examples.

For answers to commonly asked questions about sendmail or to ask a question yourself, visit the newsgroup comp.mail.sendmail (see Chapter 19 for more on reading newsgroups and posting articles to them).

Secret

Typically, a mail-transport agent is started after the system boots. The system startup files for Red Hat Linux are configured so that the sendmail mail-transport agent starts when the system is in multi-user mode. The shell script file /etc/init.d/sendmail starts sendmail.

Because the system is already set up to start sendmail at boot time, all you have to do is use an appropriate sendmail configuration file to get e-mail going on your Red Hat Linux system.

Using sendmail

To set up your system as a mail server, you must configure the sendmail mail-transport agent properly. sendmail has the reputation of being a complex but complete mail-delivery system. If you take a quick look at sendmail's configuration file, /etc/sendmail.cf, you'll immediately agree that sendmail is indeed complex. Luckily, you do not have to be an expert on the sendmail configuration file (a whole book has been written on that subject; see the sidebar "More on sendmail"). All you need is one of the predefined configuration files from this book's companion CD-ROMs.

If you have installed the *Mail/WWW/News Tools* component during Red Hat Linux installation (see Chapter 2), your system should already have a working sendmail configuration file — /etc/sendmail.cf. The default file assumes you have an Internet connection and a name server. Provided you have an Internet connection, you should be able to send and receive e-mail from your Red Hat Linux PC.

Secret

To ensure that mail delivery works correctly, your system's name must match the system name that your ISP assigned to you. Although you can give your system any host name that you want, other systems can successfully deliver mail to your system only if your system's name is in the ISP's name server.

A Mail-Delivery Test

I was able to send and receive e-mail immediately after installing Red Hat Linux because `sendmail` is installed as part of the basic operating system package. To try out the `sendmail` mail-transfer agent, I used the `mail` command to compose and send a mail message to myself at a different address, as follows:

```
mail naba@psn.net
Subject: Testing e-mail
This is from my Linux system.
.
Cc: Press Ctrl+D
```

The `mail` command is a simple mail-user agent. In the preceding example, I specify the addressee — `naba@psn.net` — in the command line. The mail program prompts for a subject line. Following the subject, I enter my message and end it with a line that contains only a period. After I end the message, the mail-user agent passes the message to `sendmail`—the mail-transport agent — for delivery to the specified address. Because my system was already connected to the Internet, `sendmail` delivered the mail message immediately.

To verify the delivery of mail, I dialed into my ISP from a Windows system and checked my mail. I also sent a short reply. (You cannot send a reply if your system does not have a host name in the ISP's DNS database.)

After I logged out of `psn.net`, I checked mail again on my Red Hat Linux PC to see if my reply made its way back to the Red Hat Linux PC. I used the `elm` program to read my mail on the Linux system. After I typed `elm`, a window appeared and `elm` displayed the current messages in my mailbox. I selected the message and pressed Enter. The output indicated that the reply from the other system had reached my system.

Thus, the initial `sendmail` configuration file that comes with Red Hat Linux should be adequate for sending and receiving e-mail, provided that your Red Hat Linux system has an Internet connection and a registered domain name.

The Mail-Delivery Mechanism

On an Internet host, the `sendmail` mail-transport agent delivers mail using the Simple Mail Transfer Protocol (SMTP). SMTP is documented in RFC 821, "Simple Mail Transfer Protocol," by Jonathan Postel, 1982.

SMTP-based mail-transport agents listen to the TCP port 25 and use a small set of text commands to interact with other mail-transport agents. In fact, the commands are simple enough that you can use them directly to send a mail message. The following example shows how I use SMTP commands to send a mail message to my account on the Linux PC from a `telnet` session running on another system on the local area network:

```
telnet lnbp200 25
Trying 192.168.1.200...
Connected to lnbp200.
Escape character is '^]'.
220 localhost.localdomain ESMTP Sendmail 8.11.0/8.11.0; Sun, 29 Oct 2000 21:51:3
7 -0500
HELP
214-2.0.0 This is sendmail version 8.11.0
214-2.0.0 Topics:
214-2.0.0       HELO    EHLO    MAIL    RCPT    DATA
214-2.0.0       RSET    NOOP    QUIT    HELP    VRFY
214-2.0.0       EXPN    VERB    ETRN    DSN     AUTH
214-2.0.0       STARTTLS
214-2.0.0 For more info use "HELP <topic>".
214-2.0.0 To report bugs in the implementation send email to
214-2.0.0       sendmail-bugs@sendmail.org.
214-2.0.0 For local information send email to Postmaster at your site.
214 2.0.0 End of HELP info
HELP DATA
214-2.0.0 DATA
214-2.0.0       Following text is collected as the message.
214-2.0.0       End with a single dot.
214 2.0.0 End of HELP info
HELO lnbp200
250 localhost.localdomain Hello lnbp75 [192.168.1.1], pleased to meet you
MAIL FROM: naba
553 5.5.4 naba... Domain name required
MAIL FROM:naba@5042-220.popsite.net
250 2.1.0 naba@5042-220.popsite.net... Sender ok
RCPT TO: naba
250 2.1.5 naba... Recipient ok
DATA
354 Enter mail, end with "." on a line by itself
Testing... 1 2 3
Sending mail by telnet to port 25
.
250 2.0.0 e9U2qkn16255 Message accepted for delivery
QUIT
221 2.0.0 localhost.localdomain closing connection
Connection closed by foreign host
```

The telnet command opens a telnet session to port 25 — the port on which sendmail expects SMTP commands. The sendmail process on the Red Hat Linux system immediately replies with an announcement.

I type HELP to view a list of SMTP commands. To get help on a specific command, I can type HELP *commandname*. The listing shows the help information printed by sendmail when I type HELP DATA.

I type HELO lnbp200 to initiate a session with the host named lnbp200. The sendmail process replies with a greeting. To send the mail message, I start with the MAIL FROM: command that specifies the sender of the message (I enter the user name on the system from which I am sending the message). sendmail requires a domain name along with the user name.

Next, I use the RCPT TO: command to specify the recipient of the message. If I want to send the message to several recipients, all I have to do is provide each recipient's address with the RCPT TO: command.

To enter the mail message, I use the DATA command. In response to the DATA command, sendmail displays an instruction that I should end the message with a period on a line by itself. I enter the message and end it with a single period on a separate line. The sendmail process displays a message indicating that the message has been accepted for delivery. Finally, I quit the sendmail session with the QUIT command.

Afterward, I log in to my Red Hat Linux system and check mail with the mail command. The following is what I see when I display the mail message that I sent through the sample SMTP session with sendmail:

```
mail
Mail version 8.1 6/6/93.  Type ? for help.
"/var/spool/mail/naba": 1 messages 1 new
>N  1 naba@5042-220.popsit  Sun Oct 29 21:53  12/440
& 1
Message 1:
From naba@5042-220.popsite.net  Sun Oct 29 21:53:46 2000
Date: Sun, 29 Oct 2000 21:53:14 -0500
From: naba@5042-220.popsite.net

Testing... 1 2 3
Sending mail by telnet to port 25

& q
Saved 1 message in mbox
```

As this example shows, the SMTP commands are simple enough to understand. This example should help you understand how a mail-transfer agent uses SMTP to transfer mail on the Internet. Of course, this whole process is automated by e-mail programs and the sendmail program (through settings in the sendmail configuration file /etc/sendmail.cf).

The sendmail Configuration File

You don't need to understand everything in the sendmail configuration file, /etc/sendmail.cf, but you should know how that file is created. That way, you can make minor changes if necessary, and then regenerate the /etc/sendmail.cf file.

To be able to regenerate the sendmail.cf file, you have to install the sendmail-cf package. This RPM file is located in the second CD-ROM bundled with this book. To install that package, log in as root and mount the second CD-ROM with the following command:

```
mount /mnt/cdrom
```

Then change to the `/mnt/cdrom/RedHat/RPMS` directory and install the package with the following:

```
cd /mnt/cdrom/RedHat/RPMS
rpm -ivh sendmail-cf*
```

The `sendmail-cf` package installs in the `/usr/lib/sendmail-cf` directory all the files needed to generate a new `sendmail.cf` configuration file. As you learn in the next few sections, the `sendmail.cf` file is generated from a number of m4 macro files. These macro files are organized into a number of subdirectories under `/usr/lib/sendmail-cf`. You can read the `README` file in `/usr/lib/sendmail-cf` to learn more about the creation of `sendmail` configuration files.

While you're at it, you can also install the `sendmail` documentation from the `sendmail-doc` package. To install that RPM, type the following command:

```
rpm -ivh sendmail-doc*
```

Note

The `sendmail-doc` package installs a number of documentation files in the `/usr/share/doc/sendmail` directory of your system. You can find a *Sendmail Installation and Operation Guide* in a PostScript file, `/usr/share/doc/sendmail/doc/op/op.ps`. You can use Ghostview to view that guide.

Now that you have taken care of the prerequisites, you can learn how to regenerate the `sendmail.cf` file.

m4 macro processor

The m4 macro processor is used to generate the `sendmail.cf` configuration file, which comes with the `sendmail` package in Red Hat Linux. The main macro file, `sendmail.mc`, is included with the `sendmail` package, but that file needs other m4 macro files that are in the `sendmail-cf` package. To be able to process the `sendmail.mc` file, you have to install the `sendmail-cf` package, as explained in the previous section. This section introduces you to the m4 macro processor.

A *macro* is basically a symbolic name for some action, or a long string of characters. A macro processor such as m4 usually reads its input file and copies it to the output, processing the macros along the way. The processing of a macro generally involves performing some action and generating some output. Because a macro generates a lot more text in the output than the macro's name, the processing of macros is referred to as *macro expansion*.

Cross-Reference

The m4 macro processor is the GNU implementation of the standard UNIX macro processor. Only a few simple m4 macros are described in this section, but there is much more to m4 than the simple examples shown here. It's essentially a new scripting language for generating configuration files. You can read the online manual about m4 by typing the command `info m4` at a shell prompt. Chapter 27 describes how to read online help using `info`.

Secret

Note that m4 is stream-based (like the sed editor, described in Chapter 11). That means it copies the input characters to the output while expanding any macros. The m4 macro processor does not have any concept of lines, so it copies newline characters to the output. That's why you see the word dnl in most m4 macro files; dnl is an m4 macro that stands for delete through newline. The dnl macro deletes all characters starting at the dnl up to and including the next newline character. The newline characters in the output don't cause any harm, they merely create unnecessary blank lines. The sendmail macro package uses dnl to avoid such blank lines in the output configuration file. Because dnl basically means delete everything up to the end of line, m4 macro files also use dnl as the prefix for comment lines.

To see a very simple use of m4, consider the following m4 macro file that defines two macros — hello and bye — and uses them in a form letter:

```
dnl #############################################
dnl #  File: ex.m4
dnl #  A simple exmapls of m4 macros
dnl #############################################
define('hello', 'Dear Sir/Madam')dnl
define('bye',
'Sincerely,


Customer Service')dnl
dnl Now type the letter and use the macros
hello,

This is to inform you that we received your recent inquiry.
We will respond to your question soon.

bye
```

Type this text using your favorite text editor and save in a file named ex.m4. You can name a macro file anything you like, but it is customary to use the .m4 extension for m4 macro files.

Before you process the macro file using m4, note the following key points illustrated by the preceding example:

- Use the dnl macro to start all the comment lines (for example, the first four lines in the example).

- End each macro definition with the dnl macro. Otherwise, when m4 processes the macro file, it will produce a blank line for each macro definition.

- Use the built-in m4 command define to define a new macro. The macro name and the value are both enclosed between a pair of left and right quotes ('...'). Note that you cannot use the plain single quote to enclose the macro name and definition.

Now process the macro file ex.m4 using m4, as follows:

```
m4 ex.m4
Dear Sir/Madam,

This is to inform you that we received your recent inquiry.
We will respond to your question soon.

Sincerely,


Customer Service
```

As you can see, m4 prints out the form letter on standard output, expanding the macros hello and bye into their defined values. If you want to save the form letter in a file called letter, use the shell's output redirection feature, like this:

```
m4 ex.m4 > letter
```

What if you want to use the words hello or bye in the letter without expanding them? You can do so by enclosing these macros in a pair of quotes ('...'). You have to do this for other predefined m4 macros, such as define. To use define as a plain word and not a macro to expand, you'd write 'define'.

sendmail.mc file

The simple example in the preceding section should give you an idea of how m4 macros are defined and used to create configuration files such as the sendmail.cf file. Essentially, many complex macros are written and stored in files in the /usr/lib/sendmail-cf directory. A top-level macro file sendmail.mc, described later in this section, brings in these macro files with the include macro (used to copy a file into the input stream).

By defining its own set of high-level macros in files located in the /usr/lib/sendmail-cf directory, sendmail essentially creates its own macro language. The sendmail macro files use the .mc extension. The primary sendmail macro file that you should configure is the sendmail.mc file, located in the /etc/mail directory.

Unlike the /etc/sendmail.cf file, the /etc/mail/sendmail.mc file is short and should be easier to work with. Here is the full listing of the /etc/mail/sendmail.mc file that comes with Red Hat Linux:

```
divert(-1)
dnl This is the macro config file used to generate the
/etc/sendmail.cf
dnl file. If you modify thei file you will have to regenerate the
dnl /etc/sendmail.cf by running this macro config through the m4
dnl preprocessor:
dnl
```

```
dnl        m4 /etc/sendmail.mc > /etc/sendmail.cf
dnl
dnl You will need to have the sendmail-cf package installed for this
to dnl work.
include('/usr/lib/sendmail-cf/m4/cf.m4')
VERSIONID('linux setup for Red Hat Linux')dnl
OSTYPE('linux')
define('confDEF_USER_ID',''8:12'')dnl
undefine('UUCP_RELAY')dnl
undefine('BITNET_RELAY')dnl
define('confAUTO_REBUILD')dnl
define('confTO_CONNECT', '1m')dnl
define('confTRY_NULL_MX_LIST',true)dnl
define('confDONT_PROBE_INTERFACES',true)dnl
define('PROCMAIL_MAILER_PATH','/usr/bin/procmail')dnl
define('ALIAS_FILE','/etc/aliases')dnl
define('STATUS_FILE', '/var/log/sendmail.st')dnl
define('UUCP_MAILER_MAX', '2000000')dnl
define('confUSERDB_SPEC', '/etc/mail/userdb.db')dnl
dnl define('confPRIVACY_FLAGS', 'authwarnings,novrfy,noexpn')dnl
dnl define('confTO_QUEUEWARN', '4h')dnl
dnl define('confTO_QUEUERETURN', '5d')dnl
dnl define('confQUEUE_LA', '12')dnl
dnl define('confREFUSE_LA', '18')dnl
FEATURE('smrsh','/usr/sbin/smrsh')dnl
FEATURE('mailertable','hash -o /etc/mail/mailertable')dnl
FEATURE('virtusertable','hash -o /etc/mail/virtusertable')dnl
FEATURE(redirect)dnl
FEATURE(always_add_domain)dnl
FEATURE(use_cw_file)dnl
FEATURE(local_procmail)dnl
FEATURE('access_db')dnl
FEATURE('blacklist_recipients')dnl
dnl We strongly recommend to comment this one out if you want to
protect
dnl yourself from spam. However, the laptop and users on computers
that do
dnl not hav 24x7 DNS do need this.
FEATURE('accept_unresolvable_domains')dnl
dnl FEATURE('relay_based_on_MX')dnl
MAILER(smtp)dnl
MAILER(procmail)dnl
```

As the comments (the lines begin with dnl) in the beginning of the file explain, you can generate the /etc/sendmail.cf file by running the sendmail.mc file through the m4 macro processor with the following command (you have to log in as root):

m4 /etc/mail/sendmail.mc > /etc/sendmail.cf

The comments also tell you that you need the sendmail-cf package to process this file.

From the previous section's description of m4 macros, you can see that the sendmail.mc file uses define to create new macros. You can also see the liberal use of dnl to avoid inserting too many blank lines into the output.

The other uppercase words such as OSTYPE, FEATURE, and MAILER are sendmail macros. These are defined in the .m4 files located in the subdirectories of the /usr/lib/sendmail-cf directory and are incorporated into the senbdmail.mc file with the following include macro:

```
include('/usr/lib/sendmail-cf/m4/cf.m4')
```

The /usr/lib/sendmail-cf/m4/cf.m4 file, in turn, includes the cfhead.m4 file, which includes other m4 files, and so on. The net effect is that, as the m4 macro processor processes the sendmail.mc file, the macro processor incorporates many m4 files from various subdirectories of /usr/lib/sendmail-cf.

Note the following points about the /etc/mail/sendmail.mc file:

- The VERSIONID('linux setup for Red Hat Linux') macro inserts the version information enclosed in quotes into the output.

- OSTYPE('linux') specifies the operating system to be Linux. You have to specify this early to ensure proper configuration. It is customary to place this macro right after the VERSIONID macro.

- MAILER(smtp) describes the mailer According to the /usr/lib/sendmail-cf/README file, MAILER declarations should always be placed at the end of the sendmail.mc file, and MAILER('smtp') should always precede MAILER('procmail'). The mailer smtp refers to the Simple Mail Transfer Protocol (SMTP) mailer.

- FEATURE macros request various special features. For example, FEATURE('blacklist_recipients') turns on the capability to block incoming mail for certain user names, hosts, or addresses. The specification for what mail to allow or refuse is placed in the access database (/etc/mail/access.db file). You also need the FEATURE('access_db') macro to turn on the access database.

Tip   The sendmail macros such as FEATURE and MAILER are described in the /usr/lib/sendmail-cf/README file. Consult that file to learn more about the sendmail macros before you make changes to the sendmail.mc file.

sendmail.cf File Syntax

The sendmail.cf file's syntax is designed to be easy to parse by the sendmail program, because sendmail reads this file whenever it starts. Human readability was not a primary consideration when the file's syntax was designed. Still, with a little explanation, you can understand the meaning of the control lines in sendmail.cf.

Each `sendmail` control line begins with a single-letter operator that defines the meaning of the rest of the line. A line that begins with a space or a tab is considered a continuation of the previous line. Blank lines and lines beginning with a pound sign (#) are comments.

Often, there is no space between the single-letter operator and the arguments that follow the operator. This makes the lines even harder to understand. For example, `sendmail.cf` uses the concept of a class — essentially a collection of phrases. You can define a class named P and add the phrase REDIRECT to that class with the following control line:

```
CPREDIRECT
```

Because everything is jumbled together, it's hard to decipher. On the other hand, to define a class named `Accept` and set it to the values OK and RELAY, you write the following:

```
C{Accept}OK RELAY
```

This may be slightly easier to understand because the delimiters (such as the class name, `Accept`) are enclosed in curly braces.

Other newer control lines are even easier to understand. For example, the line

```
O HelpFile=/etc/mail/helpfile
```

defines the option `HelpFile` as the filename `/etc/mail/helpfile`. That file contains help information used by `sendmail` when it receives a HELP command.

Table 18-1 summarizes the one-letter control operators used in `sendmail.cf`. Each entry also shows an example of that operator. This table should help you understand some of the lines in `sendmail.cf`.

Table 18-1   Control Operators Used in sendmail.cf

Operator	Description
C	Defines a class; a variable (think of it as a set) that can contain several values. For example, `Cwlocalhost` adds the name `localhost` to the class w.
D	Defines a macro, a name associated with a single value. For example, `DnMAILER-DAEMON` defines the macro n as `MAILER-DAEMON`.
F	Defines a class read from a file. For example, `Fw/etc/mail/local-host-names` reads the names of hosts from the file `/etc/mail/local-host-names` and adds them to the class w.

Continued

Table 18-1 *(continued)*

Operator	Description
H	Defines the format of header lines that sendmail inserts into a message. For example, H?P?Return-Path: <$g> defines the Return-Path: field of the header.
K	Defines a map (a key-value pair database). For example, Karith arith defines the map named arith as the compiled-in map of the same name.
M	Specifies a mailer. The following lines define the procmail mailer: Mprocmail,P=/usr/bin/procmail,F=DFMSPhnu9,S=EnvFromSMTP/HdrFromSMTP,R=EnvToSMTP/HdrFromSMTP,T=DNS/RFC822/X-Unix,A=procmail -Y -m $h $f $u
O	Assigns a value to an option. For example, O AliasFile=/etc/aliases defines the AliasFile option to /etc/aliases, which is the name of the sendmail alias file.
P	Defines values for the precedence field. For example, Pjunk=-100 sets to -100 the precedence of messages marked with the header field Precedence: junk.
R	Defines a rule (a rule has a left-hand side and a right-hand side; if input matches the left-hand side, it's replaced with the right-hand side — this is called *rewriting*). For example, the rewriting rule R$* ; $1 strips trailing semicolons.
S	Labels a ruleset that you can start defining with subsequent R control lines. For example, Scanonify=3 labels the next ruleset as canonify or ruleset 3.
T	Adds a user name to the trusted class (class t). For example, Troot adds root to the class of trusted users.
V	Defines the major version number of the configuration file. For example, V9/Berkeley defines the version number as 9.

Other sendmail Files

The /etc/mail directory contains other files that sendmail uses. These files are referenced in the sendmail configuration file, /etc/sendmail.cf. For example, here's the result of searching for the /etc/mail string in the /etc/sendmail.cf file:

```
grep "\/etc\/mail" /etc/sendmail.cf
Fw/etc/mail/local-host-names
FR-o /etc/mail/relay-domains
```

```
Kmailertable hash -o /etc/mail/mailertable
Kvirtuser hash -o /etc/mail/virtusertable
Kaccess hash /etc/mail/access
#O ErrorHeader=/etc/mail/error-header
O HelpFile=/etc/mail/helpfile
O UserDatabaseSpec=/etc/mail/userdb.db
#O ServiceSwitchFile=/etc/mail/service.switch
#O DefaultAuthInfo=/etc/mail/default-auth-info
#Ft/etc/mail/trusted-users
```

You can ignore the lines that begin with a hash mark or number sign (#)
because those lines are treated as comments by sendmail. The other lines
are sendmail control lines that refer to other files in the /etc/mail directory.

Following are the descriptions of these files (note that not all of these files
need to be present in your /etc/mail directory; and even when present, the
file may be empty):

- /etc/mail/access — Access list database to stop spam (unwanted
  mail)

- /etc/mail/helpfile — Help information for SMTP commands

- /etc/mail/local-host-names — Names by which this host is known

- /etc/mail/mailertable — Mailer table

- /etc/mail/relay-domains — Hosts that permit relaying

- /etc/mail/userdb.db — User database file

- /etc/mail/virtusertable — Database of incoming users

The .forward File

Users can redirect their own mail by placing a .forward file in their home
directory. The .forward file is a plain text file with a comma-separated list
of mail addresses. Any mail sent to the user is then forwarded to these
addresses. If the .forward file contains a single address, all e-mail for that
user is redirected to that single e-mail address. For example, suppose the following .forward file is placed in the home directory of a user named emily:

```
ashley
```

All e-mail addressed to emily is automatically sent to the user name ashley
on the same system. User emily does not receive any mail at all.

You can also forward to a user name on another system by listing the complete e-mail address. For example, I added a .forward file with the following line to send my messages (addressed to my user name naba) to the mail
address naba@psn.net:

```
naba@psn.net
```

Now suppose I also want to keep a copy of the message on this system, in addition to forwarding to the address naba@psn.net. I can do so by adding the following line to the .forward file:

```
naba@psn.net, naba\
```

I simply append my user name and end the line with a backslash. The backslash (\) at the end of the line stops sendmail from repeatedly forwarding the message (because when a copy is sent to my user name on the system, sendmail processes my .forward file again — the backslash tells sendmail not to repeatedly forward the message).

Another use of the .forward file is to run procmail to automatically handle some mail messages. For example, suppose you want to delete any e-mail message that comes from an address containing the string mailing_list. Here's what you would do to achieve that:

1. Create a .forward file in your home directory and place the following line in it:

```
"| /usr/bin/procmail"
```

This line causes sendmail to run the external program /usr/bin/procmail and send the e-mail messages to the input stream of that program.

2. Create a text file named .procmailrc in your home directory and place the following lines in that file:

```
# Delete mail from an address that contains mailing_list
:0
* ^From:.*mailing_list
/dev/null
```

3. Log in as root and set up a symbolic link in /etc/smrsh to the /usr/bin/procmail program with the following command:

```
ln -s /usr/bin/procmail /etc/smrsh/procmail
```

This step is necessary because sendmail uses the SendMail Restricted Shell — smrsh — to run external programs. Instead of running /usr/bin/procmail, smrsh will run /etc/smrsh/procmail. That's why you need the symbolic link. This is a security feature of sendmail that controls what external programs it can run.

That's it! Now if you receive any messages from an address containing mailing_list, the message will be deleted.

Tip

With procmail, you can also perform other chores, such as automatically storing messages in a file or forwarding messages to others. All you have to do is create an appropriate .procmailrc file in your home directory. To learn more about procmail, type **man procmail**; to see examples of .procmailrc, type **man procmailex**.

The sendmail Alias File

In addition to the `sendmail.cf` file, `sendmail` also consults an alias file named `/etc/aliases` to convert a name into an address. The location of the alias file appears in the `sendmail` configuration file.

Each alias is typically a shorter name for an e-mail address. The system administrator uses the `sendmail` alias file to forward mail, to create mailing lists (a single alias that identifies several users), or to refer to a user by several different names. For example, here are some typical aliases:

```
barkakati: naba
naba: naba@lnbsoft
all: naba, leha, ivy, emily, ashley
```

The first line says that mail addressed to `barkakati` should be delivered to the user named `naba` on the local system. The second line indicates that mail for `naba` should really be sent to the user name `naba` on the `lnbsoft` system. The last line defines `all` as the alias for the five users `naba`, `leha`, `ivy`, `emily`, and `ashley`.

As the next section explains, you can set up a mailing list simply by defining an alias in the `/etc/aliases` file.

A sendmail Alias Mailing List

You can implement a simple mailing list through a `sendmail` alias. In its simplest form, all you have to do is define an alias for the addresses in the `/etc/aliases` file. For example, suppose a large company has several Web sites (one in each major department), and the Webmasters decide to keep in touch through a mailing list. One of the Webmasters, Emily, volunteers to set up a mailing list for the group. To set up the mailing list, Emily (who logs in with the user name `emily`) adds the following alias to the `/etc/aliases` file:

```
webmasters: emily, webmaster@sales, webmaster@mktg,
        webmaster@appdev, ...,
        ...,
        webmaster@admin
```

In this case, the address list includes Emily and the Webmasters at all Web sites in the company (typically, mail to the Webmaster is addressed to the user name `webmaster`). If the list of addresses gets too long, end a line with a comma and then indent the next line with a tab character.

Secret

After defining an alias in the `/etc/aliases` file, you must log in as `root` and make the new alias active by typing the following command:

```
/usr/lib/sendmail -bi
```

You can use the absolute path name `/usr/lib/sendmail` to run `sendmail` because `/usr/lib/sendmail` is a symbolic link to the actual `sendmail` program file `/usr/sbin/sendmail`.

In addition to the webmasters alias, it's conventional to define two other aliases:

- The alias *listname*-request is where users send mail to subscribe to (or unsubscribe from) the list.

- The alias owner-*listname* is where errors (such as bounced messages) are sent.

In this case, because Emily sets up the webmasters list, she might define the two aliases as follows:

```
webmasters-request: emily
owner-webmasters: emily
```

For a simple mailing list, one person is usually responsible for everything about the list.

Storing the address list in a separate file

Although defining an alias with all the addresses works, the drawback is that you must edit the /etc/aliases file whenever you want to add a new name to the list. You need to log in as root to edit the /etc/aliases file (or ask the system administrator to edit the file for you). A better solution is to store the address list in a separate file in your home directory and make sendmail read that file with the :include: directive in the alias definition.

For example, Emily might put the address list for the webmasters alias in the /home/emily/mlist/webms file (assuming that /home/emily is the login directory of user emily). Then, the /etc/aliases file would reference the address list as follows:

```
webmasters: :include:/home/emily/mlist/webms
```

In the /home/emily/mlist/webms file, each address appears on a separate line:

```
emily (Emily B. -- list owner)
webmaster@appdev (Webmaster, Application Development Group)
webmaster@mktg (Webmaster, Marketing Department)
```

As you can see, you can put helpful comments in parentheses.

Every time sendmail sends a message to the webmasters alias, it reads the /home/emily/mlist/webms file. Thus, you can add a new user by simply editing this file.

If you use an address file, make sure that only the owner can modify the file. Use the command chmod 644 *filename* to set the permission properly.

Ensuring that replies go to the list

When you set up a mailing list, you want any replies to go to everyone in the list so that discussions can take place among the group. However, when you use a sendmail alias to define a mailing list, the reply goes to the person who sent the message instead of to the entire list. You can correct this problem by making the alias start a new `sendmail` process, and changing the sender's address through the `-f` option of `sendmail`.

Here's how you'd define the `webmasters` list using this approach:

```
webmasters: "|/usr/lib/sendmail -fwebmasters -oi dist-webmasters"
dist-webmasters: :include:/home/emily/mlist/webms
```

This definition of `webmasters` runs `sendmail` with the `-f` option (this option sets the From address of the message) and sends mail to another alias, `dist-webmasters`, that points to the file containing the actual addresses. The `-f` option works only when a trusted user, such as root sends mail.

Note

When mail for the list arrives from another system, `sendmail` runs under a trusted user name. Therefore, the mail is sent out with `webmasters` as the return address. Unfortunately, when a user on the local system sends mail, the `-f` option does not work because `sendmail` runs under that user's name (and the user probably is not considered a trusted user). A solution to this problem is to set up the mailing list on a system where none of the list members have an account (this ensures that mail to the list always comes from a remote system).

Summary

The Internet has become an essential part of everyday life, as Internet Service Providers have sprung up all over the United States and in much of the world. Online services, such as America Online (AOL) and Microsoft's MSN, now offer Internet mail and Web browsing, bringing even more people to the Internet. Because of its support for TCP/IP networking — the universal language of the Internet — a Linux PC is ideal as an Internet host. This chapter describes the e-mail service and shows you how to configure the `sendmail` server on a Red Hat Linux PC.

By reading this chapter, you learn the following:

▶ Electronic mail (e-mail) is one of the important services available on Internet hosts. This chapter describes e-mail service available on a Red Hat Linux PC.

▶ E-mail software comes in two parts: a mail-transport agent, which physically sends and receives mail messages; and a mail-user agent, which reads messages and prepares new messages.

▶ The companion CD-ROMs contain several mail-transfer agents and mail-user agents. This chapter describes how to use `sendmail` as a mail-transport agent.

▶ The `sendmail` configuration is complex, but you can get going with the configuration file that comes with Red Hat Linux. All you may need to do is set your Red Hat Linux PC's host name properly.

▶ To read e-mail, you can use `mail` or `elm`. Netscape Communicator also includes a mail reader that you can use.

▶ You can automatically forward messages to another address by placing a `.forward` file in your home directory. The `.forward` file should contain a comma-separated list of e-mail addresses.

▶ You can run the `procmail` mailer by invoking it from the `.forward` file. The typical use of `procmail` is to automatically delete unwanted messages and sort messages into different files.

▶ You can set up a mailing list using the `/etc/aliases` file, which stores aliases for `sendmail`.

Chapter 19

News Server

The Internet helps you communicate in many ways. With e-mail, you generally exchange messages with people whom you already know. Sometimes, however, you may want or need to participate in group discussions. If you are looking for help in setting up XFree86 on a system with the NVIDIA GeForce 256 AGP video chipset, for example, you may want to question someone who knows something about this subject. For that sort of communication, you can post a message on the appropriate Internet newsgroup; someone is likely to give you an answer.

Internet newsgroups are like the bulletin boards or forums on other online systems, such as America Online (AOL) and MSN. Essentially, the newsgroups provide a bulletin-board system that spans the globe. You'll find a wide variety of newsgroups — covering subjects ranging from politics to computers. For Linux-related questions, you can read and post articles to newsgroups, such as `comp.os.linux.networking` and `comp.os.linux.setup`. You can think of an Internet newsgroup as a gathering place — a virtual meeting place where you can ask questions and discuss various issues.

Red Hat Linux comes with the software needed to read newsgroups and to set up your own system as a news server. This chapter introduces you to newsgroups, and then describes how to configure and run the InterNetNews server, a popular news server. You also learn how to set up local newsgroups for your corporate intranet.

Using Simple News Strategies

Although using news is reasonably simple, a news server requires some effort on your part, if it is to be set up and maintained properly. Newsgroups in particular need a great deal of disk space, and access to a news server that will provide a news feed to your server. You need a large amount of disk space, because so many newsgroups exist, and the volume of messages can be quite high. In addition, the news articles must be purged periodically; otherwise, the disk will become filled. Even if you choose a small subset of newsgroups, you may need a hundred or so megabytes just to keep the news items on your system. Running a news server can be one of the most demanding Internet services you provide because of the bandwidth requirements, disk space, and the in-memory indexes and caches that news servers require for fast access to news articles.

If you get your Internet access from an ISP (Internet Service Provider), the ISP gives you access to a mail server and a news server. Then you can use mail software that downloads messages from the mail server, and a newsreader that reads newsgroups directly from the ISP's news server. If you are the sole user of your Linux PC, I strongly recommend this strategy for reading news. That way, you get to read news and post articles without the headache of having to maintain a news server.

Another option is to read news at a Web site, such as Deja.com's Usenet Discussion Service at `http://www.deja.com/usenet`. At that Web site, you can select a newsgroup to browse, and you can post replies to articles posted on various newsgroups. In this case, you don't even need access to a news server.

All these options may not be enough if you want to set up a news server for a company intranet and manage your newsgroups. You might do this to provide a forum for employees to discuss various topics and exchange knowledge with others. Internal newsgroups can be a good way to facilitate knowledge management within a company. To set up your own newsgroups, you have to set up a news server, such as `innd` that uses the Network News Transfer Protocol (NNTP). You learn about the news server later in this chapter.

The next section briefly describes the news-related software packages that you can install in Red Hat Linux.

Installing News Software

During Red Hat Linux installation from this book's companion CD-ROMs, you have the option to install the necessary packages for World Wide Web, mail, and news. As described in Chapter 2, select the *Mail/WWW/News Tools* component when you are prompted for which components to install.

Cross-Reference

If you install the mail and news software during Linux installation; you do not have to do much more to begin using the mail and news services. Otherwise, you can use the Red Hat Package Manager (RPM) to install individual packages. Chapter 24 describes how to use the `rpm` program to install new software.

To access the RPM files for news, mount the appropriate CD-ROM with the following command:

```
mount /mnt/cdrom
```

Then, change the directory to /mnt/cdrom/RedHat/RPMS. You will find the RPM files located in that directory. Following are some of the RPMs that you may want to install (I show the RPM name; the actual filename starts with the RPM name, has a version number, and ends with an .rpm extension):

- cleanfeed (a spam filter for news servers)
- inews (an Internet news program to post news)
- inn (InterNetNews, a TCP/IP-based news server)
- pine (a versatile mail and news program)
- slrn (a simple, NNTP-based newsreader)
- tin (a full-screen newsreader)
- trn (a newsreader for a remote news server)
- xrn (an X-based newsreader program for reading news from a remote NNTP server)

You probably have already installed most of these packages. For this chapter, you need only inn, tin, and trn (as well as any other mail or news reader that you want to try).

Understanding Newsgroups

Newsgroups originated in *Usenet*—a store-and-forward messaging network for exchanging electronic mail and news items. Usenet works like a telegraph in that news and mail are relayed from one system to another. In Usenet, the systems are not on any network; they simply dial up and use the UNIX-to-UNIX Copy Protocol (UUCP) to transfer text messages.

Note

Usenet is a very loosely connected collection of computers that has worked well and continues to be used because very little expense is involved in connecting to it. All you need is a modem and a site that is willing to store and forward your mail and news. You have to set up UUCP on your system, but you do not need a sustained network connection; just a few phone calls are all it takes to keep the e-mail and news flowing. The downside is that you cannot use TCP/IP services, such as the World Wide Web, Telnet, or FTP.

From their Usenet origins, the newsgroups have migrated to the Internet (even though the name Usenet is still used to refer to news). Instead of UUCP, the news is transported by means of the Network News Transfer Protocol (NNTP), which is described in RFC 977, "Network News Transfer Protocol: A Proposed Standard for the Stream-Based Transmission of News," by B. Kantor and P. Lapsley, 1986.

Although the news transport protocol has changed from UUCP to NNTP (although some sites still use UUCP), the store-and-forward concept of news transfer remains. Thus, if you want to get news on your Red Hat Linux system, you have to find a news server from which your system can download news.

Tip

If you have signed up with an Internet Service Provider, the ISP should provide you with access to a news server. Such Internet news servers communicate by using NNTP. Then you can use an NNTP-capable newsreader, such as tin, to access the news server and read selected newsgroups. You can also read news using the news reader that comes with Netscape Communicator (included with Red Hat Linux). This is the easiest way to access news on your Linux Internet host.

The following discussion about reading newsgroups assumes that you have obtained access to a news server from your ISP.

How to Read News

To read news, you need a *newsreader* — a program that enables you to select a newsgroup and view the items in that newsgroup. You also need to understand the newsgroup hierarchy and naming convention, which is described in the "Newsgroup hierarchy" section of this chapter. First, let's learn how to read news from a news server.

As with mail programs, quite a few newsreaders are available. Most newsreaders support *threading*, organizing the replies to each article as a separate thread (sequence) of articles. Of these programs, two are most popular:

- The *threaded read news* program, trn, which is an improved version of rn, the venerable *read news* program (rn). This newsreader is called "threaded" because it interconnects an article with any replies.

- The full-screen newsreader program, such as tin. Like trn, tin supports *threading*.

Red Hat Linux includes several newsreaders, including both trn and tin. Both newsreaders should already be installed, provided you selected the *Mail/WWW/News Tools* component during Red Hat Linux installation.

Setting the NNTPSERVER environment variable

To read news from a news server by using NNTP, you have to define the NNTPSERVER environment variable. Define this environment variable to your news server's name. Both tin and trn newsreaders look up the NNTPSERVER environment variable for the name of the news server to contact.

For example, my news server's name is news.psn.net. Therefore, I define the NNTPSERVER variable as follows:

```
export NNTPSERVER=news.psn.net
```

Creating a .newsrc file

Far too many newsgroups exist on the Internet. When a newsreader starts, it has to know which newsgroups you want to read. Both the `tin` and `trn` newsreaders expect to find a list of the newsgroups in a file named `.newsrc` in your home directory.

To prepare the `.newsrc` file, you need to know how to name the newsgroups. You learn more about naming newsgroups in the "Newsgroup hierarchy" section of this chapter.

If you are interested in information about Linux, create a `.newsrc` file, specifying the following newsgroups:

```
comp.os.linux.networking:
comp.os.linux.answers:
comp.os.linux.misc:
comp.os.linux.announce:
comp.os.linux.setup:
comp.os.linux.hardware:
```

Each line shows the name of a newsgroup, followed by a colon. After you begin to read news, the newsreader program fills in article numbers following the newsgroup name.

Running tin -r to read news

As long as you have set the NNTPSERVER environment variable to your news server's name, you can use either of the newsreaders — `trn` or `tin` — to read the news. Try reading the news with each of the newsreaders to decide which you like best.

To read news with `tin`, use the following command:

```
tin -r
tin 1.4.4 release 20000803 ("Vet for the Insane") [UNIX] (c) Copyright
1991-99 Iain Lea.
Connecting to news.psn.net...
Welcome to the WebUseNet Corp. NNTP Server Farm (Twister v1.2.0)
Reading groups from active file.../
Reading groups from newsrc file...|
Checking for new groups...
Reading attributes file...
Reading newsgroups file...
```

Secret

If, instead of connecting to the news server, `tin` prints an error message that says `Can't get a (fully-qualified) domain-name!`, your system does not have a host name of the form `my.company.com`. This is often the case for stand-alone hosts with dial-up, DSL, or cable modem connections to the Internet. To get around this problem, log in as root and add a bogus host name to your `/etc/hosts` file, like this:

```
127.0.0.1       localhost my.bogusdomain.com
```

Then type `hostname my.bogusdomain.com` to set your system's host name to that bogus name. Now the `tin -r` command should work properly.

The `-r` option causes `tin` to read news from a remote news server (the one that you specify through the NNTPSERVER environment variable). After `tin` starts, it connects to the news server and communicates using NNTP. The `tin` newsreader displays status messages as it progresses to the point at which it gathers the newsgroups listed in the `.newsrc` file in your home directory.

After obtaining information about the newsgroups from the news server, `tin` displays a welcome message. Press Enter to continue. Then, `tin` displays the newsgroups from your `.newsrc` file in a full-screen text menu, as shown in Figure 19-1.

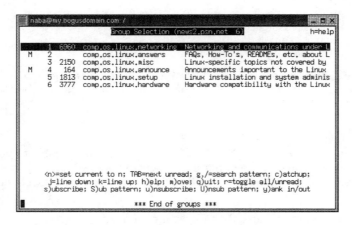

Figure 19-1: A typical newsgroup selection screen displayed by tin

The list of newsgroups that you see, of course, depends on the contents of the `.newsrc` file in your home directory. Figure 19-1 shows `tin`'s initial screen for my `.newsrc` file.

In `tin`'s newsgroup selection screen, you see the list of newsgroups in the top half of the screen, and some help information at the bottom of the screen. Initially, the first newsgroup is selected (it appears highlighted). Press **j** to go down the list; press **k** to go up. (Yes, the movement keys are the same as the ones used by the `vi` editor.) You also can press the up and down arrow keys to select a new newsgroup.

After you select a newsgroup to read, press Enter to view the list of articles in that newsgroup. Figure 19-2 shows the screen after selecting the `comp.os.linux.announce` newsgroup and pressing **j** to move down the list to an item of interest.

Figure 19-2: List of articles in a newsgroup (comp.os.linux.announce) as displayed by tin

You can then select an item, and press Enter to read that item. For example, if you press Enter with the first item selected (as shown in Figure 19-2), the tin newsreader downloads that article's text from the news server and displays it, as shown in Figure 19-3.

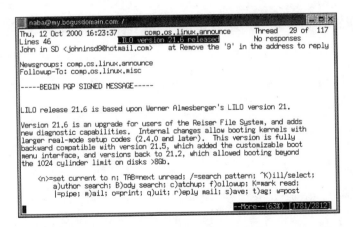

Figure 19-3: The tin newsreader displays the text of a news article.

You can read the article's text one screen at a time. To view the next screen, press the spacebar or PgDn. To return to the article selection menu, press **q**.

Pressing **q** again returns you to the newsgroup selection screen. To quit tin, press **q** in the newsgroup selection screen.

Although using `tin -r` to read news from a remote news server is simple, it can take a painfully long time for the newsreader to download news overviews and news items over a slower link. Even if you are using a PPP connection over a 56 Kbps modem, news reading over that PPP link is slow enough to make you wish for at least a 1.54-Mbps T1 link to your ISP.

Using an alternative newsreader: trn

It's also easy to read news with the `trn` newsreader. To read news from an NNTP news server, you need a version of `trn` configured for NNTP news access.

After you set the NNTPSERVER environment variable to the name of your news server, run `trn` as follows:

```
trn
Welcome to trn.  Here's some important things to remember:

    o  Trn is an extension of rn and has a similar command syntax.
    o  To access all the new features, specify the options -x and -X.  These
       options MAY be on by default, but it won't hurt to be redundant.
    o  Single-character commands don't require a carriage return -- only
       commands that let you type in an argument.
    o  At ANY prompt, you may type 'h' for help.  There are many different help
       menus, depending on the context.  Also, typing <esc>h in the middle of a
       multi-character command will list escape substitutions.
    o  Typing a space to any prompt means to do the normal thing.  You could
       spend all day reading news and never hit anything but the space bar.
    o  If you have never used the news system before, you may find the articles
       in news.announce.newusers to be helpful.
    o  Please consult the man page for complete information.

Creating /home/naba/.newsrc to be used by news programs.
Done.


To add new group use "a pattern" or "g newsgroup.name".  To get rid of
newsgroups you aren't interested in, use the 'u' command.
[Type space to continue]
Unread news in comp.os.linux.networking              6973 articles
Unread news in comp.os.linux.misc                    2147 articles
Unread news in comp.os.linux.announce                 164 articles
Unread news in comp.os.linux.setup                   1811 articles
Unread news in comp.os.linux.hardware                3775 articles
etc.

====== 6973 unread articles in comp.os.linux.networking -- read now? [+ynq]
```

The `trn` newsreader downloads information about the newsgroups listed in the `.newsrc` file in your home directory. Then `trn` displays the number of unread articles in the newsgroups.

Tip

Because of the Internet's chaotic nature, new newsgroups (especially the ones whose names begin with `alt`) are being added continually. If your `.newsrc` file does not contain the names of any recently added newsgroups, `trn` asks whether you want to subscribe to the new newsgroup. I generally press **N** (capital N) to indicate that I do not want to add any new newsgroups.

After displaying some messages about new newsgroups, `trn` prompts you with the name of the first newsgroup. To read that newsgroup, press **y** or Enter; to skip it, press **n**. To quit `trn`, press **q**.

If you select a newsgroup to read, `trn` gets an overview file for that news-group (that's the file with the list of articles in threaded order, so that each article is grouped with its replies). Then `trn` displays the list of articles in the selected newsgroup. A letter appears in the first column, identifying each thread. To view a thread, use the arrow keys to select a thread letter, and then press Enter. The `trn` newsreader downloads and displays the first arti-cle of that thread.

While you read articles, you can use several `trn` commands to navigate the articles. Typically, the commands are single letters.

To see the `trn` commands that are available at any time, press **h**.

Pressing **q** while you are reading an article returns you to the newsgroup selection level and displays a prompt for the next newsgroup. If you press **h** at this point, `trn` displays a list of article selection commands.

To quit `trn`, press **q** at the article selection prompt.

Reading newsgroups with Netscape Communicator

You can also browse newsgroups and post articles from Netscape Communicator, which comes with Red Hat Linux on this book's companion CD-ROMs. You can start Netscape Communicator by clicking the button with a big N on it, on the GNOME panel. To read newsgroups with Netscape Communicator, you must enter the name of the newsgroup server in the Netscape Preferences dialog box. To do this, select Edit ⇨ Preferences, and then select the Mail & Newsgroups item in the resulting dialog box.

After you add information about your newsgroup server, you can access newsgroups by selecting Communicator ⇨ Newsgroups, or by typing a news URL in the Location box on the toolbar (for example, type `news:comp.os.linux.announce` as the URL). In the resulting Netscape Mail & Newsgroups window, click on the newsgroup's name. This brings up a dialog box that asks you how many message headers you want to download. Once you have made your selection, Netscape starts downloading the headers for that newsgroup. From the list of headers, you can click on an item to read that item, as shown in Figure 19-4.

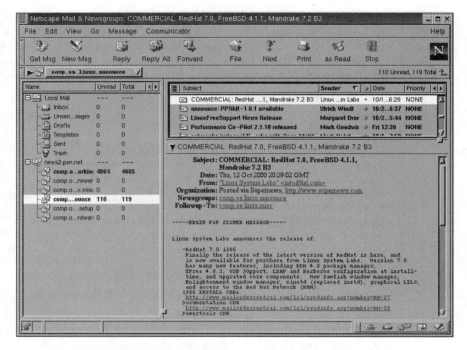

Figure 19-4: Using Netscape Communicator to read an item from comp.os.linux. announce

The newsgroup hierarchy

News items are organized in a hierarchy of newsgroups for ease of maintenance, as well as ease of use. A typical newsgroup name looks like the following:

```
comp.os.linux.announce
```

This name says that `comp.os.linux.announce` is a newsgroup for announcements (`announce`) about the Linux operating system (`os.linux`), and that these subjects fall under the broad category of computers (`comp`).

As you can see, the format of a newsgroup name is a sequence of words separated by periods. These words denote the hierarchy of the newsgroup.

To understand the newsgroup hierarchy, compare the newsgroup name with the path name of a file (such as `/usr/lib/X11/xinit/Xclients`) in Linux. Just as a file's path name shows the directory hierarchy of the file, the newsgroup name shows the newsgroup hierarchy. In filenames, a slash (/) separates the names of directories; in a newsgroup's name, a period separates the different levels in the newsgroup hierarchy.

In a newsgroup name, the first word represents the newsgroup category. The comp.os.linux.announce newsgroup, for example, is in the comp category, whereas alt.books.technical is in the alt category.

Table 19-1 lists some of the major newsgroup categories.

Table 19-1   Major Newsgroup Categories

Category	Subject
alt	"Alternative" newsgroups (not subject to any rules), which run the gamut from the mundane to the bizarre
bionet	Biology newsgroups
bit	Bitnet newsgroups
biz	Business newsgroups
clari	Clarinet news service (daily news)
comp	Computer hardware and software newsgroups
ieee	Newsgroups for the Institute of Electrical and Electronics Engineers
k12	Newsgroups devoted to elementary and secondary education
misc	Miscellaneous newsgroups
news	Newsgroups about Internet news administration
rec	Recreational and art newsgroups
sci	Science and engineering newsgroups
soc	Newsgroups for discussing social issues and various cultures
talk	Discussions of current issues (such as "talk radio")

This short list of categories is deceptive, because it does not really tell you about the wide-ranging variety of newsgroups available in each category. Because each newsgroup category contains several levels of subcategories, the overall count of newsgroups runs into several thousands. The comp category alone has more than 500 newsgroups.

Typically, you have to narrow your choice of newsgroups according to your interests. If you are interested in Linux, for example, you can pick one or more of these newsgroups:

■ comp.os.linux.admin — Information about Linux system administration.

■ comp.os.linux.advocacy — Discussions about promoting Linux.

- `comp.os.linux.announce`—Important announcements about Linux. This newsgroup is *moderated*, which means that you must mail the article to the moderator, who then posts it to the newsgroup if the article is appropriate for the newsgroup.

- `comp.os.linux.answers`—Questions and answers about Linux. All the Linux HOWTOs are posted in this moderated newsgroup. (See Chapter 10 for a list of Linux HOWTOs.)

- `comp.os.linux.development`—Current Linux development work.

- `comp.os.linux.development.apps`—Linux application development.

- `comp.os.linux.development.system`—Linux operating system development.

- `comp.os.linux.hardware`—Discussions about Linux and various types of hardware.

- `comp.os.linux.help`—Help with various aspects of Linux.

- `comp.os.linux.misc`—Miscellaneous Linux-related topics.

- `comp.os.linux.networking`—Networking under Linux.

- `comp.os.linux.setup`—Linux setup and installation.

- `comp.os.linux.x`—Discussions about setting up and running the X Window System under Linux.

You have to be selective about what newsgroups you read, because it's impossible to keep up with all the news, even in a specific area such as Linux. When you first install and set up Linux, you might read newsgroups such as `comp.os.linux.setup. comp.os.linux.hardware`, and `comp.os.linux.x` (especially if you run X). After you have Linux up and running, you may want to learn only about new things that are happening in Linux. For such information, you would read the `comp.os.linux.announce` newsgroup.

Newsgroup Subscriptions

Unlike magazines or newspapers, newsgroups do not require that you actually subscribe to them; you can read any newsgroup that is available on the news server. The news server administrator may decide to exclude certain newsgroups, however; in which case, you cannot read them.

The only thing that comes close to "subscribing" is the `.newsrc` file in your home directory. All newsreaders consult this file to determine which newsgroups you want to read. From inside the newsreader, you can use a command such as `g`, followed by the newsgroup name (in the `trn` newsreader), to subscribe to a newsgroup. When you subscribe to the newsgroup, the newsreader simply adds the name of that newsgroup to the `.newsrc` file.

How to Post News

You can use any newsreader to post a news item (a new item or a reply to an old posting) to one or more newsgroups. The exact command for posting a news item depends on the newsreader. For example, in the `trn` newsreader, follow these steps to post an article:

1. While you are reading an article in `trn`, press **f**. The newsreader asks whether you are posting an unrelated topic (unrelated to the article that you were reading when you pressed **f**). Press **y** to answer yes, as follows:

   ```
   Are you starting an unrelated topic? [ynq] y
   ```

2. The newsreader then prompts you for the subject of the new posting and the distribution. For this test posting, type a subject line with the word *ignore* in it. Otherwise, any site that receives your article will reply by mail to tell you that the article has reached the site; that's in keeping with the purpose of the `misc.test` newsgroup (which you'll shortly specify as the place to post this message). For distribution, enter **na** to indicate North America (or another distribution name that is defined in the `/var/lib/news/distributions` file), as follows:

   ```
   Subject: ignore no reply test

   Distribution: na
   ```

3. The newsreader uses the Pnews program to post an article to the news-groups. If you are posting an article for the first time, you see the following message:

   ```
   (leaving cbreak mode; cwd=/home/naba)


   I see you've never used this version of Pnews before. I will give
   you extra help this first time through, but then you must
   remember what you learned. If you don't understand any question,
   type h and a CR (carriage return) for help.


   If you've never posted an article to the net before, it is HIGHLY
   recommended that you read the netiquette document found in
   news.announce.newusers so that you'll know to avoid the commonest
   blunders. To do that, interrupt Pnews, get to the top-level
   prompt of [t]rn, and use the command "g news.announce.newusers"
   to go to that group.
   ```

4. After the preceding message, the newsreader asks whether you really want to post an article. Press **y** to continue.

   ```
   This program may post news to many machines.
   Are you absolutely sure that you want to do this? [ny] y
   ```

5. With the following prompt, the newsreader asks whether you have a file that you want to include as the news item:

```
Prepared file to include [none]:
```

Press Enter to continue.

6. The newsreader prompts you for the name of your editor (the default is vi) with the following explanation and prompt:

```
A temporary file has been created for you to edit. Be sure to
leave at least one blank line between the header and the body of
your message. (And until a certain bug is fixed all over the net,
don't start the body of your message with any indentation, or it
may get eaten.)


Within the header may be fields that you don't understand. If you
don't understand a field (or even if you do), you can simply
leave it blank, and it will go away when the article is posted.


Type return to get the default editor, or type the name of your
favorite editor.


Editor [/usr/bin/vi]:
```

Press Enter to compose the news article using vi.

7. The newsreader starts the vi editor. In the editor, you can fill in the name of the newsgroup and any other fields in the news article (including the body of the article). Following is what I filled in (I fill in the newsgroup name only):

```
Newsgroups: misc.test
Subject: ignore no reply test
Summary:
Expires:
Sender:
Followup-To:
Distribution: na
Organization:
Keywords: test ignore
```

```
Cc:
```

```
Testing ignore
```

Notice that there is no entry for the name of the organization. You can edit the field to show your organization's name or define the ORGANIZATION environment variable (set it to your organization's name) before you start trn. After you finish editing the article, save it with the :wq command.

8. The newsreader shows you the name (and a description) of the news-group to which you are about to post the article. Then trn prompts you for a command. Press **s** to send the article. The interaction with the newsreader goes like this:

```
Your article's newsgroup:

misc.test                    [no description available]


Check spelling, Send, Abort, Edit, or List? s
```

9. The trn newsreader then returns you to the article that you were reading when you started to post this article. Press **q** to quit the newsgroup that you have been reading.

10. Type **g misc.test** to subscribe to the misc.test newsgroup (that's where you just posted the new article).

11. Look at the latest article in misc.test, which should be the article that you just posted.

How to Verify Your Posting

If you post an article and read the newsgroup immediately, you'll see the new article, but that does not mean that the article has reached other sites on the Internet. After all, your posting shows up on your news server immediately, because that's where you posted the article. Because of the store-and-forward model of news distribution, the news article gradually propagates from your news server to others around the world.

Secret

The misc.test newsgroup provides a way to see whether your news posting is really getting around. If you post to that newsgroup and do not include the word *ignore* in the subject, news servers will acknowledge receipt of the article by sending an e-mail message to the address listed in the Reply-To field of the article's header.

If you have your Linux host on the Internet, try posting to the misc.test newsgroup to verify that articles are getting out. Be prepared to receive a dozen or so replies from various sites, acknowledging the arrival of your article at those sites.

Configuring and Starting the INN Server

So far, you have seen how to read news from an existing news server. Now you can turn to the subject of setting up an INN server on your system. Much of the InterNetNews (INN) software, bundled with Red Hat Linux, is already set up for you. What you need to do now is understand the various components of INN, edit the configuration files, and start innd — the INN server. I also refer to the INN server as the *news server*.

If you want to support a selection of Internet newsgroups, you also have to arrange for a *news feed* — this is the source from which your news server will get the newsgroup articles. Typically, you can get a news feed from an ISP for an additional monthly fee, to cover the cost of resources required to provide the feed. You will need the name of this *upstream* server that provides the news feed, and you have to provide that server with your server's name and the newsgroups you want to receive.

Based on the newsgroups you want to receive and the number of days you want to retain articles, you have to set aside disk space for the articles. The newsgroups are stored in a directory hierarchy (based on the newsgroup names) in the /var/spool/news directory of your system. If you are setting up a news server, you may want to devote a large disk partition to the /var/spool/news directory.

In your news server's configuration files, enter the name of the server providing the news feed. At the same time, also add to the configuration files the names of any *downstream* news servers, if any, that will receive news feeds from your server. Then you can start the news server and wait for news to arrive. Monitor the log files to ensure that the news articles are being sorted and stored properly in the /var/spool/news directory on your system.

Once you have news up and running, you must run news maintenance and cleanup scripts. These are run using the cron jobs (see Chapter 23 for more information about cron jobs). On Red Hat Linux, a cron job is already set up to run the /usr/bin/news.daily script to perform the news maintenance tasks.

Note

The following sections introduce you to INN setup, but you can learn more about INN by reading the online documentation in the /usr/share/doc directory. Type the command cd /usr/share/doc/inn* to change to the INN documentation directory. In the faq subdirectory you can find a number of HTML files with answers to frequently asked questions (FAQs) about INN. Start Netscape Communicator and open the part1.html file from the faq directory. Browse the FAQ to learn more about INN setup and use.

Another good source of information about INN is the Internet Software Consortium (ISC), a nonprofit corporation dedicated to developing and maintaining open source Internet software, such as BIND (an implementation of Domain Name System), DHCP (Dynamic Host Configuration Protocol), and INN. Rich Salz originally wrote INN; ISC took over the development of INN in 1996. You can learn more about INN, and access other resources at ISC's INN Web page (http://www.isc.org/products/INN/).

InterNetNews Components

INN includes several programs that perform specific newsgroup delivery and management tasks. It also includes a number of files that control how the INN programs work. The most important INN programs are as follows:

- innd—The news server. It runs as a daemon—a background process that keeps itself running in order to provide a specific service—and listens on the NNTP port (TCP port 119). The innd server accepts connections from other feed sites, as well as local newsreader clients, but it hands off local connections to the nnrpd.

- nnrpd—A special server, invoked by innd to handle requests from local news reader clients.

- expire—Removes old articles based on the specifications in the text file /etc/news/expire.ctl.

- nntpsend—Invokes the innxmit program to send news articles to a remote site using NNTP. The configuration file /etc/news/nntpsend.ctl controls the nntpsend program.

- ctlinnd—Enables you to interactively control the innd server. The ctlinnd program can send messages to the control channel of the innd server.

The other important components of INN are the control files. Most of these files are in the /etc/news directory of your Red Hat Linux system, but a few are in the /var/lib/news directory also. Between the two directories, there are over 30 INN control files. Some of the important files include the following:

- /etc/news/inn.conf—Specifies configuration data for the innd server. (To view online help for this file, type man inn.conf.)

- /etc/news/newsfeeds—Specifies what articles to feed downstream to other news servers. (The file is complicated, but you can get help by typing man newsfeeds.)

- /etc/news/incoming.conf—Lists the names and addresses of hosts that provide news feeds to this server. (To view online help for this file, type man incoming.conf.)

- /etc/news/expire.ctl—Controls expiration of articles, on a per-newsgroup level, if desired. (To view online help for this file, type man expire.ctl.)

- /var/lib/news/active—Lists all active newsgroups, showing the oldest and newest article number for each, and each newsgroup's posting status. (To view online help for this file, type man active.)

- /var/lib/news/newsgroups—Lists newsgroups, with a brief description of each.

■ /etc/news/nnrp.access — Lists the hosts that are permitted to read news from this news server — the default file allows only the localhost to read mail; you have to edit it if you want to allow other hosts in your local area network to read news. (To view online help for this file, type man nnrp.access.)

The next few sections describe how to set up some of the control files.

inn.conf

This file holds configuration data for all INN programs and, as such, is the most important file. Each line of the file has the value of a parameter in the following format:

```
parameter:        value
```

Depending on the parameter, the value is a string, a number, or true or false. As in many other configuration files, comment lines begin with a number, or pound sign (#).

Most of the parameters in the default inn.conf file in the /etc/news directory should not require any changes. You might want to edit one or more of the parameters shown in Table 19-2.

Table 19-2   Configuration Parameters in /etc/news/inn.conf

Parameter Name	Description
Organization	Set this to the name of your organization in the way you want it to appear in the Organization: header of all news articles posted from your system. Users may override this by defining the ORGANIZATION environment variable.
pathhost	Set this to the name of your news server as you want it to appear in the Path header of all postings that go through your server. If pathhost is not defined, the fully qualified domain name of your system is used.
domain	Set this to the domain name for your server.
allownewnews	Set this to true if you want INN to support the NEWNEWS command from news readers. Because this command can drastically reduce your server's performance, INN documentation recommends that you set this to false.
storageapi	Set this to true if you want articles to be stored using the Storage Manager API. The default setting of false causes INN to use the traditional article storage method of storing one article per file. If you set this to true, you have to choose between the storage methods timehash and cnfs, and you have to create new spool and database files (type man storage.conf to read more about cnfs and timehash storage methods). For a small number of newsgroups, you can leave this option at its default value of false.

Parameter Name	Description
hiscachesize	Set this to the size in kilobytes that you want INN to use for caching recently used history file entries. The default setting of 0 disables history caching. Because history caching can greatly increase the number of articles your server can process per second, you may want to set a value of 16384 (for 16MB), if you have enough RAM in your system.
innflags	Set this to any flags you want to pass to the INN server process when it starts up.

newsfeeds

The newsfeeds file specifies how incoming news articles are redistributed to other servers and to INN processes. If you provide news feeds to other servers, you have to list these news feeds in this file. (You also must have an entry labeled ME, which serves a special purpose explained later in this section.)

The newsfeeds file contains a series of entries, one for each feed. Each feed entry has the following format:

```
site[/exclude,exclude...]\
      :pattern,pattern...[/distrib,distrib...]\
      :flag,flag...\
      :param
```

Each entry has four fields separated by colons (:). Usually, the entries span multiple lines; and a backslash (\) at the end of the line is used to continue a line to the next. Following are the four fields:

1. The first field, *site*, is the name of the feed. Each name must be unique, and for feeds to other news servers, the name is set to the host name of the remote server. Following the name is an optional slash and an exclude list (*/exclude,exclude...*) consisting of a list of names. If any of the names in this list appear in the Path line of an article, that article will not be forwarded to the feed. You can use an exclude list if you don't want to receive articles from a specific source.

2. The second field consists of a comma-separated list of newsgroup patterns, such as *,@alt.binaries.warez.*,!control*,!local*, followed by an optional distribution list. The distribution list is a list of comma-separated keywords, with each keyword specifying a specific set of sites to which the articles are distributed. The newsgroup patterns essentially define a subscription list of sites that receive this news feed An asterisk matches all newsgroups. A pattern beginning with an @ causes newsgroups matching that pattern to be dropped. A pattern that begins with an exclamation mark (!) means that the matching newsgroups are not sent. By the way, the simple pattern-matching syntax used in INN configuration files is referred to as a *wildmat* pattern.

3. The third field is a comma-separated list of flags. These flags determine the feed entry type and sets certain parameters for the entry. There are numerous flags; you should type `man newsfeeds` and read the man page for more information about the flags.

4. The fourth field is for parameters whose values depend on the settings in the third field. Typically, this field contains names of files, or external programs that the INN server uses. You can learn more about this field from the `newsfeeds` man page.

Now that you know the layout of the `/etc/news/newsfeeds` file, you can study that file as an example. The default file contains many sample feed entries, but only two are commented out:

- `ME` is a special feed entry that's always required. It serves two purposes. First, the newsgroup patterns listed in this entry are preprended to all newsgroup patterns in all other entries. Second, the `ME` entry's distribution list determines what distributions your server accepts from remote sites.

- The `controlchan` feed entry is used to set up INN so that an external program is used to handle control messages (these messages are used to create new newsgroups and remove groups). For example, the following `controlchan` entry specifies the external program `/usr/bin/controlchan` to handle all control messages, except cancel messages (meant for canceling an article):

```
controlchan!\
        :!*,control,control.*,!control.cancel\
        :Tc,Wnsm:/usr/bin/controlchan
```

In addition to these feed entries, you would add entries for any actual sites to which your news server provides news feed. Such entries have the format

```
feedme.domain.com\
                :!junk,!control/!foo\
                :Tm:innfeed!
```

where *feedme.domain.com* is the fully qualified domain name of the site to which your system sends news articles.

incoming.conf

The `incoming.conf` file describes which hosts are allowed to connect to your host to feed articles (in versions of INN prior to 2.2.3, a file named `hosts.nntp` was used to specify remote hosts allowed to transfer articles to the local site). For a single feed, you can add an entry like

```
peer a-feed-site.domain.com {
}
```

where *a-feed-site.domain.com* identifies the site that feeds your site.

Keep in mind that simply adding a site's name in the `incoming.conf` file does not cause that remote site to start feeding your site news — it simply enables your server to accept news articles from the remote site. At the remote site, the server must be configured to actually send articles to your site.

nnrp.access

This file specifies the hosts or IP addresses from which newsreader clients (such as Netscape Communicator, `tin`, or `trn`) can retrieve newsgroups from your server. For example, the following `nnrp.access` file allows read access and post access (meaning that you can submit articles) from `localhost` and any host in the network 192.168.1.0:

```
# Default to no access
*:: -no- : -no- :!*
# Allow access from localhost and from the 192.168.1.0 network
localhost:Read Post:::*
192.168.1.0/24:Read Post:::*
```

InterNetNews Startup

In addition to the configuration files, you also need to initiate `cron` jobs that perform periodic maintenance of the news server. In Red Hat Linux, these `cron` jobs are already set up. Therefore, you are now ready to start the INN server — `innd`.

As with any other servers in Red Hat Linux, to start `innd`, log in as root and type the following command:

```
/etc/init.d/innd start
```

If you change any configuration file (such as `inn.conf` or `newsfeeds`), restart the `innd` server with the following command:

```
/etc/init.d/innd restart
```

Setting Up Local Newsgroups

If you want to use newsgroups as a way to share information within your company, you can set up a hierarchy of local newsgroups. Then you can use these newsgroups to create virtual communities within your company, where people with shared interests can informally discuss issues and exchange knowledge.

Defining a Newsgroup Hierarchy

The first task is to define a hierarchy of newsgroups and decide what each newsgroup will discuss. For example, if your company name is XYZ Corporation, here's a partial hierarchy of newsgroups that you might define:

- `xyz.general` — General items about XYZ Corporation
- `xyz.weekly.news` — Weekly news
- `xyz.weekly.menu` — The weekly cafeteria menu and any discussions about it
- `xyz.forsale` — A listing of items offered for sale by employees
- `xyz.jobs` — Job openings at XYZ Corporation
- `xyz.wanted` — Wanted (help, items to buy, and so on) postings by employees
- `xyz.technical.hardware` — Technical discussions about hardware
- `xyz.technical.software` — Technical discussions about software

Updating Configuration Files

Add descriptive entries for each of these newsgroups to the `/var/lib/news/newsgroups` file. Here are some entries from the `/var/lib/news/newsgroups` file:

```
control          Usenet control messages - DO NOT REMOVE
control.cancel   Usenet control messages - DO NOT REMOVE
junk             Articles for missing newsgroups - DO NOT REMOVE
test             A place for test posts - DO NOT REMOVE
to               Special Group for INN use - DO NOT REMOVE
```

Add a line for each newsgroup — type its name, followed by a brief description.

Next, edit the ME entry in the `/etc/news/newsfeeds` file and add the phrase `!xyz.*` to the comma-separated list of newsgroup patterns. This will ensure that your local newsgroups are not distributed outside your site.

Adding the Newsgroups

The final remaining step is to add the newsgroups. Once you have `innd` running, it's very easy to add a local newsgroup. Log in as root and use `ctlinnd` to perform this task. For example, here's how you would add a newsgroup named `xyz.general`:

```
ctlinnd newgroup xyz.general
```

That's it! That command adds the `xyz.general` newsgroup to your site. If you use the traditional storage method, the `innd` server creates the directory `/var/spool/news/articles/xyz/general` and stores articles for that newsgroup in that directory.

Once you have created all the local newsgroups, users from your intranet should be able to post news articles and read articles in the local news-groups. If they have problems accessing the newsgroups, make sure that the /etc/news/nnrp.access file contains the IP addresses or names of the hosts that should be able to access the innd server.

Testing Your Newsgroups

For example, I added a newsgroup named local.news on an INN server running on my Red Hat Linux system, using the instructions explained in he previous sections. Then I started Netscape Communicator on another system on the LAN and edited the preferences so that the news server was set to my INN server. Then I accessed the local.news newsgroup, by typing news:local.news as the URL. Figure 19-5 shows the newsgroup with the test message I posted to it.

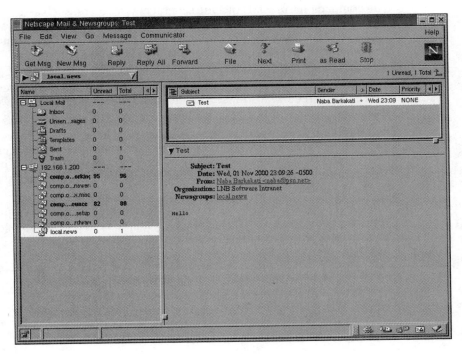

Figure 19-5: Reading the local newsgroup local.news

Summary

Internet newsgroups provide a convenient way to discuss various topics and share your knowledge with others. This chapter describes newsgroups and shows you how to set up a news server on your Red Hat Linux PC.

By reading this chapter, you learn the following:

▶ Newsgroups originated in Usenet, which is a store-and-forward network. News items travel around the world from one system to another. Nowadays, news is transported over the Internet by means of the Network News Transport Protocol (NNTP).

▶ Because thousands of newsgroups exist, storing all the news articles takes a great deal of disk space. Moreover, the articles must be purged periodically; otherwise, the disk will become filled. It's best to read news from a news server maintained by an Internet Service Provider (ISP).

▶ The companion CD-ROMs include several newsreaders, such as tin and trn. This chapter shows you how to use these newsreaders to read news from a designated news server. You can also read news with Netscape Communicator (included with Red Hat Linux on one of the CD-ROMs).

▶ To read newsgroups from a news server, you should set the environment variable NNTPSERVER to the name of the news server. You should also create in your home directory a .newsrc file that lists the newsgroups you want to read.

▶ Red Hat Linux comes with all the software and configuration files you need for the InterNetNews (INN) server. If you want to provide all Internet newsgroups, you have to find a site that is willing to provide you with a news feed. This chapter shows you how to set up the INN configuration files and start the innd server.

▶ You can use local newsgroups to provide discussion forums to employees in your company. Once innd is running, it's simple to add local newsgroups. This chapter shows you how to add such local newsgroups.

Chapter 20

FTP Server

File Transfer Protocol (FTP) is a popular client/server software for transferring files from one system to another. If you have an ISP account that provides you with a home page, you've probably used FTP to upload your Web pages to the ISP's server. Using an FTP client, you log into your ISP account and copy the files from your home system to the ISP's server.

You can also use FTP to download other files, such as open source software from Internet hosts. In this case, you don't need an account on the remote system. You simply log in using the anonymous user name and provide your e-mail address as the password. This is called anonymous FTP. If you want to enable others to download files from your system using FTP, you can set up anonymous FTP on your system so that users can log in with the user name anonymous.

Red Hat Linux comes with several FTP clients and the Washington University FTP daemon (wu-ftpd), which is a popular FTP server. Red Hat Linux also includes a package called anonftp that sets up the files you need to support anonymous FTP. This chapter introduces you to a few FTP clients and, for the command-line FTP client, describes the commands you use to work with remote directories. It also shows you how to configure the FTP server through text configuration files, and how to control access to the FTP server. Finally, this chapter describes anonymous FTP — how it's set up and how to ensure that it's secure.

Installing FTP software

During Red Hat Linux installation from this book's companion CD-ROMs, you have the option to install the necessary packages for FTP. As described in Chapter 2, select the *Anonymous FTP Server* package group when you are prompted for which packages to install.

**Cross-
Reference**

If you install the *Anonymous FTP Server* package group during Linux installation, you do not have to do much more to begin using the mail and news services. Otherwise, you can use the Red Hat Package Manager (RPM) to install individual packages. Chapter 24 describes how to use the rpm program to install new software.

To access the RPM files for FTP, mount the appropriate CD-ROM with the following command:

```
mount /mnt/cdrom
```

Then, change the directory to /mnt/cdrom/RedHat/RPMS, where you will find the RPM files. Following are some of the RPMs that you may want to install (shown is the RPM name; the actual filename starts with the RPM name, has a version number, and ends with a .rpm extension):

- wu-ftpd (the Washington University FTP daemon — an FTP server)
- anonftp (anonymous FTP setup files)
- ftp (an FTP client)
- gftp (X Window System–based graphical FTP client)
- ncftp (another FTP client)

You probably have already installed all of these packages. For this chapter, you should install wu-ftpd, anonftp, and ftp. The gftp package should be installed when you install the GNOME package group.

Understanding FTP

As the name implies, the File Transfer Protocol (FTP) enables users to transfer files between systems on the Internet. FTP is client/server software — you can use the FTP client on a system to access files on another Internet host. The FTP server on that host acts on commands you send via the FTP client.

The FTP clients and servers exchange information by using the File Transfer Protocol, which is described in RFC 959, "File Transfer Protocol," by J. Postel and J. K. Reynolds, October 1985. FTP uses two TCP ports — data is transferred on port 20, while control information is exchanged on port 21.

With FTP, you can download files from other Internet hosts, or from hosts in your local area network. Reciprocally, users on other systems also can download files from your system; typically, through a feature known as *anonymous FTP.* You learn how to set up anonymous FTP service in the section "Setting Up Secure Anonymous FTP."

The next few sections introduce you to FTP for transferring files and working with remote directories. In addition to the FTP commands, you also learn about the graphical FTP clients and how to use FTP through your Web browser.

The Command-Line FTP Client

To see how FTP works, try the command-line FTP client. You can try out the FTP commands from another system on a local area network, or on your Red Hat Linux system. For example, the following sample FTP session shows how I use the command-line FTP client to log in using my user name (naba) and browse around the directories on my system (my comments appear in italics):

```
ftp localhost
Connected to lnbp200.
220 lnbp200 FTP server (Version wu-2.6.1(1) Wed Aug 9 05:54:50 EDT
2000) ready.
Name (localhost:naba):  (I press Enter)
331 Password required for naba.
Password:        (I type my password)
230 User naba logged in.
Remote system type is UNIX.
Using binary mode to transfer files.
ftp> help        (I type help to see a list of FTP commands)
Commands may be abbreviated.  Commands are:

!           debug        mdir        sendport    site
$           dir          mget        put         size
account     disconnect   mkdir       pwd         status
append      exit         mls         quit        struct
ascii       form         mode        quote       system
bell        get          modtime     recv        sunique
binary      glob         mput        reget       tenex
bye         hash         newer       rstatus     tick
case        help         nmap        rhelp       trace
cd          idle         nlist       rename      type
cdup        image        ntrans      reset       user
chmod       lcd          open        restart     umask
close       ls           prompt      rmdir       verbose
cr          macdef       passive     runique     ?
delete      mdelete      proxy       send
ftp> help mget    (I can get help on a specific comand)
mget        get multiple files
ftp> cd /var/ftp (This changes directory to /var/ftp)
250 CWD command successful.
ftp> ls          (This command lists the contents of the directory)
227 Entering Passive Mode (127,0,0,1,177,99)
150 Opening ASCII mode data connection for /bin/ls.
total 16
d--x--x--x    2 root      root         4096 Oct  4 16:43 bin
```

```
d--x--x--x    2 root      root           4096 Oct  4 16:43 etc
drwxr-xr-x    2 root      root           4096 Oct  4 16:43 lib
drwxr-sr-x    2 root      ftp            4096 Aug 17 10:53 pub
226 Transfer complete.
ftp> bye          (This command ends the session)
221-You have transferred 0 bytes in 0 files.
221-Total traffic for this session was 2080 bytes in 2 transfers.
221-Thank you for using the FTP service on lnbp200.
221 Goodbye.
```

As the listing shows, you can start the command-line FTP client by typing the command ftp *hostname,* where *hostname* is the name of the system you want to access. Once the FTP client establishes a connection with the FTP server at the remote system, the FTP server prompts you for a user name and password. After you've supplied the information, the FTP client displays the ftp> prompt and you can begin typing commands to perform specific tasks. If you can't remember a specific FTP command, type help to view a list of them. You can get additional help for a specific command by typing help *command.*

Many of the FTP commands are similar to UNIX commands for navigating the file system. For example, cd changes directory, pwd prints the name of the current working directory, and ls lists the contents of the current directory. Two other common commands are get and put — get downloads a file from the remote system to your system, and put uploads (sends) a file from your system to the remote host.

Table 20-1 describes some commonly used FTP commands. Note that you do not have to type the entire FTP command. For a long command, you only have to type the first characters — enough to uniquely identify the command. For example, to delete a file, you can type dele; and to change the file transfer mode to binary, you can type bin.

Table 20-1   List of Commonly Used FTP Commands

Command	Description
!	Executes a shell command on the local system. For example, !ls lists the contents of the current directory on the remote system.
?	Displays list of commands (same as help)
append	Appends a local file to a remote file
ascii	Sets the file transfer type to ASCII (or plain text). This is the default file transfer type.
binary	Sets the file transfer type to binary
bye	Ends the FTP session with the remote FTP server and quits the FTP client

Command	Description
cd	Changes directory on the remote system. For example, cd /pub/Linux changes the remote directory to /pub/Linux.
chmod	Changes the permission settings of a remote file. For example, chmod 644 index.html changes the permission settings of the index.html file on the remote system.
close	Ends the FTP session with the FTP server and returns to the FTP client's prompt
delete	Deletes a remote file. For example, delete bigimage.jpg deletes that file on the remote system.
dir	Lists the contents of the current directory on the remote system
disconnect	Ends the FTP session and returns to the FTP client's prompt. (This is the same as close.)
get	Downloads a remote file. For example, get junk.tar.gz junk.tgz downloads the file junk.tar.gz from the remote system and saves it as the file junk.tgz on the local system.
hash	Turns on or off hash mark (#) printing showing the progress of file transfer. When turned on, a hash mark is printed for every 1,024 bytes transferred from the remote system.
help	Displays a list of commands
image	Same as binary
lcd	Changes the current directory on the local system. For example, lcd /var/ftp/pub changes the current local directory to /var/ftp/pub.
ls	Lists the contents of the current remote directory
mdelete	Deletes multiple files on a remote system. For example, mdelete *.jpg deletes all remote files with names ending in .jpg in the current directory.
mdir	Lists multiple remote files and saves the listing in a specified local file. For example, mdir /usr/share/doc/w* wlist saves the listing in the local file named wlist.
mget	Downloads multiple files. For example, mget *.jpg downloads all files with names ending in .jpg. If prompt is turned on, the FTP client asks for confirmation before each file is downloaded.
mkdir	Creates a directory on the remote system. mkdir images creates a directory named images in the current directory on the remote system.
mls	Same as mdir

Continued

Table 20-1 *(continued)*

Command	Description
mput	Uploads multiple files. For example, mput *.jpg sends all files with names ending in .jpg to the remote system. If prompt is turned on, the FTP client asks for confirmation before each file is sent.
open	Opens a connection to the FTP server on the specified host. For example, open ftp.netscape.com connects to the FTP server on the host ftp.netscape.com.
prompt	Turns prompt on or off. When prompt is on, the FTP client prompts you for confirmation before downloading or uploading each file during a multi-file transfer.
put	Sends a file to the remote system. For example, puT index.html sends the index.html file from the local system to the remote system.
pwd	Displays the full path name of the current directory on the remote system. When you log in as a user, the initial current working directory is your home directory.
quit	Same as bye
recv	Same as get
rename	Renames a file on the remote system. For example, rename old.html new.html renames the file old.html to new.html on the remote system.
rmdir	Deletes a directory on the remote system. For example, rmdir images deletes the images directory in the current directory of the remote system.
send	Same as put
size	Shows the size of a remote file. For example, size bigfile.tar.gz shows the size of that remote file.
status	Shows the current status of the FTP client
user	Sends new user information to the FTP server. For example, user naba sends the user name naba; the FTP server then prompts for the password for that user name.

Graphical FTP Client

GNOME comes with gFTP, a graphical FTP client. To start gFTP, select from the GNOME desktop Main Menu ⇨ Programs ⇨ Internet ⇨ gFTP. The gFTP window has a menu bar with menus for performing various tasks. Just below the menu bar is a toolbar with a number of buttons and text fields. Here you can type the name of the remote host, the user name, and the password needed to log in to the remote host. Figure 20-1 shows the gFTP window after you have filled in this information.

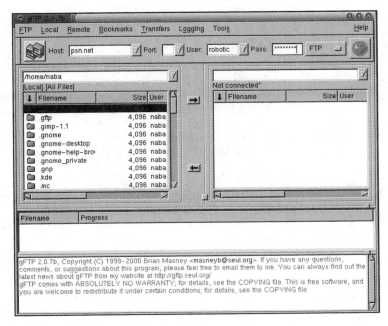

Figure 20-1: The gFTP window just before opening a connection to a remote FTP server

After you supply the host and user information, click the button with the icon of two computers to the left of the Host field. This causes gFTP to connect to that host and log in with the user name and password you have provided.

The middle part of the gFTP window is divided into two parts. The left side shows the contents of the current local directory; after establishing a connection, the right side shows the contents of the remote directory. Once the directories are listed, transferring files is simple. Simply select the desired files in the list, clicking the left arrow button to download, or the right arrow button to upload.

To disconnect, click the button on the rightmost end of the toolbar. You can then quit the gFTP application by selecting FTP ⇨ Quit from the menu.

Configuring the FTP Server

Red Hat Linux comes with the Washington University FTP daemon (wu-ftpd). The server is installed and ready to go if you install the Anonymous FTP Server package group when you install Red Hat Linux. The executable file for wu-ftpd is /usr/sbin/in.ftpd, and it uses a number of configuration files in the /etc directory. Although the default settings are adequate to begin using the wu-ftpd server, you should learn about the configuration files in case you need to customize them. You also need to know how the FTP server starts, so that you can control who can access the FTP server.

xinetd Configuration for wu-ftpd

If you type ps ax and look at the list of processes, you won't find a wu-ftpd or in.ftpd process. That's because the FTP server is started automatically by another server called xinetd — the Internet services daemon. The xinetd server listens on all the ports and then starts the appropriate server when a client request comes in. For example, clients connect to TCP port 21 when attempting to establish an FTP connection. The following line in the /etc/services file associates TCP port 21 with the ftp service:

```
ftp                21/tcp
```

This tells xinetd to look at its configuration files in the /etc/xinetd.d directory for information on what to do for the ftp service. The file /etc/xinetd.d/wu-ftpd contains the information that the FTP server uses to handle the connection:

```
# default: on
# description: The wu-ftpd FTP server serves FTP connections.
# It uses normal, unencrypted usernames and passwords for
# authentication.
service ftp
{
        socket_type             = stream
        wait                    = no
        user                    = root
        server                  = /usr/sbin/in.ftpd
        server_args             = -l -a
        log_on_success          += DURATION USERID
        log_on_failure          += USERID
        nice                    = 10
}
```

Cross-Reference

Chapter 8 explains the various attributes within curly braces. For this section, note that the server attribute specifies that the /usr/sbin/in.ftpd program be run to handle the FTP service connections. This is how xinetd starts the wu-ftpd server when a client attempts to establish connection to TCP port 21.

Secret

The xinetd server does not directly execute the server program (/usr/sbin/in.ftpd). Instead, it uses the TCP wrapper library to start the server. The TCP wrapper checks two files — /etc/hosts.allow and /etc/hosts.deny — to determine if the requested service should be allowed or denied. In the default setup, both /etc/hosts.allow and /etc/hosts.deny are empty. This has the effect of allowing all hosts access to all services.

If you want to limit access to FTP to specific hosts, first add the line ALL:ALL to the /etc/hosts.deny file. This denies all hosts access to any Internet service on your host. Now you can permit specific services to specific hosts (specified by name or IP address). For example, to allow only hosts from the 192.168.1.0 network access to the FTP service on your system, place the following line in the /etc/hosts.allow file:

```
in.ftpd: 192.168.1.0/255.255.255.0
```

You must identify the service by its program name; in this case, in.ftpd for the FTP server.

Tip

To learn more about the syntax of /etc/hosts.allow and /etc/hosts. deny, type man hosts.allow.

Before starting the service, the wrapper consults the /etc/hosts.allow file to see if the host requesting service is allowed that service. If there is nothing in /etc/hosts.allow about that host, TCP wrapper checks the /etc/hosts .deny file to see if the service should be denied. If both files are empty, TCP wrapper allows the host access to the requested service. You can place the line ALL:ALL in the /etc/hosts.deny file to deny all hosts access to any Internet services (see the "/etc/hosts.allow" and "/etc/hosts.deny" sections to learn more about these access control files).

wu-ftpd Configuration Files

The wu-ftpd server uses the following configuration files:

- /etc/ftpaccess controls operation of the wu-ftpd server and specifies which users can do what once they access the FTP server.

- /etc/ftpconversions specifies how to automatically convert tar and zip files based on filenames and extensions.

- /etc/ftpgroups lists groups of users that can access the server using a group password.

- /etc/ftphosts lists those hosts that are allowed access and those hosts that are denied access.

- /etc/ftpusers lists names of users who cannot access the FTP server.

Of these files, the most important is /etc/ftpaccess. You can usually leave the other files at the default settings. The next section explains the /etc/ ftpaccess file.

/etc/ftpaccess File

To learn what you can have in the /etc/ftpaccess file and how these lines affect the wu-ftpd server's operation, start by looking at the /etc/

ftpaccess file that comes with the wu-ftpd file in Red Hat Linux. This file contains the following lines (the line numbers in italics are not part of the actual file; I added them so that I can refer to specific lines in the text):

```
 1 class    all   real,guest,anonymous  *
 2 email root@localhost
 3 loginfails 5
 4 readme   README*    login
 5 readme   README*    cwd=*
 6 message /welcome.msg            login
 7 message .message                cwd=*
 8 compress         yes            all
 9 tar              yes            all
10 chmod            no             guest,anonymous
11 delete           no             guest,anonymous
12 overwrite        no             guest,anonymous
13 rename           no             guest,anonymous
14 log transfers anonymous,real inbound,outbound
15 shutdown /etc/shutmsg
16 passwd-check rfc822 warn
```

The following paragraphs describe each line of the ftpaccess file:

- Line 1 — class   all   real,guest,anonymous   * — defines a class of users named all of type real, guest, and anonymous. This class includes all users, as indicated by the wildcard (*) at the end of the line. The real keyword means users can access real accounts on the system using the FTP server. Similarly, the anonymous keyword enables access to anonymous FTP (described in "Setting Up Secure Anonymous FTP" section) and the guest keyword enables a guest access account (defined through the guestgroup access capability).

- Line 2 — email root@localhost — defines the e-mail address of the FTP server maintainer. In message files and README files, you can use the %E token — called a *magic cookie* because the FTP server replaces these tokens with text strings that depend on the cookie. See the description of Line 6 for more on magic cookies.

- Line 3 — loginfails 5 — specifies that after five failed login attempts, the FTP server logs a repeated login failure message and terminates the FTP connection.

- Line 4 — readme   README*   login — causes the FTP server to notify the user at login time that the README file exists and was last modified on such and such date. For example, the following is a typical message about a README file:

```
230-Please read the file README
```

```
230-  it was last modified on Sat Nov  4 10:55:09 2000 - 0 days
ago
```

- Line 5 — readme   README*   cwd=* — is similar to Line 4, except that this line causes the FTP server to notify the user about the README file whenever the user changes the current working directory (that's what cwd stands for).

- Line 6 — message /welcome.msg   login — causes the FTP server to display the contents of the /welcome.msg file (that's the welcome.msg file in the root directory) when a user logs in. In this file, you can use magic cookies, such as %U and %T, to display the user name and current time. For example, I placed the following lines in the /welcome.msg file on a system:

```
%U logged in at %T from %R.

Maximum number of users: %M

%U, you are number %N
```

When I log into that FTP server with the user name naba, here's what I see in the login message:

```
230-naba logged in at Sat Oct 21 15:10:19 2000 from lnbp400.

230-Maximum number of users: unlimited

230-naba, you are number 1
```

By comparing the messages with the magic cookies in the /welcome.msg file, you can see the expanded forms for the cookies %U, %T, %R, %M, and %N. Table 20-2 lists some of the commonly used magic cookies and their meanings. You can use these magic cookies in message files and README files.

- Line 7 — message .message   cwd=* — causes the FTP server to display the contents of the .message file from the current working directory whenever the user changes the current working directory and there is a .message file in the new working directory.

- Line 8 — compress   yes   all — enables compress capabilities for users of class all. This means that if the user downloads a compressed file bigfile.Z with the command get bigfile (without the .Z extension), the FTP server automatically decompresses the file before sending it to the FTP client. The /etc/ftpconversions file specifies how the conversion is done.

- Line 9 — tar   yes   all — enables automatic packing and unpacking of tar files (similar to how compressed files are handled, as explained in Line 8).

- Line 10 — chmod   no   guest,anonymous — causes the FTP server to disallow guest and anonymous users from changing file permissions with the chmod command.

- Line 11 — delete   no   guest,anonymous — causes the FTP server to disallow guest and anonymous users from deleting any files.

- Line 12 — overwrite   no   guest,anonymous — causes the FTP server to disallow guest and anonymous users from overwriting any files.

- Line 13 — rename   no   guest,anonymous — causes the FTP server to disallow guest and anonymous users from renaming any files.

- Line 14 — log transfers anonymous,real inbound,outbound — causes the FTP server to log all file downloads and uploads performed by real and anonymous users.

- Line 15 — shutdown /etc/shutmsg — causes the FTP server to periodically look for the file /etc/shutmsg. If that file exists, the FTP server uses the information in it to decide when to start denying users access, when to disconnect users, and when to shut down. The /etc/shutmsg file does not exist unless you create it with the intention of gradually shutting down the FTP service. The information in the /etc/shutmsg file must be in the format

  YYYY NN DD HH MM deny-HHMM disconnect-HHMM

  message to users about impending shutdown

  where *YYYY* is the year, *NN* is the month number (0 through 11), and *DD* is the day of the month (1 through 31), *HH* is the hour of the day in 24-hour format (0 through 23), and *MM* is the minute (0 through 59). The *deny-HHMM* and *disconnect-HHMM* fields specify the number of hours and minutes (in HHMM format) before shutdown that the server starts denying access and disconnecting users. For example, here's a typical content of the /etc/shutmsg file:

  `2000 10 05 21 45 0010 0005`

  `System shutdown at %s`

  This says that the FTP server will be shut down at 9:45 P.M. on April 15, 2001. Access will be denied ten minutes before shutdown, and users will be disconnected five minutes before shutdown. The message string can have magic cookies such as %s (when FTP will shut down) and %r (when connections will be denied). If this /etc/shutmsg file is present, the FTP server displays the following message when a user connects:

  `230-System shutdown at Sun Apr 15 21:45:00 2001`

  You do not have to prepare the /etc/shutmsg file yourself; simply use the ftpshut command and that program will take care of preparing the file.

- Line 16 — passwd-check rfc822 warn — causes the FTP server to ensure that the password provided by an anonymous user is an RFC822-compliant mail address of the form jdoe@someplace.com. If the address is not compliant, the FTP server displays a warning message but still lets the user log in and access files.

Table 20-2   Commonly Used wu-ftpd Magic Cookies

Magic Cookie	Meaning
%T	Local time (of the form Sat Oct 20 15:10:19 2001)
%C	Current working directory
%E	The FTP server maintainer's e-mail address from the email line in /etc/ftpaccess
%R	Remote host name
%L	Localhost name
%U	User name given at login time
%M	Maximum number of users allowed (in this class of users)
%N	Current number of users in this class

wu-ftpd Utility Programs

The wu-ftpd server comes with a few utility programs that you can use to see how many users are using the service, to see what resources they are using, and to shut down the FTP server.

ftpcount

The ftpcount utility shows you how many users are currently using the FTP server. The count is arranged by the class of users defined in the /etc/ftpaccess file. For the default ftpaccess file with the single user class named all, a typical output from ftpcount is as follows:

```
ftpcount
Service class all                      -   2 users (no maximum)
```

ftpwho

The ftpwho works like ftpcount, but shows additional details for each user in a service class. For example, the following is typical output for two users of class all currently connected to the FTP server:

```
ftpwho
Service class all:
  2485 ?        SN     0:00 ftpd: lnbp75: anonymous/naba@psn.net: IDLE
  2484 ?        SN     0:00 ftpd: lnbp400: naba: IDLE
    -   2 users (no maximum)
```

ftpshut

The `ftpshut` utility enables you to shut down the FTP server in an orderly manner. You can do this manually by setting up an `/etc/shutmsg` file and specifying the shutdown time and other information in that file (see Line 15 of the sample `/etc/ftpaccess` file described earlier). The `ftpshut` utility makes it simpler to perform this task. For example, type the following to shut down your FTP server today at 11:45 P.M.:

```
ftpshut 2145
```

This causes `ftpshut` to set up the `/etc/shutmsg` file with today's date and the shutdown time in the appropriate format. By default, `ftpshut` sets up the `/etc/shutmsg` file so that the FTP server disables new FTP connections ten minutes before shutdown, and starts disconnecting current users five minutes before shutdown.

If you want to shut down the server 30 minutes from the current time, type the following command:

```
ftpshut +30
```

On the other hand, if you want to shut it down 20 hours 45 minutes from the current time, type

```
ftpshut +2045
```

Tip

If you want to get rid of a future shutdown command, log in as root and remove the `/etc/shutmsg` file.

Setting Up Secure Anonymous FTP

Anonymous FTP refers to the use of the user name `anonymous`, which anyone can use with FTP to transfer files from a system. Anonymous FTP is a common way to share files on the Internet.

If you have used anonymous FTP to download files from Internet sites, you already know the convenience of that service. Anonymous FTP makes information available to anyone on the Internet. If you have a new Linux application that you want to share with the world, set up anonymous FTP on your Linux PC and place the software in an appropriate directory. After that, all you need to do is announce to the world (probably through a posting in the `comp.os.linux.announce` newsgroup) that you have a new program available. Now anyone can get the software from your system at his or her convenience.

Even if you run a for-profit business, you can use anonymous FTP to support your customers. If you sell a hardware or software product, you may want to provide technical information or software "fixes" through anonymous FTP.

Unfortunately, the convenience of anonymous FTP comes at a price. If you do not configure the anonymous FTP service properly, intruders and pranksters may gain access to your system. Some intruders may simply use your system's disk as a temporary holding place for various files; others may fill your disk with junk files, effectively making your system inoperable. At the other extreme, an intruder may gain user-level (or, worse, root-level) access to your system and do much more damage.

If you installed Red Hat Linux from this book's companion CD-ROMs, you already have anonymous FTP installed on your system. The default setup also employs the necessary security precautions.

Trying Anonymous FTP

To see anonymous FTP in action, try accessing your system using an FTP client. For example, in the following sample session, I accessed my system from another PC on the LAN (my input appears in boldface):

```
ftp lnbp200
Connected to lnbp200.
220 lnbp200 FTP server (Version wu-2.6.1(1) Wed Aug 9 05:54:50 EDT 2000) ready.
Name (lnbp200:root): anonymous
331 Guest login ok, send your complete e-mail address as password.
Password:            <-- I type my e-mail address as password
230 Guest login ok, access restrictions apply.
Remote system type is UNIX.
Using binary mode to transfer files.
ftp> ls -l
200 PORT command successful.
150 Opening ASCII mode data connection for /bin/ls.
total 16
d--x--x--x    2 root      root          4096 Oct  4 20:43 bin
d--x--x--x    2 root      root          4096 Nov  4 19:06 etc
drwxr-xr-x    2 root      root          4096 Oct  4 20:43 lib
drwxr-sr-x    2 root      ftp           4096 Aug 17 14:53 pub
226 Transfer complete.
ftp> bye
221-You have transferred 0 bytes in 0 files.
221-Total traffic for this session was 686 bytes in 1 transfers.
221-Thank you for using the FTP service on lnbp200.
221 Goodbye.
```

When you successfully log in for anonymous FTP, you access the home directory of the user named ftp (the default directory is /var/ftp). Place the publicly accessible files — the ones you want to enable others to download from your system — in the /var/ftp/pub directory.

Key Features of Anonymous FTP

The key features of an anonymous FTP setup are as follows:

- There is a user named ftp whose home directory is /var/ftp. The user does not have any shell assigned. Here is what you get when you search for ftp in the /etc/passwd file:

```
grep ftp /etc/passwd
```

```
ftp:x:14:50:FTP User:/var/ftp:
```

The x in the second field means that no one can actually log in with the user name ftp.

- Here is the full permission setting and owner information for the /var/ftp directory:

```
drwxr-xr-x    6 root      root        4096 Oct  4 16:43 ftp
```

As this line shows, the /var/ftp directory is owned by root, and the permission is set to 755 (only root can read and write; everyone else can only read; for more information on permission settings, see the chmod command described in Appendix A).

- You can view the contents of the /var/ftp directory with the ls -la command. The result is as follows:

```
total 24
drwxr-xr-x    6 root      root        4096 Oct  4 16:43 .
drwxr-xr-x   22 root      root        4096 Oct  4 16:43 ..
d--x--x--x    2 root      root        4096 Oct  4 16:43 bin
d--x--x--x    2 root      root        4096 Nov  4 13:15 etc
drwxr-xr-x    2 root      root        4096 Oct  4 16:43 lib
drwxr-sr-x    2 root      ftp         4096 Aug 17 10:53 pub
```

The permission settings of the bin and etc directories are 111 (execute only). All files inside the bin directory are also execute-only (permission setting 111). All files in the etc directory are read-only (permission setting 444).

- The pub directory is where you place any files that you want to enable others to download from your system through anonymous FTP.

Summary

File Transfer Protocol (FTP) is a popular Internet service for transferring files from one system to another. This chapter describes the FTP service and shows you how to configure the wu-ftpd server that comes with Red Hat Linux.

By reading this chapter, you learn the following:

▶ FTP is an important Internet service for transferring files from one system to another. FTP is documented in RFC 959.

▶ You must set up and run an FTP server if you want your system's users to transfer files to and from the system. Red Hat Linux comes with the Washington University FTP daemon (wu-ftpd), a popular FTP server.

▶ The wu-ftpd server is started by xinetd whenever an FTP client attempts to connect to TCP port 21, the default port for FTP. The configuration file /etc/xinetd.d/wu-ftpd contains the xinetd settings that control how the wu-ftpd server is started. Because xinetd uses the TCP wrappers, you can control access to FTP by placing appropriate lines in the /etc/hosts.allow and /etc/hosts.deny files.

▶ You can configure the wu-ftpd server by editing the /etc/ftpaccess file. This chapter explains the default settings in this file.

▶ The ftpcount, ftpwho, and ftpshut utility programs enable you to determine the number of FTP users and the resources they are using, and to shut down the FTP server in a graceful manner.

▶ Anonymous FTP is another popular Internet service for distributing files. With anonymous FTP, anyone can use FTP with the anonymous user ID and download files from your system. Although anonymous FTP is useful for distributing data, it poses a security risk if it is not set up properly.

▶ The default Red Hat Linux installation includes everything needed to support anonymous FTP. The default anonymous FTP setup incorporates the necessary security precautions.

Chapter 21

DNS and NIS

omain Name System (DNS) is an Internet service that converts a fully qualified domain name, such as www.redhat.com, into its corresponding Internet Protocol (IP) address. You can think of DNS as the directory of Internet hosts — DNS is what enables you to refer to a host by its name even though TCP/IP requires IP addresses for data transfers. DNS is implemented by a hierarchy of distributed DNS servers. This chapter provides an overview of DNS and shows you how to set up a caching DNS server on your Red Hat Linux system.

Network Information System (NIS) is a client/server service designed to manage information shared among several host computers on a network. Typically, NIS is used on UNIX (and Linux) systems to maintain a common set of user accounts and other system files for a group of hosts. This, among other things, enables a user to log in on all hosts with the same user name and password. This chapter describes the NIS client and server software and shows you how to use them on a Red Hat Linux system.

Domain Name System (DNS)

In TCP/IP networks, each network interface (for example, an Ethernet card on a host computer) is identified by an IP address. Because IP addresses are hard to remember, an association is made between an easy-to-remember name and the IP address — much like the association between a name and a telephone number. For example, instead of having to remember that the IP address of Red Hat's Web server is 216.148.218.195, you can simply refer to that host by its name, www.redhat.com. When you type www.redhat.com as the URL in a Web browser, the name www.redhat.com has to be translated into its corresponding IP address. This is where the concept of DNS comes in.

What Is DNS?

DNS is a distributed database that holds information about computers on the Internet. The information includes the host name, the IP address, and mail routing information. This information resides in many DNS hosts in the Internet; that's why the DNS database is called a distributed database. The primary job of DNS is to associate host names to IP addresses, and vice versa.

In ARPANET — the precursor to today's Internet, the association between host names and IP addresses was maintained in a text file named HOSTS.TXT, which was managed centrally and distributed to each host. As the number of hosts grew, it became clear that a static host table was unreasonable. DNS was proposed by Paul Mockapetris to alleviate the problems of a static host table. As formally documented in RFCs 882 and 883 (November 1983), DNS introduced two key concepts:

- Use of hierarchical domain names, such as `www.ee.umd.edu` and `www.redhat.com`

- Distributed responsibility for managing the host database using DNS servers throughout the Internet

Note

DNS, as we know it today, is an Internet standard documented in RFCs 1034 and 1035. The standard has been updated and extended by several other RFCs — 1101, 1183, 1348, 1876, 1982, 1996, 2065, 2181, 2136, 2137, 2308, 2535, 2845, and 2931. The earlier updates define data encoding, whereas later ones focus on improving DNS security. To read these and other RFCs online, visit Ohio State University's Internet RFC page at `http://www.cis.ohio-state.edu/hypertext/information/rfc.html`.

DNS defines the following:

- A hierarchical domain-naming system for hosts

- A distributed database that associates a name with an IP address

- Library routines that network applications can use to query the distributed DNS database (this library is called the *resolver library*)

- A protocol for DNS clients and servers to exchange information about names and IP addresses

Nowadays, all hosts on the Internet rely on DNS to access various Internet services on remote hosts. As you may know from personal experience, when you obtain Internet access from an Internet Service Provider (ISP), the ISP provides you with the IP addresses of name servers. These are the DNS servers that your system accesses whenever host names have to be mapped to IP addresses.

If you have a small LAN, you may decide to run a DNS server on one of the hosts, or use the name servers provided by the ISP. For medium-sized networks with several subnets, you can run a DNS server on each subnet to provide efficient DNS lookups. On a large corporate network, the corporate domain (such as microsoft.com) is further subdivided into a hierarchy of subdomains, and several DNS servers may be used in each subdomain.

The following sections provide an overview of the hierarchical domain-naming convention, and then describe BIND — the implementation of DNS used on most UNIX systems, including Red Hat Linux.

Hierarchical Domain Names

DNS uses a hierarchical tree of domains to organize the *namespace* — the entire set of names. Each higher level domain has authority over its lower level subdomains. Each domain represents a distinct block of the namespace and is managed by a single administrative authority. Figure 21-1 illustrates the hierarchical organization of the DNS namespace.

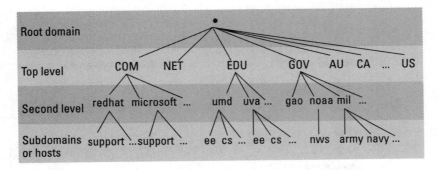

Figure 21-1: Sample domain names illustrating the hierarchical DNS namespace

The root of the tree is called the *root domain* and is represented by a single dot (.). The top-level, or root-level, domains come next. The top-level domains are further divided into second-level domains, which, in turn, can be broken into further subdomains.

The top-level domains are relatively fixed, and include well-known domains, such as COM, NET, ORG, EDU, GOV, and MIL. These are the commonly used top-level domains in the United States. These top-level domains came about as the Internet became widely used in the early 1990s.

Additionally, there is another set of top-level domain names for the countries. These domain names use the two-letter country codes assigned by the International Organization for Standardization (abbreviated as ISO, see http://www.iso.ch/). For example, the top-level country code domain for the United States is US. In the United States, many local governments and organizations use the US domain. For example, mcps.k12.md.us is the domain name of the Montgomery County Public Schools in Maryland.

The *fully qualified domain name (FQDN)* is constructed by stringing together the subdomain names, from lower to higher level, using dots (.) as separators. For example, REDHAT.COM is a fully qualified domain name; so is EE.UMD.EDU. Note that each of these may also refer to a specific host computer. Figure 21-2 illustrates the components of a fully qualified domain name.

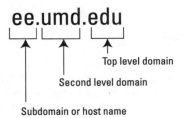

Figure 21-2: Components of a fully qualified domain name

Domain names are case-insensitive. Therefore, the domains UMD.EDU and umd.edu both represent University of Maryland's domain, as far as DNS is concerned. The norm, however, is to type domain names in all lowercase.

Berkeley Internet Domain Name (BIND) System

Most UNIX systems, including Red Hat Linux, come with the BIND system — a well-known implementation of DNS. The BIND software is installed during Red Hat Linux installation, as long as you select the *DNS Name Server* package group when selecting the packages for installation.

To see which version of BIND is installed on your Red Hat Linux system, type the following command:

```
rpm -q bind
bind-9.1.0-0.b2.1
```

As the output shows, BIND Version 9.1.0 is installed on my system.

BIND includes three major components:

- The named daemon — the *name server* — that responds to queries about host names and IP addresses
- A resolver library that applications can use to resolve host names into IP addresses and vice versa
- Command-line DNS utility programs (DNS clients), such as nslookup, dig (Domain Internet Groper), and host that users can use to query DNS

The next few sections describe these components of BIND. Later sections describe how to configure the resolver and the name server.

Learning More about DNS and BIND

This chapter only briefly describes DNS and BIND; entire books have been devoted solely to DNS and BIND. For example, **DNS and BIND, Third Edition**, by Paul Albitz and Cricket Liu (O'Reilly & Associates, 1998), can help you learn more about DNS and BIND.

BIND also comes with a lot of online documentation that's installed on your Red Hat Linux system when you install the **DNS Name Server** package group. To read the online documentation about BIND, change the current directory with the command `cd /usr/share/doc/bind*` (the directory name depends on which version of BIND is installed on your system), and then look at the files in that directory.

The Internet Software Consortium (ISC)—a non-profit corporation—supports BIND. Visit their Web site at `http://www.isc.org/` to learn more about the latest release of BIND.

To ask questions online about DNS and BIND, or to participate in related discussions, read the following newsgroups (see Chapter 19 for more information about reading newsgroups):

`comp.protocols.dns.bind`—discussions about using BIND

`comp.protocols.dns.ops`—discussions about DNS operations

`comp.protocols.dns.std`—discussions about DNS standards

named—the BIND Name Server

The `named` daemon is the name server that responds to queries about host names and IP addresses. Based on the configuration files and the local DNS database, `named` either provides answers to queries, or asks other servers and caches their responses. The `named` server also performs a function referred to as *zone transfer*, which involves copying data among the name servers in a domain.

The name server operates in one of three modes:

- *Primary*—In this case, the name server keeps the master copy of the domain's data on disk. There is one primary server for each domain or subdomain.

- *Secondary*—A secondary name server copies its domain's data from the primary server using a zone transfer operation. There are one or more secondary name servers for a domain.

- *Caching*—A caching name server loads the addresses of a few authoritative servers for the root domain, and then gets all its data by caching responses to queries resolved by contacting other name servers. Primary and secondary servers also cache responses.

A name server can be *authoritative* or not. As the term implies, the response from an authoritative name server is supposed to be accurate. The primary and secondary name servers are authoritative for their own domains, but they are not authoritative for responses provided from cached information. Caching name servers are never authoritative, because all of their responses come from cached information.

To run a name server on your Red Hat Linux system, you have to run `named` with the appropriate configuration files. Later in this chapter, you learn about the configuration files and data files that control how the name server operates.

Resolver library

The process of finding an IP address for a host name is referred to as *resolving* the host name. Network-aware applications, such as a Web browser or an FTP client, use a resolver library to perform the conversion from the name to an IP address. Depending on the settings in the `/etc/host.conf` file, the resolver library consults the `/etc/hosts` file or makes a DNS query to resolve a host name to its IP address. The resolver library queries the name servers listed in the `/etc/resolv.conf` file.

You do not need to learn much about the resolver library unless you are writing network-aware applications. To run Internet services properly, all you need to learn is how to configure the resolver. Subsequent sections in this chapter show you how to configure this, and other aspects of DNS.

DNS utility programs

You can use the DNS utility programs — `nslookup`, `dig`, and `host` — to interactively try out DNS from the shell prompt. These utility programs are DNS clients. You can use them to query the DNS database and debug any name server you might set up on your system. By default, these programs query the name server listed in your system's `/etc/resolv.conf` file.

You can use `nslookup` interactively or non-interactively. In non-interactive mode, `nslookup` enables you to look up information about a single host or IP address. For example, here's how you can use `nslookup` non-interactively to find the IP address of the host `addlab.nws.noaa.gov`:

```
nslookup addlab.nws.noaa.gov.
Server:   old-ns0.starnetinc.com
Address:  204.178.185.5

Non-authoritative answer:
Name:     addlab.nws.noaa.gov
Address:  140.90.141.131
```

Here, `nslookup` queries the name server with the IP address 204.178.185.5, because that's the first name server listed in my system's `/etc/resolv.conf` file. In this case, the non-authoritative answer for the IP address is 140.90.141.131.

Notice the trailing dot (.) in the domain name—you should append the dot when looking up hosts that are not in the current domain (the domain for your name server).

For a reverse lookup, to find the host name corresponding to an IP address, use the -query=ptr option as follows:

```
nslookup -query=ptr 131.141.90.140.in-addr.arpa.
Server:  old-ns0.starnetinc.com
Address:  204.178.185.5

Non-authoritative answer:
131.141.90.140.in-addr.arpa       name = addlab.nws.noaa.gov

Authoritative answers can be found from:
141.90.140.in-addr.arpa nameserver = netinfo.hqnoc.noaa.gov
141.90.140.in-addr.arpa nameserver = netdiag.hqnoc.noaa.gov
141.90.140.in-addr.arpa nameserver = nwrns.noaa.gov
141.90.140.in-addr.arpa nameserver = serns.noaa.gov
141.90.140.in-addr.arpa nameserver = merns.noaa.gov
141.90.140.in-addr.arpa nameserver = mwrns.noaa.gov
netinfo.hqnoc.noaa.gov  internet address = 140.90.148.33
netdiag.hqnoc.noaa.gov  internet address = 140.90.148.34
nwrns.noaa.gov  internet address = 161.55.32.3
serns.noaa.gov  internet address = 192.111.123.245
merns.noaa.gov  internet address = 192.94.173.133
mwrns.noaa.gov  internet address = 140.172.254.10
```

In this case, I am looking up the host name for the IP address 140.90. 141.131. Notice that I have to provide the address in a reverse form, 131.141.90.140, and append in-addr.arpa to that address; that's the format of a PTR record used to perform a reverse lookup. The non-authoritative answer from the name server shows that the host name is addlab.nws. noaa.gov. The last block of lines lists the name servers that can provide an authoritative answer.

You can also use nslookup in an interactive manner to perform one query after another. Here is a sample interactive session with nslookup:

```
nslookup
Default Server:  old-ns0.starnetinc.com
Address:  204.178.185.5

> help
$Id: nslookup.help,v 8.4 1996/10/25 18:09:41 vixie Exp $

Commands:        (identifiers are shown in uppercase, [] means
                 optional)
NAME           - print info about the host/domain NAME using default
                 server
NAME1 NAME2    - as above, but use NAME2 as server
help or ?      - print info on common commands; see nslookup(1) for
                 details
```

```
set OPTION       - set an option
    all          - print options, current server and host
    [no]debug    - print debugging information
    [no]d2       - print exhaustive debugging information
    [no]defname  - append domain name to each query
    [no]recurse  - ask for recursive answer to query
    [no]vc       - always use a virtual circuit
    domain=NAME  - set default domain name to NAME
    srchlist=N1[/N2/.../N6] - set domain to N1 and search list to
                   N1,N2, etc.
    root=NAME    - set root server to NAME
    retry=X      - set number of retries to X
    timeout=X    - set initial time-out interval to X seconds
    querytype=X  - set query type, e.g., A, ANY, CNAME, HINFO, MX, PX,
                   NS, PTR, SOA, TXT, WKS,SRV,NAPTR
    port=X       - set port number to send query on
    type=X       - synonym for querytype
    class=X      - set query class to one of IN (Internet), CHAOS,
                   HESIOD or ANY
server NAME      - set default server to NAME, using current default
                   server
lserver NAME     - set default server to NAME, using initial server
finger [USER]    - finger the optional USER at the current default host
root             - set current default server to the root
ls [opt] DOMAIN [> FILE] - list addresses in DOMAIN (optional: output
                   to FILE)
    -a           - list canonical names and aliases
    -h           - list HINFO (CPU type and operating system)
    -s           - list well-known services
    -d           - list all records
    -t TYPE      - list records of the given type (e.g., A,CNAME,MX,
                   etc.)
view FILE        - sort an 'ls' output file and view it with more
exit             - exit the program, ^D also exits
> set type=MX    <-- set this to query mail exchange records
> gao.gov.       <-- query this host's mail exchange
Server:  old-ns0.starnetinc.com
Address:  204.178.185.5

Non-authoritative answer:
gao.gov preference = 5, mail exchanger = gao-cp.gao.gov

Authoritative answers can be found from:
gao.gov nameserver = knock.ser.bbnplanet.net
gao.gov nameserver = vienna1-dns-auth1.bbnplanet.com
gao.gov nameserver = nic.near.net
gao-cp.gao.gov  internet address = 161.203.16.1
knock.ser.bbnplanet.net internet address = 192.239.16.129
vienna1-dns-auth1.bbnplanet.com internet address = 4.2.49.2
vienna1-dns-auth1.bbnplanet.com internet address = 4.2.49.3
vienna1-dns-auth1.bbnplanet.com internet address = 4.2.49.4
nic.near.net    internet address = 192.52.71.4
> exit
```

As you can see, the `help` command displays a brief summary of all `nslookup` commands. To end an interactive `nslookup` session, type `exit`, or Ctrl+D. The `nslookup` utility is deprecated and may be removed in future releases of BIND. Therefore, you should use `dig`, the Domain Internet Groper program to perform tasks similar to those you perform with `nslookup`. For example, to look up the IP address of `addlab.nws.noaa.gov`, type `dig addlab.nws.noaa.gov`, and `dig` prints the results of the DNS query with a great amount of detail. Look in the part of the output labeled ANSWER SECTION: for the result.

Reverse lookups (finding host names for IP addresses) are easier with `dig` than with `nslookup`, because you do not have to type the address in reverse order. For example, to find the host name corresponding to the IP address `140.90.141.131`, type the following:

```
dig -x 140.90.141.131
;; Got answer:
;; ->>HEADER<<- opcode: QUERY, status: NOERROR, id: 45240
;; flags: qr rd ra; QUERY: 1, ANSWER: 1, AUTHORITY: 6, ADDITIONAL: 6

;; QUESTION SECTION:
;131.141.90.140.in-addr.arpa.    IN      PTR

;; ANSWER SECTION:
131.141.90.140.in-addr.arpa. 86389 IN   PTR       addlab.nws.noaa.gov.

;; AUTHORITY SECTION:
141.90.140.in-addr.arpa. 86389  IN      NS
netinfo.hqnoc.noaa.gov.
141.90.140.in-addr.arpa. 86389  IN      NS
netdiag.hqnoc.noaa.gov.
141.90.140.in-addr.arpa. 86389  IN      NS        nwrns.noaa.gov.
141.90.140.in-addr.arpa. 86389  IN      NS        serns.noaa.gov.
141.90.140.in-addr.arpa. 86389  IN      NS        merns.noaa.gov.
141.90.140.in-addr.arpa. 86389  IN      NS        mwrns.noaa.gov.

;; ADDITIONAL SECTION:
nwrns.noaa.gov.         86384   IN      A         161.55.246.3
nwrns.noaa.gov.         86384   IN      A         161.55.32.3
serns.noaa.gov.         86384   IN      A         192.111.123.245
merns.noaa.gov.         86384   IN      A         192.94.173.133
mwrns.noaa.gov.         86384   IN      A         140.172.253.1
mwrns.noaa.gov.         86384   IN      A         140.172.254.10

;; Query time: 56 msec
;; SERVER: 192.168.1.1#53(192.168.1.1)
;; WHEN: Fri Feb  2 22:19:03 2001
;; MSG SIZE  rcvd: 327
```

As you can see, `dig` prints a lot of information in addition to the result. The answer you want comes right after the label ANSWER SECTION:, which in this case shows the host name to be `addlab.nws.noaa.gov`.

Finally, you can also query DNS using the host program. The host program produces output in a compact format. For example, here's a typical use of host to look up information about a host:

```
host www.gao.gov
www.gao.gov has address 161.203.16.2
www.gao.gov mail is handled (pri=5) by listserv.gao.gov
```

By default, host prints out the IP address and any MX record (these records list the names of mail handlers for the host).

For a reverse lookup, use the -t ptr option, along with the IP address as an argument, as follows:

```
host -t ptr 161.203.16.2
2.16.203.161.IN-ADDR.ARPA domain name pointer www.gao.gov
```

In this case, host prints out the PTR record that shows the host name corresponding to the specified IP address.

You can also try other types of records, such as CNAME (for canonical name), as follows:

```
host -t cname www.ee.umd.edu
www.ee.umd.edu is a nickname for www.ece.umd.edu
```

This indicates that the canonical name for www.ee.umd.edu is www.ece.umd.edu.

Another interesting type of record is HINFO (for host information). For example, you can query the HINFO record of prep.ai.mit.edu with the following command line:

```
host -t hinfo prep.ai.mit.edu
prep.ai.mit.edu host information i686 unix
```

Although most hosts do not have HINFO records, some old hosts do include this information.

Configuring DNS

You configure DNS using a number of configuration files. The exact set of files depends on whether you are running a name server, and the type of name server — caching or primary. Some configuration files are needed whether you run a name server or not.

Configuration files for resolver

You do not need a name server running on your system to use the DNS clients — nslookup, dig, and host. You can use them to query your domain's name server. Typically, your ISP would provide you with this information. You have to list the IP addresses of these name servers in the /etc/resolv.conf file — the resolver library reads this file to determine how to resolve host names. The format of this file is

```
search your-domain.com
nameserver A.B.C.D
nameserver X.Y.Z.W
```

where $A.B.C.D$ and $X.Y.Z.W$ are the IP addresses (dot-separated numeric addresses, such as 192.168.1.1) of the primary and secondary name servers that your ISP provides you.

The `search` line specifies the domains on which a host name is searched first (usually, you put your own domain in the `search` line). The domain listed on the search line is appended to any host name before the resolver library tries to resolve it. For example, if you look for a host named `mailhost`, the resolver library first tries `mailhost.your-domain.com`; if that fails, it tries `mailhost`. The search line applies to any host name you try to access. For example, if you are trying to access `www.redhat.com`, the resolver first tries `www.redhat.com.your-domain.com`, and then `www.redhat.com`.

Another important configuration file is `/etc/host.conf` — this file tells the resolver what to do when attempting to resolve a host name. A typical `/etc/host/conf` file contains the following line:

```
order hosts,bind
```

This tells the resolver to consult the `/etc/hosts` file first and, if that fails, to query the name server listed in the `/etc/resolv.conf` file. As explained in Chapter 8, the `/etc/hosts` file associates IP addresses to host names. A typical line from the `/etc/hosts` file looks like the following:

```
127.0.0.1    lnbp200  localhost.localdomain  localhost
```

This line says that the IP address 127.0.0.1 is assigned to the host names `lnbp200`, `localhost.localdomain`, and `localhost`.

In the latest version of Linux that uses GNU C Library version 2 (glibc 2) or later, the name service switch (NSS) file, `/etc/nsswitch.conf`, specifies how services such as the resolver library, NIS, NIS+, and local files such as `/etc/hosts` and `/etc/shadow` interact. For example, the following `hosts` entry in the `/etc/nsswitch.conf` file specifies that the resolver library should first try the `/etc/hosts` file, then try NIS+, and finally try DNS:

```
hosts:      files nisplus dns
```

To learn more about the `/etc/nsswitch.conf` file and what it does, type **info libc "Name Service Switch"** at the shell prompt in a terminal window.

Configuration files for a caching name server

A simple, but useful name server is one that finds answers to host name queries by using other name servers and then remembers the answer (by saving it in a cache) the next time you need it. This can shorten the time it takes to access hosts that you have accessed recently, because the answer is already in the cache.

When you install the *DNS Name Server* package group during Red Hat Linux installation, the configuration files for a caching name server are also installed. That means you can start running the caching name server without much work on your part. This section describes the configuration files and what you have to do to start the caching name server.

/etc/named.conf file

The first configuration file you need is /etc/named.conf. The named server reads this configuration file when it starts. You already have this file if you have installed the DNS Name Server when you installed Red Hat Linux in Chapter 2. Here's what the default /etc/named/conf file contains:

```
options {
        directory "/var/named";
        /*
         * Uncomment the following if you have to go through
         * a firewall to reach the name servers and the caching
         * name server is not working.
         */
        // query-source address * port 53;
};

zone "." IN {
        type hint;
        file "named.ca";
};

zone "localhost" IN {
        type master;
        file "localhost.zone";
        allow-update { none; };
};

zone "0.0.127.in-addr.arpa" IN {
        type master;
        file "named.local";
        allow-update { none; };
};
```

Comments are C-style (/* ... */) or C++-style (starts with //). The file contains block statements enclosed in curly braces ({ ... }) and terminated by a semicolon (;). A block statement, in turn, contains other statements, each ending with a semicolon.

This /etc/named.conf file begins with an options block statement with a number of option statements. The directory option statement tells named where to look for all other files that appear on file lines in the configuration file. In this case, named looks for the files in the /var/named directory.

After the options statement, the /etc/named.conf file contains several zone statements, each enclosed in curly braces and terminated by a semicolon. Each zone statement defines a zone. The first zone is named "." (root zone) and it's a hint zone that specifies the root name servers.

The next two `zone` statements in `/etc/named.conf` are master zones. The syntax for a master `zone` statement for an Internet class zone (indicated by the `IN` keyword) is as follows:

```
zone "zone-name" IN {
      type master;
      file "zone-file";
      [...other optional statements...]
};
```

The `zone-name` is the name of the zone, and `zone-file` is the zone file that contains the *resource records* (RR) — the database entries — for that zone. The next two sections describe zone file formats and resource record formats.

Zone file format

The zone file typically starts with a number of directives, each of which begins with a dollar sign ($) followed by a keyword. Two commonly used directives are `$TTL` and `$ORIGIN`.

For example, the line

```
$TTL    86400
```

uses the `$TTL` directive to set the default Time To Live (TTL) for subsequent records with undefined TTLs. The value is in seconds and the valid TTLs are in the range 0 to 2147483647 seconds. In this case, the directive sets the default TTL as 86400 seconds (or one day).

The `$ORIGIN` directive sets the domain name that will be appended to any unqualified records. For example, the following `$ORIGIN` directive sets the domain name to `localhost`:

```
$ORIGIN localhost.
```

Note

If there is no `$ORIGIN` directive, the initial `$ORIGIN` is the same as the zone name that comes after the zone keyword in the `/etc/named.conf` file.

After the directives, the zone file contains one or more resource records. These records follow a specific format, which is outlined in the next section.

Resource Record (RR) format

You have to understand the format of the resource records before you can understand and intelligently work with zone files. Each resource record has the following format (the optional fields are shown in square brackets):

```
[domain] [ttl] [class] type data [;comment]
```

The fields are separated by tabs or spaces and may contain some special characters, such as an @ symbol for the *domain* and a semicolon (;) to indicate the start of a comment.

The first field, which must begin at the first character of the line, identifies the domain. You can use the @ symbol to use the current $ORIGIN for the domain name for this record. If you have multiple records for the same domain name, leave the first field blank.

The optional *ttl* field specifies the time to live — the duration for which the data can be cached and considered valid. You can specify the time duration in one of the following formats:

N, where *N* is a number meaning *N* seconds

*N*W, where *N* is a number meaning *N* weeks

*N*D, where *N* is a number meaning *N* days

*N*H, where *N* is a number meaning *N* hours

*N*M, where *N* is a number meaning *N* minutes

*N*S, where *N* is a number meaning *N* seconds

The letters W, D, H, M, and S can also be in lowercase. Thus, you can write 86400 or 1D (or 1d) to indicate a time duration of one day. You can also combine these to specify more precise time durations, such as 5w6d16h to indicate 5 weeks, 6 days, and 16 hours.

Secret

The *class* field specifies the network type. The most commonly used value for this field is IN for Internet. Other values are CH for ChaosNet (an obsolete network used long ago by Symbolics Lisp computers), and HS for Hesiod (an NIS-like database service based on BIND).

Next in the resource record comes the *type* field, which denotes the type of record (such as SOA, NS, A, or PTR). Table 21-1 lists the DNS resource record types. The *data* field comes next, and it depends on the *type* field.

Table 21-1   DNS Resource Record Types

Type	Name	Description
SOA	Start of authority	Indicates that all subsequent records are authoritative for this zone
NS	Name Server	Identifies authoritative name servers for a zone
A	Address	Specifies the host address corresponding to a name
PTR	Pointer	Specifies the name corresponding to an address (used for reverse mapping — converting an IP address to a host name)
MX	Mail Exchanger	Identifies the host that will accept mail meant for a domain (used to route e-mail)

Type	Name	Description
CNAME	Canonical Name	Defines the nickname or alias for a host name
HINFO	Host Info	Identifies the hardware and operating system for a host
RP	Responsible Person	Provides the name of a technical contact for a domain
WKS	Well Known Services	Lists services provided by a host (this has been deprecated and is no longer used)
TXT	Text	Used to include comments and other information in the DNS database

You should learn to read the resource records, at least the ones of type SOA, NS, A, PTR, and MX, which are some of the most commonly used resource records. The following section briefly describes these records, illustrating each record type through an example.

A typical SOA record has the following format:

```
@     1D IN SOA     @ root (
                    42              ; serial
                    3H              ; refresh -- 3 hours
                    15M             ; retry -- 15 minutes
                    1W              ; expiry -- 1 week
                    1D )            ; minimum -- 1 day
```

The first field specifies the domain as an @, which means the current domain (by default, the zone name, as shown in the /etc/named.conf file). The next field specifies a TTL of one day for this record. The class field is set to IN, which means the record is for Internet. The type field specifies the record type as SOA. The rest of the fields constitute the data for the SOA record. The data includes the name of the primary name server (in this case, @, or the current domain), the e-mail address of the technical contact, and five different times enclosed in parentheses.

The NS record specifies the authoritative name servers for a zone. A typical NS record looks like the following:

```
.          3600000  IN  NS    A.ROOT-SERVERS.NET.
```

In this case, the NS record lists the authoritative name server for the root zone (notice that the name of the first field is a single dot). The time-to-live field specifies the record to be valid for 1,000 hours (3600000 seconds). The class is IN, for Internet; and the record type is NS. The final field lists the name of the name server (A.ROOT-SERVERS.NET.), which ends with a dot.

An A record specifies the address corresponding to a name. For example, the following A record shows the address of A.ROOT-SERVERS.NET. as 198.41.0.4:

```
A.ROOT-SERVERS.NET.      3600000      A      198.41.0.4
```

In this case, the network class is not specified, because the field is optional and the default is IN.

PTR records are used for reverse mapping — converting an address to a name. Consider the following example:

```
1       IN      PTR      localhost.
```

This record comes from a file for a zone named 0.0.127.in-addr.arpa. Therefore, this record says that the name associated with the address 127.0.0.1 is localhost.

An MX record specifies the name of a host that will accept mail on behalf of a specific domain. For example, here's a typical MX record:

```
naba    IN    MX    10    mailhub.lnbsoft.com.
```

This says that mail addressed to the host named naba in the current domain should be sent to mailhub.lnbsoft.com (this host is called a *mail exchanger*). The number 10 is the preference value. For a list of multiple MX records with different preference values, the ones with lower preference values will be tried first.

Now that you know a bit about resource records, you can go through the zone files for the caching name server.

/var/named/named.ca file

Information about the root name servers is in the file /var/named/named.ca, as specified in the zone statement for the root zone in the /etc/named.conf file. The following listing shows the /var/named/named.ca file from a Red Hat Linux system:

```
;        This file holds the information on root name servers needed to
;        initialize cache of Internet domain name servers
;        (e.g. reference this file in the "cache  .  <file>"
;        configuration file of BIND domain name servers).
;
;        This file is made available by InterNIC registration services
;        under anonymous FTP as
;            file                /domain/named.root
;            on server           FTP.RS.INTERNIC.NET
;        -OR- under Gopher at    RS.INTERNIC.NET
;            under menu          InterNIC Registration Services (NSI)
;                submenu         InterNIC Registration Archives
;            file                named.root
;
;        last update:    Aug 22, 1997
;        related version of root zone:   1997082200
```

```
;
;
; formerly NS.INTERNIC.NET
;
.                        3600000    IN   NS   A.ROOT-SERVERS.NET.
A.ROOT-SERVERS.NET.      3600000         A    198.41.0.4

; formerly NS1.ISI.EDU
;
.                        3600000         NS   B.ROOT-SERVERS.NET.
B.ROOT-SERVERS.NET.      3600000         A    128.9.0.107
;
; formerly C.PSI.NET
;
.                        3600000         NS   C.ROOT-SERVERS.NET.
C.ROOT-SERVERS.NET.      3600000         A    192.33.4.12
;
; formerly TERP.UMD.EDU
;
.                        3600000         NS   D.ROOT-SERVERS.NET.
D.ROOT-SERVERS.NET.      3600000         A    128.8.10.90
;
; formerly NS.NASA.GOV
;
.                        3600000         NS   E.ROOT-SERVERS.NET.
E.ROOT-SERVERS.NET.      3600000         A    192.203.230.10
;
; formerly NS.ISC.ORG
;
.                        3600000         NS   F.ROOT-SERVERS.NET.
F.ROOT-SERVERS.NET.      3600000         A    192.5.5.241
;
; formerly NS.NIC.DDN.MIL
;
.                        3600000         NS   G.ROOT-SERVERS.NET.
G.ROOT-SERVERS.NET.      3600000         A    192.112.36.4
;
; formerly AOS.ARL.ARMY.MIL
;
.                        3600000         NS   H.ROOT-SERVERS.NET.
H.ROOT-SERVERS.NET.      3600000         A    128.63.2.53
;
; formerly NIC.NORDU.NET
;
.                        3600000         NS   I.ROOT-SERVERS.NET.
I.ROOT-SERVERS.NET.      3600000         A    192.36.148.17
;
; temporarily housed at NSI (InterNIC)
;
.                        3600000         NS   J.ROOT-SERVERS.NET.
;
; housed in LINX, operated by RIPE NCC
;
```

```
.                            3600000        NS      K.ROOT-SERVERS.NET.
K.ROOT-SERVERS.NET.          3600000        A       193.0.14.129
;
; temporarily housed at ISI (IANA)
;
.                            3600000        NS      L.ROOT-SERVERS.NET.
L.ROOT-SERVERS.NET.          3600000        A       198.32.64.12
;
; housed in Japan, operated by WIDE
;
.                            3600000        NS      M.ROOT-SERVERS.NET.
M.ROOT-SERVERS.NET.          3600000        A       202.12.27.33
; End of File
```

This file contains NS and A resource records that specify the names of
authoritative name servers and their addresses for the root zone (indicated
by the ".." in the first field of each NS record).

The comment lines in the file begin with a semicolon. These comments give
you hints about the location of the root name servers. There are thirteen root
name servers for the Internet, located primarily in the United States. This file
is a necessity for any name server, because the name server has to be able to
reach at least one root name server.

/var/named/localhost.zone File

The /etc/named.conf file includes a zone statement for the localhost
zone that specifies the zone file as localhost.zone. That file is located in
the /var/named directory of your Red Hat Linux system. The /var/named/
localhost.zone file contains the following resource records:

```
$TTL    86400
$ORIGIN localhost.
@               1D IN SOA       @ root (
                                42              ; serial (d. adams)
                                3H              ; refresh
                                15M             ; retry
                                1W              ; expiry
                                1D )            ; minimum

                1D IN NS        @
                1D IN A         127.0.0.1
```

This zone file starts with a $TTL directive that sets the default Time To Live
(TTL) at one day (86400 seconds) for subsequent records with undefined
TTLs. Next, a $ORIGIN directive sets the domain name to localhost.

After these two directives, the /var/named/localhost.zone file contains
three resource records (RRs): an SOA record, an NS record, and an A record.
The SOA and the NS record specify the localhost as the primary authoritative name server for the zone. The A record specifies the address of
localhost as 127.0.0.1.

/var/named/named.local file

The third zone in the `/etc/named.conf` file specifies a reverse-mapping zone named `0.0.127.in-addr.arpa`. For this zone, the zone file is `/var/named/named.local`, which contains the following:

```
$TTL    86400
@       IN      SOA     localhost. root.localhost. (
                                1997022700 ; Serial
                                28800      ; Refresh
                                14400      ; Retry
                                3600000    ; Expire
                                86400 )    ; Minimum

        IN      NS      localhost.

1       IN      PTR     localhost.
```

The SOA and NS records specify `localhost` as the primary name server.

Secret

The SOA record also shows `root.loaclhost.` as the e-mail address of the technical contact for the domain. Note that the DNS zone files use a `user.host.` format for the e-mail address. When sending any e-mail, you have to replace the first dot with an @, and remove the final dot.

Caching name server startup and test

Now that you have studied the configuration files for the caching name server, you can go ahead and start the name server and see it in operation. To start the name server, log in as root and type the following command at the shell prompt:

```
/etc/init.d/named start
```

This starts `named` — the name server daemon.

Tip

To ensure that the server starts every time you reboot the system, use the graphical SYSV Runlevel Manager utility to automatically start `named` (log in as root and type `tksysv` in a terminal window in the GNOME or KDE desktop). The "NIS client daemon setup" section further describes how to use the SYSV Runlevel Manager.

The `named` server writes diagnostic log messages in the `/var/log/messages` file. After you start `named`, you can check the log messages, by opening `/var/log/messages` in a text editor. Following are some typical log messages from `named` when started on my Red Hat Linux system:

```
Feb  2 22:28:27 lnbp200 named: named startup succeeded
Feb  2 22:28:27 lnbp200 named[3981]: starting BIND 9.1.0b2 -u named
Feb  2 22:28:27 lnbp200 named[3981]: using 1 CPU
Feb  2 22:28:27 lnbp200 named[3985]: loading configuration from
'/etc/named.conf'
Feb  2 22:28:27 lnbp200 named[3985]: the default for the 'auth-nxdomain' option
is now 'no'
Feb  2 22:28:27 lnbp200 modprobe: modprobe: Can't locate module net-pf-10
Feb  2 22:28:27 lnbp200 named[3985]: no IPv6 interfaces found
```

```
Feb  2 22:28:27 lnbp200 named[3985]: listening on IPv4 interface lo,
127.0.0.1#53
Feb  2 22:28:27 lnbp200 named[3985]: listening on IPv4 interface eth0,
192.168.1.200#53
Feb  2 22:28:27 lnbp200 named[3985]: running
```

If there are no error messages from named, you can proceed to test the name server.

Note

Before you try the caching name server, you have to specify that name server as your primary name server. To do this, make sure that the first line in the /etc/resolv.conf file is the following:

```
nameserver 127.0.0.1
```

Now you can use nslookup to test the name server. The following sample session shows how I tested the caching name server on my Red Hat Linux system using nslookup:

```
nslookup
Default Server:  localhost
Address:  127.0.0.1
> psn.net.
Server:  localhost
Address:  127.0.0.1

Name:    psn.net
Address: 207.211.58.10
> psn.net.
Server:  localhost
Address:  127.0.0.1

Non-authoritative answer:
Name:    psn.net
Address: 207.211.58.10
```

Notice that immediately after starting, nslookup shows localhost as the default server, which is a good sign. Next I type a query for the address of psn.net. The nslookup program queries the caching name server for the answer. The caching name server starts by contacting one of the root servers and proceeds from there to find the address of psn.net. It takes a few moments, but soon nslookup prints an authoritative answer (if it's not authoritative, nslookup's output indicates this).

I immediately try looking up psn.net again. This time the caching server provides an immediate answer because the previous result was cached. However, the answer is not authoritative; therefore, the output from nslookup is shown as Non-authoritative answer:. This shows that the caching name server is working correctly. I type exit at the nslookup prompt to quit that program.

Network Information Service (NIS)

Network Information Service (NIS) was developed by Sun Microsystems as a way to share information among all computers in a local area network. The types of information most commonly shared by NIS include the following:

- User names and passwords from files such as /etc/passwd and /etc/shadow

- Group information from the /etc/group file

Normally, each system would have its own copy of information in respective files, and any changes would require updating the files on each system individually. Using NIS, you can maintain a single set of configuration files for a collection of computers in an NIS server. All other computers running NIS clients can then access the files. For example, if your user name and password are in the NIS password database, you will be able to log in on all computers on the network running NIS client programs.

Note

NIS was originally called Sun Yellow Pages (YP), but the name Yellow Pages is a registered trademark of British Telecom in the United Kingdom, so Sun Microsystems had to change the name. However, many NIS commands, and the NIS package names, begin with the letters yp.

How NIS Works

If you want to use NIS in a network, you must set up at least one computer as an NIS server. You can have multiple NIS servers in a network, each serving a different collection of computers. You can also have a master NIS server and one or more slave NIS servers that receive a copy of the master's database. The group of computers that a master NIS server supports is called an NIS *domain* or *YP domain.*

The master NIS server runs the ypserv daemon (this is the NIS server daemon) that maintains the shared information in DBM databases. (DBM refers to Data Base Management, a library of functions that maintain key-value pairs in a database.) The NIS databases are called *maps.* You can create these NIS maps directly from the text configuration files — such as /etc/passwd and /etc/group — by using the /usr/lib/yp/makedbm program that comes with the NIS server software. More accurately, the ypserv daemon uses the Makefile in the /var/yp directory to create the maps for all shared configuration files.

The master NIS server provides the maps to all NIS client computers. The clients run the ypbind daemon through which various client programs access the master NIS server. In addition to a master server, one or more NIS slave servers may be set up to provide the NIS maps, in case the master is unavailable or down. The NIS slave servers periodically copy the NIS maps from the master server (using the /usr/lib/yp/ypxfr command), and are able to provide these maps to clients when the master is down.

You can think of NIS as a way of distributing the same set of configuration files among all computers in an NIS domain. You get the benefits of sharing the same files (such as the same user name and password for all machines), yet you can still edit and maintain just one set of files — the ones on the master NIS server.

The next few sections describe how to set up your Red Hat Linux system as an NIS client and an NIS server.

NIS Client Setup

If your network uses NIS to centrally administer users and passwords, you can set up your Red Hat Linux PC as an NIS client. In fact, when you install Red Hat Linux from this book's companion CD-ROMs, you can enable NIS from the Authentication Configuration screen in the GUI installer.

Cross-Reference

During Red Hat Linux installation (see Chapter 2 for details), the Authentication Configuration screen shows you a number of different options for authenticating users — the default being shadow passwords and the MD5 password (which are discussed in Chapter 29). One of these options is a button labeled Enable NIS. You can click this button to set up your Red Hat Linux PC as an NIS client. Of course, you should do this only if your network is set up with an NIS server.

If you do select the Enable NIS option, you have to provide the following information:

- Specify the NIS domain name. The domain name refers to the group of computers that are served by the NIS server.

- Specify the name of the NIS server.

- Indicate whether you want your PC to use IP broadcast to find NIS servers in the local network.

If you did not configure your system as an NIS client during Red Hat Linux installation, you can do so by performing the following tasks:

- Define your NIS domain name.

- Set up the NIS configuration file (/etc/yp.conf). In this file, you specify the master NIS and slave servers that provide NIS maps to your Red Hat Linux PC.

- Configure the NIS client daemon — ypbind — to start when your system boots.

The next three sections show you how to perform these tasks.

NIS domain name setup

The NIS domain name is a name that identifies the group of computers that a particular NIS server supports. You can set the NIS domain name of your system by using the `domainname` command. For example, to set your NIS domain name to admin, log in as root and type the following at the shell prompt:

```
domainname admin
```

If you type `domainname` without any arguments, the command prints out the current NIS domain name.

To ensure that the NIS domain name is set as soon as your system boots, the command should be run from one of the startup scripts. You can do this by adding the following line to the `/etc/sysconfig/network` file on your Red Hat Linux system:

```
NISDOMAIN="admin"
```

Of course, you should use the NIS domain name appropriate for your network.

Caution

The NIS domain is different from the DNS domain names discussed earlier in this chapter. It's best if you pick an NIS domain name that's not related to the DNS domain name. This makes it harder for crackers to guess your NIS domain name (if they know the NIS domain name, there is a risk that they can get the NIS password database).

NIS configuration file setup

The `ypbind` daemon, described in the next section, needs information about the NIS domains and NIS servers to do its job. It finds this information in the `/etc/yp.conf` configuration file. The `ypbind` daemon reads the `/etc/yp.conf` file when it starts up, or when it receives the `SIGHUP` signal (for example, when you restart `ypbind` with the `kill -HUP` command).

To specify one or more NIS servers for the local domain (which you have already set with the `domainname` command), all you need in `/etc/yp.conf` are lines such as the following:

```
ypserver nisadmin
ypserver 192.168.1.200
```

You can use a name such as `nisadmin`, if that name is listed in the `/etc/hosts` file (that way, `ypbind` can resolve the name into an IP address, without having to use NIS). Otherwise, you should specify the NIS server's IP address.

In `/etc/yp.conf`, you can also specify specific NIS servers for specific NIS domains, like this:

```
domain sales server nissales
domain admin server nisadmin
```

A third type of entry in the `/etc/yp.conf` file specifies that `ypbind` should use IP broadcast in the local network to find an NIS server for a specified domain. To do this, add a line, such as the following to `/etc/yp.conf`:

```
domain admin broadcast
```

NIS client daemon setup

Every computer in an NIS domain, including the server, runs the `ypbind` daemon. Various NIS client applications, such as `ypwhich`, `ypcat`, and `yppoll`, need the `ypbind` daemon to obtain information from the master NIS server. More precisely, the C library contacts the `ypbind` daemon to locate the NIS server for the domain. Then the C library contacts the server directly to obtain administrative information. The client applications get the information through functions in the C library.

To interactively start `ypbind`, log in as root and type the following command:

```
/etc/init.d/ypbind start
```

If you want `ypbind` to start when the system boots, you can add the following line to the `/etc/rc.local` file:

Note

Note that `/etc/init.d` is a symbolic link to the `/etc/rc.d/init.d` directory; and `/etc/rc.local` is a symbolic link to the `/etc/rc.d/rc.local` file. These changes were made starting in Red Hat Linux 7.0 for greater compatibility across different Linux distributions.

Another way to start the `ypbind` daemon at system startup is to use the SYSV Runlevel Manager (where SYSV stands for System V — a UNIX system version). To run the SYSV Runlevel Manager, log in as root at the graphical login window, and then type `tksysv` in a terminal window. The SYSV Runlevel Manager displays the available servers, as well as which ones are started and stopped at run levels 2, 3, 4, and 5 (see Chapter 23 for a description of run levels). Four buttons — Add, Remove, Edit, and Execute — enable you to configure which servers are started and stopped at various run levels.

To start `ypbind` at a specific run level, select `ypbind` from the list of available servers and then click the Add button. A new dialog box appears, from which you can select the action (start or stop) and run level (2, 3, 4, or 5) for `ypbind`. Typically, you want to enable `ypbind` at run levels 3 and 5. Figure 21-3 shows the SYSV Runlevel Manager as it is being used to start `ypbind` at run level 5.

You can use the SYSV Runlevel Manager to automatically start the NIS server, `ypserv`, as well.

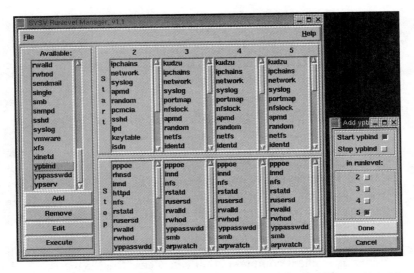

Figure 21-3: The SYSV Runlevel Manager can be used to configure servers to start automatically at various run levels.

NIS Server Setup

To set up your Red Hat Linux system as an NIS server, you should first set it up as an NIS client — set the NIS domain name, configure the /etc/yp.conf file, and configure the ypbind daemon. (Note that the ypbind daemon won't work until you have an NIS server up and running). After the client configuration, you can configure the NIS server. This requires that you perform the following tasks:

- Create the NIS maps using ypinit.
- Configure the master NIS server — ypserv
- Optionally, configure one or more slave NIS servers

The next two sections explain these steps.

NIS map creation

Creating NIS maps involves converting the text files, such as /etc/passwd and /etc/group into DBM files using makedbm. The map creation is controlled by /var/yp/Makefile, which is a file that can be used by the make command to perform specific tasks (see Chapter 27 for more information on make and Makefile).

You can configure what you want the NIS server to share with the clients in the NIS domain. You do so by editing the `Makefile` in the `/var/yp` directory. Open `/var/yp/Makefile` in a text editor and locate the line that begins with all:. Here is a typical excerpt from the Makefile showing the comments before the all: line:

```
# If you don't want some of these maps built, feel free to comment
# them out from this list.

all:  passwd group hosts rpc services netid protocols mail \
      # netgrp shadow publickey networks ethers bootparams printcap \
      # amd.home auto.master auto.home auto.local passwd.adjunct \
      # timezone locale netmasks
```

As the comment lines (the ones that begin with #) indicate, you can comment out any maps that you do not want to build. In the preceding example, the maps listed in the last three lines will not be built.

Next you should edit the `/var/yp/securenets` file to specify the IP addresses of client computers that can access the NIS maps. The default file has the following lines:

```
# securenets   This file defines the access rights to your NIS server
#              for NIS clients. This file contains netmask/network
#              pairs. A clients IP address needs to match with at
#              least one of those.
#
#              One can use the word "host" instead of a netmask of
#              255.255.255.255. Only IP addresses are allowed in this
#              file, not hostnames.
#
# Always allow access for localhost
255.0.0.0      127.0.0.0

# This line gives access to everybody. PLEASE ADJUST!
0.0.0.0        0.0.0.0
```

As the last comment line shows, the default configuration grants access to all IP addresses. For example, to limit access to the class C network 192.168.1.0, you would change the last line as follows:

```
255.255.255.0    192.168.1.0
```

This allows only those computers on the local network with IP addresses in the range 192.168.1.1 through 192.168.1.254 access to the NIS maps.

Next, you should generate the NIS map database, by running the `/usr/lib/yp/ypinit` program with the -m option. Here is a sample session with that program:

/usr/lib/yp/ypinit -m
```
At this point, we have to construct a list of the hosts which will run NIS
servers.  lnbp200 is in the list of NIS server hosts.  Please continue to add
the names for the other hosts, one per line.  When you are done with the
```

```
list, type a <control D>.
        next host to add:  lnbp200
        next host to add:  <Press Ctrl+D here>
The current list of NIS servers looks like this:

lnbp200

Is this correct?  [y/n: y]  y
We need some  minutes to build the databases...
Building /var/yp/admin/ypservers...
Running /var/yp/Makefile...
gmake[1]: Entering directory `/var/yp/admin'
Updating passwd.byname...
Updating passwd.byuid...
...lines deleted...
```

The `/usr/lib/yp/ypinit` program automatically selects your host as an NIS
server, and then prompts for the names of any other NIS servers. You can add
the server names one at a time, and then press Ctrl+D when done. Then you
have to verify that the list of NIS servers is correct (type y). After that, make
runs with the `/var/yp/Makefile` and generates the NIS maps as specified by
the `all:` line in the `Makefile`. The map files are stored in a subdirectory of
`/var/yp` that has the same name as the NIS domain name you have previously set for your system. For example, for the NIS domain admin, the map
files are in the `/var/yp/admin` directory.

Master NIS server configuration

To configure the NIS server daemon, `ypserv`, you have to prepare the configuration file `/etc/ypserv.conf`. You can learn about the syntax of this file
by reading its man page, which you can access by typing the command
man ypserv.conf. Among other options, you can use the following option
to specify that DNS should not be used to look up host names that are not in
the maps of the /etc/hosts file:

```
dns: no
```

You can also add other lines in `/etc/ypserv.conf` that specify access
rules — which hosts can access which maps. The format of the access rules
is as follows:

```
Host : Map : Security : mangle [: field_to_mangle]
```

The `field_to_mangle` is optional; it indicates which field in the map file
should be mangled (the default is the second field because the password is in
the second field of most files, such as `/etc/passwd`). To mangle a field is to
replace it with an x if the request comes from an unprivileged host. The rest
of the fields have the following meanings:

- *Host* — IP address or a wildcard (*) indicating to whom the rule applies

- *Map* — Name of the map to which the rule applies (the names of the maps
  are the same as that of the map files in the `/var/yp/domainname` directory, where *domainname* is your NIS domain name)

- *Security* — One of the following: none (to always allow access), port (to access from a port less than 1024), deny (to deny access to the map), or des (to require DES authentication — this may not be supported by all C libraries)

- *mangle* — One of the following: yes (the field specified by *field_to_mangle* should be replaced by an x, if the request is from unauthorized host), or no (do not mangle)

For example, the following lines in the /etc/ypserv.conf file restrict access to the password map to systems in the 192.168.1 network:

```
192.168.1    :    passwd.byname    : port    : yes
192.168.1    :    passwd.byuid     : port    : yes
```

If you do not specify any access rules, ypserv allows all computers to access all maps.

Once you have set up the /etc/ypserv.conf file, you can start the NIS server with the following command:

```
/etc/init.d/ypserv start
Starting YP server services: [  OK  ]
```

To ensure that ypserv starts whenever you reboot the system, you should use the SYSV Runlevel Manager and configure ypserv to start and stop at run levels 3 and 5.

Secret

To handle password changes from clients, you must also run the rpc.yppasswdd server on the master NIS server for the domain. The rpc.yppasswdd server enables users on client systems to type the yppasswd command and change their password in the NIS database. If you do not have the rpc.yppasswdd server running on the master NIS server, users will get the following error message when they type the yppasswd command:

```
yppasswd: yppasswdd not running on NIS master host
```

You can correct this problem by starting rpc.yppasswdd; log in as root and type the command /etc/init.d/yppasswdd start. To start it automatically at run levels 3 and 5, use the SYSV Runlevel Manager (type tksysv to start it).

Once you have the master NIS server up and running, you can test it using various NIS client programs, such as ypwhich, yppoll, ypcat, and ypmatch.

Slave NIS server configuration

To set up a system as a slave NIS server, first set it up as an NIS client and verify that the client works. In particular, type ypwhich -m and look for a list of NIS maps and the name of the master NIS server for each map (the next section shows how the ypwhich -m command works).

After you confirm that the system is configured as an NIS client, type the following command to set up the system as a slave NIS server:

```
/usr/lib/yp/ypinit -s nismaster
```

where *nismaster* is the name of the master NIS server for the domain.

NIS Diagnostics

If you do not have a master NIS server in your network, first perform the client configurations, and then start the master NIS server, as explained in earlier sections. Then start the ypbind daemon as follows:

```
/etc/init.d/ypbind start
Binding to the NIS domain...
Listening for an NIS domain server: lnbp200
```

Now you can try out various NIS client programs and other utilities to see if everything is working correctly.

NIS servers and clients use Remote Procedure Call (RPC) to exchange information. Network File System (NFS), described in Chapter 22, also uses RPC. RPC requires the portmap service, which maps RPC services to TCP and UDP ports. When a server that supports RPC starts up, it registers itself with portmap and lists both the services it supports, and the ports it uses. Your Red Hat Linux system should already have portmap up and running. You can check for it with the following command:

```
ps ax | grep portmap
  371 ?        S      0:00 portmap
 6755 pts/0    S      0:00 grep portmap
```

You should see a line showing the portmap process and its ID in the output. In this case, the portmap process has an ID of 371.

To see if the ypserv and ypbind processes are running on the master NIS server, use the /usr/sbin/rpcinfo program to check if ypserv and ypbind were able to register with the portmap service. For example, here is a sample output:

```
/usr/sbin/rpcinfo -p
   program vers proto   port
    100000    2   tcp    111  portmapper
    100000    2   udp    111  portmapper
    100021    1   udp   1024  nlockmgr
    100021    3   udp   1024  nlockmgr
    100024    1   udp   1025  status
    100024    1   tcp   1024  status
    100007    2   udp    647  ypbind
    100007    1   udp    647  ypbind
    100007    2   tcp    650  ypbind
    100007    1   tcp    650  ypbind
```

```
100004    2    udp    894    ypserv
100004    1    udp    894    ypserv
100004    2    tcp    897    ypserv
100004    1    tcp    897    ypserv
```

Each line shows the RPC program number, a version number, the protocol (TCP or UDP), the port number, and the service. As you can see, both ypbind and ypserv are registered.

To determine which NIS server your system is using, try the ypwhich command. Here is a typical example:

```
ypwhich
lnbp200
```

You can also use the ypwhich command to view the master NIS server for a specified map. If you want to see the master NIS server for the available maps, type the following command:

```
ypwhich -m
mail.aliases lnbp200
protocols.bynumber lnbp200
services.byservicename lnbp200
netid.byname lnbp200
services.byname lnbp200
rpc.bynumber lnbp200
rpc.byname lnbp200
hosts.byaddr lnbp200
hosts.byname lnbp200
group.bygid lnbp200
group.byname lnbp200
passwd.byname lnbp200
protocols.byname lnbp200
ypservers lnbp200
passwd.byuid lnbp200
```

The output shows a list of the available NIS maps and, for each map, the name of the master NIS server.

To view the name of the master NIS server and information about a specific NIS map, use the yppoll command. For example, here is the result of a yppoll query for the passwd.byname map:

```
yppoll passwd.byname
Domain admin is supported.
Map passwd.byname has order number 972760603. [Sat Oct 28 15:16:43 2000]
The master server is lnbp200
```

Use the ypcat command to print the values of the keys in an NIS map. For example, here is a ypcat query for the NIS map group.byname:

```
ypcat group.byname
ivy:!:503:
ashley:!:502:
emily:!:501:
naba:!:500:
```

You can use `ypmatch` to look at the entries in an NIS map that match a specific key. For example, here is a `ypmatch` command line that looks for entries that match the key `naba` in the `group.byname` map:

```
ypmatch naba group.byname
naba:!:500:
```

If you compare this with the output from `ypcat` showing all the groups, you see that `ypmatch` shows the line corresponding to the group name `naba`.

Summary

Domain Name System (DNS) is a key Internet service, one that enables us to use easy-to-remember names for Web sites and servers on the Internet, even though TCP/IP requires numeric IP addresses for data transfers. Network Information Service (NIS) is another useful service for local networks to share configuration files, such as users, groups, and passwords. Red Hat Linux comes with everything needed to run the servers and clients for DNS and NIS. This chapter describes how to use DNS and NIS in Red Hat Linux.

By reading this chapter, you learn the following:

▶ DNS is a distributed database that holds information about host names, IP addresses, and mail routing. Internet applications use DNS to convert host names, such as `www.redhat.com` into IP addresses.

▶ DNS is documented in RFCs 1034 and 1035. Many other RFCs document various updates and extensions to DNS.

▶ All hosts on the Internet use DNS. Each host needs a name server that it can query to resolve host names into IP addresses. Typically, the Internet Service Provider (ISP) provides the name servers. The IP addresses of the name servers are listed in the `/etc/resolv.conf` file.

▶ Red Hat Linux comes with the Berkeley Internet Domain (BIND) system, which is a well-known implementation of DNS.

▶ To set up a name server, you have to prepare the `/etc/named.conf` configuration files and zone files referenced in that configuration file. The zone files are usually stored in the `/var/named` directory.

▶ Red Hat Linux comes with the configuration files for a caching name server that loads the addresses of a few authoritative servers for the root domain, and then gets all its data by caching responses to queries resolved by contacting other name servers. This chapter walks you through the process of setting up the caching name server and explains the configuration files used by the server.

▶ You can use BIND utilities, such as `nslookup`, `dig`, and `host` to interactively query the DNS database.

▶ NIS was developed by Sun Microsystems as a way of sharing configuration files among a number of computers in a local area network. The password file and group information files are typically shared using NIS. This enables users to log in, using the same user name and password on all computers in the local network.

▶ NIS clients have to define their NIS domain (a name for all the computers that an NIS server serves); set up the NIS configuration file /etc/yp.conf; and run the ypbind daemon. All NIS client applications access the NIS server through the local ypbind process.

▶ To set up a master NIS server, you have to create the NIS maps — the NIS databases — by running /usr/lib/yp/ypinit; set up the configuration file /etc/ypserv.conf; and start the NIS server, ypserv.

▶ You can test the NIS server by running NIS client applications, such as ypwhich, yppoll, ypcat, and ypmatch.

▶ If you want users to be able to set or change NIS passwords using the yppasswd command, you must also run the rpc.yppasswdd daemon on the master NIS server.

Chapter 22

Samba and NFS

In This Chapter

▶ Sharing files with NFS

▶ Setting up your Red Hat Linux PC as a Windows server with Samba

▶ Accessing Windows servers with `smbclient`

▶ Configuring Samba with the Samba Web Administration Tool (SWAT)

▶ Printing from Red Hat Linux on a Windows printer

A low-end Pentium PC (or even a 486) configured with Red Hat Linux (from this book's companion CD-ROMs) makes a very capable workgroup (or office) server. By *workgroup*, I mean a small local area network (LAN) of perhaps a dozen or so PCs. You can configure the Linux PC to be the file and print server and have the other PCs be the clients. The client PCs do not have to run Linux; they can run Windows. Linux comes with the Samba package, which provides you with everything you need to set up your Linux PC as a server in a Windows network. This chapter introduces you to Samba. You also learn about file sharing through Network File System (NFS), which is built into Linux.

Sharing Files with NFS

Sharing files through NFS is simple, and involves two basic steps:

■ On the Linux server, export one or more directories by listing them in the `/etc/exports` file, and then running the `/usr/sbin/exportfs` command. You must also run the NFS server (you can do this by logging in as root and typing `/etc/init.d/nfs start`).

■ On each client system, mount the directories exported by the server, using the `mount` command.

The only problem in using NFS is that each client system must support it. Most PCs do not come with NFS. That means you have to buy NFS software separately if you want to share files using NFS. However, it makes sense to use NFS if all systems on your LAN run Linux (or other variants of UNIX with built-in NFS support).

Caution

You should also note that NFS has known security vulnerabilities. Therefore, you should not set up NFS on systems that are directly connected to the Internet.

The next subsections walk you through NFS setup, using an example of two Linux PCs on a LAN.

Exporting a File System with NFS

Start with the server system that exports — makes available to the client systems — the contents of a directory. On the server, you must run the NFS service and also designate one or more file systems that are to be exported — made available to the client systems. You can perform both tasks using the Linuxconf graphical system administration tool.

To start Linuxconf, log in as root and select Main Menu ⇨ Programs ⇨ System ⇨ Linuxconf from the GNOME desktop. From the tree menu in the Config tab, select Networking ⇨ Server tasks ⇨ Exported file systems (NFS). This brings up a tab that shows the current contents of the /etc/exports file. If that file is empty, Linuxconf displays an empty tab, as shown in Figure 22-1.

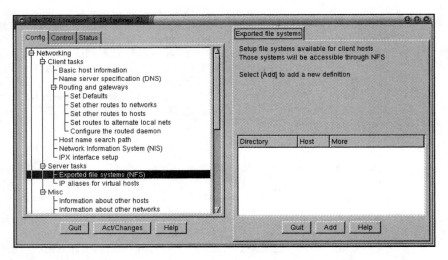

Figure 22-1: Viewing summary information about exported file systems in Linuxconf

Click the Add button. This brings up a new tab where you can specify the details of the exported file system. You specify the file system with a full path name, as shown in the Path to export field in the right-hand tab in Figure 22-2.

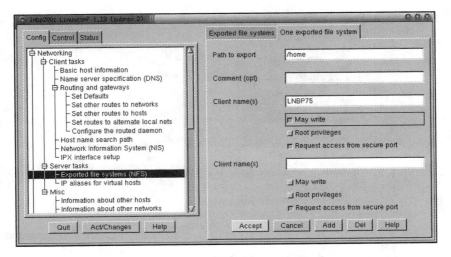

Figure 22-2: Entering information about exported file systems in Linuxconf

In this tab you should also enter the names of client systems that may mount this exported file system. In the example shown in Figure 22-2, the /home directory is being exported, and the host named LNBP75 can mount this file system for read and write operations. After entering the information, click the Accept button. Linuxconf returns to the tab shown in Figure 22-2, where it displays summary information about the exported file system. You can then click the Quit button to finish defining exported file systems.

As a result of this session Linuxconf adds the following entry to the /etc/exports file:

```
/home LNBP75(rw)
```

To verify, type cat /etc/exports in a terminal window. To manually export the files, type /usr/sbin/exportfs -a.

This command exports all file systems defined in the /etc/exports file.

Now you should turn on the NFS server. To do this, select Control panel ⇨ Control service activity from the Linuxconf window's Control tab. The Service control tab appears with a list of all the services and their status, as shown in Figure 22-3.

Each line has three fields: the first tells you the name of a service, the second whether it is enabled to run automatically or manually, and the third whether it is already running. Scroll down the list and locate the entry named nfs — this is the NFS service. In this case, the NFS service is not yet running. Click on that entry. This causes Linuxconf to display the Service nfs tab, as shown in Figure 22-4.

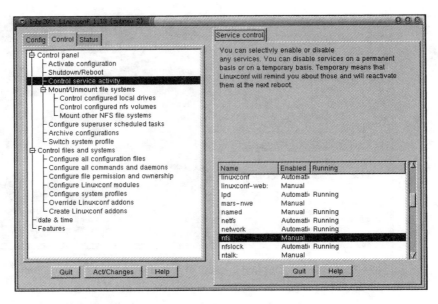

Figure 22-3: Viewing the service control tab in Linuxconf

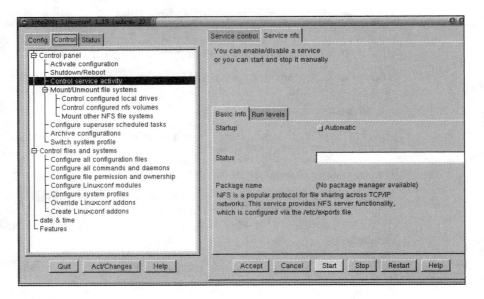

Figure 22-4: Starting the NFS service through Linuxconf

The buttons in this tab enable you to start, stop, or restart the service. In this case, click the Start button to start the NFS service. Then click Accept to return to the previous tab (Figure 22-3). Now the tab should show the status of the nfs entry as Running. Click Quit to exit this tab.

Tip

If you ever make any changes to the exported file systems listed in the /etc/exports file, remember to restart the NFS service. Click the Restart button in the Linuxconf tab shown in Figure 22-4.

If you prefer to start the NFS service using a command, log in as root and type the following command in a terminal window:

```
/etc/init.d/nfs start
Starting NFS services:  [  OK  ]
Starting NFS quotas:  [  OK  ]
Starting NFS mountd:  [  OK  ]
Starting NFS daemon:  [  OK  ]
```

To restart the NFS service, type /etc/init.d/nfs restart.

Once the NFS service is up, the server side of NFS is ready. Now you can try to mount the exported file system from a client system and access the exported file system.

Mounting an NFS File System

You can use Linuxconf on the client system to mount an exported NFS file system. From the Control tab, select Control panel ⇨ Mount/Unmount file systems ⇨ Mount other NFS file systems. Linuxconf displays a tab (see Figure 22-5) in which you can enter the information about the NFS file system.

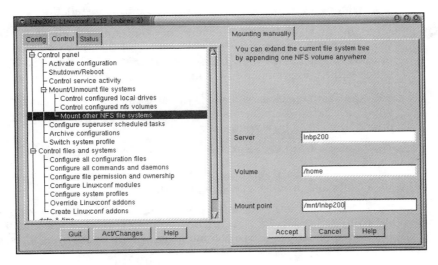

Figure 22-5: Mounting an NFS file system using Linuxconf

In the Server field, enter the host name of the system that is exporting the NFS file system. Enter the name of that file system in the Volume field. In the Mount point field, enter the name of the local directory where the NFS file system is to be mounted. (Make sure that the mount point exists; otherwise, create it with a command such as `mkdir /mnt/lnbp200`.) Then click the Accept button.

For the information shown in Figure 22-5, you can perform the mount operation by entering the following command on the client system (while logged in as root):

```
mount lnbp200:/home/public /mnt/lnbp200
```

Then you can view and access exported files from the local directory `/mnt/lnbp200`.

To confirm that the NFS file system is indeed mounted, log in as root on the client system and type `mount` in a terminal window. You should see a line similar to the following one about the NFS file system:

```
lnbp200:/home/public on /mnt/lnbp200 type nfs (rw,addr=192.168.1.200)
```

Setting Up a Windows Server Using Samba

If you rely on Windows for file and print sharing, you probably use Windows in your servers and clients. You can move to a Linux PC as your server, without losing the Windows file and printer sharing, because a Linux PC can be set up as a Windows server. When you install Red Hat Linux from this book's companion CD-ROMs you also get a chance to install the Samba software package, which performs that setup. All you have to do is select the DOS/Windows Connectivity package group during installation.

Note

After you install and configure Samba on your Linux PC, client PCs (running Windows for Workgroups or Windows 95/98/NT/2000) can access disks and printers on the Linux PC, by using the Server Message Block (SMB) protocol, which is the underlying protocol in Windows file and print sharing.

With the Samba package installed, you also can make your Linux PC a Windows client, which means that the Linux PC can access disks and printers managed by a Windows server.

The Samba software package has these major components:

- `smbd` — The SMB server, which accepts connections from Windows clients and provides file- and print-sharing services.

- `nmbd` — The NetBIOS name server, which clients use to look up servers. (NetBIOS stands for Network Basic Input/Output System — an interface that applications use to communicate with network transports, such as TCP/IP.)

- `/etc/samba/smb.conf` — The Samba configuration file that is used by the SMB server.

- `testparm` — A program that ensures that the Samba configuration file is correct.

- `smbclient` — The Windows client, which runs on Linux and allows Linux to access the files and printer on any Windows server.

- `smbmount` — A program that mounts a Samba share directory on the Linux client.

- `smbumount` — A program that unmounts a currently mounted Samba share directory.

- `smbprint` — A script that enables printing on a printer on a SMB server.

- `smbadduser` — A program that adds user to the SMB password file.

- `smbpasswd` — A program that changes the password for an SMB user.

- `smbstatus` — A command that lists the current SMB connections for the local host.

- `nmblookup` — A command that returns the IP address of a Windows PC identified by its NetBIOS name.

- SWAT — The Samba Web Administration Tool, for configuring /etc/samba/smb.conf with a Web browser.

The following subsections describe how to install Samba from the companion CD-ROM and how to set up a printer on the Linux PC to print through Windows.

Checking Whether Samba Is Installed

Check whether Samba is installed, by typing the following command in a terminal window:

```
rpm -q samba
samba-2.0.7-21ssl
```

If the `rpm` command displays a package name that begins with samba, then Samba is already installed on your system, and you should skip this subsection. Otherwise, follow these steps to install Samba from this book's companion CD-ROM:

1. Log in as root and make sure that the appropriate companion CD-ROM is in the drive and mounted. If not, use the `umount /mnt/cdrom` command to dismount the current CD-ROM, replace it with the correct CD-ROM, and then mount that CD-ROM with the `mount /mnt/cdrom` command.

2. Change the directory to the CD-ROM — specifically to the directory where the Red Hat Package Manager (RPM) packages are located — with the following command:

   ```
   cd /mnt/cdrom/RedHat/RPMS
   ```

3. Use the following `rpm` command to install Samba:

   ```
   rpm -ivh samba*
   ```

   If Samba is already installed, this command returns an error message. Otherwise, the `rpm` command installs Samba on your system by copying various files to their appropriate locations.

These steps complete the unpacking and installation of the Samba software. Now all you have to do to use Samba is configure it.

Configuring Samba

To set up the Windows file- and print-sharing services, you have to provide a configuration file named /etc/samba/smb.conf. The configuration file is a text file that looks like a Microsoft Windows 3.1 INI file.

Like the Windows INI files, the /etc/smb.conf file consists of sections, with a list of parameters in each section. Each section of the smb.conf file begins with the name of the section in brackets. The section continues until the next section begins, or the file ends.

Each line in a section specifies the value of a parameter, using the following syntax:

```
name = value
```

As in Windows INI files, comment lines begin with a semicolon (;). In the /etc/smb.conf file comments may also begin with a hash (#).

The Samba software comes with a configuration file that you can edit to get started. To prepare the configuration file, log in as root and use your favorite text editor to edit the file /etc/smb.conf. Here's a sample configuration file without any comments:

```
[global]
    netbios name = LNBP200
    workgroup = LNB SOFTWARE
    server string = LNB Software-Red Hat Linux-Samba Server
    hosts allow = 192.168.1.  127.
    guest account = naba
    log file = /var/log/samba/log.%m

# Log files can be at most 50KB
    max log size = 50

    security = user
    smb passwd file = /etc/samba/smbpasswd

# Leave the next option as is - they're for performance
    socket options = TCP_NODELAY SO_RCVBUF=8192 SO_SNDBUF=8192

    remote browse sync = 192.168.1.255
    remote announce = 192.168.1.255/LNB SOFTWARE
    local master = yes
    os level = 33

    name resolve order = lmhosts bcast

    dns proxy = no
    unix password sync = no

[homes]
    comment = Home Directories
    browseable = no
    writable = yes
```

```
[printers]
    comment = All Printers
    path = /var/spool/samba
    browseable = no
    guest ok = no
    writable = no
    printable = yes

[tmp]
    comment = Temporary file space
    path = /tmp
    read only = no
    public = yes

[public]
    comment = Public Stuff
    path = /home/samba
    browseable = yes
    public = yes
    guest ok = yes
    writable = yes
    printable = no
    available = yes
    guest only = no
    user = naba
    only user = yes
```

Change the user name from naba to your user name. Also make sure that all directories mentioned in the configuration file actually exist. For example, create the /home/samba directory with the command mkdir /home/samba.

After editing the Samba configuration file, add two users to the Samba password file. First add your user name. Here's how I add myself:

```
smbadduser naba:naba
------------------------------------------------------------
ENTER password for naba
New SMB password:          password
Retype new SMB password:   password
Password changed for user naba.
```

Tip

After making the changes to the /etc/samba/smb.conf file, type **testparm** to verify that the file is OK. Then restart the SMB services with the following command:

```
/etc/init.d/smb restart
Shutting down SMB services:                    [  OK  ]
Shutting down NMB services:                    [  OK  ]
Starting SMB services:                         [  OK  ]
Starting NMB services:                         [  OK  ]
```

Testing the Samba Configuration File

You can now try to access the Samba server on the Red Hat Linux system from one of the Windows systems on the LAN. Double-click the Network Neighborhood icon on the Windows desktop. This should open up the Network Neighborhood window (Figure 22-6) with all the other Windows systems on the LAN. Click the Lnbp200 icon to see its server string. As you can see from the comment in the lower left-hand corner of Figure 22-6, Lnbp200 is actually a Red Hat Linux system running Samba.

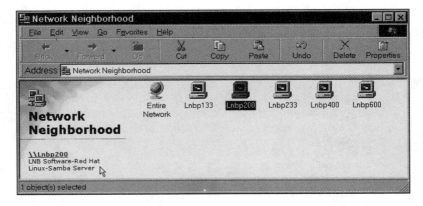

Figure 22-6: Viewing a Red Hat Linux Samba server in the Windows Network Neighborhood

If you do not see the Red Hat Linux Samba server in the Network Neighbor-hood, select Start ⇨ Find ⇨ Computer on your Windows system, enter the Red Hat Linux system's host name (in this case, Lnbp200), and click the Find Now button. The Red Hat Linux Samba server should then show up, as shown in Figure 22-7.

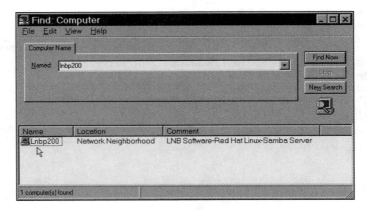

Figure 22-7: Searching for a Red Hat Linux Samba server from Windows

Once you see the Red Hat Linux Samba server, you can open it by double-clicking the icon (either in the Network Neighborhood window of Figure 22-6, or the search window of Figure 22-7). This should show folders for each shared directory in the Red Hat Linux Samba server (for the sample /etc/samba/smb.conf file shown above, you'd see two directories: tmp and public). You can then open these folders to further explore the contents of the directories.

Configuring Samba with SWAT

You have already seen how to configure Samba by editing the text file /etc/samba/smb.conf. Samba also comes with the Samba Web Administration Tool (SWAT), which enables a Samba administrator to configure the smb.conf file via a Web browser. The SWAT configuration page also has links to all help information on various configurable options in the smb.conf file.

Setting up xinetd to start SWAT

To use SWAT, you have to first configure the xinetd configuration file for SWAT, /etc/xinetd.d/swat. Log in as root and edit this file to make the following changes:

- Comment out the line disable = yes, by placing a hash (#) at the beginning of that line. This enables xinetd to start SWAT.

- Edit the line only_from = localhost so that the right-hand side lists the host names or IP addresses of systems that can access SWAT. For example, if you want all hosts in your local network with the network address 192.168.1.0 to access SWAT, change this line to:

  ```
  only_from = 192.168.1.0
  ```

Here is the /etc/xinetd.d/swat file after I made changes for my local network:

```
# default: off
# description: SWAT is the Samba Web Admin Tool. Use swat \
#              to configure your Samba server. To use SWAT, \
#              connect to port 901 with your favorite web browser.
service swat
{
        port    = 901
        socket_type     = stream
        wait    = no
#       only_from = localhost
        only_from = 192.168.1.0
        user    = root
        server  = /usr/sbin/swat
        log_on_failure  += USERID
#       disable = yes
}
```

Now restart xinetd with the following command:

```
/etc/init.d/xinetd restart
```

Now you should be able to use SWAT.

Starting SWAT

As SWAT's `xinetd` configuration file shows, the SWAT service listens on TCP port 901. Thus, you can access SWAT with a URL of the form `http://192.168.1.200:901/`, where `192.168.1.200` is the IP address of the Red Hat Linux system whose SWAT service you want to access.

After you type the SWAT URL for your system, the Web browser prompts you for a user ID and password. Enter root and the root password for your Linux system, as shown in Figure 22-8.

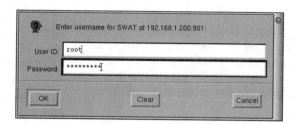

Figure 22-8: Logging in as root to administer Samba using SWAT

After you enter the root user name and password, the Web browser displays the SWAT configuration page, as shown in Figure 22-9.

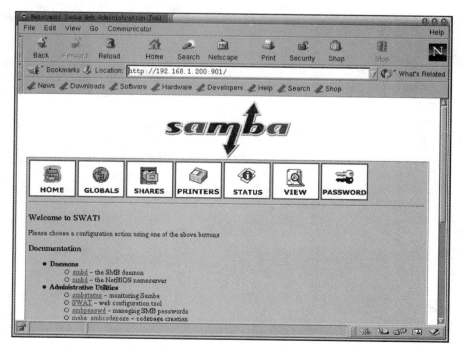

Figure 22-9: The main configuration page of the Samba Web Administration Tool (SWAT)

Now you can explore SWAT — use it to configure Samba and read online documentation about Samba.

Exploring the buttons in SWAT

The main SWAT configuration page has seven large buttons in a row along the top. When you click a button, it takes you to another SWAT page from which you can perform a specific set of tasks. In each of the new SWAT pages, the same row of buttons appears. You should explore the buttons by clicking each one, but here is a brief description of what these buttons do:

- HOME — This button takes you to the main configuration page of SWAT, the one shown in Figure 22-9.

- GLOBALS — This button takes you to the Global Variables page, where you can view and set the values of global variables in the /etc/samba/smb.conf file. These are the variables that appear in the [global] section of the file. One nice feature of SWAT is that you can get context-sensitive help for each variable you need to change. Click the Help link to the left of a variable, and a Web page appears with the help information for that variable.

- SHARES — This button takes you to the Share Parameters page, where you can define new shared directories, or edit the parameters for existing shared directories.

- PRINTERS — This button takes you to the Printer Parameters page, where you can define new shared printers, or edit parameters of existing shared printers.

- STATUS — This button takes you to the Server Status page, which contains information about the Samba servers — smbd and nmbd. This page also provides buttons for stopping or restarting the smbd and nmbd server processes.

- VIEW — This button takes you to the Current Config page, which displays the current Samba configuration (the /etc/samba/smb.conf file). If you click the Full View button on this page it displays a page containing all the Samba options, including all the default ones not explicitly set in the /etc/samba/smb.conf file.

- PASSWORD — This button takes you to a page from which you can manage the passwords for the Samba server and clients. You can add, remove, disable, or enable users. You can also change the password for a specific user name from this page.

Exploring document links in SWAT

Below the row of buttons, the SWAT configuration page provides links to documentation on various aspects of Samba. Click each of the links one-by-one to explore the documentation.

New with Samba 2.0.7 is the complete text of the book *Using Samba* by Robert Eckstein, David Collier-Brown, and Peter Kelly (O'Reilly & Associates, 1999). O'Reilly & Associates has donated the book to the Samba community to be updated collaboratively as Samba evolves. Even if you don't use SWAT to configure Samba, you can definitely use SWAT to browse the *Using Samba* book and the other documentation.

Accessing Windows Resources with smbclient

You can use the smbclient program to access shared directories and printers on Windows systems on the LAN and to check that your Linux Samba server is working. One quick way to check is to use the smbclient -L command to view the list of services on the Red Hat Linux Samba server itself. This is what I get when I run smbclient on my Linux Samba sever:

```
smbclient -L LNBP200
SSL: Error error setting CA cert locations: error:00000000::lib(0) :func(0)
:reason(0)
trying default locations.
added interface ip=192.168.1.200 bcast=192.168.1.255 nmask=255.255.255.0
added interface ip=172.16.128.1 bcast=172.16.128.255 nmask=255.255.255.0
Got a positive name query response from 192.168.1.200 ( 192.168.1.200 )
Password: (press Enter)
Anonymous login successful
Domain=[LNB SOFTWARE] OS=[Unix] Server=[Samba 2.0.7]

        Sharename      Type      Comment
        ---------      ----      -------
        tmp            Disk      Temporary file space
        public         Disk      Public Stuff
        IPC$           IPC       IPC Service (LNB Software-Red Hat Linux-Samba
Server)

        Server                   Comment
        ---------                -------
        LNBP133                  Micron Pentium 133Mhz
        LNBP200                  LNB Software-Red Hat Linux-Samba Server
        LNBP233                  Emily's NEC Pentium 233 PC
        LNBP400                  Dell Dimension XPS-400
        LNBP600                  Dell XPS T600 (2000)

        Workgroup                Master
        ---------                -------
        LNB SOFTWARE             LNBP200
```

The initial error message comes from the SSL (Secure Socket Layer) support that's linked into Samba 2.0.7. SSL is a protocol for encrypted and authenticated data transport. The error message appears because I have not configured Samba properly for SSL support.

Secret

Samba comes with documentation on configuring it for SSL support. To read this documentation, change directory with the command cd /usr/share/ doc/samba*/docs/textdocs, and then type more SSLeay.txt to browse through the text file on SSLeay — a free implementation of the SSL protocol.

The output of smbclient shows shared resources and also lists the names of the other Windows servers on the local network.

If you have other Windows servers around, you can look at their services with the smbclient program. Here is what I get when I view the shared resources on a Windows 95 PC:

```
smbclient -L LNBP133
SSL: Error error setting CA cert locations: error:00000000::lib(0) :func(0)
:reason(0)
trying default locations.
added interface ip=192.168.1.200 bcast=192.168.1.255 nmask=255.255.255.0
added interface ip=172.16.128.1 bcast=172.16.128.255 nmask=255.255.255.0
Got a positive name query response from 192.168.1.50 ( 192.168.1.50 )
Password:

        Sharename       Type        Comment
        ---------       ----        -------
        PRINTER$        Disk
        LASERJET 4M     Printer     Near Emily's desk
        C               Disk        Micron C drive
        D               Disk        LNBP133 CD-ROM
        IPC$            IPC         Remote Inter Process Communication

        Server                      Comment
        ---------                   -------

        Workgroup                   Master
        ---------                   -------
```

You can do much more than simply look at resources with the smbclient program: you can also use it to access a disk on a Windows server, or to send a file to a Windows printer. The smbclient program is like ftp — you connect to a Windows server, and then use commands to get or put files and to send files to the printer.

The following example shows how I used smbclient to access a disk on my Windows 98 PC and view its directory:

```
smbclient //lnbp400/c naba mypassword
SSL: Error error setting CA cert locations: error:00000000::lib(0) :func(0)
:reason(0)
trying default locations.
added interface ip=192.168.1.200 bcast=192.168.1.255 nmask=255.255.255.0
added interface ip=172.16.128.1 bcast=172.16.128.255 nmask=255.255.255.0
Got a positive name query response from 192.168.1.40 ( 192.168.1.40 )
smb: \> dir a*
  ATI                         D        0  Fri Apr 16 21:19:08 1999
  Acrobat3                    D        0  Sat Apr 17 15:14:10 1999
  autoexec.nav                A      230  Sat Apr 17 14:26:08 1999
```

```
AUTOEXEC.BAT              A      325  Fri Nov  3 15:55:08 2000
AUTOEXEC.BAK              A      272  Sun Apr 18 09:53:04 1999
ASD.LOG                  HR      362  Tue Feb 29 18:28:06 2000
ashley                    D        0  Thu Nov 18 21:11:18 1999

        64322 blocks of size 131072. 44931 blocks available
smb: \> quit
```

To see a list of smbclient commands, type help at the prompt. Table 22-1 is a brief summary of commonly used smbclient commands. To familiarize yourself with smbclient, try as many of these commands as you can.

Table 22-1   Common smbclient Commands

Command	Description
!	Executes a shell command (remember that you run smbclient on Linux).
c *cmd*	Displays a list of commands or help on a specific command.
cancel *id*	Cancels a print job identified by its ID.
cd *dir*	Changes the remote directory.
del *file*	Deletes the specified file.
dir *file*	Displays the directory listing.
exit	Logs off the Windows server.
get *rfile lfile*	Copies a remote file (*rfile*) to a local file (*lfile*).
help *cmd*	Provides help on a command (or displays a list of commands).
lcd *newdir*	Changes the local directory (on the Linux PC).
lowercase	Toggles automatic lowercase conversion of filenames when executing the get command.
ls *files*	Lists files on the server.
mask *name*	Applies a mask (such as $*.c$) to all file operations.
md *dirname*	Makes a directory on the server.
mget *name*	Gets all files with matching names (such as $*.doc$).
mkdir *dirname*	Makes a directory.
mput *name*	Copies files from the Linux PC to the server.
newer *file*	Gets only the files that are newer than the specified file.
print *name*	Prints the named file.
printmode *mode*	Sets the print mode (the *mode* must be text or graphics).
prompt	Toggles prompt mode off (similar to the command in ftp).
put *lfile rfile*	Copies a local file (*lfile*) to a remote file (*rfile*).

Command	Description
queue	Displays the print queue.
quit	Logs off the Windows server.
rd *dir*	Deletes the specified directory on the server.
recurse	Toggles directory recursion during file get and put operations.
rm *name*	Deletes all files with the specified name.
rmdir *name*	Deletes the specified directory.
translate	Toggles text translation (converts a line feed to a carriage return–line-feed pair).

Printing from Red Hat Linux to a Windows Printer

If you bring a Linux PC into an existing Windows environment, you may have to use the Linux PC as a Windows client, because a server may already exist. As the preceding sections explain, the Samba software package includes the smbclient program, which allows your Linux PC to be a client in a Windows network.

Cross-Reference

The next few sections show you how to set up a printer on your Red Hat Linux PC, so that print jobs are sent to a specified Windows server by means of the smbclient program. Chapter 6 describes the printing system in Linux. If you have questions about printing while reading this section, please consult that chapter. Chapter 6 describes the Red Hat print tool utilitym, which you can also use to set up your Linux PC to print on a printer on another Windows 95/98/NT/2000 PC.

Setting up the printer in two steps

The basic idea is to define a new printer on your Linux PC, so that when you use the lpr command to print on that printer, the output actually appears on a specified network printer (managed by a Windows server). This process involves two steps:

1. Add an entry for the printer to the /etc/printcap file and specify an *input filter* (a script that gets to process the file that is being printed).

2. Write the script that runs smbclient and prints the file on a designated Windows server.

Adding the printcap entry

There are two key items to notice when preparing the printcap entry that prints on a Windows printer:

- Specify /dev/null as the printer device name, because the actual printing occurs on a network printer.

- Specify an input filter that copies the input data to a file, and then uses smbclient to send that file to the printer on a selected Windows server.

Here is the printcap entry (in the /etc/printcap file) I used on my Linux PC to specify this printer:

```
lp|smbpr|Prints on a Windows printer:\
 :sd=/var/spool/lpd/lp:\
 :lp=/dev/null:\
 :if=/var/spool/lpd/lp/smbprint.tcl:\
 :lf=/var/spool/lpd/lp/smbprint.log:\
 :mx#0:\
 :sh:\
 :sf:
```

For error logging, I created the /var/spool/lpd/lp/smbprint.log file with the following commands (while I was logged in as root):

```
mkdir /var/spool/lpd/lp
touch smbprint.log
/usr/sbin/checkpc -f
```

The last command is part of LPRng, the new printing system in Red Hat Linux. The checkpc program, when used with the -f option, fixes the permission and ownership of files and creates any missing files needed for print spooling.

Writing a script to print with smbclient

The next important step is writing the input filter — /var/spool/lpd/lp/smbprint.tcl, which performs the actual printing. As the extension suggests, I used Tcl to write the input filter. You could write the script in Perl or Bash.

In the smbprint.tcl script, I decided to make a copy of the print job in a temporary file and then run smbclient to print that file. The complete /var/spool/lpd/lp/smbprint.tcl script is as follows:

```
#!/usr/bin/tcl
#
# Tcl script to print on a Windows printer using smbclient.
# Place in printer's spool directory and make it executable
# by world.

# Open the file /tmp/smbprint.out
set outfile [open /tmp/smbprint.out w]

# Read from stdin and write to outfile

while { [gets stdin line] != -1} {
 puts $outfile $line
 }
```

```
close $outfile

# Now prepare a script to run smbclient and print the file
set server "LNBP133"
set printer "LASERJET 4M"
set password "mypassword"

set outfile [open /tmp/printit w]
puts $outfile "#\!/bin/sh"
puts $outfile "echo print /tmp/smbprint.out | /usr/bin/smbclient
\"\\\\\\\\$server\\\\$printer\" $password -N -P"
close $outfile

# Make the script executable
exec chmod +x /tmp/printit

# Now execute the script
exec /tmp/printit
# Delete the script
exec rm /tmp/printit
```

The process of writing the script was fairly simple: I copied the print job to a temporary file, created a script that runs `smbclient` to print that file, and then ran that script. After preparing the script, I typed the following commands to change the ownership and permission:

```
chown lp:lp smbprint.tcl
chmod 700 smbprint.tcl
```

I have used this printer setup to print directly from Linux programs (such as Netscape) on that Windows network printer.

Note

This chapter gives you an overview of Samba, but there simply isn't enough space to provide all the available information. For more information on how to use Samba, consult the *Using Samba* book that comes with the Samba distribution. Start SWAT in a Web browser, following the instructions given earlier in the chapter, and then click the link to the *Using Samba* book. You can also consult *The Samba Book* by Olaf Borkner-Delcarlo, (SuSE Press, Hungry Minds, Inc., 2001) for information on how to troubleshoot typical Samba problems.

Summary

Red Hat Linux includes two prominent file-sharing services: NFS for sharing files with other UNIX systems (or PCs with NFS client software), and Samba for file and print sharing with Windows systems. This chapter describes both NFS and Samba.

By reading this chapter, you learn that:

▶ Network File System (NFS) enables you to mount a file system from a remote computer on your local system. Red Hat Linux includes everything you need to set up your system as a NFS server.

▶ To export a file system, you have to add that file system in the /etc/exports file, and then type /usr/sbin/exportfs -a to export the file systems. You also have to start the NFS servers by typing the command /etc/init.d/nfs start. After that, other NFS client systems on the network can mount the exported file systems with the mount command.

▶ You can use Linuxconf to export an NFS file system, start the NFS servers, and mount NFS file systems.

▶ For PC networks that use Windows networking, you can configure a Red Hat Linux PC as a Windows server: all you have to do is use the Samba software package from the companion CD-ROMs. This chapter shows you how to install and use Samba.

▶ Samba configuration is somewhat complex — you configure using settings in the text file /etc/samba/smb.conf. Samba also comes with the Samba Web Administration Tool (SWAT), which enables you to configure the smb.conf file via a Web browser.

▶ You have to edit the /etc/xinetd.d/swat file to configure and enable SWAT before you can start using SWAT.

▶ You can access Windows servers and their resources from a Samba server with the smbclient program.

▶ A Linux PC also can act as a Windows client. As an example, this chapter describes how to use a Windows printer from a Linux PC.

Part IV

Managing Red Hat Linux

Chapter 23

Advanced System Administration

Chapter 15 introduces the basics of systems and network administration on the Red Hat Linux system. In that chapter, you learn to add user accounts and use the Linuxconf graphical system administration tool. In several other chapters, you also learn many other system administration tasks, such as configuring X, setting up Internet connections, and configuring Internet services. This chapter introduces you to a number of other important system administration tasks that I do not cover elsewhere in this book.

This chapter starts with a description of how Red Hat Linux boots, so you know how to automatically start and stop services at boot time. Then you learn about automating system tasks with the `at` command, or the `crontab` facility of Linux. Next, this chapter focuses on another important system administration task — backing up and restoring files from backup storage media. Finally, the chapter discusses monitoring system performance.

Understanding How Red Hat Linux Boots

It is important to learn the sequence in which Red Hat Linux starts processes as it boots. You can use this knowledge to start and stop services, such as the Web server and Network File System (NFS). The next few sections provide you with an overview of how Red Hat Linux boots and starts the initial set of processes. These sections also familiarize you with the shell scripts that start various services on a Red Hat Linux system.

Understanding the init Process

When Red Hat Linux boots, it loads and runs the core operating-system program from the hard disk. The core operating system is designed to run other programs. A process named `init` starts the initial set of processes on your Linux system.

To see the processes currently running on the system, type the command `ps ax | more`. The first column in the output has the heading "PID"; that column shows a number for each process. *PID* stands for *process ID* (identification), which is a sequential number assigned by the Linux kernel. Right at the beginning of the list of processes, you notice a process with a process ID (PID) of 1:

```
PID TTY      STAT   TIME COMMAND
  1 ?        S      0:05 init [5]
```

As you can see, `init` is the first process, and it has a PID of 1. Also, `init` starts all other processes in your Linux system. That's why `init` is referred to as the *mother of all processes*.

What the `init` process starts depends on the following:

- The *run level*, which designates a system configuration in which only a selected group of processes exists

- The contents of the `/etc/inittab` file, a text file that specifies the processes to start at different run levels

- A number of shell scripts (located in the `/etc/rc.d` directory and its subdirectories) that are executed at a specific run level

Secret

The current run level, together with the contents of the `/etc/inittab` file, controls which processes `init` starts. Linux, for example, has seven run levels: 0, 1, 2, 3, 4, 5, and 6. By convention, some of these levels indicate specific processes that run at that level. Run level 1, for example, denotes a single-user, stand-alone system. Run level 0 means the system is halted, and run level 6 means the system is being rebooted. Run levels 2 through 5 are multi-user modes with various levels of capabilities.

The initial default run level is 3 for text-mode login screens and 5 for the graphical login screen. As the following section explains, you can change the default run level by editing a line in the `/etc/inittab` file.

To check the current run level, type the following command:

```
/sbin/runlevel
N 5
```

This command prints two alphanumeric characters as output. The first character of the output shows the previous run level (N means there is no previous run level), and the second character shows the current level (5), indicating that the system was started at run level 5.

Examining the /etc/inittab file

The /etc/inittab file is the key to understanding the processes that init starts at various run levels. You can look at the contents of the file by using the more command as follows:

```
more /etc/inittab
```

Note

To see the contents of the /etc/inittab file with the more command, you do not have to log in as root.

The following is a listing of the /etc/inittab file on my Red Hat Linux system, which is set up for a graphical login screen:

```
#
# inittab       This file describes how the INIT process should set up
#               the system in a certain run-level.
#
# Author:       Miquel van Smoorenburg, <miquels@drinkel.nl.mugnet.org>
#               Modified for RHS Linux by Marc Ewing and Donnie Barnes
#

# Default runlevel. The runlevels used by RHS are:
#    0 - halt (Do NOT set initdefault to this)
#    1 - Single user mode
#    2 - Multiuser, without NFS (The same as 3, if you do not have networking)
#    3 - Full multiuser mode
#    4 - unused
#    5 - X11
#    6 - reboot (Do NOT set initdefault to this)
#
id:5:initdefault:

# System initialization.
si::sysinit:/etc/rc.d/rc.sysinit

l0:0:wait:/etc/rc.d/rc 0
l1:1:wait:/etc/rc.d/rc 1
l2:2:wait:/etc/rc.d/rc 2
l3:3:wait:/etc/rc.d/rc 3
l4:4:wait:/etc/rc.d/rc 4
l5:5:wait:/etc/rc.d/rc 5
l6:6:wait:/etc/rc.d/rc 6
```

```
# Things to run in every runlevel.
ud::once:/sbin/update

# Trap CTRL-ALT-DELETE
ca::ctrlaltdel:/sbin/shutdown -t3 -r now

# When our UPS tells us power has failed, assume we have a few minutes
# of power left.  Schedule a shutdown for 2 minutes from now.
# This does, of course, assume you have powerd installed and your
# UPS connected and working correctly.
pf::powerfail:/sbin/shutdown -f -h +2 "Power Failure; System Shutting Down"

# If power was restored before the shutdown kicked in, cancel it.
pr:12345:powerokwait:/sbin/shutdown -c "Power Restored; Shutdown Cancelled"

# Run gettys in standard runlevels
1:2345:respawn:/sbin/mingetty tty1
2:2345:respawn:/sbin/mingetty tty2
3:2345:respawn:/sbin/mingetty tty3
4:2345:respawn:/sbin/mingetty tty4
5:2345:respawn:/sbin/mingetty tty5
6:2345:respawn:/sbin/mingetty tty6

# Run xdm in runlevel 5
# xdm is now a separate service
x:5:respawn:/etc/X11/prefdm -nodaemon
```

Lines that start with a hash mark (#) are comments. The first non-comment line in the /etc/inittab file specifies the default run level as follows:

```
id:5:initdefault:
```

Even though you do not know the syntax of the /etc/inittab file (and you really do not have to learn the syntax), you probably can guess that the 5 in that line denotes the default run level for the graphical login screen. Thus, if you want your system to run at level 3 after startup (for a plain text-mode login screen), all you have to do is change 5 to 3.

Tip

Type man inittab to see the detailed syntax of the entries in the inittab file.

Each entry in the /etc/inittab file specifies a process that init should start at one or more specified run levels. You simply list all the run levels at which the process should run. Each entry in the inittab file has four fields — separated by colons — in the following format:

```
id:runlevels:action:process
```

The fields in each entry of the inittab file have the following meanings:

■ The *id* field is a unique, one- or two-character identifier. The init process uses this field internally. You can employ any identifier you want, as long as you do not use the same identifier on more than one line. For example, si, x, and 1 are all valid identifiers.

- The *runlevels* field is a sequence of zero or more characters, each denoting a run level. The line with the identifier 1, for example, applies to run levels 1 through 5; so the *runlevels* field for this entry is 12345. This field is ignored if the action field is set to sysinit, boot, or bootwait.

- The *action* field tells the init process what to do with the entry. If this field is initdefault, for example, init interprets the *runlevels* field as the default run level. If this field is set to wait, init starts the process specified in the *process* field and waits until that process exits. Table 23-1 summarizes the valid action values you can use in the *action* field.

- The *process* field specifies the process that init has to start. Of course, some settings of the *action* field require no process field. (When *action* is set to initdefault, for example, no need exists for a *process* field.)

Table 23-1   Valid Actions in /etc/inittab

Action	Description
Respawn	Restarts the process whenever it terminates
Wait	Restarts the process once at the specified run level; init waits until that process exits
Once	Executes the process once at the specified run level
Boot	Executes the process as the system boots, regardless of the run level (the *runlevels* field is ignored)
Bootwait	Executes the process as the system boots; init waits for the process to exit (the *runlevels* field is ignored)
Off	Nothing happens for this action.
Ondemand	Executes the process at the specified run level, which must be one of a, b, or c
Initdefault	Starts the system at this run level after it boots. The *process* field is ignored for this action.
sysinit	Executes the process as the system boots before any entries with the boot or bootwait actions (the *runlevels* field is ignored)
powerwait	Executes the process when init receives the SIGPWR signal indicating that there is something wrong with the power. Then init waits until the process exits.
powerfail	Similar to powerwait except that init does not wait for the process to exit
powerfailnow	Executes the process when init receives a signal that the battery of the external uninterruptible power supply (UPS) is almost empty and the power is failing (provided that the external UPS and the monitoring process can detect this condition)

Continued

Table 23-1 *(continued)*

Action	Description
powerokwait	Executes the process when init receives the SIGPWR signal and the /etc/powerstatus file contains the word OK (indicating the power is back on)
ctrlaltdel	Executes the process when init receives the SIGINT signal, which occurs when you press Ctrl+Alt+Del. Typically, the *process* field should specify the /sbin/shutdown command with the -r option to reboot the PC.
kbdrequest	Executes the process when init receives a signal from the keyboard driver that a special key combination has been pressed. The key combination should be mapped to KeyboardSignal in the keymap file.

The *process* field is typically specified in terms of a shell script, which, in turn, can start several processes. The 15 entry, for example, is specified as follows:

```
l5:5:wait:/etc/rc.d/rc 5
```

This entry specifies that init should execute the file /etc/rc.d/rc with 5 as an argument. If you look at the file /etc/.rc.d/rc, you notice that it is a shell script file. You can study this file to see how it starts various processes for run levels 1 through 5.

The last line of the /etc/inittab file starts the graphical login process with the following entry:

```
x:5:respawn:/etc/X11/prefdm -nodaemon
```

This command runs /etc/X11/prefdm, which is a shell script that starts the graphical display manager. The display manager, in turn, displays the graphical login dialog box that enables you to log into the system.

Tip

If you do not enable the graphical login screen during Red Hat installation (covered in Chapter 2), you can do so by editing the /etc/inittab file. Locate the line containing initdefault, and make sure that it reads as follows (the run level appearing between the two colons should be 5):

```
id:5:initdefault:
```

Before you edit the /etc/inittab file, you should know that any errors in this file may prevent Red Hat Linux from starting up to a point at which you can log in. If you cannot log in, you cannot use your system. As I explain next, you can always try out a specific run level with the init command before you actually change the default run level in the /etc/inittab file.

Trying out a new run level with the init command

To try a new run level, you do not have to change the default run level in the /etc/inittab file. If you log in as root, you can change the run level (and, consequently, the set of processes that run in Linux) with the init command. It has the following format:

```
init runlevel
```

Here, runlevel must be a single character denoting the run level that you want. To put the system in single-user mode, for example, type the following:

```
init 1
```

Thus, if you want to try run level 5 (assuming your system is not set up for a graphical login screen yet) without changing the /etc/inittab file, enter the following command at the shell prompt:

```
init 5
```

The system should end all current processes and enter run level 5. By default, the init command waits 20 seconds before stopping all current processes and starting the new processes for run level 5.

Tip

To switch to run level 5 immediately, type the command init -t0 5. The number after the -t option indicates the number of seconds that init waits before changing the run level.

You can also use the telinit command, which is simply a symbolic link to init. If you make changes to the /etc/inittab file and want init to reload its configuration file, use the command telinit q.

Understanding the Red Hat Linux Startup Scripts

The init process runs a number of scripts at system startup. Notice the following lines that appear near the beginning of the /etc/inittab file:

```
# System initialization.
si::sysinit:/etc/rc.d/rc.sysinit
```

As the comment on the first line indicates, the second line causes init to run the /etc/rc.d/rc.sysinit script—the first Red Hat Linux startup script that init runs. The rc.sysinit script performs many initialization tasks, such as mounting the file systems, setting the clock, configuring the keyboard layout, starting the network, and loading many other driver modules. The rc.sysinit script performs these initialization tasks by calling many other scripts and reading configuration files located in the /etc/sysconfig directory.

After executing the `/etc/rc.d/rc.sysinit` script, the `init` process runs the `/etc/rc.d/rc` script with the run level as argument. For example, for run level 5, the following line in `/etc/inittab` specifies what `init` has to execute:

```
l5:5:wait:/etc/rc.d/rc 5
```

This says that `init` should execute the command `/etc/rc.d/rc 5` and wait until that command completes.

The `/etc/rc.d/rc` script is somewhat complicated. Here is how it works:

- It changes to the directory corresponding to the run level. For example, to change to run level 5, the script changes to the `/etc/rc.d/rc5.d` directory.

- In the directory that corresponds with the run level, `/etc/rc.d/rc` looks for all files that begin with a K and executes each of them with the argument `stop`. This kills currently running processes. Then it locates all files that begin with an S and executes each file with an argument of `start`. This starts the processes needed for the specified run level.

To see what gets executed at run level 5, type the following command:

```
ls -l /etc/rc.d/rc5.d
total 0
lrwxrwxrwx  1 root     root       15 Oct  4 17:09 K01pppoe -> ../init.d/pppoe
lrwxrwxrwx  1 root     root       14 Oct  4 16:54 K05innd -> ../init.d/innd
lrwxrwxrwx  1 root     root       13 Nov  4 15:31 K20nfs -> ../init.d/nfs
lrwxrwxrwx  1 root     root       16 Oct  4 17:09 K20rstatd -> ../init.d/rstatd
lrwxrwxrwx  1 root     root       17 Oct  4 17:09 K20rusersd -> ../init.d/rusersd
lrwxrwxrwx  1 root     root       16 Oct  4 17:09 K20rwalld -> ../init.d/rwalld
lrwxrwxrwx  1 root     root       15 Oct  4 17:09 K20rwhod -> ../init.d/rwhod
lrwxrwxrwx  1 root     root       19 Oct  4 17:18 K34yppasswdd -> ../init.d/yppasswdd
lrwxrwxrwx  1 root     root       13 Oct  4 17:10 K35smb -> ../init.d/smb
lrwxrwxrwx  1 root     root       18 Oct  4 16:43 K45arpwatch -> ../init.d/arpwatch
lrwxrwxrwx  1 root     root       15 Oct  4 16:45 K45named -> ../init.d/named
lrwxrwxrwx  1 root     root       15 Oct  4 17:15 K50snmpd -> ../init.d/snmpd
lrwxrwxrwx  1 root     root       18 Oct  4 17:02 K60mars-nwe -> ../init.d/mars-nwe
lrwxrwxrwx  1 root     root       16 Oct  4 17:18 K84ypserv -> ../init.d/ypserv
lrwxrwxrwx  1 root     root       14 Oct  4 16:54 K96irda -> ../init.d/irda
lrwxrwxrwx  1 root     root       15 Oct  4 16:59 S05kudzu -> ../init.d/kudzu
lrwxrwxrwx  1 root     root       18 Oct  4 16:54 S08ipchains -> ../init.d/ipchains
lrwxrwxrwx  1 root     root       17 Oct  4 16:43 S10network -> ../init.d/network
lrwxrwxrwx  1 root     root       16 Oct  4 16:43 S12syslog -> ../init.d/syslog
lrwxrwxrwx  1 root     root       17 Oct  4 17:06 S13portmap -> ../init.d/portmap
lrwxrwxrwx  1 root     root       17 Oct  4 17:04 S14nfslock -> ../init.d/nfslock
lrwxrwxrwx  1 root     root       14 Oct  4 16:43 S16apmd -> ../init.d/apmd
lrwxrwxrwx  1 root     root       16 Oct  4 16:43 S20random -> ../init.d/random
lrwxrwxrwx  1 root     root       15 Oct  4 16:43 S25netfs -> ../init.d/netfs
lrwxrwxrwx  1 root     root       16 Oct  4 17:05 S35identd -> ../init.d/identd
lrwxrwxrwx  1 root     root       13 Oct  4 16:44 S40atd -> ../init.d/atd
lrwxrwxrwx  1 root     root       16 Oct  4 16:58 S45pcmcia -> ../init.d/pcmcia
lrwxrwxrwx  1 root     root       16 Oct  4 17:17 S50xinetd -> ../init.d/xinetd
```

```
lrwxrwxrwx  1 root    root     14 Oct  4 17:05 S55sshd -> ../init.d/sshd
lrwxrwxrwx  1 root    root     20 Oct  4 16:43 S56rawdevices ->
../init.d/rawdevices
lrwxrwxrwx  1 root    root     13 Oct  4 17:02 S60lpd -> ../init.d/lpd
lrwxrwxrwx  1 root    root     18 Oct  4 16:45 S75keytable -> ../init.d/keytable
lrwxrwxrwx  1 root    root     14 Oct  4 16:54 S80isdn -> ../init.d/isdn
lrwxrwxrwx  1 root    root     18 Oct  4 17:11 S80sendmail -> ../init.d/sendmail
lrwxrwxrwx  1 root    root     13 Oct  4 16:53 S85gpm -> ../init.d/gpm
lrwxrwxrwx  1 root    root     15 Oct  4 16:43 S85httpd -> ../init.d/httpd
lrwxrwxrwx  1 root    root     15 Oct  4 16:43 S90crond -> ../init.d/crond
lrwxrwxrwx  1 root    root     13 Oct  4 16:45 S90xfs -> ../init.d/xfs
lrwxrwxrwx  1 root    root     17 Oct  4 16:42 S95anacron -> ../init.d/anacron
lrwxrwxrwx  1 root    root     15 Oct  4 17:15 S97rhnsd -> ../init.d/rhnsd
lrwxrwxrwx  1 root    root     19 Oct  4 17:01 S99linuxconf -> ../init.d/linuxconf
lrwxrwxrwx  1 root    root     11 Oct  4 16:43 S99local -> ../rc.local
```

As the listing of the /etc/rc.d/rc5.d directory shows, all files with names starting with K and S are symbolic links to scripts that reside in the /etc/rc.d/init.d directory — except for the last file (S99local), which is a link to /etc/rc.d/rc.local. The K scripts stop ("kill") servers, whereas the S scripts start servers. The /etc/rc.d/rc script executes these files exactly in the order that they appear in the directory listing.

Tip

Note that the last file in the directory listing is a symbolic link to the ../rc.local script. This means that /etc/rc.d/rc.local is executed after all other scripts. So you can place in that script any command you want executed whenever your Red Hat Linux system boots.

Manually starting and stopping servers

Most of the startup scripts reside in the /etc/rc.d/init.d directory. You can manually invoke scripts in this directory to start, stop, or restart specific processes — usually servers. For example, to stop the Web server (the program's name is httpd), type the following command:

```
/etc/rc.d/init.d/httpd stop
Shutting down http: [  OK  ]
```

If httpd is already running and you want to restart it, type the following command:

```
/etc/rc.d/init.d/httpd restart
Shutting down http: [  OK  ]
Starting httpd: [  OK  ]
```

Secret

Starting with Red Hat Linux 7.0, you may see documentation that tells you to use scripts in the /etc/init.d directory, instead of the /etc/rc.d/init.d directory. You can now type /etc/init.d/httpd stop to stop the Web server. That's because Red Hat Linux 7.0 introduces a set of symbolic links in the /etc directory that point to specific subdirectories of /etc/rc.d. For example, /etc/init.d is a symbolic link to /etc/rc.d/init.d. This use of symbolic links improves compatibility and portability among different Linux distributions. To see these new symbolic links, type the following command:

```
ls -l /etc | grep "rc\."
lrwxrwxrwx   1 root   root      11 Jan 13 13:39 init.d -> rc.d/init.d
lrwxrwxrwx   1 root   root       7 Jan 13 15:48 rc -> rc.d/rc
lrwxrwxrwx   1 root   root      10 Jan 13 13:39 rc0.d -> rc.d/rc0.d
lrwxrwxrwx   1 root   root      10 Jan 13 13:39 rc1.d -> rc.d/rc1.d
lrwxrwxrwx   1 root   root      10 Jan 13 13:39 rc2.d -> rc.d/rc2.d
lrwxrwxrwx   1 root   root      10 Jan 13 13:39 rc3.d -> rc.d/rc3.d
lrwxrwxrwx   1 root   root      10 Jan 13 13:39 rc4.d -> rc.d/rc4.d
lrwxrwxrwx   1 root   root      10 Jan 13 13:39 rc5.d -> rc.d/rc5.d
lrwxrwxrwx   1 root   root      10 Jan 13 13:39 rc6.d -> rc.d/rc6.d
drwxr-xr-x  10 root   root    4096 Feb  7 21:20 rc.d
lrwxrwxrwx   1 root   root      13 Jan 13 15:48 rc.local -> rc.d/rc.local
-r-xr-xr-x   1 news   news    2964 Aug 29 15:32 rc.news
lrwxrwxrwx   1 root   root      15 Jan 13 15:48 rc.sysinit -> rc.d/rc.sysinit
```

You can enhance your system administration skills by familiarizing yourself with the scripts in the `/etc/rc.d/init.d` directory. To see its listing, type the following command:

```
ls /etc/rc.d/init.d
anacron    halt       kdcrotate   named      postgresql   rwalld     syslog
apmd       httpd      keytable    netfs      pppoe        rwhod      xfs
arpwatch   identd     killall     network    random       sendmail   xinetd
atd        innd       kudzu       nfs        rawdevices   single     ypbind
crond      ipchains   linuxconf   nfslock    rhnsd        smb        yppasswdd
functions  irda       lpd         pcmcia     rstatd       snmpd      ypserv
gpm        isdn       mars-nwe    portmap    rusersd      sshd
```

The script names give you some clue about which server the script can start and stop. For example, the `nfs` script starts and stops the processes required for NFS (Network File System) services. At your leisure, you may want to study some of these scripts to see what each one does. You don't have to understand all the shell programming; the comments should help you learn the purpose of each script.

Configuring servers to start automatically at boot time

While you can start, stop, and restart servers manually by using the scripts in the `/etc/rc.d/init.d` directory, you have to set up symbolic links in the scripts for an appropriate run level. For example, to start the DNS server — `named` — in run level 5, you need an S script in the run level 5 directory (`/etc/rc.d/rc5.d`). Furthermore, that S script should be a symbolic link to the `/etc/rc.d/init.d/named` file. Setting up such symbolic links is what you do to configure servers to start automatically at boot time. Luckily, you do not have to do this job by hand. Instead, you can use the `/sbin/chkconfig` or `/usr/sbin/ntsysv` **program.**

Using chkconfig

The chkconfig program is a command-line utility for querying and updating the run-level scripts in Red Hat Linux. I introduce you to the chkconfig utility next, but you can learn more about its options by reading the chkconfig man page with the man chkconfig command.

For example, suppose you want to automatically start the named server at run levels 3 and 5. All you need to do is log in as root, and type the following command at the shell prompt:

```
/sbin/chkconfig --level 35 named on
```

To see the status of the named server, type the following command:

```
/sbin/chkconfig --list named
named    0:off  1:off  2:off  3:on   4:off  5:on   6:off
```

The output shows you the status of the named server at run levels 0 through 6. As you can see, named is set to run as run levels 3 and 5. If you now look at the directories /etc/rc.d/rc3.d and /etc/rc.d/rc5.d, you see two new S scripts that are symbolic links to /etc/rc.d/init.d/named. Both of these S scripts are symbolic links to the same script and each looks like this:

```
lrwxrwxrwx  1 root    root    15 Nov  5 21:45 S55named -> ../init.d/named
```

If you want to turn named off, you can do so with this command:

```
/sbin/chkconfig --level 35 named off
```

You can use chkconfig to see the status of all services, including the ones started through xinetd. For example, you can view the status of all services, by typing the following command:

```
/sbin/chkconfig --list | more
anacron   0:off  1:off  2:on   3:on   4:on   5:on   6:off
httpd     0:off  1:off  2:off  3:on   4:on   5:on   6:off
apmd      0:off  1:off  2:on   3:on   4:on   5:on   6:off
syslog    0:off  1:off  2:on   3:on   4:on   5:on   6:off
crond     0:off  1:off  2:on   3:on   4:on   5:on   6:off
... many lines of output deleted ...
xinetd based services:
        finger: on
        linuxconf-web:  on
        rexec:  off
        rlogin: on
        rsh:    on
        swat:   on
        ntalk:  off
        talk:   off
        telnet: on
        tftp:   off
        wu-ftpd:        on
```

The output shows the status of each service for each of the run levels from 0 through 6. For each run level, the service is either on or off. At the very end of the listing, chkconfig displays a list of the services that xinetd controls (see Chapter 8 for more information on xinetd). Each xinetd-based service is also marked on or off, depending on whether or not xinetd is configured to start the service.

Using ntsysv

If you don't like typing the chkconfig commands, a text-mode utility program called ntsysv (the full path name is /usr/sbin/ntsysv) enables you to configure the services from a dialog box.

To run ntsysv, log in as root and type /usr/sbin/ntsysv in a text console, or in a terminal in the graphical desktop. You can then select the services from the list shown in the dialog box in Figure 23-1.

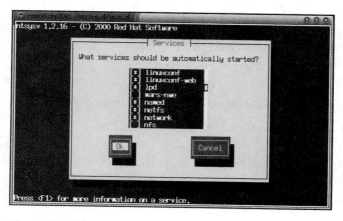

Figure 23-1: Using ntsysv to select the services that you want to start automatically

Each line in the list shows the name of a service with a square bracket prefix ([ ]). An asterisk (*) in the square bracket indicates that the service is already selected to start at boot time for the current run level. When the dialog box first appears, many services are already selected. You can use the up and down arrow keys to move around in the list, and press the spacebar to select or deselect a service. After making your selections, press Tab to select OK, and then press Enter.

Secret

By default, ntsysv configures the selected services for the current run level. That means if you are doing this while X is running, you are probably in run level 5 and the services you configure are set to start at run level 5. If you want to set up the services for levels 3 and 5, start ntsysv with the command /usr/sbin/ntsysv --level 35.

Table 23-2 shows a list of the services, along with a brief description of each one. The first column shows the name of the service, which is the same as the name of the program that has to run to provide the service.

Table 23-2 Services That You Can Configure Using ntsysv

Service Name	Description
anacron	Executes commands that are scheduled to run periodically
apmd	Monitors the Advanced Power Management (APM) BIOS and logs the status of electric power (AC or battery backup)
arpwatch	Keeps track of associations between Ethernet hardware addresses and IP addresses
atd	Runs commands scheduled by the at and batch commands
crond	Runs user-specified programs according to a periodic schedule set by the crontab command
finger	Answers finger protocol requests (for user information, such as login name and last login time)
gpm	Enables use of mouse in text-mode screens
httpd	This is the Apache World Wide Web (WWW) server.
identd	Implements the TCP/IP IDENT user-identification protocol that returns the username of the process that owns a TCP/IP connection
innd	This is the InterNetNews daemon — the Internet news server that you can use to support local newsgroups on your system.
ipchains	Automates packet-filtering firewall with IPCHAINS (I briefly describe IPCHAINS in Chapter 16, and I cover it again in Chapter 26.)
irda	Supports communications with IrDA-compliant infrared devices in Linux (IrDA is a standard for infrared wireless communication at speeds ranging from 2400bps to 4Mbps.)
kdcrotate	Rotates the Key Distribution Center (KDC) names listed in /etc/krb5.conf. The KDCs are used in Kerberos, a secure system for providing network authentication services.
keytable	Loads selected keyboard map as specified in the file /etc/sysconfig/keyboard. You should leave this service running on your system.
kudzu	Probes for new hardware and configures changed hardware
linuxconf	Performs Linux system-configuration tasks
linuxconf -web	Enables connections to Linuxconf from a Web browser
lpd	Server that manages the queue of print jobs and sends the print jobs to the printer. You need this server if you want to do any printing from the Linux system.

Continued

Table 23-2 *(continued)*

Service Name	Description
mars-nwe	This is a Novell Netware-compatible MARS file and print server. Run this server if you want to use your Linux system as a Netware server.
named	This is the Domain Name Server (DNS) that translates host names into IP addresses. You can run a copy on your system if you want.
netfs	Enables you to mount and unmount all network file systems (NFS, Samba, and Netware)
network	Enables you to activate or deactivate all network interfaces configured to start at system boot time
nfslock	Provides file-locking capability for file systems exported using the Network File System (NFS) protocol, so that other systems (running NFS) can share files from your system
ntalk	Provides support for chatting with users on different systems
pcmcia	Provides support for PCMCIA devices
portmap	Server used by any software that relies on Remote Procedure Calls (RPC). NFS requires the portmap service.
postgresql	Starts or stops the PostgreSQL server that handles database requests (PostgreSQL is a free database that comes with Red Hat Linux.)
pppoe	Server needed to support Point-to-Point Protocol over Ethernet (PPPoE), which is needed to establish PPP connections over Asymmetric Digital Subscriber Line (ADSL)
random	Server needed to generate high-quality random numbers on the Linux system
rawdevices	Assigns raw devices to block devices (needed for applications such as Oracle)
rexec	Supports remote execution with authentication based on username and password
rhnsd	Periodically connects to the Red Hat Network Services servers to check for updates and notifications
rlogind	Server that supports remote login using the rlogin command
rshd	Server that supports remote execution via the rsh command
rstatd	Returns performance statistics obtained from the Linux kernel
rusersd	Enables users on any system on the network to find out who is logged in at a system

Service Name	Description
rwalld	Enables remote users to display messages on all active terminals on a system
rwhod	Enables remote users to get a list of all users on the Linux system running the rwhod service
sendmail	Moves mail messages from one machine to another. Start this service if you want to send mail from your Linux system. If you do not plan to use your Linux system as a mail server, do not start the sendmail server because it can slow down the booting process and consume unnecessary resources.
smb	Starts and stops the Samba smbd and nmbd services that support LAN Manager services on a Linux system
snmpd	Simple Network Management Protocol (SNMP) service used for network management functions
sshd	Server for the OpenSSH (Secure Shell) secure remote login facility
swat	Server for the Samba Web Administration Tool (SWAT) used to configure Samba through a Web browser
syslog	Service used by many other programs (including other services) to log various error and status messages in a log file (usually, the /var/log/messages file). You should always run this service.
talk	Server that supports chatting with users on other systems
telnetd	Server that supports telnet remote login sessions
tftp	Server for file transfers using the Trivial File Transfer Protocol (TFTP)
wu-ftpd	Washington University FTP daemon for file transfers using the File Transfer Protocol (FTP)
xfs	Server that starts and stops the X Font Server
xinetd	This is the Internet super server, a replacement for the older inetd. It starts other Internet services, such as Telnet and FTP, whenever they are needed.
ypbind	Service needed for Network Information System (NIS). You do not need to start ypbind unless you are using NIS.
yppasswdd	Service needed for password changes in Network Information System (NIS). You do not need to start yppasswdd unless you are using NIS.
ypserv	The server for Network Information System (NIS). You do not need to start ypserv unless you are using NIS.

Scheduling Jobs in Red Hat Linux

As a system administrator, you may need to run some programs automatically at regular intervals, or execute one or more commands at a specified time in the future. Your Linux system includes the facilities to schedule jobs to run at any future date or time you want. You can set up the system to perform a task periodically, or just once. Here are some typical tasks you can perform by scheduling jobs on your Linux system:

- Back up the files in the middle of the night.
- Download large files in the early mornings when the system is not busy.
- Send yourself messages as reminders of meetings.
- Analyze the system logs periodically and look for any abnormal activities.

You can perform these tasks by using the `at` command, or the `crontab` facility of Linux. The next few sections introduce you to these job-scheduling features of Linux.

Scheduling One-time Jobs

You can use the `at` command to schedule the execution of one or more commands at a later time. The `atd` daemon — a program designed to process jobs submitted using `at` — executes the commands at the specified time, and the output is mailed to you.

Note

Before you try out the `at` command, note that the following configuration files control which users can schedule tasks using the `at` command:

- `/etc/at.allow` contains the names of the users who may submit jobs using the `at` command.
- `/etc/at.deny` contains the names of users who are not allowed to submit jobs using the `at` command.

If these files are not present, or if there is an empty `/etc/at.deny` file, then any user can submit jobs using the `at` command. The default in Red Hat Linux is an empty `/etc/at.deny` file, so anyone can use the `at` command. If you do not want some users to use `at`, simply list those usernames in the `/etc/at.deny` file.

To use `at` to schedule a one-time job for execution at a later time, follow these steps:

1. Run the `at` command with the date or time when you want your commands executed. When you press Enter, the `at>` prompt appears, as follows:

```
at 21:30
at>
```

This is the simplest way to indicate the time when you want to execute one or more commands — simply specify the time in a 24-hour format. In this case, you want to execute the commands at 9:30 p.m. tonight (or tomorrow, if it's already past 9:30 p.m.). You can, however, specify the execution time in many different ways (see Table 23-3 for examples).

2. At the `at>` prompt, type the commands you want to execute as if typing at the shell prompt. After each command, press Enter and continue with the next command. When you are finished entering the commands you want to execute, press Ctrl+D to indicate the end. Here is an example showing a single command:

```
at> ps
at> <EOT>
warning: commands will be executed using /bin/sh
job 2 at 2000-10-15 21:30
```

After you press Ctrl+D, the `at` command responds with a job number and the date and time when the job will execute.

Table 23-3   Specifying the Time of Execution with the at Command

Command	When the Job Is Run
at now	Immediately
at now + 15 minutes	15 minutes from the current time
at now + 4 hours	4 hours from the current time
at now + 7 days	7 days from the current time
at noon	At noontime today (or tomorrow, if already past noon)
at now next hour	Exactly 60 minutes from now
at now next day	At the same time tomorrow
at 17:00 tomorrow	At 5:00 p.m. tomorrow
at 4:45pm	At 4:45 p.m. today (or tomorrow, if already past 4:45 p.m.)
at 3:00 Aug 16, 01	At 3:00 a.m. on August 16, 2001

After you enter one or more jobs, you can view the current list of scheduled jobs with the `atq` command:

```
atq
4       2000-10-26 03:00 a
5       2000-10-26 21:57 a
6       2000-10-26 16:45 a
```

The first field on each line shows the job number — the same number that the `at` command displays when you submit the job. The next field shows the year, month, day, and time of execution. The last field shows the jobs pending in the queue named `a`.

If you want to cancel a job, use the `atrm` command to remove that job from the queue. When removing a job with the `atrm` command, refer to the job by its number as follows:

```
atrm 4
```

This deletes job number 4 scheduled for 3:00 a.m. October 26, 2000.

When a job executes, the output is mailed to you. Type `mail` to read your mail and view the output from your jobs.

Scheduling Recurring Jobs

While `at` is good for running commands at a specific time, it's not useful for running a program automatically at repeated intervals. You have to use `crontab` to schedule such recurring jobs. You need to do this, for example, if you want to back up your files to tape at midnight every day.

You schedule recurring jobs by placing job information in a file with a specific format and submitting this file with the `crontab` command. The cron daemon — `crond` — checks the job information every minute and executes the recurring jobs at the specified times. Because the cron daemon processes recurring jobs, such jobs are also referred to as *cron jobs*.

Any output from the job is mailed to the user who submits the job. (In the submitted job information file, you may specify a different recipient for the mailed output.)

As with the `at` command, two files control who can schedule cron jobs using `crontab`:

- `/etc/cron.allow` contains the names of the users who may submit jobs using the `at` command.

- `/etc/cron.deny` contains the names of users who are not allowed to submit jobs using the `at` command.

If the `/etc/cron.allow` file exists, only users listed in this file can schedule cron jobs. If only the `/etc/cron.deny` file exists, then users listed in this file cannot schedule cron jobs. If neither file exists, the default Red Hat Linux setup enables any user to submit cron jobs.

To submit a cron job, perform the following steps:

1. Prepare a shell script (or an executable program in any programming language) that can perform the recurring task you want to perform. You can skip this step if you want to execute an existing program periodically.

2. Prepare a text file with information about the times when you want the shell script or program (from step 1) to execute. You submit this file using `crontab`. You can submit several recurring jobs with a single file. Each line with timing information about a job has a standard format with six fields — the first five specify when the job runs and the sixth and subsequent fields constitute the actual command that runs. For example, here is a line that executes the `myjob` shell script in a user's home directory at five minutes past midnight each day:

```
5 0 * * * $HOME/myjob
```

Table 23-4 shows the meaning of the first five fields. Note that an asterisk (*) means all possible values for that field. Also, an entry in any of the first five fields can be a single number, a comma-separated list of numbers, a pair of numbers separated by a dash (indicating a range of numbers), or an asterisk.

3. Suppose the text file `jobinfo` (in the current directory) contains the job information. Submit this information to `crontab` with the following command:

```
crontab jobinfo
```

That's it! You should be set with the cron job. From now on, the cron job should run at regular intervals (as specified in the job information file), and you should receive mail messages with the output from the job.

To verify that the job is indeed scheduled, type the following command:

```
crontab -l
# DO NOT EDIT THIS FILE - edit the master and reinstall.
# (jobinfo installed on Mon Nov  6 21:22:41 2000)
# (Cron version -- $Id: crontab.c,v 2.13 1994/01/17 03:20:37 vixie Exp $)
5 0 * * * $HOME/myjob
```

The output of the `crontab -l` command shows the cron jobs currently installed in your name. To remove your cron jobs, type `crontab -r`.

Table 23-4 Specifying the Time of Execution in crontab Files

Field Number	Meaning of Field	Acceptable Range of Values*
1	Minute	0-59
2	Hour of the day	0-23
3	Day of the month	0-31
4	Month	1-12 (1 means January, 2 means February, and so on) or the names of months using the first letters (Jan, Feb, Mar, Apr, May, Jun, Jul, Aug, Sep, Oct, Nov, Dec)

Continued

Table 23-4 *(continued)*		
Field Number	**Meaning of Field**	**Acceptable Range of Values***
5	Day of the week	0-6 (0 means Sunday, 1 means Monday, and so on) or the three-letter abbreviations of the week (Sun, Mon, Tue, Wed, Thu, Fri, Sat)

* An asterisk in a field means all possible values for that field. For example, if an asterisk appears in the third field, the job is executed every day.

If you log in as `root`, you can also set up, examine, and remove cron jobs for any user. To set up cron jobs for a user, use this command:

```
crontab -u username filename
```

Here, `username` is the user for whom you install the cron jobs, and `filename` is the file that contains the information about the jobs.

Use the following form of `crontab` command to view the cron jobs for a user:

```
crontab -u username -l
```

To remove a user's cron jobs, use the following command:

```
crontab -u username -r
```

Note that the cron daemon also executes the cron jobs listed in the system-wide cron job file `/etc/crontab`. Here's the default `/etc/crontab` file in Red Hat Linux (type `cat /etc/crontab` to view the file):

```
SHELL=/bin/bash
PATH=/sbin:/bin:/usr/sbin:/usr/bin
MAILTO=root
HOME=/

# run-parts
01 * * * * root run-parts /etc/cron.hourly
02 4 * * * root run-parts /etc/cron.daily
22 4 * * 0 root run-parts /etc/cron.weekly
42 4 1 * * root run-parts /etc/cron.monthly
# sysstat
0 * * * 0,6 /usr/lib/sa/sa1 600 6 &
5 19 * * * /usr/lib/sa/sa2 -A &
```

The first four lines set up several environment variables for the jobs listed in this file. Note that the `MAILTO` environment variable specifies the user who receives the mail message with the output from the cron jobs in this file.

The line that begins with a # is a comment line. The four lines following the `run-parts` comment execute the `run-parts` shell script (located in the `/usr/bin` directory) at various times with the name of a specific directory as argument. Each of the arguments to `run-parts` — `/etc/cron.hourly`,

/etc/cron.daily, /etc/cron.weekly, and /etc/cron.monthly—are directories. Essentially, run-parts executes all scripts located in the directory that you provide as an argument (see Table 23-5).

Table 23-5   Script Directories for run-parts

Directory Name	Contents
/etc/cron.hourly	Scripts executed every hour
/etc/cron.daily	Scripts executed each day at 4:02 a.m.
/etc/cron.weekly	Scripts executed weekly on Sunday at 4:22 a.m.
/etc/cron.monthly	Scripts to be executed at 4:42 a.m. on the first day of each month

You have to look at the scripts in these directories to learn what gets executed at these periodic intervals. For example, the /etc/cron.daily directory contains the scripts shown in Table 23-6.

Table 23-6   Scripts Contained in /etc/cron/daily

Script Name	Description
0anacron	Runs anacron to process scheduled jobs that may not run because your system is not continuously running (anacron consults the /etc/anacrontab file to determine what to run)
inn-cron-expire	If the INN news server (innd) is running, executes the /usr/bin/news.daily script to expire news articles
logrotate	Automatically rotates, compresses, and mails out log files by running the /usr/sbin/logrotate program and using the configuration information stored in the /etc/logrotate.conf file
makewhatis.cron	Runs the /usr/sbin/makewhatis script to create the whatis database that the apropos and whatis commands use
slocate.crom	Runs the /usr/bin/updatedb program to create the database used by the slocate command, a security enhanced version of the GNU locate command (Unlike locate, slocate employs file permissions to make sure that users cannot see files for which they do not have access permission.)
tetex.cron	Runs the /usr/sbin/tmpwatch program to remove old font files from the /var/lib/texmf directory (used by a typesetting program called TeX)

Continued

Table 23-6 *(continued)*	
Script Name	**Description**
`tmpwatch`	Runs the `/usr/sbin/tmpwatch` program to remove old files from directories, such as `/var/cache/man` and `/var/catman`
`updatedb.cron`	Updates the filename database that the `locate` command consults (for example, try typing `locate updatedb`— this shows you all files that contain `updatedb` in their names)

Backing Up and Restoring Files

By now, you know how to perform a number of system administration tasks from automatically starting servers, to scheduling periodic jobs. The next few sections introduce you to another system administration task—backing up and restoring files. You learn about backup strategies, backup media, and how to back up and restore files, using the tape archiver (`tar`) program that comes with Red Hat Linux. You also learn how to perform incremental and automatic backups on tapes.

Selecting a Backup Strategy and Media

Your Linux system's hard disk contains everything needed to keep the system running, as well as other files, such as documents and databases that you need to keep your business running. You need to back up these files so that you can recover quickly and bring the system back to normal in case the hard disk crashes. Typically, you have to follow a strict regimen of regular backups, because you can never tell when the hard disk might fail or the file system might get corrupted. To implement such a regimen, you need to decide which files you want to back up, how often, and what backup storage media to use. This is what I mean by selecting a backup strategy and backup media.

Your choice of backup strategy and backup media depends on your assessment of the risk of business disruption due to hard disk failure. Depending on how you use your Linux system, a disk failure may or may not have much impact on you.

For example, if you use your Linux system as a learning tool (to learn about Linux or programming), all you may need are backup copies of some system files required to configure Linux. In this case, your backup strategy can be to save important system configuration files on one or more floppies, every time you change any system configuration.

On the other hand, if you use your Linux system as an office server that provides shared file storage for many users, the risk of business disruption due to disk failure is much higher. In this case, you have to back up all the files every week, and back up any new or changed files every day. You should perform these backups in an automated manner (this is where you can use the job scheduling features from earlier in this chapter). Also, you probably need a backup storage medium that can store large amounts (multiple gigabytes) of data on a single tape. In other words, for high-risk situations, your backup strategy is more elaborate and requires additional equipment (such as a tape drive).

Your choice of backup media depends on the amount of data you have to back up. For a small amount of data, such as system configuration files, you can use floppy disks as the backup media. If your PC has a Zip drive, you can use Zip disks as backup media; these are good for backing up a single user directory. To back up servers, you should use a tape drive, typically a 4mm or 8mm tape drive that connects to a SCSI controller. Such tape drives can store several gigabytes of data per tape, and you can use them to back up an entire file system on a single tape.

When backing up files to these backup media, you have to refer to the backup device by name. Table 23-7 lists device names for some common backup devices.

Table 23-7   Device Names for Common Backup Devices

Backup Device	Linux Device Name
Floppy disk	/dev/fd0
IDE Zip drive	/dev/hdc4 or /dev/hdd4
SCSI Zip drive	/dev/sda (assuming it's the first SCSI drive; otherwise, the device name depends on the SCSI ID)
SCSI tape drive	/dev/st0 or /dev/nst0 (the n prefix means that the tape is not rewound after files are copied to the tape)

Using the Tape Archiver — tar

You can use the tar command to archive files to a device, such as a floppy disk or tape. The tar program creates an archive file that can contain other directories and files and (optionally) compress the archive for efficient storage. The archive is then written to a specified device or another file. In fact, many software packages are distributed in the form of a compressed tar file.

Commercial Backup Utilities for Linux

In this chapter, you learn how to back up and restore files using the tape archiver (`tar`) program that comes with Red Hat Linux. Although you can manage backups with `tar`, a number of commercial backup utilities come with graphical user interfaces and other features to simplify backups. Here are some well-known backup utilities for Red Hat Linux:

- **BRU** — Backup and Restore Utility from EST (see www.estinc.com)

- **LONE-TAR** — Tape backup software package from Lone Star Software Corporation (see www.cactus.com)

- **Arkeia** — Backup and recovery software for heterogeneous networks from Knox Software (see www.knox-software.com)

- **CTAR** — backup and recovery software for UNIX systems from UniTrends Software Corporation (see www.unitrends.com)

The command syntax of the `tar` program is as follows:

```
tar options destination source
```

Here, *options* are usually specified by a sequence of single letters, with each letter specifying what `tar` should do. *destination* is the device name of the backup device. And *source* is a list of file or directory names denoting the files to back up.

Backing up and restoring a single-volume archive

For example, suppose you want to back up the contents of the /etc/X11 directory on a floppy disk. Log in as `root`, place a disk in the floppy drive, and then type the following command:

```
tar zcvf /dev/fd0 /etc/X11
```

The `tar` program displays a list of filenames as each file is copied to the compressed `tar` archive on the floppy disk. In this case, the options are zcvf, the destination is /dev/fd0 (the floppy disk), and the source is the /etc/X11 directory (which implies all its subdirectories and their contents). You can use a similar `tar` command to back up files to a tape — simply replace /dev/fd0 with the tape device — such as /dev/st0 for a SCSI tape drive.

Table 23-8 defines a few common `tar` options.

Table 23-8 Common tar Options

Option	Definition
c	Creates a new archive
f	Specifies the name of the archive file or device on the next field in the command line

Option	Definition
M	Specifies a multivolume archive (the next section describes multivolume archives)
t	Lists the contents of the archive
v	Displays verbose messages
x	Extracts files from the archive
z	Compresses the tar archive using gzip

To view the contents of the tar archive you create on the floppy disk, type the following command:

```
tar ztf /dev/fd0
```

You should see a list of the filenames (each begins with /etc/X11) indicating what's in the backup. In this tar command, the t option lists the contents of the tar archive.

To learn how to extract the files from a tar backup, try the following steps while logged in as root:

1. Change the directory to /tmp by typing this command:

   ```
   cd /tmp
   ```

   This is where you extract the files from the tar backup.

2. Type the following command:

   ```
   tar zxvf /dev/fd0
   ```

   This tar command uses the x option to extract the files from the archive stored on /dev/fd0 (the floppy disk).

If you check the contents of the /tmp directory, notice that the tar command creates an etc/X11 directory tree in /tmp and restores all the files from the tar archive into that directory. The tar command strips off the leading / from the filenames in the archive and restores the files in the current directory. If you want to restore the /etc/X11 directory from the archive on the floppy, use this command:

```
tar zxvf /dev/fd0 /
```

The / at the end of the command denotes the directory where you want to restore the backup files.

As you can see, the tar command enables you to create, view, and restore an archive. You can store the archive in a file, or in any device that you specify with a device name.

Backing up and restoring a multivolume archive

Sometimes the capacity of a single storage medium is less than the total storage space needed to store the archive. In this case, you can use the M option for a multivolume archive — meaning that the archive can span multiple tapes or floppies. Note, however, that you cannot create a compressed, multivolume archive. You have to drop the z option. To see how multivolume archives work, log in as root, place one disk in the floppy drive, and type the following tar command:

```
tar cvfM /dev/fd0 /usr/share/doc/ghostscript*
```

Note the M option in the option letters; it tells tar to create a multivolume archive. The tar command prompts you for a second floppy when the first one is filled. Take out the first floppy and insert another floppy when you see the following prompt:

```
Prepare volume #2 for `/dev/fd0' and hit return:
```

When you hit Enter, the tar program continues with the second floppy. In this example, you need only two floppies to store the archive; but for larger archives, the tar program continues to prompt for floppies in case more floppies are needed.

To restore from this multivolume archive, type cd /tmp to change the directory to /tmp. Then type:

```
tar xvfM /dev/fd0
```

The tar program prompts you to feed the floppies as necessary.

Tip

Use the du -s command to determine the amount of storage you need to archive a directory. For example, here's how you can get the total size of the /etc directory in kilobytes:

```
du -s /etc
9240    /etc
```

The resulting output shows that the /etc directory requires at least 9,240K of storage space to back up. If you plan to back up on multiple high-density floppies, you need about 9,240/1,200 = 8 floppies.

Backing Up on Tapes

Although backing up on tapes is as simple as using the right device name in the tar command, you do need to know some nuances of the tape device to use it well. When you use tar to back up to the device named /dev/st0 (the first SCSI tape drive), the tape device automatically rewinds the tape after the tar program finishes copying the archive to the tape. The /dev/st0 device is called a *rewinding tape device,* because it rewinds tapes by default.

If your tape can hold several gigabytes of data, you may want to write several `tar` archives — one after another — to the same tape (otherwise, much of the tape may be empty). To do this, you do not want the tape device to rewind the tape after the `tar` program finishes. To help you with this, several Linux tape devices are non-rewinding devices. The non-rewinding SCSI tape device is called /dev/nst0. Use this device name if you want to write one archive after another on a tape.

After each archive, the non-rewinding tape device writes an end-of-file (EOF) marker to separate one archive from the next. You can use the `mt` command to control the tape — you can move from one marker to the next, or rewind the tape. For example, after you finish writing several archives to a tape using the /dev/nst0 device name, you can rewind the tape with the following command:

```
mt -f /dev/nst0 rewind
```

After rewinding the tape, you can use the following command to extract files from the first archive to the current disk directory:

```
tar xvf /dev/nst0
```

After that, you must move past the end-of-file (EOF) marker to the next archive. To do this, use the following `mt` command:

```
mt -f /dev/nst0 fsf 1
```

This positions the tape at the beginning of the next archive. You can now use the `tar xvf` command again to read this archive.

Note

If you save multiple archives on a tape, you have to keep track of the archives yourself.

Performing incremental backups

Suppose you back up your system's hard disk on a tape using `tar`. Because such a full backup can take quite some time, you do not want to repeat this task every night. (Besides, only a small number of files may have changed during the day.) You can use the `find` command to list those files that have changed in the past 24 hours:

```
find / -mtime -1 -type f -print
```

This command prints a list of files that have changed within the last day. The `-mtime -1` option means you want the files that were last modified less than one day ago. You can now combine this `find` command with the `tar` command to back up only those files that have changed within the last day:

```
tar cvf /dev/st0 `find / -mtime -1 -type f -print`
```

When you place a command between single back quotes, the shell executes that command and places the output at that point in the command line. The net result is that the `tar` program saves only the changed files in the archive. Thus, you get an *incremental backup* that includes files that changed since the previous day.

Performing automated backups

Earlier in this chapter, you learn how to use `crontab` to set up recurring jobs (called cron jobs). The Linux system performs these tasks at regular intervals. Backing up your system is a good use of the `crontab` facility. Suppose your backup strategy is as follows:

- Every Sunday morning at 1:15 a.m., your system backs up the entire disk on the tape.

- On the other days of the week (Monday through Saturday), your system performs an incremental backup at 3:10 a.m. by saving only those files that have changed during the past 24 hours.

To set up this automated backup schedule, log in as `root` and type the following lines in a file named `backups` (this example assumes that you use a SCSI tape drive):

```
15 1 * * 0 tar zcvf /dev/st0 /
10 3 * * 1-6 tar zcvf /dev/st0 `find / -mtime -1 -type f -print`
```

Next, submit this job schedule with the following `crontab` command:

```
crontab backups
```

Now you should be set for an automated backup. All you need to do is place a new tape in the tape drive everyday. You should also label each tape with an appropriate label.

Monitoring System Performance

A key system administration task is to keep track of how well your Linux system performs. You can monitor the overall performance of your Linux system by gathering information such as:

- Central Processing Unit (CPU) usage
- Physical memory usage
- Virtual memory (swap space) usage
- Hard disk usage

Red Hat Linux comes with a number of utilities that you can use to monitor one or more of these performance parameters. The following sections introduce you to a few of these utilities and show you how to understand the information presented by them.

Using top

To view the top CPU processes — the ones that use most of the CPU time — you can employ the `top` program. To start this program, select Main Menu ⇨ Utilities ⇨ Top from the GNOME desktop, or type `top` in a terminal window (or text console). The `top` program then displays a text screen listing the current processes, arranged in the order of CPU usage, along with various other information, such as memory and swap space usage. Figure 23-2 shows a typical output from the `top` program.

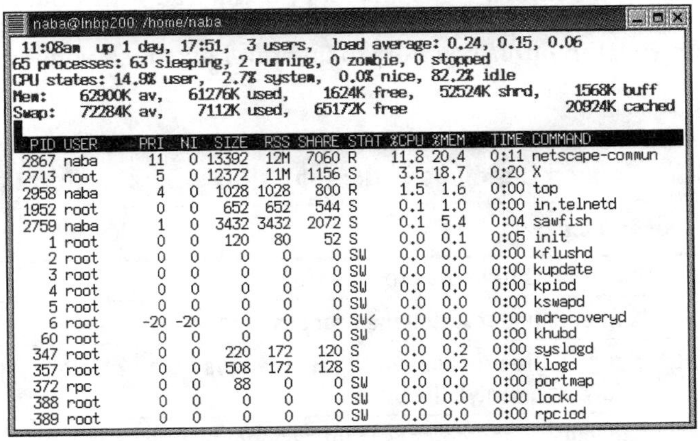

```
naba@lnbp200: /home/naba
 11:08am  up 1 day, 17:51,   3 users,   load average: 0.24, 0.15, 0.06
 65 processes: 63 sleeping, 2 running, 0 zombie, 0 stopped
 CPU states: 14.9% user,   2.7% system,   0.0% nice, 82.2% idle
 Mem:    62900K av,   61276K used,    1624K free,   52524K shrd,    1568K buff
 Swap:   72284K av,    7112K used,   65172K free                   20924K cached

  PID USER     PRI  NI  SIZE  RSS SHARE STAT %CPU %MEM   TIME COMMAND
 2867 naba      11   0 13392  12M  7060 R    11.8 20.4  0:11 netscape-commun
 2713 root       5   0 12372  11M  1156 S     3.5 18.7  0:20 X
 2958 naba       4   0  1028 1028   800 R     1.5  1.6  0:00 in.telnetd
 1952 root       0   0   652  652   544 S     0.1  1.0  0:00 top
 2759 naba       1   0  3432 3432  2072 S     0.1  5.4  0:04 sawfish
    1 root       0   0   120   80    52 S     0.0  0.1  0:05 init
    2 root       0   0     0    0     0 SW    0.0  0.0  0:00 kflushd
    3 root       0   0     0    0     0 SW    0.0  0.0  0:00 kupdate
    4 root       0   0     0    0     0 SW    0.0  0.0  0:00 kpiod
    5 root       0   0     0    0     0 SW    0.0  0.0  0:00 kswapd
    6 root     -20 -20     0    0     0 SW<   0.0  0.0  0:00 mdrecoveryd
   60 root       0   0     0    0     0 SW    0.0  0.0  0:00 khubd
  347 root       0   0   220  172   120 S     0.0  0.2  0:00 syslogd
  357 root       0   0   508  172   128 S     0.0  0.2  0:00 klogd
  372 rpc        0   0    88    0     0 SW    0.0  0.0  0:00 portmap
  388 root       0   0     0    0     0 SW    0.0  0.0  0:00 lockd
  389 root       0   0     0    0     0 SW    0.0  0.0  0:00 rpciod
```

Figure 23-2: Viewing top CPU processes

The `top` utility updates the display every five seconds. You can keep `top` running in a window so that you can continually monitor the status of your Linux system. You quit `top` by pressing q or Ctrl+C, or by closing the terminal window.

The first five lines of the output screen provide summary information about the system. Here is what these five lines show:

1. The first line shows the current time, how long the system has been up, how many users are logged in, and three load averages (the average number of processes ready to run during the last one, five, and 15 minutes).

2. The second line lists the total number of processes and the status of these processes.

3. The third line shows CPU usage — what percentage of CPU time user processes employ, what percentage of CPU time system (kernel) processes employ, and what percentage of time the CPU is idle.

4. The fourth line shows how the physical memory is used — the total amount, how much is used, how much is free, how much is shared, and how much is allocated to buffers (for reading from disk, for instance).

5. The fifth line shows how the virtual memory (or swap space) is used — the total amount of swap space, how much is used, how much is free, and how much is cached.

The table below the summary data lists information about the current processes arranged in decreasing order of CPU time usage. Table 23-9 summarizes the meanings of the column headings in the table that top displays.

Note

If the RSS field is drastically smaller than the SIZE field for a process, the process is using too little physical memory compared with what it needs. The result is a lot of swapping as the process runs. You can use the vmstat utility (which you try later in this chapter) to find out how much your system is swapping.

Table 23-9   Column Headings in the top Utility's Display Screen

Heading	Meaning
PID	The process ID of the process
USER	Username under which the process runs
PRI	Priority of the process — the value ranges from –20 (highest priority) to 19 (lowest priority); the default is 0
NI	Nice value of the process (same as negative PRI values)
SIZE	Total size of the process in kilobytes
RSS	Total physical memory used by task (typically shown in kilobytes, but an M suffix indicates megabytes)
SHARE	Amount of shared memory used by process
STAT	State of the process (S for sleeping, D for uninterruptible sleep, R for running, Z for zombies (processes that should be dead, but are still running), or T for stopped; a trailing < means the process has a negative nice value)
%CPU	Percentage of CPU time used since last screen update
%MEM	Percentage of physical memory used by the process
TIME	Total CPU time the process has used since it started
COMMAND	Shortened form of the command that starts the process

Using the GNOME System Monitor

Like the text-mode top utility, the *GNOME System Monitor* tool also enables you to view the system load in terms of the number of processes that are currently running, their memory usage, and the free disk space on your system. To run this tool, select Main Menu ⇨ Programs ⇨ System ⇨ System Monitor. You can also start the tool by typing gtop in a terminal window. The System Monitor starts and displays its output in a window, as shown in Figure 23-3.

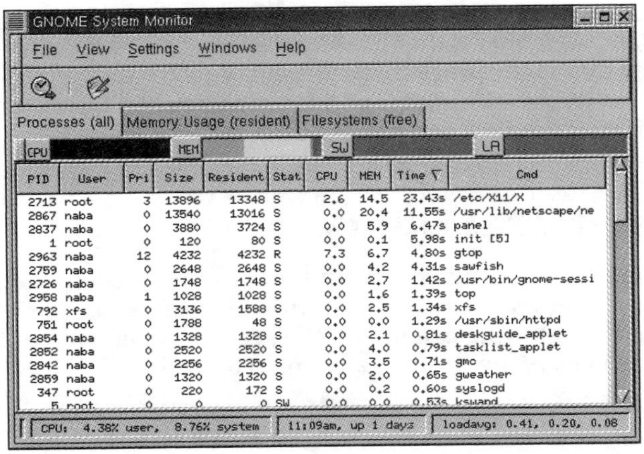

Figure 23-3: Viewing current processes in the GNOME System Monitor window

The output is similar to the output you see when you type top in a text-mode console or terminal window. In fact, the column headings in the table match what the top utility uses in its output. (See Table 23-9 for the meaning of the column headings.) As with the text-mode top utility, the display keeps updating to reflect the current state of the system.

The current processes display in descending order of CPU usage. For each process, the GNOME System Monitor shows a number of details including the process ID (PID), the user who starts the process, the priority of the process, and the command used to start the process.

The GNOME System Monitor window has two more tabs that display the memory usage and the free space on the file system. To view this information, click the appropriate tab. For example, to see how various processes use memory, click the Memory Usage tab. When you click the Memory Usage tab, the processes are listed in the order that they reside in memory. A multicolored rectangle on the left-hand side represents the physical memory. The memory used by each process is shaded with a color to help you see how much each process uses. The processes and the amount of memory used by each process are listed on the right side of the window.

The bottom of the GNOME System Monitor window shows the CPU usage summary, system up time (how long the system has been up and running), and load averages (the average number of processes that are ready to run in the last one, five, and 15 minutes).

The load averages give you an indication of how busy the system is. In addition to the top and GNOME System Monitor programs, you can also get the load averages with the uptime command, as follows:

```
uptime
   11:40am  up 2 days, 57 min,  3 users,  load average: 0.13, 0.23, 0.27
```

The output shows the current time, how long the system has been up, the number of users, and, finally, the three load averages. Load averages greater than one imply that many processes are competing for the CPU time simultaneously. You can then look at the top CPU processes and try to run these processes one after another and not all at the same time.

Using the vmstat Utility

You can get summary information about the overall system usage with the vmstat utility. To view system usage information averaged over 5-second intervals, type the following command (the second argument indicates the total number of lines of output vmstat should display):

```
vmstat 5 8
   procs                      memory     swap          io      system          cpu
 r  b  w   swpd   free  buff  cache  si  so    bi    bo   in    cs  us  sy  id
 1  0  0   4724   1620  3420  18244   0   0     2     0  129   736  27   5  68
 3  0  0   4724   2068  3420  18244   0   0     0     2  124   179   3   8  89
 0  0  0   4724   2052  3420  18244   0   0     0     2  125   301  57  13  30
 0  0  0   4724   2124  3420  18232   0   0     0     3  134   213   6   8  86
 0  0  0   4724   1980  3416  18064   0   0     4     4  182   363  54  15  31
 2  0  0   4724   1960  3416  18064   0   0     0     4  142   126  13   7  80
 0  0  0   4724   1960  3416  18064   0   0     0     3  132   183   7   9  84
 0  0  0   4724   1948  3416  18076   0   0     0     1  112    90   7   8  86
```

The tabular output is grouped into six categories of information, as indicated by the fields in the first line of output. The second line shows further details for each of the six major fields. You can interpret the six major fields, as well as the detailed fields in each category, using Table 23-10.

Table 23-10   vmstat Utility Output Fields

Field Name	Description
procs	Number of processes and their types: r = processes waiting to run; b = processes in uninterruptible sleep; w = processes swapped out, but ready to run
memory	Information about physical memory and swap space usage (all numbers in kilobytes): swpd = virtual memory used; free = free physical memory; buff = memory used as buffers; cache = virtual memory that's cached
swap	Amount of swapping (the numbers are in kilobytes per second): si = amount of memory swapped in from disk; so = amount of memory swapped to disk
io	Information about input and output (the numbers are in blocks per second; the block size depends on the disk device): bi = rate of blocks sent to disk; bo = rate of blocks received from disk

Field Name	Description
system	Information about the system: in = number of interrupts per second (including clock interrupts); cs = number of context switches per second — the number of times the kernel changes which process is running
cpu	Percentages of CPU time used: us = percentage of CPU time used by user processes; sy = percentage CPU time used by system processes; id = percentage of time CPU is idle

The first line of vmstat output following the two header lines shows the averages since the last reboot. After that, vmstat displays the 5-second average data seven more times over the next 35 seconds. In the vmstat utility's output, high values in the si and so fields indicate too much swapping. High numbers in the bi and bo fields indicate too much disk activity.

Checking Disk Performance and Disk Usage

Red Hat Linux comes with the /sbin/hdparm program that you can use to control IDE or ATAPI hard disks that are common on most PCs. One feature of the hdparm program is that the -t option enables you to determine the rate at which data can be read from the disk into a buffer in memory. For example, here's the result of the command on my system:

```
/sbin/hdparm -t /dev/hda

/dev/hda:
 Timing buffered disk reads:  64 MB in 15.18 seconds =  4.22 MB/sec
```

As you can see, the command requires the IDE drive's device name (/dev/hda) as an argument. If you have an IDE hard disk, you can try this command to see how fast data can be read from your system's disk drive.

Secret

During system startup, the /etc/rc.sysinit script runs the /sbin/hdparm program to set the hard disk parameters based on settings in the /etc/sysconfig/harddisks file. Type man hdparm to learn more about the hard disk parameters you can set. To set a parameter at boot time, you can place an appropriate line in the /etc/sysconfig/harddisks file.

To display the space available in the currently mounted file systems, use the df command. If you want a more human-readable output from df, type the following command:

```
df -h
Filesystem          Size  Used Avail Use% Mounted on
/dev/hda2           1.9G  1.4G  492M  74% /
/dev/hda1           2.0G  1.9G  176M  92% /dosc
/dev/hdc            639M  640M     0 100% /mnt/cdrom
```

As this example shows, the -h option causes the df command to show the sizes in gigabytes (G) and megabytes (M).

To check the disk space a specific directory uses, employ the du command. You can specify the -h option to view the output in kilobytes (k) and megabytes (M), as shown in the following example:

```
du -h /var/log
84k      /var/log/httpd
4.0k     /var/log/news/OLD
36k      /var/log/news
4.0k     /var/log/vbox
20k      /var/log/samba
4.0k     /var/log/sa
103M     /var/log
```

The du command displays the disk space used by each directory, and the last line shows the total disk space used by that directory. If you want to see only the total space used by a directory, use the -s option like this:

```
du -sh /home
29M      /home
```

Exploring the /proc File System

You can find out a great deal about your Linux system by consulting the contents of a special file system known as the /proc file system. Knowing about the /proc file system is useful because it can help you monitor a wide variety of information about your system. In fact, you can even change kernel parameters through the /proc file system, and thereby modify the system's behavior.

The /proc file system is not a real directory on the disk, but rather a collection of data structures in memory, managed by the Linux kernel, that appears to the user as a set of directories and files. The purpose of /proc (also called the *process file system*) is to enable users to access information about the Linux kernel and the processes that are currently running on your system.

You can access the /proc file system just as you access any other directory, but you have to know the meaning of various files to interpret the information. Typically, you can use the cat or more command to view the contents of a file in /proc; the file's contents provide information about some aspect of the system.

As with any directory, you may want to start by looking at a detailed directory listing of /proc. To do so, type ls -l /proc. In the output, the first set of directories (indicated by the letter d at the beginning of the line) represents the processes that are currently running on your system. Each directory that corresponds to a process has the process ID (a number) as its name.

Caution

Also notice a very large file named /proc/kcore; that file represents the entire physical memory of your system. Although /proc/kcore appears in the listing as a huge file, there is no physical file occupying that much space on your hard disk. You should not try to remove this file to reclaim disk space.

Several files and directories in /proc contain interesting information about your Linux system. The /proc/cpuinfo file, for example, lists the key characteristics of your system, such as processor type and floating-point processor information. You can view the processor information by typing cat /proc/cpuinfo. For example, here is what I get when I type the command on my system:

```
cat /proc/cpuinfo
processor       : 0
vendor_id       : GenuineIntel
cpu family      : 5
model           : 4
model name      : Pentium MMX
stepping        : 3
cpu MHz         : 199.615
fdiv_bug        : no
hlt_bug         : no
sep_bug         : no
f00f_bug        : yes
fpu             : yes
fpu_exception   : yes
cpuid level     : 1
wp              : yes
flags           : fpu vme de pse tsc msr mce cx8 mmx
bogomips        : 398.13
```

This output is from a 200MHz Pentium MMX system. The listing shows many interesting characteristics of the processor. Notice the line that starts with fdiv_bug. Remember the infamous Pentium floating-point-division bug? The bug is in an instruction called fdiv (for floating-point division). Thus, the fdiv_bug line indicates whether this particular Pentium has the bug (fortunately, my system's processor does not).

Note

The f00f_bug line also refers to another bug in Pentium and Pentium MMX processors. This bug gets its name from a specific instruction whose encoding starts with the hexadecimal numbers F0 0F. This bug is troublesome because it can lock up the system, regardless of the operating system. Fortunately, there is a workaround for this bug, and the Linux kernel on the companion CD-ROM implements the workaround. To see if your system has this bug, type dmesg | grep bug. You see a message about the bug if it was detected and fixed. For example, on my system, I get the following:

```
dmesg | grep bug
Intel Pentium with F0 0F bug - workaround enabled.
```

The last line in the /proc/cpuinfo file shows the BogoMips for the processor, as computed by the Linux kernel when it boots. *BogoMips* is something that Linux uses internally to time delay loops.

Table 23-11 summarizes some of the files in the /proc file system from which you can get information about your Linux system. You can view some of these files on your system to see what they contain. Note that not all the files shown in Table 23-11 are present on your system — the contents of the /proc file system depend on the kernel configuration and the driver modules that are loaded (which, in turn, depend on your PC's hardware configuration).

Tip

You can navigate the /proc file system just as you work with any other directories and files in Linux. Use the more or cat command to view the contents of a file.

Table 23-11   Files and Directories in /proc

File Name	Content
/proc/apm	Information about advanced power management (APM)
/proc/bus	Directory with bus-specific information for each bus type, such as PCI
/proc/cmdline	The command line used to start the Linux kernel (for example, auto BOOT_IMAGE=linux ro root=303)
/proc/cpuinfo	Information about the CPU (the microprocessor)
/proc/devices	Available block and character devices in your system
/proc/dma	Information about DMA (direct memory access) channels that are used
/proc/filesystems	List of supported file systems
/proc/ide	Directory containing information about IDE devices
/proc/interrupts	Information about interrupt request (IRQ) numbers and how they are used
/proc/ioports	Information about input/output (I/O) port addresses and how they are used
/proc/kcore	Image of the physical memory
/proc/kmsg	Kernel messages
/proc/ksyms	Kernel symbol table
/proc/loadavg	Load average (average number of processes waiting to run in the last one, five, and 15 minutes)
/proc/locks	Current kernel locks (used to ensure that multiple processes do not write to a file at the same time)
/proc/meminfo	Information about physical memory and swap space usage

File Name	Content
/proc/misc	Miscellaneous information
/proc/modules	List of loaded driver modules
/proc/mounts	List of mounted file systems
/proc/net	Directory with many subdirectories that contain information about networking
/proc/partitions	List of partitions known to the Linux kernel
/proc/pci	Information about PCI devices found on the system
/proc/rtc	Information about the PC's real-time clock (RTC)
/proc/scsi	Directory with information about SCSI devices found on the system
/proc/sound	Information about the sound driver module, if any
/proc/stat	Overall statistics about the system
/proc/swaps	Information about the swap space and how much is used
/proc/sys	Directory with information about the system (You can change kernel parameters by writing to files in this directory. This is one way to tune the system's performance, but it requires expertise to do it properly.)
/proc/uptime	Information about how long the system has been up
/proc/version	Kernel version number

Using sysctl to View and Set Kernel Parameters

As the entry for /proc/sys in Table 23-6 explains, you can change kernel parameters by writing to files in the /proc/sys directory. This is one way to tune the system's performance. Red Hat Linux also comes with the /sbin/sysctl program, which enables you to read and write kernel parameters without having to manually overwrite files in the /proc/sys directory.

In Chapter 16, you encounter an instruction that asks you to log in as root and enable IP forwarding in the kernel, by typing the following command:

```
echo "1" > /proc/sys/net/ipv4/ip_forward
```

This is the manual way to set the value of a parameter — using the echo command to copy the value into a file in the /proc/sys directory.

You can perform this same step by running `sysctl` as follows:

```
/sbin/sysctl -w net.ipv4.ip_forward=1
net.ipv4.ip_forward = 1
```

This `sysctl` command sets the value of the parameter and echoes the new value for your information. As you can see, you refer to the parameter using the last part of the pathname excluding `/proc/sys`, but you use periods (.) instead of slashes (/) as separators. Note that, if you prefer, you can continue to use slashes as separators and refer to this variable as `net/ipv4/ip_forward`.

You can use `sysctl` to both query and set the value of a parameter. To see the value of a parameter, use the parameter's name as an argument like this:

```
/sbin/sysctl dev.cdrom.info
dev.cdrom.info = CD-ROM information, Id: cdrom.c 3.10 2000/06/10
dev.cdrom.info =
dev.cdrom.info = drive name:              hdc
dev.cdrom.info = drive speed:             20
dev.cdrom.info = drive # of slots:        1
dev.cdrom.info = Can close tray:                    1
dev.cdrom.info = Can open tray:           1
dev.cdrom.info = Can lock tray:           1
dev.cdrom.info = Can change speed:        1
dev.cdrom.info = Can select disk:         0
dev.cdrom.info = Can read multisession:   1
dev.cdrom.info = Can read MCN:            1
dev.cdrom.info = Reports media changed:   1
dev.cdrom.info = Can play audio:                    1
dev.cdrom.info = Can write CD-R:                    0
dev.cdrom.info = Can write CD-RW:         0
dev.cdrom.info = Can read DVD:            0
dev.cdrom.info = Can write DVD-R:         0
dev.cdrom.info = Can write DVD-RAM:       0
dev.cdrom.info =
dev.cdrom.info =
```

The command `/sbin/sysctl dev.cdrom.info` displays the contents of that parameter. In this case, `dev.cdrom.info` is a structure that contains many different fields; `sysctl` shows these fields as separate lines in the output.

For a simple parameter, such as `fs.file-max`, `sysctl` displays the single value as shown in the following example:

```
/sbin/sysctl fs.file-max
fs.file-max = 4096
```

The `fs.file-max` variable denotes the maximum number of file handles the Linux kernel can allocate. If you get error messages about running out of file handles, you may want to increase this value with a command, such as `/sbin/sysctl -w fs.file-max=8192`.

Secret

To use `sysctl` to modify kernel variables and tune the kernel's performance, you need to know what each parameter means. You can find documentation on these parameters in the `/usr/src/linux/Documentation/sysctl` directory of your system (provided you install the kernel-source RPM). In particular, look at the `/usr/src/linux/Documentation/sysctl/ kernel.txt` file for information on the kernel parameters.

You can see the values of all parameters in the `/proc/sys` directory by typing the `/sbin/sysctl -a` command. It's instructive to look through the names of the parameters and their values. You should try the `/sbin/sysctl -a` command on your system.

Caution

Before you use `sysctl` to change any of the parameters listed in Table 23-12, you should know that changing some kernel parameters can adversely affect your system's performance and even cause the system to hang. You should play with these parameters only if you know what you are doing. In particular, never play around with kernel parameters on a production system.

If you have a number of parameters to alter using `sysctl`, you can place the parameters and their values in a file and then use the command `/sbin/sysctl -p` *filename* to load the settings from that file. For example, when Red Hat Linux boots, a startup script sets some parameters with the following command:

```
/sbin/sysctl -p /etc/sysctl.conf
```

On my Red Hat Linux system, the `/etc/sysctl.conf` file contains the following lines:

```
# Disables packet forwarding
net.ipv4.ip_forward = 0
# Enables source route verification
net.ipv4.conf.all.rp_filter = 1
# Disables automatic defragmentation (needed for masquerading, LVS)
net.ipv4.ip_always_defrag = 0
# Disables the magic-sysrq key
kernel.sysrq = 0
```

Table 23-12 describes some of the interesting kernel parameters from the `/proc/sys` directory, as well as the meaning of these parameters.

Table 23-12   Some Kernel Parameters in the /proc/sys Directory

Parameter Name	Meaning
`fs.file-max`	Maximum number of file handles that the Linux kernel can allocate (default value is 4096)
`fs.file-nr`	Three values representing the number of allocated file handles, the number of used file handles, and the maximum number of file handles
`fs.inode-max`	Maximum number of inode structures the kernel can allocate (default value is 8192)
`fs.super-max`	Maximum number of superblocks, and thus the maximum number of mounted file systems the kernel can support (default value is 256)
`kernel.acct`	Three values specifying *high*, *low*, and *frequency* that control the logging of process accounting information — when free space on file system goes below the *low* (percent), accounting is suspended; it resumes when free space goes above *high* (percent); and *frequency* specifies how many seconds the free space in formation is valid (default values are 4% for high, 2% for low, and 30 seconds for *frequency*)
`kernel.ctrl-alt-del`	When set to 0, a Ctrl+Alt+Del keypress is handled by using the `init` program to restart the system; when set to 1, Ctrl+Alt+Del performs an immediate reboot without even saving any dirty buffers to the disk
`kernel.domainname`	The NIS domain name of the system
`kernel.hostname`	The hostname of the system
`kernel.modprobe`	Name of the program that the kernel uses to load one or more modules (for example, `/sbin/modprobe`)
`kernel.osrelease`	The version number of the operating system (for example, `2.4.0-0.43.12`)
`kernel.ostype`	Name of operating system (for example, `Linux` for all Linux systems)
`kernel.panic`	Number of seconds the kernel waits before rebooting in case of a panic (default is 0)
`kernel.printk`	Values that affect the printing or logging of error messages by the kernel
`kernel.rtsig-max`	Maximum number of POSIX real-time signals that can be outstanding in the system (default is 1024)
`kernel.rtsig-nr`	Number of real-time signals currently queued

Parameter Name	*Meaning*
`kernel.shmall`	Total amount, in bytes, of shared memory segments that can be created (default is 33554432 bytes)
`kernel.shmmax`	Maximum size, in bytes, of shared memory segments that can be created (default is 33554432 bytes; kernel supports shared memory segments up to 1GB)
`kernel.sysrq`	When set to 0, the SysRq key is disabled; when set to 1, user can perform specific tasks by pressing Alt+SysRq and a command key (see the file `/usr/src/linux/Documentation/sysrq.txt` for more information)
`kernel.version`	The build number and the date the kernel was built (for example, `#1 Wed Dec 27 17:44:32 EST 2000`)
`net.core.netdev_max_backlog`	Maximum number of packets that can be queued on input when a network interface receives packets faster than the kernel can process them (default is 300)
`net.core.optmem_max`	Maximum size of ancillary buffer allowed per socket (default is 10240 bytes or 10K)
`net.core.rmem_default`	Default size of socket receive buffer in bytes (default is 65535 bytes or 64K)
`net.core.rmem_max`	Maximum size of socket receive buffer in bytes (default is 65535 bytes or 64K)
`net.core.wmem_default`	Default size of socket send buffer in bytes (default is 65535 bytes or 64K)
`net.core.wmem_max`	Maximum size of socket send buffer in bytes (default is 65535 bytes or 64K)
`net.ipv4.conf.all.accept_redirects`	When set to 1, the kernel accepts ICMP redirect messages (should be set to 0 for a system configured as a router)
`net.ipv4.conf.all.accept_source_route`	When set to 1, accepts source routed packets (should be set to 1 for a system configured as a router)
`net.ipv4.conf.all.forwarding`	When set to 1, enables IP forwarding for all interfaces
`net.ipv4.conf.all.hidden`	When set to 1, hides network addresses from other systems
`net.ipv4.conf.all.log_martians`	When set to 1, logs all packets with source addresses with no known route
`net.ipv4.conf.all.rp_filter`	When set to 0, turns off source validation; when set to 1, performs source validation using reverse path (as specified in RFC 1812)

Continued

Table 23-12 *(continued)*

Parameter Name	Meaning
`net.ipv4.conf.all.secure_redirects`	When set to 1, accepts ICMP redirect messages only for gateways listed in default gateway list
`net.ipv4.conf.all.send_redirects`	When set to 1, sends ICMP redirect messages to other hosts
`net.ipv4.conf.all.shared_media`	When set to 1, assumes that different subnets share the media and can communicate directly
`net.ipv4.conf.eth0.accept_redirects`	When set to 1, accepts ICMP redirect messages (must be 0 for a system used as a router)
`net.ipv4.conf.eth0.forwarding`	When set to 1, turns on IP forwarding for the `eth0` network interface
`net.ipv4.conf.eth0.hidden`	When set to 1, keeps the address hidden from other devices
`net.ipv4.conf.eth0.log_martians`	When set to 1, logs packets with impossible addresses in the log file
`net.ipv4.conf.eth0.rp_filter`	When set to 0, turns off source validation; when set to 1, performs source validation using reverse path (as specified in RFC 1812)
`net.ipv4.icmp_echo_ignore_all`	When set to 1, kernel ignores all ICMP ECHO requests sent to it
`net.ipv4.icmp_echo_ignore_broadcasts`	When set to 1, kernel ignores all ICMP ECHO requests sent to broadcast or multicast addresses
`net.ipv4.ip_always_defrag`	When set to 1, automatically reassembles all fragmented packets (this is enabled when masquerading is enabled)
`net.ipv4.ip_autoconfig`	Contains 1 if the host receives its IP address by using a mechanism such as RARP, BOOTP, or DHCP; otherwise, it is 0
`net.ipv4.ip_default_ttl`	Time-to-live (TTL) for IP packets (default value is 64; this is the maximum number of routers through which the packet can travel)
`net.ipv4.ip_forward`	When set to 1, packets are forwarded among interfaces
`net.ipv4.ip_local_port_range`	Two numbers denoting the range of port numbers used by TCP and UDP for the local port (default range 1024-4999; you can change this to 32768-61000 if you need more ports)

Parameter Name	Meaning
`net.ipv4.ip_masq_debug`	When set to 1, enables debugging of IP masquerading
`net.ipv4.ipfrag_high_thresh`	Maximum memory for use in reassembling IP fragments (default is 262144 bytes)
`net.ipv4.ipfrag_low_thresh`	When maximum amount of memory (`net.ipv4.ipfrag_high_thresh`) is already being used to reassemble fragmented IP packets, further packets are discarded until the memory usage comes down to this value (default is 196608 bytes)
`net.ipv4.ipfrag_time`	Time in seconds to keep an IP fragment in memory (default is 30 seconds)
`net.ipv4.tcp_fin_timeout`	Number of seconds to wait for a final FIN before the socket is closed — this occurs to prevent denial-of-service attacks (default is 180 seconds)
`net.ipv4.tcp_keepalive_probes`	Number of keepalive probes TCP sends out before it decides that the connection is broken (default value is 9)
`net.ipv4.tcp_keepalive_time`	Time in seconds between keepalive messages (default is 7200 seconds or two hours)
`net.ipv4.tcp_max_ka_probes`	Maximum number of keepalive probes to send in one interval of the slow timer (default is 5)
`net.ipv4.tcp_max_syn_backlog`	Length of the backlog queue for each socket (default is 128)
`net.ipv4.tcp_retries1`	Number of times an answer to a TCP connection request is retransmitted before giving up (default is 7)
`net.ipv4.tcp_retries2`	Number of times a TCP packet is retransmitted before giving up (default is 15)
`net.ipv4.tcp_sack`	When set to 1, enables select acknowledgments as specified in RFC 2018
`net.ipv4.tcp_syn_retries`	Number of times initial SYNs for a TCP connection attempt are retransmitted (default value is 10)
`net.ipv4.tcp_syncookies`	When set to 1, sends out SYN cookies when the SYN backlog queue of a socket overflows (this prevents the common SYN flood attack)
`net.ipv4.tcp_timestamps`	When set to 1, enables timestamps as defined in RFC 1323
`net.ipv4.tcp_window_scaling`	When set to 1, enables window scaling as defined in RFC 1323

Continued

Table 23-12   *(continued)*

Parameter Name	Meaning
vm.bdflush	Settings that control the operation of the bdflush daemon that handles flushing of dirty buffers; dirty indicates that a buffer's contents have changed and still remain to be written to the disk (see the file /usr/src/linux/Documentation/sysctl/vm.txt for more details)
vm.buffermem	The first value denotes the minimum percentage of memory that should be used for the buffers (default is 2%)
vm.freepages	Three values provide *minimum*, *low*, and *high* threshold values for the number of free pages that control swapping — when the number of free pages reaches the *minimum*, only the kernel can allocate more memory; if the number of free pages drops below the *low* threshold, kernel starts swapping aggressively; the *high* threshold is the number of pages the kernel tries to keep available (the default values are 128 for minimum, 256 for low, and 384 for high threshold)
vm.kswapd	The three values specify *base*, *minimum*, and *cluster* values that control the operation of kswapd, the kernel swap out daemon that frees memory when needed — the *base* value computes how many pages kswapd tries to free in one round; the *minimum* value is the minimum number of times kswapd tries to free a page; and the *cluster* value is the number of pages kswapd writes to the disk in one turn (the default values are 512 for base, 32 for minimum tries, and 32 for the cluster)
vm.overcommit_memory	If this value is set to 1, the system pretends that there is always enough memory; when it's 0, the kernel checks before each memory allocation request to determine if enough memory remains
vm.pagecache	Similar to vm.buffermem, but this one controls the amount of memory used for page cache
vm.page-cluster	If this value is n, the Linux virtual memory subsystem reads 2^n pages at once (default is 4, which means the VM subsystem reads 16 pages at a time)
vm.pagetable_cache	The range of values that specify the size of the cache for page tables — primarily used for multiprocessor systems (default is between 25 and 50)

Summary

If you use your Red Hat Linux system for production work (to run an Internet server or an office server, for example), you have to perform some advanced system administration tasks. This chapter introduces you to some system administration tasks that I do not cover elsewhere in the book.

By reading this chapter, you learn the following:

▶ After Linux boots, a process named `init` starts all the other processes. The exact set of initial processes depends on the run level, which typically is a number ranging from 0 to 6. The `/etc/inittab` file specifies the processes that start in each run level.

▶ The `/etc/inittab` file specifies that a graphical display manager starts at run level 5. In Red Hat Linux, the display manager provides the graphical login prompt.

▶ The `init` process executes Red Hat Linux startup scripts in the `/etc/rc.d` directory and its subdirectories.

▶ You can use the `/sbin/chkconfig` program to set up servers to start automatically at various run levels.

▶ You can use the `at` command to execute one or more commands at a future time and have the output mailed to you.

▶ You can use the `crontab` facility to set up periodic jobs (called cron jobs) that are executed at recurring intervals. Then you can have the output mailed to you.

▶ If you use your Red Hat Linux system for anything important, you have to back up your files. You should select a backup strategy and backup media based on your needs and your level of tolerance for the risk of business interruption from a hard disk failure.

▶ You can use the tape archiver program — `tar` — to back up and restore files. This chapter shows you how to set up cron jobs for automated full and incremental backups.

▶ Red Hat Linux comes with utilities and commands that you can use to keep an eye on your system's performance. You learn to use and interpret the displays produced by `top`, the GNOME System Monitor, and `vmstat`. You also learn some commands to check available disk space and your hard disk's performance.

▶ The `/proc` file system contains an extensive amount of information about the system. The `/proc` file system is not a disk-based file system; it is a collection of data structures in memory, managed by the Linux kernel, that appears to the user as a set of directories and files.

▶ In the `/proc/sys` directory, there are a number of files whose values you can set to modify the kernel's behavior at run time. You can either directly write to these files, or use the `/sbin/sysctl` program to view or set the parameters. If you know what you are doing, you can tune the performance of your system, by modifying the parameters in the `/proc/sys` directory.

Chapter 24

Software Installation
and Upgrade

You should know how to install or remove software packages distributed in the form of Red Hat Package Manager (RPM) files, because most Red Hat Linux software comes in RPM files. This chapter shows you how to work with RPM files.

Many open-source software packages also come in source-code form, usually in compressed archives. You have to build and install the software to use it. This chapter describes the steps you'll ordinarily follow when downloading, building, and installing source-based software packages.

Finally, this chapter briefly describes the Red Hat Network and how, after registering with it, you can use Red Hat's Update agent to update specific Red Hat Linux packages.

Working with the Red Hat Package Manager

A significant innovation from the people at Red Hat is the Red Hat Package Manager (RPM) — a system for packaging all the necessary files for a software product in a single file (referred to as an RPM file, or simply an RPM). Red Hat Linux is distributed in the form of a lot of RPMs. In the following sections you learn to install, remove, and query RPMs, using the Gnome RPM graphical tool and the rpm commands.

Using Gnome RPM

Gnome RPM is a graphical front utility for installing and uninstalling RPMs. You can perform the same kinds of operations with Gnome RPM, as with the rpm command at the shell prompt. (You learn about the rpm command later in this chapter.)

To start Gnome RPM, log in as root, and then select Main Menu ⇨ System ⇨ GnoRPM. Figure 24-1 shows the initial Gnome RPM window. Gnome RPM has a standard GNOME user interface with a menu bar and a toolbar. The toolbar has buttons for common RPM operations, such as Install a New Package, Query a Package, and Uninstall a Package. The tree menu on the left of the window shows the currently installed packages organized in a hierarchy of package groups (a *package group* contains a number of packages or RPMs). You can click the plus signs to view the hierarchy. If you click a specific package group, Gnome RPM displays all the packages in that group in the area to the right of the tree menu. For example, Figure 24-1 shows the packages in the package group named Desktops.

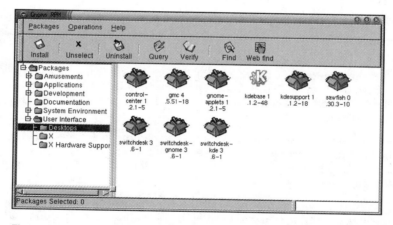

Figure 24-1: Gnome RPM displaying the contents of the Desktops package group

As Figure 24-1 shows, the Desktops package group contains the packages that make up the GNOME and KDE desktops, the Sawfish window manager, and the switchdesk utility, which enables you to change your default desktop from GNOME to KDE, and vice versa.

You typically select one or more packages, and then perform tasks, such as uninstalling the package, querying the package (to see when it was installed and the files it contains), or verifying the package (to ensure that none of the files have changed). To perform these operations, open the package group and select the package, by clicking its icon. Then click the Uninstall, Query, or Verify button to initiate the operation. Each of these operations brings up a window in which Gnome RPM displays relevant information and provides buttons with which you can initiate further action. For example, when you query the gnome-applets package, Gnome RPM displays the information in a window, as shown in Figure 24-2.

Figure 24-2: Gnome RPM querying the gnome-applets package

This window includes buttons with which you can verify or uninstall the package. As Figure 24-2 shows, you can learn a lot about a package by browsing the information in the query results. You can see when the package was installed, when it was built, its size in bytes, a brief description, and what files make up the package (including the full path name of each file). There is even a URL where you can find more information about the package. Gnome RPM displays the URL as a link that you can click to view that Web page in your Web browser.

If you want to verify a package, select the package from the main Gnome RPM window, and click the Verify button on the toolbar. For example, Figure 24-3 shows the result of verifying the apache package, which is in the System Environment ⇨ Daemons folder in the main window's tree menu.

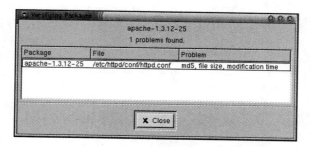

Figure 24-3: Results of verifying the apache package

The `apache` package refers to the Apache Web server, and the results of verifying the package shows that the configuration file, `/etc/httpd/conf/httpd.conf`, has changed from the default supplied with the package. As long as you know that you did indeed edit the configuration file, this is nothing to worry about. You can use Gnome RPM's Verify button to see what, if any, files in a package have changed.

To install a new package from this book's companion CD-ROMs, mount a CD-ROM with the packages (type `mount /mnt/cdrom`), and then click the Install button on the Gnome RPM toolbar. An Install dialog box appears with all the uninstalled packages on the CD-ROM. Go through the tree menu of packages, and select the ones you want to install. When you select a package, a check mark appears in the box to the right of its name, as shown in Figure 24-4.

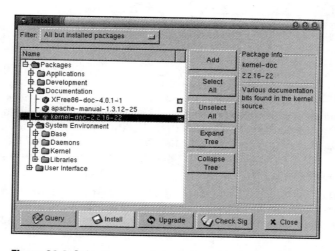

Figure 24-4: Selecting a package to install from the Install dialog box

From this dialog box, you can select packages to install — one package at a time. When you are done selecting packages, click the Install button to install them. Gnome RPM installs the packages and displays any errors it encounters. For example, if the packages are already installed, Gnome RPM tells you.

You can browse through the tree menu of packages to confirm that the selected packages were indeed installed. For example, I had selected the kernel-doc package from the Documentation package group (see Figure 24-4). After installing that package, I should see the kernel-doc package when I select the Documentation package group in the Gnome RPM main window.

You'll find Gnome RPM a handy utility for installing and upgrading various software packages for Red Hat Linux. If you want to learn more about Gnome RPM, read the online help text by selecting the appropriate item from Gnome RPM's Help menu.

Using the RPM Commands

When you install Red Hat Linux from the companion CD-ROMs, the installation program uses the rpm command to unpack the packages (RPM files) and copy the contents to appropriate locations on the disk.

Although you do not need to understand the internal structure of an RPM file you should know how to use the rpm command to work with RPM files. Specifically, you may want to perform one or more of the following tasks with RPMs:

- Find out the version numbers and other information about RPMs installed on your system.

- Install a new software package from an RPM. For example, you might install a package that you had skipped during the initial installation. In particular, you have to install the source files for the Linux kernel, before you can rebuild the kernel.

- Remove (uninstall) unneeded software that you had previously installed from an RPM. You might uninstall a package to reclaim the disk space, if you find that you rarely (or never) use the package.

- Upgrade an older version of an RPM with a new one. You might upgrade after you download a new version of a package from Red Hat's FTP server. Often, you must upgrade an RPM to benefit from the fixes in the new version.

- Verify that an RPM is in working order. You can verify a package to ensure that all necessary files are in the correct locations.

You can perform all of these tasks with the rpm command — it's just a matter of using different options. The next few subsections briefly introduce you to the rpm command.

Tip

If you ever forget the `rpm` options, type the following command to see a list:

`rpm --help | more`

You will be amazed by the number of options `rpm` has!

Understanding RPM filenames

An RPM contains a number of files, but it appears as a single file on your Red Hat Linux system. By convention, the RPM filenames have a specific structure. To see the names of RPM files that are available on the companion CD-ROMs, use the following steps:

1. Place the first CD-ROM in the CD-ROM drive, and mount it with the following command (you must be logged in as root):

   `mount /mnt/cdrom`

   This `mount` command works because there is an entry for this mount point in the `/etc/fstab` file.

2. Go to the directory in which the RPMs are located and view the listing using the `ls` command. For example to see RPMs with names that start with X, type:

   `cd /mnt/cdrom/RedHat/RPMS`

   `ls X*.rpm | more`

   `Xaw3d-1.5-8.i386.rpm`

   `Xaw3d-devel-1.5-8.i386.rpm`

   `XFree86-3DLabs-3.3.6-33.i386.rpm`

   `XFree86-4.0.2-1.i386.rpm`

   `XFree86-8514-3.3.6-33.i386.rpm`

   `XFree86-AGX-3.3.6-33.i386.rpm`

   `XFree86-FBDev-3.3.6-33.i386.rpm`

   `XFree86-I128-3.3.6-33.i386.rpm`

   `XFree86-libs-4.0.2-1.i386.rpm`

   `XFree86-Mach32-3.3.6-33.i386.rpm`

   `XFree86-Mach64-3.3.6-33.i386.rpm`

   `XFree86-Mach8-3.3.6-33.i386.rpm`

   `XFree86-Mono-3.3.6-33.i386.rpm`

   `XFree86-P9000-3.3.6-33.i386.rpm`

   `XFree86-S3-3.3.6-33.i386.rpm`

   `XFree86-S3V-3.3.6-33.i386.rpm`

   `XFree86-SVGA-3.3.6-33.i386.rpm`

   `XFree86-VGA16-3.3.6-33.i386.rpm`

   `XFree86-W32-3.3.6-33.i386.rpm`

As you might guess from the listing, all RPM files end with an `.rpm` extension. To understand the various parts of the filename, consider the following RPM:

```
XFree86-4.0.2-1.i386.rpm
```

This filename has the following parts, separated by dashes (-):

- *Package name* — `XFree86`
- *Version number* — `4.0.2`
- *Release number* — `1` (this is a Red Hat–assigned release number)
- *Architecture* — `i386` (this package is for Intel 80386–compatible processors)

Usually, the package name is descriptive enough for you to guess what the RPM might contain. The version number is the same as that of the software package's current version number (even when it is distributed in some other form, such as a `tar` file). Red Hat assigns the release number to keep track of changes. The architecture should be `i386` or `noarch` for the RPMs you want to install on a PC with an Intel x86–compatible processor.

Finding out about RPMs

As it installs packages, the `rpm` command builds a database of installed RPMs. You can use the `rpm -q` command to query this database to find out information about packages installed on your system.

For example, to find out the version number of the Linux kernel installed on your system, type the following `rpm -q` command:

```
rpm -q kernel
kernel-2.4.0-0.43.12
```

The response is the name of the RPM for the kernel (this is the executable version of the kernel, not the source files). The name is the same as the RPM filename, except that the last part — `.i386.rpm` — is not shown. In this case, the version part of the RPM tells you that the kernel is 2.4.0.

You can see a list of all installed RPMs with the following command:

```
rpm -qa
```

You will see a long list of RPMs scroll by your screen. To view the list one screen at a time, type

```
rpm -qa | more
```

If you want to search for a specific package, feed the output of `rpm -qa` to the `grep` command. For example, to see all packages with kernel in their names, type:

```
rpm -qa | grep kernel
kernel-utils-2.4.0-0.43.12
kernel-source-2.4.0-0.43.12
kernelcfg-0.6-10
kernel-headers-2.4.0-0.43.12
kernel-2.4.0-0.43.12
```

You can query much more than a package's version number with the `rpm -q` command. By adding single-letter options, you can find out other useful information. For example, try the following command to see the files in the kernel package:

```
rpm -ql kernel
/boot/System.map-2.4.0-0.43.12
/boot/module-info-2.4.0-0.43.12
/boot/vmlinux-2.4.0-0.43.12
/boot/vmlinuz-2.4.0-0.43.12
/dev/shm
/lib/modules
/lib/modules/2.4.0-0.43.12
/lib/modules/2.4.0-0.43.12/build
/lib/modules/2.4.0-0.43.12/kernel
/lib/modules/2.4.0-0.43.12/kernel/drivers
/lib/modules/2.4.0-0.43.12/kernel/drivers/atm
/lib/modules/2.4.0-0.43.12/kernel/drivers/atm/ambassador.o
/lib/modules/2.4.0-0.43.12/kernel/drivers/atm/atmtcp.o
/lib/modules/2.4.0-0.43.12/kernel/drivers/atm/eni.o
/lib/modules/2.4.0-0.43.12/kernel/drivers/atm/fore_200e.o
/lib/modules/2.4.0-0.43.12/kernel/drivers/atm/horizon.o
/lib/modules/2.4.0-0.43.12/kernel/drivers/atm/idt77105.o
(rest of the listing deleted)
```

Following are several useful forms of `rpm -q` commands to query information about a package (to use any of these `rpm -q` commands, type the command followed by the package name):

- `rpm -qc` — Lists all configuration files in a package.

- `rpm -qd` — Lists all documentation files in a package. These are usually the online manual pages (also known as *man pages*).

- `rpm -qi` — Displays detailed information about a package, including version number, size, installation date, and a brief description.

- `rpm -ql` — Lists all the files in a package. For some packages this can be a very long list.

- `rpm -qs` — Lists the state of all files in a package.

Note

These `rpm` commands provide information about installed packages only. If you want to find information about an uninstalled RPM file, add the letter p to the command-line option of each command. For example, to view the list of files in the RPM file named `LPRng-3.6.26-3.i386.rpm`, use the following command:

```
rpm -qpl LPRng-3.6.26-3.i386.rpm
```

Of course, this works only if the current directory actually contains that RPM file.

Installing an RPM

To install an RPM, use the `rpm -i` command. You will have to provide the name of the RPM file as the argument. A typical example would be to install an RPM from this book's companion CD-ROMs containing the Red Hat Linux RPMs. As usual, you have to first mount the CD-ROM and then change to the directory in which the RPMs are located. Then use the `rpm -i` command to install the RPM. If you want to view the progress of the RPM installation, use `rpm -ivh`. A series of hash marks (#) are displayed as the package is unpacked.

For example, to install the kernel-source RPM (which contains the source files for the Linux operating system) from the first companion CD-ROM, I type the following commands:

```
mount /mnt/cdrom
cd /mnt/cdrom/RedHat/RPMS
rpm -ivh kernel-source*
```

Tip

You do not have to type the full RPM filename—you can use a few characters from the beginning of the name followed by an asterisk (*). Make sure that you type enough of the name to uniquely identify the RPM file.

If you try to install an RPM that is already installed, the `rpm` command displays an error message. For example, here is what happens when I try to install the Emacs editor on my system:

```
rpm -i emacs-20*
package emacs-20.7-28 is already installed
```

To force the `rpm` command to install a package even if there are errors, just add `--force` to the `rpm -i` command, as follows:

```
rpm -i --force emacs-20*
```

Removing an RPM

You might want to remove—uninstall—a package if you realize that you don't really need the software. For example, if you installed the X Window System development package, but discover that you are not interested in writing any X applications, you can easily remove the package with the `rpm -e` command.

You will need to know the name of the package before you can remove it. One good way to find the name is to use `rpm -qa` in conjunction with `grep` to search for the appropriate RPM file. For example, to locate the X Window System development RPM, you might try the following command:

```
rpm -qa | grep XFree
XFree86-75dpi-fonts-4.0.2-1
XFree86-devel-4.0.2-1
XFree86-twm-4.0.2-1
XFree86-SVGA-3.3.6-33
XFree86-libs-4.0.2-1
XFree86-xfs-4.0.2-1
XFree86-4.0.2-1
XFree86-tools-4.0.2-1
XFree86-xdm-4.0.2-1
```

In this case, `XFree86-devel` happens to be the package name you need. To remove the package, type:

```
rpm -e XFree86-devel
```

Note that you do not need the full RPM filename; all you need is the package name—the first part of the filename up to the dash (-) before the version number.

The `rpm -e` command does not remove a package that other packages need. For example, when I try to remove the kernel-headers package, I get the following error message:

```
rpm -e kernel-headers
error: removing these packages would break dependencies:

        kernel-headers   is needed by glibc-devel-2.2-9
        kernel-headers >= 2.2.1 is needed by glibc-devel-2.2-9
```

Upgrading an RPM

Use the `rpm -U` command to upgrade an RPM. You must provide the name of the RPM file that contains the new software. For example, if I have version 4.72 of Netscape Communicator installed on my system, but I want to upgrade to version 4.75, I download the RPM file `netscape-communicator-4.75-2.i386.rpm` from Red Hat's FTP server (`ftp://ftp.redhat.com/pub/redhat/updates/` or one of the mirror sites listed at `http://www.redhat.com/mirrors.html`), and then use the following command:

```
rpm -U netscape-communicator-4.75-2.i386.rpm
```

The `rpm` command performs the upgrade by first removing the old version of the `netscape-communicator` package, and then installing the new RPM.

Tip

Whenever possible you should upgrade, rather than remove, the old package, and then install the new version. Upgrading automatically saves the old configuration files, which saves you the hassle of configuring the software after a fresh installation.

Caution

When you are upgrading the kernel and the kernel module packages that contain a ready-to-run Linux kernel, you should go ahead and install it with the `rpm -i` command (instead of the `rpm -u` command). That way you won't overwrite the current kernel.

Verifying an RPM

You may not do this often, but if you suspect that a software package is not properly installed, use the `rpm -V` command to verify it. For example, to verify the `kernel` package, type the following:

```
rpm -V kernel
```

This causes `rpm` to compare size and other attributes of each file in the package against those of the original files. If everything verifies correctly, the `rpm -V` command does not print anything. If there are any discrepancies, you will see a report of them. For example, I have modified the configuration files for the Apache Web server. Here is what I see when I verify the `apache` package:

```
rpm -V apache
S.5....T c /etc/httpd/conf/httpd.conf
```

In this case, the output from `rpm -V` shows that a configuration file has changed. Each line of this command's output consists of three parts:

- The line starts with eight characters: each character indicates the type of discrepancy found. For example, S means the size is different and T means the time of last modification is different. Table 24-1 shows each character and its meaning. A period means that that specific attribute matches the original.

- For configuration files, a c appears next; otherwise, this field is blank. That's how you can tell whether a file is a configuration file. Typically you shouldn't worry if a configuration file has changed, because you probably made the changes yourself.

- The last part of the line is the full path name of the file. From this part, you can tell exactly where the file is located.

Table 24-1   Characters Used in RPM Verification Reports

Character	Meaning
S	Size has changed
M	Permissions and file type are different
5	Checksum computed with the MD5 algorithm is different
D	Device type is different
L	Symbolic link is different
U	File's user is different
G	File's group is different
T	File's modification time is different

Building Software Packages

In the previous sections you saw how to install software packages distributed in the Red Hat Package Manager (RPM) format. RPM files bundle everything—all the executable binary files and configuration files—needed to install a software package. However, many open-source software packages are distributed in source-code form, without any executable binaries. Before you can use such software, you have to build the executable binary files by compiling, and then you have to follow some instructions to install the package. This section shows you how to build software packages from source files.

Downloading and Unpacking the Software

Open-source software source files are typically distributed in compressed `tar` archives. These archives are created by the `tar` program, and then compressed with the `gzip` program. The distribution is in the form of a single large file with the `.tar.gz` or `.tar.Z` extension—often referred to as a *compressed tarball*. If you want the software, you have to download the compressed `tarball` and unpack it.

You download the compressed `tar` file using anonymous FTP, or through your Web browser. Typically this involves no effort on your part, beyond clicking a link and saving the file in an appropriate directory on your system.

To try your hand at downloading and building a software package, practice on the X Multimedia System (XMMS)—a graphical X application for playing MP3 and other multimedia files. XMMS is bundled with Red Hat Linux and should already be installed on your system, if you selected the Multimedia Support package group during Red Hat Linux installation. However, there is no harm in downloading and rebuilding the XMMS package again.

The source files for XMMS are available from `http://www.xmms.org/download.html` in the form of a compressed `tar` archive. You can also download the files from the `xmms/1.2.x` directory of the anonymous FTP server `ftp.xmms.org`. You can try downloading from the anonymous FTP server, if you have never manually downloaded files.

Before attempting to download a file from an FTP server, make sure that your Red Hat Linux system is connected to the Internet. You should also change the directory to the location in which you want to store the downloaded file (although you can always move the file after downloading). I typically log in as root and change directory to `/usr/local/src` before typing the `ftp` command. If you are using the GNOME or KDE desktop, you'll be typing these commands from a terminal window.

Here is a sample session that you can use as a guideline when you download the compressed `tar` file for XMMS from the anonymous FTP server (the lines I typed are shown in boldface):

```
ftp ftp.xmms.org
Connected to ftp.xmms.org.
220 ProFTPD 1.2.0 Server (FTP server for awpti.org) [awpti.org]
Name (ftp.xmms.org:naba): anonymous
331 Anonymous login ok, send your complete e-mail address as password.
Password:      <-- I type my e-mail address
230 Anonymous access granted, restrictions apply.
Remote system type is UNIX.
Using binary mode to transfer files.
ftp> cd xmms/1.2.x
250 CWD command successful.
ftp> ls
227 Entering Passive Mode (204,62,193,74,15,165).
150 Opening ASCII mode data connection for file list
drwxr-xr-x   5 root     root         4096 Sep 19 22:32 rpm
drwxr-xr-x   2 root     root         4096 Jul 15 17:22 solaris
-rw-r--r--   1 root     root        89787 Sep 20 14:34 xmms-1.2.0-1.2.1.diff.bz2
-rw-r--r--   1 root     root        99757 Sep 20 14:34 xmms-1.2.0-1.2.1.diff.gz
-rw-r--r--   1 root     root      1585494 Jun 12 15:14 xmms-1.2.0.tar.gz
-rw-r--r--   1 root     root       124662 Sep 20 14:35 xmms-1.2.1-1.2.2.diff.bz2
-rw-r--r--   1 root     root       159987 Sep 20 14:35 xmms-1.2.1-1.2.2.diff.gz
-rw-r--r--   1 root     root      1605015 Jun 19 15:03 xmms-1.2.1.tar.gz
-rw-r--r--   1 root     root       339229 Sep 20 14:36 xmms-1.2.2-1.2.3.diff.bz2
-rw-r--r--   1 root     root       617273 Sep 20 14:37 xmms-1.2.2-1.2.3.diff.gz
-rw-r--r--   1 root     root      1667505 Jul 11 21:37 xmms-1.2.2.tar.gz
-rw-r--r--   1 root     root      1684542 Sep  3 19:21 xmms-1.2.3-pre1.tar.gz
-rw-r--r--   1 root     root      1785203 Sep 19 22:39 xmms-1.2.3.tar.gz
226 Transfer complete.
ftp> binary
200 Type set to I.
ftp> get xmms-1.2.3.tar.gz
local: xmms-1.2.3.tar.gz remote: xmms-1.2.3.tar.gz
227 Entering Passive Mode (204,62,193,74,15,171).
150 Opening BINARY mode data connection for xmms-1.2.3.tar.gz (1785203 bytes).
226 Transfer complete.
1785203 bytes received in 1.4e+03 secs (1.2 Kbytes/sec)
ftp> bye
221 Goodbye.
```

Notice that you have to log in with the user name anonymous — that's why the FTP server is called anonymous FTP server. For password, type your e-mail address, and then press Enter. To change directory, use the cd command; you can get a directory listing with the ls command.

You need to type the binary command to make sure that the data transfer occurs in binary mode (because the .tar.gz file is a binary file). Then you can use the get command to download the file — in this case xmms-1.2.3.tar.gz. As I mentioned earlier, the .tar.gz extension tells you that this is a compressed tar archive. After the download is complete, type bye to end the anonymous FTP session.

After downloading the compressed tar file, examine the contents with the following command:

```
tar ztf xmms*.gz | more
xmms-1.2.3/
xmms-1.2.3/Makefile.in
xmms-1.2.3/README
xmms-1.2.3/stamp-h.in
xmms-1.2.3/ABOUT-NLS
xmms-1.2.3/AUTHORS
xmms-1.2.3/COPYING
xmms-1.2.3/ChangeLog
xmms-1.2.3/INSTALL
xmms-1.2.3/Makefile.am
xmms-1.2.3/NEWS
xmms-1.2.3/TODO
xmms-1.2.3/acconfig.h
xmms-1.2.3/acinclude.m4
xmms-1.2.3/aclocal.m4
xmms-1.2.3/config.guess
xmms-1.2.3/config.h.in
xmms-1.2.3/config.sub
xmms-1.2.3/configure
xmms-1.2.3/configure.in
xmms-1.2.3/install-sh
... rest of the output not shown ...
```

The output of this command shows you what's in the archive and gives you an idea of the directories that will be created once you unpack the archive. In this case, a directory named xmms-1.2.3 will be created in the current directory, which, in my case, is /usr/local/src. From the listing, you'll also learn the programming language used to write the package. If you see .c and .h files, that means the source files are in the C programming language, which is used to write many open-source software packages.

To extract the contents of the tar archive, type the following tar command:

```
tar zxvf xmms*.gz
```

You'll again see the long list of files as they are extracted from the archive and copied to the appropriate directories on your hard disk.

Now you are ready to build the software.

Building the Software from Source Files

After you unpack the compressed tar archive, all source files will be in a directory whose name is usually that of the software package with a version-number suffix. For example, the XMMS version 1.2.3 source files are extracted to the xmms-1.0.1 directory. To start the process of building the software, change directory with the following command:

```
cd xmms*
```

You don't have to type the entire name — the shell can expand the directory name and change to the xmms-1.2.3 directory.

Nearly all software packages come with some sort of README or INSTALL file — a text file that tells you how to build and install the package. XMMS is no exception; it comes with a README file that you should peruse, by typing more README. There is also an INSTALL file that contains instructions for building and installing XMMS.

Note

Most open-source software packages, including XMMS, also come with a file named COPYING. This file contains the full text of the GNU General Public License (GPL), which spells out the conditions under which you can use and redistribute the software. If you are not familiar with the GNU GPL, you should read this file and show the license to your legal counsel for a full interpretation and an assessment of applicability to your business.

To build the software package, follow the instructions in the README or INSTALL file. For the XMMS package, the README file lists some of the prerequisites (such as libraries), and then tells you what commands you should type to build and install the package. In the case of XMMS, the instructions are to use the following steps:

1. Type ./configure to run a shell script that checks your system configuration and creates a Makefile — a file that is used by the make command to actually build and install the package. (You can type ./configure --help to see a list of options that configure accepts.)

2. Type make to build the software. This step compiles the source files in all the subdirectories.

3. Type make install to install the software. This step copies libraries and executable binary files to appropriate directories on your system.

Although these steps are specific to XMMS, most other packages follow these steps — configure, make, and then install. The configure shell script guesses system-dependent variables and creates a Makefile with commands needed to build and install the software.

Note

Usually you do not have to do anything but type the commands to build the software, but you must install the software-development tools on your system. This means that you must install the Development package when you install Red Hat Linux. To build and run XMMS, you must also install the X Window System package, because it's an X application.

To begin building XMMS, type the following command to run the configure script (you must be in the xmms-1.2.3 directory when you type this command):

```
./configure
```

The configure script starts running and prints lots of messages as it checks various features of your system — from the existence of the C compiler to various libraries that are needed to build XMMS. Finally, the configure script creates a Makefile that you can use to build the software.

Tip

If the `configure` script displays error messages and fails, review the INSTALL and README files to find any clues to solving the problem. You may be able to circumvent it, by providing some information to the `configure` script through command-line arguments.

After the `configure` script finishes, build the software, by typing **make**. This command runs the GNU `make` utility, which reads the Makefile and starts compiling the source files according to information specified in the Makefile. The `make` command will go through all the source directories, compile the source files, and create the executable files and libraries needed to run XMMS. You'll see a lot of messages scroll by as each file is compiled. These messages show the commands used to compile and link the files.

The `make` command can take 10 to 15 minutes to complete. After `make` is done, you can install the XMMS software with the following command:

```
make install
```

This command also runs GNU `make`, but the install argument instructs GNU `make` to perform a specific set of commands from the Makefile. These instructions essentially go through all the subdirectories and copy various files to their final locations. For example, the binary executable files xmms, gnomexmms, wmxmms, and xmms-config are copied to the /usr/bin directory.

Now that you have installed XMMS, try running it from the GNOME or KDE desktop, by typing xmms in a terminal window. From the XMMS window you can open an MP3 file and try playing it. Note that your PC must have a sound card and that it must be configured correctly (Chapter 5 covers sound-card configuration). Figure 24-5 shows a typical view of XMMS playing an MP3 music clip.

Figure 24-5: Playing MP3 music with XMMS

Now you've seen how to download, unpack, build, and install a typical software package. Here's an overview of the steps you follow:

1. Download the source code, usually in the form of a .tar.gz file, from the anonymous FTP site or Web site. Use the Web browser, or download manually from the anonymous FTP server.

2. Unpack the file with a tar zxvf *filename* command.

3. Change directory to the new subdirectory where the software is unpacked, with a command, such as cd *software_dir*.

4. Read any README or INSTALL files to learn any specific instructions you must follow to build and install the software.

5. The details of building the software may differ slightly from one software package to another, but typically you type the following commands to build and install the software:

```
./configure
make
make install
```

6. Read any other documentation that comes with the software to learn how to use the software and whether you must configure the software further before using it.

Upgrading Red Hat Linux with the Update Agent

If you check the process on your system with ps ax, you'll see a process named rhnsd. That's the Red Hat Network (RHN) services daemon. Its job is to connect periodically to the Red Hat Network servers and check for any updates and notifications. By default, the rhnsd daemon checks with the Red Hat Network servers every 30 minutes.

In addition to the RHN services daemon (rhnsd), Red Hat Linux also comes with an Update Agent called up2date (located in the /usr/sbin directory) that enables you to obtain updates for your Red Hat Linux system.

The idea behind Red Hat Network is to enable registered users to keep their Red Hat Linux current. The idea is that you register with the Red Hat Network and provide information about your system's hardware and the RPMs currently installed on your system. Once you've done this, the RHN services daemon, or the Update Agent, can download any new RPM files your system requires and install those files for you.

The next few sections provide an overview of how to update your system using the Update Agent and the Red Hat Network.

Registering with Red Hat Network

To take full advantage of the Red Hat Network's facilities, you must register with the Red Hat Network. To register, make sure your Internet connection is up and then double-click the RHN Registration icon on the GNOME desktop, or select Main Menu ⇨ Programs ⇨ System ⇨ RHN Registration.

The Red Hat Registration program runs and displays a message explaining the registration process, as shown in Figure 24-6.

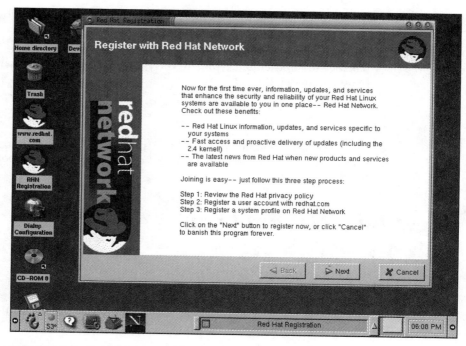

Figure 24-6: Registering with the Red Hat Network Registration program

Click the Next button to continue. The Red Hat Registration program displays a privacy statement explaining the information collected and sent to Red Hat's server during registration. The information includes an inventory of RPM files on your system and an inventory of your system hardware. Read the privacy policy, and if you want to continue, click the Next button. You are prompted for a user name and password to establish a new user account with Red Hat, as shown in Figure 24-7.

Supply the requested information and click the Next button. After some time, the Red Hat Registration program displays a screen that requests your name and address. Fill in the requested information and click the Next button.

The next screen shows the hardware information that will be sent to the Red Hat Network. Click the Next button to continue. The RHN registration software builds a list of the RPMs installed in your system and shows the list. Click the Next button to continue.

A message informs you that your system information will be sent to the Red Hat Network. Click the Next button to proceed. The Red Hat Registration program sends your information (the information mentioned in the privacy statement) to the Red Hat Network. This step can take several minutes, depending on the speed of your connection. As the information is transmitted to the Red Hat Network, a progress bar shows the percentage sent so far.

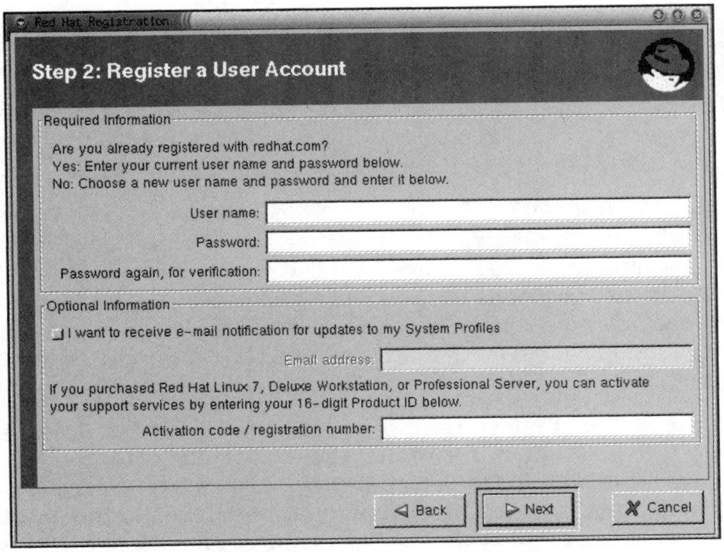

Figure 24-7: Information you provide when registering with the Red Hat Network

The Red Hat Registration program contacts a Red Hat Network server using Secure HTTP (https). You can see the connection information by typing netstat | more. For example, here are a few lines of the netstat output showing the HTTPS connection between my system and the Red Hat Network server (IP address 216.148.218.260):

```
Active Internet connections (w/o servers)
Proto Recv-Q Send-Q Local Address          Foreign Address         State
tcp       0      0 lnbp200:1825           216.148.218.160:https   ESTABLISHED
```

After the Red Hat Registration program successfully uploads your system profile to the Red Hat Network, the final window displays a message telling you to visit http://www.redhat.com/network, to log in, and access Red Hat Network. Click the Finish button to exit the Red Hat Registration program.

Once the registration is complete, you can use the up2date utility to update your Red Hat Linux system.

Updating Red Hat Linux Packages

Once you're registered with Red Hat Network, you can use up2date to update Red Hat Linux. To use the Red Hat Update Agent, log in as root, and select Programs ⇨ System ⇨ Update Agent, or type /usr/sbin/up2date from a terminal window in the GNOME or KDE graphical desktop.

When the Update Agent starts, you may see a dialog box that prompts you to install Red Hat's public key in your GPG key ring. (GPG refers to GNU Privacy Guard or GnuPG, a program for encrypting, decrypting, and signing e-mail and other data using the OpenPGP Internet standard.) Red Hat's public GPG key is used to verify that packages downloaded by the Update Agent are securely signed by Red Hat. Click the Yes button to install Red Hat's key.

The Red Hat Update Agent displays a window with a welcome message. Click the Next button to proceed. The Update Agent retrieves a list of all available packages from the Red Hat Network. (This may take a few minutes.) Then the Update Agent downloads the headers for all available packages. For each download, a progress bar shows the percentage of data downloaded so far. The header download takes quite a bit of time over a slow connection to the Internet.

After the Red Hat Update Agent downloads the headers, it displays a list of packages to be skipped. You can accept the list, and click the Next button to continue. Then the Update Agent displays a list of all the packages available for update from Red Hat Network. Scroll through the list and pick the package updates you want to download. Click the box to the left of a package's name to select it. As you select packages, the Update Agent displays the total size of the packages you have selected so far. Figure 24-8 shows a typical list of packages, with a few package updates selected for download (including the update for the `up2date` package itself).

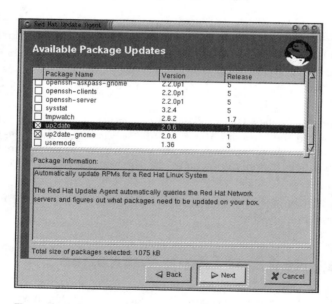

Figure 24-8: Select packages to update from the list of available package updates.

After selecting the packages, click the Next button to proceed with the download. The Update Agent then checks for any package dependencies and begins downloading the packages. Progress bars show the status of the download.

After the download is finished, click the Next button to proceed with the installation. Once again the Update Agent displays progress bars as it installs each package update.

Click the Next button when the installation is complete. The Update Agent displays a message about the package or packages that it installed success-fully, as shown in Figure 24-9.

Figure 24-9: Red Hat Update Agent window after package installation

Click the Finish button to exit the Red Hat Update Agent.

As this example shows, once you have registered with the Red Hat Network, you can use the Red Hat Update Agent to keep Red Hat Linux up to date (hence the name up2date).

Summary

Most Red Hat Linux software comes in Red Hat Package Manager (RPM) files and many open-source software packages are provided in source-code form (usually in compressed archives). Therefore, you need to know how to work with RPM files and how to build software from source code. This chapter covered both of these topics. The chapter also showed you how to use the Red Hat Update Agent to update Red Hat Linux packages.

By reading this chapter, you learned the following:

▶ Red Hat Package Manager (RPM) is a system for packaging all the necessary files for a software product in a single file. The file is referred to as an RPM file, a package, or simply an RPM. Red Hat Linux is distributed in the form of a lot of RPMs.

▶ You can use the `rpm` commands or the Gnome RPM graphical tool, to work with RPM files. You learned to use the Gnome RPM graphical RPM utility with which you can install and uninstall RPMs. You also learned the syntax of a number of RPM commands to query, install, upgrade, remove, and verify RPMs.

▶ To download and install open-source software distributed in source-code form, use `ftp` to download and `tar` to unpack, and then read the `README` file for installation instructions. Typically, you have to run a `configure` script to create a `Makefile`, and then run the `make` command to build the software. Using the X Multimedia System (XMMS) package as an example, this chapter showed you how to build the software and install it.

▶ You can register with the Red Hat Network and use the Red Hat Update Agent to download and install any updates to various packages that make up Red Hat Linux. This chapter shows you how to register and use the Red Hat Update Agent.

Chapter 25

Kernel Reconfiguration and Upgrade

One reason Linux is so exciting is because many programmers are constantly improving it. Some programmers, for example, write drivers that add support for new hardware, such as a new CD-ROM drive or a new networking card. Other programmers add support for a new bus, such as the Universal Serial Bus (USB). The Linux development community makes all these innovations available to you in the form of fixes known as *patches*, or through new versions of Linux.

Although you do not have to upgrade or modify the Linux operating system — the kernel — every time a new patch or a new version is available, sometimes you need to upgrade simply because the new version corrects some problems or supports your hardware better. On the other hand, if an earlier kernel version has everything you need, there is no need to rush out and upgrade.

Sometimes you may want to rebuild the kernel even when there are no fixes or enhancements. The Linux kernel on the companion CD-ROM is a generic kernel that uses modules to support all types of hardware. You may want to build a new kernel that links in the drivers for only those devices actually installed on your system. In particular, if you have a SCSI hard disk, you definitely want to create a kernel that supports your SCSI adapter. Depending on your needs, you may also want to change some of the kernel configuration options, such as turning on network packet filtering so that you can use your Linux system as an Internet gateway for your local area network (LAN).

Tip

Red Hat provides many of the fixes and improvements. These updates are in the form of Red Hat packages distributed from Red Hat's FTP server (try `ftp://ftp.redhat.com/pub/redhat/updates/`; if it's busy, consult `http://www.redhat.com/mirrors.html` for a mirror site near you). To install these packages, you have to use the Red Hat Package Manager (RPM), as described in Chapter 24.

This chapter explains how to apply a kernel patch and how to rebuild the Linux kernel.

Applying Kernel Patches

Like any major software product, Linux has a version number that changes as new features are added. Typically, the version number has two parts: the *major version number* and the *minor version number*. MS-DOS 6.2, for example, has a major version number of 6 and a minor version number of 2. The minor version number changes as incremental improvements are made to the software; the major version number changes only when a significant change occurs.

In addition to the customary major and minor version numbers, Linux includes a third number that denotes the current patch level. Patches typically are corrections — changes made to code to fix errors.

Finally, Red Hat adds a fourth set of numbers that denotes the Red Hat release number for the software.

Tip

The Linux login prompt at a text terminal shows you the Linux version number, the patch level, and the Red Hat release number. If you use a graphical login screen, press Ctrl+Alt+F1 for a virtual terminal that shows the text-mode login prompt. (To switch back to the graphical screen, press Ctrl+Alt+F7.) The second line of the prompt has the following form:

```
Kernel 2.4.0-0.43.12 on an i586
```

This message tells you that the Linux version is 2.4, the patch level is 0, and the Red Hat release number is 0.43.12. Kernel version 2.4.0 was originally included on the public beta version of Red Hat Linux 7.1x. However, in later versions of Red Hat Linux, Red Hat may have upgraded the kernel to a later version.

Tip

You can also use the `uname` command to determine the current kernel version number. To see how it works, type:

```
uname -r
2.4.0-0.43.12
```

The output shows the full version number of the Linux kernel. The `uname` command works on any UNIX system.

Although the version number changes relatively slowly, a version such as 2.4 may contain many patches. You generally can find out about patches if you keep up with Linux developments by periodically reading Internet news-groups that are devoted to Linux (such as comp.os.linux.announce and comp.os.linux.setup). You can also find out about the latest kernel patches from The Linux Kernel Archives at http://www.kernel.org/.

Cross-Reference You need access to the Internet to read the newsgroups. Consult Chapter 16 for more information on connecting your Red Hat Linux system to the Internet.

Installing the Kernel Source

To apply any patches to the kernel, you need the kernel source files installed on your system. The Red Hat Linux installation program installs the kernel source files, provided you select the Kernel Development component during installation. If you did not install the Kernel Development component, you can install these files from the kernel-source RPM on the companion CD-ROM.

Use the following steps to install the kernel source package on your system:

1. Log in as root and insert the first Red Hat Linux CD-ROM into the CD drive.

2. Use the mount command to mount the first CD-ROM drive on a directory in the file system:

   ```
   mount /mnt/cdrom
   ```

3. Change the directory to the RedHat/RPMS directory on the CD-ROM, and use RPM to install the kernel source files. Use the following commands:

   ```
   cd /mnt/cdrom/RedHat/RPMS
   rpm -ivh kernel-source*
   Preparing...        ###########################################
   [100%]
      1:kernel-source  ###########################################
   [100%]
   ```

RPM indicates progress by displaying a series of hash marks (#), as well as a percentage, showing how much of the installation is complete. After RPM finishes installing the kernel source package, the necessary source files appear in the /usr/src/linux-2.4 directory. Note that in earlier versions of the kernel, the source files were located in the /usr/src/linux directory.

What Is a Kernel Patch?

The term *kernel* refers to the core Linux operating system — it is the program that makes your PC a Linux PC. The term *patch* refers to corrections. Putting the two together, you can see that *kernel patch* refers to corrections to the Linux operating system.

Linux comes with the source code, so patches are alterations to the source code. When

you apply a kernel patch, you change the Linux operating system's source code. After you make the changes, you have to rebuild Linux to put the changes into effect. Rebuilding involves setting many configuration options and compiling the kernel source code.

Getting the Patches

If you read about a kernel patch that fixes some problem that you have with Linux, you typically learn about the patch number as well. When you ask for help with some Linux problem, by posting a message in a newsgroup (such as "I am running kernel version 2.2.13, and my brand-new SCSI controller does not seem to work"), you may get replies indicating that you should bring the kernel up to 2.2.17 because that new SCSI controller is supported at patch level 2.2.17.

To go from 2.2.13 to 2.2.17, you have two options:

- Get the complete Linux 2.2.17 kernel source and install it.
- Get patches 14 through 17, and apply them to the source files for kernel version 2.2.13.

Typically, the entire kernel distribution is a large file (a 13.7MB `bzip2`-compressed file for version 2.2.17), even in compressed form. Conversely, most patch files are less than 500K (although some can be over 1MB). Therefore, it makes sense to download and apply only the required patches. You can get the patches from the Internet using your Web browser.

If you do not have Internet access, Chapters 16 explains how you can connect your system to the Internet. (You have to sign up with an Internet Service Provider to gain access.)

To explain the process of obtaining the kernel patch files, I assume that your system is connected to the Internet and that you can use Netscape Communicator to access any computer on the Internet.

The Linux kernel patches (as well as the latest versions of the kernel) are available from the Web site `http://www.kernel.org/`. Follow the links on that page to reach the FTP server (`ftp.kernel.org`) that has the kernel distributions, including the patches. If the FTP site is busy, you get a list of mirror sites (organized geographically); pick a suitable site from this list. At the

FTP site, the Linux kernels and associated patches are organized by version number. All files for Linux version 2.2, for example, are in the `/pub/linux/kernel/v2.2/` directory. The kernel files and patches for version 2.2 are listed in the following manner (I show only a few representative lines from the listing):

```
linux-2.2.16.tar.bz2    13503 Kb    Wed Jun 07 21:34:00 2000
linux-2.2.16.tar.gz     16705 Kb    Wed Jun 07 21:34:00 2000
patch-2.2.17.bz2          736 Kb    Mon Sep 04 18:35:00 2000
patch-2.2.17.gz           867 Kb    Mon Sep 04 18:35:00 2000
```

The first two files are the complete distribution of Linux 2.2.16 kernel in two different formats. The last two files are the patches for version 2.2.17; by applying these patches, you can bring a 2.2.16 kernel up to version 2.2.17.

As the sample listing shows, each file has two versions — a `.bz2` file and a `.gz` file. By convention, files compressed with the `bzip2` compression program appear with the `.bz2` extension; files compressed by the `gzip` program have the `.gz` extension. The `bzip2` format is gaining popularity, because it can compress better than `gzip` (compare the sizes in the sample listing).

You should download the `.bz2` files because they are smaller than the `.gz` variants. For example, to upgrade the kernel from 2.2.13 to 2.2.17, you download the following files:

```
patch-2.2.14.bz2    1374 Kb    Tue Jan 04 00:00:00 2000
patch-2.2.15.bz2    1106 Kb    Thu May 04 00:00:00 2000
patch-2.2.16.bz2    1037 Kb    Wed Jun 07 21:34:00 2000
patch-2.2.17.bz2     736 Kb    Mon Sep 04 18:35:00 2000
```

To download each file, click the filename and save the file on your system's hard disk. Next, you have to unpack the patch files and apply the patches.

Applying the Patches

After you download the patches, you first have to decompress the file. Then you can apply the patches.

Tip

To decompress the `.bz2` files, you need the `bzip2` program, which is a freely available and fast data compressor and decompressor. The first companion CD-ROM includes `bzip2`, and the installation program should install it. If it doesn't, you can install `bzip2` by inserting the first CD-ROM in the CD-ROM drive, logging in as `root`, and typing the following commands:

```
mount /mnt/cdrom
cd /mnt/cdrom/RedHat/RPMS
rpm -Uvh bzip2*
```

After installing `bzip2`, follow these steps to apply the patches (while logged in as `root`):

1. Copy the patch files to the /usr/src directory.

2. Type the following commands to go to the /usr/src directory and decompress the patch files:

```
cd /usr/src
bzip2 -d patch*.bz2
```

3. Change to the /usr/src/linux directory and use the patch command to apply the patches, one by one (assuming you are upgrading a kernel from version 2.2.13 to 2.2.17):

```
cd /usr/src/linux
patch -p1 < ../patch-2.2.14 > err.14
patch -p1 < ../patch-2.2.15 > err.15
patch -p1 < ../patch-2.2.16 > err.16
patch -p1 < ../patch-2.2.17 > err.17
```

The first command runs the patch command with the file patch-2.2.14 as input and sends all output messages (including any error reports) to the file err.14.

After the commands finish, check the err.14, err.15, err.16, and err.17 files to see whether any of the patches failed. One good way is to use the text-search tool grep to look for any occurrence of the string FAIL, as follows:

```
grep FAIL err.*
```

If grep finds any occurrence of the string FAIL, the patch was not successful — perhaps because the kernel source files were already modified from their original form.

Cross-Reference

For a quick reference on Linux commands, including grep and patch, see Appendix A.

If the patches work without any errors, these patch commands change the source code of the Linux operating system to reflect any changes that the developers have made since version 2.2.13. After the last patch, the Linux source code should be at level 2.2.17. All you have to do next is rebuild the kernel; then your Linux system is at version 2.2.17.

Tip

These steps may not work with Red Hat Linux because Red Hat has modified some of the kernel files. If the patch command fails in Red Hat Linux, you can still upgrade the kernel to newer versions — you just have to get the newer kernels from Red Hat's FTP server. You can also download the latest version of the entire kernel distribution from http://www.kernel.org and rebuild the kernel as explained in the following section. If a Red Hat RPM for a newer kernel is not available yet, you can download the entire new kernel source and build the kernel by following the directions in the next section.

Rebuilding the Kernel

Rebuilding the kernel refers to the task of creating a new binary file for the core Linux operating system. This binary file is the file that runs when Linux boots. You may have to build the kernel for various reasons:

- After you apply kernel patches (as described in the preceding section), the operating system's source files are updated. You have to rebuild the kernel and reboot the system to use the new kernel.

- After you initially install Linux, you may want to create a new kernel that includes support for only the hardware actually installed on your system. In particular, if you have a SCSI adapter, you may want to create a kernel that links in the SCSI driver. The kernel in the companion CD-ROM includes the SCSI driver as an external module that you load at start up.

- If you have a system with hardware for which only experimental support is available, you have to rebuild the kernel to include that support into the operating system.

Tip

Before you rebuild the kernel, make sure you have the emergency boot floppy (covered in Chapter 2) that you prepared when installing Red Hat Linux. If the system does not boot after you rebuild the kernel, you can use that emergency boot floppy to start the system and repeat the kernel build process.

Caution

Never rebuild and install a new kernel without first making sure that you have an emergency boot floppy. If you did not create the boot floppy during Red Hat Linux installation, use the /sbin/mkbootdisk command to create the boot floppy. Type man mkbootdisk to learn the syntax of that command. The exact command line to build the emergency boot floppy depends on the kernel version number. For example, to create a boot floppy for version 2.4.0-0.43.12, log in as root and type the following command at the shell prompt (you have to insert a blank floppy disk when prompted):

```
mkbootdisk -device /dev/fd0 2.4.0-0.43.12
```

Replace 2.4.0-0.43.12 with the version number of your Linux kernel, as displayed by the uname -r command.

To rebuild the Linux kernel, you need the kernel source files. The kernel source files are not normally installed. If you have not done so already, you should install these files, following the steps outlined earlier in the section, "Installing the Kernel Source."

Building the kernel involves the following key phases:

- Configuring the kernel
- Building the kernel
- Building and installing the modules (if any)
- Installing the kernel and setting up LILO

The next section describes the use of modules versus linking in hardware support directly into the kernel. Subsequent sections describe the phases of kernel building.

Creating a Monolithic versus a Modular Kernel

Before you start configuring the kernel, you need to understand that you have two options for the device drivers needed to support various hardware devices in Linux:

- *Link in support*—You can link the drivers for all hardware on your system into the kernel. As you might imagine, the size of the kernel grows as device driver code is incorporated into the kernel. A kernel that links in all necessary support code is called a *monolithic kernel.*

- *Use modules*—You can create the necessary device drivers in the form of modules. A *module* is a block of code that the kernel can load after it starts running. A typical use of modules is to add support for a device without having to rebuild the kernel for each new device. Modules do not have to be device drivers; they can also serve to add new functionality to the kernel. A kernel that uses modules is called a *modular kernel.*

You do not have to create a fully monolithic or fully modular kernel. In fact, it is common practice to link some support directly into the kernel. Conversely, you can build infrequently used device drivers in the form of modules. For a company such as Red Hat, it makes sense to distribute a modular kernel. Red Hat provides a generic kernel, along with a large number of modules, to support many different types of hardware. Then, the Red Hat installation program configures the system to load only those modules that are needed to support the hardware installed in a user's system.

Tip

When you create a custom kernel for your hardware configuration, you may want to link in all required device drivers into the kernel. You can keep the size of such a monolithic kernel under control because you only link in device drivers for the hardware actually installed on your system.

Configuring the Kernel

The first phase in rebuilding a kernel is configuring the kernel. To configure the kernel, log in as `root`. Then change the kernel source directory by using the `cd` command as follows:

```
cd /usr/src/linux*
```

To configure the kernel, you have to indicate which features and device drivers you want to include in your Linux system. In essence, you build a copy of Linux with the mix-and-match features that you want.

Linux provides several ways for you to configure the kernel:

■ Type `make menuconfig` to enter the kernel configuration parameters through a text-based interface similar to the one used by the Red Hat installation program.

■ Type `make xconfig` to use an X Window System-based configuration program to configure the kernel. You have to run X to use this configuration program with a graphical interface.

■ Type `make config` to use a shell script that prompts you for each configuration option one by one. You can use this configuration program from the Linux command prompt. When you use this option, you undergo a long question-and-answer process to specify the configuration parameters.

■ Type `make oldconfig` to use a shell script to reconfigure the kernel after upgrading the sources. This configuration script keeps the existing options and prompts you only for new or changed options.

As you configure the kernel, you have to select how to include support for specific devices. Typically, for each configuration option, you have to respond with one of the following choices:

■ `y` to link in the support into the kernel

■ `m` to use a module

■ `n` to skip the support for that specific device

■ `?` to get help on that kernel configuration option

If a device does not have a modular device driver, you don't see the `m` option. For some configuration options, you may have to type a specific answer. For example, when responding to the processor type, you type `Pentium-III` to indicate that you have a Pentium III PC.

The `make menuconfig`, `make xconfig`, `make config`, and `make oldconfig` commands achieve the same end result — each stores your choices in a text file named `.config` located in the `/usr/src/linux*` directory. Because the filename starts with a period, you don't see it when you use the `ls` command alone to list the directory. Instead, type `ls -a` to see the `.config` file in the directory listing.

Note

All that the kernel configuration step does is capture your choices in the `.config` file. (In fact, the `.config` file does not exist until you configure the kernel once.) The kernel file does not change until you actually compile the kernel with the `make` command. That means you can go through the kernel configuration option as many times as you want.

Here are some lines from the `.config` file on my system (after configuring the kernel):

```
more .config
#
# Automatically generated make config: don't edit
#

#
# Code maturity level options
#
CONFIG_EXPERIMENTAL=y

#
# Processor type and features
#
# CONFIG_M386 is not set
# CONFIG_M486 is not set
# CONFIG_M586 is not set
CONFIG_M586TSC=y
# CONFIG_M686 is not set
CONFIG_X86_WP_WORKS_OK=y
CONFIG_X86_INVLPG=y
CONFIG_X86_BSWAP=y
CONFIG_X86_POPAD_OK=y
CONFIG_X86_TSC=y
CONFIG_1GB=y
# CONFIG_2GB is not set
CONFIG_MATH_EMULATION=y
CONFIG_MTRR=y
# CONFIG_SMP is not set

#
# Loadable module support
#
CONFIG_MODULES=y
CONFIG_MODVERSIONS=y
CONFIG_KMOD=y
(rest of the file not shown)
```

Essentially, each configuration option has a name, and each one is assigned a value. The name begins with CONFIG_ followed by a word that identifies the option. Each selected option has a value of y (to link in support for that feature) or m (to use a module for that feature). Lines beginning with # are comments. Comment lines list features that are not selected.

In the sample .config file, CONFIG_MODULES is set to y. This means the kernel should include support for loadable modules — drivers that the kernel can load while it is running. On the other hand, CONFIG_MATH_EMULATION is not set. That means the kernel need not include code to emulate a math coprocessor (386 and 486SX processors need a separate math coprocessor, but newer processors such as the Intel Pentium family and AMD K6 have the math coprocessor built in).

Tip

I describe the configuration process through the `make config` command. Although this approach is somewhat tedious because it walks you through each option one by one, it is ideal as a learning tool. As you step through the groups of configuration options, I provide notes explaining what most of the options mean. You can then use any configuration tool (`make xconfig`, `make menuconfig`, `make config`, or `make oldconfig`) to configure the kernel.

Starting the kernel configuration

To start configuring the kernel, type:

```
make config
rm -f include/asm
( cd include ; ln -sf asm-i386 asm)
/bin/sh scripts/Configure arch/i386/config.in
#
# Using defaults found in arch/i386/defconfig
#
*
* Code maturity level options
*
Prompt for development and/or incomplete code/drivers
(CONFIG_EXPERIMENTAL) [Y/n/?]
```

Press Enter to accept the default Yes answer. This causes the configuration process to show all experimental device drivers.

Tip

The possible answers to each prompt appear in square brackets with the default answer in uppercase. Thus, [Y/n/?] means the default answer is Yes, and two other possible answers are n and ?. To accept the default, press Enter. For help on this option, press ?. If you have questions about any option, press ? and carefully read the help text before you decide what to do.

Enabling support for loadable modules

The next group of options asks you about support for loadable modules. A loadable module is like the old DOS TSR (terminate and stay resident) programs.

```
*
* Loadable module support
*
Enable loadable module support (CONFIG_MODULES) [Y/n/?]
  Set version information on all module symbols (CONFIG_MODVERSIONS) [Y/n/?]
  Kernel module loader (CONFIG_KMOD) [Y/n/?]
```

You want to include support for modules, so answer Yes to the first question. The next question asks you about including version information in each module. If modules have version information, the module is checked for compatibility with the current kernel version. Because it is easy to unload a module that does not work, I tend to answer No to this option. However, you may

safely accept the default and press Enter. The third question asks whether
you want the kernel to be capable of loading required modules. You should
answer Yes to this option.

Configuring processor-related features

The next set of questions involve the processor type and support for specific
processor-related features:

```
*
* Processor type and features
*
Processor family (386, 486, 586/K5/5x86/6x86/6x86MX, Pentium-Classic, Pentium-
MMX, Pentium-Pro/Celeron/Pentium-II, Pentium-III, Pentium-4, K6/K6-II/K6-III,
Athlon/K7, Crusoe, Winchip-C6, Winchip-2, Winchip-2A/Winchip-3) [386] Pentium-
MMX
   defined CONFIG_M586MMX
Toshiba Laptop support (CONFIG_TOSHIBA) [N/y/m/?]
/dev/cpu/microcode - Intel P6 CPU microcode support (CONFIG_MICROCODE) [N/y/m/?]

/dev/cpu/*/msr - Model-specific register support (CONFIG_X86_MSR) [N/y/m/?]
/dev/cpu/*/cpuid - CPU information support (CONFIG_X86_CPUID) [N/y/m/?]
High Memory Support (off, 4GB, 64GB) [off]
   defined CONFIG_NOHIGHMEM
Math emulation (CONFIG_MATH_EMULATION) [Y/n/?]
MTRR (Memory Type Range Register) support (CONFIG_MTRR) [Y/n/?]
Symmetric multi-processing support (CONFIG_SMP) [N/y/?]
APIC and IO-APIC support on uniprocessors (CONFIG_X86_UP_IOAPIC) [N/y/?]
```

The first question of the set queries you about your system's processor type.
If you answer 386, the compiled kernel can run on any other processor (such
as a 486 or any type of Pentium). However, if you are creating a kernel specifically for your system, enter your processor type from the choices shown in
parentheses. If you have an older 386 or 486SX PC that does not have a math
coprocessor, you should answer Yes to the math emulation question and have
the kernel perform floating-point arithmetic in software. The Memory Type
Range Register (MTRR) support is a feature of the Pentium Pro, Pentium II,
and later processors. The X server can employ this feature for faster graphics
operations. You should answer Yes to symmetric multiprocessing (SMP) support, only if your system's motherboard has two or more processors.

Configuring general options

Next comes a set of general options that deal with networking, PCI bus, MCA
bus, and advanced power management (APM) BIOS support.

```
*
* General setup
*
Networking support (CONFIG_NET) [Y/n/?]
SGI Visual Workstation support (CONFIG_VISWS) [N/y/?]
PCI support (CONFIG_PCI) [Y/n/?]
   PCI access mode (BIOS, Direct, Any) [Any]
   defined CONFIG_PCI_GOANY
```

```
PCI device name database (CONFIG_PCI_NAMES) [Y/n/?]
EISA support (CONFIG_EISA) [Y/n/?]
MCA support (CONFIG_MCA) [N/y/?]
Support for hot-pluggable devices (CONFIG_HOTPLUG) [Y/n/?]
*
* PCMCIA/CardBus support
*
PCMCIA/CardBus support (CONFIG_PCMCIA) [M/n/y/?]
  CardBus support (CONFIG_CARDBUS) [Y/n/?]
  i82365 compatible bridge support (CONFIG_I82365) [Y/n/?]
  Databook TCIC host bridge support (CONFIG_TCIC) [Y/n/?]
System V IPC (CONFIG_SYSVIPC) [Y/n/?]
BSD Process Accounting (CONFIG_BSD_PROCESS_ACCT) [Y/n/?]
Sysctl support (CONFIG_SYSCTL) [Y/n/?]
Kernel core (/proc/kcore) format (ELF, A.OUT) [ELF]
  defined CONFIG_KCORE_ELF
Kernel support for a.out binaries (CONFIG_BINFMT_AOUT) [M/n/y/?]
Kernel support for ELF binaries (CONFIG_BINFMT_ELF) [Y/m/n/?]
Kernel support for MISC binaries (CONFIG_BINFMT_MISC) [M/n/y/?]
Power Management support (CONFIG_PM) [Y/n/?]
  ACPI support (CONFIG_ACPI) [Y/n/?]
    ACPI interpreter (EXPERIMENTAL) (CONFIG_ACPI_INTERPRETER) [N/y/?]
    Enter S1 for sleep (EXPERIMENTAL) (CONFIG_ACPI_S1_SLEEP) [Y/n/?]
  Advanced Power Management BIOS support (CONFIG_APM) [Y/m/n/?]
    Ignore USER SUSPEND (CONFIG_APM_IGNORE_USER_SUSPEND) [N/y/?]
    Enable PM at boot time (CONFIG_APM_DO_ENABLE) [N/y/?]
    Make CPU Idle calls when idle (CONFIG_APM_CPU_IDLE) [N/y/?]
    Enable console blanking using APM (CONFIG_APM_DISPLAY_BLANK) [N/y/?]
    RTC stores time in GMT (CONFIG_APM_RTC_IS_GMT) [Y/n/?]
    Allow interrupts during APM BIOS calls (CONFIG_APM_ALLOW_INTS) [Y/n/?]
    Use real mode APM BIOS call to power off (CONFIG_APM_REAL_MODE_POWER_OFF)
[Y/n/?]
*
* Memory Technology Devices (MTD)
*
Memory Technology Device (MTD) support (CONFIG_MTD) [N/y/m/?]
*
* Parallel port support
*
Parallel port support (CONFIG_PARPORT) [M/n/y/?]
  PC-style hardware (CONFIG_PARPORT_PC) [M/n/?]
    Use FIFO/DMA if available (CONFIG_PARPORT_PC_FIFO) [N/y/?]
    SuperIO chipset support (EXPERIMENTAL) (CONFIG_PARPORT_PC_SUPERIO) [Y/n/?]
  Support foreign hardware (CONFIG_PARPORT_OTHER) [N/y/?]
  IEEE 1284 transfer modes (CONFIG_PARPORT_1284) [Y/n/?]
```

You can simply press Enter to accept the default answers for these options. If you don't understand what an option means, press ? to get help on that option. Say Yes to the SGI Visual Workstation support, only if you want to build a kernel to run on SGI 320 or 540 workstations. Also, answer No to the CONFIG_APM_RTC_IS_GMT , only if your PC's real-time clock (RTC) stores time in Greenwich Mean Time (GMT).

Cross-Reference

Note that by answering Yes to `CONFIG_SYSCTL`, you enable the necessary support in the kernel so you can use the `/sbin/sysctl` program to view or set kernel parameters. Chapter 23 shows you how to use the `sysctl` program.

Enabling Plug-and-Play support

The next two questions ask if you want to enable Plug-and-Play (PnP) support in the kernel. If you enable PnP support, the kernel automatically configures Plug-and-Play devices (just as Windows 95/98 does). You should press Enter to accept the default choices for these two questions.

```
*
* Plug and Play configuration
*
Plug and Play support (CONFIG_PNP) [Y/m/n/?]
   ISA Plug and Play support (CONFIG_ISAPNP) [Y/m/n/?]
```

Configuring floppy and parallel port IDE devices

The next set of questions involves the floppy, and IDE (Integrated Drive Electronics) devices connected to the PC's parallel port.

```
*
* Block devices
*
Normal PC floppy disk support (CONFIG_BLK_DEV_FD) [Y/m/n/?]
XT hard disk support (CONFIG_BLK_DEV_XD) [M/n/y/?]
Parallel port IDE device support (CONFIG_PARIDE) [M/n/?]
```

The first question asks if you want floppy drive support. Because most PCs do have a floppy drive, your answer generally is Yes. You should press Enter to accept the default for the third question if you have any external CD-ROM or disk devices that connect through your PC's parallel port. These are IDE devices that use a parallel port IDE adapter — that's what the `PARIDE` in the `CONFIG_PARIDE` option refers to.

The next set of options are for various parallel IDE drivers:

```
*
* Parallel IDE high-level drivers
*
  Parallel port IDE disks (CONFIG_PARIDE_PD) [M/n/?]
  Parallel port ATAPI CD-ROMs (CONFIG_PARIDE_PCD) [M/n/?]
  Parallel port ATAPI disks (CONFIG_PARIDE_PF) [M/n/?]
  Parallel port ATAPI tapes (CONFIG_PARIDE_PT) [M/n/?]
  Parallel port generic ATAPI devices (CONFIG_PARIDE_PG) [M/n/?]
*
* Parallel IDE protocol modules
*
   ATEN EH-100 protocol (CONFIG_PARIDE_ATEN) [M/n/?]
   MicroSolutions backpack protocol (CONFIG_PARIDE_BPCK) [M/n/?]
   DataStor Commuter protocol (CONFIG_PARIDE_COMM) [M/n/?]
```

```
DataStor EP-2000 protocol (CONFIG_PARIDE_DSTR) [M/n/?]
FIT TD-2000 protocol (CONFIG_PARIDE_FIT2) [M/n/?]
FIT TD-3000 protocol (CONFIG_PARIDE_FIT3) [M/n/?]
Shuttle EPAT/EPEZ protocol (CONFIG_PARIDE_EPAT) [M/n/?]
Shuttle EPIA protocol (CONFIG_PARIDE_EPIA) [M/n/?]
Freecom IQ ASIC-2 protocol (CONFIG_PARIDE_FRIQ) [M/n/?]
FreeCom power protocol (CONFIG_PARIDE_FRPW) [M/n/?]
KingByte KBIC-951A/971A protocols (CONFIG_PARIDE_KBIC) [M/n/?]
KT PHd protocol (CONFIG_PARIDE_KTTI) [M/n/?]
OnSpec 90c20 protocol (CONFIG_PARIDE_ON20) [M/n/?]
OnSpec 90c26 protocol (CONFIG_PARIDE_ON26) [M/n/?]
```

You can accept the default answers and build in support for parallel port IDE devices through loadable modules. That way, the modules are there if you need them, but the kernel doesn't get bloated with extra code.

Configuring additional block devices

Next comes another set of options for *block devices*, which refers to devices that transfer in chunks (as opposed to a keyboard that transfers data one character at a time):

```
Compaq SMART2 support (CONFIG_BLK_CPQ_DA) [M/n/y/?]
Compaq CISS Array support (CONFIG_BLK_CPQ_CISS_DA) [N/y/m/?]
Mylex DAC960/DAC1100 PCI RAID Controller support (CONFIG_BLK_DEV_DAC960)
[M/n/y/?]
Loopback device support (CONFIG_BLK_DEV_LOOP) [M/n/y/?]
Network block device support (CONFIG_BLK_DEV_NBD) [M/n/y/?]
RAM disk support (CONFIG_BLK_DEV_RAM) [Y/m/n/?]
    Default RAM disk size (CONFIG_BLK_DEV_RAM_SIZE) [4096]
    Initial RAM disk (initrd) support (CONFIG_BLK_DEV_INITRD) [Y/n/?]
*
* Multi-device support (RAID and LVM)
*
Multiple devices driver support (RAID and LVM) (CONFIG_MD) [Y/n/?]
 RAID support (CONFIG_BLK_DEV_MD) [Y/m/n/?]
   Linear (append) mode (CONFIG_MD_LINEAR) [M/n/y/?]
   RAID-0 (striping) mode (CONFIG_MD_RAID0) [M/n/y/?]
   RAID-1 (mirroring) mode (CONFIG_MD_RAID1) [M/n/y/?]
   RAID-4/RAID-5 mode (CONFIG_MD_RAID5) [M/n/y/?]
 Logical volume manager (LVM) support (CONFIG_BLK_DEV_LVM) [Y/m/n/?]
    LVM information in proc filesystem (CONFIG_LVM_PROC_FS) [Y/n/?]
```

Enabling the loopback device lets Linux manipulate an entire file system inside a single large file. The multiple devices driver (CONFIG_BLK_DEV_MD option) allows Linux to combine several hard disk partitions into a single logical device. This option supports RAID (Redundant Array of Independent Disks) devices. The RAM disk support allows the kernel to use a portion of your system's memory as a disk capable of storing a file system. Typically, a RAM disk functions only during system startup when the hard disk may not be available yet. The RAM disk is essential if you are booting a SCSI disk and you haven't compiled the SCSI drivers into the kernel.

Configuring the network

The next set of options deals with networking. How you answer depends on how you want to use your Linux system in a network. Here are some guidelines:

- Answer Yes to enable `CONFIG_NETFILTER` if you want to use your Linux system as a *firewall*—an intermediary system that controls information flowing between a local area network (LAN) and the Internet. When you enable `CONFIG_NETFILTER`, you can use the Linux PC as a packet-filtering firewall. (See Chapter 26 for more information on packet filters.) You should also turn on this option if you want to use IP masquerading, which allows many systems on a private LAN to access the Internet through a Linux system with a valid IP address. You also have to turn on `CONFIG_IP_NF_CONNTRACK`, `CONFIG_IP_NF_IPTABLES`, and `CONFIG_IP_NF_NAT`. Chapter 16 explains IP masquerading.

- If you answer Yes to `CONFIG_IP_ALIAS`, you can assign multiple IP addresses to a single network interface card.

- You should always enable `CONFIG_INET` for TCP/IP networking.

- Answer Yes to `CONFIG_IP_ADVANCED_ROUTER` if you want to use your Linux system as a *router*—a gateway between two LANs.

- You should turn on `CONFIG_IP_MULTICAST` if you employ the Linux system to address several networked computers at once using IP multicasting.

- You can enable `CONFIG_SYN_COOKIES` if you want Linux to resist a type of attack known as *SYN flooding*, which can overwhelm the network connection.

- You can safely answer No to the IP tunneling (`CONFIG_NET_IPIP`) option. You need to address this option only in certain situations, such as moving a laptop from one network to another, without changing its IP address.

Here is a complete list of the networking options:

```
*
* Networking options
*
Packet socket (CONFIG_PACKET) [Y/m/n/?]
  Packet socket: mmapped IO (CONFIG_PACKET_MMAP) [Y/n/?]
Kernel/User netlink socket (CONFIG_NETLINK) [Y/n/?]
  Routing messages (CONFIG_RTNETLINK) [Y/n/?]
  Netlink device emulation (CONFIG_NETLINK_DEV) [Y/m/n/?]
Network packet filtering (replaces ipchains) (CONFIG_NETFILTER) [Y/n/?]
  Network packet filtering debugging (CONFIG_NETFILTER_DEBUG) [N/y/?]
Socket Filtering (CONFIG_FILTER) [Y/n/?]
Unix domain sockets (CONFIG_UNIX) [Y/m/n/?]
TCP/IP networking (CONFIG_INET) [Y/n/?]
  IP: multicasting (CONFIG_IP_MULTICAST) [Y/n/?]
  IP: advanced router (CONFIG_IP_ADVANCED_ROUTER) [N/y/?]
  IP: kernel level autoconfiguration (CONFIG_IP_PNP) [N/y/?]
```

```
   IP: tunneling (CONFIG_NET_IPIP) [M/n/y/?]
   IP: GRE tunnels over IP (CONFIG_NET_IPGRE) [M/n/y/?]
     IP: broadcast GRE over IP (CONFIG_NET_IPGRE_BROADCAST) [Y/n/?]
   IP: multicast routing (CONFIG_IP_MROUTE) [N/y/?]
   IP: ARP daemon support (EXPERIMENTAL) (CONFIG_ARPD) [N/y/?]
   IP: TCP Explicit Congestion Notification support (CONFIG_INET_ECN) [N/y/?]
   IP: TCP syncookie support (disabled per default) (CONFIG_SYN_COOKIES) [Y/n/?]
*
*   IP: Netfilter Configuration
*
Connection tracking (required for masq/NAT) (CONFIG_IP_NF_CONNTRACK) [M/n/y/?]
   FTP protocol support (CONFIG_IP_NF_FTP) [M/n/?]
Userspace queueing via NETLINK (EXPERIMENTAL) (CONFIG_IP_NF_QUEUE) [M/n/y/?]
IP tables support (required for filtering/masq/NAT) (CONFIG_IP_NF_IPTABLES) [M/n
/y/?]
   limit match support (CONFIG_IP_NF_MATCH_LIMIT) [M/n/?]
   MAC address match support (CONFIG_IP_NF_MATCH_MAC) [M/n/?]
   netfilter MARK match support (CONFIG_IP_NF_MATCH_MARK) [M/n/?]
   Multiple port match support (CONFIG_IP_NF_MATCH_MULTIPORT) [M/n/?]
   TOS match support (CONFIG_IP_NF_MATCH_TOS) [M/n/?]
   Connection state match support (CONFIG_IP_NF_MATCH_STATE) [M/n/?]
   Unclean match support (EXPERIMENTAL) (CONFIG_IP_NF_MATCH_UNCLEAN) [M/n/?]
   Owner match support (EXPERIMENTAL) (CONFIG_IP_NF_MATCH_OWNER) [M/n/?]
   Packet filtering (CONFIG_IP_NF_FILTER) [M/n/?]
     REJECT target support (CONFIG_IP_NF_TARGET_REJECT) [M/n/?]
     MIRROR target support (EXPERIMENTAL) (CONFIG_IP_NF_TARGET_MIRROR) [M/n/?]
   Full NAT (CONFIG_IP_NF_NAT) [M/n/?]
     MASQUERADE target support (CONFIG_IP_NF_TARGET_MASQUERADE) [M/n/?]
     REDIRECT target support (CONFIG_IP_NF_TARGET_REDIRECT) [M/n/?]
   Packet mangling (CONFIG_IP_NF_MANGLE) [M/n/?]
     TOS target support (CONFIG_IP_NF_TARGET_TOS) [M/n/?]
     MARK target support (CONFIG_IP_NF_TARGET_MARK) [M/n/?]
   LOG target support (CONFIG_IP_NF_TARGET_LOG) [M/n/?]
ipchains (2.2-style) support (CONFIG_IP_NF_COMPAT_IPCHAINS) [M/n/y/?]
ipfwadm (2.0-style) support (CONFIG_IP_NF_COMPAT_IPFWADM) [M/n/y/?]
   The IPv6 protocol (EXPERIMENTAL) (CONFIG_IPV6) [M/n/y/?]
     IPv6: enable EUI-64 token format (CONFIG_IPV6_EUI64) [N/y/?]
*
*   IPv6: Netfilter Configuration
*
IP6 tables support (required for filtering/masq/NAT) (CONFIG_IP6_NF_IPTABLES) [M
/n/y/?]
   limit match support (CONFIG_IP6_NF_MATCH_LIMIT) [M/n/?]
   netfilter MARK match support (CONFIG_IP6_NF_MATCH_MARK) [M/n/?]
   Packet filtering (CONFIG_IP6_NF_FILTER) [M/n/?]
   Packet mangling (CONFIG_IP6_NF_MANGLE) [M/n/?]
     MARK target support (CONFIG_IP6_NF_TARGET_MARK) [M/n/?]
   Kernel httpd acceleration (EXPERIMENTAL) (CONFIG_KHTTPD) [N/y/m/?]
Asynchronous Transfer Mode (ATM) (EXPERIMENTAL) (CONFIG_ATM) [Y/n/?]
   Classical IP over ATM (CONFIG_ATM_CLIP) [Y/n/?]
     Do NOT send ICMP if no neighbour (CONFIG_ATM_CLIP_NO_ICMP) [N/y/?]
   LAN Emulation (LANE) support (CONFIG_ATM_LANE) [M/n/y/?]
     Multi-Protocol Over ATM (MPOA) support (CONFIG_ATM_MPOA) [M/n/y/?]
```

```
 *
 *
 *
The IPX protocol (CONFIG_IPX) [M/n/y/?]
   IPX: Full internal IPX network (CONFIG_IPX_INTERN) [N/y/?]
Appletalk protocol support (CONFIG_ATALK) [M/n/y/?]
DECnet Support (CONFIG_DECNET) [M/n/y/?]
  DECnet: SIOCGIFCONF support (CONFIG_DECNET_SIOCGIFCONF) [Y/n/?]
   DECnet: router support (EXPERIMENTAL) (CONFIG_DECNET_ROUTER) [Y/n/?]
      DECnet: use FWMARK value as routing key (EXPERIMENTAL) (CONFIG_DECNET_ROUTE_
FWMARK) [Y/n/?]
802.1d Ethernet Bridging (CONFIG_BRIDGE) [N/y/m/?]
CCITT X.25 Packet Layer (EXPERIMENTAL) (CONFIG_X25) [N/y/m/?]
LAPB Data Link Driver (EXPERIMENTAL) (CONFIG_LAPB) [N/y/m/?]
802.2 LLC (EXPERIMENTAL) (CONFIG_LLC) [N/y/?]
Frame Diverter (EXPERIMENTAL) (CONFIG_NET_DIVERT) [N/y/?]
Acorn Econet/AUN protocols (EXPERIMENTAL) (CONFIG_ECONET) [N/y/m/?]
WAN router (CONFIG_WAN_ROUTER) [M/n/y/?]
Fast switching (read help!) (CONFIG_NET_FASTROUTE) [N/y/?]
Forwarding between high speed interfaces (CONFIG_NET_HW_FLOWCONTROL) [N/y/?]
 *
 * QoS and/or fair queueing
 *
QoS and/or fair queueing (EXPERIMENTAL) (CONFIG_NET_SCHED) [N/y/?]
```

Note that the Linux kernel now supports the next version of the Internet Protocol: IP version 6 (IPv6, also called IPng or IP next generation).

Configuring telephony support

Next come two options for telephony support in Linux. With the right hardware and software, telephony support enables you to use the Linux system for making phone calls over the Internet (also known as *voice over IP* or *VoIP*).

```
 *
 * Telephony Support
 *
Linux telephony support (CONFIG_PHONE) [M/n/y/?]
QuickNet Internet LineJack/PhoneJack support (CONFIG_PHONE_IXJ) [M/n/?]
```

You can accept the default choices to build driver modules for telephony support if you have a telephony card, such as the Internet PhoneJACK or Internet LineJACK manufactured by Quicknet Technologies, Inc. If you do not have any Quicknet telephony cards, you can safely ignore this option.

Configuring IDE devices

The next set of questions involves IDE devices, such as hard disks and ATAPI CD-ROM drives.

```
 *
 * ATA/IDE/MFM/RLL support
 *
```

```
ATA/IDE/MFM/RLL support (CONFIG_IDE) [M/n/y/?]
*
* IDE, ATA and ATAPI Block devices
*
Enhanced IDE/MFM/RLL disk/cdrom/tape/floppy support (CONFIG_BLK_DEV_IDE) [M/n/?]
```

The first question asks if you want the kernel to support IDE devices. The second question asks if you want to use the full-featured IDE device that can control up to ten IDE interfaces. Because each IDE interface can have a master and a slave device, this enables Linux to access a total of up to twenty IDE devices, such as disks or CD-ROM drives. You can press Enter to accept the default choices for both of these options.

Tip

The next set of options concerns various IDE drivers. The initial comment starts with a note that refers to the file `/usr/src/linux*/Documentation/ide.txt`. You can find many useful help files (these are all text files) in the `/usr/src/linux*/Documentation` directory.

```
*
* Please see Documentation/ide.txt for help/info on IDE drives
*
  Use old disk-only driver on primary interface (CONFIG_BLK_DEV_HD_IDE) [N/y/?]
  Include IDE/ATA-2 DISK support (CONFIG_BLK_DEV_IDEDISK) [M/n/?]
    Use multi-mode by default (CONFIG_IDEDISK_MULTI_MODE) [N/y/?]
  PCMCIA IDE support (CONFIG_BLK_DEV_IDECS) [M/n/?]
  Include IDE/ATAPI CDROM support (CONFIG_BLK_DEV_IDECD) [M/n/?]
  Include IDE/ATAPI TAPE support (CONFIG_BLK_DEV_IDETAPE) [M/n/?]
  Include IDE/ATAPI FLOPPY support (CONFIG_BLK_DEV_IDEFLOPPY) [M/n/?]
  SCSI emulation support (CONFIG_BLK_DEV_IDESCSI) [M/n/?]
*
* IDE chipset support/bugfixes
*
  CMD640 chipset bugfix/support (CONFIG_BLK_DEV_CMD640) [Y/n/?]
    CMD640 enhanced support (CONFIG_BLK_DEV_CMD640_ENHANCED) [N/y/?]
  ISA-PNP EIDE support (CONFIG_BLK_DEV_ISAPNP) [Y/n/?]
  RZ1000 chipset bugfix/support (CONFIG_BLK_DEV_RZ1000) [Y/n/?]
  Generic PCI IDE chipset support (CONFIG_BLK_DEV_IDEPCI) [Y/n/?]
    Sharing PCI IDE interrupts support (CONFIG_IDEPCI_SHARE_IRQ) [Y/n/?]
    Generic PCI bus-master DMA support (CONFIG_BLK_DEV_IDEDMA_PCI) [Y/n/?]
    Boot off-board chipsets first support (CONFIG_BLK_DEV_OFFBOARD) [N/y/?]
      Use PCI DMA by default when available (CONFIG_IDEDMA_PCI_AUTO) [N/y/?]
      ATA Work(s) In Progress (EXPERIMENTAL) (CONFIG_IDEDMA_PCI_WIP) [Y/n/?]
      Good-Bad DMA Model-Firmware (WIP) (CONFIG_IDEDMA_NEW_DRIVE_LISTINGS)
[Y/n/?]
      AEC62XX chipset support (CONFIG_BLK_DEV_AEC62XX) [Y/n/?]
        AEC62XX Tuning support (CONFIG_AEC62XX_TUNING) [N/y/?]
      ALI M15x3 chipset support (CONFIG_BLK_DEV_ALI15X3) [Y/n/?]
        ALI M15x3 WDC support (DANGEROUS) (CONFIG_WDC_ALI15X3) [N/y/?]
      AMD Viper support (CONFIG_BLK_DEV_AMD7409) [Y/n/?]
        AMD Viper ATA-66 Override (WIP) (CONFIG_AMD7409_OVERRIDE) [N/y/?]
      CMD64X chipset support (CONFIG_BLK_DEV_CMD64X) [Y/n/?]
      CY82C693 chipset support (CONFIG_BLK_DEV_CY82C693) [Y/n/?]
      Cyrix CS5530 MediaGX chipset support (CONFIG_BLK_DEV_CS5530) [Y/n/?]
```

```
    HPT34X chipset support (CONFIG_BLK_DEV_HPT34X) [Y/n/?]
      HPT34X AUTODMA support (WIP) (CONFIG_HPT34X_AUTODMA) [N/y/?]
    HPT366 chipset support (CONFIG_BLK_DEV_HPT366) [Y/n/?]
    Intel PIIXn chipsets support (CONFIG_BLK_DEV_PIIX) [Y/n/?]
    NS87415 chipset support (EXPERIMENTAL) (CONFIG_BLK_DEV_NS87415) [N/y/?]
    OPTi 82C621 chipset enhanced support (EXPERIMENTAL) (CONFIG_BLK_DEV_OPTI621)
[N/y/?]
      PROMISE PDC20246/PDC20262/PDC20267 support (CONFIG_BLK_DEV_PDC202XX) [N/y/?]

    SiS5513 chipset support (CONFIG_BLK_DEV_SIS5513) [Y/n/?]
    SLC90E66 chipset support (CONFIG_BLK_DEV_SLC90E66) [N/y/?]
    Tekram TRM290 chipset support (EXPERIMENTAL) (CONFIG_BLK_DEV_TRM290) [N/y/?]

    VIA82CXXX chipset support (CONFIG_BLK_DEV_VIA82CXXX) [Y/n/?]
  Other IDE chipset support (CONFIG_IDE_CHIPSETS) [N/y/?]
  IGNORE word93 Validation BITS (CONFIG_IDEDMA_IVB) [N/y/?]
```

You can accept the default answers for these options. Note that IDE/
ATAPI FLOPPY refers to IDE floppy drives, such as Iomega Zip drive or
Imation Superdisk LS-120 drive. The questions about CMD640 and RZ1000
bug fixes refer to some known problems with specific chipsets used in IDE
interfaces.

Configuring SCSI devices

Next follows an entire set of options that has to do with SCSI devices. If
your system has a SCSI adapter, you should start by answering Yes to the
CONFIG_SCSI option. After that, you have to answer questions about the
types of devices (disk, tape, CD-ROM) that are connected to the SCSI adapter.
Finally, you must enable support for the specific SCSI adapter model on your
system.

Tip

If your system has a SCSI adapter, always press **y** in response to all the
needed SCSI options. Do not press **m** to create SCSI modules. You have to go
through several extra steps to install a kernel that has to load modular SCSI
device drivers. The easiest approach is to simply link in the SCSI support by
answering **y** to options such as CONFIG_SCSI, CONFIG_BLK_DEV_SD, and the
configuration option corresponding to your SCSI adapter (see the following
listing).

The following listing shows the list of choices for SCSI support:

```
*
* SCSI support
*
SCSI support (CONFIG_SCSI) [M/n/y/?]
*
* SCSI support type (disk, tape, CD-ROM)
*
  SCSI disk support (CONFIG_BLK_DEV_SD) [M/n/?]
Maximum number of SCSI disks that can be loaded as modules
(CONFIG_SD_EXTRA_DEVS) [40]
  SCSI tape support (CONFIG_CHR_DEV_ST) [M/n/?]
  SCSI CD-ROM support (CONFIG_BLK_DEV_SR) [M/n/?]
    Enable vendor-specific extensions (for SCSI CDROM)
(CONFIG_BLK_DEV_SR_VENDOR) [Y/n/?]
```

```
Maximum number of CDROM devices that can be loaded as modules
(CONFIG_SR_EXTRA_DEVS) [4]
  SCSI generic support (CONFIG_CHR_DEV_SG) [M/n/?]
*
* Some SCSI devices (e.g. CD jukebox) support multiple LUNs
*
  Enable extra checks in new queueing code (CONFIG_SCSI_DEBUG_QUEUES) [N/y/?]
  Probe all LUNs on each SCSI device (CONFIG_SCSI_MULTI_LUN) [N/y/?]
  Verbose SCSI error reporting (kernel size +=12K) (CONFIG_SCSI_CONSTANTS)
[Y/n/?]
  SCSI logging facility (CONFIG_SCSI_LOGGING) [Y/n/?]
*
* SCSI low-level drivers
*
3ware Hardware ATA-RAID support (CONFIG_BLK_DEV_3W_XXXX_RAID) [M/n/?]
7000FASST SCSI support (CONFIG_SCSI_7000FASST) [M/n/?]
ACARD SCSI support (CONFIG_SCSI_ACARD) [M/n/?]
Adaptec AHA152X/2825 support (CONFIG_SCSI_AHA152X) [M/n/?]
Adaptec AHA1542 support (CONFIG_SCSI_AHA1542) [M/n/?]
Adaptec AHA1740 support (CONFIG_SCSI_AHA1740) [M/n/?]
Adaptec AIC7xxx support (CONFIG_SCSI_AIC7XXX) [M/n/?]
  Enable Tagged Command Queueing (TCQ) by default
(CONFIG_AIC7XXX_TCQ_ON_BY_DEFAULT) [N/y/?]
  Maximum number of TCQ commands per device (CONFIG_AIC7XXX_CMDS_PER_DEVICE) [8]

  Collect statistics to report in /proc (CONFIG_AIC7XXX_PROC_STATS) [Y/n/?]
  Delay in seconds after SCSI bus reset (CONFIG_AIC7XXX_RESET_DELAY) [5]
AdvanSys SCSI support (CONFIG_SCSI_ADVANSYS) [M/n/?]
Always IN2000 SCSI support (CONFIG_SCSI_IN2000) [M/n/?]
AM53/79C974 PCI SCSI support (CONFIG_SCSI_AM53C974) [M/n/?]
AMI MegaRAID support (CONFIG_SCSI_MEGARAID) [M/n/?]
BusLogic SCSI support (CONFIG_SCSI_BUSLOGIC) [M/n/?]
  Omit FlashPoint support (CONFIG_SCSI_OMIT_FLASHPOINT) [N/y/?]
Compaq Fibre Channel 64-bit/66Mhz HBA support (CONFIG_SCSI_CPQFCTS) [M/n/?]
DMX3191D SCSI support (CONFIG_SCSI_DMX3191D) [M/n/?]
DTC3180/3280 SCSI support (CONFIG_SCSI_DTC3280) [M/n/?]
EATA ISA/EISA/PCI (DPT and generic EATA/DMA-compliant boards) support
(CONFIG_SCSI_EATA) [M/n/?]
  enable tagged command queueing (CONFIG_SCSI_EATA_TAGGED_QUEUE) [Y/n/?]
  enable elevator sorting (CONFIG_SCSI_EATA_LINKED_COMMANDS) [N/y/?]
  maximum number of queued commands (CONFIG_SCSI_EATA_MAX_TAGS) [16]
EATA-DMA [Obsolete] (DPT, NEC, AT&T, SNI, AST, Olivetti, Alphatronix) support
(CONFIG_SCSI_EATA_DMA) [M/n/?]
EATA-PIO (old DPT PM2001, PM2012A) support (CONFIG_SCSI_EATA_PIO) [M/n/?]
Future Domain 16xx SCSI/AHA-2920A support (CONFIG_SCSI_FUTURE_DOMAIN) [M/n/?]
GDT SCSI Disk Array Controller support (CONFIG_SCSI_GDTH) [M/n/?]
Generic NCR5380/53c400 SCSI support (CONFIG_SCSI_GENERIC_NCR5380) [M/n/?]
  Enable NCR53c400 extensions (CONFIG_SCSI_GENERIC_NCR53C400) [N/y/?]
NCR5380/53c400 mapping method (use Port for T130B) (Port, Memory) [Port]
  defined CONFIG_SCSI_G_NCR5380_PORT
IBM ServeRAID support (CONFIG_SCSI_IPS) [M/n/?]
Initio 9100U(W) support (CONFIG_SCSI_INITIO) [M/n/?]
Initio INI-A100U2W support (CONFIG_SCSI_INIA100) [M/n/?]
IOMEGA parallel port (ppa - older drives) (CONFIG_SCSI_PPA) [M/n/?]
```

```
IOMEGA parallel port (imm - newer drives) (CONFIG_SCSI_IMM) [M/n/?]
  ppa/imm option - Use slow (but safe) EPP-16 (CONFIG_SCSI_IZIP_EPP16) [N/y/?]
  ppa/imm option - Assume slow parport control register
(CONFIG_SCSI_IZIP_SLOW_CTR) [N/y/?]
NCR53c406a SCSI support (CONFIG_SCSI_NCR53C406A) [M/n/?]
NCR53c7,8xx SCSI support (CONFIG_SCSI_NCR53C7xx) [M/n/?]
  always negotiate synchronous transfers (CONFIG_SCSI_NCR53C7xx_sync) [N/y/?]
  allow FAST-SCSI [10MHz] (CONFIG_SCSI_NCR53C7xx_FAST) [Y/n/?]
  allow DISCONNECT (CONFIG_SCSI_NCR53C7xx_DISCONNECT) [Y/n/?]
NCR53C8XX SCSI support (CONFIG_SCSI_NCR53C8XX) [M/n/?]
SYM53C8XX SCSI support (CONFIG_SCSI_SYM53C8XX) [M/n/?]
  default tagged command queue depth (CONFIG_SCSI_NCR53C8XX_DEFAULT_TAGS) [8]
  maximum number of queued commands (CONFIG_SCSI_NCR53C8XX_MAX_TAGS) [32]
  synchronous transfers frequency in MHz (CONFIG_SCSI_NCR53C8XX_SYNC) [20]
  enable profiling (CONFIG_SCSI_NCR53C8XX_PROFILE) [Y/n/?]
  use normal IO (CONFIG_SCSI_NCR53C8XX_IOMAPPED) [N/y/?]
  include support for the NCR PQS/PDS SCSI card (CONFIG_SCSI_NCR53C8XX_PQS_PDS)
[N/y/?]
  assume boards are SYMBIOS compatible (EXPERIMENTAL)
(CONFIG_SCSI_NCR53C8XX_SYMBIOS_COMPAT) [N/y/?]
PAS16 SCSI support (CONFIG_SCSI_PAS16) [M/n/?]
PCI2000 support (CONFIG_SCSI_PCI2000) [M/n/?]
PCI2220i support (CONFIG_SCSI_PCI2220I) [M/n/?]
PSI240i support (CONFIG_SCSI_PSI240I) [M/n/?]
Qlogic FAS SCSI support (CONFIG_SCSI_QLOGIC_FAS) [M/n/?]
Qlogic ISP SCSI support (CONFIG_SCSI_QLOGIC_ISP) [M/n/?]
Qlogic ISP FC SCSI support (CONFIG_SCSI_QLOGIC_FC) [M/n/?]
Qlogic QLA 1280 SCSI support (CONFIG_SCSI_QLOGIC_1280) [M/n/?]
Qlogic QLA 2100 FC SCSI support (CONFIG_SCSI_QLOGIC_QLA2100) [M/n/?]
Seagate ST-02 and Future Domain TMC-8xx SCSI support (CONFIG_SCSI_SEAGATE)
[M/n/?]
Simple 53c710 SCSI support (Compaq, NCR machines) (CONFIG_SCSI_SIM710) [M/n/?]
Symbios 53c416 SCSI support (CONFIG_SCSI_SYM53C416) [M/n/?]
Tekram DC390(T) and Am53/79C974 SCSI support (CONFIG_SCSI_DC390T) [M/n/?]
  _omit_ support for non-DC390 adapters (CONFIG_SCSI_DC390T_NOGENSUPP) [N/y/?]
Trantor T128/T128F/T228 SCSI support (CONFIG_SCSI_T128) [M/n/?]
UltraStor 14F/34F support (CONFIG_SCSI_U14_34F) [M/n/?]
  enable elevator sorting (CONFIG_SCSI_U14_34F_LINKED_COMMANDS) [N/y/?]
  maximum number of queued commands (CONFIG_SCSI_U14_34F_MAX_TAGS) [8]
UltraStor SCSI support (CONFIG_SCSI_ULTRASTOR) [M/n/?]
SCSI debugging host simulator (EXPERIMENTAL) (CONFIG_SCSI_DEBUG) [M/n/?]
*
* PCMCIA SCSI adapter support
*
PCMCIA SCSI adapter support (CONFIG_SCSI_PCMCIA) [Y/n/?]
  Adaptec AHA152X PCMCIA support (CONFIG_PCMCIA_AHA152X) [M/n/?]
  Qlogic PCMCIA support (CONFIG_PCMCIA_QLOGIC) [M/n/?]
  Future Domain PCMCIA support (CONFIG_PCMCIA_FDOMAIN) [M/n/?]
  Adaptec APA1480 CardBus support (CONFIG_PCMCIA_APA1480) [M/n/?]
*
* IEEE 1394 (FireWire) support
*
IEEE 1394 (FireWire) support (EXPERIMENTAL) (CONFIG_IEEE1394) [M/n/y/?]
```

```
Texas Instruments PCILynx support (CONFIG_IEEE1394_PCILYNX) [M/n/?]
  Use PCILynx local RAM (CONFIG_IEEE1394_PCILYNX_LOCALRAM) [N/y/?]
  Support for non-IEEE1394 local ports (CONFIG_IEEE1394_PCILYNX_PORTS) [Y/n/?]
OHCI (Open Host Controller Interface) support (CONFIG_IEEE1394_OHCI1394) [M/n/?]

Video1394 support (CONFIG_IEEE1394_VIDEO1394) [M/n/?]
Raw IEEE1394 I/O support (CONFIG_IEEE1394_RAWIO) [M/n/?]
Excessive debugging output (CONFIG_IEEE1394_VERBOSEDEBUG) [N/y/?]
```

Configuring I2O drivers

I2O, pronounced eye-two-oh, refers to *Intelligent Input/Output* — a new device driver architecture that is independent of the operating system and the controlled device. I2O functions by logically separating the part that is responsible for managing the device from the part that contains operating system-specific details (it's called the I2O Split Driver model). The two parts of an I2O driver are the OS Services Module (OSM), which works with the operating system, and the Hardware Device Module (HDM) that interfaces with the particular device that the driver manages. The OSM and HDM communicate by passing messages to each other. To learn more about I2O, visit Intel's Developer Web site at `http://developer.intel.com/design/iio/papers/`.

Linux comes with some I2O drivers for SCSI and PCI devices. You can build the I2O drivers through the following configuration options:

```
*
* I2O device support
*
I2O support (CONFIG_I2O) [M/n/y/?]
  I2O PCI support (CONFIG_I2O_PCI) [M/n/?]
  I2O Block OSM (CONFIG_I2O_BLOCK) [M/n/?]
  I2O LAN OSM (CONFIG_I2O_LAN) [M/n/?]
  I2O SCSI OSM (CONFIG_I2O_SCSI) [M/n/?]
  I2O /proc support (CONFIG_I2O_PROC) [M/n/?]
```

Configuring network adapters

The next group of options involves networking. They include the configuration of local area network (LAN) adapters such as Ethernet and Token ring cards. You can also enable dial-up and wide area network (WAN) support, using SLIP and PPP through options in this category. The following listing shows the networking configuration options:

```
*
* Network device support
*
Network device support (CONFIG_NETDEVICES) [Y/n/?]
*
* ARCnet devices
*
ARCnet support (CONFIG_ARCNET) [N/y/m/?]
```

```
       *
       * Appletalk devices
       *
       Appletalk interfaces support (CONFIG_APPLETALK) [Y/n/?]
          Apple/Farallon LocalTalk PC support (CONFIG_LTPC) [M/n/y/?]
          COPS LocalTalk PC support (CONFIG_COPS) [M/n/y/?]
             Dayna firmware support (CONFIG_COPS_DAYNA) [Y/n/?]
             Tangent firmware support (CONFIG_COPS_TANGENT) [Y/n/?]
          Appletalk-IP driver support (CONFIG_IPDDP) [M/n/y/?]
             IP to Appletalk-IP Encapsulation support (CONFIG_IPDDP_ENCAP) [Y/n/?]
             Appletalk-IP to IP Decapsulation support (CONFIG_IPDDP_DECAP) [Y/n/?]
       Dummy net driver support (CONFIG_DUMMY) [M/n/y/?]
       Bonding driver support (CONFIG_BONDING) [M/n/y/?]
       EQL (serial line load balancing) support (CONFIG_EQUALIZER) [M/n/y/?]
       Universal TUN/TAP device driver support (CONFIG_TUN) [M/n/y/?]
       Ethertap network tap (OBSOLETE) (CONFIG_ETHERTAP) [M/n/y/?]
       General Instruments Surfboard 1000 (CONFIG_NET_SB1000) [M/n/y/?]
       *
       * Ethernet (10 or 100Mbit)
       *
       Ethernet (10 or 100Mbit) (CONFIG_NET_ETHERNET) [Y/n/?]
          3COM cards (CONFIG_NET_VENDOR_3COM) [Y/n/?]
             3c501 "EtherLink" support (CONFIG_EL1) [M/n/y/?]
             3c503 "EtherLink II" support (CONFIG_EL2) [M/n/y/?]
             3c505 "EtherLink Plus" support (CONFIG_ELPLUS) [M/n/y/?]
             3c507 "EtherLink 16" support (EXPERIMENTAL) (CONFIG_EL16) [M/n/y/?]
             3c509/3c529 (MCA)/3c579 "EtherLink III" support (CONFIG_EL3) [M/n/y/?]
             3c515 ISA "Fast EtherLink" (CONFIG_3C515) [M/n/y/?]
             3c590/3c900 series (592/595/597) "Vortex/Boomerang" support (CONFIG_VORTEX)
       [M/n/y/?]
          AMD LANCE and PCnet (AT1500 and NE2100) support (CONFIG_LANCE) [M/n/y/?]
          Western Digital/SMC cards (CONFIG_NET_VENDOR_SMC) [Y/n/?]
             WD80*3 support (CONFIG_WD80x3) [M/n/y/?]
             SMC Ultra support (CONFIG_ULTRA) [M/n/y/?]
             SMC Ultra32 EISA support (CONFIG_ULTRA32) [M/n/y/?]
             SMC 9194 support (CONFIG_SMC9194) [N/y/m/?]
          Racal-Interlan (Micom) NI cards (CONFIG_NET_VENDOR_RACAL) [Y/n/?]
          Racal-Interlan (Micom) NI cards (CONFIG_NET_VENDOR_RACAL) [Y/n/?]
             NI5010 support (EXPERIMENTAL) (CONFIG_NI5010) [M/n/y/?]
             NI5210 support (CONFIG_NI52) [M/n/y/?]
             NI6510 support (CONFIG_NI65) [M/n/y/?]
          AT1700/1720 support (EXPERIMENTAL) (CONFIG_AT1700) [M/n/y/?]
          DEPCA, DE10x, DE200, DE201, DE202, DE422 support (CONFIG_DEPCA) [M/n/y/?]
          HP 10/100VG PCLAN (ISA, EISA, PCI) support (CONFIG_HP100) [M/n/y/?]
          Other ISA cards (CONFIG_NET_ISA) [Y/n/?]
             Cabletron E21xx support (CONFIG_E2100) [M/n/y/?]
             EtherExpress 16 support (CONFIG_EEXPRESS) [M/n/y/?]
             EtherExpressPro support/EtherExpress 10 (i82595) support
       (CONFIG_EEXPRESS_PRO) [M/n/y/?]
             HP PCLAN+ (27247B and 27252A) support (CONFIG_HPLAN_PLUS) [M/n/y/?]
             HP PCLAN (27245 and other 27xxx series) support (CONFIG_HPLAN) [M/n/y/?]
             ICL EtherTeam 16i/32 support (CONFIG_ETH16I) [M/n/y/?]
             NE2000/NE1000 support (CONFIG_NE2000) [M/n/y/?]
             SK_G16 support (CONFIG_SK_G16) [Y/m/n/?]
```

```
    EISA, VLB, PCI and on board controllers (CONFIG_NET_PCI) [Y/n/?]
      AMD PCnet32 PCI support (CONFIG_PCNET32) [M/n/y/?]
      Adaptec Starfire support (EXPERIMENTAL) (CONFIG_ADAPTEC_STARFIRE) [M/n/y/?]
      Ansel Communications EISA 3200 support (EXPERIMENTAL) (CONFIG_AC3200)
[M/n/y/?]
      Apricot Xen-II on board Ethernet (CONFIG_APRICOT) [M/n/y/?]
      CS89x0 support (CONFIG_CS89x0) [M/n/y/?]
      DECchip Tulip (dc21x4x) PCI support (CONFIG_TULIP) [M/n/y/?]
      Generic DECchip & DIGITAL EtherWORKS PCI/EISA (CONFIG_DE4X5) [M/n/y/?]
      Digi Intl. RightSwitch SE-X support (CONFIG_DGRS) [M/n/y/?]
      DM9102 PCI Fast Ethernet Adapter support (EXPERIMENTAL) (CONFIG_DM9102)
[M/n/y/?]
      EtherExpressPro/100 support (CONFIG_EEPRO100) [M/n/y/?]
        Enable Power Management (EXPERIMENTAL) (CONFIG_EEPRO100_PM) [Y/n/?]
      Mylex EISA LNE390A/B support (EXPERIMENTAL) (CONFIG_LNE390) [M/n/y/?]
      EtherExpressPro/100 support (alternate driver) (CONFIG_E100) [M/n/y/?]
      National Semiconductor DP83810 series PCI Ethernet support (CONFIG_NATSEMI)
[M/n/y/?]
      PCI NE2000 and clones support (see help) (CONFIG_NE2K_PCI) [M/n/y/?]
      Novell/Eagle/Microdyne NE3210 EISA support (EXPERIMENTAL) (CONFIG_NE3210)
[M/n/y/?]
      Racal-Interlan EISA ES3210 support (EXPERIMENTAL) (CONFIG_ES3210) [M/n/y/?]
      RealTek RTL-8139 PCI Fast Ethernet Adapter support (CONFIG_8139TOO) [M/n/y/?
]
      RealTek 8129 (not 8019/8029/8139!) support (EXPERIMENTAL) (CONFIG_RTL8129)
[M/n/y/?]
      SiS 900/7016 PCI Fast Ethernet Adapter support (CONFIG_SIS900) [M/n/y/?]
      SMC EtherPower II (CONFIG_EPIC100) [M/n/y/?]
      Sundance Alta support (CONFIG_SUNDANCE) [M/n/y/?]
      TI ThunderLAN support (CONFIG_TLAN) [M/n/y/?]
      VIA Rhine support (CONFIG_VIA_RHINE) [M/n/y/?]
      Winbond W89c840 Ethernet support (CONFIG_WINBOND_840) [M/n/y/?]
      Sun Happy Meal 10/100baseT PCI support (CONFIG_HAPPYMEAL) [M/n/y/?]
    Pocket and portable adapters (CONFIG_NET_POCKET) [Y/n/?]
      AT-LAN-TEC/RealTek pocket adapter support (CONFIG_ATP) [Y/m/n/?]
      D-Link DE600 pocket adapter support (CONFIG_DE600) [M/n/y/?]
      D-Link DE620 pocket adapter support (CONFIG_DE620) [M/n/y/?]
  *
  * Ethernet (1000 Mbit)
  *
  Intel PRO/1000 support (CONFIG_E1000) [N/y/m/?]
  Alteon AceNIC/3Com 3C985/NetGear GA620 Gigabit support (CONFIG_ACENIC) [M/n/y/?]

    Omit support for old Tigon I based AceNICs (CONFIG_ACENIC_OMIT_TIGON_I)
[N/y/?]
  Packet Engines Hamachi GNIC-II support (CONFIG_HAMACHI) [M/n/y/?]
  Packet Engines Yellowfin Gigabit-NIC support (EXPERIMENTAL) (CONFIG_YELLOWFIN)
[M/n/y/?]
  SysKonnect SK-98xx support (CONFIG_SK98LIN) [M/n/y/?]
  FDDI driver support (CONFIG_FDDI) [Y/n/?]
    Digital DEFEA and DEFPA adapter support (CONFIG_DEFXX) [M/n/y/?]
    SysKonnect FDDI PCI support (CONFIG_SKFP) [M/n/y/?]
  HIPPI driver support (EXPERIMENTAL) (CONFIG_HIPPI) [N/y/?]
```

```
PLIP (parallel port) support (CONFIG_PLIP) [M/n/?]
PPP (point-to-point protocol) support (CONFIG_PPP) [M/n/y/?]
  PPP multilink support (EXPERIMENTAL) (CONFIG_PPP_MULTILINK) [Y/n/?]
  PPP support for async serial ports (CONFIG_PPP_ASYNC) [M/n/?]
  PPP support for sync tty ports (CONFIG_PPP_SYNC_TTY) [M/n/?]
  PPP Deflate compression (CONFIG_PPP_DEFLATE) [M/n/?]
  PPP BSD-Compress compression (CONFIG_PPP_BSDCOMP) [M/n/?]
  PPP over Ethernet (EXPERIMENTAL) (CONFIG_PPPOE) [N/m/?]
SLIP (serial line) support (CONFIG_SLIP) [M/n/y/?]
  CSLIP compressed headers (CONFIG_SLIP_COMPRESSED) [Y/n/?]
  Keepalive and linefill (CONFIG_SLIP_SMART) [Y/n/?]
  Six bit SLIP encapsulation (CONFIG_SLIP_MODE_SLIP6) [Y/n/?]
*
* Wireless LAN (non-hamradio)
*
CIPE (Crypto IP Encapsulation) (CONFIG_CIPE) [M/n/y/?]
Wireless LAN (non-hamradio) (CONFIG_NET_RADIO) [Y/n/?]
  STRIP (Metricom starmode radio IP) (CONFIG_STRIP) [M/n/y/?]
  AT&T WaveLAN & DEC RoamAbout DS support (CONFIG_WAVELAN) [M/n/y/?]
  Aironet Arlan 655 & IC2200 DS support (CONFIG_ARLAN) [M/n/y/?]
  Aironet 4500/4800 series adapters (CONFIG_AIRONET4500) [M/n/y/?]
   Aironet 4500/4800 ISA/PCI/PNP/365 support  (CONFIG_AIRONET4500_NONCS) [M/n/?]

    Aironet 4500/4800 PNP support  (CONFIG_AIRONET4500_PNP) [Y/n/?]
    Aironet 4500/4800 PCI support  (CONFIG_AIRONET4500_PCI) [Y/n/?]
    Aironet 4500/4800 ISA broken support (EXPERIMENTAL)
(CONFIG_AIRONET4500_ISA) [Y/n/?]
    Aironet 4500/4800 I365 broken support (EXPERIMENTAL)
(CONFIG_AIRONET4500_I365) [Y/n/?]
*
* Token Ring devices
*
Token Ring driver support (CONFIG_TR) [Y/n/?]
  IBM Tropic chipset based adapter support (CONFIG_IBMTR) [M/n/y/?]
  IBM Olympic chipset PCI adapter support (CONFIG_IBMOL) [M/n/y/?]
  IBM Lanstreamer chipset PCI adapter support (CONFIG_IBMLS) [M/n/y/?]
  Generic TMS380 Token Ring ISA/PCI adapter support (CONFIG_TMS380TR) [M/n/y/?]
    Generic TMS380 PCI support (CONFIG_TMSPCI) [M/n/?]
    Madge Smart 16/4 PCI Mk2 support (CONFIG_ABYSS) [M/n/?]
  SMC ISA/MCA adapter support (CONFIG_SMCTR) [M/n/y/?]
Fibre Channel driver support (CONFIG_NET_FC) [Y/n/?]
  Interphase 5526 Tachyon chipset based adapter support (CONFIG_IPHASE5526)
[M/n/?]
Red Creek Hardware VPN (EXPERIMENTAL) (CONFIG_RCPCI) [M/n/y/?]
Traffic Shaper (EXPERIMENTAL) (CONFIG_SHAPER) [M/n/y/?]
*
* Wan interfaces
*
Wan interfaces support (CONFIG_WAN) [Y/n/?]
  Comtrol Hostess SV-11 support (CONFIG_HOSTESS_SV11) [M/n/?]
  COSA/SRP sync serial boards support (CONFIG_COSA) [M/n/?]
  MultiGate (COMX) synchronous serial boards support (CONFIG_COMX) [N/y/m/?]
  LanMedia Corp. SSI/V.35, T1/E1, HSSI, T3 boards (CONFIG_LANMEDIA) [N/y/m/?]
```

```
      Sealevel Systems 4021 support (CONFIG_SEALEVEL_4021) [M/n/?]
      SyncLink HDLC/SYNCPPP support (CONFIG_SYNCLINK_SYNCPPP) [N/m/?]
      Frame relay DLCI support (CONFIG_DLCI) [M/n/y/?]
        Max open DLCI (CONFIG_DLCI_COUNT) [24]
        Max DLCI per device (CONFIG_DLCI_MAX) [8]
        SDLA (Sangoma S502/S508) support (CONFIG_SDLA) [M/n/?]
      WAN router drivers (CONFIG_WAN_ROUTER_DRIVERS) [Y/n/?]
        Sangoma WANPIPE(tm) multiprotocol cards (CONFIG_VENDOR_SANGOMA) [M/n/y/?]
          Maximum number of cards (CONFIG_WANPIPE_CARDS) [4]
          WANPIPE Cisco HDLC support (CONFIG_WANPIPE_CHDLC) [Y/n/?]
          WANPIPE PPP support (CONFIG_WANPIPE_PPP) [Y/n/?]
        Cyclom 2X(tm) cards (EXPERIMENTAL) (CONFIG_CYCLADES_SYNC) [M/n/y/?]
          Cyclom 2X X.25 support (CONFIG_CYCLOMX_X25) [Y/n/?]
      SBNI12-xx support (CONFIG_SBNI) [M/n/y/?]
*
* PCMCIA network device support
*
PCMCIA network device support (CONFIG_NET_PCMCIA) [Y/n/?]
  3Com 3c589 PCMCIA support (CONFIG_PCMCIA_3C589) [M/n/?]
  3Com 3c574 PCMCIA support (CONFIG_PCMCIA_3C574) [M/n/?]
  Fujitsu FMV-J18x PCMCIA support (CONFIG_PCMCIA_FMVJ18X) [M/n/?]
  NE2000 compatible PCMCIA support (CONFIG_PCMCIA_PCNET) [M/n/?]
  New Media PCMCIA support (CONFIG_PCMCIA_NMCLAN) [M/n/?]
  SMC 91Cxx PCMCIA support (CONFIG_PCMCIA_SMC91C92) [M/n/?]
  Xircom 16-bit PCMCIA support (CONFIG_PCMCIA_XIRC2PS) [M/n/?]
  IBM PCMCIA tokenring adapter support (CONFIG_PCMCIA_IBMTR) [M/n/?]
  Xircom Tulip-like CardBus support (CONFIG_PCMCIA_XIRTULIP) [M/n/y/?]
  Pcmcia Wireless LAN (CONFIG_NET_PCMCIA_RADIO) [Y/n/?]
    Aviator/Raytheon 2.4MHz wireless support (CONFIG_PCMCIA_RAYCS) [M/n/?]
    Xircom Netwave AirSurfer wireless support (CONFIG_PCMCIA_NETWAVE) [M/n/?]
    AT&T/Lucent Wavelan wireless support (CONFIG_PCMCIA_WAVELAN) [M/n/?]
    Aironet 4500/4800 PCMCIA support (CONFIG_AIRONET4500_CS) [M/n/?]
*
* ATM drivers
*
ATM over TCP (CONFIG_ATM_TCP) [M/n/y/?]
Efficient Networks ENI155P (CONFIG_ATM_ENI) [M/n/y/?]
  Enable extended debugging (CONFIG_ATM_ENI_DEBUG) [N/y/?]
  Fine-tune burst settings (CONFIG_ATM_ENI_TUNE_BURST) [N/y/?]
ZeitNet ZN1221/ZN1225 (CONFIG_ATM_ZATM) [M/n/y/?]
  Enable extended debugging (CONFIG_ATM_ZATM_DEBUG) [N/y/?]
  Enable usec resolution timestamps (CONFIG_ATM_ZATM_EXACT_TS) [Y/n/?]
IDT 77201 (NICStAR) (ForeRunnerLE) (CONFIG_ATM_NICSTAR) [M/n/y/?]
  Use suni PHY driver (155Mbps) (CONFIG_ATM_NICSTAR_USE_SUNI) [Y/n/?]
  Use IDT77015 PHY driver (25Mbps) (CONFIG_ATM_NICSTAR_USE_IDT77105) [Y/n/?]
Madge Ambassador (Collage PCI 155 Server) (CONFIG_ATM_AMBASSADOR) [M/n/y/?]
  Enable debugging messages (CONFIG_ATM_AMBASSADOR_DEBUG) [N/y/?]
Madge Horizon [Ultra] (Collage PCI 25 and Collage PCI 155 Client)
(CONFIG_ATM_HORIZON) [M/n/y/?]
  Enable debugging messages (CONFIG_ATM_HORIZON_DEBUG) [N/y/?]
Interphase ATM PCI x575/x525/x531 (CONFIG_ATM_IA) [M/n/y/?]
  Enable debugging messages (CONFIG_ATM_IA_DEBUG) [N/y/?]
```

```
FORE Systems 200E-series (CONFIG_ATM_FORE200E_MAYBE) [M/n/y/?]
  PCA-200E support (CONFIG_ATM_FORE200E_PCA) [Y/n/?]
   Use default PCA-200E firmware (normally enabled)
(CONFIG_ATM_FORE200E_PCA_DEFAULT_FW) [Y/n/?]
  Maximum number of tx retries (CONFIG_ATM_FORE200E_TX_RETRY) [16]
  Debugging level (0-3) (CONFIG_ATM_FORE200E_DEBUG) [0]
```

You should enable the next option only if you need support for amateur packet radio (AX.25):

```
*
* Amateur Radio support
*
Amateur Radio support (CONFIG_HAMRADIO) [N/y/?]
```

Enabling support for infrared devices

The Linux kernel now supports IrDA-compliant infrared (IR) devices. The following set of options allows you to enable support for IrDA devices. If your PC has any IrDA interfaces, you can build the modules needed to support such devices.

```
*
* IrDA (infrared) support
*
IrDA subsystem support (CONFIG_IRDA) [M/n/y/?]
*
* IrDA protocols
*
  IrLAN protocol (CONFIG_IRLAN) [M/n/?]
  IrNET protocol (CONFIG_IRNET) [M/n/?]
  IrCOMM protocol (CONFIG_IRCOMM) [M/n/?]
  Ultra (connectionless) protocol (CONFIG_IRDA_ULTRA) [Y/n/?]
  IrDA protocol options (CONFIG_IRDA_OPTIONS) [Y/n/?]
*
*   IrDA options
*
    Cache last LSAP (CONFIG_IRDA_CACHE_LAST_LSAP) [Y/n/?]
    Fast RRs (CONFIG_IRDA_FAST_RR) [Y/n/?]
    Debug information (CONFIG_IRDA_DEBUG) [N/y/?]
*
* Infrared-port device drivers
*
*
* SIR device drivers
*
IrTTY (uses Linux serial driver) (CONFIG_IRTTY_SIR) [M/n/?]
IrPORT (IrDA serial driver) (CONFIG_IRPORT_SIR) [M/n/?]
*
* FIR device drivers
*
NSC PC87108/PC87338 (CONFIG_NSC_FIR) [M/n/?]
Winbond W83977AF (IR) (CONFIG_WINBOND_FIR) [M/n/?]
Toshiba Type-O IR Port (CONFIG_TOSHIBA_FIR) [M/n/?]
SMC IrCC (Experimental) (CONFIG_SMC_IRCC_FIR) [M/n/?]
```

Many IR interfaces are in the form of *dongles* — small adapters that typically attach to the serial port of the PC. You can use the following options to enable support for several common types of dongles:

```
*
* Dongle support
*
Serial dongle support (CONFIG_DONGLE) [Y/n/?]
  ESI JetEye PC dongle (CONFIG_ESI_DONGLE) [M/n/?]
  ACTiSYS IR-220L and IR220L+ dongle (CONFIG_ACTISYS_DONGLE) [M/n/?]
  Tekram IrMate 210B dongle (CONFIG_TEKRAM_DONGLE) [M/n/?]
  Greenwich GIrBIL dongle (CONFIG_GIRBIL_DONGLE) [M/n/?]
  Parallax LiteLink dongle (CONFIG_LITELINK_DONGLE) [M/n/?]
  Old Belkin dongle (CONFIG_OLD_BELKIN_DONGLE) [M/n/?]
```

Enabling support for ISDN

The next set of options enables you to include support for *ISDN (Integrated Services Digital Network)* — a digital telephone line that you can use to connect the Linux system to the Internet. The following ISDN-related options include the configuration of specific ISDN adapters:

```
*
* ISDN subsystem
*
ISDN support (CONFIG_ISDN) [M/n/y/?]
  Support synchronous PPP (CONFIG_ISDN_PPP) [Y/n/?]
    Use VJ-compression with synchronous PPP (CONFIG_ISDN_PPP_VJ) [Y/n/?]
    Support generic MP (RFC 1717) (CONFIG_ISDN_MPP) [Y/n/?]
  Support audio via ISDN (CONFIG_ISDN_AUDIO) [Y/n/?]
    Support AT-Fax Class 1 and 2 commands (CONFIG_ISDN_TTY_FAX) [Y/n/?]
*
* ISDN feature submodules
*
isdnloop support (CONFIG_ISDN_DRV_LOOP) [M/n/?]
Support isdn diversion services (CONFIG_ISDN_DIVERSION) [N/y/?]
*
* low-level hardware drivers
*
*
* Passive ISDN cards
*
HiSax SiemensChipSet driver support (CONFIG_ISDN_DRV_HISAX) [M/n/?]
*
*    D-channel protocol features
*
  HiSax Support for EURO/DSS1 (CONFIG_HISAX_EURO) [Y/n/?]
    Support for german chargeinfo (CONFIG_DE_AOC) [Y/n/?]
    Disable sending complete (CONFIG_HISAX_NO_SENDCOMPLETE) [N/y/?]
    Disable sending low layer compatibility (CONFIG_HISAX_NO_LLC) [N/y/?]
    Disable keypad protocol option (CONFIG_HISAX_NO_KEYPAD) [N/y/?]
  HiSax Support for german 1TR6 (CONFIG_HISAX_1TR6) [Y/n/?]
  HiSax Support for US NI1 (CONFIG_HISAX_NI1) [Y/n/?]
```

```
*
*    HiSax supported cards
*
  Teles 16.0/8.0 (CONFIG_HISAX_16_0) [Y/n/?]
  Teles 16.3 or PNP or PCMCIA (CONFIG_HISAX_16_3) [Y/n/?]
  Teles PCI (CONFIG_HISAX_TELESPCI) [Y/n/?]
  Teles SOBox (CONFIG_HISAX_SOBOX) [Y/n/?]
  AVM A1 (Fritz) (CONFIG_HISAX_AVM_A1) [Y/n/?]
  AVM PnP/PCI (Fritz!PnP/PCI) (CONFIG_HISAX_FRITZPCI) [Y/n/?]
  AVM A1 PCMCIA (Fritz) (CONFIG_HISAX_AVM_A1_PCMCIA) [Y/n/?]
  Elsa cards (CONFIG_HISAX_ELSA) [Y/n/?]
  ITK ix1-micro Revision 2 (CONFIG_HISAX_IX1MICROR2) [Y/n/?]
  Eicon.Diehl Diva cards (CONFIG_HISAX_DIEHLDIVA) [Y/n/?]
  ASUSCOM ISA cards (CONFIG_HISAX_ASUSCOM) [Y/n/?]
  TELEINT cards (CONFIG_HISAX_TELEINT) [Y/n/?]
  HFC-S based cards (CONFIG_HISAX_HFCS) [Y/n/?]
  Sedlbauer cards (CONFIG_HISAX_SEDLBAUER) [Y/n/?]
  USR Sportster internal TA (CONFIG_HISAX_SPORTSTER) [Y/n/?]
  MIC card (CONFIG_HISAX_MIC) [Y/n/?]
  NETjet card (CONFIG_HISAX_NETJET) [Y/n/?]
  NETspider U card (CONFIG_HISAX_NETJET_U) [Y/n/?]
  Niccy PnP/PCI card (CONFIG_HISAX_NICCY) [Y/n/?]
  Siemens I-Surf card (CONFIG_HISAX_ISURF) [Y/n/?]
  HST Saphir card (CONFIG_HISAX_HSTSAPHIR) [Y/n/?]
  Telekom A4T card (CONFIG_HISAX_BKM_A4T) [Y/n/?]
  Scitel Quadro card (CONFIG_HISAX_SCT_QUADRO) [Y/n/?]
  Gazel cards (CONFIG_HISAX_GAZEL) [Y/n/?]
  HFC PCI-Bus cards (CONFIG_HISAX_HFC_PCI) [Y/n/?]
  Winbond W6692 based cards (CONFIG_HISAX_W6692) [Y/n/?]
  HFC-S+, HFC-SP, HFC-PCMCIA cards (CONFIG_HISAX_HFC_SX) [Y/n/?]
*
* Active ISDN cards
*
ICN 2B and 4B support (CONFIG_ISDN_DRV_ICN) [M/n/?]
PCBIT-D support (CONFIG_ISDN_DRV_PCBIT) [M/n/?]
Spellcaster support (EXPERIMENTAL) (CONFIG_ISDN_DRV_SC) [N/m/?]
IBM Active 2000 support (EXPERIMENTAL) (CONFIG_ISDN_DRV_ACT2000) [N/m/?]
Eicon active card support (CONFIG_ISDN_DRV_EICON) [N/m/?]
CAPI2.0 support (CONFIG_ISDN_CAPI) [M/n/?]
CAPI2.0 Middleware support (CONFIG_ISDN_CAPI_MIDDLEWARE) [Y/n/?]
CAPI2.0 filesystem support (CONFIG_ISDN_CAPIFS) [Y/n/?]
  AVM B1 ISA support (CONFIG_ISDN_DRV_AVMB1_B1ISA) [Y/n/?]
  AVM B1 PCI support (CONFIG_ISDN_DRV_AVMB1_B1PCI) [Y/n/?]
  AVM B1 PCI V4 support (CONFIG_ISDN_DRV_AVMB1_B1PCIV4) [Y/n/?]
  AVM T1/T1-B ISA support (CONFIG_ISDN_DRV_AVMB1_T1ISA) [Y/n/?]
  AVM B1/M1/M2 PCMCIA support (CONFIG_ISDN_DRV_AVMB1_B1PCMCIA) [N/y/?]
  AVM T1/T1-B PCI support (CONFIG_ISDN_DRV_AVMB1_T1PCI) [Y/n/?]
  AVM C4 support (CONFIG_ISDN_DRV_AVMB1_C4) [Y/n/?]
  Verbose reason code reporting (kernel size +=7K)
(CONFIG_ISDN_DRV_AVMB1_VERBOSE_REASON) [Y/n/?]
Hypercope HYSDN cards (Champ, Ergo, Metro) support (module) (CONFIG_HYSDN)
[Y/n/?]
  HYSDN CAPI 2.0 support (CONFIG_HYSDN_CAPI) [Y/n/?]
```

You should build the ISDN driver only if your PC has an ISDN card. If you anticipate adding an ISDN card and purchase ISDN service from the phone company, you can build the driver as a module. Read the file `/usr/src/linux*/Documentation/isdn/README` for more information on how to set up and use the ISDN driver in Linux.

Configuring CD-ROM drives with proprietary interfaces

If you have a CD-ROM drive with a proprietary interface — not a SCSI or IDE (ATAPI) CD-ROM drive — you should select your CD-ROM interface from the following set of options:

```
*
* Old CD-ROM drivers (not SCSI, not IDE)
*
Support non-SCSI/IDE/ATAPI CDROM drives (CONFIG_CD_NO_IDESCSI) [Y/n/?]
  Aztech/Orchid/Okano/Wearnes/TXC/CyDROM  CDROM support (CONFIG_AZTCD) [M/n/y/?]
  Goldstar R420 CDROM support (CONFIG_GSCD) [M/n/y/?]
  Matsushita/Panasonic/Creative, Longshine, TEAC CDROM support (CONFIG_SBPCD)
[M/n/y/?]
  Mitsumi (standard) [no XA/Multisession] CDROM support (CONFIG_MCD) [M/n/y/?]
MCD IRQ (CONFIG_MCD_IRQ) [11]
MCD I/O base (CONFIG_MCD_BASE) [300]
  Mitsumi [XA/MultiSession] CDROM support (CONFIG_MCDX) [M/n/y/?]
  Optics Storage DOLPHIN 8000AT CDROM support (CONFIG_OPTCD) [M/n/y/?]
  Philips/LMS CM206 CDROM support (CONFIG_CM206) [M/n/y/?]
  Sanyo CDR-H94A CDROM support (CONFIG_SJCD) [M/n/y/?]
  ISP16/MAD16/Mozart soft configurable cdrom interface support
(CONFIG_ISP16_CDI) [M/n/y/?]
  Sony CDU31A/CDU33A CDROM support (CONFIG_CDU31A) [M/n/y/?]
  Sony CDU535 CDROM support (CONFIG_CDU535) [M/n/y/?]
```

Typically, you can ignore the CD-ROM options, unless you have one of the listed CD-ROM interfaces.

Configuring character devices

The next few options deal with configuring character devices, which include devices connected to the serial and parallel ports. These options also include configuration of multiport serial interface cards that enable you to connect multiple terminals or other devices to your Linux system. Answer No if you do not have any such devices on your system. Near the end of the list you see a question about parallel printer support (`CONFIG_PRINTER`). If you plan to connect a printer to the parallel port, answer Yes to this option.

```
*
* Input core support
*
Input core support (CONFIG_INPUT) [M/n/y/?]
  Keyboard support (CONFIG_INPUT_KEYBDEV) [M/n/?]
```

```
Mouse support (CONFIG_INPUT_MOUSEDEV) [M/n/?]
 Horizontal screen resolution (CONFIG_INPUT_MOUSEDEV_SCREEN_X) [1024]
 Vertical screen resolution (CONFIG_INPUT_MOUSEDEV_SCREEN_Y) [768]
Joystick support (CONFIG_INPUT_JOYDEV) [M/n/?]
Event interface support (CONFIG_INPUT_EVDEV) [M/n/?]
*
* Character devices
*
Virtual terminal (CONFIG_VT) [Y/n/?]
 Support for console on virtual terminal (CONFIG_VT_CONSOLE) [Y/n/?]
Standard/generic (8250/16550 and compatible UARTs) serial support
(CONFIG_SERIAL) [Y/m/n/?]
 Support for console on serial port (CONFIG_SERIAL_CONSOLE) [Y/n/?]
Extended dumb serial driver options (CONFIG_SERIAL_EXTENDED) [Y/n/?]
 Support more than 4 serial ports (CONFIG_SERIAL_MANY_PORTS) [Y/n/?]
 Support for sharing serial interrupts (CONFIG_SERIAL_SHARE_IRQ) [Y/n/?]
 Autodetect IRQ on standard ports (unsafe) (CONFIG_SERIAL_DETECT_IRQ) [N/y/?]
 Support special multiport boards (CONFIG_SERIAL_MULTIPORT) [Y/n/?]
 Support the Bell Technologies HUB6 card (CONFIG_HUB6) [N/y/?]
Non-standard serial port support (CONFIG_SERIAL_NONSTANDARD) [Y/n/?]
 Computone IntelliPort Plus serial support (CONFIG_COMPUTONE) [M/n/y/?]
 Comtrol Rocketport support (CONFIG_ROCKETPORT) [M/n/y/?]
 Cyclades async mux support (CONFIG_CYCLADES) [M/n/y/?]
   Cyclades-Z interrupt mode operation (EXPERIMENTAL) (CONFIG_CYZ_INTR) [N/y/?]

 Digiboard Intelligent Async Support (CONFIG_DIGIEPCA) [M/n/y/?]
 Hayes ESP serial port support (CONFIG_ESPSERIAL) [M/n/y/?]
 Moxa Intellio support (CONFIG_MOXA_INTELLIO) [M/n/y/?]
 Moxa SmartIO support (CONFIG_MOXA_SMARTIO) [M/n/y/?]
 Multi-Tech multiport card support (EXPERIMENTAL) (CONFIG_ISI) [M/n/?]
 Microgate SyncLink card support (CONFIG_SYNCLINK) [M/n/?]
 HDLC line discipline support (CONFIG_N_HDLC) [M/n/?]
 SDL RISCom/8 card support (CONFIG_RISCOM8) [M/n/y/?]
 Specialix IO8+ card support (CONFIG_SPECIALIX) [M/n/y/?]
 Specialix DTR/RTS pin is RTS (CONFIG_SPECIALIX_RTSCTS) [Y/n/?]
 Specialix SX (and SI) card support (CONFIG_SX) [M/n/y/?]
 Specialix RIO system support (CONFIG_RIO) [N/y/m/?]
 Stallion multiport serial support (CONFIG_STALDRV) [Y/n/?]
   Stallion EasyIO or EC8/32 support (CONFIG_STALLION) [M/n/y/?]
   Stallion EC8/64, ONboard, Brumby support (CONFIG_ISTALLION) [M/n/y/?]
Unix98 PTY support (CONFIG_UNIX98_PTYS) [Y/n/?]
Maximum number of Unix98 PTYs in use (0-2048) (CONFIG_UNIX98_PTY_COUNT) [256]
Parallel printer support (CONFIG_PRINTER) [M/n/?]
 Support for console on line printer (CONFIG_LP_CONSOLE) [Y/n/?]
Support for user-space parallel port device drivers (CONFIG_PPDEV) [M/n/?]
```

Configuring I2C protocol

I2C — pronounced eye-squared-see — is a protocol developed by Philips
for communication over a a pair or wires at rates between 10 and 100kHz.
System Management Bus (SMBus) is a subset of the I2C protocol. Many
modern motherboards have an SMBus meant for connecting devices such
as EEPROM (electrically erasable programmable read-only memory) and

chips for hardware monitoring. Linux supports the I2C and SMBus protocols. You need this support for Video for Linux. If you have any hardware sensors or video equipment that needs I2C support, answer m to the CONFIG_I2C option and then answer m to the specific driver for your hardware. For example, if you want to use a BT848 frame-grabber board (to capture video), you should answer m to the CONFIG_I2C_ALGOBIT option.

To learn more about the I2C, read the documentation in the /usr/src/ linux*/Documentation/i2c directory. In particular, the summary file briefly describes the I2C and SMBus protocols.

Here are the configuration options related to I2C protocol support:

```
*
* I2C support
*
I2C support (CONFIG_I2C) [M/n/y/?]
I2C bit-banging interfaces (CONFIG_I2C_ALGOBIT) [M/n/?]
  Philips style parallel port adapter (CONFIG_I2C_PHILIPSPAR) [M/n/?]
  ELV adapter (CONFIG_I2C_ELV) [M/n/?]
  Velleman K9000 adapter (CONFIG_I2C_VELLEMAN) [M/n/?]
I2C PCF 8584 interfaces (CONFIG_I2C_ALGOPCF) [M/n/?]
  Elektor ISA card (CONFIG_I2C_ELEKTOR) [M/n/?]
I2C device interface (CONFIG_I2C_CHARDEV) [M/n/?]
```

Specifying the type of mouse

From the next set of options, specify the type of mouse on your PC:

```
*
* Mice
*
Bus Mouse Support (CONFIG_BUSMOUSE) [M/n/y/?]
  ATIXL busmouse support (CONFIG_ATIXL_BUSMOUSE) [M/n/?]
  Logitech busmouse support (CONFIG_LOGIBUSMOUSE) [M/n/?]
  Microsoft busmouse support (CONFIG_MS_BUSMOUSE) [M/n/?]
Mouse Support (not serial and bus mice) (CONFIG_MOUSE) [Y/m/n/?]
  PS/2 mouse (aka "auxiliary device") support (CONFIG_PSMOUSE) [Y/n/?]
  C&T 82C710 mouse port support (as on TI Travelmate) (CONFIG_82C710_MOUSE)
[M/n/y/?]
```

If you have a digitizer pad on an IBM PC110 palmtop, enable the driver module for the pad from the next question:

```
PC110 digitizer pad support (CONFIG_PC110_PAD) [M/n/y/?]
```

Enabling support for joysticks

If you have a joystick or a special game controller (steering wheel, game pad, six-degrees-of-freedom controller), answer y in the CONFIG_JOYSTICK option to include joystick support.

```
*
* Joysticks
*
Joystick support (CONFIG_JOYSTICK) [N/y/?]
```

When you enable CONFIG_JOYSTICK, **you also have to build a device-specific driver by answering** m **to the option for your joystick type. You can enable support for specific joysticks from the following set of options:**

```
*
* Game port support
*
  ns558 gameports (CONFIG_INPUT_NS558) [N/m/?] (NEW)
  PDPI Lightning 4 gamecard (CONFIG_INPUT_LIGHTNING) [N/m/?] (NEW)
  Aureal Vortex and Trident 4DWave gameports (CONFIG_INPUT_PCIGAME) [N/m/?]
(NEW)
*
* Gameport joysticks
*
  Classic PC analog joysticks and gamepads (CONFIG_INPUT_ANALOG) [N/m/?] (NEW)
  Assasin 3D and MadCatz Panther devices (CONFIG_INPUT_A3D) [N/m/?] (NEW)
  Logitech ADI digital joysticks and gamepads (CONFIG_INPUT_ADI) [N/m/?] (NEW)
  Creative Labs Blaster Cobra gamepad (CONFIG_INPUT_COBRA) [N/m/?] (NEW)
  Genius Flight2000 Digital joysticks and gamepads (CONFIG_INPUT_GF2K) [N/m/?]
(NEW)
  Gravis GrIP joysticks and gamepads (CONFIG_INPUT_GRIP) [N/m/?] (NEW)
  InterAct digital joysticks and gamepads (CONFIG_INPUT_INTERACT) [N/m/?] (NEW)
  ThrustMaster DirectConnect joysticks and gamepads (CONFIG_INPUT_TMDC)
[N/m/?](NEW)
  Microsoft SideWinder digital joysticks and gamepads (CONFIG_INPUT_SIDEWINDER)
[N/m/?] (NEW)
*
* Serial port support
*
  Serial port input line discipline (CONFIG_INPUT_SERPORT) [N/m/?] (NEW)
*
* Serial port joysticks
*
  Logitech WingMan Warrior joystick (CONFIG_INPUT_WARRIOR) [N/m/?] (NEW)
  LogiCad3d Magellan/SpaceMouse 6dof controller (CONFIG_INPUT_MAGELLAN) [N/m/?]
(NEW)
  SpaceTec SpaceOrb/Avenger 6dof controller (CONFIG_INPUT_SPACEORB) [N/m/?]
(NEW)
  SpaceTec SpaceBall 4000 FLX 6dof controller (CONFIG_INPUT_SPACEBALL) [N/m/?]
(NEW)
  I-Force/Serial controllers (CONFIG_INPUT_IFORCE_232) [N/m/?] (NEW)
  I-Force/USB controllers (CONFIG_INPUT_IFORCE_USB) [N/m/?] (NEW)
*
* Parallel port joysticks
*
  Multisystem, Sega Genesis, Saturn joysticks and gamepads (CONFIG_INPUT_DB9)
[N/m/?] (NEW)
  Multisystem, NES, SNES, N64, PSX joysticks and gamepads (CONFIG_INPUT_GAMECON)
  [N/m/?] (NEW)
```

```
    Multisystem joysticks via TurboGraFX device (CONFIG_INPUT_TURBOGRAFX)
[N/m/?](NEW)
```

Many of these options are new in Linux kernel version 2.4 and they are
marked as NEW. Note that Linux now supports joysticks that connect to
the serial and parallel ports.

Enabling support for a non-SCSI tape drive

If you have a non-SCSI tape drive that uses the QIC-02 format, you should
answer Yes to the next question; otherwise, answer No:

```
QIC-02 tape support (CONFIG_QIC02_TAPE) [N/y/m/?]
```

Configuring the watchdog timer

Configuration options in the next set enable you to turn on support for the
watchdog timer. This essentially causes the kernel to create a special file; failure to open the file and write to it every minute causes the system to reboot.
There are watchdog boards that can monitor the PC's status (including the
temperature). You can also enable support for specific watchdog cards from
the following options:

```
*
* Watchdog Cards
*
Watchdog Timer Support (CONFIG_WATCHDOG) [Y/n/?]
  Disable watchdog shutdown on close (CONFIG_WATCHDOG_NOWAYOUT) [N/y/?]
  Software Watchdog (CONFIG_SOFT_WATCHDOG) [M/n/y/?]
  WDT Watchdog timer (CONFIG_WDT) [M/n/y/?]
  WDT PCI Watchdog timer (CONFIG_WDTPCI) [M/n/y/?]
    WDT501 features (CONFIG_WDT_501) [N/y/?]
  Berkshire Products PC Watchdog (CONFIG_PCWATCHDOG) [M/n/y/?]
  Acquire SBC Watchdog Timer (CONFIG_ACQUIRE_WDT) [M/n/y/?]
  SBC-60XX Watchdog Timer (CONFIG_60XX_WDT) [N/y/m/?]
  Mixcom Watchdog (CONFIG_MIXCOMWD) [N/y/m/?]
  Intel i810 TCO timer / Watchdog (CONFIG_I810_TCO) [M/n/y/?]
Intel i8x0 Random Number Generator support (CONFIG_INTEL_RNG) [N/y/m/?]
/dev/nvram support (CONFIG_NVRAM) [M/n/y/?]
Enhanced Real Time Clock Support (CONFIG_RTC) [Y/m/n/?]
Double Talk PC internal speech card support (CONFIG_DTLK) [M/n/y/?]
Siemens R3964 line discipline (CONFIG_R3964) [M/n/y/?]
Applicom intelligent fieldbus card support (CONFIG_APPLICOM) [M/n/y/?]
```

If you want access to the PC's nonvolatile (battery-backed) memory —
NVRAM — in the real-time clock, answer Yes to the CONFIG_NVRAM option.
You can get access to the real-time clock by enabling the CONFIG_RTC config-
uration option.

Configuring floppy tape drive

If you have a tape drive connected to your floppy controller, answer y or m to
the next option and then select the other parameters appropriately (or accept
the default choices):

```
*
* Ftape, the floppy tape device driver
*
Ftape (QIC-80/Travan) support (CONFIG_FTAPE) [M/n/y/?]
  Zftape, the VFS interface (CONFIG_ZFTAPE) [M/n/?]
  Default block size (CONFIG_ZFT_DFLT_BLK_SZ) [10240]
*
*   The compressor will be built as a module only!
*
  Number of ftape buffers (EXPERIMENTAL) (CONFIG_FT_NR_BUFFERS) [3]
  Enable procfs status report (+2kb) (CONFIG_FT_PROC_FS) [N/y/?]
Debugging output (Normal, Excessive, Reduced, None) [Normal]
  defined CONFIG_FT_NORMAL_DEBUG
*
* Hardware configuration
*
Floppy tape controllers (Standard, MACH-2, FC-10/FC-20, Alt/82078) [Standard]
  defined CONFIG_FT_STD_FDC
  Default FIFO threshold (EXPERIMENTAL) (CONFIG_FT_FDC_THR) [8]
  Maximal data rate to use (EXPERIMENTAL) (CONFIG_FT_FDC_MAX_RATE) [2000]
```

Configuring graphics support

The next set of options configures support for advanced video cards that can perform hardware-accelerated, 3-D graphics. You can enable the first option to build the AGP (Accelerated Graphics Port) driver, and then answer Yes to the option for your specific chipset.

```
/dev/agpgart (AGP Support) (CONFIG_AGP) [M/n/y/?]
  Intel 440LX/BX/GX and I815/I840 support (CONFIG_AGP_INTEL) [Y/n/?]
  Intel I810/I815 (on-board) support (CONFIG_AGP_I810) [Y/n/?]
  VIA chipset support (CONFIG_AGP_VIA) [Y/n/?]
  AMD Irongate support (CONFIG_AGP_AMD) [Y/n/?]
  Generic SiS support (CONFIG_AGP_SIS) [Y/n/?]
  ALI M1541 support (CONFIG_AGP_ALI) [Y/n/?]
```

Next, you have to configure a set of options for the *Direct Rendering Manager (DRM)* — a device-independent driver that supports the XFree86 *Direct Rendering Infrastructure (DRI)*. DRI is meant for direct access to 3-D graphics hardware in advanced graphics cards, such as 3Dfx Banshee and Voodoo3. To learn more about DRI, use the Web browser to visit the URL http://dri.sourceforge.net/.

If you have a 3-D graphics card, you can answer Yes to CONFIG_DRM and then build the module for the graphics card in your system. If you do not have one of the listed graphics cards, you should answer No to all of these options:

```
Direct Rendering Manager (XFree86 DRI support) (CONFIG_DRM) [Y/n/?]
  3dfx Banshee/Voodoo3+ (CONFIG_DRM_TDFX) [M/n/y/?]
  3dlabs GMX 2000 (CONFIG_DRM_GAMMA) [M/n/y/?]
  ATI Rage 128 (CONFIG_DRM_R128) [M/n/y/?]
  Intel I810 (CONFIG_DRM_I810) [M/n/?]
  Matrox g200/g400 (CONFIG_DRM_MGA) [M/n/?]
```

Configuring audio and video devices

The next set of options involves audio and video devices, including FM radio cards. For more information on these devices, consult the documentation in the /usr/src/linux*/Documentation/video4linux directory.

```
*
* Multimedia devices
*
Video For Linux (CONFIG_VIDEO_DEV) [M/n/y/?]
*
* Video For Linux
*
  V4L information in proc filesystem (CONFIG_VIDEO_PROC_FS) [Y/n/?]
  I2C on parallel port (CONFIG_I2C_PARPORT) [M/n/?]
*
* Video Adapters
*
  BT848 Video For Linux (CONFIG_VIDEO_BT848) [M/n/?]
  Mediavision Pro Movie Studio Video For Linux (CONFIG_VIDEO_PMS) [M/n/?]
  Quickcam BW Video For Linux (CONFIG_VIDEO_BWQCAM) [M/n/?]
  QuickCam Colour Video For Linux (EXPERIMENTAL) (CONFIG_VIDEO_CQCAM) [M/n/?]
  CPiA Video For Linux (CONFIG_VIDEO_CPIA) [M/n/?]
    CPiA Parallel Port Lowlevel Support (CONFIG_VIDEO_CPIA_PP) [M/n/?]
    CPiA USB Lowlevel Support (CONFIG_VIDEO_CPIA_USB) [M/n/?]
  SAA5249 Teletext processor (CONFIG_VIDEO_SAA5249) [M/n/?]
  SAB3036 tuner (CONFIG_TUNER_3036) [M/n/?]
  Stradis 4:2:2 MPEG-2 video driver  (EXPERIMENTAL) (CONFIG_VIDEO_STRADIS)
[M/n/?]
  Zoran ZR36057/36060 Video For Linux (CONFIG_VIDEO_ZORAN) [M/n/?]
    Include support for Iomega Buz (CONFIG_VIDEO_BUZ) [M/n/?]
  Zoran ZR36120/36125 Video For Linux (CONFIG_VIDEO_ZR36120) [M/n/?]
*
* Radio Adapters
*
  ADS Cadet AM/FM Tuner (CONFIG_RADIO_CADET) [M/n/?]
  AIMSlab RadioTrack (aka RadioReveal) support (CONFIG_RADIO_RTRACK) [M/n/?]
  AIMSlab RadioTrack II support (CONFIG_RADIO_RTRACK2) [M/n/?]
  Aztech/Packard Bell Radio (CONFIG_RADIO_AZTECH) [M/n/?]
  GemTek Radio Card support (CONFIG_RADIO_GEMTEK) [M/n/?]
  Maestro on board radio (CONFIG_RADIO_MAESTRO) [M/n/?]
  Miro PCM20 Radio (CONFIG_RADIO_MIROPCM20) [M/n/?]
  SF16FMI Radio (CONFIG_RADIO_SF16FMI) [M/n/?]
  TerraTec ActiveRadio ISA Standalone (CONFIG_RADIO_TERRATEC) [M/n/?]
  Trust FM radio card (CONFIG_RADIO_TRUST) [M/n/?]
  Typhoon Radio (a.k.a. EcoRadio) (CONFIG_RADIO_TYPHOON) [M/n/?]
    Support for /proc/radio-typhoon (CONFIG_RADIO_TYPHOON_PROC_FS) [Y/n/?]
  Zoltrix Radio (CONFIG_RADIO_ZOLTRIX) [M/n/?]
```

Enabling support for specific file systems

The next set of options enables you to turn on support for specific types of file systems. You can make your choices based on the guidelines shown in Table 25-1.

Table 25-1   Common File System Configuration Options

Option	Description
CONFIG_ADFS_FS	Enables Linux to read from the ADFS — the Acorn Disc Filing System — the standard file system of the RiscOS operating system that runs on Acorn's ARM-based Risc PC systems and the Acorn Archimedes systems. Answer y if you want Linux to read from ADFS partitions on hard drives and from ADFS floppy disks.
CONFIG_AFFS_FS	Enables support for the Fast File System (FFS) — the file system used by Amiga systems since AmigaOS version 1.3 (34.20). Answer y if you need to read from and write to an Amiga FFS partition on your hard drive. Note that this support does not enable Linux to read from Amiga floppy disks because of an incompatibility of the floppy controller used in an Amiga and the standard floppy controller in PCs.
CONFIG_CODA_FS	Enables support for Coda, an advanced network file system that is similar to NFS but that better supports disconnected operation (for example, laptops) and is a better security model. Answer y only if you need your Linux system to act as a Coda client. Consult the file /usr/src/ linux*/ Documentation/filesystems/coda.txt for more information.
CONFIG_EXT2_FS	Enables support for the second extended file system — the current standard file system for Linux. You should definitely answer y to turn on this option.
CONFIG_FAT_FS	Turns on support for any File Allocation Table (FAT)-based file system (including MS-DOS and Windows 95 VFAT file systems). Answer y if you want to access MS-DOS or VFAT files.
CONFIG_HFS_FS	Enables Linux to mount Macintosh-formatted floppy disks and hard drive partitions with full read/write access. Answer y if you want to access Macintosh file systems.
CONFIG_HPFS_FS	Enables your Linux system to access and read an OS/2 HPFS file system (you can only read HPFS files). Answer y if you have an OS/2 partition on your hard disk.
CONFIG_ISO9660_FS	Turns on support for the standard ISO 9660 file system used on CD-ROMs (this is also known as the High Sierra File System and is referred to as hsfs on some UNIX workstations). If you have a CD-ROM drive, answer y here.

Option	Description
CONFIG_JOLIET	Enables support for Microsoft's Joliet extension for the ISO 9660 CD-ROM file system, which allows for long filenames in Unicode format (Unicode is the new 16-bit character code that can encode the characters of almost all languages of the world.) Answer y if you want to be able to read Joliet CD-ROMs under Linux.
CONFIG_MINIX_FS	Supports the Minix file system — the original file system of Linux. This simple file system still functions on floppy disks, so you should answer m to include support in the form of a module.
CONFIG_MSDOS_FS	Supports MS-DOS file systems. Press y if you want to read an MS-DOS partition on the hard disk or an MS-DOS floppy.
CONFIG_NFS_FS	Enables you to mount Network File System (NFS) directories from other systems on a network. Answer y if you want to access NFS directories.
CONFIG_NTFS_FS	Enables Linux to read from the NT file system (NTFS) — the file system used by Microsoft Windows NT. Answer y here for read-only access to an NTFS partition on the hard disk.
CONFIG_PROC_FS	Turns on support for the /proc virtual file system through which you can get information about the kernel. (For example, type the cat /proc/interrupts command to list the IRQs used by the system.) The /proc file system does not exist on the disk; files are created when you access them. You should answer y to enable this option because it is useful and several Linux system utilities rely on the /proc file system.
CONFIG_QNX4FS_FS	Supports the file system used by the QNX 4 operating system — a popular real-time operating system (http://www.qnx.com/). Answer y if you intend to mount QNX hard disks or floppies for read-only access.
CONFIG_QUOTA	Turns on disk quota so you can limit each user's disk space. Answer y only if your system has many users and you want to implement disk quota for the ext2 file system.
CONFIG_ROMFS_FS	Turns on support for a very small, read-only, memory-resident file system used in the initial RAM disk (initrd) during Red Hat Linux installation. Answer y to include support for this file system. Consult the file /usr/src/linux*/Documentation/filesystems/romfs.txt for more information.
CONFIG_SMB_FS	Enables your Linux system to access shared directories from networked PCs running Windows 95/98/NT/2000 or Windows for Workgroups. Answer y if you want to access shared directories on Windows systems.

Continued

Table 25-1 *(continued)*

Option	Description
CONFIG_SYSV_FS	Turns on support for the System V file system used by SCO, Xenix, and Coherent variants of UNIX for Intel PCs. If you need to access a System V file system, answer y here.
CONFIG_UFS_FS	Allows your Linux system to read to (but not write to) the UFS file system used by the BSD (Berkeley Software Distribution) variants of UNIX (such as SunOS, FreeBSD, NetBSD, and NeXTstep). Answer y if you need to access any UFS file system. If you also want to write to UFS file systems, answer y to the experimental CONFIG_UFS_FS_WRITE option.
CONFIG_UMSDOS_FS	Supports the UMSDOS file system, which stores a Linux file system in an MS-DOS partition. You can safely answer n.
CONFIG_VFAT_FS	Supports Windows 95/98/NT/2000 VFAT file systems with long filenames. Answer y if your system has partitions with VFAT file systems, or you expect to read floppy disks with Windows files.

The following listing shows the available choices for these file system configuration options:

```
*
* File systems
*
Quota support (CONFIG_QUOTA) [Y/n/?]
Kernel automounter support (CONFIG_AUTOFS_FS) [M/n/y/?]
Kernel automounter version 4 support (also supports v3) (CONFIG_AUTOFS4_FS)
[M/n/y/?]
ADFS file system support (CONFIG_ADFS_FS) [N/y/m/?]
Amiga FFS file system support (EXPERIMENTAL) (CONFIG_AFFS_FS) [N/y/m/?]
Apple Macintosh file system support (EXPERIMENTAL) (CONFIG_HFS_FS) [M/n/y/?]
BFS file system support (EXPERIMENTAL) (CONFIG_BFS_FS) [M/n/y/?]
DOS FAT fs support (CONFIG_FAT_FS) [M/n/y/?]
  MSDOS fs support (CONFIG_MSDOS_FS) [M/n/y/?]
    UMSDOS: Unix-like file system on top of standard MSDOS fs (CONFIG_UMSDOS_FS)
[M/n/?]
  VFAT (Windows-95) fs support (CONFIG_VFAT_FS) [M/n/?]
EFS file system support (read only) (EXPERIMENTAL) (CONFIG_EFS_FS) [N/y/m/?]
Compressed ROM file system support (CONFIG_CRAMFS) [M/n/y/?]
Simple RAM-based file system support (CONFIG_RAMFS) [M/n/y/?]
ISO 9660 CDROM file system support (CONFIG_ISO9660_FS) [Y/m/n/?]
  Microsoft Joliet CDROM extensions (CONFIG_JOLIET) [Y/n/?]
Minix fs support (CONFIG_MINIX_FS) [M/n/y/?]
NTFS file system support (read only) (CONFIG_NTFS_FS) [N/y/m/?]
OS/2 HPFS file system support (CONFIG_HPFS_FS) [M/n/y/?]
```

```
/proc file system support (CONFIG_PROC_FS) [Y/n/?]
/dev file system support (EXPERIMENTAL) (CONFIG_DEVFS_FS) [N/y/?]
/dev/pts file system for Unix98 PTYs (CONFIG_DEVPTS_FS) [Y/n/?]
QNX4 file system support (read only) (EXPERIMENTAL) (CONFIG_QNX4FS_FS) [N/y/m/?]

ROM file system support (CONFIG_ROMFS_FS) [M/n/y/?]
Second extended fs support (CONFIG_EXT2_FS) [Y/m/n/?]
System V and Coherent file system support (read only) (CONFIG_SYSV_FS) [M/n/y/?]

  SYSV file system write support (DANGEROUS) (CONFIG_SYSV_FS_WRITE) [N/y/?]
UDF file system support (read only) (CONFIG_UDF_FS) [M/n/y/?]
  UDF write support (DANGEROUS) (CONFIG_UDF_RW) [N/y/?]
UFS file system support (read only) (CONFIG_UFS_FS) [M/n/y/?]
  UFS file system write support (DANGEROUS) (CONFIG_UFS_FS_WRITE) [N/y/?]
*
* Network File Systems
*
Coda file system support (advanced network fs) (CONFIG_CODA_FS) [M/n/y/?]
NFS file system support (CONFIG_NFS_FS) [M/n/y/?]
  Provide NFSv3 client support (CONFIG_NFS_V3) [Y/n/?]
NFS server support (CONFIG_NFSD) [M/n/y/?]
  Provide NFSv3 server support (CONFIG_NFSD_V3) [Y/n/?]
SMB file system support (to mount Windows shares etc.) (CONFIG_SMB_FS) [M/n/y/?]

  Use a default NLS (CONFIG_SMB_NLS_DEFAULT) [N/y/?]
NCP file system support (to mount NetWare volumes) (CONFIG_NCP_FS) [M/n/y/?]
  Packet signatures (CONFIG_NCPFS_PACKET_SIGNING) [Y/n/?]
  Proprietary file locking (CONFIG_NCPFS_IOCTL_LOCKING) [Y/n/?]
  Clear remove/delete inhibit when needed (CONFIG_NCPFS_STRONG) [Y/n/?]
  Use NFS namespace if available (CONFIG_NCPFS_NFS_NS) [Y/n/?]
  Use LONG (OS/2) namespace if available (CONFIG_NCPFS_OS2_NS) [Y/n/?]
  Lowercase DOS filenames (CONFIG_NCPFS_SMALLDOS) [Y/n/?]
  Allow mounting of volume subdirectories (CONFIG_NCPFS_MOUNT_SUBDIR) [Y/n/?]
  NDS authentication support (CONFIG_NCPFS_NDS_DOMAINS) [N/y/?]
  Use Native Language Support (CONFIG_NCPFS_NLS) [Y/n/?]
  Enable symbolic links and execute flags (CONFIG_NCPFS_EXTRAS) [Y/n/?]
```

Linux can read and manipulate disk partitions created by many different systems. The next option enables you to include support for specific partition types:

```
*
* Partition Types
*
Advanced partition selection (CONFIG_PARTITION_ADVANCED) [N/y/?]
```

If you press y, you can enable support for specific partitions from the following list:

```
  Acorn partition support (CONFIG_ACORN_PARTITION) [N/y/?] (NEW)
  Alpha OSF partition support (CONFIG_OSF_PARTITION) [N/y/?] (NEW)
  Amiga partition table support (CONFIG_AMIGA_PARTITION) [N/y/?] (NEW)
  Atari partition table support (CONFIG_ATARI_PARTITION) [N/y/?] (NEW)
```

```
    Macintosh partition map support (CONFIG_MAC_PARTITION) [N/y/?] (NEW)
    PC BIOS (MSDOS partition tables) support (CONFIG_MSDOS_PARTITION) [Y/n/?]
      BSD disklabel (FreeBSD partition tables) support (CONFIG_BSD_DISKLABEL)
[N/y/?] (NEW)
      Solaris (x86) partition table support (CONFIG_SOLARIS_X86_PARTITION) [N/y/?]
(NEW)
      Unixware slices support (CONFIG_UNIXWARE_DISKLABEL) [N/y/?] (NEW)
    SGI partition support (CONFIG_SGI_PARTITION) [N/y/?] (NEW)
    Ultrix partition table support (CONFIG_ULTRIX_PARTITION) [N/y/?] (NEW)
    Sun partition tables support (CONFIG_SUN_PARTITION) [N/y/?] (NEW)
```

Selecting a native language character set

Next comes a set of configuration options that requires you to select a native
language character set. The Microsoft FAT file systems use these character
sets to store and display filenames in one of several languages. The character
sets are stored in files called DOS *codepages*. You have to include the appropriate codepages so that the Linux kernel can read and write filenames correctly in any DOS partitions in the hard disk. Note that the codepages apply
only to filenames; they have nothing to do with the actual contents of files.

You can include support for as many codepages as you want. Answer Yes to
the codepages for your selection of languages from the following set:

```
*
* Native Language Support
*
Default NLS Option (CONFIG_NLS_DEFAULT) [iso8859-1]
Codepage 437 (United States, Canada) (CONFIG_NLS_CODEPAGE_437) [M/n/y/?]
Codepage 737 (Greek) (CONFIG_NLS_CODEPAGE_737) [M/n/y/?]
Codepage 775 (Baltic Rim) (CONFIG_NLS_CODEPAGE_775) [M/n/y/?]
Codepage 850 (Europe) (CONFIG_NLS_CODEPAGE_850) [M/n/y/?]
Codepage 852 (Central/Eastern Europe) (CONFIG_NLS_CODEPAGE_852) [M/n/y/?]
Codepage 855 (Cyrillic) (CONFIG_NLS_CODEPAGE_855) [M/n/y/?]
Codepage 857 (Turkish) (CONFIG_NLS_CODEPAGE_857) [M/n/y/?]
Codepage 860 (Portugese) (CONFIG_NLS_CODEPAGE_860) [M/n/y/?]
Codepage 861 (Icelandic) (CONFIG_NLS_CODEPAGE_861) [M/n/y/?]
Codepage 862 (Hebrew) (CONFIG_NLS_CODEPAGE_862) [M/n/y/?]
Codepage 863 (Canadian French) (CONFIG_NLS_CODEPAGE_863) [M/n/y/?]
Codepage 864 (Arabic) (CONFIG_NLS_CODEPAGE_864) [M/n/y/?]
Codepage 865 (Norwegian, Danish) (CONFIG_NLS_CODEPAGE_865) [M/n/y/?]
Codepage 866 (Cyrillic/Russian) (CONFIG_NLS_CODEPAGE_866) [M/n/y/?]
Codepage 869 (Greek) (CONFIG_NLS_CODEPAGE_869) [M/n/y/?]
Codepage 874 (Thai) (CONFIG_NLS_CODEPAGE_874) [M/n/y/?]
Codepage 932 (Shift-JIS, EUC-JP) (CONFIG_NLS_CODEPAGE_932) [M/n/y/?]
Codepage 936 (GBK) (CONFIG_NLS_CODEPAGE_936) [M/n/y/?]
Codepage 949 (UnifiedHangul) (CONFIG_NLS_CODEPAGE_949) [M/n/y/?]
Codepage 950 (Big5) (CONFIG_NLS_CODEPAGE_950) [M/n/y/?]
NLS ISO 8859-1  (Latin 1; Western European Languages) (CONFIG_NLS_ISO8859_1)
[M/n/y/?]
NLS ISO 8859-2  (Latin 2; Slavic/Central European Languages)
(CONFIG_NLS_ISO8859_2) [M/n/y/?]
NLS ISO 8859-3  (Latin 3; Esperanto, Galician, Maltese, Turkish)
(CONFIG_NLS_ISO8859_3) [M/n/y/?]
```

```
NLS ISO 8859-4  (Latin 4; Estonian, Latvian, Lithuanian) (CONFIG_NLS_ISO8859_4)
[M/n/y/?]
NLS ISO 8859-5  (Cyrillic) (CONFIG_NLS_ISO8859_5) [M/n/y/?]
NLS ISO 8859-6  (Arabic) (CONFIG_NLS_ISO8859_6) [M/n/y/?]
NLS ISO 8859-7  (Modern Greek) (CONFIG_NLS_ISO8859_7) [M/n/y/?]
NLS ISO 8859-8  (Hebrew) (CONFIG_NLS_ISO8859_8) [M/n/y/?]
NLS ISO 8859-9  (Latin 5; Turkish) (CONFIG_NLS_ISO8859_9) [M/n/y/?]
NLS ISO 8859-14 (Latin 8; Celtic) (CONFIG_NLS_ISO8859_14) [M/n/y/?]
NLS ISO 8859-15 (Latin 9; Western European Languages with Euro)
(CONFIG_NLS_ISO8859_15) [M/n/y/?]
NLS KOI8-R (Russian) (CONFIG_NLS_KOI8_R) [M/n/y/?]
NLS UTF8 (CONFIG_NLS_UTF8) [M/n/y/?]
```

Configuring the console drivers

After selecting the natural language support for DOS file systems, you have to configure the console drivers that the kernel can use to display text output without the X Window System. You definitely want to answer Yes to the `CONFIG_VGA_CONSOLE` option, because that allows the kernel to display output in text mode using generic VGA mode (supported by nearly all video cards). Most of the other console drivers are experimental in nature. A new feature is the `CONFIG_FB` option, which can enable support for frame buffer devices. A *frame buffer* is an abstraction for the graphics hardware so that the kernel and other software can produce graphical output without having to rely on low-level details (such as hardware registers) of a video card. As you can see from the following list of options, frame buffer support is available for a few specific video cards:

```
*
* Console drivers
*
VGA text console (CONFIG_VGA_CONSOLE) [Y/n/?]
Video mode selection support (CONFIG_VIDEO_SELECT) [Y/n/?]
Ignore bad video mode selections (CONFIG_VIDEO_IGNORE_BAD_MODE) [N/y/?]
MDA text console (dual-headed) (EXPERIMENTAL) (CONFIG_MDA_CONSOLE) [M/n/y/?]
*
* Frame-buffer support
*
Support for frame buffer devices (EXPERIMENTAL) (CONFIG_FB) [Y/n/?]
  nVidia Riva support (EXPERIMENTAL) (CONFIG_FB_RIVA) [M/n/y/?]
  Cirrus Logic support (EXPERIMENTAL) (CONFIG_FB_CLGEN) [M/n/y/?]
  Permedia2 support (EXPERIMENTAL) (CONFIG_FB_PM2) [M/n/y/?]
  Cyber2000 support (CONFIG_FB_CYBER2000) [N/y/m/?]
  VESA VGA graphics console (CONFIG_FB_VESA) [Y/n/?]
  VGA 16-color graphics console (CONFIG_FB_VGA16) [N/y/m/?]
  Hercules mono graphics console (EXPERIMENTAL) (CONFIG_FB_HGA) [M/n/y/?]
  Matrox acceleration (EXPERIMENTAL) (CONFIG_FB_MATROX) [M/n/y/?]
    Millennium I/II support (CONFIG_FB_MATROX_MILLENIUM) [Y/n/?]
    Mystique support (CONFIG_FB_MATROX_MYSTIQUE) [Y/n/?]
    G100/G200/G400 support (CONFIG_FB_MATROX_G100) [Y/n/?]
      Matrox I2C support (CONFIG_FB_MATROX_I2C) [M/n/?]
      G400 second head support (CONFIG_FB_MATROX_MAVEN) [N/m/?]
    Multihead support (CONFIG_FB_MATROX_MULTIHEAD) [Y/n/?]
```

```
ATI Mach64 display support (EXPERIMENTAL) (CONFIG_FB_ATY) [M/n/y/?]
ATI Rage 128 display support (EXPERIMENTAL) (CONFIG_FB_ATY128) [M/n/y/?]
3Dfx Banshee/Voodoo3 display support (EXPERIMENTAL) (CONFIG_FB_3DFX) [M/n/y/?]

SIS 630/540 display support (EXPERIMENTAL) (CONFIG_FB_SIS) [N/y/m/?]
Virtual Frame Buffer support (ONLY FOR TESTING!) (CONFIG_FB_VIRTUAL) [N/y/m/?]

Advanced low level driver options (CONFIG_FBCON_ADVANCED) [N/y/?]
Support only 8 pixels wide fonts (CONFIG_FBCON_FONTWIDTH8_ONLY) [N/y/?]
Select compiled-in fonts (CONFIG_FBCON_FONTS) [N/y/?]
```

Configuring the sound card

The next set of options involves sound-card support. If you have a sound
card installed, start by answering y or m to the CONFIG_SOUND option. After
that, you have to answer a number of questions about various sound cards.
You can always answer m to build the sound support in the form of modules
that you can load when needed. Here is a typical listing of sound-related
options:

```
*
* Sound
*
Sound card support (CONFIG_SOUND) [M/n/y/?]
  C-Media PCI (CMI8338/8378) (CONFIG_SOUND_CMPCI) [M/n/?]
    Enable S/PDIF loop for CMI8738 (CONFIG_SOUND_CMPCI_SPDIFLOOP) [Y/n/?]
    Enable 4 channel mode for CMI8738 (CONFIG_SOUND_CMPCI_4CH) [Y/n/?]
    Separate rear out jack (CONFIG_SOUND_CMPCI_REAR) [Y/n/?]
  Creative SBLive! (EMU10K1) (CONFIG_SOUND_EMU10K1) [M/n/?]
  Crystal SoundFusion (CS4280/461x) (CONFIG_SOUND_FUSION) [M/n/?]
  Crystal Sound CS4281 (CONFIG_SOUND_CS4281) [M/n/?]
  Ensoniq AudioPCI (ES1370) (CONFIG_SOUND_ES1370) [M/n/?]
  Creative Ensoniq AudioPCI 97 (ES1371) (CONFIG_SOUND_ES1371) [M/n/?]
  ESS Technology Solo1 (CONFIG_SOUND_ESSSOLO1) [M/n/?]
  ESS Maestro, Maestro2, Maestro2E driver (CONFIG_SOUND_MAESTRO) [M/n/?]
  S3 SonicVibes (CONFIG_SOUND_SONICVIBES) [M/n/?]
  Trident 4DWave DX/NX, SiS 7018 or ALi 5451 PCI Audio Core
(CONFIG_SOUND_TRIDENT) [M/n/?]
  Support for Turtle Beach MultiSound Classic, Tahiti, Monterey
(CONFIG_SOUND_MSNDCLAS) [M/n/?]
Full pathname of MSNDINIT.BIN firmware file (CONFIG_MSNDCLAS_INIT_FILE)
[/etc/sound/msndinit.bin]
Full pathname of MSNDPERM.BIN firmware file (CONFIG_MSNDCLAS_PERM_FILE)
[/etc/sound/msndperm.bin]
  Support for Turtle Beach MultiSound Pinnacle, Fiji (CONFIG_SOUND_MSNDPIN)
[M/n/?]
  Full pathname of PNDSPINI.BIN firmware file (CONFIG_MSNDPIN_INIT_FILE)
[/etc/sound/pndspini.bin]
  Full pathname of PNDSPERM.BIN firmware file (CONFIG_MSNDPIN_PERM_FILE)
[/etc/sound/pndsperm.bin]
  VIA 82C686 Audio Codec (CONFIG_SOUND_VIA82CXXX) [M/n/y/?]
  OSS sound modules (CONFIG_SOUND_OSS) [M/n/?]
    Verbose initialisation (CONFIG_SOUND_TRACEINIT) [N/y/?]
```

```
        Persistent DMA buffers (CONFIG_SOUND_DMAP) [Y/n/?]
    AD1816(A) based cards (EXPERIMENTAL) (CONFIG_SOUND_AD1816) [M/n/?]
    Aztech Sound Galaxy (non-PnP) cards (CONFIG_SOUND_SGALAXY) [M/n/?]
    Adlib Cards (CONFIG_SOUND_ADLIB) [M/n/?]
    ACI mixer (miroPCM12) (CONFIG_SOUND_ACI_MIXER) [M/n/?]
    Crystal CS4232 based (PnP) cards (CONFIG_SOUND_CS4232) [M/n/?]
    Ensoniq SoundScape support (CONFIG_SOUND_SSCAPE) [M/n/?]
    Gravis Ultrasound support (CONFIG_SOUND_GUS) [M/n/?]
      16 bit sampling option of GUS (_NOT_ GUS MAX) (CONFIG_SOUND_GUS16) [Y/n/?]
      GUS MAX support (CONFIG_SOUND_GUSMAX) [Y/n/?]
    Intel ICH audio support (CONFIG_SOUND_ICH) [M/n/?]
    Loopback MIDI device support (CONFIG_SOUND_VMIDI) [M/n/?]
    MediaTrix AudioTrix Pro support (CONFIG_SOUND_TRIX) [M/n/?]
    Microsoft Sound System support (CONFIG_SOUND_MSS) [M/n/?]
    MPU-401 support (NOT for SB16) (CONFIG_SOUND_MPU401) [M/n/?]
    NM256AV/NM256ZX audio support (CONFIG_SOUND_NM256) [M/n/?]
    OPTi MAD16 and/or Mozart based cards (CONFIG_SOUND_MAD16) [M/n/?]
      Support MIDI in older MAD16 based cards (requires SB)
(CONFIG_MAD16_OLDCARD) [Y/n/?]
    ProAudioSpectrum 16 support (CONFIG_SOUND_PAS) [M/n/?]
    PSS (AD1848, ADSP-2115, ESC614) support (CONFIG_SOUND_PSS) [M/n/?]
      Enable PSS mixer (Beethoven ADSP-16 and other compatibile)
(CONFIG_PSS_MIXER) [N/y/?]
        Have DSPxxx.LD firmware file (CONFIG_PSS_HAVE_BOOT) [N/y/?]
    100% Sound Blaster compatibles (SB16/32/64, ESS, Jazz16) support
(CONFIG_SOUND_SB) [M/n/?]
    AWE32 synth (CONFIG_SOUND_AWE32_SYNTH) [M/n/?]
    Full support for Turtle Beach WaveFront (Tropez Plus, Tropez, Maui)
synth/soundcards (CONFIG_SOUND_WAVEFRONT) [M/n/?]
    Limited support for Turtle Beach Wave Front (Maui, Tropez) synthesizers
(CONFIG_SOUND_MAUI) [M/n/?]
    Yamaha FM synthesizer (YM3812/OPL-3) support (CONFIG_SOUND_YM3812) [M/n/?]
    Yamaha OPL3-SA1 audio controller (CONFIG_SOUND_OPL3SA1) [M/n/?]
    Yamaha OPL3-SA2, SA3, and SAx based PnP cards (CONFIG_SOUND_OPL3SA2) [M/n/?]

    Yamaha PCI legacy mode support (CONFIG_SOUND_YMPCI) [M/n/?]
    6850 UART support (CONFIG_SOUND_UART6850) [M/n/?]
    Gallant Audio Cards (SC-6000 and SC-6600 based) (CONFIG_SOUND_AEDSP16)
[M/n/?]
      SC-6600 based audio cards (new Audio Excel DSP 16) (CONFIG_SC6600) [Y/n/?]

        Activate SC-6600 Joystick Interface (CONFIG_SC6600_JOY) [Y/n/?]
        SC-6600 CDROM Interface (4=None, 3=IDE, 1=Panasonic, 0=?Sony?)
(CONFIG_SC6600_CDROM) [4]
        SC-6600 CDROM Interface I/O Address (CONFIG_SC6600_CDROMBASE) [0]
      Audio Excel DSP 16 (SBPro emulation) (CONFIG_AEDSP16_SBPRO) [Y/n/?]
      Audio Excel DSP 16 (MPU401 emulation) (CONFIG_AEDSP16_MPU401) [Y/n/?]
  TV card (bt848) mixer support (CONFIG_SOUND_TVMIXER) [M/n/?]
```

Enabling USB support

The next set of options enables support for the *Universal Serial Bus (USB)* —
a serial bus that comes built into most new PCs. USB supports data-transfer
rates as high as 12Mbps — 12 million bits per second or 1.5 megabytes per

second—compared with 115Kbps or the 0.115Mbps transfer rate of a standard serial port (such as COM1). You can daisy-chain up to 127 devices on a USB bus. The bus also provides power to the devices, and you can attach or remove devices while the PC is running—a capability commonly referred to as *hot swapping*. USB can replace the functionality of the PC's serial and parallel ports, as well as the keyboard and mouse ports. Many PC peripherals—such as mouse, keyboard, printer, scanner, modem, digital camera, and so on—are designed to connect to the PC through a USB port.

The options for USB support are as follows:

```
*
* USB support
*
Support for USB (CONFIG_USB) [M/n/y/?]
  USB verbose debug messages (CONFIG_USB_DEBUG) [N/y/?]
*
* Miscellaneous USB options
*
  Preliminary USB device filesystem (CONFIG_USB_DEVICEFS) [Y/n/?]
  Enforce USB bandwidth allocation (EXPERIMENTAL) (CONFIG_USB_BANDWIDTH) [N/y/?]

*
* USB Controllers
*
  UHCI (Intel PIIX4, VIA, ...) support (CONFIG_USB_UHCI) [M/n/?]
  UHCI Alternate Driver (JE) support (CONFIG_USB_UHCI_ALT) [M/n/?]
  OHCI (Compaq, iMacs, OPTi, SiS, ALi, ...) support (CONFIG_USB_OHCI) [M/n/?]
*
* USB Devices
*
  USB Printer support (CONFIG_USB_PRINTER) [M/n/?]
  USB Scanner support (CONFIG_USB_SCANNER) [M/n/?]
  Microtek X6USB scanner support (EXPERIMENTAL) (CONFIG_USB_MICROTEK) [M/n/?]
  USB Audio support (CONFIG_USB_AUDIO) [M/n/?]
  USB Modem (CDC ACM) support (CONFIG_USB_ACM) [M/n/?]
  USB Serial Converter support (CONFIG_USB_SERIAL) [M/n/?]
    USB Generic Serial Driver (CONFIG_USB_SERIAL_GENERIC) [Y/n/?]
    USB Handspring Visor Driver (CONFIG_USB_SERIAL_VISOR) [M/n/?]
    USB Digi International AccelePort USB Serial Driver
(CONFIG_USB_SERIAL_DIGI_ACCELEPORT) [M/n/?]
    USB ConnectTech WhiteHEAT Serial Driver (EXPERIMENTAL)
(CONFIG_USB_SERIAL_WHITEHEAT) [M/n/?]
    USB FTDI Single Port Serial Driver (EXPERIMENTAL)
(CONFIG_USB_SERIAL_FTDI_SIO) [M/n/?]
    USB Keyspan PDA Single Port Serial Driver (EXPERIMENTAL)
(CONFIG_USB_SERIAL_KEYSPAN_PDA) [M/n/?]
    USB Keyspan USA-xxx Serial Driver (EXPERIMENTAL) (CONFIG_USB_SERIAL_KEYSPAN)
  [M/n/?]
      USB Keyspan USA-28 Firmware (CONFIG_USB_SERIAL_KEYSPAN_USA28) [N/y/?]
      USB Keyspan USA-28X Firmware (CONFIG_USB_SERIAL_KEYSPAN_USA28X) [N/y/?]
      USB Keyspan USA-19 Firmware (CONFIG_USB_SERIAL_KEYSPAN_USA19) [N/y/?]
      USB Keyspan USA-18X Firmware (CONFIG_USB_SERIAL_KEYSPAN_USA18X) [N/y/?]
```

```
        USB Keyspan USA-19W Firmware (CONFIG_USB_SERIAL_KEYSPAN_USA19W) [N/y/?]
      USB ZyXEL omni.net LCD Plus Driver (EXPERIMENTAL)
(CONFIG_USB_SERIAL_OMNINET) [M/n/?]
      USB Belkin and Peracom Single Port Serial Driver (EXPERIMENTAL)
(CONFIG_USB_SERIAL_BELKIN) [M/n/?]
       USB Serial Converter verbose debug (CONFIG_USB_SERIAL_DEBUG) [N/y/?]
    USB IBM (Xirlink) C-it Camera support (CONFIG_USB_IBMCAM) [M/n/?]
    USB OV511 Camera support (CONFIG_USB_OV511) [M/n/?]
    USB Kodak DC-2xx Camera support (CONFIG_USB_DC2XX) [M/n/?]
    USB Mustek MDC800 Digital Camera support (EXPERIMENTAL) (CONFIG_USB_MDC800)
    [M/n/?]
    USB Mass Storage support (CONFIG_USB_STORAGE) [M/n/?]
       USB Mass Storage verbose debug (CONFIG_USB_STORAGE_DEBUG) [N/y/?]
    USS720 parport driver (CONFIG_USB_USS720) [M/n/?]
    DABUSB driver (CONFIG_USB_DABUSB) [M/n/?]
    PLUSB Prolific USB-Network driver (EXPERIMENTAL) (CONFIG_USB_PLUSB) [M/n/?]
    USB ADMtek Pegasus-based ethernet device support (EXPERIMENTAL)
(CONFIG_USB_PEGASUS) [M/n/?]
    USB Diamond Rio500 support (EXPERIMENTAL) (CONFIG_USB_RIO500) [M/n/?]
    D-Link USB FM radio support (EXPERIMENTAL) (CONFIG_USB_DSBR) [M/n/?]
    USB Bluetooth support (EXPERIMENTAL) (CONFIG_USB_BLUETOOTH) [M/n/?]
    NetChip 1080-based USB Host-to-Host Link (EXPERIMENTAL) (CONFIG_USB_NET1080)
    [M/n/?]
*
* USB Human Interface Devices (HID)
*
    USB Human Interface Device (full HID) support (CONFIG_USB_HID) [M/n/?]
    USB HIDBP Keyboard (basic) support (CONFIG_USB_KBD) [M/n/?]
    USB HIDBP Mouse (basic) support (CONFIG_USB_MOUSE) [M/n/?]
    Wacom Intuos/Graphire tablet support (CONFIG_USB_WACOM) [M/n/?]
```

As the long list of options shows, the Linux kernel can support USB devices. If your PC has a USB port, you should answer y or m to the CONFIG_USB option. Then you have to answer m to the CONFIG_USB_UHCI or CONFIG_USB_OHCI option, depending on the type of USB interface — UHCI (Intel) or OHCI (Compaq and others) — that your PC has. To determine the type of USB interface, use the /sbin/lspci command and look for the USB controller's make and model in the output. For example, here's the output from /sbin/lspci for a PC with a USB port:

```
/sbin/lspci
00:00.0 Host bridge: Intel Corporation 430TX - 82439TX MTXC (rev 01)
00:07.0 ISA bridge: Intel Corporation 82371AB PIIX4 ISA (rev 01)
00:07.1 IDE interface: Intel Corporation 82371AB PIIX4 IDE (rev 01)
00:07.2 USB Controller: Intel Corporation 82371AB PIIX4 USB (rev 01)
00:07.3 Bridge: Intel Corporation 82371AB PIIX4 ACPI (rev 01)
00:0d.0 VGA compatible controller: S3 Inc. ViRGE/DX or /GX (rev 01)
```

As the fourth line of output shows, this PC has an Intel USB controller. Therefore, I need the driver module for the Intel UHCI support (CONFIG_USB_UHCI option).

After you select the UHCI or OHCI interface support, you have to build the driver modules for specific USB devices on your system. For more information on USB devices, consult the documentation in the `/usr/src/linux*/Documentation/usb` directory—especially the links in the `usb-help.txt` file.

Enabling support for kernel debugging

The next and final option enables you to use the SysRq key (equivalent to pressing Alt+PrintScreen) to get important status information right after a system crash. This information is useful if you are a Linux developer who expects to debug the kernel. Most users answer No (because most users run a stable version of the kernel and do not expect to fix kernel errors) to disable this option:

```
*
* Kernel hacking
*
Magic SysRq key (CONFIG_MAGIC_SYSRQ) [Y/n/?] n
```

The kernel configuration session ends with the following message that tells you to type the command `make dep` before building the kernel.

```
*** End of Linux kernel configuration.
*** Check the top-level Makefile for additional configuration.
*** Next, you must run 'make dep'.
```

Building the Kernel

You should initiate the next three tasks with a single command line (Linux enables you to enter multiple semicolon-separated commands on the same line) so that you can type the line, press Enter, and then take a break because this part takes a while.

Depending on your system, making a new kernel can take anywhere from a few minutes to over an hour. Type the following on a single line to initiate the process:

```
make dep; make clean; make zImage
```

The `make dep` command determines which files have changed and what needs to be compiled again. The `make clean` command deletes old, unneeded files (such as old copies of the kernel). Finally, `make zImage` creates the new kernel in a compressed file and places it in a certain directory.

Secret

If you link in too many features into the kernel (by answering Yes to configuration options), the kernel file size may be too big to fit in the 640K of memory that a PC can use as it boots up. This 640K limit exists because the Intel x86 processors start in real mode and can only access 1MB of memory, of which 640K is available for programs. This limit is a leftover from the old MS-DOS days, and it applies only as the Linux kernel is initially loaded as the PC starts. In this case, the `make` command displays an error message such as the following:

```
System is too big. Try using bzImage or modules.
```

Tip

If you get a "System too big" error, type `make bzImage` to use a different type of compressed kernel that may fit within the memory limits. Otherwise, go through the `make config` step again, and eliminate unnecessary features by answering No to those configuration questions. For other features that you really need or may want to try out, type `m` to create modules. Although the kernel size is limited at startup, the kernel can load as many modules as it needs, once the boot process is complete.

As the kernel is built, you see a lot of messages on the screen. When it's all over, there is a new kernel in the form of a compressed file named `zImage` in the `/usr/src/linux*/arch/i386/boot` directory.

To use the new kernel, you have to copy the kernel to the `/boot` directory under a specific name and edit the `/etc/lilo.conf` file to set up LILO — the Linux Loader. You learn these steps in the section, "Installing the New Kernel and Setting up LILO" later in this chapter. Before you proceed with the kernel installation, however, you have to build and install the modules.

Building and Installing the Modules

If you select any modules during the kernel configuration, you have to build the modules and install them. Perform these tasks with the following steps:

1. Type the following commands to build the modules:

   ```
   cd /usr/src/linux
   make modules
   ```

2. The current set of modules in a directory is named after the version of Linux kernel your system is running. For example, if your system runs kernel version 2.2.16-22, the modules are in the following directory:

   ```
   /lib/modules/2.2.16-22
   ```

   Move the module directory to a new location as follows:

   ```
   mv /lib/modules/2.2.16-22 /lib/modules/2.2.16-22-old
   ```

3. Install the new modules with the following command:

   ```
   make modules_install
   ```

Now you can install the kernel and make it available for booting by LILO.

Installing the New Kernel and Setting Up LILO

Red Hat Linux uses LILO to load the Linux kernel from the disk. The configuration file `/etc/lilo.conf` lists the kernel binary that LILO runs. You can examine the contents of the LILO configuration file by typing the following command:

```
cat /etc/lilo.conf
```

Here is what I see when I try this command on one of my systems with a SCSI adapter:

```
boot=/dev/hda
map=/boot/map
install=/boot/boot.b
prompt
timeout=50
message=/boot/message
linear
default=linux

image=/boot/vmlinuz-2.2.16-22
        label=linux
        root=/dev/hda2
        initrd=/boot/initrd-2.2.16-22.img
        read-only

other=/dev/hda1
        label=dos
```

You learn more about LILO and its configuration file (`/etc/lilo.conf`) in Chapter 4. For this discussion, you should note the following:

- The last two lines are for booting from a DOS partition (Microsoft Windows is installed in that partition).

- The five lines starting with `image=/boot/vmlinuz-2.2.16-22` define a specific kernel file that LILO can boot. You can make LILO boot another kernel by adding a similar section to the configuration file.

- The `image=/boot/vmlinuz-2.2.16-22` line identifies the kernel that LILO loads. In this case, the kernel file is `vmlinuz-2.2.16-22`, which is located in the `/boot` directory.

- The `label=linux` line gives a name to the kernel. In this case, you can type `linux` at the `boot:` prompt to make LILO boot this particular kernel.

- The `root=/dev/hda2` line specifies the disk partition where the root Linux file system is located. This location may differ on your system.

- The `initrd=/boot/initrd-2.2.16-22.img` line specifies a file that contains an initial RAM disk (*initrd* stands for *initial RAM disk*) image that serves as a file system before the disks are available. You can see the `initrd` line only if your system has a SCSI adapter and the kernel uses a modular SCSI driver. In this case, the kernel uses the RAM disk—a block of memory used as a disk—to get started; then it loads the SCSI driver module and begins using the SCSI hard disk. You do not need the `initrd` line if you create a kernel with the SCSI adapter support built into the kernel.

On systems that have an MS-DOS partition, the LILO configuration file may include another section with details for the operating system (perhaps Windows 95 or 98) on that partition.

To configure LILO to boot yet another kernel (the one you just built), you need to follow these steps:

1. Copy the new kernel binary to the /boot directory. The new, compressed kernel file is in the /usr/src/linux*/arch/i386/boot directory. If you typed the command make zImage, the kernel filename is zImage; if you built the kernel with the make bzImage command, the filename is bzImage. I simply copy that file to the /boot directory with the same name:

   ```
   cp /usr/src/linux*/arch/i386/boot/zImage /boot
   ```

   If the kernel filename is bzImage, make sure you use bzImage instead of zImage. You can use any other filename you want, as long as you use that same filename when referring to the kernel in the /etc/lilo.conf file in step 3.

2. Save the old System.map file in the /boot directory, and copy the new map file. (I assume that you rebuilt kernel version 2.2.16-22 after changing some configuration options):

   ```
   mv /boot/System.map-2.2.16-22 /boot/System.map-2.2.16-22-old
   cp /usr/src/linux*/System.map /boot/System.map-2.2.16-22
   cd /boot
   ln -s System.map-2.2.16-22 System.map
   ```

3. Use your favorite text editor to edit the /etc/lilo.conf file to add the following lines just after the timeout line in the file. (If you need help with a text editor, consult Chapter 14 to learn about vi and Emacs — two popular text editors for Linux):

   ```
   image=/boot/zImage
           label=new
           root=/dev/hda2
           read-only
   ```

Caution

On your system, you should make sure that the root line is correct — instead of /dev/hda2, you should list the correct disk partition where the Linux root directory (/) is located. Also, use the correct filename for the kernel image file (for example, /boot/bzImage if the kernel file is so named).

Note that I do not show the initrd line anymore, because I assume that you are no longer using a modular SCSI driver even if your system has a SCSI adapter.

4. Save the lilo.conf file and exit the editor.

5. Install LILO again by using the following command:

   ```
   /sbin/lilo
   ```

Now you are ready to reboot the system and try out the new kernel.

Rebooting the System

After you finish configuring and installing LILO, you return to the Linux prompt. While you are still logged in as `root`, type the following command to reboot the system:

```
reboot
```

When you see the LILO `boot:` prompt, type the name you assigned to the new kernel in the `/etc/lilo.conf` file. You do not have to type anything if you added the new kernel description before all other operating systems in the LILO configuration file.

After the system reboots, you should see the familiar graphical login screen. To see proof that you are indeed running the new kernel, log in as a user, open a terminal window, and type `uname -srv`. This command shows you the kernel version, as well as the date and time when this kernel was built. If you upgraded the kernel source, you should see the version number for the new kernel. If you simply rebuilt the kernel for the same old kernel version, the date and time should match the time when you rebuilt the kernel. That's your proof that the system is running the new kernel.

Tip

If the system *hangs* (nothing seems to happen—there is no output on the screen and no disk activity), you may have skipped a step during the kernel rebuild. You can power the PC off and on to reboot. This time, enter `linux` (the old working kernel's name) at the LILO `boot:` prompt.

If you cannot boot the older version of Red Hat Linux either, use the emergency boot disk (containing an earlier, but working, version of Linux) to start the system. Then you can repeat the kernel rebuild and installation process making sure that you follow all the steps correctly.

Upgrading with a Red Hat Kernel RPM

As mentioned earlier in the section, "Applying Kernel Patches", you may get errors when applying kernel patches, because of differences between Red Hat's version of the kernel files and the standard kernel source. In this case, you can get newer versions of kernels using the Red Hat Update agent or accessing Red Hat's FTP server. Red Hat distributes all software updates, including new versions of kernels, in the form of RPM files.

Cross-Reference

Chapter 24 describes how you can register with the Red Hat Network and get updates on Red Hat Linux and its components, including the kernel, by using the Red Hat Update agent (`/usr/sbin/up2date`).

If you decide to download the kernel RPMs using FTP, the basic steps to accomplish the kernel upgrade are as follows:

1. Download the kernel RPM files, if any, from Red Hat's FTP server. If you want to rebuild the kernel, you have to download the `kernel-source` and `kernel-headers` RPMs corresponding to the new version of the kernel.

2. Install the RPMs using the `rpm -i` command.

3. If you have a SCSI adapter on your system, create a new, initial RAM disk by running the `/sbin/mkinitrd` command.

4. Reconfigure LILO to boot the new kernel.

5. Try out the new kernel by rebooting the system.

The next few sections further describe these steps.

Downloading New Kernel RPMs

Red Hat makes software updates available in the form of RPMs — packages — at its FTP server (`ftp://ftp.redhat.com/pub/redhat/updates/`, or one of the mirror sites listed at `http://www.redhat.com/mirrors.html`). The updates are organized in directories according to Red Hat Linux version numbers. For example, any updates for Red Hat Linux 7.0 for Intel x86 systems reside in the `7.0/i386` directory. Use a Web browser (for example, Netscape Communicator on your Linux system) to visit the FTP site and download any kernel RPMs available at that site.

Installing the Kernel RPMs

To install the kernel and the modules, follow these steps:

1. Make sure you are in the directory where the RPM files (the ones you downloaded from Red Hat's FTP server) are located.

2. Type the following command to install the kernel RPM:

   `rpm -ivh filename.rpm`

   Here, `filename.rpm` is the name of the kernel RPM file.

You need to install the `kernel-source` and `kernel-headers` RPMs only if you want to build a new kernel. Use the `rpm -ivh` command to install these RPMs.

Making a New, Initial RAM Disk

If you have a SCSI adapter in your system and you are using a SCSI device driver module, you have to make a new, initial RAM disk image — a file that you can copy into a block of memory and use as a memory-resident disk.

To see if you have any SCSI driver modules, type the following command:

`grep scsi /etc/modules.conf`

Tip

If this command produces no output, your system is not using a SCSI module and does not need an initial RAM disk. You can skip this step and proceed to reconfigure LILO.

On one of my systems with an Adaptec AHA 1542 SCSI adapter, I get the following result when I search using the `grep` command:

```
grep scsi /etc/modules.conf
alias scsi_hostadapter aha1542
```

In this case, I have to create the initial RAM disk using the `mkinitrd` command. Usually, the initial RAM disk image is stored in a file whose name begins with `initrd`. As mentioned earlier, `initrd` is shorthand for *initial RAM disk*; the `mkinitrd` command is so named because it makes an `initrd` file.

The `mkinitrd` program resides in the `/sbin` directory; you have to use a command line of the following form to create the `initrd` file:

```
/sbin/mkinitrd /boot/initrd-filename.img  module-directory-name
```

The `initrd` file has to be in the `/boot` directory where the kernel is located. You can use any filename for *initrd-filename*. The *module-directory-name* is the name of the directory in `/lib/modules` where the module files are located. By convention, the module directory name is the same as the kernel version number. For example, if your kernel version (as reported by the `uname -r` command) is 2.2.16-22, the module directory name is `2.2.16-22`. Another common practice is to use an `initrd` filename created by appending the version number to the `initrd-` prefix. Thus, for kernel version 2.2.16-22, the `initrd` file is `initrd-2.2.16-22.img`.

To create the initial RAM disk image for kernel version 2.2.16-22, type the following command:

```
/sbin/mkinitrd /boot/initrd-2.2.16-22.img 2.2.16-22
```

This creates the file `initrd-2.2.16-22.img` in the `/boot` directory. You refer to this `initrd` file in the LILO configuration file (`/etc/lilo.conf`).

Reconfiguring LILO

After you install the RPMs and, if necessary, create the initial RAM disk image, you have to reconfigure LILO so that it can boot the new kernel. This reconfiguration step is very much like the procedure described earlier in the section, "Installing the New Kernel and Setting up LILO." The only difference is the need to include an `initrd` line if your system requires the SCSI driver module.

Use a text editor such as `vi` or Emacs to edit the `/etc/lilo.conf` file. Add the following lines near the beginning of that file right after the `timeout` line:

```
image=/boot/vmlinuz-2.2.16-22
        label=linux-new
        root=/dev/hda2
        initrd=/boot/initrd-2.2.16-22.img
        read-only
```

Caution

On the `root=/dev/hda2` line, change `/dev/hda2` to the correct device name for the disk partition where your Linux system's root directory (/) is located.

After editing and saving the `/etc/lilo.conf` file, reinstall LILO with the following command:

```
/sbin/lilo
```

Now you can reboot the system and try out the new version of kernel.

Trying Out the New Kernel

After installing the new kernel RPM, creating the initial RAM disk file, and reconfiguring LILO, you are ready to try the new kernel. To restart the system, log in as `root` and type the following command from the Linux prompt:

```
reboot
```

You may also reboot the system from the graphical login screen. Select Reboot from the Options menu on the login dialog box.

When the system reboots and you see the LILO `boot:` prompt, type `linux-new` to boot the new kernel. If you added the new kernel description before all other operating systems in the LILO configuration file, that kernel should boot even if you don't type anything at the `boot:` prompt.

After Linux starts, you should see the usual graphical login screen. Log in as a user, open a terminal window, and type the `uname -sr` command to see the version number. The response should show that your system is running the new version of the kernel.

Summary

Linux was developed through the efforts of many programmers scattered around the globe. These programmers (and many new ones) continue to enhance Linux and to release bug fixes and new versions. From time to time, you may have to get some updates or bug fixes and rebuild the Linux kernel. This chapter provides detailed information on how to apply the fixes (known as *patches*) and how to build a new kernel. It also shows you how to download and install new updates from Red Hat in the form of Red Hat Package Manager (RPM) files.

By reading this chapter, you learn the following:

▶ The term *kernel* refers to the core Linux operating system — the program that makes your PC a Linux PC.

▶ The Linux kernel is improved continually to correct errors (these are the bug fixes) or add new functionality. Such updates are distributed in the form of *patches* — changes to specific Linux source files. You have to apply the patches and rebuild the kernel to benefit from any enhancements to the kernel.

▶ You can get the Linux kernel patches from the Web site http://www. kernel.org/. Follow the links on that page to reach the FTP server that has the kernel distributions, including the patches. If the FTP site is busy, you get a list of mirror sites (organized geographically); pick a suitable site from this list. At the FTP site, the Linux kernels and associated patches are organized according to version number. Look under the current version number (for example, v2.2 for version 2.2) in the /pub/linux/kernel directory for specific patches.

▶ The patches are distributed in compressed form — recognizable by the .gz and .bz2 suffixes in the filenames. You have to use the gunzip or bzip2 programs to uncompress the patches. If bzip2 is not installed on your system, you can install it from the first companion CD-ROM.

▶ Copy the patches to the /usr/src directory, uncompress the patch files, and then use the patch command to apply the patches. This alters the kernel's source code in the /usr/src/linux directory.

▶ Before rebuilding the kernel, you should prepare an emergency boot disk so that you can restart the system if something goes wrong with the kernel rebuild process.

▶ To rebuild the kernel, change the directory to /usr/src/linux and then use the make command. You have to follow the sequence make config; make dep; make clean; make zImage (in that order). If you get a "System too big" error, you should try the make bzImage command. You also have to use the commands make modules and make modules_install.

▶ To make a new kernel available for booting, you have to copy the new kernel file to the /boot directory and edit the LILO configuration file /etc/lilo.conf so that it includes information about the new kernel file. Then, you have to run /sbin/lilo to reinstall LILO.

▶ In addition to applying patches, you can also upgrade to a new version of the kernel by downloading and installing updates from Red Hat's FTP server. These updates are distributed in the form of Red Hat Package Manager (RPM) files, which package all necessary files for a software package in a single file. You have to use the rpm command to install and use RPM files.

▶ You can download updates for Red Hat Linux from one of the mirror sites listed at http://www.redhat.com/mirrors.html. The updates are organized in directories according to Red Hat Linux version numbers. For example, any updates for Red Hat Linux 7.0 for Intel x86 systems appear in the 7.0/i386 directory.

Chapter 26

System and Network Security

In This Chapter

▶ Establishing an overall security framework

▶ Securing your Red Hat Linux system

▶ Understanding network security issues

▶ Implementing Internet firewalls

▶ Learning about packet filtering and application gateway

▶ Understanding the role of proxy servers such as SOCKS version 5

▶ Learning about the TIS Firewall Toolkit

▶ Keeping up with security

As a system administrator, you have to worry about your Red Hat Linux system's security. For a stand-alone system, or a system used in an isolated local area network (LAN), you have to focus on protecting the system from the users and the users from one another. In other words, you do not want a user to modify or delete system files, whether intentionally or unintentionally. You also do not want a user destroying another user's files.

If your Linux system is connected to the Internet, you must also worry about securing the system from unwanted accesses over the Internet. These intruders, also known as *crackers*, typically impersonate a user, steal or destroy information, and even deny access to your own system (this is known as a *denial of service* attack).

By its very nature an Internet connection makes your system accessible to any other system on the Internet. After all, the Internet connects many networks across the globe. In fact, the client/server architecture of Internet information services, such as HTTP (Web) and FTP, rely on the wide-open network access that the Internet provides. Unfortunately, the easy accessibility to Internet services running on your system also means anyone on the Net can easily access your system.

If you operate an Internet host that provides information to others, you certainly want everyone to access your system's Internet services, such as FTP and Web servers. However, these servers often have vulnerabilities that crackers may exploit in order to cause harm to your system. You need to know about the potential security risks of Internet services and the precautions you can take to minimize the risk of someone exploiting the weaknesses of your FTP or Web server.

You may also want to protect your company's internal network from outsiders, even though your goal is to provide information to the outside world through a Web server. You can protect your internal network by setting up an Internet firewall — a controlled access point to the internal network — and placing the Web and FTP servers on a host outside the firewall.

This chapter takes you through the basic steps you should follow in securing your Red Hat Linux system. You also learn about setting up an Internet firewall and running Web and FTP servers outside the firewall, where users cannot break through and access your company's internal network. As you'll see, Red Hat Linux already includes many of the tools you need to maintain system security. You can even set up a packet-filtering firewall, using the ipchains software that comes with Red Hat Linux.

Tip

To learn more about Linux security, consult the *Linux Security HOWTO* at http://metalab.unc.edu/pub/Linux/docs/HOWTO/Security-HOWTO. Another good resource is the *Linux Administrator's Security Guide*, which you can read online at http://www.securityportal.com/lasg/.

Establishing a Security Framework

The first step in securing your Linux system is to set up a security policy. The security policy is your guide to what you enable users (as well as visitors over the Internet) to do on the Linux system. The level of security you establish depends on how you use the Linux system and how much is at risk if someone gains unauthorized access to your system.

If you are a system administrator for Linux systems at an organization of any sort, you probably want to involve the management, as well as the users, in setting up the security policy. Obviously, you cannot create such an imposing policy that no one can do any work on the system. On the other hand, if the users are creating or using data that are valuable to the organization, you have to set up a policy that protects the data from disclosure to outsiders. In other words, the security policy should strike a balance between the users' needs and the need to protect the system.

For a stand-alone Linux system, or a home system that you occasionally connect to the Internet, the security policy can be just a listing of the Internet services that you want to run on the system and the user accounts you plan to set up on the system. For any larger organization, you probably have one or more Linux systems on a LAN connected to the Internet — preferably through a *firewall* (a device that controls the flow of Internet Protocol (IP) packets between the LAN and the Internet). In such cases, it is best to think of computer security across the entire organization systematically. Figure 26-1 shows the key elements of an organization-wide framework to computer security.

Figure 26-1: An organization-wide framework for computer security

The security framework outlined in Figure 26-1 starts with the development of a security policy based on business requirements and risk analysis. The business requirements identify the security needs of the business — the computer resources and information you have to protect (including any requirements imposed by applicable laws, such as the requirement to protect the privacy of some types of data). Typical security requirements might include items such as the following:

■ Enable access to information by authorized users.

■ Implement business rules that specify who has access to what information.

■ Employ a strong user-authentication system.

■ Deny malicious or destructive actions on data.

■ Protect data from end-to-end as it moves across networks.

■ Implement all security and privacy requirements imposed by applicable laws.

Risk analysis involves determining the following and performing some analysis to determine the priority of handling the risks:

- *Threats* — What you are protecting against.
- *Vulnerabilities* — The weaknesses that might be exploited (these are the risks).
- *Probability* — The likelihood that a vulnerability will be exploited.
- *Impact* — The effect of exploiting a specific vulnerability.
- *Mitigation* — What to do to reduce the vulnerabilities.

Before I describe analysis, here are some typical threats to computer security:

- *Denial of service* — The computer and network are tied up so that legitimate users cannot make use of the systems. For businesses, denial of service can mean loss of revenue.
- *Unauthorized access* — Use of the computer and network by someone who is not an authorized user. The unauthorized user could steal information or maliciously corrupt or destroy data. Some businesses may be hurt by the negative publicity from the mere act of an unauthorized user gaining access to the system, even if there is no explicit damage to any data.
- *Disclosure of information to the public* — The unauthorized release of information to the public. For example, the disclosure of a password file enables potential attackers to figure out user name and password combinations for accessing a system. Exposure of other sensitive information, such as financial and medical data, might be a potential liability for a business.

These threats come from exploitation of vulnerabilities in your organization's computer and people resources. Some common vulnerabilities are the following:

- *People* (divulging passwords, losing security cards, etc.)
- *Internal network connections* (routers, switches)
- *Interconnection points* (gateways — routers and firewalls — between the Internet and the internal network)
- *Third-party network providers* (ISPs, long-distance carriers)
- *Operating-system security holes* (potential holes in Internet servers, such as `sendmail`, `named`, etc.)
- *Application security holes* (known security holes in specific applications)

To perform risk analysis, assign a numeric value to the probability and impact of each potential vulnerability. A workable risk analysis approach is to do the following for each vulnerability or risk:

1. Assign subjective ratings of Low, Medium, and High for the probability. As the ratings suggest, a Low probability means a lesser chance that the vulnerability will be exploited; High probability means a greater chance.

2. Assign similar ratings to impact. What you consider *impact* is up to you. If the exploitation of a vulnerability will affect your business greatly, assign it a High impact.

3. Assign a numeric value to the three levels — Low = 1, Medium = 2, and High = 3 — for both probability and impact.

4. Compute the product of the probability and impact — you can think of this as the risk level. Then make a decision to develop protections for vulnerabilities that exceed a specific threshold for the product of probability and impact. For example, you may choose to handle all vulnerabilities with a product that is greater than 6.

If you want to characterize the probability and impact with a finer level of granularity, pick a scale of 1 through 5, for example, and then follow the same steps as before.

Based on the risk analysis and any business requirements that you may need to address regardless of risk level, you can craft a security policy for the organization. The security policy typically addresses the following areas:

- *Authentication* — What method will be used to ensure that a user is the real user? Who gets access to the system? What is the minimum length and complexity of passwords? How often users change passwords? How long can a user be idle before that user is logged out automatically?

- *Authorization* — What can different classes of users do on the system? Who can have the root password?

- *Data Protection* — What data must be protected? Who has access to the data? Is encryption necessary for some data?

- *Internet Access* — What are the restrictions on users (from the LAN) accessing the Internet? What Internet services (such as Web, Internet Relay Chat, and so on) can the users access? Are incoming e-mails and attachments scanned for viruses? Is there a network firewall? Are virtual private networks (VPNs) used to connect private networks across the Internet?

- *Internet Services* — What Internet services are allowed on each Linux system? Are there any file servers? Mail servers? Web servers? What services run on each type of server? What services, if any, run on Linux systems used as desktop workstations?

- *Security Audits* — Who tests whether the security is adequate? How often is the security tested? How are problems found during security testing handled?

- *Incident Handling* — What are the procedures for handling any computer security incidents? Who must be informed? What information must be gathered to help with the investigation of incidents?

■ *Responsibilities* — Who is responsible for maintaining security? Who monitors log files and audit trails for signs of unauthorized access? Who maintains the database of security policy?

Once you analyze the risks — vulnerabilities — and develop a security policy, you have to select the mitigation approach: how to protect against specific vulnerabilities. This is where you develop an overall security solution based on security policy, business requirements, and available technology — a solution that consists of the following:

■ Services (authentication, access control, encryption)

■ Mechanisms (user name/password, firewalls)

■ Objects (hardware, software)

Finally, you want to install security management that continually monitors, detects, and responds to any security incidents.

The combination of the risk analysis, security policy, security solutions, and security management provides the overall security framework. Such a framework helps to establish a common level of understanding of security and a common basis for design and implementation of the security solutions.

The remainder of this chapter shows you some of the ways in which you can enhance and maintain the security of your Red Hat Linux system and any network.

Securing the Red Hat Linux System

Once you have a security policy defined, you can proceed to secure the system according to the policy. The exact steps depend on what you want to do with the system — whether it is a server or a workstation, and how many users must access the system. The general steps for securing the system and maintaining the security are as follows:

■ When installing Red Hat Linux, select only those package groups that you need for your system. Do not install any unnecessary software. For example, if your system is a workstation, you do not need to install most of the servers (Web server, news server, and so on).

■ Create initial user accounts and make sure that all passwords are strong ones that password-cracking programs can't "guess." As you'll learn soon, Red Hat Linux includes the tools to enforce strong passwords.

■ Enable only those Internet services that you need on a system. In particular, do not enable services that are not properly configured. Later in this chapter, you learn about enabling and disabling Internet services, using Linuxconf and the chkconfig command.

■ Use secure shell (ssh) for remote logins. Do not use the "r" commands, such as rlogin and rsh.

- If you have an internal network connected to the Internet, use a firewall to control the flow of data between the internal network and the Internet.

- Use file-integrity checking tools, such as Tripwire, to monitor any changes to crucial system files and directories.

- Periodically check various log files for signs of any break-ins or attempted break-ins. These log files are in the /var/log directory of your system.

- Check security news by regularly visiting and installing updates from Red Hat, once a fix becomes available.

Securing Passwords

Historically, UNIX passwords are stored in the /etc/passwd file, which any user can read. For example, a typical old-style /etc/passwd file entry for the root user looks like this:

```
root:t6Z7NWDK1K8sU:0:0:root:/root:/bin/bash
```

The fields are separated by colons (:) and the second field contains the password in encrypted form. To check if a password is valid, the login program encrypts the plain-text password entered by the user and compares it with the contents of the /etc/passwd file. If there is a match, the user is allowed to log in.

Password-cracking programs work just like the login program, except that these programs pick one word at a time from a dictionary, encrypt the word, and compare the encrypted word with the encrypted passwords in the /etc/passwd file for a match. To crack the passwords, the intruder needs the /etc/passwd file. Often, crackers use weaknesses of various Internet servers (such as mail and FTP) to get a copy of the /etc/passwd file.

Recently, several improvements have made the UNIX passwords more secure. These include shadow passwords and pluggable authentication modules, described in the next two sections.

Cross-Reference

Red Hat Linux includes password security enhancements that you can select during installation. In Chapter 2, as you complete the Red Hat Linux installation, one step involves making selections in an Authentication Configuration screen. If you accept the default selections — Enable MD5 passwords and Enable shadow passwords — you automatically enable more secure passwords in Red Hat Linux.

Shadow passwords

Instead of being stored in the /etc/passwd file, which any user can read, passwords are now stored in a shadow password file. On Red Hat Linux, the shadow passwords are in /etc/shadow file. Only the super user (root) can read this file. For example, here is the entry for root in the new-style /etc/passwd file:

```
root:x:0:0:root:/root:/bin/bash
```

As you can see, the second field contains an x, instead of an encrypted password. The encrypted password is now stored in the /etc/shadow file where the entry for root is like this:

```
root:$1$AAAni/yN$uESHbzUpy9Cgfoo1Bf0tS0:11077:0:99999:7:-1:-1:134540356
```

The format of the /etc/shadow entries with colon-separated fields resembles the entries in the /etc/passwd file, but the meanings of most fields differ. The first field is still the user name and the second one is the encrypted password.-

The remaining fields in each /etc/shadow entry control when the password expires. You do not need to interpret or change these entries in the /etc/shadow file. Instead, you should use the change command to change the password expiration information. For starters, you can check a user's password expiration information, by using the chage command with the -l option, as follows (in this case, you have to be logged in as root):

```
change -l root
Minimum:         0
Maximum:         99999
Warning:         7
Inactive:        -1
Last Change:              Oct 30, 2000
Password Expires:         Never
Password Inactive:        Never
Account Expires:          Never
```

In this case, the output shows various expiration information: you can change the root password any time (that's what zero minimum time means), it lasts for 99,999 days, and the root user gets a warning seven days before the password expires.

If you want to ensure that the password changes every 90 days, you can use the -M option to set the maximum number of days the password stays valid. For example, to make sure that user naba is prompted to change the password in 90 days, I log in as root and type the following command:

```
change -M 90 naba
```

You can do this for each user account to ensure that all passwords expire and that all users must pick new passwords.

Pluggable Authentication Modules (PAMs)

In addition to improving the password file's security by using the shadow passwords, Red Hat Linux also improves the actual encryption of the passwords stored in the /etc/shadow file. Password encryption is now done using the MD5 message-digest algorithm to convert the plain-text password into a 128-bit *fingerprint* or *digest*. The MD5 algorithm, described in RFC 1321 (`http://www.faqs.org/rfcs/rfc1321.html`), compresses a large file securely so that you can digitally sign it through encryption with a private key. It works quite well for password encryption, as well.

Another advantage of MD5 over the older-style password encryption is that the older passwords were limited to a maximum of eight characters in length; new passwords (encrypted with MD5) can be much longer. Longer passwords are harder to guess, even if the `/etc/shadow` file falls into the wrong hands.

A clue to the use of MD5 encryption in the `/etc/shadow` file is the increased length of the encrypted password and the 1 prefix, as in the second field of the following sample entry:

```
root:$1$AAAni/yN$uESHbzUpy9Cgfoo1Bf0tSO:11077:0:99999:7:-1:-1:134540356
```

A Pluggable Authentication Module (PAM) performs the actual MD5 encryption. PAM provides a flexible method for authenticating users on Linux systems. Through settings in configuration files, you can change the authentication method on the fly, without having to actually modify programs, such as `login` and `passwd`, that verify a user's identity.

Red Hat Linux uses PAM extensively, and the configuration files are located in the `/etc/pam.d` directory of your system. Check out the contents of this directory on your system. Here's what I see on my Red Hat Linux system:

```
ls /etc/pam.d
chfn            kbdrate         other           rlogin          up2date
chsh            kde             passwd          rp3-config      up2date-config
ftp             kppp            poweroff        rsh             xdm
gdm             linuxconf       ppp             samba           xscreensaver
gnorpm-auth     linuxconf-auth  reboot          sshd            xserver
halt            linuxconf-pair  rexec           su
isdn-config     login           rhn_register    system-auth
```

As this listing shows, there is a configuration file (each one is a text file) for various programs that authenticate users. For example, there is an entry for `login`, `passwd`, and `su`. Here's the content of the `/etc/pam.d/passwd` file on my system:

```
cat /etc/pam.d/passwd
#%PAM-1.0
auth        required        /lib/security/pam_stack.so service=system-auth
account     required        /lib/security/pam_stack.so service=system-auth
password    required        /lib/security/pam_stack.so service=system-auth
```

These lines indicate that authentication, account management, and password-checking should all be done by using the `pam_stack` module (`/lib/security/pam_stack.so`) with the argument `service=system-auth`. The `pam_stack` module essentially refers to another configuration file in the `/etc/pam.d` directory. In this case, the configuration file is `/etc/pam.d/system-auth`. Here's the content of the `/etc/pam.d/system-auth` file on my Red Hat Linux PC:

```
cat /etc/pam.d/system-auth
#%PAM-1.0
# This file is auto-generated.
# User changes will be destroyed the next time authconfig is run.
auth        sufficient   /lib/security/pam_unix.so likeauth nullok md5 shadow
auth        required     /lib/security/pam_deny.so
account     sufficient   /lib/security/pam_unix.so
account     required     /lib/security/pam_deny.so
password    required     /lib/security/pam_cracklib.so retry=3
password    sufficient   /lib/security/pam_unix.so nullok use_authtok md5 shadow
password    required     /lib/security/pam_deny.so
session     required     /lib/security/pam_limits.so
session     required     /lib/security/pam_unix.so
```

Although I won't go over all the details, here's a brief explanation of these lines. The first `auth` line specifies an authentication module that checks the user's identity, by using the PAM module `/lib/security/pam_unix.so` with the argument string `likeauth nullok md5 shadow`. The options in the argument string have the following meanings:

`likeauth` Returns same value whether the module is used to set new credentials or authenticate an existing user name.

`nullok` Allows blank password.

`md5` Encrypts passwords with the MD5 hash algorithm.

`shadow` Consults the `/etc/shadow` file when checking passwords.

The second `auth` line in the `/etc/pam.d/system-auth` file denies access to the system if the authentication by the `pam_unix.so` module is unsuccessful.

The `account` lines in the `/etc/pam.d/system-auth` file check to make sure that the user account has not expired and the user is allowed to log in at a given time of day, and so on.

The two `password` lines in the `/etc/pam.d/system-auth` file specify how passwords are set. The first `password` line uses the `/lib/security/pam_cracklib.so` module to try to crack the new password (that's what the `cracklib` in the module's name indicates). The `retry=3` part indicates that the user can try to enter a new password three times at most. The second `password` line indicates that the MD5 encryption is used to store the password in the `/etc/shadow` file.

The `/etc/pam.d/passwd` configuration file applies when you use the `passwd` command to change passwords. Here's an example where I am trying to change my password:

```
passwd
Changing password for naba
(current) UNIX password: I type my current password
New UNIX password:
BAD PASSWORD: it is too short
```

```
New UNIX password:  I type "transport" as password
BAD PASSWORD: it is based on a dictionary word
New UNIX password:  I type "nabal2" as the new password
BAD PASSWORD: it is based on your username
passwd: Authentication token manipulation error
```

In this case, the passwd program is using the PAM module to check my identity (when I first type my current password), and then making sure that each of the new passwords I try are strong ones. Finally, the PAM modules abort the passwd program after I fail to select a good password in three tries.

Securing Internet Services

For an Internet-connected Linux system (or even one on a TCP/IP LAN), a significant threat is the possibility that someone will use one of many Internet services to gain access to your system. Each service — such as mail, Web, or FTP — requires running a server program that responds to client requests arriving over the TCP/IP network. Some of these server programs have weaknesses that can allow an outsider to log in to your system — maybe with root privileges. Luckily, Red Hat Linux comes with some facilities that you can use to make the Internet services more secure.

Potential intruders can employ a *port-scanning tool* — a program that attempts to establish a TCP/IP connection at a port and look for a response — to check which Internet servers are running on your system. Then the intruder can potentially exploit any known weaknesses of one or more services, to gain access to your system.

Using Linuxconf to disable stand-alone services

To avoid opening up unnecessary entry points into your system, make sure that you run only those Internet services that you need. You can enable and disable the services using Linuxconf, the graphical system-administration utility. Log in as root and select Main Menu ⇨ Programs ⇨ System ⇨ LinuxConf from the GNOME desktop. Then click the Control Panel button on the Control tab. In the next dialog box, click the button labeled Control service activity. This shows you a list with the status of the current services.

To control a service, click the service's name. For example, to control the Web server, click httpd. This causes Linuxconf to display the Service httpd tab, through which you can control the Web server.

If you do not want the Web server to automatically start at boot time, click the Automatic button to turn it off. To immediately stop the Web server, click the Stop button.

Using the chkconfig command to disable stand-alone services

Chapter 23 describes the /sbin/chkconfig program that you can use to configure the stand-alone services. You can read more about chkconfig in that chapter. For the purposes of this chapter, the key points are as follows:

- Log in as root and type **/sbin/chkconfig –list** to view all the services set to start automatically at the run levels 0 through 6 (Chapter 23 explains run levels).

- The services that are on for run levels 3 and 5 are the ones that matter most, because your Red Hat Linux system is usually at run level 3 (text mode), or 5 (graphical login). Type **/sbin/runlevel** to see the current run level.

- To stop a service, such as ypserv, from automatically starting at run levels 3, 4, and 5, type **/sbin/chkconfig –level 345 ypserv off**. Similarly, you can stop all unneeded services using chkconfig.

Configuring the xinetd server to disable other services

In addition to the stand-alone servers, such as Web server (httpd), mail (sendmail), and domain name server (named), you have to configure another server separately. That other server, xinetd (the Internet super server), starts a host of other Internet services, such as FTP, TELNET, and so on. Here you briefly look at the security aspects of the xinetd server.

The xinetd server reads a configuration file named /etc/xinetd.conf at startup. This file, in turn, refers to configuration files stored in the /etc/xinetd.d directory. The configuration files in /etc/xinetd.d tell xinetd which ports to listen to and which server to start for each port. You can browse through the files in /etc/xinetd.d directory on your system to find out the kinds of services that xinetd is set up to start. Some of these services provide information that intruders may use to break into your system. You should turn off these services, by placing a diasble = yes line in that service's configuration file. To learn more about the xinetd configuration files, type man xinetd.conf at the shell prompt in a terminal window.

Depending on what you need on your system, you may want to disable everything but the ftp and telnet services. After you make any changes to the xinetd configuration files, you must restart the xinetd server, by typing the following command:

```
/etc/rc.d/init.d/xinetd restart
Stopping xinetd: [  OK  ]
Starting xinetd: [  OK  ]
```

Another security feature of xinetd is its use of the TCP wrapper facility to start various services. The TCP wrapper provides an access control facility for Internet services. The TCP wrapper can start other services, such as FTP and TELNET; but before starting the service, it consults the /etc/hosts. allow file to see if the host requesting service is allowed that service. If nothing appears in /etc/hosts.allow about that host, TCP wrapper checks the /etc/hosts.deny file to see if it should deny the service. If both files are empty, TCP wrapper enables the host to access the requested service.

You can place the line ALL:ALL in the /etc/hosts.deny file to deny all hosts access to any Internet services on your system. Then you can add to /etc/hosts.allow the names of those hosts that can access services on your system. For example, to enable only hosts from the 192.168.1.0 network and the localhost (IP address 127.0.0.1) access the services on your system, place the following line in the /etc/hosts.allow file:

```
ALL: 192.168.1.0/255.255.255.0 127.0.0.1
```

If you want to permit access to a specific Internet service to a specific remote host, you can do so using the following syntax for a line:

```
server_program_name: hosts
```

Here *server_program_name* is the name of the server program (for example, in.telnetd for TELNET and in.ftpd for FTP), and *hosts* is a comma-separated list of hosts that can access the service. *hosts* can also take the form of a network address, or an entire domain name, such as .mycompany.com. For example, here's how you can give TELNET access to all systems in the mycompany.com domain:

```
in.telnetd: .mycompany.com
```

Tip

In summary, you should edit configuration files in /etc/xinetd.d directory to turn off unneeded services and use the /etc/hosts.deny and /etc/hosts.allow files to control access to the services running on your system. After you edit the files in the /etc/xinetd.d directory, remember to type /etc/rc.d/init.d/xinetd restart to restart the xinetd server.

Using Secure Shell (SSH) for Remote Logins

Red Hat Linux 7.1 comes with the Open Secure Shell (OpenSSH) software, a suite of programs that provide a secure replacement for the Berkeley r commands: rlogin (remote login), rsh (remote shell), and rcp (remote copy). OpenSSH uses public-key cryptography to authenticate users and to encrypt the communication between two hosts, so users can securely log in from remote systems and copy files securely.

This section briefly describes how to use the OpenSSH software in Red Hat Linux. To learn more about OpenSSH and read the latest news about it, visit http://www.openssh.com/.

The OpenSSH software is installed during Red Hat Linux installation, if you select the Networked Workstation package group. Table 26-1 lists the main components of the OpenSSH software.

Table 26-1   Components of the OpenSSH Software

Component	Description
/usr/sbin/sshd	The secure shell daemon that must run on a host if you want users on remote systems to use the ssh client to log in securely. When a connection from an ssh client arrives, sshd performs authentication using public-key cryptography, and then establishes an encrypted communication link with the ssh client.
/usr/bin/ssh	The secure shell client that users can run to log in to a host that is running sshd. Users can also use ssh to execute a command on another host.
/usr/bin/slogin	A symbolic link to /usr/bin/ssh.
/usr/bin/scp	The secure copy program that works like rcp, but securely. The scp program uses ssh for data transfer and provides the same authentication and security as ssh.
/usr/bin/ssh-keygen	The program you use to generate the public and private key pairs you need for the public-key cryptography used in OpenSSH. The ssh-keygen program can generate key pairs for both RSA and DSA (Digital Signature Algorithm) authentication.
/etc/ssh/sshd_config	The configuration file for the sshd server. This file specifies many parameters for sshd, including the port to listen to, the protocol to use (there are two versions of SSH protocols, SSH1 and SSH2, both supported by OpenSSH), and the location of other files.
/etc/ssh/ssh_config	The configuration file for the ssh client. Each user can also have a ssh configuration file named config in the .ssh subdirectory of the user's home directory.

OpenSSH uses public-key encryption where the sender and receiver each have a pair of keys — a *public key* and a *private key*. The public keys are freely distributed and each party knows the other's public key. The sender encrypts data using the recipient's public key. Only the recipient's private key can then decrypt those data.

To use OpenSSH, do the following:

- If you want to support ssh-based remote logins on a host, start the sshd server on your system. Log in as root, and then type the following command at the shell prompt to ensure that the sshd server starts at system reboot:

```
chkconfig --add sshd
```

To start the sshd server immediately, type the following command:

```
/etc/init.d/sshd start
```

- Generate the host keys with the following command:

```
ssh-keygen -d -f /etc/ssh/ssh_host_key -N ''
```

The -d flag causes the ssh-keygen program to generate DSA keys, which are used by the SSH2 protocol.

A user who wants to log in using ssh has to generate the public-private key pair also. For example, here is the command I type to generate the DSA keys for use with SSH2:

```
ssh-keygen -d
Generating DSA parameter and key.
Enter file in which to save the key (/home/naba/.ssh/id_dsa):
Enter passphrase (empty for no passphrase):
Enter same passphrase again:
Your identification has been saved in /home/naba/.ssh/id_dsa.
Your public key has been saved in /home/naba/.ssh/id_dsa.pub.
The key fingerprint is:
e5:64:9a:a2:92:7c:79:ae:a1:15:eb:35:b6:4a:24:4d naba@lnbp200
```

Next I copy my public key—the /home/naba/.ssh/id_dsa.pub file—to the remote system and save it as the ~/.ssh/authorized_keys2 file (that refers to the authorized_keys2 file in the .ssh subdirectory of the other system, assuming that the remote system is also another Linux system). Note that the 2 in the name of the authorized_keys2 file refers to the SSH2 protocol.

Once I have set up the public key file in my home directory on the remote system, I can log in to my account on the lnbp200 host, by typing the following command on the remote system:

```
ssh lnbp200 -l naba
```

I should get a shell prompt from the lnbp200 host without any prompts for a password. Note that I could also log in to this account with the following equivalent command:

```
ssh naba@lnbp200
```

If I simply wanted to securely copy a file from the lnbp200 system, I could use scp, as illustrated by the following example:

```
scp lnbp200:/etc/ssh/ssh_config .
ssh_config            100%  |*****************************|   989        00:00
```

This command copies the /etc/ssh/ssh_config file from the lnbp200 host to the system from which I type the command.

Understanding Network Security Issues

The issue of security comes up as soon as you connect your organization's internal network to the Internet. This is true even if you connect a single computer to the Internet, but the security concerns are more pressing when an entire internal network is opened up to the world.

If you are an experienced system administrator, you already know that it's not the cost of managing an Internet presence that worries the corporate management; their main concern is security. To get your management's backing for the Web site, you need to lay out a plan to keep the corporate network secure from intruders.

You might think that you can avoid jeopardizing the internal network by connecting only the external servers, such as Web and FTP servers to the Internet. However, this simplistic approach is not a wise one. It is like deciding not to drive because you may have an accident. Not having a network connection between your Web server and your internal network also has the following drawbacks:

- You cannot use network file transfers, such as FTP to copy documents and data from your internal network to the Web server.

- Users on the internal network cannot access the corporate Web server.

- Users on the internal network do not have access to any Web servers on the Internet. Such a restriction makes a valuable resource — the Web — inaccessible to the users in your organization.

A practical solution to this problem is to set up an Internet firewall, and then put the Web server on a highly secured host outside the firewall. You'll find more information about firewalls in the "Implementing Internet Firewalls" section later in this chapter.

With a firewall in place, the strategy is to run the Internet services, such as FTP server and Web server, on a system outside the firewall. That system serves as your Internet host and is openly accessible to anyone on the Internet. That means that anyone can exploit existing security vulnerabilities in the Internet information services you run. The previous sections in this chapter describe some of these vulnerabilities and what precautions you can take to avoid them.

Internet Security Terminology

Computer books, magazine articles, and experts on Internet security use a number of terms with unique meanings. You need to know these terms to understand discussions about firewalls (and to effectively communicate with firewall vendors). Here are some of the better-known Internet security terms:

Application gateway—A proxy service that acts as a gateway for application-level protocols, such as FTP, TELNET, and HTTP.

Authentication—The process of confirming that a user is indeed who he or she claims to be. The typical authentication method is a challenge-response method wherein the user enters a username and secret password to confirm his or her identity.

Backdoor—A security weakness a cracker places on a host in order to bypass security features.

Bastion host—A highly secured computer that serves as an organization's main point of presence on the Internet. A bastion host typically resides on the perimeter network, but a dual-homed host (with one network interface connected to the Internet and the other to the internal network) is also a bastion host.

Buffer overflow—A security flaw in a program that enables a cracker to send an excessive amount of data to that program and overwrite parts of the running program with code in the data being sent. The end result is that the cracker can execute arbitrary code on the system and possibly gain access to the system as a privileged user.

Certificate—An electronic document that identifies an entity (such as an individual, an organization, or a computer) and associates a public key with that identity. A certificate contains the certificate holder's name, a serial number, expiration dates, a copy of the certificate holder's public key, and the digital signature of the Certificate Authority so that a recipient can verify that the certificate is real.

Certificate Authority (CA)—An organization that validates identities and issues certificates.

Cracker—A person who breaks into (or attempts to break into) a host, often with malicious intent.

Confidentiality— Of data, a state of being accessible by no one but you (usually achieved by encryption).

Decryption—The process of transforming encrypted information into its original, intelligible form.

Denial of service (DoS)—An attack that uses so much of the resources on your computer and network that legitimate users cannot access and use the system.

Digital signature—A one-way MD5 or SHA-1 hash of a message encrypted with the private key of the message originator, used to verify the integrity of a message and assure non-repudiation.

DMZ—Another name for the perimeter network. (*DMZ* stands for demilitarized zone— the buffer zone separating North and South Korea.)

Dual-homed host—A computer with two network interfaces (think of each network as a home).

Encryption—The process of transforming information so it is unintelligible to anyone but the intended recipient. The transformation is done by a mathematical operation between a key and the information.

Firewall—A controlled access gateway between an organization's internal network and the Internet. A dual-homed host can be configured as a firewall.

Continued

(continued)

Hash—A mathematical function converts a message into a fixed-size numeric value known as a *message digest* or *hash*. The MD5 algorithm produces a 128-bit message digest, whereas the Secure Hash Algorithm-1 (SHA-1) generates a 160-bit message digest. The hash of a message is encrypted with the private key of the sender to produce the digital signature.

Host—A computer on any network (so called because it offers many services).

Integrity—Of received data, a state of being the same data that were sent (unaltered in transit).

IPSec (IP Security Protocol)—A security protocol for the network layer that is designed to provide cryptographic security services for IP packets. IPSec provides encryption-based authentication, integrity, access control, and confidentiality (visit `http://www.ietf.org/html.charters/ipsec-charter.html for the list of RFCs related to IPSec`).

Non-repudiation—A security feature that prevents the sender of data from being able to deny ever having sent the data.

Packet—A collection of bytes that serve as the basic unit of communication on a network. On TCP/IP networks, the packet may be referred to as an *IP packet* or a *TCP/IP packet*.

Packet filtering—Selective blocking of packets based on the type of packet (as specified by the source and destination IP address or port).

Perimeter network—A network between the Internet and the protected internal network. The bastion host resides on the perimeter network. Also known as DMZ.

Proxy server—A server on the bastion host that enables internal clients to access external servers (and enables external clients to access servers inside the protected network). There are proxy servers for various Internet services, such as FTP and HTTP.

Public-key cryptography—An encryption method that uses a pair of keys—a *private key and a public key*—to encrypt and decrypt the information. Anything encrypted with the public key can be decrypted with the corresponding private key, and vice versa.

Public Key Infrastructure (PKI)—A set of standards and services that enables the use of public-key cryptography and certificates in a networked environment. PKI facilitates tasks, such as issuing, renewing, and revoking certificates, and generating and distributing public-private key pairs.

Screening router—An Internet router that filters packets.

Symmetric-key encryption—An encryption method wherein the same key is used to encrypt and decrypt the information.

Virus—A self-replicating program that spreads from one computer to another by attaching itself to other programs.

Worm—A self-replicating program that copies itself from one computer to another over a network.

Implementing Internet Firewalls

An Internet firewall is an intermediary between your internal network and the Internet. The firewall controls access to and from the protected internal network.

If you connect an internal network directly to the Internet, you have to make sure that every system on the internal network is properly secured—which can be nearly impossible, because it takes only one careless user to render the entire internal network vulnerable. A firewall is a single point of connection to the Internet: you can direct all your efforts toward making that firewall system a daunting barrier to unauthorized external users.

To be useful, a firewall should have the following general characteristics:

- It must control the flow of packets between the Internet and the internal network.

- It must not provide dynamic routing, because dynamic routing tables are subject to *route spoofing*—use of fake routes by intruders. Instead, the firewall should use *static routing tables* (which you can set up with the `route` command on Red Hat Linux systems).

- It must not allow any external user to log in as root. That way, even if the firewall system is compromised, the intruder may not be able to become root from a remote login.

- It must be kept in a physically secure location.

- It must distinguish between packets that come from the Internet and packets that come from the internal protected network. This feature allows the firewall to reject packets that come from the Internet, but have the IP address of a trusted system on the internal network (an attack wherein packets use fake IP addresses is known as *IP spoofing*).

- It should act as the SMTP mail gateway for the internal network. The `sendmail` software should be set up so that all outgoing mail appears to come from the firewall system.

- It should not have any user accounts. However, the firewall system may need to have a few user accounts for those internal users who need access to external systems. External users who need access to the internal network should use SSH for remote login (see discussion of SSH earlier in this chapter).

- It should keep a log of all system activities, such as successful and unsuccessful login attempts.

- It should provide DNS service to the outside world to resolve any host names that should be known to the outside world.

- It should provide good performance, so that it does not hinder the internal users' access to specific Internet services (such as HTTP and FTP).

A firewall can take many different forms. Here are three common forms of a firewall:

- *Screening router with packet filtering*—This simple firewall uses a router capable of filtering (blocking) packets based on IP addresses.

- *Dual-homed host with proxy services* — In this case a host with two network interfaces — one on the Internet and the other on the internal network — runs proxy services that act as a gateway for services, such as FTP and HTTP.

- *Perimeter network with bastion host* — This firewall configuration includes a perimeter network between the Internet and the protected internal network. A secure bastion host resides on the perimeter network and provides various services.

Tip

In a large organization you may also need to isolate smaller internal networks from the corporate network. You can set up such *internal firewalls* the same way you set up Internet firewalls.

The next few sections describe the common forms of firewall: screening router with packet filtering, dual-homes host, perimeter network with bastion host, and application gateway.

Screening Router with Packet Filtering

If you were to directly connect your organization's internal network to the Internet you would have to use a router to ensure proper exchange of packets between the internal network and the Internet. Most routers can block a packet based on its source, or destination IP address (as well as port number). The router's packet-filtering capability can serve as a simple firewall. Figure 26-2 illustrates the basic concept of packet filtering.

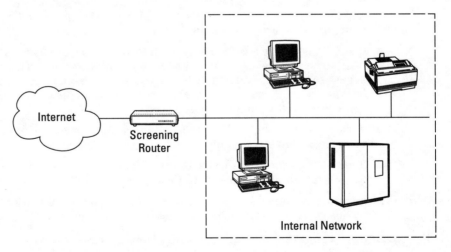

Figure 26-2: Packet filtering with a screening router provides a simple firewall.

Many router vendors, such as Cisco and 3Com, offer routers that can be programmed to perform packet filtering. The exact details of filtering depend on the router vendor, but all routers operate according to rules that refer to the basic attributes of an Internet packet:

- Source IP address
- Destination IP address
- Protocol (TCP, UDP, or ICMP)
- Source port number (if protocol is TCP or UDP)
- Destination port number (if protocol is TCP or UDP)
- ICMP message type

Additionally, the router knows the physical interface on which the packet arrived and the interface on which the packet will go out (if it is not blocked by the filtering rules).

Most packet filters operate in the following sequence:

1. You define the rules for allowing or blocking specific types of packets, based on IP addresses and port numbers. These packet-filtering rules are stored in the router.

2. The screening router examines the header of each packet that arrives for the information (such as IP addresses and port numbers) to which your rules apply.

3. The screening router applies the rules in the order in which they were stored.

4. If a rule allows the packet to be forwarded, the router sends the packet to its destination.

5. If a rule blocks the packet, the router drops the packet (stops processing the packet).

6. If none of the rules applies, the packet is blocked. This rule epitomizes the security philosophy that one should "deny unless expressly permitted."

Later in this chapter you learn how to implement a packet filter using the ipchains software that comes with Red Hat Linux.

Although packet filtering with a screening router is better than no security, packet filtering suffers from the following drawbacks:

- It is easy for the network administrator to inadvertently introduce errors into the filtering rules.

- Packets are filtered on the basis of IP addresses, which represent specific hosts. Essentially, packet filtering either blocks or routes all packets from a specific host. That means that anyone who breaks into a trusted host can immediately gain access to your protected network.

- Because it is based on IP addresses, packet filtering can be defeated by a technique known as IP spoofing, whereby a cracker sends packets with the IP address of a trusted host (by appropriating the IP address of a trusted host and setting up an appropriate route).

- Packet filtering is susceptible to routing attack programs that can create a bogus route that allows an intruder to receive all packets meant for the protected internal network.

- Screening routers that implement packet filtering do not keep logs of activities. That makes it hard for you to determine if anyone is attempting to break into the protected network. As you see in the next section, a dual-homed host can provide logging.

- A screening router does not hide the host names and IP addresses of the internal network. Outsiders can access and use this information to mount attacks against the protected network.

A more sophisticated approach is to use an application gateway that controls network traffic, based on specific applications instead of on a per-packet basis. You can implement an application gateway with a dual-homed host, or a bastion host.

Dual-Homed Host

A dual-homed host is a system with two network interfaces — one connected to the Internet and the other on an internal network that needs protection. The term *dual-homed* refers to the fact that the host "lives" in two networks.

In fact, if your operating system supports IP routing — the ability to forward network packets from one interface to another — the dual-homed host can serve as a router. However, you must turn off the IP forwarding feature to use the dual-homed host as a firewall system.

Linux supports the IP forwarding feature. If you plan to use a dual-homed host as a firewall, you have to use the `sysctl` command to disable IP forwarding.

With IP forwarding turned off, systems on both networks — the internal network as well as the Internet — can reach the dual-homed host, but no one from the Internet can access the internal network (nor can anyone from the internal network access the Internet). In this configuration, the dual-homed host completely isolates the two networks. Figure 26-3 illustrates the basic architecture of a dual-homed host.

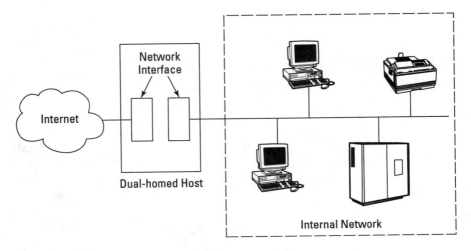

Figure 26-3: A dual-homed host as an Internet firewall

You implement the firewall function of the dual-homed host, by running application gateways — proxy services — on the dual-homed host. These proxy services allow specific applications, such as FTP and HTTP, to work across the dual-homed host. That means that you can configure the firewall so that internal clients (on the internal network) will be able to access Web and FTP servers on the Internet.

Your public Web site can run on the dual-homed host and be accessible to everyone on the Internet.

Caution

Note that you should not allow user logins on the dual-homed host. Anyone logged into the host can have access to both the internal network, as well as the Internet. Because the dual-homed host is your only barrier between the Internet and the internal network, it's best not to increase the chances of a break-in by allowing users to log in to the firewall system. By having user accounts, you increase the chances of an intruder gaining access to the firewall by cracking a user's password.

Perimeter Network with Bastion Host

An Internet firewall is often more complicated than a single dual-homed host that connects to both the Internet and the protected internal network. In particular, if you provide a number of Internet services you may need more than one system to host them. Imagine that you have two systems: one to run the Web and FTP servers and the other to provide mail (SMTP) and domain name system (DNS) lookups. In this case you'd place these two systems on a network that sits between the Internet and the internal network. Figure 26-4 illustrates this concept of an Internet firewall.

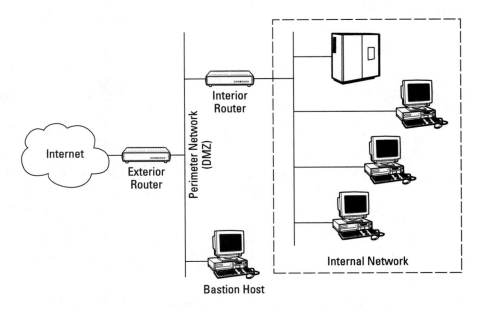

Figure 26-4: An Internet firewall consisting of a perimeter network and bastion hosts

As Figure 26-4 illustrates, the firewall consists of a perimeter network that connects to the Internet through an exterior router. The perimeter network, in turn, connects to the internal network through an interior router. The perimeter network has one or more hosts that run Internet services, including proxy services that allow internal hosts to access Web servers on the Internet.

The term *bastion host* is used to describe any system on the perimeter network, because such a system is on the Internet and has to be well fortified. The dual-homed host is also a bastion host, because the dual-homed host is also accessible from the Internet and has to be protected.

In the firewall configuration shown in Figure 26-4, the perimeter network is known as a DMZ (demilitarized zone) network because that network acts as a buffer between the Internet and the internal network (just as the real-life DMZ is a buffer between North and South Korea).

Typically you combine a packet-filtering router with a bastion host. Your Internet service provider typically provides the external router, which means that you do not have much control over that router's configuration. But you provide the internal router, which means that you can choose a screening router and employ some packet-filtering rules. For example, you would typically employ the following packet-filtering rules:

- From the internal network, allow only packets addressed to the bastion host.

- From the DMZ, allow only packets originating from the bastion host.
- Block all other packets.

This ensures that the internal network communicates only with the bastion host (or hosts).

Like the dual-homed host, the bastion host also runs an application gateway that provides proxy services for various Internet services, such as TELNET, FTP, SMTP, and HTTP.

Application Gateway

The bastion host or the dual-homed host is the system that acts as the intermediary between the Internet and the protected internal network. As such, that system serves as the internal network's gateway to the Internet. Toward this end the system runs software to forward and filter TCP/IP packets for various services, such as TELNET, FTP, and HTTP. The software for forwarding and filtering TCP/IP packets for specific applications are known as proxy services.

Figure 26-5 illustrates a proxy server's role in a firewall.

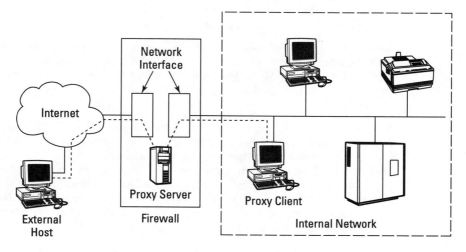

Figure 26-5: A proxy server lets internal hosts access Internet servers.

As Figure 26-5 shows, a proxy server accepts a connection for a specific protocol, such as FTP, and forwards the request to another server. In other words, the proxy server acts as a proxy for an actual server. Because it acts as a gateway for a specific application (such as HTTP or FTP), a proxy server is also known as an *application gateway*.

Unlike a screening router, which blocks packets only on the basis of information in the packet header (such as source and destination IP addresses), a proxy server actually uses the packet's data to decide what to do. For example, a proxy server does not blindly forward packets to an Internet service. The proxy server can enforce a site's security policy and disallow certain operations, depending on the specific application. For example, an FTP proxy server might prevent users from internal networks from using the FTP put command to send files to the Internet.

Accessing an Internet service through a proxy server can be a bit more involved than accessing that service directly. For example, a user on the internal network establishes a TELNET session with an Internet host with the following steps:

1. The user establishes a TELNET session with the firewall host — the system that runs the TELNET proxy. To do this, the user has to enter a user name and password so that the firewall host can verify that the user has permission to connect to the Internet.

2. The user enters a command (which the TELNET proxy accepts) to connect to the Internet host. The TELNET proxy, in turn, establishes a TELNET connection between itself and the Internet host.

3. The TELNET proxy on the firewall begins passing packets back and forth between the Internet host and the user's system (until the user ends the TELNET session with the Internet host).

Besides acting as a gateway, the TELNET proxy also logs the user's session with the Internet host. The logging is part of an application gateway's security feature, because the log file keeps track of all firewall accesses (as well as attempted accesses that may fail, because of a wrong user name or password).

Although the TELNET session involves two steps — first TELNET to the firewall host and then connect to the Internet host — the process of accessing services through a proxy need not be too cumbersome. The exact steps you take to access services through a firewall depend on the proxy software and the client program you use to access a service. With the right client program, proxies can be transparent to the user. For example, the Netscape Navigator Web browser makes it easy to access a Web site through an HTTP proxy. All you need to do is indicate through a menu choice the HTTP proxy you want to use.

Firewall Software

You need some sort of proxy or application gateway software to make the firewall work. I use the generic term *firewall software* to refer to the proxy software. The primary purpose of the proxy software is to allow internal users to access servers on the Internet.

What does SOCKS stand for?

According to the SOCKS Frequently Asked Questions (FAQ), the name SOCKS came from parts of the word *sock*ets. That name was used during the software's development and the name stuck.

If you want to read the SOCKS FAQ, you can find the latest FAQ files at `www.socks.nec.com/socksfaq.html`.

Following are some popular firewall software packages (all freely available on the Internet for non-commercial use):

■ *SOCKS* — This is a general-purpose proxy system that relays TCP data streams from a client (inside the firewall) to the Internet and back. To use the SOCKS proxy, you need versions of the client programs (TELNET, Web browser) linked with the SOCKS library.

■ *TIS Firewall Toolkit (FWTK)* — This freeware software package from Trusted Information Systems (TIS) includes several proxy servers. With TIS FWTK proxies, you can use unmodified versions of client programs to access Internet services, but the access becomes a two-step process — you must first log in to the firewall before connecting to the Internet service.

You can set up a dual-homed host with SOCKS proxy, or TIS FWTK.

SOCKS

SOCKS is a freely available software package, originally developed by David and Michelle Koblas, and currently maintained by Ying-Da Lee, that acts as a generic proxy for Internet services, such as HTTP, FTP, and TELNET. There are two well-known versions of SOCKS — SOCKS Version 4 (SOCKS V4) and SOCKS Version 5 (SOCKS V5). SOCKS V5 improves upon SOCKS V4 in the following ways:

■ SOCKS V4 can act as proxy for TCP connections only, but SOCKS V5 can provide proxy service for UDP, as well. Utilities such as `ping` and `traceroute`, use UDP (connectionless protocol), whereas services such as FTP, TELNET, and HTTP use TCP (connection-oriented protocol).

■ SOCKS V5 includes authentication, based on user name and password.

■ SOCKS V5 clients can use a SOCKS V5 server to perform DNS name lookups, whereas SOCKS V4 clients must be able to resolve any host-name (convert a hostname to an IP address) on their own.

Because of its popularity, SOCKS has become the de facto standard proxy software for Internet firewalls. The following RFCs describe the proposed Internet standards based on the SOCKS V5 protocol:

- **RFC 1928** — *SOCKS Protocol Version 5*, M. Leech, M. Ganis, Y. Lee, R. Kuris, D. Koblas & L. Jones, April 1996.

- **RFC 1929** — *Username/Password Authentication for SOCKS V5*, M. Leech, April 1996.

- **RFC 1961** — *GSS-API Authentication Method for SOCKS Version 5*, P. McMahon, June 1996.

For a host of other information that supplements this section's brief description of SOCKS, visit `http://www.socks.nec.com/`.

SOCKS V5 supports what is known as *authenticated traversal of multiple firewalls* (in fact, SOCKS V5 is also called Authenticated Firewall Traversal, or AFT). That's just a fancy way of saying that you can connect several SOCKS V5 servers in sequence and still maintain the firewall security. That means that you can build a virtual private network that connects two or more geographically separate networks by hooking up the SOCKS V5 proxy servers, as illustrated in Figure 26-6.

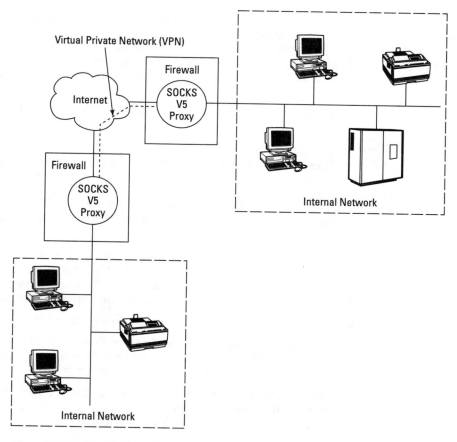

Figure 26-6: Using SOCKS V5 to build a virtual private network that spans the Internet

NEC's reference implementation of the SOCKS V5 software package is available for non-commercial use from `http://www.socks.nec.com/reference/socks5.html`. The SOCKS V5 software is available in source code form for UNIX—you can use this source to build the executable programs on Red Hat Linux. (A SOCKS V4 implementation is available through anonymous FTP from `ftp://ftp.nec.com:/pub/socks/`.)

The SOCKS software has the following components:

- *SOCKS Server*—The generic SOCKS proxy server. Clients use the SOCKS client library to communicate with the SOCKS server, which, in turn, provides access to the Internet services, such as TELNET, FTP, and HTTP.

- *SOCKS Client Library*—A nearly compatible replacement for standard Berkeley socket functions, such as `bind`, `connect`, `accept`, and `listen`.

- *SOCKS-ified Clients*—Some standard clients, such as TELNET and FTP, that have been linked with the SOCKS library. The *SOCKS-ified* adjective refers to client programs that have been linked with the SOCKS client library.

Because SOCKS provides a single generic proxy server, the basic arrangement of a SOCKS firewall is shown in Figure 26-7.

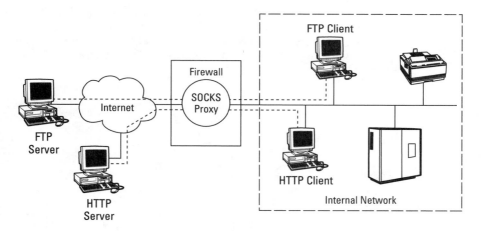

Figure 26-7: In a SOCKS firewall, all clients go through the same proxy server.

As Figure 26-7 illustrates, all clients know the protocol for communicating with the SOCKS server, and the SOCKS server can handle connections to many Internet services, including TELNET, FTP, and HTTP.

SOCKS enables users on the protected network to transparently access servers on the Internet, provided the user runs a SOCKS-ified client. (You can use the SOCKS server's configuration file to control which hosts can access the Internet.)

To SOCKS-ify a client, you must compile and link the client program with the SOCKS library. This process replaces the standard Berkeley sockets calls with the SOCKS version of calls.

Of course, you can recompile a client program only if you have the source code for the client program. Because SOCKS is popular, many vendors already include SOCKS support for their clients. For example, the Netscape Navigator Web browser includes support for SOCKS — all you have to do is specify the SOCKS server in Navigator's Network options.

TIS Firewall Toolkit

TIS Firewall Toolkit (FWTK) from Trusted Information Systems, includes a number of proxy servers that work with the standard client programs. To obtain the TIS FWTK, you first have to read the TIS FWTK software license (you can find it at `ftp://ftp.tis.com/pub/firewalls/toolkit/ LICENSE`). If you agree to abide by the conditions imposed by the license, send an e-mail message to `fwtk-request@tislabs.com` with the single word `accepted` in the body of the message (not the subject — the subject can be anything). Then Trusted Information Systems will send you a reply containing information about the location of the FWTK source code and its documentation. This section briefly discusses the TIS Firewall Toolkit.

Whereas SOCKS provides a single proxy that works for all TCP connections, TIS Firewall Toolkit provides individual proxy servers for each service. For example, `tn-gw` is the TELNET proxy and `http-gw` is the HTTP and Gopher proxy. Figure 26-8 shows the architecture of the TIS Firewall Toolkit proxy servers.

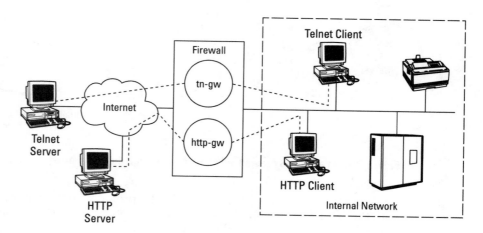

Figure 26-8: TIS Firewall Toolkit provides a proxy server for each client.

As Figure 26-8 shows, each client works through a specific proxy server dedicated to handling that client's protocol.

TIS Firewall Toolkit enables the use of standard (unmodified) client applications to access Internet services. However, users must first access the proxy server, and then initiate connection to the server on Internet. For example, when a user on the internal network wants to use TELNET to connect to an external host, he or she has to go through the following two-step process:

1. The user runs TELNET and connects to the bastion host, where the TELNET proxy (`tn-gw`) runs. The `tn-gw` proxy asks for user name and password and authenticates the user.

2. The user types `connect` *remotehost* (where *remotehost* is the external host's name) at the proxy prompt (`tn-gw>`). The TELNET proxy establishes the connection between the user's system and the external host.

The user follows similar steps to use the FTP proxy (`ftp-gw`).

Using a Red Hat Linux System as a Packet Filter

You can set up a Red Hat Linux system as a packet filter, by using the `ipchains` IP firewall software that comes with the Linux kernel. Typically you would have a Red Hat Linux system with two network interfaces — for example, an Ethernet interface for a local area network and a dial-up PPP connection to the Internet. You must first turn off IP forwarding by logging in as root and typing the following command:

```
/sbin/sysctl -w net.ipv4.ip_forward=0
```

With IP forwarding turned off, the Linux kernel does not automatically forward IP packets from one network interface to another (you want to use the `ipchains` firewall software to control what IP packets pass between the two network interfaces).

It is somewhat complex to configure `ipchains`. `ipchains` uses the concept of a chain, which is a sequence of rules. Each rule says what to do with a packet if the header contains certain information (such as the originating or destination IP address). If a rule does not apply, `ipchains` consults the next rule in the chain. By default, there are three chains:

- *Input chain* — The first set of rules against which packets are tested. The packets continue to the next chain only if the input chain does not specify `DENY` or `REJECT`.

- *Forward chain* — Contains the rules that apply to packets that are attempting to pass through this system to another system.

- *Output chain* — Includes the rules applied to packets before they are sent out.

You can add rules to these chains or create new chains of rules, by using the `ipchains` command. You can also view the current chains and save them to a file. For example, if you have done nothing else, the `ipchains -L` command should show the following:

```
ipchains -L
Chain input (policy ACCEPT):
Chain forward (policy ACCEPT):
Chain output (policy ACCEPT):
```

In this case, all three chains — input, forward, and output — show the same `ACCEPT` policy, which means everything is wide open.

Secret

If you get an error message when you try to run the `ipchains` command, log in as root and type `/sbin/insmod ipchains` to load the module that supports `ipchains`. Linux kernel 2.4 supports many different IP packet operations, such as filtering and masquerading, through loadable modules. Kernel 2.4 also comes with the `iptables` command that enables you to administer IP packet filtering. Type `man iptables` to learn more.

If you are setting up a packet filter, the first thing you do is deny everything except local loopback (the `lo` network interface) traffic with the following commands:

```
ipchains -A input -i ! lo -j DENY
ipchains -A output -i ! lo -j DENY
ipchains -A forward -j DENY
```

The first `ipchains` command, for example, appends to the input chain (`-A input`) the rule that if the packet does not come from the `lo` interface (`-i !lo`), then `ipchains` should `DENY` the packet (`-j DENY`).

Caution

Don't type `ipchains` commands from a remote login session. A rule that begins denying packets from all addresses could also stop what you type from reaching the system, and once that happens you may have no way of accessing the system over the network. To avoid unpleasant surprises, always type `ipchains` rules at the console — the keyboard and monitor that are connected directly to your Red Hat Linux PC that is running the packet filter.

You can gradually add rules to each of these chains to allow specific packets in or out. For example, to accept packets from the 192.168.1.0 network, you would add the following rule to the input chain:

```
ipchains -A input -s 192.168.1.0/24 -j ACCEPT
```

Note

I won't provide all the details of the `ipchains` commands in this section. Type `man ipchains` to read a summary of the commands. You should also read the IPCHAINS-HOWTO at `http://www.ibiblio.org/pub/Linux/docs/ HOWTO/IPCHAINS-HOWTO` for a detailed discussion of `ipchains`.

Once you define the rules using the `ipchains` command, they are in the memory and will be gone when you reboot the system. To save them for future use, use the `ipchains-save` command to store the rules in a file. For example, you can save the rules in a file named `ipchains.rules` with the following commands:

```
ipchains-save > ipchains.rules
```

Here are a few lines from the `ipchains.rules` file on a test system:

```
:input ACCEPT
:forward ACCEPT
:output ACCEPT
-A input -s 0.0.0.0/0.0.0.0 -d 0.0.0.0/0.0.0.0 -i ! lo -j DENY
-A input -s 192.168.1.0/255.255.255.0 -d 0.0.0.0/0.0.0.0 -j ACCEPT
-A forward -s 0.0.0.0/0.0.0.0 -d 0.0.0.0/0.0.0.0 -j DENY
-A output -s 0.0.0.0/0.0.0.0 -d 0.0.0.0/0.0.0.0 -i ! lo -j DENY
... lines deleted...
```

Secret

On a Red Hat Linux system, you can automate the process of setting up the rules by saving the `ipchains` rules in the file `/etc/sysconfig/ipchains` (type `/sbin/ipchains-save > /etc/sysconfig/ipchains`), and then enabling `ipchains` with the following command:

```
/sbin/chkconfig add --ipchains
```

That should ensure that the `/etc/init.d/ipchains start` command is executed at system startup. The `/etc/init.d/ipchains` script will then run the `/sbin/ipchains-restore` command to restore the `ipchains` rules from the `/etc/sysconfig/ipchains` file.

Monitoring System Security

After you set up your system securely, you have to periodically monitor the log files for any signs of intrusion. You can also install the Tripwire software to monitor the integrity of critical system files and directories.

Additionally, you should periodically check security news to learn about recently discovered weaknesses in any of your system components. If Red Hat provides an upgrade to fix a security problem, download the new RPM files, and install them on your system.

Cross-Reference

Follow the steps in Chapter 24 to download the new RPM files and install them.

Using Tripwire to Monitor the Integrity of System Files

The worst security breaches are the ones that go undetected. A savvy cracker might manage to get access to a system, replace critical system programs with Trojan horses, and then hide his or her tracks by modifying the log files. Later on the cracker could use the Trojan horse programs to access the system at will. The problem is that the system administrator may never even suspect that anything is out of the ordinary. Using software such as Tripwire to monitor file integrity can help avoid this type of problem.

This book's companion CD-ROMs include the Tripwire package. It is not installed by default, but you can easily install it and then configure it to monitor any changes to specified system files and directories.

Installing Tripwire

To install the Tripwire package, place the second CD-ROM in the CD-ROM drive and mount it with the mount /mnt/cdrom command (or, if you are running the GNOME desktop, wait until the magicdev device automatically mounts the CD-ROM). Then type the following commands to install the Tripwire package:

```
cd /mnt/cdrom/RedHat/RPMS
rpm -ivh tripwire*
tripwire    ###############################################
```

The Tripwire installation does the following:

- Installs the programs siggen, tripwire, twadmin, and twprint in the /usr/sbin directory.

- Places some files in the /etc/tripwire directory, including the shell script /etc/tripwire/twinstall.sh, which you have to run after installing the package.

- Installs the tripwire-check script in the /etc/cron.daily directory. This causes the tripwire-check script to be executed daily.

- Installs the man pages for twconfig, twpolicy, twfiles, siggen, tripwire, twadmin, twintro, and twprint. You can read these man pages with commands, such as man tripwire.

- Installs some Tripwire documentation in the /usr/share/doc directory. To change to the Tripwire documentation directory, type cd/usr/share/doc/tripwire*.

- Creates the /var/lib/tripwire/report directory in which to store Tripwire reports.

After installing the Tripwire package, you have to run the /etc/tripwire/twinstall.sh script to generate cryptographic keys. Type the following command:

```
/etc/tripwire/twinstall.sh
```

The Tripwire site and local passphrases are used to sign a variety of files, such as the configuration, policy, and database files.

```
Passphrases should be at least 8 characters in length
and contain both letters and numbers.

See the Tripwire manual for more information.

------------------------------------------------
Creating key files...

(When selecting a passphrase, keep in mind that good passphrases typically
have upper and lower case letters, digits and punctuation marks, and are
at least 8 characters in length.)

Enter the site keyfile passphrase:    <-- Select a site passphrase and type it.
Verify the site keyfile passphrase:  <-- Retype the site passphrase.
Generating key (this may take several minutes)...Key generation complete.

(When selecting a passphrase, keep in mind that good passphrases typically
have upper and lower case letters, digits and punctuation marks, and are
at least 8 characters in length.)

Enter the local keyfile passphrase:    <-- Select passphrase for local keyfile.
Verify the local keyfile passphrase:  <-- Retype the same passphrase.
Generating key (this may take several minutes)...Key generation complete.


------------------------------------------------
Signing configuration file...
Please enter your site passphrase:  <-- Type the site passphrase from before
Wrote configuration file: /etc/tripwire/tw.cfg

A clear-text version of the Tripwire configuration file
/etc/tripwire/twcfg.txt
has been preserved for your inspection.  It is recommended
that you delete this file manually after you have examined it.


------------------------------------------------
Signing policy file...
Please enter your site passphrase:  <-- Type the site passphrase from before
Wrote policy file: /etc/tripwire/tw.pol

A clear-text version of the Tripwire policy file
/etc/tripwire/twpol.txt
has been preserved for your inspection.  This implements
a minimal policy, intended only to test essential
Tripwire functionality.  You should edit the policy file
to describe your system, and then use twadmin to generate
a new signed copy of the Tripwire policy.
```

Initializing the Tripwire database

Next, you have to initialize the Tripwire database with the following command:

```
tripwire --init
Please enter your local passphrase:
Parsing policy file: /etc/tripwire/tw.pol
Generating the database...
*** Processing Unix File System ***
### Warning: File system error.
### Filename: /usr/sbin/fixrmtab
### No such file or directory
### Continuing...
...Many lines of output deleted....
Wrote database file: /var/lib/tripwire/lnbp200.twd
The database was successfully generated.
```

You might get a few error messages for files that are not in your system, but
are referred to in the Tripwire policy file /etc/tripwire/twpol.txt. At the
end of all the processing, Tripwire writes a database file named after your
system's hostname and saves that file in the /var/lib/tripwire directory.
The database file is digitally signed with the key you specified in response to
prompts from the /etc/tripwire/twinstall.sh script (a *digital signature*
is typically the one-way hash of the message text, encrypted with the local
private key — the hash is usually computed with the MD5 or SHA-1 algorithm).

Checking file integrity

Once the Tripwire database is initialized, you should periodically run
Tripwire in integrity-checking mode with the command tripwire --check.
In this mode Tripwire uses the policy file, /etc/tripwire/tw.pol, and compares the state of the current files against what's stored in the initial database. Tripwire prints a report on the standard output and also saves the
report in the /var/lib/tripwire/report directory.

For example, when I log in as root and type the following command:

```
tripwire --check
```

the tripwire --check command displays some error messages about missing files (the same ones I got when I initialized the Tripwire database with the
tripwire init command). After that, Tripwire prints the report to the standard output and also writes it to a file.

In this case, Tripwire writes the report to the file lnbp200-20001113-
211618.twr in the /var/lib/tripwire/report directory (the filename
depends on my system's hostname and the date and time I ran the tripwire
--check command). The filename is the date and time appended to the host
name, with dashes as separators, and then ending with a .twr. The report is
in binary format. To print the report, use the twprint command with the following syntax:

```
twprint --print-report -r reportfilename.twr
```

The last argument is the name of the report file. For example, to view the report I generated, I type the following command:

```
cd /var/lib/tripwire/report
twprint --print-report -r lnbp200-20001113-211618.twr
Note: Report is not encrypted.
Tripwire(R) 2.3.0 Integrity Check Report

Report generated by:          root
Report created on:            Mon Nov 13 21:16:18 2000
Database last updated on:     Never


===============================================================================
Report Summary:
===============================================================================


Host name:                    lnbp200
Host IP address:              127.0.0.1
Host ID:                      None
Policy file used:             /etc/tripwire/tw.pol
Configuration file used:      /etc/tripwire/tw.cfg
Database file used:           /var/lib/tripwire/lnbp200.twd
Command line used:            tripwire -check


===============================================================================
Rule Summary:
===============================================================================
-------------------------------------------------------------------------------

    Section: Unix File System
-------------------------------------------------------------------------------


    Rule Name                       Severity Level   Added   Removed  Modified
    ---------                       --------------   -----   -------  --------
    Invariant Directories           66               0       0        0
    Temporary directories           33               0       0        0
  * Tripwire Data Files             100              1       0        0
    Critical devices                100              0       0        0
    User binaries                   66               0       0        0
    Tripwire Binaries               100              0       0        0
  * Critical configuration files    100              0       0        2
    Libraries                       66               0       0        0
    Shell Binaries                  100              0       0        0
    File System and Disk Administraton Programs
                                    100              0       0        0
    Kernel Administration Programs  100              0       0        0
    Networking Programs             100              0       0        0
    System Administration Programs  100              0       0        0
    Hardware and Device Control Programs
... Lines deleted ...

Total objects scanned:  20324
Total violations found:  4
... Lines deleted ...
```

```
-------------------------------------------------------------------------
Rule Name: Critical configuration files (/etc/hosts.allow)
Severity Level: 100
-------------------------------------------------------------------------

  ----------------------------------------
  Modified Objects: 1
  ----------------------------------------

Modified object name:  /etc/hosts.allow
... Lines deleted ...
```

In this partial report, `twprint` reported four violations of the rules. An asterisk (*) appears next to the rules that were violated. An example of the violation is a change to the `/etc/hosts.allow` file, which I had modified between the time the Tripwire database was created and the time I typed the `tripwire --check` command. I expected to see this change included in the Tripwire report. This example shows how Tripwire detects and reports any changes to system files.

Secret

When you install Tripwire, your system is already set up to run the `/etc/cron.daily/tripwire-check` script every day. The `/etc/cron.daily/tripwire-check` script executes the `tripwire --check` command to generate a report. All you need to do is log in as root, and use the `twprint` command to review the latest report each day.

Examining Log Files

Many Linux system applications, including some servers, write log information using the logging capabilities of `syslogd`. On Red Hat Linux systems, the log files written by `syslogd` reside in the `/var/log` directory. Make sure that only the root user can read and write these files.

You should routinely monitor the following log files:

- `/var/log/messages` contains a wide variety of logging messages, from user logins to messages from services started by the TCP wrapper.
- `/var/log/secure` contains reports from services, such as `in.telnetd` and `in.ftpd`, which `xinetd` starts through the TCP wrapper.
- `/var/log/maillog` contains reports from `sendmail`.
- `/var/log/xferlog` contains a log of all FTP file transfers.

Unfortunately, there is no easy-to-use tool for viewing these log files. The best approach is to browse them routinely. You can open the log file in the `vi` editor in read-only mode by typing a command, such as `vi -R /var/log/messages`, which prevents you from accidentally overwriting the log file. In the editor, you can search for a date and begin browsing from that point.

Because many potential intruders use port-scanning tools in an attempt to establish TCP/IP connections to well-known ports on your system, you should look for messages that indicate attempted connections from unknown hosts (indicated by names or IP addresses). To do this, browse through the /var/log/secure file. For example, here's what a line in the /var/log/secure file shows when I connect to my Linux system from one of the PCs on the LAN:

```
Oct 26 20:18:19 lnbp200 xinetd[511]: START: ftp pid=23824 from=192.168.1.40
```

Notice the text pid=23824 that appears next to the word ftp. That's the process ID of the FTP server program started by xinetd. You can use this number to look at corresponding messages in the /var/log/messages file to see whether this attempt did or did not succeed. Here is a sample of how I check this:

```
grep "\[23824\]" messages
Oct 26 20:30:01 lnbp200 ftpd[23824]: FTP LOGIN FROM lnbp400 [192.168.1.40], naba
Oct 26 20:30:22 lnbp200 ftpd[23824]: FTP session closed
```

The resulting output tells me that the user naba successfully logged in and sometime later closed the FTP session.

Similarly, you should analyze any suspicious messages you find in these log files. You may be surprised by the number of attempts curious outsiders make to gain access to your system.

Keeping Up with Security News and Updates

To keep up with the latest security alerts, you may want to visit one or more of the following sites daily:

- CERT Coordination Center at http://www.cert.org
- Computer Incident Advisory Capability (CIAC) at http://www.ciac.org
- National Infrastructure Protection Center at http://www.nipc.gov

If you have access to Internet newsgroups, you can periodically browse the following:

- comp.security.announce — A moderated newsgroup that includes announcements from CERT about security.
- comp.security.unix — A newsgroup that includes discussions of UNIX security issues, including items related to Red Hat Linux.

If you prefer to receive regular security updates through e-mail, you can also sign up on, or subscribe to, various mailing lists:

- redhat-watch-list@redhat.com — Send an e-mail message to redhat-watch-list-req@redhat.com with the word subscribe in the Subject line.
- linux-security@redhat.com — Send an e-mail message to linux-security-sub@redhat.com with the word subscribe in the Subject line.

- FOCUS-LINUX — Fill out the form in `http://www.securityfocus.com/focus/linux/list/subscribe.html` to subscribe to this mailing list focused on Linux security issues.

- Cert Advisory mailing list — Send an e-mail message to `cert-advisory-request@cert.org` with `SUBSCRIBE` *myname@myisp.com* in the Subject line (replace *myname@myisp.com* with your e-mail address).

Finally, you should check Red Hat's Web site at `http://www.redhat.com/support/errata/` for updates that may fix any known security problems with Red Hat Linux.

Summary

As the system administrator, your primary concern is the security of your Red Hat Linux system and the local network. You may also have to worry about securing it from unwanted access from the Internet. This chapter introduces you to the subjects of system and network security and shows you how to use some of the security features of Red Hat Linux.

By reading this chapter, you learn the following:

- It is helpful to think of an organization-wide security framework. In such a framework you first establish a security policy based on business requirements and risk analysis. Then you develop an overall security solution based on security policy, business requirements, and available technology. Finally, you put in place the management practices to continually monitor, detect, and respond to any security problems.

- Risk analysis means identifying threats and vulnerabilities. Then you can assess the probability and impact of each vulnerability and decide to mitigate those vulnerabilities that are most likely to be exploited and whose exploitation will cause the most harm.

- To secure the Red Hat Linux system you have to secure the passwords and the network services, such as FTP, NFS, and HTTP. You can use the `/sbin/chkconfig` command to disable unnecessary services. For services started by `xinetd` you have to edit the configuration files in `/etc/xinetd.d` directory.

- Use secure shell (SSH) for secure remote logins. This chapter shows you how to use SSH.

- For a system connected to the Internet (including a local network), you can meet network security needs by setting up a firewall between the internal network and the Internet. Any publicly accessible servers, such as Web and FTP servers should be placed outside the firewall in a perimeter network, or the demilitarized zone (DMZ).

- There are many kinds of firewalls — packet filters, dual-homed hosts, and application gateways (or proxy servers). This chapter provides an overview of firewalls, including a description of SOCKS and TIS Firewall Toolkit (FWTK) software. You can implement a packet filtering firewall, by using the `ipchains` software that comes with Red Hat Linux.

- You can monitor the integrity of system files and directories, by installing and setting up the Tripwire software that comes on the companion CD-ROMs.

- You should periodically review the log files in the `/var/log` directory of your Red Hat Linux system for any signs of intrusion attempts.

- The chapter provides some on line resources from which you can learn more about securing your Red Hat Linux system. You can use these online resources to keep up with late-breaking security news.

Part V

Programming Red Hat Linux

Chapter 27

Software Development in Linux

Many Linux users happen to be software developers. If you want to develop software as a hobby or want to add features to Linux, you'll find that Linux includes everything you need to create UNIX and X applications. You can use the GNU C and C++ compilers to write conventional programs (that you compile and link into an executable). As an alternative, you can use the Tcl/Tk scripting language to write interpreted graphical applications.

This chapter discusses software development on a Linux PC. The focus is not on any specific programming language. Instead, this chapter describes how to use various software development tools, such as compilers, makefiles, and version-control systems.

The chapter also describes the implications of Free Software Foundation's GNU Public License on any plans you might have to develop Linux software. You need to know this, because you usually use GNU tools and GNU libraries to develop software in Linux.

I also discuss dynamic linking and the Executable and Linking Format (ELF), which makes dynamic linking easier. These topics are of interest to Linux programmers, because dynamic linking reduces the size of executables and may enable programmers to distribute software in binary form, even if software uses the GNU libraries.

Cross-Reference

Developing X applications that have graphical user interfaces is a complex enough subject to deserve an entire chapter. Accordingly, X programming on Linux is discussed in Chapter 30.

Software Development Tools in Linux

As expected, as a UNIX look-alike, Linux includes these traditional UNIX software development tools:

- A text editor, such as vi or emacs, for editing the source code (described in Chapter 14).

- A C compiler for compiling and linking programs written in C — the programming language of choice for writing UNIX applications (although nowadays, many programmers are turning to C++). Linux includes the GNU C and C++ compilers. Originally, the GNU C Compiler was known as GCC. The acronym GCC now stands for GNU Compiler Collection (see description in http://gcc.gnu.org/).

- The GNU make utility for automating the *software build* process — the process of combining object modules into an executable or a library.

- A debugger for debugging programs. Linux includes the GNU debugger gdb, as well as xxgdb, a graphical interface to gdb.

- A version-control system to keep track of various revisions of a source file. Linux comes with RCS (Revision Control System) and CVS (Concurrent Versions System). Nowadays, most open-source projects use CVS as the version-control system.

These tools are installed automatically if you select the *Development* package group when you install Red Hat Linux from this book's companion CD-ROMs, following the steps outlined in Chapter 2. The next few sections briefly describe how to use these tools to write applications for Linux.

info: The Authoritative Help on GNU Tools

You may have noticed that most of the Linux software development tools are from the Free Software Foundation's GNU project. The online documentation for all these tools comes as info files. The info program is GNU's hypertext help system.

To see info in action, type **info** at the shell prompt, or type **Esc-x** followed by **info** in GNU Emacs. I typically access info from GNU Emacs, because doing so enables me to use online help while editing a program. However, you can always type **info** in a separate terminal window. Figure 27-1 shows the terminal window after I type **info** at the shell prompt.

In info, the online help text is organized in nodes; each node represents information on a specific topic. The first line shows the header for that node.

Figure 27-1 shows the initial info screen, with a directory of topics. This directory is an info file: /usr/share/info/dir, a text file that contains embedded special characters. The following are a few lines from the /usr/share/info/dir file that correspond to the screen shown in Figure 27-1:

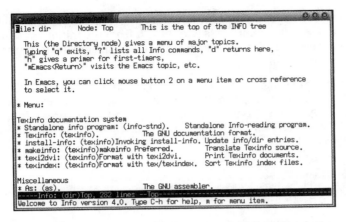

Figure 27-1: The terminal window after typing **info** at the shell prompt

```
$Id: dir,v 1.2 1996/09/24 18:43:01 karl Exp $
This is the file .../info/dir, which contains the topmost node of the
Info hierarchy.  The first time you invoke Info you start off
looking at that node, which is (dir)Top.
^_   (This is the Ctrl+_ character)
File: dir      Node: Top       This is the top of the INFO tree

  This (the Directory node) gives a menu of major topics.
  Typing "q" exits, "?" lists all Info commands, "d" returns here,
  "h" gives a primer for first-timers,
  "mEmacs<Return>" visits the Emacs topic, etc.

  In Emacs, you can click mouse button 2 on a menu item or cross reference
  to select it.

* Menu:

Texinfo documentation system
* Standalone info program: (info-stnd).    Standalone Info-reading program.
* Texinfo: (texinfo).         The GNU documentation format.
* install-info: (texinfo)Invoking install-info. Update info/dir entries.
* makeinfo: (texinfo)makeinfo Preferred.       Translate Texinfo source.
(...Lines deleted...)
```

A comparison of this listing with the screen shown in Figure 27-1 shows
that info displays only the lines that follow the Ctrl+_ character. In your
system, the /usr/share/info directory contains this info file, as well as
others, with the text for each topic. These info files usually are stored in
compressed format. You really don't have to know these details to use the
info files.

Tip

You have to use several single-letter commands to navigate info files. The best way to learn the commands is to type **h** from the initial info directory, shown in Figure 27-1. Type **d** after reading the help screens to return to the initial directory of topics.

From the directory screen of Figure 27-1, type **m**, followed by the name of a menu item (shown in boldface with an asterisk prefix). For example, to view the online help for GCC, type **m**, then type **gcc**, and then press Enter. The info system, in turn, displays the top-level menu of items for GCC, as shown in Figure 27-2.

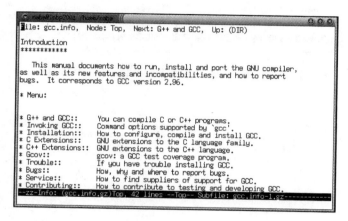

Figure 27-2: The info window, showing the top-level help on GCC

You can explore further by typing **m**, followed by one of the menu items shown in Figure 27-2.

While you're at it, you may want to type **m**, and then **copy**, and then press Enter in the screen shown in Figure 27-2. That action displays the GNU General Public License (GPL), shown in Figure 27-3.

GPL covers Linux and the gcc compiler. GPL requires distribution of the source code (that's why all Linux distributions come with source code). In the "Implications of GNU Licenses" section, you learn that you can still use GNU tools to develop commercial applications and to distribute applications in binary form (without source code), as long as they link with selected GNU libraries only.

At any time in info, you can type **d** to return to the info topic directory shown in Figure 27-1. From that screen, you can view help on other GNU tools, such as make and the GNU debugger.

To quit info, type q. If you access info from the Emacs editor, press Ctrl+X, followed by Ctrl+C, to quit the Emacs editor.

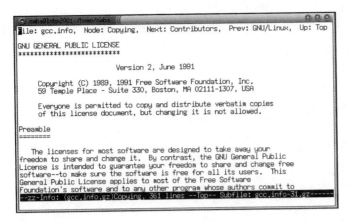

Figure 27-3: The info window, showing the first page of the GNU General Public License (GPL)

GNU C and C++ Compilers

The most important software development tool in Linux is GCC, which is the GNU C and C++ compiler. In fact, GCC can compile three languages: C, C++, and Objective-C (a language that has object-oriented extensions to C). You use the same gcc command to compile and link both C and C++ source files. The GCC compiler supports ANSI standard C, making it easy to port any ANSI C program to Linux. Additionally, if you've ever used a C compiler on other UNIX systems, you are right at home with GCC.

Invoking GCC

Use the gcc command to invoke GCC. By default, when you use the gcc command on a source file, GCC preprocesses, compiles, and links the executable. However, you can use GCC options to stop this process at an intermediate stage. For example, you might invoke gcc by using the -c option to compile a source file and to generate an object file, but not to perform the link step.

Using GCC to compile and link a few C source files is very simple. Suppose you want to compile and link a simple program made up of two source files. The following listing shows the file area.c: the main program that computes the area of a circle whose radius is specified through the command line:

```
#include <stdio.h>
#include <stdlib.h>

/* Function prototype */
double area_of_circle(double r);

int main(int argc, char **argv)
{
```

```
  if(argc < 2)
  {
    printf("Usage: %s radius\n", argv[0]);
    exit(1);
  }
  else
  {
    double radius = atof(argv[1]);
    double area = area_of_circle(radius);
    printf("Area of circle with radius %f = %f\n",
        radius, area);
  }
  return 0;
}
```

The following listing shows the file `circle.c`, which provides a function that computes the area of a circle.

```
#include <math.h>

#define SQUARE(x) ((x)*(x))

double area_of_circle(double r)
{
  return 4.0 * M_PI * SQUARE(r);
}
```

For such a simple program, of course, I can place everything in a single file, but this contrived example lets me show you how to handle multiple files.

To compile these two programs and to create an executable file named `area`, you might use this command:

```
gcc -o area area.c circle.c
```

This invocation of GCC uses the `-o` option to specify the name of the executable file. (If you do not specify the name of an output file, GCC creates a file named `a.out`.)

If there are too many source files to compile and link, compile the files individually, and generate object files (that have the `.o` extension). That way, when you change a source file, you need to compile only that file and to link all the object files. The following example shows how to separate the compile and link steps for the example program:

```
gcc -c area.c
gcc -c circle.c
gcc -o area area.o circle.o
```

The first two invocations of `gcc` with the `-c` option compile the source files. The third invocation links the object files into an executable named `area`.

In case you are curious, here's how you run the sample program (to compute the area of a circle with a radius of 1):

```
./area 1
Area of circle with radius 1.000000 = 12.566371
```

Tip

Incidentally, you have to add the ./ prefix to the program's name (area), only if the current directory is not in the PATH environment variable. There is no harm in adding the prefix, even if your PATH contains the current directory.

Compiling C++ programs

GNU CC is a combined C and C++ compiler, so the gcc command also can compile C++ source files. GCC uses the file extension to determine whether a file is C or C++. C files have a lowercase .c extension, whereas C++ files end with .C or .cpp.

Although the gcc command can compile a C++ file, that command does not automatically link with various class libraries that C++ programs typically require. That's why it's easier to compile and link a C++ program by using the g++ command, which invokes gcc with appropriate options.

Suppose you want to compile the following simple C++ program stored in a file named hello.C (it's customary to use an uppercase C extension for C++ source files):

```
#include <iostream.h>

void main(void)
{
   cout << "Hello from Linux!" << endl;
}
```

To compile and link this program into an executable program named hello, use this command:

```
g++ -o hello hello.C
```

This command creates the hello executable, which you can run as follows:

```
./hello
Hello from Linux!
```

As you see in the following section, a host of GCC options controls various aspects of compiling C++ programs.

Exploring GCC options

Following is the basic syntax of the gcc command:

```
gcc options filenames
```

Each option starts with a hyphen (-) and usually has a long name, such as -funsigned-char or -finline-functions. Many commonly used options are short, however, such as -c to compile only, and -g to generate debugging information (needed to debug the program, by using the GNU debugger).

You can view a summary of all GCC options, by using `info`. Type `info` at the shell prompt, and then press m, followed by `gcc`. Then follow the menu items: Invoking GCC ⇨ Option Summary. Usually, you do not have to specify GCC options explicitly; the default settings are fine for most applications. Table 27-1 lists some of the GCC options you might use.

Table 27-1   Commonly Used GCC Options

Option	Meaning
-ansi	Support ANSI standard C syntax only. (This option disables some GNU C-specific features, such as the asm and typeof keywords.)
-c	Compile and generate object file only.
-DMACRO	Define the macro with the string "1" as its value.
-DMACRO=DEFN	Define the macro as DEFN.
-E	Run only the C preprocessor.
-fallow-single-precision	Perform all math operations in single precision.
-fpack-struct	Pack all structure members without any padding.
-fpcc-struct-return	Return all struct and union values in memory, rather than in registers. (Returning values this way is less efficient, but is compatible with other compilers.)
-fPIC	Generate position-independent code (PIC) suitable for use in a shared library.
-freg-struct-return	When possible, return struct and union values in registers.
-g	Generate debugging information. (The GNU debugger can use this information.)
-IDIRECTORY	Search the specified directory for files you include by using the #include preprocessor directive.
-LDIRECTORY	Search the specified directory for libraries.
-lLIBRARY	Search the specified library when linking.
-m486	Optimize code for a 486. (This code also can run on a 386.)
-o FILE	Generate the specified output file (used to designate the name of an executable file).

Option	Meaning
-O0	Do not optimize.
-O or -O1	Optimize the generated code.
-O2	Optimize even more.
-O3	Perform optimizations beyond those done for -O2.
-pedantic	Generate errors if any non-ANSI standard extensions are used.
-pg	Add extra code to the program so that, when run, it generates information the gprof program can use to display timing details for various parts of the program.
-shared	Generate a shared object file (typically used to create a shared library).
-traditional	Support traditional Kernighan and Ritchie C syntax only.
-UMACRO	Undefine the specified macro.
-v	Display the version number of GCC.
-w	Don't generate any warning messages.
-Wl,OPTION	Pass the OPTION string (containing multiple comma-separated options) to the linker. To create a shared library named libXXX.so.1, for example, use the following flag: -Wl,-soname,libXXX.so.1

The GNU make Utility

When an application is made up of more than a few source files, compiling and linking the files by manually typing the gcc command is inconvenient. Additionally, you do not want to compile every file whenever you change something in a single source file. This situation is what makes the GNU make utility so helpful.

The make utility works by reading and interpreting a *makefile*: a text file you have to prepare, according to a specified syntax. The makefile describes which files constitute a program and explains how to compile and link the files to build the program. Whenever you change one or more files, make determines which files should be recompiled and then issues the appropriate commands for compiling those files and rebuilding the program.

The make utility is, in fact, specified in Section 6.2 of the POSIX.2 standard (IEEE Standard 1003.2-1992) for shells and tools. GNU make conforms to the POSIX.2 standard.

Makefile names

By default, GNU make looks for a makefile that has one of the following names, in the order shown:

- GNUmakefile
- makefile
- Makefile

In UNIX systems, using Makefile as the name of the makefile is customary, because it appears near the beginning of directory listings where the upper-case names appear before the lowercase names.

When you download software from the Internet, you usually find a Makefile, together with the source files. To build the software, you only have to type **make** at the shell prompt; make takes care of all the steps necessary to build the software.

If your makefile does not have a standard name, such as Makefile, you have to use the -f option to specify the makefile's name. If your makefile is called webprog.mak, for example, you have to run make using the following command line:

```
make -f webprog.mak
```

GNU make also accepts several other command-line options, which are summarized in the "How to run make" section of this chapter.

The makefile

For a program that consists of several source and header files, the makefile specifies the following:

- The items to be created by make — usually the object files and the executable. The term *target* is used for an item to be created.
- The files or other actions required to create the target.
- Which commands should be executed to create each target.

Suppose you have a C++ source file named form.C that contains the following preprocessor directive:

```
#include "form.h"  // Include header file
```

The object file form.o clearly depends on the source file form.C and the header file form.h. In addition to these dependencies, you must specify how make should convert the form.C file to the object file form.o. Suppose you want make to invoke g++ (because the source file is in C++) with these options:

- -c (compile only)
- -g (generate debugging information)
- -02 (optimize some)

In the makefile, you can express this with the following rule:

```
# This a comment in the makefile
# The following lines indicate how form.o depends
# form.C and form.h and how to create form.o.

form.o: form.C form.h
        g++ -c -g -02 form.C
```

In this example, the first noncomment line shows form.o as the *target* and form.C and form.h as the *dependent* files.

Secret

The line following the dependency indicates how to build the target from its dependents. This line must start with a Tab.

The benefit of using make is that it prevents unnecessary compilations. After all, you can invoke g++ (or gcc) in a shell script to compile and link all the files that make up your application, but the shell script compiles everything, even if the compilations are unnecessary. GNU make, on the other hand, builds a target, only if one or more of its dependents has changed since the last time the target was built. make verifies this change by examining the time of the last modification of the target and the dependents.

Note

make treats the target as the name of a goal to be achieved; the target does not have to be a file. You can have a rule such as this:

```
clean:
        rm -f *.o
```

This rule specifies an abstract target named clean that does not depend on anything. This dependency statement says that to make clean, GNU make should invoke the command rm -f *.o, which deletes all files that have the .o extension (these are the object files). Thus, the net effect of creating the target named clean is to delete the object files.

Variables (or macros)

In addition to the basic service of building targets from dependents, GNU make includes many nice features that make it easy for you to express the dependencies and rules for building a target from its dependents. If you need to compile a large number of C++ files by using GCC with the same options, for example, typing the options for each file is tedious. You can avoid this task by defining a variable or macro in make as follows:

```
# Define macros for name of compiler
CXX= g++

# Define a macro for the GCC flags
```

```
CXXFLAGS= -02 -g -m486

# A rule for building an object file
form.o: form.C form.h
        $(CXX) -c $(CXXFLAGS) form.C
```

In this example, CXX and CXXFLAGS are make variables. GNU make prefers to call them variables, but most UNIX make utilities call them macros.

To use a variable anywhere in the makefile, start with a dollar sign ($) followed by the variable within parentheses. GNU make replaces all occurrences of a variable with its definition; thus, it replaces all occurrences of $(CXXFLAGS) with the string -02 -g -m486.

GNU make has several predefined variables that have special meanings. Table 27-2 lists these variables. In addition to the variables listed in Table 27-2, GNU make considers all environment variables predefined variables.

Table 27-2   Some Predefined Variables in GNU make

Variable	Meaning
$%	Member name for targets that are archives. If the target is libDisp.a(image.o), for example, $% is image.o, and $@ is libDisp.a.
$*	Name of the target file without the extension.
$+	Names of all dependent files with duplicate dependencies, listed in their order of occurrence.
$<	The name of the first dependent file.
$?	Names of all dependent files (with spaces between the names) that are newer than the target.
$@	Complete name of the target.
$^	Names of all dependent files, with spaces between the names. Duplicates are removed from the dependent filenames.
AR	Name of the archive-maintaining program. (Default value: ar.)
ARFLAGS	Flags for the archive-maintaining program. (Default value: rv.)
AS	Name of the assembler program that converts the assembly language to object code. (Default value: as.)
ASFLAGS	Flags for the assembler.
CC	Name of the C compiler. (Default value: cc.)
CFLAGS	Flags to be passed to the C compiler.

Variable	Meaning
CO	Name of the program that extracts a file from RCS. (Default value: co.)
COFLAGS	Flags for the RCS co program.
CPP	Name of the C preprocessor. (Default value: $(CC) -E.)
CPPFLAGS	Flags for the C preprocessor.
CXX	Name of the C++ compiler. (Default value: g++.)
CXXFLAGS	Flags to be passed to the C++ compiler.
FC	Name of the FORTRAN compiler. (Default value: f77.)
FFLAGS	Flags for the FORTRAN compiler.
GET	Name of the program to extract a file from SCCS. (Default value: get.)
GFLAGS	Flags for the SCCS get program.
LDFLAGS	Flags for the compiler when it is supposed to invoke the linker ld.
LEX	Name of the program to convert Lex grammar to C program. (Default value: lex.)
LFLAGS	Flags for Lex.
MAKEINFO	Name of the program that converts Texinfo source files to info files. (Default value: makeinfo.)
RM	Name of the command to delete a file. (Default value: rm -f.)
TEX	Name of the program to generate TeX DVI files from TeX source files. (Default value: tex.)
TEXI2DVI	Name of the program to generate TeX DVI files from the Texinfo source. (Default value: texi2dvi.)
YACC	Name of the program to convert YACC grammars to C programs. (Default value: yacc -r.)
YFLAGS	Flags for yacc.

Implicit rules

GNU make also includes built-in, or implicit, rules that define how to create specific types of targets from various dependencies. An example of an implicit rule is the command that make should execute to generate an object file from a C source file.

GNU make supports two types of implicit rules:

■ *Suffix rules* — Suffix rules define implicit rules for `make`. A suffix rule defines how to convert a file that has one extension to a file that has another extension. Each suffix rule is defined with the target showing a pair of suffixes (file extensions). The suffix rule for converting a `.c` (C source) file to a `.o` (object) file, for example, might be written as follows:

```
.c.o:
    $(CC) $(CFLAGS) $(CPPFLAGS) -c -o $@ $<
```

This rule uses the predefined variables `CC`, `CFLAGS`, and `CPPFLAGS`. For filenames, the rule uses the variables `$@` (the complete name of the target) and `$<` (the name of the first dependent file).

■ *Pattern rules* — These rules are more versatile because you can specify more complex dependency rules, by using pattern rules. A pattern rule looks just like a regular rule, except that a single percent sign (%) appears in the target's name. The dependencies also use % to indicate how the dependency names relate to the target's name. The following pattern rule specifies how to convert any file X.c to a file X.o:

```
%.o: %.c
    $(CC) $(CFLAGS) $(CPPFLAGS) -c -o $@ $<
```

GNU `make` has a large set of implicit rules, defined as both suffix and pattern rules. To see a list of all known variables and rules, run `make` by using the following command:

```
make -p -f/dev/null
# GNU Make version 3.79.1, by Richard Stallman and Roland McGrath.
# Built for i386-redhat-linux-gnu
# Copyright (C) 1988, 89, 90, 91, 92, 93, 94, 95, 96, 97, 98, 99, 2000
#       Free Software Foundation, Inc.
# This is free software; see the source for copying conditions.
# There is NO warranty; not even for MERCHANTABILITY or FITNESS FOR A
# PARTICULAR PURPOSE.

# Report bugs to <bug-make@gnu.org>.

make: *** No targets.  Stop.

# Make data base, printed on Fri Nov 17 21:38:22 2000

# Variables
(lines deleted...)
# default
CC = cc
# default
COMPILE.c = $(CC) $(CFLAGS) $(CPPFLAGS) $(TARGET_ARCH) -c
(lines deleted...)
# default
OUTPUT_OPTION = -o $@
# default
MAKE_VERSION := 3.79.1
```

```
(lines deleted...)
# Implicit Rules
%.o: %.c
#   commands to execute (built-in):
        $(COMPILE.c) $(OUTPUT_OPTION) $<
(lines deleted...)
```

The listing shows selected parts of the output GNU `make` displays when you use the `-p` option. The output includes the names of variables, as well as implicit rules.

A sample makefile

You can write a makefile easily if you use GNU `make`'s predefined variables and its built-in rules. Consider, for example, a makefile that creates the executable `xdraw` from three C source files (`xdraw.c`, `xviewobj.c`, and `shapes.c`) and two header files (`xdraw.h` and `shapes.h`). Assume that each source file includes one of the header files. Given these facts, here is what a sample makefile might look like:

```
###############################################################
# Sample makefile
# Comments start with '#'
#
###############################################################

# Use standard variables to define compile and link flags

CFLAGS= -g -O2
# Define the target "all"
all: xdraw

OBJS=xdraw.o xviewobj.o shapes.o

xdraw: $(OBJS)

# Object files
xdraw.o: Makefile xdraw.c xdraw.h

xviewobj.o: Makefile xviewobj.c xdraw.h

shapes.o: Makefile shapes.c shapes.h
```

This makefile relies on GNU `make`'s implicit rules. The conversion of `.c` files to `.o` files uses the built-in rule. Defining the variable `CFLAGS` passes the flags to the C compiler.

Secret

The target named `all` is defined as the first target for a reason—if you run GNU `make` without specifying any targets in the command line (see the `make` syntax described in the following section), it builds the first target that it finds in the makefile. By defining the first target `all` as `xdraw`, you can ensure that `make` builds this executable file, even if you do not explicitly specify it as a target. UNIX programmers traditionally use `all` as the name of the first target, but the target's name is immaterial; what matters is that it is the first target in the makefile.

If you have a directory that contains the appropriate source files and header files, you can try the makefile. Here's what happens when I try the sample makefile:

```
make
cc -g -O2  -c xdraw.c -o xdraw.o
cc -g -O2  -c xviewobj.c -o xviewobj.o
cc -g -O2  -c shapes.c -o shapes.o
cc  xdraw.o xviewobj.o shapes.o  -o xdraw
```

As the output of `make` shows, `make` uses the `cc` command (which happens to be a symbolic link to GCC in your Linux system) with appropriate options to compile the source files and, finally, to link the objects to create the `xdraw` executable.

How to run make

Typically, you run `make` with a single command in the command line; that is, you run `make` by typing `make`. When run this way, GNU `make` looks for a file named `GNUmakefile`, `makefile`, or `Makefile`—in that order. If `make` finds one of these makefiles, it builds the first target specified in that makefile. However, if `make` does not find an appropriate makefile, it displays the following error message and exits:

```
make: *** No targets.  Stop.
```

If your makefile happens to have a different name from the default names, you have to use the `-f` option to specify the makefile. The syntax of this `make` option is the following:

```
make -f filename
```

where `filename` is the name of the makefile.

Even when you have a makefile with a default name such as `Makefile`, you may want to build a specific target out of several targets defined in the makefile. In that case, you have to run `make` by using this syntax:

```
make target
```

If the makefile contains the target named `clean`, you can build that target with this command:

```
make clean
```

Another special syntax overrides the value of a `make` variable. For example, GNU `make` uses the `CFLAGS` variable to hold the flags used when compiling C files. You can override the value of this variable when you invoke `make`. Here is an example of how you can define `CFLAGS` to be the option `-g -O2`:

```
make CFLAGS="-g -O2"
```

In addition to these options, GNU `make` accepts several other command-line options. Table 27-3 lists the GNU `make` options.

Table 27-3   Options for GNU make

Option	Meaning
-b	Ignore but accept for compatibility with other versions of `make`.
-C *DIR*	Change to the specified directory before reading the makefile.
-d	Print debugging information.
-e	Allow environment variables to override definitions of similarly named variables in the makefile.
-f *FILE*	Read *FILE* as the makefile.
-h	Display the list of `make` options.
-i	Ignore all errors in commands executed when building a target.
-I *DIR*	Search specified directory for included makefiles (the capability to include a file in a makefile is unique to GNU `make`).
-j *NUM*	Specify the number of commands that `make` can run simultaneously.
-k	Continue to build unrelated targets, even if an error occurs when building one of the targets.
-l *LOAD*	Don't start a new job if load average is at least *LOAD* (a floating-point number).
-m	Ignore but accept for compatibility with other versions of `make`.
-n	Print the commands to be executed, but do not execute them.
-o *FILE*	Do not rebuild the file named *FILE*, even if it is older than its dependents.
-p	Display the `make` database of variables and implicit rules.
-q	Do not run anything, but return zero if all targets are up to date; return 1 if anything needs updating and 2 if an error occurs.
-r	Get rid of all built-in rules.
-R	Get rid of all built-in variables and rules.
-s	Work silently (without displaying the commands as they are executed).
-t	Change the timestamp of the files.
-v	Display the version number of `make` and a copyright notice.
-w	Display the name of the working directory before and after processing the makefile.
-W *FILE*	Assume that the specified file has been modified (used with -n to see what happens if you modify that file).

The GNU Debugger

Although make automates the process of building a program, that task is the least of your worries when a program does not work correctly, or when a program suddenly quits with an error message. You need a debugger to find the cause of program errors. This book's companion CD-ROMs include gdb — the versatile GNU debugger with a command-line interface. The CD-ROMs also include xxgdb, an X Window System–based graphical front end for gdb.

Like any debugger, gdb lets you perform typical debugging tasks, such as the following:

- Set breakpoint so that program execution stops at a specified line.
- Watch the values of variables in the program.
- Step through the program one line at a time.
- Change variables in an attempt to fix errors.

The gdb debugger can debug C and C++ programs.

Preparing a program for debugging

If you want to debug a program by using gdb, you have to ensure that the compiler generates and places debugging information in the executable. The debugging information contains the names of variables in your program and the mapping of addresses in the executable file to lines of code in the source file. gdb needs this information to perform its functions, such as stopping after executing a specified line of source code.

Tip

To ensure that the executable is properly prepared for debugging, use the -g option with GCC. You can do this by defining the variable CFLAGS in the makefile as:

```
CFLAGS= -g
```

Running gdb

The most common way to debug a program is to run gdb by using the following command:

```
gdb progname
```

progname is the name of the program's executable file. After it runs, gdb displays the following message and prompts you for a command:

```
GNU gdb 5.0
Copyright 2000 Free Software Foundation, Inc.
GDB is free software, covered by the GNU General Public License, and you are
welcome to change it and/or distribute copies of it under certain conditions.
Type "show copying" to see the conditions.
There is absolutely no warranty for GDB.  Type "show warranty" for details.
This GDB was configured as "i386-redhat-linux".
(gdb)
```

To see a list of gdb commands, type `help` at the prompt:

```
(gdb) help
List of classes of commands:

aliases -- Aliases of other commands
breakpoints -- Making program stop at certain points
data -- Examining data
files -- Specifying and examining files
internals -- Maintenance commands
obscure -- Obscure features
running -- Running the program
stack -- Examining the stack
status -- Status inquiries
support -- Support facilities
tracepoints -- Tracing of program execution without stopping the program
user-defined -- User-defined commands

Type "help" followed by a class name for a list of commands in that class.
Type "help" followed by command name for full documentation.
Command name abbreviations are allowed if unambiguous.
(gdb)
```

The initial message displays the classes of gdb commands. You can get further help on a specific class of commands or a specific command, by following the instructions. To see the list of commands you use to run the program you are debugging, type `help running` at the gdb prompt.

To quit gdb, type **q**, and then press Enter.

gdb has a large number of commands, but you need only a few to find the cause of an error quickly. Table 27-4 lists the commonly used gdb commands.

Table 27-4   Commonly Used gdb Commands

Command	Description
break *NUM*	Set a breakpoint at the specified line number (the debugger stops at breakpoints).
Bt	Display a trace of all stack frames. (This command shows you the sequence of function calls so far.)
clear *FILENAME*:*NUM*	Delete the breakpoint at a specific line in a source file. For example, clear xdraw.c:8 clears the breakpoint at line 8 of file xdraw.c.
Continue	Continue running the program being debugged. (Use this command after the program has stopped due to a signal or breakpoint.)

Continued

Table 27-4 *(continued)*

Command	Description
display *EXPR*	Display value of expression (consisting of variables defined in the program) each time the program stops.
file *FILE*	Load specified executable file for debugging.
help *NAME*	Display help on the command named *NAME*.
info break	Display a list of current breakpoints, including information on how many times each breakpoint has been reached.
info files	Display detailed information about the file being debugged.
info func	Display all function names.
info local	Display information about local variables of current function.
info prog	Display the execution status of the program being debugged.
info var	Display all global and static variable names.
Kill	End the program you are debugging.
List	List a section of the source code.
Make	Run the make utility to rebuild the executable without leaving gdb.
Next	Advance one line of source code in the current function without stepping into other functions.
print *EXPR*	Show the value of the expression *EXPR*.
Quit	Quit gdb.
Run	Start running the currently loaded executable.
set variable *VAR=VALUE*	Set the value of the variable *VAR* to *VALUE*.
shell *CMD*	Execute a UNIX command *CMD*, without leaving gdb.
Step	Advance one line in the current function, stepping into other functions, if any.
watch *VAR*	Show the value of the variable named *VAR* whenever the value changes.
Where	Display the call sequence. Use this command to locate where your program died.

Command	Description
x/F ADDR	Examine the contents of the memory location at address ADDR in the format specified by the letter F, which can be o (octal); x (hex); d (decimal); u (unsigned decimal); t (binary); f (float); a (address); i (instruction); c (char); or s (string). You can append a letter indicating the size of data type to the format letter. Size letters are b (byte); h (halfword, 2 bytes), w (word, 4 bytes); and g (giant, 8 bytes). Typically, ADDR is the name of a variable or pointer.

Finding bugs by using gdb

To understand how you can find bugs by using gdb, you need to see an example. The procedure is easiest to show with a simple example, so I start with a rather contrived program that contains a typical bug.

This is the contrived program, which I stored in the file dbgtst.c:

```
#include <stdio.h>

static char buf[256];
void read_input(char *s);

int main(void)
{
  char *input = NULL; /* Just a pointer, no storage for string */

  read_input(input);

/* Process command. */
  printf("You typed: %s\n", input);

/* ... */
  return 0;
}

void read_input(char *s)
{
  printf("Command: ");
  gets(s);
}
```

This program's main function calls the read_input function to get a line of input from the user. The read_input function expects a character array in which it returns what the user types. In this example, however, main calls read_input with an uninitialized pointer — that's the bug in this simple program.

Build the program by using `gcc` with the `-g` option:

```
gcc -g -o dbgtst dbgtst.c
```

Ignore the warning message about the `gets()` function being dangerous.

To see the problem with this program, run it:

```
./dbgtst
Command: test
Segmentation fault (core dumped)
```

The program dies after displaying the `Segmentation fault` message. For this small program, you can find the cause by examining the source code. In a real-world application, however, you may not immediately know what causes the error. That's when you use `gdb` to find the cause of the problem.

To use `gdb` to locate a bug, follow these steps:

1. Load the program under `gdb`. To load a program named `dbgtst` in `gdb`, type the following:

   ```
   gdb dbgtst
   GNU gdb 5.0
   Copyright 2000 Free Software Foundation, Inc.
   GDB is free software, covered by the GNU General Public License,
   and you are welcome to change it and/or distribute copies of it
   under certain conditions.
   Type "show copying" to see the conditions.
   There is absolutely no warranty for GDB.
   Type "show warranty" for details.
   This GDB was configured as "i386-redhat-linux"...
   (gdb)
   ```

2. Run the program under `gdb` by using the `run` command. If the program prompts for input, type the input text. The program should fail as it has previously. Here's what happens with the `dbgtst` program:

   ```
   (gdb) run
   Starting program: /home/naba/rhls4e/dbgtst
   Command: test

   Program received signal SIGSEGV, Segmentation fault.
   0x4008a952 in _IO_gets (buf=0x0) at iogets.c:55
   55      iogets.c: No such file or directory.
   (gdb)
   ```

3. Use the `where` command to determine where the program died. For the `dbgtst` program, this command yields this output:

   ```
   (gdb) where
   #0  0x4008a952 in _IO_gets (buf=0x0) at iogets.c:55
   #1  0x80484e5 in read_input (s=0x0) at dbgtst.c:22
   #2  0x80484a4 in main () at dbgtst.c:10
   ```

```
#3   0x4003a790 in __libc_start_main (main=0x804848c <main>,
argc=1,
     ubp_av=0xbffffb24, init=0x8048304 <_init>, fini=0x804852c
<_fini>,
     rtld_fini=0x4000d35c <_dl_fini>, stack_end=0xbffffb1c)
     at ../sysdeps/generic/libc-start.c:111
(gdb)
```

The output shows the sequence of function calls. Function call #0 —
the most recent one — is to a C library function, gets. The gets call
originates in the read_input function, which in turn is called from
the main function.

4. Use the list command to inspect the lines of suspect source code. In
dbgtst, you might start with line 21 of dbgtst.c file, as follows:

```
(gdb) list dbgtst.c:21
16          return 0;
17      }
18
19      void read_input(char *s)
20      {
21        printf("Command: ");
22        gets(s);
23      }
24
(gdb)
```

After looking at this listing, you should be able to tell that the problem
might be the way read_input is called. Then you list the lines around
line 10 in dbgtst.c (where the read_input call originates):

```
(gdb) list dbgtst.c:10
5
6       int main(void)
7       {
8         char *input = NULL; /* Just a pointer, no storage for
string */
9
10        read_input(input);
11
12      /* Process command. */
13        printf("You typed: %s\n", input);
14
(gdb)
```

At this point, you should be able to narrow the problem to the variable
named input. That variable should be an array, not a NULL pointer.

Fixing bugs in gdb

Sometimes, you can try a bug fix directly in gdb. For the example program in
the preceding section, you can try this fix immediately after the program dies
after displaying an error message. Because the example is a contrived one, I
have an extra buffer named buf defined in the dbgtst program, as follows:

```
static char buf[256];
```

I can fix the problem of the uninitialized pointer by setting the variable input to buf. The following session with gdb corrects the problem of the uninitialized pointer (this example picks up immediately after the program has run and died, due to the segmentation fault):

```
(gdb) file dbgtst
A program is being debugged already.  Kill it? (y or n) y

Load new symbol table from "dbgtst"? (y or n) y
Reading symbols from dbgtst...
done.
(gdb) list
1       #include <stdio.h>
2
3       static char buf[256];
4       void read_input(char *s);
5
6       int main(void)
7       {
8          char *input = NULL; /* Just a pointer, no storage for string
*/
9
10         read_input(input);
(gdb) break 9
Breakpoint 1 at 0x8048499: file dbgtst.c, line 9.
(gdb) run
Starting program: /home/naba/rhls4e/dbgtst

Breakpoint 1, main () at dbgtst.c:10
10         read_input(input);
(gdb) set var input=buf
(gdb) cont
Continuing.
Command: test
You typed: test

Program exited normally.
(gdb)q
```

As the previous listing shows, if I stop the program just before read_input is called and set the variable named input to buf (which is a valid array of characters), the rest of the program runs fine.

After trying in gdb a fix that works, you can make the necessary changes to the source files and can make the fix permanent.

Implications of GNU Licenses

You have to pay a price for the bounty of Linux — to protect its developers and users, Linux is distributed under the GNU GPL (General Public License), which stipulates the distribution of the source code.

This does not mean, however, that you cannot write commercial software for Linux that you want to distribute (either for free, or for a price) in binary form only. You can follow all the rules and still sell your Linux applications in binary form.

When writing applications for Linux, be aware of two licenses:

- The GNU General Public License (GPL), which governs many Linux programs, including the Linux kernel and GCC.
- The GNU Library General Public License (LGPL), which covers many Linux libraries.

Caution

The following sections provide an overview of these licenses and some suggestions on how to meet the requirements of the licenses. Because I am not a lawyer, however, you should not take anything in this book as legal advice. The full text for these licenses is in text files on your Red Hat Linux system; show these licenses to your legal counsel for a full interpretation and an assessment of applicability to your business.

The GNU General Public License

The text of the GPL is in a file named COPYING in various directories in your Red Hat Linux system. For example, type cd /usr/share/doc/gdb*, and then type more COPYING to read the GPL.

The GPL has nothing to do with whether you charge for the software or distribute it for free; its thrust is to keep the software free for all users. GPL does this by requiring that the software is distributed in source-code form and stipulating that any user can copy and distribute the software in source-code form to anyone else. In addition, everyone is reminded that the software comes with absolutely no warranty.

The software that GPL covers is not in the public domain; such software is always copyrighted, and the GPL spells out the restrictions on the software's copying and distribution. From a user's point of view, of course, GPL's restrictions are not really restrictions; they are benefits, because the user is guaranteed access to the source code.

Caution

If your application uses parts of any software the GPL covers, your application is considered a derived work, and the GPL covers it, which means you must distribute the source code to your application.

Although the GPL covers the Linux kernel, the GPL does not cover your applications that use the kernel services through system calls. Those applications are considered normal use of the kernel.

If you plan to distribute your application in binary form (as most commercial software is distributed), you must make sure your application does not use any parts of any software the GPL covers. Your application may end up using parts of other software when it calls functions in a library. Most libraries, however, are covered by a different GNU license, which is described in the following section.

You have to watch out for only a few library and utility programs the GPL covers. The GNU dbm (gdbm) database library is one of the prominent libraries GPL covers. The GNU bison parser-generator tool is another utility the GPL covers. If you allow bison to generate code, the GPL covers that code.

Secret

Other alternatives for the GNU dbm and GNU bison are not covered by GPL. For a database library, you can use the Berkeley database library db in place of gdbm. For a parser-generator, you might use yacc instead of bison.

The GNU Library General Public License

The text of the GNU LGPL is in a file named COPYING.LIB. If you have the kernel source installed, a copy of COPYING.LIB file is in one of the source directories. To locate a copy of the COPYING.LIB file, use this find command:

```
find /usr/share/doc -name "COPYING*" -print
```

This command lists all occurrences of COPYING and COPYING.LIB in your system. The COPYING file contains the GPL, whereas COPYING.LIB has the LGPL.

The LGPL is intended to allow use of libraries in your applications, even if you do not distribute source code for your application. The LGPL stipulates, however, that users must have access to the source code of the library you use and that users can make use of modified versions of those libraries.

The LGPL covers most Linux libraries, including the C library (libc.a). Thus, when you build your application on Linux by using the GCC compiler, your application links with code from one or more libraries the LGPL covers. If you want to distribute your application in binary form only, you need to pay attention to LGPL.

Secret

One way to meet the intent of the LGPL is to provide the object code for your application and a makefile that relinks your object files with any updated Linux libraries the LGPL covers.

Note

A better way to satisfy the LGPL is to use *dynamic linking*, in which your application and the library are separate entities, even though your application calls functions in the library when it runs. With dynamic linking, users immediately get the benefit of any updates to the libraries without ever having to relink the application.

Version Control

When you write applications with a few files, it is simple enough to prepare a makefile to automate the software-build process and to not worry about keeping track of changes. Typically, for small projects, you might keep track of changes through comments at the beginning of a file.

This approach works well for a small project, but for larger software projects, you should use some tools that help manage different versions of your applications. In fact, you can benefit from version-control tools, even if you are the sole author of a small application. After time passes, you may have trouble remembering what changes you have made. Software version control can help you track these changes.

The Linux software distribution comes with RCS and CVS . Both of these products are collections of tools that help you control software revisions.

The next few sections provide an overview of RCS through some simple examples. A later section briefly discusses CVS and lists some other sources of information about CVS.

Source Control Using RCS

Source control refers to the idea of saving a version of the source code, so you can recover a specific version or revision of a file whenever you need it. Essentially, when you modify a source file, the sequence goes something like this:

1. When you have an initial version of the source file, you archive it — place it under source control.

2. When you want to make changes in the file, you first get a copy of the current revision. (When you get it this way, the tools should ensure that no one else can modify that revision.)

3. You make the changes in the source file, test the code, and store the modified file as a new revision.

4. The next time you want to make changes in the file, you start with the latest revision of the file.

RCS provides the tools that enable you to archive file revisions and update them in a controlled manner. Table 27-5 lists the tools.

Table 27-5   RCS Tools

Tool	Purpose
ci	Creates a new revision of a file, or adds a working file to an RCS file.
co	Gets a working version of a file for reading. (co -l provides a working file and locks the original so you can modify the working file.)
ident	Searches for identifiers in a file.
merge	Incorporates changes from two files into a third file.
rcsdiff	Compares a working file with its RCS file.
rcsmerge	Merges different revisions of a file.
rlog	Views the history of changes in a file.

Suppose you have just finished developing the initial working version of an application and want to use RCS to manage the revisions from now on. The following sections outline the steps to follow to use RCS for your development effort.

Creating initial RCS files

The first step in managing source-file revisions by using RCS is to enable RCS to archive the current revision of your files. Follow these steps to put the source file under the control of RCS:

1. In the directory where you keep your application's source files, create a subdirectory named RCS by typing mkdir RCS. If the RCS subdirectory exists, RCS archives file revisions in this directory.

2. In each file you plan to place under revision control, add a comment by adding the following RCS identification keyword:

   Id

   In a C source file, for example, add the following:

   ```
   /*
    * $Id$
    */
   ```

   In a makefile, on the other hand, use the following:

   ```
   # $Id$
   ```

   RCS later expands these identifier keywords to include information about the file revision and date.

3. Check in each file with RCS, use the ci command, and provide a brief description of each file as prompted by ci. Following is how you might check in Makefile:

   ```
   ci Makefile
   RCS/Makefile,v  <--  Makefile
   enter description, terminated with single '.' or end of file:
   NOTE: This is NOT the log message!
   >> Makefile for sample programs.
   >>.
   initial revision: 1.1
   done
   ```

   When a file is checked in, the ci command creates a corresponding RCS file in the RCS subdirectory. The RCS file's name is the same as the original file, except a ,v is appended to the name. Thus, the RCS file for Makefile is Makefile,v. Also, ci deleted the original source file after it created the RCS file. To use or edit the file again, you have to extract it by using the co command.

After you follow these steps, all your files are safely stored in RCS files in the RCS subdirectory.

Using the archived files

Now suppose you want to edit one of the files (for example, to add a new feature) and rebuild the application. For starters, you need all the source files and the makefile for the compile and link step.

You should extract all these files by using the `co` command for read-only access (except for the file you want to change). The `co` command is straightforward to use. To get a working copy of `Makefile` for read-only use, for example, use the following command:

```
co Makefile
RCS/Makefile,v --> Makefile
revision 1.1
done
```

By default, this command looks for an RCS file named `RCS/Makefile,v` and creates a read-only working copy of it named `Makefile`.

A copy of `Makefile` is in the directory. Examine that copy of `Makefile` to see what happens to that `$Id$` keyword that you add as a comment. Here's what my example `Makefile` shows:

```
# $Id: Makefile,v 1.1 2000/11/18 03:06:56 naba Exp $
```

As this example shows, RCS expands each identifier keyword into a string with information. The exact information depends on the identifier.

If you want to modify a file, you have to check it out by using the `-l` option. If you want to check out a copy of the file `xmutil.c` for editing, use this command:

```
co -l xmutil.c
RCS/xmutil.c,v --> xmutil.c
revision 1.1 (locked)
done
```

Compare this output with that from the previous example of `co`; the current output confirms that the RCS file is locked. No one else can modify the archived file until you check in the copy you checked out for editing.

When you check out a file and put a lock on it, no one else can check out the same file for editing. However, anyone can get a copy of the file for read-only use.

After you make changes in a file, you can check it in again by using the `ci` command, just as you do when you create the RCS file.

Using RCS identification keywords

You can use RCS identification keywords — each of which is a string delimited by dollar signs ($ . . . $) — to record information in source files. RCS expands the `$Id$` keyword, for example, into summary information about the file, including the filename, revision number, date, and author. All you have to do is put the keyword in the file; RCS takes care of expanding that keyword into the appropriate information. Table 27-6 lists the identification keywords RCS supports.

Keyword	Purpose
$Author$	Login ID of the user who checked in the revision.
$Date$	Date and time when the revision was checked in.
$Header$	Expands to summary information, including full path name of the RCS file, revision number, date, author, and the state of file revision.
Id	Same as $Header$, except the RCS filename does not have a directory prefix.
$Locker$	Login ID of the user who locked the file (empty if the file is not currently locked).
Log	Expands to a log of changes made in the file.
$RCSfile$	Name of the RCS file without the directory names.
$Revision$	Revision number of the RCS file.
$Source$	Expands to the full path name of the RCS file.
$State$	Indicates the state of the file revision (whether it is locked or not).

Table 27-6   Identification Keywords RCS Supports

Tip

At minimum, you may want to use the Id keyword in your files to include summary information about the latest revision.

RCS expands the identifier keywords anywhere in a file. Thus, you might mark an object file (and the executable that uses that object file) by placing the identifier keyword in a string variable. A common practice is to define a string named rcsid as follows:

```
static const char rcsid[] = "$Id";
```

Defining the rcsid string causes the object and executable file to contain a string such as the following:

```
$Id: xmutil.c,v 1.1 2000/11/18 03:09:56 naba Exp naba $
```

Viewing the changes made so far

Most of the time, the ci and co commands are used to maintain file revisions with RCS. RCS, however, includes several other tools for managing various aspects of version control, such as comparing two revisions, viewing the history of changes, and examining identifiers in files.

If you have checked out a file for modification, you might want to know what changes you have made thus far. You can use the `rcsdiff` program to see a list of changes. If you've been editing a file named `xmutil.c`, for example, you can compare the working file against its RCS file, by using this command:

```
rcsdiff xmutil.c
```

The `rcsdiff` program runs the UNIX `diff` utility to find the differences between the working file and the RCS file.

If necessary, you can even find the differences between two specific revisions of a file, by using a command such as the following:

```
rcsdiff -r1.1 -r1.2 xmutil.c
```

This command lists the differences between revision 1.1 and 1.2 of the file `xmutil.c`.

Discarding changes made so far

Sometimes after making changes in a file, you realize the changes are either wrong or unnecessary. In such a case, you want to discard the changes you have made so far.

To discard changes, all you have to do is unlock the RCS file, and then delete the working copy of the file. To unlock an RCS file, use the `rcs` command with the `-u` (unlock) option. The following command discards the current changes in the file named `xmutil.c`:

```
rcs -u xmutil.c
```

Another, more convenient, way to discard changes is to overwrite the current working file with a copy of the former RCS file. To do this, use the `co` command with `-u` and `-f` flags:

```
co -f -u xmutil.c
```

The `-u` option unlocks the checked-out revision, and `-f` forces `co` to over-write the working file with the former revision of that file.

Viewing the change log

As you make changes in a file and keep checking in revisions, RCS maintains a log of changes. You can view this log by using the `rlog` command. The follow-ing example shows how to view the log of changes for the file `xmutil.c`:

```
rlog xmutil.c

RCS file: RCS/xmutil.c,v
Working file: xmutil.c
head: 1.2
branch:
locks: strict
access list:
```

```
symbolic names:
keyword substitution: kv
total revisions: 2;      selected revisions: 2
description:
Motif utilities
----------------------------
revision 1.2
date: 2000/10/26 01:16:47;  author: naba;  state: Exp;  lines: +10 -6
Added new header file
----------------------------
revision 1.1
date: 2000/10/26 01:10:27;  author: naba;  state: Exp;
Initial revision
=====================================================================
```

The first part of the `rlog` output displays some summary information about the RCS file. The lines following the `description:` line show the description I enter when I create the RCS file. Following this description is an entry for each revision, with the most recent revision appearing first. Each revision's entry shows the date, the author, and a brief description the author has entered.

Examining identifier keywords

If any identifier keywords are embedded in a file, you can view them by using the `ident` command. If `Makefile` contains the `$Id$` keyword, you can examine the keyword by using this command:

```
ident Makefile
Makefile:
     $Id: Makefile,v 1.1 2000/10/26 01:06:26 naba Exp $
```

If you define a string variable with a keyword that eventually gets embedded in a binary file (an object file or an executable file), use `ident` to view those identifiers, as well. You can try `ident` in any binary file to see whether it contains any embedded keywords. This is what I find when I try `ident` on the file `/usr/bin/ident` (the executable program for the `ident` command itself):

```
ident /usr/bin/ident
/usr/bin/ident:
     $Id: rcsbase.h,v 5.20 1995/06/16 06:19:24 eggert Exp $
     $Id: ident.c,v 5.9 1995/06/16 06:19:24 eggert Exp $
     $Id: rcsmap.c,v 5.3 1995/06/16 06:19:24 eggert Exp $
```

From this output, you can tell the exact versions of source files that are used to build this version of the `ident` program.

Concurrent Version Control with CVS

CVS is another source-control tool designed to keep track of changes made by a group of developers working on the same set of files. CVS keeps track of collections of files in a shared directory. An entire collection of files is given a module name; a developer can check out an entire collection of files by using the module name.

CVS actually uses RCS to save the version-control information in RCS files stored in a directory hierarchy, called the *repository*, which is separate from the developer's working directory. Unlike RCS, CVS does not lock the files when they are checked out. In fact, CVS enables multiple developers to check out an entire collection of files. When developers commit the files back to the repository, CVS tries to merge the changes various developers have made. If CVS cannot successfully merge the changes, the developers are notified, and they have to resolve any conflicting changes manually.

To use an existing CVS repository, first set the CVSROOT environment variable to that repository. The repository can even be on a different system. For example, to work on GNOME as a developer, set CVSROOT as follows:

```
export CVSROOT=':pserver:anonymous@anoncvs.gnome.org:/cvs/gnome'
```

You also must log in to the CVS server by using this command:

```
cvs login
(Logging in to anonymous@anoncvs.gnome.org)
CVS password:  (There is no password, simply press Enter)
```

Then, use the `cvs checkout` command to extract the packages you need from the repository. When extracting files from a remote CVS server, you can specify a compression level with `-z` option (the recommended level is `-z3`). Thus, you might use the following command to get the `gnome-xml` package from the GNOME CVS repository:

```
cvs -z3 checkout gnome-xml
U gnome-xml/.cvsignore
U gnome-xml/AUTHORS
U gnome-xml/COPYING.LIB
U gnome-xml/ChangeLog
U gnome-xml/Copyright
U gnome-xml/HACKING
U gnome-xml/HTMLparser.c
U gnome-xml/HTMLparser.h
U gnome-xml/HTMLtree.c
U gnome-xml/HTMLtree.h
U gnome-xml/INSTALL
U gnome-xml/MAINTAINERS
U gnome-xml/Makefile.am
U gnome-xml/Makefile.win
U gnome-xml/NEWS
U gnome-xml/README
U gnome-xml/SAX.h
U gnome-xml/TODO
U gnome-xml/acconfig.h
U gnome-xml/acinclude.m4
U gnome-xml/aclocal.m4
```

```
U gnome-xml/autogen.sh
U gnome-xml/config.h.in
U gnome-xml/configure.in
(...Lines deleted...)
```

The copy of CVS on your system then downloads from the repository the latest version of each file in the `gnome-xml` module, creates a directory named `gnome-xml` in the current directory, and places the files in that directory. You can simply type `cd gnome-xml` to change the directory and to begin working on these files.

If you have checked out a module to a working directory, you can use the `cvs update` command to bring your copy current. The `cvs update` command essentially merges the changes in the repository with whatever changes you may have made in the working directory. If conflicting changes exist, you have to resolve the problem manually.

After you work on these files, you can use the `cvs commit` command to incorporate your changes to the files in the repository. You can either commit specific files, or commit the entire module.

When you no longer want your working copy of a module, use the `cvs release` command to indicate that you no longer need the module. To remove the files, use the `cvs release -d` command; the `-d` flag means you want to delete the files.

That, in short, is how CVS works. To learn more about CVS, consult these resources:

■ Type `info cvs` to browse help information on CVS.

■ Type `cd /usr/share/doc/cvs*` to change to the CVS documentation directory. In that directory is a file named FAQ (Frequently Asked Questions) and several PostScript files about CVS. The FAQ file may be a bit out of date, but you can still use it as a source of information about CVS.

■ Visit one of these Web sites to read the latest online information about CVS:

  • `http://www.cvshome.org/`

  • `http://www.loria.fr/~molli/cvs-index.html`

  • `http://www.delorie.com/gnu/docs/cvs/cvs_toc.html`

Linux Programming Topics

Developing software under Linux is quite similar to developing software under any UNIX system. Most C and UNIX programming issues are generic and apply to all UNIX systems. There are, however, a few topics you want to know about if you are developing software for Linux.

This section covers the most significant topic: the Executable and Linking Format (ELF) binary in Linux. The other topic — the use of dynamic linking in applications — is related to ELF. I also describe how you can exploit dynamic linking and how to create a dynamically linked library in Linux.

The Executable and Linking Format

If you have programmed in UNIX, you probably know that when you compile and link a program, the default executable file is named a.out. What you may not have realized is that a file format is associated with the a.out file. The operating system has to know this file format so it can load and run an executable. Linux has been using the a.out format for its binaries since Linux originated.

Although the a.out format has served its purpose adequately, it has two shortcomings:

■ Shared libraries are difficult to create.

■ Dynamically loading a shared library is cumbersome.

Using shared libraries is desirable, because a shared library enables many executable programs to share the same block of code. Also, the dynamic loading of modules is becoming increasingly popular because it enables an application to load blocks of code only when needed, thus reducing the memory requirement of the application.

Meanwhile, the UNIX System Laboratories (USL) had developed ELF, a new binary format, for use in System V Release 4 (SVR4). The ELF format is much more flexible than the a.out format. In particular, ELF has these advantages over the a.out format in Linux:

■ Shared libraries for the ELF format are simpler to create. You compile all source files with the gcc -fPIC -c command, and then link them by using a command such as the following, which creates the library libXXX.so.1.0:

```
gcc -shared -Wl,-soname,libXXX.so.1 -o libXXX.so.1.0 *.o
```

■ Dynamic loading (wherein a program loads code modules at runtime) is simpler. With dynamic loading, you can design an application to be extensible so that users can add new code in the form of shared libraries.

Because of ELF's increased flexibility, Linux developers (in particular, the GCC developers) decided to move to ELF as the standard binary-format Linux. By default, the new GCC compilers — gcc version 2.7 and later — generate ELF binaries.

Secret

Notice that GCC continues to use a.out as the default name of the executable file (used only if you do not specify an output filename by using the -o option). Although the executable may be named a.out, the binary format is ELF, not the a.out format.

If you want to check the binary format of an executable file, use the `file` command. The following example shows how to check the file type of `/bin/ls` (the executable file for the `ls` command):

```
file /bin/ls
/bin/ls: ELF 32-bit LSB executable, Intel 80386, version 1,
dynamically linked (uses shared libs), stripped
```

On the other hand, the file command reports the following for an older `a.out` format executable (the default name of executable files is still `a.out`, but the format is ELF):

```
file a.out
a.out: Linux/i386 demand-paged executable (QMAGIC)
```

Shared Libraries in Linux Applications

Most Linux programs use shared libraries. At minimum, most C programs use the C shared library `libc.so.X`, wherein X is a version number. When a program uses one or more shared libraries, you need the program's executable file, as well as all the shared libraries, to run the program. In other words, your program won't run if all shared libraries are not available on a system.

If you sell an application, you need to make sure all necessary shared libraries are distributed with your software.

Examining shared libraries that a program uses

Use the `ldd` utility to determine which shared libraries an executable program needs. The following is what `ldd` reports for a typical C program that uses the ELF binary format:

```
ldd a.out
        libc.so.6 => /lib/libc.so.6 (0x4001f000)
        /lib/ld-linux.so.2 => /lib/ld-linux.so.2 (0x40000000
```

For a more complex program, such as `gimp` (ELF version), `ldd` shows more shared libraries:

```
ldd /usr/bin/gimp
        libgtk-1.2.so.0 => /usr/lib/libgtk-1.2.so.0 (0x4001f000)
        libgdk-1.2.so.0 => /usr/lib/libgdk-1.2.so.0 (0x40151000)
        libgmodule-1.2.so.0 => /usr/lib/libgmodule-1.2.so.0 (0x40187000)
        libglib-1.2.so.0 => /usr/lib/libglib-1.2.so.0 (0x4018a000)
        libdl.so.2 => /lib/libdl.so.2 (0x401af000)
        libXi.so.6 => /usr/X11R6/lib/libXi.so.6 (0x401b2000)
        libXext.so.6 => /usr/X11R6/lib/libXext.so.6 (0x401ba000)
        libX11.so.6 => /usr/X11R6/lib/libX11.so.6 (0x401c9000)
        libm.so.6 => /lib/libm.so.6 (0x40297000)
        libc.so.6 => /lib/libc.so.6 (0x402b6000)
        /lib/ld-linux.so.2 => /lib/ld-linux.so.2 (0x40000000)
```

In this case, the program uses several shared libraries, including the X11 library (libX11.so.6), the GIMP toolkit (libgtk-1.2.so.0), the General Drawing Kit (GDK) library (libgdk-1.2.so.0), the Math library (libm.so.6), and the C library (libc.so.6).

Thus, almost any Linux application requires shared libraries to run. Additionally, the shared libraries must have the same binary format an application uses.

Creating a shared library

With ELF, creating a shared library for your own application is simple enough. Suppose you want to implement an object in the form of a shared library. A set of functions in the shared library represents the object's interfaces. To use the object, load its shared library, and then invoke its interface functions (you learn how to do this in the following section).

Here is the C source code for this simple object, implemented as a shared library (you might also call it a dynamically linked library) — save this in a file named dynobj.c:

```
/*------------------------------------------------------*/
/* File: dynobj.c
 *
 * Demonstrate use of dynamic linking.
 * Pretend this is an object that can be created by calling
 * init and destroyed by calling destroy.
 */
#include <stdio.h>
#include <stdlib.h>
#include <string.h>

/* Data structure for this object */
typedef struct OBJDATA
{
  char *name;
  int version;
} OBJDATA;

/*------------------------------------------------------*/
/* i n i t
 *
 * Initialize object (allocate storage).
 *
 */
void* init(char *name)
{
  OBJDATA *data = (OBJDATA*)calloc(1, sizeof(OBJDATA));
  if(name)
    data->name = malloc(strlen(name)+1);
  strcpy(data->name, name);

  printf("Created: %s\n", name);
```

```
  return data;
}
/*-----------------------------------------------------------*/
/* s h o w
 *
 * Show the object.
 *
 */
void show(void *data)
{
  OBJDATA *d = (OBJDATA*)data;
  printf("show: %s\n", d->name);
}
/*-----------------------------------------------------------*/
/* d e s t r o y
 *
 * Destroy the object (free all storage).
 *
 */
void destroy(void *data)
{
  OBJDATA *d = (OBJDATA*)data;
  if(d)
  {
    if(d->name)
    {
      printf("Destroying: %s\n", d->name);
      free(d->name);
    }
    free(d);
  }
}
```

The object offers three interface functions:

- init to allocate any necessary storage and initialize the object
- show to display the object (here, it simply prints a message)
- destroy to free any storage

To build the shared library named libdobj.so, follow these steps:

1. Compile all source files with the -fPIC flag. In this case, compile the dynobj.c file, by using this command:

   ```
   gcc -fPIC -c dynobj.c
   ```

2. Link the objects into a shared library with the -shared flag, and provide appropriate flags for the linker. To create the shared library named libdobj.so.1, use the following:

   ```
   gcc -shared -Wl,-soname,libdobj.so.1 -o libdobj.so.1.0 dynobj.o
   ```

3. Set up a sequence of symbolic links so that programs that use the shared library can refer to it with a standard name. For the sample library, the standard name is `libdobj.so`, and the symbolic links are set up by using these commands:

```
ln -sf libdobj.so.1.0 libdobj.so.1
ln -sf libdobj.so.1 libdobj.so
```

4. When you test the shared library, define and export the `LD_LIBRARY_PATH` environment variable, by using the following command:

```
export LD_LIBRARY_PATH=`pwd`:$LD_LIBRARY_PATH
```

After you test the shared library and are satisfied that the library works, copy it to a standard location, such as `/usr/local/lib`, and run the `ldconfig` utility to update the link between `libdobj.so.1` and `libdobj.so.1.0`. These are the commands you use to install your shared library for everyone's use (you have to be `root` to perform these steps):

```
cp libdobj.so.1.0 /usr/local/lib
/sbin/ldconfig
cd /usr/local/lib
ln -s libdobj.so.1 libdobj.so
```

Dynamically loading a shared library

ELF makes it simple to load a shared library in your program and to use the functions within the shared library. The header file `<dlfcn.h>` declares the functions for loading and using a shared library. Four functions are declared in the file `dlfcn.h` for dynamic loading:

- `void *dlopen(const char *filename, int flag);` — loads the shared library specified by `filename` and returns a handle for the library. The flag can be `RTD_LAZY` (resolve undefined symbols as the library's code is executed); or `RTD_NOW` (resolve all undefined symbols before `dlopen` returns and fail if all symbols are not defined). If `dlopen` fails, it returns `NULL`.

- `const char *dlerror (void);` — if `dlopen` fails, call `dlerror` to get a string that contains a description of the error.

- `void *dlsym (void *handle, char *symbol);` — returns the address of the specified `symbol` (function name) from the shared library identified by the `handle` (that was returned by `dlopen`).

- `int dlclose (void *handle);` — unloads the shared library if no one else is using it.

Here is the `dlfcn.h` file with the appropriate function declarations:

```
/*------------------------------------------------------*/
/* File: dlfcn.h
 *
 * Header file with function prototypes.
```

```
 */
void *dlopen(const char *filename, int flag);
const char *dlerror (void);
void *dlsym (void *handle, char *symbol);
int dlclose (void *handle);
```

When you use any of these functions, include the header file `<dlfcn.h>` with this preprocessor directive:

```
#include <dlfcn.h>
```

The following is a simple test program — dltest.c — that shows how to load and use the object defined in the shared library libdobj.so, which you create in the preceding section:

```
/*-------------------------------------------------------*/
/* File: dltest.c
 *
 * Test dynamic linking.
 *
 */
#include <dlfcn.h>   /* For the dynamic loading functions */
#include <stdio.h>

int main(void)
{
  void *dlobj;
  void * (*init_call)(char *name);
  void (*show_call)(void *data);
  void (*destroy_call)(void *data);

/* Open the shared library and set up the function pointers */
  if(dlobj = dlopen("libdobj.so.1",RTLD_LAZY))
  {
    void *data;

    init_call=dlsym(dlobj,"init");
    show_call=dlsym(dlobj,"show");
    destroy_call=dlsym(dlobj,"destroy");

/* Call the object interfaces */
    data = (*init_call)("Test Object");
    (*show_call)(data);
    (*destroy_call)(data);
  }
  return 0;
}
```

The program is straightforward: it loads the shared library, gets the pointers to the functions in the library, and calls the functions through the pointers.

You can compile and link this program in the usual way, but you must link with the -ldl option so you can use the functions declared in `<dlfcn.h>`. Here is how you build the program dltest:

```
gcc -o dltest dltest.c -ldl
```

To see the program in action, run `dltest`:

```
./dltest
Created: Test Object
show: Test Object
Destroying: Test Object
```

Although this procedure is not exciting, you now have a sample program that uses a shared library.

To see the benefit of using a shared library, return to the preceding section, and make some changes in the shared library (print some other message in a function, for example). Rebuild the shared library alone. Then run `dltest` again. The resulting printout should show the effect of the changes you make in the shared library, which means you can update the shared library independently of the application.

Summary

Your Red Hat Linux system comes loaded with all the tools you need to develop software. In particular, it has all the GNU software development tools, such as GCC, the GNU debugger, GNU `make`, and the RCS version-control utility. This chapter describes these software development tools and shows you how to use them.

By reading this chapter, you learn that:

▶ The GNU tools comprise the software development environment on your Linux PC. These tools include GNU Emacs for text editing; GCC for compiling C and C++ programs; GNU `make` for automating software builds; the GNU debugger for debugging; and the RCS for version control.

▶ A utility named `info` provides online help information on the GNU tools. You can run `info` alone or under GNU Emacs, by using the `Ctrl+h i` command.

▶ GCC is the GNU C and C++ compiler. You can use the `gcc` command to compile and link C programs. Use `g++` to compile and link C++ programs.

▶ GCC has a plethora of options, but you need to use only a few. Some of the common options are `-c` (for compiling only) and `-o` (for specifying the name of the output executable file).

▶ The GNU `make` utility enables you to automate the build process. You specify the modules that comprise an executable, as well as any dependencies; `make` takes care of compiling only those files that need recompilation. The input file for `make` is known as a makefile and is commonly named `Makefile`.

▶ The GNU debugger enables you to locate errors in your programs. Use the `gdb` command to run the debugger. You have to compile the program, by using GCC's `-g` option to generate debugging information the GNU debugger can use.

▶ When you use GNU tools to develop software (as you do in Linux), you should be aware of the GNU licenses: the GNU General Public License (GPL) and the GNU Library General Public License (LGPL). The LGPL covers GNU libraries. If you distribute your software in binary form, you should use dynamic linking to comply with the terms of the LGPL. You should not take anything in this book as legal advice, of course; always consult your own legal counsel for a definitive answer.

▶ Version control is an important aspect of software development. In Linux, you get the RCS (Revision Control System) to manage revisions of source files.

▶ Concurrent Versions System (CVS) is a versatile RCS-based version control system that manages multiple directories of files. CVS enables multiple developers to work simultaneously on the same set of files. Open-source projects, such as GNOME, use CVS to enable many developers to work on various parts of the project.

▶ Shared libraries are commonly used in Linux applications to reduce the memory requirements of executables. Applications are dynamically linked with a shared library at runtime, and many applications can share a single library.

▶ The Linux development community has adopted the Executable and Linking Format (ELF) for binaries. ELF makes dynamic linking simpler to program. This chapter shows an example of how to use dynamic linking in your own applications.

Chapter 28

Shell and Perl Scripting

The fundamental philosophy of UNIX, which Linux continues to follow, is to give the user many small and specialized commands, along with the plumbing necessary to connect these commands. By *plumbing*, I mean the way in which one command's output functions as a second command's input. Bash, the default shell in Linux, provides this plumbing in the form of I/O redirection and pipes. Bash also includes features, such as the if statement, which runs commands only when a specific condition is true; and the for statement, which repeats commands a specified number of times. You can use these features of Bash when writing interpreted programs called *shell scripts*.

This chapter shows you how to write simple shell scripts: a collection of shell commands stored in a file. Shell scripts are used to automate various tasks. For example, when your Red Hat Linux boots, many initialization tasks are performed by shell scripts stored in various subdirectories in the /etc directory (for example, /etc/init.d).

When it comes to writing scripts, the *Perl* language is also popular among UNIX system administrators. Because you probably are the system administrator of your Linux system, this chapter also introduces you to Perl scripting.

Cross-Reference

Chapter 29 covers Tcl/Tk, another popular scripting language you can use to build applications with a graphical interface.

Looking at Some Simple Shell Scripts

If you are not a programmer, you may feel apprehensive about programming. But shell scripting (or programming) can be as simple as storing a few commands in a file. In fact, you can have a useful shell program that has a single command.

While writing this book, for example, I captured screens from the X Window System and used the screen shots in figures. I used the X screen-capture program, xwd, to store the screen images in the X Window Dump (XWD) format. The book's production team, however, wanted the screen shots in TIFF format. Therefore, I used the Portable Bitmap (PBM) toolkit to convert the XWD images to TIFF format. To convert each file, I ran two programs and deleted a temporary file, as follows:

```
xwdtopnm < file.xwd > file.pnm
pnmtotiff < file.pnm > file.tif
rm file.pnm
```

These commands assume that the xwdtopnm and pnmtotiff programs are in the /usr/bin directory — one of the directories listed in the PATH environment variable. By the way, xwdtopnm and pnmtotiff are two programs in the PBM toolkit.

After converting a few XWD files to TIFF format, I got tired of typing the same sequence of commands for each file, so I prepared a file named totif and saved the following lines in it:

```
#!/bin/sh
xwdtopnm < $1.xwd > $1.pnm
pnmtotiff < $1.pnm > $1.tif
rm $1.pnm
```

Then I made the file executable, using this command:

```
chmod +x totif
```

The chmod command enables you to change the permission settings of a file. One of those settings determines whether the file is executable or not. The +x option means that you want to mark the file as an executable file. You need to do this, because Bash runs only executable files. (See the chmod command reference in Appendix A for more information on permission settings of a file.)

Finally, I converted the file figure1.xwd to figure1.tif, by using the following command:

```
./totif figure1
```

The ./ prefix indicates that the totif file is in the current directory — you don't need the ./ prefix if the PATH environment variable includes the current directory. The totif file is called a *shell script* or *shell program*. When you run this shell program with the command totif figure1, the shell substitutes figure1 for each occurrence of $1.

That, in a nutshell, is why you might create shell programs — to have your Linux shell perform repetitive chores.

Here is another interesting example of a shell program. Suppose that you occasionally have to use MS-DOS text files on your Linux system. Although you might expect to use a text file on any system without any problems, there is one catch: DOS uses a carriage return followed by a line feed to mark the end of each line, whereas Linux (and other UNIX systems) use only a line feed. As a result, if you use the vi editor with the -b option to open a DOS text file (for example, type vi -b *filename* to open the file), you see ^M at the end of each line. That ^M stands for Ctrl+M, which is the carriage-return character.

On your Linux system, you easily can rid the DOS text file of the extra carriage returns, by using the tr command with the -d option. Essentially, to convert the DOS text file *filename.dos* to a Linux text file named *filename.linux*, type the following:

```
tr -d '\015' < filename.dos > filename.linux
```

In this command, '\015' denotes the ASCII code for the carriage-return character in octal notation.

Note

You can use the tr command to translate or delete characters from the input. When you use tr with the -d option, it deletes all occurrences of a specific character from the input data. Following the -d option, you must specify the character to be deleted. Like many UNIX utilities, tr reads the standard input and writes its output to standard output. As the sample command shows, you must employ input and output redirection to use tr to delete all occurrences of a character in a file and save the output in another file.

If you don't want to remember all this information every time you convert a DOS file to UNIX, store the following in a file named dos2unix:

```
tr -d '\015' < $1 > $2
```

Then, make the file executable by using this command:

```
chmod +x dos2unix
```

That's it! Now you have a shell program named dos2unix that converts a DOS text file to a UNIX text file. If you have the MS-DOS partition mounted as /dosc, you can try the dos2unix shell program with the following command:

```
dos2unix /dosc/autoexec.bat aexec.bat
```

The preceding command creates a file named aexec.bat in the current directory. If you open this file with the vi -b aexec.bat command, you should not see any ^M characters at the ends of lines.

Note

If you are familiar with MS-DOS, you may notice that shell scripts closely resemble MS-DOS batch files, except for some syntax differences. Shell scripts, however, are much more powerful.

Shell scripts are popular among system administrators. If you are a system administrator, you can build a collection of custom shell scripts that help you automate tasks you perform often. If a disk seems to be getting full, for example, you may want to find all files that exceed some size (say, 1MB) and that have not been accessed in the past 30 days. Additionally, you may want to send an e-mail message to all users who have large files, requesting that they archive and clean up those files. You can perform all these tasks with a shell script. You might start with the following find command to identify large files:

```
find / -type f -atime +30 -size +1000k -exec ls -l {} \; >
/tmp/largefiles
```

This command creates a file named /tmp/largefiles, which contains detailed information about the old files taking up too much space. After you get a list of the files, you can use a few other Linux commands — such as sort, cut, and sed — to prepare and send mail messages to users who have large files that they should clean up. Instead of typing all these commands manually, you'd place them in a file and create a shell script. That, in a nutshell, is the essence of shell scripts — to gather shell commands in a file, so that you can easily perform repetitive system administration tasks.

Learning the Basics of Shell Scripting in Bash

Now that you have seen examples of simple shell scripts, the next few sections provide an overview of Bash programming.

Secret

As you try out simple shell programs, don't name your sample programs test. Linux includes an important program named test (/usr/bin/test). This program tests for various conditions in shell scripts, such as whether a file exists and whether a file is readable. If you create a sample program named test, some scripts may end up calling your program instead of the system's test program.

A Simple Shell Script

Earlier in this chapter, you learned how you can place frequently used commands in a file and use the chmod command to make the file executable. Voilà — you have a shell script. Just as most Linux commands accept command-line options, a Bash script accepts command-line options. Inside the script, you can refer to the options as $1, $2, and so on. The special name $0 refers to the name of the script itself.

Consider the following Bash script:

```
#!/bin/sh
echo "This script's name is: $0"
echo Argument 1: $1
echo Argument 2: $2
```

The first line causes Linux to run the /bin/sh program, which subsequently processes the rest of the lines in the script. The name /bin/sh traditionally refers to the Bourne shell — the first UNIX shell. In Linux, /bin/sh is a symbolic link to /bin/bash, which is the executable program for Bash. Therefore, in Linux, Bash runs Bourne shell scripts (Bash happens to be compatible with the Bourne shell).

If you save this simple script in a file named simple, and you make that file executable with the command chmod +x simple, you can run the script as follows:

```
./simple
This script's name is: ./simple
Argument 1:
Argument 2:
```

The script file's name appears relative to the current directory, which is represented by a period. Because you ran the script without any arguments, the script does not display any arguments.

Now, try running the script with a few arguments, as follows:

```
./simple "This is one argument" second-argument third
This script's name is: ./simple
Argument 1: This is one argument
Argument 2: second-argument
```

As this example shows, the shell treats the entire string within double quotation marks as a single argument. Otherwise, the shell uses spaces as separators between arguments on the command line.

Note that this sample script ignores the third argument because the script is designed to print only the first two arguments. The script ignores all arguments after the first two.

Bash Programming Overview

Like any programming language, Bash includes the following features:

- Variables that store values, including special built-in variables for accessing command-line arguments passed to a shell script and other special values

- The capability to evaluate expressions

- Control structures that enable you to loop over several shell commands, or to execute some commands conditionally

- The capability to define functions that can be called in many places within a script. Bash also includes many built-in commands that you can use in any script.

The next few sections illustrate some of Bash's programming features through simple examples. Because you are already running Bash, you can try the examples by typing them at the shell prompt in a terminal window.

Variables

You define variables in Bash just as you define environment variables. Thus, you might define a variable as follows:

```
count=12   # note no embedded spaces allowed
```

To use a variable's value, prefix the variable's name with a dollar sign ($). $PATH, for example, is the value of the variable PATH (yes, the famous PATH environment variable). To display the value of the variable count, use the following command:

```
echo $count
```

Bash has some special variables for accessing command-line arguments. In a shell script, $0 refers to the name of the shell script. The variables $1, $2, and so on, refer to the command-line arguments. The variable $* stores all the command-line arguments as a single variable, and $? contains the exit status of the last command executed by the shell.

You also can prompt the user for input and use the read command to read the input into a variable. Following is an example:

```
echo -n "Enter value: "
read value
echo "You entered: $value"
```

Tip

The -n option prevents the echo command from automatically adding a new line at the end of the string that it displays.

Shell functions

You can group a number of shell commands into a function and assign it a name. Later, you can execute that group of commands by using the single name assigned to the function. Here is a simple script that illustrates the syntax of shell functions:

```
#!/bin/sh

hello() {
        echo -n "Hello, "
        echo $1 $2
}

hello Jane Doe
```

When you run this script, it displays the following output:

```
Hello, Jane Doe
```

This script defines a shell function named `hello`. The function expects two arguments; and in the body of the function, these arguments are referenced by $1 and $2. The function definition begins with `hello()` — the name of the function, followed by parentheses. The body of the function is enclosed in curly braces — { . . . }. In this case, the body uses the `echo` built-in command (see Table 28-1 for a list of built-in commands).

Control structures

In Bash scripts, the control structures — such as `if`, `case`, `for`, and `while` — depend on the exit status of a command to decide what to do next. When any command executes, it returns an *exit status*: a numeric value that indicates whether the command succeeded. By convention, an exit status of zero means that the command succeeded. (Yes, you read it right: zero indicates success.) A non-zero exit status indicates that something went wrong with the command.

You might use a script that makes a backup copy of a file before opening it, by using the `vi` editor in the following manner:

```
#!/bin/sh
if cp "$1" "#$1"
then
    vi "$1"
else
    echo "Failed to create backup copy"
fi
```

This script illustrates the syntax of the *if-then-else* structure, and shows how the exit status of the `cp` command is used by the `if` structure to determine the next action. If `cp` returns zero, the script invokes `vi` to edit the file; otherwise, the script displays a message and exits. By the way, the script names the backup file whose name is the same as that of the original, except for a hash mark added at the beginning of the filename.

Tip

Don't forget the final `fi` that terminates the `if` structure. Forgetting `fi` is a common source of errors in Bash scripts.

Bash includes the `test` command to enable you to evaluate any expression and use the expression's value as the exit status of the command. Suppose you want a script that enables you to edit an existing file. Using `test`, you might write such a script as follows:

```
#!/bin/sh
if test -f "$1"
then
    vi "$1"
else
    echo "No such file"
fi
```

A shorter form of the `test` command omits `test` and places the command's options in brackets. Using this notation, you can write the preceding script as follows:

```
#!/bin/sh
if [ -f "$1" ]
then
     vi "$1"
else
     echo "No such file"
fi
```

Secret

The left square bracket ([) is in fact a symbolic link to /usr/bin/test. You can confirm this fact by typing `ls -l /usr/bin/[`.

Another common control structure is the `for` loop. The following script adds the numbers 1 through 10:

```
#!/bin/sh
sum=0
for i in 1 2 3 4 5 6 7 8 9 10
do
     sum=`expr $sum + $i`
done
echo "Sum = $sum"
```

This example also illustrates the use of the `expr` command to evaluate an expression.

The `case` statement is used to execute a group of commands based on the value of a variable. For example, consider the following script, based on the `confirm()` function in the /etc/init.d/functions file in your Red Hat Linux system:

```
#!/bin/sh
echo -n "What should I do -- (Y)es/(N)o/(C)ontinue? [Y] "
read answer
case $answer in
    y|Y|"")
       echo "YES"
    ;;
    c|C)
       echo "CONTINUE"
    ;;
    n|N)
       echo "NO"
    ;;
    *)
       echo "UNKNOWN"
    ;;
esac
```

Save this in a file named `confirm` and type `chmod +x confirm` to make it executable. Then try it out like this:

```
./confirm
What should I do -- (Y)es/(N)o/(C)ontinue? [Y] c
CONTINUE
```

The script displays a prompt and then reads the input you type. Your input is stored in a variable named `answer`. Then the `case` statement executes a block of code based on the value of the `answer` variable. For example, when I type c, the following block of commands is executed:

```
c|C)
   echo "CONTINUE"
;;
```

The `echo` command causes the script to display `CONTINUE`.

From this example, you can see that the general syntax of the `case` command is as follows:

```
case $variable in
   value1 | value2)
   command1
   command2
   ...other commands...
   ;;

   value3)
   command3
   command4
   ...other commands...
   ;;
esac
```

Essentially, the `case` command begins with the word `case` and ends with `esac`. In between, separate blocks of code are enclosed between the values of the variable, followed by a right parenthesis and terminated by a pair of semicolons (; ;).

Built-In Commands in Bash

Bash has more than 50 built-in commands, including common commands, such as `cd` and `pwd`, as well as many others that are not used frequently. You can use these built-in commands in any Bash script, or at the shell prompt. Appendix A describes many of the built-in commands that you typically use at the shell prompt.

Although this chapter does not have enough space to cover all built-in Bash commands, Table 28-1 describes most of these commands and their arguments. After looking through this information, type `help cmd` to read more about a specific built-in command. For example, to learn more about the built-in command `test`, type the following:

```
help test
test: test [expr]
    Exits with a status of 0 (trueness) or 1 (falseness) depending on
    the evaluation of EXPR.  Expressions may be unary or binary.
Unary
    expressions are often used to examine the status of a file.  There
    are string operators as well, and numeric comparison operators.

    File operators:

        -b FILE        True if file is block special.
        -c FILE        True if file is character special.
        -d FILE        True if file is a directory.
        -e FILE        True if file exists.
        -f FILE        True if file exists and is a regular file.
        -g FILE        True if file is set-group-id.
        -h FILE        True if file is a symbolic link.
        -L FILE        True if file is a symbolic link.
        -k FILE        True if file has its `sticky' bit set.
        -p FILE        True if file is a named pipe.
        -r FILE        True if file is readable by you.
        -s FILE        True if file exists and is not empty.
        -S FILE        True if file is a socket.
        -t FD          True if FD is opened on a terminal.
        -u FILE        True if the file is set-user-id.
        -w FILE        True if the file is writable by you.
        -x FILE        True if the file is executable by you.
        -O FILE        True if the file is effectively owned by you.
(... Lines deleted ...)
```

Where necessary, the online help from the help command includes a considerable amount of detail.

Note that some external programs may have the same name as Bash built-in commands. If you want to run any such external program, you have to explicitly specify the full path name of that program. Otherwise, Bash executes the built-in command of the same name.

Table 28-1   Summary of Built-In Commands in Bash Shell

Function	Description
. filename [arguments]	Reads and executes commands from the specified file using the optional arguments (same as source)
: [arguments]	Expands the arguments but does not process them
[expr]	Evaluates the expression expr and returns zero status if expr is true
alias [name[=value] ...]	Defines an alias

Function	Description
bg [*job*]	Puts the specified job in the background. If no job is specified, it puts the currently executing command in the background.
bind [-m *keymap*] [-lvd] [-q *name*]	Binds a key sequence to a macro
break [*n*]	Exits from a for, while, or until loop. If *n* is specified, the *n*-th enclosing loop is exited.
builtin *builtin_command* [*arguments*]	Executes a shell built-in command
cd [*dir*]	Changes the current directory to *dir*
command [-pVv] *cmd* [*arg* ...]	Runs the command *cmd* with the specified arguments (ignoring any shell function named *cmd*)
continue [*n*]	Starts the next iteration of the for, while, or until loop. If *n* is specified, the next iteration of the *n*-th enclosing loop is started.
declare [-frxi] [name[=value]]	Declares a variable with the specified name and, optionally, assigns it a value
dirs [-l] [+/-*n*]	Displays the list of currently remembered directories
echo [-neE] [*arg* ...]	Displays the arguments on standard output
enable [-n] [-*all*] [*name* ...]	Enables or disables the specified built-in commands
eval [*arg* ...]	Concatenates the arguments and executes them as a command
exec [*command* [*arguments*]]	Replaces the current instance of the shell with a new process that runs the specified command
exit [*n*]	Exits the shell with the status code *n*
export [-nf] [*name*[=*word*]] ...	Defines a specified environment variable and exports it to future processes
fc -s [*pat=rep*] [*cmd*]	Re-executes the command after replacing the pattern *pat* with *rep*

Continued

Table 28-1 *(continued)*

Function	Description
fg [*jobspec*]	Puts the specified job in the foreground. If no job is specified, it puts the most recent job in the foreground.
getopts *optstring name* [*args*]	Gets optional parameters (called in shell scripts to extract arguments from the command line)
hash [-r] [*name*]	Remembers the full path name of a specified command
help [*cmd* ...]	Displays help information for specified built-in commands
history [*n*]	Displays past commands or past *n* commands, if you specify a number *n*
jobs [-lnp] [*jobspec* ...]	Lists currently active jobs
kill [-s *sigspec* | -*sigspec*] [*pid* | *jobspec*] ...	Sends a specified signal to one or more processes
let *arg* [*arg* ...]	Evaluates each argument and returns 1 if the last *arg* is 0
local [*name*[=*value*] ...]	Creates a local variable with the specified name and value (used in shell functions)
logout	Exits a login shell
popd [+/-*n*]	Removes entries from the directory stack
pushd [*dir*]	Adds a specified directory to the top of the directory stack
pwd	Prints the full path name of the current working directory
read [-r] [*name* ...]	Reads a line from standard input and parses it
readonly [-f] [*name* ...]	Marks the specified variables as read-only, so that the variables cannot be changed later
return [*n*]	Exits the shell function with the return value *n*

Function	Description
`set [--abefhkmnptuvxldCHP]` `[-o option] [arg ...]`	Sets various flags
`shift [n]`	Makes the *n*+1 argument $1, the *n*+2 argument $2, and so on
`source filename [arguments]`	Reads and executes commands from a file
`suspend [-f]`	Stops execution until a SIGCONT signal is received
`test expr`	Evaluates the expression *expr* and returns zero if *expr* is true
`times`	Prints the accumulated user and system times for processes run from the shell
`trap [-l] [cmd] [sigspec]`	Executes *cmd* when the signal *sigspec* is received
`type [-all] [-type	-path]` `name [name ...]`	Indicates how the shell interprets each *name*
`ulimit [-SHacdfmstpnuv [limit]]`	Controls resources available to the shell
`umask [-S] [mode]`	Sets the file creation mask — the default permission for files
`unalias [-a] [name ...]`	Undefines a specified alias
`unset [-fv] [name ...]`	Removes the definition of specified variables
`wait [n]`	Waits for a specified process to terminate

Perl as a Scripting Language

Officially, *Perl* stands for *Practical Extraction Report Language*. Larry Wall created Perl to extract information from text files, and then use that information to prepare reports. Programs written in Perl, the language, are interpreted and executed by `perl`, the program. This book's companion CD-ROMs include the `perl` program; you should install it on your system in the `/usr/bin` directory.

Perl is available on a wide variety of computer systems because, like Linux, Perl can be distributed freely. In addition, Perl is popular among many users and system administrators as a scripting language, which is why I introduce

Perl and describe its strengths. In Chapter 29, you'll learn about another scripting language (Tcl/Tk) that provides the capability to create graphical user interfaces for the scripts.

As you know by now, the term *script* is simply a synonym for *program*. Unlike programs written in languages such as C and C++, you do not have to compile Perl programs; the `perl` program simply interprets and executes the Perl programs. The term *script* often is used for such interpreted programs written in a shell's programming language, or in Perl. (Strictly speaking, `perl` does not interpret a Perl program; it converts the Perl program to an intermediate form, before executing the program.)

Note

If you are familiar with shell programming or the C programming language, you can pick up Perl very quickly. If you have never programmed, becoming proficient in Perl may take a while. I encourage you to start with a small subset of Perl's features and ignore anything that you do not understand. Then, slowly add Perl features to your repertoire.

Determining Whether You Have Perl

Before you proceed with the Perl tutorial, check whether you have `perl` installed on your system. Type the following command:

```
which perl
```

The `which` command tells you whether it finds a specified program in the directories listed in the `PATH` environment variable. If `perl` is installed, you should see the following output:

```
/usr/bin/perl
```

If the `which` command complains that no such program exists in the current `PATH`, this does not necessarily mean that you do not have `perl` installed; it may mean that you do not have the `/usr/bin` directory in `PATH`. Ensure that `/usr/bin` is in `PATH`; either type `echo $PATH` or look at the message displayed by the `which` command (that message includes the directories in `PATH`). If `/usr/bin` is not in `PATH`, use the following command to redefine `PATH`:

```
export PATH=$PATH:/usr/bin
```

Now, try the `which perl` command again. If you still get an error, you may not have installed `perl`. You can install Perl from the companion CD-ROMs, with the following steps:

1. Log in as `root`.

2. Insert the first companion CD-ROM in the CD-ROM drive, and mount the CD-ROM using the following command:

   ```
   mount /mnt/cdrom
   ```

3. Type the following command to change the directory to the location of the Red Hat packages:

```
cd /mnt/cdrom/RedHat/RPMS
```

4. Type the following `rpm` (Red Hat Package Manager) command to install Perl:

```
rpm -ivh perl*
```

If you have `perl` installed on your system, type the following command to see its version number:

perl -v

Following is typical output from that command:

```
This is perl, v5.6.0 built for i386-linux

Copyright 1987-2000, Larry Wall

Perl may be copied only under the terms of either the Artistic License or the
GNU General Public License, which may be found in the Perl 5.0 source kit.

Complete documentation for Perl, including FAQ lists, should be found on
this system using `man perl' or `perldoc perl'.  If you have access to the
Internet, point your browser at http://www.perl.com/, the Perl Home Page.
```

This output tells you that you have Perl version 5.6, patch Level 0, and that Larry Wall, the originator of Perl, holds the copyright. Perl is distributed freely under the GNU General Public License, however.

The companion CD-ROM has version 5.6.0 of Perl. You can get the latest version of Perl by pointing your World Wide Web browser to the Comprehensive Perl Archive Network (CPAN). The following address connects you to the CPAN site nearest to you:

```
http://www.perl.com/CPAN/
```

Your First Perl Script

Perl has many features of C, and, as you may know, most books on C start with an example program that displays Hello, World! on your terminal. Because Perl is an interpreted language, you can accomplish this task directly from the command line. If you enter

```
perl -e 'print "Hello, World!\n";'
```

the system responds

```
Hello, World!
```

This command uses the -e option of the perl program to pass the Perl program as a command-line argument to the Perl interpreter. In this case, the following line constitutes the Perl program:

```
print "Hello, World!\n";
```

To convert this line to a script, simply place the line in a file and start the file with a directive to run the perl program (as you do in shell scripts, when you place a line such as #!/bin/sh to run the Bourne shell to process the script).

To try a Perl script, follow these steps:

1. Use a text editor, such as vi or emacs, to save the following lines in the file named hello:

   ```
   #!/usr/bin/perl
   # This is a comment.
   print "Hello, World!\n";
   ```

2. Make the hello file executable, by using the following command:

   ```
   chmod +x hello
   ```

3. Run the Perl script, by typing the following at the shell prompt:

   ```
   hello
   Hello, World!
   ```

   If you get the error message bash: hello: command not found, the current directory is not in the PATH environment variable. Type ./hello to run the script.

That's it! You have written and tried your first Perl script.

Secret

Notice that the first line of a Perl script starts with #!, followed by the full path name of the perl program. If the first line of a script starts with #!, the shell simply strips off the #!, appends the script file's name to the end, and runs the script. Thus, if the script file is named hello and the first line is #!/usr/bin/perl, the shell executes the following command:

```
/usr/bin/perl hello
```

A Perl Overview

Most programming languages, including Perl, have some common features:

- *Variables* to store different types of data. You can think of each variable as a placeholder for data — kind of like a mailbox, with a name and room to store data. The content of the variable is its value.

- *Expressions* that combine variables by using *operators*. One expression might add several variables; another might extract a part of a string.

- *Statements* that perform some action, such as assigning a value to a variable, or printing a string.

- *Flow-control statements* that enable statements to be executed in various orders, depending on the value of some expression. Typically, flow-control statements include `for`, `do-while`, `while`, and `if-then-else` statements.

- *Functions* (also called *subroutines* or *routines*) that enable you to group several statements and give them a name. This feature enables you to execute the same set of statements by invoking the function that represents those statements. Typically, a programming language provides some predefined functions.

- *Packages* and *modules* that enable you to organize a set of related Perl subroutines that are designed to be reusable. (Modules were first introduced in Perl 5).

The next few sections provide an overview of these major features of Perl and illustrate the features through simple examples.

Basic Perl syntax

Perl is free-form, like C; no constraints exist on the exact placement of any keyword. Perl programs often are stored in files with names that end in `.pl`, but there is no restriction on the filenames that you use.

As in C, each Perl statement ends with a semicolon (`;`). A pound sign (`#`) marks the start of a comment; the `perl` program disregards the rest of the line beginning with the pound sign.

Groups of Perl statements are enclosed in braces (`{...}`). This feature also is similar in C.

More on Perl

I devoted a few sections of this chapter to giving you an overview of Perl and showing a few simple examples. However, this discussion does not do justice to Perl. If you want to use Perl as a tool, consult one of the following books on Perl:

Larry Wall, Tom Christiansen, and Jon Orwant, *Programming Perl*, 3rd Edition (O'Reilly & Associates, 2000)

Randal L. Schwartz, Tom Christiansen, and Larry Wall, *Learning Perl*, 2nd Edition (O'Reilly & Associates, 1997)

Paul E. Hoffman, *Perl For Dummies* (IDG Books Worldwide, 2000)

Programming Perl, 3rd Edition, is the authoritative guide to Perl (although it may not be the best resource for learning Perl). The book by Randal Schwartz focuses more on teaching Perl programming. Paul Hoffman's book is a good introduction for nonprogrammers wanting to learn Perl.

Variables

You don't have to declare Perl variables before using them, as you do in C. You can recognize a variable in a Perl script easily, because each variable name begins with a special character: an at symbol (@), a dollar sign ($), or a percent sign (%). These special characters denotes the variable's type. The three variable types are as follows:

- *Scalar variables* represent the basic data types: integer, floating-point number, and string. A dollar sign ($) precedes a scalar variable. Following are some examples:

```
$maxlines = 256;

$title = "Red Hat Linux Secrets, 4th Edition";
```

- *Array variables* are collections of scalar variables. An array variable has an at symbol (@) as a prefix. Thus, the following are arrays:

```
@pages = (62, 26, 22, 24);

@commands = ("start", "stop", "draw", "exit");
```

- *Associative arrays* are collections of key-value pairs, in which each key is a string and the value is any scalar variable. A percent-sign (%) prefix indicates an associative array. You can use associative arrays to associate a name with a value. You might store the amount of disk space used by each user in an associative array, such as the following:

```
%disk_usage = ("root", 147178, "naba", 28547, "emily", 55);
```

Because each variable type has its own special character prefix, you can use the same name for different variable types. Thus, %disk_usage, @disk_usage, and $disk_usage can appear within the same Perl program.

Scalars

A *scalar variable* is one that can store a single value, such as a number, or a text string. Scalar variables are the basic data type in Perl. Each scalar's name begins with a dollar sign ($). Typically, you start using a scalar with an assignment statement that initializes it. You even can use a variable without initializing it; the default value for numbers is zero, and the default value of a string is an empty string. If you want to see whether a scalar is defined, use the defined function as follows:

```
print "Name undefined!\n" if !(defined $name);
```

The expression (defined $name) is 1 if $name is defined. You actually can "undefine" a variable by using the undef function. You can undefine $name, for example, as follows:

```
undef $name;
```

Variables are evaluated according to context. Following is a script that initializes and prints a few variables:

```
#!/usr/bin/perl
$title = "Red Hat Linux Secrets, 4th Edition";
$count1 = 650;
$count2 = 495;

$total = $count1 + $count2;

print "Title: $title -- $total pages\n";
```

When you run the preceding Perl program, it produces the following output:

```
Title: Red Hat Linux Secrets, 4th Edition -- 1145 pages
```

As the Perl statements show, when the two numeric variables are added, their numeric values are used; but when the $total variable is printed, its string representation is displayed.

Another interesting aspect of Perl is the fact that it evaluates all variables in a string within double quotation marks ("..."). However, if you write a string inside single quotation marks ('...'), Perl leaves that string untouched. If you write

```
print 'Title: $title -- $total pages\n';
```

with single quotes instead of double quotes, Perl displays

```
Title: $title -- $total pages\n
```

and does not generate a new line.

Secret

A useful Perl variable is $_ (the dollar sign followed by the underscore character). This special variable is known as the *default argument*. The Perl interpreter determines the value of $_ depending on the context. When the Perl interpreter reads input from the standard input, $_ holds the current input line; when the interpreter is searching for a specific pattern of text, $_ holds the default search pattern.

Arrays

An *array* is a collection of scalars. The array name begins with an at symbol (@). As in C, array subscripts start at zero. You can access the elements of an array with an index. Perl allocates space for arrays dynamically.

Consider the following simple script:

```
#!/usr/bin/perl
@commands = ("start", "stop", "draw" , "exit");

$numcmd = @commands;
print "There are $numcmd commands.\n";
print "The first command is: $commands[0]\n";
```

When you run the script, it produces the following output:

```
There are 4 commands.
The first command is: start
```

As you can see, equating a scalar to the array sets the scalar to the number of elements in the array. The first element of the @commands array is referenced as $commands[0], because the index starts at zero. Thus, the fourth element in the @commands array is $commands[3].

Two special scalars are related to an array. The $[variable is the current base index (the starting index), which is zero by default. The scalar $#*arrayname* (in which *arrayname* is the name of an array variable) has the last array index as the value. Thus, for the @commands array, $#commands is 3.

You can print an entire array with a simple print statement like this:

```
print "@commands\n";
```

When Perl executes this statement, it displays the following output:

```
start stop draw exit
```

Associative arrays

Associative array variables, which are declared with a percent-sign (%) prefix, are unique features of Perl. Using associative arrays, you can index an array with a string, such as a name. A good example of an associative array is the %ENV array that Perl automatically defines for you. In Perl, %ENV is the array of environment variables that you can access, by using the environment-variable name as an index. The following Perl statement prints the current PATH environment variable:

```
print "PATH = $ENV{PATH}\n";
```

When Perl executes this statement, it prints the current setting of PATH. In contrast to regular arrays, you have to use braces to index an associative array.

Perl has many built-in functions — such as delete, each, keys, and values — that enable you to access and manipulate associative arrays.

Operators and expressions

Operators are used to combine and compare Perl variables. Typical mathematical operators are addition (+), subtraction (-), multiplication (*), and division (/). Perl and C provide nearly the same set of operators. When you use operators to combine variables, you end up with *expressions*. Each expression has a value.

Following are some typical Perl expressions:

```
error < 0
$count == 10
$count + $i
$users[$i]
```

These expressions are examples of the *comparison operator* (the first two lines), the *arithmetic operator*, and the *array-index operator*.

Predefined Variables in Perl

Perl has several predefined variables that contain useful information you may need in a Perl script. Following are a few important predefined variables:

- @ARGV is an array of strings that contains the command-line options to the script. The first option is $ARGV[0], the second one is $ARGV[1], and so on.

- %ENV is an associative array that contains the environment variables. You can access this array by using the environment-variable name as a key. Thus, $ENV{HOME} is the home directory, and $ENV{PATH} is the current search path that the shell uses to locate commands.

- $_ is the default argument for many functions. If you see a Perl function used

without any argument, the function probably is expecting its argument in the $_ variable.

- @_ is the list of arguments passed to a subroutine.

- $0 is the name of the file containing the Perl program.

- $^V is the version number of Perl you are using (for example, if you use Perl Version 5.6.0, $^V will be v5.6.0).

- $< is the user ID (an identifying number) of the user running the script. This is useful on UNIX, where each user has an ID.

- $$ is the script's process ID.

- $? is the status returned by the last system call.

Caution

In Perl, don't use the == operator to determine whether two strings match; the == operator works only with numbers. To test the equality of strings, Perl includes the FORTRAN-style eq operator. Use eq to see whether two strings are identical, as follows:

```
if ($input eq "stop") { exit; }
```

Other FORTRAN-style string comparison operators include ne (inequality), lt (less than), gt (greater than), le (less than or equal), and ge (greater than or equal). You also can use the cmp operator to compare two strings. The return value is −1, 0, or 1, depending on whether the first string is less than, equal to, or greater than the second string.

Perl also provides the following unique operators. C lacks an exponentiation operator, which FORTRAN includes; Perl uses ** as the exponentiation operator. Thus, you can enter the following:

```
$x = 2;
$y = 3;
$z = $x**$y;  # z should be 8 (2 raised to the power 3)
$y **= 2; # y is now 9 (3 raised to the power 2)
```

You can initialize an array to null by using ( ) — the *null-list operator* — as follows:

```
@commands = ();
```

The dot operator (.) enables you to concatenate two strings, as follows:

```
$part1 = "Hello, ";
$part2 = "World!";
$message = $part1.$part2;  # Now $message = "Hello, World!"
```

A curious, but useful, operator is the *repetition operator*, denoted by x=. You can use the x= operator to repeat a string a specified number of times. Suppose you want to initialize a string to 65 asterisks (*). The following example shows how you can initialize the string with the x= operator:

```
$marker = "*";
$marker x= 65;  # Now $marker is a string of 65 asterisks
```

Another powerful operator in Perl is the *range operator*, which is represented by two periods (..). You can initialize an array easily by using the range operator. Following are some examples:

```
@numerals = (0..9); # @numerals = 0, 1, 2, 3, 4, 5, 6, 7, 8 , 9
@alphabet = ('A'..'Z'); # @alphabet = capital letters A through Z
```

Regular expressions

If you have used UNIX for a while, you probably know about the grep command, which enables you to search files for a pattern of strings. Following is a typical use of grep to locate all files that have any occurrences of the string blaster or Blaster—on any line of all files with names that end in .c:

```
cd /usr/src/linux*/drivers/cdrom
grep "[bB]laster"  *.c
```

The preceding commands produce the following output on my system:

```
cdu31a.c:   { 0x230,    0 },   /* SoundBlaster 16 card */
sbpcd.c: *              Works with SoundBlaster compatible cards and with "no-soun
d"
sbpcd.c:        0x230, 1, /* Soundblaster Pro and 16 (default) */
sbpcd.c:        0x250, 1, /* OmniCD default, Soundblaster Pro and 16 */
sbpcd.c:        0x270, 1, /* Soundblaster 16 */
sbpcd.c:        0x290, 1, /* Soundblaster 16 */
sbpcd.c:static const char *str_sb = "SoundBlaster";
sbpcd.c:static const char *str_sb_l = "soundblaster";
sbpcd.c: *              sbpcd=0x230,SoundBlaster
sbpcd.c:            msg(DBG_INF,"   LILO boot: ...
sbpcd=0x230,SoundBlaster\n");
sjcd.c: *  the SoundBlaster/Panasonic style CDROM interface. But today, the
```

As you can see, grep found all occurrences of blaster and Blaster in the files with names ending in .c.

The grep command's "[bB]laster" argument is known as a *regular expression*, which is a pattern that matches a set of strings. You construct a regular expression with a small set of operators and rules that resemble the ones for writing arithmetic expressions. A list of characters inside brackets ([...]), for example, matches any single character in the list. Thus, the regular expression "[bB]laster" is a set of two strings, as follows:

```
blaster    Blaster
```

Perl supports regular expressions, just as the grep command does. Many other UNIX programs, such as the vi editor and sed (the stream editor), also support regular expressions. The purpose of a regular expression is to search for a pattern of strings in a file. That's why editors support regular expressions.

Perl enables you to construct complex regular expressions. The rules, however, are fairly simple. Essentially, the regular expression is a sequence of characters in which some characters have special meaning. Table 28-2 describes the basic rules for interpreting the characters.

Table 28-2   Rules for Interpreting Regular Expression Characters

Expression	Meaning
.	Matches any single character except a newline
$x*$	Matches zero or more occurrences of the character x
$x+$	Matches one or more occurrences of the character x
$x?$	Matches zero or one occurrence of the character x
[...]	Matches any of the characters inside the brackets
$x\{n\}$	Matches exactly n occurrences of the character x
$x\{n,\}$	Matches n or more occurrences of the character x
$x\{,m\}$	Matches zero or, at most, m occurrences of the character x
$x\{n,m\}$	Matches at least n occurrences, but no more than m occurrences of the character x
$	Matches the end of a line
\0	Matches a null character
\b	Matches a backspace
\B	Matches any character not at the beginning or end of a word
\b	Matches the beginning or end of a word — when not inside brackets
\c$X$	Matches Ctrl-X (where X is any alphabetic character)
\d	Matches a single digit
\D	Matches a nondigit character
\f	Matches a form feed
\n	Matches a newline (line-feed) character

Continued

Table 28-2 *(continued)*	
Expression	**Meaning**
\ooo	Matches the octal value specified by the digits *ooo* (where each *o* is a digit between 0 and 7)
\r	Matches a carriage return
\S	Matches a non-white space character
\s	Matches a white space character (space, tab, or newline)
\t	Matches a tab
\W	Matches a non-alphanumeric character
\w	Matches an alphanumeric character
\xhh	Matches the hexadecimal value specified by the digits *hh* (where each *h* is a digit between 0 and f)
^	Matches the beginning of a line

If you want to match one of the characters $, |, *, ^, [,], \, and /, you have to place a backslash before them. Thus, you type these characters as \$, \|, *, \^, \[, \], \\, and \/. Regular expressions often look confusing because of the preponderance of strange character sequences and the generous sprinkling of backslashes. As with anything else, however, you can start slowly and use only a few of the features in the beginning.

So far, this section has summarized the syntax of regular expressions. But, you have not seen how to use regular expressions in Perl. Typically, you place a regular expression within a pair of slashes and use the match (=~), or not-match (!~) operators to test a string. You can write a Perl script that performs the same search as the one done with grep earlier in this section. The following steps help you complete this exercise:

1. Use an editor to type and save the following script in a file named lookup:

    ```
    #!/usr/bin/perl

    while (<STDIN>)
    {
        if ( $_ =~ /[bB]laster/ ) { print $_; }
    }
    ```

2. Make the lookup file executable, by using the following command:

    ```
    chmod +x lookup
    ```

3. Try the script, using the following command:

    ```
    cat /usr/src/linux*/drivers/cdrom/sbpcd.c | ./lookup
    ```

My system responds with this:

```
*              Works with SoundBlaster compatible cards and with
"no-sound"
        0x230, 1, /* Soundblaster Pro and 16 (default) */
        0x250, 1, /* OmniCD default, Soundblaster Pro and 16 */
        0x270, 1, /* Soundblaster 16 */
        0x290, 1, /* Soundblaster 16 */
static const char *str_sb = "SoundBlaster";
static const char *str_sb_l = "soundblaster";
*               sbpcd=0x230,SoundBlaster
            msg(DBG_INF,"   LILO boot: ...
sbpcd=0x230,SoundBlaster\n")
```

The `cat` command feeds the contents of a specific file (which, as you know from the `grep` example, contains some lines with the regular expression) to the lookup script. The script simply applies Perl's regular expression-match operator (=~) and prints any matching line.

The `$_` variable in the script needs some explanation. The `<STDIN>` expression gets a line from the standard input and, by default, stores that line in the `$_` variable. Inside the `while` loop, the regular expression is matched against the `$_` string. The following single Perl statement completes the `lookup` script's work:

```
if ( $_ =~ /[bB]laster/ ) { print $_; }
```

This example illustrates how you might use a regular expression to search for occurrences of strings in a file.

After you use regular expressions for a while, you can better appreciate their power. The trick is to figure out exactly what regular expression performs the task you want. Following is a search that looks for all lines that begin with exactly seven spaces and end with a right parenthesis:

```
while (<STDIN>)
{
    if ( $_ =~ /\)\n/ && $_ =~ /^ {7}\S/ )  { print $_; }
}
```

Flow-control statements

So far, you have seen Perl statements intended to execute in a serial fashion, one after another. Perl also includes statements that enable you to control the flow of execution of the statements. You already have seen the `if` statement and a `while` loop. Perl includes a complete set of flow-control statements just like those in C, but with a few extra features.

In Perl, all conditional statements take the following form:

```
conditional-statement
{ Perl code to execute if conditional is true }
```

Notice that you *must* enclose within braces ({...}) the code that follows the conditional statement. The conditional statement checks the value of an expression to determine whether to execute the code within the braces. In Perl, as in C, any non-zero value is considered true, whereas a zero value is false.

The following sections briefly describe the syntax of the major conditional statements in Perl.

if and unless

The Perl if statement resembles the C if statement. For example, an if statement might check a count to see whether the count exceeds a threshold, as follows:

```
if ( $count > 25 ) { print "Too many errors!\n"; }
```

You can add an else clause to the if statement, as follows:

```
if ($user eq "root")
{
    print "Starting simulation...\n";
}
else
{
    print "Sorry $user, you must be \"root\" to run this program.\n";
    exit;
}
```

If you know C, you can see that Perl's syntax looks quite a bit like that in C. Conditionals with the if statement can have zero or more elsif clauses to account for more alternatives, such as the following:

```
print "Enter version number:"; # prompt user for version number
$os_version = <STDIN>;            # read from standard input
chop $os_version;  # get rid of the newline at the end of the line
# Check version number
if ($os_version >= 10 ) { print "No upgrade necessary\n";}
elsif ($os_version >= 6 && $os_version < 9)
                                   { print "Standard upgrade\n";}
elsif ($os_version > 3 && $os_version < 6) { print "Reinstall\n";}
else { print "Sorry, cannot upgrade\n";}
```

Note

The unless statement is unique to Perl. This statement has the same form as if, including the use of elsif and else clauses. The difference is that unless executes its statement block only if the condition is false. You can, for example, use the following:

```
unless ($user eq "root")
{
    print "You must be \"root\" to run this program.\n";
    exit;
}
```

In this case, unless the string user is "root", the script exits.

while

Use Perl's while statement for *looping*—the repetition of some processing until a condition becomes false. To read a line at a time from standard input, and to process that line, you might use the following:

```
while ($in = <STDIN>)
{
# Code to process the line
    print $in;
}
```

Secret

If you read from the standard input without any argument, Perl assigns the current line of standard input to the $_ variable. Thus, you can write the preceding while loop as follows:

```
while (<STDIN>)
{
# Code to process the line
    print $_;
}
```

Perl's while statements are more versatile than those of C, because you can use almost anything as the condition to be tested. If you use an array as the condition, for example, the while loop executes until the array has no elements left, as in the following example:

```
# Assume @cmdarg has the current set of command arguments
while (@cmdarg)
{
    $arg = shift @cmdarg;   # this extracts one argument
# Code to process the current argument
    print $arg;
}
```

The shift function removes the first element of an array and returns that element.

You can skip to the end of a loop with the next keyword; the last keyword exits the loop. The following while loop adds the numbers from 1 to 10, skipping 5:

```
while (1)
{
    $i++;
    if($i == 5) { next;}   # Jump to the next iteration if $i is 5
    if($i > 10) { last;}   # When $i exceeds 10, end the loop
    $sum += $i;            # Add the numbers
}
# At this point $sum should be 50
```

for and foreach

Perl and C's for statements have similar syntax. Use the for statement to execute a statement any number of times, based on the value of an expression. The syntax is as follows:

```
for (expr_1; expr_2; expr_3) { statement block }
```

expr_1 is evaluated one time, at the beginning of the loop; the statement block is executed until expression *expr_2* evaluates to zero. The third expression, *expr_3*, is evaluated after each execution of the statement block. You can omit any of the expressions, but you must include the semicolons. In addition, the braces around the statement block are required. Following is an example that uses a for loop to add the numbers from 1 to 10:

```
for($i=0, $sum=0; $i <= 10; $sum += $i, $i++) {}
```

In this example, the actual work of adding the numbers is done in the third expression, and the statement controlled by the for loop is an empty block ({}).

The foreach statement is most appropriate for arrays. Following is the syntax:

```
foreach Variable (Array) { statement block }
```

The foreach statement assigns to *Variable* an element from the *Array* and executes the statement block. The foreach statement repeats this procedure until no array elements remain. The following foreach statement adds the numbers from 1 to 10:

```
foreach $i (1..10) { $sum += $i;}
```

Notice that I declare the array with the range operator (..). You also can use a list of comma-separated items as the array.

Secret

If you omit the *Variable* in a foreach statement, Perl implicitly uses the $_ variable to hold the current array element. Thus, you can use the following:

```
foreach (1..10) { $sum += $_;}
```

goto

The goto statement transfers control to a statement label. Following is an example that prompts the user for a value and repeats the request, if the value is not acceptable:

```
ReEnter:
print "Enter offset: ";
$offset = <STDIN>;
chop $offset;
unless ($offset > 0 && $offset < 512)
{
    print "Bad offset: $offset\n";
    goto ReEnter;
}
```

Accessing Linux commands

You can execute any Linux command from Perl in several ways:

- Call the `system` function with a string that contains the Linux command that you want to execute.

- Enclose a Linux command within backquotes (`), which also are known as grave accents. You can run a Linux command this way and capture its output.

- Call the `fork` function to copy the current script and process new commands in the child process. (If a process starts another process, then the new process is known as a *child process*.)

- Call the `exec` function to overlay the current script with a new script or Linux command.

- Use `fork` and `exec` to provide shell-like behavior. (Monitor user input and process each user-entered command through a child process.) This section presents a simple example of how to accomplish this task.

The simplest way to execute a Linux command in your script is to use the `system` function with the command in a string. After the `system` function returns, the exit code from the command is in the `$?` variable. You easily can write a simple Perl script that reads a string from the standard input and processes that string with the `system` function. Follow these steps:

1. Use a text editor to enter and save the following script in a file named `rcmd.pl`:

```
#!/usr/bin/perl
# Read user input and process command

$prompt = "Command (\"exit\" to quit): ";
print $prompt;

while (<STDIN>)
{
    chop;
    if ($_ eq "exit") { exit 0;}

# Execute command by calling system
    system $_;
    unless ($? == 0) {print "Error executing: $_\n";}
    print $prompt;
}
```

2. Make the `rcmd.pl` file executable, using the following command:

```
chmod +x rcmd.pl
```

3. Run the script by typing `./rcmd.pl` at the shell prompt. Note the following sample output from the `rcmd.pl` script (the output depends on what commands you enter):

```
Command ("exit" to quit): ps
  PID TTY          TIME CMD
  767 pts/0    00:00:00 bash
  940 pts/0    00:00:00 rcmd.pl
  945 pts/0    00:00:00 ps
Command ("exit" to quit): exit
```

You also can run UNIX commands by using fork and exec in your Perl script. Following is an example script — psh.pl — that uses fork and exec to execute commands entered by the user:

```
#!/usr/bin/perl

# This is a simple script that uses "fork" and "exec" to
# run a command entered by the user

$prompt = "Command (\"exit\" to quit): ";
print $prompt;

while (<STDIN>)
{
    chop;     # remove trailing newline
    if($_ eq "exit") { exit 0;}

    $status = fork;
    if($status)
    {
# In parent... wait for child process to finish...
        wait;
        print $prompt;
        next;
    }
    else
    {
        exec $_;
    }
}
```

The following example shows how the psh.pl script executes the ps command:

```
Command ("exit" to quit): ps
  PID TTY          TIME CMD
  767 pts/0    00:00:00 bash
  949 pts/0    00:00:00 psh.pl
  950 pts/0    00:00:00 ps
Command ("exit" to quit): exit
```

UNIX shells, such as Bash, use the fork and exec combination to run commands.

File access

You may have noticed the <STDIN> expression in various examples in this chapter. That's Perl's way of reading from a file. In Perl, a *file handle*, also known as an *identifier*, identifies a file. Usually, file handles are in uppercase characters. STDIN is a predefined file handle that denotes the standard input — by default, the keyboard. STDOUT and STDERR are the other two predefined file handles. STDOUT is used for printing to the terminal, and STDERR is used for printing error messages.

To read from a file, you write the file handle inside angle brackets (<>). Thus, <STDIN> reads a line from the standard input.

You can open other files by using the open function. The following example shows you how to open the /etc/passwd file for reading, and how to display the lines in that file:

```perl
open (PWDFILE, "/etc/passwd");   # PWDFILE is the file handle
while (<PWDFILE>) { print $_;}   # By default, input line is in $_
close PWDFILE;                   # Close the file
```

By default, the open function opens a file for reading. You can add special characters at the beginning of the filename to indicate other types of access. A > prefix opens the file for writing, whereas a >> prefix opens a file for appending. Following is a short script that reads the /etc/passwd file and creates a new file, named output, with a list of all users without any shell (the password entries for these users have : at the end of each line):

```perl
#!/usr/bin/perl
# Read /etc/passwd and create list of users without any shell

open (PWDFILE, "/etc/passwd");
open (RESULT, ">output");                    # open file for writing

while (<PWDFILE>)
{
    if ($_ =~ /:\n/) {print RESULT $_;}
}

close PWDFILE;
close RESULT;
```

After you execute this script, you should find a file named output in the current directory. Following is what the output file contains when I run this script on my Linux system:

```
bin:x:1:1:bin:/bin:
daemon:x:2:2:daemon:/sbin:
adm:x:3:4:adm:/var/adm:
lp:x:4:7:lp:/var/spool/lpd:
mail:x:8:12:mail:/var/spool/mail:
news:x:9:13:news:/var/spool/news:
uucp:x:10:14:uucp:/var/spool/uucp:
operator:x:11:0:operator:/root:
games:x:12:100:games:/usr/games:
gopher:x:13:30:gopher:/usr/lib/gopher-data:
ftp:x:14:50:FTP User:/var/ftp:
nobody:x:99:99:Nobody:/:
```

Piping Perl Filenames

One interesting filename prefix is the pipe character—the vertical bar (|). If you call open with a filename that begins with |, the rest of the filename is treated as a command. The Perl interpreter executes the command, and you can use print calls to send input to this command. The following Perl script sends a mail message to a list of users:

```perl
#!/usr/bin/perl
# Send mail to a list of users

foreach ("root", "naba")
{
    open (MAILPIPE, "| mail -s
Greetings $_");
    print MAILPIPE "Remember to
send in your weekly report
```

```
today!\n";
    close MAILPIPE;
}
```

If a filename ends with a pipe character (|), that filename is executed as a command; you can read that command's output with the angle brackets, as shown in the following example:

```perl
open (PSPIPE, "ps ax |");
while (<PSPIPE>)
{
# Process the output of the ps
command
# This example simply echoes each
line
    print $_;
}
```

Subroutines

Although Perl includes a large assortment of built-in functions, you can add your own code modules in the form of subroutines. In fact, the Perl distribution comes with a large set of subroutines. Following is a simple script that illustrates the syntax of subroutines in Perl:

```perl
#!/usr/bin/perl
sub hello
{
# Make local copies of the arguments from the @_ array
    local ($first,$last) = @_;

    print "Hello, $first $last\n";
}

$a = Jane;
$b = Doe;

&hello($a, $b);      # Call the subroutine
```

When you run the preceding script, it displays the following output:

```
Hello, Jane Doe
```

Note the following points about subroutines:

- The subroutine receives its arguments in the array @_ (the at symbol, followed by an underscore character).

- Variables used in subroutines are global by default. Use the `local` function to create a local set of variables.

- Call a subroutine by placing an ampersand (&) before its name. Thus, subroutine `hello` is called by `&hello`.

If you want, you can put a subroutine in its own file. The `hello` subroutine, for example, can reside in a file named `hello.pl`. When you place a subroutine in a file, remember to add a return value at the end of the file — just type `1;` at the end to return 1. Thus, the `hello.pl` file appears as follows:

```
sub hello
{
# Make local copies of the arguments from the @_ array
    local ($first,$last) = @_;

    print "Hello, $first $last\n";
}
1;        # return value
```

Then, you have to write the script that uses the `hello` subroutine, as follows:

```
#!/usr/bin/perl
require 'hello.pl';      # include the file with the subroutine

$a = Jane;
$b = Doe;

&hello($a, $b);        # Call the subroutine
```

This script uses the `require` function to include the `hello.pl` file that actually contains the definition of the `hello` subroutine.

Built-in functions in Perl

Perl has nearly 200 built-in functions (also referred to as *Perl functions*), including functions that resemble the ones in the C Run-Time Library, as well as functions that access the operating system. You really need to go through the list of functions to appreciate the breadth of capabilities available in Perl. Table 28-3 briefly describes each of the Perl functions.

This chapter does not have enough space to cover these functions, but you can learn about the Perl functions by pointing your World Wide Web browser to the following address:

```
http://www.perl.com/CPAN//doc/manual/html/pod/perlfunc.html
```

This address connects you to the Comprehensive Perl Archive Network (CPAN) — actually, it connects to the CPAN site nearest to you — so you can download the page with an overview of the Perl built-in functions. Then, click a function's name to view more detailed information about that function.

Table 28-3   A Quick Reference Guide to Perl Functions

Function Call	Description
abs(VALUE)	Returns the absolute value of the argument
accept(NEWSOCKET, GENERICSOCKET)	Waits for a connection on a socket
alarm(SECONDS)	Sends an alarm signal after a specified number of seconds
atan2(Y,X)	Returns the arctangent of Y/X
bind(SOCKET,NAME)	Associates a name to an already opened socket
binmode(FILEHANDLE)	Arranges for a file to be treated as binary
bless(REF,PACKAGE)	Makes a referenced item an object in a package
caller(EXPR)	Returns information about current subroutine calls
chdir(EXPR)	Changes the directory to the directory specified by EXPR
chmod(LIST)	Changes the permissions of a list of files
chomp(VARIABLE)	Removes trailing characters that match the current value of the special variable $/
chop(VARIABLE)	Chops off the last character (useful for removing the trailing newline character in a string)
chown(LIST)	Changes the owner of a list of files
chr(NUMBER)	Returns the character whose ASCII code is NUMBER
chroot(FILENAME)	Changes the root directory to the specified FILENAME
close(FILEHANDLE)	Closes the specified file
closedir(DIRHANDLE)	Closes the directory that had been opened by opendir
connect(SOCKET,NAME)	Initiates a connection to another system using a socket
cos(EXPR)	Returns the cosine of the angle EXPR (radians)
crypt(PLAINTEXT, SALT)	Encrypts a string
dbmclose(ASSOC_ARRAY)	Disassociates an associative array from a DBM file. (DBM, or data base manager, is a library of routines that manages DBM files — data files that contain key/data pairs.)

Function Call	Description
dbmopen(ASSOC, DBNAME, MODE)	Associates an associative array with a DBM file
defined(EXPR)	Returns true if EXPR is defined
delete $ASSOC{KEY}	Deletes a value from an associative array
die(LIST)	Prints LIST to standard error and exits the Perl program
do SUBROUTINE (LIST)	Calls a subroutine
dump(LABEL)	Causes a core dump
each(ASSOC_ARRAY)	Returns next key-value pair of an associative array
endgrent	Closes the /etc/group file in UNIX
endhostent	Closes the /etc/hosts file in UNIX
endnetent	Closes the /etc/networks file in UNIX
endprotoent	Closes the /etc/protocols file in UNIX
endpwent	Closes the /etc/passwd file in UNIX
endservent	Closes the /etc/services file in UNIX
eof(FILEHANDLE)	Returns true if end-of-file is reached
eval(EXPR)	Executes the EXPR as if it were a Perl program
exec(LIST)	Terminates the current Perl program by running another program (specified by LIST) in its place
exists($ASSOC($KEY))	Returns true if the specified key exists in the associative array
exit(EXPR)	Exits the Perl program and returns EXPR
exp(EXPR)	Returns e raised to the power EXPR
fcntl(FILEHANDLE, FUNCTION, SCALAR)	Performs various control operations on a file
fileno(FILEHANDLE)	Returns the file descriptor for a file handle
flock(FILEHANDLE, OPERATION)	Locks a file so other processes cannot change the file (useful when multiple processes need to access a single file)
fork	Creates a child process and returns the child process ID
format NAME = picture line value list	Defines an output format to be used by the write function

Continued

Table 28-3 *(continued)*

Function Call	Description
formline(PICTURE, LIST)	Formats a list of values according to the contents of PICTURE
getc(FILEHANDLE)	Reads the next character from the file
getgrent	Returns group information from /etc/group
getgrgid(GID)	Looks up a group file entry by group number
getgrnam(NAME)	Looks up a group file entry by group name
gethostbyaddr (ADDR, ADDRTYPE)	Translates a network address to a name
gethostbyname(NAME)	Translates a network hostname to corresponding addresses
gethostent	Gets entries from the /etc/hosts file on UNIX
getlogin	Returns current login information in UNIX
getnetbyaddr (ADDR, ADDRTYPE)	Translates a network address to its corresponding network name
getnetbyname(NAME)	Translates a network name to its corresponding network address
getnetent	Gets entries from the /etc/networks file (or equivalent on non-UNIX systems)
getpeername(SOCKET)	Returns the socket address of the other end of a socket connection
getpgrp(PID)	Returns the current process group for the specified process ID
getppid	Returns the process ID of the parent process
getpriority(WHICH, WHO)	Returns the current priority of a process
getprotobyname(NAME)	Translates a protocol name into a number
getprotobynumber(NUMBER)	Translates a protocol number into a name
getprotoent	Gets networking protocol information from the /etc/networks file in UNIX
getpwent	Gets entry from the password file (/etc/passwd in UNIX)
getpwnam(NAME)	Translates a user name into the corresponding entry in the password file

Function Call	Description
`getpwuid(UID)`	Translates a numeric user ID into the corresponding entry in the password file
`getservbyname (NAME, PROTO)`	Translates a service (port) name into the corresponding port number
`getservbyport (PORT, PROTO)`	Translates the service (port) number into a name
`getservent`	Gets entries from the `/etc/services` file in UNIX
`getsockname(SOCKET)`	Returns the address of this end of a socket connection
`getsockopt(SOCKET, LEVEL, OPTNAME)`	Returns the requested socket options
`glob(EXPR)`	Returns filenames corresponding to a wildcard expression
`gmtime(EXPR)`	Converts binary time into a nine-element list corresponding to Greenwich Mean Time (GMT)
`goto(LABEL)`	Jumps to the statement identified by the `LABEL`
`grep(EXPR, LIST)`	Searches `LIST` for occurrences of the expression
`hex(EXPR)`	Returns the decimal value corresponding to hexadecimal `EXPR`
`index(STR, SUBSTR, POSITION)`	Returns the position of the first occurrence of a string (the search begins at the character location specified by `POSITION`)
`int(EXPR)`	Returns the integer portion of `EXPR`
`ioctl(FILEHANDLE, FUNCTION, SCALAR)`	Controls various aspects of `FILEHANDLE`
`join(EXPR, LIST)`	Returns a single string by joining list elements
`keys(ASSOC_ARRAY)`	Returns an array of keys for an associative array
`kill(LIST)`	Sends a signal to a list of processes
`last(LABEL)`	Exits the loop identified by `LABEL`
`lc(EXPR)`	Returns the lowercase version of `EXPR`
`lcfirst(EXPR)`	Returns `EXPR`, after changing the first character to lowercase
`length(EXPR)`	Returns length in number of characters

Continued

Table 28-3 *(continued)*

Function Call	Description
link(OLDFILE, NEWFILE)	Creates NEWFILE as a link to OLDFILE
listen(SOCKET, QUEUESIZE)	Waits for incoming connections on a socket
local(LIST)	Makes a list of variables local to a subroutine
localtime(EXPR)	Converts binary time into a nine-element list corresponding to local time
log(EXPR)	Returns the logarithm (to base e) of EXPR
lstat(FILEHANDLE)	Returns file statistics for a file (if the file refers to a symbolic link, returns information about the symbolic link)
m/PATTERN/gimosx	Performs pattern matching
map(EXPR, LIST)	Evaluates the expression EXPR for each item of LIST
mkdir(FILENAME, MODE)	Creates the directory specified by FILENAME
msgctl(ID, CMD, ARG)	Performs message control operations on message queues
msgget(KEY, FLAGS)	Gets a message queue identifier corresponding to KEY
msgrcv(ID, VAR, SIZE, TYPE, FLAGS)	Receives a message from the message queue identifier ID
msgsnd(ID, MSG, FLAGS)	Sends a message-to-message queue identifier ID
my(EXPR)	Declares one or more private variables that exist in a subroutine or a block enclosed in curly braces ({...})
next(LABEL)	Starts the next iteration of the loop identified by LABEL
no(Module LIST)	Stops using a Perl module
oct(EXPR)	Returns the decimal equivalent of an octal number in EXPR
open(FILEHANDLE, EXPR)	Opens a file whose name is in EXPR, and associates that file with FILEHANDLE
opendir(DIRHANDLE, EXPR)	Opens a directory whose name is in EXPR, and associates that directory with DIRHANDLE
ord(EXPR)	Returns the numeric ASCII code of the first character in EXPR

Function Call	Description
pack(TEMPLATE, LIST)	Takes a list of values and returns a string containing a packed binary structure (TEMPLATE specifies the packing)
pipe(READHANDLE, WRITEHANDLE)	Opens a pipe for reading and writing
pop(ARRAY)	Removes and returns the last element of an array
pos(SCALAR)	Returns the position where the last pattern match occurred (applies when a global search is performed with /PATTERN/g)
print(FILEHANDLE LIST)	Prints a list of items to a file identified by FILEHANDLE
printf(FILEHANDLE LIST)	Prints formatted output to a file
push(ARRAY, LIST)	Appends values in LIST to the end of ARRAY
q/STRING/	Quotes a STRING, without replacing variable names with values (similar to a single quoted string)
qq/STRING/	Quotes a STRING, but replaces variable names with values (similar to a double quoted string)
quotemeta(EXPR)	Returns the value of EXPR, after adding a backslash prefix for all characters that take on special meaning in regular expressions
qw/STRING/	Quotes a word list (similar to parentheses used in patterns)
qx/STRING/	Quotes a command (similar to backquotes)
rand(EXPR)	Returns a random value between 0 and EXPR
read(FILEHANDLE, SCALAR, LENGTH)	Reads a specified number of bytes from the file
readdir(DIRHANDLE)	Reads directory entries from a directory handle
readlink(EXPR)	Returns the filename pointed to by a symbolic link
recv(SOCKET, SCALAR, LEN, FLAGS)	Receives a message from a socket
redo(LABEL)	Restarts the loop identified by LABEL
ref(EXPR)	Returns true if EXPR is a reference (a reference points to an object)
rename(OLDNAME, NEWNAME)	Changes the name of a file from OLDNAME to NEWNAME

Continued

Table 28-3 *(continued)*

Function Call	Description
require(FNAME)	Includes the file specified by FNAME, and executes the Perl code in that file
reset(EXPR)	Clears global variables
return(LIST)	Returns from subroutine with the specified values
reverse(LIST)	Reverses the order of elements in LIST
rewinddir(DIRHANDLE)	Sets the current position to the beginning of the directory identified by DIRHANDLE
rindex(STR, SUBSTR)	Returns the last position of a substring in a string
rindex(STR, SUBSTR, POSITION)	Returns the position of the last occurrence of a substring in a string
rmdir(FILENAME)	Deletes the directory specified by FILENAME
s/PATTERN/REPLACEMENT/ egimosx	Replaces PATTERN (a regular expression) with REPLACEMENT
scalar(EXPR)	Evaluates the expression EXPR in a scalar context
seek(FILEHANDLE, POSITION, WHENCE)	Moves to a new location in a file
seekdir(DIRHANDLE, POS)	Moves to a new position in a directory
select(FILEHANDLE)	Returns the currently selected file handle, and sets FILEHANDLE as the default file handle for output
select(RBITS, WBITS, EBITS, TIMEOUT)	Checks if one or more files are ready for input or output
semctl(ID, SEMNUM, CMD, ARG)	Controls the semaphores used for interprocess communication
semget(KEY, NSEMS, FLAGS)	Returns the semaphore ID corresponding to a key
semop(KEY, OPSTRING)	Performs a semaphore operation (semaphores are used for interprocess communications in UNIX System V)
send(SOCKET, MSG, FLAGS, TO)	Sends a message to a socket
setgrent	Sets group information in /etc/group
sethostent(STAYOPEN)	Opens the host database (the /etc/hosts file in UNIX)

Function Call	Description
`setnetent(STAYOPEN)`	Opens the network database (the `/etc/networks` file in UNIX)
`setpgrp(PID,PGRP)`	Sets the current process group of a process
`setpriority (WHICH, WHO, PRIORITY)`	Sets the priority for a process
`setprotoent(STAYOPEN)`	Opens the protocol database (the `/etc/protocols` file in UNIX)
`setpwent`	Opens the `/etc/passwd` file in UNIX
`setservent(STAYOPEN)`	Opens the `/etc/services` file in UNIX
`setsockopt(SOCKET, LEVEL, OPTNAME, OPTVAL)`	Sets the specified socket options
`shift(ARRAY)`	Removes the first value of the array and returns it
`shmctl(ID, CMD, ARG)`	Controls shared memory settings, such as permission
`shmget(KEY, SIZE, FLAGS)`	Allocates a shared memory segment
`shmread (ID, VAR, POS, SIZE)`	Reads from the shared memory segment identified by `ID`
`shmwrite(ID, STRING, POS, SIZE)`	Writes to the shared memory segment identified by `ID`
`shutdown(SOCKET, HOW)`	Shuts down a socket connection
`sin(EXPR)`	Returns the sine of the angle specified by `EXPR` (in radians)
`sleep(EXPR)`	Sleeps for `EXPR` seconds
`socket(SOCKET, DOMAIN, TYPE, PROTOCOL)`	Opens a socket for a specified type and attaches it to the file handle `SOCKET`
`socketpair(SOCKET1, SOCKET2, DOMAIN, TYPE, PROTOCOL)`	Creates an unnamed pair of sockets
`sort(LIST)`	Sorts a list and returns the sorted list in an array
`splice(ARRAY, OFFSET, LENGTH, LIST)`	Replaces some `ARRAY` elements with `LIST`
`split(/PATTERN/ , EXPR, LIMIT)`	Splits `EXPR` into an array of strings
`sprintf(FORMAT, LIST)`	Returns a string containing formatted output consisting of `LIST` elements formatted according to the `FORMAT` string

Continued

Table 28-3   *(continued)*

Function Call	Description
sqrt(EXPR)	Returns the square root of EXPR
srand(EXPR)	Sets the seed for random number generation
stat(FILEHANDLE)	Returns a 13-element list with statistics for a file
study(STRING)	Examines STRING in anticipation of doing many pattern matches on the string
substr(EXPR, OFFSET, LEN)	Returns a substring from the string EXPR
symlink(OLDFILE, NEWFILE)	Creates NEWFILE as a symbolic link to OLDFILE
syscall(LIST)	Calls the system function specified in the first element of LIST (and passes to that call the remaining list elements as arguments)
sysopen(FILEHANDLE, FILENAME, MODE, PERMS)	Opens a file named FILENAME and associates it with FILEHANDLE
sysread(FILEHANDLE, SCALAR, LENGTH, OFFSET)	Reads a specified number of bytes from a file
system(LIST)	Executes the shell commands in LIST
syswrite(FILEHANDLE, SCALAR, LENGTH, OFFSET)	Writes a specified number of bytes to a file
tell(FILEHANDLE)	Returns the current file position in bytes from the beginning of a file
telldir(DIRHANDLE)	Returns the current position where the readdir function can read from a directory handle
tie(VARIABLE, PACKAGENAME, LIST)	Associates a variable to a package that implements the variable
time	Returns the number of seconds since 00:00:00 GMT 1/1/1970
times	Returns time in seconds for this process
tr/SEARCHLIST/ REPLACE_LIST/cds	Translates a search list into a replacement list
truncate(FILEHANDLE, LENGTH)	Truncates the file FILEHANDLE to a specified LENGTH
uc(EXPR)	Returns the uppercase version of EXPR
ucfirst(EXPR)	Returns EXPR after changing the first character to uppercase

Function Call	Description
`umask(EXPR)`	Sets the permission mask to be used when creating a file (this specifies what operations are not allowed on the file)
`undef(EXPR)`	Undefines EXPR
`unlink(LIST)`	Deletes a list of files
`unpack(TEMPLATE, EXPR)`	Unpacks a string into an array and returns the array
`unshift(ARRAY, LIST)`	Prepends LIST to the beginning of ARRAY
`untie(VARIABLE)`	Breaks the binding between a variable and a package
`use(MODULE)`	Starts using a Perl module
`utime(LIST)`	Changes the access and modification time of a list of files
`values(ASSOC_ARRAY)`	Returns an array containing all values from an associative array
`vec(EXPR, OFFSET, BITS)`	Treats the string EXPR as a vector of integers, and returns a specified element of the vector
`wait`	Waits for a child process to terminate
`waitpid(PID, FLAGS)`	Waits for a specific child process (identified by PID) to terminate
`wantarray`	Returns if the current subroutine has been called in an array context
`warn(LIST)`	Produces a warning message (specified by LIST) on the standard error
`write(FILEHANDLE)`	Writes a formatted record to a file
`y/SEARCHLIST/ REPLACE_LIST/cds`	Translates a search list into a replacement list

Understanding Perl Packages and Modules

A Perl *package* is a way to group together data and subroutines. Essentially, it's a way to use variable and subroutine names, without conflicting with any names used in other parts of a program. The concept of a package existed in Perl 4.

The package provides a way to control the namespace — a term that refers to the collection of variable and subroutine names. Although you may not be aware of this, when you write a Perl program, it automatically belongs to a package named main. Besides main, there are other Perl packages in the Perl library (these packages are in the lib subdirectory of the Perl 5 installation directory), and you can define your own package, as well.

Perl modules, as you'll learn soon, are packages that follow some specific guidelines.

Perl packages

You can think of a Perl package as a convenient way to organize a set of related Perl subroutines. Another benefit is that variable and subroutine names defined in a package do not conflict with names used elsewhere in the program. Thus, a variable named $count in one package remains unique to that package and does not conflict with a $count used elsewhere in a Perl program.

A Perl package is in a single file. The package statement is used at the beginning of the file to declare the file as a package and to give the package a name. For example, the file timelocal.pl defines a number of subroutines and variables in a package named timelocal. The timelocal.pl file has the following package statement in various places:

```
package timelocal;
```

The effect of this package declaration is that all subsequent variable and subroutine names are considered to be in the timelocal package. You can put such a package statement at the very beginning of the file that implements the package.

What if you are implementing a package and you need to refer to a subroutine or variable in another package? As you might guess, all you need to do is specify both the package name and the variable (or subroutine) name. Perl 5 provides the following syntax for referring to a variable in another package:

```
$Package::Variable
```

Here Package is the name of the package and Variable is the name of the variable in that package. If you omit the package name, Perl assumes that you are referring to a variable in the main package.

Note

In Perl 4, you refer to a variable in another package with the $Package'Variable syntax—that's a single quote between the package name and the variable name. The double-colon syntax ($Package::Variable) is new in Perl 5. The pair of colons is more readable than a single quote. Also, C++ happens to use a similar syntax when referring to variables in another C++ class (a class is basically a collection of data and functions—a template for an object).

To use a package in your program, you can simply call the require function with the package filename as an argument. For instance, there is a package named ctime defined in the file ctime.pl. That package includes the ctime subroutine that converts a binary time into a string. The following simple program uses the ctime package from the ctime.pl file:

```
#!/usr/bin/perl -w

# Use the ctime package defined in ctime.pl file
require 'ctime.pl';

# Call the ctime subroutine
$time = ctime(time());

# Print the time string
print $time;
```

As you can see, this program uses the `require` function to bring the `ctime.pl` file into the program. When you run this program, it should print the current date and time formatted, as shown in the sample output:

```
Sun Nov 19 15:41:09 2000
```

Note that the `-w` option causes the Perl interpreter to print warning messages about any bad constructs in the Perl script. It's a good idea to include the `-w` option on the line that invokes the Perl interpreter.

Perl modules

Perl 5 takes the concept of a package one step further and introduces the *module*, which is a package that follows certain guidelines and that's designed to be reusable. Each module is a package that is defined in a file with the same name as the package, but with a `.pm` extension. Each Perl object is implemented as a module. For example, the CGI object is implemented as the CGI module, stored in the file named `CGI.pm`.

Perl 5 comes with a number of modules. You'll find these modules in the lib subdirectory of the Perl 5 installation directory. For Perl version 5.6.0, the Perl modules are in the `/usr/lib/perl5/5.6.0` directory (the last part of the path name is the Perl version number). Look for files with names that end in `.pm` (for Perl module).

Using a Module

You can call the `require` function, or the `use` function, to include a Perl module in your program. For example, there is a Perl module named `Cwd` (defined, as expected, in the `Cwd.pm` file) that provides a `getcwd` subroutine that returns the current directory. You can call the `require` function to include the `Cwd` module and call `getcwd` as follows:

```
require Cwd;  # You do not need the full file name
$curdir = Cwd::getcwd();
print "Current directory = $curdir\n";
```

The first line brings the `Cwd.pm` file into this program — you do not have to specify the full filename; the `require` function automatically appends `.pm` to the module's name to figure out which file to include. The second line shows how you call a subroutine from the `Cwd` module. When you use `require` to include a module, you must invoke each subroutine with the *Module::subroutine* format.

If you were to rewrite this example program with the `use` function in place of `require`, it would take the following form:

```
use Cwd;
$curdir = getcwd();  # no need for Cwd:: prefix
print "Current directory = $curdir\n";
```

The most significant difference is that you no longer need to qualify a subroutine name with the module name prefix (such as `Cwd::`).

You can call either `require` or `use` to include a module in your program. You need to understand the following nuances when you use these functions:

- When you include a module by calling `require`, the module is included only when the `require` function is invoked as the program runs. You must use the *Module::subroutine* syntax to invoke any subroutines from a module you include with the `require` function.

- When you include a module by calling `use`, the module is included in the program as soon as the `use` statement is processed. Thus, you can invoke subroutines and variables from the module, as if they were part of your program. You do not need to qualify subroutine and variable names with a *Module::* prefix.

Tip

You may want to stick to the `use Module;` syntax to include modules in your program, because this lets you use a simpler syntax when you call subroutines from the module.

Using Objects in Perl 5

An *object* is a data structure together with the functions that operate on that data. Each object is an instance of a *class* that defines the type of the object. For example, a rectangle class may have as data the four corners of the rectangle; and functions such as one that computes the rectangle's area, and another that draws the rectangle. Then, each rectangle object can be an instance of the rectangle class, with different coordinates for the four corners. It's in this sense that an object is an instance of a class.

The functions (or subroutines) that implement the operations on an object's data are known as *methods*. That's terminology borrowed from Smalltalk, one of the earliest object-oriented programming languages.

Classes also suggest the notion of inheritance. You can define a new class of objects, by extending the data or methods (or both) of an existing class. A common use of inheritance is to express the IS A relationship among various classes of objects. Consider, for example, the geometric shapes. Because a circle IS A shape and a rectangle IS A shape, you could say that the circle and rectangle classes inherit from the shape class. In this case, the shape class is called a parent class, or *base class.*

Note

The basic idea behind object-oriented programming is that you can package the data and the associated methods (subroutines) of an object as a black box. Programmers access the object only through advertised methods, without having to know the inner working of the methods. Typically, a programmer can create an object, invoke its methods to get or set attributes (that's another name for the object's data), and destroy the object. This section shows you how to use objects in Perl 5. With this knowledge in hand, you'll be able to exploit objects as building blocks for your Perl programs.

Understanding Perl objects

Perl 5 implements objects using modules, which package data and subroutines in a file. Perl 5 presents the following simple model of objects:

- An *object* is denoted by a reference (objects are implemented as references to a hash).

- A *class* is a Perl module that provides the methods to work with the object.

- A *method* is a Perl subroutine that expects the object reference as the first argument.

Object implementers have to follow certain rules and provide certain methods in a module that represents a class. However, you really don't need to know much about an object's implementation to use it in your Perl program. All you need to know are the steps you have to follow when you use an object.

Creating and accessing Perl objects

A useful Perl object is Lincoln Stein's CGI object, which is implemented by the Perl module `CGI.pm`. That module comes with the Perl distribution and is in the `/usr/lib/perl5/5.6.0` directory (for Perl version 5.6.0).

As the name implies, the CGI object is meant for writing Common Gateway Interface applications for World Wide Web servers. A CGI program accepts queries submitted by a user and returns a Hypertext Markup Language (HTML) document with a response (this is the document that the user sees in the Web browser).

When you create a CGI object, it automatically parses a query string submitted by the user, via an HTML form. (These are forms that you see on many Web pages; you can essentially fill in and submit information through these forms.) The CGI object provides methods to access the parameters entered by the user on a form, create headers needed for Web pages, and generate HTML code for the Web page that will be sent back by the CGI program.

To use the CGI object, you follow these general steps:

1. Place the following line to include the CGI module in your program:

   ```
   use CGI;
   ```

   You must include this line before you create a CGI object.

2. To create a CGI object, use the following syntax:

   ```
   $query = new CGI;
   ```

   where $query is the reference to the CGI object. In the case of the CGI object, creating the object automatically parses the query and sets up the internal variables of the object.

3. Invoke methods from the CGI object as illustrated by the following examples:

   ```
   print $query->header;  // Send the HTTP header
   print $query->start_html("Title of document");
   print $query->end_html; // End HTML document
   ```

   Here $query->header calls the header method of the $query CGI object. Similarly, start_html and end_html are methods in the CGI object. All of these methods return strings, which is why they are used as arguments to the print function.

You access the object's methods, using the arrow operator and the object reference that you obtain after creating the object.

How do you know which methods to call, and in what order to call them? You have to read the object's documentation before you can use the object. The method names and the sequences of method invocation depend on what the object does.

Using the English module

Perl includes several special variables with strange names, such as $_ for the default argument and $! for error messages corresponding to the last error. When you read a program, it can be difficult to guess what a special variable means. The result is that you may end up avoiding a special variable that could be useful in your program.

As a helpful gesture, Perl 5 provides the English module (English.pm), which enables you to use understandable names for various special variables in Perl. To make use of the English module, include the following line in your Perl program:

```
use English;
```

After that, you can refer to $_ as $ARG and $! as $ERRNO (these "English" names can still be a bit cryptic, but they're definitely better than the punctuation marks).

The following program uses the English module and prints out a few interesting variables:

```
#!/usr/bin/perl -w
# File: english.pl

use English;
if($PERL_VERSION ge v5.6.0)
{
    print "Perl version 5.6.0 or later\n";
}
else
{
    print "Perl version prior to 5.6.0\n";
}
print "Perl executable = $EXECUTABLE_NAME\n";
print "Script name = $PROGRAM_NAME\n";
```

When I run this script, the output appears as follows:

```
./english.pl
Perl version 5.6.0 or later
Perl executable = perl
Script name = ./english.pl
```

The English module is handy, because it lets you write Perl scripts in which you can refer to special variables by meaningful names. To learn more about the Perl special variables and their English names, type man perlvar at the shell prompt.

Summary

Scripts or interpreted programs are often used to automate various tasks in Linux. This chapter focuses on writing scripts in Bash — the Bourne Again shell — as well as in the scripting language Perl.

By reading this chapter, you learn the following:

▶ A shell script is nothing more than a sequence of Linux commands in a file. Typically, you have to place a special line at the beginning of the script file and make it executable. Then, you can run the script, by typing its name at the shell prompt.

▶ When your Red Hat Linux system boots, shell scripts stored in various subdirectories in the /etc directory (for example, /etc/init.d) perform many initialization tasks.

▶ There are many built-in shell commands that you can use in shell scripts. You already know some of the built-in commands, such as cd and pwd, but this chapter describes many more built-in shell commands.

▶ Perl is a popular scripting language that appears on this book's companion CD-ROMs. You can use Perl to write powerful scripts on your Red Hat Linux system.

▶ Perl contains features comparable to those of other programming languages, such as C. A powerful feature of Perl is its capability to use regular expressions and to search files for occurrences of a search pattern.

▶ Perl 5, the latest version of Perl (and the one that comes with Red Hat Linux), includes a number of helpful features. A key feature is the Perl *module*, which is a package of subroutines that follows certain guidelines. Modules make it possible to implement objects in Perl.

▶ You can download the latest version of Perl (as well as Perl documentation) from the Comprehensive Perl Archive Network (CPAN) at `http://www.perl.com/CPAN/`.

Chapter 29

Tcl/Tk Scripting

In This Chapter

▶ Looking at Tcl/Tk

▶ Understanding Tcl syntax

▶ Writing Tcl scripts

▶ Building graphical interfaces for Tcl scripts with Tk

▶ Learning to use Tcl/Tk through examples

I f you are already a C and X Window System programmer, you will be surprised by the ease with which you can create graphical applications with *Tcl (Tool Command Language)* and its associated X toolkit, *Tk* — collectively referred to as Tcl/Tk (pronounced "tickle/tee kay"). Tcl is a scripting language like Perl. The biggest strength of Tcl is its X toolkit, Tk, which enables you to develop scripts with graphical user interfaces.

When I started using Tcl/Tk, I was pleasantly surprised by how few lines of Tcl/Tk it takes to create a functioning graphical interface. To a newcomer, a Tcl/Tk script still looks rather complicated, but if you have used C-based toolkits, such as Xt and Motif to write programs, you can appreciate the high-level nature of Tk. Creating a user-interface component such as a button is much simpler in Tk than in Motif. You still have to tend to many details, such as how to lay out the components of the user interface, but you can see results faster than you can with a C program that calls the Motif library.

Tip

If you have never programmed, don't avoid this chapter out of fear. The examples in this chapter teach you the basics of Tcl and Tk. You are bound to become a believer in Tcl/Tk after you see how quickly you can use Tcl/Tk's interpreter to create applications with graphical interfaces.

Introducing Tcl

The creator of Tcl, John Ousterhout, intended Tcl to be a simple embeddable scripting language whose interpreter could be linked with any C program, so that the C program could use Tcl scripts. The term *embeddable* refers to this property of Tcl: the capability of any C program to use the Tcl interpreter and run Tcl scripts.

Whence Tcl/Tk?

John Ousterhout created Tcl and Tk when he was at the University of California at Berkeley. Tcl first appeared in 1989; Tk followed in 1991. Tcl/Tk are freely available for unrestricted use, including commercial use. At the time of this writing, the current Tcl version is 8.3; Tk is also 8.3. This book's first companion CD-ROMs includes Tcl/Tk.

The following sections provide an overview of Tcl, its syntax, and some of its important commands. Because Tcl underlies the Tk toolkit, you should become familiar with Tcl before jumping into Tk, although Tk undoubtedly is more fun, because you can use it to create graphical interfaces.

Your First Tcl Script

In Chapter 6, you learned how to write shell scripts and Perl scripts. You write Tcl scripts the same way. Unlike Perl, Tcl includes a shell — an interactive interpreter of Tcl commands. The Tcl shell program's name is tclsh; it should be in the /usr/bin directory.

When you log in, the PATH environment variable should include the /usr/bin directory. Thus, you can start the Tcl shell, by typing tclsh. A percent sign (%) appears on the next line; this is the Tcl shell program's prompt. To see which version of Tcl that you have, type info tclversion at the Tcl shell prompt. The Tcl shell program responds by printing the version of Tcl:

```
tclsh
% info tclversion
8.3
%
```

Now you can interactively try the following Tcl program, which prints Hello, World! on the standard output (the display screen):

```
% puts "Hello, World!"
Hello, World!
% exit
```

Type exit to quit the Tcl shell (tclsh).

Note   Note that I didn't show the shell prompt in previous chapters, but I show the Tcl prompt (%) in this chapter's listings. That's because the Tcl prompt looks different from the Bash prompt, which should tell you that you aren't working in Bash.

The Tcl shell immediately processes the Tcl command that you enter and displays the results; then it prompts you for the next input. At this point, you can type exit to quit the Tcl shell.

To prepare and run a Tcl script, follow these steps:

1. Use a text editor to enter and save the following lines in a file named `hellotcl` (this file will be the Tcl script):

```
#!/usr/bin/tclsh
# A simple Tcl script
puts "Hello, World!"
```

2. Type the following command at the shell prompt to make the `hellotcl` file executable (that's what the +x in the `chmod` command means):

```
chmod +x hellotcl
```

3. To run the `hellotcl` script, type the following at the shell prompt:

```
hellotcl
Hello, World!
```

If you receive the error message `bash: hellotcl: command not found`, the current directory is not in the `PATH` environment variable. In that case, type `./hellotcl` to execute the script.

You use these basic steps to create and run any Tcl script. You still have to learn the nuances of Tcl syntax, of course — as well as many rules. This section gets you started with an overview of Tcl.

More on Tcl/Tk

This chapter provides an overview of Tcl and Tk, highlights many key points, and shows simple examples. However, there isn't enough room in this chapter to list all the information that you need to fully exploit the power of Tcl and Tk. Because of Tcl/Tk's popularity, you can find quite a few resources about it, ranging from books to Internet sites. Following is a short list of Tcl/Tk resources:

Books — Two prominent books on Tcl/Tk are available. The first book is *Tcl and the Tk Toolkit* (Addison Wesley, 1994), by John K. Ousterhout, the originator of Tcl and Tk. John's book provides a broad overview of Tcl and Tk, including an explanation of the way that Tcl command strings are parsed. The other book is *Practical Programming in Tcl and Tk, Third*

Edition (Prentice Hall, 2000), by Brent B. Welch. This book provides more Tcl and Tk examples.

Internet resources — Several FTP and Web sites contain the latest Tcl/Tk distributions and information about Tcl/Tk development. Following are the URLs for a few key sites:

ftp://ftp.scriptics.com/pub/tcl/
(Tcl/Tk master distribution site)

http://www.scriptics.com/
(Tcl developer site)

http://www.tcltk.com/
(Tcl/Tk community Web site)

http://www.neosoft.com/tcl/
(Tcl/Tk contributed sources archive)

A Tcl Overview

True to its name (Tool Command Language), Tcl consists of a set of commands that you can combine according to a set of rules. To write Tcl scripts, you have to understand two broad subjects:

- **Tcl syntax** — Tcl syntax is the set of rules that the Tcl command interpreter follows when it interprets a *command string* (a line that contains a command and its arguments).

- **Tcl commands** — Although the syntax is the same for all commands, each individual Tcl command is meant to perform a specific task. To exploit Tcl fully, you have to know what commands are available and what each command does. The Tcl command set can be extended by applications. In fact, Tk itself is an extension of Tcl; Tk adds commands that manipulate components of graphical user interfaces.

Start by learning the Tcl syntax, a handful of rules that determine the way that each Tcl command is parsed. Because Tcl has many commands, learning all the commands can take a while. Even after you become proficient in the Tcl syntax and a small set of commands, you may need to keep a reference manual nearby so that you can check the exact format of the arguments that each command requires.

Tcl commands include the following basic programming facilities that you expect from any programming language:

- *Variables* that store data. Each variable has a name and a value. Tcl also allows you to define arrays of variables.

- *Expressions* that combine values of variables with *operators*. An expression might add two variables, for example. Tcl uses the `expr` command to evaluate expressions.

- *Control-flow commands* that enable commands to be executed in various orders, depending on the value of some expression. Tcl provides commands such as `for`, `foreach`, `break`, `continue`, `if`, `while`, and `return` to implement flow control in Tcl scripts.

- *Procedures* that enable you to group several commands, and give them a name. Procedures also accept arguments. Tcl provides the `proc` command to enable you to define procedures. You can use a procedure to execute the same set of commands (usually, with different arguments), by invoking the procedure that represents those commands.

The next few sections provide an overview of the Tcl syntax and the core Tcl commands.

Basic Tcl Syntax

To understand the basic Tcl syntax, you have to know a bit about how the Tcl interpreter processes each command string. The steps are as follows:

1. The Tcl interpreter parses (breaks down) the command string into words.

2. The Tcl interpreter applies rules to substitute values of variables and replace certain commands with their results.

3. The Tcl interpreter executes the commands, taking the first word as the command name and calling a command procedure to execute the command. That command procedure receives the rest of the words as strings.

When writing Tcl command strings, you have to use *white space* (a space or a tab) to separate a command's name from its arguments. A newline or a semicolon (;) marks the end of a command string. You can put two commands on the same line if you insert a semicolon after the first command. Thus, you can use the following:

```
% puts Hello, ; puts World!
Hello,
World!
```

The resulting output appears on separate lines, because the `puts` command adds a newline by default.

Use a backslash at the end of a line to continue that command string on the next line (this is a standard convention in UNIX). Thus, you could write a command string to print `Hello, World!` as follows:

```
puts "Hello, \
World!"
```

Substitutions

The Tcl interpreter replaces certain parts of the command string with an equivalent value. If you precede a variable's name with a dollar sign ($), for example, the interpreter replaces that word with the variable's value. As you learn in the "Variables" section, you can define a variable in a Tcl script by using the `set` command, as follows:

```
set count 100
```

This command defines a variable named `count` with the value 100. Now suppose that you type the following:

```
puts $count
```

The interpreter first replaces `$count` with its value, which is 100. Thus, that command string becomes:

```
puts 100
```

When the interpreter executes the puts command, it prints 100. This is an example of *variable substitution*.

In all, the Tcl interpreter supports three kinds of substitutions:

■ **Variable substitution** — As the preceding example shows, if the Tcl interpreter finds a dollar sign ($), it replaces the dollar sign, as well as the following variable name with that variable's value.

■ **Backslash substitution** — You can embed special characters, such as the newline and tab, in a word by using backslash substitution. You simply type a backslash, followed by one or more characters; the interpreter replaces that sequence with a nonprintable character. These sequences are patterned after ANSI Standard C's escape sequences. Table 29-1, which follows this list, summarizes the backslash sequences that the Tcl interpreter understands.

■ **Command substitution** — This type of substitution refers to the mechanism that enables you to specify that a command be evaluated and replaced by its result before the interpreter processes the command string. The command string length "Hello, World!", for example, returns 13, which is the length of the string. To set a variable named len to the length of this string, type the following:

```
set len [string length "Hello, World!"]
```

The interpreter processes the command inside the square brackets and replaces that part of the command string with the value of the command. Thus, this command becomes

```
set len 13
```

and the set command sets the len variable to 13.

Table 29-1   Backslash Sequences in Tcl

Sequence	Replacement Character *
\a	Bell character (0x7)
\b	Backspace (0x8)
\f	Form feed (0xc)
\n	Newline (0xa)
\r	Carriage return (0xd)
\t	Horizontal tab (0x9)
\v	Vertical tab (0xb)
\<newline>	Replace the newline and white space on the next line with a single space
\\	Interpret as a single backslash (\)

Sequence	Replacement Character *
\"	Interpret as double quotation marks (")
\ooo	Use the value specified by the octal digits (up to three)
\xhh	Use the value specified by the hexadecimal digits (up to two)

* Hexadecimal values are shown in parentheses (for example, 0xd means hexadecimal d)

Comments

A pound sign (#) marks the start of a comment; the Tcl interpreter disregards the rest of the line, beginning with the pound sign. Tcl does, however, have a peculiar requirement for comments: you cannot start a comment within a command. The command string must end before you start a comment.

To understand this problem, try the following Tcl command at the `tclsh` prompt:

```
% puts "Hello, World!" # This is a comment
wrong # args: should be "puts ?-nonewline? ?channelId? string"
```

Essentially, the `puts` command processes the remainder of the line and complains about the number of arguments. The solution is to put a semicolon just before the pound sign (#), as follows:

```
% puts "Hello, World!" ;# This is a comment
Hello, World!
```

Tip

If you put comments at the end of a Tcl command, remember to precede the pound sign (#) with a semicolon (;). The semicolon terminates the preceding command and enables you to start a comment.

Braces and double quotation marks

You can use braces ({ ... }) and double quotation marks (" ... ") to group several words. Use double quotes to pass arguments that contain an embedded space or a semicolon, which otherwise ends the command. The quotes are not part of the group of words; they simply serve to mark the beginning and end of a group of words. Following are some examples of using double quotes to group words:

```
% puts "Hello, World!"
Hello, World!
% puts "Enter 1; otherwise file won't be saved!"
Enter 1; otherwise file won't be saved!
```

When you group words with double quotes, all types of substitutions still take place, as illustrated by the following example:

```
% puts "There are [string length hello] characters in 'hello'"
There are 5 characters in 'hello'
```

The Tcl interpreter replaces everything inside the brackets with the result of the `string length hello` command, whose return value is the number of characters in `hello` (5). In the expression `[string length hello]` you can replace the string `hello` with any variable, to determine the length of that variable's value.

You also can use braces to group words. The Tcl interpreter does not perform any substitution when you group words with braces (if you enclose words in double quotes, the interpreter does perform substitution). Consider the preceding example with braces instead of double quotes:

```
% puts {There are [string length hello] characters in 'hello'}
There are [string length hello] characters in 'hello'
```

As the result shows, the Tcl interpreter simply passes everything, unchanged, as a single argument.

Tip

Use braces as a grouping mechanism when you have to pass expressions to control commands, such as `while` loops, `for` loops, or procedures.

Variables

Everything is a string in Tcl. Variable names, as well as values, are stored as strings. To define a variable, use the built-in Tcl command `set`. The following commands, for example, define the variable `book` as "Red Hat Linux Secrets, 4th Edition"; the variable `year` as 2001; and the variable `price` as $39.99:

```
set book "Red Hat Linux Secrets, 4th Edition"
set year 2001
set price \$39.99
```

To refer to the value of a variable, append a dollar sign ($) to the variable's name. Therefore, to print the variable `book`, use the following format:

```
% puts $book
Red Hat Linux Secrets, 4th Edition
```

If you use `set` with a single argument, `set` returns the value of that argument. Thus, `set book` is equivalent to $book, as the following example shows:

```
% puts [set book]
Red Hat Linux Secrets, 3rd Edition
```

Expressions

You can write expressions by combining variables with mathematical operators, such as + (add), - (subtract), * (multiply), and / (divide). Here are some examples of expressions:

```
set count 1
$count+1
```

```
$count + 5 - 2
2 + 3.5
```

You can use numbers, as well as variable names, in expressions. Use white space to enhance readability. Use parentheses to specify how you want an expression to be evaluated.

In addition to the basic mathematical operators, Tcl includes several built-in mathematical functions, such as `sin`, `cos`, `tan`, `log`, and `sqrt`. Call these functions just as you do in C, with arguments in parentheses, as follows:

```
set angle 1.5
2*sin($angle)
```

You also can use Boolean operators, such as ! (not), && (and), and || (or). Comparison operators — such as < (less than), > (greater than), <= (less than or equal to), == (equal to), and != (not equal to) — also are available. Expressions that use Boolean or comparison operators evaluate to 1 if true and 0 if false. You can write expressions, such as the following:

```
count == 10
angle < 3.1415
```

Expressions are not commands by themselves. You can use expressions as arguments only for commands that accept expressions as arguments. The `if` and `while` commands, for example, expect expressions as arguments.

Tcl also provides the `expr` command to evaluate an expression. The following example shows how you might evaluate an expression in a Tcl command:

```
% set angle 1.5
1.5
% puts "Result = [expr 2*sin($angle)]"
Result = 1.99498997321
```

Although Tcl stores everything as a string, you have to use numbers where numbers are expected. If `book` is defined as `"Red Hat Linux Secrets, 4th Edition"`, for example, you cannot write an expression $book+1, because it does not make sense.

Control-Flow Commands

Tcl's control-flow commands enable you to specify the order in which the Tcl interpreter executes commands. You can use the `if` command to test the value of an expression; and if the value is true (nonzero), you can make the interpreter execute a set of commands. Tcl includes control-flow commands that are similar to those in C, such as `if`, `for`, `while`, and `switch`. This section provides an overview of the control-flow commands.

Secret

A Tcl control-flow command typically has a *command block* (a group of commands) that the control-flow command executes after evaluating an expression. To avoid substitutions (such as replacing variables with their values), you must enclose the entire command block in braces. The following if-else control-flow commands illustrate the style of braces that works properly:

```
if { expression } {
# Commands to execute when expression is true
command_1
command_2
} else {
# Commands to execute when expression is false
# ...
}
```

You should follow this style of braces religiously in Tcl scripts. In particular, remember to include a space between the control-flow command (such as if) and the left brace ({) that follows the command.

The if command

In its simplest form, Tcl's if command evaluates an expression and executes a set of commands if that expression is nonzero (true). You might compare the value of a variable with a threshold as follows:

```
if { $errorCount > 25 } {
    puts "Too many errors!"
}
```

You can add an else clause to process commands if the expression evaluates to zero (false). Following is an example:

```
if { $user == "root" } {
    puts "Starting system setup ..."
} else {
    puts "Sorry, you must be \"root\" to run this program!"
}
```

Tcl's if command can be followed by zero or more elseif commands if you need to perform more complicated tests, such as the following:

```
puts -nonewline "Enter version number: "   ;# prompt user
set version [gets stdin]                    ;# read version number

if { $version >= 10 } {
    puts "No upgrade necessary"
} elseif { $version >= 6 && $version < 9} {
    puts "Standard upgrade"
} elseif { $version >= 3 && $version < 6} {
    puts "Reinstall"
} else {
    puts "Sorry, cannot upgrade"
}
```

The while command

The `while` command executes a block of commands, until an expression becomes false. The following `while` loop keeps reading lines from the standard input until the user presses Ctrl+D:

```
while { [gets stdin line]  != -1 } {
    puts $line
# Do whatever you need to do with $line
}
```

Although this `while` command looks simple, you should realize that it has two arguments inside two sets of braces. The first argument is the expression; the second argument contains the Tcl commands to be executed if the expression is true. You must always use braces to enclose both of these arguments. The braces prevent the Tcl interpreter from evaluating the contents; the `while` command is the one that processes what's inside the braces.

If you use a variable to keep count inside a `while` loop, you can use the `incr` command to increment that variable. You can skip to the end of a loop, by using the `continue` command; the `break` command exits the loop. The following Tcl script uses a `while` loop to add all the numbers from 1 to 10, except 5:

```
#!/usr/bin/tclsh

set i 0
set sum 0

while { 1 } {
    incr i                          ;# increment i
    if {$i == 5} { continue }       ;# skip if i is 5
    if {$i > 10} {break }           ;# end loop if i exceed 10
    set sum [expr $sum+$i]          ;# otherwise, add i to sum
}
puts "Sum = $sum";
```

When you run this script, it should display the following result:

```
Sum = 50
```

The for command

Tcl's `for` command takes four arguments, which you should type in the following manner:

```
for {expr_1} { expr_2} { expr_3} {
    commands
}
```

The `for` command evaluates *expr_1* once at the beginning of the loop and executes the commands inside the final pair of braces, until the expression *expr_2* evaluates to zero. The `for` command evaluates the third expression — *expr_3* — after each execution of the commands. You can omit any of the expressions, but you must use all the braces. The following example uses a `for` loop to add the numbers from 1 to 10:

```
#!/usr/bin/tclsh
for {set i 0; set sum 0} {$i <= 10} {set sum [expr $sum+$i]; incr i} {
}
puts "Sum = $sum";
```

When you run this script, it displays the following result:

```
Sum = 55
```

The foreach command

You may not have seen a command like `foreach` in C, but `foreach` is handy when you want to perform some action for each value in a list of variables. You can add a set of numbers with the `foreach` command as follows:

```
set sum 0
foreach i { 1 2 3 4 5 6 7 8 9 10} {
    set sum [expr $sum+$i]
}
puts "Sum = $sum"
```

If you have a list in a variable, you can use that variable's value in place of the list shown within the first pair of braces. Following is a `foreach` loop that echoes the strings in a list:

```
set users "root naba"
foreach user $users {
    puts "$user"
}
```

The switch command

Tcl's `switch` command is different from C's `switch` statement. Instead of evaluating a mathematical expression, Tcl's `switch` command compares a string with a set of patterns and executes a set of commands, depending on which pattern matches. Often, the pattern is expressed in terms of a regular expression.

Cross-Reference

See Chapter 28 for an introduction to regular expressions.

The following script illustrates the syntax and a typical use of the `switch` command:

```
#!/usr/bin/tclsh
# This script reads commands from the user and processes
# the commands using a switch statement

set prompt "Enter command (\"quit\" to exit): "

puts -nonewline "$prompt"; flush stdout
```

```
while { [gets stdin cmd]  != -1 } {
    switch -exact -- $cmd {
        quit    { puts "Bye!"; exit}
        start   { puts "Started"}
        stop    { puts "Stopped"}
        draw    { puts "Draw.."}
        default { puts "Unknown command: $cmd" }
    }
# prompt user again
    puts -nonewline $prompt; flush stdout
}
```

Following is a sample session with this script (user input is in boldface):

```
Enter command ("quit" to exit): help
Unknown command: help
Enter command ("quit" to exit): start
Started
Enter command ("quit" to exit): stop
Stopped
Enter command ("quit" to exit): quit
Bye!
```

As this example shows, the switch statement enables you to compare a
string with a set of other strings and then activate a set of commands,
depending on which pattern matches. In this example, the string is $cmd
(which is initialized by reading the user's input with a gets command), and
the patterns are literal strings: quit, start, stop, and draw. Following is a
case of an exact match, as indicated by the -exact flag on the first line of the
switch command:

```
switch -exact -- $cmd {
    ...
}
```

Secret

The two hyphens (--) immediately after the -exact flag mark the end of the
flags. When you use the switch command, you should always use the double
hyphens at the end of the flag to prevent the test string from matching a flag
inadvertently.

You can use the switch command with the -regexp flag to compare a string
with a regular expression, as in the following example:

```
# Assume that $cmd is the string to be matched

switch -regexp -- $cmd {
    ^q.*    { puts "Bye!"; exit}
    ^x.*   { puts "Something x..."}
    ^y.*   { puts "Something y..."}
    ^z.*   { puts "Something z..."}
    default { puts "Unknown command: $cmd" }
}
```

In this example, each regular expression has a similar form. The pattern ^z.*
means any string that starts with a single z, followed by any number of other
characters.

Tcl Procedures

You can use the `proc` command to add your own commands. Such commands are called *procedures*; the Tcl interpreter treats them just as though
they were built-in Tcl commands. The following example shows how easy it is
to write a procedure in Tcl:

```
#!/usr/bin/tclsh

proc total items {
    set sum 0
    foreach i $items {
        set sum [expr $sum+$i]
    }
    return $sum
}

set counts "5 4 3 5"
puts "Total = [total $counts]"
```

When you run the preceding script, it prints the following:

```
Total = 17
```

In this example, the procedure's name is `total`, and it takes a list of numbers as the argument. The procedure receives the arguments in the variable
named `items`. The body of the procedure extracts each item and returns a
sum of the items. Thus, to add the numbers from 1 to 10, you have to call the
`total` procedure as follows:

```
set sum1_10 [total {1 2 3 4 5 6 7 8 9 10}]
```

Secret

In a Tcl procedure, the argument name `args` has a special significance; if
you use `args` as the argument name, you can pass a variable number of
arguments to the procedure. If you change the `total` procedure's argument
name from `items` to `args`, for example, you can call `total` this way:

```
set sum1_10 [total 1 2 3 4 5 6 7 8 9 10]    ;# variable arguments
```

If you want to access a *global variable* (a variable defined outside a procedure) in the Tcl procedure, you have to use the `global` command inside the
procedure. The `global` command makes a global variable visible within the
scope of a procedure. If a variable named `theCanvas` holds the current drawing area in a Tk (Tcl's X toolkit) program, a procedure that uses `theCanvas`
must include the following command:

```
global theCanvas
```

Built-In Tcl Commands

You have seen many Tcl commands in the preceding examples. Knowing the types of commands that are available in Tcl helps you decide which commands are most appropriate for the task at hand. Although this chapter does not have enough room to cover all Tcl commands, Table 29-2 summarizes Tcl's built-in commands.

Tip

To get online help about any Tcl command listed in Table 29-2, type man n, followed by the command name. To get online help about Tcl's file command, for example, type **man n file**.

Table 29-2   Built-In Tcl Commands

Command	Action
append	Appends an argument to a variable's value
array	Performs various operations on an array variable
break	Exits a loop command (such as while and for)
catch	Executes a script and traps errors to prevent errors from reaching the Tcl interpreter
cd	Changes the current working directory
close	Closes an open file
concat	Joins two or more lists in a single list
continue	Immediately begins the next iteration of a for or while loop
eof	Checks to see whether end-of-file is reached in an open file
error	Generates an error
eval	Concatenates lists (as concat does), and then evaluates the resulting list as a Tcl script
exec	Starts one or more processes that execute the command's arguments
exit	Terminates the Tcl script
expr	Evaluates an expression
file	Checks filenames and attributes
flush	Flushes buffered output to a file
for	Implements a for loop
foreach	Performs a specified action for each element in a list
format	Formats output and stores it in a string (as the sprintf function in C does)

Continued

Table 29-2   *(continued)*

Command	*Action*
gets	Reads a line from a file
glob	Returns the names of files that match a pattern (such as *.tcl)
global	Accesses global variables
history	Provides access to the *history list* (the list of past Tcl commands)
if	Tests an expression and executes commands if the expression is true (nonzero)
incr	Increments the value of a variable
info	Returns internal information about the Tcl interpreter
join	Creates a string, by joining all items in a list
lappend	Appends elements to a list
lindex	Returns an element from a list at a specified index. (Index 0 refers to the first element.)
linsert	Inserts elements into a list before a specified index
list	Creates a list comprised of the specified arguments
llength	Returns the number of elements in a list
lrange	Returns a specified range of adjacent elements from a list
lreplace	Replaces elements in a list with new elements
lsearch	Searches a list for a particular element
lsort	Sorts a list in a specified order
open	Opens a file and returns a file identifier
pid	Returns the process identifier (ID)
proc	Defines a Tcl procedure
puts	Sends characters to a file
pwd	Returns the current working directory
read	Reads a specified number of bytes from a file. (You can read the entire file in a single read.)
regexp	Matches a regular expression with a string
regsub	Substitutes one regular expression pattern for another
rename	Renames or deletes a command
return	Returns a value from a Tcl procedure

Command	Action
scan	Parses a string, using format specifiers patterned after C's sscanf function
seek	Changes the *access position* (where the next input or output operation occurs) in an open file
set	Sets a variable's value or returns its current value
source	Reads a file and processes it as a Tcl script
split	Breaks a string into a Tcl list
string	Performs various operations on strings
switch	Processes one of several blocks of commands, depending on which pattern matches a specified string
tell	Returns the current access position for an open file
time	Returns the total time needed to execute a script
trace	Executes a specified set of Tcl commands whenever a variable is accessed
unknown	Handles any unknown command. (The Tcl interpreter calls this command whenever it encounters any unknown command.)
unset	Removes the definition of one or more variables
uplevel	Executes a script in a different context
upvar	References a variable outside a procedure. (This is used to implement the pass-by-reference style of procedure call, in which changing a procedure argument changes the original copy of the argument.)
while	Implements a while loop that executes a set of Tcl commands repeatedly, as long as an expression evaluates to a nonzero value (true)

String Manipulation in Tcl

If you browse through the Tcl commands listed in Table 29-2, you find quite a few—such as append, join, split, string, regexp, and regsub—that operate on strings. This section summarizes a few string-manipulation commands.

When you set a variable to a string, the Tcl interpreter considers that string to be a single entity, even if that string contains any embedded spaces or special characters. Sometimes, you need to access the string as a list of items. The split command is a handy way to separate a string into its components. The lines in the /etc/passwd file, for example, look like the following:

```
root:x:0:0:root:/root:/bin/bash
```

The line is composed of fields separated by colons (:). Suppose that you want to extract the first field from each line (because that field contains the login name). You can read the file one line at a time, split each line into a list, and extract the first element (the item at index 0) of each list. Following is a Tcl script that does this:

```
#!/usr/bin/tclsh

set fid [open "/etc/passwd" r]      ;# Open file for read-only access

while { [gets $fid line] != -1 } {
    set fields [split $line ":"]    ;# split the string into a list
# Just print out the first field
    puts [lindex $fields 0]         ;# extract item at a index 0
}
```

When you run this script, it should print all the login names from your system's /etc/passwd file.

The join command is the opposite of split; you can use it to create a single string from the items in a list. Suppose that you have a list of six items, defined as follows:

```
set x {1 2 3 4 5 6}
```

When you join the elements, you can select what character you want to use between fields. To join the elements without anything in between them, use the following format:

```
set y [join $x ""]
```

Now the y string is "123456".

The string command is actually a group of commands for working with strings, because the first argument of string specifies the operation to be performed. The string compare command, for example, compares two strings, returning zero when the two strings are identical. A return value of –1 indicates that the first string argument is lexicographically less than the second one, which means that it appears before the second one in a dictionary. Similarly, a 1 return value indicates that the first string is lexicographically greater than the second one. Thus, you might use string compare in an if command as follows:

```
if { [string compare $command "quit"] == 0} {
    puts "Exiting..."
    exit 0
}
```

Table 29-3 lists the operations that you can perform with Tcl's string command.

Table 29-3   Operations You Can Perform with String in Tcl

String Command	Description
string compare *string1 string2*	Returns −1, 0, or 1 after comparing strings
string first *string1 string2*	Returns the index of the first occurrence of *string1* in *string2*
string index *string charIndex*	Returns the character at index *charIndex*
string last *string1 string2*	Returns the index of the last occurrence of *string1* in *string2*
string length *string*	Returns the length of the string
string match *pattern string*	Returns 1 if the pattern matches the string, and 0 if it does not
string range *string first last*	Returns a range of characters from string
string tolower *string*	Returns the string in lowercase characters
string toupper *string*	Returns the string in uppercase characters
string trim *string chars*	Returns the string after trimming the leading or trailing characters
string trimleft *string chars*	Returns the string after trimming the leading characters
string trimright *string chars*	Returns the string after trimming the trailing characters

Arrays

In Tcl, an *array* is a variable with a string index. An array contains elements; the string index of each element is called the *element name*. In other words, you can access an element of an array, by using its name. Internally, Tcl implements arrays with an efficient data structure known as a *hash table*, which enables the Tcl interpreter to look up any array element in a relatively constant period of time.

You declare an array variable, by using the set command. The following example shows how you might define the disk_usage array that holds the amount of disk space used by a system's users:

```
set disk_usage(root)      147178
set disk_usage(naba)      28574
set disk_usage(emily)     73
set disk_usage(ivy)       61
set disk_usage(ashley)    34
```

After you define the array, you can access its individual elements by element name, as in the following example:

```
set user "naba"
puts "Disk space used by $user = $disk_usage($user)K"
```

Environment Variables

Tcl provides the environment variables in a predefined global array named env, with the environment-variable names used as element names. In other words, you can look up the value of an environment variable, by using the variable name as an index. The following command prints the current PATH:

```
puts "$env(PATH)"
```

You can manipulate the environment variable array just as you do any other variables. You can add a new directory to PATH, for example, as follows:

```
set env(PATH) "$env(PATH):/usr/sbin"
```

Any changes to the environment variable do not affect the parent process (for example, the shell from which you started the Tcl script). Any new processes created by the script by means of the exec command, however, inherit the altered environment variable.

File Operations in Tcl

Most of the examples presented so far in this chapter use Tcl's puts command to display output. By default, puts writes to the standard output, the terminal window, when you use X. You can write to a file, however, by providing a file identifier as the first argument of puts. To get a file identifier, you first have to open the file, using Tcl's open command. The following example shows how you would open a file, write a line of text to the file, and close the file:

```
set fid [open "testfile" w]   ;# open "testfile" for write operations
puts $fid "Testing 1..2..3"   ;# write to this file
close $fid                    ;# close the file
```

When you use puts to display a string on the standard output, you do not have to provide any file-identifier argument. In addition, puts automatically appends a newline character at the end of the string. If you do not want the newline, use puts with the -nonewline argument, as follows:

```
puts -nonewline "Command> "  ;# -nonewline is good for command prompts
flush stdout ;# make sure output appears right away
```

You also have seen the use of the gets command to read a line of input from the standard input. The following invocation of gets, for example, reads a line from the standard input (the command returns when you press Enter):

```
set line [gets stdin]  ;# read a line from standard input
```

The keyword `stdin` is a predefined file identifier that represents the standard input, which by default is your keyboard. Other predefined file IDs are `stdout`, for the standard output; and `stderr`, for the standard error-reporting device. By default, both `stdout` and `stderr` are connected to the display screen.

Following is a different way to call `gets` and read a line of input into a variable named `line`:

```
gets stdin line        ;# read a line of input into the line variable
```

To read from another file, you first should open the file for reading, and then use `gets` with that file's ID. To read all lines from `/etc/passwd` and display them on the standard output, for example, you would use the following:

```
set fpass [open "/etc/passwd" r]      ;# open /etc/passwd for reading
while { [gets $fpass line] != -1} {   ;# read the lines in a while loop
    puts $line                        ;# and print each line
}
```

The `gets` command is good for reading text files, because it works one line at a time; in fact, it looks for the newline character as a marker that indicates the end of a line of text. If you want to read binary data, such as an image file, you should use the `read` command instead. To read and process a file in 2,048-byte chunks, you might use `read` in the following manner:

```
# Assume fid is the file ID of an open file
while { ![eof $fid]} {                ;# Until end-of-file is reached
    set buffer [read $fid 2048]  ;# read up to 2048 bytes into buffer
# process the data in buffer      ;# and process the buffer
}
```

The second argument of the `read` command is the maximum number of bytes to be read. If you omit this argument, the `read` command reads the entire file. You can use this feature to process entire text files. After reading the contents of the file, use the `split` command to separate the input data into lines of text. Following is an example:

```
set fid [open "/etc/passwd" r] ;# open file for reading
set buffer [read $fid 100000]  ;# read entire file into buffer
split $buffer "\n"             ;# split buffer into lines
foreach line $buffer {
    puts $line                 ;# do whatever you want with each line
}
```

Secret

If you want to process several files (such as all files whose names end with `.tcl`), use the `glob` command to expand a filename, such as `*.tcl`, into a list. Then you can use the `open` command to open and process each file in the following manner:

```
foreach filename [glob *.tcl] { ;# create list of filenames
    puts -nonewline $filename    ;# print the filename
    set file [open $filename r] ;# open that file
    gets $file line              ;# read the first line
```

```
      puts $line                    ;# and print it (for testing)
# process rest of the file as necessary
      close $file                   ;# remember to close the file
}
```

This is a good example of how to use the glob command in a script.

Executing Linux Commands

Instead of duplicating the large number of Linux commands, Tcl simply provides the mechanism to run any Linux command. If you know Linux commands, you can use them directly in Tcl scripts.

You use the exec command to execute a Linux command in a Tcl script. In the command's simplest form, you provide the Linux command as an argument of exec. To show the current directory listing, for example, type the following:

```
exec ls
```

The output appears on the standard output (the monitor), just as it does when you enter the ls command at the shell prompt.

When you run Linux commands from the shell, you can redirect the input and output by using special characters, such as < (redirect input), > (redirect output), and | (pipe). These options are available in Tcl as well, because the exec command accepts a complete command line, including any input or output redirections. Thus, you can send the directory listing to a file named dirlist as follows:

```
exec ls > dirlist
```

Secret

Tcl's exec command does not expand wildcard characters (such as an asterisk) in filenames passed to a Linux command. If you use wildcards in filenames, you have to perform an additional step: You must process the filename specification through the glob command to expand it properly, before providing the command to exec. Additionally, you must pass the entire exec command to eval as an argument. To see a list of all files with names that end in .tcl, for example, you have to use the exec command with glob, and feed the entire command to eval as follows:

```
eval exec ls [glob *.tcl]   ;# this is equivalent to "ls *.tcl"
```

Introducing Tk

Tk (pronounced *tee-kay*) is an extension of Tcl. Tk provides an X Window System–based toolkit that you can use in Tcl scripts to build graphical user interfaces. As you might expect, Tk provides a set of Tcl commands beyond the core built-in set. You can use these Tk commands to create windows, menus, buttons, and other user-interface components and to provide a graphical user interface for your Tcl scripts.

Tk uses the X Window System for its graphic components, which are known as *widgets*. A widget represents a user-interface component, such as a button, scrollbar, menu, list, or even an entire text window. Tk widgets provide a Motif-like, three-dimensional appearance.

Note

If you are familiar with the Motif widgets, you may know that Motif relies on Xt Intrinsics — an X toolkit that is used to build widgets. Unlike Motif, the Tk toolkit is not based on any other toolkit; it uses only Xlib, which is the C-language library for the X Window System. The upshot is that you need only the freely available X Window System to use Tk.

As with anything new, you can best learn Tk through examples, which the following sections provide.

"Hello, World!" in Tk

Tk is a major-enough extension to Tcl to warrant its own shell, called wish (the *windowing shell*). The wish shell interprets all built-in Tcl commands, as well as the Tk commands. You must start X before you can run wish; after all, wish enables you to use X to create graphical interfaces.

The wish program should be in the /usr/bin directory, which should be in your PATH environment variable by default. To start wish, all you have to do is type the following at the shell prompt in a terminal window:

```
wish
%
```

The wish program displays its prompt (the percent sign) and a small window, as shown in the upper-right corner of Figure 29-1.

Therefore, wish provides an interactive prompt from which you can enter Tk commands to create a graphical interface. As wish interprets the commands, it displays the resulting graphical interface in the window.

To see how this interactive creation of graphical interface works, try the following commands at the wish prompt (type the part shown in boldface):

```
% label .msg -text "Hello, World!"
.msg
% button .bye -text "Bye" -command { exit }
.bye
% pack .msg .bye
%
```

Figure 29-2 shows the result of these commands; wish displays a Hello, World! label with a Bye button below it.

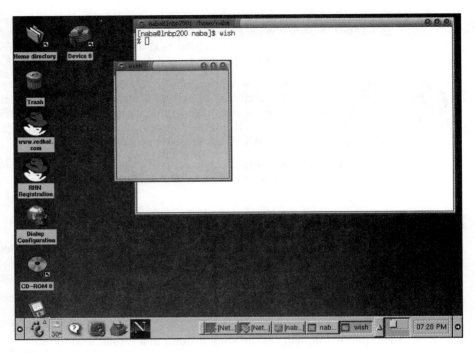

Figure 29-1: The result of running wish from a terminal window

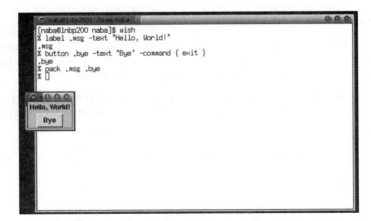

Figure 29-2: Interactively creating a label and a button in wish

Notice that the label and the button do not appear until you enter the `pack` command. In addition, the `wish` window shrinks to a size just large enough to hold the label and the button.

Click the Bye button; the wish program exits. This is because the -command { exit } argument of the button command associates the Tcl command exit with a click of the Bye button.

To create a Tk program or script that displays the Hello, World! label and the Bye button, all you have to do is place the Tk commands in a file, and add a special line at the beginning to ensure that the wish shell processes the file. To do so, follow these steps:

1. Use a text editor to enter and save the following lines in a file named hellotk:

```
#!/usr/bin/wish -f
# A simple Tk script
label .msg -text "Hello, World!"
button .bye -text "Bye" -command { exit }
pack .msg .bye
```

Notice the -f option in the first line. In Tk versions earlier than 4.0, you have to start wish with that option to ensure that it processes the script file. The flag is optional in Tk version 4.0 and later.

2. Type the following command at the shell prompt to make the hellotk file executable (that's what the +x in the chmod command means):

```
chmod +x hellotk
```

3. To run the hellotk script, type the following at the shell prompt in a terminal window:

```
hellotk
```

Figure 29-3 shows the window with a Hello, World! label and the Bye button that should appear when you run the hellotk script. Click the Bye button to close the window and end the script.

Figure 29-3: The result of running the hellotk script

As this example shows, the basic steps for writing a Tk script are the same as those for creating and running any Tcl script. The only difference is that the Tk commands generate graphical output.

Tk Widget Basics

Now that you have been exposed to Tcl, you can begin writing Tk scripts. What you need to know are the Tk commands used to create and configure widgets.

Note

The term *widget* has the same meaning in Tk as it does in an X toolkit, such as Motif — it is a user interface component, such as a push button, list box, or dialog box.

In the example in the preceding section, you used a label and a button widget. The command for creating a widget is the same as the widget's name. Therefore, the `button` command creates a button widget, `label` creates a label, and so on.

Tk has several other widget-creation commands, which are listed in Table 29-4.

Table 29-4 Tk Commands for Creating Widgets

Command	Action
Button	Creates a button widget
Canvas	Creates a canvas widget on which you can display text, bitmaps, lines, boxes, polygons, and other widgets
Checkbutton	Creates a toggle button and associates it with a Tcl variable
Entry	Creates a one-line text-entry widget
Frame	Creates a frame widget that is capable of holding other widgets
Label	Creates a read-only, one-line label widget
Listbox	Creates a list-box widget that is capable of scrolling lines of text
Menu	Creates a menu
Menubutton	Creates a menu-button widget that pops up an associated menu when clicked
Message	Creates a read-only, multiple-line message widget
Radiobutton	Creates a radio-button widget that is linked to a Tcl variable
Scale	Creates a scale widget that can adjust the value of a variable
Scrollbar	Creates a scrollbar widget that you can link to another widget
Text	Creates a text widget where the user can enter and edit text
Toplevel	Creates a top-level widget (a widget whose window is a child of the X Window System's root window)

As you create a widget, you can specify many of its characteristics as arguments of the command. You can, for example, create a blue button with a red label (test) and display the button by using the following commands:

```
button .b -text test -fg red -bg blue
pack .b
```

The `pack` command does not create a widget; rather, it positions a widget in relationship to others. Table 29-5 lists all the widget-manipulation commands.

Tip

To look up online help about any Tk command listed in Tables 29-4 and 29-5, type `man n`, followed by the command name. To get online help about the `bind` command, for example, type `man n bind`.

Table 29-5   Tk Commands for Manipulating Widgets

Command	Action
After	Executes a command after a specified amount of time elapses
Bind	Associates a Tcl command with an X event, so that the Tcl command is automatically invoked whenever the X event occurs
Destroy	Destroys one or more widgets
Focus	Directs keyboard events to a particular window (gives that window the input focus)
Grab	Confines pointer and keyboard events to a specified widget and its children
Lower	Lowers a window in the stacking order. (The stacking order refers to the order in which various windows overlap one another on the display screen.)
Option	Provides access to the X resource database
pack	Automatically positions widgets in a frame, based on specified constraints
place	Allows manual positioning of a widget relative to another widget
raise	Raises a window's position in the stacking order
selection	Manipulates the X PRIMARY selection (the standard name of a selection in X)
send	Sends a Tcl command to a different Tk application (used for interprocess communications)
tk	Provides information about the internal state of the Tk interpreter
tkerror	Handles any error that occurs in Tk applications (the interpreter calls this command when errors occur in Tk applications)
tkwait	Waits for an event, such as the destruction of a window, or a change in the value of a variable
update	Processes all pending events and updates the display
winfo	Returns information about a widget
wm	Provides access to the window manager. (You can send commands to the window manager, requesting a size for your top-level window, for example.)

Naming widgets

From the example that created a label and a button, you may have guessed that the argument that follows the widget-creation command is the widget's name. If you are wondering why all the names start with a period, which is required at the beginning of a widget's name, it is because widgets are organized in a hierarchy.

Suppose that you have a main window that contains a menu bar, a text area, and a scrollbar. The menu bar has two buttons, labeled File and Help. Figure 29-4 shows this widget hierarchy as it appears onscreen; it also shows how the widget names relate to this hierarchy.

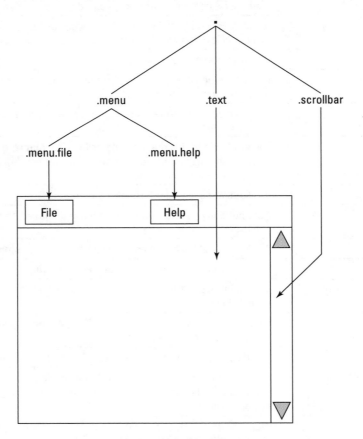

Figure 29-4: Relationship between widget names and the widget hierarchy

The root of the hierarchy is the main window of the application; a single period (dot) is used to denote the main window. This main window is a child of the root window of the X display. Each child of the main window has a name that begins with a dot. Thus, .menu is a child of the main window.

The names of other widgets depend on their positions in the hierarchy. The buttons in the menu bar have names — `.menu.file` and `.menu.help` — that indicate that they are child widgets of the `.menu` widget. As you create widgets, you specify the name of each widget, in turn defining the widget hierarchy.

If you think about it, you can see that the widget-naming scheme is similar to the path name of a file in Linux. The period (`.`) in the widget names is analogous to the slash (`/`) in a file's path name. In fact, the Tk documentation and online manual pages use the term *Tk pathname* to indicate the widget hierarchy.

Note

All widget names must start with a lowercase letter or a number. The name cannot include a period, because the period indicates the widget's location in the hierarchy. Names that start with an uppercase letter denote a class that is used in specifying resources; the meaning of the term *resources* is the same as in X.

Cross-Reference

See Chapter 12 for a discussion of X resources and how they are specified.

Configuring widgets

Tk treats each widget name as a command name. You can perform operations on a specific widget, by using that widget's name, followed by arguments that make sense for that widget. If you have a button named `.b`, for example, use the following command to set that button's background to blue:

```
.b config -fg blue
```

You can change the button's label to `Goodbye!` by using the following command:

```
.b config -text Goodbye!
```

The arguments `-fg blue` and `-text Goodbye!` specify the attributes of a widget. Each attribute name begins with a hyphen (-), as in `-text`. The next argument is that attribute's value.

Displaying widgets

Tk does not display a widget, until you use a command to position the widget in the main window. You have to use a *geometry manager* — a Tk procedure that arranges one or more child widgets in a parent widget. Tk provides two geometry-management commands:

■ The `place` command enables you to position a widget at a fixed location in the window of a designated master widget (which does not necessarily have to be a parent widget). The master widget is used as a reference — other widgets are positioned relative to the master widget. You also can specify relative positions, such as a horizontal position that is half the width of the master widget.

- The `pack` command arranges child widgets around the edges of the master window. You can specify the side of the parent on which the child widget is placed, as well as any extra space that you want to use around the child. As the name suggests, the `pack` command packs widgets together as tightly as possible.

Although the `pack` and `place` commands take many different options, their basic use is straightforward. I suggest that you start `wish`, create a few widgets, and try the `place` and `pack` commands to see their effects. After that, you can consult the online manual for the exact options whenever you need them.

Tip   The `pack` and `place` commands have a form — `pack forget` and `place forget` — that you can use to hide a widget. If you want to hide a button named `.btn1`, for example, use the command `pack forget .btn1`. To make the button reappear, use the `pack .btn1` command again.

The pack command

The `pack` command is the most commonly used geometry-management command in Tk. As some of the simple examples in this chapter show, to make a button named `.btn1` appear, you use `pack` as follows:

```
pack .btn1
```

You can specify several widget names on the same `pack` command line. To display the buttons `.btn1`, `.btn2`, and `.btn3`, arranged in a vertical line in that order, use the following:

```
pack .btn1 .btn2 .btn3
```

Table 29-6 summarizes the `pack` command's syntax. As Table 29-5 shows, you can position widgets and get information about the widget hierarchy.

Table 29-6   Different Forms of the pack Command

Command	Description
pack *widgetNames options*	Packs the listed widgets according to the specified options (same as pack configure). Table 29-7 shows the list of available options.
pack configure *widgetNames options*	Packs the listed widgets according to the specified options
pack forget *widgetNames*	Hides (*unpacks*) the specified widgets
pack info *widget*	Returns the *packing configuration* (a list of options and values) of the specified *widget*

Command	Description
pack propagate *widget* *boolean*	If *boolean* is 1, enables geometry propagation for the specified widget; otherwise, disables propagation. (When geometry propagation is enabled, the size of a widget's window is determined by the sizes of the widgets contained in that window.)
pack slaves *widget*	Returns the list of widgets managed by a specified *widget*

If you want a more complicated layout of widgets, you have to use the packing options shown in Table 29-7.

Table 29-7   Options for Packing Widgets

Option	Description
-after *widgetName*	Places the widget that is being packed after the widget specified by *widgetName*
-anchor *anchorPos*	Determines where the managed widget is placed. (This applies only when the containing widget is larger than the managed widget.) The *anchorPos* value can be center, e, n, ne, nw, s, se, sw, or w; the default is center.
-before *widgetName*	Places the widget that is being packed before the widget specified by *widgetName*
-expand *boolean*	If *boolean* is 1, the contained widget expands to use any space left over in the containing widget
-fill *style*	Indicates how to expand the containing widget, if it becomes bigger than what the widgets contained in it require. The *style* value can be both, none, x, or y.
-in *widgetName*	Indicates the widget in which the widgets specified in the pack command line are placed. If you do not use this option, widgets are packed in their parent widget (f.b is packed in .f).
-ipadx *amount*	Specifies extra horizontal space inside the widget that is being packed (in addition to the space that it already needs). The *amount* value is a number, in screen units.

Continued

Table 29-7 *(continued)*	
Option	**Description**
-ipady *amount*	Specifies extra vertical space inside the widget that is being packed (in addition to the space that it already needs). The *amount* value is a number, in screen units.
-padx *amount*	Specifies extra horizontal space outside the border of the widget that is being packed. The *amount* value is a number, in screen units.
-pady *amount*	Specifies extra vertical space outside the border of the widget that is being packed. The *amount* value is a number, in screen units.
-side *sideName*	Packs against the specified side. The *sideName* value is bottom, left, right, or top; the default is top.

Tip

If you are wondering how to remember all these options, my advice is that you *not* remember them. You usually can get by with just a few of these options, and you will begin to remember them after a while. To become familiar with what each option does, start wish, create a few widgets, and try packing them with different options. From then on, whenever you need the exact syntax of an option, consult the online manual, by typing **man n pack**, or simply **man pack**.

The place command

The place command is a simpler way to specify the placement of widgets compared to the pack command, but you have to position all the windows yourself. It is simpler than pack because the place command gives you direct control of the widget positions. On the other hand, direct control of widget placement is fine for a few windows, but it can get tedious in a hurry when you have many widgets in a user interface.

Using place, you can position a widget at a specific location. To place .btn1 at the coordinate (100, 50) in its parent widget, use the following command:

```
place .btn1 -x 100 -y 50
```

A good use of place is to center a widget within its parent widget. For this purpose, you use the -relx and -rely options of place. If .f is a *frame widget* (a widget that contains other widgets), you can display it at the center of the parent window, by using the following commands:

```
frame .f
button .f.b1 -text Configure
button .f.b2 -text Quit
pack .f.b1 .f.b2 -side left
place .f -relx 0.5 -rely 0.5 -anchor center
```

As the code fragment shows, the buttons inside the frame are packed with the `pack` command. Only the frame, `.f`, is positioned with the `place` command. The `-relx` and `-rely` options enable you to specify the relative positions in terms of a fraction of the containing widget's size. A zero value for `-relx` means the left edge; 1 is the right edge; and 0.5 means the middle.

Like `pack`, the `place` command has several forms, which are listed in Table 29-8.

Table 29-8   Forms of the place Command

Command	Description
`place` *widgetNames options*	Positions the listed widgets according to the specified options (same as `place configure`). Table 29-9 shows the list of available options.
`place configure` *widgetNames options*	Positions the listed widgets according to the specified options
`place forget` *widgetNames*	Stops managing the specified widgets and unmaps (hides) them
`place info` *widget*	Returns the list of options and their values for the specified *widget*
`place slaves` *widget*	Returns the list of widgets managed by the specified *widget*

In addition, `place` takes several options, which are summarized in Table 29-9. Use these options with the plain `place` command or `place configure` command.

Table 29-9   Options for Placing Widgets

Option	Description
`-anchor` *anchorPos*	Specifies which point of the managed widget is placed in the specified position in the managing window. The *anchorPos* value can be center, e, n, ne, nw, s, se, sw, or w; the default is nw (upper-left corner).
`-bordermode` *bmode*	Indicates how the managing widget's borders are used when the managed widgets are positioned. The *bordermode* value must be ignore, inside, or outside.

Continued

Table 29-9 *(continued)*

Option	Description
-height *size*	Specifies the height of the managed widget
-in *widgetName*	Indicates the widget relative to which the positions of the widgets specified in the place command line are specified. If you do not use this option, widgets are placed relative to their parent widgets (.f.b is positioned relative to .f).
-relheight *fraction*	Specifies the height of the managed widget as a fraction of the managing widget. The fraction is a floating-point value.
-relwidth *fraction*	Specifies the width of the managed widget as a fraction of the managing widget. The fraction is a floating-point value.
-relx *fraction*	Specifies the horizontal position of the managed widget as a fraction of the managing widget's width. The fraction is a floating-point value; 0.0 means the left edge, and 1.0 means the right edge.
-rely *fraction*	Specifies the vertical position of the managed widget as a fraction of the managing widget's height. The fraction is a floating-point value; 0.0 means the top edge, and 1.0 means the bottom edge.
-x *coord*	Specifies the horizontal position of the managed widget's anchor point in the managing widget. The *coord* value is specified in screen coordinates.
-y *coord*	Specifies the vertical position of the managed widget's anchor point in the managing widget. The *coord* value is specified in screen coordinates.
-width *size*	Specifies the width of the managed widget

Binding actions to events

When you write a program that has a graphical user interface, various program actions are initiated by events, such as the user clicking a button in the user interface. In a Tk script, you indicate what the program does, by associating actions with events. In this case, an *action* is simply a Tcl script that performs some task. In the case of a Quit button, for example, a logical action is the Tcl command exit, which ends the Tk script.

For buttons, a simple way to form this association is with a click of the button. Use the -command option of the button command to specify a

Tcl command to be executed when the user clicks the button. The `exit` command is associated with the `Quit` button as follows:

```
button .b -text Quit -command { exit }
```

Tip

The curly braces are not necessary when you have only one Tcl command, but you must enclose multiple commands inside braces.

The `bind` command is the most common way to associate an action with an event. Following is the general syntax of the `bind` command:

```
bind widgetName <eventSpecification> TclCommand
```

The *widgetName* argument is usually the path name of a widget, although you can bind an event to a class of widgets, such as all buttons. Typically, you have to consult online help to specify *eventSpecification*. (In this section, I show you an example and then explain event specifications.) The last argument — *TclCommand* — refers to the Tcl commands that you want to execute when the specified event occurs. These Tcl commands can be any Tcl script, ranging from a simple `puts` command, to a complete Tcl script stored in a separate file.

To see a more detailed example of how to bind an action to an event, consider this scenario. You may have noticed that many Microsoft Windows applications, as well as GNOME and KDE applications, sport a toolbar — essentially, a collection of buttons, each of which is meant to perform a specific task. Typically, each button bears an icon that indicates its purpose. To help users learn the meaning of a button quickly, many Windows applications have a feature called *tool help*. If you place the mouse pointer on a button, a small window pops up, displaying a short Help message that tells you what the button does.

You can use Tk to implement a similar tool-help feature. Follow these steps:

1. Create the button.

2. Prepare the Help message as a label (preferably with a bright background, such as yellow).

3. When the mouse pointer enters a button, an `Enter` event occurs. Bind the `Enter` event to a command that makes the help label visible. Use the `place` command to position the label relative to the button, so that the tool-help label always appears near the associated button.

   The following example shows how `bind` is used to associate the `place` command (shown within braces) with the `Enter` event:

   ```
   bind .f.q <Enter> { place .bh -in .f.q -relx 0.5 -rely 1.0 }
   ```

4. When the mouse pointer leaves the button, a `Leave` event occurs. Bind the `Leave` event to the `place forget` command to hide the Help message, as follows:

   ```
   bind .f.q <Leave> { place forget .bh }
   ```

The following sample `toolhelp` script demonstrates how to implement tool help in Tk:

```
#!/usr/bin/wish -f
# Demonstrates a "tool help" window that appears when you
# place the mouse pointer inside the "Quit" button.

wm geometry . 180x60

frame .f
button .f.b -text File
label .bh -text "Quit program"
.bh config -bg yellow
button .f.q -text Quit -command { exit }

bind .f.q <Enter> { place .bh -in .f.q -relx 0.5 -rely 1.0 }
bind .f.q <Leave> { place forget .bh }


pack .f.b .f.q -side left
pack .f -fill x
```

Make the `toolhelp` script file executable by using the `chmod +x toolhelp` command. Then run that script by typing `./toolhelp` at the shell prompt in a terminal window. Figure 29-5 shows the window that results after you place the mouse pointer on the Quit button.

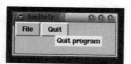

Figure 29-5: A Tk script that demonstrates how to implement tool-help messages

When you use `bind` to associate a Tcl script with an event, you need to know how to specify the event. Most events are either keyboard events or mouse events. A smaller number of events are related to the state of a widget's window. `<Map>` and `<Unmap>` events, for example, occur when a widget is managed or unmanaged (when you use `pack forget` or `place forget`).

Keyboard events

There are two keyboard events:

■ `<KeyPress>` occurs when you press a key.

■ `<KeyRelease>` occurs when you release a key.

You can specify a keyboard event for a specific key, by appending that key's *keysym* (which is the X Window System's standard name for a key) to the string `KeyPress-` and enclosing everything in angle brackets. The event associated with pressing the q key, for example, is specified by <Keypress-q>. Tk provides a shorter format for keyboard events. You can simply place the keysym inside angle brackets, as follows:

```
<q>
```

For most key presses, the event specification is straightforward. If you want to exit when the user presses Ctrl+C inside a widget named .text, use the bind command as follows:

```
bind .text <Control-c> exit
```

Table 29-10 shows some other commonly used keysyms.

Table 29-10   Some Commonly Used Keysyms

Keysym	Name of Key
BackSpace	Backspace
comma	Comma
Down	Down arrow
dollar	Dollar sign ($)
Escape	Escape
exclam	Exclamation mark
Left	Left arrow
numbersign	Number sign (#)
period	Period
Return	Enter
Right	Right arrow
Tab	Tab
Up	Up arrow

Tip

Inside the Tcl commands that are bound to a key event, use the %A keyword to refer to the printable character that the user presses. For any nonprintable character, %A is replaced by { } (a pair of empty braces). The %W keyword is replaced by the name of the widget that receives the keypress. Thus, you can use the following code to insert text into a text widget named .text1:

```
# Assume .text1 is a text widget
bind .text1 <KeyPress> {
    if { "%A" != "{}"} { %W insert insert %A}
}
```

Remember that a widget's name itself is a command, and that the command's argument depends on the type of widget. For a text widget, the command %W insert insert %A inserts the character into the text widget.

Mouse events

Use <ButtonPress> and <ButtonRelease> to denote mouse-button click and release events, respectively. You have to append the button number to make the event specific. Thus, the action of clicking the left mouse button (which is button 1 in X terminology) is denoted by <ButtonPress-1>. A shorthand notation for button presses is to omit Press; thus, you can write <Button-1> to denote the event generated by clicking the left mouse button.

Tip

In the Tcl commands that are bound to a mouse event, the keywords %x and %y denote the x and y coordinates of the mouse pointer (relative to the widget's window) at the time of the mouse event. Thus, you can track the position of mouse clicks on a widget .text1 as follows:

```
bind .text1 <Button-1> { puts "Click at (%x, %y) on widget: %W"}
```

Other mouse events include the Enter and Leave events, which occur when you move the mouse pointer into or out of a widget, respectively. These two events are denoted by <Enter> and <Leave>. The tool-help example shown in "Binding actions to events" earlier in this chapter, illustrates a way to use the <Enter> and <Leave> events.

Another event related to the mouse pointer is the <Motion> event, which occurs when you move the mouse pointer within a widget.

Window events

In addition to keyboard and mouse events, X includes many events that occur when a window is manipulated. The X server generates <Map> and <Unmap> events, for example, when a widget is displayed or hidden (by the pack or place command).

A <Configure> event occurs when the user resizes a window. Thus, you can bind a <Configure> event to a redisplay procedure that redraws the contents of a widget, based on the new size.

A <Destroy> event occurs when a window is about to be destroyed. You bind a procedure to the <Destroy> event and intercept requests to delete a window.

Summary

The combination of Tool Command Language (Tcl) and its X Window System–based graphical toolkit, Tk, is ideal for quickly developing applications with a graphical interface. This chapter introduces Tcl/Tk through simple examples.

By reading this chapter, you learn the following:

▶ Tcl is an interpreted language with a set of commands that you can combine, according to a set of rules. Tcl comes with the Red Hat Linux distribution on the companion CD-ROMs. You can install Tcl at the same time that you install Linux (see Chapter 1 for more information).

▶ You can learn the Tcl syntax and develop Tcl scripts interactively, by running the Tcl command interpreter, `tclsh`, and entering Tcl commands at the `tclsh` prompt.

▶ Tcl includes built-in commands for most routine tasks, such as reading and writing files, manipulating strings, and running any Linux command. Additionally, Tcl includes control-flow commands — such as `if`, `for`, and `while` — that enable you to control the sequence of commands processed by the interpreter. Finally, you can use Tcl's `proc` command to write new Tcl commands that use combinations of existing commands.

▶ Tk, the Tcl toolkit, is an extension of Tcl that uses the X Window System to enable you to build graphical user interfaces. Tk provides the three-dimensional appearance of Motif, but Tk does not require the Motif toolkit, or any other X toolkit. Tk is built on Xlib, which is the C-language Application Programming Interface (API) for X.

▶ Tk includes commands for creating many common widgets (user-interface elements), such as buttons, labels, list boxes, and scrollbars. A widget-naming convention specifies the widget hierarchy (the organization of the widgets).

▶ To make the graphical interface active, you have to use the `bind` command to associate Tcl commands with specific keyboard and mouse events.

▶ You can interactively experiment with and create Tk programs, by running `wish`, the windowing shell that can interpret all Tcl and Tk commands.

Chapter 30

GUI Programming

In This Chapter

▶ Understanding event-driven programming

▶ Understanding callback functions and event handlers

▶ Writing a Motif program

▶ Understanding Motif widgets

▶ Setting widget resources

▶ Using Xlib functions in Motif programs

▶ Summarizing X events

▶ Drawing text, graphics, and images in Motif programs

Chapter 27 shows you how to use the software development tools in Linux and describes how to exploit dynamic linking in your applications. Chapters 28 and 29 focus on scripting languages, such as the Bash shell, Perl, and Tcl/Tk. This chapter turns to another important programming topic: how to write applications with graphical user interface (GUI). This means writing X applications, because the X Window System is the underlying windowing system on Linux.

The primary programming interface to the X Window System is the Xlib library of C functions. You can use Xlib functions to build graphical user interfaces that have menus and buttons, by using a hierarchy of windows, display graphics, text, and images in these windows. Although you can do a great deal with Xlib, building complete programs by using Xlib functions alone is tedious. To build user interfaces, without getting mired in details, you need utility functions and a collection of prefabricated user-interface components, such as buttons, menus, and scrollbars. Several X toolkits provide tools that help you build user interfaces easily.

The current crop of X toolkits includes Open Software Foundation's (OSF) Motif toolkit, Sun's XView and OPEN LOOK Intrinsics Toolkit (OLIT), and the Athena Widgets, to name but a few (see the section "Motif Widgets" for a discussion of widgets). Motif is a popular toolkit for creating graphical user interfaces. Motif is also the GUI toolkit for the Common Desktop Environment (CDE), a popular graphical desktop that comes with many UNIX workstations.

Note

Motif used to be a licensed product of The Open Group, which formed in 1996 after the merger of the X/Open Company Ltd. and the Open Software Foundation (OSF). In May 2000, The Open Group decided to release the source code for Motif, under a public license, to the open-source community—in particular to the Linux community. In addition to *Open Motif* from The Open Group, another option for Motif for Linux is *LessTif*, a free version of Motif distributed under the GNU General Public License. Both Open Motif and LessTif are available for download from the `powertools` directory of Red Hat Linux 7.1 distribution (visit any of the mirror sites listed at `http://www.redhat.com/mirrors.html`). I cover Motif programming in this chapter because Motif is an industry standard graphical user interface (it conforms to the IEEE 1295 specification) and is used on more than 200 hardware and software platforms. Motif is the leading GUI for UNIX systems. If you are developing X applications, chances are you are using Motif.

This chapter provides a brief introduction to the Motif toolkit, which is based on the Xt Intrinsics. This chapter shows you how to create and manipulate widgets through the functions the Xt Intrinsics provides. The latter part of the chapter provides an overview of the Motif widget set and describes how to use Xlib functions to draw in a Motif application.

Tip

To try out the sample programs that I show in this chapter, you should download and install the `openmotif` and `openmotif-devel` RPMs from the `powertools` directory of Red Hat Linux 7.1 distribution from one of the mirror sites listed at `http://www.redhat.com/mirrors.html`.

Developing GNOME and KDE Applications

GNOME (GNU Network Object Model Environment) and KDE (K Desktop Environment) are two new graphical user interfaces for Linux and other versions of UNIX. Both GNOME and KDE rely on the X Window System, but each has its own toolkit of functions that programmers can use to develop graphical applications. If you have installed Red Hat Linux from the companion CD-ROMs and have used the graphical login, you may have seen many GNOME and KDE applications in action. This chapter does not cover GNOME and KDE programming, because each of these subjects needs a book of its own.

To develop GNOME applications, use the GTK+ toolkit, which was developed as part of GIMP—the GNU Image Manipulation Program. In fact, GTK stands for GIMP Toolkit. You also use GNOME widgets to implement high-level user-interface elements, such as dialog boxes, in GNOME applications. Visit the GNOME Development Site at `http://developer.gnome.org/` to find more information on how to develop GNOME applications.

KDE developers use an object-oriented toolkit named Qt—a C++ class library—to build the user interfaces. Qt provides most of the widgets, such as menus, buttons, and sliders, which you see in a KDE application. You can learn more about Qt, by visiting Troll Tech's Web site at `http://www.troll.no`. To learn more about developing KDE applications, visit the KDE homepage at `http://developer.kde.org/`.

Basic Motif Programming

The Motif toolkit provides a set of user interface components called *widgets*. You can think of each widget as a window with some associated information, such as window dimensions and color. The *Xt Intrinsics*, a layer of data structures and functions built with Xlib, provides the necessary data structures for a widget. The Xt Intrinsics also automatically handles redrawing a widget's contents when needed.

Just as windows in X are organized in a parent-child hierarchy, with child windows contained within a parent's borders, Motif widgets are organized in a parent-child hierarchy.

If you have never written applications with graphical user interfaces, you'll have to adapt to a new programming style, known as *event-driven programming,* when you write Motif applications.

Note

In event-driven programming, you do not specify the exact sequence of tasks the program must perform. Instead, you define many small functions, each of which is responsible for responding to an event, such as "user has clicked the Save button." The event-driven program waits for events, and it processes each event by calling the corresponding event-handler function.

You'll understand event-driven programming best by going through the simple example presented in the following section.

Step-by-Step Motif Programming

To write any Motif program, follow these steps:

1. Include the Motif header files:

```
#include <Xm/Xm.h>

/* Include header file of each widget you plan to use.
 * For example, here are the necessary header files
 * for Form, Label, and PushButton widgets.
 */

#include <Xm/Form.h>
#include <Xm/Label.h>
#include <Xm/PushB.h>
```

2. Call the XtAppInitialize function to initialize the toolkit and to create a top-level widget. This function returns an identifier (of the data type Widget) that represents the top-level widget.

3. Call XtVaCreateManagedWidget to create each widget and to set the widget's internal variables, known as *resources*.

4. Call `XtAddCallback` to indicate which functions should be called to handle specific events occurring in a widget. These functions are known as *callback functions*. In a Motif program, all work is done in callback functions.

5. Call `XtRealizeWidget` with the identifier of the top-level widget as the argument. This action realizes (creates) all the widgets.

6. Call the `XtAppMainLoop` function to begin processing events. This action gets the Motif program running.

A Simple Motif Program

The following listing is a simple Motif program that displays a button. The program quits when the user clicks the button.

```c
/*---------------------------------------------------------*/
/* File: xmquit.c
 *
 * An example program that displays a PushButton
 * inside a Form widget.
 *
 */

#include <Xm/Xm.h>
#include <Xm/Form.h>
#include <Xm/PushB.h>

/* Label for the push button */
static char label[] = "Press here to quit...";

/* Prototype of callback function */
static void cb_quit(Widget w, XtPointer client_data,
              XtPointer call_data);

/*---------------------------------------------------------*/
int main(int argc, char **argv)
{
  XtAppContext app;
  Widget     toplevel, quit_button, form;
  XmString   xmlabel;

/* Initialize toolkit and create the top-level widget */
  toplevel = XtAppInitialize(&app, "XMquit", NULL, 0,
                &argc, argv, NULL, NULL, 0);

/* Create the Form widget */
  form = XtCreateManagedWidget("Form", xmFormWidgetClass,
                toplevel, NULL, 0);

/* Create the push button widget as a child of the Form
 * and set its label at the same time. This also shows
 * how to create a "Motif String (XmString)" and use it.
```

```
*/

  xmlabel = XmStringCreateLtoR(label,
              XmSTRING_DEFAULT_CHARSET),
  quit_button = XtVaCreateManagedWidget("Exit",
          xmPushButtonWidgetClass, form,
          XmNlabelString, xmlabel,
          NULL);
  XmStringFree(xmlabel);

/* Set the callback function for this pushbutton */
  XtAddCallback(quit_button, XmNactivateCallback,
        cb_quit, NULL);

/* Realize the widgets */
  XtRealizeWidget(toplevel);

/* Start the event loop */
  XtAppMainLoop(app);
}
/*--------------------------------------------------------*/
/* c b _ q u i t
 *
 * Function to be called when user presses and releases
 * button in the pushbutton.
 */
static void cb_quit(Widget w, XtPointer client_data,
              XtPointer call_data)
{
  XtCloseDisplay(XtDisplay(w));
  exit(0);
}
```

Makefile for a Motif Program

Use the makefile shown in the following listing to compile and link the
xmquit program. (Motif must be installed on your system.)

```
#################################################################
# Makefile to compile and link a Motif program on Linux
# This makefile assumes that you have installed the
# openmotif and openmotif-devel packages

CFLAGS= -I/usr/X11R6/include
LDFLAGS= -L/usr/X11R6/lib -lXm -lXt -lX11 -lXext

all: xmquit

xmquit.o: xmquit.c

xmquit: xmquit.o
        cc -o xmquit xmquit.o $(LDFLAGS)
```

To test the program, first make sure X is running on your Linux PC. From an xterm window, type xmquit to run the program. Figure 30-1 shows the graphical interface the xmquit program displays.

Figure 30-1: Output of the sample Motif program xmquit

When you click the push button (by pressing and releasing the left mouse button with the pointer inside the push button's window), the program exits.

Widget Resources

When you use a Motif widget in an application, you do not need to know the details of the widget's data structure. You need information about the configurable parameters of the widget. These parameters, known as the widget's *resources*, control its appearance and behavior. A widget's resource is any configurable data the widget uses.

To be useful as a building block of user interfaces, a widget has to be highly configurable. A widget that allows the programmer to pick the foreground and background colors, for example, is much more useful than one that hardwires these values.

A programmer can set a widget's resources through an argument list. To do this, you first have to consult the widget's documentation and learn the names of the resources you want to set. The resource names are constants, such as XmNwidth and XmNheight. Use the constants XmNwidth and XmNheight to refer to the width and height resources of a widget.

To set the values of resources through an argument list, specify the value of each resource in an Arg structure, which is defined in <X11/Intrinsic.h> with this typedef statement:

```
typedef struct
{
  String  name; /* Name of resource */
  XtArgVal value; /* Its value    */
} Arg, *ArgList;
```

The value of the resource is stored as an XtArgVal — a system-dependent data type capable of holding a pointer to any C variable. If the value of a resource is less than the size of XtArgVal, it is stored directly in the value field of Arg. Otherwise, the value field is a pointer to the resource's value.

When you create a widget, you can specify an array of Arg structures with the values of the resources you want to set. You can prepare the array of resource values in two ways:

- Use a statically initialized array of Arg structures.

- Assign values at runtime by using the XtSetArg macro.

To see how to set resources, consider the PushButton widget. Suppose you want to set the push button's width and height, as well as its *label* — the text displayed on the button. The documentation of the PushButton widget tells you that the names of the resources are XmNwidth, XmNheight, and XmNlabelString. You also have to know that the string for XmNlabelString is not a simple C character array; it is a *compound string*, a special data type created by passing the string as an argument to a Motif utility routine (XmStringCreateLtoR).

With that information in hand, you can set the resource values by using an Arg array, as follows:

```
Arg    args[20];
Cardinal nargs;
XmString cstr;
.

.
  cstr = XmStringCreateLtoR("WarnGen",
                           XmSTRING_DEFAULT_CHARSET);
  XtSetArg(args[nargs], XmNwidth, 160);      nargs++;
  XtSetArg(args[nargs], XmNheight, 80);      nargs++;
  XtSetArg(args[nargs], XmNlabelString, cstr); nargs++;
  XmStringFree(cstr);
```

Secret

There is a reason why nargs++ is not used in XtSetArg to increment the count of arguments; XtSetArg is defined as a macro in such a way that it uses the first argument twice. If you use nargs++ in the first argument, the macro ends up incrementing nargs twice in each call. This result is why most toolkit applications define the argument list as shown.

After you prepare the argument list, call the XtCreateManagedWidget function to create a widget and to set its resources:

```
Arg    args[20];
Cardinal nargs;
Widget  toplevel, /*Previously-created top-level shell */
        pb1;     /* New push-button              */

pb1 = XtCreateManagedWidget("WarnGen", xmPushButtonWidgetClass,
                            toplevel, args, nargs);
```

This procedure creates a new push button named WarnGen, whose parent widget is toplevel and whose initial resource settings are in the array args.

You can avoid the tedious steps of specifying the resources one-by-one, and then creating the widget. The Xt Intrinsics library includes the XtVaCreateManagedWidget function, which enables you to specify the resources and to create the widget with a single function call. You can create a push button with specified width, height, and label, for example, by using the following call to XtVaCreateManagedWidget:

```
Widget  toplevel, /*Previously-created top-level shell */
        pb1;      /* New push-button                   */
XmString label;   /* Compound string to store label    */

/* First, create the compound string for the label */
xmlabel = XmStringCreateLtoR("WarnGen", XmSTRING_DEFAULT_CHARSET);

h_button = XtVaCreateManagedWidget("WarnGen",
            xmPushButtonWidgetClass, toplevel,
            XmNwidth,    200,
            XmNheight,   100,
            XmNlabelString, xmlabel,
            NULL);

/* Free the compound string (the Motif toolkit
   makes a copy) */
XmStringFree(xmlabel);
```

As the code fragment shows, `XtVaCreateManagedWidget` accepts a variable number of arguments:

- The first three arguments are required and are the same as those `XtCreateManagedWidget` requires. The first argument is the name of the widget, the second is the widget class, and the third specifies the parent widget.

- Following the three compulsory arguments is a list of resource specifications. Each specification is in the form of a resource name, followed by the value of that resource.

- A NULL resource name marks the end of this list.

Callback Registration

Most Motif widgets include a class of resources known as *callbacks*, which are pointers to functions. You can set such a resource to one of your functions and have the widget call that function in response to one or more events. These functions go by the name of *callback functions*; you write these functions to perform specific tasks and the Motif toolkit calls them back when appropriate.

A widget typically has more than one type of callback resource, each type meant for functions to be called in a specific situation. A widget's callback resource is a list of functions rather than a single function. The widget calls all the callbacks when the conditions for that callback resource are met. The calling order is the same as the order in which you register the callbacks.

In the program listed under the heading "A simple Motif program," the function `cb_quit` is a callback function for the push button widget's `XmNactivateCallback` resource. According to the `PushButton` documentation, the widget calls the functions in the `XmNactivateCallback` resource when the user clicks the button. In addition to XmNactivateCallback, PushButton has two more callback resources:

- XmNarmCallback functions, called when the user clicks the button.
- XmNdisarmCallback list, called when the user releases the button.

As the example shows, use the XtAddCallback function to add a function to a callback list of a widget. To add the cb_quit function to the XmNactivateCallback resource of the quit_button widget, use the following:

```
XtAddCallback(quit_button, XmNactivateCallback, cb_quit, NULL);
```

The last argument of XtddCallback—declared to be of type XtPointer—is a pointer to data to be passed to the callback function when the widget calls it. The callback function cb_quit has this prototype:

```
static void cb_quit(Widget w, XtPointer client_data,
                    XtPointer call_data);
```

When the widget calls this function, the second argument is whatever you passed to XtAddCallback as the last argument. The last argument passed to the callback function is the pointer to an XmAnyCallbackStruct structure, which is defined in <Xm/Xm.h> (refers to the file /usr/include/Xm/Xm.h) as the following:

```
typedef struct
{
   int    reason;  /* Indicates why callback was called  */
   XEvent *event; /* Info on event triggering callback  */
} XmAnyCallbackStruct;
```

Note

The reason field indicates why the widget calls the callback function. You have to consult the widget's documentation to interpret the value of this field. The event field is a pointer to an XEvent structure with information on the event that triggers the callback.

Event-Handler Registration

Suppose you want to allow the user to draw in a widget's window with the mouse. (Motif provides an XmDrawingArea widget for this purpose.) To program this capability, you want to catch the mouse click in the widget's window. The Motif toolkit enables you to do this, by using a method similar to the callback resources widgets use. Essentially, you can register your own event handler for selected events in a widget's window. Thereafter, when these events occur, the widget calls the registered event handler, giving you a chance to take action.

Use the Xt Intrinsics function XtAddEventHandler to add an event handler. To add a function named event_handler as the handler for ButtonPress events in the drawing widget, use the following:

```
XtAddEventHandler(drawing, ButtonPressMask, FALSE,
                  event_handler, NULL);
```

The first argument of XtAddEventHandler is the widget for which you are setting up an event handler. The second argument is an *event mask* (a bit pattern represented by a named constant value) that specifies the events for which the handler is invoked. The third argument is a Boolean value that should be set to True if you are setting the event handler for one of the X events — ClientMessage, MappingNotify, SelectionClear, or SelectionRequest — for which there is no event mask. In this case, set the second argument to NoEventMask. As in XtAddCallback, the last argument is a pointer to any data you want passed back to the event handler when it is called.

Note

You have to write the event_handler function according to the following prototype:

```
void event_handler(Widget w, XtPointer client_data, XEvent *event);
```

As this function prototype shows, the widget calls the event handler with three arguments: The first argument is the widget's ID. The second argument is the same pointer you pass as the last argument of XtAddEventHandler when you register this event handler. The third argument is a pointer to the XEvent structure that triggers the function call.

See the "X event summary" section for a summary of X events.

Motif Widgets

A widget set is like any toolbox; before using tools, you have to know what each does. This section provides an overview of the Motif widgets so you can learn the widget categories and what each category can do. You also should learn how to use important widgets in each category. Then you'll be able to pick the widgets that meet your needs and to use them in your application.

Three distinct categories of Motif widgets exist:

- *Shell widgets* provide the top-level window for a Motif application. Pop-up dialog boxes also use shell widgets.

- *Primitive widgets* represent the stand-alone widgets, such as labels, push buttons, and scrollbars.

- *Manager widgets* can contain other widgets as children and manage the layout of the child widgets. This category includes forms, message boxes, and scrolled windows.

All Motif widgets inherit the resources of a widget named Core. Knowing the resources of the Core widget is important, because its resources apply to every widget. The Core resources are the following:

- XmNaccelerators is the translation table that binds a sequence of keyboard and mouse events to specific actions.

- XmNancestorSensitive is a Boolean variable that indicates whether the immediate parent of a widget receives input events. To alter this resource setting, call the XtSetSensitive function.

- XmNbackground is the background pixel value for the widget's window. The pixel value translates to an actual RGB (red-green-blue) color through the current colormap.

- XmNbackgroundPixmap is a pixmap (a block of memory that stores an array of pixel values) used to tile the widget's window.

- XmNborderColor and XmNborderPixmap are the colormap and pixmap for the border of the widget's window.

- XmNborderWidth is the width of the border of the widget's window.

- XmNcolormap is the colormap to be used by the widget's window.

- XmNdepth is the number of bits used for each pixel value in the widget's window. Xt Intrinsics sets this value when the window is created.

- XmNdestroyCallback is the list of functions to be called when you destroy the widget by calling the XtDestroyWidget function.

- XmNheight and XmNwidth are the height and width of the widget's window, excluding the border width.

- XmNmappedWhenManaged is a flag that, when set to True, maps the widget's window as soon as the widget is realized and managed (the XtCreateManagedWidget function manages the widget). You can alter this flag by calling the XtSetMappedWhenManaged function.

- XmNscreen is a pointer to the Screen data structure that contains information about the physical display screen where the widget's window is displayed.

- XmNsensitive is a Boolean variable that, when True, causes Xt Intrinsics to dispatch mouse and keyboard events to the widget. To alter this resource, use the function XtSetSensitive.

- XmNTranslations is the *translation table* — a list of events with corresponding functions called when the specified events occur.

- XmNx and XmNy are the *x* and *y* coordinates of the upper-left corner of the widget's window, excluding the border. The coordinates are specified in the parent widget's coordinate frame.

Shell Widgets

A shell widget manages only one child; a shell widget's primary purpose is to set up the top-level window of an application. Xt Intrinsics provides several classes of shell widgets, the most important of which are the following:

- `TopLevelShell`
- `OverrideShell`
- `TransientShell`

When you call `XtAppInitialize`, Xt Intrinsics creates an instance of `ApplicationShell` widget, a subclass of `TopLevelShell`. The `ApplicationShell` and `TopLevelShell` widgets are used for normal top-level windows of applications. The window manager interacts with these top-level windows.

The `TransientShell` class is used for pop-up dialog boxes, which are top-level windows the user can move, but not resize to an icon. To create a dialog box, you use a subclass of `TransientShell` called `DialogShell`. Motif includes several convenience functions that enable you to create a `DialogShell` widget and place inside it another widget, such as a selection box or a message box. These convenience functions have names that start with `XmCreate` and end with `Dialog` (for example, `XmCreateFileSelectionDialog` or `XmCreateMessageDialog`).

The `OverrideShell` widget is a type of `Shell` widget that completely bypasses the window manager. The window manager does not put frames around an `OverrideShell` widget. Motif defines a subclass of `OverrideShell` — `XmMenuShell` — to display pop-up menus. You can use the function `XmCreatePopupMenu` to create a `MenuShell` with a menu inside it.

Primitive Widgets

All Motif primitive widgets are derived from the `XmPrimitive` class, which, in turn, is defined as a subclass of the `Core` class. The `XmPrimitive` class defines a standard set of resources all primitive widgets inherit. In particular, the `XmPrimitive` class is responsible for the 3D shading effect of Motif widgets.

These eight primitive widgets are derived directly from the `XmPrimitive` class:

- `ArrowButton` displays a button with an arrow. You can specify the direction of the arrow.
- `CSText` displays and edits multiple lines of compound strings. The text can include multiple fonts, colors, underlined text, and embedded tabs.
- `Label` displays a string or a pixmap inside a window.
- `List` displays a list of text items from which the user can select one or more.
- `Sash` is used as a separator between two panes. The user can drag the sash to adjust the size of the panes.

- ScrollBar is a scrollbar with arrows at the two ends and a slider. Scrollbars can be horizontal or vertical.

- Separator is used to separate items in a menu.

- Text widget acts as a single-line editor or multiple-line editor.

- TextField displays a single line of editable text.

These subclasses further specialize the functionality of the Label class:

- CascadeButton displays an associated pull-down menu when the user clicks the CascadeButton.

- DrawnButton is a button that allows you to draw on it (so you can display whatever you want on the button).

- PushButton is a standard push button.

- TearOffButton is a special push button that displays a tear-off menu.

- ToggleButton displays a string or a pixmap next to a small button. The button represents a state with two values: on or off. When the user clicks the button, the state changes.

All primitive widgets inherit the resources of the XmPrimitive class. Some of the important resources of the XmPrimitive class are:

- XmNbottomShadowColor is the pixel value used to draw the bottom and right side of a primitive widget's shadow. These two sides are collectively called the *bottom shadow*.

- XmNbottomShadowPixMap is the pixmap used to draw the bottom shadow.

- XmNforeground is the foreground color to be used in the primitive widgets.

- XmNhelpCallback is the list of callbacks that can be bound to functions that provide context-sensitive help.

- XmNhighlightColor is the color used to highlight the widget's window. A push button, for example, is highlighted when the user clicks it.

- XmNhighlightOnEnter is a Boolean variable that, when set to True, asks the widget to highlight its window when the cursor enters the window (provided that the input focus follows the pointer; the window that has the input focus gets the keyboard input). This resource is ignored if the user has to click to indicate input focus.

- XmNhighlightPixmap is the pixmap used to highlight the widget's window.

- XmNhighlightThickness is the thickness of the rectangle used to highlight the widget's window.

- XmNnavigationType is a constant that specifies how focus is assigned to the widget during keyboard traversal (keyboard traversal refers to the way the input focus moves from one widget to another as the user presses the Tab key); it can be XmNONE, XmTAB_GROUP, XmSTICKY_TAB_GROUP, or XmEXCLUSIVE_TAB_GROUP.

- XmNshadowThickness is the thickness of the shadow.

- XmNtopShadowColor is the color for the top shadow. It is used only if XmNtopShadowPixmap is NULL.

- XmNtopShadowPixmap is the pixmap for the top shadow.

- XmNtraversalOn is a Boolean value that indicates whether the widget accepts keyboard inputs.

- XmNunitType is the measurement unit used for all values that specify dimensions in the widget. The default value is copied from a manager that owns the widget. Usually, the default unit is pixels (specified by the constant XmPIXELS). Motif enables you to work in device-independent units, if you prefer. Specify the unit with one of the constants: XmPIXELS, Xm100TH_MILLIMETERS, Xm1000TH_INCHES, Xm100TH_POINTS, or Xm100TH_FONT_UNIT, defined in the header file <Xm/Xm.h>. You can set XmNunitType to Xm100TH_FONT_UNIT, for example, to indicate that all dimensions are defined in terms of one hundredth of a font's unit. You can explicitly set the font's unit with the XmSetFontUnits function.

- XmNuserData is a pointer not used internally. You can store a pointer to your own widget-specific data in this resource.

Manager Widgets

The manager widgets are derived from the XmManager class — a subclass of the Constraint class that, in turn, inherits from the Composite class. A manager widget can act as a container for other child widgets and manage the layout of the children. Some manager widgets, such as Form, enable you to specify the layout in terms of constraints such as "attach this child widget to the left edge of the container."

All manager widgets inherit their resources from the XmManager class. The XmManager resources are similar to those of the XmPrimitive class.

A few important manager widgets exist:

- The Command widget is a type of SelectionBox that provides a command history mechanism. A command entry area exists where the user can type commands. When you execute a command by pressing Enter, that command string is saved in a history buffer, which is displayed in a scrollable list area. You can use the Command widget to accept user input for your command-driven applications.

- The `DrawingArea` widget provides an empty window in which you can draw graphics or text (using Xlib functions as described in the "Xlib function overview" section later in this chapter).

- The `FileSelectionBox` widget is a special type of `SelectionBox` that displays a list of filenames in a list box. The widget has an area in which the user can enter a *file filter*, which is a search string used to locate files of interest. (`*.c`, for example, displays all filenames that end with `.c`.) The user's current selection is displayed in another box. At the bottom of the widget are four buttons labeled `OK`, `Filter`, `Cancel`, and `Help`.

- The `Form` widget supports complex layouts specified through certain resources that the widget attaches to each of its children. These resources are known as *constraint resources*; in effect, they provide a layout language you use to indicate how the child widgets are placed in the `Form`. Each constraint resource indicates the spatial relationship of a child widget to the `Form`, or to another child widget.

- The `Frame` widget displays a frame (with 3D shading) around a single child widget.

- The `MainWindow` widget provides a standard layout for the main window of an application. The `MainWindow` widget manages a combination of a menu bar, a `Command` widget, a `DrawingArea` widget, and scrollbars.

- The `MessageBox` widget displays a message and a row of three buttons labeled `OK`, `Cancel`, and `Help`.

- The `PanedWindow` widget lays out its children in panes arranged vertically.

- The `RowColumn` widget arranges its children in rows and columns. You can use `RowColumn` widgets in menu bars and pull-down menus.

- The `Scale` widget displays an elongated rectangle with a slider that enables the user to enter a numerical value. You can set the minimum and maximum values for the scale and for floating-point values, and you can specify the number of digits to follow the decimal point.

- The `ScrolledWindow` widget manages a work area (that can contain other widgets) and two scrollbars (horizontal and vertical).

- The `SelectionBox` widget displays a list of items in a scrollable box and provides an area where the current selection is displayed. The widget has three buttons labeled `OK`, `Cancel`, and `Help`. You can optionally turn on or off a fourth button labeled `Apply`.

Xlib and Motif

You can use the Motif widgets to build the user interface of a Motif application, but you cannot build most real-world applications with Motif widgets alone. Suppose that your application is for viewing satellite images for weather forecasting. You can use Motif widgets to enable the user to select a satellite image and even prepare a scrollable viewing area to display the image. To display the image, however, you have to rely on Xlib functions. You use Xlib functions for displaying images, graphics, and text in Motif applications. Additionally, you may have to write code that responds to an X event.

Note

The bottom line is that you have to learn the basics of X programming with Xlib functions, even if you use the Motif toolkit to write most of your applications. The next few sections provide an overview of Xlib and X events. You also see an example of using Xlib drawing functions in a Motif application.

An Overview of Xlib

The X Window System uses a client/server model to provide its services. The X server takes care of input and output at the display. X applications are the clients that use the capabilities of the server, by sending X protocol requests. X protocol requests are delivered over a communication link between the clients and the X server. If client and server are running on different machines, this link is a network connection. If the client and server are on the same machine, communication may occur through a shared block of memory, or some other interprocess communication (IPC) mechanism the operating system supports.

Although you can conceivably write an X application that performs all input and output by sending X protocol requests to the server, doing so is like programming a microprocessor directly in its machine language. To ease the programmer's job, the X Window System includes *Xlib*, a set of C language functions and macros that X applications can use to access the facilities of the X server.

Because Motif is based on X, a Motif application also is an X client; under the hood, a Motif application works by calling Xlib functions.

The primary purpose of Xlib is to provide an easy way for C programmers to send X protocol requests to the server. Xlib, however, is much more than just a set of functions with a one-to-one correspondence to all possible X protocol requests; it includes many convenience functions to ease the burden of handling common tasks while hiding the X protocol completely from the programmer. For example, only one X protocol request exists to create a window, but Xlib has two routines for creating windows: `XCreateSimpleWindow` and `XCreateWindow` (the first is simpler than the second). Similarly, the foreground and background colors for a window are specified in a graphics context (GC). To set these colors, simply call the Xlib routines `XSetForeground` and `XSetBackground`. Xlib takes care of setting up the proper protocol requests to change only these colors in the specified GC.

Xlib also includes many utility functions that don't have anything to do with interacting with the X server. Xlib utility functions help you get the user's choices from a resource file, manipulate screen images and bitmaps, translate names of colors to pixel values, and use the resource manager.

More information on Xlib and Motif programming

This chapter provides an overview of Motif programming and how Xlib functions are used in Motif applications. However, a single chapter is not enough to provide all the information you need to fully exploit the power of Xlib and the Motif toolkit. Quite a few books are available on Xlib and Motif programming, because of their popularity. For a more complete discussion of Xlib and the Motif toolkit, consult one of the following books:

■ Volume 1: *Xlib Programming Manual*, O'Reilly & Associates, 1993

■ Volume 2: *Xlib Reference Manual*, O'Reilly & Associates, 1993

■ Volume 6A: *Motif Programming Manual*, Second Edition, Dan Heller, Paula Ferguson and David Brennan, O'Reilly & Associates, 1994

■ Volume 6B: *Motif Reference Manual*, Paula Ferguson and David Brennan, O'Reilly & Associates, 1993

An Xlib Function Overview

Broadly speaking, Xlib functions enable an application to open the X display (connect to the X server), create windows and draw in them, retrieve events, and finally close the display. If you are developing a Motif application, you can get by with a reasonably small number of Xlib functions. You do not have to worry about opening the display, for example, if you are using the Motif toolkit. In a Motif application, you primarily use the Xlib graphics, image, and text-output functions.

Table 30-1 summarizes the commonly used Xlib functions, grouped according to task. This list is by no means complete, yet it is rather long. As a Motif programmer, you do not have to learn all these functions; this list gives you an overall view of Xlib's capabilities. For complete coverage of Xlib functions, consult the books listed in the "More information on Xlib and Motif programming" sidebar.

Table 30-1   Common Xlib Functions Grouped According to Task

Task	*Commonly Used Xlib Functions*
Open/close X display	`XOpenDisplay XCloseDisplay`
Get user's choices	`XGetDefault XrmInitialize` `XrmGetResource XrmParseCommand`

Continued

Table 30-1 *(continued)*

Task	Commonly Used Xlib Functions
Create/manage windows	XCreateSimpleWindow XCreateWindow XDestroyWindow XMapRaised XMapWindow XUnmapWindow XGetWindowAttributes XChangeWindowAttributes
Control window's size and position	XGeometry XGetGeometry XMoveWindow XResizeWindow XMoveResizeWindow XLowerWindow XRaiseWindow XCirculateSubWindows
Interact with window manager	XSetStandardProperties XGetWMHints XSetWMHints
Get and process events	XSelectInput XEventsQueued XNextEvent XPeekEvent
Synchronize with server	XFlush XSync XSynchronize
Handle errors	XGetErrorText XSetErrorHandler XSetIOErrorHandler
Manipulate graphics contexts	XCreateGC XChangeGC XCopyGC XFreeGC XSetForeground XSetState XSetBackground XSetFunction
Draw graphics	XDrawArc XDrawArcs XDrawLine XDrawLines XSetDashes XSetArcMode XDrawPoints XDrawPoint XDrawRectangle XDrawRectangles XFillArc XFillArcs XSetFillRule XFillRectangle XFillRectangles XFillPolygon XSetLineAttributes
Clear and copy areas	XClearWindow XClearArea XCopyArea XCopyPlane
Draw text	XLoadFont XLoadQueryFont XSetFont XUnloadFont XDrawString XDrawImageString XDrawText XTextWidth XListFonts
Use color	XDefaultColorMap XDefaultVisual XGetVisualInfo XParseColor XAllocColor XGetStandardColorMap XSetWindowColorMap XFreeColors

Task	Commonly Used Xlib Functions
Display images	XCreatePixmap XFreePixmap XCreatePixmapFromBitmapData XReadBitmapFile XWriteBitmapFile XCreateImage XDestroyImage XGetImage XPutImage XGetPixel XPutPixel
Handle mouse and keyboard input	XQueryPointer XTranslateCoordinates XCreateFontCursor XDefineCursor XFreeCursor XUndefineCursor XGetMotionEvents XLookupString XRefreshKeyboardMapping XRebindKeysym
Interapplication communication	XInternAtom XChangeProperty XGetWindowProperty XDeleteProperty XSendEvent XGetSelectionOwner XSetSelectionOwner XConvertSelection

Common Xlib Features

Although Xlib has many functions, the functions share some common features. Knowing these common features can help you use Xlib effectively. The common features fall into these categories:

- Common header files
- Function and data-structure naming conventions
- Order of arguments in function calls

Header files

If you use Xlib functions in a program, you have to include these header files:

```
#include <X11/Xlib.h>
#include <X11/Xutil.h>
```

The first header file declares the Xlib functions and data structures. The second header file is used by the utility functions of Xlib. Additionally, you may need to include other header files, such as <X11/cursorfont.h>, if you use the standard cursor shapes.

When a header file is named this way (<X11/Xlib.h>), the compiler expects to find the file in the X11 subdirectory of the standard location for header files: the /usr/include directory. Thus, you find the file <X11/Xlib.h> in the /usr/include/X11 directory of your system.

Naming conventions

Xlib follows a consistent naming convention for all functions, macros, and data structures. When you know this naming scheme, you can often guess function names and avoid common typing errors. The naming conventions are:

- *Functions and macros.* The names of Xlib functions and macros are built by concatenating one or more words with the first letter of each word capitalized (see Table 30-1 for examples). The names of functions begin with a capital X, but macro names never start with X. In fact, if a function and a macro work identically, the function's name is derived by adding an X prefix to the macro's name. The macro that returns the name of the current X display is DisplayString, for example, and the equivalent function is named XDisplayString.

- *Data structures.* User-accessible data structures are named just like functions; their names begin with a capital X. Data-structure members are named in lowercase, with underscore characters (_) separating multiple words. The XImage data structure, for example, has an integer field named bits_per_pixel. This rule does not apply to data structures whose members are not to be accessed by the user. An example is the Display data structure, whose name does not begin with X because the user is not supposed to access the internals of this structure directly.

You can use these conventions to select names for your own data structures and functions, so that they do not conflict with names in Xlib. You can use lowercase names for your variables and uppercase names for your macros. To be safe, you may decide to add a unique prefix (perhaps your organization's or your project's initials) to all your external functions and variables.

Argument order in Xlib function calls

In addition to the naming conventions, Xlib functions and macros order their arguments in a consistent manner. The arguments appear in this order:

- *Display.* The display is the first argument of a function or a macro.

- *Windows, fonts, and other X server resources.* X server resources — such as window, font, and pixmap — appear immediately after the display argument. When several resources are used, windows and pixmaps precede all others. The graphics context (GC) appears last among the resources.

- *Source and destination.* Many functions perform tasks that involve taking something from one or more arguments (the source) and storing the result in other arguments (the destination). In these cases, the source arguments always precede the destination arguments.

- *x, y, width, and height.* Many functions take the position (*x, y*) and size (*width, height*) of windows or pixmaps as arguments. Among *x* and *y*, the *x* argument always precedes *y*, whereas *width* always comes before *height*. When all four arguments are present, the order is *x, y, width,* and *height.*

- *Bit mask*. Xlib has some functions that selectively change one or more members in a structure. Indicate the members being changed by setting bits in a *bit mask* (an integer variable in which each bit position corresponds to a member of the structure). When a function takes a bit mask as an argument, the mask always precedes the pointer to the structure.

Tip

Knowing the convention for argument order is even more helpful than knowing how functions are named. After you become familiar with several Xlib functions, you can often guess the argument list for a function simply because you know these rules.

X Server Resources

Chapter 5 uses the term *resource* to mean user-customizable parameters in an application. In the context of the X server, however, *resource* signifies anything created at the request of an application. Thus, X resources include:

- Window
- Graphics context (GC)
- Font
- Cursor
- Colormap
- Pixmap

A large part of X programming involves creating and using these resources because this is how an X or Motif application generates output in windows and accepts input from the mouse and keyboard.

Applications create resources by calling Xlib functions. When your program creates any of these resources, the Xlib function returns a resource ID — a 32-bit identifier (of type `unsigned long` in the C programming language). For your convenience, the header file `<X11/X.h>` uses the C `typedef` statement to define several synonyms — such as `Window`, `Font`, `Pixmap`, `Cursor`, and `Colormap` — for the resource identifiers. Thus, when you create a window, you can refer to the returned resource ID as a `Window`.

Windows

Among the resources of the X server, windows are the most important. Windows are the lifeblood of the X Window System. In X, a *window* is an area of the display screen where an application displays output and accepts input (mouse and keyboard). X allows windows to be nested in a parent-child hierarchy, with all child windows clipped at the boundary of the parent. Whenever an X application draws text or graphics, it must specify a window. Also, all inputs from the mouse and the keyboard are associated with a window. Xlib includes many functions for controlling the size, color, and hierarchy of windows.

Graphics contexts (GC)

To avoid repeatedly sending graphics attributes to the server, X uses the concept of a *graphics context* (GC) — an X server resource that holds all graphics attributes, such as colors and font, necessary for drawing in a window. These graphics attributes control the appearance of the output. The advantage of this approach, is that an application can create one or more GCs at the server, initialize them, and later use them for drawing in a window. Because a GC is identified by a resource identifier, you can ask the server to use a specific set of attributes by including a single graphics-context identifier in the drawing request, instead of a variable number of graphics attributes.

To perform text output by using the Xlib text-output routine, XDrawString, you have to create the GC and set up the font and colors before calling XDrawString. You can use Xlib routines, such as XCreateGC and XChangeGC to create and manipulate GCs.

Fonts

In X, a *font* refers to a collection of bitmaps (a pattern of ones and zeros) that represent the size and shape of characters from a set. The X server uses a font to display text in a window. When you call an Xlib function, such as XdrawString, to draw one or more characters, the server retrieves and draws the image corresponding to each character from the current font.

Cross-Reference

X provides many fonts that have a standard naming convention. You have to load one of these fonts before drawing text in a window; otherwise, the server uses a default font. To specify a font, use a resource identifier of type Font. Chapter 5 summarizes the font-naming convention of X.

Cursors

The *cursor* represents the shape of the onscreen pointer that indicates the current position of the mouse. As you move the mouse, the cursor tracks the movement onscreen. A cursor is somewhat similar to a single character from a font. In fact, you can call Xlib's XCreateFontCursor function to create a new cursor, by selecting one of the characters from a special cursor font. As with any other resource, when you create a cursor, you get back a resource identifier of type Cursor. After creating a cursor, you can assign it to a window, by using the function XDefineCursor. If you do not define a cursor for a window, the X server uses the cursor of its parent.

Changing cursors is a useful way to inform users about the special purpose of a particular window. If a window manager lets you resize a window by dragging the corners of a window's frame, for example, the window manager changes the cursor when the user has the mouse at the corners.

Colormaps

An X display screen uses a block of memory, known as the *frame buffer* (or *video memory*), capable of storing a fixed number of bits (usually 8) for each pixel on the screen. This number is the so-called *pixel value*. The color displayed at each pixel, on the other hand, is the result of varying the intensities of three closely located dots of the basic colors: red (R), green (G), and blue (B). The intensity of these three components is often referred to as the *RGB value* or the *RGB triplet*.

The *colormap* is the key to generating an RGB triplet from a pixel value — it maps a pixel value to an RGB color. For example, if the video memory stores 8-bit pixel values, a pixel can take one of 2^8, or 256, possible values. Thus, the colormap must have 256 entries, and each entry must show the intensities of the R, G, and B components.

When an X application uses colors, it works with pixel values. To ensure that a pixel value appears as the correct color, the application has to identify the colormap used to translate that pixel value to a color. The application does so through the colormap resource.

The video card in most systems can use only one colormap at a time — a situation that creates the notion of installing a colormap. If multiple applications install colormaps independently, the result is chaos. The convention is that X applications should never install their own colormaps; instead, they should inform the window manager of the colormaps they need. Given the right hints, the window manager takes care of installing the right colormap for each application.

Pixmaps

A *pixmap* is a block of memory in the X server in which you can draw, just as you draw in a window. In fact, window and pixmap resources are collectively known in X as *drawables*. All drawing functions accept drawables as arguments. What you draw in a pixmap does not appear on the display; to make the contents of a pixmap visible, you have to copy from the pixmap to a window. You can think of a pixmap as an off-screen window — a two-dimensional array of pixel values that can be used to hold graphics images and fill patterns. If a single bit represents each pixel value in a pixmap, the pixmap is known as a bitmap.

X Event Summary

Everything in an X application happens in response to events received from the X server. When an application creates a window and makes it visible by mapping it, for example, the application cannot tell whether the server has finished preparing the window for output. To draw in that window, the application must wait for a specific event — an Expose event — from the server. All mouse and keyboard inputs from the user also arrive at the X application in the form of events.

Because the basic design of X does not impose any particular style of user interface, X events contain an extraordinary amount of detail. For example, you can get one mouse event when a mouse button is clicked and another when that button is released. For each event, you can find out (among other things) which button is involved, the window that contains the cursor, the time of the event, and the x and y coordinates of the cursor location. This level of detailed event reporting allows programmers to use X to implement any type of user interface.

X provides 33 events for handling everything from mouse and keyboard input to messages from other X clients. Table 30-2 summarizes the X events.

Table 30-2 Summary of X Events

Event Name	Meaning
Mouse Events	
ButtonPress	Mouse button clicked with pointer in the window
ButtonRelease	Mouse button released with pointer in the window
EnterNotify	Mouse pointer enters the window
LeaveNotify	Mouse pointer leaves the window
MotionNotify	Mouse moved after stopping
Keyboard Events	
FocusIn	Window receives input focus (all subsequent keyboard events come to that window)
FocusOut	Window loses input focus
KeyMapNotify	Occurs after an EnterNotify or FocusIn event (this is how the X server informs the application of the state of the keys after these events)
KeyPress	Key pressed (when window has focus)
KeyRelease	Key released (when window has focus)
MappingNotify	Keyboard reconfigured (the mapping of a key to a string has changed)
Expose Events	
Expose	Previously obscured window, or part of window becomes visible
GraphicsExpose	During graphics copy operations, parts of the source image are obscured (means that the copied image is not complete)
NoExpose	Graphics copy is successfully completed
Colormap Notification Event	
ColormapNotify	Window's colormap has changed

Event Name	Meaning
Interclient Communication Events	
ClientMessage	Another client has sent a message using the XSendEvent function
PropertyNotify	Property associated with the window has changed
SelectionClear	Window loses ownership of selection
SelectionNotify	Selection successfully converted
SelectionRequest	Selection needs conversion
Window-State Notification Events	
CirculateNotify	Window raised or lowered in the stacking order
ConfigureNotify	Window moved or resized, or its position in the stacking order changed
CreateNotify	Window created
DestroyNotify	Window destroyed
GravityNotify	Window moved because its parent's size changed
MapNotify	Window mapped
ReparentNotify	Window's parent changed
UnmapNotify	Window unmapped
VisibilityNotify	Window's visibility changed (became visible or invisible)
Window-Structure Control Events	
CirculateRequest	Request to raise or lower the window in the stacking order (used by window managers)
ConfigureRequest	Request to move, resize, or restack window (used by window managers)
MapRequest	Window about to be mapped (used by window managers)
ResizeRequest	Request to resize window (used by window managers)

The 33 X events shown in Table 30-2 can be broadly grouped in the following seven categories:

- *Mouse events* — The X server generates mouse events when the user clicks a mouse button, or moves the mouse.

- *Keyboard events* — The server generates keyboard events when the user presses or releases any key on the keyboard. These events are delivered to an application only if a window the application owns has the input focus. Usually, the window manager decides how the focus is transferred from one window to another. Two common focus models exist: clicking a window to type in it (used by the Macintosh and Microsoft Windows), or allowing the focus to follow the mouse pointer (which means the focus is assigned to the window that contains the mouse pointer).

- *Expose events* — Of all X events, an Expose event is the most crucial; applications draw in their windows in response to this event. Almost all X applications request and process this event. (In Motif applications, most Expose events are handled behind the scenes, but you do have to take care of Expose events in DrawingArea widgets.) The GraphicsExpose and NoExpose events involve copying from one part of a window, or a pixmap, to another. These events allow applications to handle situations in which another window obscures the source of the copy operation, and the contents of the obscured area are unavailable for copying.

- *Colormap notification event* — The server generates a ColorMapNotify event whenever an application changes the colormap associated with a window, or installs a new colormap. Well-behaved X applications should handle the colormap changes through the window manager.

- *Interclient communication events* — These events send information from one X application to another. The concepts of property and selection are used for this purpose.

- *Window-state notification events* — The server generates these events when a window is moved or resized, or when its place in the stacking order is altered. These events are useful for keeping track of changes in the layout of windows on-screen. Typically, window managers use these events for this purpose; your application can use them, too, if you want to alter the size and position of the subwindows when the user resizes the topmost window.

- *Window-structure control events* — These events are used almost exclusively by window managers to intercept an application's attempt to change the layout of its windows. By monitoring the MapRequest event, for example, the window manager can tell when an application maps its topmost window. When this happens, the window manager can add its own frame to the window and can place it at an appropriate location onscreen.

Xlib Programming Topics

When you write Motif applications, the Motif toolkit takes care of many window-creation details and event-handling details for you. All that you typically provide are callback functions that perform application-specific tasks. You need to use only a small set of Xlib functions in a Motif application. The following sections provide an overview of the types of Xlib programming you have to perform in a Motif application.

Setting cursor shape and color

The cursor determines the onscreen appearance of the mouse pointer. In X, these parameters define a cursor:

- Source bitmap
- Mask bitmap
- Foreground and background colors, specified as RGB values
- Hotspot (the point in the cursor's bitmap that defines the location of the pointer onscreen)

The bitmaps are small, rectangular arrays of ones and zeros (usually, 16×16 or 32×32). When drawing the cursor, the X server paints the pixels that correspond to ones by using the foreground color, whereas pixels at locations with zeros appear in the background color. The mask bitmap determines the outline within which the cursor shape is drawn. The hotspot determines the pointer location. For many cursor shapes, the hotspot is at the center of the cursor's bitmap. For an arrow cursor, the hotspot is the point of the arrow.

You can assign a cursor to any window in your Motif application. The following example shows how you might create a new cursor from a standard cursor font and assign it to the window of a `DrawingArea` widget in a Motif application:

```
#include <X11/cursorfont.h>
Cursor xhair_cursor;
    .
    .
    .
/* Create a cross-hair cursor for the drawing area. Assume that
"drawing_area"
 * is the name of the DrawingArea widget.
 */
  xhair_cursor = XCreateFontCursor(XtDisplay(drawing_area),
                  XC_crosshair);
    .
    .
    .
/* Change the cursor shape in the DrawingArea (call this after the
 * widgets are realized.
 */
/* Realize all widgets */
  XtRealizeWidget(top_level);

/* Set the cursor for the DrawingArea widget's window */
  XDefineCursor(XtDisplay(drawing_area), XtWindow(drawing_area),
        xhair_cursor);

/* Free the cursor */
  XFreeCursor(XtDisplay(drawing_area), xhair_cursor);
```

After this is done, the cursor shape changes to the crosshair cursor whenever the pointer enters the window `my_window`. This selection remains in effect until you undefine the cursor for that window, by calling

XUndefineCursor. When you remove the cursor from a window, the server displays the cursor of the window's parent when the pointer is in that window that has an undefined cursor.

The second argument of XCreateFontCursor specifies the cursor shape with a symbolic name. These names are defined in the header file <X11/cursorfont.h>.

After assigning a cursor to a window, if you do not intend to refer to it anymore, you can free the cursor, by calling XFreeCursor. Any window that displays this cursor continues to do so; the server gets rid of the cursor only after that cursor is not defined for any window. After you undefine a cursor, you must not refer to that cursor's ID again.

When a cursor is created, it has, by default, a black foreground and a white background. To change the color of a cursor, use the XRecolorCursor function, as follows:

```
XColor fgcolor, bgcolor; /* Colors in XColor structure */
Cursor arrow_cursor;     /* Cursor whose color is set */

XRecolorCursor(theDisplay, arrow_cursor, &fgcolor, &bgcolor);
```

You have to allocate the foreground and background colors before using them in the XRecolorCursor function call.

You also can use your own source and mask bitmaps to define a custom cursor. After you have the two pixmaps (bitmaps are pixmaps of depth 1), you can use XCreatePixmapCursor to create a new cursor. This function needs the two pixmaps, the foreground and background colors, and the coordinates of the hotspot, as shown in this example:

```
Display    *theDisplay;
Cursor     my_cursor;
Pixmap     source, mask;
XColor     fgcolor, bgcolor;
unsigned int x_hot, y_hot;

my_cursor = XCreatePixmapCursor(theDisplay, source, mask,
                     &fgcolor, &bgcolor, x_hot, y_hot);
```

Another way to get a cursor, is to select a specific character from a font and use the bitmap of that character as a cursor. Before using the font, you have to load the font by calling the XLoadFont function. Then you can create the cursor by using the function XCreateGlyphCursor.

Drawing graphics and text

To draw graphics or text in an X window, you have to create a *graphics context* (GC) — a data structure (resource) in which the X server stores graphics attributes, such as background and foreground colors, line style, and font. These attributes control the appearance of graphics and text.

Creating a GC

To create a GC, use the Xlib function XCreateGC. This function takes four arguments, in this order:

- A pointer to the X display
- The ID of a drawable (a Window or a Pixmap variable)
- An unsigned long bit mask, that indicates which attributes of the GC you want to specify
- The address of a XGCValues structure

Specify various graphics attributes in the XGCValues structure, and use the bit mask to indicate which members of the structure have valid values. Following is an example of how to call XCreateGC:

```
Display    *disp;
Drawable   win;
unsigned long mask;
XGCValues  xgcv;
GC         gc;

/* Set values of selected members of xgcv, as needed.
 * Then set mask. This example sets the foreground and
 * the background pixels to the default white and black
 * colors for the screen.
 */
xgcv.foreground = WhitePixel(disp, DefaultScreen(disp));
xgcv.background = BlackPixel(disp, DefaultScreen(disp));
mask = GCForeground | GCBackground;

gc = XCreateGC(disp, win, mask, &xgcv);
```

Because a GC is a resource, it consumes memory in the X server. Therefore, you should free a GC when it is no longer needed. You can do so with the XFreeGC function, as follows:

```
Display *disp;
GC      gc;

XFreeGC(disp, gc);
```

The X server automatically frees all your application's resources (including GCs) when the application exits, so you need to destroy a GC explicitly only when you have created one for a temporary purpose.

GC attributes

The X server maintains the GC, so you don't need to know the internal details of the GC. The values of a GC's attributes are specified through a XGCValues structure. The basic idea is to set the values of the attributes you want and then to create a bit mask to indicate which attributes you are specifying. The X server uses the XGCValues structure, together with the bit mask to determine which parts of a GC to change.

The definition of the XGCValues structure gives you an idea of which graphics attributes you can control. This is how that structure is defined in the <X11/Xlib.h> header file:

```
typedef struct
{
    int         function;          /* Operation on pixels     */
    unsigned long plane_mask;      /* Bit planes affected     */
    unsigned long foreground;      /* Foreground pixel value  */
    unsigned long background;      /* Background pixel value  */
    int         line_width;        /* Line width (0 or more)  */
    int         line_style;        /* One of: LineSolid,
                                            LineOnOffDash,
                                            LineDoubleDash   */
    int         cap_style;         /* One of: CapNotLast,
                                       CapButt, CapRound,
                                       CapProjecting          */

    int         join_style;        /* One of: JoinMiter,
                                       JoinRound, JoinBevel   */
    int         fill_style;        /* One of: FillSolid,
                                       FillTiled, FillStippled,
                                       FillOpaqueStippled     */
    int         fill_rule;         /* One of: EvenOddRule,
                                            WindingRule       */
    int         arc_mode;          /* One of: ArcChord,
                                            ArcPieSlice       */
    Pixmap      tile;              /* Pixmap for tiling       */
    Pixmap      stipple;           /* Bitmap for stippling    */
    int         ts_x_origin;       /* x and y offset for tile*/
    int         ts_y_origin;       /* or stipple operations   */
    Font        font;              /* Default font            */
    int         subwindow_mode;    /* One of: ClipByChildren,
                                            IncludeInferiors  */
    Bool        graphics_exposures;/*True=generate exposures*/
    int         clip_x_origin;     /* Origin of clip_mask     */
    int         clip_y_origin;
    Pixmap      clip_mask;         /* Bitmap for clipping     */
    int         dash_offset;       /* Controls dashed line    */
    char        dashes;            /* Pattern of dashes       */
} XGCValues;
```

To set these attributes, you also need the name of the bit mask associated with each member of the XGCValues structure. Table 30-3 lists the bit masks used to select specific members of XGCValues. When you set multiple attributes, use a bitwise-OR (indicated by the C operator |) combination of the masks corresponding to the attributes you want to set.

Table 30-3 also lists the default value of each attribute. When you create a GC without specifying any attribute values, the X server initializes the GC with the default attribute values.

Table 30-3   Bit-Mask Constants for GC Attributes

Attribute name	Bit-mask constant	Description
function	GCFunction	Operation on pixels (Default: overwrite existing pixels)
plane_mask	GCPlaneMask	Bit planes affected (Default: all bitplanes affected)
foreground	GCForeground	Foreground pixel (Default: 0)
background	GCBackground	Background pixel (Default: 1)
line_width	GCLineWidth	Line width (Default: 0)
line_style	GCLineStyle	Line style (Default: solid line)
cap_style	GCCapStyle	How lines end (Default: ends at end point without any projection)
join_style	GCJoinStyle	How lines join (Default: miter join)
fill_style	GCFillStyle	Fill style (Default: solid fill)
fill_rule	GCFillRule	How figures are filled (Default: fill using the even-odd rule, in which a point is inside if a line drawn from outside the figure crosses its edges an odd number of times)
arc_mode	GCArcMode	Appearance of filled arcs as pie slices, or closed with a chord (Default: arcs filled as pie slices)
tile	GCTile	Pixmap for tiling (Default: pixmap filled with foreground pixel)
stipple	GCStipple	Bitmap for stippling (Default: bitmap of all ones). The stipple pattern is like a stencil through which the foreground color is applied to a drawable.
ts_x_origin	GCTileStipXOrigin	x-offset for tiling or stippling (Default: 0)
ts_y_origin	GCTileStipYOrigin	y-offset for tiling or stippling (Default: 0)
font	GCFont	Default font for text output (Default: depends on X server)
subwindow_mode	GCSubwindowMode	Draw into children or not (Default: do not draw into child windows)

Continued

Table 30-3 *(continued)*		
Attribute name	**Bit-mask constant**	**Description**
graphics_exposures		GCGraphicsExposures Graphics exposure events generated if True (Default: True)
clip_x_origin	GCClipXOrigin	x-origin of clip_mask (Default: 0)
clip_y_origin	GCClipYOrigin	y-origin of clip_mask (Default: 0)
clip_mask	GCClipMask	Bitmap for clipping (Default: no clip mask used)
dash_offset	GCDashOffset	Starting point in dash pattern (Default: 0)
dashes	GCDashList	Pattern of dashes (Default: pattern of 4 pixels on and then 4 off)

Drawing points

The simplest graphics operation in X, is drawing a point in a window or pixmap. You can draw a single point at the coordinates (x, y) by using this call:

```
Display *disp;  /* The connection to the X server   */
Window win;     /* The drawable--a window           */
GC   thisGC;    /* Graphics context for the drawing */
int  x, y;      /* Point to be drawn                 */

XDrawPoint(disp, win, thisGC, x, y);
```

The pixel at the location is set to the foreground color specified in the GC. Other attributes in the GC control the final appearance of the point. For example, the point is not drawn if it lies outside the clip mask.

If you want to draw a large number of points, all using the same GC, you can use the XDrawPoints function to draw them all at the same time with a single X protocol request. Store the points in an array of XPoint structures. The XPoint structure is defined in <X11/Xlib.h>, as follows:

```
typedef struct
{
  short x, y;  /* x and y coordinates of the point */
} XPoint;
```

You call XDrawPoints in the usual manner with a display, a drawable, and a GC as the first three arguments:

```
XPoint pt[10];
int    numpt = 10;
...
XDrawPoints(p_disp, window_1, thisGC, pt, numpt,
          CoordModeOrigin);
```

The array of points and number of points follow the three standard arguments. The last argument tells the server how to interpret the coordinates of the points in the array. You can specify one of these constants:

- CoordModeOrigin means that the coordinates are relative to the origin of the window or the pixmap.

- CoordModePrevious is used when the coordinate of each point is given in terms of the x and y displacements from the preceding point. The first point is assumed to be relative to the origin of the window.

Drawing lines

Xlib includes three line-drawing functions:

- XDrawLine
- XDrawSegments
- XDrawLines

The XDrawLine function has this calling syntax:

```
XDrawLine(disp, win, thisGC, x1, y1, x2, y2);
```

This function draws a line between the points (x1, y1) and (x2, y2) in the drawable named win, using the line attributes specified in the GC (thisGC).

XDrawSegments draws several possibly disjointed line segments, using the same graphics attributes. The segments are specified by means of the XSegment structure, which is defined in <X11/Xlib.h> as the following:

```
typedef struct
{
   short x1, y1; /*Coordinates of start-point of segment*/
   short x2, y2; /*Coordinates of end-point of segment  */
} XSegment;
```

The following example shows how to use the XDrawSegments function to draw several line segments:

```
Display  *disp;
Window   window_1;
GC       thisGC;
XSegment lines[] =
{
   {50, 80, 150, 200},
   {10, 20, 35, 60},
   {250, 10, 200, 100}
};
```

```
int numsegs = sizeof(lines) / sizeof(XSegment);

XDrawSegments(disp, window_1, thisGC, lines, numsegs);
```

The XDrawLines function is similar to XDrawPoints, with one difference: XDrawPoints draws points, whereas XDrawLines connects the points with a line. Call XDrawLines with the same arguments that you use for XDrawPoints.

Drawing and filling rectangles

Xlib includes several functions for drawing rectangles. The XDrawRectangle function is for drawing a rectangle, given the coordinates of its upper-left corner and its width and height. The function call is of the following form:

```
XDrawRectangle(disp, window, thisGC, x, y, width, height);
```

To draw the outline around the rectangle, this function draws these lines:

- (x, y) to (x+width, y)
- (x+width, y) to (x+width, y+height)
- (x+width, y+height) to (x, y+height)
- (x, y+height) to (x,y)

You can use the same GC to draw several rectangles, by calling XDrawRectangles, which expects an array of rectangles and their number as arguments, as follows:

```
XRectangle rects[]; /* Array of rectangles  */
int        nrects;  /* Number of rectangles */

XDrawRectangles(disp, window, thisGC, rects, nrects);
```

The XRectangle function is a structure for storing the parameters of a rectangle. The function is defined in <X11/Xlib.h> as follows:

```
typedef struct
{
   short     x, y;                 /* Upper-left corner */
   unsigned short width, height; /* Width and height   */
} XRectangle;
```

You can draw a filled rectangle by calling the XFillRectangle function. Call this function the same way you call XDrawRectangle, with exactly the same arguments. Notice that when you draw a filled rectangle, the width and height of the filled area are exactly the width and height specified in the call to XFillRectangle.

XFillRectangles is the function for drawing multiple filled rectangles. The function is analogous to XDrawRectangles and is called with the same arguments.

Drawing polygons

A *polygon* is a figure enclosed by multiple lines. To draw the outline of a polygon, use the XDrawLines function. For filled polygons, Xlib provides the
XFillPolygon function, which has this usage:

```
int shape; /* One of: Convex, NonConvex, or Complex */
int mode;  /* One of: CoordModeOrigin or
                       CoordModePrevious            */

XPoint points[]; /* Vertices of the polygon */
int  numpoints;  /* How many vertices        */

XFillPolygon(disp, win, thisGC, points, numpoints,
             shape, mode);
```

You have to specify the vertices of the polygon in an array of XPoint structures, just as you do when drawing multiple points with XDrawPoints. Also,
the mode argument is interpreted the same way as it is for XDrawPoints.

The shape argument helps the server optimize the filling algorithm. Specify
Convex for this argument, only if your polygon is such that a line drawn
between any two internal points lies entirely inside the polygon. (Triangles
and rectangles, for example, are convex shapes.)

If the shape is not convex, but none of the edges intersect, you should use
NonConvex as the shape argument. For polygons that have intersecting
edges, use Complex. Notice that if you are not sure about a polygon, you can
safely specify Complex as the shape. The drawing process may be a bit
slower, but the result is correct.

The fill rule in the GC determines which points XFillPolygon fills. You can
set the fill rule by calling XSetFillRule.

Drawing arcs, circles, and ellipses

In X, arcs, ellipses, and circles are handled by the arc-drawing functions:
XDrawArc and XDrawArcs. You can think of the former function as being for a
single arc and the latter as being for several arcs. Call the XDrawArc function
like this:

```
XDrawArc(disp, window, gc, x, y, width, height, angle1, angle2);
```

You can think of an arc as a part of an ellipse. Drawing an arc involves specifying the *bounding rectangle*, which is the smallest rectangle that completely
encloses the ellipse to which the arc belongs. Specify the rectangle by using
the coordinates of the upper-left corner (x,y) and the dimensions of the rectangle (width and height). Indicate the angle where the arc starts (angle1),
as well as its angular extent (angle2).

The X server draws the arc by starting at a point on the ellipse along the
angle1 line, where angle1 is measured counterclockwise, with zero degrees
along the three o'clock line. Then the server traces the ellipse in a counterclockwise direction until it covers the angular extent specified by angle2.

The angles angle1 and angle2 are integer values that specify angles in units of $\frac{1}{64}$-degree. Thus, to draw a 60-degree-wide arc, starting at 30 degrees from the three o'clock direction, use this call:

```
XDrawArc(p_disp, window, thisGC, x, y, width, height, 30*64, 60*64);
```

You can draw an ellipse by starting at zero degrees and specifying an extent of 360*64. If the width and height of the bounding rectangle are equal, you get a circle.

Drawing text

To display text, you first need to select a font. In X, fonts are resources residing in the server. Applications have to load a font before using it. When the X server successfully loads a font, it returns a resource ID that the application subsequently uses to refer to that font. In Chapter 5, you learn how to name a font. When the name is known, you can load a font by calling the XLoadFont function:

```
Display *disp; /* Identifies connection to X server   */
char   fontname[]="*helvetica-bold-r*140*";/*Font Name */
Font   helvb14;                          /* Font id   */
.
.
.
if((helvb14 = XLoadFont(disp, fontname)) == None)
{
   fprintf(stderr, "Cannot load font: %s\n", fontname);
/* Handle error. Probably just use the default font */
/* ... */
}
```

When the XLoadFont function returns a nonzero value (meaning the function is successful), you can start using the 14-point bold Helvetica font, shown in the previous example, by setting the font attribute of a GC. To do this, call XSetFont:

```
XSetFont(disp, thisGC, helvb14);
```

Subsequently, whenever any text is drawn with this GC, the output is in 14-point bold Helvetica.

Because fonts are server-resident resources, when your application no longer needs a font, you should release the font by calling the XUnloadFont function, which call has this form:

```
XUnloadFont(p_disp, helvb14);
```

If you have a GC with helvb14 as the font and you unload that font, the X server does not unload the font until that GC is destroyed.

After you have a GC with the appropriate font, your application can call one of these functions to display text:

- XDrawString(Display* display, Drawable d, GC gc, int x, int y, const char* string, int length);—draws text string in foreground color only.

- XDrawImageString(Display* display, Drawable d, GC gc, int x, int y, const char* string, int length);—draws characters using both foreground and background colors.

- XDrawText(Display* display, Drawable d, GC gc, int x, int y, XTextItem* items, int nitems);—draws several text strings on a line.

Each function draws several characters on a single line. The first two functions draw all the characters by using the font specified in the GC that you provide as an argument. The functions are called in the same way, as follows:

```
char string[]; /* String to be displayed      */
int  nchars;   /* Number of characters in string */

XDrawString(disp, window, thisGC, x, y, string, nchars);
XDrawImageString(disp, window, thisGC, x, y, string, nchars);
```

You specify a starting position, where the server places the origin of the first character's bitmap. Then the server copies the foreground pixel value (from the GC) to all pixels corresponding to ones in the bitmap. XDrawString does not alter the pixels where the bitmap is zero. XDrawImageString, on the other hand, also fills the pixels corresponding to zeros in each character's bitmap with the GC's background color (using the stipple or tile, if any).

If you want to use more than one font on the same line of text, use the XDrawText function. This function accepts the information about the string segments in a XTextItem structure, which is defined in <X11/Xlib.h> as:

```
typedef struct
{
   char *chars; /* Pointer to the string to be drawn   */
   int nchars;  /* Number of characters in string      */
   int delta;   /* Dist. from last char of prev. string*/
   Font font;   /* Font = None means use GC's font      */
} XTextItem;
```

Each XTextItem structure contains information about a single block of text. The first two members identify the string and its length. The member named delta is an offset, in pixels, applied before drawing this string. The last member specifies the font to be used when drawing this string. When calling XDrawText, you have to provide the usual Display pointer, drawable, and GC, followed by the location where the string should appear and the strings in an array of XTextItem structures:

```
XTextItem text_chunks[]; /*Array of strings to display */
int numchunks;           /* Number of XTextItem structures  */

/* Initialize "text_chunks" first ... */

XDrawText(disp, window, thisGC, x, y, text_chunks, numchunks);
```

XDrawText displays each string by using the font specified in the font field of the corresponding XTextItem structure. The function does so by loading the font into the GC that you provide in the function call. If the font field in the XTextItem is set to None, XDrawText uses whatever font the GC happens to have.

Using drawing functions in Motif

To use Xlib functions in any application, you need the Display pointer, the window ID, and, for drawing functions, a graphics context (GC). Xt Intrinsics (the foundation on which Motif is built) provides macros and functions to get these parameters for any widget.

Display and window ID

Motif applications work with widgets, but most Xlib functions require a pointer to the Display structure and a window identifier as arguments. Given a widget ID, you can get the pointer to its Display structure, by using the XtDisplay function. Similarly, the XtWindow function returns the ID of the window associated with a widget.

Suppose you want to use the Xlib function XClearWindow to clear a widget's window. Given the widget ID w, you can do this by using the following code fragment:

```
#include <X11/Intrinsics.h>

Widget   w;
Display *p_disp;
Window   win;

p_disp = XtDisplay(w);
win = XtWindow(w);
XClearWindow(p_disp, win);
```

The window ID the XtWindow returns is NULL if the widget has not been realized. The Display pointer, however, is valid immediately after the widget is created, if you call XtCreateWidget, or another equivalent function.

GC creation in Motif

To draw text and graphics in a widget's window, you have to create one or more GCs. When using Xlib alone, you use functions, such as XCreateGC, XcopyGC, and XchangeGC, to create and manipulate GCs. Xt Intrinsics provides the function XtGetGC for creating GCs. This function tries to minimize the number of GC creations, by keeping track of the GCs all the widgets create in an application. Xt Intrinsics creates a new GC only when none of the existing ones has attributes that match what you request in the XtGetGC call.

When creating a GC for a widget, you should get the foreground and background pixel values from the widget's resources. That way, you use the foreground and background colors the user may have specified for that widget in a resource file.

You get the value of a widget's resources by calling XtGetValues. The steps are similar to those involved in setting resource values. Suppose you want the foreground and background colors for the DrawingArea widget named drawing_area. The following example shows how you can get these values and set up a GC, by using these attributes:

```
Arg      args[20];
Cardinal narg;
Widget   drawing_area;
XGCValues xgcv;
GC       theGC;
int      fg, bg;

/* Retrieve the background and foreground
 * colors from the widget's resources.
 */
  narg = 0;
  XtSetArg(args[narg], XmNforeground, &fg); narg++;
  XtSetArg(args[narg], XmNbackground, &bg); narg++;
  XtGetValues(drawing_area, args, narg);

/* Now, define a GC with these colors */
  xgcv.foreground = fg;
  xgcv.background = bg;
  theGC = XtGetGC(drawing_area, GCForeground | GCBackground,
                  &xgcv);
```

Notice that when you retrieve a resource's value, you provide the address of a variable in which XtGetValues places the value.

After you create the GC, you can manipulate it with Xlib functions. However, the GC XtGetGC returns is read-only; hence, you cannot change it. Use XcreateGC, if you need a GC you can change.

A Motif line-drawing program

The following listing is xmlines, a Motif line-drawing program. The program can draw rubber-band figures. When the user first clicks the left mouse button in the drawing area, one corner of the line is marked. As the user moves the mouse while holding down the mouse button, the line appears to move in keeping with the mouse's movement. The final line is drawn when the user releases the button.

```
/*---------------------------------------------------*/
/* File: xmlines.c
 *
 * A Motif program that draws lines.
 */
 /*---------------------------------------------------*/
#include <stdio.h>

#include <X11/Xlib.h>
#include <X11/Xutil.h>
```

```c
#include <X11/cursorfont.h>

#include <Xm/Xm.h>
#include <Xm/RowColumn.h>
#include <Xm/MainW.h>
#include <Xm/DrawingA.h>

#define MAXARGS    20
#define MAXLINES   100
#define WIDTH      400
#define HEIGHT     300

static char message[] =
 "Hold down left mouse button, move, and then release.";
static int msglen = XtNumber(message) - 1;

/* Array of lines */

XSegment lines[MAXLINES];
int    numlines = 0;
int    curline = 0;

GC   theGC;   /* GC for regular drawing */
GC   xorGC;   /* GC used for rubber-band drawing */

Cursor xhair_cursor;

/* Function prototypes */

/* These are callbacks */
void start_rubberband(Widget w, XtPointer data, XEvent *p_event,
          Boolean *cdispatch);
void continue_rubberband(Widget w, XtPointer data, XEvent *p_event,
          Boolean *cdispatch);
void end_rubberband(Widget w, XtPointer data, XEvent *p_event,
          Boolean *cdispatch);

void handle_expose(Widget w, XtPointer client_data, XtPointer other);

/* This function draws the lines */
static void draw_line(Display *d, Window w, GC gc, int curline);

/*-------------------------------------------------------*/
void main(int argc, char **argv)
{
  Widget     top_level, main_window, drawing_area;
  Arg        args[MAXARGS];
  Cardinal   argcount;
  int        fg, bg;
  XGCValues  xgcv;
  XtAppContext app;

/* Create the top-level shell widget and initialize the toolkit*/
```

```
top_level = XtAppInitialize(&app, "XMlines", NULL, 0,
                &argc, argv, NULL, NULL, 0);

/* Next, the main window widget */
  argcount = 0;
  XtSetArg(args[argcount], XmNwidth, WIDTH);  argcount++;
  XtSetArg(args[argcount], XmNheight, HEIGHT); argcount++;
  main_window = XmCreateMainWindow(top_level, "Main",
                  args, argcount);
  XtManageChild(main_window);

/* Create the drawing area */
  argcount = 0;
  XtSetArg(args[argcount], XmNresizePolicy, XmRESIZE_ANY);
  argcount++;
  drawing_area = XmCreateDrawingArea(main_window,
              "drawing_area", args, argcount);
  XtManageChild(drawing_area);

/* Attach the drawing area to main window */
  XmMainWindowSetAreas(main_window, NULL, NULL, NULL,
            NULL, drawing_area);

/* Create the GCs. First retrieve the background and foreground
 * colors from the widget's resources.
 */
  argcount = 0;
  XtSetArg(args[argcount], XmNforeground, &fg); argcount++;
  XtSetArg(args[argcount], XmNbackground, &bg); argcount++;
  XtGetValues(drawing_area, args, argcount);

/* Define a GC with these colors */
  xgcv.foreground = fg;
  xgcv.background = bg;
  theGC = XtGetGC(drawing_area, GCForeground | GCBackground,
          &xgcv);
/* Set up a GC with exclusive-OR mode (for rubber-band drawing)*/
  xgcv.foreground = fg ^ bg;
  xgcv.background = bg;
  xgcv.function = GXxor;
  xorGC = XtGetGC(drawing_area, GCForeground |
          GCBackground | GCFunction, &xgcv);

/* Add callback to handle expose events for the drawing area */
  XtAddCallback(drawing_area, XmNexposeCallback, handle_expose,
          &drawing_area);

/* Create a crosshair cursor for the drawing area */
  xhair_cursor = XCreateFontCursor(XtDisplay(drawing_area),
              XC_crosshair);

/* Add event handlers for button events to handle the drawing */
  XtAddEventHandler(drawing_area, ButtonPressMask, False,
          start_rubberband, NULL);
```

```
    XtAddEventHandler(drawing_area, ButtonMotionMask, False,
            continue_rubberband, NULL);
    XtAddEventHandler(drawing_area, ButtonReleaseMask, False,
            end_rubberband, NULL);

/* Realize all widgets */
  XtRealizeWidget(top_level);

/* Change the cursor for the drawing area */
  XDefineCursor(XtDisplay(drawing_area), XtWindow(drawing_area),
        xhair_cursor);

/* Set up a grab so that the cursor changes to a crosshair and
 * is confined to the drawing_area while the mouse button is
 * pressed. This is done through what is known as a "grab"
 */
  XGrabButton(XtDisplay(drawing_area), AnyButton, AnyModifier,
        XtWindow(drawing_area), True, ButtonPressMask|
        ButtonMotionMask | ButtonReleaseMask,
        GrabModeAsync, GrabModeAsync,
        XtWindow(drawing_area), xhair_cursor);

/* Free the cursor */
  XFreeCursor(XtDisplay(drawing_area), xhair_cursor);

/* Start the main event-handling loop */
  XtAppMainLoop(app);
}
/*------------------------------------------------------------*/
/* s t a r t _ r u b b e r b a n d
 *
 * Start of rubber-band line
 */
void start_rubberband(Widget w, XtPointer data, XEvent *p_event,
        Boolean *cdispatch)
{
  int x = p_event->xbutton.x,
    y = p_event->xbutton.y;

/* Crude check to ensure that we don't exceed array's capacity */
  if(numlines > MAXLINES-1) numlines = MAXLINES-1;
  curline = numlines;
  numlines++;

  lines[curline].x1 = x;
  lines[curline].y1 = y;
  lines[curline].x2 = x;
  lines[curline].y2 = y;
  draw_line(XtDisplay(w), XtWindow(w), xorGC, curline);
}
```

```
/*-------------------------------------------------------*/
/* c o n t i n u e _ r u b b e r b a n d
 *
 * Handle mouse movement while drawing a rubber-band line
 */
void continue_rubberband(Widget w, XtPointer data, XEvent *p_event,
          Boolean *cdispatch)
{
  int x = p_event->xbutton.x,
    y = p_event->xbutton.y;

/* Draw once at old location (to erase line) */
  draw_line(XtDisplay(w), XtWindow(w), xorGC, curline);

/* Now update end-point and redraw line */
  lines[curline].x2 = x;
  lines[curline].y2 = y;
  draw_line(XtDisplay(w), XtWindow(w), xorGC, curline);
}
/*-------------------------------------------------------*/
/* e n d _ r u b b e r b a n d
 *
 * End of rubber-band drawing
 */
void end_rubberband(Widget w, XtPointer data, XEvent *p_event,
          Boolean *cdispatch)
{
  int x = p_event->xbutton.x,
    y = p_event->xbutton.y;

/* Draw once at old location (to erase line) */
  draw_line(XtDisplay(w), XtWindow(w), xorGC, curline);

/* Now update end-point and redraw line in normal GC */
  lines[curline].x2 = x;
  lines[curline].y2 = y;
  draw_line(XtDisplay(w), XtWindow(w), theGC, curline);
}
/*-------------------------------------------------------*/
/* h a n d l e _ e x p o s e
 *
 * Expose event-handler for the drawing area
 */
void handle_expose(Widget w, XtPointer data, XtPointer other)
{
  XmDrawingAreaCallbackStruct *call_data =
          (XmDrawingAreaCallbackStruct*)other;
  XEvent *p_event = call_data->event;
  Window win = call_data->window;
  Display *p_display = XtDisplay(w);
```

```
   if(p_event->xexpose.count == 0)
   {
     int i;
/* Clear the window and draw the lines in the "lines" array*/
     XClearWindow(p_display, win);

     if(numlines > 0)
     {
       XDrawSegments(p_display, win, theGC, lines, numlines);
     }
   }

/* Display the message (this is an example of text output) */
   XDrawImageString(p_display, win, theGC, 50, 30, message,
           msglen);
}
/*------------------------------------------------------*/
/* d r a w _ l i n e
 *
 * Draw a specified line from the lines array.
 */
static void draw_line(Display *d, Window w, GC gc, int curline)
{
  int x1 = lines[curline].x1, y1 = lines[curline].y1,
    x2 = lines[curline].x2, y2 = lines[curline].y2;

  XDrawLine(d, w, gc, x1, y1, x2, y2);
}
```

To build the `xmlines` program, use this Makefile:

```
###############################################################
# Makefile to compile and link a Motif program on Linux
# This makefile assumes that you have installed the
# openmotif and openmotif-devel packages

CFLAGS= -I/usr/X11R6/include
LDFLAGS= -L/usr/X11R6/lib -lXm -lXt -lX11 -lXext

all: xmlines

xmlines.o: xmlines.c

xmlines: xmlines.o
        cc -o xmlines xmlines.o $(LDFLAGS)
```

Figure 30-2 shows a sample output of the `xmlines` program after I draw a number of lines.

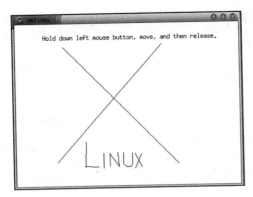

Figure 30-2: The output of the xmlines program, showing some lines

Using color

X incorporates an abstract color model that captures most of the capabilities of common color-graphics hardware. To use color in an X application, you need to understand the color model X uses.

Visuals

X encapsulates the common features of the display hardware in a data structure called the Visual. However, X adds an important twist to encourage sharing of colormaps, by allowing colormaps to be read-only or read-write. Cells in the read-write colormaps can be changed dynamically, whereas read-only colormaps are fixed.

The class member of the Visual structure indicates the color capabilities of the underlying graphics display. Based on the classification of color and grayscale displays, together with X's notion of read-write and read-only colormaps, six distinct classes of Visuals exist, identified by the following names (which are defined in <X11/X.h>):

- DirectColor visual represents a display in which the pixel value is decomposed into bit fields that index into individual colormaps for the R, G, and B components. The colormap entries can be changed dynamically. This visual class is common among displays that have 24-bit planes.

- TrueColor displays are the same as DirectColor, but their colormaps are fixed.

- The PseudoColor visual class models a common type of display hardware — one in which each pixel value looks up an RGB value and in which the colormap can be modified at any time.

- StaticColor displays are similar to PseudoColor, except that the colormap cannot be modified.

- GrayScale visual represents a grayscale monitor that allows the intensity map to be modified. The GrayScale visual is the grayscale equivalent of the PseudoColor visual.

- StaticGray is similar to GrayScale, but has a fixed gray-level map. Black-and-white (monochrome) displays are modeled by a StaticGray visual with a depth of 1.

Each screen in an X display has at least one associated visual structure. Many servers provide more than one visual for a screen. The server for an 8-bit display, for example, might provide a PseudoColor visual of depth 8 and a StaticGray visual of depth 1. Thus, windows on the same screen can be used as a color window or, in the case of StaticGray, as a monochrome window.

Note

Even if a server supports multiple visuals, one of them is the default visual. You can refer to this default visual by using the macro DefaultVisual (display, screen), which returns a pointer to the Visual structure of the specified screen in the X display identified by display.

Available visuals

To see a list of visuals the X server supports on your system, type the following command at the shell prompt in a terminal window (you must be running X for this command to work):

```
xdpyinfo -display :0.0
```

The xdpyinfo program displays a great deal of information about the X server, including the number of visuals. The X server supports six visuals, the default visual being an 8-bit PseudoColor visual.

Typically, you do not have to select a visual, because the default visual is adequate for most applications. If your system has a 24-bit graphics card and the default visual is 8-bit, however, you may want to select and use a 24-bit visual explicitly.

Secret

To use a nondefault visual in a Motif application, you have to specify three resources — visual type, colormap, and depth — of the top-level shell before the widget is realized.

X colormap

In X, each window has an associated colormap that determines how the pixel values are translated into colors (or gray levels in grayscale monitors). Although the hardware may allow only one colormap, X allows each window to have its own colormap, as long as the visual class of the screen is not TrueColor, StaticColor, or StaticGray. Before the pixel values in a window are interpreted according to such a *virtual colormap*, that colormap has to be installed in the hardware colormap. You need a window manager to take care of this chore. By convention, most window managers implement a policy of installing a window's colormap in the hardware, as soon as the window gains input focus.

A colormap is a resource of the X server. Normally, you do not have to create a new colormap for your application. When the server starts, it creates and installs a default colormap. The server normally defines only two color cells in this default colormap. Any X application can allocate and use the rest of the cells.

Note

To use colors from a colormap, you first have to find the colormap's identifier, which is a variable of type `Colormap`. When you create a new colormap, you get back an ID. For the default colormap, the colormap's ID is returned by the macro `DefaultColormap(display,screen)`, which requires that you identify the display and the screen. You can use `DefaultScreen(display)` as the screen argument for `DefaultColormap`.

Colors from a colormap

When you use color in a Motif application, you have to specify a pixel value. The pixel value implies a particular color, depending on the contents of the colormap cell it references. The first step in using a color in X is to obtain the index of a colormap cell that contains the red, green, and blue intensities appropriate for the color you want. To do this, request that the X server allocate a colormap cell (in a specified colormap) with your color. When requesting a colormap cell, you provide the desired red, green, and blue levels; the X server returns an index you can use as the pixel value corresponding to that color.

Because many applications may use similar colors, X provides two ways to allocate colormap cells:

- Shared read-only cells
- Private read-write cells

Shared read-only color cells

You can allocate shared read-only color cells in any visual class, but to allocate read-write cells, the visual class must allow the colormap to be altered. That means the visual class has to be `DirectColor`, `PseudoColor`, or `GrayScale`.

For each colormap, the X server keeps track of the cells currently in use. When the server receives a request for a shared read-only cell in a colormap, it determines the closest color the hardware can support; then it searches any previously allocated read-only cells in that colormap for a cell that may already contain that color. If the server finds such a cell, it returns information about that cell. Otherwise, if the visual class permits writing to the colormap, the server allocates a new cell for read-only use, loads the requested color into the cell, and returns that information.

Note

The nice thing about shared read-only colormap cells is that you can use them on any visual; to allocate private read-write colormap cells, you have to make sure the visual is `DirectColor`, `PseudoColor`, or `GrayScale`.

Private read-write color cells

Private read-write color cells also have some advantages. These cells enable you to alter the mapping of pixel to color at any time. This capability is useful for displaying images; you can change the colors of an image by altering the colormap entries without having to redraw the image with new pixel values.

Also, private colormap cells can be allocated in a single contiguous block, so that the pixel values are in sequence. This capability is useful if the application requires the displayed colors to relate to the pixel values in a well-defined way. An example is a satellite image displayed in a grayscale that associates a gray level to each data level in the satellite image.

XColor structure

When you allocate colors or define new colormap entries, you provide information about the color in an `XColor` structure, which is defined in `<X11/Xlib.h>` as the following:

```
typedef struct
{
  unsigned long pixel; /*Pixel value (after allocation)*/
  unsigned short red,   /* Red intensity (0 - 65,535)   */
            green,  /* Green intensity (0 - 65,535) */
            blue;   /* Blue intensity (0 - 65,535)  */
  char      flags;    /* Used when storing colors     */
  char      pad;  /* Added to make structure size even */
};
```

Note

You should specify a color by indicating the intensities of the RGB components in the fields `red`, `green`, and `blue`. These intensities range from 0 to 65,535; zero implies no intensity, and 65,535 means full intensity. The server automatically scales these values to the range of intensities the display screen's hardware needs.

The field named `pixel` is the pixel value you use to display the color corresponding to the RGB value in red, green, and blue. When allocating a color, you provide the RGB values for the color; the X server returns the pixel value corresponding to the colormap cell with that color.

Read-only color cell allocation

Xlib provides two functions for allocating shared read-only colormap cells:

- `XAllocColor`
- `XAllocNamedColor`

The `XAllocColor` function requires that you define a `XColor` structure and then fill in the red, green, and blue fields with the RGB levels for the color you want. You also have to specify the colormap in which you want to allocate the color. Typically, you use `XAllocColor` in conjunction with `XParseColor`, which accepts the name of a color and sets up the corresponding RGB values in a `XColor` structure.

To allocate a light cyan color in the default colormap and to use it as the background of a window, for example, you might use the following code (see Chapter 5 for information on naming colors in X applications):

```
Display    *disp;
XColor     color;
Colormap   default_cmap;
unsigned long bgpixel;

default_cmap = DefaultColormap(disp,
                     DefaultScreen(disp));

/* Try to allocate a "light cyan" colormap cell */

   if (XParseColor(disp, default_cmap, "light cyan",
               &color) == 0 ||
     XAllocColor(disp, default_cmap, &color) == 0)
   {
/* Use white background in case of failure */
     bgpixel = WhitePixel(disp, DefaultScreen(disp));
   }
   else
   {
/* Colormap cell successfully allocated */
     bgpixel = color.pixel;
   }
 .
 .
 .
/* Use "bgpixel" as background when creating the window */
```

First, XParseColor sets up the RGB values for the color named light cyan. Then XAllocColor requests a read-only color cell with that RGB value. If all goes well, both functions return nonzero values, and the pixel member of color contains the pixel value you should use wherever you need the light cyan color. If the functions fail, you must include some means to handle the situation. In this example, if the allocation fails, the white color is used as the background color. The server always allocates the white and black colors in the default colormap. You can refer to these colors by using the macros WhitePixel(display,screen) and BlackPixel(display,screen), respectively.

The X server provides a color database that applications can use to translate the textual names of colors into red, green, and blue intensities appropriate for that particular display screen. The functions XParseColor and XAllocNamedColor use this database.

XAllocNamedColor is similar to XAllocColor, but it directly takes the name of a color as a string. When you use XAllocNamedColor, the previous example of allocating a light-cyan cell becomes the following:

```
    XColor exact; /* Exact RGB definition of color */

    if (XAllocNamedColor(disp, default_cmap, "light cyan",
            &exact, &color) == 0)
    {
/* Use white background in case of failure */
        bgpixel = WhitePixel(disp, DefaultScreen(disp));
    }
    else
    {
/* Colormap cell successfully allocated */
        bgpixel = color.pixel;
    }
```

XAllocNamedColor requires two XColor arguments. In the XColor structure
named exact, XAllocNamedColor returns the exact RGB value for the
requested color (from the database); in color, it returns the closest color
supported by the hardware and the pixel value corresponding to the allocated colormap cell (when allocation succeeds).

Read-write color cell allocation

Some applications need colors to be allocated in the colormap in a specific
way. You can, for example, display a two-dimensional array of weather satellite data as an image in which the color of each pixel represents a data point.
When you display such an image, you may want all pixel values to appear in
sequence, so that you can easily map the data into colors. You also may want
to alter the mapping of data to colors to bring out features of the data.
Allocating a contiguous block of private read-write colormap cells best
handles this type of need.

To allocate read-write color cells, call the XAllocColorCells function.
Before you use this function, of course, you must make sure the screen's
visual class allows alterations to the colormap (the class must be
DirectColor, PseudoColor, or GrayScale).

This is how you should call XAllocColorCells:

```
Display    *disp;
Colormap   cmap;  /* Colormap where cells are allocated*/
Bool       contig; /* True = allocate contiguous planes */
unsigned long planes[]; /* Array to hold plane masks   */
unsigned int nplanes;   /* Number of planes to allocate*/
unsigned long pixels[]; /* Array to hold pixel values  */
unsigned int npixels;   /* Number of pixels to allocate*/

if(!XAllocColorCells(disp, cmap, contig, planes, nplanes, pixels,
npixels))
{
/* Error allocating color cells */
/* ... */
}
```

X requires that you specify the read-write colormap cells in a unique manner. You specify the number of pixel values (npixels) and the number of planes (nplanes); npixels must be positive, whereas nplanes can be zero or positive. In return, the server reserves npixels*2@supnplanes colormap cells and returns the information about the usable cells in the arrays named pixels and planes. npixels values are returned in pixels, and nplanes bit masks are returned in the planes array.

To allocate a single read-write color cell, call XAllocColorCells as follows:

```
Display    *disp;
Colormap   cmap;    /* Colormap where cells are allocated*/
unsigned long pixels[1];

if(!XAllocColorCells(disp, cmap, False, NULL, 0, pixels, 1))
{
/* Error allocating color cells */
/* ... */
}
/* Successfully allocated color cell. The pixel value is pixels[0] */
```

After calling XAllocColorCells to allocate private read-write color cells, you must store colors in these cells before using them. Use XStoreColor to change the RGB value corresponding to a single pixel value; you have to use an XColor structure to do this. Set the red, green, and blue fields to the desired levels of the primary color. Set pixel to the pixel value of an allocated (read-write) cell. Then call XStoreColor:

```
  Colormap colormap;
  XColor  color;
/* Assume that colorcell is a previously allocated read-
 * writecell. The following code stores "red" in
 * this cell
 */
  color.pixel = colorcell;
  color.red = 65535;
  color.green = 0;
  color.blue = 0;
  color.flags = DoRed | DoGreen | DoBlue;
  XStoreColor(disp, colormap, &color);
```

The flags field in color indicates which of the primary color levels in the colormap cell should be updated.

To set a single colormap cell with a color identified by a name, rather than by the RGB components, use XStoreNamedColor. To set pixel value colorcell to red, use this:

```
XStoreNamedColor(p_disp, colormap, "red", colorcell,
        DoRed | DoGreen | DoBlue);
```

If you have several read-write colormap cells to initialize, use XStoreColors to store colors in them at the same time. As expected, this function takes an array of XColor structures and the number of such structures as arguments, as follows:

```
XColor colors[]; /* Array of colors      */
int   ncolors;   /* Number in colors array */
.

.
/* Set up the "colors" array before calling XStoreColors */

XStoreColors(p_disp, colormap, colors, ncolors);
```

Freeing colors

Whether you use shared or private colormap cells, you should free the colors when they are no longer needed. When an application terminates, the X server automatically frees the colors that application uses. If your application allocates colors often (it may allocate colors each time an image is displayed in a window, for example), you should call XFreeColors to free the colors you no longer need:

```
Display    *disp;
Colormap    colormap;   /* Cells freed in this colormap */
unsigned long pixels[];/* Identifies cells being freed */
int        numpix;     /* Number of cells being freed  */
unsigned long planes;  /* Identifies planes being freed*/

XFreeColors(disp, colormap, pixels, numpix, planes);
```

XFreeColors frees colors that have been allocated by any of these functions: XAllocColor, XAllocNamedColor, XAllocColorCells, and XAllocColorPlanes. When you are freeing one or more read-only cells allocated by XAllocColor or XAllocNamedColor, provide the array of pixel values, their count, and a zero for the planes argument.

For private read-write cells, use a logical OR of the plane masks returned by a previous call to XAllocColorCells.

Displaying an image

The X server supports images through pixmaps and bitmaps, whereas Xlib supports the XImage structure that enables you to manipulate images locally — on the system where your application is running, not on the server.

Creating a pixmap

A *pixmap* is a drawable, which means you can draw in a pixmap, just as you draw in a window. Like a window, a pixmap can be thought of as a rectangular array of pixels (a *raster*), with each location capable of holding a pixel value. You also can view a pixmap as several rectangular bit planes, with as many planes as there are bits in the pixel value.

For windows, the pixel values in the raster are displayed constantly. The hardware reads the pixel values and translates them to colors or gray levels, depending on the capabilities of the display.

In contrast, the contents of a pixmap are not visible, until they are copied to a window. Thus, you can think of a pixmap as an off-screen drawing area — an area of memory where you can save a drawing or an image. In fact, you can prepare drawings in a pixmap and display them whenever they are needed, by using the XCopyArea function.

Pixmaps are primarily used to draw images and to store patterns for tiling. Pixmaps used as tiles are small (usually, no larger than 32 × 32 pixels), but those used to store images can be quite large.

Like windows, pixmaps are resources maintained at the X server. Before using a pixmap, you have to create it by calling the Xlib function XCreatePixmap. This function returns a resource identifier of type Pixmap you use when referring to the pixmap in subsequent drawing requests.

Suppose you want to create a pixmap to draw some figures off-screen. You can create a pixmap by using this code:

```
Display   *disp;    /* Identifies the X display  */
Window    root_win; /* Root window's ID          */
Pixmap    pmap1;    /* Pixmap being created      */
unsigned int width, /* Width of pixmap (pixels)  */
             height,/* Height of pixmap (pixels) */
             depth; /* Bits per pixel value      */
.
.
.
/* Create a pixmap */
  width = 100;
  height = 50;
  depth = DefaultDepth(disp, DefaultScreen(disp));
  root_win = RootWindow(disp, DefaultScreen(disp);

  pmap1 = XCreatePixmap(disp, root_win, width, height, depth);
```

When creating a pixmap, you specify its dimensions (*width* and *height*) and its *depth* (the number of bits in the pixel values the pixmap should be able to store).

The second argument of XCreatePixmap must be an identifier of a previously created drawable. The X server uses this argument to determine the screen for which you are creating the pixmap. You can use the ID of any valid window or pixmap. A simple solution is to use the root window's ID.

Caution

In X, every window and pixmap is created for a specific screen. In a multiple-screen X display, you cannot copy a pixmap from one screen to a window in another screen, even if both have the same depth.

Drawing in a pixmap

When a valid pixmap is available, you can draw in it just as you do in a window. Here is how you draw figures in a pixmap:

```
/* Draw in the pixmap (assume that the GC has been set up) */
  XFillRectangle(disp, pmap1, theGC, 10, 10, 20, 20);
  XFillArc(disp, pmap1, theGC, 30, 30, 20, 20, 0, 360*64);
```

As with windows, you have to provide a graphics context (GC) with all the graphics attributes, such as foreground and background colors. You use the same coordinate system with pixmaps as you do with windows — with the origin at the upper-left corner, the x-axis pointing to the right, and the y-axis pointing down.

Secret

A few minor differences exist between drawing in pixmaps and drawing in windows. The differences stem from windows being always displayed onscreen, whereas pixmaps are never displayed. A main difference is that windows have an associated background color, but pixmaps do not. Thus, you cannot fill the pixmap with the background color by calling XClearArea. Instead, you must use XFillRectangle to fill all pixels in the pixmap with the current background color. When you create a pixmap, its contents are undefined, so you should always fill it with a known value, such as the background color.

Pixmaps do not generate events, other than GraphicsExpose and NoExpose that occur during copying between windows and pixmaps.

Displaying a pixmap

After you have created and drawn in a pixmap, you can display it by using the XCopyArea function. To display the pixmap pmap1 in the window win at coordinates (x, y), for example, use this code:

```
/* Copy drawing from pixmap to the window */
  XCopyArea(p_disp, pmap1, win, theGC, 0, 0, width, height, x, y);
```

Freeing pixmaps

Because most X displays have limited off-screen memory, you should release pixmap resources as soon as you finish using them, by calling XFreePixmap:

```
Pixmap pmap1;

/* Create pixmap "pmap1" and use it */
/* ... */
XFreePixmap(p_disp, pmap1);
```

All resources (including pixmaps) your application uses are automatically freed when your application exits. You have to free pixmaps explicitly, only if you use several large pixmaps.

Using bitmaps

A *bitmap* is a pixmap of depth 1. You create a bitmap by specifying depth 1 when you call the XCreatePixmap function. Because only 1 bit exists in each location of the bitmap, a bitmap is a pattern of ones and zeros.

Bitmaps are used somewhat differently from pixmaps. Because pixmaps store the entire pixel value, they usually are copied directly into windows and displayed. Bitmaps, however, are mostly used as stencils (or stipples) through which the background and foreground pixel values are applied to a drawable's raster. First, the bitmap is laid over the raster of the drawable (repeating the bitmap, if necessary, to cover the entire raster). Then the foreground color is applied to all pixels where the bitmap (the stencil) has a one.

Another use of bitmaps is as a clip mask. The operation is similar to using the bitmap as a stencil, except that the graphics operations are performed only for those pixels in the raster that have a one in the bitmap pattern being used as the stencil.

Because of the special use of bitmaps, they are widely used even when the displays support more than one plane.

Although bitmaps are often used as stipples and clip masks, you also can display a bitmap directly in a window, or copy it into a pixmap. Because the bitmap is depth 1 and the drawable (pixmap or window) may have a depth greater than 1, you cannot use the XCopyArea function to do this. Xlib provides another function, XCopyPlane, just for this purpose.

XCopyplane requires you to specify a rectangular area in a source bitmap and a destination drawable. The server copies the bitmap to the destination pixmap as follows: It uses the bitmap as a stencil and, using the foreground color (specified in a GC), draws those pixels in the drawable where the bitmap has ones.

You can identify the bitmap as one of the planes in an arbitrary pixmap. To do this, specify a mask with exactly 1 bit set to 1. That mask identifies a bit plane in the source pixmap. This bit plane is used as the stencil for the copy operation.

Here is some code that copies the bitmap read in by XReadBitmapFile to a window, using the current foreground color in a GC:

```
Display    disp;          /* Identifies the X display  */
Window    win;            /* Destination window        */
GC        theGC;          /* GC used for copying        */
Pixmap    my_bmp;         /* Bitmap created by function*/
int       xh_bmp, yh_bmp; /* Coordinates of hotspot     */
unsigned int w_bmp, h_bmp;/* Width and height of bitmap*/
unsigned long planemask;  /* Identifies source bitmap  */
int       xsrc, ysrc;     /* Corner of source rectangle*/
int       xdest, ydest;   /* Copy to this point        */
.
.
/* Read in bitmap using "XReadBitmapFile" Assume
 * that bitmap data is in a file named "testicon.xbm"
 */
root_win = RootWindow(disp, DefaultScreen(disp));

if(XReadBitmapFile(disp, root_win, "testicon.xbm",
        &w_bmp, &h_bmp, &my_bmp,
        &xh_bmp, &yh_bmp) != BitmapSuccess)
{
  fprintf(stderr, "Failed to read bitmap file!\n");
```

```
/* Exit if you cannot proceed */
.
.
.
}
/* Bitmap "my_bmp" is ready to be used */

xsrc = 0;
ysrc = 0;
xdest = 10;
ydest = 10;
planemask = 1;

XCopyPlane(disp,my_bmp, win, theGC, xsrc, ysrc,
        w_bmp, h_bmp, xdest, ydest, planemask);
```

The mask that identifies the bitmap from my_bmp is set to 1, because my_bmp is already a bitmap and, as such, has only 1 bit plane.

Summary

Nowadays, users expect most software to come with an easy-to-use graphical user interface (GUI). In Linux, the graphical interface is the X Window System — the standard for all UNIX workstations. X provides the basic windowing capability and graphical output capability, but not much more than that. The actual "look and feel" comes from toolkits, such as Motif. Motif is the de facto, standard graphical user interface for UNIX workstations. The Open Group's Open Motif software is freely available for Red Hat Linux. Because Motif is a popular GUI toolkit, this chapter provides an introduction to Motif programming.

By reading this chapter, you learn that:

▶ Xlib is the C function library that provides access to the basic capabilities of the X Window System. With Xlib, it's tedious to create even simple user-interface elements, such as buttons and menus. You need a higher-level toolkit, such as Motif, to build graphical user interfaces easily. (Some people say you need even a higher level of abstraction than Motif provides.)

▶ Motif relies on the X Toolkit Intrinsics, or Xt Intrinsics, which is a set of convenient functions for managing widgets — graphical user interface objects. Xt Intrinsics provides a basic set of widgets on which other widget sets (such as Motif) are built.

▶ Motif programs rely on widgets to implement the user interface. The look and feel of widgets are controlled by the settings of variables, known as resources.

▶ A typical Motif program creates several widgets, sets their resources, and then runs a loop that processes events (such as input from the mouse and keyboard, or the request to redraw the contents of a window). This style of programming is known as *event-driven programming*.

▶ The Motif widgets employ an object-oriented architecture (even though they are implemented in C) that uses inheritance to build on a basic set of widgets. The three basic types of widgets are shell, primitive, and manager.

▶ Although Motif widgets make it easy to build user-interface elements, such as buttons, menu bars, and list boxes, you still need to use the basic Xlib functions for displaying text, graphics, and images.

▶ The graphics context (GC) is at the heart of any graphics output that uses the X Window System. You specify all graphics attributes, such as color and font, through the GC.

▶ Pixmaps are off-screen blocks of memory where you can draw graphics and text, just as you do in a window on the display screen. The X server manages the pixmaps.

▶ When you use Xlib drawing calls in Motif programs, you have to obtain an appropriate graphics context before making the Xlib calls.

Appendix A

Linux Commands

This appendix presents alphabetically arranged reference entries for the most important Linux commands. The goal here is to provide you with an overview of all commands needed to manage files and directories, start and stop processes, find files, work with text files, and access online help.

If you are looking for a command for a specific task, but don't know which command to use, you may find it helpful to browse through the commands by category. Table A-1 shows the Linux commands organized by categories.

Table A-1	Linux Commands
Command Name	**Action**
Getting Online Help	
apropos	Finds man pages for a specified keyword
info	Displays online help information about a specified command
man	Displays online help information
whatis	Similar to apropos, but searches for complete words only
Making Commands Easier	
alias	Defines an abbreviation for a long command
type	Shows the type and location of a command
unalias	Deletes an abbreviation defined using alias
Managing Files and Directories	
cd	Changes the current directory
chmod	Changes file permissions
chown	Changes file owner and group
cp	Copies files
ln	Creates symbolic links to files and directories
ls	Displays the contents of a directory

Continued

Table A-1 *(continued)*

Command Name	Action
mkdir	Creates a directory
mv	Renames a file as well as moves a file from one directory to another
rm	Deletes files
rmdir	Deletes directories
pwd	Displays the current directory
touch	Updates a file's time stamp
Finding Files	
find	Finds files based on specified criteria such as name, size, etc.
locate	Finds files using a periodically updated database
whereis	Finds files based in the typical directories where executable (also known as binary) files are located
which	Finds files in the directories listed in the PATH environment variable
Processing Files	
cat	Displays a file on standard output (can be used to concatenate several files into one big file)
cut	Extracts specified sections from each line of text in a file
dd	Copies blocks of data from one file to another (used to copy data from devices)
diff	Compares two text files and finds any differences
expand	Converts all tabs into spaces
file	Displays the type of data in a file
fold	Wraps each line of text to fit a specified width
grep	Searches for regular expressions within a text file
less	Displays a text file, one page at a time (can go backwards also)
lpr	Prints files
more	Displays a text file, one page at a time (goes forward only)
nl	Numbers all nonblank lines in a text file and prints the lines to standard output
paste	Concatenates corresponding lines from several files

Command Name	Action
patch	Updates a text file using the differences between the original and revised copy of the file
sed	Copies a file to standard output while applying specified editing commands
sort	Sorts lines in a text file
split	Breaks up a file into several smaller files with specified size
tac	Reverses a file (last line first and so on)
tail	Displays the last few lines of a file
tr	Substitutes one group of characters for another throughout a file
uniq	Eliminates duplicate lines from a text file
wc	Counts the number of lines, words, and characters in a text file
zcat	Displays a compressed file (after decompressing)
zless	Displays a compressed file one page at a time (can go backwards also)
zmore	Displays a compressed file one page at a time

Archiving and Compressing Files

Command Name	Action
compress	Compresses files
cpio	Copies files to and from an archive
gunzip	Decompresses files compressed with GNU ZIP (gzip) or compress
gzip	Compresses files (more powerful than compress)
tar	Creates an archive of files in one or more directories (originally meant for archiving on tape)
uncompress	Decompresses files compressed with compress

Managing Processes

Command Name	Action
bg	Runs an interrupted process in the background
fg	Runs a process in the foreground
free	Displays the amount of free and used memory in the system
halt	Shuts down Linux and halts the computer
kill	Sends a signal to a process (usually used to terminate a process)
ldd	Displays the shared libraries needed to run a program
nice	Runs a process with lower priority (referred to as *nice mode*)

Continued

Table A-1 *(continued)*

Command Name	Action
ps	Displays a list of currently running processes
printenv	Displays the current environment variables
pstree	Similar to ps, but shows parent-child relationships clearly
reboot	Stops Linux and then restarts the computer
shutdown	Shuts down Linux
top	Displays a list of most processor- and memory-intensive processes
uname	Displays information about the system and the Linux kernel
Managing Users	
chsh	Changes the shell (command interpreter)
groups	Prints the list of groups that includes a specified user
id	Displays the user and group ID for a specified user name
passwd	Changes the password
su	Starts a new shell as another user or root (when invoked without any argument)
Managing the File System	
df	Summarizes free and available space in all mounted storage devices
du	Displays disk usage information
fdformat	Formats a diskette
fdisk	Partitions a hard disk
fsck	Checks and repairs a file system
mkfs	Creates a new file system
mknod	Creates a device file
mkswap	Creates a swap space for Linux in a file or a disk partition
mount	Mounts a device (for example, the CD-ROM) on a directory in the file system
swapoff	Deactivates a swap space
swapon	Activates a swap space
sync	Writes buffered data to files
tty	Displays the device name for the current terminal

Command Name	Action
Working with Date and Time	
umount	Unmounts a device from the file system
cal	Displays a calendar for a specified month or year
date	Shows the current date and time or sets a new date and time

The rest of this appendix covers individual reference entries for each command shown in Table A-1. Each reference entry is organized as follows:

- *Purpose* tells you when to use the command.

- *Syntax* shows the syntax of the command with a few common options. Typical option values are also shown. All optional items are shown in square brackets.

- *Options* lists most options, along with a brief description of each option. For many commands, you will find all options listed in this section. However, some commands have too many options to cover here. For those commands, I describe the most commonly used options.

- *Description* describes the command and provides more details about how to use the command.

alias

Purpose	Define an abbreviation for a long command or view the current list of abbreviations.
Syntax	alias [abbrev=command]
Options	None
Description	If you type alias alone, you get a listing of all currently defined abbreviations. Typically, you use alias to define easy-to-remember abbreviations for longer commands. For example, if you type ls -l often, you might add a line with alias ll='ls -l' in the .bashrc file in your home directory. Then you can type ll instead of ls -l to see a detailed listing of a directory. alias is a built-in command of the bash shell and is described in Chapter 10.

apropos

Purpose	View a list of all man pages that contain a specific keyword.
Syntax	apropos keyword
Options	None

Description	The `apropos` command looks up the keyword in a database (known as the `whatis` database) created by the `/usr/sbin/makewhatis` program. The `whatis` database is an index of keywords contained in all of the man pages in the system. Unfortunately, when you try `apropos` with a simple keyword such as find, you may end up with a long listing of man pages because the word find appears in many man pages.

bg

Purpose	Run an interrupted process in the background.
Syntax	`bg`
Options	None
Description	After you type a command that takes a long time to finish, you can press Ctrl+Z to interrupt the process. Then, you can type `bg` to continue that command in the background while you type other commands at the shell prompt. `bg` is a built-in command of the Bash shell.

cal

Purpose	View the calendar of any month in any year.
Syntax	`cal` `cal [-jy] [[month_number] year]`
Options	`-j` displays Julian dates (days numbered between 1 and 366) `-y` displays the calendar for all months of the current year
Description	If you type `cal` without any options, it prints a calendar for the current month. If you type `cal` followed by a number, `cal` treats the number as the year and prints the calendar for that year. To view the calendar for a specific month in a specific year, provide the month number (1 = January, 2 = February, and so on) followed by the year. Thus, to view the calendar for April 2001, type the following:

```
cal 4 2001
      April 2001
Su Mo Tu We Th Fr Sa
 1  2  3  4  5  6  7
 8  9 10 11 12 13 14
15 16 17 18 19 20 21
22 23 24 25 26 27 28
29 30
```

cat

Purpose   Copy contents of a file to standard output (the screen).

Syntax   `cat [-benstvA]` *files*

Options   `-b` numbers nonblank lines

`-e` shows each end-of-line (as $) and all nonprinting characters

`-n` numbers all output lines starting with number 1

`-s` replaces multiple blank lines with a single blank line

`-t` shows tabs as `^I`

`-v` shows nonprinting characters

`-A` shows all characters (including nonprinting ones)

Description   Typically, `cat` is used to display the contents of a file or to concatenate several files into a single file. For example, `cat file1 file2 file3 > all` combines three files into a single file named `all`.

cd

Purpose   Change the current directory.

Syntax   `cd [`*directory*`]`

Options   None

Description   Typing `cd` without a directory name changes the current directory to your home directory. Otherwise, `cd` changes to the specified directory. `cd` is a built-in command of the Bash shell.

chmod

Purpose   Change the permission settings of one or more files.

Syntax   `chmod [-cfvR]` *permission files*

Options   `-c` lists only files whose permissions changed

`-f` stops any error message displays

`-v` verbosely displays permission changes

`-R` recursively changes permissions of files in all subdirectories

Description   To use `chmod` effectively, you have to learn how to specify the permission settings. One way is to concatenate one letter from each of the following tables in the order shown (*Who/Action/Permission*):

Who	Action	Permission
u user	+ add	r read
g group	- remove	w write
o others	= assign	x execute
a all	s set user ID	

To give everyone read access to all files in a directory, type chmod a+r *. On the other hand, to make a specific file executable by everyone, type chmod +x filename.

Another way to specify a permission setting is to use a three-digit sequence of octal numbers. In a detailed listing, the read, write, and execute permission settings for the user, group, and others appear as the sequence rwxrwxrwx (with dashes in place of letters for disallowed operations). Think of rwxrwxrwx as three occurrences of the string rwx. Now, assign the values r=4, w=2, and x=1. To get the value of the sequence rwx, simply add the values of r, w, and x. Thus, rwx = 7. Using this formula, you can assign a three-digit value to any permission setting. For example, if the user can read and write the file and everyone else can only read the file, the permission setting is rw-r--r-- (that's how it appears in the listing), and the value is 644. Thus, if you wanted all files in a directory to be readable by everyone but writeable by the user, you would use the command chmod 644 *.

chown

Purpose
Change the user and group ownership of a file.

Syntax
chown [cvfR] username.groupname files

Options
-c lists only files whose ownership changed

-f stops any error message displays

-v verbosely displays ownership changes

-R recursively changes the ownership of files in all subdirectories

Description
To make a user the owner of one or more files, invoke chown with the user name followed by the filenames. To change the group ownership as well, append the new group name to the user name with a period as separator. For example, to make user naba the owner of all files in a directory, I type chown naba *. Note that you have to be logged in as root to change the ownership of files.

chsh

Purpose	Change the default shell that is started at login.
Syntax	chsh [-s *shell*] [*username*]
Options	-s shell specifies the name of the shell executable to use (shell can be any program listed in the /etc/shells file, such as /bin/bash and /bin/csh)
Description	A user's default shell is stored in the /etc/passwd file. The chsh command lets you change the default shell to any of the shells listed in the /etc/shells file. If you type chsh without any arguments, chsh prompts you for the name of a shell.

compress

Purpose	Compress one or more files using Lempel-Ziv compression.
Syntax	compress [-cdrvV] *files*
Options	-c writes the compressed file to the standard output and retains the original file
	-d decompresses the file
	-r recursively compresses files in all subdirectories
	-v displays a message as each file is compressed
	-V prints the version number and exits
Description	The compress command compresses each specified file and replaces the original with the compressed version (with a .Z suffix appended to the name). You can decompress the file with the compress -d command or the uncompress command.

cp

Purpose	Copy files and directories.
Syntax	cp [*options*] *source_files destination_directory* cp [*options*] *source_file destination_file*
Options	-a preserves all file attributes
	-b makes a backup copy before copying
	-d copies a link but not the file pointed to by the link
	-i asks for confirmation before overwriting files
	-l creates hard links instead of copying files

-p preserves ownership, permissions, and the file time stamp

-R recursively copies files in all subdirectories

-s creates soft links instead of copying files

-u copies only when the file being copied is newer than the destination

-v displays verbose messages as copying progresses

--help displays a Help message about cp

Description   The cp command copies one file to another. You can also copy several files from one directory to another.

cpio

Purpose   Copy files in from, or out to, an archive that can be on a storage medium such as tape or a file on the disk.

Syntax
```
cpio [-icdv] pattern
cpio [-ocBv] pattern
cpio [-padm] pattern
```

Options   -i extracts files whose names match the *pattern*

-o copies files to archive files whose names are provided on standard input

-p copies files to another directory on the same system

-a resets access times of input files

-B copies files using 5,120 bytes per record (the default is 512 bytes per record)

-c reads or writes header information as ASCII characters

-d creates directories as needed

-m retains the previous file-modification time

-v prints a list of filenames

Description   The cpio command copies files in from, and out to, archives. There are three distinct variants of the cpio command: cpio -o creates an archive, cpio -i extracts from an archive, and cpio -p copies from one directory to another. cpio is not that popular among Linux users; tar is much more commonly used. However, some installation programs use cpio during the installation process.

cut

Purpose
Copy selected parts of each line of text from a file to standard output.

Syntax
`cut [options] file`

Options
`-b list` extracts the characters at positions specified in the `list`

`-f list` extracts the fields (assumed to be Tab-separated) specified in `list`

`-d char` specifies the character that delimits the fields (the default is Tab)

`-s` skips lines that do not contain delimited fields (see the `-f` option)

Description
The `cut` command extracts specified parts from each line of text in a file and writes those lines out to standard output. You can extract either a range of characters (specified by their positions) from each line or specific fields, where the fields are separated by a special character, such as the Tab. For example, to extract characters 1 through 11 and the fifty-sixth character onward from a detailed directory listing, use the following command:

```
ls -l | cut -b 1-11,56- | more
drwxr-xr-x CORBA
-rw-r--r-- DIR_COLORS
-rw-r--r-- Muttrc
drwxr-xr-x X11
-rw-r--r-- adjtime
-rw-r--r-- aliases
-rw-r--r-- aliases.db
-rw-r--r--  anacrontab
-rw-------  at.deny
-rw-r--r--  bashrc
(... lines deleted)
```

date

Purpose
Display the current date and time or set a new date and time.

Syntax
```
date [options] [+format]
date [-su] [MMDDHHMM[[CC]YY][.SS]]
```

Options
`-u` displays or sets the time using Greenwich Mean Time (GMT)

Description	The date command alone displays the current date and time. Using the +*format* argument, you can also specify a display format for the date and time. For a complete listing of the format specification, type man date.
	To set the date, use date followed by the date and time in the MMDDHHMM format, where each character is a digit (MM is the month, DD is the day, HH the hour, and MM the minutes). You can optionally specify the year (YY) and century (CC) as well.

dd

Purpose	Copy blocks of data from standard input to standard output (and optionally convert the data from one format to another).
Syntax	dd *option1=value1 option2=value2 option3=value3 ...*
Options	if=*file* reads from the specified file instead of standard input
	of=*file* writes to the specified file instead of standard output
	ibs=*nbytes* reads blocks of *nbytes* bytes at a time
	ibs=*nbytes* writes blocks of *nbytes* at a time
	bs=*nbytes* reads and writes blocks of *nbytes* bytes at a time
	cbs=*nbytes* converts *nbytes* bytes at a time
	skip=*nblocks* skips *nblocks* input blocks from the beginning of the input file
	seek=*nblocks* skips *nblocks* output blocks in the output file
	count=*nblocks* copies *nblocks* blocks from input to output
	conv=*code* performs conversion; *code* can be one of following:

    ascii converts EBCDIC to ASCII
    ebcdic converts ASCII to EBCDIC
    lcase converts to lowercase
    ucase converts to uppercase
    swab swaps every pair of input bytes
    noerror continues after read errors
    (Note: EBCDIC is a character-encoding format used in IBM mainframes)

Description
The dd command copies blocks of data from standard input to standard output, optionally converting the data as the copying proceeds. Typically, dd is used to copy data directly from one device to another. For example, you can copy the Linux kernel (/boot/vmlinuz) to a diskette with the following command: dd if=/boot/vmlinuz of=/dev/fd0

df

Purpose
Display the amount of free and used storage space on all mounted file systems.

Syntax
df [options] [*filesystem*]

Options
-a displays information for all file systems

-i displays inode information (the disk is organized into inodes)

-T prints the type of file system

-t *type* displays information about specified types of file systems only

-x *type* excludes specified types of file systems from the output

--help displays a Help message

Description
The df command shows the amount of free and used space on a specified file system. If you want to know how filled up all of your disks are, use the df command without any arguments. The df command then displays information about used and available storage space on all currently mounted file systems.

diff

Purpose
Show the difference between two text files (or all files with the same names in two directories).

Syntax
diff [options] *from_file to_file*

Options
-a treats all files as text even if they aren't text files

-b ignores blank lines and repeated blanks

-c produces output in a different format

-d tries to find a smaller set of changes (this makes diff slower)

-e produces a script for the ed editor to convert from_file to to_file

-f produces output similar to that of -e, but in reverse order

-i ignores case

-l passes the output to the pr command to paginate it

-n works like -f, but counts the number of changed lines

-r recursively compares files with the same name in all subdirectories

-s reports when two files are the same

-t expands tabs to spaces in the output

-u uses the unified output format

-v displays the version of diff

-w ignores spaces and tabs when comparing lines

Description   The diff command compares *from_file* with *to_file* and displays the lines that differ. The output is in a format that the patch command can use to convert *from_file* to *to_file*.

du

Purpose   Display summary information about disk usage (in kilobytes).

Syntax   du [options] [*directories_or_files*]

Options   -a displays usage information for all files (not just directories)

-b displays usage in bytes (instead of kilobytes)

-c displays a grand total of all usage information

-k displays usage information in kilobytes (default)

-s displays total disk usage without per-directory details

Description   The du command displays the disk space (in kilobytes) used by the specified files or directories. By default, du displays the disk space used by each directory and subdirectory. A common use of du is to view the total space used by the current directory. For example, here is how you might check the details of disk space used by the /var/log directory:

```
du /var/log
64        /var/log/httpd
36        /var/log/news
20        /var/log/samba
4780      /var/log
```

expand

Purpose Write files to standard output after expanding each tab into an appropriate number of spaces.

Syntax expand [options] [*files*]

Options -*n* (where *n* is a number) sets the tabs *n* spaces apart

-*n1* [*n2*, ...] (where *n1*, *n2*, ... are numbers) specifies the tab stops

-i converts only the initial tab into spaces

Description The expand command reads from the specified files (or standard input, if no files are specified) and writes them to standard output, with each tab character expanded to an appropriate number of spaces. By default, expand assumes that the tab positions are eight spaces apart (equivalent to the -8 option).

fdformat

Purpose Format a diskette specified by device name (such as /dev/fd0H1440 for a 3.5-inch, high-density diskette in drive A).

Syntax fdformat [-n] *device_name*

Options -n disables the verification that is performed after formatting

Description The fdformat command formats a diskette. Use an appropriate device name to identify the diskette drive (see Chapter 15 for naming conventions for diskette drives). After formatting a diskette with fdformat, you can use mkfs to install a Linux file system; or tar to store an archive.

fdisk

Purpose Partition a disk or display information about existing partitions.

Syntax fdisk [options] [*device_name*]

Options -l displays partition tables and exits

-s *device* displays the size of the specified partition

-v displays the version number of the fdisk program

Description The fdisk command partitions a specified hard disk (see Chapter 4 for disk-drive naming conventions). You can also use fdisk to display information about existing partitions. You should never run fdisk and alter the partitions of a hard disk while one or more of its partitions are mounted on the Linux file system. Instead, you should boot from an installation diskette (or a boot diskette), and then perform the partitioning. Remember that partitioning typically destroys all existing data on a hard disk.

fg

Purpose	Continue an interrupted process in the foreground.
Syntax	`fg`
Options	None
Description	After you interrupt a process by typing Ctrl+Z, you can continue that process in the foreground by typing the `fg` command. Note that `fg` is a built-in command of the Bash shell.

file

Purpose	Display the type of data in a file based on rules defined in the `/usr/lib/magic` file (this is known as the *magic file*).
Syntax	`file [options] files`
Options	`-c` displays a parsed form of a magic file (or the default one) and exits
	`-m file1[:file2:...]` specifies other magic files
	`-v` displays the version number and exits
	`-z` looks inside compressed files
Description	The `file` command uses rules specified in the `/usr/lib/magic` file to determine the type of data in the specified files. For example, you can use the `file` command to check the type of each file in the `/usr/lib` directory, as shown here:

```
file * | more
Mcrt1.o:                ELF 32-bit
LSB relocatable, Intel 80386, version
 1, not stripped
X11:                    symbolic link
to ../X11R6/lib/X11
apache:                 directory
appletsConf.sh:         ASCII text
aspell:                  directory
bison.hairy:            C program
text
```

```
bison.simple:                  C program
text
cappletConf.sh:                ASCII text
cracklib_dict.hwm:             data
cracklib_dict.pwd:             ASCII text
cracklib_dict.pwi:             data
(... lines deleted)
```

find

Purpose   Display a list of files that match a specified set of criteria.

Syntax   `find [path] [options]`

Options   `-depth` processes the current directory first, and then subdirectories

`-maxdepth` *n* restricts searches to *n* levels of directories

`-follow` processes directories included through symbolic links

`-name` *pattern* finds files whose names match the *pattern*

`-ctime` *n* matches files modified exactly *n* days ago

`-user` *uname* finds files owned by the specified user

`-group` *gname* finds files owned by the specified group

`-path` *pattern* finds files whose path name matches the *pattern*

`-perm` *mode* finds files with the specified permission setting

`-size` +*n*K finds files bigger than *n* kilobytes

`-type` *x* finds files of a specified type, where *x* is one of the following:

f matches files
d matches directories
l matches symbolic links
`-print` displays the names of the files found

`-exec` *command* [*options*] {} \; executes the specified command by passing it the name of the file that was found

Description   The `find` command is useful for finding all files that match a specified set of criteria. If you type `find` without any arguments, the output is a listing of every file in all subdirectories of the current directory. To view all files whose names end with `.gz`, you would type `find .
-name "*.gz"`.

fold

Purpose   Wrap lines of text to a specified width (the default is 80 characters).

Syntax   `fold [options] [files]`

Options   `-b` counts bytes instead of columns, so backspaces and tabs are counted

`-s` breaks lines at word boundaries

`-w` *N* (where *N* is a number) sets line width to *N* characters

Description   The `fold` command wraps each input line to a specified number of characters and displays the results on the screen (standard output). If you do not specify any filename, `fold` reads lines from the standard input.

free

Purpose   Display the amount of free and used memory in the system.

Syntax   `free [options]`

Options   `-b` displays memory in number of bytes

`-k` displays memory in kilobytes (default)

`-m` displays memory in megabytes

`-s` *n* repeats the command every *n* seconds

`-t` displays a line containing a summary of the total amounts

Description   The `free` command displays information about the physical memory (RAM) and the swap area (on the disk). The output shows the total amount of memory, as well as the amount used and the amount free.

fsck

Purpose   Check and repair a Linux file system.

Syntax   `fsck [options] device_name`

Options   `-A` checks all file systems listed in the `/etc/fstab` file

`-R` skips the root file system (when checking all file systems)

`-T` does not show the title on startup

`-N` shows what might be done, but does not actually do anything

-V produces verbose output

-t *fstype* specifies the file-system type (such as ext2)

-n answers all confirmation requests with no (only for the ext2 file system)

-p carries out all repairs without asking for confirmation (for ext2)

-y answers all confirmation requests with yes (only for the ext2 file system)

Description The fsck command checks the integrity of a file system and carries out any necessary repairs. Depending on the type of file system, fsck runs an appropriate command to perform the actual task of checking and repairing the file system. For example, to check an ext2 file system, fsck runs the e2fsck program. You have to run fsck when you power down your system without running the shutdown command. Typically, fsck is automatically run during system startup.

grep

Purpose Search one or more files for lines that match a regular expression (a search pattern).

Syntax grep [options] *pattern   files*

Options -*N* (where *N* is a number) displays *N* lines around the line containing *pattern*

-c shows the number of lines that contain the search pattern

-f *file* reads options from a specified file

-i ignores case

-l displays the filenames that contain *pattern*

-n displays a line number next to lines that contain *pattern*

-q returns a status code, but does not display any output

-v displays the lines that do not contain *pattern*

-w matches only whole words

Description The grep command searches the specified files for a pattern. The pattern is a regular expression, which has its own rules. Typically, you use grep to search for a specific sequence of characters in one or more text files.

groups

Purpose	Show the groups to which a user belongs.
Syntax	groups [*username*]
Options	None
Description	The groups command displays the names of groups to which a user belongs. If you do not specify a user name, the command displays your groups.

gunzip

Purpose	Decompresses files compressed by the gzip or the compress command.
Syntax	gunzip [options] *files*
Options	See the options for gzip
Description	The gunzip command decompresses compressed files (these files have the .gz or .Z extension). After decompressing, gunzip replaces the compressed files with their decompressed versions and removes the .gz or .Z extension in the filenames. The gunzip command is the same as gzip with the -d option.

gzip

Purpose	Compresses one or more files.
Syntax	gzip [options] *files*
Options	-c writes output to standard output and retains the original file
	-d decompresses the file (same as gunzip)
	-h displays a Help message
	-l lists the contents of a compressed file
	-n does not save the original name and time stamp
	-r recursively compresses files in all subdirectories
	-v displays verbose output
	-V displays the version number
Description	The gzip command compresses files using Lempel-Ziv (LZ77) coding, which produces better compression than the algorithm used by the compress command. After compressing a file, gzip replaces the original file with the compressed version and appends a .gz to the filename.

halt

Purpose   Terminate all processes and halt the system (you must log in as `root`).

Syntax   `halt [options]`

Options   `-n` does not flush out in-memory buffers to disk before halting the system

`-f` forces a halt without calling the `/sbin/shutdown` command

`-i` shuts down all network interfaces before halting the system

Description   The `halt` command lets the super user (root) terminate all processes and halt the system. The `halt` command invokes `/sbin/shutdown` with the `-h` option.

id

Purpose   List the user ID, group ID, and groups for a user.

Syntax   `id [options] [username]`

Options   `-g` displays group ID only

`-n` displays group name instead of ID

`-u` displays user ID only

Description   The `id` command displays the user ID, the group ID, and the groups for a specified user. If you do not provide any user name, `id` displays information about the current user.

info

Purpose   View online help information about any Linux command.

Syntax   `info [options] command`

Options   `-d dirname` adds a directory to a list of directories to be searched for files

`-f infofile` specifies the file to be used by `info`

`-h` displays usage information about info

Description   The `info` command displays online help information about a specified command in a full-screen text window. You can use Emacs commands to navigate the text displayed by `info`. To learn more about `info`, type `info` without any arguments.

kill

Purpose	Send a signal to a process.
Syntax	`kill [options]` *process_id*
Options	`-`*signum* (where *signum* is a number or name) sends the specified signal
	`-l` lists the signal names and numbers
Description	The `kill` command sends a signal to a process. Typically, the signal is meant to terminate the process. For example, `kill -9 123` terminates the process with ID 123. To see process IDs, use the `ps` command. To see a list of signal names and numbers, type `kill -l` (that's a lowercase "ell").

ldd

Purpose	Display names of shared libraries required to run a program.
Syntax	`ldd [options]` *programs*
Options	`-v` prints the version number of `ldd`
	`-V` prints the version number of the dynamic linker (`ld.so`)
	`-d` relocates functions and reports missing functions
	`-r` relocates both data and functions and reports missing objects
Description	The `ldd` command lets you determine which shared libraries are needed to run the specified programs. For example, to determine what you need to run the Bash shell (`/bin/bash`), type the following:

```
ldd /bin/bash
        libtermcap.so.2 =>
/lib/libtermcap.so.2 (0x4001f000)
        libdl.so.2 => /lib/libdl.so.2
(0x40023000)
        libc.so.6 => /lib/libc.so.6
(0x40026000)
        /lib/ld-linux.so.2 => /lib/
ld-linux.so.2 (0x40000000)
```

less

Purpose	View text files one screen at a time (and scroll backwards if necessary).

Syntax	`less [options]` *`filenames`*
Options	`-?` displays a list of commands you can use in `less`
	`-p` *`text`* displays the first line where *`text`* is found
	`-s` reduces multiple blank lines to a single blank line
Description	The `less` command displays the specified files one screen at a time. Unlike `more`, you can press b, Ctrl+B, or Esc+V to scroll backwards. To view the commands you can use to interact with `less`, press h while you are viewing a file in `less`.

ln

Purpose	Set up a hard or symbolic link (pseudonyms) to files and directories.
Syntax	`ln [options]` *`existing_file new_name`*
Options	`-b` makes backup copy of files about to be removed
	`-d` creates a hard link to a directory (only root can do this)
	`-f` removes the existing file with *`new_name`*
	`--help` displays a Help message
	`-s` creates a symbolic link
	`-v` displays verbose output
Description	The `ln` command assigns a new name to an existing file. With the `-s` option, you can create symbolic links that can exist across file systems. Also, with symbolic links, you can see the link information with the `ls -l` command. Otherwise, `ls -l` shows two distinct files for a file and its hard link.

locate

Purpose	From a periodically updated database, list all files that match a specified pattern.
Syntax	`locate` *`pattern`*
Options	None
Description	The `locate` command searches a database of files for any name that matches a specified pattern. Your Linux system is set up to periodically update the file database. If you are not sure about the location of a file, just type `locate` followed by a part of the filename. For example, here's how you can search for the `XF86Config` file:

```
locate XF86Config
/etc/X11/XF86Config
/etc/X11/XF86Config-4
/usr/X11R6/lib/X11/XF86Config
/usr/X11R6/lib/X11/XF86Config.98
/usr/X11R6/lib/X11/XF86Config.eg
/usr/X11R6/man/man5/XF86Config.5x.gz
/usr/X11R6/man/man5/XF86Config-3.5x.gz
```

lpr

Purpose	Print one or more files.
Syntax	`lpr [options] [files]`
Options	`-Pprinter` prints to the specified printer (the name appears in `/etc/printcap`)
	`-#N` (where *N* is a number) prints that many copies of each file
	`-h` suppresses the burst page (the first page, with user information)
	`-m` sends mail upon completion of a print job
	`-r` removes the file after printing
	`-J jobname` prints this job name on the burst page
	`-U username` prints this user name on the burst page
Description	The `lpr` command prints the specified files by using your system's print spooling system. If no filenames are specified, `lpr` reads input from the standard input. You can print to a specific printer with the `-P` option.

ls

Purpose	List the contents of a directory.
Syntax	`ls [options] [directory_name]`
Options	`-a` displays all files, including those that start with a period (`.`)
	`-b` displays unprintable characters in filenames with octal code
	`-c` sorts according to file creation time
	`-d` lists directories like any other file (rather than listing their contents)
	`-f` lists directory contents without sorting (exactly as they are in the disk)

-i shows the inode information

-l shows the file listing in the long format, with detailed information

-p appends a character to a filename to indicate type

-r sorts the listing in reverse alphabetical order

-s shows the size (in kilobytes) of each file next to the filename

-t sorts the listing according to the file's time stamp

-1 displays a one-column listing of filenames

-R recursively lists the files in all subdirectories

Description The ls command displays the listing of a specified directory. If you omit the directory name, ls displays the contents of the current directory. By default, ls does not list files whose names begin with a period (.); to see all files, type ls -a. You can see full details of files (including size; user and group ownership; and read-write-execute permissions) with the ls -l command.

man

Purpose View online manual pages (also called *man pages*).

Syntax man [options] [*section*] *command*

Options -C *cfile* specifies the man configuration file (the default is /etc/man.config)

-P *pager* specifies the program to use to display one page at a time (e.g., less)

-a displays all man pages matching a specific *command*

-h displays a Help message and exits

-w shows the location of the man pages to be displayed

Description The man command displays the man pages for the specified command. If you know the section for a man page, you can provide the section as well. For example, all Tcl/Tk man pages are in section n. Thus, you can view the man page for the Tcl/Tk command pack with the command man n pack.

mkdir

Purpose Create a directory.

Syntax mkdir [options] *directory_name*

Options	-m *mode* assigns the specified permission setting to the new directory
	-p creates the parent directories if they do not already exist
Description	The mkdir command creates the specified directory.

mkfs

Purpose	Create a Linux file system on a hard-disk partition or a diskette.
Syntax	mkfs [-V] [-t] [options] *device_name* [*blocks*]
Options	-V produces verbose output needed for testing
	-t *fstype* specifies the file system type (such as ext2)
	-c checks the device for bad blocks before creating the file system
	-l *filename* reads the bad-block list from specified file
Description	The mkfs command creates a Linux file system on a specified device. The device is typically a hard-disk partition or a diskette (that has been formatted with fdformat).

mknod

Purpose	Create a device file with specified major and minor numbers.
Syntax	mknod *device_file* {b|c} *major minor*
Options	None
Description	The mknod command creates a device file (such as the ones in the /dev directory) through which the operating system accesses physical devices, such as hard disk, serial port, keyboard, and mouse. To create a device file, you have to log in as root and you have to know the major and minor numbers of the device for which you are creating the device file. Additionally, you must specify either b or c to indicate whether the device is block- or character-oriented. Typically, you will perform this step following specific instructions in a HOWTO document.

mkswap

Purpose	Create a swap space for Linux.
Syntax	mkswap [options] *device_or_file numblocks*

Options	-c checks the device for bad blocks before creating the swap space
	-f forces creation of swap space even if there are errors, such as the requested size is greater than space available on the device
	-P *NNN* uses *NNN* as the page size for the swap space
	-v*N* (where *N* is 0 or 1) creates an old-style swap space if *N* is 0; if *N* is 1, creates a new-style swap space
Description	The mkswap command creates a swap space for use by the Linux kernel. If you are creating swap space in a disk partition, specify the partition's device name (such as /dev/hda2) as the second argument to mkswap. If you want to use a file as swap space, create the file with a command such as dd if=/dev/zero of=swapfile bs=1024 count=16384. Then type **mkswap swapfile 16384** to create the swap space. You have to use the swapon command to activate a swap space.

more

Purpose	View text files one screen at a time.
Syntax	more [options] *filenames*
Options	+*N* (where *N* is a number) displays the file starting at the specified line number
	+/*pattern* begins displaying two lines before the *pattern*
	-s reduces multiple blank lines to a single blank line
Description	The more command displays the specified files one screen at a time. To view the commands you can use in more, press h while you are viewing a file using more. For more advanced file viewing, use the less command.

mount

Purpose	Associate a physical device to a specific directory in the Linux file system.
Syntax	mount [options] *device directory*
Options	-a mounts all devices listed in the /etc/fstab file
	-h displays a Help message and exits
	-r mounts the device for read-only (no writing allowed)
	-t *fstype* specifies the file system type on the device

-v displays verbose messages

-V displays the version number and exits

Description   The mount command attaches the contents of a physical device to a specific directory on the Linux file system. For example, you may mount a CD-ROM at the /mnt/cdrom directory. Then, you can access the contents of the CD-ROM at the /mnt/cdrom directory (in other words, the root directory of the CD-ROM appears as /mnt/cdrom after the mount operation). To see the listing of the RedHat directory on the CD-ROM, type `ls /mnt/cdrom/RedHat`.

mv

Purpose   Rename files and directories or move them from one directory to another.

Syntax   `mv [options] source  destination`

Options   -b makes backup copies of files being moved or renamed

-f removes existing files without prompting

-i prompts before overwriting any existing files

-v displays the name of the file before moving it

Description   The mv command either renames a file or moves it to another directory. The command works on either plain files or directories. Thus, you could rename the file `sample` to `sample.old` with the command `mv sample sample.old`. On the other hand, you can move the file `/tmp/sample` to `/usr/local/sample` with the command `mv /tmp/sample /usr/local/sample`.

nice

Purpose   Run a program at a lower or higher priority level.

Syntax   `nice [options] program`

Options   +n (n = number) adds n to the nice value (positive values are lower priority)

-n (n = number) subtracts n from the nice value (negative nice value indicates a higher priority)

Description   The nice command enables you to run a program at lower or higher priority. By default, programs run at the nice value of zero. Adding to the nice value decreases the priority, whereas subtracting from the nice value increases the program's priority. Only root can decrease the nice value.

nl

Purpose Add line numbers to nonblank lines of text in a file and write to standard output.

Syntax `nl [options] [file]`

Options `-ba` numbers all lines

`-bt` numbers text lines only (the default)

`-sc` separates text from line numbers with the character *c* (the default is tab)

`-wn` uses *n* columns to show the line numbers

Description The `nl` command adds a line number to each non-blank line of text from a file and writes the lines to standard output. Suppose the file `sample.txt` has the following lines:

```
A line followed by a blank line and

then another non-blank line.
```

The `nl` command applied to this file produces the following result:

```
nl sample.txt
     1  A line followed by a blank line and

     2  then another non-blank line.
```

passwd

Purpose Change password.

Syntax `passwd [username]`

Options None

Description The `passwd` command changes your password. It prompts for the old password, followed by the new password. If you log in as root, you can change another user's password by specifying the user name as an argument to the `passwd` command.

paste

Purpose Write to standard output corresponding lines of each file, separated by a tab.

Syntax `paste file1 file2 [...]`

Options `-s` pastes the lines from one file at a time, instead of one line from each file

-d *delim* uses delimiters from the list of characters, instead of a tab

- causes paste to use standard input as a file

Description   The paste command takes one line from each of the listed files and writes them out to standard output, separated by a tab. With the -s option, the paste command can also concatenate all lines from one file into a single gigantic line.

patch

Purpose   Apply the output of the diff command to an original file.

Syntax   patch [options] < *patch_file*

Options   -c causes the patch file to be interpreted as a context diff

-e forces patch to interpret the patch file as an ed script

-f forces patch to be applied regardless of any inconsistencies

-n causes the patch file to be interpreted as a normal diff

-p*n* strips everything up to *n* slashes in the path name

-R indicates that patch file was created with new and old files swapped

-u causes the patch file to be interpreted as a unified diff

-v displays the version number

Description   The patch command is used to update an original file by applying all the differences between the original and a revised version. The differences are in the form of an output from the diff command, stored in the *patch_file*. Changes to Linux kernel source code are distributed in the form of a patch file. Chapter 25 discusses how to apply patches to the kernel source.

printenv

Purpose   View a list of environment variables.

Syntax   printenv

Options   None

Description   The printenv command displays a list of all current environment variables.

ps

Purpose Display status of processes (programs) running in the system.

Syntax `ps [options]`

Options Note that unlike other commands, `ps` options do not have a – prefix.

a displays processes of other users

f displays a family tree of processes

j displays output using jobs format

l displays in long format, with many details for each process

m displays memory usage information for each process

u displays the user name and start time

x displays processes that are not associated with any terminal

Description The `ps` command displays the status of processes running in the system. Typing `ps` alone produces a list of processes you are running. To see a list of all processes in the system, type `ps ax` (or `ps aux`, if you want more details about each process).

pstree

Purpose Display all running processes in the form of a tree.

Syntax `pstree [options] [pid]`

Options –a shows command-line arguments

–c does not compact subtrees

–l displays long lines

–n sorts processes by process ID (instead of by name)

–p shows process IDs

Description The `pstree` command shows all of the processes in the form of a tree, which makes it easy to understand the parent-child relationships among the processes. For example, here is a typical output from `pstree`:

```
pstree
init-+-apmd
     |-atd
     |-deskguide_apple
     |-gdm-+-X
     |      `-gdm---gnome-session
```

```
                              |-gmc
                              |-gnome-name-serv
                              |-gnome-smproxy
                              |-gpm
                              |-gweather
                              |-httpd---8*[httpd]
                              |-identd---identd---3*[identd]
                              |-kflushd
                              |-klogd
                              |-kpiod
                              |-kswapd
                              |-kupdate
                              |-lockd---rpciod
                              |-lpd
                              |-magicdev
                              |-mdrecoveryd
                              |-6*[mingetty]
                              |-named
                              |-netscape-commun---netscape-commun
                              |-panel
                              |-portmap
                              |-rpc.statd
                              |-sawfish
                              |-session-propert
                              |-sshd
                              |-syslogd
                              |-tasklist_applet
                              |-xfs
                              |-xinetd---in.telnetd---login---bash---
                       su---bash-+-more
                              |
                       `-pstree
                              `-xscreensaver---gears
```

pwd

Purpose	Display the current working directory.
Syntax	pwd
Options	None
Description	The pwd command prints the current working directory. pwd is a built-in command of the Bash shell.

reboot

Purpose	Terminate all processes and reboot the system (you must log in as root).
Syntax	reboot [options]

Options   -n reboots the system without flushing out in-memory buffers to disk

-f forces a halt without calling the /sbin/shutdown command

-i shuts down all network interfaces before rebooting the system

Description   The reboot command lets the super user (root) terminate all processes and reboot the system. The reboot command invokes /sbin/shutdown with the -r option.

rm

Purpose   Delete one or more files.

Syntax   rm [options] *files*

Options   -f removes files without prompting

-i prompts before removing a file

-r recursively removes files in all subdirectories, including the directories

-v displays the name of each file before removing it

Description   The rm command deletes the specified files. To remove a file, you must have write permission to the directory that contains the file.

rmdir

Purpose   Delete a specified directory (provided the directory is empty).

Syntax   rmdir [options] *directory*

Options   -p removes any parent directories that become empty

Description   The rmdir command deletes empty directories. If a directory is not empty, you should use the rm -r command to delete the files, as well as the directory.

sed

Purpose   Copy a file to standard output after editing according to a set of commands.

Syntax   sed [options] [*editing_commands*] [*file*]

Options   -e'instructions' applies the editing instructions to the file

-f *scriptfile* applies editing commands from *scriptfile*

-n suppresses default output

Description	The `sed` command is known as the stream editor — it copies a file to standard output while applying specified editing commands. If you do not specify a file, it reads from the standard input. To use the stream editor, you have to learn its editing commands, which are very similar to the ones used by the `ed` editor (described in Chapter 14).

shutdown

Purpose	Terminate all processes and shut down (or reboot) the system.
Syntax	`shutdown [options]` *time* `[messages]`
Options	`-t` *seconds* specifies the time between the message and the kill signal
	`-h` halts the system after terminating all the processes
	`-r` reboots the system after terminating all the processes
	`-f` performs a fast reboot
	`-k` sends warning messages, but does not actually shut down the system
	`-c` cancels a shutdown that's in progress
Description	The `shutdown` command (the full path name is `/sbin/shutdown`) brings down the Linux system in an orderly way. You must specify a time when shutdown begins; use the keyword `now` to shutdown immediately. You must be logged in as `root` to run the `shutdown` command.

sort

Purpose	Sort or merge lines from a file and then write to standard output.
Syntax	`sort [options] [files]`
Options	`-c` checks if files are already sorted, and prints error message if not
	`-m` merges files by sorting them as a group
	`-b` ignores leading blanks
	`-d` sorts in phone directory order (using only letters, digits, and blanks)

-f treats lowercase letters as equivalent to uppercase letters

-k *pos1*[,*pos2*] specifies the sort field as characters between the two positions *pos1* and *pos2*

-o *file* writes output to the specified file instead of standard output

-r sorts in reverse order

-g sorts numerically after converting the prefix of each line into a floating-point number

-i ignores unprintable characters

-n sorts numerically (used when a number begins each line)

-t*c* specifies the separator character

+*n* only considers characters from position *n* onwards (0 = first position)

Description   The sort command sorts the lines in one or more files and writes them out to the standard output. The same command can also merge several files (when used with the -m option) and produce an appropriately sorted and merged output.

split

Purpose   Split a file into several smaller files.

Syntax   split [options] *file* [*prefix*]

Options   -l *n* (where *n* is a number) puts *n* lines in each file

-*n* (where *n* is a number) puts *n* lines in each file

-b *nk* (where *n* is a number) splits the file every *n* kilobytes

-c *nk* (where *n* is a number) puts as many lines as possible in a split file without exceeding *n* kilobytes per file

Description   The split command breaks up a large file into smaller files. By default, split puts 1,000 lines into each file. The files are named by groups of letters such as aa, ab, ac, and so on. You can specify a prefix for the filenames. For example, to split a large archive into smaller files that fit into several high-density, 3.5-inch diskettes, use split as follows:

split -C 1440k bigfile.tar disk.

This creates files named disk.aa, disk.ab, and so on.

su

Purpose	Become another user.
Syntax	su [options] [*username*]
Options	-c *command* passes the *command* to the shell
	-f prevents reading the startup file (.cshrc) when the shell is csh or tcsh
	-l makes the new shell a login shell by reading the user's startup file
	-p preserves the environment variables HOME, USER, LOGNAME, and SHELL
	-s *shell* runs the specified *shell* instead of the user's default shell
Description	The su command lets you assume the identity of another user. You have to provide the password of that user before you can continue. If you do not provide a user name, su assumes you want to change to the root user.

swapoff

Purpose	Deactivate the specified swap device or file.
Syntax	swapoff *device*
Options	None
Description	The swapoff command stops Linux from using the specified device or file as a swap space.

swapon

Purpose	Activate the specified swap device or file.
Syntax	swapon [-a] *device*
Options	-a enables all swap devices listed in the /etc/fstab file
Description	The swapon command activates the specified device or file as a swap space. During system startup, all swap spaces are activated by the swapon -a command, which is invoked by the script file /etc/rc.d/rc.sysinit.

sync

Purpose	Write buffers to disk.
Syntax	sync
Options	None

Description   When you cannot shut down your Linux system in an orderly manner (for example, when you cannot execute shutdown, halt, or reboot commands), you should type sync before switching off the computer.

tac

Purpose   Copy a file, line by line, to the standard output in reverse order (last line first).

Syntax   tac *file*

Options   -b places the separator at the beginning of each line

-r treats the separator string specified by -s as a regular expression

-s *sep* specifies a separator (instead of the default newline character)

Description   The tac command displays the specified text file in reverse order, copying the lines to standard output in reverse order. By default, tac treats each line as a record and uses the newline character as the record separator. However, you can specify a different separator character, in which case, tac will copy those records to standard output in reverse order.

tail

Purpose   View the last few lines of a file.

Syntax   tail [options] *file*

Options   -*N* (where *N* is a number) displays last *N* lines

-n *N* (where *N* is a number) displays last *N* lines

-f reads the file at regular intervals and displays all new lines

Description   The tail command displays lines from the end of the specified file. By default, tail displays the last 10 lines from the file. To view the last 24 lines from a file named messages, type tail -24 messages.

tar

Purpose   Create an archive of files or extract files from an archive.

Syntax   tar [options] *files_or_directories*

Options   -c creates a new archive

-d compares files in an archive with files in the current directory

-r extends the archive with more files

-t lists the contents of an archive

-x extracts from the archive

-C *directory* extracts files into the specified directory

-f *file* uses the specified file as the archive, instead of a tape

-L *n* specifies the capacity of the tape as *n* kilobytes

-N *date* only archives files newer than the specified date

-T *file* archives or extracts the filenames specified in *file*

-v displays verbose messages

-z compresses or decompresses the archive with gzip

Description	The tar command creates an archive of files, or extracts files from an existing archive. By default, tar assumes the archive to be on a tape. However, you can use the -f option to specify a file as the archive.

top

Purpose	List currently running processes, arranged in order by their share of CPU time.
Syntax	top [q] [d *delay*]
Options	q causes top to run with the highest possible priority (you have to be root)
	d *delay* specifies the delay between updates, in seconds
Description	The top command produces a full-text screen with the processes arranged according to their share of the CPU time. By default, top updates the display every five seconds. Press q or Ctrl+C to quit top.

touch

Purpose	Change a file's time stamp.
Syntax	touch [options] *files*
Options	-c stops touch from creating a file that does not exist
	-d *time* uses the specified time
	-r *file* uses the time stamp from the specified file
	-t *MMDDhhmm[[CC]YY][.ss]* uses the specified date and time

Description   The touch command lets you change the date and time of the last modification of a file (this information is stored with the file). If you use touch without any options, the current date and time are used as the time stamp for the file. If the specified file does not exist, touch creates a new file of size 0 bytes.

tr

Purpose   Copies from standard input to standard output, while substituting one set of characters with another.

Syntax   tr [options] *string1* [*string2*]

Options   -c complements characters in *string1* with ASCII codes 001–377

-d deletes from the input all characters specified in *string1*

-s replaces repeated sequences of any character in *string1* with a single character

Description   The tr command substitutes all characters in *string1* in the input with the corresponding characters in *string2*. For example, to convert the file sample.lc to all uppercase and store in sample.uc, type the following:

tr [a-z] [A-Z] < sample.lc > sample.uc

To replace repeated occurrences of newlines in a file with a single newline character, type the following:

tr -s '\n' < infile > outfile

tty

Purpose   Display the device name of the terminal.

Syntax   tty

Options   None

Description   The tty command displays the name of the terminal connected to the standard input. This is useful in shell scripts that may need the terminal name.

type

Purpose   Display the type of a command (whether it is a built-in shell command or a separate executable program).

Syntax   type *command*

Options	None
Description	The `type` command tells you the type of a command — whether it is a built-in shell command, an alias, or an executable program. For example, I used `alias ll='ls -l'` to define the alias `ll`. Here is what I get when I check the type of the command `ll`:

```
type ll
ll is aliased to 'ls -l'
```

umount

Purpose	Disassociate a device from the Linux file system.
Syntax	umount *device*
Options	None
Description	The `umount` command removes the association between a device and a directory in the Linux file system. Only the root can execute the `umount` command.

unalias

Purpose	Delete an abbreviation defined earlier with `alias`.
Syntax	unalias *abbreviation*
Options	None
Description	The `unalias` command removes an abbreviation defined earlier with the `alias` command. `unalias` is a built-in command of the Bash shell.

uname

Purpose	Display system information, such as type of machine and operating system.
Syntax	uname [options]
Options	`-a` displays all information
	`-m` displays the hardware type (for example, `i586`)
	`-n` displays the machine's host name
	`-p` displays the processor type (this appears as `unknown`)
	`-r` displays the operating system release (for example, 2.4.0-0.43.12)
	`-s` displays the operating system name
	`-v` displays the operating system version (shown as date of compilation)

Description | The uname command displays a variety of information about your machine and the operating system (Linux).

uncompress

Purpose | Decompress one or more files that have been compressed using the compress command.

Syntax | uncompress [-cdrvV] *files*

Options | -c writes the result to the standard output and retains the original

-r recursively decompresses files in all subdirectories

-v displays a message as each file is decompressed

-V prints the version number and exits

Description | The uncompress command decompresses each specified file and replaces the compressed version with the original (also removes the .Z suffix appended to the name of the compressed file). Using the uncompress command yields the same result as running compress with the -d option.

uniq

Purpose | Write all unique lines from an input file to standard output.

Syntax | uniq [options] *file*

Options | -*n* (where *n* is a number) ignores the first *n* fields on each line

+*n* (where *n* is a number) ignores the first *n* characters on each line

-c writes the number of times each line occurred in file

-d writes only duplicate lines

-u writes only unique lines (the default)

Description | The uniq command removes duplicate lines from an input file and copies the unique lines to the standard output. If you do not specify an input file, uniq reads from standard input.

wc

Purpose | Display the byte, word, and line count of a file.

Syntax | wc [options] [*files*]

Options	-c displays only the byte count
	-w displays only the word count
	-l displays only the line count
Description	The wc command displays the byte, word, and line count of a file. If you do not specify an input file, wc reads from standard input.

whatis

Purpose	Search whatis database (see apropos) for complete words.
Syntax	whatis *keyword*
Options	None
Description	The whatis command searches the whatis database (see the entry for apropos) for the specified keyword and displays the result. Only complete word matches are displayed.

whereis

Purpose	Find the source, binary, and man page for a command.
Syntax	whereis [options] *command*
Options	-b searches only for binaries
	-m searches only for man pages
	-s searches only for sources
Description	The whereis command searches the usual directories (where binaries, man pages, and source files are located) for binaries, man pages, and source files for a command. For example, here is the result of searching for the files for the rpm command:

```
whereis rpm
rpm: /bin/rpm /usr/lib/rpm /usr/include/rpm
/usr/man/man8/rpm.8
```

which

Purpose	Search the directories in the PATH environment variable for a command.
Syntax	which *command*
Options	None

Description	The `which` command searches the directories in the PATH environment variable for the file that will be executed when you type the command. This is a good way to check what will be executed when you type a specific command.

zcat, zless, zmore

Purpose	View the contents of a compressed text file without having to first decompress the file.

Syntax	`zcat filename`
	`zless filename`
	`zmore filename`

Options	None
Description	The `zcat`, `zless`, and `zmore` commands work the same way as `cat`, `less`, and `more`. The only difference is that the z-commands can directly read files compressed with `gzip` or `compress` (without having to first decompress the files with `gunzip`). These commands are particularly useful for reading compressed text files, such as the ones in `/usr/info` directory.

Appendix B

Linux Resources

This appendix lists some resources where you can get more information about specific topics. Most of the resources are on the Internet because that's where you can get the latest information on Linux. Often, you'll be able to download the files necessary for a specific task.

Some Internet resources appear in the standard Uniform Resource Locator (URL) syntax — Chapter 17 explains URLs. If you have used a Web browser such as Netscape Communicator or Microsoft Internet Explorer, you are probably already familiar with URLs.

Instead of providing a long listing of URLs, this appendix describes a few key Web sites that you can use as a starting point for your search.

Web Pages

If you browse the Internet, you may notice that there are quite a few Web pages with Linux-related information. A good starting point for locating information about Linux is the Linux Online page at:

```
http://www.linux.org/
```

You can click the buttons to access more information about the topic identified by that button's label. At this page, you also find an organized collection of links to Linux-related Web sites.

To browse recent news about Linux, visit the Linux Resources page at:

```
http://www.linuxresources.com/
```

Specialized Systems Consultants (SSC), Inc., the publisher of the *Linux Journal*, maintains this page. You can scan the articles in the latest issue of *Linux Journal* and find out other information, such as the latest version of the kernel and links to other Linux resources.

Another popular and definitive source of Linux information is the home page of the Linux Documentation Project (LDP) at the following URL:

```
http://www.linuxdoc.org/
```

On this Web site, you can find many more pointers to other Linux resources on the Internet. In particular, you can browse and download the latest HOWTO documents from `http://metalab.unc.edu/pub/Linux/docs/HOWTO/`.

For Red Hat Linux–specific questions, you can visit Red Hat's Support Web site at:

`http://www.redhat.com/apps/support/`

This Web site provides links such as Product Updates and Errata, Hardware Compatibility List, and Installation Guides and Manuals. In particular, you can find the manuals and FAQs (Frequently Asked Questions) at `http://www.redhat.com/support/docs/howto/`.

Newsgroups

To keep up with Linux developments, you really need access to the Internet, especially to the newsgroups. You can find discussions on specific Linux-related topics in the newsgroups listed in Table B-1.

Table B-1   Linux Newsgroups on the Internet

Newsgroup	Provides the Following
comp.os.linux.admin	Information about Linux system administration
comp.os.linux.advocacy	Discussions about promoting Linux
comp.os.linux.announce	Important announcements about Linux. (This is a moderated newsgroup, which means you must mail an article to the moderator, who then posts it to the newsgroup.)
comp.os.linux.answers	Questions and answers about Linux. (All the Linux HOWTOs are posted in this moderated newsgroup.)
comp.os.linux.development	Current Linux development work
comp.os.linux.development.apps	Linux application development
comp.os.linux.development.system	Linux operating system development
comp.os.linux.hardware	Discussions about Linux and various hardware
comp.os.linux.help	Help with various aspects of Linux
comp.os.linux.misc	Miscellaneous topics about Linux

Newsgroup	Provides the Following
comp.os.linux.networking	Networking under Linux
comp.os.linux.setup	Linux setup and installation
comp.os.linux.x	Discussions about setting up and running the X Window System under Linux

You can use Netscape Communicator to read the newsgroups. For a newsgroup, use a URL of the form news://my.newsserver.com/newsgroup, in which my.newsserver.com is the fully qualified domain name of your news server (your Internet service provider should give you this name), and newsgroup is the name of the newsgroup you want to read. For example, assuming that your news server is news.myisp.net, you can browse the comp.os.linux.setup newsgroup by typing the following URL in the Location field of the Netscape Web browser:

news://news.myisp.net/comp.os.linux.setup

Tip

You can also use the Deja.com Power Search page at http://www.dejanews.com/home_ps.shtml to search for specific items in the comp.os.linux newsgroups.

FTP Archive Sites

You can download Red Hat Linux and other Linux distributions from one of several FTP sites around the world. In addition to the Linux distribution itself, these sites also contain many other software packages that run under Linux.

For the latest list of Red Hat Linux FTP sites worldwide, visit the following Web page maintained by Red Hat:

http://www.redhat.com/mirrors.html

This page displays a table of URLs of sites that maintain the Red Hat distribution for downloading. In that table, the Updates column lists the URLs for downloading specific Red Hat Package Manager (RPM) files for the latest Red Hat Linux version (for Intel-based PCs).

Tip

Red Hat provides many of the fixes and improvements — these updates are in the form of Red Hat packages distributed from Red Hat's FTP server. (Try ftp://ftp.redhat.com/pub/redhat/updates/; if it's busy, consult http://www.redhat.com/mirrors.html for a mirror site near you.) To install these packages, you have to use the Red Hat Package Manager (RPM).

Magazines

Linux Journal is a monthly magazine devoted entirely to Linux. On the Web, the magazine home page is at `http://www.linuxjournal.com/`. There you can find information about how to subscribe to this magazine.

Linux Magazine is another monthly magazine that covers everything about Linux. Visit their home page at `http://www.linux-mag.com/` to learn more about the magazine and to subscribe.

Appendix C

About the CD-ROMs

The companion CD-ROMs contain Red Hat Linux 7.1 with the Linux 2.4 kernel, which is the latest version of Linux available as of this writing (Spring 2001). Linux is a complete UNIX-like operating system for your PC. The Red Hat Linux distribution includes over 1.2GB of files. By installing Linux on a PC, you can turn that PC into a full-fledged UNIX workstation.

Note

Please note that the software contained in these CD-ROMs is distributed under a variety of license agreements. Some of the software (such as the Linux kernel) is distributed in full source and binary format under the GNU General Public License. In all cases, the software is copyrighted by the respective authors. After installing Red Hat Linux, you should consult the README.* files (or files with names such as COPYING and COPYRIGHT) in various subdirectories of the /usr/share/doc directory for information on the licensing terms for each software package.

Installation can be a tricky step in Linux. You need some specific information about hardware, such as disk controller, video card, and CD-ROM drive. Linux controls the hardware through drivers, so you need to make sure that the current release of Linux includes drivers for your hardware. Because Linux is free, you cannot really demand—or expect—support for some specific hardware. Linux is, however, continually improving through collaboration among programmers throughout the world. If your hardware is popular enough, there's a good chance that someone has developed a driver for it. In any case, the Red Hat Linux on the companion CD-ROMs already supports such a wide variety of hardware that all your PC's peripherals probably are supported.

Cross-Reference

The CD-ROM Installation Instructions that face this book's CD-ROM show the general procedure to install and configure Linux and the X Windows System.

You will find the following software on the Red Hat Linux 7.1 CD-ROM:

- Linux kernel 2.4 with driver modules for all major PC hardware configurations, including IDE/EIDE and SCSI drives, PCMCIA devices, and CD-ROMs

- A complete set of installation and configuration tools for setting up devices (such as the keyboard and mouse) and services

- A graphical user interface based on the XFree86 4.0.3 package, with GNOME and KDE desktops

- Full TCP/IP networking for Internet, LANs, and intranets

- Tools for connecting your PC to your Internet service provider (ISP) using PPP, SLIP, or dial-up serial communications programs

- A complete suite of Internet applications, including electronic mail (`sendmail`, `elm`, `pine`, `mailx`), **news** (`inn`, `tin`, `trn`), TELNET, FTP, DNS, and NFS

- Apache Web server 1.3.19, to turn your PC into a Web server; and Netscape Communicator 4.76, to surf the Net

- Samba 2.0.7 LAN Manager software for Microsoft Windows connectivity

- Several text editors (e.g., GNU Emacs 20.7; `vim`)

- Graphics and image manipulation software, such as The GIMP, XPaint, Xfig, Gnuplot, Ghostscript, Ghostview, and ImageMagick

- Programming languages (GNU C and C++ 2.96, Perl 5.6.0, Tcl/Tk 8.3.2, Python 1.5.2, GNU AWK 3.0.6) and software development tools (GNU Debugger 5.0, CVS 1.11, RCS 5.7, GNU Bison 1.28, flex 2.5.4a, TIFF, and JPEG libraries)

- Support for industry standard Executable and Linking Format (ELF) and Intel Binary Compatibility Specification (iBCS)

- A complete suite of standard UNIX utilities from the GNU project

- Tools to access and use DOS files and applications (`mtools` 3.9.7)

- Text formatting and typesetting software (`groff`, TeX, and LaTeX)

- Games, such as GNU Chess, Mahjongg, Reversi, Minesweeper, FreeCell, Gnobots, Snake Race, `fortune`, `xgammon`, and `xpilot`

Index

Symbols & Numbers

A

G

g++ command, 863
g command (sed), 370
G command (sed), 370
game controllers, 789–791
Games group, 69, 410
gasp command, 359
gateways, 249, 283
Gawk, 345
GCC, 345, 861–865
gdb, 15, 345
gdb utility, 874–880
gdbm, 345
gEdit, 412–413
Genoa chipsets, 91
geometry manager, 977–978
geometry of hard drives, 115
-geometry option, 405–406
get command
    dip, 516
    FTP, 621
    using, 747
GET command (HTTP), 548–550
gets command (Tcl), 964, 968–969
gettext, 345
getty files, 227–233
gf option, in printcap entries, 189
gFTP, 622–623
Ghostscript, 198–203, 345, 437–440
Ghostview, 181, 199, 345, 440–441
the GIMP, 9, 345, 426–429
Gimp Tool Kit, 384
glob command (Tcl), 964, 969–970
global command (Tcl), 964
global variables, 679
GlobalImageDir= (gdm), 378
GLOBALS button (SWAT), 679
GNOME
    application development, 990
    as default GUI, 302–303
    display manager, 373–381
    File Manager, 318–322
    office tools, 420–421, 423
    overview, 384–390

playing audio CDs, 167–168
purpose, 345
selecting as default, 73
switching to KDE, 381–383
text editor, 412–413
GNOME group packages, 69
GNOME RPM, 491–492, 736–739
gnotepad+, 414–416
GNU C Library, 344
GNU General Public License (GPL), 860,
    880–882
GNU Library General Public License
    (GPL), 880–882
GNU Project, 343
GNU tools
    bc, 359–361
    binary utilities, 357–359
    C compilers, 861–865
    command-line options, 329
    debugger, 874–880
    Emacs. See Emacs
    file utilities, 348–353
    find command, 353
    gzip, 361–363
    make utility, 865–873
    Midnight Commander, 363–364
    online help, 858–861
    patch, 364–365
    shell utilities, 347–348
    software overview, 344–346
    stream editor, 365–370
    text utilities, 354–357
gnuchess, 344
Gnumeric, 345, 417–419
Gnuplot, 433–437
GoldStar CD-ROM drives, 158
gopher protocol, 546
goto command (dip), 516
goto statement (Perl), 926
GPG, 754
gpm, 701
gprof, 15
gprof command, 359
Grab command (Tk), 975

continued

General Public License

Preamble

The licenses for most software are designed to take away your freedom to share and change it. By contrast, the GNU General Public License is intended to guarantee your freedom to share and change free software — to make sure the software is free for all its users. This General Public License applies to most of the Free Software Foundation's software and to any other program whose authors commit to using it. (Some other Free Software Foundation software is covered by the GNU Library General Public License instead.) You can apply it to your programs, too.

When we speak of free software, we are referring to freedom, not price. Our General Public Licenses are designed to make sure that you have the freedom to distribute copies of free software (and charge for this service if you wish), that you receive source code or can get it if you want it, that you can change the software or use pieces of it in new free programs; and that you know you can do these things.

To protect your rights, we need to make restrictions that forbid anyone to deny you these rights or to ask you to surrender the rights. These restrictions translate to certain responsibilities for you if you distribute copies of the software, or if you modify it.

For example, if you distribute copies of such a program, whether gratis or for a fee, you must give the recipients all the rights that you have. You must make sure that they, too, receive or can get the source code. And you must show them these terms so they know their rights.

We protect your rights with two steps: (1) copyright the software, and (2) offer you this license which gives you legal permission to copy, distribute and/or modify the software.

Also, for each author's protection and ours, we want to make certain that everyone understands that there is no warranty for this free software. If the software is modified by someone else and passed on, we want its recipients to know that what they have is not the original, so that any problems introduced by others will not reflect on the original authors' reputations.

Finally, any free program is threatened constantly by software patents. We wish to avoid the danger that redistributors of a free program will individually obtain patent licenses, in effect making the program proprietary. To prevent this, we have made it clear that any patent must be licensed for everyone's free use or not licensed at all.

The precise terms and conditions for copying, distribution and modification follow.

Terms and Conditions for Copying, Distribution, and Modification

0. This License applies to any program or other work which contains a notice placed by the copyright holder saying it may be distributed under the terms of this General Public License. The "Program", below, refers to any such program or work, and a "work based on the Program" means either the Program or any derivative work under copyright law: that is to say, a work containing the Program or a portion of it, either verbatim or with modifications and/or translated into another language. (Hereinafter, translation is included without limitation in the term "modification".) Each licensee is addressed as "you".

Activities other than copying, distribution and modification are not covered by this License; they are outside its scope. The act of running the Program is not restricted, and the output from the Program is covered only if its contents constitute a work based on the Program (independent of having been made by running the Program). Whether that is true depends on what the Program does.

1. You may copy and distribute verbatim copies of the Program's source code as you receive it, in any medium, provided that you conspicuously and appropriately publish on each copy an appropriate copyright notice and disclaimer of warranty; keep intact all the notices that refer to this License and to the absence of any warranty; and give any other recipients of the Program a copy of this License along with the Program.

You may charge a fee for the physical act of transferring a copy, and you may at your option offer warranty protection in exchange for a fee.

2. You may modify your copy or copies of the Program or any portion of it, thus forming a work based on the Program, and copy and distribute such modifications or work under the terms of Section 1 above, provided that you also meet all of these conditions:

a) You must cause the modified files to carry prominent notices stating that you changed the files and the date of any change.

b) You must cause any work that you distribute or publish, that in whole or in part contains or is derived from the Program or any part thereof, to be licensed as a whole at no charge to all third parties under the terms of this License.

c) If the modified program normally reads commands interactively when run, you must cause it, when started running for such interactive use in the most ordinary way, to print or display an announcement including an appropriate copyright notice and a notice that there is no warranty (or else, saying that you provide a warranty) and that users may redistribute the program under these conditions, and telling the user how to view a copy of this License. (Exception: if the Program itself is interactive but does not normally print such an announcement, your work based on the Program is not required to print an announcement.)

These requirements apply to the modified work as a whole. If identifiable sections of that work are not derived from the Program, and can be reasonably considered independent and separate works in themselves, then this License, and its terms, do not apply to those sections when you distribute them as separate works. But when you distribute the same sections as part of a whole which is a work based on the Program, the distribution of the whole must be on the terms of this License, whose permissions for other licensees extend to the entire whole, and thus to each and every part regardless of who wrote it.

Thus, it is not the intent of this section to claim rights or contest your rights to work written entirely by you; rather, the intent is to exercise the right to control the distribution of derivative or collective works based on the Program.

In addition, mere aggregation of another work not based on the Program with the Program (or with a work based on the Program) on a volume of a storage or distribution medium does not bring the other work under the scope of this License.

3. You may copy and distribute the Program (or a work based on it, under Section 2) in object code or executable form under the terms of Sections 1 and 2 above provided that you also do one of the following:

   a) Accompany it with the complete corresponding machine-readable source code, which must be distributed under the terms of Sections 1 and 2 above on a medium customarily used for software interchange; or,

   b) Accompany it with a written offer, valid for at least three years, to give any third party, for a charge no more than your cost of physically performing source distribution, a complete machine-readable copy of the corresponding source code, to be distributed under the terms of Sections 1 and 2 above on a medium customarily used for software interchange; or,

   c) Accompany it with the information you received as to the offer to distribute corresponding source code. (This alternative is allowed only for noncommercial distribution and only if you received the program in object code or executable form with such an offer, in accord with Subsection b above.)

The source code for a work means the preferred form of the work for making modifications to it. For an executable work, complete source code means all the source code for all modules it contains, plus any associated interface definition files, plus the scripts used to control compilation and installation of the executable. However, as a special exception, the source code distributed need not include anything that is normally distributed (in either source or binary form) with the major components (compiler, kernel, and so on) of the operating system on which the executable runs, unless that component itself accompanies the executable.

If distribution of executable or object code is made by offering access to copy from a designated place, then offering equivalent access to copy the source code from the same place counts as distribution of the source code, even though third parties are not compelled to copy the source along with the object code.

4. You may not copy, modify, sublicense, or distribute the Program except as expressly provided under this License. Any attempt otherwise to copy, modify, sublicense or distribute the Program is void, and will automatically terminate your rights under this License. However, parties who have received copies, or rights, from you under this License will not have their licenses terminated so long as such parties remain in full compliance.

5. You are not required to accept this License, since you have not signed it. However, nothing else grants you permission to modify or distribute the Program or its derivative works. These actions are prohibited by law if you do not accept this License. Therefore, by modifying or distributing the Program (or any work based on the Program), you indicate your acceptance of this License to do so, and all its terms and conditions for copying, distributing or modifying the Program or works based on it.

6. Each time you redistribute the Program (or any work based on the Program), the recipient automatically receives a license from the original licensor to copy, distribute or modify the Program subject to these terms and conditions. You may not impose any further restrictions on the recipients' exercise of the rights granted herein. You are not responsible for enforcing compliance by third parties to this License.

7. If, as a consequence of a court judgment or allegation of patent infringement or for any other reason (not limited to patent issues), conditions are imposed on you (whether by court order, agreement or otherwise) that contradict the conditions of this License, they do not excuse you from the conditions of this License. If you cannot distribute so as to satisfy simultaneously your obligations under this License and any other pertinent obligations, then as a consequence you may not distribute the Program at all. For example, if a patent license would not permit royalty-free redistribution of the Program by all those who receive copies directly or indirectly through you, then the only way you could satisfy both it and this License would be to refrain entirely from distribution of the Program.

   If any portion of this section is held invalid or unenforceable under any particular circumstance, the balance of the section is intended to apply and the section as a whole is intended to apply in other circumstances.

   It is not the purpose of this section to induce you to infringe any patents or other property right claims or to contest validity of any such claims; this section has the sole purpose of protecting the integrity of the free software distribution system, which is implemented by public license practices. Many people have made generous contributions to the wide range of software distributed through that system in reliance on consistent application of that system; it is up to the author/donor to decide if he or she is willing to distribute software through any other system and a licensee cannot impose that choice.

   This section is intended to make thoroughly clear what is believed to be a consequence of the rest of this License.

8. If the distribution and/or use of the Program is restricted in certain countries either by patents or by copyrighted interfaces, the original copyright holder who places the Program under this License may add an explicit geographical distribution limitation excluding those countries, so that distribution is permitted only in or among countries not thus excluded. In such case, this License incorporates the limitation as if written in the body of this License.

9. The Free Software Foundation may publish revised and/or new versions of the General Public License from time to time. Such new versions will be similar in spirit to the present version, but may differ in detail to address new problems or concerns.

   Each version is given a distinguishing version number. If the Program specifies a version number of this License which applies to it and "any later version", you have the option of following the terms and conditions either of that version or of any later version published by the Free Software Foundation. If the Program does not specify a version number of this License, you may choose any version ever published by the Free Software Foundation.

10. If you wish to incorporate parts of the Program into other free programs whose distribution conditions are different, write to the author to ask for permission. For software which is copyrighted by the Free Software Foundation, write to the Free Software Foundation; we sometimes make exceptions for this. Our decision will be guided by the two goals of preserving the free status of all derivatives of our free software and of promoting the sharing and reuse of software generally.

No Warranty

11. BECAUSE THE PROGRAM IS LICENSED FREE OF CHARGE, THERE IS NO WARRANTY FOR THE PROGRAM, TO THE EXTENT PERMITTED BY APPLICABLE LAW. EXCEPT WHEN OTHERWISE STATED IN WRITING THE COPYRIGHT HOLDERS AND/OR OTHER PARTIES PROVIDE THE PROGRAM "AS IS" WITHOUT WARRANTY OF ANY KIND, EITHER EXPRESSED OR IMPLIED, INCLUDING, BUT NOT LIMITED TO, THE IMPLIED WARRANTIES OF MERCHANTABILITY AND FITNESS FOR A PARTICULAR PURPOSE. THE ENTIRE RISK AS TO THE QUALITY AND PERFORMANCE OF THE PROGRAM IS WITH YOU. SHOULD THE PROGRAM PROVE DEFECTIVE, YOU ASSUME THE COST OF ALL NECESSARY SERVICING, REPAIR OR CORRECTION.

12. IN NO EVENT UNLESS REQUIRED BY APPLICABLE LAW OR AGREED TO IN WRITING WILL ANY COPYRIGHT HOLDER, OR ANY OTHER PARTY WHO MAY MODIFY AND/OR REDISTRIBUTE THE PROGRAM AS PERMITTED ABOVE, BE LIABLE TO YOU FOR DAMAGES, INCLUDING ANY GENERAL, SPECIAL, INCIDENTAL OR CONSEQUENTIAL DAMAGES ARISING OUT OF THE USE OR INABILITY TO USE THE PROGRAM (INCLUDING BUT NOT LIMITED TO LOSS OF DATA OR DATA BEING RENDERED INACCURATE OR LOSSES SUSTAINED BY YOU OR THIRD PARTIES OR A FAILURE OF THE PROGRAM TO OPERATE WITH ANY OTHER PROGRAMS), EVEN IF SUCH HOLDER OR OTHER PARTY HAS BEEN ADVISED OF THE POSSIBILITY OF SUCH DAMAGES.

End Of Terms And Conditions

CD-ROM Installation Instructions

Although these instructions do not provide detailed installation instructions for Red Hat Linux, you can use the following general procedures to install and configure Red Hat Linux and the X Window System, which is the graphical user interface for Linux. Follow these steps:

1. Gather information about your PC's hardware, such as graphics card, network card, and SCSI card before you install Linux.

2. Use the non-destructive repartitioning program FIPS to repartition your hard disk without destroying the existing contents. FIPS essentially creates a new partition by shrinking the existing DOS partition. Remember to defragment your hard disk before using FIPS, because FIPS can only allocate contiguous free space to a new partition. Skip this step if you plan to use Linux as the sole operating system, or if you plan to install Red Hat Linux on a DOS/Windows partition, or on an empty second hard disk.

3. Under DOS or Windows, create a Linux boot disk.

4. Boot your PC with the Linux boot disk (or start MS-DOS and run the AUTOBOOT command from the first CD-ROM, labeled "CD 1of 3"). This procedure automatically runs the Red Hat Linux installation program. From this point on, you will respond to a number of dialog boxes as the Red Hat installation program takes you through the steps. Here are some of the key installation steps:

   - Identify any SCSI adapters installed in your PC.

   - Use Red Hat's Disk Druid utility to prepare the hard disk partitions where you plan to install Linux. If you have created space for Linux by reducing the size of an existing DOS partition, this step enables you to create the partitions for Linux.

   - Configure the Ethernet network, if any. You have to specify parameters, such as the IP address and host name for your Red Hat Linux system.

   - Specify the local time zone, and set the root password.

   - Install the Linux Loader (LILO) program on your hard disk so you can boot Linux when you power up your PC after shutting it down.

   - Select the specific software packages, such as the X Window System and the GNOME graphical desktop that you want to install.

   - Configure the X Window System and enable graphical login screen so that when you boot your Linux system, it will display a login dialog and go directly into the GNOME or KDE graphical desktop after successful login.